Contemporary
Literary Criticism

Guide to Gale Literary Criticism Series

For criticism on	Consult these Gale series
Authors now living or who died after December 31, 1959	*CONTEMPORARY LITERARY CRITICISM (CLC)*
Authors who died between 1900 and 1959	*TWENTIETH-CENTURY LITERARY CRITICISM (TCLC)*
Authors who died between 1800 and 1899	*NINETEENTH-CENTURY LITERATURE CRITICISM (NCLC)*
Authors who died between 1400 and 1799	*LITERATURE CRITICISM FROM 1400 TO 1800 (LC) SHAKESPEAREAN CRITICISM (SC)*
Authors who died before 1400	*CLASSICAL AND MEDIEVAL LITERATURE CRITICISM (CMLC)*
Black writers of the past two hundred years	*BLACK LITERATURE CRITICISM (BLC) AND BLACK LITERATURE CRITICISM SUPPLEMENT (BLCS)*
Authors of books for children and young adults	*CHILDREN'S LITERATURE REVIEW (CLR)*
Dramatists	*DRAMA CRITICISM (DC)*
Hispanic writers of the late nineteenth and twentieth centuries	*HISPANIC LITERATURE CRITICISM (HLC)*
Native North American writers and orators of the eighteenth, nineteenth, and twentieth centuries	*NATIVE NORTH AMERICAN LITERATURE (NNAL)*
Poets	*POETRY CRITICISM (PC)*
Short story writers	*SHORT STORY CRITICISM (SSC)*
Major authors from the Renaissance to the present	*WORLD LITERATURE CRITICISM, 1500 TO THE PRESENT (WLC)*
Major authors and works from the Bible to the present	*WORLD LITERATURE CRITICISM SUPPLEMENT (WLCS)*

ISSN 0091-3421

Volume 127

Contemporary Literary Criticism

Criticism of the Works
of Today's Novelists, Poets, Playwrights,
Short Story Writers, Scriptwriters, and
Other Creative Writers

Jeffrey W. Hunter
EDITOR

Jenny Cromie
ASSOCIATE EDITOR

Rebecca J. Blanchard
Vince Cousino
Justin Karr
Linda Pavlovski
ASSISTANT EDITORS

GALE GROUP

Detroit
New York
San Francisco
London
Boston
Woodbridge, CT

STAFF

Jeffrey W. Hunter, *Editor*

...mie, Justin Karr, Timothy J. White, *Associate Editors*
Rebecca J. Blanchard, Vince Cousino, Linda Pavlovski, *Assistant Editors*

Maria Franklin, *Permissions Manager*
Kimberly F. Smilay, *Permissions Specialist*
Erin Bealmear and Sandy Gore, *Permissions Associates*

Victoria B. Cariappa, *Research Manager*
Corrine Boland, Wendy Festerling, Tamara Nott, Tracie A. Richardson, *Research Associates*
Tim Lehnerer, Patricia Love, *Research Assistants*

Mary Beth Trimper, *Production Director*
Cindy Range, *Production Assistants*

Barbara J. Yarrow, *Graphic Services Manager*
Sherrell Hobbs, *Macintosh Artist*
Randy Bassett, *Image Database Supervisor*
Robert Duncan and Mikal Ansari, *Scanner Operators*
Pamela Reed, *Imaging Coordinator*
Kelly A. Quin, *Image Editor*

Library of Congress Catalog Card Number 76-46132
ISBN 0-7876-3202-3
ISSN 0091-3421

Printed in the United States of America
10 9 8 7 6 5 4 3 2 1

Contents

Preface vii

Acknowledgments xi

Preface

A Comprehensive Information Source
on Contemporary Literature

Named "one of the twenty-five most distinguished reference titles published during the past twenty-five years" by *Reference Quarterly,* the *Contemporary Literary Criticism (CLC)* series provides readers with critical commentary and general information on more than 2,000 authors now living or who died after December 31, 1959. Previous to the publication of the first volume of *CLC* in 1973, there was no ongoing digest monitoring scholarly and popular sources of critical opinion and explication of modern literature. *CLC,* therefore, has fulfilled an essential need, particularly since the complexity and variety of contemporary literature makes the function of criticism especially important to today's reader.

Scope of the Series

CLC presents significant passages from published criticism of works by creative writers. Since many of the authors covered by *CLC* inspire continual critical commentary, writers are often represented in more than one volume. There is, of course, no duplication of reprinted criticism.

Authors are selected for inclusion for a variety of reasons, among them the publication or dramatic production of a critically acclaimed new work, the reception of a major literary award, revival of interest in past writings, or the adaptation of a literary work to film or television.

Attention is also given to several other groups of writers—authors of considerable public interest—about whose work criticism is often difficult to locate. These include mystery and science fiction writers, literary and social critics, foreign writers, and authors who represent particular ethnic groups.

Format of the Book

Each *CLC* volume contains individual essays and reviews taken from hundreds of book review periodicals, general magazines, scholarly journals, monographs, and books. Entries include critical evaluations spanning from the beginning of an author's career to the most current commentary. Interviews, feature articles, and other published writings that offer insight into the author's works are also presented. Students, teachers, librarians, and researchers will find that the generous critical and biographical material in *CLC* provides them with vital information required to write a term paper, analyze a poem, or lead a book discussion group. In addition, complete bibliographical citations note the original source and all of the information necessary for a term paper footnote or bibliography.

Features

A *CLC* author entry consists of the following elements:

- The **Author Heading** cites the author's name in the form under which the author has most commonly published, followed by birth date, and death date when applicable. Uncertainty as to a birth or death date is indicated by a question mark.

- A **Portrait** of the author is included when available.

- A brief **Biographical and Critical Introduction** to the author and his or her work precedes the criticism. The first line of the introduction provides the author's full name, pseudonyms (if applicable), nationality, and a listing of genres in which the author has written. To provide users with easier access to information, the biographical and critical essay included in each author entry is divided into four categories: "Introduction," "Biographical Information," "Major Works," and "Critical Reception." The introductions to single-work entries—entries that focus on well known and frequently studied books, short stories, and poems—are similarly organized to quickly provide readers with information on the plot and major characters of the work being discussed, its major themes, and its critical reception. Previous volumes of *CLC* in which the author has been featured are also listed in the introduction.

- A list of **Principal Works** notes the most important writings by the author. When foreign-language works have been translated into English, the English-language version of the title follows in brackets.

- The **Criticism** represents various kinds of critical writing, ranging in form from the brief review to the scholarly exegesis. Essays are selected by the editors to reflect the spectrum of opinion about a specific work or about an author's literary career in general. The critical and biographical materials are presented chronologically, adding a useful perspective to the entry. All titles by the author featured in the entry are printed in boldface type, which enables the reader to easily identify the works being discussed. Publication information (such as publisher names and book prices) and parenthetical numerical references (such as footnotes or page and line references to specific editions of a work) have been deleted at the editor's discretion to provide smoother reading of the text.

- Critical essays are prefaced by **Explanatory Notes** as an additional aid to readers. These notes may provide several types of valuable information, including: the reputation of the critic, the importance of the work of criticism, the commentator's approach to the author's work, the purpose of the criticism, and changes in critical trends regarding the author.

- A complete **Bibliographical Citation** designed to help the user find the original essay or book precedes each critical piece.

- Whenever possible, a recent **Author Interview** accompanies each entry.

- A concise **Further Reading** section appears at the end of entries on authors for whom a significant amount of criticism exists in addition to the pieces reprinted in *CLC*. Each citation in this section is accompanied by a descriptive annotation describing the content of that article. Materials included in this section are grouped under various headings (e.g., Biography, Bibliography, Criticism, and Interviews) to aid users in their search for additional information. Cross-references to other useful sources published by The Gale Group in which the author has appeared are also included: *Authors in the News, Black Writers, Children's Literature Review, Contemporary Authors, Dictionary of Literary Biography, DISCovering Authors, Drama Criticism, Hispanic Literature Criticism, Hispanic Writers, Native North American Literature, Poetry Criticism, Something about the Author, Short Story Criticism, Contemporary Authors Autobiography Series,* and *Something about the Author Autobiography Series.*

Other Features

CLC also includes the following features:

- An **Acknowledgments** section lists the copyright holders who have granted permission to reprint material in this volume of *CLC*. It does not, however, list every book or periodical reprinted or consulted during the preparation of the volume.

- Each new volume of *CLC* includes a **Cumulative Topic Index,** which lists all literary topics treated in *CLC, NCLC, TCLC,* and *LC 1400-1800.*

- A **Cumulative Author Index** lists all the authors who have appeared in the various literary criticism series published by The Gale Group, with cross-references to Gale's biographical and autobiographical series. A full listing of the series referenced there appears on the first page of the indexes of this volume. Readers will welcome this cumulated author index as a useful tool for locating an author within the various series. The index, which lists birth and death dates when available, will be particularly valuable for those authors who are identified with a certain period but whose death dates cause them to be placed in another, or for those authors whose careers span two periods. For example, Ernest Hemingway is found in *CLC,* yet F. Scott Fitzgerald, a writer often associated with him, is found in *Twentieth-Century Literary Criticism.*

- A **Cumulative Nationality Index** alphabetically lists all authors featured in *CLC* by nationality, followed by numbers corresponding to the volumes in which the authors appear.

- An alphabetical **Title Index** accompanies each volume of *CLC*. Listings are followed by the author's name and the corresponding page numbers where the titles are discussed. English translations of foreign titles and variations of titles are cross-referenced to the title under which a work was originally published. Titles of novels, novellas, dramas, films, record albums, and poetry, short story, and essay collections are printed in italics, while all individual poems, short stories, essays, and songs are printed in roman type within quotation marks; when published separately (e.g., T. S. Eliot's poem *The Waste Land),* the titles of long poems are printed in italics.

- In response to numerous suggestions from librarians, Gale has also produced a **Special Paperbound Edition** of the *CLC* title index. This annual cumulation, which alphabetically lists all titles reviewed in the series, is available to all customers. Additional copies of the index are available upon request. Librarians and patrons will welcome this separate index: it saves shelf space, is easy to use, and is recyclable upon receipt of the next edition.

Citing *Contemporary Literary Criticism*

When writing papers, students who quote directly from any volume in the Literary Criticism Series may use the following general forms to footnote reprinted criticism. The first example pertains to material drawn from periodicals, the second to material reprinted in books:

[1]Alfred Cismaru, "Making the Best of It," *The New Republic,* 207, No. 24, (December 7, 1992), 30, 32; excerpted and reprinted in *Contemporary Literary Criticism,* Vol. 85, ed. Christopher Giroux (Detroit: Gale, 1995), pp. 73-4.

[2]Yvor Winters, *The Post-Symbolist Methods* (Allen Swallow, 1967); excerpted and reprinted in *Contemporary Literary Criticism,* Vol. 85, ed. Christopher Giroux (Detroit: Gale, 1995), pp. 223-26.

Suggestions Are Welcome

The editors hope that readers will find *CLC* a useful reference tool and welcome comments about the work. Send comments and suggestions to: Editors, *Contemporary Literary Criticism,* The Gale Group, 27500 Drake Rd., Farmington Hills, MI 48333-3535.

Acknowledgments

The editors wish to thank the copyright holders of the excerpted criticism included in this volume and the permissions managers of many book and magazine publishing companies for assisting us in securing reproduction rights. We are also grateful to the staffs of the Detroit Public Library, the Library of Congress, the University of Detroit Mercy Library, Wayne State University Purdy/Kresge Library Complex, and the University of Michigan Libraries for making their resources available to us. Following is a list of the copyright holders who have granted us permission to reproduce material in this volume of *CLC*. Every effort has been made to trace copyright, but if omissions have been made, please let us know.

COPYRIGHTED EXCERPTS IN *CLC*, VOLUME 127, WERE REPRODUCED FROM THE FOLLOWING PERIODICALS:

Africa Today, v. 41, 1994. © Africa Today Associates. Reproduced by permission of *Africa Today,* Graduate School of International Studies, University of Denver, Denver, CO 80208.—*African American Review,* v. 32, Summer, 1998 for "Beneath the Black Aesthetic: James Baldwin's Primer of Black American Masculinity" by Andrew Shin and Barbara Judson. Copyright © 1998 by Andrew Shin and Barbara Judson. Reproduced by permission of the authors.—*American Book Review,* v. 18, October-November, 1996. Reproduced by permission.—*American Film,* v. XV, September, 1990 for "Henry and June" by Judson Klinger. Copyright 1990 by *American Film.* Reproduced by permission of the author./v. XIV, April, 1989 for "In Pursuit of Crazy Language" by Judson Klinger with Thomas McGuane. Copyright 1989 by *American Film.* Reproduced by permission of the authors.—*Ariel: A Review of International English Literature,* v. 23, April, 1992 for "Contests of Text and Context in Chinua Achebe's 'Arrow of God'" by Adeleke Adeeko. Copyright © 1992 The Board of Governors, The University of Calgary. Reproduced by permission of the publisher and the author./ v. 24, October, 1993 for "Art and Orthodoxy in Chinua Achebe's 'Anthills of the Savannah'" by Chelva Kanaganayakam. Copyright © 1993 The Board of Governors, The University of Calgary. Reproduced by permission of the publisher and the author.—*The Atlantic Monthly,* v. 209, May, 1962 for "Solace in Doing" by Edward Weeks; v. 224, July, 1969 for a review of "The Three Daughters of Madame Liang" by Edward Weeks. Both reproduced by permission of the Literary Estate of Edward Weeks.—*The Bloomsbury Review,* v. 13, July/August, 1993 for a review of "Nothing But Blue Skies" by Gregory McNamee. Copyright © by Owaissa Communications Company, Inc., 1993. Reproduced by permission of the author.—*Book World—The Washington Post,* v. XXII, October 25, 1992 for "McGuane Mellows" by David Streitfeld. © 1992 Washington Post Book World Service/Washington Post Writers Group. Reproduced by permission of the author./ v. 25, November 12, 1995. © 1995, Washington Post Book World Service/Washington Post Writers Group. Reproduced by permission.—*Buzzworm: The Environmental Journal,* v. V, January-February, 1993 for "Thomas McGuane Speaks" by Deborah Houy with Thomas McGuane. Reproduced by permission of the authors.—*Chicago Review,* v. 24, 1972. Copyright © 1972 by *Chicago Review.* Reproduced by permission.—*Chicago Sunday Tribune,* November 7, 1954; May 3, 1959. © 1954, renewed 1982; © 1959, renewed 1987 Tribune Media Services, Inc. All rights reserved. Both reproduced by permission.—*Chicago Tribune Books,* December 25, 1995 for "Barry Unsworth Rescues 'All the World's a Stage' from Cliche" by Adam Begley. © 1995 Tribune Media Services, Inc. All rights reserved. Reproduced by permission of the author./ March 9, 1997. © 1997 Tribune Media Services, Inc. All rights reserved. Reproduced by permission.—*Christian Science Monitor,* October 7, 1992. © 1992 The Christian Science Publishing Society. All rights reserved. Reproduced by permission from *The Christian Science Monitor.*—*CLA Journal,* v. XXXV, March, 1992; v. XXXVII, June, 1994. Copyright, 1992, 1994 by The College Language Association. Both used by permission of The College Language Association.—*College Literature,* v. 19, October, 1992. Copyright © 1992 by West Chester University. Reproduced by permission.—*Commonweal,* v. 104, 1977. Copyright © 1977 Commonweal Publishing Co., Inc. Reproduced by permission of Commonweal Foundation.—*Callaloo,* v. 13, 1990 for "An Interview with Chinua Achebe" by Charles H. Rowell. © 1990 by Charles H. Rowell. Reproduced by permission of The Johns Hopkins University Press.—*Critique,* v. XXXII, September, 1991; v. XXXIV, Winter, 1993. Copyright © 1991, 1993 Helen Dwight Reid Educational Foundation. Both reproduced with permission of the Helen Dwight Reid Educational

COPYRIGHTED EXCERPTS IN *CLC*, VOLUME 127, WERE REPRODUCED FROM THE FOLLOWING BOOKS:

PHOTOGRAPHS APPEARING IN *CLC*, VOLUME 127, WERE RECEIVED FROM THE FOLLOWING SOURCES:

Chinua Achebe

1930-

(Full name Albert Chinualumogu Achebe) Nigerian novelist, short story writer, poet, essayist, editor, and author of children's literature.

The following entry presents an overview of Achebe's career through 1997. For further information on his life and works, see *CLC*, Volumes 1, 3, 5, 7, 11, 26, 51, and 75.

INTRODUCTION

Widely known as "the father of the African novel in English," Achebe is one of the most significant writers to emerge from contemporary Africa with a literary vision that has profoundly influenced the form and content of modern African literature. In his novels, he has chronicled the colonization of Nigeria by Great Britain and the political turmoil following its independence. Achebe's novels represent some of the first works written in English that articulate an intimate and authentic account of African culture and mores—especially his first novel, *Things Fall Apart* (1958), which critics have proclaimed a classic of modern African fiction. A major theme of Achebe's writings is the social and psychological impact of European imperialism on indigenous African societies, particularly with respect to a distinctly African consciousness in the twentieth century. Critics have praised Achebe's novels for their insightful renditions of African history as well as balanced examinations of contemporary African politics and society. Scholars also have praised Achebe's innovative fusion of Igbo folklore, proverbs, and idiomatic expressions with Western political ideologies and Christian doctrines.

Biographical Information

Born in Ogidi, Nigeria, Achebe attended Church Mission Society School, where his Igbo (or Ibo) parents were catechists. He continued his education at Government College in Umuahia, which is considered one of the best secondary schools in West Africa. In 1948 he enrolled in the first class at the newly established University College in Ibadan, run by the University of London. As an English literature student, Achebe often contributed stories, essays, and sketches to the *University Herald.* These works eventually were collected in *Girls at War* (1972). Within a year after his graduation in 1953, Achebe began a twelve-year career as a producer for the Nigerian Broadcasting Company (NBC) in Lagos, Nigeria's capital. During these years, Achebe also began researching and writing his most famous

novel, *Things Fall Apart*, which was published two years prior to Nigerian autonomy in 1960. He followed his literary debut with three other novels—*No Longer at Ease* (1960), *Arrow of God* (1964), and *A Man of the People* (1966). By 1966, however, Nigeria's political climate worsened, deteriorating into a thirty-month civil war. Achebe quit his position at NBC and moved to the eastern region of Nigeria, which briefly seceded to become the independent state of Biafra. While there, Achebe devoted all his time to Biafran affairs and writing poetry, short stories, and essays. His most notable work during this time was his book of poetry, *Beware, Soul Brother* (1971). After the war ended in 1970, Achebe accepted a series of visiting professorships in the United States, where he founded and edited the respected African literary journal *Okike* and published *Morning Yet on Creation Day* (1975), a collection of literary and political essays written between 1962 and 1973. In 1976 Achebe returned to Nigeria where began teaching at the University of Nigeria in Nsukka. By the early 1980s, he was actively involved in Nigerian politics, serving first as the deputy national president of the People's Redemption Party and later as president of the town union in his hometown. At the same time, he also issued a polemical commentary on Nigerian leadership, *The Trouble with Nigeria* (1983). In 1987 Achebe published *Anthills of the Savannah*—his first novel after a twenty-one-year sabbatical from writing long fiction and the work that won Achebe a nomination for the prestigious Booker Prize. In 1990 Achebe nearly died from injuries sustained in an auto accident on a Nigerian highway under suspicious circumstances. Achebe spent six months recuperating in England following the accident, and moved to the United States where he continues to write and teach.

Major Works

A realistic and anthropologically informative portrait of traditional Igbo society distinguishes *Things Fall Apart*, which is named after a title from a line in Irish poet W. B. Yeats's poem "The Second Coming." Set in the village of Umuofia during the initial stages of colonization in the late 1880s, the narrative traces the conflict between Igbo and Western customs through the characterization of Okonkwo, a proud village leader whose refusal to adapt to the encroaching European influences leads him to murder and suicide. *No Longer at Ease* follows Obi Okonkwo, the grandson of the protagonist of Achebe's first novel, throughout his failure to successfully combine his traditional Igbo upbringing with his British education and affluent lifestyle in Lagos during the late 1950s. Describing Igbo village life during the 1920s, *Arrow of God* centers on Ezeulu, a spiritual leader, whose son Oduche attends a missionary school to learn about Western society and technology. When Oduche comes home, he nearly kills a sacred python, which precipitates a chain of events culminating in Ezeulu's loss of his position as high priest and his detention by British authorities. Highlighting the widespread graft and abuse of power by Nigerian leaders following its independence from Great Britain, *A Man of the People* focuses on the tribulations of a Nigerian teacher who joins a political group working to remove a corrupt bureaucrat from office. The poems of *Beware, Soul Brother*—which later was republished as *Christmas in Biafra* (1973)—reflect on the human tragedy of the Nigerian civil war, using plain language and stark imagery. Similarly, some of the stories in *Girls at War* are about aspects of imminent war. Most of the stories deal with the conflict between traditional religious values and modern, secular mores, displaying the full range of Achebe's talents for humor, irony, and political satire. Divided into two parts, *Morning Yet on Creation Day* addresses a number of literary and political themes, with special emphasis on traditional and contemporary roles of art and the writer in African society. Set in the fictional West African country of Kangan, *Anthills of the Savannah* is about three childhood friends who hold influential governmental posts. When one of them fails in his bid for election as president for life, he works to suppress his op-

position. After successfully conspiring to murder one friend, he meets a violent death during a military coup, while the third friend dies in a street riot. Generally considered Achebe's most accomplished work, *Anthills of the Savannah* illustrates the often dire consequences for society when individual responsibility and power are recklessly exploited. While retaining the use of Igbo proverbs and legends to enhance his themes, Achebe also pays more attention to the development and role of the women characters in this novel. In the book, Achebe gives women strength and composure as the agents of traditional morals and precepts. Finally, *Hopes and Impediments* (1988) gathers new and previously published essays and speeches, including a controversial essay attacking British novelist Joseph Conrad as racist. The book also includes a tribute to American novelist James Baldwin, along with several commentaries on post-colonial African society that highlight cultural forces influencing its modern-day character.

Critical Reception

Many critics regard Achebe as the finest Nigerian novelist of the twentieth century with his works often serving as the standard for judging other African literary works. Achebe's literary criticism and sociological essays also have won praise. As one of the most discussed African writers of his generation, Achebe has inspired a substantial body of criticism and scholarship about his writing and political stances. Achebe's inventive usage of Igbo proverbs and folklore in his novels is the most studied feature of his art. Scholars have mostly concentrated on the significance of proverbs in Achebe's construction of vernacular speech patterns and social conventions, as well as a way to distinguish identities of his fictional characters. Scholars also have focused on how the proverbs provide thematic control to Achebe's narrative structures. Critics note, however, that Achebe's writings have relevance beyond the borders of Nigeria and beyond the anthropological, sociological, and political concerns of post-colonial Africa. Achebe's literature also deals with the universal qualities of human nature. As Achebe has said, "My politics is concerned with universal communication across racial and cultural boundaries as a means of fostering respect for all people. . . . As long as one people sit on another and are deaf to their cry, so long will understanding and peace elude all of us."

PRINCIPAL WORKS

CRITICISM

Chinua Achebe with Charles H. Rowell (interview date 28 May 1989)

SOURCE: "An Interview with Chinua Achebe," in *Conversations with Chinua Achebe,* edited by Bernth Lindfors, University Press of Mississippi, 1997, pp. 165-84.

[*In the following interview, originally conducted on May 28, 1989, and first published in* Callaloo *in 1991, Achebe discusses the role of the writer and literature in an African context, paying particular attention to indigenous narrative traditions, the influence of the English language on the continent, and the genesis of his own identity as a writer.*]

[*Rowell:*] *Mr. Achebe, here in the United States, those of us who read twentieth-century world literature think of you as one of the most important writers in this era. We view you as an artist—and for us the word* artist *has a certain kind of meaning. In the African world, does* artist *have the same meaning as that conceptualized in the Western world? Or, more specifically, what do Nigerians conceive the writer to be?*

Is he or she thought of as an artist, a creator of the kind that we think of here in the United States when we speak about writers?

[Achebe:] Well, I think that there are obviously certain common factors when anybody talks about an artist, whether in America or in Africa. I think there are certain factors which would apply to either place—and so we can leave those aside, if you like. But there are differences definitely, in

emphasis if not absolute, and it is these that one should draw attention to. The artist has always existed in Africa in the form of the sculptor, the painter, or the storyteller, the poet. And I suppose the role of the writer, the modern writer, is closer to that of the *griot,* the historian and poet, than to any other practitioner of the arts. But I think one can find, even from the other forms of art, fundamental statements, cultural statements, made about art in general which seem to me to be peculiarly African in their emphasis.

What I mean, for instance, is this. The ceremony, which is called "*Mbari*" among the Igbo people, is a festival of art, a celebration of humanity. It is not a festival of oral arts; it is more a festival of the visual arts, the plastic arts, though drama and songs are presented there as well. There you will find, I think, what our people thought of art—and that's the reason I am referring to it. Some of the statements made by *Mbari* are very profound. One is that art is in the service of the community. There is no apology at all about that. Art is invented to make the life of the community easier, not to make it more difficult. Artists are people who live in society. The professional artist, the master artist and craftsman, is a special kind of person, but he is not the only person who is expected to practice art.

For this celebration, this *Mbari* celebration, ordinary people are brought in to work under the supervision of professional artists, because we assume that everybody has art in themselves. So ordinary people are brought in, and they are secluded with the professionals for a period—months and sometimes even years—to create this celebration of life through art. So what this says to me is that art is not something up there in the rarified reaches of the upper atmosphere but something which is down here where we live. Art is not something which is beyond the comprehension of ordinary people. It is something which ordinary people not only can understand and use, but even take part in making. So these are ideas which I don't find very much in the West, you see. These are some of the ideas we have that one should specify and draw attention to. If one looked at what we do and compared it with what our contemporaries do in the West, these ideas would explain some of the differences and some of the puzzlement that certain Western critics have, for instance, when they encounter African literature and say: "Why do they do that? Why are they so political?" And they ask these questions to the point of irritation. If only they understood where we were coming from, then perhaps they would not be so puzzled. Perhaps they would even be open to persuasion on this score.

At the University of Virginia, last April [19, 1989], you responded to a question from the audience which I think describes further what you have just said or is related to it. I can't quote you directly. However, I do remember that you implied that art, in Nigeria, is intimately linked to social responsibility and that it is connected to that which is moral, that which is ethical, that which is right, or that which is good. I think you made that statement in response to a question about Joseph Conrad—and I'm not trying to get into a Joseph Conrad discussion here. Will you say more about art?

Yes. The festival which I have just been talking about, the *Mbari* festival, is commanded from time to time by the goddess of creativity, the earth goddess, called *Ala* or *Ani* by the Igbo people. This goddess is not only responsible for creativity in the world; she is also responsible for morality. So that an abomination is described as taboo to her, as *nso-ani*. That's the word for something which is not supposed to be done—not just a wrongdoing—but an abomination, something which is forbidden by this goddess. So obviously by putting the two portfolios, if you like, of art and morality in her domain, a statement is being made about the meaning of art. Art cannot be in the service of destruction, cannot be in the service of oppression, cannot be in the service of evil. We tend to be a little apologetic about that. You know, if you talk about "good," people will get uneasy. They become uneasy. I don't know why that should be so, but we work ourselves into all kinds of corners from which we then become uneasy when certain words are mentioned. That's not the fault of the words; there is perhaps something wrong with us.

So there is no question at all, in the view of my people, that art cannot serve immorality. And morality here doesn't mean "be good and go to church." That's not what I'm talking about. I'm talking about manifest wickedness like murder. There is no art that can say that it is right to commit murder. I remember, I think it was Yevtushenko who once said that "You cannot be a poet and a slave trader." It seems to me fairly obvious that you cannot combine those particular professions, because they are antithetical. And this is not something which only the Africans or the Igbo people know, I think it is there, embedded also, in the minds of other people. The difference is that our culture makes no bones about it, and I think this comes through too in our writing. It does not mean that our heroes have to be angels. Of course not. It means, in fact, that heroes will be as human as anybody else; and yet the frontier between good and evil must not be blurred: it means that somewhere, no matter how fuzzy it may be to us, there is still a distinction between what is permissible and what is not permissible. One thing which is not permissible is to stereotype and dehumanize your fellows. That is not permissible in our art. You celebrate them, their good and their bad. You celebrate even rascals, because they abound in the world and are part of its richness.

You just said that this conceptualization of art comes

through "in our writing." Will you talk about how this is exemplified in your own work or that of other African writers, either consciously or unconsciously?

Well, I think if you took a tape recorder and went around African writers, I bet you will find them making rather large statements for what they do. You'll find them saying, for instance, "I am writing so that the life of my people will be better." I even found a modern story in Hausa which ended: "And so they married and they produced many sons and daughters who helped to raise the standard of education in the country." That's the way the story ends, imitating the format of the folk story but obviously turning it into something very practical for today, you see. And I said elsewhere, if anybody reads this story and says "oh now, this is an anticlimax," he could not possibly know anything about Africa, because the story of today has to do with raising the standards of education of the country, you see. We are engaged in a great mission, and we attempt to bring this into our storytelling. It is this mission that our storyteller brings into his tale without the slightest inclination to discuss it self-consciously in the way we are doing now. He instinctively felt a need for his story and supplied it. This is why we get letters saying, to me for instance, "Why did you let Okonkwo fail in **Things Fall Apart**? Why did you let a good man or a good cause stumble and fall?" At another time, I remember a letter from a woman in Ghana saying, "Why did Obi, in **No Longer at Ease,** not have the courage to marry the girl he loved instead of crumbling?" People are expecting from literature serious comment on their lives. They are not expecting frivolity. They are expecting literature to say something important to help them in their struggle with life.

That is what literature, what art, was supposed to do: to give us a second handle on reality so that when it becomes necessary to do so, we can turn to art and find a way out. So it is a serious matter. That's what I'm saying, and I think every African writer you talk to will say something approaching what I have just said—in different forms of words, except those who have too much of the West in them, and there are some people, of course, who are that way. But the writer I am referring to is the real and serious African writer. I think you will find them saying something which sounds as serious, as austere, or as earnest as what I have just said.

You've mentioned the griot. *I have read many things about what a* griot *is. And sometimes these texts seem to contradict each other. What is a* griot? *The word itself sounds Francophone.*

It's a word that comes from somewhere: I don't even know where it comes from. I know it certainly is not a Nigerian word. It's not an Igbo word. But it is a word which concerns us, because we know roughly what kind of person we are talking about. We are talking about the traditional poet and historian. The function of this person would not be exactly the same thing in all cultures. Where you have a monarchical system, for instance, the chances are that the *griot* or the poet, this historian, would be connected with the history of the dynasty. This is supposedly where problems immediately arise, you know. How reliable, then, is this poet, who resides in the court of the emperor, reciting the history? There are problems there. And the greatest *griots,* I think, have managed to find a way around those problems. How they do it we cannot go into here. It suffices to remind us that 700 years after the life and death of Sundiata, the first emperor of Mali, the *griots* in West Africa were still reciting the story of his birth and life and death. It was only in the fifties, the 1950s, that this story was finally put down in writing. And the person who put it down in writing went to different and widely separated places and compared the versions given by various *griots* and discovered that the core of the story remained the same, you see. This is quite remarkable: over a period of 700 years . . . because we tend to think that unless something is scribbled down on some piece of paper it cannot be true. I don't know who told us that. And we have come to believe it ourselves, that our history should be measured in terms of paper. So whenever you don't have a piece of paper, somebody says there is no history. And we seem to be quite ready to accept it. So you would find our historians going to archives in Portugal, for instance, to see what some sailor from Portugal had said when he came to Benin in the fifteenth century. We don't ask the condition of this sailor when he was making his entry, whether he was drunk or sober. He is on a piece of paper and therefore reliable—and more reliable than what you might gather in the field by asking people: "What do you remember? What do your people remember about this?"

Anyway, I think we are learning. We know a little better now than we used to. Thanks to the work of people like the late Professor Dike, who helped to create a new historiography of Africa using the oral tradition. We know now that we can find some of the truth in oral traditions. Now, to get back to the problem of the *griot,* let me tell the story of one short fable in Hausa, which I think exemplifies the way a *griot* might approach his problem obliquely, because if you are dealing with the emperor who is so much more powerful than yourself, you have to have your wits around you. If you start telling a story which puts him in a bad light or a bad mood, your career will be very short indeed! So you have to find a way of getting around this problem.

Now this is a story, a very simple animal story, from the Hausa language, which I encountered years ago. And I have used it again and again because I think it is a marvelous little story. In my own words, it goes something like this: The snake was riding his horse, coiled up in his saddle.

That's the way the snake rode his horse. And he came down the road and met the toad walking by the roadside. And the toad said to him. "Excuse me, sir, but that's not how to ride a horse." And the snake said, "No? Can you show me then?" And the toad said, "Yes, if you would step down, sir." So the snake came down. The toad jumped into the saddle and sat bolt upright and galloped most elegantly up and down the toad. When he came back he said, "That's how to ride a horse." And the snake said, "Excellent. Very good. Very good, indeed. Thank you. Come down, if you don't mind." So the toad came down, and the snake went up and coiled himself in the saddle as he was used to doing and then said to the toad. "It is very good to know, but it is even better to have. What good does excellent horsemanship do to a man without a horse?" And with that he rode away.

Now, the Hausa, who made this story, are a monarchical people. They have classes: the emir, the upper class, the nobility, etc., down to the bottom, the ordinary people, the *talakawa.* As you can see, the snake in this story is an aristocrat, and the toad a commoner. The statement, even the rebuke, which the snake issues is, in fact, saying: "Keep where you belong. You see, people like me are entitled to horses, and we don't have to know how to ride. There's no point in being an expert. That's not going to help you." Now that's very nice in that kind of political situation. And we can visualize the emir and his court enjoying this kind of story and laughing their heads off—because, you see, it's putting the commoner in his place. But also if you think deeply about this story, it's a two-edged sword. I think that's the excellence of the *griot* who fashioned it. To put this other edge to it, which is not noticed at first . . . this other side is that the snake is incompetent, the snake is complacent, the snake is even unattractive. It's all there in the story, you see, and the time will come in this political system when all this will be questioned. Why is it that a snake is entitled to a horse? Why is it that the man who knows how to ride does not have a horse to ride? You see. This questioning will come in a revolutionary time, and when it comes you don't need another story. It is the same story that will stand ready to be used; and this to me is the excellence of the *griot* in creating laughter and hiding what you might call the glint of steel. In the voluminous folds of this laughter, you can catch the hint of a concealed weapon which will be used when the time comes. Now this is one way in which the *griot* gets around the problem of telling the emperor the truth, you see. That is very, very important. Of course, if the *griot* is strong enough to say this to the emperor in his face, he will do it. But if he is not, he will find a way to conceal his weapon. Of course, there will be *griots* who sell out, but we're not talking about those, those who sing for their dinner.

After your reading-lecture at the University of Virginia last April, one of my graduate students, a native of

Mauritania, said to me: "In this culture, meaning the Western culture, you meet knowledge, you meet erudition, you meet expertise, but not wisdom. Mr. Achebe speaks and writes wisdom." That was what the student, Mohamed B. Taleb-Khyar, said, and I quote him directly.

That was very kind of him.

What I would like to ask of you is this: Does this speaking wisdom characterize, in any way, the sensibility of the African artist?

Yes. I think it does. Wisdom is as good a word to use, I think, in describing the seriousness I was talking about, this *gravitas* that I'm talking about which informs our art. We can be as jovial, as lighthearted, even as frivolous as anybody else. But everything has its place and its measure. When you are dealing with art of the level at which we are dealing with it, it's a serious matter, a matter of clarification and wisdom.

You are a teacher—in the United States we would say that you are a professor—of literature. What is the status of teaching literature in Africa? That's to say, does the teaching of literature contribute positively or negatively in the development, for example, of the new Nigeria? In other words, what is the role of the humanities in the African context?

Well, we as writers and artists have or should have a central role in the society. We are not necessarily carrying the day in that way of thinking. For instance, when I gave the National Lecture in Nigeria (which you give if you win the Nigerian National Merit Award which is our highest honor for intellectual achievement), the lecture I gave recently in Nigeria was entitled **"What Has Literature Got To Do With It?"** It was about the problem of development which concerns all of us. How do we develop, how do we raise our standard of living, how do we improve the life of our people, how do we modernize, and all of that which we aspire to like anybody else? How do we even raise the income per capita? All of these things are important. What I'm asking is: What has literature got to do with them? Has literature any relevance to all this or is it simply something we can perhaps forget for the time being? Are we to concentrate on the hard sciences, and then perhaps when we have become developed we can afford the luxury of literature. Is that what we want? There will be people who say so. There are attempts, for instance, to shift the emphasis in the universities in Nigeria from the humanities to the sciences, to limit the admissions for the humanities and increase the admissions for the sciences. Now all that, of course, may be necessary. I really don't know, but I think any people who neglect the importance of addressing the minds and hearts and the spirit of the people will find that

they will be really getting nowhere at all in their development. One of the examples I gave was a story told us in Japan.

Some years ago I was taking part in a symposium in Japan. The Japanese would bring two foreign experts to Japan to meet with about half a dozen local experts in similar disciplines. They would talk and discuss for three or four days. On this occasion, the subject was culture and development. I remember the story which a Japanese professor told. His grandfather went to the University of Tokyo and graduated, he said, I think, about 1900. All of his notes, the notes he wrote in the university as a student, were written in English. His own father graduated about 1920. Half of his notes were written in English and half in Japanese. Then he, the man who was telling us the story, graduated in 1950 or thereabouts, from the same university. All his notes were written in Japanese. Now this profile is very interesting. The Japanese were becoming giants in the modern world, in technology and so on, surpassing those who began the industrial revolution. They were also, as it were, travelling back to regain their own culture through their language, you see. This is very important; I think this is an extremely important story. It says something about the relationship between technology and the humanities.

How far can you develop without dealing with certain humanistic problems, such as who am I, why am I here, what is the meaning of life, what is my culture? I believe that the relationship is close, important and crucial.

You teach literature courses. You told me that you teach African literature frequently. But when you teach a literature course that does not include an African literary text, what are some of the creative works or texts you select?

No, I have never taught anything but African literatures, and I'm not really a professional literature teacher. The only reason I got into teaching at all is that I wanted to teach African literature. So I taught African literature from the start. I guess I've not done anything else in my teaching career.

If you were teaching a course in twentieth-century literature, what are some of the texts you'd use? And why would you select them? I guess, ultimately, I'm asking this: What are some of the twentieth-century texts you consider to be important? For example, I couldn't imagine teaching a course in twentieth-century American literature without including Ralph Ellison's Invisible Man *or William Faulkner's* Absalom, Absalom! *or Toni Morrison's* Sula. *In other words, what do you consider some of the most important texts for teaching twentieth-century world literature?*

Well, it's not really a question I can answer satisfactorily. The texts you mention are all very important—and there are other important ones as well. I wouldn't really be able to or want to rattle off a list just like that, but I would certainly try to cover the world. I would attempt to cover those writers who have written what you call "the landmarks" of the twentieth century. And I guess that would include people like T. S. Eliot, would include Ezra Pound, would include Faulkner, would include Hemingway. Then if you come nearer to our time . . . yes, yes, *Invisible Man* is an outstanding novel by any stretch of the imagination—and I would include it for that reason and also for the reason that Ellison is writing from a history and a tradition which have a unique message for us. I would include one—at least one—Baldwin text. From African literature I would include *Ambiguous Adventure* by Cheikh Hamidou Kane, I would include Camara Laye and Amos Tutuola. I would include Alex La Guma and Nadine Gordimer. Then I would attempt to find, even in translation, some Arabic writers from Egypt. Naguib Mahfouz and Alifa Rifaat, for example. Then I would attempt to include writers from India, Raja Rao for example. That doesn't cover the whole world. Then I would move to Latin America, you see. I would include Neruda and Marquez. Actually, some of the most interesting writing is taking place there. I would also go to the Caribbean which, for its size, is perhaps the most dynamic literary environment in the world in our time. There is a legion of people there I would want to include. So you see I would have really to end up with a very long list and then begin to pare it down. But the important thing I would attempt to do is not to limit myself to anybody's "Great Tradition," because that sort of thing limits you and blinds you to what is going on in the real world.

Are there other reasons that you would not include "anybody's 'Great Tradition'"?

No, no, I said I would go beyond anyone's "Great Tradition." Why? Because it is not the "Great Tradition." It cannot be. No way. One small corner of the world cannot wake up one morning and call its artifact the "Great Tradition," you see. Our people have a saying that the man who's never traveled thinks that his mother makes the best soup. Now we need to travel—with all due respect to our mothers—we need to travel. So the question of a "Great Tradition" makes sense only if you're not aware of other people's traditions.

I had a very curious experience in Holland, where I was put up to run as president of International PEN. An older, much older, man, a Frenchman, was put up also—or he put himself up after he saw my name. And he won. But the interesting thing is that he had no conception—and didn't want to have any conception—of the literature of Africa. He kept quite clearly and studiously avoiding any mention of African literature, and at some point he said something like this:

"How can we expect the Third World, with all of their problems, to produce great art?" Do you see what I mean? Now this is the kind of mind or mentality I'm talking about. It remains alien to me though I encounter it frequently. It is alien to me because my whole life has been ordered in such a way that I have to know about other people. This is one of the penalties of being an underdog: that you have to know about the overdog, you see. The overdog doesn't need to know about the underdog; therefore, he suffers severe limitations, and the underdog ends up being wiser because he knows about himself and knows about the overdog. So my reading list would be really catholic, would be catholic in every sense of the word. I haven't talked about the Far East, because I don't know enough, but I will try and find, for example, some good writers from Japan. One must read the Japanese novelists. Their own contribution to the consciousness of the twentieth century is unique.

Is the Third World writer presently participating in the ongoing revision of what one calls "the literary canon"?

Oh yes, yes. By just being there. He/she is, in fact, the reason for the revision. He/she is the very reason for the revision.

Isn't the Third World writer something else other than what we just said? The matter I'm thinking of here is linguistic. Let us assume for a moment that Percy Shelley was correct when he said that "the poet is the legislator of the world." The poet is indeed a person who shapes our vision of the world; he or she does that and provides us with a vocabulary, or new vocabulary, to describe it. I'm thinking of you and what you do for the English-speaking world as a writer, and what Jorges Luis Borges does, or did, for the Spanish-speaking world, and what Aimé Césaire does linguistically, for example, for the French-speaking world. In other words, does the Third World writer alter or adapt the medium and, through a destruction of what is out there as—I'll call it this—"the parent language or dialect" itself, revise or reinvest the medium?

Well, yes. My answer to the previous question was rather brief, but it was really intended to contain all of this. This Third World creature comes with an experience which is peculiar, including the linguistic experience. The use of French, in the case of Césaire, is the use of a French that has been in dialogue with other languages, you see. In my case, it is an English which has been in dialogue with a very rich alien linguistic milieu—that is, you have African languages strong in their own right, and an African history and experience. An English which has had this particular encounter cannot be the same as the English of Kingsley Amis writing in London. So this is something which the members of the metropolis have to deal with, and they don't always like it. But it is not really something for me to worry about. I know some people who are worried, and they say, "Look what they are doing to my language!" They are horrified.

We come with this particular preparation which, as it happens, actually enriches the metropolitan languages. But that's not why we do it; we're not doing it in order to enrich the metropolitan language. We're doing it because this is the only way we can convey the story of ourselves, the way we can celebrate ourselves in our new history and the new experience of colonialism, and all the other things. We have had to fashion a language that can carry the story we are about to tell.

It's not all so new, even though, perhaps, it's happening now on such a wide scale that we are paying more attention to it than before. But if you think, for instance, of all the great writers in English in our century, they are virtually all Irish. Why is that so? This is very important, and I think it is the same situation. James Joyce, of course, addresses it directly and talks about it in that famous passage in which Stephen Daedalus is talking about what the English language means to him and to his teacher who is English. He muses on the fact that every word he says means something different to each of them—any word, "ale" or "Christ"; no word can mean the same thing to me as it does to him. Why? Because we colonials and excolonials come to the English language with a whole baggage of peculiar experiences which the English person doesn't have. This is what has made the English language, in our time, such a powerful force in literature. This is why we're talking about the Caribbean literature and about African literature.

Will you elaborate on a statement you just made about using a new form of English? You said that it (the new form of the medium) was the only "way we can convey the history of ourselves." You said we use the language in the way we do because this is the only way we can convey the history or the story of ourselves. Apparently, you are talking about the nature of that revised form, or the new fabric, of English.

Well, take Nigeria. Nigeria is a vibrant cultural environment. It has been for a long time. It has, literally, two hundred languages—not all of them important, but some quite big. The three main Nigerian languages are spoken by at least ten million people each, and some of them, like Hausa, cross beyond Nigeria's borders to other places. The English language arrives in Nigeria, then, and is thrown into this very active linguistic environment. Of course, it has the special privilege of being the language of administration, the language of higher education—the *lingua franca,* in fact, the language in which the various indigenous political and linguistic entities can communicate among themselves. Unless he learns the Igbo language, the Hausa man will communicate with the Igbo man in English. A Yoruba man communicates with a Hausa man in English. We're talking about Nigeria. And this has gone on for a number of generations. English, then, acquires a particular position of importance. You must recognize this, unless, of course, you agree with some of my friends who have said that we should ignore this history and ignore this reality and ignore whatever advantage of mutual communication English has brought to our very complex situation. Unless you were to accept that extreme position, you would have to say, "What will we do with this English language that's been knocking around here now for so long?" Our people don't allow anything as powerful as that to keep knocking around without having a job to do, because it would cause trouble.

This is the whole point of that *Mbari* phenomenon that I was describing earlier, in which anything which is new and powerful, which appears in the horizon, is brought in and domesticated in the *Mbari* house with all the other things that have been around, so that it doesn't have the opportunity to stay out of sight and scheme to overthrow the environment. This is what art does. Something comes along and you bring it in—and even if you don't yet fully understand it, you give it a place to stand. This is the way in which we have been using the English language to tell our story. It's not the only way we can tell our story, of course. I can tell our story in the Igbo language. It would be different in many ways. It would also not be available to as many people, even within the Nigerian environment. So this is the reality: this English, then, which I am using, has witnessed peculiar events in my land that it has never experienced anywhere else. The English language has never been close to Igbo, Hausa, or Yoruba anywhere else in the world. So it has to be different, because these other languages and their environment are not inert. They are active, and they are acting on this language which has invaded their territory. And the result of all this complex series of actions and reactions is the language we use. The language I write in. And, therefore, it comes empowered by its experience of the encounter with me. One advantage it has is this: Although it is thus different, it is not so different that you would have to go to school to learn it in America or in India or Kenya or anywhere English is already spoken. So it definitely has certain advantages which we can only ignore to our own disadvantage. It is a world language in a way that Hausa, Yoruba, Igbo are not. There is no way we can change that. Now that is not to say that we should therefore send these other languages to sleep. That's not what I'm saying. I am saying that we have a very, very complex and dynamic multilingual situation, which we cannot run away from but contain and control.

No Longer at Ease *addresses the problem of communication in particular terms. There are moments in the* *novel when there's a lack of communication. This problem revolves around Obi, your central character. Will you comment on the issues related to language and its failure as a medium in modern society?*

Well, yes, language is of course a marvelous tool of communication. This is what makes us different from cattle, that we have language and we are able to communicate with the precision that language brings. But even this is not enough. We all know that. Sometimes we say, "I know what I want to say, but I just can't find the words to say it." In other words, language is not absolutely perfect; there are still things we struggle to express. Sometimes we approach fairly close to what we feel, what we want to say, but at other times no. So it's not surprising that there should be problems in communication, even though we've got language in the technical sense of just using words. But, of course, you can be using the same words and still not communicate, because of other blocks, of other factors. People can refuse to listen. People can for all kinds of reasons not want to accept the message.

That failure of communication, for instance, between Obi and Clara is interesting. They speak the same language but there is a communication breakdown. Obi is saying "just give me a little more time, my mother is sick, let's wait, we'll get married later on." Now, Clara cannot understand that, you see, and it's not because she's unreasonable. She's very reasonable. She's so reasonable that she had foreseen this problem before, and warned Obi about it, you see. She is not going to allow herself to be brutalized over and over again; this is why she'd taken the humiliating pains to say: "Do you know that you're not supposed to marry someone like me?" Obi says, "Nonsense, we're beyond that, we're civilized people." And now that Clara has invested her life in this civilization she's being told: "Let's wait a minute." So this is an example of my own view of the breakdown in communication because it's not that either party does not understand the words being used, it's just that no words can solve their predicament. There's no way you can resolve this particular problem in any kind of language; we are at an impasse, and it's now beyond language. But we have no better tool than language to communicate with one another. So when language fails, what do we do? We resort to fighting, but that, of course, is destructive. So language is very important, it is a hallmark of our humanity, one of the hallmarks of our humanity, but it is never enough, even that is not enough. We work at it, we give it all the patience we have, but we must expect that even when all is said and done there will always remain those areas, those instances when we are unable to get across.

What about Obi and communication with his family?

Well, the same kind of thing is happening but not to the same degree, obviously. Between him and his mother there is a very peculiar relationship that has been built up from birth, which he's in no position to deal with at all. He can deal with his father quite abruptly, in fact, and overwhelm him, but he doesn't even try with his mother. This is a relationship we may not comprehend unless we come from a culture like his. There's no way he can argue with his mother when she says, "well, if you're going to marry that girl, wait until I'm dead. You won't have very long to wait." In some cultures they say "to hell with that, she's had her own life, this is my life." That's not the Igbo people, you know. There's no way Obi can respond like that. So that's communication again. One part of Obi knows that he can say "mother, I can't wait." Another part of him says "you can't say that to your mother."

Critics have often described Okonkwo in **Things Fall Apart** *as representative of a kind of Aristotelian tragic hero. How do you respond to critics reading Okonkwo as a hero in terms of Aristotle's concept of tragedy?*

No, I don't think I was responding to that particular format. This is not, of course, to say that there is no relationship between these. If we are to believe what we are hearing these days, the Greeks did not drop from the sky. They evolved in a certain place which was very close to Africa. Very close to Egypt which in itself was also very close to the Sudan and Nubia which was very close to West Africa. So it may well turn out, believe it or not, that some of the things Aristotle was saying about tragedy were not really unheard of in other cultures. It's just that we are not yet ready to make these quantum leaps! For instance, it has been shown that one-third of the entire vocabulary of ancient Greek came from Egypt and the Middle East. And so obviously there were links with us which the Greeks themselves apparently had no problem acknowledging. It was only late, from the eighteenth century, that the Europeans began to find it difficult to accept that they owed anything to Africa. In any event, I think a lot of what Aristotle says makes sense. Putting it in a neat, schematic way may be peculiar to the Greek way of thinking about the hero. But that idea is not necessarily foreign to other people: the man who's larger than life, who exemplifies virtues that are admired by the community, but also a man who for all that is still human. He can have flaws, you see; all that seems to me to be very elegantly underlined in Aristotle's work. I think they are there in human nature itself, and would be found in other traditions even if they were not spelled out in the same exact way.

Would you agree that there are patterns of irony or an extensive use of irony in all of your first four novels, from **Things Fall Apart** *all the way down to* **No Longer at Ease***? If there are ironic situations or ironic characters,* *will you talk about that irony? I really don't like to ask writers to talk about their own work.*

I think irony is one of the most powerful (how does one say it?) . . . one of the most powerful conditions in human experience. And anybody who is a storyteller—I see myself as a storyteller—will sooner or later come to the realization that ironies are among the most potent devices available to them. Irony can raise a humdrum story to a totally new level of power and significance simply by the fact of its presence, the presence of ironic juxtaposition. That's really all I can say. Your question seems to me almost like asking what do I think about metaphors. Well, you can't even begin to tell a story without saying *this thing* is like *that thing.* Or even *this thing* is *that thing.* Or, as in an almost grotesque proverb of Igbo, *the corpse of another person is a log of wood.* Of course, we know that somebody else's body is not a log of wood; but it could be so for all we care. We don't seem to be able to put ourselves inside that box. We do not say "there go I but for the grace of God." We lack the imagination to leap into that box. And if we didn't the world would have been a much more wholesome place. The oppression in the world would not be as great as it is. The inhumanity we practice would be greatly reduced. But because we lack the metaphoric imagination we are unable to make that imaginative leap from out of our own skin into somebody else's. And so our storytellers jolt us with metaphor and irony, and remind us that "there but for the grace of God go I." Without metaphor and irony things would be white or black, and not very interesting. It's only when you show that this white is also black that something very interesting and important begins to happen.

In this interview, you have, I've noticed, in more than one instance, used a tale to illustrate your point. You have also used the proverb. I suddenly remember the narrator of **Things Fall Apart** *talking about the importance of proverbs in Igbo conversation.*

Proverbs are miniature tales; they are the building blocks, if you like, of tales. They are tales refined to their simplest form, because a good proverb is a short story. It is very short indeed. What it demonstrates, first of all—before we go on to the why—is the clarity with which those who made these proverbs had observed their reality. A proverb is a very careful observation of reality and the world, and then a distillation into the wisdom of an elegant statement so that it sticks in the mind. You see it, you know it's true, you tell yourself, "this is actually true, why hadn't I thought of it," and you remember it. And there is a whole repertory of these statements made by my people across the millennia. Some must have fallen out of use; others have remained and have been passed on from one generation to the next. And part of the training, of socialization of young people

in this society, is to become familiar with these statements from our immemorial past. So that when we are dealing with a contemporary situation, when we are dealing with here and now, we have the opportunity to draw from the proverbial repertory to support or refute what is said. It's like citing the precedents in law. This case before us is what we are talking about. But similar things have happened before; look at the way our ancestors dealt with them down the ages. So it gives one a certain stability, it gives one a certain connectedness; it banishes, it helps to banish the sense of loneliness, the cry of desolation: why is this happening to me, what have I done, woe is me! The proverb is saying no, it's tough, but our ancestors made this proverb about this kind of situation, so it must have happened to someone else before you, possibly even to a whole lot of other people before. Therefore, take heart, people survived in the face of this kind of situation before. So proverbs do many kinds of things. They are, just for their elegance as literary forms, interesting and satisfying; then they ground us in our "Great Tradition"; they tell us something about the importance of observing our reality carefully, very carefully.

We know you in the United States as a novelist mainly. But you're also a poet, a critic, and a short story writer. Does the poem, or the essay, or the short story do something for you that the novel cannot do?

Yes, I think so, I think so. Though, I hope you won't ask me what it is, because that would be more difficult. But suddenly I have not been writing short stories for some time; there was a period in my life when I wrote a lot of short stories. At that point I was not writing novels. There was also a period when I wrote much poetry, much for me; now I rarely write poetry and so it must mean these forms serve me at particular times or have served me at particular times. If I may be more specific, during the Biafran war, the civil war in Nigeria, I was not writing novels for years and years and years; after that I was not in a mood to write novels. I wrote most of my poetry at that period, many of the short stories. So without saying categorically that I only write poetry in times of war, I think that there is some connection between the particular distress of war, the particular tension of war, and the kind of literary response, the genres that I have employed in that period. I remember in particular one poem, **"Christmas in Biafra,"** which actually came out of the kind of desperation which you felt hearing carols on short-wave radio and being reminded that there were places in the world where people were singing about the birth of the Prince of Peace and you were trapped in this incredible tragedy. Now it's a very powerful feeling, a very powerful feeling indeed. It is analogous to that scene in **Things Fall Apart** just before those men kill Ikemefuna and they hear in the air the sound of music from a distant clan. I don't know how those men felt hearing it: the sounds of peace and celebration in the world and a horrendous event at home. So what I'm feeling at any particular time and what the world is doing impinge on the kind of writing I do, obviously.

Earlier you said, "I see myself as a storyteller." What do you mean?

Well, that's just a manner of speaking, of again relating myself in the manner of the proverbs we are talking about to something that had happened before. So even though I don't think I'll ever be in the court of the emperor, telling stories to him and his courtiers, still I am in that tradition, you see. The story has always been with us, it is a very old thing, it is not new; it may take new forms, but it is the same old story. That's mostly what I'm saying, and we mustn't forget that we have a certain link of apostolic succession, if you like, to the old *Griots* and storytellers and poets. It helps me anyway; it gives me that sense of connectedness, of being part of things that are eternal like the rivers, the mountains, and the sky, and creation myths about man and the world. The beginning was a story, it is the story that creates man, then man makes other stories, you see. And for me this is almost like Ezeulu in **Arrow of God** who before he performs important functions in his community has to go to the beginning and tell how his priesthood came into existence. He has to recite that story to his community to validate his priestly rites. They know it already but cannot hear it too often. This is how stories came into being, and this is what they did for our ancestors and we hope that they will continue to serve our generations, not in the same form necessarily, but the same spirit.

What is the role of the literary critic in the new Nigerian society?

Well, that's a good question. I didn't want to speak for critics, but I dare say that there were ancestors of literary critics in the past; I mean spectators who might get up and say: I don't like that stuff! Obviously modern critics could claim a certain apostolic succession but quite frankly I don't think the role of their ancestors was as elevated as that of the original creators. Today when the thing is down in print on paper, I think the role of the critic has become a lot more complex and thus a lot more important. It is important because there is need for mediation. Since I'm not going to go around and meet the people and answer their questions as a storyteller would do in the past, actually meet them face to face and experience their support or disagreement, somebody else is called into existence to perhaps explain difficult parts, or perform all kinds of functions of a mediating nature. Also, there is so much which is produced, there is so much that is written, all of it is not of the same quality and a certain amount of discrimination is necessary just to survive the barrage of production in the modern world, the sheer number of books. I

think therefore the role of the critic is important. Also, I think the critic is there to draw attention to this continuity that I was talking about, to the tradition. How does this new work relate to what has happened before, how does it relate to writers who were here before, how does it even relate to those who did not write their stories but told them? So I think there is a new and necessary and important role for the critic.

I'm going to ask one more question about art and literature. Then I want to turn to a handful of questions about your background. If you had to look back on your works and judge them, is there one text or one genre which allowed you to speak or write the best way you wanted to? Or is there one of them which is more representative of the kind of expression you wanted to make?

Well, I think I can only talk about the genre, and the only reason I can talk about it is that I can lean on the simple fact of numbers. I've written more novels than I've done any other thing, and therefore that must be the one that as of now seems most congenial. But I really don't even try to think about that and even if I were tempted I would resist the thought. I would go out of my way to stop it because, as I've said, everything I have written has been useful to me at the time when I needed to write it, and I wouldn't want to say that this time is more important than that time. So apart from being able to say that obviously I have written more novels, I would not bother to rank my texts and genres, or award distinctions, even secretly.

Did your education at the University of Ibadan direct you in any way toward a career in creative writing? I guess what I'm ultimately asking is how did you come to write?

Yes, well, I think I grew up in Ibadan in a way that pointed clearly in the direction of writing. That was the period when I was able to reassess what I had read and all I had to go by at that point was the colonial novel written by white people about us. And so it was a very, very crucial moment in my career, that moment when I was reading these things again with a new awareness of what was going on, the subtle denigration, and sometimes not so subtle, that I had missed before. So in that sense it's at Ibadan that I grew up, and growing up is part of the decision to write. It did not give me the taste for writing; it was always there. Even in high school and before that, because the taste for stories was always there. I think it's simply encountering myself in literature and becoming aware that that's not me, you see. A number of texts helped; one of them was Joyce Cary's *Mister Johnson*, and I suppose one of them was Conrad's *Heart of* Darkness. There were a lot of other books not so well known and not worth remembering. But what I'm talking about is encountering the colonial ideology, for the first time in fiction, as something sinister and unacceptable. So if you add to this the weakness to stories anyway, you have the possibilities, even the incitement to become a writer, somebody who will attempt to tell his own story. Because we all have a story in us, at least one story, I believe. So in my case Ibadan was the watershed, a turning point.

At the present time we have only a bit of biographical or autobiographical public information about you, the man and the writer, and I've always wondered whether or not the Christian component of your background (your father was a mission teacher) extracted you from Igbo culture in any way?

I think it intended to, but I don't think it succeeded. Certainly it had its moments of success. But with my curiosity, my natural curiosity, I didn't allow it to succeed completely. And so there I was between two competing claims but not aware of any discomfort as a child. I was certainly aware of curiosity about the non-Christian things that were going on in my community, and I was not really convinced that because they were non-Christian they were therefore bad, or evil. And even though I met a lot of Christians who seemed to operate on the basis that everything in the traditional society was bad or evil or should be suppressed, I think that slowly, little by little, they realized too that that was really a lost hope, a wrong kind of attitude to adopt. I could see that a bit in my father. I know that he became less rigid as he grew older. The things he would not tolerate, when I was very little, I saw him not pay too much attention to later on—like traditional dancing and singing, you know. I never had any problem with those things. I was in a peculiar and an interesting position of seeing two worlds at once and finding them both interesting in their way. I mean I was moved by the Christian message. I was moved by hymns in the church. I was moved by the poetry of Christianity. I was also moved by the thing that Christianity was attempting to suppress: the traditional religion, about which at the beginning I didn't know very much. But I was going to make it my business to listen and learn and go out of my way to find out more about the religion. This is how it happened. So I was not distressed at all by being born in that kind of crossroads. On the contrary, I thought it was one of the major advantages I had as a writer.

Solomon O. Iyasere (essay date March 1992)

SOURCE: "Okonkwo's Participation in the Killing of His 'Son' in Chinua Achebe's *Things Fall Apart*: A Study of Ignoble Decisiveness," in *CLA Journal*, Vol. XXXV, No. 3, March, 1992, pp. 303-15.

[*In the following essay, Iyasere explains the thematic and structural significance of the murder of Ikemefuna in*

Things Fall Apart, focusing on the character development of Okonkwo.]

No episode in Achebe's memorable novel, ***Things Fall Apart***,[1] is more shocking and heartrending as the execution of Ikemefuna, an event too dreadful to endure. Circumstances surrounding the event make it even more hideous—if that is possible—and invite our moral revulsion more intensely than the killing of the messenger. Commenting on the significance of the murder of Ikemefuna, David Caroll writes:

> The death of Ikemefuna is a turning point in the novel. The guardianship of the boy was a mark of Okonkwo's hard-won status and the highest point of his rise to power. The execution of Ikemefuna is the beginning of Okonkwo's decline, for it initiates the series of catastrophes which ended in his death. But this event is not only a milestone in the career of the hero. The sympathetic rendering of Ikemefuna's emotions as he is being marched through the forest to his death has wider implications.[2]

As crucial as this episode is to the overall thematic and structural development of the novel, especially in the development of the central character, critics have paid only cursory attention to it. With the exception of a brief study by Damian Opata, most of the comments on the killing of Ikemefuna, particularly those treating Okonkwo's participation, have been superficial and judicial, far less extensive and vigorous than the event demands.

The vexing, and paradoxical, question raised by Ikemefuna's death is why Okonkwo takes part, particularly after Oguefi Ezeudu, a respected elder in Umuofia who understands its values and traditions and the habits of the gods, warns Okonkwo against participating:

> "That boy calls you father. Do not bear a hand in his death." Okonkwo was surprised, and was about to say some things when the old man continued: "Yes, Umuofia has decided to kill him. The Oracle of the Hills and Caves has pronounced it. They will take him there. But I want [you] to have nothing to do with it. He calls you father." (59-60)

In defense of Okonkwo's participation, Damian Opata argues that Okonkwo has no choice but to comply with the monstrous decree of the gods; further, because Ikemefuna is already regarded as a sacrificial lamb, his death already a fait accomplit, Okonkwo acts only as a messenger executing the decree of the gods. To stress Okonkwo's place as a victim who deserves our sympathy instead of our vilification, Opata writes:

Okonkwo's killing of Ikemefuna is instinctive. No time was left for him to consider his actions. In other words, his killing of Ikemefuna was not premeditated. The immediate circumstances under which he had to kill Ikemefuna seem to have been forced on him by capricious fate, he was not in control of the situation. Rather, the situation was controlling him and we should not apply the principles of morality to a situation in which he was inexorably led by uncanny fate.[3]

The inaccuracies of Opata's view derive from his uninformed reading of the text; Opata disregards the particularities of the rhetoric of Achebe's controlled presentation of Okonkwo's actions throughout the novel and of the circumstances leading to his execution of Ikemefuna. For example, nowhere in the novel is it hinted that if Okonkwo had time to reflect on the execution he would have acted differently, as Opata seems to imply. In fact, a close reading of the text shows that Okonkwo was informed of the intended execution by Oguefi Ezeudu two full days before the execution was carried out (59-60); if Okonkwo had been a man of thought and not of blind action, he would have reflected on the moral consequences of his action during those two days. To demonstrate his eagerness to participate in the execution, "Okonkwo got ready quickly [when] the party set out with Ikemefuna carrying a pot of wine" (60).

To suggest, as Opata does, that Okonkwo is a victim of fate, one forced by circumstances beyond his control to kill Ikemefuna, is inaccurate. Although the capricious gods decreed that the innocent Ikemefuna should be killed, the gods did not specifically order Okonkwo to participate in the event. The fact is that Okonkwo was free to choose not to participate in Ikemefuna's execution, as the following conversation between Okonkwo and his friend Obeirika makes plain:

> "I cannot understand why you refused to come with us to kill that boy," he [Okonkwo] asked Obeirika.
>
> "Because I did not want to," Obeirika replied sharply. "I had something better to do."
>
> "You sound as if you question the authority and the decision of the Oracle, who said he should die."
>
> "I do not. Why should I? But the Oracle did not ask me to carry out its decision."
>
> "But someone had to do it. If we were all afraid of blood, it would not be done. And what do you think the Oracle would do then?
>
> "The Earth cannot punish me for obeying her messen-

ger," Okonkwo said. "A child's fingers are not scalded by a piece of hot yam which its mother puts into its palm."

> "That is true," Obeirika agreed. "But if the Oracle said that my son should be killed, I would neither dispute it nor be the one to do it." (69)

Opata's argument that Okonkwo is a victim of fate denies him his tragic stature and thereby robs him of our deepest sympathy.

More responsive to Ikemefuna's execution and Okonkwo's role in it is David Carroll, who writes:

> This incident is not only a comment on Okonkwo's heartlessness. It criticizes implicitly the laws he is too literally implementing. . . . As we watch him [Ikemefuna] being taken unsuspectingly on his apparently innocent journey, the whole tribe and its values is [sic] being judged and found wanting. For the first time in the novel, we occupy the point of view of an outsider, a victim, and from this position the community appears cruel.[4]

Carroll's comment is to the point in directing our attention to Okonkwo's heartlessness and his literal minded acceptance of the decree of the gods. However, it does not specifically address the crucial question of whether or not Okonkwo had the choice of refusing to participate in the gods' hideous decree nor why Okonkwo interprets the gods so literally.

Okonkwo was faced with a paradoxical situation in participating in Ikemefuna's death. On the one hand, his relationship with the boy had evolved into a strong paternal/filial relationship; on the other hand, the gods decreed that the boy must die—a decree which had to be obeyed without question—as did the decree that the twins must die, as Obeirika recalled:

> [W]hat crime had they committed? The Earth had decreed that they were an offense on the land and must be destroyed. And if the clan did not exact punishment for an offense against the goddess, her wrath was loosed on the land and not just the offender. As the elders saw, if one finger brought oil, it soils the others. (130)

The important question raised here is why does Okonkwo participate in executing Ikemefuna? Does he fear and respect the wrath of the gods? Judging from Okonkwo's actions, we have to say that the answer is "no"; habitually, Okonkwo acts too impulsively, too violently, to think of the consequences of his actions. This habit of impulse is made clear, for example, when Okonkwo beats his wife during the sacred Week of Peace—a week of harmony, restraint, and decorum: "And when she returned, he beat her heavily. In his anger he had forgotten that it was the Week of Peace. His first two wives ran out in great alarm, pleading with him that it was the sacred week. But Okonkwo was not the man to stop beating somebody halfway through, not even the fear of a goddess" (31). In fact, because of his excessive pride; because he would not admit his error, "people said he had no respect for the gods" (32). Though not afraid of a goddess, Okonkwo is not fearless, for he fears failure, as the narrator tells us:

> [H]is whole life was dominated by fear, the fear of fail-ure and of weakness. It was deeper and more intimate than the fear of evil and capricious gods and of magic. . . . Okonkwo's fear was greater than these. It was not external but lay deep within himself. It was the fear of himself, lest he should be found to resemble his father. (14)

Robert Wren emphasizes Okonkwo's freedom to choose not to participate in killing Ikemefuna, "[I]f a man says 'no' strongly enough, his 'chi' says 'no' also. Okonkwo had that within him which said 'no' to the killing of Ikemefuna."[5]

Does he act, then, out of his own selfish motives—his inordinate ambition to be acknowledged as one of the courageous and brave men of Umuofia? Does he perceive the decree of the gods as a challenge to his manhood and, as a result, exceeds in his actions even what the gods demand? Based on a careful analysis of Achebe's controlled presentation of Okonkwo's character, his habit of mind and action, as this paper contends, Okonkwo's participation results not from obedience to the gods. Instead, like Ezeulu in *Arrow of God,* Okonkwo is in competition with the gods and acts out of his pathological fear of being thought weak—his fear of being perceived as like his father Unoka.

Because of the centrality of the scene in which Ikemefuna is killed to our understanding of Okonkwo's role in it, it is necessary to cite the passage of length:

> At the beginning of their journey the men of Umuofia talked and laughed about the locust, about their women, and about some effeminate men who had refused to come with them. But as they drew near to the outskirts of Umuofia, silence fell upon them too.
>
> The sun rose slowly to the center of the sky, and the dry, sandy footway began to throw up the heat that lay buried in it. Some birds chirruped in the forest around. The men trod dry leaves on the sand. All was silent. Then from the distance came the faint beating of the ekwe. . . .

> They argued for a short while and fell into silence again, and the elusive dance rose and fell with the wind. Somewhere a man was taking one of the titles of the clan, with music and dancing and a great feast. . . .
>
> Thus the men of Umuofia pursued their way, armed with sheathed machetes, and Ikemefuna, carrying a pot of palm wine on his head, walked in their midst. Although he had felt uneasy at first he was not afraid now. Okonkwo walked behind him. He could hardly imagine that Okonkwo was not his real father. He had never been fond of his real father, and at the end of three years he had become very distant indeed. . . .
>
> As the man who had cleared his throat drew up and raised his machete, Okonkwo looked away. He heard the blow. The pot fell and broke in the sand. He heard Ikemefuna cry, "My father, they have killed me!" as he ran towards him. Dazed with fear, Okonkwo drew his machete and cut him down. (61-63)

This tragic event takes place during or immediately after the celebration of the coming of the locust—an occasion of joy, laughter, and excitement, especially among the children of Umuofia. "Locusts are descending" was joyfully chanted everywhere, and men, women, and children left their work or their play to run into the open to see the unfamiliar sight. Ikemefuna's death comes only two days after "Okonkwo sat in his obi cruching happily with Ikemefuna and Nwoye and drinking palm wine copiously . . ." (59), sharing with Ikemefuna the joy which enveloped the whole community. The feast of the locust thus serves as a foil for and throws into sharp relief the killing of Ikemefuna.

These contrasting events are presented as occurring almost simultaneously to underscore the brutality and inhumanity of the Umuofia society. On the very day that Ikemefuna sits happily with his "father" Okonkwo, Ezeulu reports, "Yes, Umuofia has decided to kill him" (59). The narrator's terse, mournful description of Ikemefuna's death intensifies both the horror of the event and the dastardliness of Okonkwo's participation: His "son" runs to him for protection only to be felled by the hard steel of Okonkwo's machete. Okonkwo's deliberate participation makes the death of Ikemefuna too horrible to endure.

Okonkwo is consistently presented in the novel, as in the above episode, as a man of ignoble decisiveness, one who acts strong but is mentally weak. He is a man who rushes headlong into action and will not allow himself to be contained, as he should be, by the bonds of interpersonal relationships, by the prickings of conscience, or by the customs and values of his society.

Okonkwo's predisposition to commit himself with tragic

intensity to irrevocable violence is made clear in the narrator's first description of him:

> He was tall and huge and his bushy eyebrows and wide nose gave him a severe look. He breathed heavily, and it was said that when he slept, his wives and children in their houses could hear him breathe. When he walked, his heels hardly touched the ground and he seemed to walk on springs, as if he was going to pounce on somebody. And he did pounce on people quite often. He had a slight stammer and whenever he was angry and could not get the words out quickly enough, he would use his fists. . . . (4)

Emphasis here and throughout is on Okonkwo's intimidating physical strength and his reliance on force to achieve his ends. As Eustance Palmer observes, "In a sense, Okonkwo is presented as a life-denying force. He was always associated with death, whereas his father, with all his faults is associated with life . . . always charged and tense like a loaded cannon. . . . [O]ne expects his fiery temper and nervous energy to find outlet in violent action in that he will plunge headlong into self destruction."[6] Equally important, the narrator's emphasis on Okonkwo's monstrous energy and brute strength calls attention to Okonkwo's primary weakness—his inability to think, to use language to channel and communicate his thoughts and thereby interact meaningfully with his environment.

To Okonkwo, words are mere shapes to fill a void, not prime instruments for conceptual expressions or for giving outward experience its form and making it definite and clear. According to Susan Langer, "all genuine thinking is symbolic, and the limits of expressive medium are therefore really the limits of our conceptual powers. Beyond these, we have only blind feeling, which records nothing and conveys nothing, but has to be discharged in action . . . or other impulsive demonstrations."[7] Because of his limited metacognitive power, Okonkwo habitually resorts to blind and impulsive actions; he approaches every problem—no matter how complex or paradoxical—with a single-minded, preconceived solution: force without thought, action without regard for consequence. Unlike his friend Obeirika, his uncle Uchendu, and his father Unoka, Okonkwo is too impatient, too much a man of action to deal with subtleties, with nuances that do not fit easily into his monochromatic view of life. Okonkwo's rigid use of language corresponds to his rigid approach to life. (In significant ways, his attitude towards life and language help explain why he accepts the decree of the gods literally, without questions). Okonkwo's rhetorical ineptitude further alienates him from Umuofia, further divorces him from his goal of being Umuofia's champion, because Umuofia prides itself on its rhetorical refinement. In Umuofia, as among the Ibos, the art of conversation is regarded highly, and prov-

erbs "are the palm oil with which words are eaten." As Wren observes, Okonkwo "does occasionally use a proverb—four or five times in the course of the novel—but they do not seem to flow from him. . . ."[8] In general, Okonkwo finds words poor substitutes for action. As C. L. Innes observes, "Phrases or statements which reaffirm rather than extend the existing world view of a person or his society are typical of Okonkwo. . . . His contributions to a discussion are generally short and commonplace. . . . For Okonkwo talking is never a prelude to action, it leads nowhere."[9] Lacking rhetorical skill, Okonkwo overcompensates for his deficiency in this area by being too quick to act, by doing more than Umuofia and even the gods demand.

Okonkwo possessed a monomaniacal commitment to placing success and achievement above everything else—even the need to love and be loved—and identifying his whole existence with gaining power as one of the lords of the clan of Umuofia. This commitment to and drive for power ruled his life. Worse still, this habit of mind leads tragically to Okonkwo's denial of his true self and makes inevitable his suicide. He resorts to force instead of dialogue, acts violently when flexibility and compassion are called for.

The murder of Ikemefuna, though the most dreadful, is the climax of a series of extreme actions Okonkwo takes to assert his manliness—his existence. Other key moments arise when he savagely beats his son, repudiates his father, Unoka, kills the messenger, and ultimately turns his own violent hand against himself.

Okonkwo's impulsive violence marks his relationship with his only biological son, Nwoye. The boy seeks his father's love and understanding, but Okonkwo is incapable of responding to these basic human needs; he considered them unmanly and effeminate. When Okonkwo is confronted by the failure of his own rigid code as Nwoye turns to Christianity for love and succor, Okonkwo responds in the only way he knows—with violence:

> It was late afternoon before Nwoye returned. He went into the obi and saluted his father, but he did not answer. Nwoye turned around into the inner compound when his father, suddenly overcome with fury, sprang to his feet and gripped him by the neck.
>
> "Where have you been?" he stammered. Nwoye struggled to free himself from the choking grip.
>
> "Answer me," roared Okonkwo, "before I kill you!" He seized a heavy stick that lay on the dwarf wall and hit him two or three savage blows.
>
> "Answer me!" he roared again. Nwoye stood looking

at him and did not say a word. The women were screaming outside, afraid to go in.

"Leave that boy at once," said a voice in the outer compound. It was Okonkwo's uncle, Uchendu. "Are you mad?"

Okonkwo did not answer. But he let hold of Nwoye, who walked away and never returned. (157)

In another crucial event, the final gathering of the clan, everything seems to point toward the need for dialogue and flexibility in responding to the clan's increasing fragmentation, "They have broken the clan and gone their several ways. . . . Our brothers have deserted us and joined a stranger to soil their fatherland. If we fight the stranger we shall hit our brothers and perhaps shed the blood of a clansman" (210). Okonkwo reacts predictably, decisively, violently. Early in the morning, under a somber silence, the elders of Umuofia gather in the marketplace to decide collectively what action they will need to take to stop the Reverend Smith and the District Commissioner's ruthless violations of the customs and traditions of Umuofia. A foreign judicial system has been established in place of indigenous laws; a foreign religion, Christianity, has begun to supplant the local gods. Umuofia's existence and all that gave the people's lives substance and meaning are being destroyed from within and without. As the elders deliberate, five messengers from the District Commissioner arrive, and tragic drama unfolds, with Okonkwo at center stage:

> He [Okonkwo] sprang to his feet as soon as he saw who it was. He confronted the head messenger, trembling with hate, unable to utter a word. The man was fearless and stood his ground, his four men lined up behind him.
>
> In that brief moment the world seemed to stand still, waiting. There was utter silence. The men of Umuofia were merged into the mute backcloth of trees and giant creepers, waiting.
>
> The spell was broken by the head messenger. "Let me pass!" he ordered.
>
> "What do you want here?"
>
> "The white men whose power you know too well have ordered this meeting to stop."
>
> In a flash Okonkwo drew his machete. The messenger crouched to avoid the blow. It was useless. Okonkwo's machete descended twice and the man's head lay beside his uniformed body.

> Okonkwo stood looking at the dead man. He knew that Umuofia would not go to war. He knew because they had let the other messengers escape. They had broken into tumult instead of action. He discerned fright in that tumult. He heard voices asking: "Why did he do it?"
>
> He wiped his machete on the sand and went away. (210-11)

To understand the reason why Okonkwo acts as he does, we need to examine Okonkwo's relationship with Unoka. Okonkwo's relationship with his father, Unoka, is devoid of love and marked by hate. Okonkwo violently and decisively repudiates Unoka, obliterating his father's existence from his mind because Unoka is known to be weak, a failure: "[H]e had long ago learned how to slay that ghost. Whenever thought of his father's weakness and failure troubled him, he expelled it by thinking about his own strength and success" (68-69). At his death, Unoka had no title; when he died, he was not accorded the proper traditional funeral but was buried like a dog. In trying to obliterate all Unoka represents, Okonkwo casts off not only Unoka's undignified irresponsibility but also those positive attributes—love, compassion, creativity—which Unoka embodies. What Okonkwo does not recognize is that by attempting to obliterate his father's reality, he symbolically destroys his own existence and his own place in Umuofia society and ends up, in death, just like his father. To Umuofia, Okonkwo's death by hanging is an abomination, an offense against the earth; as a result, Umuofia buries Okonkwo, as Obeirika mournfully observes, "like a dog." The clan's attitude toward Okonkwo's death is tersely summarized: "His body is evil, and only strangers may touch it. . . . We cannot bury him. Only strangers can. We shall pay you men to do it. When he has been buried, we will then do our duty. We shall make sacrifices to cleanse this deserted land" (214).

Okonkwo's fatal gift is his predisposition to violence; he commits himself with tragic intensity to become the champion of the heroic tradition of Umuofia through extreme and decisive action. These attributes appear to serve him well, especially when he channels his strength towards industry. He threw himself into whatever he did like a man possessed. For example, during the planting season, Okonkwo worked daily from cock-crow until the chickens went to roost. He was very strong and rarely became fatigued. Consequently, Okonkwo became prosperous and well known throughout the nine villages and beyond; he had a large compound enclosed by a thick wall of red earth, and his own hut, or obi, stood immediately behind the only gate in the wall. Each of his three wives had her own hut and "the barn was built against one end of the red wall and long stacks of red yam stood out prosperously in it" (15).

Okonkwo was respected for rising so suddenly from great poverty and misfortune to be one of the lords of the clan.

Paradoxically, the same qualities that contribute to Okonkwo's greatness also account for his isolation, his blindness, and his ruin. To achieve success, fame, and power, Okonkwo habitually resorts to and comes to rely on thoughtless violence. Without regard for consequences, Okonkwo acts: he kills Ikemefuna, beats his son, repudiates his father, butchers the messenger. He becomes the apotheosis of violent action and as such ultimately destroys himself.

Yet Okonkwo is not a classical Machiavellian. Although bound to violence to achieve his goals, deep down in his heart, he is not an evil, heartless man. As I have argued elsewhere,[10] he is capable of love, warmth, and compassion. To maintain the image of his "grandiose self," he struggles and succeeds in burying these positive human attributes within himself because he considers them unmanly. He allows his buried humanity to surface only in private, unguarded moments: for example, it is in the dark that he shows his spontaneous response and deep-felt anguish in saving his dying daughter Ezinma from Chielo, and it is in his private dark room that he shows *brief* remorse after his brutal killing of Ikemefuna.

On the one hand, we admire Okonkwo's heroic determination to achieve personal success and applaud his strong commitment, though futile, to preserve the legacy of Umuofia's heroic tradition. At the same time, we condemn and despise him when his determination to succeed and his commitment to preserve the tradition become an insane preoccupation leading to inhuman acts and violence, such as his slaughtering his "son" Ikemefuna.

All in all, Okonkwo is a man of uncommon achievement and uncommon failure. The overriding paradox of his life and death is that if he had not been obsessed with avoiding the life of failure which his father Unoka lived, he would have been less prone to violence, but if he had been less violent, he probably would not have achieved success as a lord in Umuofia. He is, as tragic heroes often are, a victim of the defects of his virtues.

Notes

1. Chinua Achebe, *Things Fall Apart* (New York: Astor, 1959). All subsequent quotations from the text are from this edition.

2. David Carroll, *Chinua Achebe* (New York: Twayne, 1970), pp. 48-49.

3. Damian Opatu, "Eternal Sacred Order Versus Conventional Wisdom: A Consideration of Moral Culpability in the Killing of Ikemefuna in *Things Fall Apart*," *Research in African Literature*, 18, No. 1 (1987), 75-76.

4. Carroll, p. 49.

5. Robert Wren, *Achebe's World* (Washington, D.C.: Three Continents Press, 1980), p. 44.

6. Eustance Palmer, *An Introduction to the African Novels* (London: Heinemann Educational Books, 1972), p. 54.

7. Susanne Langer, *Philosophy in a New Key*, 3rd ed. (Cambridge: Harvard Univ. Press, 1987), p. 87.

8. Wren, p. 57.

9. C. L. Innes, "Poetry and Doctrine in *Things Fall Apart*," in *Critical Perspectives on Chinua Achebe*, ed. C. L. Innes and Bernth Lindfurs (Washington, D.C.: Three Continents Press, 1978), pp. 114, 120.

10. Solomon O. Iyasere, "Narrative Techniques in *Things Fall Apart, New Letters* 40, No. 3 (1974).

Adeleke Adeeko (essay date April 1992)

SOURCE: "Contests of Text and Context in Chinua Achebe's 'Arrow of God,'" in *Ariel*, Vol. 23, No. 2, April, 1992, pp. 7-22.

[*In the following essay, Adeeko examines various manipulations of a thematic Nigerian proverb in* Arrow of God, *arguing that its intentional misuse contributes to the novel's tragedy.*]

Proverbs are so conspicuous in Chinua Achebe's novels that they constitute the most studied singular feature of his art. As it were, Achebe's use of proverbs is in itself proverbial. One can speak of two tendencies in this well-traversed area. Bold critics often tend to generate ethnic theories of cognition from the structure and nature of the proverbs, and much of the highly perceptive ones concentrate on the significance of the sayings in Achebe's creative construction of "vernacular" conversation. For the reason that proverbs usually employ concrete images, Cairns suggests, for instance, that the sayings reflect the African predilection for non-abstract thought (16). However, more perceptive Achebe scholars have revealed that he uses proverbs to add distinctively local shade to his settings, depict the speech patterns and conventions of Igbo characters who would not ordinarily speak English, define these characters by particular types of proverbs, and also exercise narrative control by changing "thematic" statements as his plots develop. In addition, such studies reveal that women and children do not cite proverbs in Achebe's Igboland and that "educated" people (ironically, like Achebe himself), more often than not, forget or misuse proverbs.[1] In spite of the large attention paid to his inventiveness in proverb usage, a lack still exists of a "rhetorical" analysis of this all-important aspect of Achebe's work.[2] Two factors could have, in the main, contributed to this neglect. First, paremiology used to be almost exclusively an anthropologist's forte wherein proverbs were defined in terms of the mores of the people that use them. Second, many critics believe that Achebe chooses the proverb as his signature idiom because he is a teacher, his novels are his lesson plans, and no other figure known to literary anthropology helps the teacher better than the proverb (Achebe, "The Novelist" 162).[3] Why is the proverb such a good friend of the teacher-novelist? It is an oral and rural manner of speaking, it is highly pragmatic, and it is unavoidably didactic. According to Patnaik,

> [c]ultures that employ the oral mode of communication are more likely to value compressed succinct expression. What better vehicle of communication than the proverb, which by its very nature penetrates to the heart of the situation and character, lending at the same time, to succinct thought a freshness of expression and ingeniousness of idea. (68)

While not disregarding the basic assumption of anthropological interpretation, I suggest in this paper that proverbs are not mere vehicles of thought. I equate them with structures that render thinking perceptible. I assume that proverbs are rhetorical not because they are simply figures of speech but because they thematize the possibility of representing speech. Much as they are about political control, the tragic conflicts in *Arrow of God* result from what I perceive to be an almost endless jostling for superiority between the authorities of message, meaning, and context. The colonial milieu provides the concrete historical and political boundaries within which these "proverbial" contests play themselves out.[4] In the ensuing "literary" reading of one thematic proverb—"a messenger does not choose its message" (158)—in *Arrow of God,* I argue that the novel dramatizes not just the well-documented monumental disaster that accompanies the colonial incursion into Umuaro but also the role that disagreements over reading (in this so-called "oral" culture) play in the development of the novel's tragedy.

A messenger's loyalty to its charge first becomes the main focus of a conversation when Ezeulu rejects Tony Clarke's orders to report to the District Headquarters for instruction on becoming a Warrant Chief.

"Do you know what you are saying, my friend?" asked the messenger in utter unbelief.

"Are you a messenger or not?" asked Ezeulu. "Go home and give my message to your master." (157)

To avert a major confrontation between the cocky imperial messenger and the tradition conscious audience, Akuebue quickly intervenes with a tacit citation of tradition on the appropriate comportment of messengers:

> In Umuaro it is not our custom to refuse a call, although we may refuse to do what the caller asks. Ezeulu does not want to refuse the white man's call and so he is sending his son. (157)

When the messenger declines this reminder of tradition, Akuebue expresses his surprise with the proverb "I have never heard of a messenger choosing the message he will carry" (158).

The messenger "chooses" his message, as Akuebue implies, not because there is no proverb prohibiting such behaviour where he comes from, but because the messenger believes he speaks for a sovereign Crown that is not subject to "local" laws. He deems it untenable that a local potentate could cite tradition to so dismiss the white master's subpoena. This little skirmish over the importance of a message as determined by the social position of its originator and courier is going to lead to unimaginable implications for Ezeulu and his community as the story unfolds.

In tracing the itinerary of the sad events that ensue, I find that most other key conflicts in the novel—even before this encounter—involve the cultural control of either messages or messengers. At several crucial moments, the plot relies on the outcome of struggles for command between the messages and messengers, and on all such occasions, the messengers succeed regardless of what the contestants think. The messengers at each of these turns demonstrates that they have minds of their own independent of the fates of their messages, their senders, and their intended receivers. In almost every instance, the messengers accept all messages dumped on them, but deliver only those that suit them. In the wake of what we may call this apparent "betrayal," tragic scenarios often result. On most occasions, the messengers appear indifferent to the incessant struggles on how to articulate the dispatchers' intentions with the receivers' wiles.

The first consequential conflict in the novel arises when a delegation, charged with negotiating a choice of settlement of a land dispute with Okperi, unwittingly botches its mission. One of the elders at the meeting specifically tells Akukalia that "we do not want Okperi to choose war; nobody eats war. If they choose peace we shall rejoice. *But whatever they say you are not to dispute with them.* Your duty is to bring word back to us" (19). As Ogbuefi Egonwanne bids here, the emissaries are to be true messengers, though, as Ezeulu argues later, not necessarily messengers of truth. The clan expects Akukalia to be a transparent messenger in whom its message could be easily read, for according to proverbial injunction, he cannot choose his message.

The message, partly because of the messenger's meddling with his commission, actually miscarries when Akukalia reaches Okperi. First, it is the market day in Okperi, and there are not too many qualified people around to receive the message. Second, Akukalia is impatient and refuses to return at a more convenient time because, according to him, his "mission could not wait" (25). The urgency, I must say, is not part of the message, and there is therefore little surprise, except for the messenger who has added the urgency, when Ebo, his Okperi host, quotes the traditional saying, "I have not yet heard of a message that could not wait" (25). A heated argument ensues, and at one point Ebo, presumably innocently, censures Akukalia: "'if you want to shout like a castrated bull you must wait until you return to Umuaro'" (26). Incidentally, Akukalia is an impotent man, "whose two wives were secretly given to other men to bear his children" (26). At this point, the hitherto wayward message totally falls through. Akukalia runs into Ebo's family shrine and breaks his *ikenga*, "the strength of his right arm" (27). By so doing, Akukalia severs Ebo's communication channel with his ancestors. To convince his primogenitors that he is still alive, Ebo murders his assailant. By virtue of this incident, the Okperi people unwittingly choose war because customarily Umuaro must draw equal compensation for Akukalia's death. Akukalia does not live long enough to pass on the options in his charge, but the message got delivered. The messenger's body, even in death, anchors the mission.

Before discussing the major singular conflict in the story, I want quickly to examine another important episode involving an argument over the supremacy of either the message or the messenger. The colonial administration wants to make Ezeulu its messenger by offering him a warrant chieftaincy. Already, Ezeulu is a messenger of Ulu and the Umuaro community, but Tony Clarke and his superiors in the colonial hierarchy do not perceive him as one. So, after making his offer through an interpreter, Clarke asks, "Well, are you accepting the offer or not?" (196). Ezeulu replies:

> "Tell the white man that Ezeulu will not be anybody's chief [messenger], except Ulu."

> "What!" shouted Tony Clarke. "Is the fellow mad?"

"I tink so sah," said the interpreter.

"In that case he goes back to prison." Clarke was now really angry. What cheek! A witch-doctor making a fool of the British Administration in public! (196)

Clarke's detention order spells doom for the community, and greater conflicts over the role of the messenger develop.

Ezeulu already sees himself as a messenger of his god, whose command he does not dispute, but Clarke and Winterbottom read him incorrectly by assuming that he is a transparently honest messenger on whom they could load their own message. They develop the wrong prompt after listening to the chief's testimony against his own clan during the Okperi-Umuaro boundary adjustment inquiries. Somehow, the colonial operatives believe that Ezeulu's deposition, which contradicted his clan's claims, marks him out as an unusually honest African who can be trusted with the Crown's directives to Umuaro citizens. The colonial administrators do not know that Ezeulu is not a dispassionate messenger on whose face they can wilfully inscribe their own messages. This singular misreading engenders the tragic conflict that occurs over the eating of two calendrical yams. Ezeulu's detention for refusing the chieftaincy prevents him from re-marking the communal schedule for two months. As the drama of how to prevent an imminent collapse of the Umuaro economy unfolds, it appears clearly that different sectors of the federation are motivated by vested methods of textual interpretation, negotiations on deciphering the will of the messenger and of the sender vis-à-vis the truthfulness of the message. It is also a battle over the "nature" of nature.

First, Ezeulu's assistants, who also "reckon" the number of months, approached the chief priest after the "twelfth moon" to make arrangements for the next New Yam Feast. One of them says:

> It is now four days since the new moon appeared in the sky; it is already grown big. And yet you have not called us together to tell us the day of the New Yam Feast— (232)

And Ezeulu responds, "I see. I thought perhaps I did not hear you well. Since when did you begin to reckon the year for Umuaro?" (233). One of the assistants, Chukwulobe, who thinks Obiesili is tactless, recasts the request: "We do not reckon the year for Umuaro; we are not Chief Priest. But we thought that perhaps you have lost count because of your recent absence—" (233). Ezeulu completely loses his temper:

> Lost count! Did your father tell you that the Chief Priest

of Ulu can lose count of the moons? No, my son . . . no Ezeulu can lose count. Rather it is you who count with your fingers who are likely to make a mistake, to forget which finger you counted at the last moon. (233)

There is no doubt that Ezeulu's incarceration in Okperi could not but result in loss in counting; in fact, that is partly the reason why tradition does not allow the chief priest to stay away from Umuaro for an extended period of time. But if counting the yams is all there is, then he has not lost count, for he has the yams to refer to, and there can be no arguments over that. But one more visit two days later by the titled elders further shows that there is more to this conversation than mere yams. The elders call on Ezeulu to urge him to amend the calendar so as not to change things as they know them to be. But to their gracious entreaties Ezeulu replies, "'I need not speak in riddles. You all know what our custom is. I only call a new festival when there is only one yam left'" (236). When the elders insist that Ezeulu should seek a way out, with one of them even suggesting that he eat up the yams, the Priest restates his position saying, "you have spoken well. But what you ask me to do is not done. Those yams are not food and a man does not eat them because he is hungry. You are asking me to eat death" (237).

Again, Ezeulu is both right and wrong, and the ambiguity is not totally of his own making. The yams are food and, of course, not food. They are food because he eats them; they are not food because these particular yams satisfy more than nutritional needs, and someone will have to eat them if the entire community is not to starve. In other words, the yams are yams and not yams at the same time. They are markers (or messengers or signifiers) of the communal calendar, and Ezeulu (another marker or signifier) is the designated reader and, arguably, the writer.

Surprisingly, Ezeulu the designated reader now takes an unprecedented stand by refusing to read according to the senders' (the community's) will. He hedges the elders and his assistants because the yams (messengers) have a will of their own (their materiality) that he exploits, knowingly or unknowingly. He denies the elders their wishes by telling them that, although they are the initial creators of the calendar, the yams and whatever they now signify are beyond their direct control. The elders, on the other hand, also recognize the yams' will, and they too seek to bend it to serve the purpose imperilled by current circumstances but for which the yams were originally invented. Ezeulu hides behind the invincibility of the messenger (signifier), and the elders wave the banner of the infallibility of the social will. The elders face a greater difficulty than Ezeulu because they have to contend with two messengers: the yams (the text) and their eater (the reader). The resultant confusion is more disconcerting because ordinary reasoning suggests that this is an open text whose letters everybody can decipher but which no one can now read.[5]

The community expects Ezeulu to count the moons with the aid of the yams and *not* the yams with the moons. Chukwulobe therefore suggests he has lost count, but Ezeulu rejects such counsel because the yams (the messenger, the signifier) say he has not. In a way, the yams carry transparent messages that neither the yams, nor Ezeulu, nor the aides and the elders can choose for them. Ezeulu accordingly rejects the pleas of his aides and the community that he should count moons and not yams. He maintains that it is impossible for him and anybody else to do so, and anyone who has a contrary opinion must actually be miscounting. The yam counter, he insists, is forever right, and the finger counter incessantly susceptible to miscounting.

The yams are relatively permanent and differentiable, and once eaten they are no more countable. Every yam eaten (thus counted) disappears, and its absence announces its conspicuousness and thereby determines the value of the remainder. On the other hand, the fingers are not removed, they are always present and so could be recounted. These facts notwithstanding, the community believes that Ezeulu is wrong in the values he assigns to the remaining yams. The citizens do not share Ezeulu's calculations that the yams represent an unalterable ("natural") number of moons.[6] Ezeulu holds everybody to ransom because the yams, like him, though messengers, and contrary to proverbial injunctions, have their own designs that are indifferent to whatever purpose for which the users (the senders and the receivers) might wish to make of them. Ironically, it is also this independence that tethers them to the schemes of whoever deems them useful.

It is also possible for us to see the Ezeulu-Umuaro fiasco as the product of a quarrel over the cultural control of nature and its signs. In Ezeulu's logic (also available to his opponents), there can be no culture (the year, the calendar) beyond the signification of the yams. The year ends only at the mercy of the calendar and not because it has a natural end. That is why, after consulting the deity over whether or not he should announce the New Yam Feast as the elders demand, he comes out with a negative result (240). But the arbitrariness of the whole marking system, the lack of organic connection between the yam (the signifier) and the New Yam Feast (the signified, the planting season and, by implication, the fiscal year) is highlighted by the elders' insistence that Ezeulu either eat the yams or substitute a sacrifice. The elders believe they made Ulu, not because Ulu "gave birth" to the yams or the harvest, but because they made it so. Anichebe Udeozo speaks to this effect when he says to Ezeulu: "I want you to look around this room and tell me what you see. Do you think there is another Umuaro outside this hut now?" (237). Ezeulu agrees with him that the elders are the creators of the Federation and the tradition. Udeozo then tells him:

> Yes, we are Umuaro. Therefore listen to what I am going to say. Umuaro is now asking you to go and eat those remaining yams today and name the day of the next harvest . . . and if Ulu says we have committed an abomination let it be on the heads of the ten of us here. (237-38)

Udeozo's plea falls on deaf ears, and Ezeulu's wish partially prevails because the same arbitrariness that the elders' entreaties hang on also permits the chief priest to read the yams his own way.

Were Udeozo talking to a messenger that had no interest in his message, his invocation of public interest might have swayed Ezeulu. But the chief priest is prosecuting a personal agenda while furthering Ulu's course. He pursues his grievance under the pretext that he is a mere messenger who does not select his messages, whereas in fact he chooses them at every turn. He could not be proved false because, "cultural" (proverbial) prohibition notwithstanding, it appears that all messengers possess the ability to bear their own messages in addition to others latched onto them.

What are the specifics of Ezeulu's grudge? Prior to his detention, Ezeulu has had a long-running disagreement with some sections of his community in the persons of the rival priest of Idemili and his active supporter, the wealthy Nwaka. The high point of this conflict occurs during the land dispute inquiry I mentioned above. Ezeulu, the Chief Priest of Umuaro's "highest" deity, almost single-handedly gives the parcel of land in question to the foreigners, who, by the way, are his mother's people. In this society, historical recollection is a reconstitution, subject to conjecture and personal interests. Ezeulu, even with his high office, does not possess the right to a *correct* historical reconstruction and as such has no right to speak *for* the community. But, acting on the belief that his is the voice of a messenger speaking only for the deity he serves, he testifies against his people. He thereby chooses his message, which he believes belongs to his deity.

Ezeulu also uses the same rationale at the acrimonious pre-war deliberations when he appeals to the people to listen to him because he speaks on behalf of a deity that never endorses unjust courses. "Ulu would not fight an unjust war," he says. To buttress this point, he informs the assembly: "My father said this to me that when our village first came here to live the land belonged to Okperi. . . .This is the story as I heard it from my father" (17).[7] At this meeting, Ezeulu maintains he does not speak for himself but as a simple messenger of truth, and Nwaka, his most notorious opponent, replies that that does not make him a *truthful* messenger.

> Wisdom is like a goatskin bag; every man carries his own. Knowledge of the land is also like that. Ezeulu has told us what his father told him about the olden days. We know that a father does not speak falsely to his son. But we also know that the lore of the land is beyond the knowledge of many fathers. . . . My father told me a different story. (17-18)

Nwaka may be right in several other unstated respects. At the least, Ezeulu's mother, of whom he has fond memories, comes from Okperi. In addition, the priest is also involved in a theological rivalry with Ezidemili. He cannot for these reasons be a messenger of unimpeachable truth.[8]

While taking refuge in the proverb of a messenger not choosing its message, Ezeulu testifies against his people and conveniently forgets another proverb: "no man, however great, can win a judgment against his clan" (148). Henceforth, the community regards itself as set against Ezeulu and so sees nothing heroic in his refusal to be the white man's chief. As fate would have it, it is this very lack of enthusiasm that Ezeulu, still using the old alibi that he is a mere messenger, now avenges on his people by refusing to bend the message of the yams. At any rate, only in Ezeulu's mind does such a notion exist, because evidence abounds that there is nothing like a mere messenger and that every messenger bears its own message, if only that of a *message bearer.*

The novel's tragedy further takes shape partly because Ezeulu does not understand that even the messenger cannot totally control the messages in its care, its own messages included. This is so because, like their carriers, messages have their own wills, and these wills are messengers in another sense. As dramatized in the pre-war meeting, Ezeulu's anti-war message, for which he claims divine guidance, can easily be interpreted against him, as Nwaka does, as "I am the voice of Okperi that also happens to be the land of your chief priest's mother" (17). In other words, Ezeulu is *not* a mere messenger although he shelters himself behind the proverbial "injunction" that says he is.[9]

To conclude this section on the apparent discrepancy between historical experience as narrated here and cultural "injunction" as "encoded" in the proverb, I want to cite one incident between Ezeulu and his son, Oduche, whom he has sent to join the local Anglican Church so as, in Ezeulu's words, "to be his eyes" among the people of the new religion. While packaging the boy, as it were, Ezeulu does not think that Oduche may like the new faith and all the benefits and prestige that come with it. Ezeulu, thoughtful as he is, never imagined that the new faith will make his son an inheritor of a legacy that empowers the boy to kill the sacred snake of Idemili (another Umuaro deity and Ulu's arch-rival), which the local teacher interprets to be a species of the serpent that deceived Adam and Eve. None of Oduche's independent but prohibited actions as a Christian surpasses his not telling his father that Umuaro citizens, in a desperate attempt to escape hunger and poverty, are sending the sacrificial yams that they normally give to Ulu on the day of the New Yam Feast to Jesus, the Christ. When Ezeulu learns about this development from his friend, he is surprised that his son (his eyes, his messenger) did not alert him earlier. He rebukes the boy:

> Do you remember what I told you when I sent you among those people? . . . I called you as a father calls his son and told you to go and be my eye and ear among those people. I did not send Obika or Edogo; I did not send Nwafo, your mother's son. I called you by name and you came here—in this *obi*—and I sent you to *see and hear for me*. I did not know at that time that I was sending a goat's skull. (251)

Again, the messenger derails the message. The messenger chooses, because of the comforts of the destination, not to fulfill his commission. He returns no answer to the sender.

One other image that aptly illustrates the itinerary I am drawing appears in the narration of Ezeulu's first night in detention at Okperi. Ezeulu has vowed not to watch for the moon while he is in detention, "but," the narrator tells us, "the eye is very greedy and will steal a look at something its owner has no wish to see" (179). Ezeulu watches for the moon that night although he did not see anything. The visual imagery, again, demonstrates the inevitable errancy of the messenger. In other words, the messenger has its own business to attend to that often might not coincide with the dispatcher's.[10]

I find the greatest support for the disparity between the proverb and the narration at the point at which Ezeulu's mind snaps. He seeks explanations for the unfortunate turns of events in proverbs that focus on the non-culpability of the messenger in the effect of its message.

> Why, he asked himself again and again, why had Ulu chosen to deal thus with him, to strike him down and cover him with mud? What was his offence? Had he not divined the god's will and obeyed it? When was it ever heard that a child was scalded by the piece of yam its own mother put in its palm? What man would send his son with a potsherd to bring fire from a neighbor's hut and then unleash rain on him? Who ever sent his son up the palm to gather nuts and then took

an axe and felled the tree? But today such a thing had happened before the eyes of all . . .

> Perhaps it was the constant, futile throbbing of these thoughts that finally left a crack in Ezeulu's mind. Or perhaps his implacable assailant having stood over him for a little while stepped on him as on an insect and crushed him in the dust. But this final act of malevolence proved merciful. It allowed Ezeulu, in his last days, to live in the haughty splendor of a demented high priest and spared him knowledge of the final outcome. (260-61)

One can hastily read these sayings as confirming that Ezeulu is a victim of the social vagaries that invariably determine the fates of messages and messengers. Lindfors, for instance, interprets the sequence of proverbs as Ezeulu's belated regret of not knowing the limits of his powers. He says, "Ezeulu, in trying to adjust to the changing times, takes certain inappropriate actions which later lead him to neglect his duties and responsibilities. Not knowing his limitations, he goes too far and plunges himself and his people into disaster" (15). Griffiths has said, rightly I think, that this interpretation is inadequate. But Griffiths's replacement is equally short on several marks. Although it might be correct to say that Ezeulu seeks help in "proverbial" knowledge and that "frantically he runs through the proverbial wisdom seeking for a clear sign that the relationship of trust which must exist between high priest and god still endures" (97), it is, however, not true that this so-called proverbial society (as opposed to modern "literate" ones) and its mores succumb to the "irresistible and incomprehensible force of the white man, a force blind to the values and meaning of tribal life" (97). The invading force is not blind to local values. Indeed, it bends over backwards to understand and manipulate them for its own purpose.

The conglomerate of proverbs running around in Ezeulu's head all centre on the unjust culpability of the messenger. Ezeulu, the ordinary messenger (though of a deity), struggles within a web of proverbs about message and messenger, and ponders why he must suffer for carrying out his duties "faithfully." His assailant is certainly not just the white man as Griffiths claims. Ezeulu is crushed by the burden of his office as both a *message* and a *messenger* at the time when a "discursive displacement" (Spivak 197) is taking place in his land. Ezeulu does not violate "tradition" if his actions are interpreted according to the letters of the proverb. But as the narration shows, proverbs do not ossify tradition. When perceived as "readable" codes, we see that proverbs expose tradition as textual constructs that can only be successfully—politically, that is—invoked by those with prevailing reading strategies.

We need to ask whether or not the proverb is wrong about

the irremediable servitude and muteness of the messenger. I believe that the proverb is, in spite of itself, correct to a very large extent because all the messengers who choose to appoint their messages, consciously or not, regardless of their purpose, lose out because everything they had hitherto perceived as controllable messages slipped out of their grips and became other messengers. The proverb seems to be wrong because each manipulator enjoys temporary successes that events usually negate later. Ezeulu makes of the yams messages of vengeance, but the yams eventually turn into messengers of change in the hands of the famished citizens, the local mission school teacher, and the Anglican catechist. The teacher, in particular, recognizes the "open" letters of the yam and fully exploits them by urging his church members to convince their fellow citizens to substitute the church harvest for the New Yam Feast. He even tells them that if the "dead" Ulu can eat one fine tuber from each family, the "living" god deserves at least two. Both the Feast and the church ceremony inhabit entirely different worlds, but Mr. Goodcountry tears them from their different universes and yokes them together because both the yam and the harvest are so usable; they are independent messengers that, so to say, conventions and trappings of particular epochs cannot hold from circulating.

It is tempting to say that Ezeulu's foresight prevails because Christianity becomes widespread and the colonial administration fully settles down in Umuaro. Yielding to such temptation will amount to crediting Ezeulu with more than he deserves, for he is certainly not clairvoyant. Events do not happen the way they do simply because Ezeulu wishes them so but in spite of his desires. Events turn around because the traditional calendar markers refuse ironically to obey Ezeulu's wishes, and respond to the mission teacher's. It is true many kids go to the mission school as Ezeulu suspects they would; even Nwaka—Ezeulu's most vociferous critic—sends his laziest son there. I submit that events turn out this way because of the yam text's favorable response to the local teacher's perceptive, though opportunistic, reading. For readers like Ezeulu, the teacher's substituted text is the anti-thesis of all that the yam was created for.

Chinua Achebe's critics often attribute his wide readership to the simplicity and clear-headedness of his language and plots. As I have shown in this essay, a "literary" reading might indicate that such interpretation need not be simplistic. Undoubtedly, Achebe's fiction provides strong tools for unearthing the relationships of language and power in colonial societies and the sociolinguistics of English language in postcolonial Nigeria. In equally poignant terms, *Arrow of God* dramatizes problems associated with the materiality of the letter even in so-called oral cultures. In all the "contests" for the manipulation of "textual" meanings in this novel, it appears as if the victor is the "openness" of reading.

Notes

1. For an overview of proverb criticism in Achebe's fiction see Azeze, Cairns, Griffiths, and Lindfors.

2. I use rhetoric here in the sense that Paul de Man employs it in the first chapter of his *Allegories of Reading*.

3. One proverb will summarize the situation thus: when the willing dancer meets a drummer with an itching palm, a dance ensues.

4. And according to C. L. Innes, Achebe's reaction to Joyce Cary's colonialist novels is central to the "fiction" of the text. "Insofar as it is the story of the interaction between colonists and colonized, *Arrow of God* can be seen as yet another response by Achebe to *Mister Johnson* and the literary and historical perspective it represents . . ." (64).

5. The calendar furor is not simply the dilemma that sometimes arises when a community thrusts and entrusts its fate in the hands of one person but, in addition, it is a dramatization of the problem of fetishization of knowledge. Every one in Umuaro *knows* it is the end of the year, but the fetish guide of knowledge says they *do not know*. The elders could not fault this argument because it is so.

6. The aides and the community could have asked, "counting yams and counting fingers, what is the difference?" and Ezeulu would have responded, "that is the only difference!"

7. Umuaro is certainly a patriarchal society, but, surprisingly it does not take any individual patriarch's words, no matter how great, as absolute. Every father, the society believes, has his own story to tell, and even the Chief Priest's father's narrative has no superior force.

8. To realize that this novel is also about the authenticity and authentication of historical narratives, see Winterbottom's retelling of this and related incidents to his assistant a few years later. "This war between Umuaro and Okperi began in a rather interesting way. I went into it in considerable detail. . . . As I was saying, this war started because a man from Umuaro went to visit a friend in Okperi one fine morning and after he'd had one or two gallons of palm-wine—it's quite incredible how much of that dreadful stuff they can tuck away—anyhow, this man from Umuaro having drunk his friend's palm wine reached for his *ikenga* and split it in two. I may explain that *ikenga* is the most important fetish in the Ibo man's arsenal, so to speak. It represents his ancestors to whom he must make daily sac-

rifice. When he dies it is split in two; one half is buried with him and the other half is thrown away. So you can see the implication of what our friend from Umuaro did in splitting his host's fetish. This was, of course, the greatest sacrilege. The outraged host reached for his gun and blew the other fellow's head off. And so a regular war developed between the two villages, until I stepped in. I went into the question of the ownership of the piece of land which was the remote cause of all the unrest and found *without any shade of doubt* that it belonged to Okperi. I should mention that every witness who testified before me—from both sides without exception—perjured themselves. One thing you must remember in dealing with natives is that like children they are great liars. They don't lie simply to get out of trouble. Sometimes they would spoil a good case by a pointless lie. Only one man—a kind of priest-king in Umuaro—witnessed against his own people." (41)

9. For example, he reflects several times on the immensity of his latent powers. In the opening chapter, soon after citing a new moon, Ezeulu, while waiting for the yam to cook, contemplates the extent of his political clout and debates with himself whether "[h]is power was no more than the power of a child over a goat that was said to be his. As long as the goat was alive it was his; he would find food and take care of it. But the day it was slaughtered he would know who the real owner was. No! the Chief Priest of Ulu was more than that, must be more than that. If he should refuse to name the day [the Feast of Pumpkin Leaves] there would be no festival—no planting and no reaping. But could he refuse? No Chief Priest had ever refused. So it could not be done. He would not dare" (3). Lest it be thought that Ezeulu is a thoroughly evil person, it is very important I remark that he thinks he is obeying social conventions when he acts, but as my discussion should have shown, it is not in the nature of things (that is, it is not conventional) that conventions control all things.

10. In one other incident, Nweke Ukpaka appeals to Moses Unachukwu, the only Umuaro citizen who speaks some English, to help his age group inquire from the white road overseer why he is not paying them for the work they do. In his appeal, he says, "a man may refuse to do what is asked of him but may not refuse to be asked . . ." (18) That is to say, a messenger does not choose which message he accepts but exercises a considerable control over that which he delivers. If Ukpaka is right, a messenger cannot just not choose a message, he also cannot not bear a message. However, he cannot choose which ones will reach their destinations.

Works Cited

Achebe, Chinua. *Arrow of God*. New York: Anchor-Doubleday, 1969.

———. "The Novelist as a Teacher," *New Statesman* 29 Jan. 1965: 161-62.

Azeze, Fekade. "Folklore in Literature: Some Aspects of Achebe's Use of Proverbs in *Things Fall Apart* and *Arrow of God*." *Studies & Documents/Etudes & Documents* 3 (1982): 1-14.

Cairns, P. "Style, Structure and the Status of Language in Chinua Achebe's *Things Fall Apart* and *Arrow of God*." *World Literature Written in English* 25:1 (1985): 1-9.

Clifford, James. "On Ethnographic Allegory." *Writing Culture: The Poetics and Politics of Ethnography*. Ed. James Clifford and George E. Marcus. Berkeley: U of California P, 1986.

De Man, Paul. *Allegories of Reading: Figural Language in Rousseau, Nietzsche, Rilke, and Proust*. New Haven: Yale UP, 1979.

Griffiths, Gareth. "Language and Action in the Novels of Chinua Achebe." *African Literature Today* 5 (1971): 88-105.

Innes, C. L. *Chinua Achebe*. Cambridge: Cambridge UP, 1990.

Lindfors, Bernth. "The Palm-Oil with which Achebe's Words are Eaten." *African Literature Today* 1 (1968): 3-18.

Patnaik, Eira. "Proverbs as Cosmic Truth and Chinua Achebe's *No Longer At Ease*." *Africana Journal* 13.1-4 (1982): 98-103.

Spivak, Gayatri. *In Other Worlds: Essays in Cultural Politics*. New York and London, Routledge, 1988.

Chris Kwame Awuyah (essay date October 1992)

SOURCE: "Chinua Achebe's *Arrow of God*: Ezeulu's Response to Change," in *College Literature*, Vol. 19, No. 3, October, 1992, pp. 214-19.

[*In the following essay, Awuyah analyzes Ezeulu's attitudes toward colonial authorities in* Arrow of God, *focusing on the significance of his decision to send Oduche to a Christian missionary school.*]

Achebe's **Arrow of God** is a multifarious work with several uncharted territories that can be explored with much reward. However, one must exercise caution in teaching this text to neophytes, lest they become befuddled within its several contours. It is with this notion in mind that I introduce *Arrow of God* to my beginning class in world literature (at West Chester University, Pennsylvania), most of whom are taking literature at the university level for the first time as a General Education requirement. Instead of engaging my students in multiple interpretations, as *Arrow of God* really demands, I find it expedient to map out and concentrate on a few significant segments that invariably lead to the core of Achebe's art.

A principal issue which unfailingly elicits enthusiastic comments from students is Ezeulu's response to changes in his social environment as a result of the presence of the white man. By focusing on this topic students gain insight into Ezeulu's character and become acquainted with the background of British colonial rule in Eastern Nigeria. Usually we engage in spirited discussions about the ambivalent roles of Ezeulu as a protector of the indigenous tradition, but one who undermines his god and antagonizes his people by openly associating with the new forces. My aim is to help students appreciate Ezeulu's complex character and the difficult choices he has to make. I also find it timely to relate Achebe's art to the larger configuration of black writing. Students who have studied some aspects of African/ African American history and politics have an advantage in understanding the continuity and tradition behind Achebe's work. There is personal satisfaction when students eventually come to appreciate the simple fact that Ezeulu is after all a human being who acts in the interest of his own society and its future, not some strange being who fits the Western prototype of the Neanderthal.

In consonance with the objective of focusing on singular subjects in *Arrow of God* I will analyze Ezeulu's perception of the sociopolitical dynamism in Umuaro and review his conception of his own experience with the colonizer. In one of the most memorable passages of African fictional writing, Ezeulu, the chief priest of Umuaro, explains why he has sent his son, Oduche, to a mission school:

> I want one of my sons to join these people [the Christian mission] and be my eye there. If there is nothing in it you will come back. But if there is something there, you will bring home my share. The world is like a mask dancing. If you want to see it well, you do not stand in one place. (46)

An intricate and sophisticated man, Ezeulu could not have been unaware that he has compromised his position by urging Oduche to join the white man's religion and school, whose practices undermine the local tradition. In the past Ulu (the supreme god) protected Umuaro against hostile neighbors. But with the presence of the white man, all their local traditions have become violable. Even Ulu seems vul-

nerable, a fact signaled by the tolling of a church bell that momentarily distracts the chief priest as he prepares an annual rite.

Ezeulu is convinced that it is only by understanding their ways that he can challenge white men. He confides in his close friend, Akuebue, in proverbial language:

> Shall I tell why I sent my son? Then listen. A disease that has never been seen before cannot be cured with everyday herbs. . . . This is what our sages meant when they said that a man who has nowhere to put his hand for support puts it on his own knee. (133)

Thus, with some ambivalence, the chief priest's response to social and political exigencies constitutes, for him, the ultimate sacrifice. It is imperative that he seeks information about the "strangers" who have come uninvited to his land.

Power relations in the Umuaro region have changed with the intervention of the colonizer. The British colonial administration suppressed a war between Umuaro and their neighbors, Okperi, propped up Okperi as the administrative center of the subregion, and established warrant chiefs (effectively cronies of the colonizers) in an acephalous society. The chief priest has assumed that the power of the white man derives largely from literacy, especially the ability to write with the left hand. Ezeulu's statement to Oduche about the need to acquire Western literacy is putatively a Fanonian discourse of language as power:

> I saw a young white man who was able to write his book with the left hand; he could shout in my face; he could do what he liked. Why? Because he could write with his left hand. . . . I want you to learn and master this man's knowledge so much that if you are suddenly woken up from sleep and asked what it is you will reply. You must learn it until you can write it with your left hand. (189)

However, judging even from his personal confrontation with the British, it is clear that though Ezeulu is highly impressed with the new forces, he is not willing to cede his authority to them. It is inconceivable that this proud chief priest would abandon his own tradition. Ezeulu is unequivocal in instructing his children about propriety and observance of local customs. He tells Oduche:

> When a handshake goes beyond the elbow we know it has turned to another thing. . . . Your people should know the custom of this land; if they don't you must tell them. (13)

It seems to me that Ezeulu seeks social equilibrium, co-existence between the indigenous tradition and the new forces. Unfortunately, he does not anticipate that the colonizer, positing his own value system as an absolute, wants to dominate the existing sociopolitical and economic structure.

Already some of the ancillary trappings of the new culture have caused discomfort in Umuaro. Oduche, unlike any other family member, wears a singlet, and owns a slate and chalk and a wooden box—supplies from the Christian mission. While the rest of his family sits together during a storytelling session, Oduche sits apart, completely absorbed, learning the alphabet from his new book, *Azu Ndu*.

But the real threat to Umuaro comes from the colonizer's utter disregard and, consequently, his attempt to impose a new order on the local society. A major case is the mission's crusade against indigenous traditions they consider anathematic to Christian faith. Fired with this zeal, the impressionable Oduche tries to harm a royal python, a symbol of ancestor worship. Oduche's attempt to suffocate this snake in a box, made by a missionary carpenter, is symbolic of the efforts of the Christian forces to subjugate the traditional religion.

Ezeulu regards himself as an equal and a friend of the British administration, and therefore may not have reckoned that he is at odds with the new forces, who are bent on dominating and destroying Umuaro. In line with their fixed definition of relations with the colonized, the British consider themselves at opposite ends with Ezeulu. However, even though they failed to recognize common grounds with the local people, the British have no hesitation about exploiting the social order of Umuaro in an attempt to legitimize colonial rule. Indeed, the head of the colonial administration in eastern Nigeria, Captain Winterbottom, is convinced that Ezeulu would be the best candidate through whom to maintain their authority over Umuaro. Having come to that conclusion, the British intimidated and coerced Ezeulu to become chief of Umuaro. But the chief priest remained unswayed, vowing he would "not be anybody's chief, except Ulu" (174). Dismayed at Ezeulu's resolution, the administration called him an insane witch-doctor and promptly imprisoned him.

Though embittered by his personal experience, Ezeulu is nevertheless determined to find out the full extent of the white man's power, declaring tersely: "a man must dance the dance prevalent in his time" (189). But first he must contend with problems within his own community. Because of his incarceration the chief priest was not able to perform two of the monthly ceremonies of eating sacred yams from the previous year's harvest. By custom, Ezeulu must perform these rituals before declaring the New Yam festival, which marks the beginning of a new harvest. Meanwhile food from the last season is exhausted. In the ensuing confusion, the Christian mission subverts Ezeulu's authority by urging Umuaros to harvest their crops once they make offering to the Christian God, who will protect them against Ulu. Initially, the response is slow, but, as the threat of starvation looms, even important members of the community openly seek the sanctuary of the church for immunity against Ulu, thereby subverting the authority of the traditional priest.

In the end, Ezeulu is destroyed. His tragedy is caused not so much by his personal pride as by his failure to determine the true objectives of the colonizer. The chief priest's authority has been undermined by the British administration, thus setting in motion a series of events that disrupt the political and social order of Umuaro. It is ironic that Ezeulu, the most enlightened member of Umuaro, the person with foresight, should be destroyed by the new forces.

Achebe's characterization of Ezeulu belies myths about Africa as a primordial world, an emptiness, where the benighted natives live in benign nature, waiting to be redeemed by Europeans. Ezeulu is a very impressive and an immensely powerful man, with a sharp intellect, and he is independent minded. He is the only opposing voice among the council of elders when Umuaro declares war on Okperi, and he fervently defends his decision to send Oduche to learn about the white man's culture. But even when he is at variance with some elders of Umuaro, Ezeulu never loses confidence in the system whereby leaders of the six villages which form Umuaro meet and debate mutual matters. As Achebe indicates in **Arrow of God**, the social fabric of Umuaro can absorb singular acts, dissensions, and personal differences, since the community has faith in the system.

However, when the British got to Igboland, they assumed that they had "discovered" a people living in a state of *tabula rasa*. These colonizers then considered it their duty to civilize the Igbos, to save them from the pervasive darkness. This sentiment was expressed by Captain Winterbottom who, with self-indulgence, noted the transformation in his houseboy, Boniface:

> He's a fine specimen, isn't he? He's been with me four years. He was a little boy of thirteen—by my own calculation, they've no idea of years—when I took him on. He was absolutely raw. (35)

Their cultural blinkers have prevented the British from relating well to the local people. The British administration do not appreciate Ezeulu's attributes since, for them, he is no more than "the Other." Ironically, however, it is the chief priest who shows openness, accommodation and desire to relate intellectually and with some objectivity to the foreigners.

The attributes of the Igbos, which Achebe attests to, had been validated nearly two centuries earlier by Olaudah Equiano, whose personal odyssey began in his native Essaka, Igboland, in eastern Nigeria, where he was kidnapped and sold into slavery, and later transported to the West Indies, America, and Europe. Equiano, whose name in Igbo means "one who is chosen" or "who has a loud voice," struggled to acquire literacy and has given a powerful written testimony of his experience not just of slavery, but also of life prior to enslavement. In *The Interesting Narrative of the Life of Olaudah Equiano*, he recalls in endearing terms details about his birth place, his family, and the social order. Equiano illuminates everyday activities, noting:

> We are almost a nation of dancers, musicians, and poets. Every great event, such as triumphant return from battle, or other cause of public rejoicing, is celebrated in public dances, which are accompanied with songs and music suited to the occasion. (14)

Even after his immersion in Western culture, Equiano speaks proudly of his African roots. He challenges Western aspersions about Africans as primitive, not quite human, and therefore deserving to be enslaved.

Akin to Equiano's testimony about the virtues of the Igbos, Frederick Douglass's *Narrative of the Life of Frederick Douglass* documents the painful experience of enslaved blacks in Maryland who, nonetheless, maintain their humanity. Douglass' autobiography is a personal triumph, manifesting the elevation of the human mind and empowerment that come with literacy. In a well-known episode that recalls the aspiration of the deformed slave, Caliban, to acquire the discourse of his master, Prospero, in order to attain freedom (in Shakespeare's *Tempest*), the enslaver, Mr. Auld, vigorously opposes his wife's attempt to teach Douglass to read. Accordingly, Douglass comes to the realization that literacy constitutes "the pathway . . . to freedom" (275).

Scholars such as Donald Wesling, James Olney, and Henry Louis Gates, Jr. have written extensively about the connections between literacy, slave narratives, and the affirmation of the humanity of black people. Suffice it here to say that the ethos of African/African American writing involves self-definitions, renunciation of mislabeling, and crossing boundaries from non-beings into beings. Writers who share the African heritage engage in these paradigmatic acts of reconstructing self-images. Some of the most eloquent expressions are by Achebe, Equiano, and Douglass.

In *Arrow of God,* although Ezeulu is physically destroyed, his vision has staying power. By learning to read and write,

Oduche acquires a powerful tool to express himself, to proclaim the richness of his culture, and even to protest against the presence of the colonizer. In a sense, the achievements of Achebe himself and others have become possible because of the foundation laid by the likes of Oduche. *Arrow of God* fits into the framework of black experience and must be linked with substantive issues of African/African American humanism.

Works Cited

Achebe, Chinua. *Arrow of God.* New York: Doubleday, 1989.

Douglass, Frederick. "Narrative of the Life of Frederick Douglass, an African Slave." *The Classic Slave Narrative.* Ed. Henry Louis Gates, Jr. New York: New American Library, 1987.

Equiano Olaudah. "The Interesting Narrative of the Life of Olaudah Equiano or Gustavus Vassa, the African." *The Classic Slave Narrative.* Ed. Henry Louis Gates, Jr. New York: New American Library, 1987.

Chelva Kanaganayakam (essay date October 1993)

SOURCE: "Art and Orthodoxy in Chinua Achebe's 'Anthills of the Savannah,'" in *Ariel*, Vol. 24, No. 4, October, 1993, pp. 35-51.

[*In the following essay, Kanaganayakam compares and contrasts Achebe's narrative technique in* Anthills of the Savannah *to that of his earlier works.*]

Twenty-one years after the publication of *A Man of the People* (1966), Chinua Achebe published *Anthills of the Savannah,* perhaps his most enigmatic and complex work to date. The years separating these two works have been significant ones in the life of the author, for they entailed a deep concern with political turmoil, disillusionment with economic and cultural life, loss of friends and property, and an undying faith in the ultimate destiny of his country. All these sentiments find expression in the short stories, poems, and essays published in the 1970s and 1980s, particularly in his work of non-fiction, *The Trouble with Nigeria* (1984). It is thus not surprising that the novel that followed this period of upheaval (and the author's concomitant silence as a novelist) should be different in many ways, although the thematic preoccupations of the previous novels still persist. What has changed is the attitude to a historical process, and that in turn has necessitated a more experimental form, one that transcends the referentiality of his earlier works and lends itself to greater complexity and syncreticity of vision.

Responses to the novel have varied from unqualified admiration to disappointment and scepticism. Emmanuel Ngara, for instance, speaks of the author soaring "to the heights of literary artistry" (128), and Elleke Boehmer claims that Achebe's "new vision is manifested in the strategic gender configurations of his central characters" (102). David Maughan-Brown is cautious about the ideology of leadership implicit in the novel and comments: "the solution Achebe's fiction here proposes to what its author sees as the problems afflicting contemporary Nigeria seem to me to be unlikely to have the durability of the anthills of the savannah, capable of enduring many seasons of grassfires" (148). The diversity of opinion points to the difficulties inherent in a narrative that self-consciously forges new directions.

Achebe has preserved a meticulous sense of historical continuum in his first four novels, beginning with the turn of the century in *Things Fall Apart* (1958) and moving to the post-independence era in *A Man of the People* (1966). In between are *No Longer at Ease* (1960), which deals with the classic been-to predicament of disillusionment and *Arrow of God* (1964), a novel about a priest who refuses to change with the times.[1] *Anthills of the Savannah* confronts the present by focussing on the oppressive military rule in the West African state of Kangan. Continuities are also present at other levels, and the author himself draws attention to his previous works through intertextual references. Beatrice's mention of Chielo, the priestess of Agbala, is, for instance, a clear reference to the relevance of *Things Fall Apart* to this work. Both novels are concerned with the idea of a hero and the implications of death. The preoccupation with tradition and the symbiotic relation between values and ritual figure prominently in both *Arrow of God* and *Anthills of the Savannah.* A concern with the predicament of the been-to informs *No Longer at Ease,* and in some ways all the major characters in *Anthills of the Savannah,* like Obi Okonkwo, are victims of a colonial and alienating education. Despite ostensible differences in the political context, the same urge to build up the nation dominate the protagonists of both novels. The cynicism of Odili as he watches the machinations of Chief Nanga in *A Man of the People* parallels the disdain of Chris, the Commissioner for Information, as he watches the ministers debase themselves in the presence of the president in *Anthills of the Savannah.*

However, the artistic impulse that informs Achebe's early novels is a tendentious and celebratory one, which the author himself documents at various points. As a writer, Achebe sees his world not as a taxonomist "whose first impulse on seeing a new plant or animal is to define, classify and file away," and not as a taxidermist "who plies an even less desirable trade" (*Morning* 49-50), but that of a teacher, committed "to help [his] society regain belief in itself and put away the complexes of the years of denigration and self-abasement" (*Morning* 44). He sees himself not merely as a social critic or historian, but as a teacher who seeks to remedy an internalized sense of inferiority. He comments that "although the work of redeeming which needs to be done may appear too daunting, I believe it is not one day too soon to begin" (*Hopes* 13). Abdul JanMohamed rightly points out that "the dilemma produced by colonialist praxis", namely "denigration and historical catalepsy" (178), leads Achebe to reject the acquired ontology and affirm the value of a culture that has been displaced and disprized. A concern with the conflict between two ontologies, as it manifests not only in a confrontation between the colonizer and the colonized but also in the inner contradictions and complexities of individuals and families, finds expression in the realistic mode. As JanMohamed observes:

> Realism, then, is his aesthetic as well as ethical response not only to colonialist views of African societies but also to the social dilemma of African cultures that are attempting to come to terms with the disorganization that is the legacy of colonialism. (178)

Anthills of the Savannah does not jettison this preoccupation. In fact it thrives on it by drawing attention to several manifestations of this conflict, including notions of exile, alienation and identity. Even more significantly, the novel draws heavily on the sentiments expressed in *The Trouble with Nigeria.* The points of contact between the two works are striking. Of the corruption in Nigeria, Achebe comments:

> Nigeria is *not* a great country. It is one of the most disorderly nations in the world. It is one of the most corrupt, insensitive, inefficient places under the sun. It is one of the most expensive countries, and one of those that give least value for money. It is dirty, callous, noisy, ostentatious, dishonest and vulgar. (*Trouble* 9)

Ikem's speech to the students in *Anthills of the Savannah* captures something of the vituperative quality of these words. The problems confronting Igbos that the author discusses at length in his non-fiction are reiterated in the secessionist desires of Abazon in *Anthills of the Savannah.* Transformed into fictive terms, distanced by different names, the political context still remains that of Nigeria.

Also, the novel is, as Fiona Sparrow quite clearly demonstrates in her review of the novel, a memorial to Christopher Okigbo, who died fighting in the Biafran war; Achebe movingly captures his greatness in the phrase "headstone on tiny debris of passionate courage" in the poem **"Mango Seedling"** (*Christmas* 16-17) written in memory of his friend. That he chooses to call his protagonist in **Anthills of the Savannah** Christopher Oriko and have him die in Abazon opposing a mindless sergeant indicates that the author intends the parallels to be made clear to the reader. Achebe has called his friend "the finest Nigerian poet of his generation" (**Don't** 8), and this novel is a fitting tribute to his life. In short, the novel, in addition to its concern with a historical dialectic, becomes a version of truth to a much greater degree than his previous works, which draw on political and social reality without insisting on an identification between art and life.

All these factors lead to the expectation of a strikingly referential surface, at least to the extent of his previous novels. Despite the quality of orality, the repetitious structures and the metaphorical underpinning, the early novels remain very much in the tradition of realism. They are novels that, despite their ambivalence, affirm and celebrate an indigenous ontology. **Anthills of the Savannah,** on the other hand, departs from this mode by foregrounding narrative form and language, creating paradigms that both complement and subvert meaning and by exploring an experience that the reader perceives as all too real while accepting the fictionality of the text. The novel thus marks a point of transition, a point of departure by concerning itself with forms of reading and perception, and with structures that make meaning more elusive and complex. Insisting on the fictionality and autonomy of the text becomes an important strategy in occupying a more fluid space that straddles both the public and the artistic. Interestingly, this is achieved, at least in part, by insisting on the political context and the sequentiality of the novel.

Despite the discontinuities and digressions, the reader never loses sight of the corrupt and corrupting political reality of Kangan. The secession of Abazon surfaces at various points, drawing attention to inner tensions and the fear of rulers. In fact, the novel begins with a delegation from Abazon to the Presidential Palace, and concludes (if one excepts the section on naming Elewa's daughter) with the death of Chris in Abazon. In between lies an attempt at sequentiality that insists on **Anthills of the Savannah** as a political novel about contemporary West Africa. Corruption, secret trials, jockeying for power and all the machinations of a corrupt political world provide the necessary backdrop for the text.

The political scene is seen as an inevitable aftermath of a historical process that involves acquired values, the role of the colonizer, and the values that colonization engenders. Repeated references to the colonizer departing with his luggage and leaving the colonized with half-formed ideas, a craving for power, and a desire to imitate the colonial master reinforce the suspicion that independence has been won only in principle and not in practice. The classic example of cultural conflict is evident in Sam whose studied mannerisms are described as an attempt to imitate an English gentleman of leisure. More specifically, images of the colonizer are present in Lou, the American journalist, and Mad Medico, the eccentric but astute hospital administrator. Lou is more overtly an exploiter, as is evident in her speech about how Nigeria should handle its economic policies, while Mad Medico is a more complex figure who combines a genuine regard for the African landscape with a contempt for the country's attempt to run itself and a penchant for essentialist statements. It is not without significance that his steward is called Sunday—recalling Friday. In Mad Medico's eulogies about the difference between England and Africa, and in Beatrice's skeptical comments about Mad Medico's double standards, the reader glimpses conflicts that have not been totally resolved, despite the departure of the colonizer.

These perceptions emerge as part of the *Weltanschauung,* in spite of the narrative that constantly parades its artifice, upsets the readers' expectations, and insists on its fictionality. The reader perceives this duality, and it is in the author's insistence on creating a form that works ostensibly against content that the uniqueness of the novel lies. As David Richards points out, the novel is "in part, an essentially optimistic manifesto of the power of 'the literary' in all its humanistic potential to offer an alternative epistemology to that of the state, another constellation of meaning and an arena for the outlawed disputation of political ideologies" (135).

Achebe's concern with form and the problematic nature of his endeavour become apparent in the metafictional comments he incorporates into his novel. In subtle ways, Achebe has found ways of commenting on his work even in his earlier novels. In **Arrow of God,** for instance, Edogo is clearly an artist-surrogate. As Edogo looks at the mask he has carved as it appears during a festival and wonders whether its features betray a weakness that he did not intend, and whether the response of the onlookers is a measure of his success, he is clearly meditating on the value and integrity of his art. And yet these comments are woven seamlessly into the novel, so that the reader perceives no disruption in the referentiality. **Anthills of the Savannah,** on the other hand, is more direct in its commentary. Soon after the humiliating episode with Sam at the Presidential Retreat, Beatrice feels the impulse to write, even at the expense of neglecting her routine chores. She is drawn by a frenzy to her writing about which the narrator comments:

> The discarded pages and the nearly spoilt meat seemed
> like a necessary ritual or a sacrifice to whoever had to

be appeased for this audacity of rushing in where sensible angels fear to tread, or rather for pulling up one of those spears thrust into the ground by the men in the hour of their defeat and left there in the circle of their last dance together. (83)

Here the distance between the immediate episode that occasioned the spurt of writing and language that draws on history, legend, and resistance foreground the metafictional comment. In a more specific manner, Ikem, the editor of the *Gazette,* observes that "a novelist must listen to his characters who after all are created to wear the shoe and point the writer where it pinches" (96). Later, after Ikem's speech to the students, the chairman, in an attempt to put out the fires caused by Ikem, says that "writers in the Third World context must not stop at the stage of documenting social problems but move to the higher responsibility of proffering prescriptions" and Ikem interjects with "writers don't give prescriptions. . . . They give headaches" (161).

No longer is the role of the writer or the purpose of writing clear. If Beatrice's attempt is therapeutic in some way, Ikem's comment strongly opposes the pedagogical role of the writer. The idea of the writer as non-conformist is dealt with in greater detail, with classic irony, in the episodes involving Mad Medico's friend and visiting poet, Dick, whose language and description of his magazine *Reject* clearly indicate the limitations of the kind of criticism that the visiting poet espouses.

As unclear as the objectives of writing are the forms that could express a complex vision. Beatrice, having alluded to the many strands—such as Christian, African, white, black—that make up her world, comments:

> World inside a world inside a world, without end. *Uwat'uwa* in our language. As a child how I thrilled to that strange sound with its capacity for infinite replication till it becomes the moan of the rain in the ear as it opened and closed, opened and closed. (85)

Her world, like a Chinese box, holds multitudes, and like the experience in the novel, needs a form that would contain it. A little later, the bearded old man talks about the significance of the storyteller:

> The sounding of the battle-drum is important; the fierce waging of the war itself is important; and the telling of the story afterwards—each is important in its own way. . . . But if you ask me which of them takes the eagle-feather I will say boldly: the story. (123-24).

Having affirmed the significance of the story, the old man concludes by recounting a tale which deals with the leopard and the tortoise—one which makes a tremendous impact on Ikem—about how the tortoise, moments before its death at the hands of the leopard, asks for a few moments to scratch the sand furiously to create the impression of a struggle. Here again is the notion of pretence, of fiction, a leap of the imagination that transforms the reality of defeat into something ennobling and positive.

The metafictional comments alert the reader to problems of form, of embedded paradigms that question and subvert and pose dualities in the novel. Paradigms of detection and legality appear very early in the novel, signalled by the titles of two chapters, namely, "First Witness" and "Second Witness." The structures suggest ways of reading and artistic intent, patterns of disclosure and gradual peeling away of layers until the truth is revealed. The pattern is reinforced by the various episodes of questioning and interrogation that take place in the novel, each time with the intention of arriving at the truth. Sam, at the beginning, questions two of his ministers to ascertain the truth about Chris's integrity. Police officers question Ikem, again ostensibly to get details about the parking offence. Beatrice undergoes a similar experience when her house is raided. When Chris disguises himself and attempts to leave Bassa, he is questioned by a soldier who wants to see if Chris is who he claims to be. Significantly, each time the attempt to arrive at the truth fails, thereby questioning the validity of the paradigm as a vehicle for probing the truth. Sam, for instance, totally misunderstands the integrity of his friends, which eventually leads to a series of rash decisions and his final downfall. The soldier believes Chris's fiction about selling motor parts and fails to perceive the truth. Significantly, the only person who sees through the disguise chooses not to expose Chris until after the shooting. Ironically, Chris succumbs to what he seeks to avoid by getting shot, but that is not a result of anyone discovering his true identity. Not unlike the story of the tortoise and the leopard, it is invariably the semblance of truth, the pretence, that appears to be significant. The legal process of questioning witnesses and examining evidence proves futile in the context of the novel.

The paradigm of legality leads to notions of judgement, with which the novel is so insistently concerned. Here again, judgement is perceived to be faulty. Ikem and Chris are both judged to be traitors and punished. The elders from Abazon are misjudged and arrested while Abazon is ostracized. Mad Medico is hastily deported for no valid reason. The structures that one would expect to support a referential reading now become suspect.

The paradigm of detection is reinforced by the process of providing clues rather than answers to the various mysteries in the novel. Anonymous phone calls, coded messages, nuances of expression promise greater revelation when the layers are finally peeled away. The anonymous phone calls, contrary to expectations, turn out to be those of a sympathetic officer. Chris's final words "The last green" allude to a private joke of no great significance except to Beatrice. The end of the novel is always predictable—in fact it is predicted by Beatrice in one of her visionary moments—and the various structures that promise meaning through a gradual process of disclosure are, in fact, deliberately rendered inadequate.

This process of subversion is underlined by the technique of revealing effects before the causes are examined. On the one hand, events are foretold long before they occur. On the other, incidents like the suspension of Ikem are mentioned before the events leading to it are revealed to the reader. In both cases, the narrative departs from its ostensible pattern of disclosure and sequentiality. In some ways, the novel works against itself by creating expectations only to subvert them. As Ikem points out in a slightly different context, drawing attention to the difficulty of leaning on absolutes, "all certitude must now be suspect" (99).

It is thus not surprising that the novel is so wilfully discontinuous in its account of the various events that take place. Climactic episodes, once they occur, are abandoned for several pages and picked up when the intensity of the moment is no longer felt by the reader. Beatrice's confrontation with the president, which the reader knows is bound to have its consequences, is abandoned for the next twenty-five pages, and continued only after a detailed account of Beatrice's life and her relations with Ikem and Chris. The intervening episodes are crucial to an understanding of the novel, but they do disrupt the linearity of the novel. At the beginning of *Anthills of the Savannah,* the reader is given an elaborate account of Ikem attempting to reach the Presidential Palace (for reasons unknown) in the midst of heavy traffic, and the causes and consequences are left unexplained for several chapters. The discontinuity has the effect of distancing the realism and compelling the reader to look at the synchronic axis in order to perceive complexities of meaning.

The constant interruptions to the linear narrative lead to what is perhaps a very significant aspect of the novel, namely, the strategy of presenting a series of micro narratives, linked together tenuously by the thread of sequentiality. The narratives are spoken by various voices: Chris, Ikem, Beatrice, and an unnamed omniscience. Each voice presents its own way of telling the narrative, thereby establishing its uniqueness and looking at various ways of dealing with the text. Interestingly enough, the president, who is a long-standing friend of the main characters, and who determines the events in the novel, is never made a narrator. He becomes the object of much discussion, and the reader hears conflicting tales about him, but his voice is never available. It is almost as if parts of the puzzle are deliberately left out for the reader to fill in.

Chris's voice, in keeping with his professed desire to remain "reasonable" at all times, is the voice of common sense looking somewhat sceptically, even cynically, at the contradictions of the present from the point of view of one who belongs to the establishment. His is the voice of the critic who chooses not to become an exile. In fact, he declares that he prefers the charade of the present over the option of lecturing in foreign lands about the oppression of his homeland. His voice, then, focusses on the present and strengthens the referentiality of the text. In some ways it is appropriate to have him do so, for he is in some ways a fictionalized version of Christopher Okigbo, whose presence in the novel mediates between historical circumstance and fictional text.

Ikem's narrative is unpredictable, for as the editor of a leading newspaper one would expect him to be committed to current affairs. Yet he deals with abstractions, more like a poet than an editor. On one occasion, he relates a story of public executions in a manner that recalls Achebe's poem **"Public Execution in Pictures"** (*Christmas* 60-61). While Achebe's poem is largely descriptive, Chris's version, which is far more complex, serves as a frame for the entire narrative. He claims his story to be real, but his narration flaunts its textuality and thus suggests the artifice of the entire narrative. The execution he describes involves four thieves, one of whom is dressed like a prince. The clothes worn by the prince are reminiscent of the president while the execution itself has obvious parallels with the crucifixion of Christ. The prince's final words "I shall be born again," reminiscent of Nicodemus, underscore the religious dimension of the novel, while the reference to four thieves clearly alludes to Sam, Chris, Ikem, and Mad Medico, all of whom are either killed or deported in the course of the narrative. If the scene is intensely real in its evocation of disgust and horror, it is also fictive in the manner in which it foretells the future and serves as a frame. Ikem's narrative, like that of Beatrice and the omniscient narrator, leads the narrative away from the immediate context into one that is non-linear and metaphoric.

Both the omniscient narrator and Beatrice employ a frame of reference that includes the referential and the mythical and a species of language that ranges from pidgin to standard English, all of which enable them to move freely in two worlds—the metonymic and the metaphoric. This fluidity of movement is at its best when the focus is Beatrice. Fiona Sparrow's comment that "Beatrice is the most important female character that Achebe has created" and that the "modern Beatrice" is "also a goddess and a muse" (58) alludes to the complexity of her portrayal. The multiplicity of her role comes through at various points, often through the language that intervenes between the actual event and the metaphoric subtext.

This duality is central to the design of the novel. At the referential/metonymic level, she is the promising civil servant, the pride of the nation, the headstrong "been-to," and the angered and disappointed lover. At this level, she is contemptuous of the visiting journalist, sceptical of Mad Medico's cynicism, and defiant of traditional notions of marriage. Her career, in referential terms, proves to be far from successful, and she is seen as a victim not merely of a corrupt political regime, but also the entire process of colonization. It is, however, at the metaphoric level that the significance of her portrayal becomes evident. Here is Beatrice's description of her "seduction" of the president:

> And was I glad the king was slowly but surely responding! Was I glad! The big snake, the royal python of a gigantic erection began to stir in the shrubbery of my shrine as we danced closer and closer to soothing airs, soothing our ancient bruises together in the dimmed lights. Fully aroused he clung desperately to me. And I took him then boldly by the hand and led him to the balcony railings to the breathtaking view of the dark lake from the pinnacle of the hill. And there told him the story of my Desdemona. (81)

Sam's essentialist assertion that "African chiefs are always polygamists" and his loss of self-respect in the presence of the American journalist, combined with Beatrice's recollection of having been abandoned by a boyfriend as a result of what is called the "Desdemona complex," are occasions for this impulsive act of humiliating the president. And yet the language insists on the mythical dimension of the episode, alluding to the goddess Idemili, the dark lake from which she rose, her punishment of a lascivious chief through the python, all of which are documented in the section entitled "Idemili." She herself is not entirely conscious of the mythical dimension, but she is aware, she declares, that "[s]omething possessed [her] as [she] told it" (81). Now she is an emblem of tradition, an angry goddess, a prophetess and a priestess.

Soon after her humiliation, she is visited by Ikem in circumstances that are not unlike a similar episode in England when Ikem, in response to a telephone call, braves the weather to visit her. Now the language distances the narrative and suggests the mystical/mythical element. Ikem comes "barging into a pillar of rain" to sing the praises of Idemili. This time Beatrice offers no shelter in her home, and Ikem, after having read his "love poem," which he calls the gift of insight, leaves, and both are aware that the parting is forever. Ikem goes as it were to obey the dictates of the goddess, leaving behind "twitches of intermittent lightning and the occasional, satiated hiccup of distant thunder"

(101). The narrator in the next section rightly points out that "Ikem alone came close to sensing the village priestess who will prophesy when her divinity rides her" (105).

Beatrice, however, is not done with her role. In response to the question posed by a bird—"Is the King's property correct?"—she responds, "You have not heard the news? The King's treasury was broken into last night and all his property carried away" (108), drawing attention to her "seduction" of the president, who, one remembers, is described as a "moral virgin" by Mad Medico. But Beatrice, as goddess seeking revenge, goes even further. She entices Chris in a scene in which once again the language intervenes between event and fictional text:

> From there she took charge of him leading him by the hand silently through heaving groves mottled in subdued yellow sunlight, treading dry leaves underfoot till they came to streams of clear blue water. More than once he had slipped on the steep banks and she had pulled him up and back with such power and authority as he had never seen her exercise before. (114)

The consummation is described in terms that resemble an archetypal quest, an initiation into a different realm. Beatrice herself comments that she is like Chielo, the priestess and prophetess of the Hills and the Caves. From this moment, Chris ceases to be "reasonable" and is quickly involved in the overthrow of the government. The consummation leads to a commitment against the political regime and eventually leads to death. He becomes, in a sense, the instrument of punishment for Sam, while becoming a victim himself for abandoning Beatrice in her moment of need.

She is both goddess and priestess, the source of authority and the witness, one who knows and does not know. The ambiguity is central to the novel for the death of Chris leaves Beatrice devastated, and when she recovers the narrator comments:

> It was rather the ending of an exile that the faces acknowledged, the return of utterance to the sceptical priest struck dumb for a season by the Almighty for presuming to set limits on his omnipotence. (220)

Beatrice's narrative includes a "love poem" written by Ikem about the plight of women who are either forced to bear the burden of guilt or become objects of veneration—either way rendered irrelevant in the process of running the world. Symbolically, the poem captures the paradox that relates to Beatrice. Ikem pays tribute to this complexity in an important passage:

> Those who would see no blot of villainy in the beloved

oppressed nor grant the faintest glimmer of humanity to the hated oppressor are partisans, patriots and party-liners. In the grand finale of things there will be a mansion also for them where they will be received and lodged in comfort by the single-minded demigods of their devotion. But it will not be in the complex and paradoxical cavern of Mother Idoto. (100-01)

At this level, Beatrice is the goddess in whom are enshrined the values of a culture. She is the source of nourishment and nemesis, the daughter of the almighty who was created "to bear witness to the moral nature of authority by wrapping around Power's rude waist a loincloth of peace and modesty" (102). At the end of the novel, her character undergoes yet another transformation as she decides to hold a naming ceremony for Elewa's daughter, and dismissing the claims of tradition, names the child herself. The name she suggests—Amaechina (Ama for short)—is, as the characters point out, both masculine and feminine. The subversion of tradition is caused by the symbol of tradition. The ceremony takes place accompanied by a dance that includes Muslim, Christian, and African elements. As Beatrice herself comments, "if a daughter of Allah could join his rival's daughter in a holy dance, what is to stop the priestess of an unknown god from shaking a leg?" (224). The multiplicity of the novel, the fusion of black, white, religious, secular, African, and European finds expression at the end, leading to a new beginning. The transformation recalls Achebe's comment in an essay entitled **"The Igbo World and Its Art"** where he says: "It stands to reason, therefore, that new forms must stand ready to be called into being as often as new (threatening) forces appear on the scene" (**Hopes** 43).

Beatrice, in fact, is as much Classical, Indian, and Christian as she is African. The Christian element is pervasive in the novel, and its complexity is hinted at the very beginning in the title "First Witness." The thread is picked up in the execution, in the references to Esther, the pillar of salt, the Book of Genesis, and the New Testament. Beatrice as the pillar of salt is likened to Lot's wife (which recalls Mad Medico's graffiti about Sodom and Gomorrah), and in her role as seductress a courtesan in the Indian temples, and as an unattainable lover and the object of quest and adoration, none other than Dante's Beatrice.

The non-referential, mythical dimension of the novel persists right through to the end, even in the latter part which lends itself so readily to a linear, sequential reading. It is significant that as Chris makes his plans to escape, two others—Emmanuel and Braimoh—join him, making a party of three and filling the spaces created by the absence of Ikem and Sam. Three continues to be a magic number, with Emmanuel giving Chris three kola nuts—a trivial detail that turns out to be significant when the latter is questioned by

the soldier—and Chris's last words refer to a private joke involving three green bottles. The symbolic reading prompted by the symmetry is reinforced by the three enigmatic inscriptions on the bus. The inscriptions suggest notions of guilt, suffering and redemption, all of which suggest that the journey is as much one of self-discovery as it is of escape. The journey needs to be seen in relation to Ikem's "Hymn to the Sun," which, unlike Donne's poem, is a hymn of lovelessness, dispossession, and loss of tradition. It describes a landscape through which Chris now travels, one in which the trees are stunted, like "anthills surviving to tell the new grass of the savannah about last year's brush fires" (30). Here Chris discovers himself in a final heroic gesture. Interestingly, the description of the scene concludes with a struggle in the sand between the Braimoh and the brutal strength of the sergeant, an encounter that is strongly reminiscent of the tale of the tortoise and the leopard. The juxtaposition underlines the relation between truth and art with which the novel is concerned, and which Achebe defines elsewhere as the truth of fiction: "Art is man's constant effort to create for himself a different order of reality from that which is given him, an aspiration to provide himself with a second handle on existence *through his imagination*" (**Hopes** 95-96).

In the final analysis, the novel defies easy classification. If, in the manner of the earlier novels, it deals with issues of contemporary relevance, it does so in a manner that projects ambiguity. While the novel does not abandon its pedagogical role, it refuses to take shelter in orthodoxy. Chinua Achebe's role as artist supersedes that of teacher. If a mimetic mode and a readily identifiable binary of ruler and ruled inform the previous works, an experimental form and an ambivalent subjective stance characterise the recent one. The writer is not removed from sociopolitical concerns, but the involvement is predicated on artistic distance. Inevitably, this space prevents a wholehearted endorsement of and alliance with power brokers. As Ikem points out, "a genuine artist, no matter what he says or believes, must feel in his blood the ultimate enmity between art and orthodoxy" (100). If the novel creates paradigms of reading only to subvert them, structures of realism only to disown them, it is because the novel is in many ways a charting of new territory, an exploration of the process of writing and the role of the artist in relation to the contemporary postcolonial reality about which he must write. Beatrice's seemingly innocent response to Ikem might well be one that Achebe, confronted with the complexity of postcolonial Nigeria, would reiterate: "wetin be my concern here?" (90).

Notes

1. Griffiths, in his article that deals with the "missing volume" in Achebe's trilogy, discusses the hiatus as "the difficulty within the hybridized poetics of a postcolonial

literature of formulating the revolutionary public conse-quences of the personal 'betrayals' of those transitional fig-ures who straddle the period of cultural onslaught and change" (21). While it might be far-fetched to assert that *Anthills of the Savannah* is the missing volume, it could certainly be argued that this novel attempts to deal with the difficulties in filling the lacunae.

Works Cited

Achebe, Chinua. *Christmas in Biafra and Other Poems.* New York: Doubleday, 1973.

————. *Morning Yet on Creation Day.* London: Heinemann, 1975.

————. *Don't Let Him Die: An Anthology of Memorial Poems for Christopher Okigbo 1932-1967.* Enugu, Nige-ria: Fourth Dimension Publishers, 1978.

————. *The Trouble with Nigeria.* London: Heinemann, 1984.

————. *Hopes and Impediments: Selected Essays.* Lon-don: Heinemann, 1988.

————. *Anthills of the Savannah.* London: Pan Books, 1989.

Boehmer, Elleke. "Of Goddesses and Stories: Gender and a New Politics in Achebe's *Anthills of the Savannah.*" *Kunapipi* 12.2 (1990): 102-12.

Griffiths, Gareth. "Chinua Achebe: When Did You Last See Your Father?" *World Literature Written in English* 27.1 (1987): 18-27.

Lodge, David. *The Modes of Modern Writing: Metaphor, Metonymy, and the Typology of Modern Literature.* Lon-don: Edward Arnold, 1977.

Maughan-Brown, David. "*Anthills of the Savannah* and the Ideology of Leadership." *Kunapipi* 12.2 (1990): 139-48.

JanMohammed, Abdul. *Manichean Aesthetics: The Poli-tics of Literature in Colonial Africa.* Amherst: U of Mas-sachusetts P, 1983.

Ngara, Emmanuel. "Achebe as Artist: The Place and Sig-nificance of *Anthills of the Savannah.*" *Kunapipi* 12.2 (1990): 113-29.

Sparrow, Fiona. Rev. of *Anthills of the* Savannah. *World Lit-erature Written in English* 28.1 (1988): 58-63.

Veit-Wild, Flora, ed. *Dambudzo Marechera 1952-87.* Harare: Baobab Books, 1988.

Simon Gikandi (essay date 1993)

SOURCE: "Chinua Achebe and the Poetics of Location: The Uses of Space in *Things Fall Apart* and *No Longer at Ease,*" in *Essays on African Writing, A Re-evaluation,* ed-ited by Abdulrazak Gurnah, Heinemann, 1993, pp. 1-12.

[*In the following essay, Gikandi analyzes the develop-ment of meaning in* Things Fall Apart *and* No Longer at Ease *in terms of narrative representations of space and location.*]

It is not an exaggeration to say that the works of Chinua Achebe have up to now been read almost exclusively in terms of time and historicity. But this privileging of tem-poral terms has not arisen because of critical oversight or theoretical blindness: Achebe seems to have written his works so close to the axis of temporality that his whole oeuvre has an uncanny way of forcing us to read it not so much in the sequence in which his novels were written, but in the progressive historical relation these texts have es-tablished *vis á vis* the African experience. In the circum-stances, even when our critical paradigms are generated by the desire to trace the formal and ideological relations be-tween Achebe's texts—as I have tried to do in *Reading Chinua Achebe*[1]—we are more likely to follow a trajec-tory from **Things Fall Apart,** through **Arrow of God,** to **No Longer at Ease,** than one which reads these novels in the order in which they appeared. It is indeed difficult to promote a programme of reading Achebe's novels that will seek their cultural and symbolic value in the genetic rela-tion between **Things Fall Apart** and **No Longer at Ease,** although the latter is considered to be a sequel to the former.

Why does it seem easier to insert **Arrow of God** in the tem-poral space that separates Achebe's first and second nov-els even when the three works are not related in any fundamental sense? Or, to put the question another way, why has **Arrow of God** become a *supplement* for the Nwoye Okonkwo story that Achebe, by his own admission, could now write? The most obvious answer to these questions has to do with our own engagement with the novel as a genre: we are still imprisoned in a critical tradition—whose most fervent advocate has been Georg Lukács—in which the his-tory and development of the novel is explicated in strictly temporal terms.[2] In addition, the peculiar condition in which Achebe's novels have been produced—the history of co-lonialism and nationalism—has affirmed the centrality of the temporal axis in our theoretical and critical reflections.

There is, in other words, such a close affinity between Achebe's narratives and his subject—the African historical experience—that it is difficult, if not impossible, not to read these texts as both representations of this experience and a metacommentary on their condition of possibility. The temporal axis offers readers a secure framework for reading Achebe's novels.

My essay seeks to propose a different approach to the epistemology of narrative in Achebe's first two novels, to pose the question of location and space and its relation to the development of meaning in both *Things Fall Apart* and *No Longer at Ease.* Can a methodical interpretation of spatial relations and what Foucault has called 'the fatal intersection of time and space' cast new insights into the epistemology that drives Achebe's works? [3] Can an interpretation of the numerous spatial and geographical metaphors that have such a palpable presence in Achebe's texts proffer us new ways of reconvening the central problems in these texts—problems about identity and location, power and knowledge, and the topography of the nation? Surely, a reconsideration of the poetics of location—and the politics of space—is warranted by the current reconfiguration of global cultures. It is warranted by the simple fact that the present period, a period in which the postcolonial cultures of formerly colonised areas are challenging older, temporal organisations of power and knowledge, has come to be defined, in the words of Foucault, as 'the epoch of space . . . when our experience of the world is less that of a long life developing through time than that of a network that connects points and intersections with its own skein' (p. 22). If this is so, how is a poetics of location exemplified in Achebe's texts, and what is its relation to the inherited nineteenth-century (colonial) discourse on the place and space of the African in the taxonomy of world cultures?

It is important to begin with the question of inherited spaces, and the geopolitics surrounding African cultures, because if metaphors of location seem to play a more prominent role in Achebe's earlier works than they do in the later ones, this has to do with his proximity to the colonial text which had deployed colonised spaces as a key element in the debate on Englishness and its domain. For Englishness, as I have argued elsewhere, defines itself through gestures of situatedness: English identity, especially in the period of high imperialism, is enacted against the backdrop of the spaces of the Other which function as what Foucault has aptly called *heterotopias.*[4] If utopias are sites that have no real places and present society in perfected form, says Foucault, heterotopias are the real spaces in which the central meanings of a culture 'are simultaneously represented, contested and inverted' (p. 24). Heterotopias are hence spaces of representation and interpretation. Such spaces, according to Foucault, are mirrors that exert 'a sort of counteraction' on the positions occupied by the writing subject; from the standpoint of this mirror, this subject, counteracting itself against the Other, comes back towards itself (p. 24). It is not by accident, then, that some of the most important colonial texts on Africa in the modern period, texts such as Conrad's *Heart of Darkness*, Cary's *Mister Johnson*, and Greene's *Journey without Maps*, are dominated by the problematic of location, of spaces, of maps and roads. As numerous critics have observed, these texts provide the English with mirrors in which to gaze at themselves; but the African is absent from such works except as a projection of European desire.[5]

Now in writing against this tradition in *Things Fall Apart,* Achebe provides us with an ingenious, but paradoxical, deployment of space; he wants, on one hand, to counter the heterotopic representation of the African in the colonial text by making Umuofia an epistemological presence, one defined not only by the process of time, but also by an ensemble of spaces; the African space hence functions as a Foucauldian 'space of emplacement' (p. 22). On the other hand, however, Achebe's narrative does not seek to represent the African space as a utopian counter to European heterotopias; if he were to do so, he would merely be valorising the romantic image of Africa to counter the western projection of the continent as a savage space. To avoid these two traps—that is, the image of Africa as the place of the savage or as the cradle of human values—Achebe invokes a double image of Umuofia: the village is shown to be both an autonomous geographical entity, and a place torn by contending social and historical forces. This doubleness accounts for the chronotopic disjuncture that leads to the triumph of colonialism at the end of the novel.

Moreover, when we consider the tension between time and space in the novel, we realise how Okonkwo's narrative is both progressive and retrogressive. From a temporal perspective, the structure of the novel, especially in the first part, encourages us to see Okonkwo's story as a progressive struggle in which he ultimately triumphs over the process of time. The wrestling match that opens the novel is the quintessential space of emplacement and empowerment because it makes Okonkwo's subjectivity parallel the character of his community and culture: his triumph takes place in 'a fight which the old men agreed was one of the fiercest since the founder of their town engaged a spirit of the wild for seven days and seven nights'.[6] Okonkwo's victory in the wrestling ring has become, over the years, one of the founding stories of the village: 'That was many years ago, twenty years or more, and during this time Okonkwo's fame had grown like a bush-fire in the harmattan' (p. 3).

But if the first part of the novel promotes a progressive narrative in which time brings fame and prosperity to the cultural hero, the second and final parts negate the temporal process. In exile, Okonkwo is forced into a historical hiatus; on his return to Umuofia, he realises that his life (and hence his story) has been reduced to zero ground. Moreover, the ending of the novel appears to be a void in which the hero is silenced and, in his abomination, is cut off from the spirit of his community. As the District Commissioner notes, Okonkwo's story, which opened the novel by being compared to the mythical narratives of Umuofia's founding father, can only be confined to 'a reasonable paragraph' (p. 148). And although it is possible to argue that the compression of the hero's story to only a paragraph in the colonial text arises from the coloniser's ethnocentric negation of the African narrative, we also need to remember that by the time Okonkwo returns to Umuofia after his exile, his story has become marginal even in his own community.

The relation between the space of emplacement and that of negation is, however, more complicated than the structure of the novel suggests. We can discern this complication if we refuse to follow the linear plotting of the novel and focus our attention on the constant juxtaposition of different spatial configurations and the uncanny ways in which the hierarchy of social spaces that emplaces Okonkwo in Umuofia is also responsible for his displacement. We need, in effect, to reconsider Okonkwo's troubled relation with his communal territory, a relation that is defined in the narrative by the tension between space and time in his engenderment. Consider, for example, how the incipient moment of the novel derives its power from the subtle evocation of the metaphorical identity between Okonkwo and Umuofia and his metonymic displacement from it; the novel surrounds the heroic character with innumerable spaces in which his relation with his community is affirmed and his hierarchy within it is denoted. In the wrestling arena of his youth, Okonkwo's identity as a powerful man is realised (p. 3); in the market place where 'the normal course of action' (p. 8) is a connotation of the norms by which the community lives, Okonkwo is recognised as Umuofia's representative man and is 'asked on behalf of the clan' to look after Ikemefuna 'in the interim' (p. 9).

In all these instances, Okonkwo's authority as the protector of the Umuofian doxa is closely related to the character of his household space: 'Okonkwo's prosperity was visible in his household. He had a large compound enclosed by a thick wall of red earth . . . The barn was built against one end of the red walls, and long stacks of yams stood out prosperously in it' (p. 10). This household is, in effect, represented as a replica of the larger social spaces that sustain a cosmos which, in turn, provides natural ground and cultural stability to the larger community. In this household, celestial power becomes symbolised in material terms (Okonkwo's prosperity is written on his household) and also functions as a spatial mirror for both idealised social production and the localisation of the communal doxa. In

other words, when we gaze at Okonkwo's social space (his household), we witness not only the materiality of 'his personal god and ancestral spirits', but also the gods that have 'built' Umuofia. Moreover, the novel provides us with a crucial juxtaposition between this individualised space and the communal space (*ilo*) that it replicates. Both function as crucial symbols of the organic community.

But even as we trace Okonkwo's advancement along the temporal axis that elevates him from the son of a pauper to one of the strongest men in Umuofia, we cannot fail to notice how his temporal progression is constantly being challenged by what would appear to be the undialectical force of space.[7] In the first part of **Things Fall Apart,** as most readers will recall, Okonkwo's struggle to succeed is a manifest struggle against the process of time, a struggle that is commented on retrospectively (p. 17). On the temporal axis, the subject has transcended his past; his suffering and penury are narrated in the past tense (Chapter 2) as a qualifying appendix to his present prosperity (Chapter 1). But in spatial terms, the present doesn't have any primacy over the past: Okonkwo remembers his first 'tragic' year as a farmer 'with a cold shiver throughout the rest of his life' (p. 17). In Okonkwo's body and psyche, the very forces he thought he had transcended rule his life, for in this internal landscape his selfhood is mapped by a repressed past association with his father.

So if in the visible space of his household we read Okonkwo's material and temporal advancement from the regime of his father, his internal landscape is defined by Unoka: his 'whole life was dominated by fear, the fear of failure and of weakness . . . It was fear of himself, lest he should be found to resemble his father'; 'he was possessed by the fear of his father's contemptible life and shameful death' (pp. 9, 13). If his household is an affirmation of masculinist power ('Okonkwo ruled his household with a heavy hand'), his masculine aggression arises in his attempt to deny the feminine forces he associates with his father (pp. 30-2).[8]

Moreover, if Okonkwo's masculine ideologies are predicated on the belief that the household (and *natio*) ruled by men is a natural entity, the Ikemefuna subtext both affirms masculinity and carefully questions the intrinsic value of the male-dominated space. Consider, for example, the process by which Ikemefuna is temporarily incorporated into Umuofia: 'For three years Ikemefuna lived in Okonkwo's household and the elders of Umuofia seemed to have forgotten about him. He grew rapidly like a yam tendril in the rainy season, and was full of the sap of life. He had become wholly absorbed in his new family' (p. 37). The images of vegetation and growth are important here: they suggest that Umuofia is an organic community with the natural capacity to absorb and assimilate those who enter it. And yet we know that Ikemefuna does not have natal rights within this community; he can only inscribe himself within it by appealing to Umuofia's implied discourse of what is 'right', especially through the evocation of masculinity (and hence homosociality). In other words, Ikemefuna becomes part of Umuofia by establishing the 'deep, horizontal comradeship' that Benedict Anderson has isolated as a key facet of nationness.[9]

It is through Ikemefuna that Nwoye is masculinised, at least temporarily, thus allowing Okonkwo to sustain his fantasy of an overarching male hegemony that will reproduce itself through his son: 'Okonkwo was inwardly pleased at his son's development, and he knew it was due to Ikemefuna. He wanted Nwoye to grow into a tough young man capable of ruling his father's household when he was dead and gone to join the ancestors' (p. 37). But no sooner has this desire been asserted than it is negated: in the Obi, the male domain, the men bond through 'masculine stories of violence and bloodshed', but in his inner space, Nwoye, eager to please his father and to conduct himself as a man, 'feigned that he no longer cared for women's stories' (p. 38). Masculine stories are hence not able to transform Nwoye's 'essential' character.

In addition, masculine ideologies are exposed as inverted—rather than natural and organic entities—at that crucial junction in the novel when Ikemefuna is 'cut down' by Okonkwo, in spite of his unconditional identification with male hegemony and masculinist spaces. We are told that Ikemefuna could 'hardly imagine that Okonkwo was not his real father', but his evocation of the name of the imagined father does not save him in the end (pp. 42, 43). Indeed, soon after Ikemefuna dies, we are left to witness the collapse of the 'deep, horizontal comradeship' that held the household together: a 'snapping' takes place inside Nwoye (p. 43) and a cold shiver descends on Okonkwo (p. 44). So, if Okonkwo seems to have reached the height of success (in temporal terms), his spaces of empowerment are shown to be in a state of crisis because they were founded on unstable male relationships.

It is in this context that Okonkwo's subsequent exile acquires several important resonances. Okonkwo's exile, it must be emphasised, is not merely the opposite of belonging, nor does it simply denote the hero's displacement from the masculine space he has dominated; it is, above all, the process that compels the hero to confront his repressed feminine space. Although exile displaces Okonkwo from his space of emplacement—'everything had been broken' (p. 92)—the maternal space, as his uncle reminds him, provides him a sanctuary in moments of distress (p. 94). The motherland, then, functions as an example of what Foucault calls a 'crisis heterotopia', a place 'reserved for individuals who are, in relation to society and

to the human environment in which they live, in a state of crisis' (p. 24).

But in this part of the novel we notice, once again, a crucial tension between temporality and spatiality. On one hand, from the perspective of time and historicity, Okonkwo's life in exile is denoted either by temporal suspense (he has to wait seven years before he resumes his place in Umuofia), or by his marginalisation in relation to the grand narrative of colonisation (he hears of the great historical events of his time second hand). In both cases, however, the narrative sustains the illusion that the hero will, in time, return to his proper place. On the other hand, Okonkwo (in exile) inhabits a heterotopic space that is at once privileged (because it is a sanctuary), but is not very different from the desecrated space occupied by the missionaries (the evil forest), or the marginal social spaces inhabited by outcasts. Indeed, when Okonkwo returns to Umuofia in the last section of the book, the narrative constantly calls attention to his loss of place in Umuofia: 'Seven years was a long time to be away from one's clan. A man's place was not always there waiting for him' (p. 121); the hero returns to a community that no longer recognises him ('Umuofia did not appear to have taken any special notice of the warrior's return'); he is forced to mourn for 'the clan, which he saw breaking up and falling apart' (p. 129).

If the novel opened with a symmetrical relationship between the hero and his communal space, they are now placed in opposition. Hence we can say that Okonkwo's exile from his natal space constitutes a radical break with his space of emplacement. In fact, the only reason why we don't read his exile as a radical form of marginalisation is because the narrative promotes the illusion that Okonkwo will be rehabilitated (in time); until the end, the narrative sustains the false belief that the space of exile is really not one of absolute loss. If we ignore this illusion, however, we can see why Okonkwo's exile is both a negation of the progressive narrative promised at the beginning of the novel and an ironic retour to the space inhabited by his father, the space from which he sought to escape.

Let us recall that Okonkwo, by killing a kinsman, has 'polluted' the earth, the source of his masculine power; his act is hence an abomination that recalls Unoka's death; the father's fatal sickness 'was an abomination to the earth, and so the victim could not be buried in her bowels' (p. 13); by committing suicide, Okonkwo, too, has committed 'an offence against the Earth' (p. 147). We may quibble about ostensible differences in the two men's deaths, but we cannot escape the similitude. Above all, we cannot escape the fact that Okonkwo, the great defender of the Umuofian doxa, has in his death (and possibly his life) gone, in Obierika's words, 'against our custom' (p. 147). But one of the questions the novel has raised at the same time is this: now that Umuofia is being challenged and transformed by the forces of colonialism, what exactly is the authority of custom and what spaces sustain it?

This is the question taken up by the asymmetrical spaces in *No Longer at Ease.* In this novel, Achebe uses as his epigraph a verse from T. S. Eliot's 'Journey of the Magi' to foreshadow the unstable places and spaces in which the poetics of identity formation are played out: 'We returned to our places, these Kingdoms. / But no longer at ease here, in the old dispensation.'[10] The theme of dislocation is also underscored by an Igbo proverb that appears strategically in the novel's moment of closure, a moment that is haunted by the dialectical tension between Obi's desire for identity and the reality of displacement: 'Wherever something stands, another thing stands beside it' (p. 145).

Now, because critical attention has often been focused on the temporal progression of this novel, that is, Obi's transformation from an idealistic young man to a corrupt bureaucrat, we have not paid enough attention to how this crisis of selfhood is generated by the contending loyalties between inherited and designated locations. Obi's inherited location is Umuofia, but far from being a place with a stable space, a natural ground that sustains a tradition, the ancestral home is a schizophrenic and transplanted locale, which is under the hegemony of colonialism, the designated space. In the circumstances Obi has to define himself in relation to, or even against, two contending spaces.

There is, first of all, an Umuofia space that exists as a marginal space in Lagos: this is a small village that subsists on 'its past when it was the terror' of its neighbours (p. 4), but it neither has the authority of the original nor can it sustain its traditions. This space speaks a deracinated language as it tries to negotiate its mythical past and its colonised present (pp. 5, 6). Obi's position, in relation to this space, is one of liminality: he belongs to a nationalistic generation that has rediscovered the value of tradition as a discursive formation, but cannot appropriate the spaces in which this tradition first emerged.

Then there is the Umuofia of colonial desires, the community that had sent Obi to England. This is not the community associated with his legendary grandfather; it does not proffer him a space in which he can fulfil his desire for the past. Indeed, this Umuofia expects him not to be a representative of its mythical history, but a custodian of its communal desire for Englishness (pp. 28-30). For the 'modern' Umuofians, power is vested in the fantasmic image of England which Obi embodies: he is praised as 'Obi who had been to the land of the whites. The refrain said over and over again that the power of the leopard resided in its claws' (p. 29). But Obi cannot identify with this given image either, because once he has lived in England for some time, he becomes convinced that if the notion of Nigeria is to have value, it has to negate the eromania associated with England and Englishness—hence his craving for 'things Nigerian' (p. 31).

And yet, Obi cannot escape from his colonial heritage because his identity is mapped, as it were, by England and Englishness in ironic ways. First, it is only in an oppositional relation to England that Nigeria 'first became more than just a name to him' (p. 11): the realities of English life ('the miseries of winter') necessitated a counteracting value that would, in turn, be imagined as the Nigerian national space; and it is around this space that memories and desires can be reorganised. In the sense of Obi's discovery of it, there would be no Nigeria if England did not exist as its geographic and cultural Other. There is even a second, more pervasive irony: even as he decries the colonial mentality, the cultural spaces that Obi inhabits are exclusively English. His technology of identity formation is English literature, which connects him to the colonial chairman of the civil service commission in ways he cannot be linked with his Umuofian kinsmen and women.[11] Above all, Englishness realises the cultural geography of England in ways that are more definitive than the Nigeria Obi wants to imagine: Housman's poetry hence seems to have a palpability which Obi's poem on Nigeria does not have (pp. 136-7).

In the end, Obi has to negotiate three spaces with contradictory claims and cultural contours: an Umuofia that is displaced from its traditions and is in a perpetual state of cultural crisis; a Nigeria that he had earlier hoped would be an erotic space of fulfilment but has become corrupted in its genesis; and an England whose cultural transcripts have shaped his character but whose function as a colonial power is a negation of the most important ingredients in his Africanity—history, home, language. All these spaces and their problems crystallise in Obi's relation with Clara and the failure of the marriage plot which, in traditional fiction, provides an ideal place for resolving problems of cultural and national identity. In quite unexpected ways, Clara confronts Obi with the problem of abomination that had plagued his ancestors. As an *osu* she inhabits what Foucault would call the 'heterotopia of deviation' (p. 25); she inhabits a place that is part of Igbo culture, but outside its norms.

Obi's intention to marry Clara forces him, in effect, to reflect on what his Umuofian compatriots consider to be his estrangement from the Igbo norm. For example, when Joseph asks him whether he knows what an *osu* is, we are told, he was saying 'in effect that Obi's mission-house upbringing and European education had made him a stranger in his country—the most painful thing one could say to Obi' (pp. 64-5). And yet there is a sense in which marrying Clara

would have been the apotheosis of Obi's desire for a Nigerian space. It would have been a willed entry into the desired nationalist space, a space transcending ethnic
traditions and family loyalties. At the same time, however,
he could not reach his desired space without evoking the
(colonial) doctrines of modernity and Christianity.

At the end of the novel, we come to realise that these are
not real options: his mother will stand up for tradition and
will even commit an abomination to stop her son from marrying an *osu*; his father will not countenance the thought
that modernity and Christianity are good enough reasons
to defy the inherited norm. So, like his grandfather before
him, Obi is left suspended in limbo. His presumed imprisonment at the end of the novel could well be Achebe's way
of valorising the split between cultural geographies that
have, at the same time, been spatialised by history. For this
reason, the way African spaces have been organised and
reorganised by Achebe's early novels points towards interesting directions in which the poetics of location can be
examined.

NOTES

1. Simon Gikandi, *Reading Chinua Achebe*, London:
James Currey, 1991.

2. Georg Lukács, *The Theory of the Novel*, trans. Anna
Bostock, Cambridge, Massachusetts: MIT Press, 1971, pp.
120-5.

3. Michel Foucault, 'In Other Spaces', trans. Jay
Miskowice, *Diacritics* 16 (Spring 1986), pp. 22ff. Further
references will be included in the text.

4. I am pursuing some of these questions in *Maps of Englishness: Postcolonial Theory and the Politics of Identity*, in progress.

5. See Abdul JanMohammed, *Manichean Aesthetics: The
Politics of Literature in Colonial Africa*, Amherst: Uni-
versity of Massachusetts Press, 1983; and Christopher
Miller, *Black Darkness: Africanist Discourse in French*,
Chicago: University of Chicago Press, 1985.

6. Chinua Achebe, *Things Fall Apart*, London: Heinemann,
1958, p. 3.

7. See Edward Soja, *Postmodern Geographies: The
Reassertion of Space in Critical Social Theory*, London:
Verso, 1989, p. 11.

8. An excellent discussion of masculinist ideologies in
Things Fall Apart can be found in Rhonda Cobham's 'Making Men and History: Achebe and the Politics of Revision-

ism', in *Approaches to Teaching 'Things Fall Apart'*, ed.
Bernth Lindfors, New York: Modern Language Association,
1991, pp. 91-100.

9. Benedict Anderson, *Imagined Communities: Reflections
on the Origins and Spread of Nationalism*, London: NLB,
1983, p. 16.

10. Chinua Achebe, *No Longer at Ease*, London:
Heinemann, 1960.

11. The relation between space and identity formation is
discussed by Caren Kaplan in 'Reconfigurations of Geography and Historical Narrative: A Review Essay', *Public
Culture* 3 (Fall 1990), p. 27.

Chinua Achebe with Eleanor Wachtel (interview date January 1994)

SOURCE: "Eleanor Wachtel with Chinua Achebe," in *The
Malahat Review*, No. 113, December, 1995, pp. 53-66.

[*Wachtel is a writer and radio personality who hosts CBC
Radio's Sunday literary program "Writers & Company."
In the following interview, originally broadcast in January, 1994, Achebe discusses his personal and literary
background, the evolution of his literary career, and his
role in and hopes for the Nigerian political economy.*]

The first book I ever read by a black African was **Things
Fall Apart** by Chinua Achebe. I read it some twenty-five
years ago, just as the Nigerian civil war was winding down.
It was often referred to as the Biafran war, because Biafra
was the name of the breakaway Ibo nation. And it was the
first time in my memory that Africa became associated with
that horrific image of starving children with distended bel-
lies. Casualties were very high—most of them Ibo civil-
ians who starved to death after federal forces blockaded the
rebel-controlled area.

Things Fall Apart provided a rare and original picture of
Ibo society in the late nineteenth century. By focusing on
a single village and its leader, the novel illustrated Nigeria's
early experience of colonialism and British rule. The book
sold millions of copies worldwide, was translated into thirty
languages, and adapted for stage, radio, and television.
It was the first novel by an African to be taught to African secondary students throughout the English-speaking
parts of the continent. By the late sixties, when I caught
up with it, **Things Fall Apart** had come to be recognized as the first "classic" in English from tropical Africa, and Achebe became known as the "father of the
African novel in English."

Achebe followed *Things Fall Apart* with three other novels in fairly quick succession: *No Longer at Ease, Arrow of God,* and in 1966, *A Man of the People.* But when the Biafran war ended in 1970, Achebe wrote poetry, short stories, and essays, but not novels. In the early 1980s, he became directly involved in Nigerian politics—first as the deputy national president of the People's Redemption Party, and then as president of the town union of his hometown, Ogidi.

Finally in 1987, twenty-one years after his previous novel, Chinua Achebe wrote a dark political work of fiction called *Anthills of the Savannah.* It was short-listed for Britain's Booker Prize.

Nigeria is Africa's most populous country—with ninety million people. It won its independence from Britain in 1960, but this oil-rich country has been run by the military for all but nine of those thirty-five years. Most recently, in June 1993, the presidential elections were declared invalid and the generals maintained control.

Five years ago, Chinua Achebe was injured in a car accident on a highway in Nigeria. The circumstances were unsettling and a military vehicle was said to be involved. Achebe spent six months in England undergoing operations and therapy, and then moved to the United States. He was very close to death. In fact, the American doctors who examined his X-rays didn't think he'd survive.

But Achebe continues to write and teach. His most recent book of essays is called *Hopes and Impediments.* In his novel, *Anthills of the Savannah,* the traditional storyteller says, "It is only the story that outlives the sound of war-drums and the exploits of brave fighters. . . . The story is our escort; without it, we are blind."

I talked to Chinua Achebe from his home in Anandale, New York, in January 1994.

[Wachtel:] *You have said that your father revered books and hoarded paper, and that when he died the family made a bonfire of his life's accumulation of paper. It's a powerful image, but did it feel strange to see all those things that he'd saved go up in smoke?*

[Achebe:] In retrospect, yes it did, but it wasn't archival material, it was old church magazines and so on. We just needed space. You know, even though I'm a writer, I don't like paper. When my table is full of paper I always like to get rid of it. So it's a matter of temperament. You are right, though, looking back; one should save what can be saved. But I do think that there's too much paper in the world.

So your father's legacy to you was a love of literature and a revulsion for paper.

Yes, that's right. It's a great paradox.

You were born in a village in eastern Nigeria to Christian missionary parents, and you've talked about "living at the crossroads of culture." Can you give me a sense of the early days in your life with those two influences, the Christian and the traditional Ibo?

It's not easy to put into words. It's like being in two worlds, or being at the confluence of two rivers, but it's never quite the confluence. The image of crossroads is a good one, because crossroads are a place where there's a lot of traffic, not just human traffic but also spirit traffic. So it's a very powerful location. That's the idea I was trying to convey. Christianity was new, strange in many ways, but it was powerful, and so was the traditional life of the people. When I was growing up, we had already passed the initial encounter, which involved fighting at times—literally, actual battles. Things had become more settled, and the advantage was that you saw a bit of the past and a bit of the future. That was where you stood. Of course, being of the Christian party, the missionary party, I was not really supposed to pay much attention to the traditional; what they did was thought to be heathenish, and I was not supposed to be interested in it, but I *was.*

You've written about how on one arm of the cross in this crossroads you sang hymns and read the Bible, and on the other there was your uncle's family, as you ironically put it, "blinded by heathenism, offering food to idols." As a child, which one were you drawn to more?

The one which I was not supposed to see. The fact that it was forbidden was part of the attraction. I wasn't evaluating the two. If anyone had asked me, I would have said that the Christian faith was the right one. But I was curious about what was going on in the other place.

Which impulse do you feel most strongly now?

The traditional, because it is the underdog; and of course I've learned more and more about it. I was not exposed to it, nor was anyone in my generation; it was not taught in the schools, and so it was always something half-understood. Now that I have had time and years to look at it, I have discovered profound truths and profound significances that are very valuable, and so I'm in a position to look at Christianity from the position of traditional religion.

Would you describe yourself as speaking three languages—Ibo, English, and Nigerian pidgin?

I've never really described myself that way but you are right. Nigerian pidgin is something which we all pick up; I didn't grow up with it, it's more a language, or dialect, of the cities, but as one grew up one encountered it and picked it up.

You use it quite a lot in your novels. How your characters speak seems to depend on a number of things: their class or level of education, the context, and how intimate they're feeling. Is this something you consciously do?

Yes and no. A closeness to life as it is lived is for me very vital. What I try to achieve in my novels is as close a version of events as would happen in real life. That's an aspect of realism that I think is valuable, so that then you can delve into magic or whatever you do.

Ibo proverbs figure prominently in your novels. Did they always resonate for you, even when you were growing up?

Yes, I loved them. The language of the Ibo people, their imagery is all very picturesque, and I always found it, and still find it, very moving and very powerful. A very simple example, for instance: in English we would say, "Two heads are better than one." The Ibos would say, "Two heads, four eyes." They always bring in a picture so you see it at once. It's not just that it's better, they tell you *how* it's better.

There's a line in your first novel that "proverbs are the palm oil with which words are eaten." It's a very vivid image. There's another one that you use and I think the idea of it really is implicit in several of your novels, and the English translation is, "To every man his due." What does that mean to you in its broadest sense?

It's extremely central to my understanding of reality, and it is so important to the Ibo that they say it in many different ways. The world is very complex, that's what they are saying. We must be aware of that complexity, and not just be aware but actually recognize it in the way we behave by according to every reality its own respect. You are not expected to admire or to love every thing, but you are expected to recognize that that thing has its own validity. That is what is meant by "To everyone his due."

For example, if you entered a hall in which Ibo elders were assembled for a meeting, if you came in and there were many, many people seated, the polite thing would be to shake hands with everybody and call them by their chosen names, not the names which they were given at birth but their titles. Everyone who becomes a titled person takes a new name, and you are supposed to know that and address them that way when you meet. Now, that's how you should deal with this crowd. But it's impossible! It would take the whole day if you were to go around shaking hands with everybody there and calling them by their names. So what you then do is greet them generally and say, "To everyone his due," which means you recognize everyone's title.

Your first novel, **Things Fall Apart,** *was published thirty-five years ago. It sold more than three million copies, and it's been translated into thirty languages. How does it feel to be described as "the father of African literature in English"?*

Oh, I don't mind that. I don't mind that at all. [*laughs*] It couldn't have even come close to my mind when I started writing. It's just one of those amazing developments, the way that my work has grown. It has been an amazing and gratifying surprise. Actually, the figure that my publishers give is not three million but eight, and it's still spreading—right now it's spreading very fast in the Far East. So I'm very happy and of course humbled by this, and that's all I can say, really.

You've said that one of the reasons you became a novelist was to tell the story from the inside. Do you remember how you felt when you first read books like Mr. Johnson, *by Joyce Cary, which was actually set in Nigeria, or when you read Joseph Conrad's* Heart of Darkness, *which was set in what was then the Congo?*

That's a long story. I encountered Conrad before I was old enough to see what was going on and so it didn't make the kind of impact that it would have made if I had been older. It was only when I reread it at college, at the University of Ibadan, as an undergraduate in the English department, that I then began to realize just what was happening there. Joyce Cary was different. The Joyce Cary was a later book; it was published in the forties, so I read it for the first time in college. Not just my response but the response of the whole class was quite definite: we didn't like what Joyce Cary was doing. I remember it was interesting because our teachers were all English and we were all Nigerian, and our teachers thought it was a marvellous book. In fact it is still called by some people in the West the greatest African novel. It's just amazing. One of my colleagues shocked our teacher by saying that the only moment he enjoyed in the book was when Johnson was shot. That was a very drastic response but it conveys the exasperation that we Africans feel when we encounter this kind of mindless racism.

When you first read Heart of Darkness, *and you say you were too young to understand it, did you identify with Marlowe?*

You identify with whom the author wants you to identify with, that's what fiction does; and until you are strong enough to break away from that, you don't see what's going on. I believe this is the problem with professors in the West today who don't see racism in *Heart of Darkness;* they are still reading like young boys and girls who are fascinated by the sound of adjectives and the creation of emotion, a cheap emotion, with fear and stereotype. That's really what's happening. But when you become experienced with literature, you should be able to get rid of that response.

Do you buy into what's called "appropriation of voice," the argument that only a black African is truly able to write about black Africa?

No, I don't. I think anybody can write about any place, even places they have never visited. Kafka wrote about America without leaving Prague. But a good writer knows just what kind of story to write about the place you don't know deeply. There are many different levels on which a story can move; you don't have to be an expert about place.

You were what's sometimes called "a been-to," in that you studied in Ibadan but you also studied in London. When you came back to Nigeria, just before independence, what were your hopes or expectations?

Actually, I wasn't a proper "been-to." I went to London, to the BBC School, for less than one year. I was already working; I was not a young student. Although it was an important experience, to spend seven months in Europe, it wasn't really formative. But as to what that period meant, it was a time of excitement; it was four or five years before our independence, and independence was very much in the air. We all felt happy and excited and hopeful, optimistic. It was the optimism that at last we would be on our own again and take hold of our history and manage our lives. It was a heady moment. About a year after I came back from London, Ghana got her independence; Ghana was the first in modern Africa. And it was so exciting! We were not Ghanaians, we were Nigerians and Nigerians and Ghanaians tend to be rivals, yet the independence of Ghana felt like our own. People stayed up at night till one a.m. in the morning, which was twelve midnight in Ghana, to hear the handing over of power. So it was that kind of heady, exciting feeling.

You once described your first novel, **Things Fall Apart,** *as "an act of atonement, the homage of a prodigal son." What did you mean by that?*

What I meant was that being a Christian, being educated in things of the West, being a university graduate and all that, one really shouldn't be any of those things. Our business should be to restore what was lost, to take on the task of redefining ourselves. That is what I tried to do in my writing, and I see that as a kind of service which is demanded of us by Africa because we betrayed her in doing all these

other things. My father, for instance, was one of the first generation of Christians; he abandoned the faith of his fathers. I'm putting it rather strongly so that what I'm trying to say will be clear. In actual fact, one's life doesn't stop because you've become a Christian; there are even some advantages in getting acquainted with another culture and all that. But basically, we were led into accepting that what our forefathers, our ancestors, had done through the millennia was somehow misguided and that somebody else who's come from afar could straighten us out, that he was the Way, the Truth and the Life, and that we had been sunk in blindness. That's an outrageous thing to accept. In retelling, in redefining ourselves, we are making amends for this betrayal.

Yet I think one of the reasons that **Things Fall Apart** *is so successful is that you don't romanticize the old Africa.*

No. Making amends doesn't mean glorifying. It simply means giving to everyone his due, you know, that salutation. This is due to Africa. At no point in the history of Africa, at no point was it inhabited by people who were less than human—we have to be absolutely strict about that. You must give it its due. Then, having said that, you have to recognize that things were not perfect. Things were not supposed to be perfect. God did not make a perfect world. The Ibo people have a different notion of creation. They have a notion in which God is constantly having a conversation with humanity on how to improve the environment. It was not finished in six days; we have a role to play. So we recognize the fact that things are not perfect, things are not even good. But that does not mean that this place is less than a human habitation.

Between 1958 and 1966 you published four novels, including your post-independence political satire **A Man of the People.** *Then in the late sixties, from '67 to 1970, there was the Nigerian Civil War, which is sometimes called the Biafran War. You've described the war as a watershed for you. Can you talk about what happened to you during that time?*

If we go back to that spirit of euphoria I described, when we got our independence—the feeling that we were new people, that we were reinventing ourselves—all that hope and promise seemed smashed in the catastrophe of the civil war, in which Nigerians set upon one another and people were massacred in the thousands, hundreds of thousands. It was a war in which perhaps a million people died in the short period of two-and-a-half years. It seemed as if everything we had planned for and looked forward to was going to be taken away and that independence itself was perhaps a hoax. It was a very savage war. Beginning to deal with that reality was very difficult.

I was quite involved in the war, not in the sense of going to the front or anything, but it was close, it was close to everybody. Everyone lost friends and relations, their homes; we all became refugees, running from one place to another. So at the end of it you had to reassess what you'd been doing in this redefining of yourself. You realized that it had perhaps been too optimistic, and that now you had to look more closely at what happened. And that was why I virtually put aside the novel I had been planning. Actually, I didn't put it aside, the novel just refused to come. Again and again I wrestled with this novel that I'd had in mind for years, and it just wouldn't make itself available. I realized that this was understandable, that what had happened to us was so devastating that we couldn't just get up and say, now it's business as usual again. Some people thought, when the war ended and the leader of Biafra and the leader of Nigeria were seen embracing, that the whole thing was over. That's not true. You don't lose a million people and shake hands and just go back to business as usual.

Was there a way in which you felt you had to heal yourself as well?

Yes, and I wasn't sure just what to do. One of the things I did was leave the country, though not right away; I felt that my role during the war was so well known that I couldn't run away. If there was going to be any punishment, it would be right that I would be one of those punished. So I sat around for two years after the war ended and when it was clear that I could go away, then I left the country for four years.

What was your role during the war?

I was more of a traveller. I travelled to the United States, to Europe, to other parts of Africa, and spoke about what was happening. I gave lectures, but I always came right back, to the fighting itself and to the war. And my family was there, my wife and three little children. My role was described as diplomatic in some places, but that's a very grand way of putting it, because I didn't really have any official position. I was simply a writer who travelled and spoke about what was going on.

More than twenty years elapsed between the last novel of your earlier period, **A Man of the People,** *and the publication of* **Anthills of the Savannah** *in 1987. The poet in* **Anthills of the Savannah** *is a man poised between action and reflection, and at one point he's addressing a group of students and, in answer to a question about what the country should do, he says, "Writers don't give prescriptions, they give headaches." When I read that I felt it was you. Is that true?*

Yes, I think you are right. Just at that point, as long as you

don't take it that that character is me; no characters of mine are allowed to be me. They may reflect, they may share some common ideas here and there with me. On that point, yes, he is talking like me, that's exactly what I would say in that circumstance.

That whole dilemma of action or reflection seems to be one that you have alternated between in your own life. You were involved in actual Nigerian politics in the 1980s. Then you published a novel. Do you find yourself going back and forth on this issue?

Yes, I think there's an inevitable seesaw position for someone like me, because you get so frustrated that things are not working out, and you want to go in and do something. Then you find that it isn't really that kind of action where your best work can be done. I discovered, for instance, that party politics was really going to be a waste of my time. I got into it because I felt so desperate to indicate that, out of all the bad leaders we had, this particular man was least bad and our people should know that and recognize it. There is a certain amount of value in that kind of work, but it's time-consuming and it's also energy-consuming. In the end you say, no, I really should be writing my books. So one does alternate in that kind of desperate way in our situation, and our situation is very desperate.

The novel **Anthills of the Savannah** *is in some ways a very political book. It's set in a fictional country called Kangan, but it feels as if it's probably not a very distant relation from a country like Nigeria, and it's a place where corruption is everywhere. Have people in Nigeria ever criticized you for being disloyal to your country by painting such a bleak picture?*

They have on and off, yes. But Nigerians are very critical of themselves, generally. I think you will find more people who regard me as a truthful witness and as a seer and prophet rather than as somebody who is disloyal. You will find some who take the other position, maybe among the leaders, but even there I'm not so sure. Nigerians tend to recognize their faults and it's amazing that we don't do very much with that recognition.

Has there been any personal price that you've had to pay for being a writer who speaks the truth?

Oh, little ones. I wouldn't really bother even to discuss them because I got off very lightly. For instance, at the end of the Biafran War, someone who was on the other side, who was very powerful on the federal side, told me that I personally gave Nigeria more trouble than all the other Biafrans put together. That was of course an exaggeration, but even so I got off very lightly. Having one's passport seized is not something one can complain about when one could have been charged with high treason. I think by and large my political work has been accepted as valid and valuable for Nigeria.

You were involved in a terrible car accident in Nigeria in 1990, which necessitated surgery and many months of therapy. Did you ever feel that the accident wasn't an accident?

We have not bothered to pursue any investigation along those lines, but it did cross our minds. There were a few strange things that happened just before the accident. But we are very lucky, we are very lucky that it wasn't worse than it was, and so we have simply left it there. Also, the outpouring of love and sympathy that we saw, from all over Nigeria, makes it unnecessary for us to pursue what happened.

What is your physical condition now?

It's more or less where it was when I left the hospital. I broke my spine and so, as you know, I am a paraplegic. I'm in a wheelchair and it looks as if that's the way it's going to be.

The anthills of your novel's title, **Anthills of the Savannah,** *stand as a powerful metaphor, some indication of hope. Can you tell me what that metaphor means?*

It's about hope, promise, but most importantly it's about memory. The grassland, the savannah, is generally consumed by a fire at the end of every year in the dry season, and all the grass is burnt. If you came there you would see nothing except these anthills dotted across the landscape. That's all that survives until the rains return and the new grass comes up. But that new grass wasn't there when this disaster happened, it doesn't know anything about it, and if it's going to find out what happened last year, the only person it can ask is the anthill, that's all that was there. So that's the image. It's hope, it's survival, and it is memory, because if you survive without knowing who you are, then it really doesn't make any sense. You have to be told the importance of the story. It's the anthill that has the story. If the grass is wise, it will ask, what was it that happened? And then the story will be told.

Nadine Gordimer has described you as a moralist and an idealist, but it would seem to me that your idealism has had to weather some very difficult things over the years. How is your idealism faring these days?

It's still alive and well, because without it the business of the writer would be meaningless. I don't think the world needs to be told stories of despair; there is enough despair

as it is without anyone adding to it. If we have any role at all, I think it's the role of optimism, not blind or stupid optimism but the kind which is meaningful, one that is rather close to that notion of the world which is not perfect, but which can be improved. In other words, we don't just sit and hope that things will work out; we have a role to play to make that come about. That seems to me to be the reason for the existence of the writer.

You have distanced yourself from your parents' Christianity, but in your essays especially and even in talking to you, I feel that you assign to literature and the imagination almost the same kind of spiritual or even religious value, that fiction is a kind of salvation, or can be a salvation.

Yes. And so one hasn't really moved all that far away. We have a proverb which says that the little bird that flies off the ground and lands on an anthill may think it's left the ground, but it hasn't.

How do you convince people of the redemptive powers of fiction?

I don't think it needs a lot of heavy work. I think good stories attract us and good stories are also moral stories. I've never seen a really good story that is immoral, and I think there is something in us which impels us towards good stories. If we have people who produce them, we are lucky. I can't make a very large claim for what I do, I just make a modest claim because we really don't know.

I feel that there has to be a purpose to what we do. If there was no hope at all, we should just sleep or drink and wait for death. But we don't want to do that. And why? I think something tells us that we should struggle. We don't really know why we should struggle, but we do, because we think it's better than sitting down and waiting for calamity. So that's my sense of the meaning of life. That's really how I would put it, that we struggle, and because we struggle, that struggle has to be told, the story of that struggle has to be conveyed to another generation. You have struggle and story, and these two are quite enough for me.

You're giving me a variation of a story that's told in the novel **Anthills of the Savannah,** *which is about a leopard and a tortoise, and it's a story that's told twice, first in a village and then to university students. It's about what you're saying, the meaningfulness of the struggle itself, that to have struggled is important, so your children will know that you struggled. Can you tell that story, the story of the leopard and the tortoise?*

It's a very short one. The leopard had been looking for the tortoise to deal with him for something or other, and hadn't found him for a long time. On this day, on a lonely road, he suddenly chanced upon Tortoise, and so he said, "Aha! at last, I've caught you. Now get ready to die." Tortoise of course knew that the game was up and so he said, "Okay, but can I ask you a favour?" and Leopard said, "Well, why not?" Tortoise said, "Before you kill me, could you give me a few moments just to reflect on things?" Leopard thought about it—he wasn't very bright—and he said, "Well, I don't see anything wrong with that. You can have a little time." And so Tortoise, instead of standing still and thinking, began to do something very strange: he began to scratch the soil all around him and throw sand around in all directions. Leopard was mystified by this. He said, "What are you doing? Why are you doing that?" Tortoise said: "I'm doing this because when I'm dead, I want anybody who passes by this place to stop and say, "Two people struggled here. A man met his match here."

You've been living in the United States on and off over the last twenty or so years. Do you think of yourself now as living in exile?

No, I don't. I spare myself that luxury, and as a matter of fact, I'm constantly planning for my return. I've been here now three years, since my accident, and it's partly medical, but I'm making arrangements to get back home. It's very important to me that I get back home. People at home also expect me back.

Despite the recent coup?

Perhaps *because* of the recent coup. The situation is so bad—

The fact that it's so bad means you feel a greater compulsion to be there?

Yes. People in fact do call or write me and say, when are you coming? I am very much involved in what's going on in Nigeria and I'd like to keep it that way.

Do you need to go back to Nigeria in order to write more about it?

I think so, though that's not an immediate problem. I have enough knowledge about the place to write the kind of fiction I want to write. I may not know what's happening politically this week, but that's never been my need; I've never really needed that kind of topical knowledge. I have enough residual information and knowledge to keep working for a time. What I need is the spiritual sense of connectedness one gets by being there.

I understand the way in which you are hopeful about the

possibilities of literature, but are you also hopeful about Nigeria?

That's a tough question. I have said, and more than once, that always, even in my reincarnation, I would like to be a Nigerian. But as more and more bizarre situations occur, you sometimes wonder whether you haven't spoken too positively. I still think that we *might* just make it. We have squandered so much time and money and people, but I still hope. Here it's hope rather than belief. Even if we don't make it, then we'll have other arrangements. A country is simply an area or territory defined and called one thing and if the people there don't really want to live together in that definition, then they can make other arrangements. I think we should give Nigeria at least one more chance to see if we can make it as a country.

NOTE: In November 1994, Nobel Prize winning writer Wole Soyinka had his passport taken away when he was leaving the country, and he was forced into involuntary exile. Also in 1994, writer and environmental activist Ken Saro-Wiwa was arrested. For more than a year, international groups such as PEN campaigned for his release. On November 10, 1995, Ken Saro-Wiwa was executed along with eight other activists for the Ogoni people.

Saro-Wiwa had been president of the Association of Nigerian Authors, an organization founded by Chinua Achebe in 1988 expressly in order to protect writers by banding together. When reached for comment, Chinua Achebe said that even though he had little faith in the Nigerian military, he was stunned by the execution. "It was not only a terrible thing to do, but a stupid thing to do. But the way I read it is that nothing is impossible once you depart from government by consultation. It will simply get worse and worse. What we have seen in the last thirty years is an increasing wickedness within the military and at the same time a complete collapse of Nigeria. Nobody is talking about the suffering, the agony of millions of Nigerians on a day-to-day basis at all levels."

Andrew E. Robson (essay date June 1994)

SOURCE: "The Use of English in Achebe's *Anthills of the Savannah*," in *CLA Journal*, Vol. XXXVII, No. 4, June, 1994, pp. 365-76.

[*In the following essay, Robson examines various types of English that appear in* Anthills of the Savannah, *demonstrating how each reflects differences in education, social status, and cultural context.*]

The language question, that is to say the question of

whether Third World writers should write in indigenous languages or the international language of the former colonizer, is most commonly political in nature. Ngugi Wa Thiong'o, the Kenyan writer, illustrates this point very clearly when he describes his decision to change from English to Gikuyu as his preferred literary language as "part and parcel of the anti-imperialist struggles of Kenyan and African peoples."[1] The language question may also be seen, however, as part of a debate in the fields of linguistics and culture, or the ethnography of communication. In this context, the question alludes not to political realities and/or fantasies, but to the nature of the relationship between language and culture. If language shapes our perception of the world, and if to be part of a language group is, in the linguist Whorf's phrase, to share a common "thought world," then to write a novel whose characters are Nigerian, for example, but whose thoughts and words are presented in English, might be said to be risking a certain lack of authenticity. Ngugi seems to be thinking along these lines when he asserts that "Language . . . has a dual character: it is both a means of communication and a carrier of culture,"[2] but he politicizes the sociolinguistic point by insisting that to write in English would be, for him and other Third World writers, to help perpetuate cultural imperialism. Taken to one extreme, of course, this kind of thinking, which sees language in proprietary terms, and which sees language choice as being equivalent to political choice, fails to take into consideration other aspects of the ethnography of communication, particularly in the area of code mixing and bilingualism. The world is not as simple as Ngugi seems to suggest, especially in the tumultuous areas of language and politics, where one symbol of modernity is the exile, the emigrant, the refugee, and others who live daily in a cultural and linguistic montage, a point made so effectively by Salman Rushdie. Ngugi's thesis leads us almost to the same unhappy conclusion as is reached in one version of the Sapir-Whorf hypothesis, namely that literature is, in its very essence, untranslatable because language shapes the thought worlds of its users, and each linguistic thought world is different from all others.

The proposition that one's language of choice betrays one's political values, while it may in certain cases be true, is too narrow. We speak the language of our society first, and Third World writers usually speak the language of their former colonizers second. In neither case do we have much choice in the matter. Of course, we may ask why Chaucer or Conrad decided to write in English, or why Beckett chose to write in English, and it is possible that in both cases the answer is political in nature (certainly, much in human affairs can be said to have a political context), but it is also possible that such decisions have some other motivation—aesthetic, practical, mercenary, or quirkily individualistic. Chinua Achebe has observed that the language issue is unnecessarily sensationalised; he writes: "The is-

sue is, I'm bilingual. This is the advantage we have—why turn it into a liability?"[3]

It is the purpose of this paper to describe how Achebe uses this "advantage" in his 1987 novel, *Anthills of the Savannah*.[4] We shall see that in this work his use of English reflects the reality of language varieties and code switching reflecting educational background, social status, and context, as well as his characteristic flair for representing the dignity of indigenous languages in English words. Achebe, like Rushdie but in a different context, demonstrates the significance of language within contemporary culture in a way that is more telling and more relevant than the narrow obsessiveness of Ngugi who, after all, translates his work into English and who lives in the world of Salman Rushdie far more than the world of Franz Fanon.

Chinua Achebe's *Anthills of the Savannah* is set in a fictional West African state called Kangan. A civilian government has been overthrown, landing "unloved and unmourned on the rubbish heap" (11), and a military man has assumed the presidency. His closest advisers, members of his cabinet, are close friends, all of whom have overseas educations, mostly in England. The president himself is a graduate of Sandhurst, England's prestigious military academy. The privileged education of these people is reflected in their language. They and their friends are all bilingual and have a perfect facility in English, which is, indeed, their usual medium of communication. The language they use is indistinguishable from educated English anywhere in the world, except for the occasional local references. Christopher Oriko, the Commissioner for Information, describes his longtime friend, now His Excellency the President, and those around him with ironic detachment:

> He is in mufti as he now tends to be more and more within the precincts of the Presidential Palace: a white dashiki tastefully embroidered in gold, and its matching trousers. By contrast many of my colleagues, especially the crew from the Universities, aspire to the military look. Professor Okong wears nothing but Khaki safari suits complete with epaulettes. It is amazing how the intellectual envies the man of action. (4)

The words here are those of educated English speakers everywhere: "within the precincts," "tastefully embroidered," "the crew from the Universities," with the latter having perhaps a rather British sound. The final sentence—"It is amazing how the intellectual envies the man of action"—is also interesting, because it is characteristic of this novel that the philosophical, the reflective, the ironic voices of the narrators employ standard educated English. Ikem Osodi, editor of the *National Gazette* and, with Christopher Oriko, one of the two principal characters in the novel, both of whom are eventually murdered by security or military men, uses this same voice after witnessing public executions held before a grotesquely festive crowd and state television cameras:

> I had never expected that Authority should excel in matters of taste. But the ritual obscenities it perpetrated that afternoon took me quite by surprise—from the pasting of a bull's eye on the chest of the victim to the antics of that sneaky wolf of a priest in sheep's clothing whispering God knows what blasphemies into the doomed man's ear, to the doctor with his stethoscope rushing with emergency strides to the bull's eye and then nodding sagely and scientifically that all was finished. Call him tomorrow to minister genuine human distress and see how slow he can be! And how expensive! Authority and its servants far exceeded my expectations that day. (37)

A certain self-consciousness about English appears among this group also, with Christopher Oriko noting that one moment of crisis "threw the Chief Secretary into utter confusion and inelegance of speech" (6). Oriko even goes so far as to correct the English of the Attorney-General:

> "Your Excellency, let us not flaunt the wishes of the people."
>
> "Flout, you mean," I said.
>
> "The people?" asked his Excellency, ignoring my piece of pedantry. (5)

In these circles, the language of the elite is spoken, and this emphasizes the distance between the powerful and the powerless. This distance is suggested more directly when the Chief Secretary opens the palace window in order to hear what is going on outside: "And the world surges into the alien climate of the Council Chamber on a violent wave of heat and the sounds of the chanting multitude" (8).

In the "alien" world of the elite, there is a little room for the language of the ordinary people. The use of traditional proverb is characteristic of the national culture, but the President, impatient with Professor Okong's obfuscations, tells him to "Please cut out the proverbs, if you don't mind" (18). The President is happier with the language and values of Sandhurst:

> I certainly won't stand for my commissioners sneaking up to me with vague accusations against their colleagues. It's not cricket! No sense of loyalty, no esprit de corps, nothing! And he calls himself a university professor. (19)

This, then, is the world of educated soldiers, of a certain

disdain for the masses, of people trained in foreign universities, and of public relations. The President tells Okong to "humour" the masses outside: "Gauge the temperature and pitch your message accordingly" (16). In response to these and other remarks by the President, Okong makes the first successful use of traditional proverbs in the novel, putting himself and his colleagues in the role of students, with the President being teacher:

> We are always ready to learn. We are like children washing only their bellies, as out elders say when they pray. (17)

This flattery, along with the self-abasement that it involves, is expressed in traditional proverb form and is appropriate for this moment of deference to authority. In general, the representation of the idiom, notable particularly for its use of proverbs, for its ornate formality, and for its elegance, reminds us of the traditional society from which it springs. Thus, deference to the chief may be expressed in such a form, although the reader may be aware of the rather fawning effect of this particular speech in the political context in which it takes place. There is something paradoxical, even incongruous, about the use of such language in the palace, and this explains the President's impatient demand, shortly thereafter, that Okong "cut out the proverbs."

No such sense of the inappropriateness of traditional oratory attaches itself to the use of such language at the gathering of Abazon elders and their supporters, who are hoping to petition the President for relief from certain reprisals which he imposed on them following their rejection of a proposal to make him President-for-Life. Ikem, the editor, is also from the Abazon region and is the guest of honor at a gathering near the palace. Ikem is criticized by one speaker for his failure over the years to attend ceremonies and monthly meetings of the urban Abazonian community. At this point, one of the elders, a member of the delegation from the province itself, far from the urban center, speaks in defense of Ikem:

> "I have heard what you said about this young man, [Ikem] Osodi whose doings are known everywhere and fill our hearts with pride. Going to weddings and naming ceremonies of one's people is good. But don't forget that our wise men have said also that a man who answers every summons by the town-crier will not plant corn in his fields. So my advice to you is this. Go on with your meetings and naming ceremonies because it is good to do so. But leave this young man alone to do what he is doing for the Abazon and for the whole of Kangan; the cock that crows in the morning belongs to one household but his voice is the property of the neighborhood. You should be proud that this bright

cockerel that wakes the whole village comes from your compound."

There was such compelling power and magic in his voice that even the MC who had voiced the complaints was now beginning to nod his head, like everybody else, in agreement. (112)

Here, in the more tribal, more traditional context of village elders and a gathering of the community at a moment of crisis, the cadence and imagery of traditional speech is powerful. The image of Ikem, the news editor, as the cockerel whose early morning voice belongs to the whole community, is one which is compelling in any context, but it is particularly appropriate when used among people whose village lives make them intimately familiar with the early morning crowing alluded to.

The use of such images and proverbs is also interesting in the context of the struggle between the master-of-ceremonies and the elder for the audience's sympathy. This oratorical struggle becomes a battle of proverbs, with the MC couching his sarcasm in the terms of traditional oratory:

"When you hear Ikem Osodi everywhere you think his head will be touching the ceiling. But look at him, how simple he is. I am even taller than himself, a dunce like me. Our people say that an animal whose name is famous does not always fill a hunter's basket." (111)

This contest is, as we have seen, won by the elder, and Achebe uses this character to deliver some of the most poignant messages in the novel. The wisdom of the elder is used to assert the supreme value of the storyteller's art compared with "the sounding of the drum" and "the fierce waging of the war":

"[I]t is only the story [that] can continue beyond the war and the warrior. . . . It is the story, not the others, that saves our progeny from blundering like blind beggars into the spikes of the cactus fence. The story is our escort; without it, we are blind. . . . It is the thing that makes us different from cattle; it is the mark on the face that sets one people apart from their neighbors." (114)

Here, the author's voice may be heard in that of the elder. The novel is a continuation of Achebe's brave condemnations of corruption and failure of leadership in Nigeria and elsewhere; the writer, as we have seen recently in Eastern Europe, as well as in parts of Africa and around the world, may articulate the present pain and the future promise, may be a moral voice in a frightened or indifferent world. Such is Ikem in the novel, and such is the novelist himself. The elder may articulate the significance of history, or the

story, for the reader, but he also gives his people a way of seeing the circumstances of the present that are both true and painful:

"It is proper that a beggar should visit a king. When a rich man is sick a beggar goes to visit him and say sorry. When the beggar is sick, he waits to recover and then goes to tell the rich man that he has been sick. It is the place of the poor man to make a visit to the rich man who holds the yam and the knife."

"That is indeed the world," replied the audience. (117)

The people's recognition of the realpolitik of their situation does not lessen the bitter irony of what is being said, and the language itself expresses this poignancy; to those in the palace, the crowd outside is a rabble to be dealt with in the noncommittal language of public relations, but to the crowd itself, those in the palace hold both the yam and the knife, and the poor are supplicants.

The third variety of English used in *Anthills of the Savannah* is the *lingua franca* of the urban masses; it may be referred to as pidgin English, described by Brosnahan in 1958 as "spoken by those without any formal education," and by Banjo, in 1971, as "marked by wholesale transfer of phonological, syntactic, and lexical features of Kwa or Niger-Congo to English. Spoken by those whose knowledge of English is very imperfect. Neither socially acceptable in Nigeria nor internationally intelligible."[5]

We are first introduced, in a mild way, to this variety when Ikem calls Chris Oriko's office and is told that he is "not on seat, sir" (25). This, of course, is not the full-blooded pidgin of the taxi drivers, but it gives us a local idiom, meaning that the person is not in the office at present, used by a secretary of intermediate education. Elewa, Ikem's uneducated girlfriend, speaks the real thing, and, in talking with her, Ikem and others switch codes constantly, depending on the purpose of the context. We are repeatedly made aware of the gaps that yawn between different codes, as when Ikem is remembering an argument with Elewa:

That was the night I first tried to explain my reason for not letting her sleep in my flat. . . . "Your compliment to my stamina notwithstanding," I said totally and deliberately over her head, "the reason is really quite simple, I no want make you join all the loose women of Bassa who no de sleep for house." She stared at me with her mouth wide open, quite speechless. Thinking to press home my point and advantage I said something like: "I wouldn't want a sister of mine to do that, you see." She fired back then: "Anoder time you wan' poke make go call dat sister of yours, you hear?" (33)

Beatrice, the English-educated girlfriend of Chris, is similarly at ease in both codes, as when she talks with her maid, Agatha. A soldier has come to her door:

> When Agatha had whoever it was as long to herself as she thought necessary she came to the door of the bedroom to inform me that one soja-man from President house de for door; he say na President sendam make he come bring madam. "Tellam make he siddon," I said, "I de nearly ready." (65)

The pidgin code is also used between Beatrice and Chris in moments of banter, especially when the context is sexual (32).

Among the masses, therefore, and in certain contexts among educated people, the language of the streets is used. It is the language of banter but is also the language of confrontation and danger in encounters with police and soldiers. Chris Oriko's last exchange, as he attempts to evade capture by security forces, pits him against a police sergeant who is abusing a young woman. Chris cannot stand by and ignore the brutality, and his decency and his frame of reference are in stark contrast to the lawlessness and casual violence of the policeman:

> Chris bounded forward and held the man's hand and ordered him to release the girl at once. As if that was not enough he said, "I will make a report about this to the Inspector-General of Police."
>
> "You go report me for where? You de craze! No be you de ask about President just now? If you no commot for my front now I go blow your head to Jericho, craze-man." The other said nothing more. He unslung his gun, cocked it, narrowed his eyes while confused voices went up all some asking Chris to run, others the policeman to put the gun away. Chris stood his ground looking straight into the man's face, daring him to shoot. And he did, point-blank into the chest presented to him. (189)

Throughout the novel, Achebe describes the violence of the country in the most formal English. Educated English is also often used to score points over the less educated, either for momentary gratification, as with Ikem and Elewa, or to confuse and intimidate less-educated but armed antagonists, as when Ikem is confronted by police on a set-up charge, and decides that a counter-attack, in legalese, might help:

> "Do you know it is an offence to operate a vehicle without interior lights according to the Criminal Code chapter forty-eight section sixteen subsection one hundred and six?"

> "Na today—even na jus' nou as I de come here de light quench out."

> His lie is as good as mine but I have an advantage: I know he is lying; he doesn't know I am, and he is scared. (34)

Educated English is, furthermore, also the language of reflection on the important issue raised in the novel. Ikem's set-pieces, as when he lectures the students towards the end of the novel, are addressed to the widest audience possible, the readers of the novel, and the language is articulate, educated, and unambiguous. He speaks for human decency and against hypocrisy and unthinking dogmatism. The students are not always pleased by what they hear:

> "I regret to say that students are in my humble opinion the cream of the parasites." Redoubled laughter. "The other day, did not students on National Service raze to the ground a new maternity block built by peasants? Why? They were protesting against their posting to a remote rural station without electricity and running water. Did you read about it?" The laughter had died all of a sudden. "Perhaps someone can show one single issue in this country in which students as a class have risen above the low, very low, national level. Tribalism? Religious extremism? Even electoral merchandising. Do you not buy and sell votes, intimidate and kidnap your opponents just as the politicians used to do? . . . So what are we talking about? Do you not form tribal pressure groups to secure lower admission requirements instead of striving to equal and excel any student from anywhere? Yes, you prefer academic tariff walls behind which you can potter around in mediocrity. Are you asking me to agree to hand over my life to a democratic dictatorship of mediocrity? No way!" (147-48)

In this voice Ikem seems to be the medium through which Achebe's vision is articulated. He is brave indeed, not pandering to the worst instincts of his audience, nor seeking refuge in the conventional wisdom, but challenging anyone who cares to listen to put behind them the squalid factionalism, corruption, and violence of the past and seek a better path, based on traditional civility ("At this point the normal courtesies which the prevalence of armed robberies had virtually banished from Bassa could no longer be denied" one of the narrators notes elsewhere in the novel [124]), democratic processes, and a humanity that ameliorates suffering and rewards merit in national affairs.

In some ways this is a bleak novel, except that it is filled with characters from all sectors of society who, given a chance, could help realize this humane vision. The novel ends with a naming ceremony for Elewa's baby girl, and the ceremony is Beatrice's idea; thus the future is anticipated, a new start possible. The naming is celebrated by two women from opposite ends of the educational spectrum, both of whom have lost their male companions to state-sponsored brutality and lawlessness, and by a cross-section of men, civilian and military, of various religions, young and old, all of whom participate in a kola-nut ceremony for the baby, and, of course, for themselves and their country. Beatrice, the English major, cannot resist a reference to Keats' "Truth is beauty" (216), and this spirit of cultural pluralism, where wisdom from any source remains wisdom, where life is celebrated, not murder and mayhem, is also represented in Ikem's "Hymn to the Sun," a prose-poem in which the central image of the novel, from which the title is derived, is articulated:

> The trees had become hydra-headed bronze statues so ancient that only blunt residual features remained on their faces, like anthills surviving to tell the new grass of the savannah about last year's brush fires. (28)

This admixture of Western and African images, like the representation of different groups and individuals through a range of English language varieties, conveys the view of someone who embraces the best of these various worlds and who sees the best hope for the future in nurturing a sense of a common humanity among the population, from soldier to intellectual to market woman to taxi driver to politician to policeman. The use of English in the novel, that is to say the use of different English language varieties, is perfectly appropriate, reflecting sociolinguistic realities and being a superb device for realizing a dangerous world in which the way characters use language reveals much about their status and their ability to survive and function.

Notes

1. Ngugi Wa Thiong'o, *Decolonizing the Mind* (London: James Currey, 1986) 28.

2. Ngugi 13.

3. Robert Moss, "Writing and Politics: An Interview with Chinua Achebe," *West Africa* 11 August 1986: 1677.

4. Chinua Achebe, *Anthills of the Savannah* (New York: Anchor, 1987). All page references are to this edition.

5. Qtd. in Ayo Bamgbose, "Standard Nigerian English: Issues of Identification," *The Other Tongue,* ed. Braj Kachru (Oxford: Pergamon, 1983) 100.

Anthonia C. Kalu (essay date 1994)

SOURCE: "The Priest/Artist Tradition in Achebe's *Arrow of God,*" in *Africa Today*, Vol. 41, No. 2, 1994, pp. 51-62.

[*Kalu is an American educator whose research interests include multiculturalism, women in the African diaspora, African and African-American literary theory construction, and African development issues. In the following essay, Kalu demonstrates how Achebe's use of traditional Igbo religious, political, philosophical, and artistic motifs in* Arrow of God *combine to illumine the abstract notion of duality.*]

In his efforts to validate the African literary artist's vision, Chinua Achebe has frequently spoken out against art for art's sake. He insists that

> art is, and was always, in the service of man. Our ancestors created their myths and legends and told their stories for a human purpose (including no doubt, the excitation of wonder and pure delight); they made their sculptures in wood and terra cotta, stone and bronze to serve the needs of their times. Their artists lived and moved and had their beings in society and created their works for the good of that society.[1]

In this functional view of art, he appears to agree with Ernst Fischer[2] that the arts express a higher purpose in man's existence. Achebe considers himself and other African artists teachers and recorders of African history and culture. He feels a need "to look back and try to find out where we went wrong, where the rain began to beat us."[3] He uses Igbo society to demonstrate that the arts contribute to man's sensitivity about a "fullness of life of which individuality with all its limitations cheats him."[4]

He argues in his works that the Igbo art tradition is based on Igbo thought which contemplates an inscrutable order that humanity constantly attempts to reorder and control. In his works, Achebe identifies certain major characters and situations in Igbo life, using these as the people do in their oral art tradition to portray their perception of the harmonizing principles in their lives. Achebe's interpretation of Igbo thought through art reveals a relationship between political and religious institutions. It is in these relationships that the Igbo artist and art traditions are most important. In recreating and revealing these connections, Achebe assumes the venerable role of Igbo priest and artist.

Achebe's initial exploration of this relationship is in *Things Fall Apart* where Chielo, the priestess, is portrayed in her performance of her duties to Agbala. However, this presentation of Chielo does not allow analysis adequate to the purposes of this work. His demonstration of this link is most fully realized in *Arrow of God* [5] in which he uses Ezeulu, the priest of Ulu, to explore these institutions in an Igbo community. Ezeulu's priestly functions, and his involvement, through Ulu, in making and implementing plans for the security of Umuaro are combined with his attitude toward life and understanding of Igbo thought to give an insight into Igbo society. In the performance of his duties to Ulu and Umuaro, he shows a desire to preserve both for posterity. Ulu, created by the people in a time of stress, is Umuaro's god of protection and symbolizes the Igbo's emphasis on the group. Ezeulu's desire to preserve this concept becomes the core of Achebe's portrayal of duality in Igbo thought. The depiction of this concept in *Arrow of God* revolves around Ezeulu and his responsibilities as the priest of Ulu, facilitating Achebe's exploration of Igbo traditions and art.

In his work, Achebe participates in group preservation in a way that is normally the responsibility of only priestly elders. The difference is the location of emphasis. In his direct involvement with the traditional society, Ezeulu tries to bring everything together under religion, while Achebe explains the society, including Ezeulu, through art. Achebe's exploration of the many facets of Igbo life in *Arrow of God* simultaneously delineates the complementary discourses that inform their significance within Igbo thought. The locus of his presentation, the priest/artist tradition, will be used here to show how Igbo traditional religion, politics, philosophy, and art were combined to give meaning to the abstract notion of duality, a concept central to most of Achebe's work and most deliberately explored in *Arrow of God.*

Community Sanction

The traditional Igbo priest bridges the real and supernatural worlds, striving to maintain harmony between them. He is able to do this because he has a special relationship with the people and is perceived by them as having special powers. The priest and his functions must be sanctioned by the community. The man who becomes a priest has to demonstrate that he is in harmony with his environment. He must exhibit an understanding of Igbo thought. The priest of Ala, the earth goddess, for instance, must manifest *Agwu*, divination force, in his life. In an article in which the *Ala* priesthood is discussed, M. S. O. Olisa says that

> one of the initial signs that a man is "called" to assume Ala Priesthood is the manifestation of "*Agwu*" in his life, a mild display by him of mental abnormality in which he sees visions and has supernatural communications with all sorts of spiritual forces. After undergoing this experience the Igbo often initiate and confer on him the title of Ezeani.[6]

Community sanction of such manifestations involves the people in the relationship that this individual now has with the supernatural world. When Boi Adagbom, a chief priest in Ika, was asked about his calling to the priesthood, he replied, " . . . if you were chosen, you would just know. Certain violent changes occur in you and you would 'answer the spirit's voice'."[7] The changes enable the individual to act as a link between the two worlds. He is then able to perform rituals and sacrifices to the god who has called him. He becomes an instrument of mediation between the community and its god. Like Wole Soyinka's singer of Yoruba tragic music, he becomes

> a mouthpiece of the chthonic forces of the matrix and his somnambulist "improvisations"—a simultaneity of musical and poetic forms—which are not representations of the ancestor, recognitions of the living or unborn, but of the no man's land of transition between and around these temporal definitions of experience.[8]

At moments when he communes with the gods, during sacrifices and divinations, he becomes like spirits, unknown. Then he dresses and acts the part, becoming the concrete interpretation and evidence of the people's relationship with the gods and each other. He interprets and balances and briefly becomes the major, visible part of the abstract principle governing these relationships. At all other times, he is an ordinary man, though this does not detract from his importance in the community. As a result of his special powers, the priest plays an important role in the making and execution of laws, becoming the direct connection between the gods and the elders. He guides the elders in their efforts to communicate with the gods in the maintenance of a harmonious society. Additionally, the rest of the community uses him to seek the god's will through sacrifices and divinations. This is not to say that Igbo society is theocratic, however, " . . . gods and the supernatural do play dominant roles in its political life."[9]

Role of Traditional Institutions and Rituals

In traditional society, the functions and attributes of the priest are taken for granted because of the assumption of shared beliefs and experiences. This is most evident in the art tradition. In Igbo oral narrative performance, for instance, the performer does not need to explain any images from the people's traditions when they occur in the story. The narratives become coded carriers of such information. In the contemporary and literate society, writers of Igbo fiction make assumptions similar to those that govern oral narrative performance traditions. Some of these assumptions are based on Igbo aesthetics, others are part of the norms and values of Igbo life. Consequently, the intersection of orality and literacy in Igbo life remains a location for interrogation of the conflict between Igbo and Western thought.

Frequently, Igbo writers during the early part of the colonial period rejected or ignored the significance of Igbo thought in their works. For instance, J. U. T. Nzeako[10] and Leopold Bell-Gam,[11] who have written of some aspects of Igbo traditions, often reflect a Westernized and Christian point of view, portraying traditional customs as backward and pagan. In *Omenuko*[12] and *Elelea Na Ihe O Mere*,[13] the functions of traditional priests are portrayed but unexplained. Achebe, in his first novel, ***Things Fall Apart,*** also presupposes the reader's familiarity with such information. He only briefly mentions the priestess Chielo's authority in relation to the Oracle of the Hills and Caves. Her brief appearance during Ezinma's illness provides scant insight regarding the existence and significance of the Oracle or its role in the lives of the people of Umuofia. When Ikemefuna's death is announced, one learns from Ezeudu that,

> Yes, Umuofia has decided to kill him. The Oracle of the Hills and Caves has pronounced it. They will take him outside Umuofia as is the custom and kill him there. . . .[14]

The reader has to know more about Igbo traditional religion, religious beliefs and political systems to fully understand Chielo, her Agbala and Ezeudu's announcement.

It is in ***Arrow of God*** that Achebe offers interpretations and explanations for the existence of such institutions, merging their complexities in Ezeulu. In his office as the priest of Ulu, he is portrayed as half-man, half-spirit. Achebe invests him with special powers, rights and privileges which give him a strong voice among the elders of Umuaro. His thoughts and actions strongly affect the rest of the community.

Even the actions of the members of his household, because they are close to him, become important to the people; this is the case when Oduche is sent to the new church and when he tries to suffocate the sacred python. Both incidents become major issues for discussion and action in the community because of Ezeulu's status. In ***Arrow of God*** Achebe interprets most aspects of Igbo traditional priesthood through Ezeulu. He discusses the rivalry between Ezeulu's sons over succession to the priesthood, and also Ezeulu's eldest son's apprehension about becoming a priest at his father's death. However, it is Nwafo, Ezeulu's youngest son, whom Achebe uses to show how one may be called to the priesthood. Nwafo's closeness to Ezeulu and his interest in the rituals mark him as a possible choice, among Ezeulu's sons, as successor to his father.

> His youngest son Nwafo now came into the *Obi*, saluted Ezeulu by name and took his favorite position on the mud-bed at the far end, close to the shorter thresh-

old. Although he was still only a child it looked as though the deity had already marked him out as his future Chief Priest. Even before he had learnt to speak more than a few words he had been strongly drawn to the god's ritual.[15]

Nwafo is strongly attracted to the service of the god, Ulu. When Ezeulu is detained at Okperi, it is Nwafo who wonders what should be done about announcing the new moon.

> However as dusk came down Nwafo took his position where his father always sat. He did not wait very long before he saw the young thin moon. It looked very thin and reluctant. Nwafo reached for the *ogene* and made to beat it but fear stopped his hand.[16]

Although he takes "his position where his father always sat," he is old enough to know that his father's successor has to be appointed by Ulu and endorsed by the people of Umuaro.

During the festival of the First Pumpkin Leaves, Ezeulu re-enacts the first coming of Ulu, showing how the people's support made it possible for him to lead them through his priestly office.

> "At that time," he said, "when lizards were still in ones and twos, the whole people assembled and chose me to carry their new deity. I said to them: 'Who am I to carry this fire on my bare head? A man who knows that his anus is small does not swallow an Udala seed.' They said to me: 'Fear not. The man who sends a child to catch a shrew will also give him water to wash his hand.' I said: 'So be it.'"[17]

As Ezeulu continues with the retelling of the legend of the first coming of Ulu, the duties that go with his priesthood become apparent. He is expected not only to stand between the people and the things that threaten them, but also to eliminate the sources of these threats. He derives strength and confidence from the knowledge that the people support him at all times. Also, Ezeulu's role as buffer between his people and their god is comparable to that of the priests/medicine men in *Omenuko* and *Elelea Na Ihe O Mere* who cleanse the land and the people of abominations. However, Ezeulu's office differs from theirs in that he is also involved in decision-making in Umuaro. The nature of Ulu makes it necessary for him to be concerned with Umuaro's safety and to play an important philosophical role in the socio-political welfare of the people.

Ezeulu demonstrates his awareness of the possible results of the changing times when he tries to secure Umuaro's future by sending Oduche to the new religion. Conscious of the Igbo's concern for preservation of the community, he sees the need to be in control of the present as well as anticipate events of the future. In the past, this consciousness in the people's worldview led to the amalgamation of the villages that make up Umuaro. Ezeulu therefore makes Oduche his ambassador to the new religion, Christianity: "I want one of my sons to join these people and be my eye there. If there is nothing in it you will come back. But if there is something there you will bring home my share."[18] Some analysts of this novel have tended to agree with Ugoye, Oduche's mother, in her assertion that Oduche was sacrificed to the white man's religion.[19] This is true only to the extent that Oduche is the first person from his family to get involved with the new religion. From Ezeulu's point of view, as the keeper of the people's god of protection, he is using Oduche to maintain a balance in their lives. Achebe points this out in Ezeulu's reply to Ugoye,

> . . . Do you not know that in a great man's household there must be people who follow all kinds of strange ways? There must be good people and bad people, honest workers and thieves, peace-makers and destroyers; that is the mark of a great *Obi*. In such a place, whatever music you beat on your drum there is somebody who can dance to it.[20]

It may be true that historically such a decision may not have been made by a man of Ezeulu's social status, but the point here is that this type of thinking made it possible for the Igbo to tolerate their own people who joined the new group. Since they could neither chase away nor kill the strangers without harming or even losing their own people, the best approach was to fit the phenomenon into a known and existing world view. Achebe points this out several times in **Arrow of God.** When Obika is whipped by Mr. Wright, for instance, instead of confronting Mr. Wright or doing anything else that might make him angrier, the young men quickly reactivate an already existing quarrel, and Achebe comments: "It was much easier to deal with an old quarrel than with a new and unprecedented incident."[21] The meeting ends with Nweke Ukpaka's speech, which begins, "What a man does not know is greater than he. . . . "[22] Nweke Ukpaka advises his age-mates to let Unachukwu, the carpenter who interprets for Mr. Wright, stay during their deliberations because he is their only link with the white man. Unachukwu is allowed to stay for the same reason that Ezeulu sends Oduche to the new church—both are a way of controlling, from a distance, an unprecedented threat to their well being:

Transitions and the New Dispensation

Ezeulu's use of Oduche as his "eye" in the new culture parallels the people's authorization of his own priestly responsibilities to Ulu. He can be seen as the people's "eye" in the supernatural world of spirits and gods which is beyond their human vision. The most obvious physical demonstration of this is evidenced in Ezeulu's function as watchman for the new moon. Apart from this visible calendar-keeping function of his watch, there is also the symbolic but unemphasized function of the priest as the person who keeps the people alert to changes in nature. He keeps an eye on nature, and as a result the people are kept aware of the passing of the seasons. This duty is so ritualized that even his house is built in a special way, emphasizing his distinctness in this regard.

> His *obi* was built differently from other men's huts. There was the usual long threshold in front but also a shorter one on the right as you entered. The eaves on this additional entrance were cut back so that sitting on the floor, Ezeulu could watch that part of the sky where the moon had its door.[23]

Achebe here describes a physical relationship based on an abstract principle: Ezeulu, the priest, watches for the moon through the cutting in the eaves of his house. In Ezeulu's words to Oduche when the latter is sent to join the new religion, the priest is the "eye" of Umuaro. The cutting in the eaves of his house constitutes another eye, linking Ezeulu to the universe which is symbolized in the moon. The people see the approach of the seasons through the moon. This arrangement constitutes one aspect of Ezeulu's bridging function between the people and their world. He becomes one of the tools which Umuaro uses in its attempt to live harmoniously with nature. It is an important manifestation of his priestly responsibility.

Ezeulu, more than anybody else, realizes the symbolic nature of this arrangement and of his duties to Umuaro through Ulu. However, he becomes politically involved in Umuaro's affairs beyond the requirements of his priestly office. He wants Ulu to become a nature god like Idemili or Udo, with his priest in complete command of choosing and naming the days of all Umuaro's feasts. Achebe uses Ezeulu's interests in politics to explore the priest's human attributes, the other aspect of his duality. He pushes him into a position where even though Ezeulu recognizes his duties to the people, he is forced to choose between them and their god. He chooses to listen to the voice of Ulu, knowing that the people are no longer behind him. Caught between gods and men, he lets his human side assert itself, and forgets that the gods came into being to serve men. He disregards his favorite proverb: "When an adult is in the house, the she-goat is not left to bear its young from the tether." Ezeulu, the adult in the Umuaro household, allows his people to suffer, and like the man who brings home ant-infested faggots, he should have expected the visit of lizards.

However, Achebe strikes a balance between Ezeulu, the

priest, and Ezeulu, the man. The priest in Ezeulu remains conscious of his duties toward Ulu and Umuaro's safety. He sees clearly the limits of the authority of his office. As the priest of Ulu, conscious of the people's voice supporting him, he warns against the dangers of fighting a "war of blame" against Okperi. His vision in this regard remains clear in spite of opposition from Nwaka and his group.

Duality, Politics, and Igbo Art

It is, however, at the peak of the performance of his priestly duties that Ezeulu's duality and that of the people's worldview are best expressed. This is portrayed during the festival of the First Pumpkin Leaves. Ezeulu, in his full regalia as Ulu's priest, comes into the village square.

> He wore smoked raffia which descended from his waist to the knee. The left half of his body—from forehead to toe—was painted with white chalk. Around his head was a leather band from which an eagle feather pointed backwards. On his right hand he carried *Nne ofo,* the mother of all staff of authority in Umuaro. . . . [24]

The figure of the priest embodies in artistic form the people's perception of their world. His painted body symbolizes his ability to bridge the gap between reality and the supernatural, reaffirming for them the harmonious existence of the two. It is also a concrete, visible way of bringing together the people's view of duality as it makes that which is intangible visible. In Ezeulu's hand is the staff of authority, which orders their lives, and on his head is the eagle feather, a symbol of affluence.[25] Artistically, this image brings together the apparently unrelated institutions of politics and religion. The harmonious merging results in plenitude, a mark of social and economic stability. It is significant that this symbol is manifested during the Festival of the First Pumpkin Leaves, the first food-related item to be harvested in the year. The harmonious society works together to produce life-giving food. The abundant green leaves, carried by the women, symbolize life and good health. Continuity of the group is reaffirmed and assured.

Another important aspect of this image involves Ezeulu as a work of art. In full priestly regalia, he visually refers to such ritual art objects as the *ofo,* the ancestral staff of authority and justice, and the *okposi,* carved representations of renowned departed ancestors. Like Ezeulu in priestly regalia, these are fashioned by the people to aid them in their communication with their gods and ancestors. As the priest moves in the circle made by the people, the women throw pumpkin leaves at him. He becomes the scapegoat which must carry away and bury their sins of the past year. The only difference between him and other ritual art objects is that he is living. Consequently, he becomes both

intermediary and representation; a combination of reality and art. However, as with other ritual situations, the emphasis is on the priest as representation rather than on the priest as an individual, reflecting the people's concern for the expression of community will over that of the individual. This concern in Igbo thought led to their intolerance of recalcitrant individuals, priests or even gods. Achebe refers to this aspect of Igbo thought when he portrays Ezeulu's attempts to attach too much importance to himself and his god. This individualistic tendency in Ezeulu allows Achebe's in-depth exploration of dualism within the society's systems and in the person of the priest in *Arrow of God.*

Achebe: The Artist/Priest

His use of Ezeulu to illustrate such aspects of Igbo thought parallels the traditional narrators' use of characters who are not allowed to win in confrontations between themselves and either their *chi* or the community. Such characters are usually portrayed as achievers who are discouraged from indulging in excesses but are encouraged to work towards the good of their families and communities. This theme has also been explored in more or less depth in early written Igbo literature.[26] Its importance in Igbo thought is evidenced by its continued expression even in works like Leopold Bell-Gam's *Ije Odumodu Jere* which is not primarily concerned with the celebration of Igbo world view or art tradition. Achebe's *Arrow of God* is possibly his most deliberate attempt at the celebration of Igbo traditions. Most Igbo authors working within the novel or short story forms portray characters which, because of shared beliefs and experiences, become reaffirmations of aspects of Igbo thought. Oral traditional genres range from the oral tale to the reenactment of myth during festivals in which many different art forms are employed. Contemporary and written Igbo literature uses most of the oral narrative techniques but has yet to achieve the unity of festival drama. Achebe tries to achieve this unity through explanations of the people's worldview, descriptive images of customs and traditions, transliteration of the Igbo language into English, and a combination of Igbo oral narrative techniques with those of the Western novel.

In *Arrow of God,* for instance, he demonstrates the various uses of proverbs in Igbo language and culture. They serve as points of reference and linguistic signposts which in the novel serve the artistic objective of unifying the story line. Proverbs are repositories of the wisdom of the ancestors. However, they, like any other aspect of Igbo thought, are open to manipulation. As Achebe demonstrates, one can explicate issues using proverbs, or they can become a starting point, a premise to an argument. Since their meanings are dynamic, they can work backwards or forwards, for, or against, a given argument. Hence, the assumption among the

Igbo of their applicability in rhetoric. In using the proverb, "When an adult is in the house the she-goat is not left to suffer the pain of parturition on its tether,"[27] for instance, Achebe is able to show Ezeulu as protecting the people's interest in the Okperi land case but he also gets angry enough to hurt them when they refuse to act like adults during his confrontation with the British. The alternate interpretation makes him out as the goat; thus, he reacts by inverting the situation (with Ulu's help?) and making the elders suffer. This proverb works in an oblique way with the other frequently quoted proverb in the novel: "a man who brings home ant-infested faggots should expect the visit of lizards."[28] When Ezeulu and the elders refuse to act like knowledgeable adults, that is, like wise statesmen whose titles bequeath elegance in manner, the best behavior and the responsibility to rational action, they become subject to the balancing natural principles of which they are supposed to be guardians.

In none of the known works of fiction by writers of Igbo origin has the Igbo art tradition and worldview been as exhaustively treated as in Arrow of God. The portrayal of Ezeulu shows Achebe's understanding of Igbo society and thought, paralleling him to the traditional elders of the land. His interpretations of Igbo life place him among the artists and philosophers of Igbo tradition. Achebe has claimed to be an ancestor worshipper[29] and insists that the African novelist is a teacher.[30] He contends that

> the writer cannot expect to be excused from the task of re-education and regeneration that must be done. In fact he should march right in front. For he is after all—as Ezekiel Mphahlele says in his *African Image*—the sensitive point of his community.[31]

This assertion makes his role similar to Ezeulu's, the priest of Umuaro's god of protection, whose charge is to march in front of the people leading and confronting all threats to the community. Like Ezeulu, the writer has to be able to find ways of maintaining balance in the community. However, Achebe the artist emphasizes the Igbo art tradition more than the religion. This does not mean that Igbo religion is absent in his works; rather, he uses descriptions of aspects of the people's religion to delineate the role and significance of traditional religious objects as art objects. His explanation of Igbo worldview emphasizes the need for those familiar with the background, setting and characters to begin to see the utility and application of traditional wisdom and its possibilities in the reassessment of current experiences and problems. As with the priest/artist's religious objects, Achebe's works demonstrate the artist/priest's commitment to the well being of the society.

NOTES

1. Chinua Achebe, *Morning Yet On Creation Day* (New York: Anchor Press/Doubleday, 1975), p. 29.

2. Ernst Fischer, *The Necessity of Art*, Anna Bostock trans., (New York: Penguin Books, 1963).

3. Achebe, *op. cit.*, p. 70.

4. Fischer, *op. cit.*, p. 8.

5. Chinua Achebe, *Arrow of God* (New York: Doubleday and Company, 1969).

6. M.S.O. Olisa, "Political Culture and Stability in Igbo Society," *Conch*, vol. 3, no. 2 (Sept. 1971), p. 20.

7. Elizabeth Islchei, *Igbo Worlds* (Philadelphia: Institute for the Study of Human Issues, 1978), p. 20.

8. Wole Soyinka, *Myth, Literature and the African World* (Cambridge: Cambridge University Press, 1976), p. 148.

9. M. S. O. Olisa, *op. cit.*, p. 22.

10. J. U. T. Nzeako, *Okuko Agbasaa Okpesi* (London: Thomas Nelson and Sons Ltd., 1964).

11. Leopold Bell-Gam, *Ije Odumodu Jere* (Lagos: Longmans, 1963).

12. Pita Nwanna, *Omenuko* (London: Longmans, 1933).

13. D. N. Achara, *Elelea Na Ihe O Mere* (London: Longmans, 1953).

14. Chinua Achebe, *Things Fall Apart* (London: Heinemann, 1958), p. 40.

15. Achebe, *Arrow of God, op. cit.*, p. 4.

16. *Ibid.* p. 187.

17. *Ibid.*

18. *Ibid.* p. 51.

19. See Bernth Lindfors, "The Palm Oil with which Achebe's Words are Eaten," in C. L. Innes and Bernth Lindfors, eds., *Critical Perspectives on Chinua Achebe* (Washington, D.C.: Three Continents Press, 1978), p. 58; Emmanuel Obiechina, "The Human Dimension of History in *Arrow of God,*" in Innes and Lindfors, eds., p. 176.

20. Achebe, *Arrow of God, op. cit.*, p. 51.

21. *Ibid.* p. 94.

22. *Ibid.*

23. *Ibid.* p. 1.

24. *Ibid.* p. 80.

25. Donatus J. Nwoga, "The Igbo World of Achebe's Arrow of God," *Research in African Literatures*, vol 12, no. 1 (Spring, 1981), p. 26.

26. See D. N. Achara, *Ala Bingo* (London: Longmans, 1954); Pita Nwanna, *Omenuko, op. cit.*, D. N. Achara, *Elelea Na Ihe O Mere, op. cit.*

27. Achebe, *Arrow of God, op. cit.*, p. 20.

28. *Ibid*, p. 148.

29. C. O. D. Ekwensi, "African Literature," *Nigeria Magazine*, no. 83 (Dec. 1964), p. 286.

30. See Achebe, *Morning Yet on Creation Day, op. cit.*, pp. 67-73; Achebe, "The Uses of African Literature," *Okike*, no. 15, (Aug. 1979), pp. 8-17.

31. Achebe, *Morning Yet On Creation Day, op. cit.*, p. 72.

Neil ten Kortenaar (essay date January 1995)

SOURCE: "Beyond Authenticity and Creolization: Reading Achebe Writing Culture," in *Publications of the Modern Language Association of America*, Vol. 110, No. 1, January, 1995, pp. 30-42.

[*Ten Kortenaar has written other scholarly articles on Achebe. In the following essay, he compares similarities in the narrative strategies of the colonized and the colonizer to define their respective cultural identities in Arrow of God.*]

The discussion of culture in postcolonial literary criticism revolves around the twin poles of authenticity and hybridization. One response to the experience of colonialism and the concomitant denigration of cultural identities has been to call for a return to precolonial authenticity. In current debates the standard of fidelity to origins is often Ngũgĩ wa Thiong'o's rejection of English in favor of Gĩkũyũ for the language of his novels. Such authenticity contrasts with the acceptance by other writers of some measure of interfertilization (or creolization or mongrelization or *métissage*). In the French Caribbean, for instance, the negritude of Aimé Césaire stands against the *créolité* celebrated by Patrick Chamoiseau. Advocates of creolization denounce colonialism but believe that it is irreversible. That position does not leave the former colonized without a culture: they have a hybrid or creole culture that has borrowed from the metropolitan culture and in the process subverted and indigenized it. Creolization celebrates the exuberant mutual contamination of styles that is characteristic of Salman Rushdie's and Wilson Harris's writings.

Advocates of creolization often argue that authenticity is quixotic, that, as Françoise Lionnet writes, "[c]ross- or transcultural exchange has always been 'an absolute fact' of life everywhere" (104). When conceived as a peculiarly postcolonial condition, however, creolization is open to the same objection that is levied against authenticity: that cultures have always been characterized by fluidity and exchange. Hybridization, like authenticity, is unintelligible without a notion of cultural purity. Both authenticity and creolization ascribe the significance of cultural elements to national provenance: where a thing is from is what it means.[1]

If, as Walter Benn Michaels writes, there "are no anti-essentialist accounts of identity," reifications of culture (including not only authenticity but also creolization) are rhetorical in intention: they manipulate shared symbols in order to win consent for political action. Although purporting to describe what people are and what they do, authenticity and creolization actually challenge people to identify with a certain image of themselves and so to adopt a certain identity. These constructions are what Anthony Cohen calls attempts "to represent the person or group in terms of a reified and/or emblematized culture" (195). To accept the validity of either authenticity or creolization as a description of oneself is to accept certain modes of dressing, speaking, and writing as belonging properly to oneself and to reject other styles as false. Such definitions of identity create a world not only of members and nonmembers but also of loyalists and traitors. Implicit in such a world is the assumption that there are people who have lost their identity.[2]

To say that authenticity and creolization serve rhetorical purposes is not to say that these constructs are false. They are the metaphors by which a communal identity is fashioned; identities have always been constructed by such means. People give reasons for what they do, invest what they do with meaning, and identify what they do as belonging properly to themselves; by this ascription of meaning to actions people declare who they are. Communities are constituted not by the possession of a shared culture that shapes the individual and makes him or her a replicate in miniature of the whole but rather by the ongoing debate over what the shared culture is, how members should behave, and what children should be taught (see Cohen 195-96). Like Cohen, I presume that culture "does not exist apart from what people *do*, and therefore what people do cannot be explained as its product" (207). People fashion their identity by identifying with cultural symbols and by narrating a place in the world. Of course, a community's narratives are shaped according to conventions, and narrative conventions change from age to age and differ from clime to clime. Narratives and symbols are social institutions that outlast the lives of individuals, and cultural agents must construct their lives within these inherited parameters. But individuals do not therefore merely replicate their inheritance. Culture, Jean-Loup Amselle argues, is not a prescriptive grammar but rather a reservoir of often contradictory potential practices that social actors can make use of when communal identity is being renegotiated, as it always is (10).

David Laitin rightly distinguishes between two faces of culture. The first face, which Laitin relates to the social systems theory of Clifford Geertz, is a symbolic system that establishes values and horizons of common sense. The second, associated with the positivist anthropology of Abner Cohen, locates the significance of cultural symbols not so much in their meaning, about which there is always disagreement, as in the fact that they are shared and can be used to summon a community to collective action. This face is shown when, as with authenticity and creolization, "[c]ultural identity becomes a political resource" (Laitin 11).

The first face establishes the limits of the thinkable, whereas people self-consciously shape the second. Laitin suggests how these two faces can be reconciled. The second face acknowledges that symbols serve the political and rhetorical ends of cultural agents; it cannot predict, however, what those ends will be. For an understanding of ends, the first face of culture needs to be considered—as well as the narrative conventions available within a community at any particular juncture. The inherited symbolic system does not determine who will win in any given conflict, but it directs community members to "what is worth fighting about" (Laitin 174).

This essay examines how the two faces of culture are related in Chinua Achebe's novel ***Arrow of God,*** which depicts the cultural crisis that accompanied the consolidation of British colonialism in Igboland in the early 1920s. Achebe's depiction of cultural redefinition at the time of the colonial encounter facilitates understanding of contemporary postcolonial communities. Achebe represents culture in Africa as Paulin Hountondji argues that it should be represented: as something invented and in constant need of reinvention (233).

I

Arrow of God, Achebe's third novel and many would say his best, was published in 1964, six years after ***Things Fall Apart,*** and revised in 1974. The novel depicts a fictional community of Igbo speakers grouped in six villages collectively known as Umuaro, which falls within the larger colonial territory baptized Nigeria, where the colonial administrative and military apparatus and the missionary presence are only beginning to make themselves felt. Achebe presents a community that defines itself by shared symbols (local deities and established rituals, as well as a proverbial wisdom) and by symbolic boundaries. Individuals invest shared symbols with various meanings, about which there is disagreement. The British intrusion forces Umuaro to redefine itself, but its culture has always been subject to redefinition. Umuaro did not have a homeostatic, holistic culture that fell apart when the Europeans came. The villages invented the god Ulu to unite them when they were threatened by Abam slave-raiders (15). If ever things were in danger of falling apart, it was then; instead a new identity was constructed and given religious legitimacy. Umuaro is best understood through the will of its members to narrate a collective identity.

The presence of the colonizers occasions an internal debate in Umuaro. The crisis in the novel is a contest between rival interpretations that are also rival strategic responses to the historical moment. Umuaro illustrates what Amselle has argued, that debate on the values of a community is what constitutes the community:

> Pour qu'il y ait identité, société, culture ou ethnie, il n'est pas nécéssaire que les agents se mettent d'accord sur ce qui définit cette culture: il suffit qu'ils s'entendent pour débattre ou négocier sur les termes de l'identité, sur ce qui la fonde comme problème. En d'autres termes, on peut avancer que l'identité c'est l'accord sur l'objet même du désaccord. (65)

> For there to be an identity, society, culture, or ethnicity, it is not necessary for the members to agree on what defines that culture: it is enough that they agree to debate or negotiate the terms of that identity. In other words, identity is an agreement about the object of disagreement. (trans. mine)

The terms of the debate resemble the poles of tradition and change, as the novel's critics have often said. The novel shows, however, that tradition and change are not absolute positions but the rhetorical means whereby a community fashions itself. All rivals in the debate make use of proverbs and appeal to the ancestors; the winner is neither the one who is closest to the opinion of the ancestors nor the one who is closest to objective reality but the one who can persuade the audience.

Ezeulu, the priest of the patron deity Ulu, assumes the mantle of upholder of tradition, but the novel makes clear that Ezeulu invents the tradition that he upholds. His devotion to Ulu is not the culture of Umuaro waiting to be interpreted and judged; it is already Ezeulu's own interpretation of Umuaro culture, with a judgment inscribed within it. Authenticity is a rallying cry in the community's internal debate. My reading here differs from that of Simon Gikandi, who emphasizes the crisis in traditional authority provoked by colonialism and the gap that colonialism opened in Igbo culture.[3] Gikandi considers two examples of this gap: the headstrong young Akukalia's destruction of another man's *ikenga,* the symbolic manifestation of a person's life and strength, in a burst of unreasoning temper and the imprisonment of the sacred python in a box by Ezeulu's son Oduche. These two examples of sacrilege are certainly parallel, but the novel contrasts them. Achebe signals the difference between the two incidents by setting Akukalia's breaking of the *ikenga* in the past, five years before the narrative opens, and Oduche's imprisonment of the python in the narrative present. When the *ikenga* is broken, the elders can still debate communal strategy without taking the British into account. Akukalia's act is symptomatic not of a newly opened gap but of gaps that have always existed. The imprisonment of the python, however, is a sacrilege that would have been inconceivable before the coming of the missionaries, one that marks a change in the order of debate.

Five years before the events in the novel's present, Umuaro debates going to war with its neighbor Okperi over a land dispute. At stake is communal identity: specifically, whether or not Umuaro's relation to Okperi is a filial one. The boundary between Umuaro and Okperi does not separate those who are known from strangers who are not but divides two symmetrically constituted communities. The category of stranger does not operate; there is instead either alliance and intermarriage or hostility. But Umuaro and Okperi's parallel relation does not make the boundary between them any less necessary. Those who straddle the boundary are regarded as potential traitors to Umuaro—Nwaka is quick to hint that Ezeulu opposes the war because Ezeulu's mother was from Okperi—and the boundary dispute is serious enough that people are willing to go to war over it.

Akukalia is sent to Okperi with the sensitive assignment of offering the choice of war or peace. He has been specifically warned against losing his temper—the elder who warns him recognizes anger as an inevitable temptation for a young man full of the importance of his mission. The elder's fears are realized, for temper moves Akukalia to do what he recognizes as sacrilegious: he breaks another man's *ikenga* because he believes that it is sacred. The transgression implies acknowledgment of the boundary between the sacred and the profane. Sacrilege is not always foreign.

The British colonial administration puts an end to the fighting that breaks out between Umuaro and Okperi and then sits in judgment on the rivals in the land dispute. Captain Winterbottom is proud of the title "Breaker of Guns" that he has earned in establishing the Pax Britannica in this corner of the world. Of course, the presence of an outside arbiter changes the significance of the war for all concerned: the British intervention draws attention to a previously unconsidered external boundary that Umuaro and Okperi share. Winterbottom's account of the war to his newly arrived subordinate Tony Clarke shows that however much Winterbottom understands the facts, he does not understand the significance of the war. Winterbottom is sure that there must exist an absolute border that the two communities know but that they are lying about, because he assumes that African identities are fixed and absolute. He does not recognize the war's ritual function as a means of establishing identity. From the British perspective, the war is only a marker of a generalized African or Igbo identity: Africans are always fighting among themselves *because* they are Africans, and they require the British presence to maintain peace.

The British want fixed, easily understood identities for their colonial subjects, and Winterbottom values Ezeulu as the one such subject who will not prevaricate. But even those colonizers who are concerned about "respecting" local cultural conditions cannot agree what those conditions are and how they are to be respected. Winterbottom has been passed over for promotion precisely because he disagrees with the precepts of indirect rule as they are being applied in Igboland. Indirect rule was intended to preserve indigenous frameworks of control, but the model developed in northern Nigeria was inappropriate in Igboland, where the British had to invent "traditional" rulers because there were no absolute chiefs to assume local authority. Colonialism was riven with such contradictions. On the one hand, indirect rule imposed an unnatural stabilizing of identities among the colonized (see Young 79); on the other, the missionaries who accompanied the colonizers worked to destabilize those identities. John Goodcountry, the missionary in Umuaro, is dedicated to erasing traditional identities, abolishing pagan practices, and converting Umuaro to Christianity.[4]

Goodcountry has a disciple in Oduche, the son whom Ezeulu sends to be his eyes and ears at the mission school. Oduche imprisons a python to show that the sacred python has no power over Christians or at least to test its power. He acknowledges the symbolic boundary between the sacred and the profane, but his transgression is also a would-be redrawing of that boundary. The transgression provokes a crisis because any attempt to redraw the boundary requires that the boundary indeed be redrawn, even if only to be restored.

An explicit prohibition against interfering with the python exists, so it must always have been possible to imagine a transgression. What is new is that Oduche's transgression of the boundary between the sacred and the profane also challenges the boundary between the self and the other. The line that Oduche seeks to draw does not distinguish separate selves that are symmetrically constituted; it defines a new self, radically different from and completely opposed to an old self, which it also defines. The significance of Oduche's sacrilege is not that it contravenes an established set of values—all sacrilege does so, though without necessarily provoking a crisis—but that it shifts the debate and draws attention to new points of concern.

The process of collective self-redefinition is only partly influenced by the hegemonic definitions imposed by the British; it largely follows a dynamic within the community, a dynamic determined by available cultural resources. The sociologist Robert Wuthnow describes three common symbolic distinctions that delineate a social identity (71-75) and that can be observed in the structure of Umuaro. The Umuarans illustrate the first distinction, between moral objects and real programs, when they raise yams for subsistence but tell themselves that they do so to comply with the will of Ulu. What they must do to survive also fulfills the higher end of uniting them in a community. Wuthnow draws a second distinction between the self and the roles that the self must play. There is no essential self that is the repository of authenticity, but symbolic distinctions bring the self into being by demarcating what is self and what are the roles that are not the self but that the self must perform. Even though Ezeulu's name suggests an absolute identification with his role, his family and his neighbors distinguish between the man and the priest of Ulu. Wuthnow's third distinction is between intentionality and inevitability. The members of a social structure are given the sense that they are free to act, but moral responsibility is hemmed in by a sense of inevitability, which allows absolution for failure. In Umuaro, where the realm of freedom encompasses even mortality, a dying man is asked what he has done to deserve to die and is urged to refuse the spirit forces that seek his death (114). At the same time human freedom is limited by the intractability that characterizes the world and the human body. Akukalia's sacrilege can be attributed to his temper, a part of himself beyond his control, or to "Ekwensu, the bringer of evil" (24). In this way final responsibility for the sacrilege is removed from human hands.

When Ezeulu defends an authentic identity based on the worship of Ulu, the "tradition" that he upholds blurs the consensual internal distinctions between moral order and real programs, self and roles, intentionality and inevitability. Ezeulu wants to punish his fellow villagers for having insisted that he obey a white man's summons and travel to Okperi even though they know that the priest of Ulu is never to leave Umuaro. Ezeulu refuses to eat the sacred yams that as priest of Ulu he is supposed to eat at each new moon and that he has failed to eat during the thirty-two days that he has been detained by the British for refusing their offer of a warrant chieftaincy. Since the eating of the last of the yams is the signal that the time has come to harvest, Ezeulu's obstinate adherence to the letter of the law calls famine down on the community. The distinction between moral objects and real programs is thereby dissolved: the object of complying with the will of Ulu conflicts with the community's program of raising yams for subsistence. Ezeulu's totalizing impulse also provokes the collapse of the distinction between intentionality and inevitability, between freedom and necessity, as the priest identifies his own will with the god Ulu's. Ezeulu imagines himself to be an arrow of God and erases the realm of freedom. He also identifies his self too absolutely with one of its roles: he forgets the man and allows the priest to subsume his whole identity.

Ezeulu's dogmatic defense of the cult of Ulu is not the response of a whole, integrated world to the violence of a hegemonic alien culture but a redefinition of the world of Umuaro that erases other internal distinctions. The British impose contradictory definitions on the colonized: the administrators seek conformity to fixed definitions that the missionaries in turn condemn. The response of the colonized is also conflicted: Ezeulu does away with internal symbolic distinctions and makes identity fixed and unchanging.[5]

II

Both the Umuarans and the British are more concerned about internal distinctions than about the external boundary between the two peoples: Ezeulu regards Nwaka as a greater personal threat than Winterbottom is, the god Ulu is engaged in a wrestling match with Idemili rather than with the Christian God, and Winterbottom worries more about proving something to his superiors than about the control of Umuaro. The novel illustrates the idea that when faced with a threat to its external boundaries, a community shores up its internal boundaries and seeks greater certainty about the status, loyalties, and values of its own members (Wuthnow 117).

Readers of Achebe's postcolonial novel, however, are most interested in the external boundary between the colonizers and the colonized. The boundary dividing the Igbo of Umuaro from the British is an internal division in the world of the novel, which contains both groups. At first colonizer and colonized are allocated separate chapters, but even that segregation breaks down. Although the differences between the groups are never minimized, the text evokes a world larger than the microworld of either one. Readers are invited to sympathize with the Umuarans, while the British are drawn with bolder strokes and are mildly satirized—the people of Umuaro have a story, while the British are relegated to a somewhat static background, a reversal of the strategy of imperialist texts. Nevertheless, the simultaneous presentation suggests that the two groups are located on a sociocultural continuum and that only confrontation makes them appear internally coherent and irreconcilably different.[6]

Both the colonized and the colonizers observe formal rituals: the lieutenant governor's dinner party (33-34) is as rigidly ruled by convention as is the breaking of kola nuts among the Igbo. Members of both groups jockey for status in a hierarchy that exists only in the eyes of others within the cultural community. Like the Umuarans, the British are defined by symbolic distinctions. But the distinction that the British make between the sacred and the profane inevitably comes into conflict with that made by the Umuarans, and Assistant Superintendent Wade finds it blasphemous that an English florin with the head of George V is part of a local sacrifice intended to ward off malevolent powers (161). An implicit distinction also exists between moral objects and real programs: Tony Clarke, who imprisons the "witch-doctor" Ezeulu for having embarrassed the administration, suffers from a guilty conscience until he can find a "reasonable explanation" for the detention, one that he can put down in his log (178). So, too, the British distinguish between the self and roles that the self must play: Clarke and Wright mock Winterbottom the captain for his pomposity but pity Winterbottom the man, whose wife has deserted him (102-03).

Distinctions are also drawn between intentionality and inevitability. The experience of imperialism encourages the British to exaggerate the arena in which they are free to act: an imperialist text that Clarke finds a little too smug celebrates "those who can deal with men as others deal with material, who can grasp great situations, coax events, shape destinies and ride on the crest of the wave of time" (33). At the same time stalled careers and other failures must be attributed to an intractability beyond human control. Africa's resistance to imperialist control is figured in terms of heat and discomfort and measured by morbidity rates. The British response to the intractability of Africa is to stress self-discipline and moderation; for example, Winterbottom would prefer cold baths but believes that he must take hot ones, since "Africa never spared those who did what they liked instead of what they had to do" (29). As Philip D. Curtin explains, the British in Africa found that "rules of conduct, whether sensible or not, were psychologically necessary. Where death was both common and mysterious, it was essential to lay out an area of personal responsibility, so that each could consider 'all men mortal but himself'" (354).

If Wuthnow's categories make possible a comparison between the Umuarans and the British, the differences between the two communities are significant. They go beyond the use of symbols and the drawing of boundaries to differences in the possession and exercise of power. The authority of the British has its basis in violence, as is made manifest when Wright the road builder strikes Ezeulu's son Obika and when Ezeulu is detained for refusing to cooperate with the administration. Umuaro, in contrast, is democratic. Indeed, the community accords with Mazi Elechukwu Nnadibuagha Njaka's depiction of Igbo political culture as "para-democratic": no individual wields uncontested authority in the public forum, and the most anyone can hope for is to influence decision making (59). Ezeulu's desire to command the obedience of others can be fulfilled only in his own compound; there, however, he tyrannizes his wives and sons. The colonizers regard Nigeria much as Ezeulu regards his compound; they claim to determine the place of Umuaro and Okperi within a larger order that only they, the British, can perceive.

The redefinition of identities in Achebe's Umuaro and by extension in Igboland is a response to British power. The powerful other inevitably frames the terms in which debates about identity are conducted. The community of Umuaro seems more concerned, however, about establishing internal loyalties than about marshaling external resistance, partly because the British never had as much power in West Africa as they thought they had. As Kwame Anthony Appiah has written, the West African situation differed from the New World or the southern African situation in that "the experience of the vast majority of these citizens of Europe's African colonies was one of essentially shallow penetration by the colonizer" (7). The Umuarans' relative indifference to the British can also be explained by the assertion that colonial authorities set the grounds for the debate but could not take away the villagers' capacity to tell their own story. Political imperialism should be differentiated from cultural imperialism.

III

How did the British acquire power over Africans? A common Weberian explanation attributes European ascendancy to peculiar cultural qualities. If culture and identity are constantly being invented through a process of negotiation, the most successful negotiators are those who can make unforeseen circumstances and even foreign ideological structures fit their own narratives. Stephen Greenblatt describes improvisation as the dual ability "to capitalize on the unforeseen and to transform given materials into one's own scenario" (227). Greenblatt argues that improvisation is a skill that is not valued everywhere and that came into its own during the European Renaissance. The second British Empire, which included Nigeria, was explicitly founded on improvisation in Greenblatt's sense. The policy of indirect rule presumed that the British could enter into African political and psychic structures and use those structures to rule Africans.

Greenblatt's notion of improvisation assumes both a structural homology between the improviser and the improviser's other, such as the one that exists between the cultures of the British and the Umuarans, and an absence of reciprocity: the British study the Igbo and fit them into a British narrative, not the other way around. Achebe makes clear, however, that the psychic structures of Africans are not fixed and that both the British and the Africans attempt to fit the other into a self-serving narrative. The problem Winterbottom encounters in his attempts to manipulate Igbo culture is that the "natives . . . are great liars" (38).[7] How can one enter into another's psychic structures if the other will not stand still long enough for those structures to be defined? Winterbottom recognizes that the system of warrant chiefs, the linchpin of British improvisation in Igboland, is a terrible failure, for the appointed men exploit the British power structures for their own ends. One chief, James Ikedi, threatens to demolish compounds to make way for new roads in order to extract bribes from wealthy villagers (57). He even uses his British-awarded title to have himself declared king among a people who have always abominated kings (58).

Inserting oneself into the consciousness of another, which is part of Greenblatt's definition of improvisation, is not the sole preserve of the colonizer. Ezeulu recognizes the need to enter into British structures; thus the defender of the worship of Ulu sends his son Oduche to the missionary school. The colonized who fulfills British expectations for natives and the colonized who imitates British codes both play roles, and sometimes the same person plays both roles. This role-playing may take the form of selfish manipulation, as with James Ikedi, and it may also serve larger, political purposes. Moses Unachukwu, who has lived for ten years among the whites in Onitsha before his return to Umuaro to take up the role of translator, knows how to address different audiences. At the end of the novel, Unachukwu gets a clerk in Okperi to write a letter on behalf of the priest of Idemili to the bishop on the Niger: "Being the work of one of the knowledgeable clerks on Government Hill the petition made allusions to such potent words as law and order and the King's peace" (214).

Like Greenblatt's improviser, the British and the Umuarans fit the unforeseen, the apparently random, and the meaningless into their own narratives. In *Arrow of God* the unforeseeable is figured by sudden illness and death. The people of Umuaro interpret sickness as a wrestling match between the patient and the forces that seek to do the patient harm. The British think of sickness as the product of

an imbalance, the result of intemperance. When Winterbottom is struck down by fever after having Ezeulu arrested, there are rival interpretations: "Perhaps it was Captain Winterbottom's rage and frenzy that brought it on; perhaps his steward was right about its cause [and the fever was Ezeulu's revenge]" (149). Achebe's narrative dwells less on whether the fever is the result of personal immoderation or an enemy's magical power than on the fever's function as an unforeseen event that tests the characters' ability to fit the world into their own narrative. The person closest to Winterbottom, the missionary doctor Mary Savage, breaks down in tears and panic, but others respond strategically. Winterbottom's incapacity thrusts Tony Clarke into a position of authority and aggravates an existing crisis in Umuaro. Ezeulu is able to turn his prolonged incarceration to his own account: he fits the British into his own narrative of divine retribution for Umuaro.

At the end of the novel Ezeulu's son Obika dies suddenly and unexpectedly while carrying the mask of the *ogbazulobodo*. Those closest to Obika do not know how to react: Ezeulu despairs, believing that the death presages "the collapse and ruin of all things" (229). The rest of Umuaro sees in Obika's death the abandonment of the stubborn priest by his god. The death is clearly overdetermined. Shortly before his death, Obika challenges the power of a feared medicine man, lifting him up and throwing him into the bush in front of a great crowd gathered for a festival (198). The festival is subsequently marred by a bad omen when a ram offered in sacrifice is not killed with the first blow (201). There is, however, another possible explanation. Obika agrees to carry the mask despite a fever, goaded by the thought that the villagers will blame him if he does not (224): the suggestion is that the fever kills him. The significance of an unforeseen event such as Obika's death is precisely that it can be fitted into rival narratives.

Ezeulu is unable to respond to Obika's death, for it comes at a moment of great stress—"At any other time Ezeulu would have been more than a match to his grief. He would have been equal to any pain not compounded with humiliation" (229)—and he is driven mad. In Achebe's novel madness can be defined as the incapacity to insert oneself into the consciousness of others: Ezeulu ends his days isolated from others and from the world. Ezeulu's demise is open to multiple interpretations, however: "Perhaps it was the constant, futile throbbing of these thoughts that finally left a crack in Ezeulu's mind. Or perhaps his implacable assailant . . . stepped on him as on an insect and crushed him under the heel in the dust" (229). Moreover, since Ezeulu's mother has also gone mad, it is possible to view his behavior as hereditary.

Ezeulu's collapse is fitted into narratives that serve others' purposes. The Christians, led by Goodcountry, invite the disenchanted and hungry worshipers of Ulu to join the church and to eat the yams that Ezeulu has forbidden. The people of Umuaro agree so that they can harvest their yams and preserve the community. Who is using whom? Under pressure to redraw its boundaries, the community risks splitting apart. The mass conversion to Christianity conspicuously redraws the boundary between the sacred and the profane; however, other boundaries are subtly redrawn along reassuringly familiar lines. The distinction between real programs and moral objects, for instance, is strengthened: the community turns from Ulu to a god that will bless the harvest of the yams. So, too, the distinction between intentionality and inevitability remains relatively constant. Ezeulu's demise allows the community to evade direct responsibility for the mass apostasy by blaming the gods. It is not the community that abandons Ulu but Ulu who abandons his people: "For a deity who chose a moment such as this to chastise his priest or abandon him before his enemies was inciting people to take liberties; and Umuaro was just ripe to do so" (230).

Another way the community avoids final responsibility for its apostasy is by redrawing the boundary between reason and madness that defines the space in which meaningful discourse takes place. At the end Ezeulu really is mad; that is, he is unable to insert himself into the consciousness of others. Yet both Clarke and Nwaka believe that Ezeulu was already mad when he refused the position of warrant chief (175-76). At the same time most Umuarans consider Ezeulu's rejection of the British offer a courageous model of meaningful discourse. Afterward, however, they interpret Ezeulu's final madness not as a break with what has come before but as the fulfillment of something that has always been at least potentially present. Midway through the novel the priest's laugh disturbs his friend Akuebue because it sounds like a madman's: Akuebue "was given no chance to examine this strange feeling of fear closely. But he was to have it again in future and it was only then he saw its meaning" (131). Akuebue does not at first understand that Ezeulu's laughter is a sign of madness for the good reason that the laughter of deities can be equally fearful. Eventually, however, the meaning of the laugh is understood, and Ezeulu's final madness is traced back to his tenure as priest of Ulu. Although Ezeulu's sanity is shattered by the silence of his god when his son dies, others later assume that Ezeulu was already mad when he conversed with his god. Two different kinds of madness are conflated here: that of the absence of God and that of the presence of God.

The distinctions that constitute identity are created by rituals, symbolic acts "performed for expressive rather than purely instrumental purposes" (Wuthnow 140). Two kinds of ritual are depicted in *Arrow of God*. Organized, regularly recurring ritual occasions, such as the Festival of the Pumpkin Leaves, provide participants with the opportunity to discharge moral obligations and thereby to acquire a sense of moral worth. This kind of ritual is not a means of knowing but an expression of what is already known: for some, like the five wives of Nwaka, the festival is as much an occasion to display wealth as it is an opportunity to fulfill moral duties (68). When the moral order comes under stress, however, extemporized rituals that dramatize the crisis are felt to be more meaningful than organized, recurring rituals are. Oduche's imprisonment of the python is a ritual in this second sense, a symbolic-expressive dramatization of the conflict that engulfs the community. Responses to this ritual event, which derives its meaning from the particular historical moment, are stronger (and less unanimous) than are responses to the annual Festival of the Pumpkin Leaves.

Ezeulu's final madness is also a ritual of this second kind, an expressive manifestation of the passing of the old and the drawing of new symbolic boundaries. Ezeulu recapitulates at a single unrepeatable moment the scapegoat role that he plays every year at the Festival of the Pumpkin Leaves: taking the sins of the community on himself so that the community can be renewed. Ezeulu makes possible the community's mass conversion to Christianity by conspicuously drawing onto himself all the cultural features that stand in the way of that move and then suffering immolation.

The community interprets Ezeulu's final madness and expulsion as a ritual tragedy. Umuaro and its leaders read in Ezeulu's fate the gods' punishment of his ambition and stubbornness and the vindication of the wisdom "that no man however great [is] greater than his people" (230). Casting Ezeulu's story as a tragedy allows the community to render intelligible its own changing identity at a moment of historical crisis. What is at stake in *Arrow of God* is not any particular cultural values but the capacity of a collectivity to generate a satisfying narrative.

As Achebe says in his preface to the second edition of the novel, Ezeulu's defeat operates like a rite of passage. For Wuthnow, "[r]ites of passage . . . dichotomize the continuous progression of real time into two distinct periods as far as social time is concerned" (113-14), a division that is artificial. Ezeulu's defeat is not the death of a single complete and internally consistent culture, but the story is told that way. The validity of this telling lies not in its correspondence to objective reality but in its status as a symbolic expression of an Umuaran self that has been reinvented in colonial times.

The conversion to Christianity does not necessarily mark the death or falling apart of a culture, for culture does not have an ontological existence apart from what cultural agents do. John Tomlinson argues against the conception of cultural imperialism as the spread of false behavior and false consciousness, against the presumption that people are something more than what they do. More accurately, cultural imperialism deprives cultural agents of the spiritual resources or institutional space necessary to generate meaningful collective narratives. Achebe's Igbo suffer political imperialism but are able to resist cultural imperialism, for they retain a "collective will-formation" (Tomlinson 165) and a capacity to account for their experience and their place in the world through narrative.[8]

The Umuaran narrative is, of course, a tragedy about the loss of authenticity. Tragedy, however, is not the only possible mode for the community's story. If continuity rather than discontinuity were stressed, the experience of colonization might be figured as a heroic narrative of resistance, or if the discontinuity were rendered more absolute, the narrative might trace the integration of a subsistence economy into a capitalist world order. Tragedy is accepted as the most appropriate narrative configuration because it is that part of the reservoir of available cultural elements that proves most useful for Umuaran self-definition.

IV

Greenblatt writes that improvisation, the manipulative role-playing favored by the West ever since the Renaissance, requires seeing the other's culture as an ideological construct but does not risk—and may actually strengthen—one's own worldview. And yet the narrative strategies of Achebe's Igbo characters presume a self-conscious awareness of the constructed nature of all cultural systems: the people of Umuaro never forget that Ulu is their own creation.

Andrew Apter contends that the deep or secret knowledge of the guardians of Yoruba ritual is the human invention of their practices. Achebe's model of double consciousness among the Igbo in *Arrow of God* represents a more democratic view: the guardian of ritual forgets that Ulu is a human creation, but the rest of the community remembers.[9]

Achebe's model more closely reflects Karin Barber's analysis of Yoruba religion, which focuses not on the priests' deep knowledge but on the devotees' worship. In Barber's study of praise songs Yoruba devotees of an *orisa*, or god, are well aware that their god is a function of human belief and acknowledge that the relation between god and devotee is characterized by mutual dependence. Devotees rely on the *orisa* to answer their needs; the *orisa* in turn requires worship for prestige and existence. If one *orisa* fails, the devotee is always free to experiment with another; there is plenty of room for innovation and adjustment. For Barber, the reception of Christianity and Islam in Yorubaland was facilitated by this openness. The presence of other religions enlarged the devotee's choices instead of inspiring skepticism, as a religion's claims to a complete and all-inclusive account of the world might have done. Barber's account of elastic paganism can be usefully applied to *Arrow of God*,[10] which illustrates not the collapse of one religion and the triumph of another but the flexibility of Igbo beliefs. Gods are abandoned and in effect cease to exist when they do not satisfy their devotees; other, more accommodating gods are adopted if they can better answer the needs of worshipers.

I do not mean to suggest that Igbo religion is a consistent whole resilient enough to triumph over all vicissitudes. The tragic narrative told by the people of Umuaro makes possible the redrawing of symbolic boundaries and distinctions necessary for the community's survival. Yet it is inaccurate to speak of the survival of the community, because that phrase implies an internally consistent identity. At the end of the novel, worship is addressed no longer to a local patron deity but to the Christian God, and the identity of the people of Umuaro is subtly dissolving within a more general Igbo identity. In Njaka's terms, the *ikwu* 'field of which one is a member' is expanding to include Igboland and perhaps even all of Africa, while the *ibe* 'world of the other' is shifting from Okperi to the British and the white man more generally (54). Cultural agents change who they are as they change what they do. *Arrow of God* describes how the people of Umuaro become Igbo and African. Umuaro is only a fictional place, but Igboland and Africa define identities that Achebe shares with many readers.[11]

Although *Arrow of God* celebrates a paganism sufficiently elastic to contain Christianity, Achebe's novel is not itself pagan, any more than Barber's or Apter's anthropological analyses are.[12] Only once is Ulu shown speaking to his priest, and on that occasion Ulu's laughter suggests that the god is the projection of a madman: "I say who told you that this was your own fight to arrange the way it suits you? You want to save your friends who brought you palm wine he-he-he-he-he!" (191). And in the second edition of the novel Achebe adds the comment that "[o]nly the insane could sometimes approach the menace and mockery in the laughter of deities." (191). Achebe's world is made by humans, not by gods or by transcendental forces

V

Ezeulu's tragedy is the narrative configuration that the people of Umuaro give to colonization. The configuration that Achebe gives is more radically self-reflexive: colonization is a tragedy *because* the colonized write it as a tragedy, complete with cathartic release, and the capacity of the colonized to fit their experience into a narrative indicates the community's resilience. Writing for the citizens of the newly independent Nigeria, Achebe in turn constructs a narrative that explains their low status in the world order but that also offers possibilities for collective self-definition and action. *Arrow of God* presents self-fulfilling evidence that Nigerians are capable of generating a meaningful narrative. Achebe's narrative is not a tragedy but a realist novel about the telling of a tragedy, a novel in which Africans are not the victims but the makers of their own history. They do not always make what they intend, of course—"Our eye sees something; we take a stone and aim at it. But the stone rarely succeeds like the eye in hitting the mark" (171)—but then neither do the British.

Although Achebe makes changes in the second edition of *Arrow of God* that implicitly side with reformers rather than purists, in the introduction to that edition he declares himself ready to "salute those who stand fast, the spiritual descendants of that magnificent man, Ezeulu." Achebe admires Ezeulu's steadfastness even though *Arrow of God* shows that the priest himself has drawn the line at which he stands fast. Achebe explores how people use appeals to tradition or to change to invent themselves.

Authenticity and creolization are accounts of culture that do what Walter Benn Michaels calls "cultural work" (682). Michaels argues that attributing a culture to someone who does not practice it implicitly ascribes culture to·genes, blood, or the collective unconscious and commits a racist fallacy. My point is related but different: neither authenticity nor creolization has ontological validity, but both are valid as metaphors that permit collective self-fashioning.

In rejecting the notion of pure, uncontested cultures, I may appear to side with advocates of creolization against supporters of authenticity. Objections to authenticity's ontological status do not, however, negate its force as an enabling metaphor. One may not be able to return to the world of one's ancestors, but one can claim to be doing so, with political effect. Tradition has an ontological existence, not in the past but in the present, where it affects people's self-images and their behavior. Uzo Esonwanne writes that "[a}s with the history of any other peoples, the history of Africa's 'past' derives its ideological and cultural valence from the current struggles of its peoples" (124); this assertion has always been true.

Appeals to authenticity are neither regressive nor progressive in themselves. Ezeulu's "tradition" serves his own will to power, in opposition to that of his rival Nwaka, but can also advance the purposes of those in Umuaro who are more democratic. In the service of, say Mobutu in Zaire, authenticity is mere obfuscation in the service of tyranny. But Ng g 's call for a return to the language that he learned at his mother's knee, made in the name of decolonizing the mind, serves a Marxist-inspired project of social change

by directly addressing the classes who could not read his novels if they were written in English.

Like authenticity, hybridization is a metaphor that does not define a particular political program. Hybridization is most often invoked by advocates of pluralism and tolerance, but it can also underwrite imperialism. "The intersection of races and the blending of opposed civilizations are the most powerful auxiliaries of liberty," writes Jules Michelet, a nationalist and believer in France's imperial mission (Todorov 241). Michelet claims that the blending of races makes France manifestly superior to other nations, which are less exposed to outside influences, purer, and therefore weaker. Creolization, like authenticity, is a rallying standard in intracommunal debate. What is really at stake in such debates is not authenticity or creolization but democracy as opposed to totalitarianism (Amselle 11).

My own attempt to subsume authenticity and hybridization within a single discussion is, of course, part of a current North American debate that has uncertain meaning for African debates. That I have eschewed the division usually drawn between imperialist capitalist modernity and precapitalist tradition makes possible a vision of the equality of cultural identities but precludes explanation of why some collectivities achieve power over others. A neo-Marxist narrative of late capitalist modernity's expansion and its integration of the globe in an unjust order might offer a response. What my own narrative offers is a reminder that political and economic imperialism is not necessarily synonymous with the overtaking of one national *culture* by another. Authenticity and creolization are best regarded as valuable rhetorical tools that can be made to serve liberation. It may also be liberating to remember that these constructions are effectively rhetorical.

NOTES

1. It will be obvious to readers that this essay is indebted to James Clifford's *The Predicament of Culture* and to the essays collected by Clifford and George Marcus in *Writing Culture*.

2. In postcolonial literary circles, the epitome of the false self is often V. S. Naipaul. Françoise Lionnet argues that there is a binary opposition between assimilation and authenticity, between sameness and difference, that creolization or "transculturation" is able to transcend. I am sympathetic to her values, but I would point out the binary opposition between authenticity and creolization. Creolization cannot be understood without a notion of cultural purity to which it stands opposed. Assimilation, however, is a position that is usually attributed to others and rarely espoused. Writers who are prepared to accept the label "assimilationist," such as Naipaul and Nirad Chaudhuri,

are lone pessimists who signal that they have left behind a community.

3. Gikandi acknowledges that the novel illustrates "Achebe's concern with contradictions and cosmic dualities," a concern informed by the Igbo process of artistic production known as *mbari*, but he believes that the novel is essentially predicated on "the loss of narrative and linguistic authority" (52).

4. Goodcountry is from the Niger Delta (46), an area that suffered colonization decades earlier than Igboland but that Achebe's readers in 1964 would have thought of as close to Igboland and falling within the same national and even state divisions.

5. Amselle would go so far as to say that nothing is less traditional than so-called primitive societies (57); tradition is the result of contact with the literate European ethnographer.

6. "It is not the existence of different cultures that produces comparative ethnology, but comparative ethnology that constitutes cultures as different" (Amselle 51).

7. For Winterbottom to see the Igbo as truth tellers would require that the truth be singular and stable and that colonizer and colonized agree on that truth. Of course Winterbottom believes that the colonized are liars before they open their mouths.

8. I do not deny the possibility of cultural imperialism (slavery, dispossession, and genocide have deprived people of the ability to generate meaningful narratives). I am suggesting that political imperialism is not always cultural imperialism.

9. Apter points to a critical practice at the heart of ritual that "sanctions self-conscious awareness of the role of human agency in rewriting official illusions of legitimacy, of the practical role which ritual fulfils in the unmaking and remaking of hegemony" ("*Que Faire?*" 100).

10. If an analogy can be drawn between Barber's description of Yoruba beliefs and Achebe's depiction of the worship of Ulu in Umuaro, it is not because the Yoruba and the Igbo are Africans and therefore the same. Barber herself contrasts the Yoruba beliefs she describes with the beliefs of the Tallensi of northern Ghana. I apply Barber's analysis because it is suggestively parallel to the depiction of Umuaro in ways that Apter's analysis of Yoruba religion, for instance, is not.

11. The notion that ethnic identity in Africa is an invention can be found in the essays collected by Jean-Loup Amselle and Elikia M'bokolo. For the argument that Africa and the Negro race are inventions, see V. Y. Mudimbe, as well as Kwame Anthony Appiah.

12. In *Black Critics and Kings* Apter does suggest what a pagan critical philosophy would look like.

Works Cited

Achebe, Chinua. *Arrow of God*. 1964. London: Heinemann, 1986.

Amselle, Jean-Loup. *Logiques métisses: Anthropologie de L'identité en Afrique et ailleurs*. Paris: Payot, 1990.

Amselle, Jean-Loup, and Elikia M'bokolo, eds. *Au coer de l'ethnie: Ethnies, tribalisme et état en Afrique*. Paris: Découverte, 1985.

Appiah, Kwame Anthony. *In My Father's House: Africa in the Philosophy of Culture*. New York: Oxford UP, 1992.

Apter, Andrew. *Black Critics and Kings: The Hermeneutics of Power in Yoruba Society*. Chicago: University of Chicago, 1992.

———. "*Que Faire*? Reconsidering the Inventions of Africa." *Critical Inquiry* 19 (1992): 87-104.

Barber, Karin. "How Man makes God in West Africa; Yoruba Attitudes towards the *Orisa*." *Africa* 51 (1981): 724-45.

Clifford, James. *The Predicament of Culture*. Cambridge: Harvard UP, 1988.

Clifford, James, and George E. Marcus, eds. *Writing Culture*. Berkeley: U of California P, 1986.

Cohen, Anthony P. "Culture as Identity: An Anthropologist's View." *New Literary History* 24 (1993): 195-209.

Curtin, Philip D. *The Image of Africa British Ideas and Action, 1780-1850*. Madison: U of Wisconsin P, 1964.

Esonwanne, Uzo. "The Madness of Africa(ns); or, Anthropology's Reason." *Cultural Critique* 17 (1990-91): 107-26.

Gikandi, Simon. *Reading Chinua Achebe*. Portsmouth: Heinemann, 1991.

Greenblatt, Stephen. *Renaissance Self-Fashioning*. Chicago: U of Chicago P, 1980.

Hountondji, Paulin. *Sur la "philosophie africaine."* Paris: Maspero, 1977.

Laitin, David D. *Hegemony and Culture: Politics and Religious Change among the Yoruba.* Chicago: U of Chicago P, 1986.

Lionnet, Françoise. "*Logiques métisses*: Cultural Appropriations and Postcolonial Representations." *College Literature* 19 (1993): 100-20.

Michaels, Walter Benn. "Race into Culture: A Critical Genealogy of Cultural Identity." *Critical Inquiry* 18 (1992): 655-85.

Mudimbe, V.Y. *The Invention of Africa.* Bloomington: Indiana UP, 1988.

Ng g wa Thiong'o. *Decolonising the Mind: The Politics of Language in African Literature.* Portsmouth: Heinemann, 1986.

Njaka, Mazi Elechukwu Nnadibuagha. *Igbo Political Culture.* Evanston: Northwestern UP, 1974.

Todorov, Tzvetan. *Nous et les autres.* Paris: Seuil, 1989.

Tomlinson, John. *Cultural Imperialism: A Critical Introduction.* Baltimore: Johns Hopkins UP, 1991.

Wuthnow, Robert. *Meaning and Moral Order.* Berkeley: U of California P, 1987.

Young, Crawford. "Patterns of Social Conflict: State, Class, and Ethnicity." *Daedalus* 3.2 (1982): 71-98.

Stephen Criswell (essay date 1995)

SOURCE: "Okonkwo As Yeatsian Hero: The Influence of W. B. Yeats on Chinua Achebe's *Things Fall Apart,*" in *The Literary Criterion*, Vol. XXX, No. 4, pp. 1-14.

[*In the following essay, Criswell traces thematic parallels between* Things Fall Apart *and Yeats's play* On Baile's Strand, *focusing on conceptual similarities that characterize the tragic hero in each work.*]

The title of Chinua Achebe's first novel, *Things Fall Apart,* is taken from W. B. Yeats's poem, "The Second Coming." Many critics, such as Judith Gleason and A. G. Stock, have commented on the influence of Yeats's view of history and time (his notion of the cyclical nature of existence symbolized by his "gyres," or intertwining cones, illustrated in

such poems as "The Double Vision of Michael Robartes," "The Phases of the Moon," and "The Second Coming") on Achebe's novel. However, Chinua Achebe may have found in the writings of W. B. Yeats more than merely a shared view of the rise and fall of civilizations (as A. G. Stock suggests); it is possible that Achebe was influenced by the way Yeats utilized Irish folklore to dramatize his interpretation of the historical process. Yeats found the legends of the Irish hero, Cuchulainn, to be an especially useful vehicle for his cosmological paradigm and his notion of the tragic hero's place within that cosmology. One such legend, "The Death of Aife's One Son," seems to have served as the inspiration for certain events in *Things Fall Apart.* Several parallels between the Irish legend and Achebe's novel suggest that the Nigerian novelist was inspired by the "The Death of Aife's One Son" and, more specifically, by Yeats's version of the legend, and in comparing Yeats's play as well as certain poems with Achebe's novel, it appears that in creating Okonkwo, his novel's hero, Achebe has constructed an Igbo version of the Yeatsian tragic hero.

"The Death of Aife's One Son," from the Ulster cycle of Irish myths, legends, and tales, began as an orally-transmitted legend and was eventually recorded in the Yellow Book of Lecan (a fourteenth-century monastic manuscript) as one of the pre-tales, or *remscela,* of the Irish Epic, the *Tain Bo Cuailnge* (Kinsella x). The legend recounts an episode in the life of the *Tain's* hero, Cuchulainn, who according to Ulster legends was trained in arms in by Scathach, the warrior queen of Alba (Scotland). While under Scathach's tutelage, Cuchulainn aids his teacher in defeating a rival warrior queen, Aife, whom Cuchulainn defeats in single combat. In exchange for her life, Aife agrees to bear Cuchulainn's child. Cuchulainn returns to Ulster before the child is born, but before departing, he tells Aife to name the child Connla (or Conloach). He gives her a gold ring and tells her that when the boy's finger has grown to fit the ring, she must send him to Ulster.

Years pass, and Aife receives word that Cuchulainn has married someone else. Jealous, Aife vows to get revenge through her and Cuchulainn's son. She sends Connla, who by now has grown into a young man and, like his father, possesses extraordinary strength and ability, to Ulster. Before Connla leaves, Aife gives him three commands:

> The first never to give way to any living person, but to die sooner than be made turn back; the second, not to refuse a challenge from the greatest champion alive, but to fight him at all risks, even if he [is] sure to lose his life; the third, not to tell anyone his name on any account, though he might be threatened with death for hiding it. (Gregory 658)

When Connla arrives on Ulster's shore, the high-king,

Conchubar, sends one warrior after another to intercept the boy and get his name. When he refuses to reveal his name, the boy is challenged to single combat by the warriors, each of whom Connla easily defeats. Finally, Cuchulainn, seeing that the young man should prove to be a worthy opponent, challenges Connla. The two warriors fight equally in strength and skill, but Cuchulainn eventually uses his secret weapon, the *gae bolga,* the terrible javelin that only Cuchulainn can use. The *gae bolga's* blow is fatal, but before the young man dies, he reveals his name and shows his father the gold ring that Cuchulainn had given to Aife. Cuchulainn becomes maddened with rage and grief. Fearing that the crazed hero will turn on his fellow warriors, King Conchubar orders his druids to bewitch Cuchulainn into taking his rage out on the sea. The druids' spell takes hold of Cuchulainn, and he fights the waves for three days and nights until he is eventually exhausted.

W. B. Yeats retells this legend in his play, *On Baile's Strand* (1903), making several changes to the story in order to use the legend to dramatize his conception of history. In *A Vision,* which Yeats published in 1925, the poet outlines his complicated and at times mystical system of history. According to his system, history moves in cycles, or gyres, from objectivity (the "primary gyre") to subjectivity (the "antithetical gyre") and from subjectivity back to objectivity. The period of the subjective age emphasizes the individual, the heroic, passion, worldly glory, and human achievement; the objective age is marked by service to others, passivity, civil concerns, conformity, and uniformity. When the objective age reaches its zenith and soon begins its decline, the subjective age begins its ascension, and vice-versa. As Yeats explains in *A Vision*:

> Each age unwinds the thread another age has wound, and it amuses one to remember that before Phidias, and his westward-moving art, Persia fell, and that when full moon came round again, amid east-ward moving thought, and brought Byzantine glory, Rome fell; and that at the outset of our westward-moving Renaissance Byzantium fell; all things dying each other's life, living each other's death. (271)

According to Yeats, as one civilization or age begins to fall (for example, the Greco-Roman period), an age or civilization with opposing or antithetical concerns (in this case, Christianity) begins to grow.

In *On Baile's Strand* Yeats reworks the legend of "The Death of Aife's One Son" to illustrate the decline of one age—the subjective age, represented by the self-determined, physically powerful Cuchulainn—and the rise of another—the objective age, represented by the civic-minded leader of the society, King Conchubar. While the plot of Yeats's play superficially follows the ancient Irish

legend, Yeats makes specific deliberate alterations to the story. In his version, the story opens with Conchubar's having called Cuchulainn to a meeting of the kings of Ireland. Conchubar convinces Cuchulainn to swear obedience to him and his state. In the growing objective age, the subjective hero is feared and distrusted and must be brought under civil control. Conchubar explains to Cuchulainn:

> Look at the door and what men gather there—
> Old counselors that steer the land with me,
> And younger kings, the dancers and harp-players
> That follow in your tumults, and all of these
> Are held there by one anxiety.
> Will you be bound into obedience
> And so make this land safe for them and theirs? (29)

Cuchulainn yields to Conchubar's command, reflecting on the days when men "praised whatever life could make the pulse run quickly," and realizing "that's all over" (32). Cuchulainn understands that the gyre of the heroic age is winding down.

The first order that Conchubar gives Cuchulainn is to defeat the young man who has just arrived on Ulster's shore. As in the legend, Yeats's Cuchulainn does not know that the boy is his son, but he admires his strength and prowess. At first the hero refuses Conchubar's command, but his warrior's pride soon gets the better of him. He fights and kills the boy. When he soon discovers that he has killed his own son, he flies into a rage. But in Yeats's version it is unclear if Cuchulainn is tricked into attacking the waves, or if he chooses to do so, having no one else upon whom to exact his revenge. The play ends with the image of Cuchulainn foolishly but tragically, even heroically, fighting the sea, the "invulnerable tide" (*Poems* 36) which serves as a symbol of the endless process of change. It is this process, or cycle, that is the source of Cuchulainn's pain. Cuchulainn, in the ultimate heroic act, takes up arms against the eternal process that potentially makes all heroism meaningless. He cannot stop the rise of the objective age, but he can remain true to his heroic nature and stand against the process of change, though it means his defeat.

Yeats takes this heroic, but often futile, stand against the inevitable as his theme in a number of his poems and plays. Some of his most memorable, and anthologized, poems honour doomed but determined heroes. Probably Yeats's most famous doomed hero, Major Robert Gregory, the airman of "An Irish Airman Foresees His Death," knows his fate; he knows that his death will not change the lives and futures of his countrymen:

> My country is Kiltartan Cross,
> My countrymen Kiltartan's poor,
> No likely end could bring them loss

Or leave them happier than before.

(Poems 135)

However, Gregory confronts death freely for one moment of self-determination:

> A lonely impulse of delight
> Drove me to this tumult in the clouds;
> I balanced all, brought all to mind,
> The years to come seemed waste of breath,
> A waste of breath the years behind
> In balance with this life, this death. (135)

As Jahan Ramazani has pointed out in *Yeats and the Poetry of Death,* "The airman affirms this intense life of death as his chosen fate and freedom" (85). Otto Bohlmann has noted that Yeats's Cuchulainn is "of the same breed as Robert Gregory" (145), as are the tragic heroes of the Easter Rising commemorated in Yeats's "Easter 1916." In an age and place "where motley is worn" and people spend their days at "counter or desk" (85), Yeats celebrates the doomed leaders of the seemingly futile Easter Rebellion, who displayed the heroism of an earlier age:

> And what if excess of love
> Bewildered them till they died?
> I write it out in verse—
> MacDonagh and MacBride
> And Connolly and Pearse
> Now and in time to be,
> Wherever green is worn,
> Are changed, changed utterly:
> A terrible beauty is born. (180)

The heroic act transcends and transfigures history. Standing courageously with self-determination even in the face of death, the Yeatsian hero rises above the endless gyres of existence that inevitably seem to make all heroism meaningless. In *On Baile's Strand* Yeats's Cuchulainn, in Maeve Good's words, "battle[s] against a world hostile to the heroic temperament" (13), but like the leaders of the Easter Rebellion, he behaves heroically in an unheroic age and stands against the inevitable process that has created this age.

It is this tragic-heroic stand against change, along with the motif of infanticide, that most clearly links Yeats's play with Achebe's *Things Fall Apart.* Obviously, Achebe was inspired to some degree by Yeats, taking the title of his novel from Yeats's "The Second Coming" A. G. Stock, in her article "Yeats and Achebe," examines the relationship between *Things Fall Apart* and the poem that provided the novel's title. She notes specifically the similarities between Yeats's and Achebe's concept of history:

> It is startling to find the Yeatsian pattern traced most closely where Yeats himself was least likely to look for it, in an imaginary village of the lower Niger. . . . [Yeats] looks at Europe with its two-thousands-year-old tradition of Christian civilization, which itself once made chaos of the values that proceeded it and is now collapsing before the onset of something new, something more frightening because it is nameless, being all that our inherited civilization has incapacitated us from understanding. Achebe is . . . primarily interested in Europe; from the standpoint of Umuofia the western world is itself the fabulous formless darkness. But his instrument of interpretation is the same; his Umuofia is a civilization in miniature, and the chaos finds its way in through slight flaws in its structure, murmurs that might have remained inaudible if they had not found an echo in the darkness. (106)

While she makes the important observation that Christianity and, more significantly, the British raj, are to Okonkwo's village "mere anarchy let loose on the Umuofian world" (110) and she shows how this idea is played out in the novel, Stock limits Yeats's influence on Achebe's novel to a shared view of history and, of course, to the novel's title. Judith Gleason in her study of African novels, *This Africa,* also notes the influence of Yeats's conception of the historical process on Achebe's first novel: "For *Things Fall Apart* comes from the world of Yeats' cataclysmic vision, and how the Irish Poet would have appreciated the wild Old Nigerian" (132). While most critics acknowledge, at least to some degree, the influence of Yeats's concept of history on *Things Fall Apart,* few if any see Yeats as having any further influence. However, if it is clear that in writing his first novel, Achebe had in mind Yeats's poem and the view of history which it dramatizes, then it is reasonable to assume that Achebe was familiar with and possibly inspired by Yeats's other works, particularly *On Baile's Strand.* Both works contain the key plot elements of the hero murdering his own son (or in the case of Okonkwo his foster-son), which in thematic terms becomes, for both works, the destruction of the future of the protagonists' way of life and the hero's final futile stand against inevitable change. While these motifs are by no means limited to these two stories, the pairings of the motifs and the theme which they both develop seem unique to these two works.

The first motif, the murder of the hero's son at the hands of the hero himself, plays itself out in *Things Fall Apart* somewhat differently than in Yeats's play; however, the contexts and results of the action are similar. Okonkwo does not kill his own son, Nwoye, but rather Ikemefuna, the hostage-child who becomes part of Okonkwo's family and, for all practical purposes, his foster-son. Achebe describes Ikemefuna's feelings for Okonkwo, stating "he could hardly imagine that Okonkwo was not his real father" (58). Like Cuchulainn with his son, Okonkwo admires Ikemefuna's qualities ("manly" qualities that Okonkwo himself possesses and that he fears are lacking in his own son, Nwoye) and regrets having to kill him. Unfortunately the village has decided that the boy must die, and fearing that the community might think him weak, Okonkwo refuses not to participate in Ikemefuna's execution. Okonkwo, like Cuchulainn, is so driven by his pride that he willingly kills his own foster-son, and in the process he destroys the possibility of continuing his way of life. Ikemefuna, like Connla, embodies, if only in rudimentary form, many of his father's ideals of manhood, ideals antithetical to those of the fast-approaching new order. Though killing Ikemefuna does not drive him mad, Okonkwo's participation in this act seems to initiate his eventual downfall, culminating in his final actions—the killing of the messenger and his subsequent suicide—actions which could be perceived as insane, but which nevertheless have tragic-heroic quality to them.

These final actions of the novel's protagonist closely parallel, thematically, the actions of Cuchulainn at the conclusion of *On Baile's Strand*. Okonkwo is faced with the collapse of his whole way of life. The arrival of the Christian missionaries signals the beginning of a new way of life contrary to Umuofia's old order. The process of change that Okonkwo faces is "incomprehensible, uncomprehending, invincible" (Stock 109), and completely unsympathetic toward Okonkwo's old ways. The District Commissioner best represents not only the power of the British Empire, but also this indifference of the process of change; he tells Okonkwo and others in his community:

> We shall not do you any harm . . . if only you agree to cooperate with us. We have brought a peaceful administration to you and your people so that you may be happy . . . in the dominion of our queen, the most powerful ruler in the world. (178)

Okonkwo must choose between accepting this powerful new order or standing firmly, but perhaps futilely, against it. He chooses to fight though he realizes that the days of Umuofia's heroes are over. Like Cuchulainn, Okonkwo recalls the "days when men were men," but realizes "worthy men are no more" (184). He takes the only opportunity for action open to him and kills one of the "white man's" messengers. His actions seem unreasonable to the other villagers: "He heard voices asking: 'Why did he do it?'" The only response Okonkwo gives to their questions is to hang himself. However, Okonkwo's friend, Obierika, provides the answer, telling the British officials, "That man was one of the greatest men in Umuofia. You drove him to kill himself" (191). The source of Okonkwo's suffering and his seemingly incomprehensible actions lies in the coming of the British to Umuofia, or more accurately to the process of change their arrival represents. Like Yeats's Cuchulainn, Achebe's Okonkwo recognizes the inevitable end of his old

way of life, but he chooses to act against the process of change and commit some act of self-determination, even if his only choice is suicide. Charles E. Nnolim has pointed out that "in committing suicide Okonkwo displays another Igbo characteristic—a characteristic that slave traders discovered to their chagrin—that of resorting to suicide as a way out of difficulties in which every other alternative leads to personal humiliation and defeat" (60). While suicide is an offence against the Earth-goddess, it does not seem to have for the Igbo the same sense of weakness or shame often associated with it in the West (In fact, Nnolim, in arguing that *Things Fall Apart* is an Igbo epic, cites Okonkwo's suicide as one of the characteristics that makes him an epic hero.), and in the novel Okonkwo's suicide has an air of martyrdom, like Yeats's description of the Rebellion leaders' suicidal stand against the British, or his description in "Parnell's Funeral" of the deaths of Irish nationalists Robert Emmet, Lord Edward Fitzgerald, and Wolfe Tone (Emmet was executed by the British, Fitzgerald wounded and eventually died, and Tone committed suicide while awaiting execution).

One further element connects Achebe's novel with Yeats's works: the effects of colonialism. Much of Yeats's work is, in tone and substance, often nationalistic and even at times propagandistic. Yeats's poetry and plays, like Achebe's works, are situated historically in a colonial and post-colonial context, and as Edward Said has noted, "It is helpful to remember that 'the Anglo-Irish conflict' with which Yeats's poetic œuvre is saturated was a 'model of twentieth-century wars of liberation'" (235). While A. G. Stock criticizes Yeats for his "nostalgia for the lost Hellenic world" (111), Said argues that Yeats's historic concerns were for his country's present situation, its struggle against colonial oppression:

> His greatest decolonizing works concern the birth of violence, or the violent birth of change . . . Yeats situates himself at that juncture where the violence of change is unarguable but where the results of the violence beseech necessary, if not always sufficient, reason. His greatest theme . . . is how to reconcile the inevitable violence of the colonial conflict with the everyday politics of an ongoing national struggle." (235)

Said points out that one of the ways that Yeats treats this theme is by taking the "inevitable violence" and the "disorder" of the colonial conflict "back to the colonial intervention in the first place—which is what Chinua Achebe did in 1959 in his great novel *Things Fall Apart*" (235). One of the purposes of both writers' works is to reconnect their countrymen and women with their pre-colonial past and restore their dignity and identity, for as Frantz Fanon has noted:

Colonialism is not simply content to impose its rule upon the present and the future of a dominated country. Colonialism is not satisfied merely with holding a people in its grip and emptying the native's brain of all form and content. By a kind of perverted logic, it turns to the past of the people, and distorts, disfigures and destroys it. (210)

Yeats attempted to reconnect himself and his fellow Irish to their past and their culture, in part, through his use of Irish folklore and mythology, especially the tales of Cuchulainn, and his celebration of those Irish men and women who stood against British rule. Achebe, in much the same way, has dealt with this issue; he has said:

> African people did not hear of culture for the first time from Europeans; . . . their societies were not mindless but frequently had a philosophy of great depth and value and beauty, . . . they had poetry, and above all, they had dignity. It is this dignity that many African people all but lost during the colonial period and it is this that they must regain. The worst thing that can happen to any people is the loss of their dignity and self-respect. The writer's duty is to help them regain it by showing them in human terms what happened to them, what they lost. (**"The Role of the Writer"** 8)

In *Things Fall Apart,* Achebe succeeds in showing "what happened," and in creating Okonkwo, Achebe gives his Nigerian readers a pre-colonial hero who is the epitome of dignity and self-respect, and as Judith Gleason notes, "Okonkwo alone defies the disintegrative effects of colonial occupation" (81). Achebe has constructed a figure like Yeats's Cuchulainn, a warrior from "the heroic past" (Nnolim 56), who, though defeated in the end, tragically and heroically confirms "the fundamental worth of the personality of the nation" (55).

While A. G. Stock seems to suggest that Yeats and Achebe are too different in "their minds, their perspectives, and their fields of vision" for Yeats to have had a direct effect on Achebe's novel (She makes a point of stating that *Things Fall Apart* does not "smell of discipleship" [106]), the parallels between Achebe's novel and Yeats's *On Baile's Strand* suggest that *Things Fall Apart* owes something to Yeats's play and its ancient Irish source, and the thematic similarities—from their shared concepts of history to their similar portrayals of the tragic hero to their concern with the effects of colonialism—between Achebe's novel and much of Yeats's work suggest that Achebe found in Yeats's poetry more than just the title of his first book. More importantly, however, examined together Achebe's novel and Yeats's poetry and plays illuminate each other, bringing out in both the essential idea of the tragic-heroic stand against the inevitable eternal processes of history.

Clayton G. Mackenzie (essay date Summer 1996)

SOURCE: "The Metamorphosis of Piety in Chinua Achebe's *Things Fall Apart,*" in *Research in African Literatures*, Vol. 27, No. 2, Summer, 1996, pp. 128-38.

[*In the following essay, Mackenzie details the transformation of indigenous religious beliefs and practices in* Things Fall Apart, *comparing it to the relatively static portrayal of religion in* Arrow of God.]

Matters of religion are thematically central to *Things Fall Apart* and *Arrow of God.* Both novels reflect revisions in the nature of traditional worship, and both attest to the demise of traditional mores in the face of an aggressive and alien proselytizing religion. The disparities between the two novels are equally significant. Possibly for reasons of historical setting, *Things Fall Apart* differs from *Arrow of God* in its presentation of the status of indigenous beliefs and in its precise delineation of the evolutionary process of those beliefs—a process not articulated in any detail in the later novel. The shifts of belief in *Things Fall Apart* are marked by the pragmatic transference of old pieties for new, a metamorphosis demanded by the realities of a revised socio-economic hierarchy.

The first mention of the religious beliefs of Umuofia in *Things Fall Apart* is a reference to the Oracle of the Hills and the Caves. It is a decisive allusion, correlating the will of the Oracle with the life and direction of the clan, and leaving no doubt as to the significance of the divine agency and of the necessity of obedience to it:

> . . . in fairness to Umuofia it should be recorded that it never went to war unless its case was clear and just and was accepted as such by its Oracle—the Oracle of the Hills and the Caves. And there were indeed occasions when the Oracle had forbidden Umuofia to wage a war. If the clan had disobeyed the Oracle they would surely have been beaten, because their dreaded *agadi-nwayi* would never fight what the Ibo call *a fight of blame.* (9)

That the Oracle is perceived as supreme there can be no doubt. The sacrifice of the boy Ikemefuna is undertaken expressly because the "Oracle of the Hills and the Caves has pronounced it" (40). Though the execution may run counter to clan feelings of attachment to the youngster, a profound sense of individual and collective religious belief lends to the sacrifice an inexorable determination. It is a mysterious decision but the Umuofia, for the maintenance of the universal well-being, must comply with it. Not even the most powerful paternal feelings of Okonkwo can stand in the way of the expression of religious duty and faith.

Opposition of a sort comes only from Obierika who asserts a defiant passivity in response to Okonkwo's charge that he appeared to be questioning the authority of the Oracle: " . . . [I]f the Oracle said that my son should be killed I would neither dispute it nor be the one to do it" (47). Lekan Oyeleye suggests this indicates that "Obierika's loyalty to the community gods is not as over-zealous and thoughtless as Okonkwo's brand of loyalty" (22). But the issue of Obierika's exceptionalism is stronger than this. Achebe's narrative characterizes Obierika's inaction as being not only at variance with Okonkwo's view of things but with the received canon of traditional deific lore. Obierika claims that "the Oracle did not ask me to carry out its decision" (46), but this is a spurious absolution since, as a member of the clan, he is as responsible as the next clansperson for the execution of the Oracle's instructions.

His impiety is further censured by the source of the rebuke, since even the iron-willed Okonkwo, who has by this time himself transgressed against the earth goddess Ani in the beating of his wife, has duly and humbly atoned for his crime.[1] Had Obierika's unapologetic misgivings found any sympathetic ear one might have thought it would have been that of his friend—but not so. True, part of Okonkwo's interrogative tone stems from his own inner turmoil about the death of Ikemefuna but, on a more significant level, as a penitent transgressor he speaks for the devotional mores of the clan in asserting the preeminence of collective obedience and action.

Okonkwo has been mentioned and, since he tends to dominate most critical deliberations on *Things Fall Apart,* it is worth offering an explanation of his diminished role here. Undoubtedly, Okonkwo's relation to the deific system is important, but it may not be as pivotal as some critics have contended. Bonnie Barthold, for example, believes that the "narrative structure of *Things Fall Apart* is defined by Okonkwo's relationship with the earth goddess, Ani, and the ever-increasing seriousness of the offenses he commits against her" (56).[2] The Ani-Okonkwo colloquy is intriguing but in fact most of the novel's allusions to deities come from persons other than Okonkwo and, as shall be argued, Achebe goes to some lengths to construct a religious pantheon that ranges beyond any single god or goddess. It is significant, too, that the initial religious allusions of the novel locate themselves firmly in the territory of an Oracle-clan discourse, and that, subsequently, the spiritual experiences of individuals are repeatedly referenced to that all-pervading dialogue.

Elsewhere in the novel, the strength of other oracles is attested. A group of fugitives who have found sanctuary in Umuofia recount the story of the arrival of the first white man in their village. The elders of the village consulted their Oracle. It foretold the demise of the clan and the ar- rival of more strangers: "It said that other white men were on their way. They were locusts, it said, and that first man was their harbinger sent to explore the terrain. And so they killed him" (97-98). All true, of course, and all the more reason for the clan to believe in the efficacy of oracular worship and counsel. The role of the Oracle in Umuofia at the outset of *Things Fall Apart* is unambiguous, unequivo- cal, certain.

In Achebe's other novels there is little reference to oracles. *Arrow of God,* the most religious of these, is steeped in traditional belief but focuses essentially on the Chief Priest, Ezeulu. He is given some oracular functions: for in- stance, it is for him to name the day of the Festival of Pumpkin Leaves (3)—but for the most part, there is articu- lated no elaborate ritual of oracular consultation. The world of *Arrow of God* has the feel of a monotheistic world, as its title suggests. Personal "chi" are mentioned, but Ulu stands firmly as the tutelary god; and Ezeulu is, essentially, the agent of Ulu rather than an intermediary priest who brings back divine messages from places of holy confer- ence.

This may seem a minor, even insignificant, distinction be- tween the two novels but it is important. After all, it is made clear in *Things Fall Apart* that Chielo, who at first domi- nates belief and worship in Umuofia, is the priestess of Agbala. Yet, the religious pantheon of *Things Fall Apart* is essentially polytheistic. Agbala is divine, but the novel explicitly styles him as only one of many divinities who are material to the life of the clan. Achebe, in fact, goes to some lengths to reveal a cosmology of deities in the novel. The notion of personal gods, or "chi," is established early (10); the narrator offers an account of the dispute be- tween the sky and earth (38); their presence and that of Amadiora, the divine thunderbolt, is forcefully reiterated (102-3); the gods and goddesses of the traditional system are a source of disparagement on the part of the Christian intruders (103); a group of converts derisively repudiates the clan's worship of more than one god (110); the clans- man Okika reminds the clan of their constellation of gods and goddesses: Idemili, Ogwugwu, Agbala, "and all the oth- ers" (143).

This is not necessarily to infer that the setting of *Things Fall Apart* is a more "traditional" setting or a more authen- tic religious setting than that of *Arrow of God.* But it does indicate differences in the indigenous theistic designs of the two works. These may be traced further. In *Arrow of God,* the powers of the Chief Priest of Ulu, Ezeulu, are con- siderably less than his equivalent in *Things Fall Apart*— the priestess of Agbala, Chielo. On the question of going to war, an option expressly raised in both novels, oracular authority of the priest in *Arrow of God* is notably less se- cure than it is in the earlier work. Here, for example, is how

Nwaka advocates war against the Okperi (a course of action opposed by Ezeulu):

> Nwaka began by telling the assembly that Umuaro must not allow itself to be led by the Chief Priest of Ulu. 'My father did not tell me that before Umuaro went to war it took leave from the priest of Ulu,' he said. 'The man who carries a deity is not a king. He is there to perform his god's ritual and to carry sacrifice to him. . . .' (27)

In *Things Fall Apart* we are told that there can be no war without validation from the Oracle of the Hills and the Caves. This, as Cook rightly maintains, "is not a rationalisation of weakness but takes its stand from a position of strength" (72). In *Arrow of God,* the oracular right of Ezeulu to forbid war is diminished by personal slanders as to his true earthly intentions. Obligations of divine belief have been weakened by the doubts and meanderings of mortal integrity. That Nwaka is at least partially successful in his argument is evidenced by the narrator's assertion that "Umuaro was divided in two" (27) on the matter.

The disparities between the two novels may be partially explained by the variant time frame that separates the events they describe. *Things Fall Apart* is located at points immediately before and after the arrival of the colonialists. The work is a third over before white people are even mentioned (51), and even there the allusion is merely a trivial speculation about whether they have toes or not. The novel is more than two-thirds over before a white person actually appears in Umuofia—an occasion that brings out every man and woman in the village (101). *Arrow of God,* on the other hand, presents not simply a single white missionary but an entire colonial community within the opening three chapters. Here, white people are not fantastical rumors but a familiar and integral part of the social landscape. Their leader, Captain T. K. Winterbottom, has already spent fifteen years in the African colonial service and is now firmly entrenched in his bungalow atop "Government Hill" (29).

Clan attitudes towards the indigenous religion in *Arrow of God* have been tempered, before the novel has even started, by contact with a dominant, monotheistic creed—and one which, though regarded with hostility by many clanspeople, has not yet seriously challenged the supposedly inviolate nature of indigenous belief and worship. By way of contrast, *Things Fall Apart* presents the process of attitudinal beliefs in relation to the indigenous religion prior to the socio-historical point at which *Arrow of God* begins. It appears that the arrival of Christianity not only secures native converts but also distorts, even among hostile clan non-converts, responses to and perceptions of indigenous beliefs. This goes beyond what some critics have called a

simple "hybridization of culture" (Ashcroft 129). Hybridization implies a compromise of differences, a common meeting ground. It cannot of itself encapsulate the spirit and movement of Achebe's representation. Homi Bhabha has written incisively of "the cultural and historical hybridity of the postcolonial world . . . as the paradigmatic *place of departure*" (21; emphasis added). It is that point of "departure" in which Achebe seems acutely interested. He seeks to move beyond espousal of a dualist model of cultural attrition and inter-adaptation, to a delineation of the metamorphosis of faith-oriented traditional pieties into economically-driven "new world" pieties.

Once the first white person has arrived in Umuofia (101), a repudiation of indigenous clan religious beliefs follows almost immediately:

> At this point an old man said he had a question [for the white man]. 'Which is this god of yours,' he asked, 'the goddess of the earth, the god of the sky, Amadiora of the thunderbolt, or what?'. . .
>
> 'All the gods you have named are not gods at all. They are gods of deceit who tell you to kill your fellows and destroy innocent children. There is only one true God and He has the earth, the sky, you and me and all of us.' (102-03)

After this, the notion of the traditional "Oracle," so strong hitherto, disappears without a trace from the novel. It is never again mentioned, or even intimated. There are many opportunities when it could have been. The killing of the royal python is one. Achebe makes clear to us that the python is "the emanation of the god of water" (12) and therefore sacred. Accidental killing of such an animal could be atoned through sacrifices and an expensive burial ceremony. But because no one has ever imagined that someone would knowingly kill a python, there is no statutory sanction for the crime. A decision about action, even if it is to be that no action should be taken, is required by the clan. What is interesting is the nature of the consultative process leading to that decision, and what does not happen rather than what does.

Chielo, the priestess, is not consulted. In fact, after she has called the clan's Christian converts "the excrement of the clan" (101), we hear nothing more from or about her in the novel. A priestess, the high priestess of Agbala, who has hitherto played a central role in the process of traditional life, takes no further part in the story or the events it describes. Certainly no one suggests that the Oracle of the Hills and the Caves should be consulted over the killing of the python. The clan's first instinct is to resolve the issue through human discussion:

. . . the rulers and elders of Mbanta assembled to decide on their action. Many of them spoke at great length
and in fury. The spirit of war was upon them. . . . (112)

We know from the first chapter of the novel that the clan
never went to war unless its cause was confirmed as just
by the Oracle (9). Why is it that consultation of the Oracle
is now not even mooted as an option? Indeed, divine conference with the Oracle, once so integral a part of clan life,
is suddenly abandoned to a new order of things—to a secular consultative context in which those wishing to go to war
are opposed by those who do not wish to go to war. The
reasons put forward by the latter are interesting:

'It is not our custom to fight for our gods,' said one of
them. 'Let us not presume to do so now. If a man kills
the sacred python in the secrecy of his hut, the matter
lies between him and the god. We did not see it. . . . '
(113)

In other words, the gods can look after themselves, why
should we do their fighting for them? A fascinating modi-
fication of devotion has occurred here. The cosmology of
deities, the very cornerstone of clan being, has suddenly
become distanced from the actuality of the existence of
Umuofia. At one time an integral weave in the fabric of clan
life, the indigenous religious order has abruptly become
remote and distant. It is now located in a schemata of parallel activities in which the divinities of an ordered universe
and the mortals of an ordered world function independently,
avoiding interference in each other's affairs and linked only
by a respectful cordiality of verbal oblation on the part of
the traditional worshipper.

The transformation is dramatic and arresting. But is the new
equation of relation plausible? In a sense and for a time,
yes. It looks as if it is working in the case of the slaying
of the royal python, an act which has apparently precipi-
tate consequences. Okoli, a prime suspect in the crime, falls
ill and dies: "His death showed that the gods were still able
to fight their own battles. The clan saw no reason then for
molesting the Christians" (114). Perhaps Obierika's thesis
of godly acceptance and human inertia, of belief and oblation without enactment, was a credible modus vivendi after all?

The assumption is false. The narrative rapidly and subtly
undermines any thoughts that divine sanction comes without a reciprocation of mortal action. Okoli had, in fact, denied the crime and Achebe is careful to present no evidence
against him. Not long after, we learn that Enoch was most
likely the real offender (131). What is significant is not
whether Okoli is guilty or innocent but that his death enables the clanspeople to seize upon a bogus exemplar of
divine self-help in order to reassert the new order of

things—to withdraw to the sanctuary of a piety that is passive, undemanding and removed, one which places no burden of sacrifice or atonement or forceful action upon the
celebrant.

To the chagrin of Okonkwo, the spokesperson of the old
faith now as he had been earlier in the face of Obierika's
heretical passivity, the most the clan can offer against the
Christians for the slaying of the emanation of the god of
water is ostracization. It is an action calculated not to
avenge the outrage against the god, but rather to distance
the village from the crime that has been committed: "We
should do something. But let us ostracise these men. We
would then not be held accountable for their abominations"
(113). And the death of Okoli, be it fortuitous or not, removes from a grateful clan even that necessity.

This sense of wily self-preservation which now characterizes the clan may be usefully compared, for example, to
their response earlier in the novel to Okonkwo's beating
of his youngest wife. During the beating, his first two wives
and a host of neighbors beg him to stop since this is a sacred week—and "it was unheard of to beat somebody during the sacred week" (21). Ezeani, the priest of the earth
goddess, Ani, visits Okonkwo to rebuke him, and refuses
to eat "in the house of a man who has no respect for our
gods and ancestors" (21). His is not a humanitarian concern but a religious one:

'The evil you have done can ruin the whole clan. The
earth goddess whom you have insulted may refuse
to give us her increase, and we shall all perish.' His
tone now changed from anger to command. 'You
will bring to the shrine of Ani tomorrow one she-
goat, one hen, a length of cloth and a hundred cow-
ries.' (22)

The whole episode is marked by certainties of transgression, of censure, of atonement. At the center of this process stands the priest, the intermediary between deity and
mortal. There is no questioning of his position, no doubt
about his authority, no possibility of his denial. Just as in
the killing of Ikemefuna, there is no ambiguity or blurring
of responsibilities and significances. The progress of the
clan, divinely guided and humanly effected through the collective obedience of the clanspeople, is distinct and em-
phatic.

How rapidly things change. The only decisive communal
action that occurs in the last third of the book is the burning of Mr Smith's church (130-35). This act, in revenge for
the unmasking of an egwugwu (131), an ancestral spirit and
therefore part of the indigenous religious cosmology, fills
Okonkwo with something approaching happiness (136). We
are told:

When the egwugwu went away the red-earth church which Mr Brown had built was a pile of earth and ashes. And for the moment the spirit of the clan was pacified. (135)

The destruction of the church is framed in terms of a human victory. Immediately after the burning of the building, we learn that Okonkwo's clan "which had turned false on him appeared to be making amends" (136); Okonkwo himself rejoices that it was "like the good old days again, when a warrior was a warrior" (136); and a few lines later we learn that "[e]very man in Umuofia went about armed with a gun or a machete" (136). There is a sense of the clan's human destiny having been reasserted as the prerogative of the clan itself. No one thanks the gods for the building's destruction; no one even credits them with a hand in it.

Yet, why should this be? It is, after all, the egwugwu who have burned down the church. The egwugwu are explicitly linked, through their patronizing deity, with the world of the godly immortals:

'All our gods are weeping. Idemili is weeping. Ogwugwu is weeping, Agbala is weeping, and all the others. . . .' (143)

Technically, it is not the living clanspeople at all who have been responsible for the action. Though the egwugwu masks are worn by living beings, according to traditional doctrine a transmigration of flesh and spirit occurs in which the human impersonators become unearthly spirits. If the victory over the church is a victory of the deific world (and we are told, after all, that "the spirit of the clan was pacified") how is it that the clan itself interprets the destruction of the church as a human act and never alludes to it in terms of divine intervention?

One explanation may be that they are no longer convinced of the divinity of the egwugwu, regarding the ritual of the nine spirits as no more than an historic re-enactment of people and actions from times past. Whether this is the case or not, the clanspeople appear not to covet further the idea that the path to community survival is traceable irrevocably to the cosmology of indigenous gods. If they did they would surely have left the issue of the egwugwu unmasking to the gods. Instead, they take up arms, apparently without any kind of oracular consultation, and steel themselves for the worst.

Adewale Maja-Pearce has speculated that one of Achebe's purposes in *Things Fall Apart* is to assert that "the spiritual values of pre-colonial Africa were in no way inferior to those of Europe, merely different" (10). That difference became a source of vulnerability. The religious codes and practices of Umuofia, unchallenged for centuries and perhaps millennia, had not evolved strategies for adaptation or confrontation. Like the sacred python, no one ever thought their sacredness would or could ever be challenged. The real power of missionary proselytization lay in the breaking down of community norms. The evil forest became no longer evil; the outcasts became no longer outcasts; the objects and rituals of traditional sacrament were destroyed.

Despite this, some Umuofians yet seek an accommodation, a hybridization perhaps, with the new theology. As he struggles to find a compromise between the religion he has always known and that which has suddenly arrived, the village elder Akunna debates the issue of the gods with the missionary Mr. Brown:

'You say that there is one supreme God who made heaven and earth,' said Akunna on one of Mr. Brown's visits. 'We also believe in Him and call Him Chukwu. He made all the world and the other gods.'

'There are no other gods,' said Mr. Brown. 'Chukwu is the only God and all others are false. . . .' (126-27)

Mr. Brown is no intercessor, no hybridizer. He spurns the idea that he is the earthly representative of his God, leading Akunna to exclaim, aghast, "but there must be a head in this world among men" (127). There is no compromise on offer. Mr. Brown rejects not only the central indigenous notion of a multi-deity system, but also the pivotal function of a high priest or priestess within a religious framework.

It may be possible to see in *Arrow of God* how both of these crucial tenets of traditional worship—polytheism and priestly intercession—have been corrupted in the revised perception of traditional lore. As noted earlier, not only is Ulu a rather "singularized" god, but his earthly messenger, Ezeulu, is emphatically disrobed of the trappings of infallible or absolute authority by the clanspeople. Further, the clan's attitude towards Ulu becomes less than coherent in the latter stages of the novel. When Ezeulu says he cannot enact a ritual that will enable new yams to be planted because Ulu has not sanctioned it, a clan delegation urges him to perform the rites anyway and to lay the blame on them (208). When he refuses, a new choice is mooted:

So the news spread that anyone who did not want to wait and see all his harvest ruined could take his offering to the god of the Christians who claimed to have power of protection from the anger of Ulu. (216)

The contest is styled as a battle of singularities, one god versus another. It is an essentially Biblical construct; a binary contest between feast and famine, between protection and threat, between the knight and the dragon—and, implicitly, between good and evil. Traditional theology has been undermined by Christian mythology, and subsumed into a Biblical schemata of loss and salvation. Gone are the ordinances of seasonal and festive celebration; gone the multiplicities of divine representation, of elemental hierarchies, of ancestral phantasm and conference. The shape and detail of traditional beliefs have evaporated. Ulu, disconnected from his deific order, must battle for authority in the pavilion of his foe. Of course Ulu will lose. He may offer only the mysterious piety of suffering; Christianity, as it is unfolded and displayed in *Arrow of God,* offers the clear piety of economics, a simple exchange of spiritual faith for material prosperity.

Joseph Swann speculates that the demise of Ulu may have been self-willed, "not for any reason of cultural dissatisfaction, but as a simple historical necessity, to safeguard the bare existence of the clan" (194). But what is existence without faith? In the clan's ancient frame of things it should be as nothing. The fact that it is now feasible attests to a shift in the devotional perspective of the clan members. Knowingly or otherwise, they are trapped into a revisionist interpretation—in effect, a Christianization—of their traditional beliefs. Where once they might have accepted the ruling of the divinity, and starved in the certainty of a mysterious but painful purpose, now an alien creed offers an alluring alternative.

Things Fall Apart reveals a time when this was not so, and goes on to present the temporal nexus point between the ways of the old religion and the ways of a new world order. On the face of it, the new order seems more logical and democratic, and, to contemporary sensibilities, humane. The clanspeople meet and discuss their tactics; the imperatives of action are no longer handed down to them by unseen deities who communicate imperiously through their human emissaries. It is, of course, a superficial freedom. In truth, they now act under a new and equally powerful imperative, a colonial imperative. This new relationship, however, is not founded on mystical ordination or divine machination. It is a relationship of pragmatism and commodity.

That point is made abundantly clear in the abduction of the six clanspeople by the District Commissioner's officers (137-39). This may be compared with the abduction of Okonkwo's child, Ezinma, by Agbala's priestess Chielo (70-76). After a bizarre odyssey, the child is returned unharmed, and without explanation (77). The six men, on the other hand, are ransomed. Either the clan pays up the requisite cowrie fine or the six will be hanged. Just as no one questions the motives of Chielo, so no one questions the motives of the District Commissioner. But the reasons for the silences are quite different. Chielo is not challenged because the ways of the gods are beyond mortal comprehen-

sion; the District Commissioner is not challenged because, by contrast, his position is abundantly comprehensible. He goes to some lengths to explain the readily discernible economics of commodity transfer: the freedom of six human beings for two hundred bags of cowrie shells. It is a logical, business transaction, and the clan finds it as compelling as it did obedience to the Oracle of the Hills and the Caves.

There is no talk of gods or goddesses or holy wars. The clan's financial penance is part of the new order that has enveloped their traditional life. An egwugwu has been unmasked; their six leaders have been captured through false promises of parley; an extortionate ransom demand has been made—yet the response of the clan is pragmatic. The men of the clan meet at the marketplace and agree to raise the fine without delay (139). The matter is settled on a commodity basis. Faith in oracular arbitration has been replaced by faith in a new kind of fiscal logic. This eclipse is signed by the fact that the night preceding their decision is a night of the full moon. Normally a time of sacred and secretive communal ritual, it is on this occasion presented as a time of desolation and emptiness (139).

The economics of religious school education provide momenta no less forceful than the exchange of prisoners for money. This is how the novel describes the impact of Mr. Brown, a missionary educator, on the life and times of the village:

> Mr. Brown's school produced quick results. A few
> months in it were enough to make one a court mes-
> senger or even a court clerk. Those who stayed longer
> became teachers; and from Umuofia labourers went
> forth into the Lord's vineyard. New churches were es-
> tablished in the surrounding villages and a few schools
> with them. From the very beginning religion and edu-
> cation went hand in hand. (128)

Mr. Brown's school offers advantages to its enrolment and to the work of the missionary himself. For the local participants it promises advancement within the prevailing socio-economic system; for Mr. Brown it accords the opportunity to convert to Christianity those who have entrusted their education to his care. But the benefits come at a price. The need for court messengers or court clerks, or indeed for people who can read or write, is one generated by the demands of a colonial hegemony, not by the requirements of clan administration. The knowledge and understanding that Mr. Brown's school seeks to promulgate is openly abrasive to the organization and culture of the clan.

Eustace Palmer argues that "[a]s long as a reasonable person like Mr. Brown is in charge of the mission station, co-existence is possible between the new religion and traditional society" (58). In fact, the interrelation between the two can never be characterized in terms of co-existence, because the economics of Mr. Brown's religion demand ideological substitution, not concurrence or hybridization. In *Things Fall Apart,* Christianity, like colonialism in general, is depicted as offering a clear rationale of "exchange" for Umuofia. In return for adherence to Christian doctrine, the church offers explicit routes for individual economic advancement.

As the meaning and decisiveness of that interaction dawns on the clan it corrupts the ancient way of things. What use is there in praying to Agbala for the white people to go away when the new order presents so persuasively the dimensions of its power that only co-operation and attempted advancement within its structure seems practicable? Achebe's irony, of course, is that the Umuofia come to believe in the supremacy of the missionary colonizers as devoutly as they once had in their own theater of gods. But these are devotions engendered by quite different experiences: the former, through the compulsion of physical aggression and economic inducement; the latter, through the magnificence and munificence of faith. In the end, the metamorphosis of piety is not a change from belief in one religious system to belief in another religious system but rather a switch from faith in a world where life is given, to commitment to one where security and achievement are measured and earned very differently.

Authors write novels for a multiplicity of reasons, not all of them obvious or cogent. It is possible, as Theo D'haen has suggested, that some postcolonial literatures seek to "take revenge upon the mother country, among other things by means of their shared post-colonial literatures" (16). But *Things Fall Apart* is not about revenge—though Achebe misses few opportunities to satirize the colonial presence. The Nigerian poet Tanure Ojaide offers another possibility:

> Literature might be devoted to leisure in other cultures, but for us Africans who are experiencing the second half of the twentieth century, literature must serve a purpose: to expose, embarrass, and fight corruption and authoritarianism. . . . It is understandable why the African artist is utilitarian. We do not have the luxury of some Western writers, who are apolitical and can afford to write art for art's sake and be confessional (a euphemism for self-therapy). (17)

While no one may accuse Achebe of complacency, Ojaide's premise of utilitarianism is more difficult to decipher in *Things Fall Apart.* The problem is that once things have irrevocably fallen apart, once a unique and intricate construct of a matured civilization has been irreversibly dis-

mantled, then rehearsing the indiscretions of the past can easily be regarded as motiveless reminiscence. Yet, there is clearly a purpose to *Things Fall Apart* and it may be discernible as much in the need for personal therapy as in the quest for historical truth. Achebe perceives a gap between how things were and how things are. The intercessionary phase has been typically fashioned as the sublimation of one culture by another. This is a neat enough postcolonial aphorism but without the detail and minutiae of human circumstance, its veracity can remain only intuitive.

Things Fall Apart, and *Arrow of God* after it, provide the detail, the historical glimpses, of a traditional and colonial past. These are not concurrent glimpses, and not even consecutive. But, in a sense, their temporal dislocations are all the more informative. In particular, the shifting time frame of Umuofia in *Things Fall Apart* delineates not only how things fell apart but theorizes on why they fell apart. It bestows no ebullient credit; it lays no absolute onus of blame. As Aijaz Ahmad has written, history cannot decisively resolve theoretical debate because "[t]he difficulty with theoretical debate . . . is that it can neither ignore the facts nor be simply settled by them; thought . . . tends always to exceed the facts" (287). Obscurities of absolution and blame are of themselves the ironically definitive truths of history. The decline of Umuofia was a decline effected by a concatenation of unfortunate and calamitous and mysterious circumstances. It cannot be argued that the learning of this past is overtly utilitarian for what has been lost will not exist again and therefore cannot be lost again. What can be said is that the novel reconstructs the detail of grand and momentous events, rejecting nineteenth-century ahistorical polarities of Africa and Occident, and asserting a process of metamorphosing piety against a backdrop of seemingly irresistible social and economic imperatives.

NOTES

1. For a discussion of Okonkwo's transgressions against the earth goddess, see Maja-Pearce 10-16 and Barthold 56-58.

2. See, as well, Lindfors, who explores Okonkwo's relationship with his chi (78-79).

WORKS CITED

Achebe, Chinua. *Arrow of God.* London: Heinemann, 1974.

———. *Things Fall Apart.* London: Heinemann, 1962.

Ahmad, Aijaz. *In Theory.* London: Verso, 1992.

Ashcroft, Bill, Gareth Griffiths, and Helen Tiffin. *The Empire Writes Back.* London: Routledge, 1989.

Barthold, Bonnie J. *Black Time: Fiction of Africa, the Caribbean and the United States.* New Haven, CT: Yale UP, 1981.

Bhabha, Homi K. *The Location of Culture.* London: Routledge, 1994.

Cook, David. *African Literature: A Critical View.* London: Longman, 1977.

D'haen, Theo. "Shades of Empire in Colonial and Post-Colonial Literatures." *Shades of Empire In Colonial and Post-Colonial Literatures.* Ed. C. C. Barfoot and Theo D'haen. Amsterdam: Rodopi, 1993. 9-16.

Lindfors, Bernth. *Folklore in Nigerian Literature.* New York: Africana, 1973.

Maja-Pearce, Adewale. *A Mask Dancing: Nigerian Novelists of the Eighties.* London: Hans Zell, 1992.

Ojaide, Tanure. "I Want To Be An Oracle: My Poetry and My Generation." *World Literature Today* 68 (1994): 15-21.

Oyeleye, A. Lekan. "*Things Fall Apart* Revisited: A Semantic and Stylistic Study of Character in Achebe." *The Question of Language in African Literature Today.* Ed. Eldred Durosimi Jones. Trenton, NJ: Africa World, 1991. 15-23.

Palmer, Eustace. *An Introduction to the African Novel.* London: Heinemann, 1972.

Swann, Joseph. "From *Things Fall Apart* to *Anthills of the Savannah*: The Changing Face of History in Chinua Achebe's Novels." *Crisis and Creativity in the New Literatures in English.* Ed. Geoffrey V. Davis and Hena Maes-Jelinek. Amsterdam: Rodopi, 1990. 191-203.

Richard Begam (essay date Fall 1997)

SOURCE: "Achebe's Sense of an Ending: History and Tragedy in *Things Fall Apart*," in *Studies in the Novel*, Vol. XXIX, No. 3, Fall, 1997, pp. 396-411.

[*In the following essay, Begam describes three distinct conclusions to* Things Fall Apart *in relation to three different conceptions of history produced by reading the narrative in a post-colonial context, arguing that the novel offers various responses to tragedy as an art form as well.*]

One of the more notable consequences of cultural global-ization has been the exchange that has occurred over the last decade or so between what we have come to call postmodernism and postcolonialism.[1] This meeting of First World and Third World has inspired more controversy than consensus, but on one point there seems to have been wide agreement: if we want to understand colonialism, then we must understand how it is represented. As Hayden White has argued, speaking of historiography in general, the "form" is the "content," and this means that the language, vocabulary, and conceptual framework in which the experience of colonialism is produced inevitably determine what can and cannot be said about it.[2] To borrow Homi K. Bhabha's formulation, "nation" and "narration" are not easily separated—the one implies the other.[3]

The present paper explores the intersection between narrative construction and colonial representation by focusing on an aspect of literary form that has received little attention in postcolonial studies—namely, the question of closure or ending. It is puzzling that this subject, which has generated so much commentary in modern and postmodern studies, has gone virtually unexamined in the area of postcolonial literature. Yet it is certainly reasonable to assume that a literature that identifies itself as *post*colonial and defines itself in terms of the aftermath of colonialism, will have a passing interest in the way endings are narratively achieved, in what they mean and how they are fashioned. Of particular interest in this regard is the highly problematic relation that postcolonial literature has to its own past and, more specifically, to the writing of its own history.[4]

We may begin to appreciate some of the difficulties entailed in this relation by considering a number of connected questions. First, where do postcolonial writers locate their past? Is it to be found in the colonial, precolonial, or postcolonial period? Second, can we neatly separate the different historical strands that traverse and intersect these various epochs? Can we confidently assign to them decisive beginnings and conclusive endings? Third, what historical stance should postcolonial writers assume toward their own history, especially if they wish to forge a sense of national identity after colonization? To what extent does "critical history," of the sort described by Nietzsche, become a luxury that the postcolonial writer cannot afford?[5]

In examining these questions, I want to take up the case of Chinua Achebe's ***Things Fall Apart*** because, as an exercise in historical recuperation, it is necessarily concerned with issues of formal shaping and narrative closure. Of course, at first glance, the novel appears to have a perfectly transparent narrative line: it tells the tragic story of Okonkwo's rise and fall among the Igbo people, concluding with that least ambiguous of all endings, the death of the hero. With only a few exceptions, critics have understood the novel in precisely these terms, seeing its closing pages as entirely unproblematic.[6] Yet any straightforward reading of Achebe's ending must reconcile itself with the fact that the novel describes a situation of profound cultural entropy, a society in which the norms of conduct and institutions of governance are in the process of "falling apart." What is more, while Achebe's novel movingly elegizes the passing away of traditional Igbo culture, the long view it adopts—looking ahead to the future establishment of Nigeria—suggests that Achebe's own position on the modernization of Africa is, at the very least, complicated. Given the subject of Achebe's novel and his own divided response to it, we would expect a fairly open-ended conclusion, one that acknowledges its own closure as tentative, even contingent.

In what follows, I will argue that *Things Fall Apart* resists the idea of a single or simple resolution by providing three distinct endings, three different ways of reading the events that conclude the novel. At the same time, I will relate these endings to three different conceptions of history, especially as it is produced within a postcolonial context. First, Achebe writes a form of nationalist history. Here the interest is essentially reconstructive and centers on recovering an Igbo past that has been neglected or suppressed by historians who would not or could not write from an African perspective. As Achebe observed in 1964, four years after Nigerian independence: "Historians everywhere are re-writing the stories of the new nations—replacing short, garbled, despised history with a more sympathetic account."[7] Nationalist history tends to emphasize what other histories have either glossed over or flatly denied—namely that "African people did not hear of culture for the first time from Europeans; that their societies were not mindless but frequently had a philosophy of great depth and value and beauty, that they had poetry and, above all, they had dignity."[8] Second, Achebe writes a form of adversarial history. Here the emphasis falls not on the reconstruction of an authentic past that has been lost, but on the deconstruction of a counterfeit past that has been imposed. Adversarial history enables Achebe to write against what he himself has called "colonialist" discourse, against the attitudes and assumptions, the language and rhetoric that characterized British colonial rule in Nigeria. Third, Achebe writes a form of metahistory. This kind of history calls attention to itself as a piece of writing, a narrative construction that depends on principles of selection (what material will be included?), emphasis (what importance will be attached to it?) and shaping (how will it be organized and arranged?).[9]

Yet *Things Fall Apart* is concerned not only with writing history, but also with fashioning tragedy. Achebe himself made this point in an interview with Robert Serumaga, in which he discussed the political implications of tragedy and explicitly referred to his novel as an example of that genre.[10] A good deal of the critical literature has focused on this issue, addressing the question of whether the novel is indeed a tragedy and, if so, what kind of tragedy. Thus, Bruce Macdonald and Margaret Turner maintain that *Things Fall Apart* fails as an Aristotelian tragedy; Alastair Niven asserts that it succeeds as "modern" tragedy; while Afam Ebeogu treats it as an example of Igbo tragedy, and Abiola Irele considers it more generally as an instance of cultural and historical tragedy.[11] It will be my contention that much of the disagreement over generic classification has resulted from a failure to identify Achebe's multi-perspectival approach to the problem—a failure to recognize that he has written three distinct endings. Hence, I also want to argue that the novel offers us a variety of responses to tragedy, as well as history. According to the model I shall develop, nationalist history is associated with classical or Aristotelian tragedy; adversarial history is associated with modern or ironic tragedy; and metahistory is associated with critical discourse. My larger purpose in pursuing this line of analysis is to suggest that *Things Fall Apart* demands what is, in effect, a palimpsestic reading, a kind of historical and generic archaeology, which is designed to uncover, layer by layer, those experiences that have accreted around colonialism and its protracted aftermath.

The first of the novel's three endings centers on Okonkwo's killing of the messenger, his failed attempt to rouse his people to action, and his subsequent suicide. This ending presents the events of the novel largely from an African perspective, equating Okonkwo's demise with the collapse of Igbo culture. The idea that Okonkwo is a great man whose destiny is linked with that of his people is immediately established in the novel's celebrated opening:

> Okonkwo was well known throughout the nine villages and even beyond. His fame rested on solid personal achievements. As a young man of eighteen he had brought honor to his village by throwing Amalinze the Cat. Amalinze was the great wrestler who for seven years was unbeaten, from Umuofia to Mbaino. He was called the Cat because his back would never touch the earth. It was this man that Okonkwo threw in a fight which the old men agreed was one of the fiercest since the founder of their town engaged a spirit of the wild for seven days and seven nights. (p. 7)

In this passage history recedes into myth, as the narrator presents the seven-year reign of Amalinze and the seven-day struggle of the founder of the village in epic terms (here seven obviously functions as a conventional rather than a naturalistic number[12]). The passage also serves both to connect Okonkwo with the beginnings of Umuofia (through his wrestling exploits he is compared with the village's symbolic progenitor) and to look forward to his own and his people's end (the "spirit of the wild," representing Nature, will be replaced by the more powerful alien force of British imperialism.) In a few deft strokes, Achebe illustrates how Okonkwo has come to personify the destiny of his community, extending from its earliest origins to its final destruction.[13]

The larger effect of Achebe's opening is to establish Okonkwo as a particular kind of tragic protagonist: the great warrior who carries with him the fate of his people. Seen from the standpoint of the first ending, he is, as Michael Valdez Moses has argued, a Homeric hero cast in a distinctly Achillean mold:

> Like Achilles, Okonkwo is "a man of action, a man of war" (p. 7). His "fame" among the Igbo rests "on solid personal achievements" (p. 3), foremost of which are his exploits as the greatest wrestler and most accomplished warrior of the nine villages. He is a man renowned and respected for having brought home from battle five human heads; and on feast days and important public occasions, he drinks his palm wine from the skull of the first warrior he killed.[14]

Okonkwo is, in other words, identified with his community to the extent that it esteems the martial ethos he embodies, and while his village certainly does more than make war, it especially prizes those men who win distinction on the battlefield ("in Umuofia . . . men were bold and warlike" [p. 151]).

This is not to say, however, that Okonkwo epitomizes all the virtues of Igbo culture, or that he is himself without fault. On the contrary, Achebe himself understands that, within an Aristotelian framework, his hero is necessarily a flawed character, guilty of errors in judgement—guilty, to use the Greek term, of *hamartia*. As Achebe has observed in an interview with Charles Rowell: "[The tragic protagonist is] the man who's larger than life, who exemplifies virtues that are admired by the community, but also a man who for all that is still human. He can have flaws, you see; all that seems to me to be very elegantly underlined in Aristotle's work."[15] Obviously Okonkwo is "larger than life" ("He was tall and huge, and his bushy eyebrows and wide nose gave him a very severe look" [p. 7]) yet his epic proportions carry a figurative as well as a literal significance: they indicate the difficulty he experiences fitting within the boundaries of any social order. So it is that as a "man of action," a great athlete and warrior, he is excessive both in his high-spiritedness, what the Greeks called *thymos* ("whenever he was angry and could not get his words out quickly enough, he would use his fists" [p. 8]), and in his prideful arrogance, what the Greeks called *hybris* ("The oldest man present said sternly [to Okonkwo] that those whose palm-kernels were cracked for them by a benevolent spirit should not forget to be humble" [p. 28]). Indeed,

like many of the heroes of classical tragedy, Okonkwo's immoderate behavior consistently places him at cross-purposes not merely with his fellow Umuofians, but with the gods themselves ("Okonkwo was not the man to stop beating somebody half-way through, not even for fear of a goddess" [p. 31]), and it comes as no surprise when, in the second part of the novel, he is sent into temporary exile for offending Ani, the Earth deity. Nevertheless, if we are to appreciate the tragedy of the first ending—something that Achebe clearly intends—then we must recognize that Okonkwo's faults are essentially virtues carried to an extreme, and that while he is obviously not perfect, he nevertheless represents some of the best qualities of his culture.[16] As Obierika remarks near the novel's end, "That man was one of the greatest men in Umuofia" (p. 191).[17]

The crisis of the novel comes in the penultimate chapter when an impudent messenger, sent by the colonial authorities, orders a tribal meeting to disband. Okonkwo the warrior is moved to action:

> In a flash Okonkwo drew his machete. The messenger crouched to avoid the blow. It was useless. Okonkwo's machete descended twice and the man's head lay beside his uniformed body.
>
> The waiting backcloth jumped into tumultuous life and the meeting was stopped. Okonkwo stood looking at the dead man. He knew that Umuofia would not go to war. He knew because they had let the other messengers escape. They had broken into tumult instead of action. He discerned fright in that tumult. He heard voices asking: "Why did he do it?"
>
> He wiped his machete on the sand and went away. (p. 188)

The scene is presented with a devastating simplicity. From the perspective of the first ending, the people of Umuofia have deserted Okonkwo and in the process betrayed themselves, but the wiping of the machete is the only eloquence he permits himself. It is an ordinary and everyday gesture, yet in the present context it acquires special significance: Okonkwo remains true to the martial ethos that his people have abandoned, here represented by the warrior's care of his weapon; at the same time, he symbolically dissolves his connection with his people, wiping away the blood bond that has joined them. This gesture is especially resonant because, as critics have pointed out, in killing the messenger he is shedding the blood of a fellow Igbo.[18]

The suicide that follows is itself a profound violation of Igbo law, which strictly prohibits acts of self-destruction. The question of how we should respond to Okonkwo's final deed has been examined in detail by Kalu Ogbaa and

Damian Opata, but with strikingly different results. For Ogbaa the suicide grows out of Okonkwo's failure to act with sufficient piety toward the Igbo gods and traditions, while for Opata it is a consequence of the Igbos' refusal to rally around Okonkwo and join him in resisting the British.[19] As was the case with discussions of the novel's tragedy, the disagreement arises in the first place because the reader has difficulty establishing Achebe's position on a number of issues—difficulty knowing, for example, where he stands on the question of violent resistance to the British. Of course, this interpretive problem largely disappears once we begin to read the novel palimpsestically as a layering of diverse perspectives on history and tragedy. Hence, understood within the terms of the novel's first ending, Okonkwo's suicide is the logical and necessary consequence of an idealistic and absolutist position. Both nationalist history and heroic tragedy demand that he remain unyielding and that the Igbos honor their cultural heritage by refusing assimilation. Even in this final gesture, then, Okonkwo functions as the true representative of his people. For, as he sees it, Igbo culture has willingly succumbed to its own annihilation, committing what is a form of collective suicide by submitting to the British. In taking his own life, Okonkwo has simply preceded his people in their communal destruction. Once again he has led the way.

The novel's second ending, which I associate with adversarial history, views events from the heavily ironized perspective of the District Commissioner. Igbo culture is now presented not from the inside as vital and autonomous, but from the outside as an object of anthropological curiosity, and its collapse is understood not as an African tragedy but as a European triumph. As the final scene of the novel unfolds, the Igbos take the District Commissioner to the place where the suicide was committed:

> Then they came to the tree from which Okonkwo's body was dangling, and they stopped dead.

> "Perhaps your men can help us bring him down and bury him," said Obeirika. "We have sent for strangers from another village to do it for us, but they may be a long time coming."

> The District Commissioner changed instantaneously. The resolute administrator in him gave way to the student of primitive customs.

> "Why can't you take him down yourselves?" he asked.

> "It is against our custom," said one of the men. "It is an abomination for a man to take his own life." (p. 190)

What is particularly noteworthy in this episode is the way the District Commissioner effortlessly shifts from the "resolute administrator" to the "student of primitive customs." Here Achebe demonstrates that, within a colonial context, the Foucauldian power-knowledge nexus is much more than a speculative theory—it is an inescapable and omnipresent reality. Thus, those who wrote historical and anthropological accounts of the Igbos were typically either representatives of the British government or their semi-official guests, and the colonial administration not only helped to enable such research by "opening up" various regions, but also relied upon it in determining local policy.[20] In the case of Igboland, the earliest anthropological studies were written by P. Amaury Talbot, himself a District Commissioner, and G. T. Basden, a missionary whose safety and well-being literally depended on the colonial office. As Robert M. Wren has shown, both Talbot and Basden were, by the standards of the day, sympathetic observers of the Igbos—indeed, the latter was a personal friend of Achebe's father—but this did not prevent them from expressing in their published writings typically European attitudes towards the Africans.[21] By way of illustration we might consider how the scene with the District Commissioner continues:

> "Take down the body," the Commissioner ordered his chief messenger, "and bring it and all these people to the court."

> "Yes, sah," the messenger said, saluting.

> The Commissioner went away, taking three or four of the soldiers with him. In the many years in which he had toiled to bring civilization to different parts of Africa he had learned a number of things. One of them was that a District Commissioner must never attend to such undignified details as cutting a hanged man from the tree. Such attention would give the natives a poor opinion of him. In the book which he planned to write he would stress that point. (p. 191)

Achebe makes much the same point himself, though obviously to very different effect, in his essay, **"Colonialist Criticism"**:

> To the colonialist mind it was always of the utmost importance to be able to say: "I know my natives," a claim which implied two things at once: (a) that the native was really quite simple and (b) that understanding him and controlling him went hand in hand—understanding being a pre-condition for control and control constituting adequate proof of understanding.[22]

Yet notice how carefully Achebe has chosen his words: it is important for the colonialist mind not to know the natives but to be able to *say* "I know my natives." What the

District Commissioner ultimately achieves is not genuine understanding but the illusion of understanding that comes with the power to control:

> Every day brought him some new material. The story of this man who had killed a messenger and hanged himself would make interesting reading. One could almost write a whole chapter on him. Perhaps not a whole chapter but a reasonable paragraph, at any rate. There was so much else to include, and one must be firm in cutting out details. He had already chosen the title of the book, after much thought: *The Pacification of the Primitive Tribes of the Lower Niger.* (p. 191)

With these words, *Things Fall Apart* completes its passage from the heroic tragedy of the first ending to the biting irony of the second ending. In his well-known essay on *Heart of Darkness*, Achebe argues against European accounts of Africa that have reduced its people to—I quote Achebe quoting Conrad—"rudimentary souls" capable only of "a violent babble of uncouth sounds."[23] In presenting Okonkwo's epic story, epitomized by the first ending, Achebe offers a powerful counter-statement to the "dark continent" idea of Africa. But with the second ending he does something more. By ironically undermining the perspective of the District Commissioner, by exposing the latter's personal ignorance (not a "whole chapter" but a "reasonable paragraph") and political interests (the "pacification" of the Lower Niger), Achebe seeks to confront and finally to discredit the entire discourse of colonialism, those quasi-historical, quasi-anthropological writings that have treated Africa as nothing more than—again I quote Achebe—"a foil to Europe, a place of negations."[24]

At the same time, the second ending begins to redefine our point of view on the tragic events of the novel. Although this ending is clearly meant to undermine the District Commissioner's position, indeed to portray him as a fool, it nevertheless substantially alters the tone and mood of Achebe's resolution. Obviously the novel would read very differently—and its tragedy function very differently—if it concluded with, say, a heroic recitation of Okonkwo's suicide by Obeirika. In other words, the final chapter of *Things Fall Apart* serves not as a simple denouement— one that helps us sort out a rather messy climax—but as a significant qualification of what has gone before, a distinctly new ending that complicates our sense of Achebe's approach to both history and tragedy.[25] In this regard, it is important to remember what Achebe himself has observed in interviews and essays: that while the passing away of traditional Igbo culture involved profound loss, it also held out the possibility of substantial gain. Thus, when he was asked about returning to pre-colonial society, the kind of world Okonkwo inhabited before "things fell apart," Achebe responded, "It's not really a question of going back. I think

if one goes back, there's something wrong somewhere, or else a misunderstanding."[26] In another interview, he pushed this position further, arguing that colonization was a multi-faceted phenomenon, which had produced benefits as well as burdens: "I am not one of those who would say that Africa has gained nothing at all during the colonial period, I mean this is ridiculous—we gained a lot."[27] Finally and most tellingly, he has insisted that, despite his own ambivalence on the subject, modernization is a necessary and essential part of Africa's future: "The comprehensive goal of a developing nation like Nigeria is, of course, development, or its somewhat better variant, modernization. I don't see much argument about that."[28]

What all of this means is that Achebe's response to colonization is far more nuanced, far more complex, than most critics have recognized or been willing to acknowledge. How such complexity expresses itself, and how it modifies Achebe's sense of tragedy, is further explored in the third ending.

What I shall identify as the third ending is located in *No Longer At Ease,* the sequel to *Things Fall Apart.* No doubt, the assertion that one text contains the ending of another will immediately strike some readers as dubious. Such a claim begins to gain credibility, however, when we remember that Achebe originally conceived of his two novels as the first and third sections of a single work.[29] In other words, the compositional history of *Things Fall Apart* and *No Longer At Ease* provides some justification for treating the latter as a continuation of the former, an extension that qualifies Okonkwo's story, even redirects its course. Indeed, there is good reason to argue that *No Longer At Ease* is not only a continuation of *Things Fall Apart* but also a rewriting of it, one that essentially recapitulates the action of the earlier novel, though in a markedly different setting. Hence, both novels tell the story of a representative of the Igbo people who takes a stand on a question of principle and is destroyed in the ensuing collision between African and European values. To paraphrase one critic, the fall of Okonkwo's machete is replaced by the fall of the judge's gavel, as we are transported from a heroic to a legalistic world, but the narrative outline remains essentially the same. The very structure of *No Longer At Ease* indicates, then, that Okonkwo's story has not reached its end, that the tragic destiny it implies continues to be lived out.

This does not mean, however, that in writing *Things Fall Apart* and *No Longer At Ease* as independent works Achebe somehow betrayed the internal logic of his own narrative. On the contrary, the decision to treat Okonkwo's and Obi Okonkwo's stories separately contributes to what I have called Achebe's palimpsestic effect, the sense that the same or similar events acquire new meanings in different contexts. It is therefore not surprising that in moving from the first novel to the second, we observe Okonkwo's traditional tragedy transform itself into Obi's modern tragedy, as the heroic gives way to the ironic.

The point of intersection between the two novels, the scene in which I locate the third ending of *Things Fall Apart,* occurs when Okonkwo's grandson, Obi, a university-educated civil servant, finds himself discussing tragedy with a British colonial officer. Obi advances the opinion—of special interest given the first ending of *Things Fall Apart*—that suicide ruins a tragedy:

> Real tragedy is never resolved. It goes on hopelessly forever. Conventional tragedy is too easy. The hero dies and we feel a purging of the emotions. A real tragedy takes place in a corner, in an untidy spot, to quote W. H. Auden. The rest of the world is unaware of it. Like that man in *A Handful of Dust* who reads Dickens to Mr. Todd. There is no release for him. When the story ends he is still reading. There is no purging of the emotions for us because *we are not there.*[30]

Obi draws a distinction in this passage between two kinds of tragedy. In traditional or Aristotelian tragedy, there is a clear resolution, an aesthetic pay-off that comes in the form of *catharsis*; but in modern or ironic tragedy, the tragedy described in Auden's "Musée des Beaux Arts," the fall from a high place is likened to Brueghel's famous painting of Icarus. In the foreground the ploughman ploughs his field; in the background a ship sails on its way. And it is only after careful inspection that we are able to discover the place of tragedy: there in the corner, barely perceptible, we see Icarus's two legs breaking the surface of the water, sole testimony of his personal catastrophe.

While the point of departure for Obi's discussion of tragedy is Graham Greene's *The Heart of the Matter,* his observations have an obvious application to *Things Fall Apart.* Okonkwo's story as viewed from the Igbo perspective presents history in the form of classical or heroic tragedy. Okonkwo's story as viewed from the District Commissioner's perspective presents history in the form of modern or ironic tragedy. One of Obi's remarks is particularly apposite: there is no purging of the emotions in modern tragedy, because "we are not there." These words perfectly describe the situation of the District Commissioner. He "was not there" in the sense that he was never in a position genuinely to understand Okonkwo, to appreciate who he was and what he represented.

It is important to stress, however, that the novel's first ending is not in some way compromised because it is associated with the "conventional," while the novel's second ending is in some way enhanced because it is associated

with the "real." Indeed, if Achebe provides us with any controlling point of view, it comes with the third ending, which illustrates the vexed and ambiguous relation in which the postcolonial stands to its own past. For with his remarks on tragedy, Obi is offering a narrative analysis of what is *literally* his own past. In describing a tragedy that ends in suicide, he is describing his grandfather's tragic fall and its significance for Igbo culture after it was lost, after "things fell apart."

What the novel's third ending illustrates, then, is that the boundaries between the "conventional" and the "real," the heroic and the ironic, are not clearly or cleanly drawn. From Obi's perspective—and, for that matter, the reader's—Okonkwo functions both as a literary persona and a living person, an epic hero and an historical anachronism. Yet the novel does not invite us to select one of these alternatives so much as to understand the various, though decidedly distinctive, truths they articulate. In other words, we are not meant to choose from among three possible endings, but to read all of them, as it were, simultaneously and palimpsestically. If we are able to do this, we shall see how Achebe's sense of an ending is intimately bound up with his sense of cultural loss; how the tragedy of the past necessarily depends on the perspective of the present; and how history is inevitably written for both the "they who were there" and the "we who are not there."

At the beginning of this paper I asked three questions about the relation of postcolonial literature to the writing of history. I would now like to propose, however provisionally, some answers to these questions. First, where do postcolonial writers locate their past? There is certainly no single or definitive response to this question, but a writer like Achebe is acutely aware of how problematic are the issues it raises. For this reason *Things Fall Apart* and *No Longer At Ease* not only situate themselves in periods of historical transition (Nigeria at the turn of the century and in the late 1950s) but also superimpose these periods on each other through a series of intertextual connections, suggesting that postcolonial writers are the products of all the historical periods through which their cultures have lived. Second, can we confidently assign decisive beginnings and conclusive endings to the various epochs of colonial and postcolonial history? It is not immediately apparent how Achebe would answer this question, but his experiment in extended closure reminds us that the narrative shaping that necessarily comes with beginnings and endings in a human creation—a product of what Richard Rorty calls "contingency"—rather than a naturally occurring or divinely given reality.[31] So it is that each of the three endings with which Achebe concludes *Things Fall Apart* grows out of different interests, different assumptions, different intentions, and none of these is, ultimately, true in itself. Finally, what historical stance should postcolonial writers assume toward their own history? This is a particularly difficult problem and one that cannot be fully treated in the space that remains. Still, it is worth observing that Achebe has not only qualified the kind of nationalist history with which his work is so often associated, but also that he has shown a willingness to criticize traditional Igbo culture. While Achebe urgently feels the need to recuperate an African past that has been lost or overlooked, to tell the story that has not been told, he nevertheless recognizes the importance of maintaining a sense of intellectual and historical integrity:

> The question is how does a writer re-create this past? Quite clearly there is a strong temptation to idealize it— to extol its good points and pretend that the bad never existed . . . [But] The credibility of the world [the writer] is attempting to re-create will be called into question and he will defeat his own purpose if he is suspected of glossing over inconvenient facts. We cannot pretend that our past was one long technicolour idyll. We have to admit that like other people's pasts ours had its good as well as its bad sides.[32]

The last general point I would like to make touches upon methodology. Too often the literature we call postcolonial has been read as little more than an exercise in political thematics. Such an approach is not surprising, given the enormous historical pressure out of which this literature was born, but it has led many critics to ignore crucial issues of form and technique. Yet, as I have sought to show, we can only begin to appreciate how a writer like Achebe envisions his past, both as history and tragedy, if we understand how he narratively shapes his material, how he achieves his sense of an ending. Attention to formal organization is particularly important in the case of Achebe, because he conceives of history neither in teleological nor positivistic terms, but as something human beings create, a series of stories built around beginnings and endings, a narrative construction. This is not to say that Achebe is fundamentally a postmodern writer, but neither is he exclusively a postcolonial writer. Or rather, to put the matter more precisely, he is a postcolonial writer insofar as he is a product of cultural globalization, insofar as he is an African who has grown up and continues to live at "the crossroads of cultures."[33]

Obviously, life at the crossroads is not easy. As a student of classical tragedy—not to mention a sometime rebellious son—he is aware of the perils, as well as the possibilities, that await us at those places of Oedipal intersection: "the crossroads does have a certain dangerous potency; dangerous because a man can perish there wrestling with multiple-headed spirits, but also because he might be lucky and return to his people with the boon of prophetic vision."[34] But if forebears like Okonkwo, and al-

ter egos like Obi, have been vanquished wrestling the demons of multiplicity, Achebe has emerged from these spiritual contests with a deeper and more comprehensive sense of what it means to inhabit the alternate worlds of postcolonialism, worlds that are at once aristocratic and democratic, heroic and ironic, ancient and contemporary. We are all of us the heirs of Achebe's prophetic vision, grappling with the problems and promises of a globalized modernity, working our way through its diverse scenarios, its different endings.

NOTES

1. For a discussion of "globalization" and "postcolonialism," see Michael Valdez Moses, *The Novel and the Globalization of Culture* (New York: Oxford Univ. Press, 1995). The relation between "postmodernism" and "postcolonialism" has produced an exhaustive, not to say exhausting, bibliography: some of the better known essays are Kwame Anthony Appiah's "The Postcolonial and the Postmodern." in Appiah's book *In My Father's House: Africa in the Philosophy of Culture* (New York: Oxford Univ. Press, 1992); Reginald Berry's "A Deckchair of Words," *Landfall* 40 (1986): 310-23; Diana Brydon's "The Myths that Write Us: Decolonising the Mind," *Commonwealth* 10.1 (1987): 1-14; Simon During's "Postmodernism or post-colonialism today," *Textual Practice* 1.1 (1987): 32-47; Linda Hutcheon's "'Circling the Downspout of Empire': Post-Colonialism and Postmodernism," *Ariel* 20.4 (1989): 149-75; and Helen Tiffin's "Post-Colonialism, Post-Modernism and the Rehabilitation of Post-Colonial History," *Journal of Commonwealth Literature* 23.1 (1988): 169-81.

2. See Hayden White, *The Content of the Form: Narrative Discourse and Historical Representation* (Baltimore: The Johns Hopkins Univ. Press, 1987).

3. Bhabha discusses the connection between "nation" and "narration" in the introductory essay of *Nation and Narration* (London: Routledge, 1990).

4. On narrative closure and postcolonial history, see Homi K. Bhabha, *Nation and Narration,* pp. 1-3 and Robert Young, *White Mythologies* (London: Routledge, 1990), pp. 33-41, 65-67, 137-40, 156: on historiography and postcolonialism, see Stephen Slemon, "Post-Colonial Allegory and the Transformation of History," *The Journal of Commonwealth Literature* 23.1 (1988): 157-68 and Helen Tiffin, "Post-Colonialism, Post-Modernism and the Rehabilitation of Post-Colonial History."

5. In "On the Uses and Disadvantages of History for Life," the second section of *Untimely Meditations* (Cambridge: Cambridge Univ. Press, 1983), Nietzsche argues that there

are three different species or kinds of history: the "monumental," which celebrates the past; the "antiquarian," which investigates the past; and the "critical," which condemns the past.

6. Helen Tiffin, Simon Gikandi, and Michael Valdez Moses are among the few critics who have seen the ending of Chinua Achebe's *Things Fall Apart* (New York: Fawcett, 1969) as less than straightforward. In "Post-Colonialism, Post-Modernism and the Rehabilitation of Post-Colonial History," Tiffin maintains that Achebe's novel "resists linear narrative techniques" (p. 174) until the British appear in Umuofia and asserts that the novel as a whole works against "closure" and "British textual containment" (p. 174). While I am not persuaded that the novel may neatly be divided into a linear, European narrative vs. a non-linear, African narrative, I agree with Tiffin's larger argument—namely, that the novel deliberately plays with the narrative conventions of linearity, chronology, and closure. While neither Gikandi nor Moses has focused on the novel's ending, both have suggested how the narrative shift to the District Commissioner's perspective introduces important complications into the novel's closing pages; see Gikandi, *Reading Chinua Achebe: Language and Ideology in Fiction* (London: James Currey, 1991), pp. 49-50 and Moses, pp. 132-33.

7. Chinua Achebe, "The Role of the Writer in a New Nation," *African Writers on African Writing*, ed. G. D. Killam (Evanston: Northwestern Univ. Press, 1973), p. 7.

8. *Ibid.*, p. 8.

9. Such a conception of history may initially appear to be more postmodern than postcolonial, but it is closely related to the figure of the *griot*, the African storyteller who combines the functions of historian and poet. Achebe discusses the *griot* in an interview with Charles Rowell: "the role of the writer, the modern writer, is closer to that of the *griot*, the historian and poet, than any other practitioner of the arts"; Charles H. Rowell, "An Interview with Chinua Achebe," *Callaloo* 13.1 (1990): 86.

10. Robert Scrumaga, "Interview," *African Writers Talking: A Collection of Interviews*, Dennis Duerden and Cosmo Pieterse, eds (London: Heinemann, 1972), pp. 16-17.

11. For a discussion of tragedy in *Things Fall Apart*, see Afam Ebeogu, "Igbo Sense of Tragedy: A Thematic Feature of the Achebe School," *The Literary Half-Yearly* 24.1 (1983): 69-86; Abiola Irele, "The Tragic Conflict in Achebe's Novels," *Introduction to African Literature: An Anthology of Critical Writing from "Black Orpheus"*. ed. Ulli Beier (Evanston, IL: Northwestern University Press, 1970); Roger L. Landrum, "Chinua Achebe and the Aristo-

telian Concept of Tragedy," *Black Academy Review* 1.1 (1970): 22-30; Bruce F. Macdonald, "Chinua Achebe and the Structure of Colonial Tragedy," *The Literary Half-Yearly* 21.1 (1980): 50-63; Michael Valdez Moses, *The Novel and the Globalization of Culture*; Alastair Niven, "Chinua Achebe and the Possibility of Modern Tragedy," *Kunapipi* 12.2 (1990): 41-50; Chinyere Nwahuananya, "Social Tragedy in Achebe's Rural Novels: A Contrary View," *Commonwealth Novel in English* 4.1 (1991): 1-13; Clement A. Okafor, "A Sense of History in the Novels of Chinua Achebe," *Journal of African Studies* 8.2 (1981): 50-63; Margaret E. Turner, "Achebe, Hegel, and the New Colonialism," *Kunapipi* 12.2 (1990): 31-40.

12. Both Gikandi and Innes observe how Achebe's manipulation of time in the novel's opening scene points the reader toward issues of history and myth; see Gikandi, pp. 29-30 and C. L. Innes, *Chinua Achebe* (Cambridge Univ. Press, 1990), pp. 36-37.

13. I am of course referring to the fact that colonization destroyed the premodern culture described in Umuofia. Obviously the Igbo people survived the arrival of the British, but their ethical, social, and religious systems ceased to exist as they had in the nineteenth century.

14. Moses, pp. 110-11.

15. Rowell, "An Interview With Chinua Achebe," p. 97. Achebe's views on Okonkwo as an example of an Aristotelian tragic hero are complicated, suggesting that any single theory of tragedy is not adequate to describe how the novel handles its tragic material. Thus, while Achebe rejects the idea that Okonkwo is, *tout court*, an Aristotelian hero, he goes on to explain at length how *Things Fall Apart* can be read in Aristotelian terms: "Rowell: How do you respond to critics reading Okonkwo as a hero in terms of Aristotle's concept of tragedy?" "A: No. I don't think I was responding to that particular format. This is not, of course, to say that there is no relationship between these. If we are to believe what we are hearing these days the Greeks did not drop from the sky. They evolved in a certain place which was very close to Africa . . . I think a lot of what Aristotle says makes sense" (p. 97). Achebe then proceeds to make the comment I quote in the body of this paper.

16. A number of critics, arguing against the tragic elements of *Things Fall Apart* and, reading the novel from a postheroic, Western perspective, contend that Okonkwo is not representative of his tribe—indeed, that he is fundamentally hostile to its interests and traditions; see, for example, Harold Scheub, "'When A Man Fails Alone,'" *Présence Africaine* 72.2 (1970): 61-89.

17. I agree with Moses when he maintains that Obierika's

"assessment of Okonkwo's end is only partially correct" (p. 132); it is "correct" within the terms of the novel's first ending.

18. Kalu Ogbaa, "A Cultural Note on Okonkwo's Suicide," *Kunapipi* 2.3 (1981): 133-34.

19. See Kalu Ogbaa's "A Cultural Note on Okonkwo's Suicide," pp. 126-34, and Damian Opata's "The Sudden End of Alienation: A Reconsideration of Okonkwo's Suicide in Chinua Achebe's *Things Fall Apart*," *African Marburgensia* 22.2 (1989): 24-32.

20. Achebe offers a memorable example of the power-knowledge nexus in *Arrow of God* (New York: Anchor Books, 1989, [pp. 32-33]) when he shows a colonial officer reading *The Pacification of the Primitive Tribes of the Lower Niger* by George Allen, the District Commissioner in *Things Fall Apart*. For Michel Foucault's treatment of power-knowledge, see *Discipline and Punish*: *The Birth of the Prison*, trans. Alan Sheridan (New York: Vintage Books, 1979), and *Power/Knowledge: Selected Interviews and Other Writings 1972-1977*, ed. Colin Gordon (New York: Pantheon Books, 1980); for critiques of Foucault's application of this idea to Western democracies, see Richard Rorty, "Moral Identity and Private Autonomy: The Case of Foucault," *Philosophical Papers*, *Vol. 2: Essays on Heidegger and Others* (Cambridge: Cambridge Univ. Press, 1991), and Michael Walzer, "The Lonely Politics of Michel Foucault," *The Company of Critics: Social Criticism and Political Commitment in the Twentieth Century* (New York: Basic Books, 1988).

21. Robert M. Wren, *Achebe's World: The Historical and Cultural Context of the Novels* (Washington, DC: Three Continents, Press, 1980), pp. 17-20.

22. Achebe, *Hopes and Impediments: Selected Essays* (New York: Anchor Books, 1989), p. 71.

23. Achebe, "An Image of Africa: Racism in Conrad's *Heart of Darkness*," *Heart of Darkness: An Authoritative Text, Backgrounds and Sources, Essays in Criticism*, edited by Robert Kimbrough (New York: W.W. Norton and Company, 1988), p. 255.

24. *Ibid.*, pp. 251-52. As Simon Gikandi has written, "whenever [Achebe] looked around him, he was confronted by the overwhelming hegemony of colonialist rhetoric on Africa—what he called 'the sedate prose of the district-officer-government-anthropologist of sixty or seventy years ago'—which the African intellectual has had to wrestle, like Jacob and the angel, at almost every juncture of our contemporary history. To invent a new African narrative was then to write against, and decentre, this colonial discourse

as a prelude to evoking an alternative space of representation"; *Reading Chinua Achebe*, p. 6.

25. Moses is the only critic who has argued that Achebe is not *simply* ironizing the District Commissioner: "While Achebe's irony invites us to dismiss the District Commissioner as the unfeeling and pompous representative of a racist and imperialist perspective, the novel ultimately *subsumes* rather than rejects the official British view" (p. 133).

26. Kalu Ogbaa, "An Interview with Chinua Achebe," *Research in African Literatures* 12.1 (1981): p. 6.

27. Interview with Serumaga, p. 13.

28. Achebe, *Hopes and Impediments*, p. 155.

29. See, for example, Achebe's interview with Serumaga, p. 16.

30. Achebe, *No Longer At Ease* (New York: Fawcett, 1969), pp. 43-44, my emphasis.

31. For a discussion of "contingency," see Rorty, *Contingency, Irony, and Solidarity* (Cambridge Univ. Press, 1989), especially Chapter One, "The Contingency of Language."

32. Achebe, "The Role of the Writer in a New Nation," p. 9.

33. Achebe, *Hopes and Impediments*, p. 34.

34. *Ibid.*

FURTHER READING

Criticism

Aji, Aron and Kirstin Lynne Ellsworth. "Ezinma: The *Ogbanje* Child in Achebe's *Things Fall Apart*." *College Literature* 19, No. 3 (October 1992): 170-5.

Details the narrative significance of Ezinma in *Things Fall Apart*, emphasizing the feminine principles and cultural resilience that informs the character's purpose in the novel.

Brooks, Jerome. "The Art of Fiction CXXXIX: Chinua Achebe." *Paris Review* 36 (Winter 1994): 142-66.

An interview with Achebe in which he discusses his education, his work as a broadcaster in Nigeria, his views on other writers, his audience, and the political situation in Nigeria.

Carey-Webb, Allen. "*Heart of Darkness, Tarzan,* and the 'Third World': Canons and Encounters in World Literature, English 109." *College Literature* 19, No. 3 (October 1992): 121-41.

Addresses the reception and contextualization of "Third World" or "post-colonial" literature by comparing the contemporary canonical significance of *Heart of Darkness, Tarzan,* and *Things Fall Apart.*

DePriest, Tomika. "Women's Social Roles in the Novels of Chinua Achebe." *Mount Olive Review* 8 (Winter-Spring 1995-1996): 138-43.

An examination of the social roles of women and Achebe's treatment of female characters in his various novels.

Fabre, Michel. "Chinua Achebe on *Arrow of God.*" In *Conversations with Chinua Achebe,* edited by Bernth Lindfors, pp. 45-51. Jackson, MS: University Press of Mississippi, 1997.

An interview with Achebe in which he discusses his work *Arrow of God.*

Fleming, Bruce. "Brothers under the Skin: Achebe on *Heart of Darkness.*" *College Literature* 19, No. 3 (October 1992): 90-9.

Reevaluates Achebe's charge of racism against Conrad in his essay, "An Image of Africa," focusing on similarities between the novelists' representational techniques.

Gikandi, Simon. *Reading Chinua Achebe: Language and Ideology in Fiction (Studies in African Literature),* 176 p. London: James Currey, 1991.

Gikandi reveals the nature of Achebe's creativity, its complexity and richness, and its paradoxes and ambiguities in his book. He places Achebe's writing in a wider context than former books by integrating Achebe's critical and theoretical writings.

Hall, Tony. "I Had to Write on the Chaos I Foresaw." In *Conversations with Chinua Achebe,* edited by Bernth Lindfors, pp. 18-26. Jackson, MS: University Press of Mississippi, 1997.

An interview originally published in *Sunday Nation* (Nairobi, Kenya), on January 15, 1967, in which Achebe addresses his literary reputation in Africa, political aspects of his novels, his personal politics, and the literary challenges of representing Africa.

Lindfors, Bernth. *South Asian Responses to Chinua Achebe,* edited by Bala Kothandaraman, 198 pp. New Delhi: Prestige, 1993.

Critical articles by South Asian scholars on Chinua Achebe.

Ogede, "Ode S. Achebe and Armah: a unity of shaping visions." *Research in African Literatures* 27 (Summer 1996): 112-27.

A comparison of the literary strategies employed by Achebe in *A Man of the People* and Ayi Kwei Armah in *The Beautyful Ones Are Not Yet Born.* Ogede argues that although much of the tone of Armah's work is bitter, trenchant, and somber, its vision of rebirth and renewal offers a more positive picture than Achebe's novel.

Quayson, Ato. "Realism, Criticism, and the Disguises of Both: A Reading of Chinua Achebe's *Things Fall Apart* with an Evaluation of the Criticism Relating to It." *Research in African Literatures* 25 (Winter 1994): 117-36.

Quayson evaluates criticism relating to Achebe's work in general, and then offers a reading of *Things Fall Apart,* examining the treatment of patriarchy, women, and femininity in the novel.

Sengova, Joko. "Native Identity and Alienation in Richard Wright's *Native Son* and Chinua Achebe's *Things Fall Apart*: A Cross-Cultural Analysis." *The Mississippi Quarterly* 50 (Spring 1997): 327-51.

Sengova explores the use of "native" identity and "alienation" as literary themes in Wright's novel *Native Son* and in Achebe's novel *Things Fall Apart.* Sengova examines the case of Achebe's hero, Okonkwo, in a comparison with Wright's hero, Bigger Thomas, both of whom are alienated from their society and community.

Thomas, Clara. "Close Encounters: Margaret Laurence and Chinua Achebe." *Journal of Canadian Studies* 32 (Spring 1997): 163-66.

Thomas discusses the differences between the perspectives of the mid-1970s and mid-1980s, drawing on her involvement in and memory of the encounters between authors Margaret Laurence and Chinua Achebe.

Watford, Joyce. "Techniques of the Fantastic in Two West African Novels." In *Contours of the Fantastic,* edited by Michele K. Langford, pp. 65-74. New York: Greenwood Press, 1990.

Compares various uses of traditional Nigerian fantasy elements in Amos Tutuola's *The Palm-Wine Drinkard* and *Things Fall Apart* as the means to dramatize real-world concerns.

Additional coverage of Achebe's life and career is contained in the following sources published by Gale: *Authors and Artists for Young Adults*, Vol. 15; *Black Literature Criticism*, Vol. 1; *Black Writers*, Vol. 2; *Contemporary Authors* First Revision Vols. 1-4R; *Contemporary Authors New Revision Series*, Vols. 6, 26, 47; *Children's Literature Review*, Vol. 20; *DISCovering Authors*; *DISCovering Authors: British*; *DISCovering Authors: Canadian*; *DISCovering Authors: Most-studied Authors Module, Multicultural Authors Module, Novelists Module*; *Dictionary of Literary Biography*, Vol. 117; *Major Authors and Illustrators for Children and Young Adults*; *Major Twentieth Century Writers*, Vols. 1, 2; *Something about the Author*, Vols. 38, 40; and *World Literature Criticism*.

James Baldwin
1924-1987

(Full name: James Arthur Baldwin) American novelist, essayist, playwright, scriptwriter, short story writer, and children's book author.

The following entry presents an overview of Baldwin's career. For further information on his life and works, see *CLC*, Volumes 1, 2, 3, 4, 5, 8, 13, 15, 17, 42, 50, 67, and 90.

INTRODUCTION

Baldwin is considered one of the most prestigious writers in contemporary American literature. Since the publication of his first novel, *Go Tell It on the Mountain* (1953), Baldwin has exposed the racial and sexual polarization of American society and challenged readers to confront and resolve these differences. Baldwin's influence and popularity reached their peak during the 1960s, when he was regarded by many as the leading literary spokesperson of the civil rights movement. His novels, essays, and other writings attest to his premise that the African-American experience, as an example of suffering and abuse, represents a universal symbol of human conflict.

Biographical Information

Baldwin was born in New York City's Harlem on August 2, 1924, the illegitimate child of Emma Berdis Jones. Due to his mother's inaccessibility and his stepfather's stern and remote manner, Baldwin felt isolated and retreated into the world of literature. Baldwin attended school in Harlem where one of his teachers was the Harlem Renaissance poet Countee Cullen, who encouraged Baldwin's involvement in the school's literary club. Baldwin continued developing his interest in writing until undergoing a religious conversion when he was fourteen years old. Baldwin then turned his attention to preaching, but at seventeen, left the church and his home. Baldwin continued supporting his family financially by working in a defense plant and a meat-packing plant in New Jersey. When his stepfather died in 1943, Baldwin moved to Greenwich Village to pursue his literary dreams. It was during this period that Richard Wright befriended Baldwin and encouraged him to write *Go Tell It on the Mountain*, Baldwin's highly acclaimed first novel. Baldwin also wrote book reviews to help support himself even though he felt limited by editors who wanted book reviews only by African Americans. Unhappy in America, Baldwin moved in 1948 to Paris, where he found a blurring of racial lines and greater acceptance of his homosexuality. Baldwin continued writing fiction and essays, eventually settling in St. Paul de

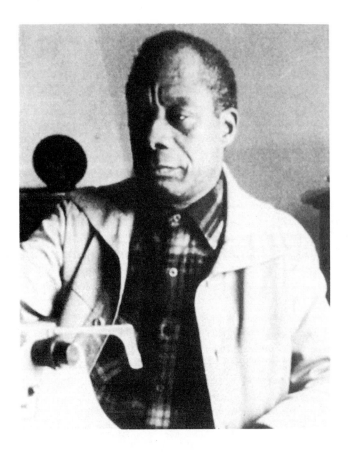

Vence, the French countryside town where he lived until the end of his life.

Major Works

Baldwin's novels tackle personal issues in his life as well as larger social issues, including race relations and sexuality. Baldwin's first novel, *Go Tell It on the Mountain*, is a semi-autobiographical account of Baldwin's adolescence. The main character, a thirteen-year-old boy named John, is saved in the Baptist church where his stepfather is a preacher. As John undergoes conversion, his stepfather and the rest of the characters recall their past sins, struggling with questions of faith as well. In *Giovanni's Room* (1956), Baldwin moves on from adolescence to confront his homosexuality. Set in Paris, this controversial novel tells the story of an ill-fated love affair between a white American student and an Italian bartender. In Baldwin's *Another Country* (1962), the protagonist is Rufus Scott, a jazz musician who makes friends with a group of whites. The novel traces Scott's relationships with his best friend Vivaldo and his white lover Leona. There are further subplots that trace the sexual interactions of the other homosexual and heterosexual characters. The novel, *Tell Me How Long the Train's Been Gone* (1968), tells the story of Leo Proudhammer, a famous black artist who becomes trapped in his public persona, losing his personal identity and convictions along the way. *If Beale Street Could Talk* (1974) is about Fonny Hunts, another artistic and intellectual protagonist. The story is narrated by Tish, Hunts's nineteen-year-old fiancee who is pregnant with his child. Hunts is imprisoned after he is falsely accused of raping a Puerto Rican woman. In the end, Hunts finds his salvation in love and in the birth of his son. Baldwin used essays to examine race relations. In his collection of essays, *The Fire Next Time* (1963), he argues that the lives and futures of whites and African Americans are inextricably intertwined. Although he respected Malcolm X, Baldwin was opposed to Malcolm's ideas about separation of the races and the superiority of African Americans. Baldwin's essays underwent a change in position with *No Name in the Street* (1972), which asserts the independence of African Americans and the possible necessity of violence against whites. In this book, Baldwin also asserts that an African American—by virtue of his powerlessness—could never be racist.

Critical Reception

Critics often discuss the fire-and-brimstone nature of Baldwin's prose even though his relationship to Christianity remains ambiguous. For part of his career during the early 1960s, Baldwin was considered "the" voice for African-Americans. However, Baldwin never intended to be a spokesman for his race. He saw himself as an intellectual who explored ideas and did not espouse a certain message. This disappointed many readers and reviewers, who dismissed Baldwin because he appeared opposed to the ideals of African-American liberation. Baldwin's ideas were seldom straightforward, and critics often accused him of espousing conflicting ideas. However, Henry Louis Gates, Jr. asserted, "As an intellectual, Baldwin was at his best when he explored his own equivocal sympathies and clashing allegiances." Many critics—including younger African American artists—accused Baldwin of hating himself, African Americans, and capitulating to whites. Others saw more subtlety in Baldwin's work, viewing his writing as a contribution to intellectual discourse on the subject of race relations. Reviewers often criticized Baldwin's fiction for its lack of artistic merit. Hilton Als argued, "It was in Baldwin's essays, unencumbered by the requirements of narrative form, character, and incident, that his voice was most fully realized." However, others—including Andrew Shin and Barbara Judson—disagreed. Shin and Judson said, "The novels, however, despite their poor critical reception, are interesting because they rarely capitulate to the urge for a simplified rhetoric that characterizes the essays of the early 1970s, persistently retaining the unresolved tension and complex-

ity of a writer—a gay black writer no less—divided between his role as a popular spokesman for the race and his role as an artist whose imaginative life encompasses aesthetic standards that may alienate a popular audience." Baldwin's homosexuality also was a sticking point with many who reviewed his work. Many saw his sexuality as an attack on black masculinity. Baldwin's supporters even turned on him after he changed his position, recanting his previous work and realigning his opinions to mirror mainstream African American discourse. Nevertheless, many reviewers still found ambivalence in Baldwin's fiction in his portrayal of African Americans. Following the publication of Baldwin's collected works, *The Price of the Ticket* (1985), critics now find his early essays an important contribution to the discourse of race relations in America.

PRINCIPAL WORKS

Go Tell It on the Mountain (novel) 1953

The Amen Corner (play) 1955

Notes of a Native Son (essays) 1955

Giovanni's Room (novel) 1956; also published as a play, 1957

Nobody Knows My Name: More Notes of a Native Son (essays) 1961

Another Country (novel) 1962

The Fire Next Time (essays) 1963

Blues for Mister Charlie (play) 1964

Going to Meet the Man (short stories) 1965

This Morning, This Evening, So Soon (novella) 1967

Tell Me How Long the Train's Been Gone (novel) 1968

Black Anti-Semitism and Jewish Racism [with others] (essays) 1969

Menschenwurde und Gerechtigkeit [with Kenneth Kaunda] (essays) 1969

No Name in the Street (essays) 1972

A Deed from the King of Spain (play) 1974

If Beale Street Could Talk (novel) 1974

The Devil Finds Work (essays) 1976

Little Man, Little Man: A Story of Childhood (novel) 1976

Just above My Head (novel) 1979

Jimmy's Blues: Selected Poems (poetry) 1983

The Price of the Ticket: Collected Nonfiction (nonfiction) 1985

Harlem Quartet (novel) 1987

CRITICISM

Wilfrid Sheed (essay date 1977)

SOURCE: "The Twin Urges of James Baldwin," in *The Good Word & Other Words*, 1978, pp. 194-200.

[*In the following essay, which was published in 1977 in Commonweal, Sheed complains that the tone of Baldwin's* The Devil Finds Work *sounds false and that the subject of movies does not support the book's religious undertone.*]

When James Baldwin goes wrong (as he has taken to doing lately), it usually seems less a failure of talent than of policy. Of all our writers he is one of the most calculating. Living his life on several borderlines, he has learned to watch his step: driven at the same time by an urge to please and a mission to scold.

In his early days, the twin urges came together to make very good policy indeed. White liberals craved a spanking and they got a good one. But then too many amateurs joined in the fun, all the Raps and Stokelys and Seales, until even liberal guilt gave out. And now the times seem to call for something a little different. **The Devil Finds Work** shows Baldwin groping for it—not just because he's a hustler, at least as writers go, but because he has a genuine quasi-religious vocation. In the last pages he richly describes a church ceremony he went through as a boy, akin to attaining the last mansions of mysticism: and you have to do *something* after that. Your work, even your atheism, will always taste of religion.

And this is the first problem we come across in the new book. Because the subject is movies, and most movies simply do not accommodate such religious passion. So his tone sounds false. He may or may not feel that strongly about movies (it's hard to believe), but sincerity isn't the issue. A preacher doesn't have to feel what he says every Sunday: rhetoric is an art, and Baldwin practices it very professionally. But the sermon's subject must be at least in the same ball park as the style, or you get bathos, the sermon that fails to rise.

Since Baldwin is too intelligent not to notice this, we get an uneasy compromise between old habits and new possibilities. The folks pays him to preach (to use his own self-mocking language), so he turns it on mechanically, almost absentmindedly, lapsing at times into incoherence, as if he's fallen asleep at the microphone. But since getting mad at the movies is only one step removed from getting mad at the funnies, he escapes periodically in two directions, one bad and one good.

The bad one is to change the subject outrageously in order to raise the emotional ante: thus there are several references to how white people like to burn babies that totally stumped me. A prophet should disturb all levels of opinion and must therefore be something of a precisionist. But this stuff passes harmlessly overhead. Blacks have been known to kill babies too, in Biafra and elsewhere, but nobody said they like it. People apt to be reading Baldwin at all have long since graduated from this level of rant. He may write for the masses, but he is read by the intelligentsia.

But his second escape at times almost makes up for the first: which is simply to talk about movies according to their kind, with amusement, irony, and his own quirky insights. More writers should do this: we were raised as much in the movie house as the library, and it's pretentious to go on blaming it all on Joyce. In Baldwin's case a movie case history is doubly valuable because his angle is so solitary, shaped by no gang and deflected by no interpretation, and shared only with a white woman teacher, herself a solitary. Nobody ever saw these movies quite the way he did, or ever will.

Unfortunately the childhood section is tantalizingly short, and the adult's voice horns in too often, but some fine things come through: in particular the way the young Baldwin had to convert certain white actors into blacks, even as white basketball fans reverse the process today, in order to identify. Thus, Henry Fonda's walk made him black, and Joan Crawford's resemblance to a woman in the local grocery store made her black, while Bette Davis's popping eyes made her not only black but practically Jimmy himself.

This is vintage Baldwin: and if he lacks confidence in his softer notes he shouldn't (his sentimental notes are another matter). He does not automatically *have* to lecture us on every topic he writes about. In this more urbane mode, his racial intrusions often make good sense. For instance, in checking *A Tale of Two Cities* against what he has learned in the streets he perhaps inadvertently suggests to this reader, at least, how Dickens might have veered away from what *he* had learned in the streets. In fact, Baldwin's whole treatment of this story suggests a potential literary critic, if he'd calm down for a minute.

This section ends with a valuable addition to Baldwin's early autobiography: a corpus to which one had thought no further additions were possible. He discovers the theater and loses his religion almost at the same moment. The reality of stage actors playing Macbeth is enough to blow away even that encounter with the Holy Ghost. And as if to symbolize this, he literally tiptoes out of church one Sunday and heads downtown for a show: taking, as he says in another context, his church with him.

If stage acting could transplant God, it utterly demolished screen acting for him. "Canada Lee [in *Native Son*] was Bigger Thomas, but he was also Canada Lee: his physical presence, like the physical presence of Paul Robeson, gave me the right to live. He was not at the mercy of my imagination as he would have been, on the screen: he was on the stage, in flesh and blood, and I was, therefore, at the mercy of *his* imagination." If you're raised an incarnational Christian (and it's hard to image another kind), flesh and blood can easily become food and drink to you. Henceforth in even the silliest play, the actors' presence would thrust reality through at Baldwin; conversely, only the greatest of actors could insert physicality into a movie, and that fleetingly.

His own course was set. Embodied reality, thick, hot, and tangible, is Baldwin's grail, even jerking him loose from his own rhetoric. So he became a man of the stage, dealing with real people and not their images; and he wrote some of his best work for it—including my own favorite, *The Amen Corner,* in which he uses the stage to exorcise the Church once and for all. Only to come out more religious than ever—only at random now, passionately foraging for Good and Evil in race, in sex, even in Norman Mailer.

Perhaps, then, not the ideal man to write about movies. The magic element which is their particular genius is precisely what maddens his fundamentalist soul the most. Like Pascal at the real theater, he sees nothing but lies up there. Although he seems to know something about the craft of movies, it doesn't interest or charm him in the least. His book has no pictures, which is unusual in a film book, but quite appropriate for this one. Because even the stills would be lies.

Specifically lies about race. And here we have a right to expect the latest news from Baldwin and not a rehash. I assume he is still a black spokesman in good standing. Although his book is disarmingly datelined from France, which is nearer the *pied-noir* country, there must be a victims' network of information which keeps him up to date. But his personal witness, his strength, has begun to sound tentative. He talks of being terrorized in some Southern town, but he can't remember what year or, apparently, the distinction between one town and another. "It is hard to be accurate concerning the pace of my country's progress." Very hard from St. Paul de Vence. We can get fresher testimony than that every day of the week.

Anyhow for Baldwin there is still just something called the South, unchanging and indivisible, and the liberals down there might as well pack up shop. It's a bleak picture and if Baldwin sees any lift in the clouds he either isn't telling or he rejects it as a dangerous illusion, an invitation to drop one's guard. For instance, in the dopey film *In the Heat of the Night,* there is a scene where the white sheriff humbles himself to carry Sidney Poitier's bags, and Baldwin sees for a moment something "choked and moving" in this, only to round on it sternly as a dangerous daydream. "White Americans have been encouraged to keep on dreaming, and black Americans have been alerted to the necessity of waking up."

So paranoia, as before, is his message to blacks, and a white reviewer is in no position to question it. Since no improvement is to be trusted, the implicit solution is revolution, and

Baldwin talks airily of seizing property as if this were still the slaphappy sixties when all seemed possible. For the moment, revolutionary rant seems as remote as the evangelism that used to pacify blacks: but again, Baldwin isn't quite calling for it, only toying with it. His new position is still very much in the works.

Meanwhile, offscreen, geographical distance may have obscured some of the social nuances Baldwin usually pounces on so swiftly and surely. He talks, for instance, of whites being terrified of blacks, and blacks being enraged by whites, as if this blanketed the case. But one of the odd things that happened in the sixties was that the blacks became largely de-mystified, for better or worse. By accepting such drugstore rebels as Rap Brown and Stokely Carmichael at their own valuation, we let ourselves in for one of the greatest letdowns in memory. The black enigma was transformed overnight into the black chatterbox. Although, as Claude Brown once said privately, these men could not have rounded up ten followers in Harlem, they told us they were leaders, so we took them for leaders. And we were relieved to find they were not the brooding giants that Baldwin had conjured, but just average publicity hounds.

Because of this comical misunderstanding, many whites ceased being impressed by blacks altogether, except such as carried knives, and a new psychic alignment occurred that Baldwin should come home and tell us about. The problem now is not so much fear as deepening indifference. Baldwin still writes as though our souls were so hag-ridden by race that even our innocent entertainments reflect it. And he gives us the old castration folderol as if it were piping hot. But the news I hear is different. Many whites now go for years without thinking about blacks at all. The invisible man has returned. And as *de facto* segregation continues to settle like mold, his future seems assured.

On the black side of the fence, one simply has to take him on trust. Young blacks today *seem* more confident than Baldwin's prototypes but it might only take a few full-time bigots plus some ad hoc recruits—as in South Boston—to chip the paint off this. What one can question, by the current division of racist labor, is his account of the white psyche. Because here again he simply says nothing that a contemporary reader can use. His white men sound at times exactly like Susan Brownmiller's rapists, whom that author also transformed into Everyman, and in fact like all the hyperaggressive bullies you've ever met: and these surely come in all colors.

Of such movies as *Death Wish* or *Straw Dogs* or the worst of Clint Eastwood (if such there be) or black exploitation films—in short all the movies that validate bullying on one side or another and make it chic—he says nothing except, tantalizingly, of the latter that they "make black experience irrelevant and obsolete" (his own, or everyone's?). If by chance he has not seen the others, in particular *Death Wish,* the mugger-killing wet dream, he has wandered unarmed into the one subject Americans really know about.

Baldwin's weakness as a prophet is to suppose that the rest of us experience life as intensely as he does; and his strength is roughly the same. If his overall sociology is suspect right now, his ability to enlarge a small emotion so that we can all see it is not. And this perhaps rescues him even as a writer about movies.

Throughout, his eyes swarm greedily over the screen, scavenging for small truths. And although brotherhood epics like *In the Heat of the Night* and *Guess Who's Coming to Dinner* were flailed insensible by white critics, leaving precious little to pick on, in each case he finds some scene or other even richer in phoniness, or closer to truth, than we suspected. For instance, in the latter film, he has a passage on a successful black son's relation to his father that probably no one else would have thought of. While for the former, he provides such a droll plot summary that the absurdity jumps a dimension.

He is also good on *The Defiant Ones* and *Lawrence of Arabia* though here one senses that he is not saying all he knows. He talks at one point of the seismographic shudder Americans experience at the word "homosexual," but he handles it pretty much like a hot potato himself: talking around and around it without quite landing on it. Again this is policy (the word homosexual does go off like a fire alarm, reminding us to put up our dukes) but in this case, I think, too much policy. When Baldwin holds back something it distorts his whole manner. The attempt to seduce is too slick. And this, just as much as his compulsion to preach when there's nothing to preach about, diverts him from his real lover, truth. He is not seeing those movies as an average black man, but as a unique exile, and the pose is beginning to wear thin.

So, the tension remains. He has been away a long time and I'm sure he has a story to tell about that, perhaps his best one yet. It is hard to believe that in Paris and Istanbul his mind was really on American movies: but they might have been something in the attic that he wanted to get rid of. And the attempt is worthwhile if only for the sake of some sprightly lines, to wit, "J. Edgar Hoover, history's most highly paid (and most utterly useless) *voyeur,*" and random bangs and flashes. He even talks several times of *human* weakness (as opposed to white weakness)—including his own: which suggests that the hanging judge may be ready to come down from his perch and mix it with us.

But for now he remains up there wagging his finger sternly at the converted and the bored. And with so many clergy-

men, he too often deduces Reality solely by intelligence in this book, and while he has more than enough of that quality, it tends to fly off in bootless directions unless anchored by touch. He is right to love the stage. His art needs real bodies. But anyone who sees reality as clearly as Baldwin does must be tempted at times to run like the wind; and perhaps, for just a little while, he's done that. After all, that's what movies are for—even for those preachers who denounce them the loudest.

James Baldwin with Quincy Troupe (interview date 1987)

SOURCE: "The Last Interview," in *James Baldwin: The Legacy,* edited by Quincy Troupe, Simon and Schuster, 1989, pp. 186-212.

[*In the following interview, Baldwin discusses his relationships, his writing, other writers, and America.*]

[Baldwin]: It all comes back now.

[*Troupe*]: *When did you first meet Miles?*

Oh, a long time ago, on West Seventy-seventh Street at his house.

What were the circumstances?

I'm trying to remember, I was living on West End Avenue then, early sixties. What was I doing at his home? I hadn't met him, but I admired him very much. But I think I met him before that. Yes, I remember. I first met him in the Village, when he was playing at the Café Bohemia. Then I met him at Club Beverly, on Seventy-fifth Street. But that was a long time ago, too, But, I'm trying to remember what I was doing at Miles's house. I don't remember. Anyway, it was a Sunday afternoon and Miles had invited me, he was having a kind of brunch. So there I was, there in Miles's presence. It was, at first, overwhelming, because I'm really shy. I remember there being a whole lot of people. Miles was at the other end of the room. At first he was upstairs, invisible. Then he was downstairs talking to someone he knew as Moonbeam. Still, he was visible, but barely. Finally he was standing in the room, visible, and so I went over to him. Miles looked like a little boy at the time, he looked about ten. So there I was trying to figure out what to say. Finally I told him how much I liked and admired him. I told him I liked his music very much and he said something like, "Are you sure?" He kind of smiled. Then he talked with me. Then we sort of knew each other. So the ice had been broken, so that ah, you know, how it is with friends, though I don't know if he thinks of me as a friend. I don't know what other people see. But I could see that there was something in Miles and me which was very much alike. I can see much of myself in Miles. And yet, I don't know what it is, can't explain it, but I think it has something to do with extreme vulnerability.

Extreme vulnerability? In what sense?

First of all, you know, with what we look like, being black, which means that in special ways we've been maltreated. See, we evolve a kind of mask, kind of persona, you know, to protect us from, ah, all these people who are carnivorous and they think you're helpless. Miles does it one way, I do it another.

How do you do it?

I keep people away by seeming not to be afraid of them, by moving fast.

And how does he do it?

In his language, by saying "bitch." Miles said when he saw me signing an autograph, "Why don't you tell the motherfuckers to get lost? What the fuck makes you think I think you can read?" I never saw him very often, but there was always a kind of shorthand between us, that nothing would ever change between us. Like Miles has come to visit me, here in St. Paul on a number of occasions when he's over here in France, playing. And you know Miles doesn't visit people. And even when he visits, he never says much, he doesn't say anything. Not all the time, however; it depends on how the spirit moves him.

So he just shows.

He just shows up here, knocks at the door. Sometimes he calls, but he may just show.

When was the last time?

A couple of summers ago.

He called and said, "I'm coming."

No. I think what happened, he was staying in Nice, so his French manager called and asked me to come and have dinner and cocktails. It was a nice night. And afterwards, he came back here.

He came out here?

Yeah. We sat around and talked about nothing.

You think he came because he feels safe with you.

Yeah. We talked about nothing and everything and we would have a little sip and we would talk about whatever. But I do the same with some people I know.

Why do you think he feels this way with you, since he's afraid of writers?

I don't think Miles thinks of me as a writer. He knows I'm a writer, but he doesn't look at me that way. He doesn't look at me that way at all. I think he thinks of me as a brother, you know? In many ways I have the same difficulty as he has, in terms of the private and public life. In terms of the legend. It's difficult to be a legend. It's hard for me to recognize *me*. You spend a lot of time trying to avoid it. A lot of the time I've been through so many of the same experiences Miles has gone through. It's really something, to be a legend, unbearable. I could see it had happened to Miles. Again, it's unbearable, the way the world treats you is unbearable, and especially if you're black.

What is that?

It's unbearable because time is passing and you are not your legend, but you're trapped in it. Nobody will let you out of it. Except other people who know what it is. But very few people have experienced it, know about it, and I think that can drive you mad; I know it can. It had a terrible effect on him and it had a terrible effect on me. And you don't see it coming.

You don't see it coming? Explain why?

No way to see it.

How do you realize it?

You have to be lucky. You have to have friends. I think at bottom you have to be serious. No one can point it out to you; you have to see it yourself. That's the only way you can act on it. And when it arrives it's a great shock.

To find out?

It's a great shock to realize that you've been so divorced. So divorced from who you think you are—from who you really are. Who you think you are, you're not at all. The only thing is that Miles has got his horn and I've got my typewriter. We are both angry men.

I want to ask you what you were trapped in and how did you come to see it. I mean, did you come through friends?

I know what you're saying but it's hard to answer, it's hard.

I know it's hard.

I don't know how to answer that.

But you saw yourself trapped?

I saw myself trapped. I think it happened to Miles, too.

What did you think you were, before you knew?

Ah, that's even more interesting. I don't know who I thought I was. I was a witness, I thought. I was a very despairing witness, though too. What I was actually doing was trying to avoid a certain estrangement, perhaps, an estrangement between myself and my generation. It was virtually complete, the estrangement was, in terms of what I might have thought and expected—my theories. About what I might have hoped—I'm talking now in terms of one's function as an artist. And the country itself being black and trying to deal with that.

Why do you think it occurred. That estrangement between you generation and the country?

Well, because I was right. That's a strange way to put it.

That's not strange, at least not to me.

I *was* right. I was right about what was happening in the country. What was about to happen to all of us really, one way or the other. And the choices people would have to make. And watching people make them and denying them at the same time. I began to feel more and more homeless in terms of the whole relationship between France and me and America, and *me* has always been a little painful, you know. Because my family's in America I will always go back. It couldn't have been a question in my mind unless it absolutely really came to that. But in the meantime you keep the door open and the price of keeping the door open was to actually be, in a sense, victimized by my own legend. You know, I was trying to tell the truth and it takes a long time to realize that you can't—that there's no point in going to the mat, so to speak, no point in going to Texas again. There's no point in saying this again. It's been said, and it's been said, and it's been said. It's been heard and not heard. You are a broken motor.

A broken motor?

Yes. You're a running motor and you're repeating, you're repeating, you're repeating, and it causes a breakdown, lessening of will power. And sooner or later your will gives out, it has to. You're lucky if it is a physical matter. Most times it's spiritual. See, all this involves hiding from something else—not dealing with how lonely you are. And of course, at the very bottom it involves the terror of every artist confronted with what he or she has to do, you know, the next

work. And everybody, in one way or another, and to some extent, tries to avoid it. And you avoid it more when you get older than you do when you're younger; still there's something terrifying about doing the work. Something like that. But it happened to Miles sooner than it happened to me. I think for me it was lucky that it was physical, because it could have been mental.

It could have been mental?

Yes. It could have been mental debilitation instead of my present physical one. I prefer the physical to the mental. Does that make sense?

It makes good sense, it makes fantastic sense. Now let me ask you something else. Now with Miles, you both were born close to each other?

Just about. I think I'm a year older. I was born in '24.

He was born in '26. So then, probably both of you, black men, geniuses, born close together, probably see the world very similar—you through your typewriter and him through his horn. Both vulnerable. So when you met you were brothers because you expected to meet each other or were you looking for each other?

Yes. We were looking for each other. Neither he nor I would have said it that way but we were; we knew that the moment we saw each other.

You were hoping?

Oh yes. That's why I was watching him before he watched me, you know.

But he knew you.

He knew about me. Yes.

He knew you when he saw you.

There's no question about that at all. We knew each other at once.

That's wonderful.

Yes it is, discovering someone very much like yourself. It was wonderful.

And that's a wonderful connection. Because he's also estranged somewhat from his musical generation.

He has to be, at least it makes sense to me that he would

be, because he's always trying to be on the cutting edge of his art. That's certainly true for me.

In the windows of your eyes, you and Miles remind me of each other. It's a certain distinctive juju.

Shit, I love that.

It's a certain distinctive juju that in Miles you recognize and you see a face that you have not seen before. And when I look at you and since I've always looked at you, I've always felt that. A certain juju, witch doctor, priest, high priest look of timelessness or representative of a certain tribe, point of view, mysticism, magic.

That would cover my father certainly. He was not really my father, because I was born out of wedlock, but that's the difference, my father. He did give me something. Don't you see, he taught me how to fight. He taught me how to fight. But it would be better to say he taught me what to fight for. I was only fighting for safety, or for money at first. Then I fought to make you look to me. Because I was not born to be what someone said I was. I was not born to be defined by someone else, but by myself, and myself only.

So when you were younger, you didn't have the pen as a weapon, as a defense, a shield. How did you fight then?

Any way I could.

What would you do?

It's hard to remember. The pulpit was part of it, but that came later.

Before the pulpit.

It was the streets.

How did you fight? Any way you could?

Well, if you wanted to beat me up, okay. And, say, you were bigger than I was, you could do it, you could beat me, but you gonna have to do it every day.

Every day? Because you would fight to the death.

You'd have to beat me up every single day. So then the question becomes which one of us would get tired first. And I knew it wouldn't be me.

You would always fight.

Oh, yes, indeed. So then the other persons would have to begin to think, and to be bugged by this kid he had to beat up every day. And some days perhaps he just didn't feel like doing it. But he would have to, yeah, because he said he was going to do it. So then come beat me up. But of course something happened to him, something has to happen to him—because someone beating someone else up is not so easy either. Because I would be standing in the schoolyard with a lead pipe as a deterrent. So, you know, eventually, it was just too dangerous. People began to leave me alone. Some of the big boys who were my friends got together and decided that they had to protect me, you know? So after that I was really protected. Because it was funny to them after a while. But that's what happened. That was the beginning of it and then later on it was cops, you know. It became just a nightmare. Especially cops. I knew that they knew that I was seven or eight or nine and they were just having fun with me. They wanted me to beg. And I couldn't beg, so I got my ass kicked. But I learned a lot, a lot about them. I learned there were very few who were humane; they just wanted you to say what they wanted you to say. They wanted to be confirmed in something by you. By your face, by your terror of them.

What about the pulpit, the idea of the pulpit? Would you talk about it as an idea?

That's a very complex idea really. I joined the Church, but my joining it was very complex, though I meant it, the purely religious part that is, the spiritual part. In a way that was very important to me, that whole time in the pulpit, because it gave me a kind of distance that was kind of respected; that was a reason I was in the pulpit, to put distance between people and myself. I began to see my people, so to speak, both ethnically and otherwise. And in the time that I was in the pulpit I learned a lot about my father. And later on, I thought, perhaps, I'd moved into the pulpit in order to arrest him. Because I thought that he had to be arrested, had to be stopped. He was having a terrible effect on everybody in the family. I could go as far as to say I thought he was crazy. But I knew with myself and the pulpit I cut a lot of his power. He couldn't fight me in that arena. He fought me, but he couldn't fight me in that arena. And I say during that time that it taught me a lot about him and myself and about the people who were in the congregation, whom I couldn't lie to. And that was why I left the pulpit.

Is that where you started to learn about the truth? I mean you knew about the truth when you were talking about when you knew you weren't going to give in.

I couldn't.

So then in the pulpit you learned another truth. And in the writing you take it . . .

I knew that was where I had to go. That I was not going to

become another fat preacher, you know? I was not going to, ah, lie to my congregation. I was not allowed to do that. I couldn't believe in what I had anymore. I didn't believe in the Christian Church anymore, not the way I had; I no longer believed in its spirituality, its healing powers.

Oh? Was it the Christian Church that disturbed you?

The way people treated each other. In the Church and outside, but especially in the Church.

How did they treat each other?

Well, they were so self-righteous. They didn't come with real deep love, for example. The people in the Church were very cruel about many things.

How old were you when you were involved in the Church?

Fourteen, fifteen.

Okay. I want you now to talk about two extraordinary women that your brother David told me about. Jeanne Fauré, who used to own the house you live in now, and Tintine. I want you, at first, if you can, to talk to me about how you came to this house. And how you came to receive the medal of honor.

Oh, that's a long story.

I know. But can you talk about it, if you can, how she came to accept you, why she accepted you, and what it was that you saw in each other?

I came here to St. Paul in 1970. It was Malcolm X's and Martin Luther King's death really. After Martin's death I sort of wandered and indeed didn't know where to go. I was in Turkey for a while, then I ended up here. I didn't want to leave; I had to. I ended up across the street from this house in a hotel. I came in the wintertime, nineteen years ago. Anyway, I and a friend of mine came down to St. Paul from Paris. We didn't have anything because it was terribly expensive at the hotel and so we settled here because at the time it also served as a roominghouse. Later I got sick, you know, and much of my family came over to see me. I rented almost all of the house. So I thought why not buy it. It was forty-three, forty-six thousand and I had been very ill so I didn't know how much longer I had to live. So I bought it. But Madame Fauré had offered to sell it to me.

This was earlier?

Yes. When I first came, nineteen-some odd years ago.

What was wrong with you, can you remember what was the illness?

Nobody knew. Nobody knew. But anyway, I needed some money to buy the house. That occupied me for a while that occupied me considerably. But I was just busy working. And I got to know Jeanne Fauré, who was a very strange lady, solitary, very strange.

How would you describe her strangeness?

In her solitude. She was a kind of legend, she was very old, you know, quite. And anyway, she and I had very little in common, it seemed to me, except I liked her very much. She was a refugee from Algeria, raised in Algeria, I believe, and then the French had to leave. And she was very bitter about that. That meant we had very little in common politically. And very little in common in what I could see in any other way. And yet there was something else beneath that made her my friend. She decided to sell the house to me; she refused to sell it to anybody else.

She decided to sell the house to you? Why do you think she picked you? Do you know to this day?

No.

Was it spiritual?

Yes.

Cosmic.

I wasn't the best candidate; in fact, I was the worst. Something in her, I don't know. We also had a very stormy relationship.

Stormy?

Politically speaking we did. In many other ways we did, too. She knew something I didn't know. She knew about Europe, she knew about civilization, she knew about responsibility. A million things that I as an American would not know, that were alien to me. And I was very slow to learn these things. In fact, it was a very expensive lesson, one that I haven't learned entirely just yet. But she was a valuable kind of guide and a kind of protection. And Tintine Roux was the old lady that ran La Colombe D'Or, which is a world-famous restaurant and inn. She became my guardian. I never lived in a small town before, which is not so easy, and she protected me. I could come in and have lunch at her restaurant. And I didn't realize it at first, that she had picked herself to be my protector.

What do you think she saw in you?

I don't know.

What do you think?

I knew Tintine liked me. Still she must have thought I was crazy, you know, at least a little strange, in any event. But both these women liked me. It was as thought they recognized where I came from. That I was a peasant, and I am. But I've only found this out over time.

Why do you say that?

I'm a peasant because of where I really come from, you know. My background, my father, my mother, the line. Something of the peasant must be in all of my family. And that's where Madame Fauré and Tintine come from, too. And the color of my skin didn't add into it at all. Both these women were watching something else besides my color. And they protected me and loved me. They're both dead now and I miss them both terribly. Because with Jeanne I truly learned a lot from her, from her European optic in regard to others; but she also had an optic that came from Algeria. What I liked about it was that she was willing to be my guide; willing and unwilling: in fact, she was a hard guide. But mostly she was willing. And so it seemed like she was my guide to something else.

What?

To a way of life, to a potential civilization she had seen only from a height.

Didn't they know about your fame?

No, not really. They'd heard of me. But beyond that, nothing.

You were comfortable with that.

Yes. Because my fame did not get in the way because by the time they knew it didn't make any difference. It was just one more aspect of this crazy kid. That's the best way to put it. They were my guides, and they were very good guides.

David told me a story about an incident that happened when her brother died, and Madame Fauré picked you to be at the head of the funeral procession.

He told you that? Well, she was the last of kin and she made me lead her brother Louis's funeral procession. Yes she did. She put her arm in mine and I had to lead. I had to. It was an incredible scene. I had to lead the funeral procession with her or she with me. It was fascinating.

I think it's a great image. Tell me about it. How did you feel?

I was in a state of shock. I didn't know what to do. And of course the people of St. Paul were shocked, too. This was in either 1974 or '75. But I was in a state of shock. I didn't quite know what to think; in fact, the town was in a state of shock.

What was the reason?

Well, they knew who I was by then, of course, but they couldn't understand why I was representing the family. When we were at the cemetery everybody had to say goodbye to me, too. Because I was standing there with her at the head of the family, under the gates of the cemetery. Because what it meant, symbolically speaking, is that I was the next in line, when she died. That's what it meant.

Do you think that could have happened in America?

I can't imagine where. I really cannot imagine where.

So in a sense that was a comforting, human experience. A remarkable spiritual connection, bond.

A very great thing, very great. At least for me. I want to write about it one day. Yes, sometime I'll have to talk about it.

When you received the Legion of Honor of France? Who did you take with you to the ceremony?

David came over. Jeanne Fauré was there and my housekeeper Valerie was there too.

Why did you pick them?

Because they had seen me through so much and I'd promised to take Jeanne and Valerie to Paris one day. Jeanne had been to Paris but she hadn't been there for a long time. I thought that would be nice for her to go. So I took them and because I owed it to them, but especially to Jeanne Fauré. Because she'd seen me through.

And how did she feel?

She was very proud. She didn't say anything to me; she never said much to me about it. But I could see it—how proud she was—in her face, in her eyes.

What year was this?

Last year, 1986.

Was that right before she died?

Yes. She died in the winter of 1987.

What month was that?

I received the award in June, and she died in January 1987.

And how did you feel with her being there?

I was very pleased. It was very nice. It was something that gave her a great pleasure and that meant a lot to me.

I thought that was a great story when he told me. I said I was definitely going to ask you about that. Because I thought that was fundamentally fantastic and so fundamentally, in a sense, spiritually right; but it's something which you don't expect to happen.

No, you don't, not at all.

Who gave you the award?

The president, the president of France, François Mitterrand. The ceremony was at the Élysée in Paris.

What other people received the award that year?

Leonard Bernstein. Leonard Bernstein and me. It was a very nice ceremony, very nice.

Okay. Let's change the subject and talk about some writers. What is your opinion of Amiri Baraka?

I remember the first time I met Amiri Baraka, who was then Le Roi Jones. I was doing **The Amen Corner** and he was a student at Howard University. I liked him right away. He was a pop-eyed little boy, a poet. He showed me a couple of his poems. I liked them very much. And then he came to New York a couple of years later. He came to New York when I came back to New York from Paris. And by this time I knew the business. I'd been through the fucking business by that time. I was a survivor. And I remember telling him that his agent wanted him to become the young James Baldwin. But I told him, "You're not the young James Baldwin. There's only one James Baldwin and you are Le Roi Jones and there's only one Le Roi Jones. Don't let them run this game on us, you know? You're Le Roi Jones, I'm James Baldwin. And we're going to need each other." That's all I said. He didn't believe it then but time took care of that.

He believes it now?

Yes, he knows it now.

What person has hurt you the most recently?

Ishmael Reed.

Why?

Because he is a great poet and it seemed to be beneath him, his anger and his contempt for me, which were both real and not real. He ignored me for so long and then he called me a cocksucker, you know what I mean? It's boring. But I always did say he was a great poet, a great writer. But that does not mean I can put up with being insulted by him every time I see him, which I won't.

What do you think about Toni Morrison?

Toni's my ally and it's really probably too complex to get into. She's a black woman writer, which in the public domain makes it more difficult to talk about.

Have you read Beloved?

Not yet. She sent it to me but I haven't read it yet.

What do you think are her gifts?

Her gift is in allegory. *Tar Baby* is an allegory. In fact all her novels are. But they're hard to talk about in public. That's where you get in trouble because her books and allegory are not always what it seems to be about. I was too occupied with my recent illness to deal with *Beloved*. But in general she's taken a myth, or she takes what seems to be a myth, and turns it into something else. I don't know how to put this—*Beloved* could be about the story of truth. She's taken a whole lot of things and turned them upside down. Some of them—you recognize the truth in it. I think that Toni's very painful to read.

Painful?

Yes.

Why?

Because it's always or most times a horrifying allegory; but you recognize that it works. But you don't really want to march through it. Sometimes people have a lot against Toni, but she's got the most believing story of everybody—this rather elegant matron, whose intentions really are serious and, according to some people, lethal.

I remember you saying that Alex Haley's Roots *had another title. What was it called first?*

It was called *Before the Anger*. But let me change the subject and just say this. It's very important for white Americans to believe their version of the black experience. That's why they have white and black commentators telling all those lies about us. You see, it's very important for the nigger to suffer. Therefore, they, white people, can feel guilty. Therefore, they can do something about it in their own good time. Let me again explain further. Once, after I published **Go Tell It on the Mountain** and **Giovanni's Room,** my publisher, Knopf, told me I was a "Negro writer" and that I "reached a certain audience." So, they told me, "you cannot afford to alienate that audience. This new book will ruin your career because you're not writing about the same things and in the same manner as you were before and we won't publish this book as a favor to you."

As a favor to you?

So I told them fuck you. My editor, whose name I won't mention here, is dead now, poor man. Later on, Bennett Cerf and I tangled too, but that was about a Christmas boycott of books we were planning.

So what did they say after you told them "fuck you"?

I told them I needed a boat ticket. So I took a boat to England with my book and I sold it in England before I sold it in America. You see whites want black writers to mostly deliver something as if it were an official version of the black experience. But the vocabulary won't hold it, simply. No true account really of black life can be held, can be contained in the American vocabulary. As it is, the only way that you can deal with it is by doing great violence to the assumptions on which the vocabulary is based. But they won't let you do that. And when you go along, you find yourself very quickly painted into a corner; you've written yourself into a corner. Because you can't compromise as a writer. By the time I left America in 1948 I had written myself into a corner as I perceived it. The book reviews and the short essays had led me to a place where I was on a collision course totally with the truth; it was the way I was operating. It was only a matter of time before I'd simply be destroyed by it. And no amount of manipulation of vocabulary or part would have spared me. It's like I think that Al Murray and Ralph Ellison are totally trapped. It's sad, because they're both trapped in the same way, and they're both very gifted writers. Ralph certainly, and Al, I thought. But you can't do anything with America unless you are willing to dissect it. You certainly cannot hope to fit yourself into it; nothing fits into it, not your past, not your present. The *Invisible Man* is fine as far as it goes until you ask yourself who's invisible to whom? You know, what is this dichotomy supposed to do? Are we invisible before each other? And invisible why, and by what system can one hope to be invisible? I don't know how anything in American life is worthy of this sacrifice. And further, I don't see anything in American life—for

myself—to aspire to. Nothing at all. It's all so very false. So shallow, so plastic, so morally and ethically corrupt.

We were talking once about the claustrophobia among writers. You said you prefer actors and painters to writers.

Yes. Well, first of all when I was coming up there weren't any writers that I knew. Langston Hughes was far away. The first writer I met was Richard Wright and he was much older than me. And the people I knew were people like Beauford Delaney and the women who hung out with him; it was a whole world that was not literary. That came later; then it wasn't literary. It came later in Paris, with Sartre and others. But there was something else. And in Paris it had nothing whatsoever to do with race for one thing. It was another kind of freedom there altogether. It had nothing to do with literature. But we can't talk about that. But when I looked back on it years and years later, looked back at myself on the American literary scene, I could see that what almost happened to me was an attempt to make myself fit in, so to speak, to wash clean for the American literary academy.

You mean they wanted you scrubbed and squeaky clean?

Exactly. You have to be scrubbed and squeaky clean and then there's nothing left of you. Let me tell you a story. When Ralph Ellison won the National Book Award in 1953 for *Invisible Man*, I was up for it the next near, in 1954, for **Go Tell It on the Mountain**. But at the time I was far from scrubbed. I didn't win. Then, years later, someone who was on the jury told me that since Ralph won it the year before they couldn't give it to a Negro two years in a row. Now, isn't that something?

A judge told you that? Can you tell us his name?

No, I wouldn't want to do that.

Okay. Do you have any comments on Norman Mailer?

Well the answer to that question is very short and very simple. Not simple, but short. Norman decided not to be a writer. He decided to be a celebrity instead and that's what he is now. Now let me tell you a story about Norman. Out of my father's first marriage there is a sister and a couple of sons, you know, a few sons. My sister had a brother who lives in California. He's a senior citizen now. But he lived with Norman Mailer when Norman was writing *The White Negro*. He was taking the pages out of Norman's typewriter, changing his clothes—they wore the same clothes, exchanged cars, and his car was better than Norman's at the time. He was like the second husband in a way. They lived together. They lived close together. Norman doesn't know I know this. No one knows this. This story took place in the forties, the early forties, in California. I've kept quiet about this all these years that Norman was living with one of my step-brothers when he wrote the book. No one knows it, though. You're the first one, outside of the family, that I have mentioned it to. His name is Osby Mitchell. Osby did something in show business, hung out with Frank Sinatra, Charlie Chaplin, that crowd.

Okay. That's something. Now, what do you think of the great praise you have received in France for **Just Above My Head**, *that it has gotten in translation. How does that make you feel?*

As you know the French call the book *Harlem Quartet.* I don't know how to answer that, Quincy, because it was written here almost ten years ago. It was the hardest book I'd ever written until then.

Why?

I had to face my own legends, too.

Which were?

It had something to do about my brothers, my relationship to my brothers. And that implied relationship to my whole life really. The key to one's life is always in a lot of unexpected places. I tried to deal with what I was most afraid of. That's why the vehicle of the book is music. Because music was and is my salvation. And when the book was done, I was glad it was over. It got the usual stormy reception in America, but by that time I was used to it. In any case, by that time I was in a different kind of trouble altogether. The reception of *Harlem Quartet* here in France didn't mean as much as it might have meant if I had gotten the praise earlier. I never thought I'd see the book again. But its translation came about after my book on the Atlanta murders was published here in France. It was hard to get the Atlanta book published in America for complex and political reasons.

Can you talk about them?

I don't quite know what they are. It's difficult for me to talk about a book that involves a possible lawsuit. It's just another example of American business, the ways in which Americans, the American publishers, attempt to control and to demolish the American writer, regardless of color, but especially a black one. I had to fight that, so I brought the book here. And it was published by Stock. And it did better than anyone thought it would do in France. So Stock already had a contract for *Just Above My Head (Harlem Quartet).* And so they published it. Stock had gone through all kinds of publishing problems—it had gone through a breakup and a reorganization. The Atlanta book won a couple of awards, and a German writer and I won the Human Rights Award of France two years ago, in 1985. But the

German writer, poor man, had to leave Germany. Anyway, behind all of this came this book *Just Above My Head,* or *Harlem Quartet.* And I think that the French for the first time really looked at my writing; the Atlanta book was something of a shock to them.

Why?

Because it demolishes, so to speak, the American myth of integration, you know, by using Atlanta, which is supposed to be the model of integration in the Deep South and exposes it for what it is; shit, you know? So the French reader goes through all of that in terms of those twenty-eight dead black children. And so it was a shock, you know. And it sort of set up, I don't know what, exactly, but it did set up expectations, or fears, whatever for the novel. It may have set up an audience for the novel. And so *Just Above My Head* turns out to be somewhat of a revelation for the French. So you know, I'm considered somewhat of an intellectual in Paris. I mean in France. For a black writer, you know? Essentially as an essayist. But the novel was a great revelation; it gave me another kind of reputation altogether. Because now, instead of an essayist, what they saw in me was a novelist. I'm much better known as an essayist in France and elsewhere, too, than I am as a novelist. Before, the translation of my novels in France have been so bad. But this was a good translation, a marvelous translation, which makes a tremendous difference. And the subject, my handing of the subject, they liked. So it's simply a matter of something happening at the right time, and that can never be foreseen, you know.

What's the award **Harlem Quartet** *is up for now?*

The best foreign novel published in France, the Prix Femina. We will know about that in a week.

Let me ask you about the difficulty the American press and critics might have had in getting into your fiction.

Well, probably the American legend of black life. It's one thing to be aware of a Miles Davis and quite another thing to know where he comes from and what sustains him. Hollywood should be sued for libel, it's true. So that the book, my book, and others come as a direct opposition of the myth by Americans of black life and black music. It's not like what they, the press and critics, say it is, not at all. But the books prove them wrong, so they ignore the books. You see what I mean? Like I very much liked the film 'Round Midnight, which is a very important film. It fills in something that is important in our lives, a gap that was once there, that one might have thought about but didn't know about.

Why do you say it's important?

Well, first of all the personality of Dexter Gordon, he gives at least a reading of what happens to the musician. The black musician inside the music industry in Paris, you know? The ruin that they met which they brought with them and which wasn't brought about by Paris.

You mean the black musicians brought the ruin with them?

Yes, that's precisely what I mean. And *'Round Midnight* makes that point in some ways very clearly.

Can you talk about the neglect of the black painter Beauford Delaney?

That's hard to do because people are still lying about Beauford. Let's talk about that over supper.

Okay. You said something to me once about how people shouldn't be jealous of someone's success. Do you recall that?

Well, what I was really trying to say was that people don't know what it is sometimes to be very successful. Don't know what it is. What I meant to say was that you can't be jealous of somebody else's success because you have no idea what it means, you know? It looks like success to you, but you're not the one that's paying for it.

And there's a price?

Of course there's a price, are you kidding? It's definitely not easy. It's rough. But for most great black writers in general, "they"—meaning white and black Americans—won't read us until they have nothing else to read.

Why do you think that is?

Well, because of the entire way of American life, the marrow of the American bone. Now today it's a *fait accompli*. There's nothing to be done about it. The whole American optic in terms of reality is based on the necessity of keeping black people out of it. We are nonexistent. Except according to their terms, and their terms are unacceptable.

Let me ask you this, since you said that. How do you look at the American society as it was during Dr. King's time and now? Any changes? Do you think it is worse, or what?

Certainly, in my opinion, it's worse. I'm not sure it's the society, I don't know what it is now.

What do you think that Ronald Reagan represents to white America?

Ronald Reagan represents the justification of their history, their sense of innocence. He means the justification of *Birth of a Nation*. The justification, in short, of being white.

How do you think white Americans feel now that they're in this economic crisis?

They're not thinking about it.

What?

They're not thinking about it. Americans don't think of such things. They try and get out of it. They hope it'll go away. And luckily they began to realize that maybe Reagan has to go, too. But they hope it all goes away. Because it's like a bad dream for them.

Won't they do anything to help it go away?

No. Because they don't know how. They don't know how they got into it or, worse, won't recognize how. I don't know. They don't know how they got into the chaos of their cities, for example. But they did it. Now how and why did they do it? They did it because they wanted their children to be safe, to be raised safely. So they set up their communities so that they wouldn't have to go to school with black children, whom they fear, and that dictates the structure of their cities, the chaos of their cities and the danger in which they live.

"They" being white.

"They" being white and their believing that they're white. But they did it; niggers didn't do it. They did it. Inch by inch, stone by stone, decree by decree. Now their kids are deeply lost and they can't even blame it now on the nigger, you know what I mean?

Yes.

That's what happened, I don't care who says what. I watched it happen, I know because I watched it happen. And all this, because they want to be white. And why do they want to be white? Because it's the only way to justify the slaughter of the Indians and enslaving the blacks—they're trapped. And nothing, nothing will spring the trap, nothing. Now they're really trapped because the world is present. And the world is not white and America is not the symbol of civilization. Neither is England. Neither is France. Something else is happening which will engulf them by and by. You, Quincy, will be here, but I'll be gone. It's the only hope the world has, that the notion of the supremacy of Western hegemony and civilization be contained.

Do you have any feelings about yuppies?

I saw them coming. I knew them. They can't, I'm afraid, be taught anything.

You don't think they can be taught anything?

No. Because you can't be taught anything if you think you know everything already, that something else—greed, materialism, and consuming—is more important to your life. You know, I taught the yuppies before they were called yuppies. And then what happened to them, really? Perfectly sound young men came out of college, went to work for Nixon, and were hardened criminals on Wall Street before you knew it. Now, is it true or not?

It's true.

And here I've only mentioned Nixon. But it's true for Reagan, too. So that's that. It's the fiber of the nation, unfortunately.

Sondra A. O'Neale (essay date 1988)

SOURCE: "Fathers, Gods, and Religion: Perceptions of Christianity and Ethnic Faith in James Baldwin," in *Critical Essays on James Baldwin*, edited by Fred L. Standley and Nancy V. Burt, G. K. Hall & Co., 1988, pp. 125-43.

[*In the following essay, O'Neale "explores the complexities of Baldwin's concepts of fatherhood and how they impinge on his search—for a sympathetic Father/God—an odyssey that he deliberately identifies as the collective historic experience of the race and its artists."*]

In a 1965 television interview for the BBC, British author Colin MacInnes said to James Baldwin: "You spoke just now of the soul, the soul of the black man, the soul of the white man. I never have been able to make out, Jimmy, whether you are or are not a religious writer. Does the concept of God mean something to you? Are you a believer in any sense, or not?" As he has done so often when people have tried to pin him down to traditional modes of religious persuasion, Baldwin answered MacInnes in ambiguities based on his own redefinitions of "the church as church," salvation as that which "we must do to save each other," and love as that which is not passive but "something active, more like a fire, like the wind."[1] Perhaps not realizing that Baldwin's "fire-wind-energy" simile alludes to Acts 2, where it is recorded that the Holy Spirit came down "like a violent, rushing wind and tongues as of fire rested on seventy fearful disciples,"[2] MacInnes did not steer Baldwin toward acknowledging the debt that his literature owes to a deep intellectual contemplation of black America's centuries-old struggle to formulate a Christian faith that would assuage

and reconstitute the evil-oriented identity that white Christian culture had imposed upon them (i.e., interpretations of the Cain and Ham curses and interpolations of the significance of skin color, predestination, heathenism, sin, and hell).[3] Nor did MacInnes acknowledge that Baldwin's relationship to what the critic called "religion"—presumably the traditional European-centered view that is the basis of American Protestantism: belief in a God whose holiness is imbued in puritanical white; a written word that calls for redemptive purging of nonpure, vis-à-vis nonwhite, phenomena from His world; and an orthodox, spiritless, liturgical form keeping strict legalistic step with a deterministic force that assures white believers of spiritual, political, and economic superiority—is, like that of all black American writers since 1760, an inherently different idea of religion. On the surface one cannot ascertain whether or not Baldwin is a "religious writer" because his works do not reflect the traditional treatment of Christianity in black American literature. Instead, Baldwin examines the enigmas of human affections absent in Christian professors; the failure of the Christian God to thwart the persistent onslaught of His African children; and the insistence of those children to forge a "normal" dependent interaction with that God. These witnesses are empirical evidences of God in Baldwin's world, and he exploits them to excess so that he can mold a composite God, discover His personality, and fathom His intentions toward black people.

Although scholarship has touched upon the recurrent father-son motif in Baldwin's works,[4] there has been little discussion of those images for an understanding of his (and black America's) search for God and for an iconography that is not totally and suicidally antipathetic to the dominant culture. Baldwin often codifies his variable perceptions of a puritanical, unloving God as a woman-mother (e.g., Margaret Alexander in *Amen Corner*); however, his use of female characters and feminine symbolism to conceptualize these possibilities is a study in itself. This essay explores the multifarious complexities of Baldwin's concepts of fatherhood and how they impinge on his search—for a sympathetic Father/God—an odyssey that he deliberately identifies as the collective historic experience of the race and its artists.

Indeed, a close critical and theological exegesis—that includes traditional religious consciousness in the canon of black American literature—of Baldwin's writings reveals these themes and gives credence to what is already suspected: that more than the heritage of any other black American writer, Baldwin's works illustrate the schizophrenia of the black American experience with Christianity. Much of the symbolism, language, archetypal rhythm, and thematic call for justice in his essays are so steeped in Christian ethics that his readers may become deafened to the tragicomic Christian pathos that is agonizing at the heart of the Baldwin message. Agonizing because, in ways similar to those of the transformed biblical disciples, the experiential anointing and ethereal vision that fourteen-year-old Baldwin received on the threshing floor of a Harlem storefront church in 1938 is at constant warfare with the unremitting oppression he receives from the world. When he sought relief in art, the divisiveness of this apparently irreconcilable dichotomy dominated his world view, his theology, and his writing. By that time, however, Baldwin also knew that by wrestling with that dichotomous angel in the public arena of his own written word, he was unveiling the agony of simultaneous disappointment and hope in the psyche of the race. That agony is evident in the earliest offerings to the canon of black American literature. Even in the mid-eighteenth century, Africans enslaved in America, while sincerely acknowledging their own conversions to Christianity, nonetheless deplored the white man's use of the same Bible both to convert and to enslave them. They also haltingly revealed their various inabilities to reach satisfactory faith-embracing conclusions (or at least to express them in a manner palatable to doubting black readers) on such doctrines as color symbolism; predeterminism; the infinite, omnipotent sovereign will of God; the Old Testament curses placed on Cain and Ham, presumably in perpetuity; and the New Testament reenslavement of Philemon.[5] For instance, in his poem "A Dialogue Between the Kind Master and the Dutiful Servant" eighteenth-century New York slave, poet, and essayist Jupiter Hammon, the first black to publish in America, craftily tells his religious master that he cannot follow him for life's guide and example because the master himself is not a true Christian; yet he is reduced to telling his slave audience in a sermon, "As Black and despised as we are," that nevertheless, God, "Our Father," will save "us" (i.e., from hell and slavery—concepts merged as one in the literature up to the 1870s) if "we" obediently trust in Christ. Hammon promised that this same God will also eventually judge (i.e., in eternity) the white man for his unjust behavior.[6] But Hammon's faith was firm. His admissions were not to engender doubt but to establish belief.

Phillis Wheatley continued the tensions of faith in, among other salient poems, her famed poetic lines, "Remember, *Christians, Negroes,* black as *Cain,* / May be refin'd, and join th' angelic train."[7] Other black poets, essayists, and narrative authors of the period, such as Briton Hammon, Olandah Equiano, Benjamin Banneker, John Marrant, and George Moses Horton—all slaves—expressed themselves in similar fashion.[8] In the nineteenth century, freed or escaped slaves, such as David Walker, J. W. C. Pennington, James Whitfield, Nat Turner (who led a slave revolt based on his faith in the righteous judgment of the Old Testament God), Sojourner Truth, William and Ellen Craft, Frances E. W. Harper, and, most prominently, Frederick Douglass, expressed complete faith in the reality of the conversion experience, in the inerrant totality of Scripture, and in the absolute love and fatherhood of their God.[9] While their stance as freed men and women was more militant than that of enslaved writers of the earlier period, their militancy involved a clear distinction between Christianity as they knew it and Christianity as it was practiced in the white world. Their faith in God, as reflected in the literature, was unswerving, and their relationship with Him could not be violated by injurious whites.[10] In the epilogue of his shorter *Autobiography,* Douglass clearly distinguishes between black Christian faith and white Christian practice:

> What I have said respecting and against religion, I mean strictly to apply to the *slaveholding religion* of this land, and with no possible reference to Christianity proper; for, between the Christianity of this land, and the Christianity of Christ, I recognize the widest possible difference—so wide, that to receive the one as good, pure, and holy, is of necessity to reject the other as bad, corrupt, and wicked. To be the friend of the one, is of necessity to be the enemy of the other. I love the pure, peaceable, and impartial Christianity of Christ: I therefore hate the corrupt, slaveholding, women-whipping, cradle-plundering, partial and hypocritical Christianity of this land. Indeed, I can see no reason, but the most deceitful one, for calling the religion of this land Christianity.[11]

In the secularized Harlem Renaissance of the 1930s, God is either absent from artistic expression or mentioned (i.e., as the saving grace and artistic folk source of the black church) with reverence. Doubt or rejection is for an unredeemed, oppressive society. Representative works include James Weldon Johnson's *God's Trombones,* Zora Neale Hurston's *Their Eyes Were Watching God,* Langston Hughes's "Cross," "Bound No'th Blue," and "Brass Spittoons," and the third section of Jean Toomer's *Cane,* with the wise, though blind, preacher, Father John.[12] Perhaps the most cogent example of the black American writer's slight but expanding distancing from traditional racial concepts of God in that period occurs in a poem, "Yet Do I Marvel," by Baldwin's high school teacher Countee Cullen (Baldwin attended DeWitt Clinton High School in the Bronx from 1938 to 1942, during which time Cullen was employed as a teacher and supervisor of the school magazine, the *Magpie,* of which Baldwin was editor and to which he contributed):[13]

> I doubt not God is good, well-meaning, kind,
> And did he stoop to quibble could tell why
> . . . .
> Inscrutable His ways, are, and immune
> . . . .
> What awful brain compels His awful hand,
> Yet do I marvel at this curious thing:

To make a poet black, and bid him sing![14]

These were Baldwin's black literary progenitors, in whose works he was well read. In their volume entitled *Dialogue,* he tells Nikki Giovanni:

> Now I can see what I owe to Richard [Wright] and what I owe to Chester [Haines], what I owe to Langston Hughes and what I owe to W. E. B. DuBois and what I owe to Frederick Douglass. But I could not see that when I was twenty. I don't think anybody can see that at twenty. But you see they were, on one level, simply more exalted victims. . . . And it takes a long time before you accept what has been given to you from your past. What we call black literature is really summed up for me by the whole career, let's say, of Bessie Smith, Ray Charles, Aretha Franklin, because that's how it's been handed down, since we couldn't read or write, as far as they knew. And it was at one time a crime to be able to read if you were black. It was punishable by law. We had to smuggle information, and we did it through our music and we did it in the church. You were talking before about the church you went to visit. I thought about the Apollo Theater. The last time I saw Aretha, what did she do at the Apollo Theater but turn it into a gospel church service—! And that's true religion. A black writer comes out of that; I don't mean he has to be *limited* to that. But he comes out of that because the standards which come from Greece and Rome, from the Judeo-Christian ethic, are very dubious when you try to apply them to your own life.[15]

Baldwin's position in *The Fire Next Time* is in the tradition of black Christian protest:

> Negroes in this country—and Negroes do not, strictly or legally speaking, exist in any other— are taught really to despise themselves from the moment their eyes open on the world. This world is white and they are black. White people hold the power, which means that they are superior to blacks (intrinsically, that is: God decreed it so), and the world has innumerable ways of making this difference known and felt and feared.[16]

He joins the black church in search of at least spiritual kinship: "My friend was about to introduce me when she looked at me and smiled and said, 'Whose little boy are you?' Now this, unbelievably, was precisely the phrase used by pimps and racketeers on the Avenue when they suggested, both humorously and intensely, that I 'hang out'

with them. Perhaps part of the terror they had caused me to feel came from the fact that I unquestionably wanted to be *somebody's* little boy."[17] But then he posits that the deity's historic treatment through His white representatives renders Him a nihilistic, loveless icon that cannot or will not proffer comfort at black men's altars. His rhetoric is strikingly atypical of ethnic conversion experience:

> All I really remember is the pain, the unspeakable pain; it was as though I were yelling up to Heaven and Heaven would not hear me. And if Heaven would not hear me, if love could not descend from Heaven—to wash me, to make me clean— then utter disaster was my portion. Yes, it does indeed mean something—something unspeakable—to be born, in a white country, an Anglo-Teutonic, antisexual country, black. You very soon, without knowing it, give up all hope of communion.[18]

Instead of finding cardinal faith on the threshing floor, he concludes that God is indeed white and that the black man cannot obtain redemption in the universe:

> The universe, which is not merely the stars and the moon and the planets, flowers, grass, and trees, but *other people,* has evolved no terms for your existence, had made no room for you, and if love will not swing wide the gates, no other power will or can. And if one despairs—as who has not?—of human love, God's love alone is left. But God—and I felt this even then, so long ago, on that tremendous floor, unwillingly—is white. And if His love was so great, and if He loved all His children, why were we, the blacks, cast down so far? Why? In spite of all I said thereafter, I found no answer on the floor—not *that answer,* anyway—and I was on the floor all night.[19]

As his writing develops, he not only continues the thematic ambiguity between possibilities of individual faith in and societal practice of Christianity as a religious system, he goes beyond the point of doubt about white practice to question the validity of life-alternating salvation in the black church, and he imperiously accuses God of being at best a weak, powerless, detached, "watch-maker" creator and at worst a white-skinned being who truly does (as slave masters and Puritans declared) hate and predetermine His non-white creation for servitude. No black American writer before Baldwin had quite the literary nerve (i.e., to risk separating himself from the mainstream of Christian black America) or the agnostic impertinence (i.e., his frequent self-recriminations for slipping toward blasphemy)[20] to question openly the justice, judgment, and sincerity of God.

Yet Baldwin claims to have had a traumatic Christian conversion. He was an ardent licensed preacher of the Gospel for three years, during which time he absorbed all facets of Christian doctrine, denominational practice, and, most importantly, biblical image, symbol, narrative, and meaning. His biblical allusions and references to the black nation's spiritual consciousness are innumerable. Today he claims membership in one of the largest Baptist churches in Washington, D.C.[21] He reveres as much today the Christian commitment of Martin Luther King and Medgar Evers as he did when he joined hands with them in the civil rights movement.[22] The unfailing optimism, seen in the entirety of his works, that only love within and between the races will ultimately save America and its black citizens is rooted in the philosophy of Christian faith.[23]

In spite of the above claims, an objective look at the constantly apposed treatment of his own experience and of the collective black Christian experience, leads to the suspicion that Baldwin really does not believe in the possibility of a spiritual epiphany to life the black man above the environment of his anguish. At least he seems to accept the prevailing social theories that treat Christianity as simply a force to keep black people insensitive to the need for more immediate freedom. Both aspects can be seen in John Grimes's conversion, in *Go Tell It on the Mountain* under the jealous eye of his cruel, oppressive stepfather, an un-Christian minister; in the tawdry, fractious, loveless relationships in the midst of "devout" religious fervor in *Amen Corner*—wretched "saved saints" who will not stoop to save the dying father, Luke Alexander; likewise in the spineless father, Rev. Henry, in *Blues for Mr. Charlie,* whose prayers and example of Christian meekness are powerless against the congregation of white "Christian" lynchers, who kill his son in the name of God; and in that very precise essay "**Many Thousands Gone,**" he sardonically says that even the white man knows his "Negroes" got "real" religion. The smug white persona expresses what the mainstream really feels about the "Negro":

> In the case of the Negro his shameful history was carried, quite literally, on his brow. Shameful; for he was heathen as well as black and would never have discovered the healing blood of Christ had not we braved the jungles to bring him these glad tidings. As he accepted the alabaster Christ and the bloody cross—in the bearing of which he would find his redemption, as, indeed, to our outraged astonishment, he sometimes did—he must, accept that image we then gave him of himself. . . .
> [24]

The persona concludes that his simple dilemma must be borne in mind if one wishes to comprehend Negro psychology.

Today, thirty-eight years after the appearance of Baldwin's first successful, quasi-religious novel, *Go Tell It on the Mountain,* critics are displeased with his continuing reliance upon religious themes. They want him to leave the arena of the black church and the black family portrayed again in his latest work, *Just Above My Head,* and "write about something more in keeping with the contemporary problems of Black America."[25] Such advice misses Baldwin's point altogether, for he believes that understanding the black man's dilemma with Christianity is axiomatic to dealing with these contemporary problems—a position that on many levels is no different from the beloved Dr. King's admonishments or those of Malcolm X, who, because of the untenable hypocrisy of practiced Christianity, disavowed his father's Baptist faith; or of the contemporary black writers of the seventies and eighties who for the most part have rejected Christianity as a basis for moral standard and have turned to Islam and other African religions.[26] Baldwin says in "**Everybody's Protest Novel**": "The African, exile, pagan, fell on his knees before that God in Whom he must now believe; Who had made him, but not in His image. This tableau, this impossibility, is the heritage of the Negro in America: *Wash me*, cried the slave to his Maker, and I shall be whiter, whiter than snow! For black is the color of evil; only the robes of the saved are white. . . . This reality, in the same nightmare notion, he both flees and rushes to embrace."[27]

Although Martin insisted that the black man was made in God's image and Malcolm and Elijah Muhammed held that there definitely must be two gods—one white and one black, with the white one and his white offspring being indisputable devils—Baldwin concluded that at the core of the question was an unsolved mystery with an illusive, incomprehensible God, sometimes white, sometimes black, with variant earthly fathers as representatives of the origins of man's being and causality. Perhaps one reason that they could be so absolute and he could not was that they had at least the psychological security of knowing a true father in the flesh while he did not. Surely, the Reverend David Baldwin was not his real father. Not only had his mother finally confessed that James was born out of wedlock, the boy spoken of in *Go Tell It on the Mountain, The Fire Next Time,* and *Nobody Knows My Name* intuitively knew that this mean, insecure, spiteful man could not be his father. In his constant daily behavior, the elder Baldwin made it clear that James was not among his chosen sons.

Within the cosmology of biblical narrative is of course the Cain story in which God and his image, Adam, denied Cain the honor of an elder son because he had murdered his younger brother Abel. They gave the inheritance of the lineage to a third son, Seth, and banished Cain from the familial community to wander as a vagabond on the earth. To support slavery, white theologians said that the mark God put upon Cain to establish his identity on the earth was black skin.[28] A thorough student of ancient lore, Baldwin was aware that the rejection he suffered from Mr. Baldwin made him quite analogous to Cain. As mimicked in the interpersonal relations in *Go Tell It on the Mountain,* David Baldwin, the younger son, was the reverend's beloved namesake. Thus, the harsh father—most succinctly because of his ministerial profession—becomes a symbol of the Calvinistic God, who had likewise cursed the African to a base position of sonship.

The young Baldwin yearned to know his "real" father. Why had he deserted him, denied him name and legitimization? Was it a matter of an unworthy son or of an irresponsible father? In either case, again as with Mr. Baldwin, the alienation becomes a representative allegory for the absence of an adequate protective father in the black man's life. The sociological implications, both in black American experience and in Baldwin's works, are obvious. The awesome limitations of a racist society will not allow any of his male characters to be economically or socially functioning fathers, or serve as role models for young men to follow. Both in life and as a personal source for his young black male characters, the steps of initiation thus presume that other "fathers" in the community are available as viable substitutes. In both his life and his work, Baldwin turns first to the church and then—discarding all but its spiritually artistic forms (i.e., its music as the cradling forerunner of jazz and the blues as contrasted in **"Sonny's Blues"**)—to the world of art and literature.

Thus, Baldwin's chaotic, essentially orphaned childhood, his conversion, and the symbolic relationship with his "earthly" fathers are merely his metaphors for the religiously inconclusive psyches of the race. The black man's relationships with the Father-God of Christianity early became a central Baldwin thesis. For him, there is no other moral standard by which whites can be judged and through which, in vindicating black peoples, the Christian God can absolve himself as the moral center of the universe. In a commentary of the black preacher's socialization of the Gospel, Baldwin makes the assumption that the confessed spiritual piety has always been an ambiguous veneer veiling demands for social justice:

> The word "belief" has nearly no meaning any- more, in the recognized languages, and ineptly approaches the reality to which I am referring: for there can be no doubt that it is a reality. The blacks had first been claimed by the Christian church, and then excluded from the company of white Christians—from the fellowship of Chris- tians: which taught us all that we needed to know about white Christians. The blacks did not so much use Christian symbols as recognize them—

recognize them for what they were before the Christians came along—and, thus, reinvested these symbols with their original energy. The proof of this, simply, is the continued existence and authority of the blacks: it is through the cre- ation of the black church that an unwritten, dis- persed, and violated inheritance has been handed down. The word "revelation" has very little mean- ing in the recognized languages: yet, it is the only word for the moment I am attempting to ap- proach.[29]

An innate perfectionist, the younger Baldwin found these absolutes quite compatible with the orderings of causal existence offered by the church. After his "conversion" experience, the directions for life were quite easy: "An eye for an eye and a tooth for a tooth." "Do unto others as you would have them do unto you." God, on behalf of the suffering saints, would quickly punish the wicked. Although such simplistic answers presented ideal solutions, Baldwin soon learned that they were not easily transferable into his expanding world. He notes in *The Fire Next Time* that all authority appeared to come from God to subversive white representatives, without whose permission the Harlemites indeed did not seem to be able to "live, move, or have their being."[30]

Even more perplexing, it became equally evident during Baldwin's three years in the ministry that although God did not seem to be doing His part, perhaps God's moral stan- dard was operating in justifiable judgment against black Christians. They themselves were not fulfilling the laws nec- essary to receive the savior's blessings. Baldwin confesses in *The Fire Next Time:*

> There was no love in the church. It was a mask for hatred and self-despair. When we were told to love everybody, I had thought that that meant *everybody.* But no. It applied only to those who believed as we did, and it did not apply to white people at all. But what was the point, the pur- pose of *my* salvation if it did not permit me to behave with love toward others, no matter how they behaved toward me?[31]

Therefore, all external truths that were supposed to comple- ment the new Christian's internal ecstatic experience—the Christian church and the Christian community—were in complete contradiction to it. White Christians, to the shout- ing black pentecostal church, were devils to be exorcised, not brethren to be loved. Yet the blacks themselves were either humble inheritors of some future earth or heaven; or pitiful imitators of the hypocritical whites whom they de- spised. Herein were the seeds planted for his agonizing mes- sage. For the next forty years, Baldwin examined these polarities in his fiction, drama, and prose. He looked into, if not resolved, the mystery that the "Church Fathers" had left untouched, and he wrote to influence a national reconciliation between the hope of Christian love that he may have tasted as a young man and the intolerable realities of hate in professing disciples. The ensuing philosophy of his dilemma is best stated in his denial of faith in the **"Down at the Cross"** essay, in which he states that the black man's experiential condition rendered it impossible for him (Baldwin in particular and the race in general) to find salvation in the black church.

Because Baldwin knew such a theorem was heretical to the Christian doctrine he was supposed to preach, he searched for a medium other than the pulpit in order to work out and affirm both a proper communal response for those who had valid spiritual experience and a proper holocaust judgment for those who profess salvation without manifesting universal love. This reordering becomes the philosophical foundation on which he creates. In all of his works, he emphasizes these extremes in a multileveled metaphor that has the ultimate vortex of estrangement from the father.

Baldwin's call for the reunion of fathers and sons is a modern continuation of the cosmic replay, both in the Bible and in America's religious culture, of the Trinity. The father—"white," light, pure, righteous judge of the universe—had to forsake, to "blacken" with the stain of sin, to sacrifice his only son. It was a necessary sacrifice. Mankind, black or white, could not be saved without it. But the gift of universal, unpredestined salvation for which Christ died on the cross has, in succeeding generations, been stolen by evil forces and persons who want to gain wealth and power. In much popular antebellum American literature, most sympathetically in *Uncle Tom's Cabin*, in steps the black man, chosen from eternity as the type of Christ. Through loving self-sacrifice, in obedience to his heavenly father's will, the black sacrificial son must redeem that gift for his own generation and for the salvation of the nation. He must in love lay down his freedom, his dignity, his life for his "lost" white brother. It is also so much of an archetypal pattern in American literature and theology, a pattern that Baldwin hates. But as much as he despised it in Stowe's novel, which he read over and over as a boy, it is nonetheless one of the solutions that he sets forth to reconcile America. This is why he could not espouse the Moslem faith of Elijah Mohammed—it was a doctrine of hate. As deeply as he understands the racial foundations of American power, Baldwin has never been able to hate the white man.

Herein lie additional levels of depth in the "father" symbolism. Baldwin advocates a reunion between white fathers and black sons—an action that is not only incredibly idealistic and in most cases impossible, but one that blacks as well as whites probably find repulsive. Historically in the literary canon, awareness of the specific identity of white parentage only intensifies the bitterness of black disinheritedness and heightens the sense of schizophrenia.[32] Additionally, with this thesis, Baldwin transgressed a movement in black aesthetics that demanded that black writers turn away from the tragic mulatto theme that had dominated white authorial portrayal of blacks as well as the post-Civil War birth of black American literature. In the historicity of these issues, Baldwin was well versed. Nevertheless, he insisted, especially in his early works, that for total self-discovery and purgation, blacks, indeed, all Americans, must face the horror of "The Great White Father."

Continuing aspects of the mulatto theme, he says in *The Fire Next Time* that the American Negro must accept the history of his white parentage, that he is neither totally African, nor Moslem, but "a unique creation; he has no counterpart anywhere, and no predecessors. . . . I am called Baldwin . . . because I was kidnapped by a white Christian named Baldwin, who forced me to kneel at the foot of the cross. I am, then, both visibly and legally the descendant of slaves in a white, Protestant country, . . . this is what it means to be an American Negro."[33] There is also the poignant prayer by Meridian Henry, in *Blues for Mr. Charlie,* lamenting the murder of his only son at the hands of a white pseudo-Christian terrorist: "But can I ask the children forever to sustain the cruelty inflicted on them by those who have been their masters, and who are now, in very truth . . . their parents? What hope is there for a people who deny their deeds and disown their kinsmen and who do so in the name of purity and love, in the name of Jesus Christ?"[34] That parentage is both physical and spiritual. Baldwin wants the white religious zealot who placed the African on the auction block to be held accountable for his failure to demonstrate the Christian protectorate that he promised in Christ. Further, he wants the white biological forefather, through the repentance of his heirs, to face the retribution of damnation for the heinous crime of denying, enslaving, and murdering his own sons.

Another point that violates the black aesthetic endeavors to reverse the images of Africans in American culture is set forth in Baldwin's generic identification of the black self as "Devil":

> In our church, the Devil had many faces, all of them one's own. He was not always evil, rarely was he frightening—he was, more often, subtle, charming, cunning, and warm. So, one learned, for example, never to take the easy way out: whatever looked easy was almost certainly a trap. In short, the Devil was that mirror which could never be smashed. One had to look into the mirror every day—*good morning, blues / Blues, how do you do? / Well, I'm doing all right Good morn-*

ing / How are you:—check it all out, and take it all in, and travel. The pleading of the blood was not, for us, a way of exorcising a Satan whom we knew could never sleep; it was to engage Satan in a battle which we knew could never end.[35]

If, as he repeated to Margaret Mead in *A Rap on Race*, the "good" Christian God is white and is vengeful toward black persons, is he saying later in *The Devil Finds Work* (as indicated in the title and the theme of the book) that blacks indeed represent God's opposite? Or is he merely speaking of that tiger to be tamed within the universal self that transcends race and color?

Aspects of the metaphor that most fill Baldwin's cup of anguish are the angry, self-depreciating relationships between black fathers and sons as a necessary insulation against the white world. He suspected that it was shame at having created a black son to perpetuate the myth that caused his natural father to disown him. Likewise, the ambivalent love-hate memories of his religiously violent stepfather were a vehicle for apprehending a causal iconography symbolic of the black man's relationship with God and society. Ultimately, one who is brought up to expect that any tender mercy can turn to cruelty cannot be disillusioned. In *The Devil Finds Work,* he acknowledges the effectiveness of the elder Baldwin's negativistic training and patriarchy:

> The pride and sorrow and beauty of my father's face: for that man I called my father really was my father in every sense except the biological, or literal one. He formed me, and he raised me, and he did not let me starve: and he gave me something, however harshly, and however little I wanted it, which prepared me for an impending horror which he could not prevent. This is not a Western idea, but fathers and sons arrive at that relationship only by claiming that relationship: that is, by paying for it. If the relationship of father to son could really be reduced to biology, the whole earth would blaze with the glory of fathers and sons.[36]

This image culminates in a father's acrimonious disapproving of Anglicized theories of black manhood. But, ultimately, Baldwin's texts and personal direction indicate that neither his religious stepfather nor other ministers in the church provided significant answers for an initiate whose questions were more than superficial. In *Notes of a Native Son,* he reminisces about the variety of the old man's life:

> "But as for me and my house," my father had said, "we will serve the Lord." I wondered, as we drove him to his resting place, what this line had meant for him. I had heard him preach it many times. I had preached it once myself, proudly giving it an interpretation different from my father's. Now the whole thing came back to me, as though my father and I were on our way to Sunday school and I were memorizing the golden text. . . . I suspected in these familiar lines a meaning which had never been there for me before. All of my father's texts and songs, which I had decided were meaningless, were arranged before me at his death like empty bottles, waiting to hold the meaning which life would give them for me. This was his legacy: nothing is ever escaped.[37]

In his move from biological, familial, and church fathers, Baldwin—and, consequently, those among his black male characters who achieve reconciliation—eventually finds ostensibly compatible generative role models among the black artists and intellectuals who fostered his artistic development. His subsequent art became a journal of his search in self and society for evidence of God and His love. In that other world of the unseen black spirit—literature, art, jazz, black language, and blues—he finds authority figures who can guide him and other thoughtful young men unable to adjust to the holocaustic horror into which they had been born: "the American despair, the search, in our country for authority. . . . The streets of my native city were filled with youngsters searching desperately for the limits which would tell them who they were, and create for them a challenge to which they could rise."[38]

As seen earlier in a discussion of the strand of biblical symbolism in the works of black American writers since the eighteenth century, the racial literary heritage gave Baldwin at least a transitional basis on which to move from religious "principling" into modern secularized art and philosophy. Although he mastered the latter, he never fully renounced the former, which for his purposes was the more functional form. But he realizes that he is attempting to "marry" incompatible elements in agnostic art and traditional black Christian faith. His conflicting emotions when in late adolescence he moved away from the church and his ministerial calling are explored not only in *The Fire Next Time* and *Notes of Native Son,* but are perhaps most eloquently expressed in both Sonny's (**"Sonny's Blues"**) and David's (*Amen Corner*) experiences when they suffer parental rejection because they must steal away to discover nonecclesiastical epiphanies in the ethereal grasp of black music.

Biographically, Baldwin's earliest artistic mentor was not really Countee Cullen but the prolific (and, even now barely recognized) genius, visual artist Beauford DeLaney. He was the first adult to assure Baldwin that the world of art and thought did not freakishly separate him from acceptable ethnic experience. When Baldwin visited Beauford's studio and lamented his abject poverty, the restricting duty to support eight younger brothers and sisters, and his inherent failure to maintain employment at any of the menial tasks he continually tried to swallow, he found in Beauford an understanding, compassionate friend. Beauford finally told Baldwin, who had lost his umpteenth dishwasher's job, "Perhaps you simply don't belong there," and encouraged him to pursue his writing instead.[39] When the often sick and ultimately incompetent ministerial stepfather died, it was DeLaney—not black churchmen—to whom James Baldwin turned. The elder artist provided a haven for the young man, now freshly terrified at the prospect of total responsibility for the family. Beauford appealed to the neighborhood for donations to supplement his own generous cash gift, which was needed for the funeral because the impoverished family lacked the money to bury the father. Baldwin's brother David; his associate, dancer and choreographer Bernard Haskell; and distinguished black American literary critic Dr. Richard Long (who himself was strongly influenced by DeLaney and who first began his lifelong friendship with Baldwin through DeLaney) all agree with Baldwin's claim that DeLaney was the true father of Baldwin's art. In later years, Baldwin, after an intermittent but compatible association with DeLaney, was able to repay the artist's gracious gesture when he, Long, and Haskell not only buried DeLaney, who died in neglect and obscurity in Paris, but withstood the attempts of an avaricious French government to confiscate his paintings.[40] Later Baldwin and Long coedited ***Beauford DeLaney Retrospective Exhibition: Harlem Studio Museum*** as a final tribute to a talented "father" who had encouraged them to let nothing inhibit their creative dreams.

Apart from Beauford's support, Baldwin was primarily on his own; though his quixotic initiative was also influenced by the world of black music, which beckoned him from Harlem's streets, as well as the consummate neighborhood and the downtown Forty-Second Street New York libraries (with their titular attempts at integration). In one interview, his brother David painfully recalls the benignly discourteous treatment that Baldwin received from Richard Wright and other members of the post-Renaissance New York circle. Later, the venerable Sterling Brown was one of the few prominent black writer/scholars who had published during the Harlem Renaissance to support Baldwin or his works when ***Amen Corner*** opened at Howard University in 1956. Brown single-handedly withstood the irate reaction of conservative black scholars who were deeply disturbed at Baldwin's portrayal of black life and language and at his irreverence for the black church.[41] Although Wright interceded to get the budding writer an early fellowship to work on ***In My Father's House*** (the first title of the novel that later became ***Go Tell It on the Mountain***), the true character of their relationship and of Wright's refusal to sponsor or associate with the younger writer is barely seen in "Alas, Poor Richard" or "Everybody's Protest Novel."

Like many black writers and artists who failed to find a congenial environment for their work in America, Baldwin set sail for France in 1948. He found some respite with white expatriots, but Beauford and Hoyt Fuller—the founder of *Negro Digest* and *Black World*, which were the major sources for publication of black writers in the fifties and sixties, and *First World* in the seventies—were mainstays of solace and encouragement. After hearing about his work, Hoyt wrote to Baldwin from Chicago to encourage him and to invite submissions. Through their correspondence and later acquaintance, Baldwin grew to respect Fuller as one of the few men who understood what he was trying to do.

Any conceptualization of Baldwin's quest for fathers must, of necessity, include a discussion of his own influence as an innovator in the mainstream of black American literature. Historically, Baldwin should be seen as the last black American writer to exploit as a major theme the black man's relationship with Christianity. Conversely, he may be considered the first black American writer to distance himself from the lone enduring black institution, the black church, not by its notable absence (as with Wright, Ellison,[42] and other blacks writing in the first half of this century; for example, Ann Petry, Nella Larsen, Sterling Brown, Chester Himes, Paule Marshall, Robert Hayden, and William Demby), but by his overtly persistent portrayal of its lack of authentic Christian commitment. In this and his subsequent treatment of homosexuality as an acceptable form of human love (in ***Giovanni's Room*** and, most recently, in ***Just Above My Head***)—a position he knew was not compatible with orthodox Christian behavior and thus utterly shocking even to black sophisticates—Baldwin opened the floodgate for contemporary anti-Christian, nonbiblically based black American literature. In most of his works, he only questions divine existence while still courting its allegiance, but his boldness invited younger writers to complete the schism between black art and black faith.

The schism between white-practiced Christianity and black American art was always axiomatically present. For two hundred years, black writers examined the Bible and indicted white society for the incorrigible refusal to love oppressed people (as the Bible commands); however, they agreed with the black preacher that faith in the true God and in His deliverance of them was the only accessible power upon which an enslaved or oppressed people could rely. In their works, the black church itself and faith as exercised in the hearts of black believers were sacrosanct.

Ironically, Baldwin intended his literature to influence national and personal reunification. He hoped that white fathers would repent and acknowledge their sons: that black fathers would be men of strength and love while throwing off the shackles of Tomism and that God the Father, indicated in even those oft-repeated prayerful exclamations,

"God knows," would reveal the black man as an equally chosen son. The Trinity would then be restored. The trust of his message is that the validity of Christianity can best be measured by how it has affected the colored peoples of the world. That effect "seems" instead to resolve solely in oppression. I say "seems" because Baldwin still attempts to separate the visible history of black America's experience with Christianity from the spiritual, visionary experience that both he and the race may have internalized. The reality of that unseen spiritual truth, codified in his novels by the suffering blues and tarring spiritual motifs, enables him to keep advocating that the demonstrable love of Christ will bring to earth that paradise revealed on the threshing floor and fulfill that prophecy in Amos 9:7, "Are ye not as children of the Ethiopians unto me, O children of Israel?" Then Baldwin can have peace with the heritage of his forefathers. Then and only then will his quest end and he can unhesitantly acknowledge oneness with the Christian God, his father. Until that essence of true Christianity is revealed, Baldwin's dissociation from variant fathers tempts him to withhold absolute commitment. The totality of his theme is a cosmologically oxymoronic statement in both language and philosophy that sensible faith in an unseen God cannot transcend experience in self, race, or society. Faith, even in one's own soul, is difficult to capture in artistic medium. In an uncontrived moment, Baldwin jocularly confessed to Nikki Giovanni, "Well, it depends on what you mean by God. . . . I've claimed Him as my father and I'll give Him a great time until it's over because God is our responsibility."[43] Although that is not belief, it at least indicates that his search for God, his primal father, is not abandoned.

NOTES

1. "Race, Hate, Sex, and Colour: A Conversation," By James Baldwin with James Mossman and Colin MacInnes, *Encounter* 25 (1965): 55-60.

2. Acts 2:1-5. The allusion has more a pentecostal than fundamentalist flavor, as this, the more emotional mold, is essentially Baldwin's church background.

3. Most basic texts on American slavery deal with theological supports manipulated to support that institution. Studies going into the greatest detail are Winthrop D. Jordan, *The White Man's Burden: Historical Origins of Racism in the United States* (New York: Oxford University Press, 1974), and *White Over Black: American Attitudes Toward the Negro, 1550-1812* (Chapel Hill: University of North Carolina Press, 1968); and Roger Bastide, "Color, Racism, and Christianity," in *Color and Race*, ed. John Hope Franklin (Boston: Houghton Mifflin, 1968).

4. See Michel Fabre, "Fathers and Sons in James Baldwin's *Go Tell It on the Mountain*," in *James Baldwin: A Collec-*tion of Critical Essays, ed. Keneth Kinnamon (Englewood Cliffs, N.J.: Prentice-Hall, 1974); see also Therman B. O'Daniel, "James Baldwin: An Interpretive Study," *College Language Association* 7 (1963): 37-47.

5. See the entries of ex-slaves in Roger Burns, *Am I Not a Man and a Brother: The Anti-Slavery Crusade of Revolutionary America, 1688-1788* (New York: Chelsea House, 1977); and Dorothy Porter, *Early Negro Writing, 1760-1837* (Boston: Beacon, 1971). The story of Philemon is in the New Testament epistle bearing his name.

6. Jupiter Hammon, "A Dialogue Entitled the Kind Master and a Dutiful Servant," in *America's First Negro Poet: The Complete Works of Jupiter Hammon of Long Island*, ed. Stanley Austin Ransome, Jr. (Port Washington, N.Y., Kennikat, 1970).

7. Phillis Wheatley, "On Being Brought from Africa to America," in *The Poems of Phillis Wheatley*, ed. Julian D. Mason (Chapel Hill: University of North Carolina Press, 1966), 7.

8. Briton Hammon, *A Narrative of the Uncommon Sufferings and Surprising Deliverance of Briton Hammon, a Negro Man* (Boston, 1760); John Marrant, *A Narrative of the Lord's Wonderful Dealings with John Marrant, a Black, 1785*, in *Narratives of North American Indian Captivities*, vol. 17 (New York: Garland, 1978). See *Black Writers of America* for other authors cited.

9. The most inclusive anthology is Richard Barksdale and Keneth Kinnamon, *Black Writers of America* (New York: Macmillan, 1972). Hammon's poem is in *America's First Negro Poet*, ed. Ransome. The Crafts' narrative is William Craft and Ellen Craft, *Running a Thousand Miles for Freedom or The Escape of William and Ellen Craft from Slavery*, collected in *Great Slave Narratives*, ed. Arna Bontemps (Boston: Beacon, 1969). Sojourner Truth's most famous speech is in the Burns Collection.

10. See Benjamin E. Mays, *The Negro's God as Reflected in His Literature* (New York: Russell & Russell, 1938).

11. Frederick Douglass, *Narrative of the Life of Frederick Douglass: An American Slave* (Boston: Anti-Slavery Office, 1845; reprint ed., Garden City, New York: Anchor/Doubleday, 1973).

12. James Weldon Johnson, *God's Trombones: Seven Negro Sermons in Verse* (New York: Viking, 1927); Zora Neale Hurston, *Their Eyes Were Watching God* (Urban: University of Illinois Press, 1978). Hughes's poems are in Barksdale and Kinnamon. Jean Toomer, *Cane* (New York: Liveright, 1975).

13. See Carolyn Wedin Sylvander, *James Baldwin* (New York: Ungar, 1980), 1-7. See also chapter 1 of Fern Marja Eckman, *The Furious Passage of James Baldwin* (New York: M. Evans; distributed by J. B. Lippincott, Philadelphia, 1966).

14. Countee Cullen, "Yet Do I Marvel," in *Black Writers of America*, 531.

15. James Baldwin and Nikki Giovanni, *A Dialogue* (New York: Lippincott, 1973), 36-38.

16. James Baldwin, *The Fire Next Time* (New York: Dell, 1962), 39-40.

17. Ibid., 43.

18. Ibid., 45.

19. Ibid., 46.

20. See Baldwin and Giovanni, *Dialogue*, 36-38. See also "Down at the Cross," in *The Fire Next Time.*

21. Interview (April 1981) with James Baldwin and Dr. Eleanor Traylor of Washington, D.C., one of the organizers of an appreciation day of James Baldwin's mother in 1979 at the Baptist church that Baldwin subsequently joined.

22. Baldwin is currently working on a studied biography of the lives of Martin Luther King, Malcolm X, and Medgar Evers. His esteem for Martin is mentioned often in his works. See, for example, *Dialogue*, 25.

23. Baldwin admitted at various times that Christianity, not the church but the religion itself, was one basis of his own moral philosophy. See Margaret Mead and James Baldwin, *A Rap on Race* (New York: Lippincott, 1979), 85-59.

24. James Baldwin, "Many Thousands Gone," in *Notes of a Native Son* (Boston: Beacon, 1955), 29-30.

25. Critical reception of *Just Above My Head* has been mixed. These remarks were included in a BBC broadcast on National Public Radio in 1982. See also *Booklist,* 1 October 1979, 216; *New York Times Book Review,* 23 September 1979, 3; *Times Literary Supplement,* 21 December 1979, 150.

26. Dr. Martin Luther King, "Letter from a Birmingham Jail," in *Why We Can't Wait* (New York: New American Library, 1963), 76-95.

27. Baldwin, "Everybody's Protest Novel." *Notes,* 21.

28. Genesis, 4.

29. James Baldwin, *The Devil Finds Work* (New York: Dial, 1976), 114.

30. Baldwin, *Fire,* 40.

31. Ibid., 57-58.

32. The tragic mulatto theme and its attendant schizophrenic psychosis are treated variously and continually in black American fiction, beginning with such early novels as William Wells Brown's *Clotel; or The President's Daughter* (London: Partridge & Oakley, 1853) and Francis E. W. Harper's *Iola Leroy; or Shadows Uplifted* (Philadelphia: Garringgues Brothers, 1892). See Robert Cone's *Negro Novel in America,* rev. ed. (New Haven: Yale University Press, 1965), for a discussion of the theme.

33. Baldwin, *Fire,* 114.

34. James Baldwin, *Blues for Mr. Charlie* (New York: Dial, 1964), 77.

35. Baldwin, *Devil,* 116.

36. Baldwin, *Devil,* 30.

37. Baldwin, *Notes,* 112-13.

38. James Baldwin, "The Northern Protestant," in *Nobody Knows My Name* (New York: Dell, 1954), 180.

39. I am preparing a biography of James Baldwin. Much of the material in this section of the essay was obtained from conversations and interviews with Mr. Baldwin, his family, and associates, I am indebted to the Emory University Grants and Research Committee for a fellowship for support in obtaining these interviews and documentation in the course of this research.

40. Interviews with James Baldwin, Bernard Haskell, David Baldwin, and Richard Long, April 1980 and August 1980.

41. Interview, James Baldwin, June 1981.

42. Richard Wright's bitter exposure to Christian dogma was through his overbearing grandmother's relationship with the Seventh-Day Adventist Church, a denomination that had no historical axis in black American historical traditions. Thus, other than his hatred of her religious hypocrisy in *Black Boy,* his scenes are not religious and certainly did not reflect a church experience of his own. In *Invisible Man,* religion is confined to the rhetoric of the college campus and others political forums. Other than metaphors of groupism that also allude to the Communist party. Ellison avoids condemnation of the black church.

43. Baldwin and Giovanni, *Dialogue*, 38.

Chinua Achebe (essay date 1989)

SOURCE: "James Baldwin," in *James Baldwin: The Legacy*, edited by Quincy Troupe, Simon & Schuster, 1989, pp. 213-17.

[*Chinua Achebe is a novelist whose works include* Things Fall Apart *and* Anthills of the Savannah. *In the following essay, he asserts the value of James Baldwin's legacy.*]

The many and varied tributes to Jimmy Baldwin, like the blind men's version of the elephant, are consistent in one detail—the immensity, the sheer prodigality of endowment.

When my writing first began to yield small rewards in the way of free travel, UNESCO came along and asked where I would like to go. Without hesitation I said, "U.S.A. and Brazil." And so I came to the Americas for the first time in 1963.

My intention, which was somewhat nebulous to begin with, was to find out how the Africans of the diaspora were faring in the two largest countries of the New World. In UNESCO files, however, it was stated with greater precision. I was given a fellowship to enable me to study literary trends and to meet and exchange ideas with writers.

I did indeed make very many useful contacts: John O. Killens, Langston Hughes, Ralph Ellison, Paule Marshall, Le Roi Jones (now Amiri Baraka), and so on; and for good measure, Arthur Miller. They were all wonderful to me. And yet there was no way I could hide from myself or my sponsors my sense of disappointment that one particular meeting could not happen because the man concerned was away in France. And that was the year of *The Fire Next Time.*

Before I came to America I had discovered and read *Go Tell It on the Mountain*, and been instantly captivated. For me it combined the strange and the familiar in a way that was entirely new. I went to the United States Information Service Library in Lagos to see what other material there might be *by* or *on* this man. There was absolutely nothing. So I offered a couple of suggestions and such was the persuasiveness of newly independent Africans in those days that when next I looked in at the library they had not only Baldwin but Richard Wright as well.

I had all my schooling in the educational system of colonial Nigeria. In that system Americans, when they were featured at all, were dismissed summarily by our British administrators as loud and vulgar. Their universities, which taught such subjects as dishwashing, naturally produced half-baked noisy political agitators, some of whom were now rushing up and down the country because they had acquired no proper skills.

But there was one American book which the colonial educators considered of sufficient value to be exempted from the general censure of things American and actually to be prescribed reading in my high school. It was the autobiography of Booker T. Washington: *Up from Slavery.*

This bizarre background probably explains why my first encounter with Baldwin's writing was such a miraculous experience. Nothing that I had heard or read or seen quite prepared me for the Baldwin phenomenon. Needless to say, my education was entirely silent about W. E. B. DuBois, who, as I later discovered, had applied *his* experience of what he called "the strange meaning of being black" in America to ends and insights radically different from Washington's.

A major aspect of my reeducation was to see (and what comfort it gave me!) that Baldwin was neither an aberration nor likely to be a flash in the pan. He brought a new sharpness of vision, a new energy of passion, a new perfection of language to battle the incubus of race which DuBois had prophesied would possess our century—which prophecy itself had a long pedigree through the slave revolts back into Africa where, believe it or not, a seventeenth-century Igbo priest-king, Eze Nri, had declared slavery an abomination. I *say believe it or not* because this personage and many others like him in different parts of Africa do not fit the purposes of your history books.

When at last I met Jimmy in person in the jungles of Florida in 1980, I actually greeted him with "Mr. Baldwin, I presume!" You should have seen his eyes dancing, his remarkable face working in ripples of joyfulness. During the four days we spent down there I saw how easy it was to make Jimmy smile, and how the world he was doomed to inhabit would remorselessly deny him that simple benediction.

Baldwin and I were invited by the African Literature Association to open its annual conference in Gainesville with a public conversation. As we stepped into a tremendous ovation in the packed auditorium of the Holiday Inn, Baldwin was in particularly high spirits. I thought the old preacher in him was reacting to the multitude.

He went to the podium and began to make his opening statements. Within minutes a mystery voice came over the public address system and began to hurl racial insults at him and me. I will see that moment to the end of my life: the happiness brutally wiped off Baldwin's face; the genial manner gone; the eyes flashing in defiant combativeness; the voice incredibly calm and measured. And the words of remorseless prophecy began once again to flow.

One of the few hopeful examples of leadership in Africa was terminated abruptly when Captain Thomas Sankara, leader of Burkina Faso, was murdered in his fourth year of rule by his second-in-command. The world did not pay too much attention to yet another round of musical chairs by power-hungry soldiers in Africa. In any event Sankara was a brash young man with Marxist leanings who recently had the effrontery to read a lecture to a visiting head of state who happened to be none other than President Mitterrand of France himself. According to press reports of the incident, Mitterrand, who is a socialist veteran in his own right, rose to the occasion. He threw away his prepared speech and launched into an hour-long counterattack in which he must have covered much ground. But the sting was in the tail: "Sankara is a disturbing person. With him it is impossible to sleep in peace. He does not leave your conscience alone" (*New York Times*, August 23, 1987, p. 10).

I have no doubt that Mitterrand meant his comment as some kind of praise for his young and impatient host. But it was also a deadly arraignment and even conviction. Principalities and powers do not tolerate those who interrupt the sleep of their consciences. That Baldwin got away with it for forty years was a miracle. Except, of course, that he didn't get away; he paid dearly every single day of those years, every single hour of those days.

What was his crime that we should turn him into a man of sadness, this man inhabited by a soul so eager to be loved and to smile? His demands were so few and so simple.

His bafflement, childlike—which does not mean simple-minded but deeply profound and saintly—comes across again and again and nowhere better perhaps than in his essay **"Fifth Avenue, Uptown"**: "Negroes want to be treated like men: a perfectly straightforward statement containing seven words. People who have mastered Kant, Hegel, Shakespeare, Marx, Freud and the Bible find this statement impenetrable." This failure to comprehend turns out to be, as one might have suspected, a willful, obdurate refusal. And for good reason. For let's face it, that sentence, simple and innocent-looking though it may seem, is in reality a mask for a profoundly subversive intent to reorder the world. And the world, viewed from the high point of the pyramid where its controllers reside, is working perfectly well and sitting firm.

Egypt's Pharaoh, according to the myth of the Israelites, faced the same problem when a wild-eyed man walked up to him with a simple demand, four words long: "Let my people go!" We are not told that he rushed off to his office to sign their exit visa. On the contrary.

So neither history nor legend encourages us to believe that a man who sits on his fellow will some day climb down on

the basis of sounds reaching him from below. And yet we must consider how so much more dangerous our already very perilous world would become if the oppressed everywhere should despair altogether of invoking reason and humanity to arbitrate their cause. This is the value and the relevance, into the foreseeable future, of James Baldwin.

As long as injustice exists, whether it be within the American nation itself or between it and its neighbors; as long as a tiny cartel of rich, creditor nations can hold the rest in iron chains of usury; so long as one third or less of mankind eat well and often to excess while two-thirds and more live perpetually with hunger; as long as white people who constitute a mere fraction of the human race consider it natural and even righteous to dominate the rainbow majority whenever and wherever they are thrown together; and—the oldest of them all—as long as the discrimination by men against women persists, the words of James Baldwin will be there to bear witness and to inspire and elevate the struggle for human freedom.

Henry Louis Gates, Jr. (essay date 1 June 1992)

SOURCE: "*The Fire Last Time,*" in *New Republic*, Vol. 206, No. 22, June 1, 1992, pp. 37-43.

[*In the following essay, Gates traces the course of Baldwin's thought and importance throughout his career.*]

"I am *not* in paradise," James Baldwin assured readers of the *Black Scholar* in 1973. "It rains down here too." Maybe it did. But it seemed like paradise to me. In 1973 I was 22 years old, an eager young black American journalist doing a story for *Time*, visiting Baldwin at his home just outside the tiny, ancient walled village of St. Paul de Vence, nestled in the alpine foothills that rise from the Mediterranean Sea. The air carried the smells of wild thyme and pine and centuries-old olive trees. The light of the region, prized by painters and vacationers, at once intensifies and subdues the colors, so that the terra-cotta tile roofs of the buildings are by turns rosy pink, rust brown, or deep red.

Baldwin's house was situated among shoulder-high rosemary hedges, grape arbors, acres of peach and almond orchards, and fields of wild asparagus and strawberries; it had been built in the eighteenth century and retained its frescoed walls and rough-hewn beams. And yet he seemed to have made of it his own Greenwich Village café. Always there were guests, an entourage of friends and hangers-on, and always there was drinking and conviviality. The grape arbors sheltered tables, and it was under one such grape arbor, at one of the long harvest tables, that we dined. The line from the old gospel song, a line that Baldwin had quoted toward the end of his then latest novel, suggested itself: "I'm going to feast at the welcome table." And we did—Baldwin, and Josephine Baker, well into her 60s but still with a lean dancer's body and the smooth skin that the French called "café-au-lait," and Cecil Brown, author of *The Life and Lovers of Mister Jiveass Nigger* and one of the great hopes of black fiction, my fiancée, Sharon Adams, and I.

At that long welcome table under the arbor, the wine flowed, food was served and taken away, and Baldwin and Baker traded stories, gossiped about everyone they knew and many people they didn't know, and remembered their lives. They had both been hurt and disillusioned by the United States and had chosen to live in France. They never forgot or forgave. At the table that long, warm night they recollected the events that led to their decisions to leave their country of birth, and the consequences of those decisions: the difficulty of living away from home and family, of always feeling apart in their chosen homes; the pleasure of choosing a new life, the possibilities of the untried. A sense of nostalgia pervaded the evening. For all their misgivings, they shared a sense, curiously, of being on the winning side of history.

People said Baldwin was ugly; he himself said so. But he was not ugly to me. There are faces that we cannot see simply as faces because they are so familiar, so iconic, and his face was one of them. And as I sat there, in a growing haze of awe and alcohol, studying his lined visage, I realized that neither the Baldwin I was meeting—mischievous, alert, funny—nor the Baldwin I might come to know could ever mean as much to me as James Baldwin, my own personal oracle, the gimlet-eyed figure who stared at me out of a fuzzy dust jacket photograph when I was 14. For that was when I first met Baldwin, and discovered that black people, too, wrote books.

It was the summer of 1965, and I was attending an Episcopal church camp in eastern West Virginia, high in the Allegheny Mountains. This was no ordinary church camp. Our themes that year were "Is God dead?" and "Can you love two people at once?" (Episcopalians were never ones to let grass grow under their feet.) After a solid week of complete isolation, a delivery man, bringing milk and bread to the camp, told the head counselor that "all hell had broken loose in Los Angeles," and that the "colored people had gone crazy." Then he handed him a Sunday paper, screaming the news that Negroes were rioting in some place called Watts. I, for one, was bewildered. I didn't understand what a riot was. Were colored people being killed by white people, or were they killing white people? Watching myself being watched by all of the white campers—there were only three black kids among the hundreds of campers—I experienced that strange combination of power and powerlessness that you

feel when the actions of another black person affect your own life, simply because both of you are black.

Sensing my mixture of pride and discomfiture, an Episcopal priest from New England handed me a book. *Notes of a Native Son,* it was called. Was this man the author, I wondered to myself, this man with a closely cropped "natural," brown skin, splayed nostrils, and wide lips, so very Negro, so comfortable to be so? This was the first time I had heard a voice capturing the terrible exhilaration and anxiety of being a person of African descent in this country. From the book's first few sentences, I was caught up thoroughly in the sensibility of another person, a black person. Coming from a tiny and segregated black community in a white village, I knew that "black culture" had a texture, a logic, of its own, *and* that it was inextricable from "white" culture. That was the paradox that Baldwin identified and negotiated, and that is why I say his prose shaped my identity as an Afro-American, as much by the questions he raised as by the answers he provided.

I could not put the book down. I raced through it, then others, filling my commonplace book with his marvelously long sentences that bristled with commas and qualifications. The biblical cadences spoke to me with a special immediacy, for I, too, was to be a minister, having been "saved" in a small evangelical church at the age of 12. (From this fate the Episcopalians—and also Baldwin—diverted me.) Eventually I began to imitate Baldwin's style of writing, using dependent clauses whenever and wherever I could. Consider a passage from *Nobody Knows My Name.*

> And a really cohesive society, one of the attributes, perhaps, of what is taken to be a "healthy" culture, has, generally, and I suspect, necessarily, a much lower level of tolerance for the maverick, the dissenter, the man who steals the fire, than have societies in which, the common ground of belief having all but vanished, each man, in awful and brutal isolation, is for himself, to flower or to perish.

There are sixteen commas in that sentence. And so in my essays at school I was busy trying to cram as many commas into my sentences as I could, until my high school English teacher forbade me.

Of course, I was not alone in my enthrallment. When Baldwin wrote *The Fire Next Time* in 1963, he was exalted as *the* voice of black America; and it was not long before he was spoken of as a contender for the Nobel Prize. ("Opportunity and duty are sometimes born together," he wrote later.) Perhaps not since Booker T. Washington had one man been taken to embody the voice of "the Negro." By the early '60s his authority seemed nearly unchallengeable. What did the Negro want? Ask James Baldwin.

The puzzle was that his arguments, richly nuanced and self-consciously ambivalent, were far too complex to serve straightforwardly political ends. Thus he would argue in *Notes of a Native Son* that

> the question of color, especially in this country, operates to hide the graver question of the self. That is precisely why what we like to call "the Negro problem" is so tenacious in American life, and so dangerous. But my own experience proves to me that the connection between American whites and blacks is far deeper and more passionate than any of us like to think. . . . The questions which one asks oneself begin, at last, to illuminate the world, and become one's key to the experience of others. One can only face in others what one can face in oneself. On this confrontation depends the measure of our wisdom and compassion. This energy is all that one finds in the rubble of vanished civilizations, and the only hope for ours.

One does not read such a passage without a double take. By proclaiming that the color question conceals the graver questions of the self, Baldwin leads you to expect a transcendence of the contingencies of race, in the name of a deeper artistic or psychological truth. But instead, with an abrupt swerve, he returns you precisely to those questions:

> In America, the color of my skin had stood between myself and me; in Europe, that barrier was down. Nothing is more desirable than to be released from an affliction, but nothing is more frightening than to be divested of a crutch. It turned out that the question of who I was was not solved because I had removed myself from the social forces which menaced me—anyway, these forces had become interior, and I had dragged them across the ocean with me. The question of who I was had at last become a personal question, and the answer was to be found in me.

> I think there is always something frightening about this realization. I know it frightened me.

Again, these words are easily misread. For Baldwin was proposing not that politics is merely a projection of private neuroses, but that our private neuroses are shaped by quite public ones. The retreat to subjectivity, the "graver questions of the self," would lead not to an escape from the "racial drama," but—and this was the alarm-

ing prospect that Baldwin wanted to announce—a rediscovery of it.

That traditional liberal dream of a non-racial self, unconstrained by epidermal contingencies, was hopefully entertained and at last, for him, reluctantly dismissed. "There are," he observed,

> few things on earth more attractive than the idea of the unspeakable liberty which is allowed the unredeemed. When, beneath the black mask, a human being begins to make himself felt one cannot escape a certain awful wonder as to what kind of human being it is. What one's imagination makes of other people is dictated, of course, by the laws of one's own personality and it is one of the ironies of black-white relations that, by means of what the white man imagines the black man to be, the black man is enabled to know who the white man is.

This is not a call for "racial understanding." On the contrary, we understand each other all too well, for we have invented one another, derived our identities from the ghostly projections of our alter egos. If Baldwin had a central political argument, it was that the destinies of black America and white were profoundly and irreversibly intertwined. Each created the other, each defined itself in relation to the other, each could destroy the other.

For Baldwin, America's "interracial drama" had "not only created a new black man, it has created a new white man, too." In that sense, he could argue, "The history of the American Negro problem is not merely shameful, it is also something of an achievement. For even when the worst has been said, it must also be added that the perpetual challenge posed by this problem was always, somehow, perpetually met." These were not words to speed along a cause. They certainly did not mesh with the rhetoric of self-affirmation that liberation movements, including those masquerading as a newly "Afrocentric" science of man, require. Yet couldn't his sense of the vagaries of identity serve the ends of a still broader, braver politics?

As an intellectual, Baldwin was at his best when he explored his own equivocal sympathies and clashing allegiances. He was here to "bear witness," he insisted, not to be a spokesman. And he was right to insist on the distinction. But who had time for such niceties? The spokesman role was assigned him inevitably. The result was to complicate further his curious position as an Afro-American intellectual. In those days, on the populist left, the favored model of the oppositional spokesman was what Gramsci called the "organic intellectual," who participated in, and was part of, the community, which he would not only analyze but also uplift. And yet Baldwin's basic conception of himself was formed by the older but still well-entrenched ideal of the alienated artist or intellectual, whose advanced sensibility entailed his estrangement from the very people he would represent.

Baldwin could dramatize the tension between these two models, especially in his fiction, but he was never to resolve it. A spokesman must have a firm grasp on his role and an unambiguous message to articulate. Baldwin had neither, and when this was discovered a few short years later, he was relieved of his duties, summarily retired, shunted aside as an elder statesman. Indeed, by the time I met him, on that magical afternoon in St. Paul de Vence, he had become (as my own editor subsequently admonished me) passé. Anyone who was aware of the ferment in black America was familiar with the attacks. And nothing ages a young Turk faster than still younger Turks; the cruel irony was that Baldwin may never have fully recovered from this demotion from a status that he had always disavowed.

If Baldwin had once served as a shadow delegate for black America in the congress of culture, his term had expired. Soldiers, not delegates, were what was wanted these days. "Pulling rank," Eldridge Cleaver wrote in his essay on Baldwin, "is a very dangerous business, especially when the troops have mutinied and the basis of one's authority, or rank, is devoid of that interdictive power and has become suspect." He found in Baldwin's work "the most grueling, agonizing, total hatred of the blacks, particularly of himself, and the most shameful, fanatical, fawning, sycophantic love of the whites that one can find in any black American writer of note in our time." According to Amiri Baraka, the new star of the Black Arts Movement, Baldwin was "Joan of Arc of the cocktail party." His "spavined whine and plea" was "sickening beyond belief." In the eyes of the young Ishmael Reed, he was "a hustler who comes on like Job."

Cleaver attacked Baldwin on more than racial grounds. For the heated new apostle of black machismo, Baldwin's sexuality, that is, his homosexuality, also represented treason: "Many Negro homosexuals, acquiescing in this racial death-wish, are outraged because in their sickness they are unable to have a baby by a white man." Baldwin was thus engaged in "a despicable underground guerrilla war, waged on paper, against black masculinity." Young militants referred to Baldwin, unsmilingly, as Martin Luther Queen. Baldwin, of course, was hardly a stranger to the sexual battlefield. "On every street corner," Baldwin would later recall of his early days in the Village, "I was called a faggot." What was different this time was a newly sexualized black nationalism that could stigmatize homosexuality as a capitulation to alien white norms, and in that way accredit homophobia as a progressive political act.

A new generation, so it seemed, was determined to define itself by everything Baldwin was not. By the late '60s Baldwin-bashing was almost a rite of initiation. And yet Baldwin would not return fire, at least not in public. He responded with a pose of wounded passivity. And then, with a kind of capitulation: the shift of political climate forced him to simplify his rhetoric or risk internal exile.

As his old admirers recognized, Baldwin was now chasing, with unseemly alacrity, after a new vanguard, one that esteemed rage, not compassion, as our noblest emotion. "It is not necessary for a black man to hate a white man, or to have particular feelings about him at all, in order to realize that he must kill him," he wrote in *No Name in the Street*, a book he began in 1967 but did not publish until 1972. "Yes, we have come, or are coming, to this, and there is no point in flinching before the prospect of this exceedingly cool species of fratricide." That same year he told *The New York Times* of his belated realization that "our destinies are in our hands, black hands, and no one else's."

It is a stirring sentiment—and a sentiment that the earlier Baldwin would have been the first to see through. How far he had come from the author of *The Fire Next Time,* who had forecast the rise of black power and yet was certain that

> we, the black and the white, deeply need each other here if we are really to become a nation—if we are really, that is, to achieve our identity, our maturity, as men and women. To create one nation has proved to be a hideously difficult task: there is certainly no need now to create two, one black and one white.

All such qualms were irrelevant now. In an offhanded but calculated manner, Baldwin affected to dismiss his earlier positions: "I was, in some way, in those years, without entirely realizing it, the Great Black Hope of the Great White Father." If there was something ominous about this public display of self-criticism, it was because we could not forget that the forced recantation had no value that does not purport to be freely given.

In an impossible gambit, the author of *No Name in the Street* sought to reclaim his lost authority by signaling his willingness to be instructed by those who had inherited it. Contradicting his own greatest achievements, he feebly borrowed the populist slogans of the day, and returned them with the beautiful Baldwinian polish. "The powerless, by definition, can never be 'racists,'" he writes, "for they can never make the world pay for what they feel or fear except by the suicidal endeavor that makes them fanatics or revolutionaries, or both; whereas those in power can be urbane and charming and invite you to those houses which they know you will never own." This view—that blacks cannot be racist—

is today a familiar one, a platitude of much of the contemporary debate. The key phrase, of course, is "by definition." For this is not only, or even largely, an empirical claim. It is a rhetorical and psychological move, an unfortunate but unsurprising attempt by the victim to forever exempt himself from guilt.

The term "racism" is here redefined by Baldwin, as it has been redefined by certain prominent Afro-American artists and intellectuals today, to refer to a reified system of power relations, to a social order in which one race is essentially and forever subordinated to another. (A parallel move is common in much feminist theory, where "patriarchy"—naming a social order to which Man and Woman have a fixed and opposed relation—contrasts with "sexism," which characterizes the particular acts of particular people.) To be sure, it does express, in an abstract and extreme manner, a widely accepted truth: that the asymmetries of power mean that not all racial insult is equal. (Not even a Florida jury is much concerned when a black captive calls his arresting officer a "cracker.") Still, it represents a grave political error.

For black America needs allies more than it needs absolution. And the slogan—a definition masquerading as an idea—would all too quickly serve as a blanket amnesty for our own dankest suspicions and bigotries. It is a slogan that Baldwin once would have debunked with his devastating mock-detachment. He would have repudiated it not for the sake of white America—for white America, he would have argued, the display of black prejudice could only provide a reassuring confirmation of its own—but for the sake of black America. The Baldwin who knew that the fates of black and white America were one also knew that if racism was to be deplored, it was to be deplored *tout court*, without exemption clauses for the oppressed.

Wasn't it this conviction, above all, that explained Baldwin's own repudiation of Malcolm X? I should be clear. His reverence for Malcolm was real, but it was posthumous. In a conversation with Kenneth Clark recorded in 1963, a year and a half before Malcolm's assassination, Baldwin ventured that by preaching black supremacy, "what [Malcolm] does is destroy a truth and invent a myth." Compared with King's appeal, he said, Malcolm's appeal was

> much more sinister because it is much more effective. It is much more effective, because it is, after all, comparatively easy to invest a population with false morale by giving them a false sense of superiority, and it will always break down in a crisis. That is the history of Europe simply—it's one of the reasons that we are in this terrible place.

Still, he cautioned, the country "shouldn't be worried about

the Muslim movement, that's not the problem. The problem is to eliminate the conditions which breed the Muslim movement." (Five years later, under contract with Columbia Pictures, Baldwin began the task of adapting Malcolm to the screen.)

That ethnic scapegoating was an unaffordable luxury, moreover, had been another of Baldwin's own lessons. "Georgia has the Negro," he once pithily wrote, slicing through the thickets of rationalization, "and Harlem has the Jew." We have grimly seen where the failure of this more truthful vision has led: to the surreal spectacle of urban activists who would rather picket Korean grocery stores than crack houses, on the assumption that sullen shopkeepers with their pricey tomatoes, and not smiley drug dealers with their discount glass vials, are the true threat to black dignity.

As I say, by 1973 the times had changed; and they have stayed changed. That, I suppose, is our problem. But Baldwin wanted to change with them. That was his problem. And so we lost his skepticism, his critical independence. Baldwin's belated public response to Cleaver's charges was heartbreaking, and all too symptomatic. Now he would turn the other cheek and insist, in *No Name in the Street,* that he actually admired Cleaver's book. Cleaver's attack on him was explained away as a regrettable if naive misunderstanding: the revolutionary had simply been misled by Baldwin's public reputation. Beyond that, he wrote,

> I also felt that I was confused in his mind with the unutterable debasement of the male—with all those faggots, punks, and sissies, the sight and sound of whom, in prison, must have made him vomit more than once. Well, I certainly hope I know more about myself, and the intention of my work than that, but I *am* an odd quantity. So is Eldridge, so are we all. It is a pity that we won't, probably, ever have the time to attempt to define once more the relationship of the odd and disreputable artist to odd and disreputable revolutionary. . . . And I think we need each other, and have much to learn from each other, and, more than ever, now.

It was an exercise in perverse and willed magnanimity, and it was meant, no doubt, to suggest unruffled strength. Instead it showed weakness, the ill-disguised appeasement of the creature whose day had come and gone.

Did Baldwin know what was happening to him? His essays give no clue; increasingly they came to represent his official voice. But his fiction became the refuge of his growing self-doubts. In 1968 he published *Tell Me How Long the Train's Been Gone.* Formally speaking, it was his least successful work, but in its protagonist, Leo Proudhammer,

Baldwin created a perfectly Baldwinian alter ego, a celebrated black artist who, in diction that matched the eloquence of Baldwin's essays, could express the quandaries that came increasingly to trouble his creator. "The day came," he reflects at one point, "when I wished to break my silence and found that I could not speak: the actor could no longer be distinguished from his role." Thus did Baldwin, our elder statesman, who knew better than anyone how a mask could deform the face beneath, chafe beneath his own.

Called to speak before a civil rights rally, Proudhammer ruminates on the contradictions of his position:

> I did not want others to endure my estrangement, that was why I was on the platform; yet was it not, at the least, paradoxical that it was only my estrangement which had placed me there? . . . It was our privilege, to say nothing of our hope, to attempt to make the world a human dwelling place for us all; and yet—yet—was it not possible that the mighty gentlemen, my honorable and invaluable confreres, by being unable to imagine such a journey as my own, were leaving something of the utmost importance out of their aspirations?

These are not unpolitical reflections, but they are not the reflections of a politician. Contrast Leroi Jones's unflappable conviction, in an essay called "Reflections of Two Hotshots" published in 1963, that "a writer must have a point of view, or he cannot be a good writer. He must be standing somewhere in the world, or else he is not one of *us,* and his commentary then is of little value." It was a carefully aimed arrow, and it would pierce Baldwin's heart.

The threat of being deemed obsolete, or "not one of *us,*" is a fearful thing. *Tell Me How Long* depicts a black artist's growing sense that (in a recurrent phrase) he no longer belongs to himself, that his public role may have depleted the rest of him. Of course, "the burden of representation," as Baldwin once called it, is a common affliction in Afro-American literature, an unfair condition of hardship that black writers frequently face; but few black writers have measured its costs—the price of this particular ticket to ride—as trenchantly as Baldwin. He risked the fate, and in some ways finally succumbed to the fate, that Leo Proudhammer most feared, which was to be "a Jeremiah without convictions."

Desperate to be "one of us," to be loved by his own, Baldwin allowed himself to mouth a script that was not his own. The connoisseur of complexity tried his hand at being an ideologue. To be sure, he could still do anything he wanted with the English essay. The problem was that he no longer knew quite what he wanted, and he cared too much about what others wanted from him. For a generation had arrived that didn't want anything from him—except, perhaps,

that he lie down and die. And this, too, has been a consistent dynamic of race and representation in Afro-America. If someone has anointed a black intellectual, be assured that someone else is busily constructing his tumbril.

We stayed in touch, on and off, through the intervening years, often dining at the Ginger Man when he was in New York. Sometimes he would introduce me to his current lover, or speak of his upcoming projects. I did not return to St. Paul de Vence until shortly after his death four-and-a-half years ago at the age of 63. This time I came to meet his brother David. The place had changed remarkably in the twenty or so years since Baldwin settled there. The grape arbors are now strung with electric lights. Luxury homes dot the landscape on quarter-acre plots, and in the midst of this congestion stands Baldwin's ten-acre oasis, the only undivided farm acreage left in St. Paul.

When I recounted for David Baldwin the circumstances of my meeting his brother for the first time, his wide eyes grew wider. He rose from the table, went downstairs into the study—where a wall of works by and about Henry James faces you as you enter—and emerged with a manuscript in hand. "This is for you," he said. He handed me a play. It was the last work that James Baldwin completed as he suffered through his final illness, and it was called **"The Welcome Table."** It was set in the Riviera, at a house much like his own, and among the principal characters were "Edith, an actress-singer/star: Creole, from New Orleans," "Daniel, ex-black Panther, fledgling playwright" with more than a passing resemblance to Cecil Brown, and "Peter Davis, Black American journalist." Peter Davis—who has come to interview a famous star, and whose prodding questions lead to the play's revelations—was, I should say, a far better and more aggressive interviewer than I was; Baldwin, being Baldwin, had transmuted the occasion into a searching drama of revelation and crisis.

Narratives of decline have the appeal of simplicity, but Baldwin's career will not fit that mold. "Unless a writer is extremely old when he dies, in which case he has probably become a neglected institution, his death must always seem untimely," he wrote in 1961, giving us fair warning. "This is because a real writer is always shifting and changing and searching." Reading his late essays, I would like to imagine him embarking on a period of intellectual resurgence. Despite the unfortunate pronouncements of his later years, I believe that he was finding his course again, and exploring the instability of all the categories that divide us. As he wrote in **"Here Be Monsters,"** an essay published two years before his death, and with which he chose to conclude *The Price of the Ticket,* his collected nonfiction: "Each of us, helplessly and forever, contains the other—male in female, female in male, white in black, and black in white. We are part of each other. Many of my countrymen appear to find this fact exceedingly inconvenient and even unfair, and so, very often, do I. But none of us can do anything about it." We needed to hear those words two decades ago, and we especially need to hear them now.

Now we are struggling in this country to fathom the rage in Los Angeles; and slowly we are realizing how intertwined, as Baldwin insisted, are the destinies of black and white America, and how easily one can lay waste to the other in the fury of interracial fratricide. Thirty years ago, Baldwin believed that an effort by the handful of "relatively conscious" blacks and whites might be able to avert the prophecy of the old spiritual: "God gave Noah the rainbow sign, No more water, the fire next time!" The belief proved difficult to sustain. Good intentions—increasingly scarce these days—seem easily defeated by the cycles of poverty, the structural as well as the cultural determinants of urban decay, alienation, and hopelessness. Today, as black intellectuals try to sort outrage from opportunism, political protest from simple criminality, they may wonder if the sense of mutuality that Baldwin promoted can long survive, or if his "elegant despair" alone will endure.

But perhaps times are due to change again. An influential black intellectual avant-garde in Britain has resurrected Baldwin as a patron saint, and a new generation of readers has come to value just those qualities of ambivalence and equivocality, just that sense of the contingency of identity, that made him useless to the ideologues of liberation and anathema to so many black nationalists. Even Baldwin's fiercest antagonists seem now to have welcomed him back to the fold. Like everyone else, I guess, we like our heroes dead.

Terry Rowden   (essay date January 1993)

SOURCE: "A Play of Abstractions: Race, Sexuality, and Community in James Baldwin's *Another Country*," in *Southern Review*, Vol. 29, No. 1, January, 1993, pp. 41-50.

[*In the following essay, Rowden analyzes racial and sexual identity in Baldwin's* Another Country, *focusing on the character of Rufus, his relationships, and his place in the community.*]

Of the many blindnesses that have characterized critical readings of James Baldwin's work, one of the most consistent has been the critical failure to consider seriously the lack of continuity uniting the persona of racial spokesman that Baldwin adopts in many of his essays and that of sexual utopian that he develops in his fiction. Although it is usually the completely whitewashed *Giovanni's Room* to which Baldwin critics point when they want to strip him of his race-

man credentials, it is actually in Baldwin's novel *Another Country,* with its general exclusion of black men and its racial scapegoating of the only one that it allows, that we are given the most explicit evidence of how ambivalent was Baldwin's relationship not only to the sexuality of the black man, but to the simple fact of the existence of black men in society.

Most works of fiction rely on some implied notion of community in order to maintain their narrative and normative coherence. They achieve this coherence by the explicit scapegoating of some person (or persons) who, by extension, become representative of something whose eradication would bring about the kind of communal situation that I am calling "utopian." The scapegoated character exists as the point in relation to which an anti-utopian or dystopian alternative can be glimpsed and textually activated, thereby making possible the normative coding of the various characters and their actions. It is as reactive movement away from this implicitly dystopian alternative that the narrative is constructed.

Of all of James Baldwin's novels, *Another Country* is the most important for a consideration of this narrative dynamic. In *Another Country* this dystopianism is enacted by, or perhaps I should say projected onto, the figure of Rufus. At best, Baldwin's Rufus is the depiction of a pathology that is never explicitly acknowledged, a case of internalized racism of almost Frankensteinian proportions. Contextualized by his unlikely group of middle-class white friends, Rufus's life and suicide can best be read not as the acts of a tragically self-aware black man destroyed by the inescapable forces of white racism, but as those of a racially alienated white/black man fatally frustrated by a lack of recognition from the only people whose recognition he can perceive as being of any value, the white bourgeoisie.

As both a self-proclaimed homosexual and a burgeoning literary superstar, by the time *Another Country* was published Baldwin was, socially, a very strangely situated man. Unfortunately, the more critics and black radicals commented on the dichotomy between the particulars differentiating Baldwin's own life from those of the people he claimed to represent, the more desperate he became to take on the mantle of race-man extraordinaire. The resulting contradictions explain perhaps better than anything else the problematic aspects of the fiction that he wrote after *Go Tell It On the Mountain*.

The observation that Baldwin's Rufus is, regardless of his other antecedents, in some sense a response to Richard Wright's Bigger Thomas is a critical commonplace, but whereas the claim can plausibly be made that, as Irving Howe put it in his essay "James Baldwin: At Ease in Apocalypse," Wright successfully deployed Bigger as "not so much a distinctive human being as an elemental force through which to release the rage black men had not dared to express," Rufus's sketchiness is much more problematic and ineffective. Rufus's suicidal response to racist oppression, the opening salvo in Baldwin's turn to the kind of protest writing for which he had previously chided Richard Wright, is supposedly the only option available to him in the unremittingly racist society of which he is a part. Unfortunately, we are never actually given any sense of the process that creates what Baldwin describes as "colored men who wanted to beat up everyone in sight, including, or perhaps especially, people who had never one way or another, given them a thought." In *Another Country* Baldwin never establishes a believable social ellipse upon which we can situate Rufus. What Baldwin wrote of Richard Wright's narrowness of focus in *Native Son* could more pertinently have been written about this aspect of *Another Country:*

> What this means for the novel is that a necessary dimension has been cut away; this dimension being the relationship that Negroes bear to one another, that depth of involvement and unspoken recognition of shared experience which creates a way of life. What the novel reflects— and at no point interprets—is the isolation of the Negro within his own group and the resulting fury of impatient scorn.

The Rufus section of the novel fails to do the kind of textual work that would justify its privileged position in the novel. In order for it to function formally in the way that Baldwin wanted it to, i.e., to resonate throughout the rest of the book, elevating the whole to the level of a serious social critique, Rufus's representativeness and his special sensitivity to the racist dynamics of American society would have to have been established with a much greater degree of realism and social specificity. This is, unfortunately, exactly what Baldwin fails to do. Although Baldwin tells us that Rufus is "part of an unprecedented multitude," he is, in fact, presented as being almost totally isolated from any recognizable section of the black community. We are repeatedly told of how well loved and respected Rufus is by his fellow jazzmen, but he is never shown actually relating to them as one black man, or more specifically as one black artist, among others. Instead Rufus's position as an artist, a jazz drummer, is used to justify his friendships with the "artsy" group of whites by whom he has been taken up as a mascot.

From the start, the idea of Rufus as exemplary black man is consistently undercut. By depriving Rufus's plight of any social context beyond casually polemical references to a state of oppression whose particulars Baldwin seems to think are so well known as to be unworthy of delineation, Baldwin fails to provide the kind of social detail that would narra-

tively validate the relationships that take place in the rest of the book. Regardless of how rhetorically seductive individual episodes in *Another Country* may be, the kind of social detail that could link these set pieces into the coherent or even comprehensive social vision that Baldwin was trying to articulate is lacking. The attention that Rufus's line "You took the best, so why not take the rest?" has received suggests that it has for many people some special expressive force as an agonized cry from the heart of the racially dispossessed urban "subproletariat." When read in the context of the novel itself, however, it is almost impossible to figure out exactly what Rufus is talking about. Nevertheless, one soon realizes that given the narrative trajectory that Rufus will travel in the novel, this isolation has an absolute strategic necessity. Only this kind of social alienation could explain both the belatedness of Rufus's recognition of the social significance of his blackness and the destructiveness and self-hatred to which this recognition gives rise.

Despite the narrative prominence and popular notoriety that the sexual and racial dynamics in *Another Country* have been granted, dramatically they are vitiated by Baldwin's fundamental lack of familiarity with the systematic particulars of the bourgeois white world that he attempts to depict and in which he tries to situate Rufus. Baldwin's inability to adequately conceptualize this social milieu makes it impossible for it and the under-depicted black one to narratively coexist and critically interrogate each other. Baldwin's attempt to delineate the emotional and ethnic tensions that might actually be operative among the sexually and racially heterogeneous group of people with whom he populates the book backfires, primarily because he never provides any plausible reasons, beyond Rufus's marginal position as a musician, for these characters to be emotionally involved or even personally aware of each other in the first place. The social landscape upon which the story is played out can only make sense if one thinks about it solely in terms of its narrative utility. Only by going completely outside of the framework that Baldwin sets up and reading the novel as the depiction of the goings-on among a self-consciously experimental group of sexual radicals can this particular collection of people be rendered believable.

This brings full circle the charge that Rufus does not represent black men. Because *Another Country's* utopianized image of homosexuality as represented by the sexually messianic figure of Eric is, as many critics have pointed out, coded as being exclusively white and male, Rufus cannot be a homosexual. Still, because (at least emotionally) his relationship with Vivaldo is so obviously homoerotic, he can't, given the novel's racial calculus, be genuinely black either. The best he can do is to represent or theatrically enact the kind of black male that Baldwin needs to serve his ideological purposes. This is the black male as bearer of a kind of heterosexual dystopianism that will throw the homosexual utopia with which the novel ends into even brighter relief. The very formlessness and social pessimism of the two novels in which Baldwin actually tried to situate socially the openly homosexual black man, *Tell Me How Long the Train's Been Gone* and *Just Above My Head,* indicate Baldwin's investment in the idea of this homosexual utopia and, implicitly, of positive community itself as something that was for whites only.

It is this dynamic of internalized racism that catalyzes the only genuinely well-drawn relationship in *Another Country,* the one between Rufus and Leona, the pathetic white southern woman whom he destroys. Although the fact of the white male's sexual exploitation of black women had been recognized since the beginnings of African-American fiction, it was not until Oscar Micheaux's *The Homesteader* that a black writer risked presenting a full-blown romance between a black man and a white woman. Charles Stember's book *Sexual Racism: The Emotional Barrier to an Integrated Society,* one of the best-known products of a strand of racist but not necessarily valueless sexology, reflects fruitfully on the master-idea of the Rufus section of *Another Country* and of many of the black novelists who have dealt with such relationships. This is the idea, best expressed by Calvin Hernton, that there is on the part of black men a "sociosexually induced predisposition for white women." If, as Stember has perhaps too sweepingly suggested, "Among men in our society sex is in fact closely associated with a feeling of defilement, and women, especially of the dominant culture tend to be seen as superior creatures," this imagined superiority may explain why the possession of or inability to possess a particular white woman is such an explosive issue for the men in *Another Country.*

In *Sexual Racism* Stember suggests that, "[w]hile the majority man attains maximum gratification only in situations where the woman is especially attractive according to cultural criteria, the black man can experience a strong feeling of conquest with almost any white woman." Bearing out this assertion, in *Another Country* the white woman seems to occupy a place squarely at the center of the black man's, Rufus's, consciousness. She occupies it, however, not as a woman but simply as an instrument, as the catalyst that sets into motion a sociosexual dynamic that seemingly involves not just this particular black man and white woman, but this man, this woman, and all of the men, black and white, to whom the relationship supposedly represents the ultimate act of social transgression. Just as, after a while, to think of Rufus is to think of Rufus and Leona, all of the culturally specific aspects of Rufus's experience that would have to be represented if Rufus were to have some force as an individual are reduced to peripheral elements which are subordinated, if not completely invalidated, by his desperate need, as a deindividualized black man, to acquire an equally deindividualized white woman. "You'd never even have

looked at that girl, Rufus, if she'd been black," the imagined voice of his sister says to Rufus at one point. "But you'll pick up any white trash just because she's white." Correspondingly, throughout their time together, Rufus almost never refers to Leona by her real name. She is among other things "Honeychild," "Miss Anne," "Little Eva," "a funny little cracker," and "a splendid specimen of Southern womanhood," but rarely simply Leona.

The Rufus-Leona relationship for most of its course is simply a play of abstractions, one in which any real psychological contact is, obviously on Rufus's part and more subtly on Leona's, systematically evaded. This dynamic can be seen at work even in the initial moments of their relationship. After Leona's first words to Rufus, Baldwin tells us:

> She had said enough. She was from the South. And something leaped in Rufus as he stared at her damp, colorless face, the face of the Southern poor white, and her straight pale hair. She was considerably older than he, over thirty probably, and her body was too thin. Just the same, it abruptly became the most exciting body he had gazed on in a long time.
>
> "Honeychild," he said and gave her his crooked grin, "ain't you a long ways from home?"
>
> "I sure am," she said, "and I ain't never going back there."
>
> He laughed and she laughed. "Well Miss Anne," he said, "if we both got the same thing on our mind let's make it to the party."

Both the simple fact that Leona is a white woman and the equally important fact that she is a white woman from the South immediately create a sense of double scapegoating that decisively excises this relationship from the utopian drama that will be played out in the novel's remaining 288 pages. For example, soon after meeting Leona, Rufus:

> remembered suddenly his days in boot camp in the South and felt again the shoe of a white officer against his mouth. He was in his white uniform, on the ground, against the red, dusty clay. Some of his colored buddies were holding him, were helping him to rise. The white officer, with a curse, had vanished, had gone forever beyond the reach of vengeance.

Leona's sexual availability as a woman enables her to stand in for and ground Rufus's relationship with Vivaldo, the white man with whom Rufus is involved in an unspoken game of racial and sexual competition, while her unique position as a southern woman enables Rufus to turn her into a surrogate for the white men against whom he cannot effectively express his resentment.

Leona, on the other hand, can scapegoat herself by "loving" and then allowing herself to be destroyed by the dangerous "other" that Rufus represents, just as another part of her had loved and been destroyed by the equally abusive relationship that her marriage to a hyperracist southern "cracker" had been. In fact, it is exactly Rufus's otherness, his blackness, that Leona must deny in order to perform her role in the drama that they are enacting. At one point Rufus asks, "Didn't they warn you down home about the darkies you'd find up North?" and she answers, "They didn't never worry me none. People's just people as far as I'm concerned." This response reveals her denial of both racial and sexual difference and, thereby, her repression of the distinctly sexual nature of her interest in Rufus. Being a product of the particular racial and sexual hierarchies which organize southern society, Leona could in fact never be unaware of the transgressive nature of her involvement with Rufus. She, perhaps more than any other character in *Another Country,* would know that people are not just people, and that there are real and potentially dangerous social implications in the sexual choices people make. Just as Rufus's self-hatred stems from his inability either to enact or reject the roles that have been socially validated for white men and made inaccessible for blacks, Leona's self-hatred is the result of a similar failure to fulfill internalized social expectations. She has "failed" as a wife and as a mother, and because of this failure has marked herself as someone deserving of destruction.

The catalyst in the Rufus/Leona relationship is the homoerotically charged presence of Rufus's best friend, Vivaldo. Because it is Rufus's status as a black man and not his sexual identity, whatever it may be, that makes him essentially unacceptable and places him outside of the positive community that Baldwin is conceptualizing in *Another Country,* whether Rufus can best be coded as homosexual, heterosexual, or bisexual is finally unimportant. As the glimpses Baldwin offers into Rufus's relationship with Eric make clear, exactly the same kind of racial abstractions that will characterize Rufus's relationship with Leona would come into play if the homosexual aspects of the relationship between Rufus and Vivaldo were allowed to take their "natural" course. Tellingly, Rufus is the only character in the book whom Eric's love cannot save.

In a way comparable to the dynamics of the relationships that Eve Kosofsky Sedgwick examines in her book *Between Men,* Rufus's relationship with Leona provides the means by which the idea of the white woman as the mediating factor linking black and white men can be dealt with. This mediation is one in which, despite the narrative prominence

accorded to Rufus's sister Ida, black women play no part other than as sexual objects, as the sources of a sexual release that is peripheral to any status concerns that a man, especially a white man, might have. Emotionally and hierarchically, only white women can situate black and white men in relation to each other. Baldwin writes:

> Vivaldo was unlike everyone else that he [Rufus] knew in that they, all the others, could only astonish him by kindness or fidelity; it was only Vivaldo who had the power to astonish him by treachery. Even his affair with Jane was evidence in his favor, for if he were really to betray his friend for a woman, as most white men seemed to do, especially if the friend was black, then he would have found himself a smoother chick, with the manners of a lady and the soul of a whore. But Jane seemed to be exactly what she was, a monstrous slut, and she thus without knowing it kept Rufus and Vivaldo equal to one another.

By forgoing sexual access to the kind of white women to whom Rufus as a poor black man could never have access, Vivaldo creates an equality that enables his friendship with Rufus. The continuum along which white women are placed in the novel goes from Jane who, according to Rufus, is "a monstrous slut" who "dresses like a goddam bull dagger" to the "frail and fair" upper-class Cass who, for Rufus, is thoroughly mysterious and unattainable. By aligning himself sexually with Jane, a white woman who has been coded as undesirable, Vivaldo becomes, symbolically, exactly the kind of black/white hybrid that Rufus envisions himself as being, thereby enabling their relationship.

Because relationships with black women are not in any way a constitutive part of Rufus's sexual self-image and because (given the dictates of the heterosexual codes that he resents but still feels compelled to follow) he knows that he must eventually choose some woman as his woman, Rufus thinks of Leona at the beginning of the novel as simply another disposable sexual conquest, but soon she becomes the woman upon whom his entire sense of himself hinges. Having revealed herself to be one of the few white women to whom a poor black man like Rufus has access, Leona's value as a sexual object is for that very reason suspect, and Vivaldo's response to her becomes a source of tremendous anxiety for Rufus. Rufus thinks:

> Perhaps Vivaldo was contemptuous of her because she was so plain —which meant that Vivaldo was contemptuous of him. Or perhaps he was flirting with her because she seemed so simple and available: the proof of her availability being her presence in Rufus's house.

At one point, after his relationship with Leona has become an unceasing round of domestic violence, he snarls at Vivaldo, "I guess you don't think she's good enough for you" and Vivaldo's reply, "Oh, shit. You don't think she's good enough for you," goes straight to the heart of Rufus's dilemma. As long as his relationship with Leona remains the stereotypic interaction of two neurotic social misfits, what I have called a play of abstractions, Rufus is secure, but when he realizes that the oppositions that have characterized his notion of sexual difference and of female sexual value do not really reflect the reality of the flesh-and-blood, pitifully human woman for whom he feels a growing affection, his world collapses.

As Murray Davis has suggested in his book *Intimate Relations*, "when an individual acquires a new intimate, he is acquiring an identity appendage that is large enough to alter his social group's reaction to him in general and their evaluation of him in particular. Intimates, that is, affect each other's reputations." From Rufus's perspective, Leona's willingness to align herself permanently with a black man reveals her essential limitations. Of all of the white women who would be willing to do so, she is probably one of the best, and she is no Cass. She is not the "princess" that Rufus had half-facetiously and half-longingly called her soon after their first meeting. In fact, at best, Leona would be situated midway between Jane and Cass on the objectifying continuum of sexual value that men like Rufus and, perhaps, Vivaldo use to gauge a woman's attractiveness, and this knowledge is more than Rufus's ego can withstand. Leona instantiates neither the pole represented by Vivaldo's grossly physical Jane or that represented by the princesslike and, for Rufus, untouchable Cass. Tragically, because of Rufus's inability to think outside of these all-or-nothing, virgin/whore dichotomies, these two antithetical female images are the only ones available to him and the only ones by way of which he can orient himself emotionally in relation to Vivaldo and, by extension, to white men in general. His realization that Leona is not Cass, a realization most forcefully brought about by his recognition of the pleasure she takes in sex, forces him to attempt to drag her to the other end of the scale if for no other reason than to relieve the unbearable emotional tension that her unplaceableness creates. Leona cannot be worshipped, and Rufus is incapable of actually loving a woman. Therefore, Rufus's only option is to defile or, as Stember would say, "animalize" her. Having finally attempted to maintain a socially visible relationship with a white woman, rather than just another covert and simply sexual one, Rufus has been forced to see exactly what his romantic options are. He realizes that he and Vivaldo are equals only in private.

The dynamic that I have been describing is borne out most forcefully by the fact that Vivaldo's "abandonment" of Rufus occurs when, for the first time in Rufus's presence, Vivaldo seriously considers taking advantage of the kind of romantic possibility that Rufus is denied:

> A tall girl, very pretty, carefully dressed—she looked like an uptown model—came into the room, looked about her, peered sharply at their table. She paused, then started out.
>
> "I wish you were looking for me," Vivaldo called.
>
> She turned and laughed. "You're lucky I'm not looking for you!" She had a very attractive laugh and a slight Southern accent. Rufus turned to watch her move daintily up the steps and disappear into the crowded bar.
>
> "Well you scored, old buddy," Rufus said, "go get her."
>
> "No," said Vivaldo, smiling, "better leave well enough alone." He stared at the door where the girl had vanished. "She's pretty isn't she?" he said partly to himself, partly to the table. He looked at the door again, shifting slightly in his seat, then threw down the last of his drink.
>
> Rufus wanted to say, Don't let me stop you, man, but he said nothing. He felt black, filthy, foolish. He wished he were miles away, or dead.

The fact that Rufus feels not only "filthy" and "foolish," but specifically "filthy," "foolish," and "black" represents one of the most telling moments in the novel. By recognizing both the physical specificity of his blackness and its social implications, Rufus must at last face his repressed awareness of the fact that Vivaldo, his best friend, is a white man with all of the advantages that this entails, and that he, Rufus, is not. Baldwin's strangest achievement in *Another Country* is that he creates a world in which, when Rufus says of the brutalized Leona, "she's the only chick in the world for me," it makes perfect sense.

Finally, despite his limitations, Rufus is the most complex and important character in *Another Country*. This is because he is the only one who actually seems to grow not only in self-awareness, but in the awareness of himself as a specific self in the specific world in which Baldwin has placed him. His suicide functions as an overwrought but existentially respectable manifestation of his desire to live and die in accordance with the one "truth" that his history has taught him. This truth is that, appearances to the contrary, James Baldwin's world at this point just didn't have enough room for everyone.

Yoshinobu Hakutani (essay date 1995)

SOURCE: "If the Street Could Talk: James Baldwin's Search for Love and Understanding," in *The City in African-American Literature*, edited by Yoshinobu Hakutani and Robert Butler, Farleigh Dickinson University Press, 1995, pp. 150-67.

[*In the following essay, Hakutani traces the protagonist's search for love and salvation in* If Beale Street Could Talk, *and contrasts Baldwin's optimistic view in this novel with the pessimism of other African-American writers, including Richard Wright.*]

No Name in the Street, a book of essays Baldwin wrote immediately before *If Beale Street Could Talk,* is about the life of black people in the city just as the story of Beale Street takes place in the city. While *No Name in the Street* is a departure from Baldwin's earlier book of essays in expressing his theory of love, *If Beale Street Could Talk* goes a step further in showing how black people can deliver that love. In *No Name in the Street,* Baldwin does not talk like an integrationist; he sounds as if he is advocating the ideas of a militant separatist who has no qualm about killing a white enemy. Although the book turns out to be a far more sustained examination of the falsehood to which Americans try to cling than his previous works, it still falls short of a vision in which love can be seized and recreated as it is in *If Beale Street Could Talk.*

Whenever Baldwin wrote about American society, he became the center of controversy, for his career coincided with one of the most turbulent eras in American history, marked by the civil rights movement at home and the Vietnam War abroad. A realist as he was, he was forced to take a stance in dealing with the current issues of society and of race in particular. He has been both extolled and denounced for his unique vision of racial harmony in America. Praising him for his ideas is not difficult to understand, because he is not only an eloquent writer but an acute historian. Modern American society is predominantly urban; black and white people live and work together in the city. Those who look forward to the future embraced him as a prophet; those who want to place politics over history and impose the past on the future dismissed him as a dreamer.

Some black readers also disparaged Baldwin's work. "The black writer," Joyce Carol Oates observed in her review of *If Beale Street Could Talk,* "if he is not being patronized simply for being black, is in danger of being attacked for not being black enough. Or he is forced to represent a mass of people, his unique vision assumed to be symbolic of a collective vision."[1] A black writer like Richard Wright is seldom assailed because he not only asserts being black but openly shows his anger as a black man. To Baldwin, Wright's portrayal of the life of black people seems to be directed toward the fictional but realistic presentation of a black man's anger. Although sympathetic to this rage, Baldwin sees a basic flaw in Wright's technique, contending that the artist must analyze raw emotion and transform it into an identifiable form and experience.[2] Baldwin cannot approve of Wright's use of violence, which he regards as "gratuitous and compulsive because the root of the violence is never examined. The root is rage."[3]

This basic difference in vision and technique between Wright and Baldwin has a corollary in the difference between the two types of novels exemplified by *Native Son* and *If Beale Street Could Talk.* Both stories take place in the city, Chicago of the thirties in Wright's novel and New York of the sixties in Baldwin's. Bigger Thomas is accused of murder in the first degree for the accidental death of a white girl, and Fonny Hunts is imprisoned for the rape of a Puerto Rican woman, which he did not commit. Behind similar scenes of racial prejudice, lie fundamentally different ideas about the existence of black people in American society. During his act of liberation, Bigger becomes aware of his own undoing and creation, but he achieves his manhood through murdering his girl friend. Fonny, an artist and an intellectual, consciously aware of the primacy of love, is able to revive that relationship and achieve his deliverance. Wright's novel, whether it is *Native Son* or *The Outsider*, ends tragically with the death of its hero, and neither of the victims can lead others to the discovery of love. Fonny's search for love and liberation, on the other hand, is accomplished through his sense of love, which others can emulate and acquire. Not only does he survive his ordeal, but his child is to be born.

Baldwin's technique of elucidating this idea of love and deliverance differs with that of a protest novel. *Native Son* was intended to awaken the conscience of white society, and Wright's strategy was necessarily belligerent. To survive in his existence, Bigger is forced to rebel, unlike Fonny who defends himself in the interior of his heart. Bigger learns how to escape the confines of his environment and gain an identity. Even before he acts, he knows exactly how Mary, and Bessie later, have forced him into a vulnerable position. No wonder he convinces himself not only that he has killed to protect himself but also that he has attacked the entire civilization. In contrast to *If Beale Street Could Talk,* *Native Son* departs from the principles of love and sympathy which people, black or white, have for their fellow human beings. In "How 'Bigger' Was Born," Wright admits that his earlier *Uncle Tom's Children* was "a book which even bankers' daughters could read and weep over and feel good about."[4] In *Native Son*, however, Wright could not allow for such complacency. He warns that the book "would be so hard and deep that they would have to face it without the consolation of tears" (xxvii).

The salient device in *If Beale Street Could Talk* is the narrative voice of a nineteen-year-old black girl named Tish. She is Fonny's fiancée and is pregnant with his child. Not only is she a compassionate and lovable woman, but the reality of her pregnancy inspires others to generate love and hope. Baldwin's concept of love and liberation is conveyed realistically by many of those involved in the story, her husband-to-be, their relatives, the lawyer, the landlord, the restaurant owner, and others regardless of their race. But what makes Baldwin's concept vibrant is Tish's voice through which it grows enriched and spiritualized. Her manner of speech is warm but calm and completely natural. Only through her vision can the reader learn to know the meaning of love and humanity.

By contrast, Wright's authorial voice, as Baldwin noted, succeeds in recording black anger as no black writer before him has ever done, but it also is the overwhelming limitation of *Native Son.* For Baldwin, what is sacrificed is a necessary dimension to the novel: "the relationship that Negroes bear to one another, that depth of involvement and unspoken recognition of shared experience which creates a way of life . . . it is this climate, common to most Negro protest novels, which has led us all to believe that in Negro life there exists no tradition, no field of manners, no possibility of ritual or intercourse, such as may, for example, sustain the Jew even after he has left his father's house."[5]

What Baldwin calls "ritual or intercourse" in black life is precisely the catalyst for the attainment of love and deliverance in *If Beale Street Could Talk.* To see the relationship of Tish and Fonny as spiritual rather than sexual, genuine rather than materialistic, is commonplace, but to make it thrive on the strength of the communal bond in black life is Baldwin's achievement. Baldwin seizes upon this kinship in family members, relatives, friends, and associates. Tommy in Saul Bellow's *Seize the Day,* like Fonny, falls a victim of circumstance, and changes his family name to Wilhelm but retains his Jewish heritage in his battle of life. "In middle age," Bellow writes about Tommy, "you no longer thought such thoughts about free choice. Then it came over you that from one grandfather you had inherited such and such a head of hair . . . from another, broad thick shoulders; an oddity of speech from one uncle, and small teeth from another, and the gray eyes . . . a wide-lipped mouth like a statue from Peru. . . . From his mother he had gotten sensitive feelings, a soft heart, a brooding nature."[6]

The antithesis to Baldwin's idea of bondage is the focus of an existentialist novel of Richard Wright's. Cross Damon in *The Outsider*, rejecting his heritage, wishes to be renamed. His mother, the product of the traditional Christianity in the South that taught black children subservient ethics, tries to mold her son's character accordingly. He thus rebels against his mother, who moans, "To think I named you Cross after

the Cross of Jesus."[7] As he rejects his mother because she reminds him of southern black piety and racial and sexual repression, he, in so doing, discards genuine motherly love altogether. He resembles Meursault in Albert Camus's *The Stranger*, who stands his trial for the murder of an Arab.[8] Meursault is not only accused of murder, but condemned as immoral because he did not weep at his mother's funeral. Damon's action, like Meursault's, derives from his nihilistic belief that "man is nothing in particular" (135). At the end of the story, however, Wright expresses a sense of irony about Damon's character. Tasting his agonizing defeat and dying, Damon utters:

> "I wish I had some way to give the meaning of my life to others. . . . To make a bridge from man to man . . . Starting from scratch every time is . . . no good. Tell them not to come down this road. . . . Men hate themselves and it makes them hate others. . . . Man is all we've got. . . . I wish I could ask men to meet themselves. . . . We're different from what we seem. . . . Maybe worse, maybe better. . . . But certainly different . . . We're strangers to ourselves." (439)

As if to heed Damon's message, Baldwin challenged the climate of alienation and estrangement that pervaded black life. Not only did he inspire black people to attain their true identity, but, with the tenacity and patience seldom seen among radical writers, he sought to build bridges between black and white people. In contrast to African-American writers like Richard Wright and John A. Williams, who fled the deep South to seek freedom and independence in the northern cities, Baldwin always felt that he was a step ahead in his career. "I am a city boy," he declared. "My life began in the Big City, and had to be slugged out, toe to toe, on the city pavements."[9] For him the city was a place where meaningful human relationships could evolve through battle and dialogue. As in any confrontation of minds, there would be casualties but eventually a resolution and a harmony would emerge. In *Another Country,* a novel of black life in the city, Rufus Scott, once a black drummer in a jazz band but now lonely and desperate, meets with a poor white girl from Georgia. They are initially attracted to each other, but eventually she becomes insane and he commits suicide. Even though hate overrules love in their relationship, it is the traditional southern culture in which she was ingrained rather than the estranged environment of New York City that ruins their relationship.

Because *Another Country* is not a polemical tract but a powerful novel, as Granville Hicks recognized,[10] it seems to express a subtle but authentic dilemma a black man faces in America. The novel suggests not only that the South is not a place where black people can have their peace of mind and happiness, but also that the city in the North is not a place where they can achieve their identity and freedom. And yet the novel is endowed with an ambivalent notion that America is their destined home. It is well known that Baldwin loved to live in another country. Paris was his favorite city, where he felt one was treated without reference to the color of skin. "This means," he wrote, "that one must accept one's nakedness. And nakedness has no color" (*No Name* 23). But Baldwin returned home, as did American expatriates in the twenties, and trusted his fortune in America.[11] In "**Many Thousands Gone**," he stated, "We cannot escape our origins, however hard we try, those origins which contain the key—could we but find it—to all that we later become" (*Notes* 20).

In search of home, black writers quite naturally turn to the city in the North, where black and white citizens live side by side and talk to one another. In *No Name in the Street,* Baldwin intimated his sentiments: "Whoever is part of whatever civilization helplessly loves some aspects of it, and some of the people in it. A person does not lightly elect to oppose his society. One would much rather be at home among one's compatriots than be mocked and detested by them" (194-95). The black citizen would be drawn to city living only because the interracial relationship in a melting pot could thrive on mutual respect and understanding, the lack of which has historically caused black people's exodus from the South. Such a relationship, as Baldwin quickly warns, is possible only if white people are capable of being fair and having goodwill and if black people themselves are able to achieve their true identity.

The burden that falls upon the shoulders of both white and black citizens is poignantly expressed with a pair of episodes in *No Name in the Street.* For the white people's responsibility, Baldwin recounts a white juror's attitude toward the American system of justice. The juror spoke in court:

> "As I said before, that I feel, and it is my opinion that racism, bigotry, and segregation is something that we have to wipe out of our hearts and minds, and not on the street. I have had an opinion that—and been taught never to resist a police officer, that we have courts of law in which to settle . . . that I could get justice in the courts"—And, in response to Garry's [the defense attorney's] question, "Assuming the police officer pulled a gun and shot you, what would you do about it?" the prospective juror, at length, replied, "Let me say this. I do not believe a police officer will do that." (159-60)

The juror's reply not only provides a "vivid and accurate example of the American piety at work," as Baldwin observes, but also demonstrates the very honesty in Baldwin that makes his feeling credible to the reader.[12]

Baldwin calls for responsibility on the part of black people as well. In the middle of the chapter "**Take Me to the Water**," he now plunges himself into the dreary waters of urban society. This part of the narrative, in contrast to the personal and family episodes preceding it, abounds with experiences that suggest impersonality and superficiality in human relationships. After a long sojourn in France, Baldwin saw his school chum, now a U.S. post office worker, whom he had not seen since graduation. At once Baldwin felt a sense of alienation that separated the one who was tormented by America's involvement in Vietnam and the one who blindly supported it. Baldwin felt no conceivable kinship to his once friend, for "that shy, pop-eyed thirteen year old my friend's mother had scolded and loved was no more." His friend's impression of the famous writer, described in Baldwin's own words, is equally poignant: "I was a stranger now . . . and what in the world was I by now but an aging, lonely, sexually dubious, politically outrageous, unspeakably erratic freak?" What impressed Baldwin the most about this encounter was the fact that despite the changes that had occurred in both men, nothing had touched this black man. To Baldwin, his old friend was an emblem of the "white-washed" black who "had been trapped, preserved, in that moment of time" (*No Name* 15-18).

No Name in the Street is an eloquent discourse intended for all Americans to attain their identity and understanding. It takes its title from the speech by Bildad and Shuhite in the Book of Job that denounces the wicked of his generation:

> Yea, the light of the wicked shall be put out,
> And the spark of his fire shall not shine.
> His remembrance shall perish from the earth,
> And he shall have no name in the street.
> He shall be driven from light into darkness,
> And chased out of the world.[13]

Baldwin sees in Bildad's curse a warning for Americans: without a name worthy of its constitution, America will perish as a nation. "A civilized country," he ironically observes, "is, by definition, a country dominated by whites, in which the blacks clearly know their place" (177). He warns that American people must remake their country into what the Declaration of Independence says they wanted it to be. America without equality and freedom will not survive; a country without a morality is not a viable civilization and hence it is doomed. Unless such a warning is heeded now, he foresees that a future generation of mankind, "running through the catacombs: and digging the grave . . . of the mighty Roman empire" (178) will also discover the ruins of American cities.

The responsibility for American people to rebuild their nation, Baldwin hastens to point out, falls upon black people as heavily as upon white people. This point echoes what he has said before, but it is stated here with a more somber and deliberate tone. It sounds comfortable to hear Baldwin speak in *Notes of a Native Son* that "blackness and whiteness did not matter" (95). He thought then that only through love and understanding could white and black people transcend the differences in color to achieve their identity as human beings and as a nation. In *No Name in the Street,* such euphoria has largely dissipated; the book instead alludes to the reality that black Americans are descendants of white Americans. "The blacks," Baldwin stresses, "are the despised and slaughtered children of the great Western house—*nameless* and *unnameable* bastards" (185, my italics). A black man in this country has no true name. Calling himself a black and a citizen of the United States is merely giving himself a label unworthy of his history and existence. To Baldwin, the race problem is not a race problem as such; it is fundamentally a problem of how black Americans perceive their own identity.[14]

No Name in the Street also addresses their cultural heritage. Baldwin admonishes the reader that the term *Afro-American* does not simply mean the liberation of black people in this country. The word, as it says, means the heritage of Africa and America. Black Americans, he argues, should be proud of this heritage. He demands they discard at once the misguided notion that they are descendants of slaves brought from Africa, the inferiority complex deeply rooted in the American psyche. An Afro-American, in Baldwin's metaphysics, is defined as a descendant of the two civilizations, Africa and America, both of which were "discovered" not by Americans but by European settlers.

Baldwin's prophecy, moreover, is rendered in epic proportion. "On both continents," Baldwin says, "the white and the dark gods met in combat, and it is on the outcome of this combat that the future of both continents depends" (194). The true identity of an Afro-American, the very term that he finds the most elusive of all names, is thus given a historical light. To be granted this name, as he stresses, "is to be in the situation, intolerably exaggerated, of all those who have ever found themselves part of a civilization which they could in no wise honorably defend—which they were compelled, indeed, endlessly to attack and condemn—and who yet spoke out the most passionate love, hoping to make the kingdom new, to make it honorable and worthy of life" (194). Historically, then, Baldwin bears out his old contention that both black and white citizens on this continent are destined to live together on the same street and determine their own future.

No Name in the Street, however, ends on a dark note, as some critics have suggested,[15] precisely because Baldwin had not yet discovered the true name for American people. The most painful episode in the book that influences his outlook on the racial question is his journey into the deep South. There he discovered not only a sense of alienation between black and white people, who had lived together over the generations, but an alienation within the white man himself. While a Southerner was conceived in Baldwin's mind as a man of honor and human feeling like a northern liberal, he struck Baldwin as a man necessarily wanting in "any viable, organic connection between his public stance and his private life" (53-54). Baldwin was in fact conscious that white people in the South always loved their black friends, but they never admitted it. This is why Baldwin characterizes the South as "a riddle which could be read only in the light, or the darkness, of the unbelievable disasters which had overtaken the private life" (55).

But Baldwin's search for a national identity in the name of brotherhood and love does not end in the South. Baldwin returns to the streets of the North. In the eyes of a middle-aged black writer, the potential for a truly American identity and understanding emerges in the city of the North through the black and white coalition with the radical students, and even in the black and white confrontation in the labor unions. Moving to Chicago in the thirties, Wright witnessed a coalition that existed between black men and white underground politicians, but this interracial cooperation, as he realized, did not arise out of the brotherhood on the part of the white men but out of their political and economic motives.[16] Such a white and black relationship as Baldwin envisioned in the sixties was a rallying cry for the black people who have seized the opportunity to make the once pejorative term *black* into what he calls "a badge of honor" (189). Although this encounter may entail hostile and dangerous reactions, it is, he asserts, a necessary crucible for black people to endure in achieving their identity. In the context of the late sixties, this is what he meant by the experience which a person, black or white, must face and acquire so that the person might attain identity. Baldwin hoped that the estrangement he witnessed in the South would not repeat itself in the North.

His most romantic quest in *No Name in the Street* involves the "flower children" he saw walking up and down the Haight-Ashbury section of San Francisco in the late sixties. Observing the young black men putting their trust not in flowers but in guns, he believed that the scene brought their true identity to the threshold of its maturity. The flower children, in his view, repudiated their fathers for failing to realize that black Americans were the descendants of white fathers; they treated the black children as their denied brothers as if in defiance of their elders. "They were in the streets," he says in allusion to the title of this work, "in the hope of becoming whole" (187). For Baldwin, the flower children were relying upon black people so that they could rid themselves of the myth of white supremacy. But he was undeniably a realist. He had no confidence in the black men who were putting their trust in guns, nor did he trust the flower children. In this episode he is quick to warn black listeners: "this troubled white person might suddenly decide not to be in trouble and go home—and when he went home, he would be the enemy" (188). In Baldwin's judgment, the flower children of the city in America became neither true rebels nor true lovers, either of whom would be worthy of their name in their quest for a national identity. In either case, he says to chide himself, "to mistake a fever for a passion can destroy one's life" (189).

The spectacle of the flower children thus figures as one of the saddest motifs in *No Name in the Street.* Although the vision of the young Baldwin was centered in love and brotherhood, the sensibility of the older Baldwin here smacks of shrewdness and prudence. Idealism is replaced by pragmatism, and honesty and sincerity clearly mark the essential attitude he takes to the problem of identity in America. His skeptical admiration for the flower children casts a sad note, for the encounter symbolizes the closest point to which black and white Americans had ever come in their search for love and understanding.

But at heart Baldwin was scarcely a pessimist. These pages, filled with love and tenderness, vividly express his feeling that, through these children, black Americans have learned the truth about themselves. And this conviction, however ephemeral it may have been, contributes to his wishfulness and optimism of the seventies. He has come to know the truth, stated before,[17] that black Americans can free themselves as they learn more about white Americans and that "the truth which frees black people will also free white people" (129). Baldwin's quest continues in *If Beale Street Could Talk,* for the novel is the catalyst for disseminating the truth. Even though Baldwin stresses the human bondage that exists within the black community, he also recognizes, in his imagination at least, the deep, universal bonds of emotion that tie the hearts of people regardless of their color of skin.

For Baldwin, the bondage that exists on Beale Street is hardly visible from outside. City life, as depicted by American realists from Stephen Crane and Theodore Dreiser down to James T. Farrell and Richard Wright, often brings out isolation and loneliness to the residents. The city is a noisy, crowded place, yet people scarcely talk to one another. New York City, Baldwin's home town, also struck Baldwin as emblematic of the impersonality and indifference that plagued city life in America. On his way to the South on a writing assignment, he stopped by the city to rest and to readjust his life, spent on foreign soil for nearly a decade. But all he heard was "beneath the nearly invincible and despairing noise, the sound of many tongues, all struggling for dominance" (*No Name* 51). The scene is reminiscent of what Crane, in the guise of a tramp, faces at the end of "An Ex-

periment in Misery": "The roar of the city in his ear was to him the confusion of strange tongues, babbling heedlessly; it was the clink of coin, the voice of the city's hopes, which were to him no hopes."[18]

Unlike an existentialist in search of individual autonomy in the face of the void, chaotic, and meaningless universe, Baldwin seeks order, meaning, and dream in one's relation to others. A critic has dismissed *If Beale Street Could Talk* as "pretentious and cloying with goodwill and loving kindness and humble fortitude and generalized honorableness."[19] But because Baldwin is a confirmed romantic, his concept of love and honor is expressed with a sense of idealism. Neither the turbulence that embroils the urban ghetto nor the indifference that sweeps over it can disperse his dream.

It is ironic that the impersonality and estrangement which permeate Beale Street compel its residents to seek a stronger and more meaningful relationship with others. Tish, separated from her fiancé in jail, reflects on her happy childhood days, "when Daddy used to bring me and Sis here and we'd watch the people and the buildings and Daddy would point out different sights to us and we might stop in Battery Park and have ice cream and hot dogs."[20] Later in the story, Baldwin portrays the crowded subway, an epitome of city life, and suggests the notion that city inhabitants are forced to protect themselves. When a crowded train arrives at the platform, Tish notices her father instinctively puts his arm around her as if to shield her from danger. Tish recalls:

> I suddenly looked up into his face. No one can describe this, I really shouldn't try. His face was bigger than the world, his eyes deeper than the sun, more vast than the desert, all that had ever happened since time began was in his face. He smiled: a little smile. I saw his teeth: I saw exactly where the missing tooth had been, that day he spat in my mouth. The train rocked, he held me closer, and a kind of sigh I'd never heard before stifled itself in him. (52)

This motif of human bondage also appears as a faint noise coming from Tish and Fonny's unborn child. Tish hears it in the loud bar where she and her sister Ernestine talk about their strategy to get Fonny out of jail:

> Then, we are silent. . . . And I look around me. It's actually a terrible place and I realize that the people here can only suppose that Ernestine and I are tired whores, or a Lesbian couple, or both. Well. We are certainly in it now, and it might get worse. I will, certainly—and now something almost as hard to catch as a whisper in a crowded place, as light and as definite as a spider's web, strikes below my ribs, stunning and astonishing

my heart—get worse. But that light tap, that kick,
that signal, announces to me that what can get
worse can get better. (122)

The bondage of black and white people in *If Beale Street
Could Talk* could also be solidified, as could the black kinship, if the relationship were based upon a mutual understanding of others as individual human beings rather than
as blacks who have typically been victimized by white society, or as whites who have habitually oppressed blacks under the banner of racial supremacy. No sooner does one treat
another human being for an economic or political purpose
than such a relationship ceases to exist. To show the possibility of a prosperous relationship between black and white
people in the city, Baldwin has created many sympathetic
portraits of white people. The Jewish lawyer the black families hire to defend Fonny is initially an ambitious man bent
on advancing his career but later becomes an altruistic individual. The Italian woman who owns a vegetable stand informs the police of a racial harassment committed by a white
hoodlum, thereby helping Fonny to be exonerated of his action to protect Tish, a victim of the white man's insult. The
owner of a Spanish restaurant willingly allows Tish and
Fonny to have dinner on credit out of his compassion for
their unjust plight.

For Baldwin, black people in the North, in contrast to those
in the South, can move freely and talk frequently with fellow residents. His white characters, unlike those in Wright's
fiction, are seldom stereotyped. Whether they are prejudiced
or fair-minded, materialistic or humanistic, they are always
individuals capable of making their own judgments. It seems
as though the spirit of individualism in which they have
grown up becomes, in turn, contagious among the black
people. In *No Name in the Street,* Baldwin shows why black
men living in Paris were treated as individuals as Algerians
were not. "Four hundred years in the West," he argues,
"had certainly turned me into a Westerner—there was no
way around that. But four hundred years in the West had
also failed to bleach me—there was no way around *that,* either" (42).

The westernization of black people in America, as Baldwin
would have agreed with Wright, has taken place by far at a
swifter pace in the North than in the South. Southern life
for black people, as vividly portrayed in *No Name in the
Street,* was not only stagnant and dark, but it created terror.
Baldwin traveled down the Southland at the time of the racial turmoil in Little Rock, Arkansas, in the late fifties, when
black children attempted to go to school in front of a hostile army and citizenry to face the white past, let alone the
white present. During his stay he encountered one of the
most powerful politicians in the South, who made himself
"sweating drunk" to humiliate another human being.
Baldwin distinctly recalls the abjectness of this incident:

"With his wet eyes staring up at my face, and his wet hand
groping for my cock, we were both, abruptly, in history's
ass-pocket." To Baldwin, those who had power in the South
still lived with the mentality of slave owners. The experience
convinced him that a black man's identity in the South was
defined by the power to which such white men tried to cling,
and that a black man's humanity was placed at the service
of their fantasies. "If the lives of those children," he reflects,
"were in those wet, despairing hands, if their future was to
be read in those wet, blind eyes, there was reason to
tremble" (61-62). It is characteristic of his narrative that the
height of terror, as just described, is set against the height
of love the child Baldwin felt when his life was saved by
his stepbrother. His narrative thus moves back and forth
with greater intensity between the author's feelings of abjectness and exaltation, of isolation and affinity.

Baldwin's style becomes even more effective as his tendency toward rhetorical fastenings and outbursts is replaced
by brief, tense images that indicate a control of the narrative voice. For instance, one summer night in Birmingham,
Baldwin met in a motel room one Rev. Shuttlesworth, as
marked a man as Martin Luther King, Jr. Gravely concerned
with Shuttlesworth's safety for fear that his car might be
bombed, Baldwin wanted to bring it to his attention as
Shuttlesworth was about to leave the room. But the minister would not let him. At first, there was only a smile on
Shuttlesworth's face; upon a closer observation, he detected
that "a shade of sorrow crossed his face, deep, impatient,
dark; then it was gone. It was the most impersonal anguish
I had ever seen on a man's face." Only later did he come to
realize that the minister was then "wrestling with the mighty
fact that the danger in which he stood was as nothing compared to the spiritual horror which drove those who were
trying to destroy him" (*No Name* 67). A few pages later, this
shade of dark and sorrow is compensated for by that of light
and joy. Baldwin now reminisces about his Paris days—how
little he had missed ice cream, hot dogs, Coney Island, the
Statue of Liberty, the Empire State Building, but how much
he had missed his brothers, sisters, and mother: "I missed
the way the dark face closes, the way dark eyes watch, and
the way, when a dark face opens, a light seems to go on
everywhere." (71).

Unlike W. E. B. Du Bois and Jean Toomer, who viewed the
South with deep nostalgia, Baldwin, like Richard Wright and
John A. Williams, was repulsed by it. Even though at times
he felt an affinity with the black people in the South and
found his home there, he also found, as does Richard Henry
in *Blues for Mister Charlie,* that once he had lived in the
North he could not go home again. Baldwin's quest for humanity in *If Beale Street Could Talk* is not merely to seek
out affinity with black people; it is to search the interior of
city life. He is in search of a human bond in the hearts and
souls of people. It stresses the conventional and yet uni-

versal bondage innate in man, a human affinity that can grow between man and woman, members of a family, relatives, friends—any group of individuals united in the name of love and understanding.

Fundamental to Baldwin's concept of human bondage is the relationship of love between a man and a woman that yields posterity. What saves Fonny and Tish from loneliness and despair is their expecting the child in her womb. Every time she visits him in jail, they focus their talk on the unborn baby. Whenever he sees her face during the visit, he knows not only does she love him, but "that others love him, too. . . . He is not alone; we are not alone." When she looks ashamed of her ever expanding waistline, he is elated, saying, "Here she come! Big as *two* houses! You sure it ain't twins? or triplets? Shit, we *might* make history" (162). While at home, she is comforted by Ray Charles's voice and piano, the sounds and smells of the kitchen, the sounds and "blurred human voices rising from the street." Only then does she realize that "out of this rage and a steady, somehow triumphant sorrow, my baby was slowly being formed" (41).

However crowded, noisy, and chaotic Baldwin's city may be, one can always discover order, meaning, and hope in one's life. The street talks as though conflict and estrangement among the residents compel them to seek their ties with smaller human units. Not only does the birth of a child, the impending birth of Tish and Fonny's baby, constitute the familial bond, but it also signals the birth of new America. Baldwin has earlier conceived this idea in *No Name in the Street*, in which the first half of the book, "Take Me to the Water," depicts the turmoil of American society in the sixties and the second, "To Be Baptized," prophesies the rebirth of a nation. In the epilogue he writes: "An old world is dying, and a new one, kicking in the belly of its mother, time, announces that it is ready to be born." Alluding to the heavy burden falling upon American people, he remarks with a bit of humor: "This birth will not be easy, and many of us are doomed to discover that we are exceedingly clumsy midwives. No matter, so long as we accept that our responsibility is to the new born: the acceptance of responsibility contains the key to the necessarily evolving skill" (196).

Baldwin's extolment of the relationship between Tish and Fonny also suggests that the interracial relationships of love and sex as seen in *Another Country* are often destroyed by the forces of society beyond their control. In such a relationship, genuine love often falls a victim of society, a larger human unit. Baldwin's love story in *If Beale Street Could Talk* also suggests that a homosexual relationship is an antithesis to the idea of rebirth. Levy, Fonny's landlord, is a personable, happily married young man. Being Jewish, he values the closeness in family life and the offspring marriage can produce. He willingly rents his loft to Fonny, who

needs the space to work on his sculptures, because he is aware of his own happiness in raising children and wants his tenants to share the same joy. "Hell," Levy tells Fonny, "drag out the blankets and sleep on it. . . . Make babies on it. That's how *I* got here. . . . You two should have some beautiful babies . . . and, take it from me, kids, the world damn sure needs them." Out of sympathy for Fonny's situation, he even forgoes payment of the rent while Fonny is in jail, saying, "I want you kids to have your babies. I'm funny that way" (133-34).

As urban society disintegrates because of its indifference and impersonality, the love and understanding that can unite smaller communities, couples, families, relatives, and friends become essential to the pursuit of happiness. Those who are deprived of such relationships cannot survive. Daniel Carty, Fonny's childhood friend, who is also arrested by the D.A.'s office, is a loner. Without ties to his family and relatives, he is doomed.

Tony Maynard, Baldwin's former bodyguard, who appears in *No Name in the Street,* is reminiscent of Daniel Carty. Tony is imprisoned on a murder charge arising from a mistaken identity.[21] Since the title "To Be Baptized" in *No Name in the Street* suggests the idea of rebirth, Baldwin's motif of alienation, which Tony's episode illustrates in the latter portion of the book, seems incongruous. In any event, Tony is treated as a victim of the indifference and hatred that exists in society; like Daniel, he is without the protection of his family and relatives. Ironically, he is a professional bodyguard for a man but no one else can guard him.

While Baldwin often evokes the idea of rebirth in *No Name in the Street* by biblical references, he has a penchant to assail, in *If Beale Street Could Talk,* those who find their haven in the church. To him, a long history of the Christian church has partly resulted in the enslavement of black people in this country, and the black people "who were given the church and nothing else"[22] have learned to be obedient to the law of God and the land but failed to be independent thinkers.[23] Mrs. Hunt, Fonny's mother, like Cross Damon's mother in *The Outsider,* has a blind trust in Christ. She even believes that Fonny's imprisonment is "the *Lord's* way of making my boy think on his sins and surrender his soul to Jesus" (64). Her doctor convinces Mrs. Hunt, who has a heart problem, that her health is more important than her son's freedom. By contrast, Fonny's father Frank is a defiant disbeliever. "I don't know," Frank tells his wife, "how God expects a man to act when his son is in trouble. *Your* God crucified *His* son and was probably glad to get rid of him, but I ain't like that. I ain't hardly going out in the street and kiss the first white cop I see" (65). Although it is tragic that Frank commits suicide when he is caught stealing money to raise funds to defend his son, Frank's action suggests the genuine feeling of love and tenderness a father can have for his son.

Baldwin ends *If Beale Street Could Talk* on a triumphant note. Fonny is out of jail, however temporary it may be, because of the efforts by those who are genuinely concerned about his welfare. Not only has he been able to endure his ordeal, but his experience in jail has renewed his human spirit. The last time Tish visits him in jail, he tells her: "Listen, I'll soon be out. I'm coming home because I'm glad I came, can you dig that?" (193). The final scene once again echoes the voice that conveys Baldwin's idea of love and rebirth. Fonny is now a sculptor at work in his studio: "Fonny is working on the wood, on the stone, whistling, smiling. And, from far away, but coming near, the baby cries and cries and cries and cries and cries and cries and cries and cries, cries like it means to wake the dead" (197).

Baldwin completed this scene of freedom and rebirth on Columbus Day, 12 October, as indicated at the end of the book. The reference to Columbus Day may easily remind one of Pudd'nhead Wilson's calendar note for that day in the conclusion of Mark Twain's classic novel of racial prejudice: "October 12, *the Discovery. It was wonderful to find America, but it would have been more wonderful to miss it.*"[24] While Twain's intention in the book is a satire on American society and on slavery in particular, Baldwin's in *If Beale Street Could Talk* is to discover a new America. When Baldwin declares in the epilogue for *No Name in the Street* that "the Western party is over, and the white man's sun has set. Period" (197), one can be puzzled. The question remains whether or not Baldwin had come away from the turbulent sixties as a disillusioned American. Throughout *No Name in the Street* he has fluctuated between his feelings of love and hatred as his episodes betray. From the perspective of his hatred and resignation, the book clearly bodes ill; from the perspective of his love and understanding, though avowedly less frequent, it nevertheless suggests its author remains hopeful. But in *If Beale Street Could Talk* Baldwin's ambivalence has largely disappeared, and the book tells that the sun will also rise in America, this time for black citizens as well as for white citizens.

NOTES

1. Joyce Carol Oates, "A Quite Moving and Very Traditional Celebration of Love," *New York Times Book Review*, 26 May 1974, 1-2.

2. I agree with Kichung Kim, who advances the theory that the difference between Wright and Baldwin arises from the two different concepts of man. Kim argues that the weakness Baldwin sees in Wright and other protest writers "is not so much that they had failed to give a faithful account of the actual conditions of man but rather that they had failed to be steadfast in their devotion . . . to what man might and ought to be. Such a man . . . will not only survive oppression but will be strengthened by it." See Kim, "Wright, the Protest Novel, and Baldwin's Faith," *CLA Journal* 17 (March 1974): 387-96.

3. James Baldwin, "Alas, Poor Richard," *Nobody Knows My Name* (New York: Dial, 1961), 151.

4. Richard Wright, "How 'Bigger' Was Born," *Native Son* (New York: Harper, 1966), xxvii.

5. James Baldwin, *Notes of a Native Son* (New York: Bantam Books, 1968), 27-28.

6. See Saul Bellow, *Seize the Day* (New York: Viking, 1956), 25. Tish in *If Beale Street Could Talk* often wonders if their baby would inherit Fonny's narrow, slanted, "Chinese" eyes.

7. Richard Wright, *The Outsider* (New York: Harper, 1953), 23.

8. Albert Camus, *The Stranger*, trans. Stuart Gilbert (New York: Vintage Books, 1942).

9. James Baldwin, *No Name in the Street* (New York: Dell, 1972), 59.

10. See Granville Hicks, "Outcasts in a Caldron of Hate," *Saturday Review* 45 (1962): 21.

11. Saunders Redding observed that Wright, who paid homage to Africa, failed to find home there. See Redding, "Reflections on Richard Wright: A Symposium on an Exiled Native Son," *Anger and Beyond: The Negro Writer in the United States*, ed. Herbert Hill (New York: Harper, 1966), 204. Like Wright, John A. Williams, who hailed from Mississippi, has said, "I have been to Africa and know that it is not my home. America is." See Williams, *This Is My Country Too* (New York: New American Library, 1956), 169.

12. To reveal this kind of malady in society as Baldwin attempts to do in *No Name in the Street* requires an artist's skills. The juror's response is reminiscent of Aunt Sally's to Huck Finn, who reports that a steamboat has just blown up a cylinder-head down the river:

> "Good gracious! Anybody hurt?"
> "No'm. Killed a nigger."
> "Well, it's lucky; because sometimes people do get hurt."

See Mark Twain, *Adventures of Huckleberry Finn*, ed. Henry Nash Smith (Boston: Houghton, 1958), 185. What Twain and Baldwin share is the genuine feeling an intense individualist possesses; both writers feel their own great powers and yet recognize the hopelessness of trying to change the world overnight.

13. *Prose and Poetry from the Old Testament*, ed. James F. Fullington (New York: Appleton, 1950), 77.

14. In a later volume of essays, Baldwin makes a similar assertion about black Americans' somber realization of themselves: "This is why blacks can be heard to say, *I ain't got to be nothing but stay black, and die!:* which is, after all, a far more affirmative apprehension than *I'm free, white and twenty-one.*" See *The Devil Finds Work* (New York: Dial, 1976), 115.

15. See, for example, Benjamin DeMott, "James Baldwin on the Sixties: Acts and Revelations," in *James Baldwin: A Collection of Critical Essays*, ed. Keneth Kinnamon (Englewood Cliffs, N.J.: Prentice-Hall, 1974), 158.

16. See Richard Wright, *12 Million Black Voices* (New York: Viking, 1941), 121-22.

17. In 1961 Baldwin wrote in his essay "In Search of a Majority:" "Whether I like it or not, or whether you like it or not, we are bound together. We are part of each other. What is happening to every Negro in the country at any time is also happening to you. There is no way around this. I am suggesting that these walls—these artificial walls—which have been up so long to protect us from something we fear, must come down" (*Nobody Knows My Name:* 136-37). In 1962 he wrote in "My Dungeon Shook": "Well, the black man has functioned in the white man's world as a fixed star, as an immovable pillar: and as he moves out of his place, heaven and earth are shaken to their foundations. . . . But these men are your brothers—your lost, younger brothers. And if the word *integration* means anything, this is what it means: that we, with love, shall force our brothers to see themselves as they are, to cease fleeing from reality and begin to change it." See *The Fire Next Time* (New York: Dial, 1963), 23-24.

18. *See Great Short Works of Stephen Crane* (New York: Harper, 1968), 258.

19. John Aldridge, "The Fire Next Time?" *Saturday Review*, 15 June 1974: 24-25.

20. James Baldwin, *If Beale Street Could Talk* (New York: Dial, 1974), 9.

21. I agree with Benjamin DeMott, who regards Tony Maynard as an undeveloped character despite much space given for that purpose, but the weakness of Baldwin's characterization results from his use of a sterile man in the con-

text of creation and rebirth (DeMott, "James Baldwin on the Sixties," 158).

22. See Baldwin's interview by Kalamu ya Salaam, "James Baldwin: Looking towards the Eighties," *Critical Essays on James Baldwin*, ed. Fred L. Standley and Nancy V. Burt (Boston: Hall, 1988), 40.

23. Sandra A. O'Neile observes in her essay, "Fathers, Gods, and Religion: Perceptions of Christianity and Ethnic Faith in James Baldwin," that "more than the heritage of any other Black American writer, Baldwin's works illustrate the schizophrenia of the Black American experience with Christianity." Black people, she argues, needed a distinction "between Christianity as they knew it to be and Christianity as it was practiced in the white world." See *Critical Essays on James Baldwin*, 125-43.

24. Mark Twain, *Pudd'nhead Wilson* and *Those Extraordinary Twins*, ed. Sidney E. Berger (New York: Norton, 1980), 113.

Valerie Rohy (essay date 1996)

SOURCE: "Displacing Desire: Passing, Nostalgia, and *Giovanni's Room*," in *Passing and the Fictions of Identity*, edited by Elaine K. Ginsberg, Duke University Press, 1996, pp. 218-33.

[*In the following essay, Rohy analyzes how the questions of origin and identity in Baldwin's* Giovanni's Room *relate to the concepts of passing and nostalgia.*]

"America is my country and Paris is my hometown," writes Gertrude Stein in "An American in France" (61). Placing in question the very notion of place, this transatlantic crossing relies on the terms—origin and identity—that it will expose as most unreliable. In the American expatriate tradition, the trope of nationality comes unfixed from its geographical moorings to become an emblem of other, more arbitrary identifications, producing a rhetoric of displacement that extends from national identity to ideology, subjectivity, sexual desire, and, in this case, "home." Stein's "Paris is my hometown" sets the scene for a performance of identity in which trappings of nationality and culture are put on by the expatriate in an act that becomes more "real" than the "real" and in which the fact of the matter—that Gertrude Stein, for example, was born in Allegheny, Pennsylvania—itself comes to seem a piece of stage scenery, a pretext for her Parisian "hometown."

Questions of origin and identity are central to James Baldwin's **Giovanni's Room,** a text which not only participates in the tradition of the American expatriate novel exemplified by Stein and, especially, by Henry James but which does so in relation to the African American idiom of passing and the genre of the passing novel. As such, *Giovanni's Room* poses questions of nationalism, nostalgia, and the constitution of racial and sexual subjects in terms that are especially resonant for contemporary identity politics. After all, the trope of "home" which Stein invokes and which proves central for Baldwin as well can hardly escape political inflection in a culture that, today as in Baldwin's 1950s, champions the white, heterosexual, bourgeois home as icon of a mythical and sentimentalized family whose "values" reflect those of the dominant culture. And at a time when attempts to intervene in the imposition of such values frequently present themselves under the rubric of "identity politics," the intersection of notions of "home" with nationalism, identity, and essentialism has taken on a particular urgency. In addressing the question of identity through the metaphorics of "passing," *Giovanni's Room* articulates the ways in which identities, including "nationality," "race," and "sexuality," are retrospective, indeed nostalgic, constructions, subject to a pathos of lost origins and demanding, on the part of the dominant culture, the violent disavowal and projection of its own contingent identity. The logics of homophobia and racism, Baldwin suggests, are each rooted in the nostalgia of an impossible essentialism whose desire for coherent identity is barred by an ineluctable passing.

The term *passing* designates a performance in which one presents oneself as what one is not, a performance commonly imagined along the axis of race, class, gender, or sexuality. Although the American passing novel typically concerns an African American who successfully presents herself or himself as white to escape the virulent effects of racism or to enter into exclusively white social circles, *passing* means, in addition, the impersonation of one sex by another. In American literature, passing across race and across gender are thoroughly imbricated—most famously, perhaps, in the narrative of William and Ellen Craft (1860), who escaped from slavery, she dressed as a white man and he posing as her servant, and in Harriet Beecher Stowe's *Uncle Tom's Cabin* (1852), when Eliza, traveling to Canada, disguises herself as a white man and her young son as a girl. In the twentieth century, novels such as Nella Larsen's *Passing* and James Weldon Johnson's *Autobiography of an Ex-Coloured Man* add to the discourse of racial passing a third important sense of passing: the appearance of "homosexual" as "heterosexual." *Giovanni's Room* may be read as a passing novel in both racial and sexual senses: appearing a generation after the Harlem Renaissance, it restages the doubling of disguises performed in earlier African American novels—*The Autobiography of an Ex-Coloured Man* and *Passing* in particular—which allows racial passing to figure (homo)sexual passing.[1] Yet how does the vocabulary of passing make it possible to set tropes of racial identity along-

side and against those of sexual identity? What would it mean to read *Giovanni's Room* "as" a passing novel or through the tropology that passing provides? Although race and sexuality by no means function in identical ways, in Baldwin's novel as in other texts, passing names a crucial nexus: a site of the relation between notions of racial and sexual identity whose intersection becomes a productive space in which to interrogate identity itself.

In America, Baldwin has said, "the sexual question and the racial question have always been intertwined" (qtd. in Goldstein 178), and in *Giovanni's Room* these questions are most clearly articulated through the discourse of nationality and nationalism. Not only does nationality stand in for race in the novel—as Giovanni's darker coloring and lower-class status contrast with David's blondness and privilege—but perhaps more important, the rhetoric that would equate "race" with "blackness" is suppressed, and the "whiteness" of the stereotypically Anglo-Saxon hero, foregrounded. In this text's extraordinary beginning, David's reflection on his own image signifies "white" with indelible quotation marks and invites, even insists on, a reading of his race in the context of his homosexuality and his homophobia: "My reflection is tall, perhaps rather like an arrow, my blond hair gleams. My face is like a face you have seen many times. My ancestors conquered a continent, pushing across death-laden plains, until they came to an ocean which faced away from Europe into a darker past."[2] Producing the narrator as a representative of white American dominant culture—its history of colonial conquest, its arrow-straight posture, even the banality of its familiarity—this meditation on culture and identity takes shape in terms of history and temporality. It is appropriate enough that a novel so committed to a reading of nostalgia and retrospection should present its own narrative as retrospection by beginning at the story's end, with Giovanni condemned to death and David about to leave home once again. But the terms in which the novel first frames race and sexuality—through the introduction of its narrator—themselves perform a kind of metaleptic reversal: in attempting to push back the frontier that emblematizes American futurity, David's ancestors have traveled not back to the future, but forward into the past. And for white America to confront its "darker past" is here, one suspects, to come face to face with the darkness or difference that its own light face—the face of an ideology we have all, in one way or another, "seen many times"—seeks to deny.

"The whole American optic in terms of reality," Baldwin has said, "is based on the necessity of keeping black people out of it. We are nonexistent. Except according to their terms, and their terms are unacceptable" (qtd. in Troupe 210). Yet Baldwin will appropriate passing, a trope that seems to literalize that "nonexistence" or invisibility, as a means of reading and resisting dominant constructions of race, gender, sexuality, and identity as such. Although no figure in

Giovanni's Room passes across the color line, David produces himself as heterosexual with Hella and as gay with Giovanni, who is himself passing, for the moment, as a gay man. Even Hella, as Baldwin makes clear, performs the rigorously scripted role of the heterosexual woman, passing as feminine through the gender performance that Joan Riviere has termed "masquerade."[3] While Baldwin as author does not attempt to pass for white, he may, outfitted in what some readers have persistently construed as a sort of Henry James drag, pass into the white literary tradition, whose conventions of first-person narrative require that an author always pass as his or her protagonist, as Baldwin does when he speaks in David's voice the "I" that is the novel's first word.[4]

These displacements of identity, the hallmark of passing, are juxtaposed in *Giovanni's Room* with a desire for placement seen as the retrograde movement of a nostalgia that remembers and longs for "home." In imagining nostalgia, Baldwin calls on both spatial and temporal metaphors: notions of "going back" to a place of origin on the one hand, and to a historical past on the other. I want to return to the relation between nostalgia and passing to suggest the ways in which spatial and temporal figures describe what amounts to the same logic of return, but let me begin by examining Baldwin's rhetoric of distance and placement and his figures of home, homeland, and nationality. If nationality, in *Giovanni's Room,* is an allegory of sexual and racial identity, "home" comes to represent sexual orthodoxy: when David finds himself "at home" neither in Paris nor in the United States, neither with his Italian lover nor with his American fiancée, his distance from father and fatherland suggests his venture into a space outside American bourgeois heterosexuality. When his father attempts to return the expatriate to his ideological, if not literal, homeland by recuperating for him the heterosexual masculine roles of wage earner, father, and married man, David has to admit that he "never felt at home" in the place where his father, reading a newspaper, would assume the stereotypical pose of the bourgeois American male. What is at stake in the return to, or resistance to, all things "American" is clear: "Dear Butch," his father writes, "aren't you ever coming home?" Yet only after he is brought "home" to heterosexual masculinity, here phobically opposed to homosexual effeminacy, can David be "Butch" (*GR* 119-20).

More persistently than his father's nagging letters, David's own homophobia pulls him back toward the America that constitutes his nostalgic ideal of secure gender and sexual identity. Prompted not only by his relocation in Paris but by the possibility of relocation in what he imagines to be a homosexual space, his nostalgia for home and homeland is a desire for an imagined site of heterosexual meaning. It is, after all, while breakfasting with Giovanni that David experiences his first bout of homesickness and "ache[s] abruptly,

intolerably" with the desire to go "home across the ocean, to things and people I knew and understood . . . which I would always, helplessly, and in whatever bitterness of spirit, love above all else" (*GR* 84). In that moment the strangeness of the city, of Giovanni, and of their love seems to reanimate the promise of epistemological security that "home" holds out. David's knowledge of the knowability of American "things and people," however, depends on a denial of difference, as his admission of "bitterness of spirit" suggests. His "bitterness" toward America marks the difference *within* the American "homeland"—a difference that is, for David, his own homosexual desire. Homosexuality is understood here, as in Freud, as the *unheimlich* return of a desire that gives the lie to homesickness and to the hope of a return to American orthodoxy; like the uncanny, that is, homosexuality appears as the return of something familiar that has been repressed—in David's case his adolescent love for Joey, which is all the more *unheimlich* for being, in fact, so close to home.

The note of "bitterness" in this discussion of differences between American and European "things and people" points to two distinct systems of difference that operate simultaneously in *Giovanni's Room.* Although the text conspicuously compares David as American with Giovanni as European, the more telling differences are those within "the American," within David himself, and within the always permeable boundaries of identity. Lacan's notion of the split subject bears repeating here: "In any case man cannot aim at being whole . . . once the play of displacement and condensation to which he is committed in the exercise of his functions, marks his relation as subject to the signifier" (*Feminine Sexuality* 81-82). Because subjectivity is lacking or divided within the symbolic, the effect of coherence depends on the expulsion of difference, yet efforts to police boundaries can produce *only* the effect of "inside" and "outside"—an effect that nonetheless makes itself felt as a continual tension between the claustrophobic "inside" of identity and its dangerous "outside." Thus David both hates to be labeled an American and is horrified by the possibility of being anything else. When Giovanni calls him a "*vrai américain,*" David responds, "I resented this: resented being called an American (and resented resenting it) because it seemed to make me nothing more than that, whatever that was; and I resented being called *not* an American because it seemed to make me nothing" (*GR* 117). Outside the putative safety of "America" is a territory so phobically overdetermined that it appears wholly evacuated, a "nothing." Producing this cipher as placeholder for a famously unspeakable love, David is as unwilling to imagine being anything other than a heterosexual as he is unwilling to imagine being anything other than an American. Yet "America," of course, is itself "nothing": it emerges as a locus of identification only by distinguishing itself from the foreign—or the perverse. In the narrative of *Giovanni's Room,* the space of that "nothing," alternately emptied out and filled up by representation, will also become, in the service of defining "America," an all too substantial abjected "something." Even so, being an American, "whatever that was," is never certain; indeed, there is perhaps no better illustration of the difference within, or impossibility of, identity than the way "nothing" haunts the phrase "nothing more than" an American.

Biddy Martin and Chandra Talpade Mohanty read "home" and identity in terms that usefully describe this mapping of culture's "outside" as a "nothing" or "nowhere":

> When the alternatives would seem to be either the enclosing, encircling, constraining circle of home, or nowhere to go, the risk is enormous. The assumption of, or desire for, another safe place like "home" is challenged by the realization that "unity"—interpersonal as well as political— is itself necessarily fragmentary, itself that which is struggled for, chosen, and hence unstable by definition; it is not based on "sameness," and there is no perfect fit. (209)

Just so, Baldwin acknowledges the uncertainty of "home"— that is, of identity as such—yet admits its persistent attraction in David's reluctance to "risk" locating himself elsewhere. Of course, risk is not only found outside those encircling walls; home is always as uncanny as the foreign, for it is itself the foreign. For dominant ideology to produce itself as the natural, not the *unheimlich*, it must repudiate its other as "nothing"; the coherence of "home" is thus purchased at great cost—a cost literalized, in Baldwin's novel, as David's repudiation of Giovanni, Guillaume's murder, Giovanni's flight and execution, and David's own homelessness.

But while the violence demanded by, and inherent in, the identity formation of the dominant culture may suggest the need for a gay "home" or community, the maid's room that David shares with Giovanni feels like a prison to him for most of the novel and seems an "Eden" only after it is lost. Though Guillaume's bar functions as a kind of gay "household" of which Guillaume is himself the founding father, the possibility of gay community and of essential gay identity is largely foreclosed in the novel. When the men who openly identify as gay, like Guillaume and Jacques, are called "disgusting old fairies" and worse, one hardly wonders why the only "homosexual" relationship validated here takes place between two bisexual men whose masculinity is continually and anxiously affirmed. But if *Giovanni's Room* implies that the best gay man is, in effect, a straight man—or at least one who mimics "straightness" impeccably—the novel also recognizes that something like gay identity, if not self-chosen, can be homophobically imposed. That is, though David

is sickened by the barroom queens who legibly signify their desire, he is himself read as gay on the street by a sailor who gives him a look of obscene contempt, "some brutal variation of *Look, baby, I know you*" (*GR* 122). This knowing gaze, seeming to recognize in David the identity he has so assiduously denied, engenders in him what Eve Kosofsky Sedgwick has termed "homosexual panic" at his inability to contain the public signification of his body (*Between Men* 83-96).[5] This fixation of homophobic fantasy and anxiety on the supposed legibility of the gay body recalls the "I know you" of the racial gaze represented in African American passing novels in scenes of recognition and exposure. In Larsen's *Passing,* for example, when Clare and Irene meet accidentally at Drayton's restaurant, the phantasmatic epistemology of passing is all too clear: to see is to know. This is equally true in *Giovanni's Room,* where even the object of the gaze is enjoined to "look," as if only by looking at himself being looked at can he fully be interpolated as the other whom this scene labors to produce.

In reading the relation of race and sexuality in *Giovanni's Room,* it may be useful to consider the somewhat different ways Baldwin frames sexuality and race elsewhere. Although his observation on the blindness of the "American optic"— as a discourse "based on the necessity of keeping black people out" except on "their terms"—remains true if the word "gay" is substituted for "black," Baldwin does not, for the most part, imagine sexual identity as symmetrical with racial identity. Race is essential, communal, and public, whereas sexuality is contingent, individual, and private. Asked in a 1984 interview with Richard Goldstein about the meaning of writing homosexuality "publicly," Baldwin said, "I made a public announcement that we're private, if you see what I mean" (175). The act of publicly announcing one's privacy, something of a contradiction in terms, suits Baldwin's vision of homosexuality as an identity that is not properly an identity, a "we" that cannot be adequately named. Saying of the term *gay,* that "I was never at home in it," Baldwin echoes David's confession that he was "never at home" in his father's house (qtd. in Goldstein 174). His response construes homosexuality, however "private," as that which can only aspire to the status of "home" and, associating homosexuality with the failure of "home" and the failure of identity, seems to return "gay" to the "unacceptable terms" of dominant representation.

Giovanni's Room and other passing narratives, however, counter Baldwin's published remarks on race and sexuality; they suggest instead that both racial identity and sexual identity always rest on "passing," and they reveal the often brutalizing consequences of attempts by the dominant culture to deny identity's contingency. In the world of the novel, "true" identity is radically inaccessible: one can never not pass, just as one can never go home, for both homeland and identity are revealed as retrospectively constructed fantasies. Like the binary logic of "coming out," passing can suggest an hypostatized opposition, but it also marks "race" and "sexuality" as fictions of identity. As Henry Louis Gates Jr. writes, "Race has become the trope of ultimate, irreducible difference . . . because it is so very arbitrary in its application" ("Writing 'Race'" 5). Race is, however, not the only trope of difference: despite the ways in which racial and sexual identities are differently constituted, policed, and performed, both homosexuality and heterosexuality are themselves tropes of difference that, not despite but because of their arbitrariness, wield enormous social power. If difference is a trope and if the distinction that is supposed to exist before comes into being only after the naming of identity, passing is not a false copy of true identity but an imitation of which, to borrow Judith Butler's account of gender, "there is no original" (*Gender Trouble* 25).

To unfold more fully the relation of identity to passing and nostalgia, I'd like to return to some ways in which the tropes of passing in *Giovanni's Room,* as in Johnson's *The Autobiography of an Ex-Coloured Man,* Jessie Redmon Fauset's *Plum Bun,* and Larsen's *Passing,* speak to identity's essential difference from itself. Such novels, clearly engaged with issues of race, community, and what we would now call identity politics, have to varying degrees been read as denouncing imposture and defending "original" or "true" identity. In Larsen's novel, Mary Helen Washington writes, "'Passing' is an obscene form of salvation" (164). If passing, that is, for Larsen provides no "salvation" at all, it appears "obscene" in threatening the negation of identity and in transgressing the boundaries that constitute "truth" or meaning in opposition to the abject, the meaningless. As a figure, passing insists that the "truth" of racial identity, indeed of identity as such, relies on the presence or possibility of the false. Yet passing is not simply performance or theatricality, the pervasive tropes of recent work on sex and gender identity, nor is it parody or pastiche, for it seeks to erase, rather than expose, its own dissimulation.[6] Passing, in other words, is only successful passing: unlike drag, its "performance" so impeccably mimics "reality" that it goes undetected as performance, framing its resistance to essentialism in the very rhetoric of essence and origin.[7]

To *pass* for is, according to the *OED,* "to be taken for, to be accepted, received, or held in repute as. Often with the implication of being something else." This formulation, flat and uninflected as it is, executes a sort of turn in a phrase that sounds like a redundancy: "Often with the implication of being something else." Here "being" or essence, the stuff of "true" identity, is reduced to, or endowed with, the status of "something else." Passing, however, must be understood as double: the gesture that can uncannily make what we think we know of "race" and "sexuality" into "something else" also represents the reversal of "being" and seeming that causes the dominant culture's self-presentation to be

"accepted" as the natural. Passing, then, exerts rhetorical or political force not primarily as the betrayal that must be disavowed for an oppressed group to claim its own essential identity but as a betrayal of "identity" that offers one way of reading the production of the dominant culture's own identifications.

In matters of race as well as sexuality, passing both invokes and unravels the logic of primary and secondary, authenticity and inauthenticity, candor and duplicity, by placing in question the priority of what is claimed as "true" identity. The discourse of racial passing reveals the arbitrary foundation of the categories "black" and "white," just as passing across gender and sexuality places in question the meaning of "masculine" and "feminine," "straight" and "gay." Racial passing is thus subject to an epistemological ambiguity; from the beginning, the discourse of passing contains an implicit critique of "identity" precisely because what constitutes "the beginning" of identity remains in question. Born into passing, Frances Harper's mulatto heroine in *Iola Leroy* is raised as a white child without the knowledge that her mother is black or that she is, in the eyes of the law, a slave of her father, whereas Johnson's *Autobiography of an Ex-Coloured Man* relates the disjunction between the narrator's childhood experience of himself as white and the eventual revelation of his "true" race, whose definition is enforced by white juridical authority.[8] Such texts' most salient question is the possibility or impossibility of predicating both identity and "politics" on a racial subject who stands before culture, before community, and before a relation to passing. But they also ask whether the law is not itself passing when it plays the role of authority so effectively that its own dissimulation or contingency is erased.

To recognize the masquerade of "natural" identity is also to reveal the unnaturalness of what the dominant culture would have us most take for granted: the ontological status of heterosexuality and whiteness. The rhetoric of passing brings into relief the inauthenticity of "authentic" identity by bringing to the fore the passing of heterosexuality and of whiteness as themselves—which is to say, the contingency at the heart of identity that engenders, in the dominant culture, endless attempts to naturalize its own position by positing the inauthenticity or secondariness of what it will construe as its others.[9] As Baldwin himself has suggested in a published conversation, the constitution of the deviant or marginal subject is the paradigmatic gesture through which the subject position of the dominant culture is defined: "People invent categories in order to feel safe: White people invented black people to give white people identity. . . . Straight cats invented faggots so they could sleep with them without becoming faggots themselves" (Baldwin and Giovanni 88-89). That is, the white or straight world invents its other in order to recognize itself, making the "inauthentic" define the authentic. The instability of heterosexuality and whiteness is projected onto, and reified in, the passing subject, people of color, and gay men and lesbians, all of whom constitute what Judith Butler, in her reading of homosexuality and miscegenation in Larsen's *Passing,* calls the "constitutive outside" of regimes of sexual and racial purity (*Bodies That Matter* 167).

If passing, then, invokes origins only to displace origins, the passing of the law itself is manifest in its nostalgia for a point of origin that, in fact, it has never known. This nostalgia takes shape, both in **Giovanni's Room** and in other discourses of race and sexuality, not only in terms of home and displacement but in terms of retrospection and the past. Like David's nationalistic fantasy of his American homeland, subjectivity—and the various identificatory mechanisms by which we recognize ourselves as subjects—is always a story told from the vantage point of the present and projected into the past, where it gains the status of an origin. In order to think further about nostalgia, I'd like to return to some ways in which metalepsis, the displacement of the secondary into the site of the primary, has been imagined in recent criticism. While the deconstructive logic of these readings is no doubt familiar, they make it possible to trace more clearly the politics of a certain cultural nostalgia in relation to the retroactive construction of individual subjectivity.

Judith Butler has persuasively described the construction of the subject "before the law" by the very agency of the law, whose part in that history is retroactively erased: "the law produces and then conceals the notion of a 'subject before the law' in order to invoke that discursive formation as a naturalized foundational premise that subsequently legitimates the law's own regulatory hegemony" (*Gender Trouble* 2).[10] As in Kafka's story of the same name, Butler's "before the law" at once suggests a space prior to juridical discipline and the very space organized under that discipline. To recognize such retrospective projections of the dominant culture, Butler cautions, is not enough if oppositional projects will also subscribe to a politics of representation that assumes a priori an essential sameness among its constituents; nor is it productive for coalitional or "representational" politics to decide in advance what the contours of their coalitions will be and thus to invent, through "description," the constituency they come to represent.[11] Metalepsis is thus centrally a part of the ways we imagine politics as such and the ways that both hegemonic and oppositional institutions take shape; but no less "political" is the nostalgia of the subject within the symbolic—indeed, nostalgia articulates the relationship of social law to psychological subject.

Insofar as it is anchored by proleptic and retrospective projections, political "identity" comes to resemble subjectivity as Lacan understands it. Having suffered a splitting of self or loss of a presence-to-himself as a result of his entrance into the symbolic order, the subject confronts a "radical fissure, and a subjective impasse, because the subject is called on to face in it the lack through which he is constituted" (*Feminine Sexuality* 116). Unable ever to face its own constitutive lack, culture itself, not unlike the Lacanian subject, attempts to "cover over" or deny lack by positing an origin, a "before." Thus the pre-Oedipal state is produced as a site of wholeness, multiplicity, or indifferentiation–as the outside of the symbolic—only within the symbolic order, by whose agency we are able retrospectively to posit the pre-Oedipal as the prediscursive realm. And yet, for Lacan, the subject owes as much to anticipation as to retrospection: the mirror stage depends on the projected image in which the child misrecognizes himself in a proleptic fantasy of his future bodily wholeness and assumes, as "the armour of an alienating identity," the template or "rigid structure" that determines subjectivity ever after (*Écrits* 4).

Just as the image of the fragmented body that precedes the mirror stage can be only metaleptically imagined, even beyond the mirror stage, as Jane Gallop notes, individual subjectivity is thoroughly indebted to projections into the past and future: it is "a succession of future perfects, pasts of a future, moments twice removed from 'present reality' by the combined action of an anticipation and a retroaction" (82). That is, the effect of identity's coherence is generated in part by endless reference to an irrecoverable origin, an *elsewhere.* If nostalgia, like passing, gestures toward an absent "something else," it does so not to displace but to locate and confirm individual or institutional "identity." Thus what Susan Stewart has called "the social disease of nostalgia" designates not an aberration in society but the disease of the social as such, the enabling "disease" or condition that, by looking backward, allows culture to progress or persist (23).

The nostalgia of the social works to vivify, and is in turn represented by, the particular desires of individuals: in **Giovanni's Room,** David's longed-for home in American heterosexual ideology is, like identity itself, revealed to be deeply nostalgic, retroactively produced as an origin from a position of belatedness and lack. The object of David's desire exists only in fantasy, as Giovanni recognizes: "you will go home and then you will find that home is not home anymore. Then you will really be in trouble. As long as you stay here, you can always think: One day I will go home" (**GR** 154-55). "Home" becomes possible only after identity and the possibility of meaning are recognized as lost, when the contingency of the origin is erased by nostalgia and "home" is naturalized as an object of desire. As a condition of desire that, as Gallop says of the image of "the body in bits and pieces," *the corps morcelé "comes after . . . so as to represent what came before"* (80), the nostalgia designated in Baldwin's novel by "homesickness" does not so much represent a disturbance of desire as the fate of all subjects within the symbolic order. Nostalgia, "a desire constitutively unsatisfied and unsatisfiable because its 'object' simply cannot ever be defined," becomes a fundamental condition of subjectivity—and of culture (Gallop 151). More than a retroactive effect, nostalgia is an effect which, unable to name what it experiences as lost, can only misrecognize the object it desires, for although its etymology refers back to *nostos,* or return, Gallop notes, nostalgia is a "transgression of return: a desire ungrounded in a past, desire for an object that has never been 'known'" (151). In racist and homophobic discourse, the "desire for an object that has never been known" is the desire for the coherence of whiteness or heterosexuality, an impossible ideal that nevertheless must be sustained if dominant culture is to "reproduce" itself, as Butler recognizes, as distinct from its "constitutive outside."

To name this effect "nostalgia" is to suggest as well the pathos that colors its backward glance—a pathos that may mean the masking or misrecognition of the more coercive aspects of the ideology "home" represents. It means, too, the misrecognition of identity as such figured not only in Lacan's mirror stage but in Baldwin's: when David examines his reflection in the first page of *Giovanni's Room,* his misrecognition of himself *as* self, however problematic his whiteness and straightness have and will become, seems the precondition of speech, even the precondition of narrative. David's desire to return to America is insistent and deeply felt, but as the novel's brutal conclusion suggests, nostalgia and violence go hand in hand as inseparable aspects of the positing and policing of identity. That is, nostalgia's inevitability in no way means its effects are symmetrical, for it is precisely the nonidentity of the white, bourgeois, heterosexual culture that David represents in *Giovanni's Room* that must be phobically projected onto an other who, like Giovanni, will bear the burden of that nostalgia even to his death.

Baldwin's ambivalent revision of the passing novel both exposes, through David, the operations of nostalgia and trades on a pathos of lost origins. As Baldwin observes in *Giovanni's Room,* agency and self-consciousness are never fully ours: the effect of identity continually and repetitively produced by the subject to recognize itself as a subject is imbued with the pathos of David's misrecognition of his own agency and subjectivity. "Nobody can stay in the garden of Eden," Jacques says, after the news of Giovanni's sentencing, "I wonder why." David thinks: "Perhaps everybody has a garden of Eden, I don't know; but they have scarcely seen their garden before they see the flaming sword. Then, perhaps, life offers only the choice of remembering the garden or forgetting it. Either, or: it takes strength to remember, it takes another kind of strength to forget, it takes a hero to do both" (35-36). The allusion to prelapsarian bliss appropriately represents the subject prior to the imposition of the

law and the symbolic order; indeed, as Gallop has noted, Lacan's account of the mirror stage is the story of a "paradise lost" (85).[12] Just as we can understand Eden only in the language of exile, we can imagine pre-Oedipal presence only in the Oedipalized language of lack. If Eden, in this particular myth of origin, is a paradigmatic home, whether the original heterosexual household or the short-lived pleasures of Giovanni's room, it is, Baldwin suggests, always already lost. The "either, or"—to remember Eden or to forget—is, as *Giovanni's Room* makes clear, no choice at all, for to remember is to engage in a nostalgic gesture that, to posit home as the originary site of identity, must simultaneously erase its retrospective construction, and to forget is to accept the nonexistence of this Eden—or, if you will, identity—a renunciation the subject can never wholly make. Thus each decision, and each performance of identity, is necessarily a double bind: David is condemned never to remember or forget Giovanni, never to get "home" or give it up.

It is easy enough, perhaps all too easy, to say that the answer to the question of identity politics is a politics of identity that insists on the contingency of identity. Such a politics, taking its cue from the discourse of passing, might seek to de-essentialize "identity" so as not to impose, through anticipation or retrospection, an illusionary and exclusionary coherence on those it "represents" and in order not to accede in its own right to the logic of the dominant culture. Yet what Baldwin's novel brings home to us most forcefully and most poignantly is the danger not only of the exercise of nostalgia but also of the fantasy that one can ever escape it. No less than the desire for an impossible return, the denial of nostalgia is itself nostalgic, for the ending of nostalgia and the accomplishment of placement is precisely the impossible object that nostalgia forever pursues. No politics, then, can ever fully overcome the passing or impersonation of its own identity or disavow the nostalgia that sustains subjectivity in the imaginary. Instead, a "politics"—which is to say, a reading—of "race" and "sexuality" might work to uncover the constitutive nostalgia of the dominant culture, for about the notions of passing, nostalgia, and desire whose effects *Giovanni's Room* traces, there is still a great deal to be said.

NOTES

1. For a reading of racial and sexual passing in Larsen, see the essay by Cutter in this collection. See also Deborah McDowell's "Introduction" to *Quicksand* and *Passing* and Blackmore, "'That Unreasonable Restless Feeling': The Homosexual Subtexts of Nella Larsen's *Passing*." Cheryl Wall discusses passing in relation to gender in "Passing for What? Aspects of Identity in Nella Larsen's Novels."

2. Baldwin, *Giovanni's Room* 7. All further quotations from

this novel will be from the Dell edition (1988) and will be cited in the text as *GR*.

3. See Riviere, "Womanliness as Masquerade," and Judith Butler's discussion of Riviere and the performance of gender in *Gender Trouble* 24-25, 50-57.

4. On Baldwin and Henry James, see Newman, "The Lesson of the Master: Henry James and James Baldwin."

5. See also Sedgwick's *Epistemology of the Closet*. For further discussion of the legibility of the gay male body, see Edelman, *Homographesis* 5-6.

6. In addition to Butler's work on performativity in *Gender Trouble*, see also Sedgwick's "Queer Performativity: Henry James's *The Art of the Novel*."

7. Marjorie Garber describes gender passing as "a social and sartorial inscription which encodes (as treason does) its own erasure" (234). For a concise formulation of the relation of drag to passing, see also Robinson, "It Takes One to Know One" 727.

8. The title of *The Autobiography of an Ex-Coloured Man* suggests that the man in question is originally "coloured," although the narrative begins with his perception of himself as a white child. See the discussion of this novel by Kawash in this collection.

9. For a useful discussion of the construction of racial hegemony, in which passing figures as "a model for the cultural production of whiteness," see Mullen, "Optic White" 72-74.

10. Whether the "nonhistorical 'before'" is invoked by the dominant culture or by feminists, Butler argues, its effect is conservative.

11. See Butler, *Gender Trouble*, on the contingency of gender (38) and the anticipatory logic of political coalitions (14).

12. On nostalgia and the prelapsarian, see also Stewart, *On Longing* 23. Lee Edelman offers an incisive reading of identity, narcissism, and *Paradise Lost* in *Homographesis* 101-04.

Hilton Als (review date 16 February 1998)

SOURCE: "The Enemy Within: The Making and Unmaking of James Baldwin," in *New Yorker*, February 16, 1998, pp. 72-80.

[*In the following review, Als presents an overview of Baldwin's life and career.*]

Twenty-two years ago, when I was fourteen, I was given James Baldwin's second collection of essays, *Nobody Knows My Name* (1961), by his friend and my mentor the writer Owen Dodson, who was one of the more ebullient survivors of the Harlem Renaissance. The dust jacket of the book featured a photograph of Baldwin wearing a white T-shirt and standing in a pile of rubble in a vacant lot. It was this photograph that compelled me to read the book. I had never seen an image of a black boy like me—Baldwin looked as if he could have been posing in my old neighborhood, in East New York—gracing anything as impressive as a collection of essays. In fact, shortly after Owen gave me the book I began to pretend that the photograph of Baldwin was of me, or the writer I meant to be, and that the book's contents were my spiritual autobiography, or a record of the life I longed to lead. I was living in a roach-infested apartment in Crown Heights, along with my mother, my older sister, my younger brother, and the wearying fear that I would never escape from it. Baldwin, though, had grown up in circumstances not so different from my own, and he had gone on to become one of the most eminent writers America had ever produced. In the book, there was Baldwin in Paris attending a conference at the Sorbonne, Baldwin in Sweden interviewing Ingmar Bergman, Baldwin grappling with the exigencies of the life of the writer. And there was Baldwin realizing that, no matter how hard he had tried to separate himself from that black boy picking his way through the rubble of Harlem, he would always be regarded by some as a "nigger."

I didn't believe that I was a nigger, but I was certainly viewed with contempt by friends and family whenever my differences—which took the form of reading and writing, and hanging out with boys who called one another "girlfriend"—declared themselves. In reading Baldwin, then, I was listening to my secret voice, the voice of someone who wasn't afraid to describe who he was and where he'd come from and what he'd seen. Baldwin was also able to convey, in his labyrinthine, emotional prose, the persistent guilt that I felt toward my family—the family I would need to leave in order to become myself. And what compounded the guilt was the vague suspicion that in leaving them behind I would be leaving my blackness behind as well, to join the white world—a world that more often than not hurt and baffled my mother and siblings. Baldwin understood these things, because he'd survived them.

During the following year, I spent many hours in the main branch of the Brooklyn Public Library, hunched over bound volumes of old magazines featuring stories about Baldwin. I was struck, in some photographs, by his enormous eyes, like dark poppies in bloom, raised in mock or serious consternation; in others, by his enormous grin, with the "liar's space" between the two front teeth. And then there were the interviews, during which he spoke with great candor and wit:

> [Journalist]: When you were starting out as a writer, you were black, impoverished, and homosexual. You must have said to yourself, "Gee, how disadvantaged can I get?"
>
> [Baldwin]: No, I thought I had hit the jackpot. It was so outrageous, you had to find a way to use it.

When I was older, and had become a writer myself, my feelings about Baldwin grew ambivalent. I have never been comfortable being identified as a black writer, particularly when that description comes from a white audience, which knows nothing of the limitations imposed by the term. Nor have I ever been comfortable with the presumed fraternity of black writers, academics, and intellectuals: I have spent my entire life trying to come to grips with my feelings for my own family, and had little interest in being adopted by another—one with its own provincialism, competitiveness, and misapprehensions. Baldwin, at one point in his life, felt the same. In 1959, when he was thirty-five, he wrote from his self-imposed exile in Europe that he had left America because he wanted to prevent himself from becoming merely "a Negro writer." He went on to become exactly that: the greatest Negro writer of his generation. Perhaps none of us escape the whipping post we've carved our names on. But Baldwin's career became a cautionary tale for me, a warning as well as an inspiration.

I recently returned to Baldwin, prompted by the Library of America's just-published two-volume selection of his novels, short stories, and essays, edited by Toni Morrison. And I found that what I identified with in his work—the high-faggot style of his voice, the gripping narrative of his ascent from teen evangelist to cultural icon—had not changed for me since the days when I devoured his books like "some weird food" (as Baldwin once described his own early love of reading). My admiration for the way in which he alchemized the singularity of his perspective into art had not diminished. Neither had my discomfort with the way he had finally compromised that perspective. But I came to recognize something I'd missed during both my early infatuation and my later disaffection: no matter how much I tried to resist my identification with Baldwin, we were uneasy members of the same tribe.

James Baldwin was disenfranchised from the start. Born James Arthur Jones, in Harlem Hospital, on August 2, 1924, he was the illegitimate child of Emma Berdis Jones, who worked as a cleaning woman to support herself and her son.

He never knew his biological father. In 1927, his mother married a Baptist preacher named David Baldwin; together, they reared eight other children, in a series of Harlem tenements. "My mother's strength was only to be called on in a desperate emergency," Baldwin wrote in 1972 in **"No Name in the Street."** Her eldest child soon learned that his mother "scarcely belonged to us: she was always in the hospital, having another baby." His stepfather was an unforgiving man with a terrible temper, who eventually lost his mind: "Between [the] children, who were terrified of him, the pregnancies, the births, the rats, the murders on Lenox Avenue, the whores who lived downstairs, his job on Long Island—to which he went every morning, wearing a Derby or a Homburg, in a black suit, white shirt, dark tie, looking like the preacher he was, and with his black lunchbox in his hand—and his unreciprocated love for the Great God Almighty, it is no wonder our father went mad."

In the midst of the anger and chaos of this household, the young Baldwin developed an insatiable appetite for literature. He writes in the introductory "Autobiographical Notes" to his first collection of essays, entitled *Notes of a Native Son* and published in 1955, "I read *Uncle Tom's Cabin*, and *A Tale of Two Cities*, over and over and over. . . . In fact, I read just about everything I could get my hands on—except the Bible, probably because it was the only book I was encouraged to read." And, reading in the larger world of books, Baldwin began to see the smallness of the world in which he lived, and to devise ways of escaping. "I knew I was black, of course, but I also knew I was smart," he once said. "I didn't know how I would use my mind . . . but I was going to get whatever I wanted that way, and I was going to get my revenge that way."

Escape was intimately bound up with issues of race. In *Notes of a Native Son* Baldwin recalls that when he was nine or ten he wrote a play that was directed by a young white schoolteacher—"a woman, who then took an interest in me, and gave me books to read, and, in order to corroborate my theatrical bent, decided to take me to see what she somewhat tactlessly referred to as 'real' plays." He goes on, "Theater-going was forbidden in our house, but, with the really cruel intuitiveness of a child, I suspected that the color of this woman's skin would carry the day for me." And it did. David Baldwin could not object to Jimmy's education, because he could not contradict the power that the white woman's skin held in his imagination:

> He would have refused permission if he dared. The fact that he did not dare caused me to despise him. . . . In later years, particularly when it began to be clear that this "education" of mine was going to lead me to perdition, he became more explicit and warned me that my white friends in high school were not really my friends and that

I would see, when I was older, how white people would do anything to keep a Negro down. . . . The best thing was to have as little to do with them as possible. I did not feel this way and I was certain, in my innocence, that I never would.

And so his stepfather's resistance proved a goad to his ambition, spurring him to reconfigure his world by turning difference into strength.

During Baldwin's years at Frederick Douglass Junior High School—from 1935 to 1938—his early ambitions were encouraged by one of the teachers there, the black homosexual writer Countee Cullen, who had enjoyed a vogue during the Harlem Renaissance. Baldwin went on to De Witt Clinton High School, a distinguished—and racially integrated—public school in the Bronx. Among his classmates were the future writer Emile Capouya, the future editor Sol Stein, and the future photographer Richard Avedon, with whom Baldwin coedited the school magazine, *The Magpie*. And as Baldwin began to venture—both literally and metaphorically—out of the neighborhood, some of his stepfather's forebodings began to be realized. Avedon remembers bringing Baldwin home to his family's apartment on the Upper East Side: "The elevator man looked at Jimmy and said, 'You have to go up the back stairs.'"

But even as Baldwin was travelling beyond the boundaries of the black community he was also trying to find his place in it. He underwent a religious conversion when he turned fourteen, began preaching shortly afterward, and proved to be good at it. In the small world of Harlem's Pentecostal churches, he had his first experience of fame, but he took little pleasure in it. "At this time of my life, Emile was the only friend I had who knew to what extent my ministry tormented me," Baldwin wrote many years later, in **"The Devil Finds Work"** (1976). Capouya believed that his friend remained in the church out of cowardice:

> Therefore, on the coming Sunday, he would buy two tickets to a Broadway matinee and meet me on the steps of the 42nd Street Library, at two o'clock in the afternoon. He knew that I spent all day Sunday in church—the point, precisely, of the challenge. . . . I had hoped for a reprieve, hoped, on the marked Sunday, to get away unnoticed: but I was the "young" Brother Baldwin, and I sat in the front row, and the pastor did not begin his sermon until about a quarter past one. Well. At one-thirty, I *tiptoed* out. . . . That was how I left the church.

He was seventeen. Shortly afterward, he left home, but he continued to help support his large family, working first at a defense plant in New Jersey, and then at a meatpacking plant

in Manhattan. The racism he encountered during this period was debilitating in its unthinking brutality: twelve years later, he described the visceral response it evoked as being like "some dread, chronic disease, the unfailing symptom of which is a kind of blind fever, a pounding in the skull and fire in the bowels," and he added, "It can wreck more important things than race relations. There is not a Negro alive who does not have this rage in his blood."

David Baldwin died in 1943, several days before his adopted son's nineteenth birthday. Baldwin buried his stepfather, moved to Greenwich Village, and embarked on a new life as a bohemian. A year later, he met Richard Wright, who championed Baldwin's early efforts at fiction, recommending him to an editor at Harper & Brothers. It was Wright who first gave voice to Baldwin's experience of racism. "He was the greatest black writer in the world for me," Baldwin later recalled, in "Alas, Poor Richard." "In *Uncle Tom's Children*, in *Native Son*, and, above all, in *Black Boy*, I found expressed, for the first time in my life, the sorrow, the rage, and the murderous bitterness which was eating up my life. . . . His work was an immense liberation and revelation for me."

Through Eugene Worth, a black friend who committed suicide in 1946 (and who inspired the character of Rufus in Baldwin's 1962 novel, ***Another Country***), Baldwin was introduced to leftist politics, and in short order the nineteen-year-old writer was a card-carrying Trotskyist, but he didn't remain one long. ("It was useful in that I learned that it may be impossible to indoctrinate me," he wrote in the introduction to his collection of pieces ***The Price of the Ticket***.) Still, during that time he became acquainted with the intellectuals who would greatly influence the beginning of his career as a writer: Saul Levitas, of *The New Leader*; Randall Jarrell, of *The Nation*; Elliott Cohen and Robert Warshow, of *Commentary*; and Philip Rahv, of *The Partisan Review*. These editors supported Baldwin's growth as a critic and allowed him access to the social world of New York intellectuals, but their patronage was not without its restrictions: as a black, he was expected and encouraged to review black books. "As for the books I reviewed—well, no one, I suppose, will ever read them again," Baldwin mused. "It was after the war, and Americans were on one of their monotonous conscience 'trips': be kind to niggers, for Christ's sake, be kind to Jews!"

To some extent, Baldwin used his blackness as a kind of surrogate Jewishness: it was his "difference" that sold, and the Jewish intellectuals who knew persecution at first hand could understand racism as persecution of a different hue. Baldwin described the connection himself, in his essay **"The Harlem Ghetto,"** which was published in 1948:

> Though the notion of suffering . . . is based on the image of the wandering, exiled Jew, the con-

text changes imperceptibly, to become a fairly obvious reminder of the trials of the Negro. . . . At this point, the Negro identifies himself almost wholly with the Jew. The more devout Negro considers that he *is* a Jew, in bondage to a hard taskmaster and waiting for Moses to lead him out of Egypt.

It is likely that this connection in suffering was clear to him as a citizen of Harlem, where the Jew was stigmatized for his whiteness, just as blacks were marked in the larger world for their blackness. But such observations must have also strengthened his sense of belonging to his new intellectual community.

Certainly this community helped to redefine Baldwin. By 1948, he was no longer the ugliest boy his father had ever seen but a promising young writer who was considered "very smart" by the older editors he worked for. And nothing is more necessary to a writer than attention. "Though it may have cost Saul Levitas nothing to hurl a book at a black boy to see if he could read it and be articulate concerning what he had read, I took it as a vote of confidence. And I loved him . . . and I think . . . that he was proud of me, and that he loved me, too." It is a touchingly vulnerable statement.

The reviews and essays Baldwin wrote for *The Nation* and other magazines are models of linguistic precision and critical acuity. In them he laid the groundwork for the themes he would explore and develop in his later essays: the tensions between blacks and Jews; black stereotypes in film; the effect of poverty on everyday life. At the same time, he was developing a style as a writer—a style that blended a full-throated preacherly cadence with the astringent obliquities of a semi-closeted queen.

Baldwin was also struggling to embrace a wider racial vision. At the end of his review of a biography of Frederick Douglass—a review published in *The Nation* in 1947, when Baldwin was only twenty-two—he wrote, "Relations between Negroes and whites, like any other province of human experience, demand honesty and insight; they must be based on the assumption that there is one race and that we are all part of it." At the same time, however, he wasn't trying to "transcend" his race: he was assuming the role of its spokesperson. In a review of Chester Himes's novel *The Lonely Crusade* Baldwin states, "On the low ground where Negroes live something is happening: something which can be measured in decades and generations and which may spell our doom as a republic and almost certainly implies a cataclysm."

In November, 1948, Baldwin decided to leave the country. Unwilling to end up like his stepfather, "sitting at the window, locked up in his terrors," he used the money from a literary fellowship he'd won to book passage to Paris. He arrived with just over forty dollars to his name and few contacts other than Richard Wright, who had arrived there two years earlier. But postwar Paris proved to be a refuge for a number of black Americans. And the Parisians, as Baldwin's friend Maya Angelou has said, were delighted with them: they were neither *les misérables* nor Algerians. "France was not without its race prejudices," she recalled in an interview. "It simply didn't have any guilt vis-à-vis black Americans. And black Americans who went there, from Richard Wright to Sidney Bechet, were so colorful, and so talented, and so marvellous, and so exotic. Who wouldn't want them?"

In Paris, Baldwin lived in a variety of hotels, some "ludicrously grim," and he supported himself in a variety of ways. His first summer, he worked as a clerk for a lawyer and he wrote pieces for French and American periodicals. And, for the first time in his life, he borrowed from friends and acquaintances. To live off the largesse of friends takes charm, but that was one resource he had in abundance. "He was able to really charm you, and entertain you, and beguile you, and I suppose seduce you if you were at all ready for it," the poet Richard Howard remembers.

Through Wright, Baldwin was introduced to the editors of the Paris-based magazine *Zero*, and for them, in 1949, he wrote his first critical piece about his former mentor—a devastating essay entitled **"Everybody's Protest Novel."** In it Baldwin argued that American protest literature simply confirmed stereotypes about blacks, and that Bigger Thomas, the anti-hero of Wright's 1940 novel, *Native Son*, was the spiritual and ideological twin of Harriet Beecher Stowe's Uncle Tom—a victim used as a vessel to project the author's self-righteousness. Baldwin felt confined by political fiction; as he later explained, he wanted to be a writer "instead of a pamphleteer."

Owen Dodson told me that when Baldwin attacked Wright's aesthetic most black intellectuals and academics felt that he had gone too far. Disdainful of intellectual protectionism among blacks, I replied that I guessed that we were not only supposed to look alike but like alike, too. Today, however, as I read Baldwin's essays on Wright and sort through my own jumbled feelings, the truth seems a bit more complicated. Certainly both **"Everybody's Protest Novel"** and Baldwin's later essay **"Alas, Poor Richard"** (1961) expressed real misgivings that the younger man had about Wright's work. But these essays—as the title of the second one suggests—also constituted a very personal attack. Baldwin meant not only to bury the tradition of black letters which had its roots in a Communism supported by white dilettantes but also to supersede Wright as the one black writer worth reading in the largely white world of American letters. The Oedipal nature of their relationship was not lost on Baldwin, who once described Wright as "my ally and my witness, and alas! my father."

It is a similar desire for a father—and an ultimate distance from him—that accounts for most of the pathos of ***Go Tell It on the Mountain,*** Baldwin's first and best novel, which was published, finally, in 1953. (Baldwin had worked on ***Mountain***—originally entitled **"In My Father's House"**— in one form or another for a decade.) The story takes place in the course of a day—the day John, its hero, turns thirteen and is "saved" in the Baptist church where his father preaches. Sharing the stage with John are the dark, troubled "vertical saints." They are his immediate elders: his mother, Elizabeth; his stepfather, Gabriel; and Gabriel's sister Florence. While John writhes and moans on the "threshing floor," each of them recounts, in flashback, the sins of his or her own past. John's sins—his blackness and his gayness—are part of the filth that he lives in and from which he cannot imagine how to escape. John's "ugliness" is also part of his sin. "His father had always said his face was the face of Satan—and was there not something—in the lift of the eyebrow, in the way his rough hair formed a V on his brow—that bore witness to his father's words? In the eye there was a light that was not the light of Heaven, and the mouth trembled, lustful and lewd, to drink deep in the winds of Hell."

The extraordinary power of ***Mountain*** arose from Baldwin's ability to convey the warping intensity of an elder's judgment and a child's inability to protect himself from it. John cannot understand why his father despises him, because the fact that the father despises himself does not occur to John. Nor can John imagine being able to escape him: there will never be any reprieve from the memory of his cruelty and its effect.

The psychic tug-of-war between attraction and rejection was also destined to play itself out in Baldwin's relationships with other men. Shortly after his arrival in Paris, Baldwin met a seventeen-year-old Swiss artist named Lucien Happesberger. The fact that Happesberger was white and Baldwin black was less of a transgression than it would have been back in the States. "In Paris," Baldwin said, "I didn't feel socially attacked, but relaxed, and that allowed me to be loved."

"He was this rather silly, giddy, predatory fellow who was extraordinarily unattractive-looking," Richard Howard recalls. "There's a famous eighteenth-century person who used to say, 'I can talk my face away in twenty-five minutes.' And Jimmy could do that." To a point, perhaps. In the gay demimonde, where looks count for a great deal, Baldwin was not a success, even after he became famous, and he tended to be attracted to straight and bisexual men, who increased the sense of isolation he fed on. Even Lucien, his great love,

was primarily attracted to women. For Baldwin, the first principle of love was love withheld; it was all he had ever known.

His second novel, ***Giovanni's Room*** (1956), traces a tragic affair between two men—a white American drifter and an Italian bartender amid the bars and *hôtels particuliers* of postwar Paris. The melodramatic plot—in which each man really does kill the thing he loves—creates, in microcosm, the sentimental, histrionic tone of Baldwin's later, unwieldy novels, notably ***Another Country.***

Giovanni's Room isn't exactly self-affirming, but the fact that he wrote about the world of his sexuality at all is extraordinary, given the year and his race. (So intense was the stern Puritanism of most blacks I knew while I was growing up that one was not simply a faggot but a damned faggot.) When ***Giovanni's Room*** was published, Howard recalls, "it was regarded as an exceptional book, and gay people were proud that such a thing existed. And that it should have been written by a black person was kind of phenomenal."

It was in Baldwin's essays, unencumbered by the requirements of narrative form, character, and incident, that his voice was most fully realized. And his attacks on the straight-white-boy gatekeepers of culture and politics remain appropriately vicious. In the nineteen-fifties, his most pugnacious contemporary was Norman Mailer. In 1959, the thirty-six-year-old Mailer published *Advertisements for Myself,* which contained his essay "Evaluations—Quick and Expensive Comments on the Talent in the Room." In it, he declares his admiration for James Jones and other major novelists of the time. But of Baldwin he says:

> James Baldwin is too charming a writer to be major. If in ***Notes of a Native Son*** he has a sense of moral nuance which is one of the few modern guides to the sophistications of the ethos, even the best of his paragraphs are sprayed with perfume. Baldwin seems incapable of saying "F— you" to the reader; instead he must delineate the cracking and the breaking and the melting and the hardening of a heart which could never have felt such sensuous growths and little deaths without being emptied as a voice.

Baldwin's subsequent essay about Mailer—**"The Black Boy Looks at the White Boy,"** published in 1961—deflates Mailer's macho posturing with his "perfumed" wit: "Norman, I can't go through the world the way you do because I haven't got your shoulders," he writes. He also pits his de-facto cool credentials against what he depicts as Mailer's privileged white petulance:

> The anguish which can overtake a white man comes in the middle of his life, when he must make

the almost inconceivable effort to divest himself of everything he has ever expected, or believed, when he must take himself apart and put himself together again, walking out of the world, into limbo or into what certainly looks like limbo. This cannot yet happen to any Negro of Norman's age, for the reason that his delusions and defenses are either absolutely impenetrable by this time, or he has failed to survive them. "I want to know how power works," Norman once said to me, "how it really works, in detail." Well, I know how power works, it has worked on me, and if I didn't know how power worked, I would be dead.

In the same place, Baldwin slyly makes fun of Mailer's infatuation with the predominantly black jazz world. "Negro jazz musicians . . . really liked Norman," he writes. But they "did not for an instant consider him as being even remotely 'hip.' . . . They thought he was a real sweet ofay cat, but a little frantic." Baldwin did not, however, own up to his reciprocal fascination with straight white boys and their privilege. Certainly *Another Country,* Baldwin's own "hip" book about interracial sex, gay sex, pot smoking, and nihilism, turned out to be an artistic disaster.

By the time Baldwin published *Another Country* and the essay collection *Nobody Knows My Name,* both in 1962, he had become America's leading black literary star. Both books were commercially successful, but the reviews of *Another Country* were mixed. The novel centers on Rufus, a black male artist, who falls in love with a white Southern woman he meets at a party, and has sex with her on the hosts' balcony. ("He forced her beneath him and he entered her. For a moment she thought she was going to scream, she was so tight. . . . Then, from the center of his rising storm, very slowly and deliberately, he began the slow ride home. And she carried him, as the sea will carry a boat.") After becoming involved with her, Rufus is tormented by the world that cannot understand their love. He beats her; she ends up in a mental ward; he commits suicide. The subplots, about adultery, bedhopping, and ambition, are equally melodramatic. Elizabeth Hardwick astutely observed in her review for *Harper's,* "In certain respects this novel is a representation of some of the ideas about American life, particularly about the Negro in American life, that Baldwin's essays have touched upon. But what is lacking in the book is James Baldwin himself, who has in his non-fictional writing a very powerful relation to the reader."

In 1962, Baldwin's incantatory voice reached its largest magazine audience. Baldwin had agreed to write a piece about Africa for William Shawn, who was then the editor of *The New Yorker;* instead, he gave Shawn the essay that came to be known as **"The Fire Next Time,"** which had originally been assigned him by Norman Podhoretz, of *Commentary.*

The peculiar power of **"The Fire Next Time"** was intensified by the cultural moment at which it appeared, just as Martin Luther King's nonviolent movement was being overtaken by the violent nationalism of Malcolm X and the Nation of Islam.

"The Fire Next Time," which appeared as a Letter from a Region in My Mind, detailed Baldwin's evangelical upbringing and his views on Christianity as a form of slavery forced on and then embraced by blacks: oppression as the condition of black American life. In order to escape "the ghetto mentality" and be a "truly moral human being," it was necessary for anyone, white or black, to first "divorce himself from all the prohibitions, crimes, and hypocrisies of the Christian church," Baldwin wrote. "If the concept of God has any validity or any use, it can only be to make us larger, freer, and more loving. If God cannot do this, then it is time we got rid of Him." The godhead with whom many blacks were replacing that Christian god was Allah, as represented by the Honorable Elijah Muhammad. When Baldwin visited him at his home in Chicago, he was impressed by the Nation of Islam's ability to transform some of Harlem's more disreputable characters into Allah-abiding men.

Baldwin was able to maintain a skeptical view of the militancy of the Nation of Islam in his essay, and yet his admiration for strong black men is palpable. At one point, he confesses that upon encountering the Honorable Elijah Muhammad's "marvellous smile" he was reminded of the day, twenty-three years earlier, when he first met the female pastor of what would become his church. "Whose little boy are you?" she asked him. And Baldwin's orphaned heart cried out, "Why, yours!"

With the publication of *The Fire Next Time* in book form, in 1963, Baldwin became something of an intellectual carpetbagger. He undertook a lecture tour for the Congress on Racial Equality; he registered voters in Alabama for the Student Nonviolent Coordinating Committee; he travelled to Nairobi with Harry Belafonte and Sidney Poitier to celebrate Kenya's independence. On May 17th, he appeared on the cover of *Time.* William Styron recalls seeing Baldwin in an airport shortly after the book came out: "He was being followed by crews of TV reporters with microphones. He saw me from a distance, and waved, and then he was swept along by the great media wave." An essayist once known for his ability to question any party line had become the official voice of black America, and almost immediately his voice as a writer was compromised.

In 1964, Baldwin was asked by Lee Strasberg, then the director of the Actors Studio, to stage a play about the Emmett Till case, which the writer had been working on intermittently since 1958. As originally conceived, by Baldwin and Frank Cosaro, who was slotted to direct it, the play, *Blues for Mis-*

ter Charlie, was to be a "balanced view" of America's racial scene. Baldwin, Cosaro says, wanted as objective a view of Mister Charlie—the white man—as of his victim, and Cosaro was impressed by that. But Baldwin couldn't ignore the political influence of the black leaders he was becoming friendly with. "He then came back to me and Strasberg," Cosaro recalls, "and said that he had to go after Mister Charlie." The result was dutiful, turgid, and unconvincing.

Baldwin had always been a preacher of one sort or another, and preaching imminent earthly damnation to liberal white folks became increasingly irresistible. Even as early as 1960, Baldwin, standing in front of Styron's fireplace in Connecticut, told his host, "Baby, we are going to burn your motherfucking houses down." By 1968, Baldwin found impersonating a black writer more seductive than being an artist. That year, he went to Hollywood to write a screen adaptation of *The Autobiography of Malcolm X.* The producer, Marvin Worth, recalls, "White liberals were thrilled to have him come into their Beverly Hills houses and beat them up, say they were shit. He was a star who played on white masochism."

The irony, however, was that no matter how much Baldwin sacrificed his gifts to gain acceptance from the Black Power movement, his gestures went unrequited: while Baldwin may have been seen as a "bad nigger" by liberal whites, back in the hood he was just another twisted white boy in blackface. Eldridge Cleaver, in his 1968 "Soul on Ice," called Baldwin "a self-willed, automated slave" and "the white man's most valuable tool in oppressing other blacks." And yet, even after he'd been vilified by Cleaver, his response was appeasing and reverential. In *No Name in the Street* (1972) Baldwin referred to Cleaver as "valuable and rare," and excused his intolerance as the vigilance of "a zealous watchman on the city wall." And it is difficult to read Baldwin's description of Huey Newton in the same essay without wincing:

> There is in him a dedication as gentle as it is unyielding, absolutely single-minded. I began to realize this when I realized that Huey was always listening and always watching. No doubt he can be fooled, he's human, though he certainly can't be fooled easily; but it would be a very great mistake to try to lie to him. Those eyes take in everything, and behind the juvenile smile, he keeps a complicated scoreboard.

Baldwin's biographer, David Leeming, told me that many of the civil-rights leaders didn't want to be associated with Baldwin, because he was so openly gay; it seems to have been why the organizers of the 1963 March on Washington pointedly ignored him. In the end, Martin Luther King and Malcolm X and Eldridge Cleaver were reincarnations of his withholding and judgmental preacher father.

By the time the Black Power movement had started to ebb, Baldwin was adrift not only politically but aesthetically. Throughout the nineteen-seventies, Styron and Mailer were working on ambitious books like *Sophie's Choice* and *The Executioner's Song,* Thomas Pynchon was breaking new ground with *Gravity's Rainbow,* and a prolific new generation of black women—Toni Cade Bambara, Gayl Jones, Alice Walker, Toni Morrison—was claiming the public's imagination. Baldwin's fastidious thought process and his baroque sentences suddenly seemed hopelessly outdated, at once self-aggrandizing and ingratiating. Nevertheless, up until his death, in 1987, at the age of sixty-three, Baldwin continued to harbor the hope that he would be embraced as an important literary figure by the army of his desire: the black men who had forsaken him.

What became clear to me as I reread Baldwin's work (the Library of America selection mercifully excludes his ill-conceived and poorly written plays, *The Amen Corner* and *Blues for Mister Charlie,* and the novels written after *Another Country*) is that he never possessed a novelist's imagination or sense of structure—or, indeed, a novelist's interest in the lives of other people. Nor was he a reporter: most of his reporting pieces were stiff and banal. He was at his best when he was writing about some aspect of life or politics that reflected his interior self: he contained a multitude of worlds, and those worlds were his true subject.

But I also realized that my acute awareness of Baldwin's weaknesses as a writer stemmed from my sense of kinship with him. Certainly Baldwin understood this particular kind of ambivalence, having written the following at thirty-six, the age I am now:

> One of my dearest friends, a Negro writer now living in Spain, circled around me and I around him for months before we spoke. One Negro meeting another at an all-white cocktail party . . . cannot but wonder how the other got there. The question is: Is he for real? Or is he kissing ass? . . . Negroes know about each other what can here be called family secrets, and this means that one Negro, if he wishes, can "knock" the other's "hustle." . . . Therefore, one "exceptional" Negro watches another "exceptional" Negro in order to find out if he knows how vastly successful and bitterly funny the hoax has been.

Baldwin had been eyeing the competition long before he was paid to do so by any white editor. In *Notes of a Native Son* Baldwin writes that he and his stepfather circled around each other endlessly before they had their only significant conversation. One Sunday afternoon, they were walking home from church when David Baldwin broke their habitual silence:

My father asked me abruptly, "You'd rather write than preach, wouldn't you?"

I was astonished at his question—because it was a real question. I answered, "Yes."

But in the end Baldwin could not distinguish between writing sermons and making art. He eventually returned to the pulpit—just where his stepfather had always wanted him to be.

Yet there is one great Baldwin masterpiece waiting to be published—one that was composed in an atmosphere of focused intimacy rather than in the stiff black preacher suit that was his legacy—and that is a volume of his letters. A number of them were lent to me while I was doing research for this article; they have the force and wit of his early essays and the immediacy of something written for an audience of one.

After Baldwin's death, the family's relation to their prodigal son continues to reflect the hazards of uttering family secrets. When I asked David Leeming why the Baldwin family would not allow his letters to be published, he explained that the family felt he shed a negative light on them, particularly on David Baldwin, who was their father and not his; and they were uncomfortable with his homosexuality. "They have no interest in further exploring who he was," Leeming says. The family's unease with the private Baldwin is something that he himself always understood. And yet he left his legacy in their hands. In the end, even a bastard may be reclaimed by his family.

Andrew Shin and Barbara Judson (essay date Summer 1998)

SOURCE: "Beneath the Black Aesthetic: James Baldwin's Primer of Black American Masculinity," in *African American Review*, Vol. 32, No. 2, Summer, 1998, pp. 247-61.

[*In the following essay, Shin and Judson analyze the change in Baldwin's presentation of homosexuality between* Giovanni's Room *and* Just Above My Head.]

It has become commonplace to suggest the similarities in the histories of the black and feminist consciousness movements of the 1960s and '70s, especially the critical blindnesses that threatened to undermine the very solidarity crucial to political identity.[1] The conspicuous elision of women from black nationalism's struggle to achieve political recognition for its people was matched by feminism's inability to countenance the interests of ethnic women in its vision of cultural renovation. Just as the Black Panthers

lorded it over their women, middle-class white feminists failed to recognize the different needs of women of color—especially Black women—who served in their very households as domestic help. Although leading white feminists might have entertained the political possibilities of a gender-based alliance between white women and women of color, insofar as they understood black female activism as part of the broader struggle for racial liberation, they tacitly committed black women to a marginal role in an essentially masculinist enterprise. While ostensibly struggling against racial oppression, black nationalism cultivated an overt sexism; meanwhile feminism, in its battle with gender oppression, perpetuated an indifferent racism. Indeed, if all the men were black, then all the women were white.[2]

How interesting, then, that James Baldwin's voice has been both silenced and lost—silenced by the sexual politics of an emergent black left, lost because critics like Irving Howe decried Baldwin's putative aestheticism in favor of Richard Wright's militancy. But from our perspective, Baldwin's is a voice ahead of its time, one that explicitly addresses the implication of race and gender and, even more, attempts to articulate a gay ethic well before "gay" entered common parlance and certainly before the work of writers and scholars like Barbara Smith, Audre Lorde, Michael Lynch, Eve Kosofsky-Sedgwick, and Lee Edelman legitimated "queer theory" as a critical discourse. Baldwin's position is especially interesting because he synthesizes race and gay consciousness during some of the most politically volatile decades of the twentieth century. Moreover, Baldwin's career strongly suggests the influence of feminism on his gay aesthetic, the insights of which he subsequently recontextualized in the struggle for black liberation.

African American literature from approximately 1940 to the mid-1970s was primarily a masculinist enterprise dominated by Richard Wright's protest novel and Ralph Ellison's literary pluralism. Along with Alice Walker's re-discovery of Zora Neale Hurston and the pastoral tradition, the last two decades have witnessed an explosion of writing by black women and the recuperation of a black female literary history that dramatizes a specifically urban sensibility suggested by the novels of, among others, Nella Larsen, Ann Petry, and, of course, Toni Morrison. In the process, Baldwin's novels have been relegated to the archives of the unread, cast aside in favor of the lapidary, famously polemical essays. The novels, however, despite their poor critical reception, are interesting because they rarely capitulate to the urge for a simplified rhetoric that characterizes the essays of the early 1970s, persistently retaining the unresolved tension and complexity of a writer—a gay black writer no less—divided between his role as a popular spokesman for the race and his role as an artist whose imaginative life encompasses aesthetic standards that may alienate a popular audience. The novel form partially liberated Baldwin from the pressures that he felt as an essayist answerable to frequently hostile audiences, both black and white. Baldwin's work, moreover, suggests a cultural space where the trend in black literary history to polarize itself along gender lines might be reversed.[3] Ours, then, is an especially compelling moment in both literary and social history to reassess Baldwin's importance in matters of black liberation.

Baldwin's famous rejoinder to Norman Mailer's manifesto of hipster culture, "The White Negro," specifically addresses the sexual mythology that obtains to black men living in America: "I think that I know something about the American masculinity which most men of my generation do not know because they have not been menaced by it in the way that I have been" (*Price* 290). Here, Baldwin suggests the straitjacket of black virility that he struggled to liberate himself from throughout his career. A legacy of the antebellum South, celebrated by 1920s primitivism and consumer culture, this cultural mythology was perpetuated in the 1960s by the radical black left and white liberals like Mailer and Norman Podhoretz. Baldwin, who challenged this orthodoxy, became the whipping boy of a cultural establishment that understood the black man as, in Baldwin's words, "a kind of walking phallic symbol" (*Price* 290). Thus the question "What does it mean to be a man in America?" became Baldwin's donnée, inflecting virtually all of his literary production.[4]

Baldwin resisted an uncritical embrace of black nationalism, developing instead a vision of the homosexual as the chief instrument of cultural renovation. Indeed, bodily pleasure between men functions as a paradigm for the body politic—two men lying together spoon-fashion becomes an image of the just society. The black man as fetishized phallus gives way to an image of wholeness, of reintegrated bodies and of community. David Leeming, Baldwin's friend and recent biographer, suggests that much of Baldwin's early work can be characterized in terms of a family romance, as elaborating a search for an absent, idealized father (Leeming 3), as though the restored authority and centrality of the father could redress the history of slavery, an institution enabled by the codification of illegitimacy, defining black children as bastards. Indeed, for Baldwin, personal and familial redemption is political; but the rhetoric of family and the inherited view of a body politic organized around paternal privilege and masculine autonomy give way to the more egalitarian ideal of brotherhood—of a society founded upon the love between men. Baldwin thus redefines the discourse of family grounded in biology and posits alternative social structures in its place.[5]

Throughout Baldwin's oeuvre, the ideal of brotherhood displaces the idea of redemption through the restored centrality of the father: Horizontal equity supplants verticality. Brotherhood in this instance, however, is not exclusive but all-encompassing, suggesting egalitarian relations between men and women as well. Cora Kaplan, for one, distinguishes Baldwin's fictional treatment of sexuality, the family, and women as much more sympathetic to women than Wright's or Ellison's, but still qualifies her judgment: "Although Baldwin is one of the first and major analysts of the intimate relationship between dominant notions of masculinity and oppression within the Black family, his view of women as somehow inevitably confined to heterosexual relations is one of the historical limitations of his writing" (185). But Kaplan here raises issues that Baldwin tacitly engages, to the degree that he emphasizes the historical limitations of heterosexual relationships for women. Additionally, it should go without saying that homosexual relationships, whether gay or lesbian, are vulnerable to hierarchy.[6]

Baldwin begins his enterprise of reimagining the body politic in the largely autobiographical *Go Tell It On the Mountain* (1952) and extends it in *Another Country* (1962) and *Tell Me How Long the Train's Been Gone* (1968), works in which homosexuality acquires an increasingly striking political dimension, but he elaborates his position most clearly through the change in his disposition toward homosexuality from *Giovanni's Room* (1956) to *Just Above My Head* (1978), the two works we will consider in depth. Baldwin dramatizes this shift in orientation iconographically by displacing the autonomous, middle-class, white-male body with the erotic, feminized, black-male body. *Giovanni's Room* invokes the expatriate experiences of a white man to make the case for the homosexual as hero, a possibility foreclosed by the construction of black American masculinity. But in *Just Above My Head,* Baldwin confronts the taboo of black homosexuality on his home ground.

Baldwin had good reason to be alienated from the contemporary literary scene. With the publication of *Native Son* (1940), Richard Wright was unquestionably the dominant black writer in postwar America, and he became the cynosure of an intense debate over the question of what it meant to be a black writer. Although Wright initially assumed the role of mentor to Baldwin and helped him win several prestigious fellowships, Baldwin quickly differentiated himself from the protest tradition with which Wright was associated. For Baldwin, the idea of protest necessitated an overly narrow conception of the black writer, restricting him to a racial category that preempted the exploration of a more expansive and imaginative notion of human potential. In other words, to be a protest writer both limited artistic expression and perpetuated the very stereotypes that the genre aimed to dismantle. Ironically, as Baldwin's career progressed, his greatest distinction lay in the almost universal praise bestowed on his skill as an essayist; on the other hand, he was repeatedly castigated for producing literature that was overly didactic and propagandistic, a literature that could not elevate itself to the level of the imagination. Indeed, the prophetic strain in Baldwin came increasingly to assume the stridency of protest as he became caught up in the Civil Rights Movement, but, importantly, his voice persistently challenges the sexism that was a prominent element of Wright's.

Liberal white critics like Irving Howe championed Wright, suggesting that the lived experience of blacks, as if by default, could only express itself oppositionally: "The program which the young Baldwin set for himself—a program of aesthetic autonomy and faithfulness to private experience, as against ideological noise and blunt stereotype—was almost impossible for the Negro writer to realize" ("James Baldwin" 97). In Howe's view, if one were black, to write was to protest. Ralph Ellison, whose *Invisible Man* (1952) rewrites *Native Son* and is the only mid-century novel by an African American to enjoy a stature comparable to Wright's, responded to Howe by suggesting that Bigger Thomas, the protagonist of *Native Son*, exemplifies the limitations of the protest novel, precisely to the extent that Bigger Thomas is utterly incapable of imagining a character as complex and enigmatic as his creator Richard Wright.[7] Wright himself offers perhaps the most interesting interpretation of the literary debates that he inspired. In his famous essay "The Literature of the Negro in the United States," Wright argues that the proliferation of a literature directed "toward strictly racial themes" bespeaks a period of heightened racial oppression; conversely, a turn toward a literature that "assumes the common themes and burdens of literary expression which are the heritage of all men" (149-50) presumes an amelioration of racism in society. Accordingly, *Native Son* might be interpreted as the legacy of an economically depressed but politically charged decade that witnessed the expanding influence of Marxism and the dissemination of an oppositional populism, a philosophy that Wright himself embraced; on the other hand, Baldwin and Ellison speak for the 1950s, a decade that basked in postwar euphoria and witnessed the inception of the Civil Rights Movement, which offered the promise of significant racial progress as realized in Brown v. Board of Education (1954).

These literary debates aside, Wright left a far more insidious legacy of misogyny, which the radical black left embraced during the 1960s. That Baldwin even imagined the homosexual as the instrument of social change was no mean feat, given that homosexuality was still being censured both by mainstream culture and by black nationalists who equated blackness with heterosexual virility. Eldridge Cleaver, for one, who was famous for suggesting that he raped black women as a preamble to raping white women, characterizes Baldwin's homosexuality as a "racial death-wish" typical of the black bourgeoisie (103), who have rejected their blackness, their African heritage: "The cross they have to bear is that, already bending over and touching their toes for the white man, the fruit of their miscegenation is not the little

half-white offspring of their dreams . . ." (102). Although Cleaver felt he had been racially oppressed, he embraced the hierarchy of traditional heterosexuality, convinced that it was his privilege to dominate women. Hence Baldwin's homosexuality struck him as a betrayal, because Baldwin presented a public image of the black man as castrated, the black man as woman. Cleaver saw no brave new world in Baldwin's vision, only the resurrected old world in which black men were lynched, their manhood desecrated.

Cleaver's homophobic observations were fueled by Norman Mailer's "The White Negro," which in a late Romantic gesture primitivized the Negro as a source of authenticity in an overly refined Western world. Likewise, LeRoi Jones, one of the most important figures of the Black Arts Movement, repudiated his early bohemianism, as exemplified by his plays *The Baptism* (1964) and *The Toilet* (1964), to join in the general condemnation of Baldwin's sexual politics, though later, Jones, in his 1987 eulogy for Baldwin, identified Baldwin's play **Blues for Mr. Charlie** (1964) as the inception of the Black Arts Movement. Thus, Baldwin occupied a complex position in the politics and culture of the sixties: An outspoken advocate of civil rights, he was nevertheless viewed as a subversive and fractious element by many of its leaders. Though Mailer cast him as the embodiment of virility by virtue of his color, he was, paradoxically, vilified by fellow blacks for not being black (read *masculine*) enough. And although Baldwin could assert his cultural authority over Mailer—"I could have pulled rank on him precisely because I was black and knew more about that periphery he so helplessly maligns in 'The White Negro' than he could ever hope to know" (**Price** 290)—he was himself characterized as a "Pussy Cat" by Cleaver (104).[8]

For his part, Baldwin tried to resist the erosion of his cultural authority by reinventing himself in the language of the new vanguard—in the very terms of the black left which composed jeremiads against a view it regarded as outmoded. Two essays published a decade apart witness Baldwin's shift from a vision of a unitary culture to a more separatist stance. The philippic **The Fire Next Time** (1963) argues the interconnected destinies of black and white America, resisting the separatist philosophy of Malcolm X, Elijah Muhammad, and the Nation of Islam, and locates the possibility of black salvation in cooperation: " . . . we, the black and the white, deeply need each other here if we are really to become a nation—if we are really, that is, to achieve our identity, our maturity, as men and women. To create one nation has proved to be a hideously difficult task; there is certainly no need now to create two, one black and one white" (**Price** 375-76).[9] But the character of the Civil Rights Movement had changed, from the unassailable working-class dignity of Rosa Parks in 1955 to the hyperbole of the Black Panthers in 1968. A decade later, cast as a political Uncle Tom and facing tribal excommunication, a somewhat resigned Baldwin sounded a different note in *No Name in the Street* (1972), as protest displaced compassion as the agent of social change: "It must be remembered that in those great days I was considered to be an 'integrationist'—this was never, quite, my own idea of myself. . . . I was, in some way, in those years, without entirely realizing it, the Great Black Hope of the Great White Father. . . . not only were no white people needed; they posed, *en bloc*, the very obstacle to black self-knowledge and had to be considered a menace" (*Price* 497-99). But the mantle of apologist and ideologue ill-suited Baldwin, and, in spite of his burgeoning militancy, by 1973, as Henry Louis Gates suggests, Baldwin was considered passé.[10] Significantly, even as Baldwin was succumbing to the rhetoric of black nationalism as an essayist during this period, his novels assumed greater and greater risks in their exploration of black homosexuality.

Although Baldwin rejected the aggressive virility of both the white liberal intelligentsia and the radical black vanguard, he did celebrate the male body, not as a juggernaut of power but as a sensorium of comfort—the body as harbor and refuge, recapitulating the infant's relation to the mother, enjoying an amorphous, passive sexuality, a luxuriant dependency, played out, however, between men. Baldwin's emphasis on the pleasures of nurturance as opposed to mastery was anathema to black radicals who feared and despised such imagery as a return to childish dependence, a soft-pedaling of agency and activism. But Baldwin repudiates masculine autonomy as the instrument of a repressive social order by reveling in the sensate, celebrating the messiness of bodily odor and fluid—a convergence of bodies that opposes the formulations of white liberalism and black radicalism. He does not invoke the cult of the primitive as a reservoir of primal energy capable of bursting through social restraint; instead, he marshals love as the glue of a just society. The exchange of odors between men cuts across racial, class, and sexual lines.

The amorphous body figures Baldwin's vision of social progress founded upon the unrestricted expression of human sexuality, a view that contrasts with Booker T. Washington's program of racial uplift based on industrial and agricultural education for young blacks, which is linked to the discrete, clean body. *Up From Slavery* is replete with Washington's injunctions regarding the importance of personal hygiene and the utility of the clean body—cleanliness as a kind of currency. Indeed, Washington discovers that his passage through life, from his early employment as a houseboy to his admission to Hampton, is greatly facilitated by his embracing of the habits of his white employers and teachers, foremost among them the attributes of cleanliness and routine:

> Life at Hampton was a constant revelation to me; was constantly taking me into a new world. The matter of having meals at regular hours, of eating on a tablecloth, using a napkin, the use of the bathtub and of the toothbrush, as well as the use of sheets upon the bed were all new to me. I sometimes feel that almost the most valuable lesson I got at the Hampton Institute was in the use and value of the bath. (59-60)[11]

Washington accordingly emphasizes the values of this "new world" upon returning to Malden to teach at the colored school:

> In addition to the usual routine of teaching, I taught the pupils to comb their hair and to keep their hands and faces clean, as well as their clothing. I gave special attention to teaching them the proper use of the tooth-brush and the bath. In all my teaching I have watched carefully the influence of the tooth-brush, and I am convinced that there are few single agencies of civilization that are more far-reaching. (69)

Although his philosophy of the toothbrush is moving, it was unfortunately tied to the whole ethos of the houseboy and the structure of racial oppression that thinkers like Du Bois decried. Radical blacks did not view self-management of the body as crucial to political agency, but as the program of Uncle Tom.[12] Washington here invokes the middle-class values delineated by the white male body, which was constructed throughout the course of the French Revolution and which elaborated the republican ideals that claimed the right to liberty, equality, and fraternity for every man. But while Washington imagined his program of racial uplift through the symbolism of the white male body, he was unable or unwilling to acknowledge that, in the early twentieth century, the black community did not have access to the attendant rights of citizenship, a state of affairs that arguably persists to this day, even after the vaunted gains of the Civil Rights Movement. Where Washington offered an image of the hyper-regulated body as an ideal, Baldwin suggested that this ideal capitulated to an oppressive social order, offering in its stead the indiscreet body of funky armpits, drunkenness, and sexual arousal, expressions of the feminized, bohemian body that achieved greater and greater political significance in the context of the Civil Rights Movement in which Baldwin became increasingly involved.

Baldwin's early novel *Giovanni's Room* dramatizes the consequences of self-deception through the experiences of a young expatriate American who is unable to come to terms with his sexuality. The novel opens with a proleptic image of the end—David, alone in an empty house in the south of France, staring at his reflection in a window pane, through which we learn, interestingly, that he is white, the son of an affluent father. That Baldwin ventriloquizes his story through a white protagonist is instructive, as though Baldwin wishes to distance himself from the autobiographical elements of the novel. Robert Bone suggests that, when Baldwin "attempts a novel of homosexual love, with an all-white cast of characters and a European setting, he simply transposes the moral topography of Harlem to the streets of Paris" (38). Bone's observation, however, elides how this "moral topography" is inflected by race.[13] That David's experiences are largely expatriate underlines the untenability of black homosexuality as a lifestyle in America. David is socially unmarked by virtue of his color, a privilege that Baldwin himself enjoyed to a much greater degree in France than in America, but David's experiences in Paris nonetheless reinforce the web of self-deception that characterizes his life in America.

At its broadest reach, *Giovanni's Room* asks: What does it mean to be a man? This is the burden from which David takes refuge in flight but cannot escape, and it dominates his reflections on two formative experiences: a homoerotic childhood friendship that he terminates in deference to an internalized cultural homophobia, and his relationship with his parents marked by a sense of filial debt. Through the metaphor of a "cavern" (*Giovanni's* 15), Baldwin brilliantly condenses David's story as a dead-end, the cul-de-sac in which we find him at the end of the novel. The cavern of innuendo and rumor refers to the discourse of mortification in which the homosexual is pilloried, but it also symbolizes an intensity of pleasure so acute as to culminate in self-dissolution.

In suppressing his homoerotic impulses, however, David finds no solace in a more conventional heterosexuality, figured here through the activities of a philandering father and the memories of a mother who, Medusa-like, haunt David's dreams: ". . . she figured in my nightmares, blind with worms, her hair as dry as metal and brittle as a twig, straining to press me against her body; that body so putrescent, so sickening soft, that it opened, as I clawed and cried, into a breach so enormous as to swallow me alive" (17). Here, in contrast to the discrete male body, Baldwin presents the maternal body as monstrous, as an amorphous, enveloping softness that devours rather than nurtures. For David, compulsory heterosexuality is not the ground of phallic power but, as with all male infants, is potentially castrating, an orientation that defines his future relationships with women. David's fear of castration occurs, however, not through the process of heterosexual desire and the feelings of inadequacy generated in the presence of the powerful paternal phallus, but through a fear of a demonic female sexuality—the "cavern" transformed into a carnivorous "breach." In this scenario, the dream symbolizes a kind of wish-fulfillment in which David desires not to possess but to inhabit the eroticized female body and experience its dissolution, an untenable subject position in a homophobic culture. Here, Baldwin dra-

matizes the vexed identity of a man unable to countenance a sexual identity elaborated through the symbolism of the female body, when it is the very condition he desires.[14]

The novel subsequently situates David in various contexts which become vehicles for the exploration of identity: David's attempt to find himself becomes a search to discover a social space that will accommodate his sexual ambivalence. From the family dynamics of his household, David projects various potential futures for himself, all of them limiting: Taking little comfort in his aunt's ideal of masculine responsibility, an ideal of oppressive duty typically imagined in the context of marriage, he is nevertheless imprisoned by the social codes militating against the expression of his homosexual impulses. Faced with this double bind, a prisoner of both society and his own nature, repulsed both by social convention and by his own errant desires, David takes refuge, as he suggests, in "constant motion" (31), journeying to France, where he meets Giovanni.

Through an American acquaintance, Belgian-born Jacques, David readily gets caught up in the bohemian subculture of Paris, which, for him, revolves around Guillaume's bar, where Giovanni bartends, drinking and smoking into the early hours. Eventually, David finds himself living in Giovanni's room, where the cavern becomes literalized. The room is both the new world of avowed homosexuality as well as, sadly, the closet. As David suggests, "I remember that life in that room seemed to be occurring beneath the sea. Time flowed past indifferently above us; hours and days had no meaning. . . . Life in that room seemed to be occurring underwater, as I say, and it is certain that I underwent a sea change there" (99, 112). Removed from the demands of the world, the room becomes a "garden of Eden" (35), but also a prison. Baldwin believes in an ethic of love, and briefly this room provides a space for the efflorescence of desire, but precisely because it is a world apart, cut off from social and political demands, this aesthetic space becomes cloying, suffocating. With its closed and whited out windows and its "courtyard malevolently press[ing], encroaching day by day" (112), this is a room without a view; and the novel goes on to imply that love cannot be enacted meaningfully except in a social and political context.

David's sea-change is not a conversion to a homosexual identity; instead, the sea-change acquires ironic overtones. Despite Giovanni's overtures of love, David cannot imagine a life together with him, taking flight instead in his fiction of an imminent marriage with his fiancée Hella and the occasional liaison with a woman. For Giovanni, David's repudiation of their love is a symptom of a more generalized fear of intimacy expressed as a loathing of disorder and the uncleanliness of one body in contact with another body: "'You never have loved anyone, I am sure you never will! You love your purity, you love your mirror. . . . You want to be *clean.* . . . you do not want to *stink,* not even for five minutes . . .'" (186-87). David's rejection of Giovanni's love leads to Giovanni's demise as, desperate and indigent, Giovanni returns to the sordid world of Guillaume's bar. Giovanni's love, in contrast to David's, is uncompromising, and in a fit of rage after having been sexually manipulated by Guillaume, Giovanni murders Guillaume, for which he is sentenced to death. Giovanni's imminent execution merely realizes the fate that David has projected for himself all along—". . . I look at my body, which is under sentence of death" (223)—and which still awaits him, as the image of the torn execution notice blown back upon him at the end of the novel suggests. For a critic like Charlotte Alexander, the reflection that David sees at the end of his "lean, hard, and cold" body "trapped in [his] mirror" (223) attests to the rigor mortis of an emotionally and physically crippling narcissism. But David's narcissism is merely the symptom of a more deeply rooted political anomie—the incapacity of a self to imagine a socio-political context in which it might express itself. What Alexander types as narcissism we might read as heterosexism. David has internalized heterosexual norms based on the discrete, masterful, masculine body that he cannot eject. The messiness of intimate exchange is tantamount in his mind to the femininity he finds repulsive—because it is the very condition he unconsciously desires but cannot express—as well as the darkness of socially stigmatized homosexuality.[15]

Ultimately, David's existentialist quest—to find himself—fails, not because, confined by walls and mirrors, he has been unable to extricate himself from the malaise that plagues him at the beginning of the novel, but because, read in the light of Baldwin's subsequent career, the novel suggests that this quest is futile in the first place. Baldwin believes that Paris—a world of intellectual fertility and sexual outlawry emblematized by Sartre's lionization of Genet—is a milieu more tolerant of homosexuality than he can find in black America or the white liberal America of Norman Mailer. But the Paris of existentialism, of Camus and Sartre, in which the individual takes responsibility for constructing the rules of his own life, ironically defeats Baldwin's purpose, precisely because of its emphasis on the individual, its alienation from politics and collective action. David is unable to construct a gay identity for himself because this Paris is too aesthetic and its mandarin pleasures eventually degenerate into the grotesque lust of old fairies like Guillaume. In this context, Giovanni's room, both a haven from and a symbol of society's oppressive strictures, comes to sum up the impotence of the aesthetic ideal. In *Giovanni's Room,* homosexual relations cannot epitomize the new society because Baldwin cannot realize this vision apart from political commitment: Politics allows the gay man to rationalize his desires, and, in turn, his non-mainstream sexuality enables him to articulate a more egalitarian form of political protest. Ironically, Baldwin finds that his ability to mobilize the power of love depends upon the politics of American life, and he returns to this scene in *Another Country* and *Tell Me How Long the Train's Been Gone*, with mixed results, and again in *Just Above My Head,* which we read as the culmination of his career.

Just Above My Head contextualizes Baldwin's exploration of black masculinity in the most volatile decade of the Civil Rights Movement, a decade that witnessed the rage of Watts, the Voting Rights Act of 1965, the Moynihan Report, and the inception of the Black Panthers. Baldwin invokes the sphere of intimate relations to dramatize the pernicious mythology of black virility perpetuated by black nationalism, suggesting instead the power of brotherhood, an orientation rooted in the novel's very conception.[16] As Barbara, a character in *Tell Me How Long the Train's Been Gone,* explains, "We felt that it [a scene in a play] made a connection—between a private love story—and—a—well, between a private sorrow and a public, a *revolutionary* situation" (296)—and, likewise, the relationship between Arthur and his older brother Hall, the two protagonists of *Just Above My Head.*

The novel begins with news of Arthur's death, as his utopian quest for a more sexually tolerant society comes to a violent end in the bathroom of a London pub, which becomes the occasion for Hall's meditation on the meaning of Arthur's life. In the process Hall attempts to come to terms with his own identity as a black man in America. Arthur's quest is thus realized through Hall, who reminisces, "Your life can now be written anew on the empty slate of his. . . . I saw myself in Arthur" (*Just* 89). The novel becomes a kind of elegy in which Hall, too, becomes a blues singer, trying to redeem his brother's life from the squalor of his murder in a men's toilet. In a powerful image of the claustrophobic nature of the closet Arthur is described lying prone, while with the last remnants of consciousness he imagines the ceiling descending ominously upon him. Hall realizes that there never was a place for Arthur in society, and his elegy is an attempt to make such a space.

Early on, the novel introduces the interactions among members of the Miller and Montana families, whose stories dramatize the impotence of black religion, which is portrayed as otherworldly, indifferent to civic duty. Through the Miller family Baldwin examines the dark underside of the black church, traditionally conceived as the heart of black communities and an integral element of the Civil Rights Movement, as well as the source of forms of indigenous black expression. As Hall suggests, "Somebody was jiving the public, and I knew it had to be . . . [Julia's] father and mother, who surely did not look holy to me" (69). Julia, who is called to preach when she is seven years old, is the cynosure of the Miller family, but she is merely the instrument of a dominating father—"the zoot-suited stud of studs" (70)—whose familial authority has its analogue in the institutional power of the church. Julia is possessed of a beauty and voice that is coopted by a system of hieratic privilege: "... as a child and as a preacher, she had not belonged to herself, nor had the remotest idea who she was. She had then been at the mercy of a force she had had no way of understanding" (524). Julia's precociously charismatic style enthralls parishioners everywhere, and her father exploits this talent to make money—she is ultimately raped by him, symbolizing her assimilation to his despotic power.

For Julia's mother Amy, religious enthusiasm assumes the form of sexual display: "Julia's mother put up the better show, though her hats were flaunting, and her skirts were tight. . . . she always wore high heels—just to make sure you didn't miss those legs" (69). Baldwin here presents the church as incapable of organizing and using the energy of sexual desire to work for social and political change. Instead, this specifically feminine charisma is dissipated, channeled into the minutiae of sexual conquest, visual display, and vain enthusiasm, as witnessed by the erotic spectacle Amy makes in church: "When she got happy," Hall reports, "she would stroke her breasts" (69-70). Baldwin is not denigrating or ridiculing women; rather, he is dramatizing the tragic waste of Amy's spiritual energy, which, in the absence of a worthy political object to give it direction, ends by devouring her, consuming her from within—hence her death from breast cancer. In the Miller family, Amy's sphere of influence is limited to her ability to please her husband; thus, she is inevitably pitted against the charms of the daughter, who desires unconsciously to displace Amy in her husband's affections. Through Amy and Julia's fates Baldwin suggests that in the absence of political organization—like the Civil Rights Movement—female sexuality exhausts itself in invidious competition and aesthetic gesture. Baldwin does not aim to trivialize women in his depiction of Amy and Julia but rather to criticize the social structures that disempower them.

The relationship between Hall and Arthur Montana supplants the patriarchal incest of Joel and Julia Miller, a relationship based on coercion, violence, and rivalry. The boys take their cue from their father Paul, a jazz pianist who, unlike Julia's father, refuses to play the role of mentor, deeming it too authoritarian, allowing Arthur instead to cultivate his own voice in gospel music and the blues. Arthur develops into a fine singer and with his friends Crunch, Peanut, and Red tours the South, a trip that is also an excursion back in time; significantly, it is the site of Arthur's first fulfilling homosexual experience as well. From Tennessee to Atlanta and Birmingham, Baldwin presents a series of erotic images that rewrite the cultural mythology of the South, a mythology responsible for Peanut's lynching on a subsequent trip. Here, Baldwin challenges the sexual iconography that white Southerners consciously vilify and unconsciously imagine, offering in its place the tableau of two black men embrac-

ing: "They curled into each other, spoon fashion, Arthur cradled by Crunch" (207). This image of two musicians side by side offers a utopian vision of gay sexuality that challenges the figurations of a dystopic homophobia, destabilizing the culture's oppressive imagining of a fetishized black phallus. Through these images, Baldwin generates an alternative vernacular of black American masculinity.

This grammar rewrites the heterosexual assumptions of black music as it is traditionally conceived. In the transitional *Another Country,* Baldwin attempted to evoke the bohemian world through a sequence of riffs and montages, fractured forms that express the brilliance and movement of improvisation. The late-night world of jazz clubs, endless talk, and sexuality—this is the milieu that Baldwin depicts, but he debunks the popular representations of bohemian élan, extending his public argument with Mailer here through the novel from instead of the polemical essay. Baldwin contends that white liberals' celebration of jazz as a form of oppositional cultural power has in effect robbed black bohemianism of its vanguard potential, holding it hostage to the misguided hero-worship of white consumer culture. Positions like Mailer's construct the black musician as stud, making his artistic authority a function of his sexual potency, a rhetorical move that epitomizes unconscious liberal racism. For Baldwin, the black musician is the intellectual, the restless experimenter who takes apart dominant musical forms and recasts them; the sexual lionizing of the black musician merely appropriates him for white consumption, and, Baldwin warns, if black musicians embrace this myth, they will be destroyed by it, as demonstrated by the case of Rufus Scott, the tragic character at the center of *Another Country.*[17]

Understood in terms of mourning, blues and jazz typically express the desire of a masculine subject for a lost feminine object.[18] *Just Above My Head* revises this formulation by interspersing scenes of gospel performances with explicitly homoerotic tableaux, highlighted by Arthur and Crunch's harmonious antiphony in Birmingham, their voices witnessing their love and desire for one another, a sexual longing that will be consummated shortly thereafter. Mourning is the psychosexual process that connects an individual to the past, insofar as the ego is constituted by a history of its losses—through linguistic substitution, the introjection of lost objects. Yet here Arthur, the itinerant bluesman who sings of love and loss, transforms the traumatic history of African Americans into a prophecy of the future, and his voice becomes the oracle of a new world. Hall recognizes Arthur as the instrument of a religious tradition that makes itself felt in social protest: "He sang, he had to sing, as though music could really accomplish the miracle of making the walls come tumbling down. He sang: as Julia abandoned her ministry, Arthur began to discover his" (219). In this view the blues singer embodies political and cultural agency, the opportunity to change society through participating in a vision that can raise the political consciousness of an audience.

But although Arthur enjoys the refuge of a shared space with Crunch and, later, with Jimmy, Julia's jazz pianist younger brother, the walls do not so much come tumbling down as implode upon him. Arthur's song may be his confession, but it is left to his brother Hall to redeem Arthur by passing on his story. Arthur's legacy remains in the memories of his friends and brother, who, at the end of the novel, imagines Arthur's voice raised in song and understands that redemption lies in interconnectedness, in living relationships, and in the memories of loved ones: ". . . ain't nothing up the road but us, man" (559).

Although Arthur's quest for a homosexual utopia fails, Baldwin suggests that feminist self-determination is a crucial step toward achieving it. For her part Julia is finally able to recreate herself through Crunch's intervention and, by journeying to Africa, realizes her story is part of a larger history. Julia's trip to Africa offers a kind of secular redemption for the religious hypocrisy that she unwittingly contributed to as a child, as she discovers there a larger family, symbolized by the family of an African diplomat, a father figure who, in her words, is "*really* black, black in a way [she'd] never encountered" (526) and the only male who "understood something" (528). Africa provides a form of sustenance that the religious life never did, but although Africa enables Julia to understand something about herself, Baldwin suggests that pan-Africanism is not really a viable solution for the problems of American blacks. As Julia realizes, "A black girl in Africa, who wasn't *born* in Africa, and who has never seen Africa, is a very strange creature for herself, and for everyone who meets her. . . . they don't know who they are meeting. *You* don't know who they are meeting either" (529). Baldwin here debunks the notion of an authentic blackness, as Julia realizes she has very little in common with the villagers she meets in Africa. Instead, she realizes that her future lies in America, for it is her home, however racially divided; she comes to recognize the need for a new vocabulary that will accommodate a culture of refugees, rather than merely reproduce the language of the fathers.[19]

By virtue of their experiences as sexual outlaws, Julia shares such a language with Arthur: ". . . she was, also, the only person in the world, now, who spoke his language. They knew the same things. And his jealousy had evaporated" (263). Here, love and the recognition of mutual need displace sexual competition over Crunch's affections. Later, Julia, the single woman, and Hall, the devoted husband, enact this love, as Hall realizes, "We looked like lovers. . . . in truth, at last, we were" (534). This is not a sexual relationship, but an agreement to "'watch over those [they] love'" (534), an assumption of responsibility to others untainted by the co-

ercive rhetoric of family: They are lovers, not fathers or mothers. The remaining members of the Miller and Montana families who come together at the welcome table—including Jimmy, Arthur's last lover—constitute a group bound by love rather than simply by blood or filial duty. But this idyllic community does not come without a cost: Crunch goes mad, Peanut is lynched, and Red becomes a junkie—all three the victims of a society that insists on casting black men as icons of virility. Arthur's violent death is especially poignant, for the bathroom of the London pub in which he dies symbolizes the world of odors and bodily exchange that Arthur embraces, as well as the squalor to which the homosexual is relegated. That he dies in such a context extends the example of Giovanni, who is ultimately executed as a consequence of his unflagging commitment to a homosexual lifestyle. Giovanni's death, however, changes nothing for the larger society; Arthur's sacrifice, on the other hand, makes possible a new order of relations based on equality rather than on the hierarchy of the paternal family. Whereas *Giovanni's Room* dramatizes a protagonist who is imprisoned by his sense of obligation to a model of heterosexual life, in *Just Above My Head,* Arthur is the agent who ultimately reintegrates family and community through his fight for civil rights. And for Arthur, social protest assumes the form of an unfettered expression of his sexuality. *Just Above My Head* thus dramatizes a family album that displaces the terms of *Giovanni's Room.*

This culturally constructed family, moreover, signifies the resolution of loss through the work of mourning—not however, through the reinstatement of positive parental images, but through the introjection of the lost brother, a process that displaces patriarchal authority in favor of a more horizontal structure of relations. The picture of the extended family with which *Just Above My Head* concludes is the social manifestation of transformed consciousnesses: The rehabilitation of Julia's psychic health begins with her trip to Africa, but culminates with her turn toward America, a reconstitution of a shattered ego that takes place in republican America, not in the land of the primordial father; so too, Hall comes more fully to understand his identity as a black man in America, for him realized through the memory of his brother's tragic life. Julia and Hall project a society informed by the lost object that dominates their consciousnesses, a culture figured through the metaphor of the contingent, feminized black body that Baldwin most poignantly depicts in *Just Above My Head.*

Arthur's legacy lives on in Hall and Julia, for whom life in 1960s America as a black man or woman demands that you watch over the people you love. This statement is as close to political commitment as Baldwin gets in this novel: On the one hand, it sounds cliché—a simple expression of fealty to one's family; but coming at the end of the novel, this homily acquires a political resonance, allowing Hall and Julia to articulate the beginnings of their commitment to Black liberation, and thus to the people they love.

NOTES

1. See, for example, Showalter 347-69.

2. As early as the mid-nineteenth century, Elizabeth Cady Stanton recognized the political possibilities of an alliance between black men and all women, a solidarity undermined by republican advocacy of black male suffrage. See hooks, *Ain't I* 3-4; and Hodes 59-74. For a cogent critique of the assumptions of contemporary black and white feminism, see McDowell, "New Directions" 186-99.

3. McDowell suggests the polarization of black American writers along gender lines as a struggle over discursive space. See "Reading" 75-97.

4. For an interesting discussion of the centrality of the black phallus in the sexual politics of black male writers and critics, and of its subversion in the work of black female writers and critics, see duCille 559-73.

5. Since the publication of Daniel Moynihan's report *The Negro Family: The Case for National Action* (1965), many scholars have elaborated both the potential and limitations of the family metaphor to conceptualize social and literary experience. Houston A. Baker, Jr., specifically invokes the idea of a family romance to describe the relationship between contemporary writers and the writers of the Harlem Renaissance, tacitly endorsing the importance of the absent father (*Modernism*). Hortense Spillers suggests that the very inadmissibility of white paternal origin perpetuates the transmission of human flesh as property ("Mama's Baby"). Anna Wilson discusses the ways that Audre Lorde's reconceptualization of family in *Zami* both challenges and reproduces conventional social structures ("Audre Lorde"). See also McDowell, "Family Matters."

6. For an extended discussion of Baldwin's treatment of women, see Harris.

7. We do not discuss this debate in great detail, as it has already inspired much spilled ink. Nevertheless, it establishes an important context for an understanding of Baldwin's work. See Baldwin, "Everybody's Protest Novel" and "Many Thousands Gone" (*Price* 27-34, 65-78); Howe, "Black Boys"; and Ellison. See also "Liberalism and the Negro: A Round-Table Discussion."

8. Mailer, although perhaps the most prominent, was not alone in primitivizing black males. See Podhoretz. For a critique of Mailer and the sexual politics of these black revolutionaries, see Dickstein 154-82.

9. Baldwin ultimately returns to this idea in an essay published two years before his death, assimilating gender to his vision of a racially unified culture: "But we are all androgynous, not because we are all born of a woman impregnated by the seed of a man but because each of us, helplessly and forever, contains the other—male in female, female in male, white in black and black in white" ("Freaks and the American Ideal of Manhood," *Playboy* Jan. 1985; rpt. "Here Be Dragons," *Price* 690).

10. See Gates 53.

11. Compare the lessons that Washington learns here with Zora Neale Hurston's observations of rural Negro life in "Characteristics of Negro Expression"—among other things, angularity, asymmetry, the will to adorn, and the jook. Although Hurston's representation of "the folk" has been questioned as a white pastoral fantasy—for example by Richard Wright and Hazel Carby–her observations here nevertheless offer an interesting contrast to Washington's cooptation by white middle-class values defined by the clean, hyper-regulated body and household. See Hurston 49-68. Wright, himself, in "The Literature of the Negro in the United States," distinguishes between "The Narcissistic Level"—borrowed forms of culture that middle-class African Americans try to make their own—and "The Forms of Things Unknown"—the native expressions developed from the experiences of migratory, working-class blacks. And it is Wright's conceptualization of "The Forms of Things Unknown" that provides the ideological justification for the Black Arts Movement as it is elaborated by thinkers like Amiri Baraka, Stephen Henderson, and Larry Neal.

12. In the 1970s and early 1980s, the ill-fated, Philadelphia-based back-to-Africa group MOVE actively resisted all forms of self-management.

13. In his essay, Bone subjects *Giovanni's Room* and *Another Country* to a scathing review, singling out Baldwin's elevation of the homosexual as redeemer for special censure. For a more sympathetic reading of *Giovanni's Room* and its ambivalences, see Adams. For a densely theoretical (read *poststructuralist*) approach that discusses Baldwin's work in the context of a more general theorization of the homosexual underpinnings of writing—what the author calls "homographesis," synecdoche as master trope—see Edelman.

14. Baldwin's metaphors anticipate the tropes that Leo Bersani invokes in his discussion of homosexuality and that Neil Hertz examines in his analysis of accounts of the 1848 Paris uprising. For Bersani, the homosexual, like the woman, desires to be penetrated, a position tantamount to self-dissolution that Bersani finds problematic ("Is the Rectum a Grave?"). Even more problematic, in the era of AIDS, is the

persistent literalization of rectal penetration and death. Baldwin, however, through the metaphor of the "cavern" suggests a more ambivalent orientation toward penetration and dissolution. Hertz invokes Freud's Medusa in a brilliant analysis of the iconography of the 1848 Paris uprising, mapping the psychological/political fear of radical change in terms of a fear of castration (*The End of the Line* 161-91). The specular power of David's dead mother, both through the photograph and the nightmarish iconography of the body, likewise attests to David's fear of castration, but here without the overt political dimensions.

15. Alexander ("The 'Stink' of Reality") argues that David's distaste for uncleanliness dramatizes his fear of physical and emotional intimacy, a trait characteristic of the narcissistic personality. Although insightful, Alexander's discussion is somewhat limited because it does not address a political context, a dimension that is central to this essay.

16. Baldwin suggests that the novel originated in a dream of his about a ceiling descending just above his head, a dream that converged with his brother David's dream about the two of them sitting on a porch presciently observing the lives of all their friends (see Leeming 345). The novel, which takes its title from a traditional gospel song—a song that Ida sings repeatedly throughout *Another Country*—thematizes the relationship between two brothers, Hall and Arthur Montana.

17. Baldwin responded to early critics of *Another Country* by suggesting that he wanted to write the way jazz musicians like Miles Davis and Ray Charles sound. In "Hip, and the Long Front of Color," Andrew Ross offers a useful discussion of postwar intellectuals' response to popular culture, specifically in the context of black music and the culture industry. See also Jones and Hebdige. In *Another Country*, Ida Scott's relationship to Steve Ellis reproduces the relationship between black music and the culture industry in the 1920s. But arguably, Ida "changes the joke and slips the yoke" by exploiting Ellis's sexual attraction to her in promoting her career.

18. Compare this with Adomo's famous observation: "The aim of jazz is the mechanical reproduction of a regressive moment, a castration symbolism. 'Give up your masculinity, let yourself be castrated,' the eunuchlike sound of the jazz band both mocks and proclaims, 'and you will be rewarded, accepted into a fraternity which shares the mystery of impotence with you, a mystery revealed at the moment of the initiation rite'" (129).

19. Baldwin most clearly elaborates his resistance to the allure of pan-Africanism as a potential solution for the problems of black Americans in "Princes and Powers," *Price* 41-63.

WORKS CITED

Adams, Stephen. "*Giovanni's Room:* The Homosexual as Hero." *James Baldwin.* Ed. Harold Bloom. New York: Chelsea House, 1986. 131-39.

Adorno, Theodor. *Prisms.* 1967. Cambridge: MIT P, 1986.

Alexander, Charlotte. "The 'Stink' of Reality: Mothers and Whores in James Baldwin's Fiction." Kinnamon 77-95.

Baker, Houston A., Jr. *Modernism and the Harlem Renaissance.* Chicago: U of Chicago P, 1987.

Baldwin, James. *Giovanni's Room.* 1956. New York: Dell, 1988.

———. *Just Above My Head.* 1978. New York: Dell, 1990.

———. *The Price of the Ticket.* New York: St. Martin's/Marek, 1985.

———. *Tell Me How Long the Train's Been Gone.* New York: Dial, 1968.

Bersani, Leo. "Is the Rectum a Grave?" *October* 43 (Winter 1987): 197-222.

Bone, Robert A. "James Baldwin." Kinnamon 28-51.

Cleaver, Eldridge. *Soul on Ice.* New York: McGraw-Hill, 1968.

Dickstein, Morris. *Gates of Eden.* New York: Basic, 1977.

duCille, Ann. "Phallus(ies) of Interpretation: Toward Engendering the Black Critical 'I.'" *Callaloo* 16.3 (1993): 559-73.

Edelman, Lee. "The Part For The (W)hole: Baldwin, Homophobia, and the Fantasmatics of 'Race.'" *Homographesis.* New York: Routledge, 1994, 42-75.

Ellison, Ralph. "The World and the Jug." *Shadow and Act.* New York: Random, 1964. 107-43.

Gates, Jr., Henry Louis. "The Welcome Table." *English Inside and Out: The Places of Literary Criticism.* Ed. Susan Gubar and Jonathan Kamholtz. New York: Routledge, 1993. 47-60.

Harris, Trudier. *Black Women in the Fiction of James Baldwin.* Knoxville: U of Tennessee P, 1985.

Hebdige, Dick. *Subculture: The Meaning of Style.* New York: Routledge, 1979.

Hertz, Neil. *The End of the Line.* New York: Columbia UP, 1985.

Hodes, Martha. "The Sexualization of Reconstruction Politics: White Women and Black Men in the South after the Civil War." *American Sexual Politics: Sex, Gender, and Race since the Civil War.* Ed. John C. Fout and Maura Shaw Tantillo. Chicago: U of Chicago P, 1993. 59-74.

Hooks, Bell. *Ain't I a Woman: Black Women and Feminism.* Boston: South End P, 1981.

Howe, Irving. "Black Boys and Native Sons." *A World More Attractive.* New York: Horizon P, 1963. 98-122.

———. "James Baldwin: At Ease in Apocalypse." Kinnamon 96-108.

Hurston, Zora Neale. "Characteristics of Negro Expression." *Negro.* Ed. Nancy Cunard and Hugh Ford. 2nd ed. 1934. New York: Ungar, 1984. 49-68.

Jones, LeRoi. Blues People: *Negro Music in White America.* New York: Morrow, 1963.

Kaplan, Cora. "Keeping the Color in *The Color Purple.*" *Sea Changes: Essays in Culture and Feminism.* London: Verso, 1986. 177-87.

Kinnamon, Keneth, ed. *James Baldwin: A Collection of Critical Essays.* Englewood Cliffs: Prentice, 1974.

Leeming, David. *James Baldwin.* New York: Knopf, 1994.

"Liberalism and the Negro: A Round-Table Discussion." *Commentary* 37 (Mar. 1964): 25-42.

Mailer, Norman. "The White Negro: Superficial Reflections on the Hipster." *Advertisements For Myself.* New York: Putnam's, 1959. 337-58.

McDowell, Deborah E. "New Directions for Black Feminist Criticism." *The New Feminist Criticism: Essays on Women, Literature & Theory.* Ed. Elaine Showalter. New York: Random, 1985. 186-99.

———. "Reading Family Matters." *Changing Our Own Words.* Ed. Cheryl Wall. New Brunswick: Rutgers UP, 1989. 75-97.

Podhoretz, Norman. "My Negro Problem and Ours." *Commentary* 35 (Feb. 1963): 93-101.

Ross, Andrew. "Hip, and the Long Front of Color." *No Re-spect: Intellectuals and Popular Culture.* New York: Routledge, 1989. 65-101.

Sedgwick, Eve Kosofsky. *Epistemology of the Closet.* Berkeley: U of California P, 1990.

Showalter, Elaine. "A Criticism of Our Own: Autonomy and Assimilation in Afro-American and Feminist Literary Theory." *The Future of Literary Theory.* Ed. Ralph Cohen. New York: Routledge, 1989. 347-69.

Spillers, Hortense. "Mama's Baby, Papa's Maybe: An American Grammar Book." *Diacritics* 17 (Summer 1987): 65-81.

Washington, Booker T. *Up From Slavery.* 1901. *Three Negro Classics.* New York: Avon, 1965.

Wilson, Anna. "Audre Lorde and the African-American Tradition: When the Family is Not Enough." *New Lesbian Criticism.* Ed. Sally Munt. New York: Columbia UP, 1992. 75-93.

Wright, Richard. "The Literature of the Negro in the United States." *White Man, Listen!* New York: Doubleday, 1957. 105-50.

FURTHER READING

Criticism

Cohen, William A. "Liberalism, Libido, Liberation: Baldwin's *Another Country.*" *Genders* (Winter 1991): 1-21.
  Explores the roles of race, sexual identity, and liberal ideology in Baldwin's *Another Country.*

DeGout, Yasmin Y. "Dividing the Mind: Contradictory Portraits of Homoerotic Love in *Giovanni's Room.*" *African American Review* 26, No. 3 (Fall 1992): 425-35.
  Discusses the conflicting images of homosexuality as both natural and deviant in Baldwin's *Giovanni's Room.*

Olson, Barbara K. "'Come-to-Jesus Stuff' in James Baldwin's *Go Tell It on the Mountain* and *The Amen Corner.*" *African American Review* 31, No. 2 (Summer 1997): 295-301.
  Analyzes how Baldwin's *The Amen Corner* functions as a response to the reception of his novel *Go Tell It on the Mountain.*

Porter, Horace. "The South in *Go Tell It on the Mountain*: Baldwin's Personal Confrontation." In *New Essays on* Go Tell It on the Mountain, edited by Trudier Harris, pp. 59-75. Cambridge: Cambridge University Press, 1996.
  Traces the role of the South in Baldwin's *Go Tell It on the Mountain* and asserts that Baldwin's experience of the South was derived secondhand from other sources.

Reid-Pharr, Robert F. "Tearing the Goat's Flesh: Homosexuality, Abjection and the Production of a Late Twentieth-Century Black Masculinity." *Studies in the Novel* XXVIII, No. 3 (Fall 1996): 372-94.

Discusses James Baldwin's *Giovanni's Room*, Eldridge Cleaver's *Soul on Ice*, and Piri Thomas' *Down These Mean Streets*, concept of black masculinity.

Tsomondo, Thorell. "Other Tale to Tell: 'Sonny's Blues' and *Waiting for the Rain.*" *Critique* 36, No. 3 (Spring 1995): 195-209.

Asserts that Baldwin and Charles Mungoshi operate as artists and historians in "Sonny's Blues" and *Waiting for the Rain*, respectively, because of the multiple stories which arise out of the narratives.

Additional coverage of Baldwin's life and career is contained in the following sources published by Gale: *Artists and Authors for Young Adults,* **Vol. 4;** *Black Literature Criticism,* **Vol. 1;** *Black Writers,* **Vol. 1;** *Concise Dictionary of American Literary Biography,* **1941-1968;** *Contemporary Authors,* **Vols. 1-4R, 124;** *Contemporary Authors Bibliographical Series,* **Vol. 1;** *Contemporary Authors New Revision Series,* **Vol. 3, 24;** *Dictionary of Literary Biography,* **Vols. 2, 7, 33;** *Dictionary of Literary Biography Yearbook,* **Vol. 87;** *DISCovering Authors; DISCovering Authors: British; DISCovering Authors: Canadian; DISCovering Authors Modules: Most-Studied, Multicultural, Novelists,* **and** *Popular Fiction and Genre Authors; Drama Criticism,* **Vol. 1;** *Major Twentieth-Century Writers, Vols. 1, 2; Something About the Author,* **Vols. 9, 54;** *Short Story Criticism,* **Vols. 10, 33; and** *World Literature Criticism.*

Djuna Barnes

1892-1982

(Also wrote under the pseudonym of Lydia Steptoe) American novelist, dramatist, short story writer, poet, and journalist.

The following entry presents an overview of Barnes's career. For further information on her life and career, see *CLC*, Volumes 3, 4, 8, 11, 29.

INTRODUCTION

Barnes is most associated with the modernists of the early twentieth century. She shared the primary ideals of modernism—to revitalize language, express the unconscious mind and the alienation of the modern individual, and to reject the modes of realism. Barnes's writing was difficult to read because she stressed imagery and symbolism in her works rather than realistic or naturalistic descriptions. Although Barnes was an infamous public figure and well-known journalist, her fiction was never widely read. She had a small cult following, including some of the best-known modernist writers of the century, such as T. S. Eliot. Nevertheless, Barnes described herself as "the most famous unknown of the century."

Biographical Information

Barnes was born in 1892 to Wald and Elizabeth Chappell Barnes. While a child and teenager, Barnes was a victim of incest. As a result, sexual abuse is a frequent subject of her work, but is sometimes buried in the subtext of her fiction. Barnes's home life was further complicated by her mother who ignored and denied Barnes's victimization, and allowed Wald's mistress and their children to move in with the family. Barnes escaped the household, becoming a freelance journalist in the 1910s. Her work ranged from the serious to the ridiculous. She interviewed famous actors, statesman, and carnival sideshow freaks. In 1921, *McCall's* magazine sent Barnes to Paris, where she remained for several years after completing of her assignment. While in Paris, Barnes met and fell in love with Thelma Wood. The relationship was destructive for Barnes because Wood strung her along for eight years before ending the relationship permanently. During her career, Barnes befriended several notable literary and political figures, including playwright Eugene O'Neill, writer James Joyce, and Secretary General of the United Nations Dag Hammarskjold. Throughout her writing career, Barnes published a series of early plays, poetry, and short stories, but the novel *Nightwood* (1936)—her most significant work—had a difficult publishing history. Several publishers

turned the manuscript down until a friend showed it to T. S. Eliot, who edited the book while working for Faber & Faber. After publishing *Nightwood*, Barnes experienced a series of personal crises, including failed relationships, money trouble, and excessive drinking. She moved into a small apartment in New York's Greenwich Village, where she remained secluded for the rest of her life. Barnes continued to write, but not prolifically, and it took her years to complete her obscure verse drama, *The Antiphon* (1958). Barnes died in 1982 at the age of ninety.

Major Works

The play, *The Dove* (1926), is about two aging sisters, Amelia and Vera Burgson, and a young woman they meet in the park whom they name "The Dove." The sisters invite the woman to move in with them, and the play reveals the sisters' voyeuristic tendencies and preoccupation with violence and sexuality. The woman becomes increasingly agitated with events in the household and her treatment until she takes a stand. The ending and the woman's fate remain ambiguous. *Ryder* (1928) is considered an autobiographical novel that tells Barnes's family story, but is unclear about how many details are factual. The Ryder family is headed by Wendell Ryder, who believes in polygamy, free love, free thinking, and idleness as an occupation. His mother runs a scam targeted toward rich, philanthropic men to support the family's needs because of Wendell's refusal to work. Wendell sexually abuses and oppresses females in the household, and although state officials step in to question Wendell's polygamy and home schooling, the family's deepest secrets are never revealed. *Nightwood* (1936) is Barnes's exploration of her relationship with Thelma Wood. The novel centers on American expatriates in Europe. There are two main story lines about Robin Vote and Matthew O'Connor. Vote's character is based on Wood. Matthew O'Connor comments on the other characters' actions. The two plots converge when O'Connor tries to counsel Felix and Nora, two characters who have both fallen in love with Vote. The novel is theme-driven, not plot-driven. In depicting the anguish of several characters who have distinct sexual, spiritual, and social identities, Barnes uses dreams, animals, and nocturnal images as metaphors for unconscious and irrational obsessions. The novel's comic depictions of terrifying events represents an early manifestation of black humor. *The Antiphon*, is a verse drama written in the Elizabethan and Jacobean traditions with a contemporary setting. The novel is about Miranda, a girl who is sexually abused by her father and left unprotected by her mother's collusion. The play is highly autobiographical and explores the feelings of exploitation and betrayal Barnes experienced during her youth.

Critical Reception

Many of the discussions and critical commentaries on Barnes's work focus on speculation about her sexuality and sexual politics. This limited commentary on her fiction has contributed to a limited readership. Georgette Fleischer said, "Zealotry has spawned gross factual errors and irrational readings that have inflated within an insular critical field and emerged as full-blown myths. This has cheapened Djuna Barnes." Many reviewers assess Barnes's *Nightwood* as one of the most important modernist works of the twentieth century. Miranda Seymour concluded, "Admired by Joyce, *Nightwood* is as important to the history of 20th-century novel as *Finnegans Wake*—and more readable." It is by far her most respected work, although there is controversy among reviewers over the quality and lasting impact of the novel. Many critics point out the mysterious and difficult nature of Barnes's prose, complaining there is no substance behind Barnes' difficult writing. However, Anne B. Dalton asserted, "I would argue that Barnes's work is more like Pandora's box: once one manages to open it, the contents stream out irrepressibly." The author herself believed her drama *The Antiphon* to be her most important work. However, many critics found *The Antiphon* difficult and obscure.

While some critics praised Barnes for carrying on the efforts of Eliot and W. B. Yeats to revive verse drama, others contended the meaning of the play was obscured by its wording. This difference of opinion characterizes the general response to virtually all of Barnes's work. She has inspired acclaim and disdain for her daring methods and bleak, fragmented depiction of modern existence.

PRINCIPAL WORKS

The Book of Repulsive Women: 8 Rhythms and 5 Drawings (poetry and drawings) 1915
An Irish Triangle (play) 1919; published in *A Book,* 1928
Kurzy of the Sea (play) 1919; published in *A Book,* 1928
Three from the Earth (play) 1919; published in *A Book,* 1928
A Book (verse and plays) 1923; enlarged edition published as *A Night among the Horse* 1929 *To the Dogs* (play) 1923
The Dove (play) 1926
She Tells Her Daughter (play) 1926
Ladies' Almanack (poetry) 1928
Ryder (novel) 1928
Nightwood (novel) 1936
The Antiphon (verse drama) 1958
Spillway (short stories) 1962
Vagaries Malicieux: Two Stories (short stories) 1974
Smoke and Other Early Stories (short stories) 1982

CRITICISM

Robert Giroux (essay date 1 December 1985)

SOURCE: "'The Most Famous Unknown in the World'—Remembering Djuna Barnes," in *New York Times,* December 1, 1985, p. 3.

[*In the following essay, Giroux discusses his experience as an editor working with Djuna Barnes.*]

"You have to trust someone, Miss Barnes. Why not trust me?" Only an author as aggravating as Djuna Barnes could have goaded me into making such a desperate plea, during a meeting in our publishing office. I was unaware I had nearly shouted these words until my assistant, in the outer room, repeated them to me. "Do you think she trusts you now?" she asked after Miss Barnes's departure. "Did it work?" Of course it didn't work. Nothing worked with Djuna Barnes, whose distrust of all book publishers seemed to be pathological, the product of her long and unhappy history with many companies here and abroad. She even rejected the word "publishers"; they were "printers" to her. She was now almost 70 years old. She took advice only from her longtime friend and admirer T. S. Eliot, who happened to be her English publisher, and he told me that occasionally even his advice was flatly rejected.

It was Eliot who had sent me the typescript of her verse play, *The Antiphon,* which our company published in 1958, three years before this meeting. We imported 1,500 English sheets from Faber & Faber, the publishing house with which Eliot was associated. Happily, the book received the critical praise we had all hoped for, and the edition sold out eventually. In *The New York Times Book Review*, Dudley Fitts called the work "dramatic poetry of a curious and high order," pointing out that the pleasure to be found in *The Antiphon* is "the pleasure of language. Not spoken language; Miss Barnes has no ear for the stage, but the intricate, rich, almost viciously brilliant discourse, modeled more or less on the murkier post-Elizabethans." The names of the Jacobean playwrights John Webster, Cyril Tourneur, Thomas Middleton and John Ford were cited in the reviews. The anonymous reviewer in *The Times Literary Supplement* wrote, "There will always be one or two eccentrics who think *The Antiphon* gives its author first place among women who have written verse in the English language."

In light of these reviews, Miss Barnes and I had a very pleasant meeting. She told me she considered *The Antiphon* her most important work. She was in unusually good spirits because of the reviews but even more because Dag Hammarskjold, the Secretary General of the United Nations, had told her he admired the work so much he wanted to translate it into Swedish. I was impressed by his willingness to take on such an arduous task; the play was difficult enough in English. W. H. Auden, who edited Hammarskjold's spiritual autobiography, *Markings*, rated his poetic judgment highly: "His knowledge and understanding of poetry, the only field in which I was competent to judge the quality of his mind, were extraordinary." Miss Barnes told me she had dined with Hammarskjold at his home and found him to be one of the most perceptive and sensitive men she had ever met; she readily gave her consent. He was now firmly established in her pantheon of heroes, alongside Eliot and Edwin Muir, the English poet who said of her play, "I feel myself that *The Antiphon* is one of the greatest things that have been written in our time, and that it would be a disaster if it were never to be known."

Hammarskjold, in this new undertaking, had the good sense to use the help of a theater man, collaborating with Karl Ragnar Gierow, the director of the Swedish Royal Dramatic Theater, known as the Dramaten. Early in 1961, under Mr. Gierow's direction, *The Antiphon* had its world premiere in Stockholm at this unusual theater, which also had the distinction of having premiered Eugene O'Neill's *Long Day's Journey Into Night* and having given Greta Garbo her earliest training in its drama school. Miss Barnes was unable to attend the opening because of her health. Hammarskjold missed it as well because the crisis in the Congo made it impossible for him to leave United Nations headquarters, but that night he sent her a bouquet of roses.

A few weeks later she phoned to tell me that the Dramaten had mailed her a packet of photographs of its production. Would I like to see them? I said I would and, having in mind that she was elderly and walked with a cane, suggested that I stop by for them at her home in Patchin Place in Greenwich Village, since I often lunched in the neighborhood. She could even bridle on the phone: "No, I prefer not to have visitors here. I'll bring them to your office tomorrow." The futility of disagreeing with her about matters small or large, especially if one was a publisher, was obvious. I respected Miss Barnes as an artist and admired her as a writer. We took pride in having her play on our list, and if we could possibly accommodate her wishes, we did so. I told her I looked forward to seeing the photos the next day.

Marianne Moore once told Elizabeth Bishop she had run into Djuna Barnes on the steps of the New York Public Library. "I was curious," the younger poet wrote, "and asked her what Djuna Barnes was 'like.' There was a long pause before Marianne said, thoughtfully, 'Well, she looked very smart, and her shoes were beautifully polished.'" My own view of Miss Barnes was equally subjective and colored by what I had learned from Eliot, who had known her for decades. He greatly enjoyed her company. Whenever he was in New York, he took her to Charles, a French restaurant on the east side of Sixth Avenue, directly across from the old Jefferson Market and Patchin Place. He told me she had been "disowned" by her family because of her rather notorious life in Paris during the 1920s and 30s, as a member of the circle that gravitated around the wealthy American expatriate Natalie Barney. (This group of artists, writers and actresses, many of whom were homosexual, was vividly depicted by Colette in her book *The Pure and the Impure*.) Occasionally I saw Miss Barnes walking in the neighborhood of our office at Union Square. She held her tall and thin frame as straight as a ramrod, using a silver-headed ebony walking stick and favoring her left side. Her most striking feature in her younger years had been a fine head of glossy auburn hair, which began to turn gray, thin out and frizzle in the 1960's. She was always smartly groomed and often wore black suits with a brightly colored or polkadot scarf at her throat.

The limited earnings from her books—including her best-known work, the novel *Nightwood,* which Eliot had published in London in 1936—were insufficient to sustain her. She depended on the generosity of patrons, and her chief supporter during the 50's and 60's was Peggy Guggenheim, a cousin of the publisher Roger Straus. I learned from Eliot the surprising fact that her four brothers were well-to-do, and I seem to recall that at least one was a banker. Her unconventional father, Wald Barnes, was born Henry Budington. He was 14 years old in 1870, when his mother, Zadel Barnes Budington, an early feminist, divorced her husband—an unusual event then—and went back to her own name, which the son then adopted.

Young Wald Barnes married Elizabeth Chappell of Oakham, England, and they gave exotic names to their five children—Thurn, Djuna, Zandon, Saxon and Shangar. Djuna, the second child and only daughter, was born in 1892 and grew up in Cornwall-on-Hudson, N.Y., in a house her father built on the Storm King mountain estate owned by their uncle, Justin Budington. Wald Barnes refused to send his children to school. According to her account, Djuna Barnes was "educated at home, and received some of her first paychecks from New York newspapers," including *The Morning Telegraph* and *The World*. In 1915 her first book, *The Book of Repulsive Women,* was brought out as a chapbook by Guido Bruno of Greenwich Village fame. The Provincetown Players produced three of her plays in 1919; four years later Boni & Liverwright published her collection of stories, plays and verses, *A Book.* Horace Liverwright issued her novel *Ryder* in 1928 and her book of short stories, *A Night Among the Horses,* the following year. Her *Ladies Almanack* was privately published also in 1928. With the appearance of *Nightwood,* she achieved an international reputation. And after a gap of 22 years, she published her play. *The Antiphon* is impossible to understand without knowing the family background that inspired it. Its odd and sometimes archaic language adds to the difficulty: Dag Hammarskjold confessed to Miss Barnes that when he first read it, he was frequently baffled but, "having worked with *The Antiphon,* I now share your view that there is nothing obscure in it." The play centers on a mortal combat between an aged and widowed mother, Augusta, and her daughter, Miranda, "a tall woman in her late fifties" who has "a distinguished but failing air." Their duel, the author says, "should be waged with style." The play ends with their deaths, the mother killing her daughter with a large brass bell, falling dead herself from the effort.

It is as fantastic a play as the stage set Djuna Barnes prescribes for it, with a balustrade on which hang "flags, gonfalons, bonnets, ribbons and all manner of stage costumes. . . . A long table with a single settle facing front, at either end of which is set the half of a gryphon, once a car in a roundabout." All this is "surrounded by music stands, horns, fiddles, guncases, bandboxes, masks, toys and broken statues, man and beast." This unlikely setting, to which members of the family have journeyed from the four corners of the earth for a reunion, serves as a kind of baroque courtroom in which we are the spectators while the whole family is put on trial. Miranda, the outcast daughter, is both prosecutor and defendant. At one point she makes an accusation against her mother for some obscure act that jolts the reader who grasps that she is describing her own birth: "The salt spilled, the bread broke. Unmuzzled bone / Drew on the hood of flesh, entombing laughter: / Tongues came forth, and forth the hissing milk / Its lashing noose, and snared the gaping mouth. / A door slammed on Eden, and the Second Gate, / And I walked down your leg." A play of brilliant recrimination, *The Antiphon* is a version of the author's family history from her view, a dramatic parallel to another American playwright's long day's journey into night. When Miss Barnes came and spread the photos of the Dramaten production on my desk, she also brought along a rave review by the drama critic of the Stockholm newspaper *Espressen.* I had never seen her look so happy. "I owe Dag Hammarskjold everything," she said. "If it hadn't been for translation, none of this would have happened." That there were no plans for a New York or London production she attributed, quite unfairly, to the disastrous tryout—in fact, it was a reading without sets or costumes—that Eliot had arranged for the Poets' Theater Company to put on for her at Harvard University in 1956, before *The Antiphon* was even published. In addition to Eliot, his friends I. A. Richards, Edwin Muir and Robert Lowell were in the audience. Everything about the Harvard tryout displeased her—the actress playing Miranda was not thin enough, all. the performers mouthed difficult lines whose meanings had not been sufficiently clarified for them. Since this was merely a reading, they interrupted themselves from time to time, reasonably enough, to ask Miss Barnes what certain lines and words meant. This had enraged her. In her view, no poet should be subjected to such questioning, especially in public. To her the tryout was a wounding breach of good manners.

H. D. Vursell, my gifted editorial colleague, entered the office at this juncture to have a look at the Dramaten photos. Hal, as he was called, had lived in Paris in the late 20s and knew many of the people Miss Barnes had known. They hit it off instantly, speaking of Natalie Barney, Mina Loy, Nancy Cunard, Virgil Thomson, Gertrude Stein, Raymond Mortimer, Romaine Brooks and even the original of Dr. O'Connor, the famous character in *Nightwood.* (Eliot, in his introduction to the novel, refers to him as "Dr. Matthew-Mighty-grain-of-salt-Dante-O'Connor," whose Irish eloquence and verbal ingenuity make him one of the most memorable characters in the book.) After Hal left, Miss Barnes lingered momentarily in the past. "Everyone in Paris knew him," she said, and at first I thought she meant Hal, but she was thinking of the original of Dr. O'Connor. "He'd been a sailor in the U.S. Navy. In Paris he went everywhere, and he talked all night long. When I put him in my books, I didn't invent a thing."

This was the most tension-free meeting I had ever known with Djuna Barnes. I might have guessed it couldn't last.

At the end she casually mentioned that she had numerous corrections and revisions for **The Antiphon.** My heart sank, since we had no plates of her book, only the imported sheets. I merely nodded as I escorted her to the elevator. If there was to be a wrangle, and it was inevitable, I preferred to face it another day.

When I alerted Roger Straus to the impending crisis, he had an inspiration. Why not collect several different examples of her work—some of her stories, her best-known novel and the revised text of her play—into a single book, **The Selected Works of Djuna Barnes**? There was a whole new generation of readers who had never heard of her and to whom such an anthology might appeal. Eventually the copyrights were cleared, and my friend James Laughlin of New Directions readily gave his consent to our use of **Nightwood.** It took several meetings with Miss Barnes—including the one at which I shouted that she had to trust someone—before we worked it all out. Publication of the collection was finally scheduled for the spring of 1962. When the galley proofs came to my desk in mid-September, I phoned to ask if I could bring them over. "You know I do not have visitors," she said. But I did not want to visit; I simply wanted to see the proofs safely delivered. "Are you aware that we have no nameplates or mailboxes and that my buzzer doesn't work?" No, but couldn't I call out her name in the courtyard? "Very well. Come tomorrow, if you wish, but don't expect me to ask you in." I said I understood perfectly. Patchin Place is a small enclave of 10 brick houses converted into small apartments in two rows on either side of a narrow, tree-shaded courtyard off West 10th Street between Sixth and Greenwich Avenues. An iron gate, usually ajar, secludes it from outsiders. Over the years it has been home to such writers as John Reed, Theodore Dreiser, Padraic Colum and Jane Bowles. I first visited it in the early 50s, when I was editing the collected edition of the poems of E. E. Cummings, who lived on the ground floor of No. 4 Patchin Place. He was a good friend and neighbor of Miss Barnes, who lived across from him at No. 5. If she was ill, he brought her chicken soup, and her reclusive behavior made him call up to her second-floor window every few weeks, "Djuna, are you still alive?"

When I arrived with her proofs, I realized that something was wrong. She was standing at the first-floor banister and in a voice much more hoarse and tired than usual said, "Bring them up." To my surprise, when I got to her door she said faintly, "Please come in." Her face was pale and drawn, and I was amazed to see that she was wearing a nightgown of pleated muslin, longer than floor length, with a ruffed collar tied with a black ribbon up to her chin. It reminded me of an old photograph of Sarah Bernhardt in the last act of *Camille,* except that this costume was transparent and she was wearing nothing beneath it. To avoid tripping, she had gathered up the folds in front of her. Wholly distracted, she seemed

unaware of my embarrassment. This was so unlike the Djuna Barnes I was accustomed to, always smartly turned out and in control, that I decided she was ill. The night table beside her bed held dozens of vials of pills and capsules in different colors.

"I haven't slept a wink," she said. "I had ears glued to the radio all night. They've murdered him!"

For a moment I thought she had gone mad. "Who's been murdered?"

"Don't you know that they've killed Dag Hammarskjold? He flew on a peace mission to the Congo, and his plane was sabotaged. He's been burned to death."

"My God, how awful!" I had not seen the papers or heard this shocking news and said so. "I know he was your friend. I'm so very sorry, Miss Barnes."

"He was a saint. I've called the U.N. office, but they don't seem to know anything except that he's dead." She said that when she first heard the news, she felt as if she had been blinded. She motioned me to a chair. I placed the package of proofs on her desk, behind which stood a thronelike curule chair in which she now sat. After a while she seemed a little less agitated, and her voice grew stronger. "His death is one of the worst crimes against civilization ever committed. Dag Hammarskjold did nothing but good, and look what they've done to him. And he really believed in the goodness of man. Well, not I!" It did not seem to be the time for proofs and publishing business, and I said I'd phone her in a day or so. "No," she said. "You're here now, and let's get on with it." I showed her the proofs, gave her the deadline for corrections and asked her how she liked the design for the jacket. It featured a handsome photograph that Berenice Abbott had taken of her around the time of *Nightwood.* I expected her to fuss and fume over every aspect of the design, but she simply said, "It's rather good," and handed it back.

"I know you're trying to take my mind off this terrible tragedy, but you needn't," she said. "I have lived with suffering all my life, and I expect to do so until the day I die." I looked around her one-room apartment, which I had never thought I would see. She had lived alone in this room since 1940—21 years. I did not know and could not have imagined that she would occupy it for another 21 years, during which I would never see her again, though we exchanged letters.

With the passing years, it was her fate to become more and more of a legend. She even called herself "the most famous unknown in the world." Books would be written about her. In her later years she would be appointed a trustee of the

Dag Hammarskjold Foundation, elected to the National Institute of Arts and Letters and awarded a grant by the National Endowment for the Arts. A group of admirers, including young writers and editors and some residents of Greenwich Village, devoted themselves to her welfare and tried to help her when she would let them. But her suffering did not cease. She was briefly hospitalized for malnutrition, apparently through self-neglect. In 1971 *The New Yorker* published her poem **"The Walking-mort,"** whose theme was the living death of old age. Her editor at the Dial Press, Frances McCullough, saw the last book she wrote, **Creatures in an Alphabet,** through press just before Miss Barnes's death in 1982.

Djuna Barnes might have learned from the authorized biography of Dag Hammarskjold by Brian Urquhart, published in 1972, that the Secretary General's death was an accident, not murder. (This does not necessarily mean that she would have changed her mind about sabotage.) When *Markings* was published posthumously, I found that one of Hammarskjold's entries was this quotation from **The Antiphon:** "Be not your own pathetic fallacy, but be / Your own dark measure in the vein, / For we're about a tragic business." The gallant woman who wrote these lines lived for three days after her 90th birthday.

Nancy J. Levine (essay date 1991)

SOURCE: "'Bringing Milkshakes to Bulldogs': The Early Journalism of Djuna Barnes," in *Silence and Power: A Reevaluation of Djuna Barnes*, edited by Mary Lynn Broe, Southern Illinois University Press, 1991, pp. 27-34.

[*In the following essay, Levine traces how Barnes's early journalism influenced her fiction, especially* Nightwood.]

Judging by her early career as a journalist, one could say that Djuna Barnes had a taste for "the bawdy, cheap cuts from the beast life," not unlike her character Felix Volkbein of *Nightwood,* who haunts the dressing rooms of Europe's actresses, acrobats, and sword swallowers (*N*, II). Barnes combined the public demands of a career with a private fascination for the strange and bizarre. The assignments she drew as a "newspaperman" (her term) during the eight years before she left for Europe in 1920 led her inevitably to the grotesque. Barnes' tabloid journalism is elegant, witty, and surprisingly undated. Because her career as a journalist was the seedbed of her greatest novel, *Nightwood,* her early essays, interviews, and works of fiction are worth considering, setting aside questions of merit. The motif of the sideshow freak emerged from this early work and found its way into *Nightwood.*

In 1913 Djuna Barnes began working as a reported and illustrator for the Brooklyn *Daily Eagle.* She free-lanced for the *Press*, the *World*, and the *Morning Telegraph* between 1914 and 1917, eventually writing for most of the other major New York papers. In addition to straightforward news reports, such as her page-one story for the *Daily Eagle*, **"Stage Opens Case in New Delfer Trial"** (1913), Barnes wrote interviews and feature articles on a startling variety of subjects. Tango dancers, chorus girls, Greenwich Village bohemians, and British suffragettes engaged her sharp-eyed, amused attention. She talked to out-of-work servant girls and to Lillian Russell in her opulent retirement. David Belasco the playwright, Diamond Jim Brady the financier, and Billy Sunday the evangelist responded to her questions with surprising openness and eloquence. Her early newspaper career kept her in touch with the popular entertainments of the 1910s—the circus, the vaudeville, the boxing ring, and the movies. Scattered among the big names she interviewed are these oddities: an Italian actress billed as "the Wild Aguglia," who kept monkeys in her dressing room; an "Indian" snake dancer named "Roshanara" (actually an English girl with a busy imagination); and a painless dentist, "Twingeless Twitchell," whose office was any Brooklyn street corner.

By 1917 Djuna Barnes was earning five thousand dollars a year as a free-lance feature writer. Fifteen dollars for an article was considered good payment in the 1910s; Barnes could, and often did, write several a day. By the time she left for Europe in 1920, she had published more than a hundred articles and over twenty-five short plays and fictions. The New York *Tribune* employed her as a stringer during her early years in Paris, Berlin, and the south of France. *McCall's*, *Vanity Fair*, *Charm*, and the *New Yorker* commissioned articles and interviews that featured personages famous, rich, or royal. *McCall's* editor, Harry Payne Burton, for example, sent Barnes a $500 check to a Barcelona address in 1925 for an article on international marriage among the elite.[1] During the 1920s, Barnes' popular journalism was an uncertain source of income, allowing her to publish her serious fiction and poetry in literary journals with small budgets. The *Little Review*, the *Dial*, and *transition* gladly took her work in return for the glory of the thing; occasional financial assistance from friends helped keep her afloat between checks.[2] From January 1929 to September 1931 she wrote articles and a gossipy monthly column, "Playgoer's Almanac" (retitled "The Wanton Playgoer"), for *Theatre Guild Magazine*. The big assignments became scarcer in the 1930s, however, and finally stopped altogether. But in the 1920s Barnes was known as a brilliant figure in literary and social circles on both continents. In May 1924 a young upstart named Ernest Hemingway warned the readers of the Paris-based *Transatlantic Review* that Djuna Barnes, "that legendary personality that has dominated the intellectual night-life of Europe for a century, is in town." It may well have been her reputation as a literary legend that finally ended her career as a popular journalist. By the late 1930s she had too much stature to write about what the crowned heads of Europe liked for dinner.

At the beginning of her career, however, there were few things Barnes would not do for the sake of a story, from risking the loss of "all dignity out of our lives as far back as our great grand uncles" on the slides, chutes, and whirling disks of Luna Park Steeple Chase to allowing herself to be lowered at the end of a rope from the top of a building for an article on firemen's rescues. Barnes' range in the 1910s was remarkably wide, but in almost every one of her light and engaging feature articles and interviews the real subject is the unexpected presence of the bizarre embedded in the everyday.

Sometimes the bizarre was not buried very deeply. For example, Barnes found Twingeless Twitchell, the dentist who pulled teeth for free, on a street corner in Brooklyn. The banner that headed her interview with Twitchell was the alliterative exuberance of a Coney Island "talker's" spiel: **"Digital Dexterity of the Dental Demonstrator Holds Audience in Awe."**[3] The point of the article is that Twingeless Twitchell's act, however odd, is not tucked away in a freak show. One could encounter him or others like him on any municipal highway. One of Barnes' first assignments for the *Daily Eagle* was to explore the streets for **"Types Found in Odd Corners Round about Brooklyn"** (1913), as the heading for a series of her drawings proclaimed. Sometimes her searching eye picked out the unusual only to deflate it; in an interview with Ruth Royce, the comedienne, Barnes called her "the greatest 'nut' in vaudeville, eccentric beyond the limits of belief unless you have seen her."[4] But more frequently her goal was to make the reader aware of the strange and contradictory nature of the quotidian world. If one could "live each day apart," she wrote in **"Found in the Bowery"** (1917), "then and only then should we see something at once beautiful and real and perhaps not beautiful at all."[5]

In these early pieces Barnes is flexing muscles she will use when she creates the characters of *Nightwood.* In a voice that recalls Dr. Matthew O'Connor's verbal dexterity, Dr. Twitchell declaims to his audience, "I'm the man that put the 'dent' in dentist and the 'ees' in teeth." O'Connor himself gives a good imitation of a medicine show spieler when he tells the café crowd, "I was standing listening to a quack hanky-panky of a medicine man saying: 'Now, ladies and gentlemen, before I behead the small boy, I will endeavour to entertain you with a few parlour tricks'" (*N,* 163). Barnes was particularly drawn to high-talking charlatans. When it came time to write the doctor's monologues, she had more than one prototype on whose mode of speech she could have drawn.[6] The evangelist Billy Sunday may have suggested the doctor's favorite rhetorical device, attack by anal-

ogy. Side-stepping the question "Is war good or bad for religion?" Billy Sunday responds aphoristically: "Through ammunition one attains immunity: through battle one locates the knees. The eyes do not necessarily have to be acquainted with the Bible; the knees must be acquainted with the floor."[7] The balanced repetition of the preacher's language ("through ammunition . . . through battle") is echoed in the doctor's speech: "we all go down in battle, but we all go home" (*N,* 129). To a certain extent, Barnes invented *all* the people about whom she wrote. Since she seldom took notes, she may have had to depend on the cadenced language of her Methodist background to recreate the ecclesiastical rhythms of Billy Sunday's oratory. Her memory was copious; as she told the actress Helen Westley during an interview, she could always "make a paragraph out of a note automatically." No doubt Barnes drew on her past for the interviews, as later she drew on the interviews for *Nightwood.*

Djuna Barnes also wrote about: a seal trainer in Brooklyn; the above-mentioned snake dancer, "Roshanara, the Reincarnation of the Ancient East"; and a baby gorilla at the Bronx Zoo named Dinah, whom she "interviewed."[8] In words that Barnes, acting as "translator," put in Dinah's mouth, the "bush-girl" expresses a wish to try chewing gum so that she can find out "what it is that keeps so many people rotatory beneath their hats."

Most of Barnes' interviewees are in Dinah's position, at least some of the time, of having words—witty, alternately racy and orotund, but unmistakably Barnes' own—placed in their mouths. The Broadway producer Arthur Voegtlin, whom Barnes interviewed for the *Press,* sounds curiously like Billy Sunday, for example, and both men recall Dr. O'Connor. She even made a spokesperson out of Roshanara, whose verbal talents are rather unexpected coming from a snake dancer; "skill," Barnes remarks in *Nightwood,* "is never so amazing as when it seems inappropriate" (*N,* II). Addressing a stumbling American public, enamored of such violent, mechanical dances as the turkey trot and the bunny hug, Roshanara says: "Incidentally, you don't know anything about dancing. That's why my act is a risk; it is moonlight to madness, and it is dream steps to the death charge. It is a hazy, calm, peaceful interpretation of a calm, peaceful race. Well, it's like bringing a milkshake to a bulldog."

In these early essays Djuna Barnes is always trying to bring milkshakes to bulldogs. The attempt to confound her readers' blunted expectations by mixing modes and forcing incongruous juxtapositions is an essential part of her style, both as a writer and as an artist. The drawings that accompanied most of her articles and interviews are an improbable but successful combination of the daily funnies and Aubrey Beardsley. One of Barnes' specialties was the vamp, a type that had its vogue in the 1910s. The pages of popular magazines were filled with drawings of slant-eyed women, dressed in sinuous wraps and wearing the bland, standardized expressions of fashion models. Barnes eschewed anodyne effects; her females are anything but bland. A fashionably dressed woman in a typical Barnes sketch of this period goes for a walk with her pet, but the animal at the end of the leash is a cubistic chicken. Barnes' first published graphic work owes a debt to the whiplash linearity of art nouveau. The prose style she employed in her feature articles for the *Daily Eagle* and the *Press* is harder to categorize. The term "euphuistic" hardly does justice to the deliberate campiness of her description of an ice cream soda as "cheerful chemicals in chiffon." There is an element of Coney Island burlesque in such a contradictory construction that makes the usual critical terminology seem stuffy.

Coney Island, not unexpectedly, was another Barnes specialty. From 1913 to 1917 she wrote four articles about her visits to that garish, red-painted amusement park. Built in 1904, Coney Island was the inspiration of two alert showmen, Elmer S. Dundy and Frederick Thompson, who also built the Hippodrome, thereby making themselves sleek fortunes. Barnes was more interested in the people who visited and worked in Coney Island than she was in the park itself. The following passage is from a piece she wrote for the *Press* in 1914:

> I heard emanating from one of the sideshows a noise that was half-way between a melody and a regret; there were also inside some torrid war cries and a glimpse of some turbans. . . . [The performers] had a lot of sheeting wound around them and a good many spears, which they occasionally threw at one another or at the crowd, or sometimes at a target which, in spite of the fact that they never do anything else, they never hit in the right place. They showed us how they cleaned their teeth, how they nursed their babies, and how they chewed gum.
>
> The last exhibit was rather the best.[9]

In an essay that appeared in the *Press* three years later, Barnes' impressions are still as sharply focused, but her response to the sideshow has tilted from outside to inside, from the position of the observer to that of the observed:

> A sideshow attracts attention. Great posters of the "Fattest Fat Lady," of the "Ossified Man," of the "Snake Charmer," and of that unfortunate fellow who has legs like whips and who is advertised as the "Cigarette Fiend." You look down upon these people as from the top of an abyss, they are the bottom of despair and of life. The demonstrator comes forward, cane in hand, he

touches the nearest freak on the shoulder and begins turning him around as if this turning were all that the unfortunate had been born for. He begins to enumerate this man's misfortunes as though they were a row of precious beads.

> An explosion in the mines, a falling of stones and coal, a man pitching forward in the darkness, a stumbling foot, a prayer to God, and then a pick through the body—"You see," he gives the young man another turn, tapping him upon the stomach, "here is where the pick thrust its head out." He smiles, rubbing his hands. The young man turns again, a fixed look upon his face, neither pleasant or otherwise, a cool self-possessed stare, a little uncertain, perhaps, whether to be proud or sorry for the accident that has made him of interest to the gaping throng.[10]

These two passages could be read as evidence that between 1914 and 1917 a development, a deepening of the character of their author, took place. Such things happen in fiction, if not in the fiction that Barnes happens to have written. Actually, these two passages illustrate two perspectives she had mastered from the start: an objective and a subjective approach to reporting.

Barnes, who began her career writing front-page news items, always retained the ability to record the facts of a story with detachment and economy. Sent to the Bowery in 1917 by the *Telegraph* to dig out hidden pockets of grand opera, she noticed the poisonous colors of the cakes in an Italian bakery and wondered about their effect on the digestion—without losing sight of her reporter's obligation to tell how, when, and where the public could attend a performance of *Salome*.

Her best journalism is subjective, however. She had what Louis Kannenstine called "a gift for uncommon observation."[11] The facts that mattered to her were the marginal, concealed, but vital details that allowed her to respond to the atmosphere of an assignment, to what one might call its psychological environment. Her essay on the playwright John Millington Synge is "an atmospheric article on an atmosphere."[12] The introduction contains an important demurral: "I am not a critic; to me criticism is so often nothing more than the eye garrulously denouncing the shape of the peephole that gives access to hidden treasure." After this graceful hesitation, we are offered a selection of homely vignettes: the Irish playwright cooking a frugal meal of tea and eggs on a small stove, wandering alone in the windy dusk, playing the penny whistle for a few friends. Perhaps these are made-up "facts"—in any case, details no "critic" would find important. But they create the illusion of a presence, palpable and intense, that owed little of its effect to the historical facts, arranged in chronological order, around which her essay is discreetly constructed. Barnes has evoked an atmosphere of loneliness, detachment, and mystery. Most of the feature articles she wrote between 1913 and 1919 have a similar subjectivity.

Barnes' Synge is sad and a bit rumpled; in spite of his celluloid collar and his lyric genius, he resembles the tramps, barflies, and laid-off workers she sketched in the **"Types Found in Odd Corners"** series she did for the Brooklyn *Daily Eagle* in 1913. Above the high-flown caption "Because the Road He Took Was Wrong," a man in a rough cap and jacket sits in a chair with his face hidden in the crook of his arm. Barnes gave the same posture of weary suffering to a young prostitute whom Nora encounters after she and Robin are separated (*N,* 157). Such outcasts of society are valuable, we are told, although "their good is incommunicable, outwitted, being the rudiment of a life that has developed, as in man's body are found evidences of lost needs" (*N,* 52). *Nightwood* is a gathering of the distressed, people she terms "*détraqués*"—O'Connor's "Tuppeny Upright," the boys and girls who hang around public toilets at night, the freak Mademoiselle Basquette, "built like a medieval abuse," and, above all, Dr. O'Connor himself. As a journalist, Barnes learned how to communicate the incommunicable good inherent in such people by studying the workers and actors she found on the margins of social "acceptability."

If much of Djuna Barnes' early newspaper work is "subjective journalism" rather than straight reportage, it was mainly because there was a demand for that work at which she, above others, excelled. She had, however, a reputation for reportorial energy and toughness, as well. "Djuna Barnes, the femme writer," Walter Winchell wrote in the late 1920s, "can hit a cuspidor twenty feet away." That particular talent belonged to someone else, but Barnes had earned the reputation. "Baby Face" Nelson and his girl friend gave her an interview at her Waverly Place apartment while nervous bodyguards patrolled the doors and windows. Once she climbed into an upstairs window to photograph the body of a murdered girl. She snapped the picture but failed to get an interview with the distraught father, who threw her out the first time she tried to enter the house. "This was the kind of thing that made me get out of the newspaper business," Barnes told a friend more than sixty years later. Between 1916 and 1918 her flow of articles diminished considerably. What ended her career as a news reporter (but not as a journalist) was her refusal to divulge to her editor the facts about a rape case she had investigated. He fired her on the spot.[13]

Barnes also earned her living by describing to a sedentary public how it felt to be a carefree young vamp, a comic or satiric persona she donned in the 1920s when she signed the pseudonym "Lydia Steptoe" to articles she wrote for *Vanity Fair, Charm,* and *Shadowland.* For a few years she gave it her all, until the role must have sickened her. Coming briefly out of deep seclusion in 1971 to give Henry Raymont of the *New York Times* an interview, she said: "Years ago I used to see people. I had to, I was a newspaperman, among other things. And I used to be rather the life of the party."[14] It is tempting to imagine a moment when, her bravado faltering, Barnes felt like the young man with the perforated stomach, "a little uncertain perhaps whether to be proud or sorry for the accident" that made her of interest to the throngs. But this is impertinent speculation. Her own terse words to Raymont will have to suffice: "I used to be invited by people who said, 'Get Djuna for dinner, she's amusing.' So I stopped it."

Barnes discovered fairly early that "subjective journalism" could be made to serve the needs of a personal and artistic, as well as a professional, integrity. The account of her experiment with force-feeding, which she wrote for the *World Magazine* in 1914, is graphically detailed, but it is not coolly detached. Her goal is to inspire the readers of the Sunday supplement with a sense of outrage on behalf of English suffragettes on a hunger strike. She writes: "If I, play-acting, felt my being burning with revolt at this brutal usurpation of my bodily functions, how they who actually suffered the ordeal in its acutest horror must have flamed at the violation of the sanctuaries of their spirit?"[15] "Empathy" has rarely been taken further by any writer.

For the average reader, the man who earned his living by displaying his perforated stomach in a sideshow would have seemed no more of a freak than the suffragette willing to risk having a tube forced into hers. What Barnes is looking for in her early pieces is a way to narrow the distance between the freakish unfortunates she encountered in "odd corners" of the city and the audience who "look[s] down upon these people as from the top of an abyss." One way is to enter the abyss herself. Thus she allowed the prison doctors and nurses to strap her to the infirmary table: "This," she thought quizzically as she looked up into their faces, "is one picture that will never go into the family album." Another way is to produce snapshots of the event that turned a human being, like ourselves, into a freak: "a stumbling foot, a prayer to God, and then a pick through the body." The world she introduces by these means is alien and threatening, but full of fascination. Unable to turn away, one experiences direct contact with the grotesque.

During the years she wrote for the daily papers, Barnes developed an eye for the diamond embedded in slug's meat. James Joyce, whom she met in Paris, told her, "A writer should never write about the extraordinary; that is for the journalist."[16] Fortunately, she was not that kind of journalist. Her extraordinary fact was almost always buried in the heart of the everyday, whether she was writing about the strange people she met in Greenwich Village and the Bowery, the circus acts at the Hippodrome, or the freak shows at Coney Island.

Nightwood is proof that Barnes absorbed, retained, and used what she had seen as a newspaper writer. The most obvious echo from her past is that collection of circus performers with suggestive names—the trapeze artist Frau Mann, for example, known onstage as "the Duchess of Broadback"—whose presence on the novel's periphery caused some early reviewers to label the book "a sideshow of freaks," to T. S. Eliot's dismay. Barnes would not have tried to duck the phrase. Frau Mann, after all, is "eccentric beyond the limits of belief unless you have seen her."

The word "freaks" appears nowhere in *Nightwood.* That Barnes would refrain from using the term marks a change in her attitude towards the use to which subjective journalism might be put. In some of her early work, she clearly itches to force the complacent to acknowledge their affinity with anomalous, marginal people. By the time she wrote *Nightwood,* the teacher had become an author without ceasing to be a humanist. Barnes herself would "never use the derogatory in the usual sense" (a "great virtue" she shared with Dr. O'Connor [*N*, 116-17]): she seems, rather, to have decided to trust her audience to summon up similar powers of discrimination. "Freaks," to be sure, is a word that recoils upon the reader who would use it for the nonheterosexual characters in *Nightwood.* If some still do, that fact only proves that Barnes continues to bring milkshakes to bulldogs, even though the "milkshake" has turned to headier stuff.

NOTES

1. Harry Payne Burton, letter to Djuna Barnes, 2 November 1925, the Djuna Barnes Collection, McKeldin Library, University of Maryland, College Park.

2. Matthew Josephson, in *Life among the Surrealists, a Memoir* (New York: Holt, Rinehart, 1962), 83, recalls that at one period Barnes was living on a monthly stipend of fifty dollars, given to her by a rich American woman (probably Natalie Clifford Barney).

3. "'Twingeless [*sic*] Twitchell' and His Tantalizing Tweezers, etc.," Brooklyn *Daily Eagle,* 27 July 1913, 6.

4. "Ruth Royce, Greatest 'Nut' in Vaudeville," *New York Press,* 19 May 1915, sec. 4, p. 4.

5. "Found in the Bowery: The Italian Drama," *New York Morning Telegraph,* 21 January 1917, sec. 2, p. 1.

6. The prototype usually cited for Dr. Matthew O'Connor is Dr. Dan Mahoney. For accounts of this friend of Barnes' expatriate years, see John Glassco, *Memoirs of Montparnasse* (New York: Oxford Univ. Press, 1970); Robert McAlmon, *Being Geniuses Together* (Garden City, NY: Doubleday, 1968); and Andrew Field, *Djuna: The Life and Times of Djuna Barnes* (New York: Putnam's, 1983).

7. "Billy Sunday, a Fire-Eater in Pulpet, etc.," *New York Press,* 12 February 1915, sec. 5, p. 2.

8. "Training Seals in Stage Stunts, etc.," *Brooklyn Daily Eagle,* 31 August 1913, 30; "Roshanara, a Wraithlike Reincarnation of the Ancient East," *New York Press,* 14 June 1914, sec. 5, p. 3; "The Girl and the Gorilla; Dinah at the Bronx Zoo etc.," *New York World Magazine,* 18 October 1914, 9.

9. "If Noise Were Forbidden at Coney Island, a Lot of People Would Lose Their Jobs etc.," *New York Press,* 7 June 1914, sec. 5, p. 5.

10. "Surcease in Hurry and Whirl," *New York Morning Telegraph,* 15 July 1917, 2.

11. Louis Kannenstine, *The Art of Djuna Barnes: Duality and Damnation* (New York: New York Univ. Press, 1977), 5-6.

12. "The Songs of Synge: The Man Who Shaped His Life as He Shaped His Plays," *New York Morning Telegraph,* 18 February 1917, 8.

13. I am indebted to Hank O'Neal's memoirs (excerpted in this volume) for Barnes' account of her newspaper experiences and for her denial of Walter Winchell's "spittoon" anecdote.

14. Henry Raymont, "From the Avant-Garde of the '30's, Djuna Barnes," *New York Times,* 24 May 1971, 24.

15. "How It Feels to Be Forcibly Fed," *New York World Magazine,* 6 September 1914, sec. 5, p. 17.

16. "Vagaries Malicieux," *Double Dealer* 3 (1922): 253; reprinted in *Vagaries Malicieux: Two Stories by Djuna Barnes* (New York: Frank Hallman, 1974).

Jeanne Campbell Reesman   (Winter 1992)

SOURCE: "'That Savage Path': *Nightwood* and *The Divine Comedy,*" in *Renascence,* Vol. XLIV, No. 2, Winter, 1992, pp. 137-58.

[*In the following essay, Reesman compares Barnes's* Nightwood *to Dante's* The Divine Comedy.]

Among the many interesting problems raised by Djuna Barnes's *Nightwood* (1936), is that of placing this complex and mysterious novel in a literary-historical context. Many critics describe *Nightwood* as an example of the post-modernist "new novel." Joseph Frank, for example, views it as a striking example of literary spatialism, a "richly experimental" novel that goes beyond other similar works in its post-cubist exploration of narrative form and narrative consciousness (Frank 46). Following Frank, Sharon Spencer calls it an "architectonic" novel that attempts "to liberate character from the restrictive traditional unities by means of new structural principles based upon juxtaposition in space" (Spencer 39). Yet although *Nightwood* clearly emerges out of the literary attitudes and trends of its time, it also progressively assimilates and coordinates itself with the literature of the past. T. S. Eliot, for example, whose introduction to *Nightwood* drew favorable attention to a relatively unknown author, praises the novel's "great achievement of a style, the beauty of phrasing, the brilliance of wit and characterisation," but adds to these virtues "a quality of horror and doom very nearly related to that of Elizabethan tragedy" (*Nightwood*, xvi).

Indeed, like Eliot himself and like James Joyce, who, as George Steiner puts it, produced works "crammed with quotations from, allusions to, pastiches and parodies of the best art, music and literature of the previous two thousand years" (Steiner 134), Barnes should be regarded as both custodian of tradition and innovator, and *Nightwood*'s experimental form should not be set apart from the rich literary tradition that informs it. As Louis F. Kannenstine notes, *Nightwood* is "steeped in the literary-historical past as thoroughly as it is grounded in its concrete present." It particularly draws upon the sacred literature of Christian and pre-Christian tradition, as does Barnes's first novel, *Ryder* (Kannenstine xi). By re-presenting the past in the present, *Nightwood* addresses all that has gone before it as well as that culture in which and for which it was composed, but its jarring juxtapositions of past and present become even more meaningful as it also becomes part of a literary past. Indeed, now, after fifty years, *Nightwood*'s juxtaposition of contemporary cultural concerns with broader themes and archetypes can be more clearly seen and described. Despite its revolutionary chic, many of the important questions about *Nightwood*—and it is a novel that has baffled and even outraged literary critics—can be taken up in light of its relation to much older literary modes. It is fitting that a cunning book like *Nightwood* should present such a paradoxical universalism.

Perhaps in part because the reclusive Barnes was so unavailable for questioning about her life and career,

Nightwood's sources in past literature have never been adequately addressed. There are tantalizing suggestions, however, of such sources in various critics' comments. Besides Eliot's and Kannenstine's remarks, Frank, for example, despite his post-modernist approach, writes that this "amazing book" combines "the simple majesty of a medieval mystery play with the verbal subtlety and refinement of a Symbolist poem" (Frank 46). Others have noted the book's significant references to the poetry of John Donne. Yet the one name which emerges repeatedly in the criticism is that of Dante Alighieri, though it comes up casually and without explanation. Kannenstine says of Dr. Matthew O'Connor (whose full name is Dr. Matthew-Mighty-grain-of-salt-Dante-O'Connor) that "the Dante in O'Connor is a chronicler of purgatory" (Kannenstine 95). Similarly, in his 1937 *New Yorker* review of *Nightwood*, Clifton Fadiman calls the characters of the novel "the denizens of Dante's Inferno" (Fadiman 103), and Stanley Edgar Hyman describes Dr. O'Connor as "the mad, tormented Dante of our sexual underworld" (Hyman 61). An examination of *Nightwood* with Dante's *The Divine Comedy* in mind confirms the association sensed by these critics and reveals the Dantean influence in theme, structure, characterization, and imagery. The much-disputed meaning of the last chapter of *Nightwood*, in particular, is made clearer through the comparison with *The Divine Comedy*. The likenesses appear to indicate a conscious memory of Dante's poem, but I have been unable to locate any biographical evidence to indicate Barnes's knowledge of it. It is, however, their significance not their origin that concerns me. To see Barnes's novel as a mirror for Dante's poem is to see it illuminated in a significant way.

As in *The Divine Comedy*, in *Nightwood* duality is the overriding thematic as well as structural pattern. To begin with, it is and is not a novel: "only sensibilities trained on poetry can wholly appreciate it," as Eliot remarks (xii). Dr. O'Connor describes the unusual structure and development of the book when he claims that he has a narrative, "but you will be put to it to find it" (97). The eight chapters of *Nightwood* each focus on a single character, and this preference for multiple points of view formally contextualizes the novel's other dichotomies of day and night, of dual forms of being, of sexuality, of love and hate, consciousness and unconsciousness, descent and ascent, spirituality and bestiality, soul and flesh, salvation and damnation, linear and simultaneous time. Most importantly, a "reverse morality" pervades every aspect of the book. What is usually considered "good" is no longer in *Nightwood*. What is grotesque is beautiful. Morality and aesthetics are problematic and even dangerous in this dualistic universe, as Doctor O'Connor warns:

> "Have you," said the doctor, "ever thought of the peculiar polarity of times and times; and of sleep? .... Well, I ... will tell you how the day and the night are related by their division. The very con-

stitution of twilight is a fabulous reconstruction of fear, fear bottom-out and wrong side up. Every day is thought upon and calculated, but the night is not premeditated. The Bible lies the one way, but the nightgown the other. The night, 'Beware of that dark door!'" (80)

The characters of *Nightwood* occupy a "middle condition" that seems to presuppose a lack of understanding as a condition of tentative existence in a seemingly empty universe. How odd and how oddly appropriate, then, is Barnes's use of the moral architecture—the resolved *and* unresolved dualisms—of *The Divine Comedy*.

Like *The Divine Comedy*, *Nightwood's* thematic focus is on love, human and divine, and this is informed throughout by the insistence on duality and reversal. Love is generally inversion in *Nightwood*. Nearly all of Barnes's love relationships in all her works involve a search for self-completion—this love is symbolized in relationships that are either strictly familial or homosexual. In *Nightwood* the most "perfect" love thus appears to be that which allows the lovers to be mirror-images of each other. As Barnes wrote in **"Six Songs of Khalidine,"** an early elegy to a dead lover:

> It is not gentleness but mad despair
> That sets us kissing mouths, O Khalidine,
> Your mouth and mine, and one sweet mouth
>   unseen
> We call our soul. . . . (Barnes, *A Book*, 145)

Similarly, in *Nightwood,* Nora remarks that " . . . a woman is yourself, caught as you turn in panic; on her mouth you kiss your own" (143). Indeed the story of *Nightwood* traces how Nora's obsessive love for Robin is revealed as a selfish personal design on Nora's part. Her sin is that she treats Robin not as another human being but as a facet of herself. In *Nightwood,* whether between man and woman, woman and woman, or man and man, love that could be joy fails because of narcissistic self-containment. Nora's attempt to become one soul with Robin, to abolish their duality, is her great failing, and she painfully learns that when one "loves" anyone in a possessive, egotistical way—that is, when one's love is a demand on the loved one to function as a mirror of one's own personality and desires—the love is doomed. *Nightwood* thus suggests that all love is in danger of becoming merely a selfish, auto-erotic quest, but it also just hints in its conclusion at awareness of another kind of love, a love that would not be the less for allowing the "other" her identity and freedom. As *The Divine Comedy* portrays the limits and possibilities of Dante's and Beatrice's relations as they occur in Dante's spiritual journey, *Nightwood* similarly explores such possibilities and limits of human and Divine love; much more tentatively than *The Divine Comedy*,

Nightwood offers a redefinition of love as salvation from self-absorption.

Perhaps like Dante at the beginning of the *Inferno*, the characters of *Nightwood* are in revolt against the facts of their physical realities as human beings; these "perpetual protagonists" of Barnes's represent to Alan Williamson an extreme form of "the tragic encounter between an aspiring hero and a limiting universe, in that the antagonist is the protagonist's own nature rather than some external force pitted against him" (Williamson 61-62). The great sins of *The Divine Comedy*, Incontinence, Violence, and Fraud, are also the sins of *Nightwood:* all the characters are morally incontinent, but they come to represent individual besetting sins as well, all involving failures to love brought on by their self-absorption and alienation. As Ulrich Weisstein comments, "sooner or later in the novel, the characters of *Nightwood* are judged according to their spiritual age" (Weisstein 9). For both Dante and Barnes, the theme is that of "the agonized heart" (Hyman 62), the pilgrim soul on its way to death—or salvation—on the "grim path of 'We know not' to 'We can't guess why'" (101). "Agony" in *Nightwood* takes on the meaning of a struggle between well-defined but seemingly impossible choices. Like Faulkner's portrayal of the "human heart in conflict with itself," the struggles of Barnes's heroes and heroines suggest that if understanding within the self is next to impossible, how much more difficult is communication—especially loving communication—between oneself and others. Language is suspect; it can falsify reality by substituting "a word [for everything seen, done or spoken] and not its alchemy," as the Doctor puts it. "We swoon with the thickness of our own tongue when we say 'I love you . . .'" (83), he adds. Since in our modern wasteland, our "night wood," one cannot know the beloved's inner life, the Doctor suggests, one cannot love or be loved.

It is this seemingly insurmountable condition of ignorance of self and others in *Nightwood* which has furnished the evidence for the standard reading of Barnes's novel as utterly despairing, but to read the novel this way would be like reading only Dante's *Inferno* and not the complete *Comedy*. *Nightwood* is an *Inferno* for the modern world; like the *Inferno* it offers in its mysterious conclusion an enhancement of the possibility of hope by leaving the issue of interpretation, of belief, up to the reader. There is hope in *Nightwood's* savage portrait of modern failures at love, but it is like the hope offered at the end of Eliot's *The Waste Land*—it is subtly suggested, not directly presented. Such "incompleteness" actually offers the more "complete" reading of *Nightwood*.

Barnes's "negative" method specifically reflects the novel's dependence upon the Christian myth of a redemptive Fall: love is possible here on earth, but paradoxically one must first face one's failures at love. Fittingly, Spencer calls

Nightwood a "form of the Christian message in disguise" (Spencer 39), and Williamson suggests that in *Nightwood,* because love seeks "to heal fragmentation, to overcome solitude, and to deny mortality," love is the most perfect act of revolt against earthly despair (Williamson 65). But the Doctor says it best: "We were created that the earth might be made sensible of her inhuman taste; and love that the body might be so dear that even the earth should roar with it" (83).

The love so great "that even the earth should roar with it" is the same love Dante beholds in *The Divine Comedy*, "The love that moves the sun and the other stars" (*Pur.,* XXXIII, 145). The structures of *The Divine Comedy* and *Nightwood* seek to trace the way of the soul on the path through damnation and purgatory to paradise. *Nightwood* stops short at purgatory, just at the precise moment, in fact, of the turn from hell into purgatory and the beginning of the way to salvation, while *The Divine Comedy* portrays the soul's ascent as well as descent. Dante encounters all manners and degrees of degradation and despair, but ends with a vision of God as changeless Light. Led by the wise Virgil and then taken into heaven by his projected soul, the animal figure Beatrice, the pilgrim is in the end united with himself and with God. His mission now, we are given to understand, is to return to earth and tell the tale of his salvation. Although *Nightwood*'s inhabitants trudge the "savage path" (*Inf.,* II, 142) Dante's pilgrim started down, it reverses the moral structure of *The Divine Comedy* and confirms it at the same time. Both works are full of inversions (as in Canto XIX of the *Inferno*, which describes the upside-down popes), perversions, and, as Kenneth Burke theorized about *Nightwood,* "con-versions" as well. In both works, one's puzzling out these structural movements and counter-movements causes one to participate fully to the very end of possibilities, or, particularly in *Nightwood*'s case, to their real beginning.

The structures of *The Divine Comedy* and *Nightwood* exhibit movement not so much through plot but through an overall spatial design. Dante's readers have always delighted in trying to "draw" in their minds his amazing geography of hell, purgatory, and heaven, and some editors have gone further. The Dorothy Sayers translation, for example, contains complicated notes and diagrams explaining where the poet and his guide are at a particular moment. The basic mythic description of death and destruction as downward and of new life and resurrection as upward emerges in *The Divine Comedy* as the structural statement of the Middle Ages, but modern *Nightwood*'s metaphorical structures are also dominated by these Dantean features of images of descent, ascent, and turning. Characters in *Nightwood* are always falling down (for example, the "go down" or "bow down" phrase so often repeated refers to several things at the same time—it is a naughty joke, a suggestion of bowing down to an aristocratic past, a sleep, a falling, a dream,

a death, a prayer). Like stage directions, *Nightwood*'s frequent movements of turning call attention to the book's spatial relationships as well as its gradual abandonment of chronology (Kannenstine 124). Such a spatial organization calls for a reconstructive reader who is willing to put together what is presented as fragmentary, to build what is smashed, to find meaning where meaning seems at best confused or illusory or, at worst, absent.

Like *The Divine Comedy*, *Nightwood* presents a "static situation" in addition to its logical/chronological narrative; according to Frank, the reader will find facets of the situation explored from different angles: "The eight chapters of *Nightwood* are like searchlights, probing the darkness each from a different direction yet ultimately illuminating the same entanglement of the human spirit" (Frank 31-32). Much the same could be said of Dante's Cantos: the sins he sees in hell, for example, may be meticulously differentiated but are all the same human weaknesses in different guises—it may even be suggested that they are all Dante's sins. Dante carries several image clusters throughout his trilogy, as Sayers notes, including the Wood, the City, the Path, the Fall, and the Ascension. In a similar way, *Nightwood* contains patterns of meaning connected independently of time-sequence. What Frank says of *Nightwood* is just as true for *The Divine Comedy*: meaning is generally located in "reference and cross-reference of images and symbols that must be referred to each other spatially throughout the time-act of reading" (Frank 49).

And yet it is not true that *Nightwood* is "timeless," that if one is lost in the night wood the year and city do not matter (Spencer 43). These things *do* matter very much: *Nightwood* tells us, especially with Dante as a background, that the traditional kinds of salvation (Dr. O'Connor's Catholicism, for example) seem utterly impossible in the modern world. In spite of what some critics claim about the book's "timelessness," *Nightwood* is set in a very particular time, precisely in "the cosmopolitan world of displaced Europeans and expatriated Americans in the post World War I years," as Walter Sutton describes it. The world of *Nightwood* is largely Djuna Barnes's world. Yet *Nightwood*'s structure is also "flexible and adaptable, accommodating itself to every altered perspective in time" (Sutton 117, 120). Similarly, Dante tells his readers in Cantos I and II of the *Inferno* exactly what time of day it is, "Day was departing and the dusk drew on" (*Inf.,* II, 1), and further that the day is his thirty-fifth birthday, "Midway this way of life we're bound upon" (*Inf.,* I, 1). It is Easter Week, 1300. Dante continues throughout the entire poem to label each Canto with the time of day—"Good Friday, a.m.," or "Holy Saturday, p.m."—emerging from hell into purgatory at precisely 5 a.m. Easter Sunday. Dante means for his readers to realize that his universal and timeless poem also occurs in their own time.

The time overlay in **Nightwood,** though buried, is also very precise: one finds a chronology scattered throughout the 170 pages of **Nightwood** that begins with Felix, born in 1880 and married to Robin in 1922. Robin goes to live with Nora until she leaves for America with Jenny, whom she first meets in 1929. The final portions of the book take place in the 1930s. But time in **Nightwood** is charted very carefully up to the point of the separation of Robin and Nora, after which occurs a descent into a world "ultimately preconscious and ahistorical" (Kannenstine 94). This movement parallels Dante's leaving off of his careful chronology as he gets further and further into heaven, and perhaps the doctor in **Nightwood** thinks of Dante's redeeming dawn: "Dawn, of course, dawn! That's when she came back frightened. At that hour the citizen of the night balances on a thread that is running thin" (139).

In both works, the night wood is the scene of the descent of the soul, and the novel's whorled, rococo pattern of descent is carefully connected to its wood imagery—such a connection exists in the chapter title, "Where the Tree Falls," for example. In the **Inferno,** the image of woods appears at regular intervals in the descent into deeper and deeper rings of hell. At the very entrance to hell appears the frightening Dark Wood in which the pilgrim is lost:

> Ay, me! How hard to speak of it—that rude
> And rough and stubborn forest! the mere breath
> of memory stirs the old fear in the blood;
>
> It is so bitter, it goes nigh unto death
> Yet there I gained such good, that, to convey
> The tale, I'll write what else I found therewith.
> (*Inf.,* I, 4-9)

Turned aside from escape to the "right road" by three animals symbolic of the sins he will have to face in Hell, a Leopard (Incontinence), a Lion (Violence), and a Wolf (Fraud), and fleeing back into the wood, Dante meets the shade of Virgil, who tells him that one day a Greyhound (Christ) will come to drive the beasts away. For now the only escape is to travel a longer way, led by Virgil through hell and purgatory to be finally guided by Beatrice through heaven.

The woods reappear in Canto IV, when Dante describes the Limbo of the Great Pagans and Poets as "the wood (as'twere) / Of souls ranged thick as trees" (II. 65-66). Canto XIII, which takes place in Circle VII, Ring ii, of hell, the Violent Against Self, portrays the Wood of the Suicides, a dismal, pathless wood of withered trees that enclose the souls of suicides:

> No green here, but discolored leaves and dark,
> No tender shoots, but writhen and gnarled and
>   tough,

> No fruit, but poison-galls on the withered bark.
> (II. 4-6)

The gloom of the woods is disturbed by the shades of two profligates, flying through the forest eternally pursued and torn by black hounds and screeching Harpies. In this night wood of total despair Dante, urged by Virgil, tests the trees to discover what they are:

> So I put forth my hand a little way,
> And broke a branchlet from a thorn-tree tall;
> And the trunk cried out: "Why tear my limbs
>   away?"
>
> Then it grew dark with blood, and therewithal
> Cried out again: "Why dost thou rend my bones?
> Breathes there no pity in thy breast at all?
>
> We that are turned to trees were human once;
> Nay, thou shouldst tender a more pious hand
> Though we had been the souls of scorpions."
> (II. 31-39)

As the Florentine explains, "I am one that made my own roof-tree my scaffold" (II. 151). The denizens of the Wood of the Suicides committed the same sin the characters of **Nightwood** commit: they wantonly destroyed their own lives "turning to weeping what was meant for joy" (*Inf.,* XI, 45). Perhaps this is what O'Connor has in mind when he declares, ". . . now *nothing, but wrath and weeping*" (166). The connection between **Nightwood** and the Wood of the Suicides becomes clearer when one realizes that Dante and Virgil's next stop is the Burning Sand and the woods that fringe it—there they discover the Sodomites, located after the suicides in hell and just before the crossing of the Great Barrier into the lower third of hell, which contains those who committed the sin of Fraud. Violence and Incontinence are left behind, but these sins form a backdrop to the Sins of Fraud which will come. The Suicides and Sodomites in *The Divine Comedy* and **Nightwood** symbolize the sin of lovelessness, and lovelessness, we learn, underlies Fraud in both works as well.

In order to make the transition from Violence to Fraud, at the edge of the barrier cliff Virgil instructs Dante to throw down his rope girdle, which Dante remembers he had used earlier to capture the Leopard. The girdle is a symbol of his last holding onto and subsequent shedding of the lesser two sins he has so far faced. When the monster Geryon is called up by the girdle from the depths of hell, Dante and Virgil climb on his back and descend into the pit of Fraud. Geryon is an image of duality, his man's face belied by his "wyven's trunk." He is "painted with ring-knots and whorled tracery," "such dyes in warp and woof" as "Arachne's web." He is propelled by his tail, "twisting the venom fork in air /

Wherewith, like a scorpion's tail, its point was tipped" (*Inf.*, XVII, 10-27). Geryon continues *The Divine Comedy*'s pattern of turning and serves as a figure of Satan as well. He also has a correspondent in *Purgatorio*: the Gryphon of Canto XXXI in whom duality of form is resolved.

But resolution does not mean stasis in either *Nightwood* or *The Divine Comedy.* Each work has at the center a static, still figure around which the other characters and action move; for human beings, movement, not stasis, is offered as the life-giving force in both works. In hell, Dante finds the strange, three-sided, frozen figure of Satan, immobile in the center of the earth, caught forever in a vast lake of ice. Dante and Virgil actually climb down his trunk and at his center, his loins, find themselves reversed and climbing up to purgatory. As Virgil explains:

> "Thou think'st," he said, "thou standest as before
> You side the centre, where I grasped the hair
> Of the ill Worm that pierces the world's core.
>
> So long as I descended thou wast there;
> But when I turned, then was the point passed by
> Toward which all weight bears down from every
>   where.
> The other hemisphere doth o'er thee lie—
> Antipodal to that which land roofs in. . . ."
>
> (*Inf.*, XXXIV, 106-13)

The still center that paradoxically causes movement, reversal, even elevation, appears again as the Vision of the Light at the center of the Heavenly Rose: the Unmoved Mover, God Himself. Dante has gone down through hell to get to the still Satan, up through purgatory to get to the still God. Ironically, Satan furnishes Dante the avenue upwards; God sends him back down to earth to sing of heaven.

Robin Vote is the still center of *Nightwood.* All characters act through her and against her and because of her. She is something different to each character, and, although she is "La Somnambule," the unmoving sleeper, she is a catalyst for either damnation or salvation, a frightening figure to those who behold her. As Dante turned in disgust away from the frozen Satan, Nora sees in Robin her own worst designs of wrongful domination of another. She cannot stand to view Robin—and yet craves the sight of her. Perhaps Nora eventually learns merely to accept what she cannot assimilate, just as Dante tells us he accepts the too-bright Light of God without being able to stare into its secrets, but *Nightwood* ends on the "down note" of the climb down Satan's torso, before everything reverses and the possibilities of purgation are revealed.

I shall return to the question of *Nightwood*'s ending, but first I wish to address exactly how the novel's characters enact their Dantean journeys. Some characters are central: Dr. O'Connor, Nora, Robin. Others are representatives of the larger world of the story. Jenny and Felix, Robin's other lovers, stand out most clearly from the rest of the inhabitants of the might wood, the freaks, whores, transvestites, circus actors, and midgets. But as noted earlier, like Dante's characters, all of the characters of *Nightwood* are symbolic and must always be viewed in relation to one another; because of their symbolic nature, they take on reflexive meaning like the parts of a poem, a meaning found only in juxtaposition and cross-reference, not in logic. It is possible to arrange the major characters of both works in such a way as to point out their echoing interrelations:

O'Connor	*Nora*	*Robin*
Speaker	Heroine	Soul
Virgil/Prophet	Dante/Pilgrim	Beatrice/Satan
Sin of Incontinence	Sin of Violence	Sin of Fraud
Leopard	Lion	Wolf

Dr. O'Connor has been singled out as the hero of *Nightwood* by some writers, but although he is heroic in his attempt to hold onto his Catholicism in order to be saved, he knows he has failed and can only interpret his failure as instruction for others. His constant sin of Incontinence damns him, as does his condemnation of the others at the end of the chapter called "Go Down, Matthew." And yet perhaps he is not so much damned as set apart from salvation. The doctor is a prophet who can show the way but who cannot live in the Promised Land, a priest who can hear confession but who cannot grant absolution, a Virgil who can lead Dante only as far as the gate of heaven before returning to his Limbo. Dr. O'Connor is strongly associated with Tiresias, the blind hermaphroditic prophet of Greek mythology who was damned by Zeus for his garrulousness, particularly his foretelling of Zeus's own downfall. Like Tiresias, O'Connor sees the future but cannot change it; he must wander in his horrible awareness of the other souls through a wasted earth, as does Tiresias in Eliot's *The Waste Land.* Nora recognizes this role: "Doctor, I have come to ask you to tell me everything you know about the night" (79). Dr. O'Connor is the "Watchman of the Night."

Eliot emphasizes the doctor's "hypersensitive awareness" of other people's pain, his "desperate disinterestedness" and "deep humility." What "sends him raving" in the end is his "squeezing himself dry" and getting no sustenance in return (Introduction to *Nightwood* xiii). Frank sees the doctor as damned (by his excessive knowledge of evil, "which condemns him to a living death") and innocent at the same time (Frank 44-47). O'Connor's despair allows him to recognize despair in others and to help them, but there is nothing else he can do but talk to them. The doctor attempts to save Nora from her obsessive attachment to Robin through talk when she visits him in his one-room flat. She surprises him, finding him in tawdry dress and wig in his filthy, cramped bed. He speaks in long, chapter-length monologues on the state of the soul in the night world; at his feet sits a pail of excrement, fitting accompaniment to his spewing of words. As a chorus chants, as a prophet raves, O'Connor goes on and on—his woman's gown, symbol of his sexual disorientation, becoming the "natural raiment of extremity" worn by "infants, angels, priests, the dead" (80).

The doctor's agony is genuine, his lack of self-consciousness laudable. Yet too often his talk is not offered as the way to salvation, but merely as a distraction to help the listener endure. The doctor's monologue is not about how to overcome a loss, but how to bear it to death. Dr. O'Connor's Catholicism is much the same to him, since for him it offers comfort but no hope. He cannot attain the state Eliot prays for in "Ash Wednesday": "Teach us to care and not to care / Teach us to sit still." His deep involvement in the sufferings of others binds him to their fates, despite the pain that bond causes him:

> "Look here!" said the doctor.... "the liar I am!
> .... I talk too much because I have been made
> so miserable by what you're keeping hushed....
> Do you think, for Christ's sweet sake!" he said,
> and his voice was a whisper. "Now that you have
> all heard what you wanted to hear, can't you let
> me loose now, let me go? I've not only lived my
> life for nothing, but I've told it for nothing—
> abominable among the filthy people—I know, it's
> all over, everything's over, and nobody knows it
> but me—drunk as a fiddler's bitch—lasted too
> long—"He tried to get to his feet, gave it up.
> "Now," he said, "the end—mark my words—now
> *nothing, but wrath and weeping!*" (165-66)

The doctor has failed because he has found selfless love impossible to maintain toward other people and has long ago given up as hopeless any other kind of love.

Before turning to the other characters of *Nightwood,* let us note the position of Dr. O'Connor in *Ryder,* Barnes's first novel, since his spiritual agony there is carried over and expanded in *Nightwood.* His role as spiritual guide is formed in *Ryder;* his one monologue (the Doctor is a minor character) recalls the words of a priest, Father Lucas, at the funeral of the Doctor's younger brother:

> Look up, he says, and there you will see the Lamb
> of the Lord trampling out the small clouds and
> the great clouds and the indifferent clouds of
> heaven, grazing without sin, go thou and do like-
> wise. I'll do that, Father, says I, and please Moses

it's in my strength, but what with a dilator on my hip and the disease and distresses and distempers of man, and what they are prone to, coming into my mind, and before my eyes, and me restless, it's a devil bit of peace I'll get, says I, banging my head against the scrofula and the tapeworm and the syphilis and the cancer and the pectoris and the mumps and the glut and the pox of mankind, I says, and me with my susceptible orbs staring down into and up through the cavities and openings and fissures and entrances of my fellowman, and following some, and continuing others, and increasing many, and them swelling and opening and contracting and pinching like the tides of the sea, and me a mortal like the sea with my ebb and flow, and my good heart, and my thundering parts and my appetites and my hungers. (Barnes, *Ryder*, 174)

The doctor enters all the orifices of the human body as the Earth itself, leading as Virgil does down tunnels and up fissures to the very gate of heaven. His eyes become the searchlights to guide others; his knowledge of the deep allows him to show other lost souls the way out. Father Lucas answers:

> Visit me often, he says, and I'll give you comfort
> and kind words and a little consolation that shall
> inch thee on thy way a bit, and bring thee nearer
> the Celestial Gate, slip by slop, cleansing your
> soul as you go, that you may not enter altogether
> dusty and dirty and mucked before the Judgment
> Seat, with its two in front and its two behind and
> the four singing Holy! Holy! Holy! God save the
> behind, I said, and staggered out into the life and
> traffic of my days. . . . (Barnes, *Ryder,* 174)

In *Nightwood,* if the doctor himself does not discover hope, he at least helps Nora to the path of purgation, for Nora is the real pilgrim. A seeker of the Word held back by her sin of selfish Violence, Nora is fascinated by depravity, repressive in response perhaps to a Puritan ethic. Nora's fascination with degradation is rather like Dante's open-mouthed awe of hell's various grisly sins and punishments, and, like Dante, she identifies strongly with the sinners, and she finds harsh judgment of them difficult to abandon. Nora's selfish identification with Robin, her clutching recognition of the "double" she finds in Robin, leads eventually to Robin's annihilation. O'Connor warns Nora against her attentions to Robin, especially her giving Robin dolls and other toys to play with: "We give death to a child when we give it a doll—it's the effigy and the shroud; when a woman gives it to another woman, it is the life they cannot have, it is their child, sacred and profane . . ." (142). Nora and Robin represent the paradox that only through another can the pilgrim find herself, and yet if she does not find the strength to continue her search for her soul alone—alone in the last extremity and freed of her selfish personal designs on the other—she will destroy the other person, the vessel of her search. But Nora is afraid to let go of Robin. Attempting to convince her of this, the doctor calls up Dante's handling of Beatrice, which for him apparently represents a notable attempt to love and yet to continue the search for selfhood separately from the beloved:

> The doctor brought his palms together. "If you, who are bloodthirsty for love, had left her alone, what? Would a lost girl in Dante's time have been a lost girl still, and he had turned his eyes on her? She would have been remembered, and the remembered put on the dress of immunity. . . . The uninhabited angel! That is what you have always been hunting!" (148)

Nora loves in the only way she knows, and she loves too much; eventually, unlike Dante with Beatrice, she violently forces Robin into reacting to her possessive needs.

But like Dante, the pilgrim Nora's need for a journey downward to a confrontation with a demonic Robin is a need for confrontation with her soul. "Robin disfigured and eternalized by the hieroglyphics of sleep and pain" (63) becomes Nora's love object. Frustrated by Robin's lack of response to her designs and particularly irritated at Robin's immersion in a numbing round of night-time partying with people whom Nora considers depraved, Nora attempts the psychological rape of Robin. She forces Robin into a moment of intense contact in which Robin suddenly feels overwhelming guilt towards Nora. Nora then cruelly tries to "slap her out of it." Nora becomes for Robin an inaccessible Madonna of redemption and unspoken accusation, and Robin feels she must leave Nora to escape insanity—which condition overtakes her anyway, as one critic emphasizes, by the end of the book (Williamson 71).

After Robin leaves Nora for Jenny, Nora turns to the Doctor, who, in spite of himself, does shed light on Nora's predicament and helps her gain insight on what has happened to her. Like Dante with Virgil, Nora begins to assert herself more and more during the course of the Doctor's monologues—these monologues finally become dialogues in which Nora speaks as much as the Doctor, defining more and more clearly the nature of her problem. She seems much better able to address her guilt, loneliness, and failure by the end of their talks than when she first came to him in a broken state. What happens to her after she leaves him furnishes the last chapter of *Nightwood.*

Waking into consciousness in the first chapter of the novel and slipping down into darkness in the last chapter, Robin

is immobile like Satan in his ghastly ice; but she is also a Beatrice shining with the eternal light of heaven. She is whatever the other characters of *Nightwood* perceive her to be, for, as Frank notes, she is a "creation" symbolizing a state before good and evil—she is "meet of child and desperado." She is a "sleepwalker living in a dream from which she has not awakened—for awakening would imply a consciousness of moral value—Robin is at once completely egotistical and yet lacking in a sense of her own identity" (Frank 32-34). Felix says Robin is looking for someone to tell her she is innocent. Robin needs "permission to live" as a human being, for in the story she never rises above the state of moral possibility. Seemingly, only in the others', especially Nora's, acting through her can she effect any progress at all, and then only for the person associated with her. Robin's fall is the reverse of Nora's rise; Robin's role as inverted *exemplum* makes her very similar indeed to the sinners of Dante's hell.

In *Nightwood* Robin embodies the legend of humankind's "true history"—she is the carrier of the primal past nearly forgotten by civilized people. In her transformative state, however (she is Geryon *and* Gryphon), she also represents the possibility of a future, good or evil, for Robin suggests the soul in all its possibilities. This helps explain why she is so often presented in animal images. Her sin is Fraud, the sin of the Wolf in Dante's scheme; and yet because she herself is not capable of moral or immoral action, her Fraud occurs through another person—Jenny, the woman who steals her away from Nora. It is really Jenny's fraud which pervades Robin's personality, just as Nora's love is harmfully thrust upon her from outside. The doctor is right to contrast Nora's love for Robin to Dante's immortalizing of Beatrice and to recognize that Nora must learn to release Robin, as Dante learns not to desire conventional control over Beatrice as he did on earth, but to love her and himself in a new way.

As Dante's and Barnes's characters portray humanity debased and elevated, the image patterns uphold the dualism and simultaneous interconnectedness thematically and structurally implied. As I have mentioned, both Dante and Barnes weave a pattern of reflexively related symbols and images throughout their work; in their fragmented worlds, identity is an unstable process, a becoming instead of a having become. Meaning thus occurs through the juxtaposed, not the synthesized image: "An image is a stop the mind makes between uncertainties," as the Doctor defines it (III), and there are many of them. Images echo and reflect allusively instead of speaking in single certainties. Uncertain, and even dark, such an insight helps explain the situation in which the characters of *Nightwood* find themselves caught. Meaning will be, but will be as open to possibility as is Nora's spiritual state.

Nightwood evokes Dante's use of *figurae* that present an event or figure in sacred history as prefiguring another, as the burning bush is a *figura* of the Virgin Mary, the Virgin a *figura* of the spotless tomb. Such images illustrate what Jacques Maritain calls "intuitive" meaning to be found in the "preconceptual life of the intellect and the imagination. Two things are not compared, but rather one thing is made known through the image of another . . . . by the same stroke their similarity is discovered" (Maritain 329). James B. Scott discovers *figurae* in **Nightwood** when he calls the novel's imagery an "apprehended tableau" (Scott 106), which also describes Dante's vast setting for the salvation of a human soul.

The most significant shared image patterns of **Nightwood's** and *The Divine Comedy*'s "tableaus" are the night and wood images and the striking animal images. Dante's woods, I noted, form an extensive pattern in the *Inferno* and are carried over to the *Purgatorio*. The woods images are equally important in **Nightwood.** The characters are lost in the night wood of the novel's title, but beyond that wood in **Nightwood** is the wood of the cradle, church door, cross, and coffin. It is further associated with the "feminine principle of matter and mother (*materia, mater*)" (Burke 339). This association calls for attention, for in its link with blood, wood takes on greater mythic meanings. In Eliot's "Sweeny Among the Nightingales," Agamemnon "cries aloud within the bloody wood," and in **Nightwood,** wood is also tragic and deadly. It appears as a symbol of the loss of spiritual life in the richly carved furniture (such as Frau Mann's "bloody wood" cabinet, the toys, and the picture frames of **Nightwood**) (Weisstein 6). Kannenstine suggests further meanings for wood: it carries the connotation of "being out of one's mind, a condition which merges with being beyond or out of time." The night wood is in short "the medium for recurrence of all lost phenomena" (Kannenstine 125-26).

Images of animals remarkably similar to those of *The Divine Comedy* haunt Djuna Barnes's night wood. Like *The Divine Comedy*, the novel is full of descriptions of people as snakes, of bestial acts, of animals evolving into humans. Most significantly, Dante's Leopard, Lion, and Wolf take human forms in **Nightwood.** The doctor daubs himself with gaudy makeup like the Leopard with "painted skin" in Dante's poem (*Inf.,* XVI, 108). Like the gamboling Leopard, the doctor incontinently talks away in empty speculation his real chance to help those who call out to him. Nora is associated with the Lion of Violence. When she first meets Robin at the circus she leads her away from a lioness:

> . . . she turned her furious great head with its yellow eyes afire and went down, her paws thrust through the bars and, as she regarded the girl, as if a river were falling behind impassable heat, her eyes flowed in tears that never reached the surface. At that the girl rose straight up. Nora took her hand. "Let's get out of here!" the girl

said, and still holding her hand Nora took her out. (54)

The image comes up again when Nora is trying to explain herself to O'Connor. He responds to her "explanations" of her feelings towards Robin that "Lions grow their manes and foxes their teeth on that bread" (151). The Doctor refers to these two animals in their Biblical comparisons to Satan, whom the prophets call a raging lion and whom Jesus calls a wily fox. As Robin's animal is the Wolf of Fraud, she is repeatedly associated with dogs, especially in the conclusion. Nora fears to rearrange anything in their house, for fear that "if she disarranged anything Robin might lose the scent of home" (56). Mythologist Erich Neumann characterizes the dog as the animal of the Great Mother in her guise as Gorgon, or Artemis/Hecate, "mistress of the night road, of fate, and of the dead." The Gorgon's principal animal is "the dog, the howler by night, the finder of tracks, . . . the companion of the dead"; as "mistress of the way down and of the lower way," the feminine Goddess keeps by her side the Cerberus-like dog (Neumann 170).

There are other important parallels in the animal imagery of *The Divine Comedy* and **Nightwood.** The Harpies in Dante's Wood of the Suicides are remarkably like the characters Barnes describes as haunting the underworld of Paris and preying on the unwary traveller in its depths; furthermore, Jenny's association with birds of prey casts her as the novel's most destructive "Harpy." The dualistic Geryon/Gryphon figures, as I have noted, are quite significant to **Nightwood.** The Gryphon, an apocalyptic animal, is Dante's first sight after his immersion in the River Lethe:

> Thus did they chant, and thus they led me, right
> Up to the Gryphon's breast, where watchfully
> Beatrice gazed, and we stood opposite.
>
> "Take heed," said they, "spare not thine eyes, for we
> Have set thee afore the orbs of emerald
> Whence Love let fly his former shafts at thee."
>
> Myriad desires, hotter than fire or scald
> Fastened mine eyes upon the shining eyes
> That from the Gryphon never loosed their hold.
>
> Like sun in looking-glass, no otherwise,
> I saw the Twyform mirrored in their range,
> Now in the one, now in the other guise.
>
> Think Reader, think how marvellous and strange
> It seemed to me when I beheld the thing
> Itself stand changeless and the image change.
> (*Pur.,* XXXI, 112-26)

Dante stares into the eyes of Beatrice, which individually mirror the Gryphon; when the duality is reconciled, the divine and human Gryphon proceeds in a pageant to a newly flowering Tree of Knowledge on the way to the gate of heaven. Interestingly, Barnes alludes to this Canto when in her poem *The Antiphon* she describes a wooden table decoration which consists of the two halves of a gryphon which had once been a carousel car. This symbol of childhood was halved by the father in the poem with his saw, but it becomes the vehicle of the mother and daughter's "voyage" to mystical union. Dante's "beast / Which in two natures one sole person is," we recall, is a symbol of incarnation, of divine and human natures in the process of resolving themselves. In *Nightwood* Nora furnishes her house with Robin with "circus chairs, wooden horses bought from a ring of an old merry-go-round, . . ." and she sits in them, staring out of the window for Robin's return and crying for forgiveness (55). Robin, on the other hand, thinks of her life with Nora and her life in the streets as a "monster with two heads" (59).

Thus it seems Nora cannot forget her sin, as Dante forgets his in the River Lethe. But what happens to Nora in "The Possessed," the final scene of *Nightwood*? The description in this short coda is deliberately sparse and difficult to follow. We know Nora has been living for some time alone in America. Apparently, Robin has left Jenny and has been circling around Nora's house for days. Nora hears odd noises outside and follows "things rustling in the grass" to a chapel on top of a hill, described as a modern Chapel Perilous. "[C]ursing and crying," Nora "blindly, without warning, plunged into the jamb of the chapel door" (169). There she sees Robin cavorting before the altar with a frightened dog, then grovelling on the wooden floor of the church with the dog, "whining and waiting." All we hear of Nora is that "at the moment Nora's body struck the wood, Robin began going down." What is the outcome of these two falls?

Though this "sacrament" Nora witnesses in the lonely church seems an unusually bleak vision of despair, not everyone reads this ending as completely dark. Donald J. Greiner, for example, argues that Barnes's use of black humor, nowhere more explicit than in the final pages, offers a more positive reading of *Nightwood* than most approaches: black humor in *Nightwood* ". . . uses comedy to encourage sympathy as well as to expose evil; it suggests futurity; it celebrates comic distortion as an indication that anything is possible. . . . " Black humor provides the opportunity to face up to ugliness and failure in the post-World War I world of *Nightwood,* and in so doing it offers hope for the characters' central thematic struggle *to become* human beings (Greiner 44-45). Alan Singer's analysis of metaphor and narrative claims that the act of creating artistic language itself offers hope in *Nightwood;* he suggests that "the true 'tragedy' of *Nightwood* lies not in the characters' failures but in

the critical interpretation that fails to acknowledge the reconstructive possibilities latent in authorial self-consciousness" (Singer 87). Lynn DeVore claims, in a similar attempt to redress the "unbalanced and tarnished image" *Nightwood* has retained, that a biographical study of the novel, particularly the identification of Nora with Barnes herself, allows the reader to "humanize" the novel. He also mentions the positive ramifications of the conclusion's "allegorical intentions," though he does not specify what these intentions are (DeVore 71, 86-89). Despite these insights, however, Nora's reaction to her vision of Robin in the conclusion has not been fully addressed.

One needs the Dantean context to read the ending. In the conclusion Barnes orchestrates all the dualisms of the descent/ascent pattern in the book with the Dantean wood and animal imagery; Robin's going down is carefully linked to Nora's hitting the wooden door of the church. What happens is simultaneously very precise and quite unresolved. Doorways have been important throughout *Nightwood* and *The Divine Comedy.* Nora earlier describes the streets of Marseilles, Tangiers, and Naples: "In open doorways nightlights were burning all day before gaudy prints of the Virgin" (157). The action of the last chapter takes place "on a contrived altar, before a Madonna, two candles . . . burning" (169). The doorway suggests the chapel as a place of transition, a place of hope—a new kind of wood. While Robin·is lost, Nora falls not into death but into a transformative state which leaves open the possibility that she has come to terms with her own sin, her abuse of Robin's freedom. She is at last able to fall down, to "bow down" or "go down"; symbolically she is ready to enter purgatory and move towards the cleansing waters of forgetfulness and salvation. The wood of the chapel door is no longer the Wood of the Suicides, but the wood of the Gryphon, the Tree of Knowledge Dante rises to behold on the way from purgatory to heaven. There is even a suggestion in the narrator's "struck the wood" of the phrase "knock on wood," which comes from the belief that the wood of the True Cross could protect the person who touched it. Nora has left the haunted night wood and entered the woods of the transformative Gryphon, a wood that becomes a garden.

This reading of the ending of *Nightwood* is prefigured by several earlier statements in the book. Nora thinks thoughts of the "resurrection, when we come up looking backward at each other . . ." (58). We are reminded in the ending of the Doctor's statements that "A man is whole only when he takes into account his shadow as well as himself—and what is a man's shadow but his upright astonishment?" (119-20) and "The unendurable is the beginning of the curve of joy" (117). Nora's vision of Robin's fall may serve to lift her up and free her from her selfish misunderstanding of Robin's nature—and more importantly of her own soul's nature. She may become a real self through self-knowledge—instead of through possessive, designing self-satisfaction. Earlier the Doctor tells Felix that " . . . [A]ll dreadful events are of profit" (119), and here in the conclusion he recognizes what Nora will eventually comprehend when she awakens: "O Widow Lazarus! Arisen from your dead!" (137).

The last paragraphs of *Nightwood* ask, "What happens now?" It seems that Dante will return to earth to write his poem of heavenly love, while we do not know what will become of Nora. But in this last scene, the Dantean model teaches us that, after this fall in the transformative wood of the church door, Nora can rise to continue living—and perhaps, if we take the metafictive view suggested by DeVore, to write the story itself. The act of turning, of movement upwards and outwards, is there for the reader, too, who is forced to turn away from the dual vision of the end, of Robin collapsed with a dog on the floor, of Nora held in the church door in a trance of stillness, just as Dante turns away abruptly from his supreme evil, the motionless Satan, *and* his supreme good, the motionless God. There is hope for reader as well as character in *Nightwood*'s Dantean dualities, for its end is clearly a call for a movement towards futurity.

WORKS CITED

Alighieri, Dante. *The Comedy of Dante Alighieri, The Florentine: L'Inferno, Il Purgatorio, Il Paradiso*. Trans. Dorothy L. Sayers. Baltimore, MD: Penguin Books, 1949.

Barnes, Djuna. *The Antiphon*. New York: Farrar, Straus & Cudahy, 1958.

———. *A Book*. New York: Boni and Liveright, 1923.

———. *Nightwood*. Introduction by T. S. Eliot. 1937; rpt. New York: New Directions, 1961.

———. *Ryder*. New York: St. Martin's Press, 1956.

Burke, Kenneth. "Version, Con-, Per-, and In-: Thoughts on Djuna Barnes's Novel, *Nightwood*." *Southern Review* 2 (1966-67): 329-46.

DeVore, Lynn. "The Backgrounds of *Nightwood*: Robin, Felix, and Nora." *Journal of Modern Literature* 10 (1983): 71-90.

Fadiman, Clifton. Review of *Nightwood* by Djuna Barnes. *The New Yorker* (13 March 1937): 83-84.

Frank, Joseph. "Spatial Form in Modern Literature." In his *The Widening Gyre: Crisis and Mastery in Modern Literatures*. Bloomington: Indiana UP, 1963. 3-62.

Greiner, Donald J. "Djuna Barnes' *Nightwood* and the American Origins of Black Humor." *Critique: Studies in Modern Fiction* 17 (1975): 41-54.

Hyman, Stanley Edgar. "The Wash of the World (Djuna Barnes)." In his *Standards: A Chronicle of Books for Our Time*. New York: Horizon Press, 1966. 58-62.

Kannenstine, Louis F. *The Art of Djuna Barnes: Duality and Damnation*. New York: New York UP, 1977.

Maritain, Jacques. *Creative Intuition in Art and Poetry*. New York: Pantheon, 1953.

Neumann, Erich. *The Great Mother*. Trans. Ralph Manheim. Princeton: Princeton UP, 1963.

Scott, James B. *Djuna Barnes*. Boston: Twayne, 1976.

Singer, Alan. "The Horse Who Knew Too Much: Metaphor and the Narrative of Discontinuity in *Nightwood*." *Contemporary Literature* 25 (1984): 66-87.

Spencer, Sharon. *Space, Time and Structure in the Modern Novel*. Chicago: The Swallow Press, 1971.

Steiner, George. "The Cruellest Months." *The New Yorker* (22 April 1972): 134-42.

Sutton, Walter. "The Literary Image and the Reader: A Consideration of the Theory of Spatial Form." *Journal of Aesthetics and Art Criticism* 16 (1957): 112-23.

Weisstein, Ulrich. "Beast, Doll, and Woman: Djuna Barnes's Human Bestiary." *Renascence* 15 (1962): 3-11.

Williamson, Alan. "The Divided Image: The Quest for Identity in the Works of Djuna Barnes." *Critique: Studies in Modern Fiction* 7 (1964): 58-74.

Ahmed Nimeiri (essay date Winter 1993)

SOURCE: "Djuna Barnes's *Nightwood* and 'the Experience of America,'" in *Critique*, Vol. XXXIV, No. 2, Winter, 1993, pp. 100-12.

[*In the following essay, Nimeiri discusses the symbolic significance of the Americanness of the characters in Barnes's* Nightwood.]

Since the American publication of Djuna Barnes's *Nightwood* in 1937, critics have focused on the formal aspects of the novel and have paid little attention to its content. This tendency has prompted Lynn DeVore to complain that "The book's linguistic complexities . . . have . . . directed critics to analyze especially the form and structure of the text as well as to speak only of its verbal tapestry in terms of imagistic, expressionistic, cubistic, or surrealist affinities while slighting its altogether human dimensions" (71). Even when critics find meaning in the novel, it is often abstract with no bearing on any particular situation, as if the story occurs in a void or a dream-world where the characters move about in a landscape of metaphors, images, and myths. This view of the novel ignores, regards as irrelevant, or even denies the existence of the obvious experiential context and its decisive effect on determining the theme. Leslie Fiedler, who virtually dismisses *Nightwood* as being little more than verbosity and expressionism, in his brief discussion of it in *Love and Death in the American Novel*, exemplifies this kind of criticism in its extreme form. Noting "the dislocated lyricism, hallucinated vision, and oddly skewed language of Miss Barnes's black little book," he concludes that "Linguistically, *Nightwood* is too complex, and thematically, it is too little concerned with the experience of America to achieve even the belated and limited success of West's work" (490). This reading of the novel, which is paraphrased and only slightly modified in the majority of subsequent criticism, is more appropriate to John Hawkes's *The Cannibal*, a book that portrays, in difficult personal idiom, Europe after the Second World War and that deals minimally with America, than it is to *Nightwood*. But what Fiedler says about Barnes's novel is still important because he inadvertently draws attention to its main theme. A careful reading will show that *Nightwood* is primarily concerned with "the experience of America" and that its real achievement is in expressing an original though dark and desperate vision of this experience. Gerald Nelson is the only critic who sees *Nightwood* as centrally concerned with America. Yet his "versions of America" in *Nightwood* are more abstractions than real expressions of the "experience of America." O'Connor, for example, represents "the entire history and soul of mankind in one body" (103).

The novel pictures the American, who migrates to Europe to find the nourishment for and fulfillment of the humanity he is deprived of at home, as encountering and embracing, in Europe, forms of the American experience that oppose his efforts to achieve a human stature and that finally strip him of his humanity. American expatriation, therefore, is not a pilgrimage to a new life away from America but an experience that ends in a retreat and entrapment into a life more sinister than that which has initially prompted the American to leave his country.[1]

Barnes gives enough clues to her concern with America so that the careful reader will not miss it. The major characters, with the exception of Felix, are American and their Americanness is not incidental but the hallmark of their per-

sonalities and the aspect that explains their actions and relations. Robin's Americanness, for example, draws Felix to her. When Matthew O'Connor asks him about the woman he wants to marry, Felix says "the American" and explains that "with an American anything can be done" (39). Thus he indicates that innocence is the essence of the American character. Similarly, Nora's Americanness is obviously central to an understanding of her character and role. She is described in terms that recreate the characteristic images of the American past (although Barnes may be making fun of Nora and what she represents):

> She was known instantly as a Westerner. Looking at her, foreigners remembered stories they had heard of covered wagons; animals going down to drink; children's heads, just as far as the eyes, looking in fright out of small windows, where in the dark another race crouched in ambush. . . .

> At . . . meetings [in Nora's salon] one felt that early American history was being re-enacted. The Drummer Boy, Fort Sumter, Lincoln, Booth, all somehow came to mind; Whigs and Tories were in the air. (50-51)

The significance of Jenny's Americanness becomes clear when she takes Robin back to America and thus makes a significant part of the action shift and conclude there. With such a conclusion it is difficult not to consider the effect of the specific identity of the characters on the meaning of the book.

O'Connor seems to be the one character whose nationality is irrelevant to his role as seer, commentator, and interpreter of experience. But O'Connor himself insists, occasionally, on being an American and describes himself in a way that indicates that, in essence, he is not different from the other American characters. When Felix says to him, "But you are American, so you don't believe," the doctor answers, "because I'm American I believe anything . . ." (40). This qualification of himself becomes meaningful when we have a deeper sense of his role, and the aspect of his personality he stresses here will be seen as more real and permanent than other aspects. His Catholicism, homosexuality, and intellectualism give the sense of being assumed to protect him against the chaos in the middle of which he lives.

A more important clue to Barnes's concern with "the experience of America" is in the conversation between the doctor and Nora in "Watchman, What of the Night" where the doctor speaks of the night and the realities excluded from normal civilized life. He contrasts two ways of apprehending reality, one American and the other French or European; he argues that unlike Europe, America banishes from its life some of the essential aspects of experience and consciousness because it cannot tolerate them. Later in the novel when O'Connor discusses Robin with Felix and, in another conversation, with Nora, we realize that this contrast is an index to both Robin's character and the novel.

But perhaps the most important clue is that the introduction of Robin, as a somnambulist and an American, marks the dramatic beginning of the book. The account of the marriage of Guido and Hedvig, which T. S. Eliot in his introduction to *Nightwood* calls the "opening movement" that is "slow and dragging" (xii), is a prologue to a story that really begins when their son, Felix, meets and marries the American somnambulist. The complications in the narrative develop after this point. The marriage and its breakdown lead to the series of actions, relations, and speculations that makes up the main body of *Nightwood.*

The structure of the novel clarifies the meaning that these clues only hint at or refer to broadly. Critics of *Nightwood* have observed that its structure rests on the relationship between two plots: one centers around Robin Vote and the people who are attracted to her, and the other deals with Dr. Matthew O'Connor and his effort to bring Felix and Nora to an awareness of the magnitude of their predicaments and to help them free themselves of the traumatic effects of their love of Robin. But the structure of the book is more complex than this. In addition to the two plots, there is the story of Felix that begins as a separate story, then merges into the Robin plot, but reaches a separate resolution in the final "bowing down" of Felix, which presages O'Connor's disintegration and Robin's descent into bestiality. Nora and Jenny each have chapters ("Night Watch" and "The Squatter") that, because of their focus on the characters of the two women, are almost complete in themselves. This fragmentariness has induced Joseph Frank to claim that *Nightwood* lacks a narrative structure in the ordinary sense and that its eight chapters "are like searchlights, probing the darkness each from a different direction, yet ultimately focusing on and illuminating the same entanglement of the human spirit" (438). The narrative in *Nightwood* is a complicated one that defies efforts to find coherence in it. Sharon Spencer expresses a typical reaction when she remarks that "there is absolutely no explanation of surprising or even bizarre events or relationships" (41) in the novel. This, however, is only partially true. The book may lack logical development, yet its parts are bound together by the thought and meaning that its story only insinuates but that come out more clearly in the speeches and conversations. Barnes concentrates on ideas and develops them carefully and in such a manner that the novel reads like an argument that moves from one chapter to the next achieving coherence gradually.

The progression of the novel is thematic. Narrative, which is subordinated to theme, illustrates and clarifies ideas and gives them logical form. O'Connor who says, "I have a narrative but you will be put to it to find it" (97), draws attention to the peculiar character of *Nightwood.* He acts minimally and talks all the time; although his conversations and monologues are sometimes vague and incomprehensible, they reveal clearly the novel's emphasis on ideas and stress the precedence of thought over action. In "Watchman, What of the Night," O'Connor spouts a long disquisition on the night in answer to Nora's inquiry about the subject. What he says provides the groundwork of ideas on which the novel stands. But in another and more immediate sense O'Connor's dissertation on the night paves the way for the story that O'Connor tells when Jenny steals Robin from Nora. He says, reminding Nora of the purpose of his talk: "'But I'm coming by degrees to the narrative of the one particular night that makes all other nights seem like something quite decent enough . . . '" (99). The implication here is that without O'Connor's exposition, that is, without a prior statement of ideas, his narrative is incomprehensible because it has no inherent meaning. The elucidated narrative reciprocally clarifies the ideas in O'Connor's speech. This strategy is employed repeatedly and makes the novel virtually locked in thought.

Nightwood may best be described in the terms that Melville uses to distinguish two modes of expression in *The Confidence-Man*, a book that resembles Barnes's novel in many ways, as a "comedy of thought" rather than a "comedy of action" (71). This dominance of thought and the sense of the novel's developing an argument rather than a narrative gives the characters clear symbolic roles. When the symbolism of the characters is examined, one understands that *Nightwood* cannot be explained completely without taking into consideration the fact that the characters are American. The novel is structured in such a way that the characters, in their symbolic roles, reveal aspects of and make statements about the American experience. This is why Nora and Jenny are given whole chapters and greater prominence than they would have in a realistic novel. The difficulties *Nightwood* poses are resolved when one sees its structure as deliberate and necessary. The first chapter seems redundant and not part of the novel unless we see the pathetic situation of the Jew as providing an appropriate explanation and a frame of reference for the predicament of the American innocent who strives to transcend his innocence and achieve a human identity. The Jew and the innocent, being close to each other in their positions on the periphery of history and experience, come together in a doomed union that inevitably fails in "La Somnambule." The American is then thrust back into his native experience represented by Nora and Jenny in the following two chapters. The next chapter, in which O'Connor discourses on the night, provides insights into the preceding chapters and expresses ideas that form the philosophical basis of the novel. At this point O'Connor emerges as the alternative to Robin, representing the American intellectual who has gone through experience but only in his mind. The rest of the novel—the last three chapters—constitutes a resolution and reveals the failure and disintegration of the main characters. The fall of Felix in "Where the Tree Falls" prefaces that of O'Connor in "Go Down, Matthew" and Robin in "The Possessed." It is notable that, at the end of their tragic experiences, the American characters return to America. Twice Barnes specifically concludes chapters with Robin's going back to America to start a new life after failing to find fulfillment in Europe. Following the breakdown of her marriage, Robin returns to America where she meets Nora; "La Somnambule" concludes with O'Connor explaining that during her three or four months' absence from Paris Robin has been "In America, that's where Nora lives" (49). Again after breaking up with Nora, Robin goes to America with Jenny and "The Squatter" ends with: "it was not long after this that Nora and Robin separated; a little later Jenny and Robin sailed for America" (77). At the end of "Go Down, Matthew," when the doctor breaks down, the ex-priest who has bought him a drink twice offers to take him home: "The ex-priest repeated, 'Come, I'll take you home'" (165). In the context of the novel, "home" becomes more than the doctor's dingy room.

The structure of *Nightwood* conveys strongly the sense of the inevitable return of the American to America, which, translated into thematic terms, expresses the failure of American expatriation. At the end of the novel we become aware of two related images of the American in search of a meaningful experience outside America: one case ends in a retreat to America and regression into the most primitive forms of the self, and the other case, ends in total estrangement from himself and from other human beings and a fall into a void of meaninglessness. In both cases the questing American discovers that he is as constricted in Europe as he has been in America. Barnes indicates the tragic consequences of expatriation from the beginning through nature imagery, especially animal imagery that illustrates the descent into bestiality and the retreat to a primitive life as the end result of American expatriation. The central image is that of the "tree of night", which gives the novel its title. The image comprehends the realities that are excluded from American life and suppressed in the American consciousness. O'Connor argues that

> To think of the acorn it is necessary to become the tree. And the tree of night is the hardest to mount, the dourest tree to scale, the most difficult of branch, the most febrile to the touch, and sweats a resin and drips a pitch against the palm that computation has not gambled. (83-84)

Nightwood delineates the effort of the American expatriate to climb the "tree of night," his plight and failure, and the final draining of his humanity as a result of the endeavor. The sense that the American in his country faces a dearth of experience that threatens to make his life vacuous and senseless is strongly suggested not through realistic details or drama, because the novel obviously eschews realism, but in general through its form, language, and mode. The thin plot with its scanty action and the heightened language that blurs what little narrative there is combine with the self-reflexivity to produce a distinct impression that the world the characters inhabit has little significant life and much mental activity. O'Connor's incessant talk has the added structural function of filling the recurring gap created frequently by the absence of story, but his words only make what is missing conspicuous.

The plight of the American expatriate is prepared for by a description of the predicament of the Jew in "Bow Down" that serves to put the position of the expatriate in proportion.[3] By characterizing Guido and Felix Volkbein in extreme terms Barnes illustrates the futile effort of the alienated Jew to come into history and experience. Guido's life expresses "the sum total of what is the Jew" (2), that is, the degradation and dehumanization that have made up the fate forced on the Jew. The image, in Guido's memory, of Jews in 1468 led with ropes about their necks into the Corso for the amusement of Christians sums up that fate and is an image that foreshadows Robin's transformation into a beast at the end of the novel. Guido's endeavor to free himself from this fate is a costly venture that leads to the distortion and effacement of his character. His marriage to "a Viennese woman of great strength and military beauty" (1) should earn him a place in society and history but only makes his position sad and ridiculous: "He tried to be one with her by adoring her, by imitating her goose-step of a stride that by him adopted became dislocated and comic" (3). He lives in a sham world of deception and gives the unmistakable sense of burlesquing life rather than living it. The son fares worse than the father and expresses the hopelessness of ending the alienation of the Jew. Felix is a degenerate version of Guido and more emphatically an outcast. Described as a Wandering Jew who goes everywhere without belonging to any place, he mixes, in his perception of the world, history and experience with make-believe and legend and avoids the rigor of his father's life by associating himself with the "pageantry of the circus and the theatre" where "he had neither to be capable nor alien" (11).

The pathetic situation of the Jew anticipates a worse and more tragic fate for the American. Felix's attraction and marriage to Robin and his steadfast friendship with O'Connor expresses the connection of the Jew and the American. The role of the Jew in *Nightwood* is similar to that of the Jew in Hemingway's *The Sun Also Rises*. Both characters are placed at the beginning of stories of American expatriation, thus indicating an affinity between the Jew and the expatriate. In both novels the Jew represents the fate that the American strives to avoid by leaving his country in quest of life and awareness; instead he falls into a worse one. Felix Volkbein is more complex than Robert Cohn and represents the historical experience of the Jew more clearly, but the two characters do not go beyond the stereotype of the Jew.

The first chapter of **Nightwood** also describes the milieu in which American expatriation exists. It teems with images of extreme alienation and decadence: Guido walking "incautious and damned" (2), Hedvig "moving toward him in recoil" (3), Frau Mann who "was as unsexed as a doll" (13), and the false barons, duchesses, princes and kings of the circus and theatre. Such a description makes clear from the beginning that the American who seeks to replace America by Europe as his right and proper experience is inadvertently opting for spiritual death and is doomed to be an outsider in Europe allying himself with the alien and decadent. This condition finally brings out the primitive in him—the aspect of himself he strives to transmute into human qualities—and allows it to dominate his character. This is precisely what Robin is ensnared in and cannot escape.

Robin represents a simple and common form of American expatriation. She is the American innocent (somnambulist) who goes or is taken to Europe to be free of the parochialism of her country and to get a cosmopolitan experience, a descendant of Henry James's innocent migrants exemplifying the trait in its most extreme form. Robin is first introduced in a fainting fit from which she cannot be brought out until Dr. O'Connor is summoned. Later the doctor and Nora characterize her innocence more clearly. O'Connor, referring to Robin, states that "to be utterly innocent . . . would be to be utterly unknown, particularly to oneself" (138), and Nora remarks that "Robin can go anywhere, do anything . . . because she forgets" (152). This lack of awareness of the self and the world indicates that Robin is, as the doctor describes her, "outside the 'human type'" (146). Hers is a state of being that precedes human experience and that is connected with animal and plant life. The room where she faints, which is a jungle of exotic plants and flowers, symbolically expresses this connection, and the description of Robin in the room emphasizes her relationship to primitive life. "Her flesh was the texture of plant life, and beneath it one sensed a frame, porous and sleep-worn, as if sleep were a decay fishing her beneath the visible surface" (34). Barnes speaks of Robin's innocence as mixed with depravity—Robin is "meet of child and desperado" (35)—and presents it as inert and almost lifeless. These are perhaps the normal features of innocence given an extreme form, but Barnes adds to the familiar picture the suggestion that the trait has now lost its human content. The general manner and the poetic language she uses to describe Robin in "La Somnambule" have the effect of abstracting human qualities from the character and insinuating that Robin has no palpable presence

in the world. Barnes wraps her in an anonymity that effaces her almost completely and, instead of referring to her directly and specifically, she speaks of "the woman," "such a woman" and "such a person." The rest of the novel continues to suggest that Robin does not exist independently in her own right, although she is often the fulcrum of the story. She is never characterized clearly; instead we have mediations on her by the author and the other characters.[4] In this way, Barnes shows that American innocence in the twentieth century has become so entrenched in itself and so removed from human intercourse that it has turned into an inhuman condition.

Robin cannot attain humanity in America and thus has to become an expatriate because America condemns and excludes the dark realities that are associated with her innocence and that are represented in the novel by such metaphors as the night, the forest, the beast and "filthiness." Conversely, Europe accommodates and regards these traits as an integral part of man's being. This is, in fact, the main point of O'Connor's discourse on the night in "Watchman, What of the Night." He tells Nora:

> The night and the day are two travels, and the French . . . alone leave testimony of the two in the dawn; we tear up the one for the sake of the other; not so the French . . . because they think of the two as one continually. (82)

and

> The French have made a detour of filthiness— Oh, the good dirt! Whereas you are of a clean race, of a too eagerly washing people, and this leaves no road for you. (84)

Robin's tragedy, however, is that her expatriation does not vindicate and accommodate her essential innocence. Like most American expatriates in the 1920s, she lives in Europe without being involved in its life, associating mainly with other American expatriates, and therefore never experiencing Europe.[5] Her significant relationships in Europe are limited to Felix, O'Connor, Nora, and Jenny. None of these characters is truly European.

Robin's marriage to Felix and the breakdown of the marriage indicate that, outside America, the American is doomed to share the perpetual alienation of the outcast and never to become a part of a meaningful experience. The marriage is a traumatic affair for Robin because, instead of realizing herself in it, she is more terribly exploited than her antecedent, Isabel Archer in Henry James's *A Portrait of a Lady*. Felix wants to reproduce and perpetuate himself without bowing down, that is, without the effort of adjusting himself to forms and conventions. But at the same time he wants Robin to give up her otherness and become part of him. This negation of her otherness, which is repeated in a sinister form in her relationships with Nora and Jenny, becomes the main feature of her experience in Europe. Felix only offers her a travesty of the values that make life meaningful; and, unlike his father, he is not even good at deception. The perversity and the futility of the marriage are evidenced by its product, the sickly child Guido, the most alienated character in *Nightwood* and the one associated with death more than life.

Awareness of the reality of her situation after the birth of her child does not prompt Robin, as in the case of Isabel Archer, to put her life in order. She sinks into despair and moves about blindly and purposelessly, thus exposing the inadequacy and helplessness of her innocence before the complexity of life. Felix sums up her position later in the novel when he describes her as one "who must get permission to live, and if [she] finds no one to give her that permission, she will make an innocence for herself; a fearful sort of primitive innocence" (117). Robin, indeed, makes for herself "a fearful sort of primitive innocence" after her separation from Felix. The trauma of her marriage throws her back to the American experience and into herself: she relates to her own race and sex. A lesbian affair, as described by Nora, is a relation to oneself that precludes otherness: "A man is another person—a woman is yourself, caught as you turn in panic; on her mouth you kiss your own" (143). Robin's lesbian affairs with American women are endeavors to attain humanity by identifying with aspects of the American experience represented by Nora and Jenny.

Nora, who is presented in "Night Watch" in such a way as to suggest a composite image of early America (Puritan, pioneer, and, in a sense, romantic and transcendentalist), represents the persistence of the past in the present. By this symbolic role she demonstrates that the past is not an invigorating influence on the present and that its immanence in the present does not bestow firmness and solidity on the fluid and, perhaps, volatile, living reality. At first Nora offers Robin an apparently meaningful life, but soon this life becomes senseless and empty because of Nora's protean and alienated character. Her love for Robin is really self-love. She tells the doctor that Robin "is myself" (127) and that "I thought I loved her for her sake, and I found it was for my own" (151). This possessiveness sometimes takes the form of an intolerance of Robin's occasional displays of vitality and joy, especially when these occur in contexts that Nora condemns as corrupt and evil. She tells O'Connor that she has tried to save Robin when Robin was drunk and gay and people were laying "dirty hands" on her. The scene ends in Nora's house where Robin falls asleep, and Nora is kissing her and saying, "Die now, so you will be quiet, so you will not be touched again by dirty hands, so you will not take my heart and your body and let them be nosed by dogs—

die now, then you will be mine forever (144-145). The same idea of Robin's death being a condition of Nora's love has been expressed before in "Night Watch": "Nora knew . . . that there was no way but death. In death Robin would belong to her" (58). Nora is like Emily Grierson in Faulkner's "A Rose for Emily" in conceiving of love as the negation of freedom and otherness. But Nora's spiritual necrophilia, which is more extreme than Emily's because of Nora's rationalization of it, becomes meaningful when seen as stemming from her symbolic role as a representative of the American past. This past is pictured in *Nightwood* as a life-killing legacy that destroys all the vestiges of humanity in the American. Significantly, the last scene in the novel takes place in Nora's estate and describes Robin's transformation into a beast. The sense of an America dominated by the past and dehumanizing its people is unmistakable and strong.

In opposition to Nora, Jenny has no sense or relation to the past. Presented in extreme terms, she has no real being; what she has is either borrowed or stolen. Four times a widow, she is not a giver but a robber of life. She stands for emptiness and vacuity and represents a persistent reality in America that is mediocre and lethal. Barnes maintains a steady invective tone in presenting and describing Jenny Petherbridge as if she is disclaiming her and wants to purge the narrative of her.[6] Robin's choice of Jenny, in spite of what Jenny represents, expresses a despair that speeds her to her end as a human being. The forfeiture of her humanity is prefigured in "The Squatter" when Jenny strikes and scratches her until she bleeds and sinks down. That the scene ends in Nora's garden indicates that Nora's repression is responsible for Robin's falling into Jenny's grip.

O'Connor seems at first to avoid Robin's fate of being trapped in certain positions and disintegrating as a result. Unlike the other characters he appears in control of experience and of his destiny. The compound name that he gives himself, Dr. Matthew-Mighty-Grain-of-Salt-Dante-O'Connor and his characterization of himself as one who knows everything suggest an effort to be all-encompassing. But we realize from his first appearance that his character is assumed and his situation unreal. He is introduced as taking the place of Count Onatorio Altamonte, who is "related to every nation" (14), as host to a group of people. The Count shows up only to dismiss the party, and the fatuity of O'Connor's situation becomes apparent. Later in the novel Felix is shocked to see the doctor looking old and exhausted. Then "the Baron hailed him, and instantly the doctor threw off his unobserved self, as one hides hastily, a secret life" (110). O'Connor is engaged most of the time in cultivating an image of himself as a sage and seer. Although he talks a great deal about himself, he seems concerned with great and universal experiences. Sometimes this contradiction makes him absurd, especially when he turns simple common remarks into poetic statements charged with meaning. When Felix asks him, in their first meeting: "Are you acquainted with Vienna?" He answers: "Vienna . . . the bed into which the common people climb, docile with toil, and out of which the nobility fling themselves, ferocious with dignity—I do but not so well but that I remember some of it still" (17). He frequently presents his opinion "with such conviction and in such general terms that the reader has little cause to doubt it" until the author expresses its fallaciousness by presenting instances of the truth (Greiner 51). We realize at the end, when O'Connor breaks down, that his speeches are carefully worked out to produce a calculated effect. He describes himself as being "damned and carefully public" (163), suggesting that he strives by talk and expatriation to avoid falling into particular experiences and becoming limited by them. He implicitly justifies his expatriation—in the contrast he makes between Europe and America—as an option for the right way of living and apprehending life. In his speeches he endeavors continuously to demonstrate his apprehension by transforming particular experiences into abstract ideas.

O'Connor's talk is the hallmark of his character and an important clue to understanding his role. He brings to mind at once Melville's confidence-man who is described (125) by a character he meets as "a talking man—what I call a wordy man. You talk, talk," and as a "punster" who puns "with ideas as another may with words."[7] Like Melville's protagonist he assumes different guises. Even his profession, compulsions, and sexual inclinations suggest that they are parts of a persona more than real aspects of a character. O'Connor is a degenerated and vulgarized form of the confidence-man as conceived by Melville. He lacks the control and mastery over experience and people and the sense of purpose that distinguishes the original character. The difference between the two characters appears in the way their talk functions in each novel and the effect it produces on the ethos of their world. In *The Confidence-Man*, talk takes the form of a colloquy in which the confidence-man, by the adept use of words, brings a person to his position and persuades him to accept his assumptions about the human condition or, failing this, exposes the inconsistency and absurdity of the other's situation. By this procedure the confidence-man strips the community of its prejudices and pretensions and brings out the evil in man's heart, revealing at the same time the snares of language and thought that lay waiting to trap and lead astray the unwary and the simple. But the confidence-man's activity and its result imply that there is shared language and values between the trickster and his victims—even if they are revealed to be false values. Not so in *Nightwood*. There is no true communication between the novel's confidence-man and those he tricks into listening to him. Sometimes we feel that Barnes deliberately intends that the difficulty and vagueness of O'Connor's speeches should alienate the reader in order to stress the absence or impossibility of communication in the modern world. The doctor often seems to be speaking to himself even when he is addressing other people, and we get the impression that his talk is developed independent of and uninfluenced by his listener. But if we take his talk seriously and examine it carefully, we discover that it addresses current topics and the plights of his listeners, although in an abstract manner, often commenting on them obliquely. For example, his stories and parables of Nikka, Mademoiselle Basquette, and his parents and his views of the Catholic and Protestant churches in the first chapter express in imaginative and intellectual terms the sense of Felix's predicament as a Jew and an outcast, which has been presented in the preceding pages. O'Connor's main effort, however, is to comprehend and contain experience so that he is not swallowed by it. He is, finally, a confidence-man who plays his own tricks on himself. He says, characterizing himself effectively: "I am my own charlatan" (96).

By serving as the alternative to Robin, O'Connor completes the picture of American expatriation. Whereas the motive of Robin's expatriation is to embrace the experience that would awaken her humanity, the purpose of O'Connor's expatriation is to live and maintain a free and uninhibited life and, at the same time, by rationalization and the exercise of pure reason, to endeavor to keep it from overwhelming and shattering his being. O'Connor is the American intellectual and artist who seeks to be free of the American repression of the mind and the imagination by migrating to Europe, accomplishing, at best, an intellectualism unconnected to any meaningful experience and a verbalism that blunts the mind and dims the imagination. But O'Connor, aware of the futility and desperate essence of his position, is ill at ease in it. His desire to be a woman, expressed practically and verbally several times, indicates this uneasiness as well as a yearning for the self-contained innocence of Robin. The strongest expression of his longing for innocence occurs when he treats Robin for her fit of fainting. He engages in a series of "honesties" while using her perfume and rouge and stealing her money. Symbolically O'Connor attempts to rob Robin of her innocence and identity and wear them himself.

O'Connor's concentration on himself, which his talk and his homosexuality express, shows that he is, as alienated in Europe as Robin and the other American characters. This fact stares him in the face when his American compatriots and Felix bring their miseries to him. In the end, pursued and touched by the American experience as when Nora comes to him with her questions about the night, he disintegrates. His volubility proves useless before the onslaughts of reality, and he finally breaks down when he realizes the emptiness and senselessness of his life. The spiritual and emotional hollowness that O'Connor reaps from his expatriation is no better a fate than Robin's bestiality, because it, too, implies a forfeiture of one's humanity.

In drawing O'Connor's character Barnes clearly echoes T. S. Eliot, especially in "The Waste Land" and "The Hollow Men," and the writers that influenced these poems, notably Dante and Conrad. O'Connor's Tiresias-like character is an appropriation to modern experience and a vulgarization of the ancient seer. Barnes uses Tiresias similarly to Eliot's use in "The Waste Land": as a consciousness that comprehends the experience she deals with.[8] O'Connor owes his hollow character—his "deliberate disguises" and his end "not with a bang but with a whimper"—to "The Hollow Men." The similarities to Eliot's poems are abundant, and the debt to Eliot is obvious. But such a comparison is not the important point. It is significant that *Nightwood* does not end with O'Connor and Europe to compel us to give these similarities great weight and to conclude that the novel is another modernist text that repeats the characterization of life between the two wars and the apocalyptic sense peculiar to modernist literature. That the novel ends with Robin and Nora in America indicates that it is more concerned with the experience of the United States during a time of crisis after the old certainties and values have been tested and proved inadequate.

NOTES

1. A number of critics refer to expatriation in *Nightwood* without seeing it as the main theme of the novel. Walter Sutton maintains that the "chief burden is the oppressive time-consciousness of a particular place and time in history—the cosmopolitan world of displaced Europeans and expatriated Americans in the post-World-War-I years—the place and time which also formed the poetry of Eliot and Pound to a very marked degree" (120). Sharon Spencer states that "Expatriation is another life condition that is shared by Miss Barnes's characters and is revealed by their drifting from one European capital to another, and from Europe to America and back again" (43). Louis F. Kannenstine observes that *Nightwood* "holds up as a rendering of continental bohemia of the twenties, a distillation of the despair and estrangement of expatriation ..." (103-104).

2. See Charles Baxter 1176 and Alan Williamson 66.

3. Andrew Field reports that "Berenice Abbott asked Barnes why she had chosen to open the novel with this strongly etched portrait of someone who turns out to be so unimportant in the novel. She answered quite directly that it was done simply to confuse and draw some attention away from the lesbian love between Nora and Robin that looms so large in *Nightwood*" (78). Surely, Barnes's view of the first chapter of her novel cannot be taken seriously. It is obvious, as I argue in this essay, that, when placed in the context of the novel, Felix's story is an appropriate and necessary introduction to a tale of alienation and disintegration. If *Nightwood* were a realistic novel, then not only Felix but

also O'Connor would be unnecessary distractions. Andrew Field, making this fundamental error, remarks: "Given what we know about the way in which Barnes used the story of Felix Volkbein as a distraction from the too painful centre of her short tale, it may well be that the figure of Dr. O'Connor was strategically deployed to be a distraction as well" (140).

4. Kannenstine notes that "Robin is seldom directly available to the reader but is nearly always presented in terms of the sensations she arouses in those with whom she becomes involved" (91).

5. "The majority of expatriates did not read European writers and did not have or use the opportunity to meet them, either. William Carlos Williams asked Robert McAlmon to present him to some young French modern poets when he came to France in 1924 and was puzzled when McAlmon replied that he didn't know any" (Field 39).

6. Kenneth Burke says of the fourth chapter of *Nightwood*: "built upon the portrait of Nora's rival, Jenny Petherbridge, 'The Squatter' is most accurately characterizable as *invective*" (340).

7. A. Robert Lee describes *The Confidence-Man* in a way that suggests its obvious similarity and relevance to *Nightwood*: "*The Confidence-Man*, willfully (or knowingly, at least) eschews plot, character in any conventional sense, even action; it offers instead talk, irrepressible, necessary human talk, as plausible yet as inconsistent and equivocal as human kind at large, and all of it worked into a superb dissonance of voices, a colloquium at once literal-seeming and fantastical ..." (159).

8. Cf. T. S. Eliot's note to line 218 of "The Waste Land": "Tiresias although a mere spectator and not indeed a 'character' is yet the most important personage in the poem, uniting all the rest. ... What Tiresias *sees*, in fact, is the substance of the poem" (72).

WORKS CITED

Barnes, Djuna. *Nightwood*. New York: New Directions, 1961.

Baxter, Charles. "A Self-Consuming Light: *Nightwood* and the Crisis of Modernism," *Journal of Modern Literature*, 3 (1974).

Burke, Kenneth. "Version, Con-, Per-, and In- (Thoughts on Djuna Barnes's Novel, *Nightwood*," *Southern Review*, 2 (April 1966).

De Vore, Lynn. "The Backgrounds of *Nightwood*: Robin, Felix, and Nora," *Journal of Modern Literature* 10 (March 1983).

Eliot, T. S. *Collected Poems, 1909-1962.* New York: Harcourt, 1966.

Fiedler, Leslie. *Love and Death in the American Novel.* New York: Stein, 1982.

Field, Andrew. *Djuna: The Life and Times of Miss Barnes.* New York: Putnam's, 1983.

Frank, Joseph. "Spatial Form in Modern Literature," *Sewanee Review* 53 (1945).

Greiner, Donald J. "Djuna Barnes' *Nightwood* and the American Origins of Black Humor," *Critique* 17 (1975).

Kannenstine, Louis F. *The Art of Djuna Barnes: Duality and Damnation.* New York: New York UP, 1977.

Lee, Robert A., Ed. *Herman Melville: Reassessments.* London and Totowa, N.J.: Vision and Barnes, 1984.

Melville, Herman. *The Confidence-Man: His Masquerade.* Evanston and Chicago: Northwestern UP and the Newberry Library, 1984.

Nelson, Gerald. *Ten Variations of America.* New York: Knopf, 1972.

Spencer, Sharon. *Space, Time, and Structure in the Modern Novel.* New York: New York UP, 1971.

Sutton, Walter. "The Literary Image and the Reader: A Consideration of the Theory of Spatial Form," *Journal of Aesthetics and Art Criticism*, 17 September 1957.

Williamson, Alan. "The Divided Image: The Quest for Identity in the Works of Djuna Barnes," *Critique,* 17 (1975).

Anne B. Dalton   (essay date Fall 1993)

SOURCE: "'This Is Obscene': Female Voyeurism, Sexual Abuse, and Maternal Power in *The Dove,*" in *Review of Contemporary Fiction,* Vol. 13, No. 3, Fall, 1993, pp. 117-39.

[*In the following essay, Dalton discusses the role of incest and child abuse in Barnes's work, especially in her play,* The Dove.]

In 1963 when she was seventy-one, Djuna Barnes referred to herself as "the most famous unknown of the century."[1] By old age, Barnes was profoundly aware that while she had been respected decades earlier as an innovative modernist writer, her work remained largely unread. Worse still, when

it *was* read, it typically provoked a mixture of admiration and bafflement or outright rejection. One critic stated that her writing "suffers from that most irritating offense of difficult writing—the mysterioso effect that hides no mystery, the locked box with nothing in it."[2] I would argue that Barnes's work is more like Pandora's box: once one manages to open it, the contents stream out irrepressibly. Yet the long-standing critical confusion makes sense since Barnes focused on exploring the position of daughters within incestuous families. Until the past decade, such discursive terrain has remained mostly uncharted, in keeping with the social taboos barring discussion of both the subject of childhood sexual abuse and the vulnerability of daughters within patriarchal structures.

Barnes's work seems to have been all the more mystifying because she was remarkably ambitious in her exploration of the forms and effects of incest. While portraying incidents of father-daughter incest and their aftereffects throughout her oeuvre, she also explored how every member of a dysfunctional family can become implicated in and/or vulnerable to physical, emotional, and sexual abuse. In the course of this lifelong examination, Barnes's scrutiny of mother-daughter relationships and grandmother-granddaughter incest was particularly perceptive and critically confounding.

In **The Antiphon,** the last play that Barnes published, the daughter, Miranda, describes herself as a stunned insect saved up for fodder to articulate the effects that the father's incestuous abuse, and the mother's collusion with him, had upon her. Unlike her namesake in Shakespeare's last drama, whose mother is long lost, this Miranda exhorts her mother to hear her and nurture her in spite of their long estrangement:

> Hear me:
> And if you hear, when you hear
> The infinitely distant, pining voice
> Of any creature punished in the web
>
> . . . .
> Find her, if you find her, turn her:
> Stroke out misfortune's fortune.[3]

Like "the creature punished in the web," the daughters in many of Barnes's earlier texts feel that they are inseparably linked to maternal figures by the traumatic past, even as they are estranged by the older women's denial of it. When Miranda says these lines, she could speak them on behalf of the many abused children and young women Barnes depicts throughout her works.

I will first analyze the nexus of abuse Barnes herself experienced as a child and young woman and then focus on her early drama **The Dove,** which has received little critical attention.[4] This play is crucial to examine because in it Barnes began to explore the ties and estrangements between daughters and maternal figures within dysfunctional households. By delving into the meaning of domestic violence, repressed lesbian desire, voyeurism, sexual exploitation, and maternal collusion in *The Dove,* Barnes began to investigate the issues that would preoccupy her throughout her literary career.[5]

Writing the Best-Kept Secret

Djuna Barnes's father, Wald, was both bizarre and abusive.[6] Both Andrew Field and Mary Lynn Broe have written about some of the violence Barnes confronted while young. Field suggests that Djuna's mother, Elizabeth Chappell Barnes, divorced Wald in 1912 after (and partially because) he had given Djuna as a sexual sacrifice to Percy Faulkner, his mistress's brother.[7] Broe refers to a constellation of traumatic events, including "the father's attempted rape, his 'virginal sacrifice' of the daughter, then his brutal barter of his daughter-bride" to Faulkner.[8] All of these events most likely occurred when Barnes was between sixteen and eighteen, and Barnes was to grapple with their aftereffects throughout her life, depicting versions of them and the trauma they engendered in her major works, *Ryder* (1928), *Nightwood* (1936), and *The Antiphon* (1958). The central father figures within these texts are violently destructive, and in keeping with these fictionalized portrayals, the few descriptions of Barnes's father that exist in her letters also characterize him as persistently invasive.[9]

During his marriage to Djuna's mother, Wald had at least one long-term mistress who, along with her children fathered by him, lived in the family's Cornwall-on-Hudson household. Wald's mother, Zadel Barnes, was also a permanent member of first the Cornwall and then the Long Island farm household. Zadel Barnes was a powerful member of the family, providing much of the financial support and the bulk of material necessities for the household during Djuna's childhood. She also supervised Djuna's education. However, Zadel most often used her power not to protect the children from her son's abusive practices but to shore up his authority within the polygynous household, and to wield her own.[10]

Barnes was intensely affected by her family members during her childhood, in part because her father isolated her and the other children from outside influences, including public schooling. At the same time, Barnes's father, mother, and paternal grandmother had a wide range of artistic interests and they encouraged the children to write, draw, and study music; to some extent, these activities may have served as a creative release in face of the abuse within the family. Responsible for a range of farm work, Barnes also labored hard during these years, since "What Wald Barnes didn't or wouldn't do, his women and his children did for him. As a young girl Miss Barnes not only

sewed and baked, but also planted and plowed fields" (Field 184).

The evidence in the family papers suggests that Barnes's mother colluded with Wald during Djuna's childhood, perhaps out of a sense of her own powerlessness and out of fear of losing her already tenuous position in the polygynous household. Like many mothers in dysfunctional families, for years Elizabeth Chappell Barnes was apparently willing to sacrifice the welfare of her children to maintain her relationship with her husband. Elizabeth's letters to Djuna (her only daughter), written after the breakup of her relationship with Wald, are punctuated by covert displays of her envy at her daughter's artistic success and by manipulative and detailed reports of her own suffering, sacrifice, and hopelessness.

As is often the case in recent research concerning mothers in incestuous households,[11] Barnes characterizes the maternal figures throughout *Ryder, Nightwood,* and *The Antiphon* as women who choose to deny and repress their memories of the past, and who feel threatened by the daughter's desire to remember and exorcise the trauma engendered by the family. In keeping with these dynamics, the letters Barnes received from her mother reveal similar tensions: "No! I do not have any wish to go back into the past to recover any of the memories I have and am trying [to] put behind me. And even if I did do so, the best facts are enof [*sic*]. Uppermost I have forgotten so much. What I do remember is not worth the trouble to put on paper and then too, I do not feel after Ryder, that I want anymore of me exploited" (Elizabeth Chappell Barnes to Djuna Barnes, 30 April 1941, McKeldin). Like Augusta, the mother in *The Antiphon,* Elizabeth seems to have been an expert at repression. Since Djuna had what Emily Coleman called "a fearful tie"[12] to her mother, it is not surprising that she found her mother's denial alienating and destructive. As is often the case with abused children grown to adulthood, the mother's subsequent denial of past trauma could easily constitute another betrayal, intensifying the effects of the original ones.[13]

The children in Barnes's natal household confronted a powerful nexus of abuse; the father isolated them from outside influences, intensifying the effect of his self-aggrandizement as prophet, his physical and sexual abuse, and both parents' inability to provide material security. The mother's acquiescence in face of these dynamics, and the grandmother's sanctioning of the father's practices through her economic and emotional support of him, left the children remarkably vulnerable to the father's power. The fact that Barnes struggled for decades to portray the father's sexual abuse, and the ways in which her mother and paternal grandmother colluded with him, suggests the profound degree to which these events traumatized her. At a much earlier point in her career, however, Barnes was able to depict, albeit in masked form, the sexual abuse to which her grandmother Zadel subjected her, as well as her mother's collusive role in these transgressions.

Although father-daughter incest is a problem of epidemic proportions, and mothers and other female relatives often collude with the fathers' transgressions, cases of mother-daughter or grandmother-granddaughter incest seem to be relatively rare (see Russell 71-74). In their groundbreaking analysis of father-daughter incest, Herman and Hirshman offer an explanation for this disparity:

> It is the refraction of the incest taboo through the institutions of male supremacy and the sexual division of labor which results in the asymmetrical application of the taboo to men and women. . . .
>
> The greater the domination of the father, and the more the caretaking is relegated to the mother, the greater the likelihood of father-daughter incest. The more democratic the family and the less rigid the sexual division of labor, the less likely that fathers will abuse their daughters. (62-63)

Barnes's post-1927 work illustrates and supports many of the issues discussed by feminist theorists writing about father-daughter incest. However, Barnes's earlier portrayals can serve as a reminder that victim disclosure rates in cases of incest perpetrated by female relatives could be quite low.

Disclosure in cases of father-daughter incest has increased dramatically in recent years, in part due to the increased support for victims stemming from social and legal reform (Russell 76-84). But with the culturally ingrained resistance to acknowledging childhood sexual abuse, and the idealization of maternal figures in Western culture, it is possible that even if a child reported incestuous abuse by a female relative, the disclosures might not register. Of course, the difficulty of indicting maternal figures[14] itself could also be prohibitive.[15] In Barnes's case, most critics seem not to have registered the indictments of either her grandmother or her father that she made in her fiction and plays.[16]

The distinct record through letters of Barnes's abuse by her grandmother is unusual in cases of incest; although only one letter from Djuna to Zadel is currently in the collection, many letters from Zadel to Djuna are available.[17] Written over a period of eighteen years, from the time Djuna was six to twenty-four, the letters reveal the grandmother's conflated efforts to nurture and exploit her granddaughter. Zadel's letters are a peculiar mélange—of advice to Djuna on how she should eat, exercise, study, and subordinate her will to ensure the well-being of the family; of practical advice on groceries and chores; of lavish endearments that seem carefully designed to manipulate; and of a regressive, highly euphe-

mistic language that expresses her erotic desire for her granddaughter, referring in detail to past sexual encounters between them. As early as 1903, when Barnes was eleven and when she and her grandmother shared the same bed, Zadel referred to sexual interactions between them and expressed the erotic nature of her desire for Djuna.[18] Not only do the letters reveal the way in which Zadel colonized Djuna to serve her sexual needs, but they also provide evidence that the other adults in the family had a matter-of-fact attitude towards this abuse.

Zadel Barnes's sexual discourse in letters addressed to Djuna is often preceded or followed by instructions Djuna was asked to pass on to her mother and father about household matters. The juxtaposition implies that the letters to Djuna may have been read by her parents. At times, Zadel would send messages for the other children in the letters to Djuna–which reinforces the impression that the letters were shared with others. The fact that the parents, Wald and Elizabeth, mention in their own letters one of the nicknames, "Flitch" (a euphemism for genitalia), that Zadel used for herself when writing to Djuna, further suggests that they were aware of the grandmother's transgressions.

The letters are especially jarring because of the ways in which Zadel would juxtapose practical instructions about such matters as supplies she was sending to the farm household with passages about her own breasts, erotic pleasure, and her desire for access to Djuna's body. Zadel often illustrated her letters with drawings of disembodied breasts to express her desire; she also used a range of euphemisms to refer to her own and Djuna's breasts–at times calling them "Misriss Pink Tops" or "Quick Tops," while referring to her aroused nipples as "pebblums on the beachums."

In one letter, sent when Djuna was seventeen, Zadel writes:

> Oh Misriss! When I sees your sweet hands a huggin' your own P.T.'s [Pink Tops]—I is just crazy and I jumps on *oo*! X like dis–(Zadel to Djuna Barnes, 4 March 1909, McKeldin)

The first drawing shows a pair of disembodied breasts approaching a thin female figure sitting upright in a chair, and the second shows the young girl and the chair knocked flat on the ground, the figure's arms spread downward as if she has no means to resist the disembodied breasts looming above her. The cartoonish drawings depict the granddaughter as she is overwhelmed by a force she cannot resist while the grandmother's regressive prose masks her authority in the exchange (cf. Broe 1989, 42).

Although Zadel's erotic discourse was mostly breast-centered, she used a whole panoply of sexual euphemisms, especially in the closing of her letters. To give just one example, she closed a letter dated 1 October 1908 to Djuna by writing, "Bless my Sexes . . . Dorations, Snickerterbitz—Corkerdit–Pink Tops and your own loving thatch of Bacon Cakes." The reference to the "thatch of Bacon Cakes" is easier to decode than some of the others; thatch refers to the granddaughter's pubic hair, while "Bacon Cakes" is a metaphor for the girl's labia, likening them to strips of pork.

Zadel's letters to Djuna show that she conditioned the child to serve her own erotic needs at a young age; they also suggest *the means by which* Zadel may have done so. For example, while Barnes was growing up, Zadel was intermittently away from the family, and often during these periods, she would arrange for food stuffs to be delivered to the Cornwall-on-Hudson household. Zadel's letters show that she used her power as the family's provider of groceries to purchase special foods for Djuna (see also Broe 1989, 42). Mention of treats often precedes the erotic passages, and the juxtapositions suggest that Zadel used her power as provider to bribe Djuna into acquiescing to the sexual abuse.

In light of this breast-centered sexual abuse, it seems especially significant that Zadel's and Wald's letters reveal that Djuna had an eating disorder during her childhood and young adulthood. It may be that Barnes tried symbolically to protest her grandmother's use of her body for oral gratification by curtailing her own oral consumption. Many of Zadel's and Wald's letters instruct Djuna on the importance of eating sufficient amounts of food, implying that she would not eat if they did not remind her. Barnes's eating problems make sense, since during her childhood she was figuratively and literally treated as a commodity to be consumed by the adults in her family.

Barnes's eating disorder is also in keeping with some of the lifelong aftereffects typically suffered by survivors of incest (Blume 151-56). As is the case for many survivors, it seems that when Barnes felt she was losing control of her life, she would try to impose a sense of order by strictly limiting her food intake. In both her young adulthood and old age when she was living on insufficient funds, Barnes would try to "manage" the financial difficulties by eating less.

One of Barnes's first professional assignments casts further light on the dynamics concerning orality, consumption, and power at work in her relationship to her family and her writing. During the first years after she left the household headed by Wald and Zadel, Barnes allowed herself to be force-fed as research for writing a newspaper article "in simulation of the force-feedings which the English suffragists were then undergoing" (Field 53). The fact that Barnes underwent the procedure and wrote the article suggests that she may have been more successful at *describing* and locating the forces that control women than at *protecting* herself from them. By participating in the force-feeding, Barnes was engaged

in a destructive, yet revealing, form of acting out. Barnes's position in the "voluntary simulation" was a symbol of her former position in her family—in which the father and grandmother conflated nurture and violence in their violation of her bodily integrity. Physicians force-fed suffragists ostensibly "for their own good," but also to break their spirit; the dynamics in this oral-centered form of ritual rape reverberate with the oral dynamics involved in Zadel's use of her role as family provider to coerce Djuna into submitting to her breast-centered sexual abuse.

By participating in the simulation, then writing an account of it for publication, Barnes publicly exposed a form of abuse that was remarkably similar to what she had suffered as a child and adolescent. However, Barnes's public exposure of the horror of force-feeding is an extreme contrast to the silencing she experienced in her family. By participating in the "simulation," Barnes may have been covertly testing her family members to see if they would recognize the parallels between the two forms of abuse. We can only speculate on what Barnes's reaction may have been when she received a letter from her father in which he congratulated her on the article, paternalistically expressed concern for her, and wrote that he wished he could beat up the physicians who force-fed her, seemingly oblivious to the parallels between the doctors' actions and his own (Wald Barnes to Djuna Barnes, 12 September 1914, McKeldin).

In most families in which there is incestuous abuse, children face a range of silencing forces; molesters may threaten to kill their victims or condition children to believe they will be to blame for the breakup of the family if they disclose the abuse. Often, sexual abusers can silence children by suggesting that they will lose the adult's love if they do not behave as required.[19] Many of the letters Zadel wrote to Djuna during her childhood show that the grandmother used similar tactics to condition her to subordinate her interests to maintain the status quo in the family. Highlighting this dynamic, one letter from Zadel instructs Djuna to be silent about family problems *even if they directly affect her.* She then explains that through such silence Djuna will not only "be happier," but also more fully loved.

> You will *please me very much* . . . if you will take yourself strongly in hand, *not* to "*butt in*" in *anything* that is not really your *very own* business and not *even then,* unless it is *very important.* If you overcome this bad habit, you will escape a lot of trouble—*prevent* a lot of trouble,—you will be *happier* and be really a much nicer girl and be more beloved. *Try hard* my darling x I believe you can do anything you really resolve to. (Zadel to Djuna Barnes, 20 February 1906, McKeldin)

It is not clear how Barnes felt about her grandmother's sexual abuse while she was a child and teenager living in the Cornwall and then the Long Island households. But by the time Barnes published *The Dove* in 1923, she had written several works that portray relationships between older women who are maternal figures and young women or children.[20] These fictional accounts suggest that Barnes felt profoundly ambivalent about her grandmother's molestation, and that, at least at times, she felt overwhelming rage as a result of the trauma.

There is one piece of direct biographical evidence, dating back to the period of Zadel's sexual abuse, showing Barnes's response to her grandmother's demands. . . . Zadel's letters frequently urged Djuna and other family members to write more often when she was away from the household on business. On one occasion, she complained bitterly:

> Imagine my emotion this morning when the morning mail brought *nothing* from *you*! And after spending nearly all day Sunday writing to you and "ma" and "pa" and Fanny [Wald's live-in mistress]! If that is to be the effect of such devotion, I'll hang my pen on the willow tree, and I'll off to the deuce again—the writer's life has no charms for me. (Zadel to Djuna Barnes, 23 February 1909, McKeldin)

Djuna's response was deeply conflicted, marked by a mixture of rage, despair, and fear; her immediate retraction of her expression of hatred suggests that she could not bear the consequences of expressing her anger to Zadel. The letter also demonstrates a form of "splitting off" common among incest survivors (Bass 42-43), as Djuna addresses Zadel both as "Grandmother" and through metonymic references to her nipples and breasts.

> Dear Pink Top Pebblums and Grandmother:
>
> Imagine *my* feelings when the mail brought *nothing* from *you,* for me!!! This is the way I looked immediately, You is a *nasty* Pink Tops and Grandmother Flitch and I hate you—oh no I don't I love yer! ha! ha! Now really wouldn't that give you a "pain"? (Djuna Barnes to Zadel Barnes, 26 February 1909, McKeldin)

Barnes's letters to and from family and friends repeatedly show that she was caught in a matrix of forces—pressured not to protest the transgressions within the family, threatened with loss of love if she did not behave as her father and grandmother willed, and conditioned by the adults to serve the sexual needs of the father and grandmother. Since many survivors of childhood sexual abuse struggle throughout their lives to remember what they have suffered, it is not surprising that it took Barnes decades to tell the story

of her father's sexual abuse in *Ryder, Nightwood,* and *The Antiphon.* What is surprising is that as early as 1923 she was able to explore the meaning of Zadel's sexual abuse and her deeply conflicted relation to her grandmother and mother in her play *The Dove.*

"The Creature Punished in the Web": Domesticity, Maternal Power, Voyeurism, and Sexual Abuse in *The Dove*

Although Barnes published *The Dove* in 1923 as part of *A Book,* the play was first staged at Smith College in 1926. The characters within the play are two sisters, Amelia and Vera Burgson, and a young woman whom the sisters name "The Dove" after they meet her in the park and invite her to live with them (148-50). The highly charged name appropriately signals The Dove's situation in the older women's household. The Christian tradition associates doves with peace, holiness, and purity. However, Barnes may also have had another meaning in mind. During the pre-Christian era, the dove "was a primary symbol for female sexuality. In India, the name of the dove-goddess meant 'lust.'"[21] These connotations are appropriate, since The Dove is the object of desire for the two sisters. As is often the case with Barnes, it is an obscure meaning of the word that proves the most revealing. In keeping with the Christian imagery, "dove" can be a term for a "gentle, innocent, or loving woman or child."[22] This definition may have been uppermost in Barnes's mind, much as it was in Tennyson's, when he wrote, "O somewhere, meek unconscious dove / . . . Poor child, that waitest for thy love!"[23] The polysemic associations generated by the young woman's name contribute to sexualizing her, while also stressing her purity and vulnerability, foreshadowing the tensions at work when the Burgson sisters attempt forcibly to incorporate her into their erotic practices. The description of The Dove, an accurate one for the playwright herself, signals that the character is Barnes's fictionalized representative: "a slight delicate girl . . . as delicate as china with almost dangerously transparent skin. Her nose is high-bridged and thin, her hands and feet are also very long and delicate. She has red hair, very elegantly coiffured" (148).[24] The stage directions also suggest that The Dove expects danger at any moment: "When she moves [seldom] the slightest line runs between her legs, giving her the expectant waiting air of a deer" (148).

The opening dialogue indicates that the two Burgson sisters are significantly older than The Dove. Although the sisters are not related to the younger woman, the age difference, coupled with the fact that they take her in, casts them as her adopted maternal figures. Throughout Barnes's writing, as in folktales about child theft, adoption by pseudomaternal figures often proves ominous.[25] Certainly, in this case, the way in which the older women "mother" the girl seems sinister at best.[26]

The stage directions indicate that as soon as the curtain rises, the set reveals some of the major tensions within and among the characters.

> The decoration is garish, dealing heavily in reds and pinks. There is an evident attempt to make the place look luxuriously sensual. The furniture is all of the reclining type.
>
> The walls are covered with a striped paper in red and white. Only two pictures are evident, one of the Madonna and child, and one of an early English tandem race.
>
> There are firearms everywhere. Many groups of swords, ancient and modern, are secured to the walls. A pistol or two lie in chairs, etc. There is only one door, which leads out into the back hall directly back centre. (147)

Symbolically, the set seems to be a perverse womb—one which conflates the relations among sensuality, violence, and mothering.[27] As the play opens, Vera and The Dove are talking while The Dove polishes "the blade of an immense sword." The dialogue reveals that Amelia had asked the girl to clean "blood stains" off of it. Although Vera's comments suggest that Amelia had imagined the stains and would in fact be afraid to use the sword, the exchange implies that someone may have been abused before the action of the play began.

Vera's speeches reveal that the two older women are extremely repressed voyeurs, at once obsessed with sexuality and violence and with denying their obsession. In fact, Vera's speech reveals that their "entire education" has consisted of a discourse on sexual expression, perversion, violence, domesticity, and repression. In spite of their obsession with sexuality, the passage makes clear that both women do not engage in any active form of sexual practice except for the voyeuristic. The final image in the paragraph suggests that Amelia's violence is linked to repressed lesbian desire:

> "[W]e collect knives and pistols, but we only shoot our buttons off with the guns and cut our darning cotton with the knives, and we'll never, never be perverse though our entire education has been about knees and garters and pinches on hindquarters—elegantly bestowed—and we keep a few animals—very badly—hoping to see something first-hand—and our beds are as full of yellow pages and French jokes as a bird's nest is full of feathers— . . . It's wicked! She keeps an enormous blunderbuss in the corner of her room, but when I make up her bed, all I find is some

Parisienne bathing girl's picture stuck full of pin holes." (151, 153)

When Vera questions The Dove about why she remains in the peculiar household, the young woman's comments about her "unnatural" life with family members on a farm echoes Barnes's own rural childhood—again signaling that The Dove is a fictionalized representative for the author. During the course of this exchange between Vera and The Dove, while Amelia is out on an errand, Vera recounts a dream, one similar in content to passages from Barnes's other works in which a mother speaks to a daughter about sexuality and danger: "I dreamt I was a Dresden doll and that I had been blown down by the wind and that I broke all to pieces—that is, my arms and my head broke all to pieces—but then I was surprised to find that my china skirt had become flexible, as if it were made of chiffon and lace" (153).

Although the play condemns the older women's voyeurism, this dream suggests that a range of forces beyond their control may have alienated the women from themselves and from their own desire. The dream reveals that Vera's subjectivity has been undercut to such an extent that she sees herself as a doll, a thing without feelings and without the power to control its body. Rather than suggesting that the women have imposed "restrictions upon themselves" (Scott 57), such passages imply that a range of forces outside the domestic situation have affected the psyches of the sisters and The Dove. In the dream, the wind seems to be a metaphor for an overwhelming erotic force, one which blows the doll down and breaks it "all to pieces" (153). As the head and the arms of the doll break, symbolizing the destruction of the woman's identity and means of resistance, the china skirt becomes "flexible," implying that it could then be manipulated by others.

Vera's dream reverberates most fully with a story Julie's mother in *Ryder* tells her daughter about two sister-dolls who die after they are molested. This thinly veiled (and often prophetic) terrorism under the guise of instruction is emblematic of the relations between all the maternal and daughter figures throughout Barnes's work. In *Ryder*, the mother's bedtime story is a frightening cautionary fable about the dangers of girlhood and of aspiring to feminine ideals. She describes an eerie process of biological and cultural destruction in which two sisters become more perfectly feminine and doll-like until both are dead.

> Felice had little hands, Alix had smaller; Felice had a tiny waist and two breasts as delicate as the first setting of blanc mange. Alix's waist was only a hand's span and her bosom was no greater than two tears set low. Felice had golden hair, Alix's was fine and thin and curling.

Felice had a little skeleton as chipped of angles as a Ming, and as light as ash. Alix's flesh covered her bones as thinly as ice on a tree. Felice's ankles were faultless, Alix's were as weightless as cuttlebone and as fragile. (155)

As in Vera's dream, the story implies that the production of women is a process of systematic destruction. The story in *Ryder* seems especially gruesome because it is told to the daughter by her mother, who is being systematically destroyed by her husband's demands. Much as in Vera's dream in which her head is broken "all to pieces," symbolizing the loss of her identity, the molestation of the two sisters also results in their erasure, since the story leads to their death. By saying "And that's the end of the two little sisters, thank God," after their molestation leads to their simultaneous pregnancies and destruction, the mother in *Ryder* implies that she finds the sisters in her story shameful because they were abused:

> Felice cried for a tiny doll, Alix got a smaller. They sat together in bed and the two dolls sat up before them. . . .
>
> The manager called and took Felice in his right arm and Alix in his left. He pinched them both at once and equally, and they both kissed him at the same moment, and he put them back to bed.
>
> Felice said:
>
> "At twenty minutes past ten, on April fourth, I shall be a mother."
>
> Alix said:
>
> "At twenty-one minutes past ten, on April fourth, I shall be a mother." . . .
>
> They had four little circles under their four blue eyes.
>
> And on April fourth, at twenty minutes past ten, Felice died.
>
> One minute later Alix died. (155-56)

Amelia's fantastical report of the abuse of the sisters connects imagistically with Vera's description of herself as the shattered Dresden doll. When the mother describes the sisters as becoming increasingly doll-like and then reduces the impregnating events to the manager's "pinch" and his "put[ting] them back to bed," her rendering implies that the sisters are helpless to resist their manipulation and that their bodies can betray them without Alix and Felice comprehending the significance of what has transpired. When the two sisters die after their molestation, their fate ironically predicts that of Julie, the daughter in *Ryder,* who dreams repeatedly of her death after she is molested by her father.[28] The maternal figures' revelations in both the novel and the play are followed by a symbolic reenactment of the abuse of the daughter figures.

In *The Dove,* soon after Vera describes her dream, Amelia returns from errands. She then tries to draw The Dove and Vera into participating in her voyeuristic habits by inviting them to look at her reproduction of Carpaccio's *Deux Courtisanes Vénitiennes,* but she fails to do so. Just as lines earlier in the play reveal that Amelia displaces her desire for an interactive sexual practice by staring at "farm animals" and playing in bed with "some Parisienne girl's picture," in this scene, gazing at the portrait functions as a substitute for erotic encounters in which her power, particularly her controlling gaze, might be compromised. Of course, by drawing attention to the way Amelia gazes at the portrait, attempting to derive erotic pleasure from the spectacle, Barnes also makes an implicit and sly comment on her audience's position, gazing upon the spectacle of the play as a whole.

Carpaccio's *Deux Courtisanes Vénitiennes* functions as a key element in *The Dove* in other ways as well. Barnes's imagination seems to have been fired by its conflation of domestic, violent, and erotic symbols, and by the central figures' attention to an eerily unrepresented drama. The original painting was cut on both the right and left sides some time before the nineteenth century,[29] and what remains of it, with its strikingly absent sections is structurally similar not only to *The Dove,* but to Barnes's many renderings of her family history in which central elements are obscured, edited out, or only metaphorically represented. Like *The Dove,* the painting has three central figures: two middle-aged women who appear to be related dominate the canvas, while near the left edge is a young boy who might be a page. Commentary on the two women in the painting is remarkably similar to some of the first critical commentary on Vera and Amelia; one art historian noted that "Their vacant, apathetic faces, devoid of any spiritual animation and individuality, possess a strange fascination for the modern onlooker; the mask of studied indifference seems to hide vice and perversion."[30] Animals fill the scene: doves on the balustrade, dogs in the foreground, and a peacock and a dark crowlike bird near the left center; yet the two women are oddly detached from the animals that surround them. In much the same way, *The Dove*'s references to animals highlight the fact that Amelia's and Vera's lives are marked by repressions as they are at once obsessed with and surrounded by, yet separate from, creatures within the world around them. Deep maroonish reds and pinks dominate Carpaccio's canvas, most likely inspiring Barnes's comment that such colors should "heavily" mark *The Dove*'s setting. Carpaccio's use of the deep red tones contributes to the painting's sexually laden atmosphere and forms a jarring contrast to the apparent boredom and apathy of the two female figures. By having one of the female figures tug on a crop or whip clenched in the teeth of a feral dog, while both of the women gaze fixedly past this spectacle, Carpaccio reinforces the feeling that a violent or visually arresting event is taking place beyond the edge of the canvas. But ultimately, because the painting is truncated, the nature of this central, yet unfigured, drama is impossible to decipher.

At points throughout **The Dove,** Vera and Amelia refer to the painting's place in their entryway, but it is not until the final moments of the action that Amelia brings it onstage. Then, in much the same manner as the figures' and the viewers' gaze reaches beyond the limits of the canvas, transfixed by some action that is not represented, the audience's gaze in **The Dove** is directed beyond the limits of the stage by The Dove's unrepresented and mysterious final acts.

The end of the play is like a vision from a dream. Instead of resolving tension, the climax serves as a summarizing symbol defining the conflicts within and among the women. In the course of the final action, The Dove confesses to Vera that she loves Amelia; the girl's attraction to the woman who asks her to polish enormous swords and who sticks pins in pictures of Parisienne bathing girls reveals that she has been conditioned into desiring her own victimization. As the three women talk, Amelia becomes agitated and eventually begins a long speech in which she expresses her rage and her narcissism: "I'm in an excellent humour–I could talk for hours, all about myself—to myself, for myself. God! I'd like to tear out all the wires in the house! Destroy all the tunnels in the city, leave nothing underground, or hidden, or useful . . ." (162). Amelia's speech leads to the final events on stage; she insists that The Dove give her the sword and her frantic demands imply that she intends to use it on herself or on The Dove. As she attempts to find the sword, she instead grasps The Dove's hand, and "clutches it convulsively." Slowly, The Dove "bares Amelia's left shoulder and breast and leaning down, sets her teeth in. Amelia gives a slight, short stifled cry. . . . The Dove stands up swiftly, holding a pistol. She turns in the doorway hastily vacated by Vera." A moment later, The Dove shouts out, "For the house of Burgson!" and fires the pistol offstage. Amelia runs out, presumably to see if The Dove has killed herself, leaving Vera alone onstage. Amelia reappears "in the doorway with the picture of the Venetian courtesans, through which there is a bullet hole" (163). Responding to Vera's question, "What has she done?", Amelia refers to the picture, then says, "*This* is obscene" (168).

The meaning of the scene is multilayered and ambiguous. The young woman's action of baring and biting the older woman's breast suggests that she craves nurture from the maternal figure, while also expressing The Dove's anger at Amelia for having threatened her with the sword (and perhaps for other abuses as well).

After attacking Amelia, The Dove may leave with the pistol because she intends to commit suicide, but it remains uncertain at the end of the scene whether or not The Dove has either injured or killed herself. In fact, as Amelia rejoins Vera onstage during the final moment of the play, The Dove's continued absence suggests a wide range of possibilities. She may have shot the picture and left the household, perhaps permanently; she may have simply shot the picture and remained near the entry, just out of the audience's view; or she may have injured or killed herself at the same time the bullet punctured the picture.

Amelia's final line, "*This* is obscene!", is also polysemic. In one sense, Amelia's comment suggests that she may have realized the obscene nature of her own voyeurism; but the fact that The Dove does not appear on stage again implies that Amelia may have had her realization at the cost of the young woman's life. Even if we interpret the final events on stage in the most positive manner possible, they still seem to signify disaster for The Dove.

If Amelia's final line does mean that she has realized the implications of her voyeurism, and if we conclude that The Dove did not shoot herself, but only the picture, the end of the play still indicates that Amelia's actions have had tragic consequences. Even if The Dove has left the household after the gunshot, ultimately, The Dove's violent exit suggests that she may not be able to escape from the patterns of violence and displacement learned from the sisters.

On a symbolic level, by having The Dove shoot the picture, Barnes shows the young girl adopting the older woman's role, but in a more extreme form. Instead of ending Amelia's voyeurism, The Dove's gesture recalls the older woman's habit of sticking pins in and putting holes through "some Parisienne bathing girl's picture." Not only is The Dove's act of shooting the gun psychosexually charged with phallic implications, but so is the description of Amelia "sticking pins in and putting holes through" to express her lesbian desire. Of course, the imagery concerning Amelia's voyeurism also seems jarringly domestic—as it calls to mind crewelwork or the process of tatting. The descriptions suggest that in the world of the play, Amelia's, as well as The Dove's, lesbian desire can only be expressed in a form that merges the conventionally phallic, the domestic, and the perversely destructive. The use of the phallic images also hints at the patriarchal regulation that forms the bedrock supporting domestic abuse.

A far more dire reading is also possible; in this case, The Dove's absence at the end of the play signals that she has killed herself, puncturing the picture in the process. Then, Amelia's exclamation, "*This* is obscene!", made after seeing the girl's body, would show her more concerned with the picture than with the dead girl. In finding the damaged representation, rather than the girl's corpse, "obscene," Amelia would be revealing the profound degree of her repression and peculiar voyeuristic fixation. In spite of the ambiguity of the ending, *The Dove* as a whole nonetheless shows that for Amelia the symbols are more important than the things themselves. She is perversely fixated on something once removed from reality like a traumatized patient obsessed with a symbolic screen memory that occludes the true source of trauma.

It seems especially fitting that Barnes transgressed injunctions against disclosing incestuous abuse through the creation of what amounts to a dramatic reenactment. Indeed, in light of the biographical evidence about Zadel Barnes's sexual abuse of Djuna, it is impossible not to see The Dove's final biting of Amelia's breast as a sign of Barnes's fury at her grandmother; and, of course, The Dove's ambiguous exit suggests the disruption of subjectivity Djuna, the child, might have experienced as a result of Zadel's sexual colonization. By writing and publishing *The Dove* as an adult, Barnes responded to her grandmother's attempts to manipulate her into lifelong silence. Describing The Dove's destruction may have enabled Barnes to begin unearthing her buried grief and rage resulting from incest.

The Critical Key to the Locked Box

The Dove can encourage critics not only to reread Barnes, but also to raise questions about the significance fictionalized portrayals of childhood and young adulthood might have in understanding modernist texts as well as contemporary incest theory. What Barnes's work suggests is that the roles of maternal figures (both as molesters and as those who collude with them) may be more complex than previous analyses have shown. Barnes's life and work also offer support for recent developments in psychological theory that argue that incest is a sign of a dysfunctional structure within the family as a whole and not just a dynamic between the molester and the victim. Barnes's oeuvre confirms and yet also adds a caveat to the arguments of some recent social scientists concerning "mother blame," a phrase used in describing the fact that female incest victims tend to direct blame and hostility at their *mothers* for their victimization by their *fathers*. Janet Jacobs argues that

> In the case of incest victims, the need for separation becomes crucial because the daughter has internalized her mother's sense of powerlessness. . . . Anger at the mother provides a means through which separation and individuation can be facilitated, with rage and rejection acting as a

> source of empowerment for the victimized child. . . . The mother-directed rage represents a first stage in coping with the intense feelings engendered by the abuse. A later stage, in which anger is appropriately focused on the perpetrator, is more likely to occur once the daughter acknowledges and understands her initial reaction to the mother's perceived role.[32]

Since Barnes was molested by her father and her grandmother, some might attribute the antimaternal hostility in *The Dove,* in keeping with Jacobs's argument, to her first stage of coping. However, both the biographical evidence and the complexity of the dynamics in *The Dove* suggest that such an explanation cannot adequately account for the hostility. The dynamics in Barnes's family and in *The Dove* suggest that we should interpret the hostility in more concrete terms—as anger towards someone who was, in fact, guilty of collusion with a molester and/or guilty of molestation itself. In other words, although ascribing antimaternal feelings to the process of separation described in ego psychology may often be useful, Barnes's writing and life can remind us that, in some cases, mother blame, or grandmother blame, is an appropriate response to actual transgressions by women.

The fact that many critics found Barnes's texts to be "the locked box" ultimately reveals more about cultural conditioning—and the unspoken injunctions against discussing or even perceiving the prevalence of incest or its aftereffects—than it does about Barnes's writing. In this sense, Barnes's dramatization of incest, which has been culturally unspeakable, created a text which was culturally unreadable. Only recently, with the proliferation of scholarship and popular works dealing with sexual abuse, has the cultural climate permitted rereadings of texts like Barnes's. As Louise DeSalvo's recent book on Virginia Woolf and the effects of childhood sexual abuse eloquently shows, scholars need to confront the meaning of critical silences and rechart the patterns within turn-of-the-century families if we are to account for the ways in which childhood experience shaped the lives of modernist writers and had enduring effects on the texts they produced.[33]

Ironically, the very factors responsible for the critics' misreading or inability to read Barnes's texts may account for why she was able to write about grandmother-granddaughter incest at an early point in her career; this particular form of sexual abuse was so culturally unimaginable that it did not fit into any extant category of taboo, and thus was practically invisible. For Barnes, such "invisibility" created a situation in which she could dramatize an incident based on personal trauma, and yet deny it at the same time, because the latent content would have been indecipherable to her audience. On the other hand, perhaps it took Barnes longer to write about father-daughter incest because of the strong and explicit cultural injunctions both against this form of sexual abuse and against indicting the father.[34]

The lesbian relationships in Barnes's work contrast with the more celebratory (albeit often coded) portrayals by Stein, H. D., and Woolf. Perhaps feminists have been slow to investigate the meaning of Barnes's work, in contrast to the feminist reevaluation of other modernist women's texts that has taken place during the past decade, because of this difference. Barnes's repeated portrayals of sexual violence in lesbian relationships can be mystifying unless we keep in mind that they are often examining some aspect of the grand-mother-mother-daughter constellation of her childhood. For example, *Nightwood,* in the course of telling the story of the lovers Robin and Nora, explores the complex dynamics of repetition compulsions stemming from childhood abuse. Nora projects the repressed elements of her family trauma onto Robin, reexperiencing her molestation by her father and grandmother through her. Just as Amelia, in *The Dove,* is a symbol for Barnes's abusive grandmother, Nora's key dream in *Nightwood,* of the leering grandmother figure in a billycock and corked mustache, further explores the effects of incestuous abuse and the resulting longing for maternal nurture.[35]

In cases of father-daughter incest, "focusing anger on the mother allows the daughter to externalize her feelings" (Jacobs 512). *The Dove,* with its role-playing elements, dramatized, and in a sense actualized, Barnes's repressed feelings about both her grandmother's and mother's betrayals. Paradoxically, depicting the destruction of The Dove thus constituted the first stage of what was to become Barnes's lifelong writing cure.

Like a seed crystal that starts the formation of an intricate structure, this articulation of the mother's and grandmother's role in her family constellation enabled Barnes to write about the father's molestation and its aftereffects later in her career. In fact, Barnes's oeuvre constitutes a progressive investigation of incest trauma. Following the thinly veiled representations of the grandmother-mother-daughter relationship, *Ryder* tells the story of Barnes's childhood, presenting fictionalized versions of each of her family members. Through dream sequences and euphemistic language, the novel shows a young girl unconsciously grappling with the effects of father-daughter incest and maternal collusion. In *Nightwood,* Nora, an adult survivor of incest, explores on both the conscious and unconscious levels the lifelong effects of her grandmother's and father's molestation. Finally, *The Antiphon* is Barnes's most explicit rendering of the family dynamics involved in incest trauma. The play summarizes all the issues that Barnes grappled with throughout her literary career; it refers both explicitly and symbolically to the incest traumas in Barnes's own life as well as those she

had presented in masked form in earlier texts. By portraying a "family reunion" and stylized reenactments of incestuous abuse, Barnes writes the abused daughter's therapy.

Although critics such as Broe and DeSalvo have begun to address the issue of critical misreadings and silence regarding Barnes's treatment of incest, further work remains. Perhaps only by assessing the relationships among Barnes's cross-textual portrayals of incest and its aftereffects may the import and intricacies of her oeuvre become clear—that her works as a whole constitute one of the most compelling explorations of the lifelong effects of childhood trauma in all of modern literature. Throughout her career Barnes created works that scrutinize the meaning of silences, repressions, and denials within families and especially within those abused by their families. With *The Dove,* Barnes began to reveal her vast knowledge of the many meanings of what one dare not tell, as well as the many meanings and tremendous power of silence.

NOTES

1. Djuna Barnes to Natalie Barney, 31 June 1963, Correspondence of Djuna Barnes, Special Collections, McKeldin Library, University of Maryland, College Park; hereafter designated as McKeldin. Unpublished material used by permission of Herbert Mitgang of the Authors League Fund and University of Maryland, College Park.

2. Review of Djuna Barnes's *Selected Works, Time,* 20 April 1962, 108.

3. Djuna Barnes, *The Antiphon* (London: Faber and Faber, 1958), 79-80.

4. There are brief discussions of *The Dove* in Louis Kannenstine, *The Art of Djuna Barnes* (New York: New York University Press, 1977), 135-37; James Scott, *Djuna Barnes* (Boston: Twayne Publishers, 1976), 56-59; Cheryl Plumb, *Fancy's Craft: Art and Identity in the Early Works of Djuna Barnes* (Selinsgrove, PA: Susquehanna University Press, 1986), 35, 40, 45-48. In Mary Lynn Broe's *Silence and Power: A Reevaluation of Djuna Barnes* (Carbondale: Southern Illinois University Press, 1991). Ann Larabee (37, 40, 42-44) and Joan Retallack (48-49) also comment on *The Dove* in essays on Barnes's early plays.

5. *The Dove* appears in *A Book* (New York: Boni and Liveright, 1923). Further references to this edition are noted parenthetically in the text.

6. Unless otherwise indicated, the description of conflicts within Barnes's natal family is informed by my reading of the Djuna Barnes Papers at the University of Maryland, par-

ticularly letters to and from Djuna Barnes and her immediate family members.

7. Andrew Field, *Djuna: The Formidable Miss Barnes* (Austin: University of Texas Press, 1985), 43; hereafter cited parenthetically.

8. Mary Lynn Broe, "My Art Belongs to Daddy: Incest as Exile, The Textual Economics of Hayford Hall," in *Women's Writing in Exile*, ed. Mary Lynn Broe and Angela Ingram (Chapel Hill: University of North Carolina Press, 1989), 56. Further citations noted parenthetically as Broe 1989.

9. For example, in a letter to Emily Coleman written in adulthood, Barnes made an oblique reference to her father's physical abuse. Her use of the word *naturally* suggests that such behavior was probably commonplace, while her use of the endearment is typical of her irony when describing family trauma: "[S]till its [*sic*] the way the rope went out in a long leaping line and the open loop at the end taking the quarter you had decided on that was fun. [N]aturally, my dear dad caught me and the rest of the children in loops with his, and dragged us about" (25 June 1939, McKeldin).

10. Throughout her writing, Barnes explores the complicated allegiances of paternal grandmothers—to their son's authority and desires, to the grandchildren's well-being, to their own erotic desires and will to power, and to daughters-in-law. As was the case in Barnes's own life, in *Ryder* and *Nightwood* there is a notable conflation of paternal authority and maternal presence whenever paternal grandmother figures appear. Zadel's correspondence suggests that she cast herself as a maternal figure, both within the Barnes household and without, in order to manipulate others to her will, much as does Sophia, the paternal grandmother in *Ryder.*

11. For example, see Sue E. Blume, *Secret Survivors: Uncovering Incest and Its Aftereffects in Women* (New York: John Wiley and Sons, 1990); Judith Lewis Herman and Lisa Hirschman, *Father-Daughter Incest* (Cambridge: Harvard University Press, 1981); and Diana Russell, *The Secret Trauma: Incest in the Lives of Girls and Women* (New York: Basic Books, 1986).

12. Emily Coleman to Djuna Barnes, 16 November 1935, McKeldin.

13. Ellen Bass and Laura Davis, *The Courage to Heal: A Guide for Women Survivors of Child Sexual Abuse* (New York: Harper & Row, 1988), 133-48.

14. The use of the term "maternal" is meant broadly, connoting any older female figure (not necessarily a relative) who casts herself in a nurturing, protective, or caretaking role in relation to a younger woman. It is in this sense that

Barnes's paternal grandmother, and the characters Barnes based upon her, may be defined as "maternal figures."

15. Russell discusses the many reasons why reported cases of incest only comprise "the tip of the iceberg" (85). She also discusses a range of factors that affect incest disclosure rates (31-37).

16. Lynda Curry's 'Tom Take Mercy': Djuna Barnes' Drafts of *The Antiphon*" and Louise DeSalvo's "'To Make Her Mutton at Sixteen': Rape, Incest, and Child Abuse in *The Antiphon*" in Broe's *Silence and Power* discuss Barnes's treatment of incest in *The Antiphon,* Barnes's most explicit and final published work on the subject. My own forthcoming analysis *The Book of Repulsive Women: Childhood Sexual Abuse in the Work of Djuna Barnes* also addresses this critical silence.

17. I am grateful to Jane Marcus for bringing the Zadel Barnes letters to my attention and for Mary Lynn Broe's "My Art Belongs to Daddy," the first essay to assess the relations between Antonia White, Emily Coleman, and Djuna Barnes at Hayford Hall, and the Zadel—Djuna Barnes correspondence.

18. Broe sketches the range of abuse Barnes experienced in her natal household and points out a range of aftereffects that Djuna may have experienced as a result. However, she offers an optimistic assessment of the meaning and effects of the erotic correspondence between Zadel and Djuna Barnes. Broe argues that it formed "a purification ritual of sorts within the family, a matriarchal text in the margins outside time. Their only syntax is that of the eternal present where a mythical world of breasts merges with breasts in the fullness of *puissance feminine.* Zadel and Djuna are empowered to triumph imaginatively over all outside threats. Temporarily safe from the violations of the patriarchal household, Zadel and Djuna played in their symbolic, marginalized world, a queendom of 'nanophilia'" (1989, 53).

19. See Bass and Davis, and Blume, for multiple examples of these dynamics.

20. A range of Barnes's short stories, most notably "Cassation" and "The Grande Malade," use a narrative frame in which a younger woman is recounting her experiences to an older woman. These works are similar to *The Dove* in their thematic emphasis on voyeurism, explorations of sexual and emotional violence, veiled attention to incest dynamics, and scrutiny of relationships between young women and pseudomaternal figures. See Carolyn Allen's "Writing Towards *Nightwood:* Djuna Barnes' Seduction Stories" in *Silence and Power*, 54-65, for the most thorough discussion of these dynamics to date.

21. Barbara Walker, *The Women's Dictionary of Symbols and Sacred Objects* (San Francisco: Harper & Row, 1988), 399.

22. *The Compact Edition of the Oxford English Dictionary* (New York: Oxford University Press, 1971), 621. See also Plumb (48) for her comments on the Christian symbolism.

23. *In Memoriam* 6: 25-28.

24. See Field, 37, 103, and 119 and Shari Benstock, *The Women of the Left Bank* (Austin: University of Texas Press, 1986), 234, 239, and 253-54 for their descriptions of Barnes's appearance.

25. As I refer to Amelia and Vera of *The Dove* as maternal figures, it is important to remember that in Barnes's oeuvre maternal figures are not simply nurturing, older women, but symbols that include their own opposites, often to a perverse degree. Such contradictory and polysemic associations were strikingly apparent in Zadel Barnes's behavior, as she simultaneously cast herself as her granddaughter's spiritual and intellectual mentor, loving protector, provider, and authority figure, while also molesting her and manipulating her into silence about abuses within the family.

26. Amelia's voyeuristic fixation on a set range of images, her attraction to instruments of violence, and her use of them as decorations in the domestic setting cast her as a figure parallel to Sophia, the paternal grandmother in *Ryder*, Barnes's most straightforwardly biographical work. One of the oddest details relating to Sophia concerns the pictures she displays on her walls: "There were prints of all she abhorred, the rack, the filling of the belly, known as the Extreme Agony, the electric chair, the woman-who-died-of-fright, the woman-who-could-no-longer-endure-it, the man-with-the-knife-in-his-heart . . . " (*Ryder* [Elmwood Park, IL: Dalkey Archive Press, 1990], 13; hereafter cited parenthetically).

27. I am using the term "perverse" as defined by Kaja Silverman in "Masochism and Male Subjectivity," *Camera Obscura* 17 (1988): 31-66. As she notes, "Perversion also subverts many of the binary oppositions upon which the social order rests; it crosses the boundary separating food from excrement (coprophilia); human from animal (bestiality); life from death (necrophilia); adult from child (pederasty); and pleasure from pain (masochism)" (33).

28. For further exploration of these dynamics, see my "Escaping from Eden: Djuna Barnes' Revision of Psychoanalytic Theory and Her Treatment of Father-Daughter Incest in *Ryder*," *Women's Studies* 22.2 (1993): 163-80.

29. Jan Lauts, *Carpaccio: Paintings and Drawings*, trans. Erica Millman and Marguerite Kay (London: Phaidon Press, 1962), 251.

30. Lauts 28; Scott 57-58.

31. I am indebted to Morton Levitt for suggesting this interpretation.

32. Janet Jacobs, "Reassessing Mother Blame in Incest," *Signs* 15.3 (Spring 1990): 512. Additional citations are noted parenthetically as Jacobs.

33. Louise DeSalvo, *Virginia Woolf: The Impact of Childhood Sexual Abuse on Her Life and Work* (New York: Ballantine Books, 1990).

34. The very fact that Zadel Barnes expressed her sexual desire for her granddaughter through letters may also help explain why Barnes was able to fictionalize the grandmother-granddaughter relationship at an earlier point than she could the father-daughter dynamics. Unlike many incest survivors who doubt the validity of their memories of abuse and are left desiring proof after they leave their families, Barnes had proof: Zadel's letters functioned as a form of concrete testimony to her past experience. Also, through the letters, Zadel had transgressed cultural injunctions against textualizing incest; although these were limited disclosures directed only to her granddaughter, they may have nonetheless provided Barnes with a sense that it was possible to transgress family and cultural injunctions against disclosing the grandmother's incestuous abuse.

35. *Nightwood* (New York: New Directions, 1961), 63.

Peter Mailloux (essay date Fall 1993)

SOURCE: "Djuna Barnes's Mystery in Morocco: Making the Most of Little," in *Review of Contemporary Fiction*, Vol. 13, No. 3, Fall, 1993, pp. 141-48.

[*In the following essay, Mailloux uses Barnes's correspondence to reconstruct a significant period in the writer's life.*]

Djuna Barnes would seem in most ways to be an ideal subject for a biography. First of all, she lived a fascinating life. She did important things, she knew important people, she lived in exotic places. Second, she provided a record of that life, both in her fiction and in her extensive personal correspondence. (It helps too that many of her friends were comparably logocentric.) And third, she presents "problems" to the biographer, questions that are difficult to answer but that also seem extraordinarily suggestive, questions that guarantee new ground to be uncovered and new centers around which to construct a personality. One of Emily Dickinson's poems begins "The Riddle we can guess / We speedily despise." Djuna Barnes was never one to be despised.

The major problems for her would-be biographers are fairly well-known. There is, for instance, the question of why Barnes, at the apparent height of her creative power, should suddenly withdraw from life and writing, turning herself, in her own description, into a kind of Trappist monk. Or there is the question of whether or not she was sexually abused by her father, or whether or not she was married and how many times, or what èxactly happened during her relationship with Thelma Wood. These, moreover, are just the beginning. The more one learns about Barnes, the more the questions seem to proliferate.

One of the minor mysteries is a problem that this would-be biographer first stumbled upon while examining the Emily Coleman papers at the University of Delaware. I was reading a letter Barnes had written Coleman on 30 August 1935, one of the long and sometimes delightful, sometimes painful, letters that Barnes then wrote Coleman, usually in response to the always incredibly long and often less delightful letters that Emily wrote her. Emily's letters picked at and probed every scab and sore spot she could find on her own psyche. Barnes's were usually more gossipy and if they told of troubles, told of physical troubles. (The particular physical "trouble" in this letter was that Barnes felt she was fat, having gone from 118 pounds to 140 pounds, even though, as she also complained in the letter, her poverty prevented her from eating breakfast.) But she also occasionally revealed herself in ways that she never did to any other correspondent. In this letter, for instance, along with news of friends, including the sad news that Dan Mahoney (the model for Matthew O'Connor in *Nightwood*) had cancer of the stomach, and worrying about *Nightwood,* which was still called *Bow Down* then, there was a peculiar passage in which Barnes claimed, apropos of nothing in particular, that she should have been the "Madame" of a poorhouse where drink would be passed out to the men while she, "like a carrion crow," would take notes from the balcony on what they said. This thought then led her to think of writing as scavenging and to wonder what exactly had turned her into a scavenger, into someone at home in the night. "Thelma?" she wondered. "Dan?" "Or Morocco?" She then concluded, "All my horrors have been good."[1]

Thelma Wood and Dan Mahoney were familiar to me even at that point in my research: Djuna had lived with Thelma for ten years in Paris and claimed that she was the one significant love of her life; Mahoney was a friend from essentially the same period. The conjunction of them with horrors was not new either. But the allusion to Morocco was less clear, and therefore intriguing. It became still more intriguing when I discovered two more references to Morocco in

later letters, both making the same point. In the first, after telling Emily that her praise for and help with *Nightwood* during the past year had saved her mind, Barnes wrote: "I thought I was dead and done for. I thought the same, in a different way, in Tangier, and behold, here I still am, and trying another book."[2] A little later in the same letter, while talking about Emily's attitude toward bullfights, Barnes wrote further: "I should see one, a bull fight, just because I don't want to, it's the way we learn anything—like Morocco." A few sentences later still she added, "So you are right, no one should go through a horror unless they can make something of it." "Everything horrible seems to be the chief value," she reiterated in a letter from 20 March 1936. "Look what I learned with Morocco and other horrors."

That something had happened in Morocco, something horrible, was now fairly clear, and that alone made it interesting. (Of course, Barnes's insistence that she had learned something important from the experience made it more interesting—and potentially significant—still.) The question was what had happened. In the remainder of the Delaware letters there were no further clues, not even to when the what might have happened. But when I looked back at the notes that I had taken while examining the huge Barnes collection at the University of Maryland I found several references that were suggestive. The first was in a letter from her mother dated 12 February 1926, which congratulated Djuna on finding a house "to suit your peculiar needs." "But how about insects, dear," the letter went on. "Africa swarms with every kind of ugly bug ànd vile reptile. . . . " Another letter to her mother sent in April confirmed that Djuna was indeed in Africa[3] (a squib in the Paris edition of the *Chicago Tribune*, dated 27 April 1926, that mentioned that Djuna Barnes had just returned from Africa was further confirmation still), and there was finally a daybook entry from 7 April, which suggested that Thelma was then in Algiers and a photograph, supposedly taken in March, that showed Thelma and Djuna together. But that was the end of the trail. No mention of Morocco. No mention of horrors. No solution to the problem. At best, in fact, there was only another small problem. In the same daybook, Barnes wrote on 28 April: "My new lover is not much to look at cross eyed but I think he's grand—he has such innocent teeth. . . . " She also referred several times to a mysterious Harry, in entries going forward as far as late July. Was this truly mention of a new lover, or just a stab at the beginning of a story? And who was Harry? And what, for heaven's sake, were innocent teeth? There remained, meanwhile, only three other references to Morocco in the material. One was in an October 1934 letter from Charles Henri Ford, a man who would eventually be a novelist, a poet, an editor, a photographer, and a filmmaker, and who had been a friend (and, occasionally, nurse and lover) of Barnes since at least 1930. He answered, vaguely, a question about Tangier that Barnes had, for reasons unknown, apparently asked him. The second item was three typed pages of notes on Tangier, written in 1930, giving a brief history and description of the place, also for reasons unknown. And the third was an article on Arab marriage, published in *Cosmopolitan* in 1934. Although what it described was far from ideal, it seemed to reveal nothing about Barnes's personal horror.

Fortunately, there were still other sources. Letters from Barnes to Ezra Pound, Edmund Wilson, Gertrude Stein, and Robert McAlmon were at Yale. Other letters, mostly to Charles Henri Ford, were at the Humanities Research Center at the University of Texas. And there were also secondary sources, books or articles by and about her friends, which turned out to provide several interesting clues. Jacqueline Weld's biography of Barnes's friend Peggy Guggenheim, for instance, mentioned that Barnes, after a summer with Guggenheim and other friends, had left for Tangier in the fall of 1932, the manuscript of *Nightwood* tucked neatly under her arm.[4] Parker Tyler, in his biography of Charles Henri Ford's lover Pawel Tchelitchew (the search for answers can sometimes carry one rather far afield), provided more information. He said that Ford had gone to Tangier with a lady friend sometime after the summer of 1932, but that she had "lost her heart" to another while there. Ford therefore had invited Barnes to join him, which she did, a romance had sprung up between them, and the two had eventually moved back to Paris together. This, Tyler said, occurred in midsummer of 1932, after "rats ate the poor lady's clothes" in Tangier.[5] (The denouement, for those interested, was that Ford soon became re-interested in Tchelitchew and moved in with him in the fall of 1933.)

The problem with Tyler's story, aside from his vagueness about dates, was that he provided no documentation, but his account was corroborated somewhat by Paul Bowles's version of the story in his autobiography, *Without Stopping.* He too claimed that Ford invited Barnes, although he said that before her arrival Ford was with a couple, not a woman (the story gets murkier; the sexual arithmetic starts to become higher mathematics). He added that Ford and Barnes stayed at first at his house, a house he used only to work in, with the understanding that they would always be out by 1:30 in the afternoon, but that they soon moved to a house a few hundred feet away, where they lived Moroccan-style (in other words, on the floor). Bowles also mentioned that Djuna liked to appear at a café in Tangier wearing blue, purple, and green makeup, and to startle patrons and passersby with an impromptu imitation of the painter Sir Francis Rose.[6]

This was a certain amount, except that it still didn't answer what had happened, or even exactly when. The when became clearer when I learned that Bowles was not in Tangier in the fall of 1932, when Weld had Barnes there, but was there in the spring of 1933.[7] As for the what, Andrew Field

in his biography of Barnes provided the first explanation I had seen, an explanation fully as startling as Djuna Barnes must have been in her blue, purple, and green makeup. He agreed that Ford and Barnes were in Tangier together in early 1933, although he had them living in three houses, not two, the third being a splendid two-level house overlooking the bay and built around a magnificent inner courtyard dominated by a giant fig tree. It was in this house, according to Field, that Barnes realized that at the age of forty-one she was pregnant. The father, still according to Field, was not the obvious suspect, Charles Henri Ford, although Ford did propose to Barnes that they have the child together. Rather, it was the French painter Jean Oberle, with whom Barnes had supposedly had an affair in late 1932. Once she learned that she was pregnant, Field concluded, Barnes and Ford left Morocco for Paris, where Barnes had an abortion.[8]

Although I would have felt more comfortable with Field's story if he had provided a few footnotes to explain how he had learned it (instead, he only mentioned a letter from Barnes to Mina Loy, and hinted at interviews with Ford, Janet Flanner, and perhaps another, as he described her, "expatriate, lesbian lady"), the events he described were certainly disturbing enough to justify Barnes's later reaction. The mystery was close to solution, I thought, until I examined the letters from Yale and Texas. The Yale letters included one from Barnes to Robert McAlmon, dated 22 April 1933, and sent from Tangier; leaving out the possibility of some inexplicable subterfuge, that took care of the when, although the letter was still vague about the what. "'Goings' with me are fairly lousy just at the moment," Barnes began. She then said that she had been in Tangier for about a month, and described the place as "not particularly amusing, nor comfortable, nor so cheap considering what one gets for it." Nevertheless, she was planning to stay, working on her book on the Baroness Elsa von Freytag-Loringhoven (a friend from Barnes's Greenwich Village days), until July, if she could afford it.

Except for mentioning that she was depressed because "everyone seems to be dying" (she was thinking particularly of the death of a former lover, and perhaps husband, Courtenay Lemon, on 2 April, and of Hart Crane's recent suicide), Barnes gave no further hints in this letter about her condition. But four letters in the Texas collection, all to Charles Henri Ford, fleshed out the story a bit more. The first to mention Tangier was sent in September 1933 from on board the ship *Augustus* which Barnes was taking back to America. It said simply, "Three days out nearing that awful Tanger, which I had hope of never seeing again," and was signed, "Always, D." The second, sent a month later from New York, was short and concluded: "I miss Europe like the devil! No one here as poor, apparently, as they have an idea they are; at least to me, who survived Tanger, it looks like God's left foot." The third sounded the same note. Again she mentioned the "rumors" of people starving in the gutters, something she had not seen, she said, and again she contrasted this supposed poverty with what she had experienced in Morocco: ". . . [S]o I am contented," she concluded. "In fact I am so contented with nothing since I've been back—having had so much less in Morocco—that everyone thinks I am a little mad. . . ."[9]

Finally, in the fourth letter, from July 1934, Barnes asked Ford a series of questions about Morocco, for a story she said she was writing about Tangier. (This was the letter to which I had read the answer, way back at the beginning of my search.) She could, it seemed, remember none of the details she needed, causing her to lament: "My God, what a condition I must have been in, was in."

So where does that leave one? The discrepancies between Field's conclusions and these letters are clear. The problem the letters suggest is squalor, not sex. Even the tone Barnes adopts with Ford is surprisingly casual, given the presumed circumstances. But there is nothing definitive, nothing that would either prove or disprove that Barnes had an abortion, that would solve, for now and forever, the mystery of what exactly happened in Morocco. Of course, a few options still remain. One might talk with Charles Henri Ford. One might find still other letters. One might consult a Ouija board.

Or . . . one might accept the mystery as a mystery and go on from there. A few conclusions are, after all, possible, even at this stage. It seems clear, for instance, after looking so closely at this minor problem, that there are no minor problems. Everything connects, as E. M. Forster might have said: begin with Morocco and whatever happened there, look for links to other events in Barnes's life, and you can end up almost anywhere. You can go back to Thelma Wood, who on the one hand led to Charles Henri Ford (and Morocco), and on the other led to *Nightwood,* which Barnes just happened to begin rewriting immediately after returning from Morocco, even though she had announced to McAlmon in April that it was finished. You can also go back, given the coincidence of his dying at just this time, to Courtenay Lemon, the supposed husband, who followed from Percy Faulkner, another supposed husband, who followed from Wald Barnes, father and supposed abuser. Or, if you prefer, you can go forward, from Charles Henri Ford (and perhaps Oberle) to Peter Neagoe to Scudder Middleton to Silas Glossup, a litany of failed loves. Or you can connect the horror of Morocco with the horrors that were still to come, particularly the breakdown of 1939, that was followed by the return to America and the self-imposed isolation that would extend for the rest of Djuna Barnes's life.

Another conclusion, only slightly more speculative, is that the questions that arise so frequently about Djuna Barnes, questions like what happened in Morocco, may themselves be answers. The mysteries, without being solved themselves, could in fact provide the key to understanding Djuna Barnes. There is no doubt, after all, that the mysteries are not just historical accidents. Barnes's later-life dislike of biographers and their questions (not to mention what she called "idiot children working on Ph.D.'s"[10]) is legendary. "Biographies sadden me," she wrote to Willa Muir in 1967. "Expositions write us away, commentaries have killed us all."[11] To stop the carnage, she made it a point never to help those who wanted to write about her or even about people she knew or had known. (At the same time, interestingly, she was often curious about these works. She inevitably demanded to see books about her before they were published; she also seems to have checked the indices of books about friends and in at least one case penciled in her name where it should have been.[12]) On several occasions she describes in letters a day spent destroying notes and letters.[13] She spent a good part of one autumn trying (unsuccessfully, as it turned out, which is how we know she tried) to retrieve her letters from Emily Coleman so she could destroy them.[14] And if all else failed, she simply changed the record. Her insistence to Hank O'Neal at the end of her life that she had never lived with Charles Henri Ford is just one example of this.[15]

As Barnes grew older, her addiction to obfuscation also grew, but her reticence actually started long before biographers began their presumptuous probing. Margaret Anderson claims that the Barnes she knew in the twenties would never talk and would never allow herself to be talked to, that she was in fact "not on speaking terms with her own psyche."[16] John Holms, who met Barnes at Hayford Hall in 1932, thought much the same, and even Emily Coleman, to whom Barnes eventually revealed so much, began by complaining constantly in her diary that Barnes would not talk about herself, would not write about herself, would not be honest even with herself. "There's a vacuum in her head,"[17] she said then, although she later amended her opinion. Djuna Barnes, one of the foremost writers of the twentieth century, could think, she decided. She just wasn't willing to express what she thought.

Of course, part of this was probably Barnes keeping herself for herself. Like Kafka, she was her own best subject, particularly as she progressed as a writer. (It is ironic that both Kafka and Barnes, although obsessed with privacy, at one point considered writing their life stories, although neither did.[18]) No matter how often or how profoundly she explored her life in her fiction, however, Barnes made sure that she revealed as little as possible as obscurely as possible, at least on the surface. Her procedure when writing *Nightwood* (as far as we can tell from the manuscripts that survive, at any rate) is representative. With each draft, she pared more scenes and more details. The novel became shorter and, perhaps more to the point, the story became more muted, more implicit. To put it another way, Barnes, by making her art more obvious, made herself less obvious. That she eventually, in editing the manuscript, had the "help" of T. S. Eliot, himself no stranger to hiding behind a text, is (depending on one's perspective) just one more historical accident, one more irony, or one more complication to add to the plot.

So where does that leave one, I ask yet again. The pattern that emerges is clear, I think: Barnes was someone who spent, not just the last years of her life, but nearly all of it, obfuscating her own past. The result is that what we know, what she lets us know, may very well be the least important things about her. Perhaps, to return to our beginning, the questions, the events she tried to conceal from others, that she may even, whether consciously or unconsciously, have tried to conceal from herself, are the real answers. If, despite the vast amount of material available to help us understand her, Djuna Barnes remains an especially elusive prey, a pleasure to pursue certainly, but also a constant warning of the limitations of biography, of the care that must be taken in trying to track her, perhaps the better strategy is to look at what we don't know, to create what might be called a biography of gaps. After all, as Barnes herself is always there to remind us: "Facts? Where are facts? Who remembers a life, even his own?"[19]

NOTES

1. All quotations from the copyrighted letters of Djuna Barnes are used with the permission of the Authors League Fund. The letters I have quoted are housed in four main collections: The Barnes Papers at McKeldin Library, University of Maryland at College Park; The Emily Holmes Coleman Papers at the University of Delaware; The Humanities Research Center at the University of Texas at Austin; The Beinecke Rare Book and Manuscript Library at Yale University. I wish to thank all of them for their assistance, and especially Dr. Blanche Ebeling-Koning at Maryland and Timothy Murray at Delaware.

2. Djuna Barnes to Emily Coleman, 8 November 1935.

3. Djuna Barnes to Elizabeth Chappell Barnes, 7 April 1926.

4. Jacqueline Weld, *Peggy, the Wayward Guggenheim* (New York: Dutton, 1986), 97.

5. Parker Tyler, *The Divine Comedy of Pawel Tchelitchew* (London: Hammond, Hammond, 1961), 356, 358.

6. Paul Bowles, *Without Stopping* (New York: Ecco Press, 1985), 165-66.

7. Michelle Green, *The Dream at the End of the World* (New York: Harper Collins, 1991), 6.

8. Andrew Field, *Djuna* (Austin: University of Texas Press, 1985), 165-66.

9. Djuna Barnes to Charles Henri Ford, 16 December 1933, Ford Papers.

10. Djuna Barnes to Natalie Barney, 28 March 1967, Barnes Papers.

11. Djuna Barnes to Willa Muir, 23 January 1967, Barnes Papers

12. Djuna Barnes's personal library included a copy of Peter Butter's biography of Edwin Muir in which she had thus altered the index.

13. See, for instance, Djuna Barnes to Emily Coleman, 6 November 1950, Barnes Papers.

14. Letters from Djuna Barnes to Emily Coleman, 22 October, 9 November, 11 December 1967, Barnes Papers.

15. Hank O'Neal, "*Life is painful, nasty and short . . .*" (New York: Paragon House, 1990), 152.

16. Margaret Anderson, *My Thirty Years' War* (Westport, CT: Greenwood Press, 1971), 181.

17. Emily Coleman's diary, 2 December 1932, 210, Coleman Papers.

18. See, for instance, Djuna Barnes to Emily Coleman, 8 September 1936, Coleman Papers.

19. Djuna Barnes to Louis Sheaffer, 9 July 1962, Barnes Papers.

Frann Michel (essay date Fall 1993)

SOURCE: "'I Just Loved Thelma': Djuna Barnes and the Construction of Bisexuality," in *Review of Contemporary Fiction*, Vol. 13, No. 3, Fall, 1993, pp. 53-61.

[*In the following essay, Michel analyzes the role of sexual identity in Barnes's life and works.*]

When asked about her sexuality, Djuna Barnes is reported to have answered, "I'm not a lesbian, I just loved Thelma."[1] Given Barnes's apparent uneasiness with categorization, it is perhaps not surprising that readers of her work are divided over whether she is best read as a lesbian or as a homophobic writer. In particular, critics have debated whether *Ladies Almanack* celebrates or attacks lesbians. But the current move to include the identity "bisexual" within queer politics may provide a new way of approaching these questions. Although Barnes never identified herself as bisexual, her position was fluid throughout her life and from book to book.

Moreover, there are some intriguing similarities between characterizations of Barnes's writing and recent characterizations of bisexuality. Critics interested in the sexuality manifest in Barnes's works, and activists concerned with the place of bisexuality in queer politics, seem both to have been working from similar ideas about form, content, and the production of meaning. Because of the stylistic complexity of Barnes's works, it can sometimes be useful to translate those texts into more easily comprehensible summaries, finding a linear narrative of a young girl's development in **Ryder,** for instance, or an autobiographical correlative for the incest narrative in **The Antiphon.** To rest with these translations, however, can be to accept an implicit division of form and content, to posit form as the container or the disguise of content or meaning. But as I will argue, Barnes's presentations of sexuality posit meaning not as contained in a stable form, but as produced by a vibrant interplay of varied forms.

The discussion of Barnes's sexuality, as well as of the sexuality of her work, has gravitated toward dichotomous positions. In 1973 Bertha Harris celebrated Barnes as a lesbian role model; in 1984 Tee Corrine described Barnes as homophobic.[2] **Ladies Almanack,** in particular, has been characterized by Susan Sniader Lanser as the work of an insider to the lesbian Natalie Barney circle, and by Karla Jay as the "venomous" work of an outsider.[3] Like much of the critical commentary on Barnes's work, these discussions tend to assume a division between form and content. In such views, Barnes was *really* a lesbian, but denied this true identity because of homophobia. Similarly, Catharine Stimpson has described Barnes's style as "evasive," Marie Ponsot has called its charms "superficial," and Louise DeSalvo has found in Barnes's work a style "which simultaneously masks and reveals."[4] What is masked or evaded, revealed or hidden beneath a superficial style is apparently the true identity of the text, the real story, the content.

Yet Barnes insisted, in a notebook entry, that "The truth is *how* you say it, and to be 'one's self' is the most shocking custom of all."[5] The ironic stance of **Ladies Almanack,** in particular, illustrates that unity of matter and manner. **"July,"** for example, consists of a complaint about the excesses of women's love language to each other, "the Means by which she puts her Heart from her Mouth to her Sleeve, and from her Sleeve into Rhetorick, and from that into the Ear of her beloved."[6] The chapter thus suggests a double disdain for the idea of being "one's self" both in its critique of an earnest, humorless sincerity, a "witless" pouring out of one's heart, and in its elaboration of the lengthy route the heart actually takes through mouth, sleeve, and rhetoric.

The chapter ends: "twittering so loud upon the Wire that one cannot hear the Message. And yet!" (46). The narrator's complaint implicitly includes the love letter of her own text: ornate, elaborate, Barnes's style might seem to obscure a clear message. And yet the irony of the chapter's complaint depends upon its sly ostentation. To omit the "And yet!" or to translate it into a direct statement would obscure precisely the "Humor" that the chapter critiques women's love letters for lacking. The "truth" of the chapter lies precisely in *how* it is written.

Further, the quotation marks Barnes places around "one's self" call our attention to the discursive status of this construct. Being "one's self" is a performance; the pose of sincerity can become a way of shocking others. For Barnes, then, one chooses the role one plays, and while the pose of sincerity or identity may be useful, there is no stable identity outside these roles. As a discursive construct, "one's self" exists only in a larger context, an exchange with present interlocutors or future readers.

If Barnes's work repeatedly warns us away from dichotomizing its form and content in service of arguments that it is "really" lesbian or homophobic, then we need other ways of discussing the sexuality manifest in that work. Recent bisexual activism and consequent public discussions on bisexual identity make available conceptual tools useful in mediating debates on the sexuality of Barnes and her work. Barnes herself is known to have been sexually involved with both men and women, and by some accounts loved men as well as women. In that sense, the most apt identification of Barnes would be bisexual.

There are, of course, multiple ways of understanding bisexuality. It can be characterized and critiqued in ways that divide form and content, preserving the analogous binarism of heterosexual and homosexual, or queer and straight. Yet if bisexual positioning is understood as one way of acknowledging the complexity of sexuality—of the interplay of desire, fantasy, behavior, social affiliation, emotional connection—then it serves as a challenge to essentializing dichotomies, a challenge also evident in Barnes's works.

Some arguments both "for" and "against" including bisexuality in queer movement can fall prey to problems of the same form/content divisions that vex accounts of Barnes's writing. Anxious lesbians and gay men insist that bisexuals are *really* just not out of the closet; earnest bisexuals claim that sex between bi men and bi women is nonetheless queer.[7] But both of these positions neglect the production of meaning in ongoing social discourses.

If the truth is *how* you say it, then bisexuals are not just stuck on the threshold of the closet. If being "one's self" is a "custom," then it is not simply the declaration of an individual monad free of culture and context. Some queer observers have been rightly skeptical of the way the bisexual label can be used to reinterpret queer figures in heterocentric ways. As Rebecca Ripley notes, the "idea that anybody is essentially, basically, really gay doesn't go down easily with straight Americans. They'd rather think that everybody is bi and therefore 'partially straight.'"[8] In a September 1992 *Nation* review, for instance, Charlotte Innes critiques recent representations of Vita Sackville-West, Violet Trefusis, and Harold Nicolson that have glorified the Sackville-West-Nicolson marriage at the expense of their same-sex relationships, and that have thus obscured as well as recapitulated the impact of homophobia on their stories. Identifying a writer as lesbian, or celebrating a lesbian text, can help provide the conceptual leverage needed to break free of such heterocentric readings.

But ideas about who or what is a lesbian or a lesbian text are as culturally and historically specific as are the dangerous uses to which a bisexual identification can be put. Indeed, if "to be 'one's self' is the most shocking custom of all," we would do well to keep in mind the risks entailed in any essentializing claims to authenticity of identity, even as we keep in sight the more palpable dangers entailed in presenting a self that for many still has the power to be shocking.

The distinction I am drawing here between a critical approach based on questions of identity and one moving toward increasingly textured understandings of sexuality can also be understood as a distinction between lesbian-feminist and queer theory. Anti-foundationalist, queer theory moves through poststructuralist articulations of the construction of subjectivity by diverse systems of power. Thus, whereas lesbian-feminist theory postulates an unproblematic continuity between the terms on either side of its hyphen, queer theory, in contrast, disarticulates sexual and gender politics. Yet while queer theory promises a movement beyond identity politics, the queer movement is pulled back to questions of identity by immediate political battles.

Opposition to the recent spate of measures that would block or rescind legal recognition of gay and lesbian rights has tended to crystallize around appeals to the idea of a genetic basis for sexual identity. Like arguments for the "real" content of a literary work, this genetic argument presumes an unchanging, essential identity. It has presumably had the tactical value of reassuring straight parents that gays in the schools are not going to be recruiting their children, and indeed of assuring all heterosexuals that their sexual identities are secure. Yet the genetic account of sexual identity has precluded the possibility of arguing that it would be OK

to choose one's sexual identity if one felt such a choice was possible, and has excluded from public discourse the possibility of arguing that heterosexuality, too, is a constructed institution rather than a biological inevitability.

These exclusions of choice and of construction constitute an exclusion of bisexuality, which is frequently associated with the possibility of choosing one's sexuality. One lesbian-identified woman reports in an interview with Dvora Zipkin, "I suppose in some kind of pure sexual sense, I am bisexual. . . . it really does feel like a choice. I know that *choice* is a bad word in queer circles these days, but I think there's a lot of choice involved in our sexual identity."[9] Bisexual activists also frequently stress the experience of sexual identity as fluid rather than fixed, the product of ongoing social construction rather than of a roll of the genetic dice. Amanda Udis-Kessler notes that "Constructionism . . . [posits] that everyone has, if not the experience of living a bisexual life, at least the potential to do so" and "that one's sexuality is not necessarily firmly set at age five, or even at age fifty."[10] Indeed, the public emergence of bisexuality as an issue in queer movement is partly a result of prominent lesbians like writer Jan Clausen becoming involved with men. The woman who writes under the name "Eridani" states that she uses the word "bisexual" as "shorthand for 'not having a sexual orientation.'"[11] The term "bisexuality," then, despite its nominal stability, still points toward a more flexible and finely grained understanding of all sexuality. While the polarization of political positions for or against legal measures is inevitable, the polarization of available sexualities into homosexual or heterosexual is not, and indeed misses the full shape of the construction of female sexuality in Barnes's works.

In ***Ladies Almanack,*** Evangeline Musset, "developed in the Womb of her most gentle Mother to be a Boy" (7), approximates the sexological accounts, dominant in the twenties, of female homosexuality as innate gender inversion—the precursor to the genetic argument, as it were. But Saint Musset's role as evangelist for the sect demonstrates that she can win converts. Indeed, the ease with which she comes to do so suggests the historical variability of women loving women.

> "In my day," said Dame Musset . . . "I was a Pioneer and a Menace, it was not then as it is now, *chic* and pointless to a degree, but as daring as a Crusade. . . . What joy has the missionary, . . . when all the Heathen greet her with Glory Halleluja! before she opens her Mouth, and with an Amen! before she shuts it!" (34)

While Musset's comments might indicate that some opponents of lesbian and gay rights are correct in their suspicions that social acceptance of same-sex eroticism can lead to more of it, her dismay at its newly chic status is differently motivated. Despite her disappointment at the ease of her recent seductions, however, the text does not confirm the view of her Crusade as "pointless." The frontispiece to the text depicts Dame Musset "out upon that exceeding thin ice to which it has pleased God, more and more, to call frail woman, there so conducting herself that none were put to the chagrin of sinking for the third time!" One of the drowning women appears to be drowning with a man, and Dame Musset's salvation of women from the frigid waters of heterosexual relations appears both heroic and, as the caption informs us, "endearing."

Think now of the narrator of the Buffalo Oral History Project who pointed out that in the 1940s "There was a great difference in looks between a lesbian and her girl."[12] The comment calls our attention to a range of positions historically available to women who have been retrospectively recast as uniformly "lesbian." Think of Stephen Gordon and Mary Llewellyn in *The Well of Loneliness*. Think of Thelma Wood calling herself "Simon" when writing to Barnes.[13] Is the lesbian's girl a lesbian? Is Stephen's? Is "Simon"'s? Well, no, not exactly. But to describe her as somehow "really" heterosexual would seem equally to miss the point.

That the category "lesbian" was not always defined, understood, and experienced as it is today should remind us that sexual identity is culturally constructed and historically variable. There may be more value in making use of any formulations that challenge heterosexism and heterocentrism than in determining what constitutes a "real" lesbian identity or in pursuing dichotomized debates about Barnes's relation to the closet. Even if a work enacts patterns of what we would today recognize as homophobia, even if its representation of same-sex desire is less complete or complex than some readers would prefer, still it may offer its queer audience considerable readerly pleasures and powers. Thus, for example, the catalytic node of what Barnes called "the Proustian chronicle" is a chapter that, as Eve Sedgwick points out, most readers find reductive and sentimental, and that invites as well as repels what Sedgwick calls "the by now authentically banal exposure of Proust's narrator as a closeted homosexual."[14]

Barnes's 1972 foreword to *Ladies Almanack* describes the work as

> Neap-tide to the Proustian chronicle, gleanings from the shores of Mytilene, glimpses of its novitiates, its rising "saints" and "priestesses," and thereon to such aptitude and insouciance that they took to gaming and to swapping that "other" of the mystery, the anomaly that calls the hidden name. (3)

The description of this almanac of female same-sex eroticism as "gleanings from the shores of Mytilene" alludes of course to Sappho, who represents, as Susan Gubar observes, "all the lesbian artists whose work" has been lost or misread, and more specifically to the Sappho whose legend provided the background for the relationship between Renée Vivien and Natalie Barney, who traveled together to Mytilene.[15] Embracing lesbianism as a kind of geographical identity, moreover, seems to put in question essentializing models of sexual inversion or innate sexuality. If, as we learn later in *Ladies Almanack,* "The very Condition of Woman is so subject to Hazard, so complex, and so grievous, that to place her at one Moment is but to displace her at the next" (55), then perhaps any Woman might choose to displace herself to the shores of Mytilene. Asking Richard Aldington to publish *Ladies Almanack,* Natalie Barney wrote to him that "All ladies fit to figure in such an almanack should of course be eager to have a copy, and all gentlemen disapproving of them. Then the public might, with a little judicious treatment, include those lingering on the border of such islands and those eager to be ferried across."[16] The idea of sapphic sexuality as a location suggests that it may be understood as a position, a perspective from which one might critique the whole map of sexuality as it is currently drawn.

Barnes's "Foreword" also calls into question the borders of that map. Shari Benstock identifies "that 'other' of the mystery" with the Lacanian Other and with the "woman of man's dreams."[17] But its relation of apposition with "the anomaly that calls the hidden name" seems to connect it with "the love that dare not speak its name." The anomalous "other," then, seems rather to be the figure Matthew O'Connor and Nora Flood in Barnes's *Nightwood* discuss as "the third sex," the invert who, like Evangeline Musset, is born that way. But then who is gaining "aptitude and insouciance" and doing the "gaming" and "swapping"? In the "Foreword," as in the text, Barnes's presentation of the residents of Mytilene is broadly inclusive.

Even in *Nightwood,* which seems to deploy the geneticist model of the "third sex" more fully than does *Ladies Almanack,* definitions of the content of sexuality are uncertain. Though Nora and the Doctor discuss Robin as an exemplum of the third sex, it is Robin who marries and has a child. Nora, in contrast, is *not* discussed as a member of the "third sex," though she is the only major female character whose only sexual relationship in the book is with another woman. Thus *Nightwood,* too, indicates the explanatory limits of essentialist, identity-based models of sexuality. If Robin "has come from place that we have forgotten and would give our life to recall," perhaps she's come from Mytilene.[18]

If the emergence of bisexuality as a description of sexual identity helps put into question essentialist, genetic models that permitted an analogy between sexual and racial identity, Barnes's partially constructionist model in **Ladies Almanack** opens up the possibility of another politically useful analogy. The language of "saints," "priestesses," and "novitiates" might remind us that religious freedom is also a civil right. Beliefs, like desires, cannot be chosen by a simple act of will, but they may change and evolve. Not everyone has a religious vocation, of course, but then, as Eridani suggests, not everyone has a sexual orientation, either.

The discussion of the sexuality manifest in Barnes's life and works has, of course, not been entirely dichotomous or always rested with a division of form and content. Those critics who have attended most closely to the finely grained presentation of female sexuality in Barnes's work and who have examined the ways that it produces meaning have pointed the most fruitful directions for Barnes scholarship. Frances Doughty, for instance, suggests the "issue is not whether Barnes was a lesbian or a heterosexual, but that she was neither."[19] Carolyn Allen notes that the biographical record reveals Barnes's assertion that she was not a lesbian, she "just loved Thelma," but observes that some of Barnes's works remain "classics of lesbian imagination" nonetheless.[20] In these views, Barnes becomes a lesbian writer, and might arguably become a bisexual writer, not because of what she or her writings *really* did or said, but because of their apprehension by critics and other readers for whom Barnes provides productive critiques of compulsory heterosexuality and generative imaginings of alternative sexualities.

NOTES

1. Andrew Field, *Djuna: The Life and Times of Djuna Barnes* (New York: Putnam, 1983), 37.

2. Cited in Carolyn Allen, "Writing Toward *Nightwood*: Djuna Barnes' Seduction Stories," in *Silence and Power: A Reevaluation of Djuna Barnes*, ed. Mary Lynn Broe (Carbondale: Southern Illinois University Press, 1991), 54.

3. Lanser, "Speaking in Tongues: *Ladies Almanack* and the Discourse of Desire," in Broe, 156-68; Karla Jay, "The Outsider among the Expatriates: Djuna Barnes' Satire on the Ladies of the *Almanack*," in Broe, 186.

4. Stimpson, "Afterword," in Broe, 371; Ponsot, "A Reader's *Ryder*," Broe, 94; DeSalvo, "'To Make Her Mutton at Sixteen': Rape, Incest, and Child Abuse in *The Antiphon*," Broe, 301.

5. Barnes, quoted in Broe, front jacket flap.

6. Djuna Barnes, *Ladies Almanack* (New York: New York University Press, 1992), 43; hereafter cited parenthetically.

7. Ara Wilson, "Just Add Water: Searching for the Bisexual Politic," *Out/Look: National Gay and Lesbian Quarterly* 4.4 (Spring 1992): 27.

8. "The Language of Desire: Sexuality, Identity and Language," in *Closer to Home: Bisexuality and Feminism*, ed. Elizabeth Reba Weise (Seattle: Seal Press, 1992), 95.

9. "Why Bi?" in Weise, 59.

10. "Bisexuality in an Essentialist World," in *Bisexuality: A Reader and Sourcebook*, ed. Thomas Geller (Ojai, CA: Times Change Press, 1990), 58.

11. "Is Sexual Orientation a Secondary Sex Characteristic?" in Weise, 174.

12. Quoted in Madeline D. Davis and Elizabeth Lapovsky Kennedy, "Oral History and the Study of Sexuality in the Lesbian Community: Buffalo, New York, 1940-1960," in *Unequal Sisters: A Multi-Cultural Reader in U.S. Women's History*, ed. Ellen Carol DuBois and Vicki L. Ruiz (New York: Routledge, 1990), 388.

13. Cited in Shari Benstock, *Women of the Left Bank: Paris, 1900-1940* (Austin: University of Texas Press, 1986), 256.

14. *Epistemology of the Closet* (Berkeley: University of California Press, 1990), 223.

15. "Sapphistries," in *The Lesbian Issue: Essays from "Signs,"* ed. Estelle B. Freedman et al. (Chicago: University of Chicago Press, 1985), 94, 95-96.

16. Cited in Benstock, 249.

17. Benstock, 247.

18. Djuna Barnes, *Nightwood* (New York: New Directions, 1946), 118.

19. "Gilt on Cardboard: Djuna Barnes as Illustrator of Her Life and Work," in Broe, 149.

20. Allen, in Broe, 54.

Michael Dirda (review date 12 November 1995)

SOURCE: "A Legend in Her Own Time," in *Washington Post Book World*, Vol. 25, No. 46, November 12, 1995, p. 5.

[*In the following review, Dirda discusses Phillip Herring's*

Djuna: The Life and Work of Djuna Barnes *and the reprinting of Barnes's* Nightwood.]

As it happens, a friend of mine lives in Patchin Place, the little courtyard in Greenwich Village where Djuna Barnes (1892-1982) spent the last 40-some years of her amazing life. Two decades ago, when Barnes was still alive, I used to think of ringing her doorbell and genuflecting or kissing her hand or presenting her with a bottle of Scotch. After all, she was one of the last surviving giants of 20th-century literature, author of the legendary *Nightwood,* and a woman who counted James Joyce among her drinking buddies and T. S. Eliot among her admirers. Make that fervent admirers: Eliot kept her picture above his desk (next to that of Yeats), addressed her as "dearest" in letters, and once declared her the greatest living writer.

Moreover, Eliot was hardly alone in his enthusiasm. Dylan Thomas used to read from *Nightwood* on his speaking tours of America. Samuel Beckett, whom Barnes scarcely knew, sent her part of the royalties from *Waiting for Godot.* Even Dag Hammarskjold, secretary general of the United Nations, valued her work so highly that he helped translate her verse-drama, *The Antiphon,* into Swedish. Rumor has it that he was pulling strings to get her the Nobel Prize when his plane was shot down over Africa.

I never saw her, and doubtless she would have growled at me to go away even if she bothered to open the door. For most of her life Barnes was essentially a "cult" author, esteemed by a small coterie that kept *Nightwood* in print, savored the brocaded prose of her early autobiographical novel *Ryder,* and guffawed over the Rabelaisian lesbians of *Ladies Almanack* (its various ribald characters were based on Parisian notables like salon-keeper Natalie Barney, journalist Janet Flanner, and poets Romaine Brooks and Renee Vivien). In recent years, feminist scholars have begun to mine Barnes's work—the University of Maryland, which houses her papers, held a major conference a few years back. (Unfortunately, those talks, reprinted in a special issue of the *Review of Contemporary Literature,* are, for the most part, dully academic when comprehensible.) It is, thus, clearly the right time for both a good new biography and a modestly priced scholarly edition of Barnes's greatest prose work.

Phillip Herring, a Joyce expert by training, provides a straightforward chronological account of this once-neglected writer's family, friends and career. By comparison with the ill-organized, highly anecdotal 1983 life produced by Andrew Field (oft vilified—sometimes justly—for his early biography of Nabokov), Herring's work seems a little pedantic, the product of a sabbatical rather than the spillover from a passion. The phrase "thoroughly sound" comes irresistibly to mind and might normally be enough to sink the

book, except for one small fact: If the soaps ever need any new plot lines, Djuna Barnes's life and work will supply plenty of naughty ideas.

For starters, Barnes's father, Wald, lived with wife, mistress and mother, not to mention assorted offspring, in a big, unhappy family. As a believer in the freest sorts of free love, Dad either raped the teenaged Djuna and/or gave her as a present to an elderly neighbor to deflower. Through most of her childhood the future author slept in the same bed with her grandmother and would seem to have engaged in some level of sexual play with the older woman (surprisingly graphic letters exist). At 17 she was even talked into a common-law marriage with a 52-year-old soap peddler. It only lasted a few months.

Not surprisingly, Barnes was happy to escape from her family to New York, where in the years just before and after World War I she became a well-paid, sought-after young journalist (and occasional illustrator, all too obviously in thrall to Aubrey Beardsley). In one stunt piece she described the ordeal of being force-fed through a tube shoved down her throat, a then common method for preserving the life of fasting suffragettes. Soon she was hanging out with the Provincetown Players, where she came to know Eugene O'Neill, John Reed and other bohemian notables. But, eventually, like so many of the artistically ambitious, the would-be novelist hied herself to Paris and the Left Bank, where she got to know . . . everybody, including Pound, Stein, Hemingway and Joyce—or Jim, as she was allowed to call him.

In her youth Barnes was a striking, if somewhat severe auburn-haired beauty, attractive to both men and women. Although most of her affairs were heterosexual, she always called Thelma Wood the central passion of her life. "I'm not a lesbian. I simply loved Thelma." The liaison lasted eight or so years, and when it was over, Barnes memorialized her lost love in a great work of lamentation, *Nightwood.* In prose of haunting musicality and splendor, she describes the havoc wreaked by Robin Vote, i.e., Wood, on the people who care for her. Here is the book's August and intricately wrought opening sentence:

> Early in 1880, in spite of a well-founded suspicion as to the advisability of perpetuating that race which has the sanction of the Lord and the disapproval of the people, Hedvig Volkbein, a Viennese woman of great strength and military beauty, lying upon a canopied bed, of a rich spectacular crimson, the valance stamped with the bifurcated wings of the House of Hapsburg, the feather coverlet an envelope of satin on which, in massive and tarnished gold threads, stood the Volkbein arms,—gave birth, at the age of forty-

five, to an only child, a son, seven days after her physician had predicted that she would be taken.

Barnes doesn't always write with such oracular, slightly humorous gravity; she can also be quite vulgarly funny, as when a character describes another "whipped with impatience, like a man waiting at a toilet door for someone inside who had decided to read the *Decline and Fall of the Roman Empire.*" In fact, most of the novel's grandest rhetorical flights belong to Dr. Matthew O'Connor, a drunken Irish Tiresias and advisor to the disconsolate, at once swishy, witty and pitiful. As O'Connor explains, "just being miserable isn't enough—you've got to know how." When Nora, the Barnes stand-in, complains about her loneliness, the doctor quickly one-ups her: "A broken heart have you! I have falling arches, flying dandruff, a floating kidney, shattered nerves *and* a broken heart." O'Connor is quite unforgettable, as are the book's starting final pages; Robin, always associated with beasts, is glimpsed in an abandoned chapel, down on her hands and knees, making strangely sexual overtures to her former lover's pet dog.

Shocking, confusingly structured, lyrical and haunting, *Nightwood* didn't precisely sell itself to prospective publishers. Indeed, Cheryl Plumb provides an enthralling account of its publishing history in her introduction to the novel's "original version," crediting Barnes's friend Emily Coleman with astute editorial advice and great cleverness in persuading T. S. Eliot to read the manuscript. Eliot, then working as an editor for the British publishers Faber and Faber, insisted on some 13 pages of cuts, which are here restored. In general, his editing "blurred sexual, particularly homosexual, references and a few points that put religion in an unsavory light. However, meaning was not changed substantially, though the character of the work was adjusted, the language softened." Besides presenting Barnes's original vision of her masterpiece, Plumb's edition also provides useful textual and explanatory notes, as well as reproductions of the surviving typescript pages.

Soon after *Nightwood* appeared in 1936 Barnes's life fell apart: She started to drink heavily, love affairs went sour, money nearly dried up. Back in New York she rented a small apartment on Patchin Place and settled down to years of crankiness, alcohol and writer's block. Perhaps not the normal kind of block, for she composed reams of poetry and worked sporadically on various projects, but it wasn't until 1957 that she was able to finish *The Antiphon,* a play that virtually no one could understand. Written in a kind of Elizabethan blank verse and reminiscent, by turns, of *Waiting for Godot, The Family Reunion* and *Long Day's Journey into Night,* this sorrowful drama builds on its author's unresolved anger toward her family, her persistent sense of betrayal and sexual exploitation. It ends with a mother crushing the skull of her Barnes-like daughter.

Barnes thought *The Antiphon* her masterpiece. Maybe. Sometimes it seems brilliantly Shakespearean in its diction, rhythm and syntax; at other times, it seems as kitschy as Ronald Firbank. In either case, I find it quite irresistible. What's a little thing like meaning compared to such word-music as this:

> Yet corruption in its deft deploy
> Unbolts the caution, and the vesper mole
> Trots down the wintry pavement of the prophet's head.
> In the proud flesh of the vanished eye
> Vainglory, like a standing pool,
> Rejects the thirsty trades of paradise.
> The world is cracked—and in the breach
> My fathers mew.

Elsewhere Barnes evokes her father "flanked by warming-pans, bassoons and bastards" and gives her murderous brothers these conspiratorial lines: "We'll never have so good a chance again; / Never, never such a barren spot, / Nor the lucky anonymity of war." I think a production of *The Antiphon* could be a triumph. Or a hoot.

Djuna Barnes died in 1982 one week after her 90th birthday. Even now, I wish that I had had the courage to ring her doorbell at No. 5, Patchin Place. Real creators, no matter how wayward their genius, deserve our thanks and our homage.

Georgette Fleischer (review date 20 November 1995)

SOURCE: "Light on *Nightwood,*" in *Nation,* Vol. 261, No. 17, November 20, 1995, pp. 628-32.

[*In the following review, Fleischer praises Phillip Herring's* Djuna: The Life and Work of Djuna Barnes *for its accuracy, but complains that Cheryl Plumb makes too many assumptions about the editing of Barnes's* Nightwood *in her republication of the original version.*]

We've never known what to do with our literary geniuses, particularly blasphemous parodists like Emily Dickinson (coy) and Gertrude Stein (mannish), who subvert gender conventions and radically alter literary forms—perhaps the former is prerequisite to the latter. Djuna Barnes is no exception.

Or is she? Unlike Dickinson and Stein, almost everything Barnes wrote that she considered complete was published in her lifetime, and her 1936 novel *Nightwood* has never since its 1946 reissue by New Directions been out of print. Then why, when Dickinson's stature matches Walt

Whitman's and Stein's cachet supersedes Ernest Hemingway's, does the name Djuna Barnes—"the most famous unknown of the century," she dubbed herself—still evoke perplexed expressions? (Like Stein, who welcomed Hemingway in her rue de Fleurus salon but snubbed Barnes, she was an American expatriate in Paris during the 1920s.)

The first wave of feminist criticism largely passed Barnes by, but since her death in 1982, she has become a feminist cause célèbre: "Canonization" by male Modernists such as T. S. Eliot had been "[mis]appropriation," but "lesbian cult status" had minimized her; her brilliance had been underrated, but her work had also been "reduced to stylistics." In the midst of this maelstrom of contrary currents, the most vocal feminists extol *Nightwood* as the representative text of the "modernism of marginality" or of "sapphic modernism." Have these co-optings done right by Barnes?

They limit the appeal and therefore the readership for Barnes's work in ways that her work itself is not limited. They impute to Barnes politics she did not profess. Zealotry has spawned gross factual errors and irrational readings that have inflated within an insular critical field and emerged as full-blown myths. This has cheapened Djuna Barnes. It never would have happened in her lifetime. (Offended by Kenneth Burke's reading of *Nightwood,* Barnes told him off in several letters and withheld permission to quote.)

Both books under review are the products of extensive, painstaking research and go a long way toward correcting the factual errors that have so vexed Barnes scholarship in the thirteen years since she died, a week after her 90th birthday, in the company of a nurse, in a tiny Patchin Place apartment in Greenwich Village where for more than forty years she had increasingly withdrawn. Her early life was contrastingly lurid.

By the time Barnes was 5 years old, her father's mistress, Fanny Faulkner, had joined their household—which had relocated from Barnes's birthplace, Storm King Mountain, near Cornwall-on-Hudson, to a Huntington, Long Island, farm—and was producing half-siblings in tandem with mother Elizabeth, both women often pregnant at the same time, once giving birth twelve days apart. "Father and his bastard children and mistresses had thrown me off marriage and babies," Barnes wrote in 1938. In addition to helping care for her prodigal father's offspring, there were other pressures.

For years Barnes shared her father's mother's bed, and correspondence dating from when she was 13 years old is illustrated by grandmother Zadel with cartoons of breasts stretched out like penises and one nude woman atop another breast-to-breast. Here Phillip Herring provides fresh perspective, though he does so in a frustratingly mild manner:

> It is not necessary to go as far as to argue, as Mary Lynn Broe does, that the Zadel-Djuna relationship was incestuous and therefore beneficial as a refuge against patriarchal violence. Broe confuses a number of issues. She says: "Temporarily safe from the violations of the patriarchal household, Zadel and Djuna played in their symbolic, marginalized world, a queendom of 'nanophilia.'"

Here Broe's jubilant "marginality" and "sapphism" crash through the looking glass where irrationality reigns. In a perverse double standard, a father's penis is patriarchal violence but a grandmother's breast stretched out like a penis is loving protection. In the six years since this piece was published no critic has ever in print pointed out that it is improper and injurious for any family member to press sexual needs on a child, physically or emotionally, actually or in pornographic cartoons. This is not a gender issue.

Aside from exhaustive archival research, Herring's *Djuna* has the benefit of fresh material provided by Barnes's "cooperative but cautious" family. The new material is a strength but gives rise to a persistent bias. For example, a later chapter describes Barnes's alcoholism after her return from Europe:

> In March [1940], at their wits' end, her family sent her to a sanatorium in upstate New York, thus perpetrating what Djuna Barnes considered to be yet another violation of her person. Zendon [second of four brothers] had led her to believe she would be going to Arizona [where her friend Emily Coleman lived], then Saxon [third brother] brought her to Tratelja, on Diamond Point, Lake George. Outrageous! To Thurn [elder brother] she was just a "drunkard" who must be made to come to her senses. Nobody seemed sympathetic. Djuna contemplated revenge in a family biography.

Was deceptively luring Barnes to a sanatorium not a violation? (Once there, Barnes refused to "talk" to the psychiatrist, though she was amenable to discussing Proust.) Other of Herring's commentaries are downright puritanical. Regarding her first book of poems: "If one truly cared for Djuna Barnes, one would say very little indeed about *The Book of Repulsive Women,* for she and others often wished that these eight disgusting 'rhythms' accompanied by five drawings had never been published." Yet despite censorious residues, *Djuna* is a strong and in other respects generous biography: "This biography derives from a particular moment in time, when, in 1988, I was looking for more novels by women for my Modernism course. I wanted to teach *Nightwood* but felt frustrated by my futile efforts to understand it; before I could understand the novel, I believed, I had to understand Djuna Barnes." It is to be hoped that the modesty of his feminism will not be scoffed at. Herring spent seven years on this project, and with few exceptions he has gotten the facts right. While I frequently disagree with his assessments of Barnes's work, Herring has integrated her life and work persuasively, delivering a full-fledged critical biography and a fascinating read.

It was in Paris in the 1920s that Djuna Barnes fell in love with Thelma Wood—another American expatriate, a sculptor and silverpoint artist—because, Barnes would later say, Thelma reminded her of grandmother Zadel. "She was that terrible past reality," Barnes wrote in 1936, "over which any new life can only come, as a person marching up and over the high mound of a grave. . . . I have *had* my great love, there will never be another."

Barnes worried that after *Nightwood,* which she wrote about Thelma Wood, there would never be another great artistic achievement either. And there never was, not that great. Composing *Nightwood* was an arduous process undertaken during one of the most peripatetic periods of Barnes's life: six years of writing at least three versions, only to have her efforts repeatedly rejected on both sides of the Atlantic, including three rejections from the editor who had published three of her previous books. Then T. S. Eliot stepped in.

Eliot's role as Barnes's editor has been the single greatest controversy in Barnes criticism, which is why Cheryl Plumb's *Original Version and Related Drafts* is so important to scholars. Repeated assertions of Eliot's "text bashing" that "reduced *Nightwood* to a third of its original size" are immediately put to rest. Working from the version Eliot accepted for publication, Plumb restores eight pages of 139. Her introduction identifies several lobbyists for pruning the character Dr. Matthew-Mighty-Grain-of-Salt-Dante O'Connor's "raffish going on," as Barnes called it. The restored passages deepen our understanding of *Nightwood.* I do not think the restored version should supplant but should rather supplement the published one. I concur with T. S. Eliot's judgment here:

> Not that the Doctor's conversation flags at all, but simply because I think that *too much of it distorts the shape of the book.* There is a good deal of the book besides the Doctor, and we don't want him to steal everything. [August 12, 1936, to Barnes. Emphasis added. Reprinted with permission of Valerie Eliot.]

Dr. O'Connor is one of the most flamboyant characters in literature, and one of the most poignant. He is a homosexual

and transvestite, afflicted by being a woman trapped in a man's body. An illegal abortionist who haunts the *pissoirs* when looking for love, a liar and a thief, he is a glorious raconteur. Ultimately frustrated, all his speeches in the published version are meant to solace his variously afflicted friends. The restored speeches are without exception onanistic. Nor do they have, except in brief, the verbal and imagistic intensity of the published version. The following account of a visit to the palace of King Ludwig II ("the mad Wittelsbach"), a Roman Catholic and homosexual like O'Connor, comes closest:

> Up there in the palace there's an attendant wandering the great empty rooms with their plush chairs and pillars, throne-room and ballroom (that seems like a terrific terminal and no trains coming in), who remembers him still and for a mark will tell you how he was his valet—and you look out of the corner of your eye to see if he knows what that might mean—and if he knew, if he remembers. He said the king was so tall that he himself, six foot three, had to stand on the tips of his shoes to get at his tie. So suddenly I myself rose on tip-toes, right in the middle of that great fine room, and whispered, "Was he large?" and it went echoing and bellowing through all those rooms like a great bull getting madder and madder the harder he ran; there had been no grandeur in that place for so long that echo couldn't be stopped. I stood there all dumbfounded, my eyes getting frightened, and he said, "Oh very!" but did he know what I meant or was he thinking of character? To draw his mind off I said in a little whisper, "Now my good man, where are the toilets? For dear's sake, I don't see so much as a toureen or a tea caddy, much less a pot."
>
> "*Lesen Sie österreichische Geschichte,*" he says, giving me a look of utter contempt. A bit of imperial and secret commode work I'll never know anything about.

There are many things we will never know about *Nightwood*: what transpired in three meetings between Barnes and Eliot in London during June of 1936 when most of the editorial decisions were made, what the early manuscripts of *Nightwood* were when whole. Cheryl Plumb's edition, which also appends all surviving pages of the early drafts, contains almost everything we can know.

Her textual notes and annotations are helpful, but the latter could have been more sumptuous and more accurate. Morpheus is not the "Greek god/personification of sleep" but one of the sons of old Somnus, able to assume the shape of any man, announcing a drowning in Ovid's *Metamorpho-*

ses by appearing naked and dripping from the sea at the bedside of the bereft wife. "Girls that the dreamer has not fashioned himself to want, scatter their legs about him to the blows of Morpheus" has far more interesting connotations than the one implied by the mistaken identification. The care taken to "restore" Barnes's punctuation in the textual emendations is, really, much ado about not too much. Barnes herself edited different proofs differently, so Eliot's and proofreaders' corrections of her punctuation are nothing like the egregious bowdlerizations of Emily Dickinson's poems; yet they are treated as such. There is a related and equally questionable assumption underlying the commentaries on the restorations:

> This three-page passage was deleted by Eliot, a deletion suggested by Coleman. In the margin of TSC2 Barnes had written [a note to Eliot], "From here to 32 can be cut if you think there are too many doctor's stories—see Coleman on other ms." The block has been included in this edition because letters to Coleman indicate her reluctance to have anything deleted, unless Eliot confirmed it. Presumably, then, she acquiesced in the decision, but regretted the deletion.

To say that Barnes regretted this and other deletions presumes too much. (There is not a shred of evidence in her subsequent correspondence that she did.) Besides, the interest of the restored passages needs no further justification. Why portray this as a rescue mission?

It comes down to the penis, I suspect; anatomy as critical destiny. Eliot has been reviled as the high priest of patriarchal Anglican High Modernism, and Barnes shall be rescued from him, whether she would or no. "We got on like a couple of priests with only one robe," Barnes wrote at the start of their alliance, which became a friendship that lasted thirty years. Must this be seen as a misalliance?

What are the consequences for the field of Barnes criticism, and consequently her readership, and consequently future alliances, literary and otherwise, that cross gender lines?

"A little-known genius," I now explain, whenever I mention Djuna Barnes and encounter yet another blank stare.

Miranda Seymour (review date 26 November 1995)

SOURCE: "So Much Genius, So Little Talent," in *New York Times Book Review*, November 26, 1995, p. 12.

[*In the following review, Seymour asserts that while*

"[*Barnes*] *has been partly revealed* [*in Phillip Herring's* Djuna: The Life and Work of Djuna Barnes]; *a bigger and bolder exposure is still needed.*"]

Few authors have achieved so much celebrity with one novel as the elegant, exotic Djuna Barnes, without whom no account of Greenwich Village in the teens, or the Left Bank in the 1920's, is complete. That one novel was *Nightwood.* Overwritten and self-indulgent, it carries off its flaws with splendid nonchalance. Admired by Joyce, *Nightwood* is as important to the history of the 20th-century novel as *Finnegans Wake*—and more readable.

It was published in 1936, when Barnes was 44 and still overwhelmed by the departure of her lover, Thelma Wood. Wood appears in the book as the elusive, promiscuous Robin Vote, reduced in the final chapter to letting herself be seduced at an altar by a dog. Barnes never makes clear whether Robin is obsessed by self-degradation or simply reverting to her instinctive level; throughout the novel, Barnes stresses the narrowness of the line between humankind and animals. A circus girl catches the eye of a dilettante aristocrat, not for her beauty but because he relishes her similarity to the lion she tames. The grotesque cabaret performers who act as a chorus and audience in the book are "gaudy, cheap cuts from the beast life, immensely capable of that great disquiet called entertainment."

The aristocrat, Baron Felix Volkbein, languid, melancholy and preoccupied with the history and culture of nobility, was Barnes's private nod to Proust. The character of Dr. Matthew-Mighty-grain-of-salt-Dante-O'Connor owed everything to the extraordinary raconteur and abortionist Daniel A. Mahoney. In his biography, *Djuna,* Phillip Herring has much to say about her friendship with Mahoney and the care with which she recorded his pronouncements in her notebooks. In *Nightwood,* the funny, horrifying monologues of Dr. O'Connor seem at first no more than a device to unify the wandering narrative. A closer reading shows that O'Connor uses his fantastic imagination to keep reality at bay. His outpourings are a lifeline he throws to his desperate friends. When, finally, he goes mad, he does so recognizing that he has failed to save them from themselves. "I've not only lived my life for nothing, but I've told it for nothing," he whispers for his own grim epitaph.

T. S. Eliot, who edited *Nightwood,* was the first to notice the significance of O'Connor's role. But readers hoping to discover from the Dalkey Archive Press edition more about Eliot's contribution to the book are in for a disappointment. In a 75-page appendix, the editor, Cheryl J. Plumb, who teaches English at Pennsylvania State University, includes some unpublished drafts from the original 670-page manuscript, but the 1995 *Nightwood* is unexcitingly close to the 1936 version. Most of the emendations are picky; a few are revealing, but at the end of the day I shall continue reading my old copy of *Nightwood,* not least because the long, cramped, asterisked lines of the annotated edition hide the flow of a prose that stands at the brink of poetry.

Mr. Herring, a professor of English at the University of Wisconsin, Madison, is, astonishingly, only the second biographer of Barnes. (The first was Andrew Field.) His book is less gossipy and more reliable than its predecessor, but the reader is still left with an awful lot of questions about their witty, beautiful, difficult subject.

Barnes's novel was only slightly more bizarre than her life. Her father, Wald, treated procreation as a religious duty and went on riding expeditions with a sponge to clean himself up after random sexual encounters. At home, his wife and children lived with his mistress and his second brood.

Wald, a weak man, was authorized to live in this way by his remarkable mother, Zadel, a spiritualist who believed in free love. Correspondence between Zadel and her granddaughter suggests that she and Djuna may have had an incestuous relationship. Certainly Barnes worshipped her. "I always thought I was my grandmother, and now I am almost right," she wrote in 1935. There are hints in her work that she thought her father had raped her, but Mr. Herring concludes that Wald is more likely to have acted as a spectator after procuring her for a friend. With Zadel's support, Barnes fled home at the age of 17 in 1909 to live—for two months—with a middle-aged suitor. At 21, she arrived in Greenwich Village.

Nightwood led many of Barnes's admirers to suppose she was an evangelist for lesbianism. Given that the novel was devoted to an obsessive love affair between two women, Lady Ottoline Morrell could hardly be blamed for writing to praise Barnes's courage in defending same-sex love. Barnes was furious. She had never regarded herself as a lesbian. Her first great love affair was with Ernst Hanfstaengl, the grandson of a Yankee general in the Civil War, to whom she was engaged from 1914 in 1916. His rejection of Barnes as an unfitting mother for his German child was painfully recorded in a section deleted from *Nightwood* that is included in Ms. Plumb's edition.

In 1921, some months after being sent to Paris on a lucrative commission for *McCall's* magazine, Barnes met and fell in love with Thelma Wood, a tall, seductive woman to whom all the pleasure was in conquest. Vanquished, Barnes condemned herself to eight years of trailing after Wood through a variety of bedrooms and bars. Wood was an alcoholic; Barnes took to drink for solace and did not shake the habit until she was almost 60. By then, Thelma had been exorcised in *Nightwood,* and Barnes was ready to embark on her most autobiographical work, *The Antiphon.* Dag

Hammarskjold thought enough of this curious play to arrange a Swedish premiere; Eliot, who published it, contributed a blurb (later withdrawn), noting that "never has so much genius been combined with so little talent." Barnes, who acknowledged only the genius, was understandably displeased.

Next to Baron Corvo, it is hard to think of a writer who so ferociously bit every extended hand. As Mr. Herring notes, Peggy Guggenheim, Barnes's most consistent supporter, was regularly informed that the rich had a duty to provide for great writers, who in turn could do as they pleased. To Guggenheim's credit, she remained unwaveringly supportive. Eliot also remained helpful and affectionate; some of the most intriguing pages of *Djuna* concern Barnes's friendship with his second wife, Valerie, and describe a 1969 reunion arranged by her between the elderly Barnes and a former admirer, Ezra Pound. The account is Mrs. Eliot's own, and it conveys the quality in Djuna Barnes that gives Mr. Herring the most trouble—her wit.

Barnes's elegant asperity was legendary. Her wit was of the spontaneous, topical, punning kind, which does not convert to reported speech. Sadly, in trying to celebrate it, Mr. Herring only leaves us wondering how anybody could have laughed at such weak jokes. But laugh they did. Joyce, who greatly influenced Barnes's style, was devoted to her. Samuel Beckett was fond enough to send a check for $3,400 when she was short of money. Her photograph was one of the five Eliot kept in his Faber & Faber office.

One of Barnes's blacker observations was that at the age of 75 she had become "the most famous unknown of the century." To younger writers, obscurity seemed to have been her choice. When she died 15 years later, in 1982, she was best known as a poverty-stricken recluse. Mr. Herring does valuable work in reassessing this image. Barnes was neither so poor nor so misanthropic as has been supposed. Approached with several lucrative offers for the film rights to her work, she lost them only by insisting on total personal control of the productions. She could afford to be highhanded. The sale of her papers in 1972 to the University of Maryland had been profitable: she had some $180,000 in the bank. A series of young men (including Mr. Field, the first biographer) readily consented to act as her secretaries, her shoppers and—most important to a woman who delighted in talking—her audience. Her nurses, however, left in droves, unable to bear her insults.

"Nothing is so abominable as a sweet old lady," Barnes wrote in *Nightwood.* There was no danger of her becoming one. "Make sure they pay you!" was one of her last recorded comments (to a young illustrator) before her death.

Enjoyable though Mr. Herring's biography is, I have reservations about it. We are told far too much about Barnes's friends and acquaintances, even when they have only a faint connection to her; they are the pillars and supports of a book in which the main figure is only glimpsed as a shadow flitting from arch to arch. It is particularly frustrating to find that the last 30 years of her life have been so hastily dismissed. It is as if, having reported on the failure of *The Antiphon* in 1958, Mr. Herring had reached the limits of his interest. Yet Barnes wrote poems until almost the end of her life, and she was, as Mr. Herring clearly indicates, not a wholehearted hermit. She has been partly revealed here; a bigger and bolder exposure is still needed.

Corinne Robins (review date October-November 1996)

SOURCE: "Stop, Look and Reread," in *American Book Review*, Vol. 18, No. 1, October-November, 1996, p. 24.

[*In the following review, Robins discusses what the drawings in* Poe's Mother: Selected Drawings of Djuna Barnes, *edited by Douglas Messerli, say about society during Barnes's era.*]

What is style besides being fashion's blood?—a distinctive look, a phrase evocative of a time, an attitude. Douglas Messerli's *Poe's Mother: Selected Drawings of Djuna Barnes* at first glance is replete with all of the above. Drawn tongue-in-cheek, a stylized Poe's mother as a slightly naughty vision of the 19th-century actress she was, adorns the book's elegant jacket cover and also occupies the next to last page of its more than a hundred drawings, including quick sketches, wood cuts, and black-and-white caricatures all displaying the professionalism and talent of a facile 1920s newspaper reporter/illustrator possessed of no coherent style except for an occasional out and out homage to Beardsley. These drawings were done to order for newspapers and the *Theater Guild Magazine,* and their chief appeal today lies in the fact that they were executed by the writer Djuna Barnes and, in turn, are the occasion for Messerli's exquisite explanatory notes, many of which end by serving up potent examples of the Barnes wit. And, as such, they have the charm, consistency, and staying power of an after dinner mint.

Douglas Messerli tells us in his introduction that, "The drawings of Djuna Barnes must be understood within the context of her other writings. In particular, her masterpiece *Nightwood* . . . in which Barnes creates a hierarchical world." In an effort to do justice to *Poe's Mother*, I took out my copy of Barnes's New Directions classic, published in 1937 reprinted in 1949, with endorsements on the jacket cover by Dylan Thomas calling it one of the three great prose works ever written by a woman" and an excerpt from T. S. Eliot's introduction that reads, "What I would leave the reader prepared to find is the great achievement of a style, the brilliance of wit and characterization." Today, rereading Barnes's masterpiece thirty years later, I find the book's brilliance something of a mixed bag. The novel begins in the 1890s and ends sometime in the 1920s. The first chapter, "Bow Down," introduces one of the book's secondary characters, Guido Volkein, a Jew of Italian descent, and his son Felix, both of whom read like characters who have wandered out of the 19th-century classic of anti-Semitism *The Protocols of the Elders of Zion.* On page three, Barnes's authorial voice tells us, "Guido lived as all Jews do, who, cut off from their people by accident or choice, find that they must inhabit a world whose constituents being alien, force the mind to succumb to an imaginary populace. When a Jew dies on a Christian bosom he dies impaled." As for Felix, Barnes tells us, "No matter where and when you meet him you feel that he has come from some other place—no matter from what place he has come—some country that he has devoured rather than resided in, some secret land he has been nourished on but cannot inherit for the Jew seems to be everywhere from nowhere." And three pages on, apropos of Felix, Barnes continues in this vein: "A Jew's doing is never his own, it is God's; his rehabilitation is never his own, it is a Christian's etc., etc."

Nightwood, a kind of Elizabethan classic of inversion, centers upon the history of an unhappy love affair between two women, Norah and Robin, which has masochistic overtones woven into the author's descriptions of the streets of Paris and Vienna, and a weird demimonde of circus performers mixing with a falsely titled European royalty. Male characters are secondary witnesses to the main drama of Robin and Norah's unhappy affair. The book's most important male character, Dr. Matthew O'Connor, is, I suspect, Barnes's answer to the genius of James Joyce. Dr. O'Connor, giving his take on a decadent Europe, speaks in a marvelous quasi-Elizabethan cadence. For example, he treats us to the following disquisition on race:

> "The Irish may be as common as whale-shit—excuse me—on the bottom of the ocean—forgive me—but they do have imagination and," he added, "creative misery, which comes from being smacked down by the devil and lifted up again by the angels. Misericordioso! Save me, Mother Mary, and never mind the other fellow! But the Jew, what is he at his best? Never anything higher than a meddler—pardon my wet glove—a supreme and marvelous meddler often, but a meddler nevertheless." He bowed slightly from the hips. "All right, Jews meddle and we lie, that's the difference, the fine difference."

Barnes, born in upstate New York, was educated at home, one presumes by a fine Christian family, who evidently taught her prose cadences courtesy of the King James Bible. Barnes's sentences, as above and throughout the novel, have a unique rhythm as witnessed by Messerli's quotes from her early stories that accompany the drawings. As reproduced in *Poe's Mother*, aside from the newspaper quick sketches of Irvin Cobb, Marsden Hartley, James Joyce etc., Barnes's drawings all borrow from Art Nouveau with a soupçon of 19th-century illustration, and lack the individualism to achieve the level of becoming visual curiosities in the way *Nightwood* has achieved its status of literary curiosity and/or classic. For example, accompanying the Barnes heading "She had read to a world Ruled by Fairies," Barnes draws a stylized Japanese-type female figure with a fantastic hairdo emerging from the naked head of a sad aging woman. The drawing is, to say the least, flaccid compared to Barnes's accompanying note: "She was always finding herself in love with the hero and heroine of some novel. She came out of them into her own life with a little gasp of sorrow, and she went back into them with a sigh of content."

Djuna Barnes and T. S. Eliot were literary gods while I was growing up, and one ignored their matter and worshipped their manner or tried to. Thus, reading *Poe's Mother* and reexamining *Nightwood* is for me an act of reparation to a younger Jewish self who read and glossed over that book's content feeling at once confused, ashamed, and slightly afraid.

I am grateful, nevertheless, to Douglas Messerli for the dedicated professionalism with which he addressed the task of gathering and in some cases literally rescuing this material. The drawings in *Poe's Mother* allow us to examine from our own perspective the manners and mores adhering to the geniuses and instant celebrities of another era.

Susan Edmunds (essay date Winter 1997)

SOURCE: "Narratives of a Virgin's Violation: The Critique of Middle-Class Reformism in Djuna Barnes's *Ryder*," in *Novel*, Vol. 30, No. 2, Winter, 1997, pp. 218-36.

[*In the following essay, Edmunds asserts in a discussion of Barnes's* Ryder, *that "Barnes makes repeated, figurative use of the narrative of a virgin's violation to foreground the ultimate complicity between middle-class reformers and the structures of oppression they would reform, while eschewing the scandalous appeal to fact on which such projects depend."*]

In her first novel, *Ryder* (1928), Djuna Barnes recasts her own family history as the story of the freewheeling Ryder family, whose outrageous actions at once parody and overturn the conventions of middle-class domestic fiction. Embracing the maverick ideals of polygamy, idleness, and freethinking, the Ryders not only fail to exemplify dominant norms of domestic conduct; they actively dispute the social mandate to uphold such norms. This dispute largely takes place in rural New York during the period between 1890 and 1910. As I will argue in some detail, it takes form as a complex battle over the legacy of middle-class reformism. Wendell Ryder and his mother Sophia defend a long-standing reformist tradition of social experimentation in the face of contemporary reformist efforts to bring their domestic practices under the rule of the wage economy and the welfare state. In this battle between reformers, no party emerges unsullied. Instead, Barnes uses the action of the novel to call the whole project of middle-class reformism into question.

In reading the novel as a satire on the checkered history of middle-class reformism, this essay both engages and disrupts existing trends in the critical reception of *Ryder* and Barnes criticism more generally. Critics have long regarded *Ryder* as a protest novel, though there is significant disagreement as to what, exactly, the novel is protesting against. Cheryl J. Plumb sums up one position in characterizing the novel as "a protest against a repressive middle-class ethic" of conformity (86).[1] Anne B. Dalton, on the other hand, contributes to a growing body of Barnes criticism in her reading of the novel as an encoded incest narrative written in protest against Barnes's own early history of sexual abuse.[2] Taken together, these readings pose a contradiction which my own argument seeks to historicize: in one, Wendell Ryder stands as an emancipatory hero of nonconformity, while in the other, he stands as a domestic and sexual predator whose practices merit suppression.

The metamorphosing impulse to read *Ryder* as a protest novel has gone hand in hand with an insistence on the novel's basis in autobiographical fact. Indeed, feminist analyses of the incest theme in Barnes's work must posit a proliferating series of connections between her autobiography and her art as the necessary ground for their own critical project of sociopolitical protest and reform. Yet here again, scholars disagree about where and how to locate the factual in a highly mannered work of fiction. Phillip Herring detects autobiographical fact everywhere at the surface of Barnes's first novel and consequently "take[s] the liberty of drawing on *Ryder* for biographical information" not available elsewhere (*Djuna* 1, 313 n2).[3] In contrast, Dalton proposes that in *Ryder* Barnes buries the most significant autobiographical events—and her protest against them—in cryptic metaphorical passages which the critic must unearth and translate back into fact (Dalton, "Escaping" 163-67).

No historical approach to Barnes's novel can divest itself

entirely of a faith in historical fact. But in shifting the frame of reference from biography to social history, my reading of *Ryder* reopens the question of the relation between fact and figure which previous critics have closed rather quickly. I propose that the defining events of the Ryder family history participate in and comment critically upon wider sociopolitical discourses associated with the history of middle-class reformism, and that they do so in ways that exceed and destabilize the strict status of autobiographical fact currently assigned to the novel's contents. The "facts" of the plot—in particular, the shadowy fact of a young girl's sexual violation—take on symbolic and figural functions which help to define and organize the critique of middle-class reformism which the novel presents. Reversing the move to read from the fictive and figural to the factual, I track the shifting and/or multiplying targets of the novel's protest in the unstable play of its figurations; through the patterning of such play, Barnes mobilizes the uncertain details of a particular family history to call society at large to account.

Barnes is able to use the story of the Ryder family in this way because she positions its antinormative domestic project at the intersection of a number of wider sociohistorical struggles. As Michel Foucault and Jacques Donzelot persuasively demonstrate, the family has served as a crucial site of social struggle and social control throughout the modern period. Foucault argues that the family becomes "the privileged locus of emergence for the disciplinary question of the normal and the abnormal" with the rise of the modern state (216). In turn, Donzelot has worked out for the French case the process by which the state came to present the middle-class family with a choice: it could preserve its "autonomy through the observance of norms that guarantee . . . social usefulness" or "become an object of surveillance and disciplinary measures in its own right" (91-92, 85). A similar process was well underway in the United States by the 1890s. This process was furthered, but also significantly complicated, by a strong and heterogeneous tradition of social experimentation and moral crusading on the part of private citizens. For as Barnes dramatizes quite vividly, the U.S. reformist tradition generated a number of competing models of what could and should constitute normative domestic and social conduct.

Ryder stages the competition between divergent models of normative conduct by condensing diffuse and long-ranging sociohistorical struggles into a series of direct and densely symbolic confrontations between representative individuals. Through such acts of condensation, the unorthodox home-life of the Ryder family comes to stand as the site at which old and new reformist philosophies vie for the authority to determine social norms. Throughout the novel, powerful representatives of capital and the state attempt to expose the Ryders' domestic activity as a set of secret and deviant practices in scandalous need of reform. But Wendell and Sophia successfully combat this threat to their autonomy by turning the same charges against their attackers. They parodically invoke the reformist philosophies of an earlier era in order to refigure their antinormative domestic practices as alternative and even superior models of normality. And they use these earlier philosophies to demonstrate that it is not they, but their attackers, whose secret misconduct should be exposed and disciplined.

Barnes performs a further act of condensation on her materials by making the narrative of a virgin's violation central to each of the struggles staged between rival reformers. The narrative of violation serves a dual figurative function in these episodes. On the one hand, sexual violation serves as a figure for the reformer's act of penetrating and scandalizing the secret of another person's purported misconduct. On the other hand, sexual violation serves as a figure for the deviant and/or wrongful contents of the secret itself. In this way, Barnes locates a disturbing symmetry at the heart of her critique, whereby the targets and the agents of social reform are assigned an equal power to abuse. The mirroring relation thus established is further evidenced in the structure of the struggles staged in the novel, in which reformers vie to reform one another, if only to elude reform themselves.

In this essay, I examine four episodes in which the narrative of a virgin's violation figures decisively in the action of the larger plot. In the first three episodes I consider, the dramatic question of whether a virgin has been or will be violated is linked to local skirmishes in the more general historical struggle between old and new philosophies of reform. Thus, a major part of my purpose in considering these episodes will be to analyze their complex historical resonances. As I indicate above, my further purpose lies in demonstrating the distinctly figurative uses to which Barnes puts the narrative of sexual violation in these scenes. This demonstration provides a necessary context for evaluating the more ambiguous and troubling relationship between fact and figure posed by the fourth episode I consider. In this last episode, Wendell Ryder's eldest daughter, Julie, has a cryptic dream of violation in which her father stands obscurely accused.

Here, I take issue with a feminist-psychoanalytic method of reading, most fully developed by Dalton, which refers the encoded contents of Julie's dream to postulated incidents of abuse which Barnes suffered at her own father's hands.[4] In contesting this reading, I do not dispute the substantial evidence which suggests that Barnes was sexually abused in childhood and/or adolescence (perhaps by her father, almost certainly with his consent), and that she labored to give representation to such abuse in her art. My objections lie elsewhere. In its confident appeal to fact, such a reading discloses a scandalous autobiographical truth lurking inside all the secrets which characters negotiate throughout the novel. But this shocking act of disclosure reproduces a long-standing reformist strategy which the novel examines only to reject. Furthermore, it shuts down the figural play of meaning through which the novel's narratives of violation indict the very project of middle-class reformism.

Barnes's indictment of middle-class reformers complicates, although it need not invalidate, a feminist evaluation of her work. Rather, it might induce us to inspect more closely the assumptions and aims of our own critical project. Much of the interest and the challenge that *Ryder* poses to its feminist readers, I would argue, lies in its historically acute analyses of reformers' vexed implication in the oppressive structures they would reform. Resisting appropriation as a text that proleptically affirms the reform agendas of contemporary academic feminists, *Ryder* engages its readers in an unsettling and open-ended process of social and self-critique that refuses univocal positions and clearly charted political solutions. If the severity of this refusal makes Barnes a poor champion of liberal and/or radical social causes (feminist or otherwise), it also makes her a provocative interlocutor in an ongoing conversation about the envisioned ends and unenvisioned consequences of organized social change.

Sophia's Nothing

As Barnes's narrator points out early in the novel, the reformist spirit of New England runs in the Ryder's very blood. Sophia Ryder is a descendent of "a great and a humorous stock" of "the early Puritan," and she has "in her the stuff of a great reformer or a noisy bailiff" (*Ryder*, 9). Like Barnes's grandmother, Zadel Barnes, on whom she is closely modeled, Sophia divides her time between an eclectic assortment of utopian ventures, radical causes, and reform efforts: during her years in London, she moves "among the Pre-Raphaelites" and befriends Oscar Wilde (34, 18); in the States, she writes "manly editorials for the *Springfield Republican*" and accompanies Elizabeth Cady Stanton on her public speaking tours (154, 18).[5] But Sophia manifests her greatest commitment to the cause of reform in her unstinting support for her son's "noble philosophy in the home" (168).

This philosophy has several components. First, there is the commitment to polygamy and free love, which leads Wendell to take a second wife, Kate-Careless, upon returning to the States with his British bride, Amelia. After the two women reluctantly set up housekeeping together on the family's Long Island farm, Bulls'-Ease, Wendell busies himself seducing as many more women as wit and circumstance permit. Second, there is the commitment to freethinking, which leads Wendell and Sophia to educate his many children at home. Finally, there is the commitment to idleness. Disenchanted with his brief, youthful employment as "a drug-

clerk," Wendell vows "never, never again to battle as a self-supporting unit!" (18). As a result, the family does its best to survive outside the wage economy. What Wendell's wives cannot produce through subsistence farming, Sophia procures on lucrative begging trips to the city.

Sophia keeps "her family from ruin" through an ingenious writing scheme which she conducts on the sly. She addresses "hundreds" of heartbreaking appeals to wealthy capitalists and statesmen, and then drops by in person, disguised as an old beggar woman, to collect their alms. "[A] mendicant of the most persistent temerity," she has thus "lied and wept and played the sweet old woman to the partial undoing of every rich man in the country, and of one of the Presidents of the States" (14). On the whole, her scheme works very well. But when she tries it out on a magnate named Boots, he fights back. Correctly suspecting that she's only pretending to be poor, he prepares to lift up the skirts of her beggar costume to reveal the layers of expensive petticoats beneath. It is at this point that Sophia invokes the narrative of a virgin's violation, both to protect her own ruse from scandalous exposure and to discredit the motives of the man who assaults her.

Sophia's begging act and the crisis to which it gives rise comment satirically on the long and divided history of the social benevolence movement in the United States. In the showdown between Sophia and Boots, rival philosophies of relief work vie for authority. Sophia parodically revives mid-nineteenth century scripts of charitable giving associated with the sentimental cult of domesticity, while Boots works from a later cultural script in which social and moral supervision of the poor takes precedence over the distribution of alms. The condensations at work in their encounter are multiple and will take some unraveling.

In the antebellum period of Sophia's youth, the sentimental cult of domesticity provided middle-class women with the rationale for their escalating participation in all the philanthropic reform movements of the day. During these years, women's benevolent work was rhetorically equated with housework; divinely appointed to set God's house in order, women reformers sought to reconstruct society on the Christian principles of love and charity (Ginzberg 5, 59-60). Like other reform-minded women of her day, Sophia models her conduct on sentimental ideals, though usually to grotesque effect. For instance, in her first act as a young married woman, she lays down "the foundations . . . of relief" which will define her role throughout the novel. These foundations turn out to be a set of "five fine chamber-pots," which spell out in succession: "Needs there are many, / Comforts are few, / Do what you will / Tis no more than I do / . . . Amen" (11). As the rhyme suggests, Sophia founds her domestic order on "a passionate and precarious love of family" and a healthy tolerance for the natural man (16).

Decades later, Sophia comes to her family's rescue with the bold decision to recruit the nation's richest men into her domestic order in the capacity of loyal sons. To this end, she deploys the sentimental script of virtuous maternity to deliver an appeal that only a brute could resist. Her letters of beggary master all the tear-jerking conventions of sentimental fiction, "and always, with unerring faithfulness to her original discovery of the way to the heart of man, they were signed 'Mother'" (15). In these letters, sentimental altruism serves as a cover for Sophia's actual motives of self-gain in much the same way that her beggar costume serves as a cover for her expensive petticoats; both the letters and the costume reach back to dominant discursive strategies of her youth in order to cast a thin normative sheen over her decidedly antinormative plan to preserve her family in idleness. As Boots's assault will demonstrate, neither cover is impenetrable. Yet Sophia is able to maintain the upper hand in her encounters with her wealthy "sons" because the sentimental script of benevolence has come to serve their interests as much as it serves her own.

This point becomes clear when we examine the shift in the history of the social benevolence movement which takes place after the Civil War. During the 1870s and 1880s, the movement underwent reorganization, strengthening its recently forged ties with the state as well as its widely recognized ties with corporate capitalism. These alliances gave rise to arguments favoring fewer handouts and greater surveillance of the poor, who were newly suspected of faking their distress.[6] Nevertheless, the sentimental script of benevolent self-sacrifice continued to legitimate the activities of reformers and capitalists alike, allowing the wealthy to recast their own schemes for personal gain as loving service to the public good.[7]

In posing literal, blood relations between the sentimental fiction writer and the corporate capitalist, Sophia's letters of beggary circulate a fiction of virtuous maternity that cuts both ways: it is impossible for her unlucky "sons" to expose the fraudulence and dishonesty of her investment in such a fiction without simultaneously exposing their own. This is the bind in which Boots finds himself when Sophia enters his corporate "sanctum" "to sweep up her gains" (176, 15). Given the nature of her advantage, the episode is best read not as an errand of charity but as the delicate encounter between a blackmailer and her victim.

Ranked by his twelve "disciples" in an enterprise which uneasily conflates the Gospel of Christ with the Gospel of Wealth, Boots confronts a woman whose business sense and religious piety match his own. Sophia opens her petition by offering Boots a vacuous, if vaguely menacing, sentimental blessing: "there is a world without end, and I fully believe in it. And what is there in that world for you, my dear, what shall I promise you?" (177). The very emptiness of the gesture suggests that Sophia here offers Boots a mother's blessing not to provide him with any practical benefit which he would otherwise lack, but to threaten him with the disaster that would ensue should such a blessing be withdrawn. In effect, she proposes that if Boots and his ilk want to insure her anonymous assent to the transparently false sentimental script of the capitalist's and the statesman's filial piety and benevolence, they will have to pay for it—up front and in person.

Boots responds, somewhat rashly, by attempting to deploy the more recent philanthropic script which casts the poor as undeserving impostors. When his twelve disciples recommend that he "toss" Sophia "from wall to wall, and from the midst of her nefarious skirts you'll hear the mother cry," Boots agrees:

> An there be a battle and no old woman found among her clothes, connivance and no mother look,—for even praying you can tell the mother bottom,—why, we will set her out at the gate, that the citizens may witness so heinous a thing! I am all charity an the supplicant be truly tattered to the skin and the skin well parched, but whole cloth estranges me, as a patch of well-fed stomach throws me off scent! (178)

As Boots detects, the "double set of real Irish linens" which Sophia wears under her "pauper's cloak" gives the lie to her posture of indigence (177, 15). Yet when he and his men finally resolve "to try her," Sophia is able to exploit the proposed scenario of her own exposure for its unsuspected power to reestablish her dissembling body as newly, if grotesquely, truthful. Should her body be turned upside down and inside out before the citizens "out at the gate," her bottom would back up her face as a portrait of helpless and deserving poverty. Thus, Sophia supplies her genital lack, which must also come to view in any attempt to "tell the mother bottom," as the culturally indisputable sign of a motherly "need" and "nothing else." "This is the hour when men seek a girl among your skirts!" she cries out in conference with herself, before addressing Boots:

> Why, find her then, catch her on the flicker, for she asks forever only help, and reeks of that condition. Tear her into pieces adequate for the glutting of your suspicion, and every rag will speak the selfsame story, for there's nothing else about. (178)

Unable to expose Sophia's worldly all without also revealing her sexual "nothing," Boots and his men find themselves trapped by appearances if not by intent in the scandalous scenario of gang-rape implied by their desire to try her. When Sophia calls out in warning to "the girl" among her skirts, she invokes the narrative of a virgin's violation to refigure the meaning of Boots's proposed investigation in two ways. The reformist project to expose a pauper as a fraud reappears as the criminal project to rob an honest woman of her virtue. At the same time, the crime of rape serves as an all too fitting figure for the rapacious greed at work beneath capitalists' own show of benevolence and warm family feeling. In this way, Sophia uses the narrative of a virgin's violation to deflect the threat of scandal away from her family's antinormative scheme to live off the labor of others, and onto corporate capitalism's all too acceptable scheme to do exactly the same thing.

The ultimate success of Sophia's venture in this scene lies in her ability to seize the power of publicity from her would-be attackers. For while it would cost Boots very little to violate the girl among her skirts in the privacy of his office sanctum, coverage of the event in the contemporary sensationalist press would cost him a lot.[8] The implicit threat of exposure through newspaper coverage is, in the end, what structures the chiastic doubling of safely kept secrets in this scene, insuring that neither party will tell on the other. Once again, the "nothing" of Sophia's genitals embodies the terms of their pact, standing as the grotesque bodily emblem of a self-serving hollowness at the center of both their investments in the sentimental script of benevolence. For Sophia such hollowness proves to be the key to her gain, for it unlocks the purse of corporate charity without opening her family to the intrusions of public surveillance. But for Boots such hollowness is only emasculating. As he extracts from his "left trouser pocket" "a bill of no mean proportions," Sophia exclaims,

> Who is pauper here now? Not I, though I've been, so the two conditions have buzzed within the hour. I bring you, Boots, my most dear, many things therefore. Farewell, then, and cry, "Mother, mother, mother!" for it is a word that comes up to me ever. (178-79)

Wendell's All

Sophia's funds, procured like so much in the Ryders' lives through a love of family, allow her son Wendell to throw body and soul into his philosophy, unhampered by the petty routines of wage-earning. The scope of his leisurely endeavors is considerable, for, as Anne Dalton remarks, Wendell "imagines himself to be the new Adam and casts himself as artist, social iconoclast, and prophet and founder of a new religion" ("Escaping" 166). In this, he too stands as the direct descendent of several mid-nineteenth-century social reformers and social philosophers. The tenets of his philosophy perhaps stand closest to those of the Transcendentalists. Wendell shows more sympathy for Thoreau's aversion to labor than for Emerson's endorsement of indus-

try and ambition, and he rejects both men's valorization of self-reliance. But he amply shares their regard for nature, their impatience with the shackles of social custom, and their high hopes for the world-transformative power of original genius. Where both Emerson's and Thoreau's enthusiasm for the natural man carefully skates above a condoning of his baser impulses, Wendell's regard for nature embraces all that is low in man and beast alike. In this sense, Wendell's philosophy can be read as a grotesque parody of Transcendentalism, one which both degrades and revives its loftier sentiments (see Bakhtin 21).

"He is nature in its other shape," confides his wife Amelia, who thinks him "great oftener than anything else"; "[h]e is a deed that must be committed" (241). His mother agrees, telling Wendell, "[Y]ou are nature, all of you, all of you, and nature is terrible when law hunts it down" (238). "The world is nothing, the man is all; in yourself is the law of all nature," Emerson says, and repeats: "No law can be sacred to me but that of my nature." "There are no fixtures in nature," he proposes further. "The only sin is limitation" (Emerson 70, 262, 403, 406).[9] To his mother Wendell explains, "I sport a changing countenance. I am all things to all men, and all women's woman" (164). And to one of many lovers, he confides, "I, my love, am to be Father of All Things." With this latter declaration, he announces his intention to give rise to a "Race" of Ryders which will encompass the earth in its human variety, "though never one" shall be "bourgeois or like to other men as we now know them" (210).

Blending sex and religion in his visionary ideas of a world to come, Wendell moves away from Emerson and Thoreau and closer to such prophets as Ann Lee, John Humphrey Noyes, and Joseph Smith, who all founded utopian communities built around alternative religious and sexual norms in the mid-nineteenth century. The "complex marriage" practices of Noyes's Oneida Community and the Mormon endorsement of polygamy offer direct parallels to Wendell's domestic philosophy.[10] But they also play a central role in the creation of historical conditions that severely limit his ability to practice it.

Thus, in an 1879 ruling on Mormon-initiated test case, the U.S. Supreme Court outlawed polygamy, arguing that monogamy stood as "the very foundation of the democratic state." The Oneida Community gave up the practice of complex marriage in the same year. The Mormon response was less compliant, and female reformers initiated a vigorous, nationwide antipolygamy crusade in the wake of the Court's ruling. The fruit of this crusade was the passage of laws that opened the way for systematic federal intervention in Mormon private life. In 1890, the Mormon Church withdrew its endorsement of plural marriage, conceding defeat in its battle for the legal right to promote alternative norms of sexual and domestic conduct.[11]

This historical context lends urgency and poignancy to Wendell's conversation with Sophia about his practice of polygamy, undertaken in the very years when lawmakers and reformers aggressively organized against it. Sophia notes, "It is very advanced, very old, and very nice, perhaps . . . but we must keep it from the public, at all costs." In his reply, he wonders, "[W]ho is to eat me? The authorities of the state and the wiseacres of the nation?" (168-69). Wendell's principled refusal to conform his sexual practices to the dictates of monogamy makes him an enemy of the state. His only weapon of self-defense is obscurity, and this weapon is understandably hard to wield when his overarching ambition is to people the world anew. As Barnes's narrator reports, Wendell has "trouble in keeping [his] life out of the papers," and the mayor wants him in jail. Eventually, the law hunts him down in his own home. When a "delegation . . . headed by a social worker" arrives to inquire about his two wives, Wendell rightly predicts, "I am about to be infested with scrutiny" (213).

In the meantime, however, it is not Wendell's extra wife but his children's truancy that runs him afoul with the state. Where the social worker's visit spells doom for the Ryder philosophy, forcing one wife and her children out on the street, Wendell emerges as the victor in his encounter with the school authorities. Once again, this success is due to his skillful deployment of the narrative of a virgin's violation to discredit the charges lodged against him. Like his mother before him, Wendell forecloses the scandalization of his private life by threatening the public domain with scandal in kind. Like her, he does so by taking up reformist arguments of an earlier era in order to resist and condemn the leading reform agendas of the present-day.

Wendell's battle with the public school system occurs after a shift in its organization that parallels the shift reviewed above in the social benevolence movement. The common schooling movement began in the 1830s as a middle-class reform effort; however, it was only after 1890, when a quiet bureaucratic revolution took place, that adequate procedures were in place nationwide to enforce attendance laws and hold schools to a single standard. At the same juncture, different strands in the ideology of public education took on new strength as states secured their control of the system. This ideology has been variously interpreted. Some point to public education's role in creating an efficient and tractable workforce, others to its role in promoting religious piety and loyalty to the state (see Tyack and Gordon).

Wendell incorporates many of these points in a speech he delivers to an investigating school authority and a crowd of his neighbors after he is called to the town schoolhouse to account for his children's truancy. Rejecting the ideological aims of the latest wave of educational reform, he reaches back to the ideas of an earlier reformer, Ralph Waldo Emerson, to defend his own position. In "Self-Reliance," Emerson grows impatient with a system of education built upon the principle of imitation rather than originality. "Every great man is a unique," he insists; "Shakespeare will never be made by the study of Shakespeare" (279). Similarly, Wendell condemns the school authorities for "trying to make scrub-oak of my sons' trees" through an uninspired curriculum devoted to rote memorization of religious and state propaganda. He complains, "The Board of Education" would have children memorize "dates and speeches, half forgotten, of dead statesmen," and learn to "render Hamlet backward, and the Commandments sideways." And he defends his children's truancy on the grounds that it offers them "[i]mmunity . . . from the common and accepted conditions of life, as taught in the parochial schools" (130-31).

Yet it is the beauty of the investigating official's self-sought mediocrity that such arguments are "Greek and a tomb to him"; any success that Wendell might hope to have in this encounter must be sought on other ground. The school's case against the Ryders, on the other hand, is simple and predictable. The investigating official informs Wendell that "there are laws in this country, and one of them is that children must attend school." And he contends that children who don't go to school "will grow up . . . deflowering women, and defaming God" (130). With this latter charge, virginal violation comes to stand for the more general threat of social havoc posed by children whose upbringing is not supervised by the state. In his reply, Wendell adroitly takes up the same figure and uses it to represent a moral threat which the state itself poses to the children it ostensibly guides and protects.

In making his second critique, Wendell concedes the need to send his children to school for the new leverage it allows him as a concerned parent. "[I]f you insist," he tells his interlocutor, "I, being but a humble citizen, can but submit, but I may warn you that Ryder as an outlaw is less trouble than citizen Ryder" (131). He goes on to play the part of a good citizen scandalized by the hidden pockets of corruption he finds on state property. He first focuses attention on the school drinking well, whose common cup communicates the taint of "three rats and one cat" festering in its depths (132). He then turns to the school privy: "its double-seated grandeur two black pits, the wood carved over with hearts and arrows, and successive generations' initials twined therein." Positioned in front of the schoolhouse's only window, the "gaped, doorless" structure of the privy offers its graffiti as a rival scene of instruction to the blackboard within (129).

In his new role as public watchdog, Wendell reveals the school's pure well of knowledge to be an "abyss of disease and filth." And he indignantly refuses to "permit my daughter to learn of love as it is written on yonder privy ring"

(132). With the latter remark, Wendell conjures up the image of a young girl violated by lessons in love learned with her pants down in a public privy in order to expose an ineradicable moral threat emanating from the public domain. The Emersonian complaint originally lodged against the school's blackboard curriculum—that it will infect his children with "the common and accepted conditions of life"—reemerges as mock outrage against the degrading commonness and defiling vulgarity of the privy's adjoining pedagogy. Wendell here reveals the public school system as the propagator of the very kind of common viciousness that it was designed to reform. In doing so, he draws public attention to scandalous instances of neglect and hypocrisy on the part of the school authorities. But he also points to a more deep-seated eagerness on the part of the state-educated public to constitute itself *as a public* by reading and writing about the very activities it would forbid him to practice in private.

Faced with these disclosures, the crowd rushes forward to attack the school official. In the ensuing tumult of righteous indignation, Wendell makes a quiet escape, resuming the role of outlaw which his unexpected success in the role of citizen newly affords him. The next time the law catches up with him, however, he is not so lucky. In a midnight conference with his mother held shortly after the social worker's visit, he decides to ask Amelia, his legitimate wife, to leave with her five children so that he might bring his marriage practices in line with federal law. Unsurprisingly—for she has always been "good and dependable"—she agrees (241).

It is at this point in the plot that Barnes's disillusionment with the whole project of middle-class reformism becomes most clear. In a late interview, Barnes comments disparagingly on Wendell: "Ryder is one of those impossible people who are going to save the world—how can anyone save the world?" (qtd. in Field 185).[12] Wendell and Sophia offer to save the world from the dubious salvation foisted upon it by a reform-minded state and corporate bureaucracy. For most of the novel, they successfully resist and expose the hypocrisy and self-interest underwriting their opponents' ostensibly altruistic devotion to the public good. But in the last pages of the novel, they too succumb to new depths of hypocrisy and self-interest, sacrificing family for the sake of family. As far as Amelia and her children are concerned, Wendell, Sophia, and the state finally appear as identical dispensers of ruin. In the Ryders' ultimate complicity with the social worker's delegation, Barnes points up the continuity between the mid-nineteenth-century models of reform that the Ryders embrace and the turn-of-the-century reform measures that they would ostensibly use such models to overcome or defy.

Julie's Share

In their brutal bargain with the social worker, Wendell and

Sophia abandon their own policy of principled resistance to the state. They also seem to close off possibilities of successful resistance for Amelia and her children. But in fact this foreclosure begins much earlier, when Wendell and Sophia appoint themselves to act as the family's sole representatives in the public sphere. In the last section of the essay, I want to turn attention to two characters who are particularly ill-served by this arrangement: Amelia herself, the good wife who gets thrown out on the street, and her daughter Julie, namelessly invoked in her father's debate with the school authorities. They too bear potentially scandalous secrets that gain representation through narratives of a virgin's violation. Yet they fail to deploy these secrets, even momentarily, as a means of personal gain or political protest. Cut off almost entirely from the outside world, they lack the free passage across the public/private divide on which scandal depends. Consequently, their secrets fail to empower them, but instead enforce and deepen their initial lack of power.

Hemmed in by the "magnificen[ce]" of Sophia's nothing and Wendell's all (9, 168), the remaining women in the Ryder household command a share of the family's greatness only insofar as they grow great with child. The illegitimate wife, Kate-Careless, a lusty and affable woman, finds the terms of such a bargain to her taste. "I've become infatuated with the flavour of motherhood," she tells Wendell; "you poked it under my nose, and I've learned to like it" (170). But Amelia and Julie never learn to like it, which may be why the pregnancies they bear in the novel are both, in some sense, false. These pregnancies also serve as vehicles for muffled protest, providing the occasion and the terms through which each woman attempts to speak the secret of her own resistance. At the time of Amelia's lying-in, she is convinced she will die and warns Julie never to "let a man touch you, for their touching never ends, and screaming oneself into a mother is no pleasure at all" (95). When the baby is born, Wendell cries out, "The babe is black!" But the transvestite midwife, Dr. Matthew O'Connor, assures him, "Bile alone is father of its colour" (97).

The scandalous possibility that Amelia has taken a black man as her lover, though quickly invalidated by O'Connor, returns in the next chapter. There, Amelia dreams of a virgin's averted violation. In her dream, she stands at the key-hole before an ornate chamber lined with the trophies of Western culture. Inside the chamber, a black ox approaches the bed of a white woman, asking that he be given "a place in your Savior." She refuses, saying "Go away and do not try to defile me, for I have time in which to think, but you must labour." The ox replies that her God "will damn himself in me," but when he kneels before Christ's crucifix at the end of the dream, he says simply, "Remember the woman" (99).

This dream of averted violation, like most dreams, gives representation to a contradictory assortment of hidden wishes. And it borrows two preexisting cultural scripts, both associated with the cause of racial reform, in order to do so. Thus, the narrator initially aligns Amelia's dream with the Christian and sentimental discourse of the antebellum abolitionist movement, glossing the dream as an attempt to "set a mighty wrong to rights, to get the black man the attention of the Lord, and a place in his mercies" (98). Yet the text of the dream, with its transparent allusion to the threat of miscegenation, exposes the limits of white abolitionists' merciful love for black slaves. Indeed, in its recourse to images of black defilement, the dream is more readily aligned with the racist discourse of white supremacy which flared up violently during and after Reconstruction. Linking the imminent fall of Western civilization to black men's bestial lust for white women, Amelia's dream reproduces the major contemporary script used to revoke the fragile political, social, and economic gains which blacks had accrued since the Civil War.[13]

Why does Amelia have such a dream at such a juncture? What does the plight of the black man have to do with her fear of childbirth or her aversion to her husband's touch? Matthew O'Connor's comment that "bile alone is father" of the baby's color provides a place to begin. O'Connor's diagnosis refers back to the medieval theory of the four humors, in which bile denotes irascibility, gloominess, and ill humor. In this sense, Amelia's black baby grotesquely embodies and renders visible its mother's "bilious" unhappiness within her marriage. In the overdetermined and contradictory logic of the dream's imagery, this unhappiness takes further form as a fantasy of protesting against the injustice of her fate through sexual and political union with a black man. At the same time, however, Amelia's dream calls upon the racist script of a pure white woman resisting defilement by a black beast to condemn and punish her own husband's amorous advances. In the figure of the black ox at the bedside, the black man's mythical offense—interracial rape—and his exacted punishment—castration—find simultaneous representation.[14] Once again, the narrator suggests that this ready-made cultural script serves as a cover for protests more properly lodged elsewhere: the dream represents "an effort to retake Wendell," king of the yard at Bulls'-Ease, "in his own colours" (98).

In the two explanations of her baby's color, Amelia finds a way to connect her individual anger and suffering with the group anger and suffering of African-Americans. But the contradictions in the dream that follows (born of the black ox's double status as wronged victim and punished sexual aggressor) lead her to reject the very alliance which gives voice to her own resistance. Through the body of her newborn child, Amelia's bilious anger at her lot takes on the sign of miscegenation, while her dream's adherence to the taboo against miscegenation signals her unwillingness to acknowl-

edge and act upon that anger. Her baby's dark coloring invokes the historic suffering of blacks to make the secret of her marital suffering scandalously visible; but her subsequent dream of a virgin's averted violation refuses the potential union between black grievances and her own.

The text of Amelia's dream, like the texts of Sophia's encounter with the magnate and Wendell's encounter with the school official, stages a confrontation between old and new scripts of social reform. But the external, interpersonal conflicts dramatized in those episodes reappear in Amelia's dream as an internal conflict waged over the very question of whether or not she will speak out in protest on her own behalf. Ironically, it is precisely the virgin's successful resistance to violation in the dream's narrative which comes to represent Amelia's self-defeating resolve to keep quiet. Appropriating and conflating central tropes drawn from competing discourses of racial (or racist) reform, Amelia's dream ultimately betrays its own aim to "set a mighty wrong to rights." Fittingly, the dream occurs in a self-contained chapter. Amelia, a country-girl "well rounded in restrictions," reports its contents to no one (98).

Julie is less willing to remain silent on her mother's account. At one point, she lashes out against Kate-Careless who manifests the "disease . . . emanating directly from her father" "to the torment of her mother" (143). But when Julie gives representation to her own torment, she, like Amelia, resorts to a false pregnancy and a grotesquely deformed sentimental dream. As such a parallel would suggest, her protest has no great effect on her position within the Ryder household. In Chapter 24, "Julie Becomes What She Had Read" (106). Schooled at home on the literary diet of Sophia's youth, she dreams of tiny Arabella Lynn: another beautiful Little Eva dying a sentimental death, but with a grotesquely exaggerated bad conscience because she has doubted the existence of God. By the end of the dream, Arabella joins a parade of pregnant "little girls" as they fall through the sky. Julie then wakes to find Sophia protecting her from Wendell's blows as he bitterly rejects her, crying, "she is none of mine. Did I not hear her deriding me greatly?" (109-10).

Anne Dalton's feminist-psychoanalytic reading of Julie's dream plausibly establishes it as an encoded incest narrative. But the larger claims of her argument cannot be derived from a reading of the dream-text alone, depending instead on a projected second narrative (to which, she claims, Barnes herself may or may not have had conscious access) concerning Barnes's own father's sexually abusive treatment of her. Dalton's argument includes an account of why incest narratives are encoded in the first place, and what social and moral obligations fall to the literary critic in the face of such encoding. She contends that the "metaphorical descriptions of father-daughter incest" in Julie's dream reflect the pressures of psychic and social censorship; unable to accuse her father directly, Barnes resorts to fiction and to figuration to convey her traumatic life story. The responsible critic must read past the dream-text's figures to uncover and condemn the "real" acts of violation (to Julie and to Barnes herself) that lie behind them. Anything less, according to Dalton, serves "to perpetuate the silencing of those who have suffered from child abuse" ("Escaping" 167-68).

If we accept the terms of Dalton's argument, we might read Julie's dream as the final secret which the text presents, one which lends its narrative to all the other secrets in the novel. Yet Julie's secret, like her mother's, has been forcibly displaced from the social border between secrecy and scandal to the psychic border between fantasy and fact. We might thus understand Julie's anger as the anger of a young girl with a secret she cannot publish. Julie lives in a house papered over with literary and newspaper images of incest and rape (14). But where her grandmother Sophia can silently rely on newspaper clippings of "the pretty girl untimely raped" to guard her skirts during her encounter with Boots in the public domain,[15] such a clipping provides Julie with no protection in the private domain of her family. Julie's experience, like her mother's troubles the otherwise very gratifying fantasy of unregulated middle-class privacy which Wendell and Sophia fight to defend. The pain of these two women reminds us that privacy is never a reliable privilege for those who lack firm access to a public voice and a public hearing.

But as soon as we get this far in such a line of argument, problems arise. Dalton assumes that the critic can (indeed must) supply what Julie lacks in the text itself. She offers a reading that speaks out publicly on behalf of the abused child and on behalf of the facts, and she "corrects . . . misreadings and 'nonreadings'" by earlier critics which have failed to do likewise ("Escaping" 168). In effect, she rescues Barnes's novel from both its silences and its silencers. In Dalton's reading, the interpretive strategies of the literary critic fuse with the self-authorizing strategies of the social reformer: the appeal to fact, the exposure of secrets, the declared devotion to another's welfare, and the self-appointed mission of correction equally characterize both enterprises. Yet *Ryder* itself meticulously examines these discursive strategies and the reformist agendas they legitimate, only to reject them.

Dalton's act of reading uncovers evidence that "incriminate[s]" Wendell Ryder (or Wald Barnes) as a child molester ("Escaping" 165). Within the novel itself, however, Wendell's and his mother's own acts of reading incriminate social reformers for interventions in family life which shore up the coercive and exploitative power of the wage economy, heterosexual monogamy, and the welfare state. The novel does not lend itself to stable oppositions between criminal projects and projects of correction. Indeed, it repeatedly foregrounds the morally suspect and historically variable nature of that very distinction.

Moreover, two episodes in the novel openly question how well justice is served by the combined forces of scandalous publicity and moral reformism in cases of alleged sexual misconduct. As we have seen, *Ryder* uses the dream-text of Julie's mother, Amelia, to dramatize a dangerous readiness to cast the black man, sooner than the white, as the offending "bull" in the rape scenarios of the nation's cultural imagination. The only other "bull" to be publicly condemned for a sexual crime in the novel is Oscar Wilde, tried and imprisoned on charges of sodomy. In the same conversation with his mother in which she reiterates the need to keep his polygamous practices secret, Wendell remembers seeing Wilde in London after

> [t]he scandal had burst, and though he was the core, the fragrant centre of a rousing stench, in a month he was a changed man, not changing, sitting within his cell, weeping, writhing, plotting 'De Profundis,' . . . a bull caught and captured, sentenced, hamstrung, marauded, peered at, peeped upon, regarded and discovered to be a gentle sobbing cow. (166)

For Barnes, who dedicated *Ryder* to "T. W." in cloaked tribute to her lesbian lover Thelma Wood, the memory of Wilde's fate and its testimony to the quality of justice served in the name of guarding sexual innocence, was likely to have been quite chilling.

The extent to which Barnes distrusted the efficacy of public exposure as a tool for justice in cases of sexual misconduct is further suggested by an anecdote she reported to Hank O'Neal in her old age. Between the time she left her parents' farm and the time she wrote *Ryder*, Barnes herself had a successful career in sensationalist journalism. According to O'Neal,

> She finally quit the papers because of a rape case in which a girl in her teens had been raped six times. The editor of the *Journal American* wanted an interview with the victim and suggested that Miss Barnes contrive a story to gain access to the girl. She managed to sneak past the guards at the hospital, entered the girl's room, made up some wild tale, and got an interview, but when it was over felt guilty about what she had done. When she told her editor she would never cover another rape case and would not write a story about this one or give the information to anyone else, he fired her on the spot. (52)

In this anecdote, Barnes narrates a moment of protracted and painful decision in which she finally chooses to perpetuate the silence of a victim of sexual abuse rather than publish the facts on her behalf (and against her will). At this moment, she seems to expose and refuse the suspect nature of her own moral, political, and/or economic investment in the reformist potential of scandalous publicity. Of course, until the anecdote is repeated, such an exposure carries little critical force for anyone other than Barnes herself since it finds its medium in silence. Yet we might use the grim choice of total silence with which Barnes marked her departure from investigative journalism better to measure what she achieves through the porous silences, the paraded secrets, which distinguish the investigative forays of her fiction.

In *Ryder*'s narratives of a virgin's violation, Barnes creates a third alternative to the limiting choice of total silence or full factual disclosure presented in her anecdote to O'Neal. It is important, I believe, to examine this alternative for what it achieves in its own right, rather than reading it as a product of compromise or failure, an index of the debilitating effects of social and psychic censorship. For *Ryder* calls into question the assumption that full factual disclosure is the best (because most therapeutic, most politically progressive) way to narrate a story of sexual violation. One can argue further that the figural and fictive deployment of the narrative of violation provides Barnes with the means for commenting critically on this very assumption.

In keeping secret the exact nature of Julie's relationship to the novel's proliferating narratives of a virgin's violation, Barnes refuses to disclose a "real" originary event to which the figural play of her text might be referred and through which it might be contained. Lodging formal accusations against no single attacker on Julie's behalf, *Ryder* conducts no trial and brings no guilty party to justice. But by the same token the novel resists the sensationalist impulse to confine the sources of social horror to the supernaturally corrosive effects of isolated agents whose practices fail to conform to the current dictates of normality.

Barnes pays a price, both for her refusal to moor Julie's dream of protest in a verifiable scene of wrongdoing, and for her wider refusal to ground her protest novel in a coherent and circumscribed set of social and political grievances. Withholding final judgment on where blame is to be laid—and for what—her novel cannot lend the weight of its critique to a specific program of change. But this is only to say that Barnes writes her protest novel to lambast, rather than serve, the cause of social reform. Indeed, the very impossibility of pinning down a "real" crime of incest or rape against Julie in *Ryder* makes possible a metaphorical widening of the field of suspects and of crimes in the recurring dream-scene of her violation. Barnes makes repeated, figurative use of the narrative of a virgin's violation to foreground the ultimate complicity between middle-class reformers and the structures of oppression they would reform, while eschewing the scandalous appeal to fact on which such projects depend. Instead, she promotes figure over fact to implicate society at large in a scandal that cannot be localized.

NOTES

1. For related discussions, of *Ryder* and *Nightwood* respectively, see J. Scott and Marcus.

2. See Dalton, "Escaping." For related discussions of the incest theme in Barnes's other works, see Broe, "Art"; Curry; Dalton, "*This*"; and DeSalvo, "Make" and *Conceived*, ch. 4. For the leading biographical evaluation of Barnes's abusive sexual history (whose details, in key areas, are still uncertain and/or disputed), see Herring, *Djuna* 53-64, 268-71.

3. In justification of his decision, Herring cites Barnes's own comment to "James Scott and others that her novel *Ryder* was completely autobiographical" (313-14 n2).

4. See Dalton, "Escaping." For an earlier reading of Julie's dream which hints at the possibility of Wendell's abuse, see Ponsot.

5. For an account of the reform efforts which Barnes's grandmother supported through her journalism, see Herring, "Zadel" 108, 111.

6. Thus, a leading philanthropic reformer, Josephine Shaw Lowell, declared that society should "refuse to support any except those whom it can control." Her colleague S. Humphreys Gurteen concurred, declaring that the "fundamental law" of charity organization "is expressed in one word: INVESTIGATE." See Boyer 145-49 and Ginzberg 189-93, 197-200.

7. In a 1915 interview with Mother Jones, Barnes reports the famous labor activist's low opinion of postbellum philanthropy: "It's relief work made possible through slavery, it's charity through chains. It's a rotten system, kept up by your high-class robbers." See Barnes *Interviews* 102. Barnes's grandmother also criticized the "narrow charity" of this period in print. In an 1873 piece for *Harper's* she contrasts the sentimental ideal of "love-ruled, intelligently regulated *homes*" for the urban poor to the black contemporary landscape of "almshouses, prisons," "asylums" and "hospitals." See Buddington 239.

8. Sophia pays tribute to the power of the press on the walls of her writing room back home, which are "covered over," like her petticoated body, with a thick layer of images. The uppermost layer consists of "clippings from newspapers"

and includes the photo of a "pretty girl untimely raped" (13-14).

9. These citations are drawn from "The American Scholar," "Self-Reliance," and "Circles."

10. For an account of these religious communities, see Foster. For biographical material linking Wald Barnes to the Mormons, see Herring, *Djuna* 31-32.

11. See Clayton 51; Iverson 126-27; and Lyman 22-26, 124-43.

12. Field goes on to note Barnes's declaration that the breakup of the family through state intervention was the one part of her novel she made up (185). This adjustment to her family history further underlines Barnes's distrust of reformist efforts to save the world.

13. Fredrickson links the increasing prevalence of the construct of "the Negro as beast" to "the ideology of extreme racism that . . . engulf[ed] the South after 1890" (256, 262).

14. As B. Scott notes, the dream ox is a castrated bull (111). For an analysis of the frequent recourse to castration in the lynching of black men, see Wiegman. For a complementary historical account, see Hodes.

15. See my footnote 8.

WORKS CITED

Bakhtin, Mikhail. *Rabelais and His World.* Trans. Hélene Iswolsky. Bloomington: Indiana UP, 1984.

Barnes, Djuna. *Interviews.* Ed. Alyce Barry. Washington: Sun and Moon, 1985.

———. *Ryder.* 1928. Lisle, IL: Dalkey Archive, 1990.

Boyer, Paul. *Urban Masses and Moral Order in America, 1820-1920.* Cambridge: Harvard UP, 1978.

Broe, Mary Lynn. "My Art Belongs to Daddy: Incest as Exile, The Textual Economics of Hayford Hall." *Women's Writing in Exile.* Eds. Mary Lynn Broe and Angela Ingram. Chapel Hill: The U of North Carolina P, 1989. 41-86.

Broe, Mary Lynn, ed. *Silence and Power: A Reevaluation of Djuna Barnes.* Carbondale: Southern Illinois UP, 1991.

Buddington, Mrs. Zadel B. "Where is the Child?" *Harper's New Monthly Magazine* 46 (1873): 229-39.

Clayton, James L. "The Supreme Court, Polygamy and the Enforcement of Morals in Nineteenth Century America: An Analysis of *Reynolds v. United States.*" *Dialogue: A Journal of Mormon Thought* 12.4 (1979): 46-61.

Curry, Lynda. "'Tom, Take Mercy': Djuna Barnes's Drafts of *The Antiphon.*" Broe, *Silence* 286-98.

Dalton, Anne B. "Escaping from Eden: Djuna Barnes' Revision of Psychoanalytic Theory and Her Treatment of Father-Daughter Incest in *Ryder.*" *Women's Studies* 22 (1993): 163-79.

———. "'*This* is obscene': Female Voyeurism, Sexual Abuse and Maternal Power in *The Dove.*" *The Review of Contemporary Fiction* 13.3 (1993): 117-39.

DeSalvo, Louise A. *Conceived with Malice.* New York: Dutton, 1994.

———. "'To Make Her Mutton at Sixteen': Rape, Incest, and Child Abuse in *The Antiphon.*" Broe, *Silence* 300-15.

Donzelot, Jacques. *The Policing of Families.* Trans. Robert Hurley. New York: Pantheon, 1979.

Emerson, Ralph Waldo. *Essays and Lectures.* New York: Literary Classics, 1983.

Field, Andrew. *Djuna: The Formidable Miss Barnes.* Austin: U of Texas P, 1985.

Foster, Lawrence. *Women, Family and Utopia: Communal Experiments of the Shakers, the Oneida Community, and the Mormons.* Syracuse: Syracuse UP, 1991.

Foucault, Michel. *Discipline and Punish: The Birth of the Prison.* Trans. Alan Sheridan. New York: Vintage, 1979.

Fout, John C., and Maura Shaw Tantillo, eds. *American Sexual Politics: Sex, Gender, and Race Since the Civil War.* Chicago: The U of Chicago P, 1993.

Fredrickson, George M. *The Black Image in the White Mind: The Debate on Afro-American Character and Destiny, 1817-1914.* Middletown: Wesleyan UP, 1987.

Ginzberg, Lori D. *Women and the Work of Benevolence: Morality, Politics, and Class in the Nineteenth-Century United States.* New Haven: Yale UP, 1990.

Gordon, Mary McDougall. "Patriots and Christians: A Reassessment of Nineteenth-Century School Reformers." *Journal of Social History* 11 (1978): 554-73.

Herring, Phillip. *Djuna: The Life and Work of Djuna Barnes.* New York: Viking, 1995.

————. "Zadel Barnes: Journalist." *The Review of Contemporary Fiction* 13.3 (1993): 107-16.

Hodes, Martha. "The Sexualization of Reconstruction Politics: White Women and Black Men in the South after the Civil War." Fout and Tantillo 59-74.

Iversen, Joan Smyth. "A Debate on the American Home: The Antipolygamy Controversy, 1880-1890." Fout and Tantillo 123-40.

Lyman, Edward Leo. *Political Deliverance: The Mormon Quest for Utah Statehood.* Urbana: U of Illinois P, 1986.

Marcus, Jane. "Laughing at Leviticus: *Nightwood* as Woman's Circus Epic." Broe, *Silence* 221-50.

O'Neal, Hank. *"Life is painful, nasty and short—in my case it has only been painful and nasty": Djuna Barnes 1978-1981: An Informal Memoir.* New York: Paragon, 1990.

Plumb, Cheryl J. *Fancy's Craft: Art and Identity in the Early Works of Djuna Barnes.* Selinsgrove: Susquehanna UP, 1986.

Ponsot, Marie. "A Reader's *Ryder.*" Broe, *Silence* 94-112.

Scott, Bonnie Kime. *Refiguring Modernism: Postmodern Feminist Readings of Woolf, West, and Barnes.* Vol. 2. Bloomington: Indiana UP, 1995.

Scott, James B. *Djuna Barnes.* Boston: Twayne, 1976.

Tyack, David B. "Ways of Seeing: An Essay on the History of Compulsory Schooling." *Harvard Educational Review* 46 (1976): 355-89.

Wiegman, Robyn. "The Anatomy of Lynching." Fout and Tantillo 223-45.

FURTHER READING

Criticism

Allen, Carolyn. "The Erotics of Nora's Narrative in Djuna Barnes's *Nightwood.*" *Signs* 19, No. 1 (Autumn 1993): 177-200.

> Presents Nora's narrative in Barnes's *Nightwood* as "a narrative of lesbian erotics" and then "argue[s] how such an erotics critiques Freud's influential writings on narcissism and desire."

Bockting, Margaret. "Performers and the Erotic in Four Interviews by Djuna Barnes." *Centennial Review* XLI, No. 1 (Winter 1997): 183-95.

> Explores the identity of women and actors in the early twentieth century by looking at four interviews conducted by Barnes with Mimi Aguglia, Gaby Deslys, Yvette Guilbert, and Alla Nazimova.

Broe, Mary Lynn. "'A Love from the Back of the Heart': The Story Djuna Wrote for Charles Henri." *Review of Contemporary Literature* 13, No. 3 (Fall 1993): 22-32.

> Studies Barnes's story "Behind the Heart" and what it tells about Barnes's relationship with Charles Henri Ford.

Castricano, Jodey. "Rude Awakenings: or What Happens When a Lesbian Reads the 'Hieroglyphics of Sleep' in Djuna Barnes' *Nightwood.*" *West Coast* 28, No. 3 (Winter 1994-95): 106-16.

> Traces the configuration of desire in Barnes's *Nightwood,* especially focusing on the last chapter.

Dalton, Anne B. "Escaping from Eden: Djuna Barnes' Revision of Psychoanalytic Theory and Her Treatment of Father-Daughter Incest in *Ryder.*" *Women's Studies* 22 (1993): 163-79.

> Analyzes Barnes's presentation of incest in *Ryder* and how her portrayal went against the prevailing psychoanalytic theories of father-daughter sexuality.

Kent, Kathryn R. "'Lullaby for a Lady's Lady': Lesbian Identity in *Ladies Almanack.*" *Review of Contemporary Fiction* 13, No. 3 (Fall 1993): 89-96.

> Explores lesbian identity in Barnes's *Ladies Almanack.*

Michel, Frann. "Displacing Castration: *Nightwood, Ladies Almanack,* and Feminine Writing." *Contemporary Literature* 30, No. 1 (Spring 1989): 33-58.

> Asserts that "Barnes's works suggest that the value of ideas of the feminine and feminine writing consists less in their postulation of a new language or their call for a revolutionary future than in the possibilities they offer for new ways of thinking language, ways that recognize the subversive and potentially revolutionary elements already operative within the languages of the past and present."

Scott, Bonnie Kime. "Barnes Being 'Beast Familiar': Representation on the Margins of Modernism." *Review of Contemporary Fiction* 13, No. 3 (Fall 1993): 41-52.

> Discusses Barnes's use of the bestial in her work, and what that means to her portrayal of women.

Stevenson, Sheryl. "*Ryder* as Contraception: Barnes v. the

Reproduction of Mothering." *Review of Contemporary Fiction* 13, No. 3 (Fall 1993): 97-106.

> Provides a female-centered reading of Barnes's *Ryder* asserting that the novel "constitutes Djuna Barnes's strongest statement against women's enslavement to reproduction."

Winkiel, Laura. "Circuses and Spectacles: Public Culture in *Nightwood.*" *Journal of Modern Literature* 21, No. 1 (Summer 1997): 7-28.

> Analyzes the role of the circus and spectacle in Barnes's *Nightwood,* the main characters' relationship to the circus, and how the circus affects the public culture.

Additional coverage of Barnes's life and career is contained in the following sources published by Gale: *Contemporary Authors,* **Vols. 9-12R, 107;** *Contemporary Authors New Revision Series,* **Vols. 16, 55;** *Dictionary of Literary Biography,* **Vols. 4, 9, 45;** *Major Twentieth-Century Writers, Vols. 1, 2;* **and** *Short Story Criticism,* **Vol. 3.**

Pearl S. Buck

1892-1973

American novelist, short story writer, playwright, essayist, editor, biographer, autobiographer, author of juvenile literature, and translator.

The following entry presents an overview of Buck's career. For further information on her life and works, see *CLC*, Volumes 7, 11, and 18.

INTRODUCTION

Buck is best known for her lifelong mission to ease tensions in East-West relations and increase understanding between the two sides. Through fiction and autobiographical accounts of her life in both worlds, Buck achieved her goal. Many Western readers have learned about the East by reading Buck's work.

Biographical Information

Buck was born in the United States in 1892, but her parents moved to China when she was only three months old. Her parents were Presbyterian missionaries who made the unusual decision to live among the Chinese instead of isolating themselves behind the protective walls of the missionary. Buck grew up living a dual life in a formal English home with Chinese playmates. The Boxer Rebellion forced Buck's family to flee to Shanghai, changing Buck's relationship with China and its people. After leaving China for four years of college at Randolph-Macon Women's College in Lynchburg, Virginia, Buck returned to China after marrying an American agriculturalist stationed in the Far East. When she returned, Buck noticed a distinct rift between Chinese and whites. Constant wars and revolutions in the country, along with her divorce, convinced her to return to America. Once home, Buck began writing about her experiences in China. Buck married her editor, Tom Walsh, and adopted five children in addition to her daughter from her first marriage. Buck's *The Good Earth* (1931) won the Pulitzer Prize in 1932. In 1938, she was awarded the Nobel Prize for literature, becoming the first American woman to earn that distinction.

Major Works

My Several Worlds: Personal Record (1954) is Buck's autobiography, which is about her experiences in China and America. *Imperial Woman* (1956) is a fictional account of the reign of China's Empress Dowager, Tzu Hsi, that speculates about life behind the walls of the Forbidden City. The

novel follows the Empress's humble beginnings as a servant in her uncle's household, as an imperial concubine, and finally as regent for her son and nephew. *Letter From Peking* (1957) tells the story of Elizabeth and her son, Rennie, who comes with her to America after leaving her half-Chinese husband because of the dangerous Communist upheaval in China. Her husband Gerald decides to remain in China instead of abandoning his post as the head of a university. The story follows Gerald's letters home and change Elizabeth's life forever. *Friend to Friend: A Candid Exchange between Pearl S. Buck and Carlos P. Romulo* (1958), is an exchange between Buck and Carlos P. Romulo on the subject of East-West relations. The book attempts to unmask some of the myths about both sides, in hopes that better understanding will promote better relations. With *Command the Morning* (1959), Buck mixes historical figures and events with a fictional story about development of the atom bomb. The story revolves around personal lives of the scientists and how they balance them with their careers—including how they keep their work secret from their wives. The novel is historically accurate about the bomb's development. Buck's *A Bridge for Passing* (1962) is an autobiographical account of Buck's trip to Japan to film her book, *The Big Wave* (1948). During her journey, Buck observes changes in Japan that happened during her twenty-five absence. Most significantly, Buck's second husband Tom died from a protracted illness while the author was in Japan. The book describes the dichotomy of her life at this time: dealing with producers during the day, while working through grief and loneliness at night. *Death in the Castle* (1965) departs from Buck's usual setting and genre. In this novel Buck tells the story about an English noble family forced to sell their family castle to an American industrialist. In *The Three Daughters of Madame Liang* (1969), Buck combines the story of a modern Chinese woman who runs a Shanghai restaurant with the love stories of her three daughters.

Critical Reception

Most reviewers note Buck's underlying impulse to teach her readers and show them the universality of mankind. Fanny Butcher said, "Pearl Buck is obviously a woman of uncommon good will, a believer in man's inherent potentialities for understanding and loving his fellow men even when his actions belie those possibilities." Many reviewers credit Buck with using a light hand and humor—a trait that saves her work from a preachy tone. Margaret Parton said that, "she is far removed from a severe schoolmarm. An old hand at this sort of thing, she knows well how to combine instruction with entertainment. . . . " However, many of Buck's critics feel her art suffers because of her focus on her message. Some have even accused the author of didacticism. Reviewers found the characters weak in *Command the Morning*, and felt the personal stories of the scientists to be out of scale with the subject of the nuclear bomb. Earl W. Foell complained that "The characters for the most part remain wooden, or at best become symbols." Critics credit Buck most for her splendid depictions that make the East familiar and accessible to Western readers.

PRINCIPAL WORKS

The Good Earth (novel) 1931, reprinted 1982
Sons (novel) 1932, reprinted 1975
The Young Revolutionist (juvenile literature) 1932
The First Wife, and Other Stories (short stories) 1933, reprinted, 1963
A House Divided (novel) 1935, reprinted, 1975
The Proud Heart (novel) 1938, reprinted, 1965
The Chinese Children Next Door (juvenile literature) 1942
The Big Wave (juvenile literature) 1948; reprinted, 1973
My Several Worlds: A Personal Record (autobiography) 1954; reprinted, 1975
Imperial Woman (novel) 1956; reprinted, 1977

Letter From Peking (novel) 1957; reprinted, 1975
Friend to Friend: A Candid Exchange between Pearl S. Buck and Carlos P. Romulo (nonfiction) 1958
Command the Morning (novel) 1959; reprinted, 1975
A Desert Incident (drama) 1959
A Bridge for Passing (autobiography) 1962
The Living Reed (novel) 1963; reprinted, 1979
Death in the Castle (novel) 1965
The People of Japan (nonfiction) 1966
The Time Is Noon (novel) 1967
The Good Deed, and Other Stories of Asia, Past and Present (short stories) 1969
The Three Daughters of Madame Liang (novel) 1969
Mandala (novel) 1970
Pearl S. Buck's America (nonfiction) 1971
Secrets of the Heart: Stories (short stories) 1976
The Old Demon (short stories) 1982
Little Red (short stories) 1987

CRITICISM

Kirkus Reviews (review date 1 September 1954)

SOURCE: A review of *My Several Worlds*, in *Kirkus Reviews*, Vol. XXII, No. 17, September 1, 1954, p. 603.

[*In the following review, the critic praises the message and impact of the personal narrative in Buck's* My Several Worlds.]

Not only Pearl Buck's most important book, but—on many counts—her best book, this autobiographical account of more than half a century comes at a time when its message is a challenge to all thoughtful readers. Born of missionary parents and brought up in a China that suffered successive internal upheavals and areas of peace and repose, Pearl Buck knew the Chinese as few white people have been privileged to know them. It took the defeat of Chiang Kai-Shek to determine the permanence of her residence in her American home, though her identification with China today is rooted in a China that she feels will triumph ultimately over Communism. The major portion of her book treats her Chinese years and opens new windows of comprehension, appreciation and knowledge to those who will read. It is an absorbing tale, personal to the extent that one shares with her the impact of what she saw and knew and experienced. On the level of her personal relations she is singularly objective, almost detached, though one knows the facts, one does not enter into the intimacy of the details. ***Fighting Angel*** and ***The Exile,*** superb tributes to her parents, published some years ago, are further set in the perspective by this her own story, and together give an extraordinary portrait of China from the time of the reign of the old Empress Dowager, through the Boxer Rebellion, on up to today. Almost inevitably the last part of the book, her twenty years of putting her roots down in her native land, suffers by being less dramatic, less pictorial, but they add to the sum total of a rounded personality. A good deal of space is devoted to her absorption in the problem of the unwanted children of the world and the constructive action she has taken in the founding of Welcome House; there is a running account of her various homes, of the children of her adoption, of her second marriage, of her journeyings, her friendships, the people of many lands that came and went. And always there is the deepening of a philosophical outlook, an inward searching, and a tempered view of what should be our goals, our responsibilities, in relation to Asia today and tomorrow. On Pearl Buck's name this should reach an audience that might otherwise sidestep a book which challenges our thinking. Don't miss it.

Margaret Parton (review date 6 November 1954)

SOURCE: "The Call of China," in *Saturday Review*, Vol. 37, No. 45, November 6, 1954, p. 17.

[*In the following review, Parton praises the delicacy and restraint of Buck's writing in* My Several Worlds.]

"Two worlds, two worlds, and one cannot be the other, and each has its ways and blessings, I suppose," Pearl Buck sighs, as she visits a lonely farm woman in a mechanized South Dakota kitchen and remembers nostalgically the chatter of Chinese women beating their laundry by the edge of the communal pond.

Of these two worlds Mrs. Buck has made a magnificent synthesis, writing of the world of China from the perspective of twenty years in the United States, of the world of America from the perspective of forty years in China. Those who have read all her books—as this reviewer has not—may feel that *My Several Worlds* is her finest achievement. Those who have not can take it as the rich autumnal flowering of a varied and sensitive mind whose roots are in the common soil of all humanity.

"We have no enemies, we for whom the globe is home," she writes, "for we hate no one, and where there is no hate it is not possible to escape love." With love, then, she has written her autobiography, and where there was hate or at least discord she writes with delicacy and a restraint almost too noble for contemporary taste, grown used to malice and vindictiveness.

If there are any toward whom Mrs. Buck reserves her anger, it is those who sowed the seeds which the innocent

must reap today in whirlwind: the English who immobilized China for a century with opium wars and condescension and who for three centuries exploited India while giving nothing in return; the French in Indo-China, the Dutch in Indonesia, the Americans who must share guilt by the very reason of their silence. And Chiang Kai-shek too, with his limited military mind and his government of contemptuous young intellectuals who failed to understand the people they governed and most particularly failed in understanding that nationalism must be supplemented by idealism if a government is to survive.

As everyone knows, Mrs. Buck is well qualified to write of these matters, to tell us of the China that is gone, and why it went. The daughter of missionary parents who first went to China in 1880, she was born in the United States but taken to China to live when she was three months old. And there, in the idyllic days before the Boxer Rebellion, she grew up in the strange dual world of the missionary child, slipping easily from Chinese patter with playmates to formal English with her parents, from a poached-egg breakfast in the dining room to rice dumplings in the kitchen, from Mark Twain to Confucius. Then the Rebellion forced the family to flee to Shanghai, and in 1909 the observant little girl saw the signs in the parks: "No Chinese, No Dogs." Seeds for the whirlwind.

China was never quite the same afterward. Each time the young Pearl returned from a trip to America, and particularly after her four years at college, she found the rift widened between Chinese and white. And yet she lived on, because it was her home, because she had undertaken a marriage "which continued for seventeen years in its dogged fashion" to an American agriculturalist stationed in China, and most of all because she loved the country about which she was at last beginning to write.

These China years are really the meat of the book, absorbing in their detail of friends, food, literary life, glimpses of Chinese history and philosophy, and the constant, tragic movement of current history. In the end the history, the continual wars and revolutions so ominous of the future, drove her from China as surely as did the dissolution of her own marriage, and her life broke in two, as does the book.

In America she found a Pennsylvania farmhouse, a happy second marriage, four new children to be adopted, and a host of new interests. But like so many Americans who have returned home after years in Asia, one thing she sought and did not find: and that was any curiosity on the part of most Americans about the life of the common man of Asia—a disinterest which is reflected in the ignorance of our statesmen and politicians.

Ah well, says Mrs. Buck with philosophical Chinese acceptance, "a nation, like a child, cannot comprehend beyond the capacity of its mental age. To teach calculus to a child of six is absurd. One has to begin at the beginning, one has to wait for maturity and it cannot be hastened."

While Mrs. Buck is, of course, giving a lesson in mature world thinking to beginners, it should be hastily added that she is far removed from a severe schoolmarm. An old hand at this sort of thing, she knows well how to combine instruction with entertainment—as witnessed by the fact that this reviewer tried conscientiously to skip here and there, and found it impossible to do.

Florence Hanton Bullock (review date 7 November 1954)

SOURCE: "Pearl Buck's Full, Rich Life," in *New York Herald Tribune*, November 7, 1954, sec. 6, p. 1.

[*In the following review, Bullock discusses the juxtaposition of Buck's life in China and her life in America.*]

In *My Several Worlds* Pearl Buck, with attractive humility and grace of spirit, gives us a step-by-step account of her pilgrim's progress, in China and the United States, from little girlhood into mature and effective womanhood. Mrs. Buck's writings have had a wide and enthusiastic acceptance and her literary honors include the Pulitzer Prize, the Nobel Prize for Literature, and membership in the American Academy of Arts and Sciences. But it becomes evident in *My Several Worlds* that all the novels, biographies and other more obviously purposeful volumes that she has turned out over the years have been but the season-to-season fruit of her development as a woman and a human being. "Life," she says, "must be lived full tilt for its own sake before it becomes material for a novel." Seventeen years of close association with the Chinese peasants—whom she profoundly loves and admires, and whose humor, wisdom, philosophical acceptance of life she has made essentially her own—went into *The Good Earth.* Yet the actual writing of that long, full, immensely rich novel took but three months.

Born in West Virginia, into a family rich in the traditions of the ministry and teaching—her father was "a severe man of God and a missionary"—Pearl Sydenstricker was transplanted early to China, and put down deep roots into that "old and sophisticated" civilization. Her parents, loyal to their spiritual insights and democratic principles, refused to live—as most missionary families lived—within the shelter of a white man's compound, and their small daughter's earliest—often her only—friends were the children of their Chinese neighbors whom she loved and ac-

cepted, as they accepted her in spite of her white skin and golden hair. So it was a rude shock to an affectionate eight-year-old when the growing hostility against "foreign devils" in the days just preceding the Boxer Rebellion alienated her from her playmates. Pearl's mother explained that her friends had not ceased to love her: they were merely afraid to be seen playing with her. And her father made it clear that he did not blame the Chinese for resenting the arrogance of the white men toward them in their own country.

The lesson was well learned. For during half a lifetime spent in China, as a child, as the wife of a man who was trying, without too much success, to teach Western methods of farming to the peasants, and as a teacher in the Chinese University in Nanking when that city was Chiang Kai-shek's bloody capital, Mrs. Buck suffered both danger and loss from looting, murdering anti-Western mobs. But she was always able to accept with genuine sympathy the point of view of the Chinese. "As a child I had watched so often the Chinese bearers trembling under the weight of too-heavy loads carried up from the English ships in port . . . I was troubled because the load was too heavy and the white man did not care that it was . . . and that trouble has followed me all the days of my life." In *My Several Worlds,* without bitterness and with only a sorrowful regret, Mrs. Buck points out the mistakes that the white man has made which have led to a divided world in which the Chinese who are, basically, she thinks, so much like ourselves, are not on our side but against us.

How successfully was such a woman able to transplant herself into the United States of the 1930's? "Roots," she says, "must be put down if one is to live." After a few months spent floundering about among the literati in Manhattan—she had dinner *a deux* with Alexander Woollcott at Wit's End, and Chris Morley took her to her first speakeasy, which she hated—she consciously and deliberately took steps which any social psychologist would approve: she bought herself an old house in a part of the country where her forefathers had lived, and settled into it. She began to study—and grow deeply fond of—her fellow Americans and some, at least, of their ways. The American pattern, she thinks, is to be patternless. She finds us "wonderful in emergency . . . a generous, impulsive, emotional people, unstable, not only from nature but from environment. . . . The years are rich with living, but life does not flow in a river as it did in China."

She speaks out frankly about several matters of interest to Americans: our way of rearing our children, of which she does not greatly approve and (angrily) of the obstructive methods of social workers in the adoption of children. (She and her husband rejoice now in a whole houseful of much-loved adopted children.) And she has wise words to say about divorces, including her own.

Mrs. Buck's great fecundity as a writer has resulted, it seems to me, from her wonderful faculty for participation, imaginative and actual, plus an unusual feeling for beauty and meanings, and a remarkable capacity for retaining her vivid impressions.

My Several Worlds has a deep humanity. For Mrs. Buck's approach to life–and writing–is one of rich and loving tenderness quite untinctured with sentimentality. And her basic creed runs through every line she writes.

Fanny Butcher (review date 7 November 1954)

SOURCE: "Memoirs of Genius at Large," in *Chicago Sunday Tribune Magazine of Books*, November 7, 1954, p. 1.

[*In the following review, Butcher asserts that "Pearl Buck has a genius for making readers see pictures and know human beings, often with humor. Nowhere has she used that genius more tellingly than in parts of* My Several Worlds."]

There are few writers who could so aptly use the title, *My Several Worlds,* for an autobiography. Few have lived so close to so many worlds. To most Americans Pearl Buck is best known as the first American woman to receive the Nobel prize for literature, the author of an unremembered number of books [39]—especially *The Good Earth,* which touched readers deeply.

To those who have read any of those books, Pearl Buck is obviously a woman of uncommon good will, a believer in man's inherent potentialities for understanding and loving his fellow men even when his actions belie those possibilities. Readers sense, even if they do not know, that in her life there must have been reagents—different from those in most lives—which have clarified her philosophy—the way that a cloudy test tube is chemically clarified.

In *My Several Worlds,* Pearl Buck tells of those reagents—literally different worlds in which she has lived. The book is subtitled, "A Personal Record," and personal it is in the sense of being a record of what her very seeing eyes saw and what her heart understood. It is not personal in the sense of being outspokenly self-revealing.

Her autobiography is in a new pattern, with no personal intimacies, but surprisingly intimate in its revelations of man's relationship to man in the world of yesterday as well as of today and tomorrow.

Pearl Buck has a genius for making readers see pictures and know human beings, often with humor. Nowhere has she used that genius more tellingly than in parts of *My Several Worlds.* Not only the Chinese, but, more briefly, Indian, Japanese, Indo-Chinese. All Asia lives in these pages as it has lived in few books of our day. The more familiar American scenes and people in the book are, perhaps by their very familiarity, less vivid.

Miss Buck's Chinese world is only one of her several worlds. There are her worlds as a writer, a teacher, a farmer, a mother of her own retarded child [whose future as much as China's upheaval brought her back to America to live] and five adopted sons and daughters; her world of helping despondent parents of other retarded innocents and of finding homes for unwanted babies of mixed blood; and over all her world of friendships.

Silence Buck Bellows (review date 1 January 1956)

SOURCE: "Inside the Forbidden City," in *New York Herald Tribune*, January 1, 1956, p. 1.

[*In the following review, Bellows discusses the difficulties of developing a fictional story around an historical figure, and how Buck approaches the problem in her* Imperial Woman.]

General events in the Chinese Empire from the early 1850's to the early 1900's are now a matter of history. What went on in the separate world inside the walls of the Forbidden City is less well known and subject to conjecture and dispute. What went on in the mind of Tzu Hsi, Empress Dowager of China, strong ruler and unpredictable woman, is anybody's guess and a challenge to the imagination. She was not a person to share her private thoughts with another, or to leave a record of them; and any attempt to cast her as the point-of-view character in a novel must necessarily be a matter for speculation.

Imperial Woman begins with the summoning of Orchid (her girlhood name), one of 60 Manchu maidens, to the palace of Emperor Hsien-Feng, there to become "Yehonala," his favorite concubine. It follows her elevation, upon the birth of her son, to the rank of Empress, her assumption of the power behind the weak throne, her regency over three child emperors, her absolute and tyrannical rule as Tzu Hsi the Empress Dowager, her final concessions to the Western powers, and the tottering of the Manchu dynasty.

Where there is so much uncertainty concerning the private life of a prominent figure, a novelist assumes a considerable responsibility in deciding which "facts" to accept as true. Pearl Buck has not evaded this responsibility. Her development of the Empress' story and character tallies closely enough with most accounts of historians and memoirs of close associates of the Dowager. But in each instance where the facts are uncertain, the author has made a clear-cut decision. She could hardly do otherwise, since her story purports to take the reader into the Empress' mind and heart and to follow her private acts; and in most cases the decision seems the logical one, judged in the light of other books.

Even so, it was an arbitrary and spectacular choice to assume that the royal heir, Tung Chin, was in reality the son of Jung Lu, the Empress' Manchu kinsman, childhood sweetheart, trusted adviser, and lifetime adorer in an idealistic love which was only once consummated; especially since historians in general seem not to have advanced this theory, although they recognize, in varying degrees, some sort of liaison between the Empress and her kinsman.

The atmosphere and the authenticity of era and conditions are beyond criticism. The reader is taken inside the walls of the Forbidden City. He threads the terrifying mazes of court intrigue. He meets Tzu Hsi in all her contradictory charm, beauty, gentleness, rage, relentlessness and cruelty. There are accounts of debauchery and atrocity that may offend some readers. But there could be no authentic picture of the Forbidden City without them.

The style is eminently suited to the tale. Some of the scenes have all the dramatically static quality of Chinese figures painted on porcelain.

To mold an historical character to the form of a novel is always a little precarious, especially when the figure has not yet receded so far into the past as to be almost legendary. In the case of so persuasive a writer as Pearl Buck, the casual reader may find himself accepting as factual history incidents and conversations which must be imaginary. *Imperial Woman* is enhanced and clarified, rather than otherwise, by the use of supplementary reading.

Fanny Butcher (review date 1 April 1956)

SOURCE: "Pearl Buck Recreates the Last Empress of China," in *Chicago Sunday Tribune Magazine of Books*, April 1, 1956, pp. 1-2.

[*In the following review, Butcher asserts that only Pearl Buck could have written* Imperial Woman.]

Perhaps in all of history there never was a woman whose life was more of her own making, whose power was more absolute, whose fate was more spectacular than the life pattern of Tzu Hsi, the mortal woman so revered that she was called "The Old Buddha" and worshipped as a living god. The world knows much from books of other great empresses, like Catherine II of Russia and Victoria of England, and of the many court favorites whose hands guided history through the men who succumbed to their beauty, their wit, or their intelligence [or a combination of those qualities]. But no one, before Pearl Buck wrote *Imperial Woman,* has told fully the amazing story of the life of the last empress of China.

Imperial Woman is a novel which probably no other pen in the world today except Pearl Buck's could have produced. No Chinese writer could have written it dispassionately, nor could anyone who had not lived in China and absorbed, with the air she breathed, its ways of life and thought and action. And probably no man would have seen the heroine of this historic novel in the revealing light in which Pearl Buck shows her, driven by relentless ambition, often ruthlessly and often uselessly cruel, and yet true [after her fashion] to the one love of her life.

This fabulous heroine starts as almost a drudge in the household of an uncle who, when her father died, had taken her and her mother into the family quarters. She was deeply in love with her kinsman, Jung Lu, but, because she was beautiful and a Manchu maiden, she was sent with her cousin to the imperial court as a concubine. Her own cousin was the imperial consort, she merely a prisoner in the imperial palace until one day the weakling emperor summoned her and from that moment was under her spell.

The imperial consort's child was a weakling girl, but when her own was a son who, the author suggests, was her lover's, not the emperor's, her power began and never until she died in her seventies did it really fail. It tottered precariously, however, many times; when the weakling emperor died; during her years of regency for her son, who became emperor; in treacherous days just before and after his death; in the regency of her nephew, whom she put upon the imperial throne; and most seriously when China was invaded by angry foreign troops protesting the massacre of their nationals, the foreigners whom the Old Buddha hated.

The history of these 46 years of absolutism of the Old Buddha is a panoramic background for an intimately detailed study of Manchu imperial life lived against it. It is also an intimate study of a beautiful, imperious woman who was an enigma even to herself at times, cruel with much of mankind but a lover of helpless animals and birds, a poet, an artist, a musician sensitive to beauty but often as cold of heart as one of the marble bridges which she insisted on building.

Pearl Buck's descriptions of fabrics, of embroidery, of jewels, of golden and bronze chrysanthemums in a courtyard are so vivid that one can almost feel the golden dragons on the imperial yellow satin or the cooling comfort of a piece of jade held in the hand on a hot day.

Everyone, of course, will want to know whether *Imperial Woman* is as great a book as *The Good Earth.* That is a question which each reader will answer himself. That it is the great obverse of her literary medallion of a China of the past everyone will agree.

Virgilia Peterson (review date 9 November 1958)

SOURCE: "All in the Family of Man," in *New York Times Book Review*, November 9, 1958, p. 4.

[*In the following review, Peterson asserts that "The people in Buck's* Letter From Peking *are informed with magnanimity; and it is this magnanimity, inherent in Miss Buck herself as well as in her characters, that lifts* Letter From Peking *far above the level of a treatise on understanding and makes it a moving and memorable tale."*]

Throughout her writing life, Pearl Buck has been building bridges of understanding between an old and a new civilization, between one generation and another, between differing attitudes toward God and nationality and parenthood and love. Not all Miss Buck's bridges have withstood the freight of problems they were designed to bear. But *The Good Earth* will surely continue to span the abyss that divides East from West, so long as there are people to read it.

Now, once again, in her latest novel, it is primarily as a builder of bridges that Miss Buck should be judged. *Letter From Peking,* taut, spare and nobly wrought, stretches from Vermont to China to link the loyalties and longings, the joys and sufferings that constitute the endless variety and the unchanging sameness of the family of man. *Letter From Peking* is one of the best of Miss Buck's bridges.

The story begins in 1950. Five long years have passed since Elizabeth, the narrator, and her son Rennie, left Peking and her beloved half-Chinese husband, Gerald MacLeod, to wait on a Vermont farm for the Communist upheaval in China to die down. Gerald himself had made them go, and had decided, as the head of a university, that he must stay behind. After months of silence, the twelfth letter from Peking, the last she will have from Gerald—as she knows when she opens it—arrives. It is, and it is not, what Elizabeth has so patiently and painfully awaited, for while it brings her reassurance of love, it seals her fate.

There was much that Elizabeth had never learned about her husband, about his Chinese mother, about his Scottish father from Virginia, and about his inmost reasons for the decision that had torn them apart. Little by little, as the story unfolds, she acquires the knowledge she lacked. Little by little, she comes to understand not only the husband who chose a Communist China that he did not believe in rather than the American wife he loved, but also his son who, at 18, cannot accept what he is or what his parents have done to him.

> "You don't understand," Rennie cries to his mother, in an agony of rebellion. "You are American, your ancestry is pure—"
>
> "O pure–" Elizabeth cries back at him, "the rebels of half a dozen nations in Europe—"
>
> "None of that matters," Rennie replies. "You are all white."

This book is peopled with men and women incapable of self-pity and unwilling to blame life for their allotted pain. They are informed with magnanimity; and it is this magnanimity, inherent in Miss Buck herself as well as in her characters, that lifts *Letter From Peking* far above the level of a treatise on understanding and makes it a moving and memorable tale.

Huston Smith (review date 22 November 1958)

SOURCE: "Empire of the Mind and Heart," in *Saturday Review*, Vol. 41, No. 47, November 22, 1958, pp. 15-6.

[*In the following review, Smith argues that Buck's half of* Friend to Friend *is more penetrating than that of Carlos Romulo because it adds something new to the East-West dialogue.*]

Toward the close of [*Friend to Friend*] Pearl Buck quotes an Asian as reminding her that "the criticisms of enemies need not be regarded, but faithful are the wounds of a friend." The civil but open criticism that pervades this entire attempt by an Oriental and an American to explore the troubled psychological relations between the United States and the Afro-Asian world makes of its brief pages two deep, reciprocally-inflicted, faithful wounds.

Carlos Romulo, Philippine Ambassador to the United

States, opens the discussion. His thesis is not unexpected. America's relations with the Afro-Asian nations are of decisive importance. Consequently it is imperative not only that Americans shed all feelings of superiority over these peoples and inclinations to dominate them, but also that they remedy their "underdeveloped" understanding of the East. Understanding does not require agreement, but it does require knowledge of what makes other peoples tick (the author's colloquialism).

Specifically, with respect to Asians and Africans it requires awareness of the psychological scars left by generations of Western colonialism and the mental set of peoples flexing their muscles for the first time in modern history. It demands an appreciation of "the grinding power of poverty, which has new meaning every mealtime to angry human beings who care little for ideological disputes when their stomachs are empty; and the heritage of pride and resentment, the curious mixture of self-reliance and inferiority complex, the dreams of glory and the days of disappointment, the ambition and the fatalism, all of which are combined in the Asian and African world."

All this is true, so true that to many readers it is likely to sound obvious. I disagree. What Ambassador Romulo says along these lines we still very much need to hear.

A few points which relate to the complexity of the problems considered in Ambassador Romulo's half of *Friend to Friend* are:

1. Mr. Romulo's message adds up to a plea for understanding. I have just affirmed that this is desperately needed. But what else? When psychologists got to the point of reducing virtually everything in child care to love, a Bettelheim was needed to write *Love Is Not Enough*. A parallel volume is now needed in international relations titled *Understanding Is Not Enough*. Did our own Civil War spring essentially from misunderstandings between North and South?

Or suppose we were to understand Communism perfectly, would this resolve our conflict with it? Mr. Romulo is excellent on understanding, but on what is needed in addition he is cursory. Equality and respect seem to be his only other general recommendations; but would observance of these settle the problems of power politics? Our respect for the Russians has risen astronomically, but this does not seem to have quieted our difficulties with them.

2. One of Mr. Romulo's brief chapters deals with myths he thinks are clouding America's understanding of the world situation. One of these—the notion that the American way is the only way to freedom—is most pertinent. But for the rest it is not a perceptive list. Some beliefs—*e.g.*, that ab-

solute weapons are so terrible that we ought not to fight to defend our freedom, or that the United States and the Soviet Union will be socially indistinguishable before long—are not sufficiently widespread to be classed as important American myths. With others his analysis is too summary to show that they are myths instead of truths.

3. In providing aid Mr. Romulo thinks the United States should not require "that the recipient country should conform to certain concepts and practices that may be valued in America but are irrelevant to the recipient country's institutions." Granted. But the inclusion of the word "irrelevant" suggests that there may be some conditions the United States should require. What are they? Capitalism? Democracy? Free institutions? Honest administration? Benefit to the masses? Feasible plans for national economic progress? Can a nation insist on *any* conditions without opening itself to charges of interference and domination?

4. Mr. Romulo thinks it is desperately important for the United States to take the initiative in making peace. "The peoples of the world must be shown that America really wants peace and to do that she must not content herself by replying to Bulganin's or Khrushchev's letters." But how Mr. Romulo can pass in five sentences from this statement to praising "the inflexibility . . . and uncompromising . . . position of Secretary of State John Foster Dulles in dealing with the Kremlin [as] a tower of strength of the free world" I cannot understand. I thought it was this posture more than anything else that is making Asians and Africans wonder if the United States is actually the world's leader with respect to peace.

Pearl Buck's half of the book is more penetrating. One of the real blessings of genuine friendship is the conditions it provides for self-understanding. In this sense Mr. Romulo's contribution serves its purpose admirably, for it prompts Mrs. Buck to one of the most insightful brief probings of the American temper I have seen. It is here, in asking *why* we appear as we do to the rest of the world, that *Friend to Friend* actually advances the East-West dialogue. Where Mr. Romulo says things more Americans need to hear, Mrs. Buck says some new things. What things, specifically, may appropriately be left for the reader to discover from the book itself. Here I will only say that they add up to a strong justification of America—a bit too strong, I am inclined to think. But this flaw, if it be such, is outweighed by two virtues: the freshness of Mrs. Buck's observations which I have just mentioned, and their healthy antidote to the excessive self-condemnation into which many Americans, this reviewer included, tend periodically to slip.

Mr. Romulo thinks that if America were ever to found an

empire it would have to be "an empire of the mind and heart." Regardless of who founds it, this book looks toward such an empire.

Taliaferro Boatwright (review date 3 May 1959)

SOURCE: "A Novel of the Atom Bomb," in *New York Herald Tribune Book Review*, May 3, 1959, p. 4.

[*In the following review, Boatwright argues that, "This essentially romantic portrayal of life weakens and diffuses the force of the author's moral argument [in* Command the Morning], *which is foursquare on the side of life and against the use of the bomb for destruction. . . ."*]

Since the second world war, Pearl Buck tells us, she has been increasingly preoccupied by the atom bomb. This absorption, which has embraced the theories of nuclear physics, the construction of the bomb and the nature and problems of the men who designed and developed it, has resulted in short stories, a play, *A Desert Incident,* which appeared briefly on Broadway earlier this year, and now a full-scale novel, which she has called, in recognition of the illimitable potentialities of nuclear power, *Command the Morning.* As might be expected of a writer of Mrs. Buck's sensibility, the principal concern of the book is the moral issue that confronted the scientists who worked on the bomb: whether they could in conscience devote their talents to the building of an instrument of destruction, a device which would cause untold death and suffering and, conceivably, might trigger the extinction of man.

In some ways "novel" is a misnomer for her book, for it is in large part a factual and accurate history of the construction of the bomb, and includes as characters a number of real persons. Most, including Presidents Roosevelt and Truman, Vice-President Wallace and Vannevar Bush, are identified obliquely, as are the settings—the University of Chicago, Oak Ridge, Hanford, Los Alamos. Some are thinly disguised; a few, notably the late Enrico Fermi, play their own parts. However, the principals, Burton Hall, the fiftyish scientist who organizes and spearheads the project, Stephen Coast, the brilliant young physicist who is his chief lieutenant, and Jane Earl, the beautiful Anglo-Indian who becomes Hall's assistant, are completely fictional.

In so far as the book sticks to the exciting and still not widely known story of the making of the bomb it is excellent. The in-gathering of the scientists, the decision to proceed, the dramatic first self-sustaining chain reaction at Stagg Field, the construction of Oak Ridge and Hanford, the first mushroom cloud over the mesa, the agonizing

qualms of the scientists over dropping the bomb on Hiroshima—all these are ably handled.

Not as much can be said for the "human interest," which seems to have been conceived with an eye to a bonbon and chaise lounge readership. This is true not only of the plot, which is concerned with such questions as whether a scientist can find happiness if he cannot share his innermost thoughts with his wife and whether a woman scientist can be both a woman and a scientist, but also of the book's general tone, that is, its system of values and its portrayal of contemporary behavior and motivation. Thus we are presented with a society of superhuman scientists and their loyal wives, a world in which the only sin is neglect, and that only as a consequence of service to the all-demanding god Science, a world from which malice and evil have been banished, along with passion, in any sense other than the romantic love of the troubadours. A few nods are made in the direction of sex: Burton Hall is represented as lustful, Coast's wife has an affair with a defecting English scientist, Jane Earl comes close to falling in love with both Coast and Hall. But Hall is all talk, Helen Coast's affair is bloodless, and Jane's loves turn out to be mostly renunciations.

This essentially romantic portrayal of life weakens and diffuses the force of the author's moral argument, which is foursquare on the side of life and against the use of the bomb for destruction, but cannot dim the story of the achievement of the scientists and the possibilities unleashed by the unlocking of secrets of nuclear power, the "divine fire" which, as Mrs. Buck rightly points out, will enable us to "ride into space on the wings of power" to command the morning, indeed.

Fanny Butcher (review date 3 May 1959)

SOURCE: "Pearl Buck's New Novel a Tour de Force," in *Chicago Sunday Tribune Magazine of Books*, May 3, 1959, p. 1.

[*In the following review, Butcher calls Buck's* Command the Morning *"one of the most memorable and rewarding reading experiences of our day."*]

The title of this commanding novel [*Command the Morning*] by our country's first woman to receive the Nobel award in literature, comes from the Bible: "The Lord answered Job out of the whirlwind and said . . . 'Hast thou commanded the morning?'" The question implied in these unforgettable pages is one which every thinking human being must be asking: Did the discovery of atomic power command the morning or the night of mankind?

This is a novel about the most past-shattering and future-building period of modern times, the months of secret research which culminated in the dropping of the atomic bomb over Hiroshima. Were those months to destroy or to free mankind? That is the question posed here.

Pearl Buck does not offer the answer. What she does is to tell the story of those momentous days in terms of the scientists through whose brains, whose chemical retorts, and whose hearts the world has changed. One of them, the only woman in a key position in the project, was uncompromisingly opposed to the use of atomic power as a weapon—ever. One young scientist, who was as violently in opposition to its use as she, changed his mind when he was convinced that the evolvement of such a weapon was inevitable and could have been used for, not against, Hitler.

There are real people in *Command the Morning.* The great Enrico Fermi appears often. The hero of the book, the scientist who had over-all charge of the entire project, is on first name terms with Washington personalities, including Vice President "Harry" and "the Chief." Real places come alive—Oak Ridge and Los Alamos from their beginnings, and that fantastic spot under a University of Chicago football stadium where the tensest of all of the moments took place, when it was found that chain reaction could be controlled and, therefore, the world-shattering power could be used.

The author's finest powers of giving intimacy to reality are evident here. Never has she had a more difficult task or a more momentous one. To most of her readers the secret of the atom will still remain esoteric despite her simplified explanations of the sciences involved. For, let's face it, how many casual readers know or can understand even the basic principles of fission? However, everyone will leave the book with a mind sharpened to the future, with the question plaguing him: Shall it be the annihilation of man or a better life for all mankind?

The story of the epochal discovery is told as a great novelist always records fact, in terms of human beings. *Command the Morning* is a magnificent fictional history of the days which could preface a new morning for the world, but it is primarily a story of men and women. It is, too, a subtle explanation of the power of creative work in men's lives. These creators were scientists, but what Miss Buck has written is true also of writers, musicians, painters, anyone dedicated to the thing he is creating. Creators really live, in the truest sense of that word, within the walls of their art or their science. They may find love, companionship, stimulation, even a kind of understanding, in those who don't know what they are talking about. But with those who do there is a tie, no matter how tenuous, which is essentially the nourishment of the soul.

Already, as the book ends, the characters feel their day is past. "The kids of today have their sights on soaring off into space," one says, just as "the kids" of the beginnings of the atomic age had theirs on harnessing the atom. "Space travel is the coming thing," is said to one of the head nuclear scientists. "It'll keep us too busy to think about wars maybe. I'll say this for the big blast you men made in the desert—it's sent us ahead a thousand years."

Command the Morning is no quick and easy book to read. It must have been a terrific one to write. But it is one of the most memorable and rewarding reading experiences of our day.

Richard Sullivan (review date 3 May 1959)

SOURCE: "Science and the Bomb," in *New York Times Book Review*, May 3, 1959, p. 29.

[*In the following review, Sullivan complains that the prose is limp and the characterization is weak in Buck's* Command the Morning.]

No question about it, since the writhing, mushroom-shaped cloud first rose over the original burst of The Bomb, we have all lived in a changed world. Regardless of race, sex, religion, age or income bracket, we are all instantly subject to reduction to cosmic dust. The means seem to be at hand to crack this old planet, like an aged croquet ball, right in two. And ironically, wonderfully, we possess these means out of our innate tendency to know and capacity to learn and find out and discover.

What Pearl Buck writes about in *Command the Morning* is inexpressibly important. This novel deals with the making of The Bomb and the dropping of The Bomb. Grave moral questions abound in both activities. The ideas which this book will cause its readers to ponder are serious. The intention of the author is obviously and most honorably serious. Yet this is a poor novel.

Any novel is first of all a stretch of words set down. It is desirable that these words be fresh, bright, alive and illuminating. The words have to captivate the reader, somehow. The prose of *Command the Morning* is limp and colorless.

The principal characters include an organizing-type scientist who has an eye for pretty women, an ingrown-quiet-type scientist whose wife doubts him because he thinks in equations, a couple of anxious-type European scientists, a spy-type, an industry-type, a military-type, and as a kind of topper a gorgeous beautiful-girl-type scientist. If any of these broadly conceived scientist-types had been individually characterized, this novel might have come alive. If all of them had been seen as persons rather than as thin caricatures, this might have been a fine novel.

As it stands, **Command the Morning** remains a bland and dull scenario for—with photogenic casting and some sharpening of the dialogue—a movie to make us all think.

Eleazar Lipsky (review date 16 May 1959)

SOURCE: "Man and Mushrooms," in *Saturday Review*, Vol. 42, No. 20, May 16, 1959, p. 31.

[*In the following review, Lipsky asserts that the scientific story dwarfs the human story of Buck's* Command the Morning.]

In Laura Fermi's account of her life with Enrico Fermi, *Atoms in the Family,* there appears a photograph of Fermi waiting to receive the Nobel Prize for science in 1933 at Stockholm. In that same picture, there also appears Pearl Buck, waiting to receive the prize for literature. The scientist seems unimpressed by the occasion, but Mrs. Buck appears tense and deeply affected.

Perhaps it was this encounter that first aroused Mrs. Buck's interest in science, for Fermi looms large in her latest novel, **Command the Morning,** which deals with the human side of the quest for nuclear energy. Her concern for the problem is well known. She has spent many days at Oak Ridge, and Los Alamos, she has studied atomic physics from textbooks and talked with the wives as well as the men who developed the first sustained nuclear chain reaction and the bomb dropped on Japan.

Inevitably Mrs. Buck has turned her interest in nuclear physics to play and novel form. Closely following the historical facts, she deals here with the special problems— emotional and domestic and moral—which arise when the arts of peace are turned to war. The central characters are fictitious, but actual scientists and political figures appear under their own names, or thinly disguised, to express contrasting views regarding the central moral issue: whether or not to develop and drop the bomb. Against this larger story, Mrs. Buck describes marriage strains and unhappy love affairs leading to the decision of her protagonist, a woman scientist, to return to her birthplace in India and the ways of peace. It is a solution not open to everyone.

Of course, all this is not really a scientific problem at all, except in the central sense that the quest for knowledge calls for an initial choice of the field of exploration. Once the scientific process has begun, the remaining problems, moral and political, are those common to humanity. Properly speaking, no scientist either dropped the bomb or made the decision: It was a soldier who executed an order of the political and military head of the nation. All those who supported or approved that order shared the responsibility. The bomb is merely one example of the more generalized problem of our times.

Mrs. Buck is earnest and intelligent and her science is accurate. The crucial episodes showing the explosion of the first bomb are charged with excitement. But, through no fault of hers, the science fails to support the human story. The atomic blast over New Mexico seems to destroy by overexposure the more truly significant, but (in this context) petty problems of the scientists. That one scientist should see in that first blinding explosion the resolution of a problem in marital infidelity is inappropriate to say the least.

It is not true (as a leading critic has suggested . . .) that the novel of science should deal only with the "big bang" to achieve contemporary significance, for the proper field of the novel is humanity, and the cosmic stage may be too large for its dwarfed actors. It is all a matter of scale. For all the author's intellectual discipline and technical accuracy, one cannot say that this novel reaches its goals, or that it satisfies the appetite for greater insight into the matter.

Elizabeth Gray Vining (review date 15 April 1962)

SOURCE: "Encounter With Grief," in *New York Times Book Review*, April 15, 1962, pp. 18-20.

[*In the following review, Vining discusses the different strands that weave together to create Buck's* A Bridge for Passing.]

This lovely book[, **A Bridge for Passing,**] is woven of three distinct strands: the making of a moving picture in Japan, an encounter with grief, and the gradually revealed portrait of a man of heart, vision and integrity. Each strand is separate, yet from the weaving there emerges a firm fabric with a pattern of the whole.

The unnamed "he" of the book, the man of the portrait, died while his wife was in Japan at work on the filming of her novel, **The Big Wave.** After an interlude at home Pearl Buck returned to Japan to finish the picture and there, in that land of beauty and disaster, to assimilate her sorrow and to find a bridge over which to pass back again to life.

The Japan that we see in the book is the authentic Japan of

today, with people whom one knows as real, not the paper dolls and caricatures of so many books about that currently much visited and much be-written country. They are people of all kinds: the movie magnate, the diplomat's wife, the actor, the writer, the simple folk of the little fishing village in the southern island of Kyushu. All of them are experiencing the conflict between the old and the new in Japan today.

Miss Buck, who had not visited the country for twenty-five years, is alive to the changes. Not all of them are pleasing. The brown permanent curls that have replaced "the smooth straight black hair which was once the glory of the Japanese woman," the "bold looks, frank speech and frankly sexual approach to any available man" which have succeeded the modest downcast face, repelled her, but as she came to know better the bevies of pretty girls in the offices she decided that the modern Japanese woman, though she had lost her "ancient sadness," was at least "vivacious and delightful." Her special friend, the mature woman executive, she found "cosmopolitan and sophisticated in the true sense of the word . . . One could never mistake her for any but a Japanese and yet this national saturation of birth and education was only the medium through which she communicated universal experience, and with wisdom and charm."

The movie, which involved a live volcano and a tidal wave, was a story of human hope and courage in the midst of natural disasters. An American film company was making it in Japan with a Japanese firm as co-producer. People who work in the theatre, comments Miss Buck, are "a group apart by temperament, whatever their race, color or nationality." There is humor as well as drama in the account of the interplay of personalities, of the casting, of the filming of the picture as they found first the volcano and then, moving south, the perfect fishing village; absorbing interest in all the details of actors and villagers, in the glorious beauty of the scene, excitement in the final trip to the volcano and a near-shipwreck.

Woven in and out is the moving experience of the woman who after a rarely happy marriage of twenty-five years must meet sorrow and learn to live with it. After the days of intense activity on location came the lonely evenings walking the Ginza or tramping the seashore, spending long healing hours in the embrace of a hollow rock looking out to sea. It was a life "lived on two separate levels, one by day, the other by night; one upon earth, the other in search of habitation not made with hands."

During the hours of reflection, of longing, of seeking for a communication that cannot be found, memories return of the man for whom she mourns, and bit by bit, a flash here and there, the portrait emerges, clear and admirable. All

who know the aching loss of a beloved person can read here their own story, can walk again the path of loneliness. Here, once again, is the recognition of inexorability, of acceptance—in Wordsworth's phrase of the burden of the mystery. "Science and religion," she concludes, "religion and science, they are two sides of the same glass, through which we see darkly until the two focusing together, reveal the truth."

Edward Weeks (review date May 1962)

SOURCE: "Solace in Doing," in *Atlantic Monthly*, Vol. 209, No. 5, May, 1962, p. 119.

[*In the following review, Weeks states that* A Bridge for Passing *"will be a touchstone for those made desolate by sorrow, and in writing it Mrs. Buck lifts our spirits as she revives her own."*]

Pearl Buck is one of those rare Americans who knows the Orient as well as she knows her homeland. She has lived through three careers and is now actively engaged in a fourth. As a child of missionary parents, she learned to speak Chinese and to love her foster country. After college, her first marriage to her missionary husband brought her back to China but not to happiness: their eldest daughter was retarded; the home ties were disrupted; and China itself became increasingly hostile. Back in the United States, struggling to find her feet as a writer, she came under the sympathetic editorship of Tom Walsh. She was determined not to commit herself emotionally, and she turned him down again and again, but when they were married and set up their home together in Pennsylvania, she entered a third career of more than two decades which was to bring her the triumph of the Nobel Prize and a companionship beatific, marred only by Tom's long last illness. The doctors finally held out no hope. It is against this background that Mrs. Buck has written her new, compassionate book, *A Bridge for Passing.*

She first passes over the bridge on her way to Tokyo, where she is to assist a Japanese company in the filming of her book *The Big Wave.* This is her first sight of Japan in twenty-five years, and although she had been here often in her girlhood, she is unprepared for the startling changes that have occurred since the American occupation. She gets on famously with the burly Japanese producer who is strenuously turning out a new picture every week; she joins in the casting and in the search for the sets that are needed, including a fishing village, a live volcano, and a tidal wave. Then comes the long-distance telephone call telling her of Tom's death, and back over the bridge she hurries. When she is released from the shock, she returns to Japan a different woman, lonelier, more given to reverie and to walking by herself. By day she is a buffer in the tense struggle between the Japanese producer and the American director; by night in the empty hotel room she finds consolation in reliving her happiness with her editor. At all times she is observing and judging the Japanese character, and these findings fill some of the most fascinating pages in the book.

"The Japanese woman," says Mrs. Buck, "has always been stronger than the Japanese man, for, like the Chinese woman, she has been given no favors." Mrs. Buck notes the effect of American courtship, of intermarriage between Japanese girls and American soldiers, and of the orphans who are cared for in organizations run by her friend Miki. She cites the courage of these people living on their dangerous islands, where there is an average of four earthquakes or tremors a day; and she remarks the combination "of delicacy and strength, of tenderness and cruelty . . . usual in the work of Japanese writers." This book will be a touchstone for those made desolate by sorrow, and in writing it Mrs. Buck lifts our spirits as she revives her own.

J. C. Long (review date 14 July 1962)

SOURCE: "In Japan, Relief from Grief," in *Saturday Review*, Vol. 45, No. 27. July 14, 1962, p. 31.

[*In the following review, Long traces the three interwoven elements of Buck's* A Bridge for Passing.]

Pearl Buck's beautifully written book [, ***A Bridge for Passing,***] contains in its short compass a triple message, and the three elements are so interwoven that no one theme predominates.

The springboard of Miss Buck's narrative is her experience as a participant in the American-Japanese motion picture production of her book ***The Big Wave,*** and in that connection she notes that movie executives and actors are of the same breed the world over. Nevertheless, Miss Buck found a special charm in the modern Japanese: their customs, kindliness, artistic qualities, and technical skills. She regards the brutal era, when the military dragged Japan into World War II, as a passing and uncharacteristic phase. Also she reports that the American Occupation was carried on in a way to encourage friendship and confidence between the two peoples. Here is a message for international good will.

However, Miss Buck undertook this film to assuage her agony over the death of her husband. Anyone who has suffered the loss of a loved one knows that desperate feeling of finality and rebellion against fate. For them the novelist's

experience reveals that time and active, sympathetic interest in the lives of others are the great healers.

Her book is in the tradition of widows who have a compulsion to exorcise the pain of their bereavement by public tribute to the one who has passed beyond. (There does not seem to have been the same compulsion in male writers.) Some may recall *An American Idyll*, by Cornelia Parker, or, again, *Death of a Man*, by Lael Wertenbaker. Those two women write in the spirit of stoical endurance. In contrast, in *A Man Called Peter* Catherine Marshall testifies to a great strength and benediction coming from the grace of God and assurance of the divine purpose.

Pearl Buck's attitude lies somewhere between resignation and hope of heaven. She considers herself to be scientific rather than religious; in fact, she seems hardly to have heard of the Christian affirmation of immortality. However, she accepts a belief in eternal life as a reasonable working hypothesis fully as reasonable as a negative insistence.

She writes:

> I am trained in science. There are two schools in the approach. One is to believe the impossible an absolute unless and until it is proved the possible. The other is to believe the possible an absolute unless and until it is proved the impossible. I belong to the latter school. Therefore all things are possible until they are proved impossible—and even the impossible may only be so, as of now.

There is a third message in this book, namely, that for the man or woman who has had a disastrous first marriage the future nevertheless may hold romance. Both Pearl Buck and her husband, Richard J. Walsh, who had been president of The John Day Company which publishes Miss Buck, had been married previously and unsatisfactorily, and yet for twenty-five years they had a union of the greatest mutual devotion.

William Clifford (review date 5 October 1963)

SOURCE: "Descendants on the Ascendance," in *Saturday Review*, Vol. 46, No. 40, October 5, 1963, pp. 41-2.

[*In the following review, Clifford discusses Buck's* The Living Reed *and "regrets that this greatly respected author's use of the arts of fiction can hit so much farther from the mark than her feeling for Asians and her detailing of Asian history."*]

In 1883 the United States ratified a treaty of amity and

commerce with Korea, recognizing Korea's independence and promising "an amicable arrangement" in case of outside interference or oppression. Chinese influence in Korea had recently declined, and Korea was looking for someone to protect her from the Japanese and Russians. We were looking for trade.

Japan soon won the struggle with Russia and moved into Korea. In 1905 Secretary of War William Howard Taft signed a secret agreement in Tokyo giving Korea to Japan, provided Japan kept hands off the Philippines and did not try to stop American trade in Manchuria. President Theodore Roosevelt declared openly: "Korea is absolutely Japan's."

Woodrow Wilson aroused the hopes of Koreans, as he did of other small nations, when he declared the self-determination of peoples, but the promise was not fulfilled. During the Second World War, which Koreans regarded as their war of liberation from half a century of Japanese occupation, Franklin Roosevelt proposed that Korea be placed under the trusteeship of China, the United States, and one or two other nations, rather than restored to freedom. (Russia as usual had other plans.) When the American military government arrived in 1945, the surrendering Japanese forbade Koreans to meet with Americans, and they shot down a group that appeared at Inchon with flowers and flags to welcome the liberators. The American general commended the Japanese for "controlling the mob."

Anyone who thought that our involvement in Korea began with the Korean War needs to know this much of recent history. In Pearl Buck's fifty-sixth published book, a novel called *The Living Reed,* this is a small part of a panoramic story of a modern Korea told with impressive documentation, authentic background, and sympathy.

Any unfamiliarity in setting and historical event may for most readers be compensated for by the novel's familiar, old-fashioned style of storytelling. Four generations of a noble Korean family are portrayed, from 1881, when they were advisers to the king and queen, down to their unhappy division on the eve of the Korean War, when one grandson is a Mission-trained doctor and another a Russian-trained agitator. "Living Reed" is the name given to the father of the Communist, a man who fought for freedom during the Japanese occupation. It symbolizes the faith that a new supply of men to continue the struggle will spring up, like bamboo reeds, in the place of those who are cut down.

One regrets that this greatly respected author's use of the arts of fiction can hit so much farther from the mark than her feeling for Asians and her detailing of Asian history. It isn't very important that she makes the mistake of saying that Pearl Harbor Day was December 7th in Korea. (As in Japan, it was the 8th.) It is more difficult to have to accept, at the end of *The Living Reed,* a character named Mariko who seems to belong in *Terry and the Pirates.* She is a kind of Dragon Lady, part Japanese, part Chinese, and part English, who dances in the Japanese theatre in Seoul during wartime, sometime around the winter of 1944-45, yet can leave when she likes to fly direct to London, Paris, and New York, carrying letters to Korean leaders in exile. "I speak the language wherever I am . . . I dance. I am an artist . . . I belong to no country—and every country."

Josh Greenfield (review date 9 October 1966)

SOURCE: "Picture Post Cards," in *World Journal Tribune Book World*, October 9, 1966, p. 8.

[*In the following review, Greenfield complains that in Buck's* The People of Japan, *she "mostly serves up the usual blend of picturesque pap and old saws."*]

Not the least of the effects of the American victory in the Pacific is that we were spared the back-breaking, mind-reeling chore of having to learn the Japanese language. Instead, the burden of language learning fell upon the vanquished: each Japanese student has to face six years of classroom English before he graduates from high school. And Americans in Japan, laughing lustily, rather than nervously, at this race of little Jerry Lewises, bespectacled and back-teethed, malaproping and mispronouncing our language, could lean back upon the counsels of *experts* if they wished insights into the "special" Japanese culture and character.

This was one of those unfortunate developments which result in our getting dramatically involved in situations from which we don't quite know how to get out of. For experts, once established, function like Civil Service servants, their moistened fingers in the air detect the wind currents around their own position rather than the drifts of a problem; they tend to fit policy instead of shaping it, producing tired justifications rather than new analyses.

Our Japanese experts, for example, functioning in the rough Asian League not only boast a competitively high average of post-war bumbles—from the urging of the retention of the emperor system through the rebuilding of the *zaibatsu* (the giant interlocking corporations) down to the current encouragement of militarization—but they have even managed to convince many of us in masterful exercises of double expertise that some of their biggest bungles have been strokes of brilliance.

But then Japan has long been a natural mark for experts. Not only is the language difficult but the people differ from us radically and the living there is easy—comfortable with good pay—because one can pile up expert points through residency. First, there were the churches funneling funds to their Christian soldiers in the rice fields; and now there are Rockefellers and Fords and Wilsons, foundation grants and fellowship handouts aplenty for those who would structure their disciplines around an exotic country. The Japan business, much like any other specialization, offers both rich rewards and a power base because it is the only game in town. The expert stakes out a field, builds a knowledge barrier around it, and then lays claim to all the secrets within it; in time he proceeds to traffic in the mystique the market demands.

The resultant misinformation about Japan, not surprisingly, is staggering. The experts busily fill the orders for the image our society demands, and a two-week excursion to Japan arranged by the Japan Travel Bureau provides mostly cultural feedback that enhances the image. Yet each time a new book about contemporary Japan appears, I turn to it hoping that now the kidding will stop, the myth will be cracked, and the simple light of truth will break through.

Although an old China hand, Pearl Buck is not professionally in the Japan business. A Nobel laureate, she is also a noble woman, a grande dame, given to the right passions and supporting the right causes; she is also sensitive and tries to be sensible. But *The People of Japan,* which is subtitled "A perceptive portrait of their life today," only occasionally lives up to that billing. Too often it is a collection of uninspected clichés and is only fitfully discerning. Miss Buck falls into the quaint-cute trap that affects so much of the writing about Japan, and in this way her book is more revealing to us of the American attitude as reflected in even liberal opinion than it is of anything else.

Take the Japanese woman. Again she is suffering and scraping, bowing and submissive, always administering dutifully to men. Take the Japanese man. Again he is haughty and proud, manly and regal, with a license to be licentious with bar girls and *geisha.* And so it goes. The Japanese are inscrutable, polite, imitative, neat, clean, beauty lovers, lonely, sentimental, gentle, rigid, etc. Superficial generalities are spun relentlessly, and soon the picture of a people swims into fixed focus, ethnic characteristics are assigned, and prototypes not only emerge but are expected. Sound familiar? We don't do it with the French (are the French *gentle*?) or the British (are the British basically neat or *sloppy*?), but we always do it with the Japanese. We patronize them. For our attitude toward them we are guilty of racism.

And how do the Japanese react to this attitude? Why naturally, we're told by the experts, as Miss Buck tells us now, they love us. For if they love us how can we *really* be guilty of racial prejudice toward them. After all didn't we bestow upon them the honor of being the world's first recipient of a nuclear attack? Didn't we intern the Nisei in America in *ersatz* concentration camps? Didn't we show our true respect for Japan as a conquered power by giving her a MacArthur and his GHQ to preside over her occupation rather than a mere educator such as HICOG's Conant as we gave to Germany? And don't we still have restrictive and discriminatory legislation against their emigration to America? Of course they love us.

Miss Buck is perceptive in her discussion of student demonstrations, in realizing that they articulate a widespread feeling of the populace at large. And she is capable of sweeping aside her good-hearted sentimentality to recognize that the Japanese are not ideologues in any way, that they are guided more by the logic of simple pragmatics than by the moralism of a philosophy or by the pull of blind emotion. She is also open-eyed in her reportage of Japanese prejudice toward the Koreans and the Eta (a remnant of the attempt to impose *caste* in Japan) and all Eurasians, but particularly those fathered by Negroes—areas of coverage that are usually slurred over.

But mostly she serves up the usual blend of picturesque pap and old saws. Her "explanation" of the Japanese character, for example, is but still another rewording of the old web of *giri* mesh—the responsibility of obligation—and her recurring description of Japanese life is a simplistic "change that is not really a change." Which may sound good but means just about as much—or as little—as the two pennies in my pocket.

If we are to deal meaningfully with Japan—in fact, with all of Asia—we must first come to grips with ourselves. We must realize, no matter how difficult it is for us to accept, that we begin any confrontation there with a racist approach which our experts have always carefully catered to. That a Pearl Buck, who is no parlor Orientalist, who is full of genteel humanity and obviously loves Japan, lands in most of the familiar traps is further sad evidence of the inscrutable blinders we still wear.

Horace Bristol (review date 5 November 1966)

SOURCE: "From Tea to Transistors," in *Saturday Review*, Vol. 49, No. 45, November 5, 1966, pp. 44, 74.

[*In the following review, Bristol asserts that Buck's* The People of Japan *is more of a sentimental look at the country than an in-depth study.*]

Pearl Buck unreservedly adopted China for her spiritual home when her parents, missionaries with more than a decade of experience in that sprawling, disorganized country, brought her there to live as a child. Later, when she was old enough to visit Japan, she took China's cultural offspring to her heart.

In her latest book, [*The People of Japan,*] a collection of memories of prewar Japan, historical facts, and more modern observations—the last based largely on a three-month tour in 1960 of Korea and Japan—Mrs. Buck takes a grandmotherly look at a country that is admittedly only a stepchild: loved, but at times very naughty. It was a country, however, that sheltered her and her family from China's advancing Communism on two occasions, and, since its disastrous defeat in World War II, has reformed and renounced its reprehensible past.

Reading *The People of Japan* is not unlike being in a window-seat of the world's fastest and perhaps finest express train—the "Hikari" or "Light"—and watching the passing scene at 150-plus miles per hour. The verdant, ageless farms with their quaint little thatched-roofed houses flash by, almost too fast, to observe the kimono- or "mompe"-clad farm women—stooped and bent as they patiently plant each rice shoot in minuscule paddy fields—suddenly give way to a dazzling complex of immaculate white ferro-concrete factories, whose automated assembly lines turn out millions of transistors, TV sets, and sophisticated computers for both the domestic and foreign markets. Disembodied, modern-day industrial Taj Mahals, apparently floating in the center of rice fields, they represent graphically what has happened and is happening to Japan today. Pearl Buck has simply, and sympathetically, put this into words.

That Mrs. Buck does not speak or understand Japanese in no way invalidates either her memories—which are obviously, and justifiably, tinged with sentiment—or the historical facts making up the major part of her text. Nevertheless the lack places at least some sections of the book in the category of, for want of a better word, "intuitive" reporting, rather than in-depth study. It means that she was not only dependent upon her interpreter, but had to rely entirely on surface observations, for no foreigner who is not fluent in the admittedly difficult Japanese language and its idioms can hope to meet and understand the Japanese people in their natural habitat.

Few if any authors with the stature, tenderness, and sensitivity of Pearl Buck have attempted it, and those who have have all too often been taken in by the charming outward manners and mannerisms of these acknowledgedly "charming" individuals (when they want to be). Perhaps that is why one of the best, if not *the* best book on modern Japan was written by a woman who had never set foot in the country—

Ruth Benedict. *The Chrysanthemum and the Sword* was not influenced by surface charm. Although Miss Benedict's wartime study of the complexities of the Japanese character may be out of date, *The People of Japan* is too loving and indulgent to update it. An honest, fundamentally accurate description of Japan today, it is, in the final analysis, also a rosy-hued picture of the country and its inhabitants seen through the eyes of a warm-hearted and forgiving grandmother.

Edward Weeks (review date July 1969)

SOURCE: A review of *The Three Daughters of Madame Liang,* in *Atlantic*, Vol. 224, No. 1, July, 1969, pp. 104-06.

[*In the following review, Weeks praises Buck's* The Three Daughters of Madame Liang *as "compassionate, elucidating, and wise."*]

Pearl Buck is an old China hand who cannot accept without protest what is going on between her native land and her country of adoption. She has a singular knowledge of China, of the Empress Dowager, and Sun Yat-sen, and from this, and from her secondhand sources about the China that is, she has written a novel, *The Three Daughters of Madame Liang,* which is compassionate, elucidating, and wise.

Madame Liang is a matriarch in her mid-fifties as the story opens; slim, lovely, and discreet, she runs a gourmet's dream of a restaurant in modern Shanghai, patronized by officials and protected by one of her old suitors, Chao Chung, a minister in Peking. In pre-Communist days she had been attracted to the Americans in the concessions, particularly to the Brandons of San Francisco, to whom after Mao's ascendancy she sent her three daughters to be educated in America. In her youth Madame Liang and her then loyal husband were fiery adherents of Sun Yat-sen; now in her privacy she repents of the ten-year chaos that followed Sun's Revolution, and has deep misgivings about the new order. "It was we who were wrong," she says, ". . . we destroyed the achievement of thousands of years. We thought what the West had was all good, and what we had was all useless." With dismay she watches the ruthless new order imposed by Chairman Mao. She hopes to live to see the liberation; meantime she awaits her daughters' return, and with her culinary art she bends to the wind.

Of the three girls, Grace, the oldest and a doctor, is the first to come home. Fresh from her research in South America, where she has been studying the health-giving properties of plants, she is ordered back to Peking to help prepare a synthesis of Chinese and Western medicine. Warned by her mother that she must listen and not speak out in the American way, the girl is first taken in hand by an old primitive, Dr. Tseng, who instructs her in the ancient herbal cures which she finds surprisingly relevant. In her adaptation she is rewarded with a small house of her own, and here she is politically—as he calls it "philosophically"—instructed by Dr. Liu Peng, a man of her own age whose square features, black brows, and strong hands are more exciting than his arguments.

Mercy, the second to return, is prettier and more maternal than her elder sister: she arrives on her honeymoon, determined that her children shall be born on Chinese soil, she and her husband, John Sung, a young nuclear physicist, having escaped from security relations by flying to London and then transshipping through the Chinese embassy. Their arrival coincides with the Great Leap Forward, and while John's knowledge is needed, he soon proves to be too "individualistic," and his punishment is severe.

The youngest daughter, Joy, is more painter than patriot, and she needs only the dissuasion and adoration of the famous artist in exile with whom she is studying to remain where she is in New York.

The skeins of these three love stories are wound together in Madame Liang's heart as, isolated and in increasing danger, she observes the desolation which famine and the Red Guards have brought to the land she loves. It is she who speaks for Miss Buck. It is she who in her reverie weighs the greatness and the weakness of China, the achievements and the moderation of centuries leading in time to a complacency completely isolated from the new knowledge. It is she who, remembering China's former love for Americans, says, "There is no hate so dangerous as that which once was love." And it is Madame Liang who in her loneliness as she reviews the skill and cunning of the god-hero Mao still places her faith in the rocklike tenacity of the Chinese people, remembering the ancient saying of Lao Tzu, "Throw eggs at a rock, and though one uses all the eggs in the world, the rock remains the same."

Aileen Pippett (review date 8 August 1969)

SOURCE: "New Rulers Stalk the Land, But the Good Earth Remains," in *New York Times Book Review*, August 8, 1969, p. 26.

[*In the following review, Pippett discusses the China portrayed in Buck's* The Three Daughters of Madame Liang.]

Pearl Buck's great novel, *The Good Earth,* described the life of Chinese peasants. Published in 1931, it was written out of intimate knowledge of actual conditions and mental attitudes; as an imaginative but truthful interpretation of East to West it deservedly won its author the Nobel Prize.

Now, 38 years and many books later, Mrs. Buck again interprets East to West in *The Three Daughters of Madame Liang,* a story of China today, a country vastly changed from the land she knew. Yet the barriers to communication between the United States and Mainland China seem to disappear as we read a novel that convinces us it is a true tale about real people.

Madame Liang's past reflects the changes in her country since her birth, in the time of the last Empress. Her progressive father objected to the cruel custom of binding girls' feet; she was educated in France, married a fellow-student at the Sorbonne and left him when he reverted to old ways and brought home a concubine. Once an ardent supporter of Sun Yat-sen, now disillusioned and regretful, she runs one of the few private enterprises remaining in the People's Republic, a luxury restaurant for foreigners in Shanghai.

She knows that the limited freedom she enjoys depends on the continuing goodwill of the powerful Minister who was once her close friend and would-be lover during their student days in Paris. And she hopes that her three daughters, who have grown up happily in America, will heed her secret warnings not to return to China. Her hopes are shattered when the eldest daughter, Grace, obeys a command from the Minister to give her country the benefit of her researches into the medicinal value of rare plants. She is allowed to spend a few days with her mother before proceeding to Peking, where she must study traditional Chinese medicine before she gets a home and laboratory of her own—and, eventually, a doctor husband. (Frankly, most American women would find Grace's young man hard to take, but it seems that love is love wherever it occurs.)

The second daughter, Mercy, does not have such good luck as adjustable Grace. A determined young woman, she smuggles herself and her husband into China on their honeymoon. He is a brilliant scientist, and far more Californian than Chinese in thinking. The efforts of the Communists to use him in nuclear weaponry result in a large-scale disaster at the site of a bomb test that failed. Later, he is exiled to a remote province for refusing to cooperate with the militarists. Even here, he keeps his faith in the Chinese people, his belief that their freedom will be achieved when current fanaticism gives way to practical techniques for better living.

A gentler alternative is offered by the experience of the

youngest daughter, Joy. An artist, she loves and marries an older, wiser artist who paints abstracts yet remains distinctively Oriental. The character of this kindly visionary has all the allurement of a Chinese scroll, depicting a vast landscape with two human beings in just the right spot to fix the harmony of the whole.

FURTHER READING

Foell, Earl W. "Mrs. Buck's Bomb-Makers." *New York Herald Tribune* (3 May 1959): 4.

> Foell complains that "in concentrating on getting this formula for scientific endeavor scrupulously accurate [in *Command the Morning*], Mrs. Buck has somehow managed to turn her characters into types that fit the research equation but not the human equation."

Rennert, Maggie. "Blue-Blood Pudding." *Sunday Herald Tribune Book Week* (4 July 1965): 11.

> Rennert asserts that although Buck's *Death in the Castle* is often cliché and unbelievable, it is still an enjoyable read.

Rogers, W. G. "Pastor's Brood." *New York Times* (19 February 1967): 44.

> Rogers concludes that Buck's strength in *The Time Is Noon* is her well-drawn good characters, but her weakness is in the unbelievability of her villains.

Rogers, W. G. A review of *Mandala. New York Times Book Review* (25 October 1970): 57.

> A brief review of *Mandala,* in which Rogers states, "The appeal of [the book], I suppose, lies in the mysticism that fills its last half."

Additional coverage of Buck's life and career can be found in the following sources published by Gale: *Authors in the News,* **Vol. 1;** *Contemporary Authors,* **Vols. 1-4R, 41-44R;** *Contemporary Authors New Revision Series,* **Vols. 1, 34;** *DISCovering Authors; DISCovering Authors: British; DISCovering Authors: Canadian; DISCovering Authors Modules: Most-Studied* **and** *Novelists; Dictionary of Literary Biography,* **Vols. 9, 102;** *Major Twentieth-Century Writers,* **Vols. 1, 2;** **and** *Something About the Author,* **Vols. 1, 25.**

Thomas McGuane
1939-

(Full name Thomas Francis McGuane III) American novelist, screenwriter, short story writer, essayist, and film director.

The following entry provides an overview of McGuane's career through 1997. For further information on his life and works, see *CLC*, Volumes 3, 7, 18, and 45.

INTRODUCTION

McGuane is known as a novelist of manners who uses satire to criticize the emptiness and meaninglessness of America's "declining snivelization." He is considered a regionalist writer—especially of the American West—whose environmental concerns are expressed through his fiction and political activism. Satirically drawn characters who are experiencing male crises is a constant theme in his fiction and screenplays. His male protagonists either leave the comforts of suburbia in a proverbial quest for America and themselves, or return to family ranches in a vain attempt to rekindle patriarchal family traditions. Whether attempting to recapture the myth of the West or embarking on an undefined quest for an America lost to its own materialism, dissipation, and mass cultural kitsch, McGuane's characters function as a critique of the self-destructive implications of masculine bravura and competition. His characters also simultaneously express nostalgia for an outmoded brand of masculinity associated with the heroic Western cowboy.

Biographical Information

Thomas Francis McGuane III was born in Wyandotte, Michigan, on December 11, 1939. He attended the University of Michigan, Olivet College, and Michigan State University, where he received a B.A. in 1962. McGuane then attended the Yale University School of Drama, earning an M.F.A. in 1965. From 1966 to 1967, McGuane had a Stegner Fellowship at Stanford University. McGuane has been married three times: to Portia Rebecca Crockett, from 1962 to 1975; briefly to actress Margot Kidder from 1976 to 1977; and to Laurie Buffett (sister of singer/songwriter Jimmy Buffett) in 1977. In the 1970s, McGuane earned a reputation as an alcoholic, a drug abuser, and a womanizer—a reputation that has been difficult for McGuane to change. McGuane, however, often reminds interviewers that he was a disciplined, prolific, and successful writer during those years of supposed dissipation. When three close members of his family died within a thirty-month period in the late 1970s—including his father and sister—McGuane was profoundly affected by the

losses. In middle age, he moved to a large ranch in Montana, where he lives with his wife and children, balancing the demands of family and ranching with a steady writing career.

Major Works

Critics have frequently compared McGuane to Ernest Hemingway, who also grew up in Michigan. Jerome Klinkowitz has said that in McGuane's first novel, *The Sporting Club* (1969), set in northern Michigan, McGuane "adapts the Hemingway code of sportsmanship and grace under pressure to contemporary times." And, while McGuane himself both denies the validity of this comparison and generally considers it an insult, his friendship with novelist Jim Harrison, also from Michigan, places him firmly in a tradition of masculinist writers who both celebrate and critique male camaraderie and competition in wilderness settings. As Beverly Lowry points out, "Mr. McGuane has never pretended to write from any other point of view than that of our manliest of American men." In *The Sporting Club*, a group of men—descendants of a one-hundred-year-old sporting club—go on a hunting trip in northern Michigan. During the trip, masculine bravado and competition lead to their self-destruction. McGuane's next three novels, *The Bushwhacked Piano* (1971), *Ninety-Two in the Shade* (1973), and *Panama* (1978), take place primarily in the Florida Keys, where, according to Klinkowitz, "within this context of intermingled exoticness and shabbiness he conducts his most thorough survey of manners." In *The Bushwhacked Piano*, Nicholas Payne leaves his family in suburbia, taking off with nothing but the motto, "I am at large," and hooking up with a self-proclaimed "floozy" girlfriend. In *Ninety-Two in the Shade*, Thomas Skelton leaves college to become a fishing guide, where his association with a fellow guide eventually leads to his self-destruction. In *Panama*, often considered McGuane's most autobiographical work, Chester Pomeroy is a burned-out rock star on the downside of his career path. A central characteristic of Pomeroy is his tendency to confuse his father with the late Western outlaw hero Jesse James. Pomeroy also attempts to win back his estranged wife through extreme tactics such as nailing himself to her door.

Subsequent McGuane novels take place primarily in the American West, specifically Montana. In *Nobody's Angel* (1982), Patrick Fitzpatrick, an army officer, returns to his family's ranch, where he falls in love with a married woman and eventually flees to Seville, Spain. In *Something to Be Desired* (1984), Lucien Taylor is a painter who also owns a tourist resort in Montana that attracts a host of eccentrics. Joe Starling of *Keep the Change* (1989) is a painter who returns to Montana to save his family ranch, where he discovers that the painting in an abandoned old house—his lifelong artistic inspiration—is merely an empty frame hanging against a plaster wall. In *Nothing But Blue Skies* (1992), Frank Copenhaver, a failing middle-aged businessman whose wife has just left him, turns to the American West in order to make sense of his life.

McGuane's work in Hollywood includes four screenplay credits and one directorial effort. His first screen credit, *Rancho Deluxe* (1973), is a comedic Western starring Jeff Bridges and Sam Waterston as two small-time cattle ranchers. The cast includes Slim Pickins and Harry Dean Stanton, as well as a cameo by country singer Jimmy Buffet. McGuane directed and wrote the screenplay for *Ninety-Two in the Shade* (1975), which is based on his 1973 novel and involves two feuding fishing boat captains in Florida. The cast for this wild comedy includes Peter Fonda, Warren Oates, Margot Kidder, and Harry Dean Stanton. *The Missouri Breaks* (1975), McGuane's third screenplay, is a revisionist Western, which was directed by Arthur Penn, and stars Jack Nicholson as an outlaw and Marlon Brando as a bounty hunter. *Tom Horn* (1980), McGuane's most recent screenplay credit and revisionist Western, stars Steve McQueen as a bounty hunter.

McGuane published a collection of non-fiction essays, *An Outside Chance*, in 1980, and a collection of short stories, *To Skin a Cat*, in 1986.

Critical Reception

McGuane's novels are fairly consistent in their characterizations, use of language, and central themes. As a result, critics have tended to review McGuane's work as a whole, not individually. His novels are especially noted for their eccentric characters and cutting use of language to parody and satirize the vulgarity and emptiness of an America drowning in its own excesses of materialism and mass culture. John Leggett describes McGuane as "a satirist with a taste for the American oddball." Jerome Klinkowitz said, "most impressive is McGuane's ability to convey the characteristics of his culture within the words and syntax of his narrator's own speech." McGuane is likewise known as a chronicler of the dissipation and empty quests associated with the 1960s and 1970s in America. "Above all, McGuane is a novelist of manners because of his ability to single out the characteristics of an age and to know his characters through them," Klinkowitz said. Many critics say McGuane's prose stands out from works by other fiction writers of the early 1970s. McGuane's prose is "like a hot pink hearse in a funeral procession," Judson Klinger said in one review. According to Klinger, McGuane's first three novels display "outrageous wit, hallucinatory prose and comic-romantic-violent vision." McGuane's regionalist fiction and revisionist Westerns have been noted by many critics. Mark Harris, who invokes the author's media image as "a counterculture cowboy," points out that "A hallmark of McGuane's writing is its sense of location; the physical world is deeply important to his characters and his prose." Gregory L. Morris asserts that "the pervasive, informing influence of the American West is always at the heart of McGuane's writing." Morris defines McGuane's protagonists as "dislocated cowboys," asserting that, "What McGuane does is open—or re-open—the West to definition, reformation, reinvention." McGuane's concern for environmental issues, as expressed in his later novels, also has captured attention from several critics. "The recent writings of Thomas McGuane show a particular interest in environmentalist concerns, examining the role played by inherited mythologies of the frontier in the ecology and politics of the contemporary American West," said David Ingram. "McGuane's explorations reveal complex and ambivalent responses to these subjects, in part liberal, radical and conservative." However, critics have questioned the depth of McGuane's characters in his later novels. *Keep the Change* has been criticized for its characterization of Joe Starling, the novel's protagonist, whom some critics find to be shallow and distancing. Richard Russo sums up the disjuncture between the novel's theme and protagonist in a biting critique: "it's ironic that in a novel that questions the validity of 'distant' ownership and urges passion, not detachment, the author himself should be so hard to locate. For all its virtues, one comes away from *Keep the Change* feeling that a writer in full possession of his themes and techniques is leasing, not owning, the character whose story this is supposed to be." Other reviewers also have criticized McGuane for the similarities between his novels. "Perhaps it is McGuane's misfortune that he has written so many books, because after four or five the generic familiarity of the plots and the similarities of the heroes become very evident," noted a *New York Review of Books* critic of *Nothing But Blue Skies* (1992). The same work, however, won praise from Brad Knickerbocker, who in a review of the 1992 novel praises McGuane for his characters, which he describes as "deep, real, funny, and intelligent."

PRINCIPAL WORKS

The Sporting Club (novel) 1969
The Bushwhacked Piano (novel) 1971
*Ninety-Two in the Shade (novel) 1973
Rancho Deluxe (screenplay) 1973
The Missouri Breaks (screenplay) 1975
Panama (novel) 1978
An Outside Chance: Essays on Sport (essays) 1980
Tom Horn (screenplay) 1980
Nobody's Angel (novel) 1982
Something to Be Desired (novel) 1984
To Skin a Cat (short stories) 1986
Keep the Change (novel) 1989
Nothing But Blue Skies (novel) 1992

* *Ninety-Two in the Shade* also was published as a screenplay in 1975.

CRITICISM

Thomas McGuane with Kay Bonetti (interview date 1984)

SOURCE: "Interview with Thomas McGuane," in *Conversations with American Novelists*, edited by Kay Bonetti, et al., University of Missouri Press, 1997, pp. 56-75.

[*In the following interview conducted in 1984, McGuane discusses how he integrates his lifestyle as a Montana Rancher with his writing career.*]

Tom McGuane's writing career began in the sixties. This interview catches him at age forty-five, looking back on a rebellious youth and forward toward the issues of middle age. He speaks of his enduring fascination with comic writing. He says that the subject of his early novels was the expression of the American dream in the wild West of the 1960s and 1970s, and the realization that acting on those ideals could not be survived. The author of ten books, McGuane writes about brooding protagonists, displaced people, characters who cannot seem to put down roots or reach out to things beyond themselves. These characters are often ironically connected and shaped by their relationships to landscape and place. **Ninety-two in the Shade** *(1973) and* **Panama** *(1978) are set in Key West, Florida.* **The Bushwhacked Piano** *(1971) tells of an eccentric peregrination through Michigan, Montana, and Florida.* **Something to be Desired** *(1984) is set partly in Montana. In many ways his novels are harrowing contemporary novels of manners, about taking drugs, sexual peccadilloes, and chaotic mobility.*

McGuane's personal journey from the drug-taking sixties to the life of a responsible citizen and parent is reflected in his novels. The western stories still retain some of the humor of the Florida novels, but the dilemmas of McGuane's protagonists become increasingly serious: divorces, multiple families, tricky business deals, the desperation to settle down. These themes can be seen especially in his novel **Nothing But Blue Skies** *(1992). Other acclaimed works include* **Nobody's Angel** *(1981) and* **The Sporting Club** *(1968).*

[*Bonetti:*] *Can you tell us a little about your life and upbringing?*

[McGuane:] I was raised in the Middle West, in Michigan, but my parents were both Boston-area Irish. Except when we were in school, we were always back there in Massachusetts in the big kind of noisy, Irish households of the forties and fifties. My parents were upward-striving, lower-middle-class people who had a facility for English. They both were English majors in college. My father was a scholarship student at Harvard; my mother went to a little school called Regis. Books and talk and language in general were a big part of growing up for me. My family was not excited about me wanting to be a writer; they thought that was very unrealistic.

It is difficult to support yourself as a serious writer.

I think any writer, even an unserious writer, has a bad time of it; a pulp writer or a sold-out writer or a hack has a hard time making a living. To understand the economics of writing is to know that writing and publishing and acquiring some kind of esteem in your community of peers is merely a key to your finances. For example, prestigious writers whose reputations are confined to the literary all live pretty well. They are getting grants and teaching jobs. I would say the people I've seen who teach writing are underworked. Other writers, like me, have been able to find work in film or journalism. There's also a way to get along. I think it's inevitable for writers to sort of feel sorry for themselves and to feel sorrier the more serious they perceive themselves to be.

In the introduction to last year's summer fiction edition of Esquire, *Rust Hills claimed that the academy has become the patronage system for writers . . . and was defending it, moreover. What did you think of that?*

I thought it was silly. I think patronage, especially homogenous patronage of the kind that academic writers receive, is exceedingly dangerous and leads to trafficking in reputations.

What do you mean by homogenous?

The colleges are, to a great degree, alike in their form of protection. I think it's good for writers to be in the world, not talking to the converted in English departments day after day—scrambling for survival, having to talk to illiterate neighbors. Obviously mine is a minority voice; this point of view is going to lose. The camp that Rust Hills describes is obviously the camp of sweeping victory.

Because the writers who teach are living pretty well . . . financially?

When I've been on campus I notice that everybody seems to be getting along better than ranchers in Montana are. There is great security there, the kind of security that the civil service or the post office provides and it goes hand in hand with complacency.

I take it you feel that this situation has a measurable impact on the kind of writing that is being done.

Well, you get these books like the latest Alison Lurie book that is built around sabbaticals. I think John Barth has suffered from being around colleges. To me the most interesting work that Barth did was the earliest work, before he knew what was going to happen to him—*The Floating Opera* and *The End of the Road*—books which I think he now kind of repudiates. His stuff lately has been less lifelike, less exciting.

So you disagree with Hills's notion.

I think Rust Hills needed to make a case for the situation now and I think that he felt he needed to overstate it. I think Rust and *Esquire* are excited about making categories, the new realism or the revival of fantasy, the kind of categories they come up with for the purposes of pigeon-holing writers.

So you feel that it's the type of writing that working within the academy encourages that has the negative effect; you aren't saying that because somebody teaches he is going to end up just writing about other teachers . . .

No . . . no . . . I'm not saying that, but I do think that kind of life, that kind of support, is going to limit the access to information and material writers might otherwise have, obviously. I think maybe the best writer we have had in a long time is Saul Bellow and being a chronic teacher hasn't hurt him at all.

So there are obviously exceptions to the rule.

There are, yes, but there is also a kind of academic writer who meters out his publications, who measures himself and politicizes against other academic writers, and that writer is of no use to readers. I think the kind of thing Hills describes in that article represents a severing of the connection between writers and readers.

To be fair, we should think of some notable exceptions; one thinks of Stanley Elkin.

He scarcely seems like an academic writer in any way. There are writers in the outside world who are vastly more academic than Elkin. But when I think of Norman Mailer in the outside world, or of Walker Percy, I think of more adventurous spirits reporting to us from the whole world rather than one of its hyperspecific laminates. This is a purely personal reaction, but I am just more interested in people who have not gone to campuses.

Your books are full of work, aren't they? And skills? Useful information?

Little odds and ends of that sort. Jim Harrison used to needle me because I would hang around the repair bay of a gas station—it really wasn't research. I like to watch people do their thing and I don't care what it is. I like to watch ladies sew, I like to watch people cook, I like to watch people fix cars, I like to watch people commercially fish. I would have to suppress that by some fiat to keep it out of my writing.

At what point did you start thinking of yourself as a writer?

Very early. It was really all I have ever wanted to do.

Did your parents ultimately support you?

Well, my father had a nice rule—and it's the same ruling I take with my children, to the degree I can afford to do it— he basically took the position he didn't want to argue with me about what I wanted to do. He would support me educationally. I was a premed major, I was a prelaw major, I went to the Yale Drama School. I was finally an English major, but I waffled around knowing that I was free to do that. Going to school kept me writing. Then I got a grant at Stanford and that extended another year and in fact when I finished there, I was publishing.

Do you value the Stegner experience?

Not really, no. I value having had the time. I didn't get much out of the Stegner thing; I didn't think he was a good teacher. It was the middle sixties—most of the other writers were thinking that writing was dead and they wanted to march on the electrical engineering building or war contractors; they just weren't interested in literature. I remember Allen Ginsberg coming up in those years and talking to people and finding they hadn't read Ezra Pound and hadn't read Whitman, didn't care, didn't want to know the names. It was an illiterate age and Stanford was just a place to get out of the weather and work on a book.

Is there some particular break that enabled you to start supporting yourself by writing?

Well, yes. I had a book on submission to Dial for six or eight months and was working pretty closely with them. I was encouraged to think that we were close to being able to publish the book. Then, suddenly from overhead the book was killed by the then editor-in-chief, E. L. Doctorow. It was just completely out of the blue and it was the most complete devastation I ever received. I remember thinking that I was going to snap. I had been writing daily for ten years and I didn't really think I could go on. And then . . . and then I suddenly realized, God, I didn't know how to do anything else. I had had minor menial jobs, but I just didn't really know what else to do. So I kind of holed up and wrote **The Sporting Club** in about six weeks and sent it to Jim Harrison. Then I lit out for Mexico thinking that I would figure out my life down there. While I was down there a cable came to this little town where I was camped out on the beach in a sleeping bag. This Mexican came out—he had a gun strapped on his waist and he came walking down to my camp and he strode right up and I thought, My God, this guy is going to shoot me. I thought I was going to be placed under arrest or something. I was pretty paranoid. He walked up and thrust out his hand and said in bad English, "Congratulations, your book is accepted." We went hooting and drank beer and had a big celebration. So I came back up and even though the book was accepted there was still work to be done on it. I moved to Montana and worked on the book, and when it came out it did pretty well. Then it was sold to the movies and was made into the worst movie in history.

What was the name of it?

The Sporting Club.

Never saw it.

If you blinked, it was gone. But I was paid for it. I had been accustomed to living on two to four thousand dollars a year and to suddenly get a movie check, man, I was looking at a decade's writing. All of a sudden I realized that if I did nothing but fill up scraps of paper I was gonna be a writer for a while.

The only real money in fiction now seems to be movie money. I know several writers who have managed to buy their first house because of their movie options.

Well, I'm one of those writers for sure . . . I came out and bought a little ranch here and then it quadrupled in value. I resold it and bought another ranch out east of town and resold it. That turned into my land base and that's what my security derives from now. But when I look around I see these kind of writers—I won't name names—who published one exquisite book of short stories twenty years ago, and have had pretty remunerative academic jobs for twenty years on the basis of that one tiny volume. I would say those writers have made a lot of money off their books.

I hadn't really thought about it that way.

Look what you have to do to get a comparable teaching job on the straight and narrow road: get a doctorate, fight your way through the MLA conventions, hope to get the nod from some backwater school, fight your way for tenure. I think writers have it very easy in colleges. Don't you think so?

In a way, you could say that. And it is unfortunate, because being a good teacher is one skill, being a writer is another. They are not necessarily the same thing at all.

I spoke to that issue at a writers' conference. I said, teaching ideally requires considerable pedagogical abilities and just because you're not making a living entirely by your writing does not mean you have to become a teacher. I've had some miserable writer teachers; they thought they were purely totemic value sitting at the head of a class monosyllabically reacting to students' questions.

Yet some writers feel that it was extremely beneficial to have that community of other writers . . .

Oh, I give you that . . . and the Stanford thing was quite interesting that way, the drama school was great that way, but where that was truest for me was as an undergraduate at Michigan State. I had three or four chums there who were really driven to write. Chief among them was Jim Harrison, of course. But there were others of us there, some of whom were very good and didn't make it. We had a really passionate literary situation. It was really beyond anything that I saw thereafter.

I don't think I have ever talked to a writer who didn't agree that writing is a very lonely profession.

I don't think loneliness is the word. John Graves said writing is "anti-life." I'm forty-five years old, I've been writing full-time since I was sixteen, I've been writing almost every day for thirty years; and as I look back with a degree of resentment, I realize that I literally lifted chunks of my life out for drafts of things, some of which got published and some didn't. And there is no experience to show for it, there is nothing but sitting in front of a legal pad for what now must amount to a third of my life. It's as though that was a hole in my life.

But you have had this friendship with another writer, Jim Harrison, all these years. Has it had an impact on your work?

I'm sure we've had an impact on each other's lives and thinking. We've managed to bolster one another in a fairly high view of the mission of writing, so that in lean years and blocked times it still felt that it was kind of a religious commitment. I don't know what writing is seen to be now, but I know that I continue to believe sort of what I believed then; I'm like someone who is intensely and successfully raised as a Catholic or a Lutheran; it just didn't go away from me. And now as I look on a future of freedom from the kinds of worries I used to have, my only vision of excitement is to be able to read and write harder and do what I wanted to do in 1955 or 1956. I am sure that the fact that Harrison and I have been writing back and forth for a quarter of a century almost entirely about writing has been one of the things that keeps that thread intact. Having a handful of writers around the country whose reality is there for you, knowing they are out there, knowing they might get what you are doing, makes you independent a little bit.

Are they the people you write for in a sense of an ideal reader?

There are some writers whose opinion really matters to me—who could really hurt my feelings if they said the book was terrible, who could make me excited by liking it. The three or four people whom you respect thinking that you're not a complete fool can really keep you going.

Who else do you want your books to be accessible to? In the sense of Virginia Woolf's "common reader"?

Let me wind back a little bit by saying I think that the sort of burnt-earth successes of modernism have left prestigious writing quite inaccessible to normal readers. There used to be a perennial *New Yorker* cartoon where some yahoo from Iowa was standing in front of a painting at the Museum of Modern Art saying, "All I can say is I know what I like" and I think it was meant to show how stupid the average guy is. I actually think that the average guy is right in saying I know what I like. I'm a little bit dour now when it comes to books which are terribly brilliant by some sort of smart-set consensus, but which nobody I know can read.

How important is the language of a novel to you, the joy of words?

There is a thrill to be had in language viewed as music, but I think for that tail to wag the dog is a mistake. Obviously there's an infinite mix and there is no right and wrong about it. At this point in my life the writing that I really like has clarity and earned and rendered feeling as its center. Writers who have done that most successfully leave you feeling experientially enlarged, rather than awed or intimidated—those things which have been the basis of the modernist response in writing.

*It seems to me that **Nobody's Angel** and **Something to be Desired** are moving towards a simpler and cleaner style than your earlier work. Do you think anything in the earlier work prepared you for this?*

I think there has inevitably been some kind of an evolution for me in the rise of emotional content. It's also been a moving away from comedy. I set out to be a comic novelist and that's become not clear to me as time has gone on. Things have happened—you can't live forty-five years without things happening to jar and change you. The biggest change for me was a tremendous uproar in my life during the seventies. My mother, father, and sister died in about thirty months flat. I remember very specifically feeling that it was a watershed, that I would never be the same again after that happened. When you have attended that many funerals that fast it's very hard to go back to a typewriter and say, "What is my next comic novel?" You simply don't do that. But reviewers think you do. Reviewers say, "Why isn't he still as funny as he was before all those deaths?" Reviewers are endlessly obtuse. And that makes you shrink away from what they represent; it makes you shrink away from publication in a funny way because you realize there's this dreadful stupor that you are going to have to march through with your latest infant in your arms.

I'm gathering from what you're saying that the "word-drunk" style in your earlier work was tied in with the fact that it was comic.

Well, yes. I wanted then and will want again to write comic novels. I love comic fiction.

Do you see comic fiction as a tradition and if so, what are some of the elements of it?

Good comic writing comes from a very nearly irrational center that stays viable because it is unexplainable. It often disports itself in a kind of charged language. That is to say it is not appropriate to use exactly the same prose style for writing an all-out comedy as it is for writing a rural tragedy. Each book demands its own stylistic answers. At the same time, one has the right to expect a writer to have a style. I don't think a writer has to be as transparent as the phone book. I don't want to be that. I think, though, as you perfect your style you should hit the target on the first shot rather than on the fourth, and a good writer should get a little bit cleaner and probably a little bit plainer as life and the oeuvre go on.

But it seems to me that there is a charged plainness in your last two books. The simplicity has under it all the skills that went into the others.

Oh, I sure hope so. You want something that is drawn like a bow and a bow is a simple instrument.

There is a lot of wit in **Something to be Desired.** *It's sad in some ways but it's also got a satirical edge. Was that intended?*

It wasn't intended to be satirical, but it was intended to be comic. I wanted to take a piece of crazy venture capitalism and show how desperate a private business really is. For some people getting their backs to the walls and starting a successful business can be as desperate an action as taking drugs. The guy says, "My God, I don't know what I'm going to do, I think I'll open a pizza parlor. My life is at an end, I'm going to start a dry cleaners." That seems to be a wholly American approach to desperation.

It also is pretty funny.

It's hilarious. But once you spot it, you can go into a town and all you see is desperation. You see some sad lady with a fashion outlet in downtown Livingston, Montana. You know, the wind is blowing through the town and the town is filled with snow as she is standing behind the plate glass, with a lot of imitation French clothes. What could be more frantic?

Critics talk about you as a comic novelist but always with the implication that this is heavy social comment, social satire and that sort of thing.

Well, there was an old Broadway producer who said, "Satire is what closes on Saturday night" and I think he is exactly right. I think satire has as its fatal component an element of meanness. It more or less says, look at what those awful people are doing. I'd never do anything like that, but by pointing them out I hope that you people will change them. Comedy, on the other hand, says, look at the awful things those people are doing. I could be doing the same thing, but for this moment I'm just going to describe it.

It strikes me that you have a lot in common with Mark Twain.

I find that hugely flattering. Nothing could please me more. I see him as immersed in a well-loved American milieu, schizphrenically rural and urban, inclined to bursts of self-pity as the autobiography would suggest and also inclined . . .

In wild and hairy business schemes . . .

Wild business schemes which I have been guilty of.

That always failed.

I'm a better businessman than he was.

His always failed.

And also an element of anger and rage disguised as comedy as in "The Man Who Corrupted Hadleyburg." Some of them are more bitter than anything else and the bad side of Twain is something I identify with, too.

One subject that seems to unify all your books is what happens to people who get hung up on an untested idea.

One of the great themes of Irish-American literature, if I can pretend to be Irish-American professionally for a moment, is spoiled romance. Scott Fitzgerald was the master of this and while the elements were in balance he was marvelous. But when it became something as ugly and pusillanimous as *The Crack-Up*, which to me is one of the most loathsome pieces of writing in the language, you see the Irish-American stance fall apart. What frustrates me when I think about Fitzgerald is it seems, from the evidence of *The Last Tycoon*, that he was about to go into a thrilling middle phase; having survived drunkenness and shattered romance, he was now going on to be a grown-up writer. We never get to find out about that.

I remember one time meeting Gore Vidal and he sort of stared at me and said, "Funny thing about all you Irish writers, you're all social climbers." And I think that is kind of true, the ease with which the Irish could move in American society once they got going. True of John O'Hara and Scott Fitzgerald for sure.

In many ways, especially in their endings, your last two novels, **Something to be Desired** *and* **Nobody's Angel,** *remind me of Henry James. They're similar in the sense of the psychological violence, the cross-currents of violence that leave people wiped out. They come to the place where they see too much, they see too clearly.*

I, of course, come to it from a sort of cruder perspective. Partly from being in the horse business, I've spent a lot of time in the Oil Belt and I've gotten to know a lot of petro-chemical zillionaires who breed horses and do things like that. I have also gotten to see a lot of people on what was recently the American frontier who are now living in the world of answered prayers. They go down to the 7-Eleven store in helicopters; they go to Scotland and buy the winner of the dog trials to bring back to keep around the house; they jet around the world and things get very, very accelerated for them. All of a sudden they are up against the accumulated values of the civilization to that point, but they have to deal with them because money, drugs, speed, and airplanes have brought them to a point of exhaustion. Sooner than it ever did before. They are up against the American dream as it's expressed in western America in a way that makes it something that can't really be survived.

But, when you think of the material James dealt with— nouveau riche Americans. The pattern of **Something to be Desired** *reminded me so much of the pattern of John Marcher in* The Beast in the Jungle, *who at the end replaces obsession with obsession on top of obsession.*

It really is a case of a man discovering that a narcissistic crisis is going to bear penalties which are permanent. I think that the nature of the age, say the sixties, the seventies, and the eighties, has been the indulgence of the "me" figure without suitable precautions. People should understand that, yes, it might be marvelous for you to go on a mission of self-discovery, but understand that people will not necessarily be here when you get back. I don't think Timothy Leary ever told anybody that; I don't even think Ken Kesey told anybody that. I think they more or less said that you paint your bus psychedelic colors and you take off, and when you come back the things that you wanted to be there will still be there. That turns out not to be the case. My book is about that. Its implications are not tragic because the narcissist is not a good tragic figure.

You've said a couple of interesting things about your earlier books; I wonder if you would care to comment about them.

I see the progress of those first three books as technological jumps from each other. The first, **The Sporting Club,** was meant to be a really controlled acid comic novel of the kind that I was then appreciating. Henry Green and Evelyn Waugh

. . . Your first two or three books represent all that you wanted to do during the previous twenty-eight years . . . you come out and want to write *Hamlet,* and then you want to write *Don Quixote* and then you want to write *The Divine Comedy.* Then you begin to simmer down a little bit. My second, **The Bushwacked Piano,** reflected my fascination with picaresque novels. The third book really derives from my interest in surrealism, juxtaposition. **Ninety-Two in the Shade** has more jagged layering of voices and situations than any book I wrote before or since. When I was writing it I was trying to not write a protagonist-centered novel. I was trying to take a different whack from a different angle and not write a Jamesian novel and not confine the information to what could be seen from a single point of view. And when I look back I realize that I must have gotten so aloft in this project I wonder how I could find the bathroom at the end of the day's work.

That book has been called a giant pun on Hemingway, and your earlier books were compared to Faulkner. Were you in any sense conscious of that element?

That is just absurd. Hemingway is a figure that casts a tremendous shadow for better or for worse. In the United States, it's a cottage industry to produce books about how terrible Ernest Hemingway was. So when Harry Crews or Jim Harrison or I are called Hemingwayesque, it's merely a way of saying, "We don't like this writer."

The criticism that I've read implied that you were writing the anti-Hemingway novel, turning the Hemingway mystique or code of behavior upside down.

I would say that the gist of the Hemingway comparison over the years has been by way of belittling my work. But I don't feel singled out. When I talked with Gore Vidal, he said, "I've been rereading Ernest Hemingway, and he is so scriptural and dull," and I said, "Well, I don't know what it is, Gore, but the people of the world go on wanting to read Ernest Hemingway." He said, "Not this people of the world." I think that is a kind of stance. There is a deep, deep hatred of Ernest Hemingway in the American literary community. And they should just admit it.

But you do admire his work?

I don't like all of his work. Actually, in fact, I don't like maybe more than half of it. But, the thing that is obviously interesting is that Hemingway can acquit himself in prose. Nothing needs to be said in defense of him; his influence will continue to erode his enemies' bastions.

How does a novel come together for you?

There are two ways a novel can come together for anybody.

One is answering to a plan. I've found over the years that that doesn't work very well for me. I'll outline everything and then the outline becomes irrelevant. The writing I like the best is when I don't know what I'm doing. This is another way of saying, if I can foresee the shape of a book and if I can foresee the outcome of things I've set in motion, then that is almost a guarantee of its being too limited. I would rather be a sort of privileged reader in that I get to write what I get to read, and chance having to write six or seven hundred pages to produce a two-hundred-page book. Then there is an element of real, deep-down excitement about the process. It is the harder way to write a book, the wilder way. It's the Indian way to write a book.

Can you identify the place where an identifiable voice, a narrator or protagonist, takes over?

Yeah, but that comes up from within. It's like metal. You heat it and you heat it and then light comes out of the metal. You can't just go right up to the thing and say, "Happen." It has to arise from some level of your *self* that you don't control.

I'm thinking of what Stanley Elkin has often said, that the first thing he hears is a voice and then the next thing that comes to him is an occupation.

Sherwood Anderson, who is by way of being my favorite writer these days, always used to try to get the pitch right. He would keep writing and writing on his first sentence until the pitch was right and then he could write it. That sounds very familiar to me. On the other hand, Peter Taylor, who is a superb writer, said one of the wiliest things that I've heard in a long time. He said that when he begins to hear the voices in a story and the story begins to write itself, he tears it up and throws it away. So there you have it. These things are highly personal. I know lots of fine horse trainers who use systems that are diametrically opposite to one another; they would seem to cancel each other, but they all end up making really fine horses.

Do you think people reading your books tend to confuse you with your characters?

Oh, yes, I'm sure they do, and I'm sure that's partly my doing. I don't think I would have much luck writing a book from a stance or a point of view which I didn't share at all. But you want to separate yourself from your narrow focus in order to broaden the geometry of the book. I used to think in terms of these utterly perverse plans for books. I was once going to write a detective novel in the form of a cookbook. I was hellbent just to shake up the kaleidoscope. I don't feel that way anymore. I find it hard enough to write interestingly and to write well, giving myself all the tools I can handle. I no longer think it is necessary to make it crazy or

write a six-hundred-page novel that takes place in two minutes.

*A lot of critics and a lot of readers seemed to think **Panama** was autobiographical. When the narrator says, "I'm working without a net, for the first time," is that you giving away yourself?*

First of all, that's a strategy to draw the reader into my web. There is nothing more handy to an author's purposes than to have a reader say, "Aha, now I'm going to find out." Then you can take him anywhere. In fact, it was tonally very much autobiographical; in specific incident, it was partly autobiographical. At the same time I wanted the reader to believe what I was saying, because sometimes one could make up something that would better illustrate an emotional point than the actual thing that happened. All of us have gone into a store and looked at a plastic doll or something that doesn't mean a thing and suddenly been overwhelmingly depressed by it. I can remember when the McDonald people brought out Egg McMuffins and there were Egg McMuffin signs all over Key West. I looked at it and I thought life was not worthwhile anymore if I had to share the planet with Egg McMuffin. Well, that doesn't translate, it's not usable.

*But does the experience described in **Panama**, this narrator who's been in the fast lane and gotten totally burned out, at all reflect what happened to you after **Ninety-Two in the Shade** and the film?*

Yes, I think I got pretty burned out . . .

You got in big trouble?

Yes, I did. It was big trouble, but it was good trouble, in some ways, because I often revert to being a control freak, as they say. And you know, I really had been such a little monk trying to be a writer for so long that I was sick of that. I saw all of these wonderful social revolutions going on around me and I wasn't part of them. Everybody was having such a wonderful time and I was always in the damn library and I was getting tired of it. And so, in 1973 when suddenly I was on the front page of the *New York Times* and movie producers wanted to give me money and people wanted me, I just said, "Yes." I said, "I'm going to go do this for a while," and I did and at the end of it, I was pretty played out. It was a bad time to be at the end of it because that was when my family started dying off. That was not a happy time. At the same time, I could hardly repudiate it; you know I wanted, as the girls used to say in the romantic dramas, to live a little. I wanted to go out and do a lot of things and I certainly did. I got out and I saw just about everything that was going on.

And did a little of it, too?

I did *all* of it.

And you did it in the seventies instead of the sixties. You were a late bloomer.

I still am.

You seem to be a person for whom a rich family life and your work out here on the ranch is very important.

Yes. I'll stick to my guns on that one. You'll find me doing this twenty-five years from now if I'm lucky enough to be alive. I have eliminated a lot of things now, and I really like my family life. I'm married to a wonderful, tough girl who knows what she wants to do. I don't have to prop her up, she's just fine, she fights back. It's great. My kids like me.

How many times have you been married?

I've been married three times really, but I was married very, very briefly the second time. I was married for fourteen or fifteen years in my first marriage. Then I was married for eight months or something like that. I've been married for eight or nine years now.

Did the burnout you went through in the seventies have anything to do with the breakup of your first marriage?

I think so . . . I think so. But it also had sort of run its course. It was not an acrimonious conclusion to a first marriage. I very much admire my first wife. She and I continue to be friends. In fact, she and my present wife are great friends.

Your second wife was an actress, wasn't she?

Margot Kidder. It was just an arbitrary event, has nothing to do with any . . . The record speaks otherwise so I can't say this, but I'm really kind of a monogamist.

What do you do here on the ranch? Can you tell us a little bit about the cutting horses?

Well, we have a band of broodmares, twenty or twenty-five mares that we use for breeding purposes. Then we run anywhere from 75 to 125 yearling cattle. We raise and sell and break and train cutting horses. Which is actually a bit of a monster; it takes up more time than I want it to.

What is a cutting horse?

In the West, cattle are sorted horseback, at least they always were. Horses are getting replaced by motorcycles and feedlots and weird things, but still a cutting horse has always been a valuable tool to a cowman for sorting cattle. They take diseased cattle out, or nonproductive cows or in-

jured cattle. To go into a herd and bring a single individual out requires an incredibly smart, skillful, highly trained horse and a very knowledgeable rider. That situation has produced a contest animal, just as range roping has produced rodeo roping, and horse breaking has produced bronco riding. That's what we raise here. We have probably one of the better small breeding programs in the nation. We work hard at it. It's not a hobby. We raised the reserve champion of the Pacific Coast in the cutting-horse futurity, we raised the national futurity reserve champion, and I've been Montana champion three years in a row, and we've had the open champion up here.

What relationship does it bear to your writing life?

It keeps me thrown among nonliterary people a big part of my life. I spend a lot of time with cattle feeders and horse trainers and breeders and ranchers, and I like that. It also has made me sort of the village freak in their world. When I rode at the national finals at the Astrodome, it was horrifying. As I rode toward the herd, I could hear these blaring loud-speakers: "Novelist, screenwriter," quack, quack, quack. It is as though this geek has come in to ride, you know. That is kind of disturbing. I'm really not one of the boys in that sense. On the other hand, I can compete against them and beat them and they respect our breeding program.

Does it keep you sane?

Well, it's the outer world. You know you can't go out there and mope around and be narcissistic and artistic in a band of broodmares with colts on their sides who all need shots and worming and trimming and vaccinating.

How do you schedule the two different things?

It goes up and down seasonally. For example there's not a lot to do in the winter. All we can do is feed. And then about now, as soon as things really get going in the spring, it gets to be too much and sometimes I kind of resent it, because I'm working on a book, and I don't want to be out there doing that all day long.

One thing we haven't talked about is the father-son and son-father element in your work.

Yes, I would like to say something about that. It seems funny. My father's been dead for almost a decade and I'm forty-five; it seems I should stop thinking about that. But it has never really seemed to quite go away. When I was a little boy, my father and I were very close and as I got older and he got more obsessed with his business and became more of an alcoholic, he kind of drifted away from me. I think I've been inconsolable about that for a big part of my life. Inconsolable. I mean when I look at a blank piece of paper, all of a sudden Dad comes out. It's there and all I've been able to do is write about it. Try to get it down. I think maybe I got it clear in **Panama** and I'm not obsessed with it anymore. I'm more obsessed with my relationship to my children and trying to feel that I've made some progress. If I could write as long as I want to, and I can think of maybe ten books that I want to write right now, I think it will be seen that this is sort of the end of that father-son era in my writing.

What about the business of games people play as an organizing principle in your work?

Once you leave subsistence, you enter the world of games, whether you move from subsistence to warfare or you move from subsistence to art. They can all be viewed as a situation where people say, "I'll tell you what, you take that position and I'll take this one . . ."

And we'll see what happens . . .

And we'll see how it turns out. For some reason it is quite automatic for me to see that interpretation of what's going on. I don't mean it in a reductive way. When I see games in life I don't say that life is just a game, that's not what I mean at all.

You do tend to write about people who aren't necessarily against the wall economically. They have the means by which to enter the realm of games.

In fact, even ranchers, like the people next door here who just barely make it financially every year, have time to do anything they want to do. You talk to people in Livingston, which is kind of a blue-collar town, and they'll often say, "You've got time to ride horses and do all the things you want to; we're really up against it." Yet they'll pay five thousand dollars for a snowmobile and they'll go buy these campers, but they see that as their necessity material. As opposed to silly stuff like horses, they've got serious stuff like campers and snowmobiles.

It's not a valid point, but one of Reagan's henchmen said, "How can we as a government address the problem of poverty when the number one nutritional problem in the United States is overeating?" And it was a real snarky remark, but at the same time I see a lot of people who say "I have a dishwashing job, and you get to be a writer." They don't have to have that job. And it makes it boring for me to write about dishwashers, because I don't see why they do it or why they want to do it.

I take it at some point you've got a character and you say, let's see what happens to him if we put him in this situation. That's in a sense sort of . . .

. . . a game. In fact it seems to me that life is like that. I mean, that makes the Lewis and Clark expedition a game.

Yes.

That makes democracy a game. Maybe even first-strike capability is a game. I don't know, I mean I think this game idea gradually moves into meaning nothing. It just means life, charged life versus passive life.

But you do see it as an organizing principle and it certainly shows up in your work.

I love play. Playfulness is probably the thing that marks our household.

You said something earlier about this Irish family you came from.

My grandmother was orphaned at thirteen. She was the oldest of the family and she raised all these children, her brothers and sisters. My father came from a small town, and had very little means. He was so astonished he went to Harvard that, to him, life became "before" and "after" Harvard, so we never revisited his origins. But I looked into the stuff. My grandfather's mother died of tuberculosis and malnutrition at twenty-nine with five children. They really didn't have much of a chance. All the girls in the family listed occupation: weaver, address: boardinghouse. You know, all the way down through these records. I just realize how terribly hard they really had it. And then, by the time I knew any of those people, I realized that's why life seemed so exciting to them. They were very optimistic people, and they had it as tough and as mean as you can have it.

You remember the thing that Galbraith said years ago, "There is a vast difference between not having enough and having enough, but there is very little difference between having enough and having too much"? I think that there are a few sectors of this country that really have too much. Certainly the country has too much. That makes me believe that our burning our candle at both ends, while much of the world has no candle, must represent at least the prospects for decline. I sometimes think I see signs of that, though my view of life is not entirely that dour.

Why not? How do you accommodate the discrepancies?

Well, for example, I have a five-year-old daughter who is very excited about the orchard and the horses, the new colts. I don't really think I need to beleaguer her with information right now about Biafra, nor do I think that the activities of a Bernard Goetz underline the reality of her pleasure in new colts. All those things aren't necessarily connected. Some people feel they are, and maybe they're right, you know. It's a sort of religious loftiness that I don't have. I think, though, that the people who do have that sensibility don't seem to ever see anything in the foreground.

Do your books stand, in and of themselves, as a defense against what you see around you that's subject for despair?

Everybody has a responsibility to develop some sort of island theory. I think that life kind of hurtles forward in a massive way for the world, but within it, people invent islands—islands of sanity, islands of family continuity, islands of professional skills and powers, islands of craft, art, and knowledge. Those islands basically are contributors toward a cure for despair, in ways that we probably cannot quite understand.

Thomas McGuane with Liz Lear (interview date March 1984)

SOURCE: "A Conversation with Thomas McGuane," in *Shenandoah*, Vol. XXXVI, No. 2, 1986, pp. 12-21.

[*In the following interview conducted in March of 1984, Lear and McGuane discuss the metaphysical implications of McGuane's fiction, ending with a focus on the recurrent imagery of wild dogs, wolves. and coyotes in his novels. To McGuane, these symbolize the threat of an apocalyptic end to humanity.*]

McGuane lives mostly on a ranch in Montana with his wife Laurie, and various children: his, hers and theirs. In prosperous years he spends some of the winter in Key West, where he keeps a sailboat. He is an accomplished and avid sportsman, with a preference for hunting, fishing, sailing, and riding cutting horses, which he also raises. Looking every inch the rancher/sportsman, he is tall, dark and ruggedly handsome.

This conversation took place in a house in Key West that McGuane had rented from fellow writer Bill Wright. It was a warm tropical night in March of 1984. We sat around a dining room table piled with books and the just completed manuscript of **Something To Be Desired.** *Through the open French doors a lighted pool glimmered and the soft breeze carried the floral scent of something nameless but sweet. From an adjacent room, the clear young inquiring voice of McGuane's daughter Anne occasionally interrupted the story being read to her.*

[*Lear:*] *I have always been intrigued with what attracts creative people to certain places. I wonder what or who brought them here and what makes them stay. Why are you in Key West?*

[McGuane:] I first came to Key West as a boy with my father to go fishing. When I decided to come back here as an adult, it was because I associated the island with writers, reading and writing.

American writers love exotic atmospheres, and yet really don't want to live outside of the country. Key West is one of those places that allow them to have it both ways. It's a southerly town without the burden of southern history. It's intrinsically a nice place. I enjoy the ambience of a place where Spanish is spoken. I like that fecund smell that the island has. I love to be out on the ocean: for better or worse, I'm still a sportsman and the ocean is one of the last frontiers where we can live in a civilized way next to that great wilderness.

Did you always want to be a writer? When did you start?

Yes. I always wanted to be a writer and I began when I was ten—at least to try.

Did you ever do any other work?

I never really made a living, of course. I worked as a boy and young man at odd jobs, the same kind of things other kids did. I worked at a gas station. I worked as a cowboy—cowboy is too big a word for it: I worked on a ranch in an unskilled way. Then I went off to school and was just hell bent to write, to read and write, and that's it.

I have just finished an intense McGuane re-read. I found your books just as fresh and vital now as they were at the time of publication. Most first books are supposedly heavily autobiographical. Is this true of your first book, **The Sporting Club,** *and in reality did such a place exist?*

Absolutely not to the first part of your question. There was a club that was loosely the physical model, but in reality it was a very innocent little club: hunting and fishing. Quite a few Michigan people belonged to it, as did my family. I had very happy times there. I invented a "ship of fools" type environment—of course, the real thing never was that.

The Sporting Club reflected a lot of literary preoccupations of those times: the interest in comic writing and black humor. There was a great wish for serious comic literature in those years. I know I craved it tremendously. I read people like Evelyn Waugh, Kingsley Amis, J. P. Donleavy and Terry Southern. My book reflected that atmosphere, plus my own interest in rivalry and my morbid but comic fascination with violence.

I was intrigued with the Stanton-type character, a person who has cut the moorings and is really going too far; the madman fool so wonderfully portrayed by Marlowe,

Cervantes, Gogol and Melville, who have turned their world upside-down and tried to reassemble themselves. The only way I could see to handle it without getting a long face was to see its comic possibilities. I don't think the truth is diminished because one finds it funny.

Panama *I feel, was actually about six years ahead of its time. I found it even more disturbing the second time around, possibly because I came to it with more understanding. Reading the book I felt made me privy to the dark recesses of someone else's mind. It was both exciting and frightening. I was glad I had the experience but I was relieved when it was over. Are you relieved that those times are over, and in writing the book did you release yourself from a lot of psychological burdens, guilts and hurts?*

Yes, in both instances. I'm glad that era is over for me. One transmutes some of that into fiction and gets a form of release from doing so. It's funny, Bill Wright has a copy of **Panama** here, and I was reading in it today. I haven't done that in a long time.

For a couple of reasons I still have pride in that book. The personal era, which may or may not have been shared by others, was announced in **Ninety-Two in the Shade** and drew its final curtain in **Panama** the hope of certain things as announced in **Ninety-Two** and the despair for its accomplishment as announced in **Panama**. I'm excited that in two thirds of a decade one could examine the rise and fall of a dream, and that's what those two books do. Even if that's only known to me, I'm completely happy that I got it down.

I find it interesting that you think the book was ahead of its time. It was roundly attacked when it came out. It also received two of the best reviews I ever got, one in the *Village Voice* and the other in the *New Yorker*, so it had people who felt strongly and positively about it. You know, it's never been out of print and it seems to gain momentum and a wider readership all the time. I would say that with the almost epidemic spread of cocaine throughout American society, that book is going to seem scriptural to more and more people.

I also saw a lesson in the book which I hope some will heed: don't go down that road too far because it only leads to despair.

It doesn't really turn on drugs, it turns on egotism, stardom, or cocaine, whatever it is that keeps you from looking out and seeing the world and the people around you. That's the thing that will get them in the end, just as it got Chester.

You mention a writer friend in the book who provides a little sanity and good advice. At one point he says, "I'm getting off the rock. I love the rock but it's a bad rock." In real life you apparently shared his sentiments. In fact you sold your house and left town. Was this character based on Jim Harrison, to whom you dedicated the book?

No. The burnt-out writer with little skeletal hands sitting watching the hotel burn, that's me. Pomeroy is another part of me, it was one part of me talking to another.

What about Don, the guardian angel. Was he another alter ego?

Yes, this was my shadow.

Why did you dedicate the book to Jim Harrison?

Because Jim, as you know, is one of my oldest friends.

You know, I really can hear him saying "get off the rock, I love it, but you've got to get off it."

Peculiarly, I think Jim is one of the people who didn't "get" the book. I dedicated it to him, and do you know he never acknowledged that. It was years before I even knew whether he had read it or not.

We all worry about the threat of nuclear war and the possible annihilation of the human race. In one of your books, I think **Ninety-Two**, *your hero says, "God, if they will only leave the ocean alone I can handle anything," and, "who on earth, slipping it to a truly desirable woman, can seriously interest himself in the notion that the race is doomed." As a real survivor, Tom, do you honestly believe that?*

The language is comic of course, but within that, I acknowledge that in human questions there are orders of magnitude. On one hand it seems mathematically predictable that we are going to blow ourselves up and yet part of us insists that we will wriggle out of it somehow.

So you see a glimmer of hope?

There is ample evidence for continuance. In some perverse way we don't buy the doom bit, maybe that in itself becomes a self-fulfilling prophesy and we will survive.

Do you revise as you go along?

I revise as I go along. Sometimes I think I write so that I can revise. Revision is two-thirds of the effort.

Do you write every day on a set schedule?

No. When the project has come to life for me, then I write every day. Then there are long unhappy periods when I don't write every day, these are unquestionably times to be avoided. Nothing goes well for me if I'm not writing.

Do you keep a notebook or diary?

Yes. I scribble things down, notions, things I think will be of great utility. They never are.

Do you ever suffer from writer's block and if so how do you overcome it?

Yes. I think all writers do. I overcome it by forcing myself to adhere to regular work practices. Showing up to work at the same place and time every day, sooner or later this works for me; but for a time there it is painful.

Some writers find starting the day confronted with an empty page very disconcerting, they will always try to leave half a page with which to start the new day. How do you handle this?

I try to leave off on a good note with the feeling that I've left something living there that will still be alive the next day. I try not to leave on a note of discouragement.

Who are your favorite writers?

I'm such an eclectic reader that I can't give a fast answer to that. In the past, my heros have been Twain, Stendhal, Aristophanes and Stephen Crane. Among the contemporaries, of course, I read my friends, Jim Harrison, an Indian writer named Jim Welch—I'm talking about my favorites now—Robert Stone and Phil Caputo. I don't want to leave anyone out, but when I'm writing a book I forget everything . . . Walker Percy, Norman Mailer, Styron and Raymond Carver.

What about new ones, the young ones coming up, any that give you hope for the future of literature?

It's funny, the ones that seem young and coming up, like Raymond Carver, are close to my age. Barry Hannah, Raymond Carver and Jayne Ann Phillips, they seem to me to be the newer voices coming up that I'm most excited about.

Do you enjoy the company of other writers?

Immensely.

Have other writers been supportive of your work or do you sense any feelings of competitiveness?

Yes, they have been supportive *and* competitive—yes, but mostly in an invigorating way, not in an abrasive one.

Flaubert said that we must love each other in our art the way mystics love each other in God. Do you think this sentiment exists today, or indeed do you think it ever has?

I don't think it exists today and I suspect that it never did. I think that writers, in so far as they feel beleaguered within society, have a sort of comradeship that disappears when they are in a situation where they are entirely within their own world. For example, when we are in Montana we are all madly in love with each other because there a writer isn't a highly esteemed individual. When we are in a place that is writer-dense, like Key West or New York, we tend to have our fangs out for each other to a degree, like any other competitive group. Every one wants to be acknowledged in that strange kind of writer's pecking order. Maybe this statement is a bit strong; I think it's both true and not true.

Do you think it's possible for a person to write like an angel and yet on every other level be a despicable person?

It's highly possible and in many instances a fact.

If you had the opportunity to sit down with any writer either living or dead and discuss his or her writing and yours, who would that be?

Socrates.

Are you a social creature?

It's kind of a moth and candle thing. I have spells when I feel quite social, then I'm overwhelmed and exasperated very suddenly and unpredictably, and want to get away from people entirely and think. I find that I can't get much thinking done in an intense social situation. I get almost hunger jitters to get off and figure things out. I don't think I'm unusual in that way. As I become more focused on absolutely what I want, in terms of my friends, my family and my work, I've become more impatient with things that don't fall into that category. I have figured out that life is short and I have a lot of work to do, and things that I want to do with my family. I often get maddened when I'm derailed unnecessarily by a not particularly interesting social situation.

Someone once said that we go through life with a diminishing portfolio of enthusiasms.

F. Scott Fitzgerald. I'm not sure, but I think it's either from that nauseating thing he wrote called *The Crack-Up* or his letters. Scott Fitzgerald went through life with a diminishing portfolio of enthusiasms. As an Irishman I recognize that as a sort of racial failure of the Irish, which is the horrible disappointment that youth passes and one's dreams have not been fulfilled. I think the Irish are very prone to that, and the drinking Irish, the absolute worst. I don't think there's a more pusillanimous document in American literature than Fitzgerald's *The Crack-Up.* The gist of it is, "you all let me down and I'm going to be pathetic because you did this to me and I'll do it on cue."

I think it's impossible not to go through life without some diminished enthusiasms, in the sense that they are diminished in their quality. Obviously, one discovers things you don't want to do any more, so you stop doing them; presumably, the ones that remain, you do with greater skill, concentration and ability.

In one of your books, I forget which one, you used that Fitzgerald quote.

I might once have thought of that line with approval. I probably did. I now think we are supposed to rise above that. I mean a forty-four year old man can't wander around among his friends and family and tell everyone how disappointed in life he is. I think that's terrible.

I get the distinct impression from your books that they are more than a little autobiographical. Are they?

No. I'm using myself insofar as I think I'm good material, things that have happened to me or things I've seen, but I really use those as points of departure. We all start out with an image, something always catches the eye, the mind, it's usually something that has happened to us, something out of our own lives and it might sustain us for half a book, but the art is there to be served and we go where that's supposed to go, not where the paltry details of one's life might dictate. I often use things that I've seen, that are true of me, a place to sort of lift the edge of the material so that I can enter.

You are then always aware of the art?

That's part of the job.

Someone said that you share a genius with Celine for seeing the disparate materials of everyday life as a highly organized nightmare. Is this true and do you continue to see things that way?

I think that's a polite way of saying "paranoia." Yes, I think that's true. In the book I'm working on now the narrator reflects that the natural state of the universe isn't heat, but cold. I think we all exist on a very fragile tissue of life and vitality. I've seen a lot of death close up; it can happen instantaneously. Remember last year when Annie was so ill. She was only four years old. The doctors said that one end of the spectrum of what she had was death. She was in perfect health when I left and a week later Laurie telephoned to say, hurry home, Annie's in an oxygen tent. One realizes

that you can walk out of a door—or that people you love can disappear like a puff of smoke. We are surrounded with that realization. I believe that very strongly. The other day a group of writers assembled for a photograph; this time next year probably some of them will have gone on to the next world. That's not really paranoia, but at the same time I feel the pressure of it as a day to day reality. I remember the dates when people close to me died as if they were only a few hours ago. A favorite aunt died, then a week later her namesake, my sister, died; ten months later my father died and a short time ago my mother died. In the meantime several friends have died. I don't really feel threatened by a sense of my own mortality, though I suppose we all are to a certain extent. I'm forty-four years old and I'm at the middle or end of my life. I don't know which. I've experienced much and had a lot of years to feel full about. What really bothers me is that the people who haven't had much chance to do things are just as subject to the arbitrary fall of the ax as I am. The sense of all that is a continuing force for me, the idea that we are all on the brink of eternity.

Re-reading your books in quick succession brought to my attention something I might otherwise have missed. There's a rather frightening image that develops from book to book. It starts very subtly in **Bushwhacked Piano,** *suddenly it's there and then it's gone, like something seen out of the corner of the eye. You speak of hearing the pad of feet in the darkness downstairs and the sound of dogs or wolves or coyotes drinking out of the toilet bowl. In successive books, there is reference to unseen dogs barking or coyotes howling like some kind of death knell. The climax comes in* **Nobody's Angel** *with that hideous scene of a house littered with slaughtered and skinned coyotes.*

How marvelous! That's very perceptive of you. That was something that crept up on me. I hadn't realized that the man and wolf thing ran so deep in me. I love dogs and I know that they belong to humans, and yet they also belong to the wild, to the jackal side of the world that preys on humans when things fall apart. We have a very deep bond with dogs, but I know that if the bomb drops there will be packs of dogs feeding on our dead, charred bodies. I see this as a powerful image of what happens to our basic hard-won deals when the rest of the planet is falling apart.

It doesn't have any personal psychological significance that culminated in **Nobody's Angel;** *something you had finally worked out?*

I think it's one of those things one never works out, either it's there or it isn't. Average people like Tio and his coyote hunting friends in **Nobody's Angel** turned on the dogs of the world before disaster struck. They anticipated Armageddon.

I have never thought of dogs in that context, pigs maybe. I remember reading that pigs were a common sight, rooting among the dead on the battlefields of the Civil War.

I read a wonderful book last year by Franklin Russell called *The Hunting Animal*. There are some passages in it about hyenas that are just unbelievable; you recognize the dog family. Packs of hyenas will pull down an antelope on the plains; they are complete feeding machines. The minute they have slowed the creature to anything like a stop, they begin to feed; they don't kill. The antelope just stands there gazing around at this mob of ravenous creatures who are literally eating it before it has had time to die.

People love dogs and dogs love people. Until people absolutely drop the ball; when dogs realize people have lost civilization, then they will become wild again and feed on people.

Jerome Klinkowitz (essay date 1985)

SOURCE: "Thomas McGuane: The Novel of Manners Radicalized," in *Literary Subversions: New American Fiction and the Practice of Criticism*, Southern Illinois University Press, 1985, pp. 104-115.

[*In the following essay, Klinkowitz discusses McGuane's fiction as "the new American novel of manners." He maintains that McGuane has the ability to single out the characteristics of an age and know his characters through them.*]

A tea biscuit crumbles, and in its fragments Henry James can read the fortunes of a social world. "Her voice sounded like money," Nick Carraway says of Daisy Buchanan, and in that manneristic notation we sense the compelling illusion of Gatsby's life. There's even a touch of it in Faulkner: young Thomas Sutpen is turned away by a servant at the rich man's door and forever vows to build himself an equal domain. Despite our relative incivility and egalitarian beliefs, who says there is no novel of manners in America?

But then come the American 1960s. On both social and artistic fronts, the old hierarchies crumble. Down with the establishment, and death to the novel. The politics of Berkeley, Madison, Columbia, and the 1968 Democratic Convention find their match in the communal rites of Woodstock and the anti-illusionistic fiction of Brautigan and Vonnegut. Apparent anarchy dislodges the old truths. The novelist's study of society now takes place in a madhouse, and the decade's most reliable narrator is Ken Kesey's Chief Broom, who in *One Flew Over the Cuckoo's Nest* warns

us, "It's still hard for me to have a clear mind thinking on it. But it's the truth even if it didn't happen."

Yet in Chief Broom's words can be found a clue to the new American novel of manners. *Why* is his narrative the truth, even though it may not have happened? Look back a few lines, as he characterizes his experience in Kesey's asylum. "I been silent so long now it's gonna roar out of me like flood-waters and you think the guy telling this is ranting and raving my *God*. . . ." The truth is in the telling, and for every step within the careful structure of janitors-orderlies-practical nurses-RNs on up to The Big Nurse herself, the Chief has a perfect image. Their manners are, in terms of this novel, a matter of his transforming language, finely tuned to each.

Kesey's novel helped signal a decade's revolution, and there are many writers who follow his example and in some cases even his lifestyle in the previously unwriterly northwest corner of the United States. Richard Brautigan, for example. Jim Harrison. Guys who know their way around a trout stream or high range better than through the pubs of Greenwich Village or midtown bars near their editors.

How this all translates into a new novel of manners, however, falls to Thomas McGuane. In his twenties during the 1960s, McGuane wrote his first published novel in 1968, that year of social and political turmoil which Michael Herr (in *Dispatches*) described as "so hot that I think it shorted out the whole decade, what followed was mutation." Through the next dozen years, as presidential candidates were assassinated, rock stars OD'ed, and the culture at large underwent a transformation whose sudden thoroughness was unknown in previous American history, McGuane produced four more novels plus a book of essays, while paying off his Montana ranch with oddball Western filmscripts for *Rancho Deluxe*, *The Missouri Breaks*, and *Tom Horn*. His fiction includes the full cast of counterculture characters, from dropouts to heavy dopers and theatrical rock stars. These protagonists both form and are formed by their cultural milieu, of which McGuane is a sharp observer. But it is in their language that they become true agents of fiction, factors in the new American novel of manners.

Although his first novel, *The Sporting Club*, is almost biblical in its microcosmic annals of a rich men's hunting and fishing lodge, McGuane's sharpest attention to manners comes with his introduction of young protagonists out searching for America and themselves. Nicholas Payne from *The Bushwacked Piano*, Thomas Skelton of *Ninety-Two in the Shade*, and Chet Pomeroy who narrates *Panama* catalogue the manners of McGuane's three residencies since childhood: Michigan, Montana, and the Florida Keys. Payne has an ear for people's speech; a girl who thumbs a ride on his motorcycle out West complains, "I'll take a car any day. . . . You cain't play the radio own this." Skelton, heavy into drugs, hallucinates while hitching with a silent-majority-type salesman who can nevertheless find common ground and share perceptions: "When Skelton told the hardware salesman that the paint had just lifted off the whole car in a single piece, the hardware salesman agreed with him about how Detroit put things together. This was the epoch of uneasy alliances." But most impressive is McGuane's ability to convey the characteristics of his culture within the words and syntax of his narrator's own speech. Listen to Chet Pomeroy, the burned-out rock star, explain why he owns a pistol:

> Something about our republic makes us go armed. I myself am happier having a piece within reach, knowing if some goblin jumps into the path, it's away with him. Here in Key West, we take our guns to parties. My pedal steel player had one on a clip underneath his instrument: it said "Death to Traitors" on the backstrap and was stolen by a fan in Muscle Shoals, Alabama, on New Year's Day.

This paragraph makes its point entirely by its conflux of manneristic references within the verbal rhythm of our era's popular idiom. Before it is a gun, it's "a piece." Adversaries are not individualized beyond a spooky presence, nor are they shot at or killed—they're just swept away by the cadence of the sentence. From here, the notations turn to rock culture: not just any music, but that from a steel guitar. And not just anywhere, but in Muscle Shoals, home of a major recording studio famous for the Southern Blues sound, and stomping grounds of the Allman Brothers Band, two of whose members died on motorcycles. Chet's way of narrating helps define the time in which he writes. *Panama* is the new American novel of manners.

Florida. "Drugs, alligators, macadam, the sea, sticky sex, laughter, and sudden death"—these are the elements out of which Chet constructs his novel. In his essays collected in ***An Outside Chance,*** McGuane explains his own fascination with what another of his protagonists calls "America's Land's End." Both essayist and novelist must be sensitive to the little elements of atmosphere which typify a place, such as "the ground swell of Latinate noise—that first of all things that make Key West another country." The town is "both an outrageous honky-tonk and a momento of another century," and even its biosphere is such that one gets the sense of living on another planet, where at a drive-in movie "the column of light from the projectionist's booth is feverish with tropical insects" blurring the image on its way to the screen, and when "driving home, palmetto bugs and land crabs pop under the tires." That's from McGuane's essay on tarpon hunting for *Sports Illustrated.* For his fictional protagonists, Key West is a springboard to history

and prophecy, but all based in the country's manners which have their toe hold in this extreme piece of land. As Nicholas Payne observes,

> He was happy to be in Key West. It was Harry Truman's favorite town and Harry Truman was fine by Payne. He liked Truman's remark about getting out of the kitchen if you couldn't stand the heat. Payne thought that beat anything in Kierkegaard. He also liked Truman's Kansas City suits and essential Calvinized watch-fob insouciance of the pre-Italian racketeer. He enjoyed the whole sense of the First Lady going bald while the daughter wheedled her way onto the Ed Sullivan show to drown the studio audience in an operatic mudbath of her own devising.

In just over one hundred words—quickly enough to leave undisturbed his narrative's progress through Payne's business in south Florida—McGuane evokes thirty years of American popular history. Double-breasted suits, the President's snappish wit, long-suffering Bess, daughter Margaret on Sunday night TV: such is the Americana of Payne's childhood which he rediscovers in such cultural time pockets as the Keys.

Florida yields an apocryphal vision as well. Chet notes that a clip-joint parking lot is dug up to reveal the grave of an ancient Calusa seagoing Indian, who for decades has been "staring up through four inches of blacktop at the whores, junkies, and Southern lawyers." In ***Ninety-Two in the Shade,*** Thomas Skelton takes his skiff out during a solar eclipse, glancing upward to see hundreds of birds circling a black hole in the sky, the same vacuity he finds in human relations. Times are bad. "Nobody knows, from sea to shining sea," this novel begins, "why we are having all this trouble with our republic," but McGuane's protagonists are determined to find out why. Their investigations take them to the heart of "hotcakes land," where the streets are lined with "franchized outrages" and "everything is for sale." But they can also locate themselves comfortably within an ambience constructed from the counterculture and uniquely local elements, as the author explains for Skelton:

> Intelligent morning: Indian River orange juice, thousand-times-washed Levi's, perfect Cuban guayabera shirt, Eric Clapton on the radio, sunlight swimming the walls, cucarachas running a four-forty in the breadbox, mockingbirds doing an infinitely delicate imitation of mockingbirds. Yes, gentlemen, there is next to nothing; but I'm going to have fun anyway.

Skelton's trick is to "look askance and it all shines on." His two closest studies are the fishing guides Faron Carter and

Nichol Dance. Carter is the less distinguished, known best for his pink wedding cake of a wife Jeannie, a former baton-twirler whose titillating half-time act has been a monument to "a whole civilization up shit creek in a cement canoe without a dream of a paddle." Dance is more original, at home in Key West as America's terminal man who has fled a murder rap up North to see his car, smoking from a jammed brake drum, ignite and explode on the town's main street—"Nothing to do but stand back and watch her go."

Skelton measures the distance between these two guides and their methods, computing an average of manners for the Key. But in the end, he favors Dance's extreme and becomes himself America's terminal man, burned out by the 1960s and murdered off Barracuda Key.

Nicholas Payne of **The Bushwacked Piano** is a more comprehensive hero, touching base with all three of McGuane's favorite regions. For him, Michigan is a place to escape: upper-middle-class parents who would suck him into the "Waring blender" of their homogenized lives, future in-laws who'd keep him out of their family unless he finishes law school, a rival boyfriend who's a perfect dud of a junior GM exec but who can dress like a department store mannequin, and so forth.

When Payne takes off, it is *to experience* things: a paragraph in which he drives his motorcycle along the California coast matches image-for-image a description McGuane included in his *Sports Illustrated* essay on riding the Matchless 500. His girlfriend and her family have taken off for their Montana vacation home; crossing its entryway, Payne feels compelled to mimic Ernest Hemingway's shotgun suicide. But as always McGuane has a sharp eye for manners and is an artist at summing up a character, even when with the girlfriend Ann Fitzgerald it's making the decision simply to inventory her room:

> Protractors, lenses, field guides, United States Geodetic Survey topographical maps, cores of half-eaten apples, every photograph of Dorothea Lange's ever reproduced, tennis shorts, panties, a killing jar, a mounting board, fatuous novel, a book about theosophy, a bust of Ouspensky, a wad of cheap Piranesi prints, her diplomas and brassieres, her antique mousetraps, her dexamyl and librium tablets, her G-string, firecrackers, bocci balls and flagons, her Finnish wooden toothbrush, her Vitabath, her target pistol, parasol, moccasins, Pucci scarves, headstone rubbings, buffalo horns, elastic bandages, mushroom keys, sanitary napkins, monogram die for stationery, Elmer Fudd mask, exploding cigars, Skira art books, the stuffed burrowing owl, the stuffed, rough-legged hawk, the stuffed tanager, the stuffed penguin,

the stuffed chicken, the plastic pomegranate, the plaster rattlesnake ashtray, the pictures of Payne sailing, shooting, drinking, laughing, reading comics, the pictures of George smiling gently in a barrera seat at the Valencia Plaza de Toros, an annotated *Story of O,* the series of telephoto shots of her mother and father duking it out beside the old barge canal in Washington, D.C., Payne's prep school varsity jacket, an English saddle, a lid of Panama Green, Charlie Chaplin's unsuccessful autobiography, dolls, a poster from the movie *Purple Noon,* a menu from the Gallatoire restaurant, one from the Columbia in Tampa, one from Joe's Stone Crab in Miami and one from Joe Muer's in Detroit, and one rolled skin from a reticulated python curled around the base of a stainless steel orbiting lamp from Sweden—in short, a lot of stuff lay wall to wall in a vast mess, upon which she threw herself with energy born of her separation from Nicholas Payne.

Why is this important? Not for *tour de force* writing, though it takes that talent to get the job done. Structurally there's the narrative need for an explanation—why won't Ann simply move in with Payne?—which that laborious inventory now makes clear. "Ann didn't want to pair off," we're told. "She wanted to play in her room with all that junk for a few more years."

Sharp-eyed and sharp-eared Nicholas adapts to Montana, jawboning it with a backcountry mechanic and studying the rodeo riders' techniques until he's figured out how to stay on a bronc for fifty seconds, winning Ann's esteem. But there's still more of America that he needs to immerse himself in before a true sense of himself can be found. Therefore it's on the road—less of a Kerouac tradition than an homage to Huck Finn, whose shore-bound troubles become things of the past once he's back in flow with the river. Highway A1A to Key West, a river of concrete which like Huck's Mississippi takes you to the extreme terminus before it all vanishes into nothing.

McGuane's facility with manners is evident once more in his ability to use them for parody. *The Bushwacked Piano's* narrative follows parallel paths as Payne celebrates these cultural idiosyncracies while Ann mocks them. She writes poetry, shoots arty photographs, and reads D.H. Lawrence seeking to be "at one" with things; with Payne as her guide, she finds the best chances for identification in the "simple national archetypes like floozies, bowlers, and rotarians." In *Ninety-Two in the Shade,* McGuane himself is partial to such caricatured types, notably Faron Carter's baton-twirler wife: "Twirling, dropping to one knee for the catches, then prancing downfield in a mindlessness now growing culturally impossible, she was a simple pink cake with a slot." Jeannie Carter is a natural at this, but the effect is heightened when

Ann adopts it as a role. As with McGuane's protagonists, her motives are fiendish: "In an epoch in which it was silly to be a druid or red Indian, there was a certain zero-hour solace in being something large enough to attract contempt." And so Ann looks forward to being a floozy "as another girl might have anticipated her freshman year at Vassar. With almost Germanic intentness, she had set her sights on being cheap and available and not in the least fussy." Pulling out the peroxide, hair spray, and heavy make-up, she faces the mirror. "Call me Sherri," she squeaks.

Other elements of satire abound. The American entrepreneur is caricatured in C. J. Clovis, who sells multi-storied bat towers for ridding areas of their mosquito problems. The folks on Mente Chica Key who buy one are in turn satirized as the typical country bumpkins eager to be chiseled by this gentle grafter from up North. Proof of the parody is that none of these cameo shots is held in focus for long. Clovis vanishes like the fly-by-night he is, the gulled townsfolk fade away into the sunset of their gumbo manners, while Ann picks up and leaves Nicholas Payne for the finer styles of her GM junior executive, pausing only to stop at Neiman-Marcus first for a quick change back from floozy-hood. George meets her at the Detroit airport, she in an Oscar de la Renta ensemble complemented with sandals by Dior, he in jacket by J. Press, Pucci cravat, and seamless cordovans from Church of London. "See them" the narrative section concludes, "running thus toward one another, perfect monads of nullity."

With **Panama,** McGuane comes to the point where he can trust his protagonist with the narration. Chet Pomeroy is a rock performer, adept at theatricalizing his culture's dark desires, "paid to sum up civilization or to act it out in a glimmer." On stage he's done this with his music; in **Panama** the effect is verbal, where Chet is no less a singer of his country's songs. Sometimes the quotations are direct, as when he's mourning the loss of his girlfriend and acknowledges that he's got heartaches by the million, or listening to another girl explain that "bad luck and trouble is getting to be my middle name." If I didn't have bad luck, I wouldn't have no luck at all, and happiness is a thing named Joe. *Watch the words*, his girlfriend cautions him, and Chet appreciates how "the occupational hazard of making a spectacle of yourself, over the long haul, is that at some point you buy a ticket too." In terms of manners, Chet has become a communal catalyst, having "poured blood from my head so that strangers could form a circle."

In the tropical atmosphere and shabby economics of Key West, Chet finds it easy to be the poet of decay. Everything's for sale and nothing's worth buying. What good there's been is swept away by dubious progress, reminding Chet of the manners of his time: "Today an old family jewelry store had become a moped rental drop; a small bookstore was a taco stand; and where Hart Crane and Stephen Crane had momentarily coexisted on a mildewed shelf was now an electric griddle warming a stack of pre-fab tortillas." Nature itself seems ready to rebel, and the air reeks decadence. Chet's narrative eye is on present manners and their long-term consequence, a vision both timely and millenial—here, with its lyric language, is another key to the new American novel of manners. "When they build a shopping center over an old salt marsh," Chet approvingly observes, "the seabirds sometimes circle the same place for a year or more, coming back to check daily, to see if there isn't some little chance those department stores and pharmacies and cinemas won't go as quickly as they'd come."

Self-consciously the artist, and so ingratiated in the reader's mind, Chet can introduce lines of poetic imagery without disrupting his ongoing sense of story. Offbeat characters can be introduced with a savor for their individuality, and examples of extreme behavior blend easily with Chet's manner of storytelling. Take Marcelline, his girlfriend's girlfriend, distinguished by her scandalous habits and kinky sexuality. She robs graves, blackmails sugar daddy lovers, and is as ready to jump into bed with Chet's girlfriend as with him. A perfect counterculture extra who herself doubts she's a survivor: "I might be gone in the next reel." How does the new American novelist sum this all up? In the perfectly concise sentence capped with a image unique to Marcelline's innocently charming idiosyncracy, as "a leggy, otherwordly beauty, trailing her dubious dreams and pastel whoredom like a pretty kite."

Above all, Thomas McGuane is a novelist of manners because of his ability to single out the characteristics of an age and to know his characters through them. Coupled with his narrative ability to blend these details into a convincing pitch, such aptness of notation helps create the spirit of the times and of his protagonists. Listen to Chet complain, with a style and vision which give us a feeling of his woes:

> For some reason, scarcely anything seems to bespeak my era so much as herpes simplex. Oddly, it appears as—what?—a teensy blister. Then a sore, not much, goes away, a little irritant. It's infectious. When your girl gets it, from you, it is not at all the same thing. For instance, she screams when she pisses. She won't put out. She demands to know, "Where did you get this one?" The answer is: *From the age*.

From the cultural conflux, Chet has drawn inward to the most intimate physical details and then suddenly reached outwards again, just when his girlfriend asks for a specific explanation. The specific is explained by the general *when each is closely realized*; in his ability to modulate the two within a convincing narrative, McGuane becomes the surprising heir to Fitzgerald and James.

Thomas McGuane with Judson Klinger (interview date April 1989)

SOURCE: "In Pursuit of Crazy Language" in *American Film*, Vol. XIV, No. 6, April, 1989, pp. 42-44 and 63-64.

[*In the following interview, McGuane discusses his experiences as a Hollywood screenwriter and the details of his work on films, including* The Missouri Breaks, Tom Horn, Rancho Deluxe, 92 In the Shade, *and* Cold Feet.]

Thomas McGuane is accustomed to rough weather. He's lived and ranched for the better part of 20 years on the wide, open rangeland of southwest Montana, and nothing much surprises him. But what's going on outside his window today is, to lift a line from one of his books, "worse than real different." A fierce winter Chinook is blowing gusts up to 100 mph, forming impenetrable snowdrifts in a matter of minutes.

In his book-lined study is a desk occupied by a lap-top computer and the manuscript of his latest novel, *Keep the Change.* The window overlooks his ranch, and, if it weren't for the snow, we would be able to see 6,000 acres of soft hills, wide river valleys, snowcapped mountains and a huge sky that's seven clean shades of blue.

When McGuane's novels arrived in the early '70s, the country was wallowing in post-'60s disillusionment. Nihilism was the philosophy of the era, ennui was the mood, and James Taylor was the soundtrack to it all. Many novelists of the time chose to reflect that mood with cold stories about detached, alienated characters, written in a controlled, minimalist style. McGuane's writing, by comparison, stood out like a hot pink hearse in a funeral procession. In *The Sporting Club, The Bushwhacked Piano* and *92 in the Shade*, his outrageous wit, hallucinatory prose and comic-romantic-violent vision drew critical comparisons to everyone from Faulkner and Hemingway to the Marx Brothers. The characters that filled his novels were half-crazy, unforgettable people who spoke the most skewed, arch dialogue you'd ever read. But none of his books sold terribly well, so by the mid '70s, like many a novelist before him, he hired out to Hollywood as a screenwriter.

McGuane's literary reputation had grown quietly, but with his immediate success in Hollywood, his "gonzo cowboy" lifestyle acquired real mystique. A tall, rugged outdoorsman with a black-Irish streak, McGuane ran wild for a few years: he carried on with famous actresses, crashed a Porsche at 140 mph, drank and fought with both fists. Still, somewhere along the way, he managed to write his best novel, *Panama*—as well as almost a dozen screenplays.

His intricate, offbeat comedy, *Rancho Deluxe* (1975), starring Jeff Bridges and Sam Waterston as laconic, chain-saw-toting rustlers in Montana, has become a cult favorite in, among other places, prisons. McGuane then directed an adaptation of his book *92 in the Shade,* which he brought in on time and under its roughly $1 million budget. It featured a dazzling ensemble of Peter Fonda, Warren Oates, Margot Kidder and William Hickey, and bears the distinction of being one of the few major studio films released with two radically different endings. "That's called not having the final cut," says McGuane. Barbra Streisand was impressed enough by *92* to ask McGuane to direct *A Star is Born*, but he wisely refused the opportunity.

McGuane's best-known screen work is the high-budget Western, *Missouri Breaks* (1976)—which might have been called *Dueling Egos in the Sun*—starring Marlon Brando and Jack Nicholson. The emotional turbulence he gathered on that movie, and on *Tom Horn* in 1980, drove McGuane out of show business and back to the literary life.

His chosen homestead of Livingston, Montana (he was raised in Michigan suburbia), attracted many other show-business friends like Peter Fonda, the late Sam Peckinpah and Warren Oates. Remote as it was, Livingston was still crowded enough that he and his wife, Laurie, recently moved out to a spread at the foot of the Absaroka Mountains, a 20-minute drive from the nearest town. There he raises cattle, trains championship-caliber cutting horses and writes books (*Nobody's Angel, Something to be Desired* and *To Skin a Cat*). And, in need of timely injections of Hollywood cash to maintain the ranch, he has lately been contemplating a return to writing and directing movies. The producers have never stopped calling.

A Tom McGuane screenplay is always news, and two of his projects are currently stirring up dust. The Mount Company is preparing his Civil War-era comedy, *Flying Colors*, and *Cold Feet* is about to be released by Avenue. Directed by Robert Dornhelm (*Echo Park*), and starring Keith Carradine, Tom Waits, Sally Kirkland and Rip Torn, the script was a collaboration between McGuane and novelist Jim Harrison, who have been close friends for 30 years, since their college days at Michigan State.

McGuane's choice to deal with Hollywood on his terms, from his picturesque outpost, is considered nothing short of heroic by the legions of unhappy screenwriters who have chosen instead to lock themselves in 8-by-12 rooms all over the Los Angeles basin and wrestle with compromise.

"At the age of 49," he says, "I don't want to spend a lot of my time in situations about which I'm cynical.

"I think that the respect the industry's given writers has been so minimal that it's created a situation in which good writers are going to keep that writing which produces their self-esteem elsewhere."

Sitting in an armchair by his stone fireplace, McGuane is a soft-spoken, friendly, at times effusive host and a natural storyteller who slips effortlessly from the subject of contemporary Italian literature to an old Andy Kaufman comedy routine. With his wit and biting irony, he comes off as sort of a one-man Algonquin round table.

[*Klinger:*] *You've lived up here in Montana for 20 years and managed to have a successful screen-writing career, in spite of the industry notion that it's hard to sustain a high-level career without living at least part-time in Los Angeles.*

[McGuane:] You know, there used to be an American fantasy not so long ago that everybody would go off to Colorado, live in a log cabin and have a computer terminal. That's one of the fantasies that came after the Abraham Lincoln fantasy of cutting fence posts and becoming president. (*laughs*)

But nothing happens unless people are actually in a room. It's like AA tells people: it doesn't matter what your motivation is, it's important that you get your body to a meeting. It doesn't matter what you think. You know, fuck your brain. Your brain got you into trouble in the first place.

Unproduced screenplays usually have a very short shelf life. How did **Cold Feet** *get made 12 years after you wrote it?*

I have to credit Robert Dornhelm, who ferreted this script out of some musty closet, liked it and wanted to do it. Cassian Elwes was the original producer on this thing, and somehow or another it went to Avenue. So its long shelf life is sort of an accident.

Did you or Jim Harrison rewrite the shooting script?

I rewrote it. The original Buck was very unlike the character whom Bill Pullman played. He was an almost pure denizen of the '70s. (*laughs*) He was right out of the whiniest of the Eagles music. He was a bit of a doped-out photographer who was working in New York and hanging out with models. We couldn't wait to get him by his little pointed ears and lift him out of the script.

What was the inspiration for Tom Waits' character, Kenny, the health-conscious hit man in **Cold Feet**?

I went out to Los Angeles one time and met some people who were hit men. And, you know, we think about the sort of hideously awful human being who would be a hit man. Literary types like to talk about nihilism and things like that, but hit men are as devoid of what we call "the human" as it's possible to be. I mean, they literally see the taking of life as a job. But since their dossier is so completely strange, we assume they would stand out sharply from the culture around them if we could ever get to meet them. In point of fact, they're just like everybody else, and they even have these little fetishistic hobbies. I got interested in this work-out boom, this health-conscious era that we live in, and I happen to know that these guys have the same kind of petty fetishes as the people at *Self* magazine. So the irony of someone who makes his living killing people, and whose real interest is in health, sort of appealed to me.

Reading the screenplay, I assumed that Rip Torn had the part of Monte, rather than Keith Carradine.

That's what I wanted. Rip Torn would have been a terrific Monte. But the feeling out there is that people Rip's age have sex less often than people Keith's age. And since movies, in this country, have become a basic tits-and-ass medium, at some point in the process of going from a script to a film, the question of what's sexy becomes the ruling issue.

I'm almost prepared to think that what the American movies want to be about is fucking and shooting, and that you're simply fighting city hall to write about anything else.

You can't really be that cynical, can you?

I'm overstating to be humorous, but my experience, over and over, has been that sexiness is imperative, and to ignore that is to court heartbreak. Why else would you cast Gregory Peck as Captain Ahab? (*laughs*)

I know of one major producer who won't consider any screenplay that doesn't contain at least one gunfight with Uzis.

We had a situation like that in **The Missouri Breaks.** Nicholson felt that he never got to "go through with anything"—that was his phrase—and that Brando had all the action stuff. Jack was kind of intimidated by Brando. So when Brando left the scene, Jack suddenly came on strong and wanted changes, right now. Arthur Penn called me and asked me if I was willing to make changes on Jack's behalf, and I said no. So they brought in Robert Towne to help the ending. [As a result] you have this extraordinary moment where the father is getting a haircut in the ranch house, and Nicholson comes in, and the father's got a gun under his barber apron, and so there's this thing where Jack gets to shoot the father. Towne wrote that scene.

In the shooting script of **Rancho Deluxe,** *there's a scene in which Harry Dean Stanton's character is weeding a garden. But in the film, he's vacuuming giant rugs on the ranch lawn—the famous "Hoovering-the-Navajos" scene. How did that change come about?*

There was a production problem—somebody got hurt or something. That scene, which I love, I wrote about 20 minutes before they shot it. I had to write it that morning, but I can't remember exactly why. That's what's nice about those situations—in that air of necessity, you really get some great ideas.

That scene has the kind of arch, lyrical, comedic language your early novels and screenplays are famous for.

I wish there was a greater call for it, frankly. You know, Paul Schrader, among other people, has criticized that side of my writing.

Right. He said that your movies have so many great lines that you start listening for the great lines, which breaks the narrative thread. He also thinks too many great lines make a movie unrealistic.

In general, I think what he says it true. But I think the age of the kind of writing that Paul Schrader's done—that modernist, flattened-out kind of writing—is passing. I like very charged language. I wish we could all write this incredibly vivid stuff, because art is not life. I like language that makes me crazy, that's like tidal movement—it sweeps you into some other district.

How long, on average, does it take you to complete a screenplay?

There's really no average. Some of them took *forever* to do, and some of them just wrote themselves. **Rancho Deluxe** wrote itself. It was just a matter of trotting into the backroom and fluttering the keys in a pleasurable way for about three weeks. There was no strain, no work, no struggle. Nothing but amusement.

Wouldn't it be nice if they were all that easy.

Yeah, right! *(laughs)* Others have made me want to hang myself.

Since you consider yourself primarily a novelist, is it worth it to put yourself through hell over a screenplay?

I think it's kind of a bad sign. Cocteau said, and I'm always

quoting this: "A writer should never do anything hard." *(laughs)* When I look back on **Rancho Deluxe**, I look back on a time when my motivation was rather more simple than it is now, which was: I thought the world was sort of funny, and I wanted to prove it. And I wish I still felt that way as clearly as I did. I really long for those moments, which do occasionally come, when things seem to me to be extremely funny.

After serving as the location for both **Rancho Deluxe** *and* **The Missouri Breaks,** *this little town, Livingston, Montana, was the focus of a lot of media attention as a late '70s "in" spot—a new artists-celebrity colony, with your ranch as the hub of the action.*

I used to be quite a bit more sociable than I am now, and I didn't mind being the center of this kind of . . . commune.

Twelve years ago or more, I kind of out-grew that. It wasn't what I wanted to do anymore. It's interesting, you know, wildness kind of takes the place of work. I had worked pretty hard most my life, and I had a period, much shorter than commonly supposed, where I just kind of ran the streets. But that, sooner or later, will devour work. The work I like to do requires long-term concentration—every day, good hours. It doesn't quite fit that chaotic lifestyle.

So that lifestyle was exaggerated in the press?

Yes. I did have friends who were always welcome. But what happens is, the nation is so utterly gaga about celebrities that, though you and I may know that Jeff Bridges is a normal human being who's fun to have around, if it gets in the papers, suddenly the two of you are in this intense *life drama*, where celebrities *encounter* on the high plains of Montana. Then, in New York, they get quite worked up about it, because they're all foaming to get out of that septic hellhole where they live. *(laughs)*

How often do you go down to L.A. to pitch ideas or discuss projects offered to you by producers?

I haven't done either one for at least a decade. I certainly would, you know. I'm thinking now that I might want to do something again, and I'll do whatever it takes. I wouldn't direct a movie unless I was going to stay and be in their faces until the thing was done. You don't want to phone it in on any level.

I had a deal with Sydney Pollack that fell apart during the [writers] strike . . . we were just going to make a movie. We weren't going to dog-ear it by running around town and boring everybody with an outline. We were just going to get on the same wavelength, and then I was going to try to put my heart and soul in it because I had all this *freedom*. But that's the closest I ever came to a movie deal I'd really loved to have had.

Sydney has hired a number of good writers over the years and not gotten good screenplays from them. He asked me why I thought that was, and I said because people who get into his position, generally, are masters at controlling the agenda. When you control the agenda of an artist, you cancel his being an artist.

You once described Brando, Nicholson and Penn as being "Kissingeresque in moving other people around for their own plans."

Movies are always described as a "collaborative medium," but all the key players are famous for being uncooperative. The higher up the ladder they get, the more they specialize in controlling the agenda. By the time you got all those guys together, you were closing in on a very, very narrow unoccupied field of control. (*laughs*) At that point, it appeared to be absolutely Chinese, the minute gestures that would shift power around the situation.

When I was first working with Arthur, I strongly felt his attention to the matters of the screenplay. As soon as the first movie star arrived, I was startled by how my status in the project just evaporated. I remember one day Arthur and I were talking about something that was intensely interesting to me, and Jack Nicholson came in, and suddenly Arthur seemed to be incredibly interested in how *blue* Jack's eyes were. And Nicholson's standing there like this little balding fireplug, and we're really trying to think about how blue his eyes were! At that point, my interest in the project literally went out the window. I said to myself, "What am I going to do next, because I ain't gonna do this anymore."

You seemed to have lost your enthusiasm for filmmaking after **The Missouri Breaks.**

I'd have to say that I'm only now getting over **The Missouri Breaks.** I wrote it as something that I could direct, that would star my old buddies—Warren Oates and Harry Dean Stanton and those kind of guys. It was going to be an ensemble movie about a little gang of outlaws who outlived their time. Then, all of a sudden, this star casting came in, and it went from being prospectively a very interesting genre movie to this kind of *monster.*

I went to see a screening of it, and everyone was euphoric at the studio. I came out of the screening and tried to sell my [net profit] points to [producer] Elliot Kastner. I eventually traded two-and-a-half points of **The Missouri Breaks** for an $800 saddle horse before the movie came out. (*laughs*) That's how much I thought of it.

Forty years ago, Westerns were an American Myth exported to the rest of the world. A lot of foreigners still think Americans all wear cowboy hats and settle their disputes with gunfights at high noon.

I'll tell you—it's worse than that. The Western is the *only* mythology we've ever produced. I'm always surprised that the commonly exploited mythological-origin story of America is not the Civil War, which is the thing that sets America apart from all other nations. But for some reason or another, the myth of the cowboy, which [John] Milius sees as the final version of the Aryan Herdsman Myth, is the one that's been our central myth. And for some reason, it seems to have disappeared.

Nobody wants Westerns anymore. I'd love to write another Western. More than anything.

What are some of your favorite Westerns?

I love just about everything John Ford did. I love a lot of the early Sam Peckinpah movies:

Ride the High Country and *The Wild Bunch*. I absolutely loved *Hud* and *The Last Picture Show*. To me, *The Last Picture Show* was so good, I remember exactly where I was sitting, what day it was and what the weather was when I saw it.

Didn't you get into a fistfight with Peckinpah that started out as an argument about Westerns?

That's a funny story. What happened was, we were at a table of really boring people, one of whom was a journalist, but we didn't know she was writing about us. And Sam leaned over to me and said, "What can we do to get out of here?" I said, "Why don't we pretend we're having an argument, stand up and say, 'Let's step outside,' and we'll step outside and leave." So I made some phony remark to him, and he *exploded*. Scared me to death—he was such a good actor. About two months later, an article comes out in a magazine about how Peckinpah and I had this fatal falling out and stepped outside for a fistfight in a parking lot. All we wanted to do was go home. (*laughs*)

You once called your script for **Tom Horn** *"the Western to end all Westerns."*

Gee, what an arrogant youngster I was! I wonder if I said that before the movie came out? Because I really did try to write this killer Western. It was this enormous thing, a 200-page screenplay. It was this huge, inclusive version that I wrote by myself before Bud Shrake became part of it.

How much research was involved in **Tom Horn**?

Enormous research! God. Endless research. By research, I mean a lot of fascinating reading about the period. [Horn] lived in a hugely interesting era. He was an abused child out of a Pennsylvania Dutch family. Spoke German as his first language. He jumped on a freight wagon and ran away from home. Ended up in Santa Fe, learning Indian languages, working as a translator. Went through all of the bloody and disillusioning things that happened in that era to the Indians among whom he lived, and ended up being deprived of the usual civilized morals of the day—ended up being a very dangerous character. I thought it was a great story, seen that way.

I wanted to do that project for years and years. Tom Horn was the perfect subject, and Steve McQueen was the perfect actor for it. I thought he was a terrific actor. He was not any fun at all to work with as a producer.

You had a terrible time with him, didn't you?

Yeah. His word wasn't any good. He woke up in a different world every morning—absolutely no continuity from day to day.

I went out [to L.A.] with a long script to meet with him, and he didn't want me to change a *word* of it. He made me promise I wouldn't change anything! By the time I'd been there two days, he didn't like anything in it. But this was a guy who just smoked dope 24 hours a day. The most wide-open pothead I've ever been around.

I didn't know what kind of ill health he was in at the time. But he had a nice side. It was like being around a thug: there was a terrific side to him, and then there was a side you absolutely couldn't trust. Apart from that, I thought the camera loved him.

When did he turn the script over to Bud Shrake?

The night my phone rang out there in California at about three o'clock in the morning. I picked it up, and I seemed to have a heavy breather on the other end. And this voice said, "You can take your macho bullshit and go back to Montana." (*laughs*) I knew Steve and I were not as happy as we'd once been together.

Who has the film rights to **Nobody's Angel**?

It was bought by Warner Bros. There was some kind of a development relationship between them and Robert Redford's company, and I worked with Redford fairly closely till we did a script and at least one revision—and really enjoyed it; he's very bright. Then it just went into that vast, intricate filing system which is the prospective films of Robert Redford.

Why do you think so many of his projects are condemned to development hell?

I think that he has the same problems that anyone faced with an infinity of choices has. What an infinity of choices produces in most cases is indecision. Indecision and procrastination are probably the two greatest sources of unhappiness known to man. I actually think that procrastination and boredom are the two great evils of modern man. (*laughs*)

Was Redford planning to play Patrick Fitzpatrick [the book's hero] and produce and direct?

Yes, as I understood it. He plays his cards very close to his chest, even in the most intimate work meetings. So you really never know what he's thinking of doing.

Again, it's a strategy meant to maintain the infinity of choices. The infinity of choices might make you unhappy, yet you spend all your working time to make sure the infinity is maintained. It's unbelievable.

In a recent interview, Redford mentioned that the two of you have become pretty good friends.

I wish we did see more of him. He has come up and visited us, and he's really a good fellow. As opposed to most actors I've known, I would have to say that Redford is pretty much of a grown-up. He could go on with his life in a very high-powered way without acting at all.

As one way of getting back into directing, have you considered taking a script through the Sundance Institute and having Redford produce it?

No, I never have. To be perfectly honest, I think writing novels is a more important thing for me to do. In terms of my usefulness on earth, it's a higher degree of usefulness for me to figure out how to write these unremunerative novels.

Asked why he writes screenplays instead of novels, Paul Schrader said, "Films are the medium of my time." He thinks a novelist has to wait too long for feedback from his audience.

I think he's right about that. He's talking about something that's very painful about the novel process. This latest novel has taken two-and-a-half years, and it won't be out for a year. But this business about "the medium of my time" — can you even say such a thing? He's a Michigan boy, as I am; maybe the medium of our time is car manufacturing! (*laughs*)

So there's little chance that you'll ever direct another movie.

Right now, I've actually been thinking a lot about trying to write and direct a movie. My biggest reservation is that I live in a very tiny town in Montana. I don't know if I know what's going on in the industry. . . And the either/or thing between movies and literature has been set up so firmly in this country that if I thought about directing now, I'd have to think seriously about not writing novels anymore.

Do you really get that much abuse from the literary community for directing a movie?

Yeah. You get really hammered over it. . . . You know, it used to hurt my feelings. *Panama* came out and everyone said it was just a prototype for a screenplay. Well, I knew when I wrote *Panama* that it could never be a movie. The ideal now in American Literature is to write a really grim, unadaptable feminist novel. (*laughs*) That keeps your credentials in tact.

As a writer, what qualities do you hope for in a director?

The thing I like in filmmakers is the same thing I like in novelists—I like the sense that they have some sort of personal vision that is independent of their second-guessing markets. When you're watching a marketeer masquerading as a director, it's an unsavory spectacle.

And who do you like?

I thought Hal Ashby was a marvelous director. I like Nick Roeg. I have an appreciation for big, strong-minded directors who sweep all the materials into their own uses. That's why Ford seems to be such a model. Bertolucci has such a tremendously strong view of things, and Altman, at his best, has that, too. I know he's sort of fallen on hard times, but I think his films are just terribly interesting. *McCabe and Mrs. Miller* seems to me to be a model of new cinema.

Altman would have been a terrific director for **92 In the Shade**. I'd have liked Ashby to direct **Rancho Deluxe**, Peckinpah to have done **Tom Horn**.

Of the directors you worked with, who came the closest to capturing the spirit of your writing?

Nobody's come close enough to make it a discussible issue. (*laughs*)

Any other directors you'd like to mention?

Yes. I love Terry Malick. I thought *Badlands* was superb. I know everyone else thought *Days of Heaven* was boring;

I couldn't see *anything* boring about it. I loved it. Malick's talent is so enormous, it's kind of like watching Raymond Carver work. He has to come back, or come back to the place he's welcome. Maybe he should be a writer.

But my all-time favorite American director is John Huston. I look down the list of the films he made and get a warm feeling.

I've heard that Malick's absence is partially due to the fact that he had a hard time handling the compromises and emotional abuse that come with the territory.

You know, I think it would really be healthy if writers would just get a little bit tougher—slightly more savage in our dealings with the other elements—and start fighting for stuff.

It seems as though you've done that more often than a lot of writers.

But to tell you the truth, I feel guilty about not doing more of it. I'm sorry I didn't go over to Red Lodge and break a fucking chair over Robert Towne's head when he was in there fucking up the end of **The Missouri Breaks**. I'm sorry that I didn't tell Jack Nicholson that when you make deals like [bringing in Towne], you deprive yourself of your own claims of being an artist—that you're just another filthy little hustler like the ones you complain about. I'm really sorry I didn't do it. But next time, I will do it. Next time, I'm gonna be absolutely right in people's faces, from A to Z. You have to care enough to do that.

Eric Larsen (review date 17 September 1989)

SOURCE: "A Literary Quilt of Faded Colors," in *Los Angeles Times Book Review*, September 17, 1989, pp. 3, 10.

[*In the following review, Larsen criticizes McGuane's novel* Keep the Change, *calling it a "half-hearted work," of "tossed-together leftovers."*]

The irrepressible Thomas McGuane strides forth once again, in [**Keep the Change**], his 10th book and seventh novel, to take on nothing less than the breadth and troubled essence themselves of native life in end-of-the-century America. In the McGuane mode, it's a book that seems to set out to do all things—dazzle, satirize, embrace, lament, and perhaps at end to salvage the pieces of a lesser world. The work disappoints, though seeming itself, by the finish, to be less an antidote to that world than another piece of it.

The literary energies of the indefatigable McGuane can put a reader in mind of something like a many-colored quilt—

there's the outdoor flavor and manliness of Hemingway over there, of course (and there, and there), here are some swatches of the ribald and word-happy picaresques of J. P. Donleavy, others of the anti-hero comics of Amis and the Angry Young Men; there's the bold and nervy strain of the American satirists of class and commerce, from Sinclair Lewis on down; and here's the poetic and telling observer of baffled small lives in backwater places, the imager of quietly despairing Americana descending from, say, Sherwood Anderson and the early regionalists.

These are noble antecedents, to a one, and their emergence in the uneven fabric of McGuane's work--now here, now there—can result in moments of brief and captivating, sometimes hilarious, brilliance. But the whole cloth that's woven from them, the overall result, the book itself and the inner spirit of it—these can be another matter. Not quite satire that's held at a level of sustained effectiveness, not quite a non-satiric novel of felt experience, not quite a successful blending of the two, **Keep the Change** reads instead, echo of its own title, like disappointingly half-hearted work, tossed-together leftovers, a project without the ability or inner conviction to find out what it really is or what it's really for.

What feels empty and perfunctory at the heart of the book may be a result of what's empty and perfunctory at the core (intentionally or not is another question) of McGuane's chosen hero this time around. Born and reared on a cattle ranch in Montana, Joe Starling Jr. is portrayed from the start as being unsure whether or not he wants to inherit his birthright of open land. His heavy-drinking father ranched it, went on to become a banker and then "an agricultural executive," but nevertheless is presumed still to love the land, and in the early pages of the book he counsels son Joe, in the sped-up tropes of comic Western parody, not to "let that old s.o.b. Overstreet get it. He tried to break me when I came into this country and he darn near got it done. We get along okay now but his dream is to make his ranch a perfect square and this is a big bite out of his southeast corner."

That Joe's father soon dies without having properly clarified Joe's title to the ranch will provide later plot complications, but more centrally at issue is Joe's attitude toward his would-be inheritance. "Joe loved the place but he didn't expect or really want to end up on it altogether," we read. And, considering the probable fact that the land "would one day be his," Joe concludes this to be "not precisely a soaring thought. He really wondered how he would put his heritage in play. He found the future eerie and he already wanted to paint."

All could be well with the book if a reader were actually able to feel the truth of either side of the double premise—that Joe "loved the place" on the one hand, and that he "wanted to paint" on the other. But both ideas, in spite of

McGuane's often desultory efforts to pull them into vitality, stubbornly remain more like identifying labels on a string-operated figure than like inner convictions deriving from a genuine psychological life. Given this limitation, the author gains free license to move his character around at will to send him (after a summer of working—and losing his virginity—on the ranch) out East, where he graduates from Yale, strives half successfully (so McGuane says, but never shows) to become a serious painter, and ends up in Florida, and then allows the author just as freely to send him fleeing again back to Montana on a putatively spiritual quest to reclaim his heritage and roots.

It's as though, again and again, Joe were less a real character than a pre-made and movable device to let McGuane write about whatever he might want to write about: the jaded and decadent tackiness of Florida; the flamboyantly and yet conventionally sexy Astrid, whom Joe hooks up with in Florida and stays half-involved with throughout the book; the worn-out town of McGuane's Deadrock, near the ranch; the sleazy and boundless opportunism of cheap entrepreneur Ivan ("Man was meant to consume") Slater, ex-Yale classmate; or the restaurant of the Yale Club in New York, where there's a hilarious moment in a scene that is, as it happens, wholly extraneous narratively.

It's unarguably true that a novel could succeed perfectly well in this way—as a purely linear comedy, aiming first for brightness and maybe not at all for depth, exploiting a character who's primarily just a narrative convenience; but McGuane's book struggles uneasily against the limits of just these traits, leading the author, to telegraph to the reader again and again, as if in nagging after-thoughts, the thematically deeper sides of what Joe is supposedly thinking or feeling, as in banal and empty lines such as "Joe was maddened by joy at being in the country of the West. He felt that he would find a restored condition for his life here."

McGuane's eye is sharp and his quick aim often perfect, especially in small things, as when Joe is on the road from Florida to Montana ("A radio preacher shouted, 'Satan is playing hardball!'"), or when he notices in a tidy residential part of Deadrock that "On most lawns, a tiny white newspaper lay like a seed," or in describing the Dickensian figure of Joe's Uncle Smitty, a shell-shocked alcoholic still living (or so he lets on) in the world of 1945—who himself makes a wily grab for the money tied up in the ranch.

But the book as a whole labors both for meaning and material descends at one moment to farce appeals at the next to high melodrama; allows Joe for long sections to forget important things like his (he thinks) illegitimate daughter, then suddenly hyperbolizes their urgency and significance; at one moment romanticizes the land and Joe's desire for it, at the next suggests that there wasn't much certainty of will there anyhow, concluding with half wistful toss-aways such as the one suggested when Astrid, who followed him to Montana, turns away from Joe: "It had been lovely, anyway," he muses. "It was a provisional life."

It may be, of course, that McGuane is a jump ahead of the reader, intending all along, against odds, to make something, anything, out of half abandoned, worn, or leftover material: to write, as part of the message, only a provisional book. At one point, when they are still in Florida, Astrid asks Joe why it is that he doesn't paint anymore. His answer is: "Paint what?" It's a question that seems to speak to the whole of this often skilled yet self-consciously jaunty and oddly mechanical book that, purposely or otherwise, is about the absence of things and emptiness.

Mark Harris (essay date 29 September 1989)

SOURCE: "Tom McGuane," in *Publishers Weekly*, September 29, 1989, p. 50, 52.

[*In the following essay, McGuane talks about his writing career, his novel* Keep the Change, *and life on his Montana ranch.*]

"The heir to Hemingway"; "Captain Berserko"; "macho pig"—Thomas McGuane has had plenty of labels to live down and just as many to live up to in his nine-book career, and none of them seems to do him justice.

Barely 30 when he burst onto the literary scene with *The Sporting Club,* he saw his star as a novelist soar with *The Bushwacked Piano* and *92 in the Shade.* Lyrical, coruscating and subtly political, his books made him a media darling—the counterculture cowboy. By 1975 he was writing *and* directing the film of his third novel, and careening toward celebrity and its gossip-page trappings: affairs, divorce, remarriage (to Margot Kidder), another divorce, remarriage, prodigious drinking and a reputation for excess in just about every area but his lean, acute prose. But with his fourth novel, *Panama* (1978), the critics who had made McGuane a hit "couldn't even remember what they had in mind," he recalls. The crash-and-burn reviews were more personal than literary; they took the author to task as much as they did the book.

But McGuane's private life has long been stable, alcohol- and trauma-free, and his critical fortunes have resurged in the last decade. With the novels *Nobody's Angel* (1982) and *Something to be Desired* (1984) and the short story collection *To Skin a Cat* (1986), the author pursued his concerns with an ever-stronger and more reflective voice. His first

novel in five years, *Keep the Change,* is likely to keep him on the ascendant.

A hunter, avid fisherman and cutting-horse champion rider, McGuane meets *PW* on a stopover in New York City before continuing on to Labrador to fish for Atlantic salmon. Settling in for dinner after a long day of flying, he begins with espresso: "I need to get some IQ points back." Six-foot-two, long-limbed and darkly tanned, he approaches what he wryly calls "deep middle age" with undiminished enthusiasm and good humor.

Born in 1939 and raised in Michigan, McGuane felt the desire to write early on; his first attempt at a novel came at age nine, and "by the time I was a junior in high school, it was all I could think about," he recalls. As a young man, he thrived in the company of other writers; his classmates and friends have included Edmund White in high school, Jim Harrison in college and William Hjortsberg at Yale Drama School, where McGuane took an abortive stab at playwriting.

Until his late 20s, McGuane lived nomadically, spending time in Salinas, Key West, Spain, Italy and Ireland. In the late '60s, longing for a more permanent home, he settled in Montana, where his cattle and horse ranch in tiny McLeod now houses a blended family that includes his wife Laurie, their young daughter and, intermittently, three older children from earlier marriages.

Professionally, he's roved almost as much. First published at Simon & Schuster (where "editors kept leaving *me*"), he decamped for Farrar, Straus, where he stayed for three books with Michael di Capua. What he calls "a business dispute" precipitated a move to Random House, where, he says, "I was just not at home." His last two books have been with the Seymour Lawrence imprint, first at Dutton and, with *Keep the Change,* at Houghton Mifflin. There, he says, "I'm off on another happy relationship, and I hope this one lasts."

Although its tone—a precisely calibrated balance of sensitivity, restiveness, passion and irony—is a departure from much of his previous work, *Keep the Change.* will be instantly recognizable as a McGuane novel to his loyalists: its territory, thematically and geographically, is purely his own. With a hero returning to his Western roots to puzzle out his feelings for two wildly different women and a conclusion brought on by no more than a careful unfolding and discovery of desires, the novel reverberates with his past writing to offer a wholly new effect. And characteristically, it's trim—under 250 pages.

"I know it's not exactly in the tradition of post-World War II American writing," says McGuane, "but I think that you should use as few scenes and paragraphs and words to achieve your effects as possible. If you're building fishing rods or shot-guns or yachts, the standard is lightness that is as much as possible commensurate with strength. I think that's a universal aesthetic, and the kind of rich overwriting which has become the standard in a certain kind of American fiction is really a mistaken idea. Accretional monument-building as a style is not one I've ever liked."

Unsurprisingly, McGuane's redrafting consists largely of excision. "For me to write a book that ended up being 400 pages, the first draft would have to be 2000. That's part of the excitement of revising, to find something that stands on its own strength rather than depending on the buttressing I thought it had to have."

As for the labels, McGuane ingenuously brushes most aside. The Hemingway comparison (in terms of both writing style and productive/destructive lifestyle) has dogged him throughout his career. Of that persistent identification he says, "either I'm outgrowing the issue or it's going away." On the antics in the 1970s that won him the "Berserko" sobriquet: "By comparison with today's dour, money-crazed climate, it does look like it was one great party. Everyone was in a slightly more festive mood. But in the '70s, I also published four or five books, wrote about eight screenplays and about 40 articles. I was getting a lot done."

Only the accusation of insensitivity (or short shrift) to women in his prose still rankles him, although he laughs when discussing the female editor who'd been "told that I was one of the macho pigs—me and Harry Crews and Jim Harrison." (After reading McGuane's works, she reported to him, "I don't think you're a macho pig at all!")

While not fond of answering for his characters—whose records with women are fairly unenviable—the author admits that "I don't think I'm ever going to make a certain type of women's literature proponent happy. A lot of women are extremely angry. For those people, who are conscious of the depth of the bad debt that has been owed to women for a long time, almost anyone [can] have some of the features they associate with the enemy. It's like having a German accent in 1919. But I have three daughters, and I'm extremely sensitive to what I perceive as their rights in the world."

A hallmark of McGuane's writing is its sense of location; the physical world is deeply important to his characters and his prose. Most frequently, it's been the town of Deadrock (a fictional gloss on Livingston), Mont. "I require that writing seem to belong somewhere," he says. "If it's floating and I can't attach it to the earth at some point, frustration sets in." Is he a late-arriving regionalist? "I object to the term officially. But in a funny way I sort of like it. Finding people who think of me as a Montana writer reinforces my wish to have succeeded in putting down roots there."

In recent years, McGuane's home state has been the site of a flourishing literary and cultural community—Richard Ford, William Kittredge, James Crumley, David Quammen and a host of other writers, actors and artists make their homes in Paradise Valley and Missoula. While McGuane jokingly refers to the Montana literary renaissance as "five guys with hardcover sales of 8000 each," he admits it pleases him. "I love Montana, but at the same time there's a certain kind of cultural deprivation that I would like to see changed. People who are born and grow up there love it so much they don't ever leave. They aren't liable to produce Márquez characters, and you go around sort of pining for that, wishing that they'd be just a tad more flamboyant."

McGuane's ranch, which keeps him completely busy for about half of every year, has taught him that "there are other circadian rhythms besides the semester system. Like it or not, you get tied into seasons, not just seasons of the planet, but breeding seasons. . . . " During the winter months, when the ranch more or less runs itself, McGuane's schedule is an idyllic-sounding confluence of writing and reading, done in "a comfortable little log house. You're there, you can't go anyplace else and you can just make a pot of coffee, go back to bed and read and read." His passion for literature seasons his conversations, and his enthusiasms are generous and global: Chekhov, Cheever, Raymond Carver, Joyce Cary, Graham Greene and uncountable others. Although he's more reserved in criticism, his assessments can be mercilessly pithy: with scalpel precision, he dismisses a contemporary's prize-winning novel as "Micheneresque."

For a time in the 1970s, McGuane was a prolific if almost consistently dissatisfied screenwriter whose credits included *Rancho Deluxe, The Missouri Breaks, Tom Horn* and his own *92 in the Shade.* Last spring his name turned up on the cult comedy *Cold Feet,* which he had written with Jim Harrison in 1976. "I literally couldn't remember what it was about," he admits, and adds that he has no plans to return to film writing. "It's menial work," he says.

McGuane begins his novels with a sense of outline and structure, but all of the big issues in his fiction are resolved in the writing itself. "It's nice to decoy oneself by making outlines and planning, but all the writing you're able to keep comes up just the way phrases come up for musicians. But for some reason, you have to pretend that it's plannable and go through a certain number of mnemonic devices just to get started."

The process was somewhat different when McGuane was younger; writing *92 in the Shade* in 1973, he says, "I felt as if I had a fuel tank strapped on my back; I felt we were on the cultural nosecone of America, and I had to write about it." While many of his contemporaries became casualties of the era, McGuane survived, and views those years without sentiment or cynicism. "In the mid-'70s, we didn't think in terms of taking a life raft on a boat. A kind of Whitmanesque optimism was afloat," he remembers, "and it's definitely gone. Even then there was a sense that it might end in tragedy, and to some extent it did. There were irreversible misunderstandings between generations that were never repaired, and left an unhealed wound in American life."

That belief resounds in many of his novels, in which wars between sons and their fathers are brutal, futile and fought unto—and after—death. But the fierce cynicism of some of his earlier writing has given way to something more ambiguous, and perhaps hopeful. "I like the more recent novels better," he says bluntly; when he "squints into" his older novels, he "wants to change everything and start rewriting. You say, gee, I wish I saw everything from a constant stance, like a lighthouse. Going back to a 1955 novel is a little like looking at a 1955 Ford—kind of cute, but tailfins just don't mean today what they did then."

In December, the former angry young man of the American West will turn 50. With his family life "semi-euphoric," McGuane can pour his boundless energy into his fiction. "The only thing that fills up the work hole in my sphere of need is writing," he says. "Between me and me in the dark of night, I consider everything else a fib, even my ranching. I love to do that—it gives me a physical grounding in the world and an orderly way to say, I'm not gonna use the old head now; I'm gonna get in the pickup truck and go look at fences. But then I say, That's enough now. My real job is as a writer and I've got to get back to work."

Gregory L. Morris (essay date Spring 1991)

SOURCE: "How Ambivalence Won the West: Thomas McGuane and the Fiction of the New West," in *Critique*, Vol. XXXII, No. 3, Spring, 1991, pp. 180-89.

[*In the following essay, Morris praises McGuane as one of a number of regional fiction writers of "the new West."*]

Writing in 1980, in a special issue of *TriQuarterly* dedicated to new writers of the American West, William Kittredge and Steven M. Krauzer declared

> The current status of western writing is similar to that of southern American writing in the early 1930s when a major regional voice, in the persons of such authors as William Faulkner, Robert Penn Warren, Eudora Welty, Andrew Lytle, and Katherine Anne Porter, was beginning to be heard. Just as the old south was gone, the old west is

gone. Free of the need to write either out of the mythology or against it, the writers of the new west, responding to the variety and quickness of life in their territory, are experiencing a period of enormous vitality. (13)

That period of vitality has sustained itself partly on the sheer strength of landscape, partly on the imaginations of writers like Thomas McGuane who have been busy redefining the shape of the "new West" in their fictions. I would contend that in many ways, McGuane is responsible for this resurgence, this renaissance; that he has worked hard to open up the new West to its newest writers such as Patricia Henley, David Long, John Keeble, Rick Bass, and others by removing layer after layer of myth, stripping away the accumulated patterns of story and legend and belief that have transformed the West into an anachronism.

Paradoxically, all of this noble work has been done under a measure of protest. The concept of place, which for McGuane translates into regionalism, is one not especially dear to his heart: "The vulgarity we call the 'sense of place' is a fairly nelly sub-instance of schizophrenia, saving up facts, preferably inherited, about locale. It's like when Southerners talk about losing the war; you want to puke" (*An Outside Chance* 221). As a writer, McGuane has always insisted upon the idea of an "American space," of an undiminished, unpartitioned landscape; in the same essay, **"Roping, from A to B,"** he says he was a writer trained by Kerouac "in the epic idea that the region was America." Therefore, things especially American—images, obsessions, dreams, deficiencies—are things held in common across that landscape. To be American is to travel well.

As a writer, McGuane favors certain portions of this region that we call America; certain locales in this republic are more familiar, more comfortable, more promisingly troublesome than others. Therefore, we have come to know McGuane's Michigan and McGuane's Key West and McGuane's Louisiana and Alabama. And, clearly, we have come to know McGuane's Montana, McGuane's Deadrock. All of these places figure significantly in his fiction and in the ideas contained within that fiction; but the pervasive, informing influence of the American West is always at the heart of McGuane's writing.

This condition is particularly interesting for a number of reasons. McGuane works hard to dismiss the notion of region, of localized landscape; yet he insists upon returning to those specific American geographies (one might stress the *American* here), and in doing so helps to define more clearly what others might easily perceive as region, as the specifics of place. For much of his career, McGuane has written out of an ambivalence that is at once personal, political, and aesthetic. In a 1975 interview, talking of having to divide his time between Key West and Montana, McGuane remarked: "I never want to leave one place for the other, but I don't feel like a real Key-Wester, or a real anything. Nabokov's been referring to himself lately as a 'friendly outsider,' and I find that a salubrious phrase. If I feel anything, it's a writer, a space man who's just landed. I'm pretty rootless, however sad that may sound" (Carter 54). For the past ten years or so, McGuane has been writing without a sense of place, denying a sense of place, but writing *about* a sense of place and, I think, *desiring* a sense of place. Apparently he now has discovered and accepted that place: "Montana is my home, my adopted home," McGuane writes in **"Roping, from A to B"** (*An Outside Chance* 213).

What has taken McGuane so long in adopting that place as home has been his political ambivalence to the American West and to its attendant mythology. It is as if he has been carrying on a love-hate affair with the region, embracing certain elements of the West, rejecting others, all the time trying to identify the true nature of the beast. On the one hand, he portrays the West as an exhausted landscape, all its myth used up, all its historical exchange spent. It is a played-out landscape inhabited by played-out characters. These characters come expecting, or hoping for, the old West, and find instead a new West, one that cannot, *will* not sustain their worn-out personalities and their worn-out beliefs.

On the other hand, however, the high lonesome does persist. The West will not disappear. It insists upon accommodation. What McGuane does is open—or re-open—the West to redefinition, reformation, reinvention. McGuane, in his heart of hearts, loves the old West, loves its ethic, its myth; but he understands that what he loves has, for the most part, vanished—that is one of the things he sets out to prove in his fiction, and it is a necessary proof. However, as he dismantles the apparatus of the old West, McGuane is careful to leave in place particular elements of that apparatus. Instead of the total extinction of myth, we have the revision of myth. Ultimately, McGuane seems to suggest that the tradition of the West sustains itself in a reformulated environment.

McGuane refashions this new West, moreover, out of an equally ambivalent aesthetic, one that allows him to move between a love for the region itself and a disdain for what that region has become, for what has been worked upon that region. First, McGuane must unmask the West, reveal the mythic imposture, strip away the pretense that clings to the West out-of-time and essentially out-of-place. Thus, he exaggerates both condition and character, magnifies the flaw, the imposture. Among McGuane's many talents as a writer is his brilliant use of satire, his vision comic, dark, and painful. Thus, character often turns into caricature, funhouse-mirror images that both distort and deflate the

historical perception of what these characters traditionally should be.

Against these caricatures McGuane opposes his protagonist-outsiders, his "dislocated cowboys"—men who come to the high lonesome to find themselves, to locate the myth, and their place within it. These heroes usually float for awhile, their self-discovery often mirroring their discovery of place, or placelessness. Sometimes they remain, content with new self, new West; sometimes they escape, unsettled, misplaced, seeking relocation.

While they are there, however, these characters help reveal McGuane's profound, though underplayed, affection for the West they temporarily inhabit. For although McGuane's method is predominantly satiric, and he generally keeps a cool distance between himself and the West he looks to demystify, the language he uses consistently betrays his real feeling for the region. Specifically, there is a significant shift in tone and perspective when McGuane gets caught up in the description of landscape *and* of work, two elements of the West that survive the changes in place and culture, two elements that link old with new. The high lonesome, the Absarokas, the Crazies—though touched by change, by the new West of "coyotes, schemers, venture capitalists" (as Lucien Taylor describes the situation in *Something to Be Desired*)—these features of landscape overwhelm the puny, often pathetic shadows of men who attempt to corral, exploit, capitalize the region.

These same shady, shadowy figures are shown up by the work that other men do, work that is authentic, full of meaning and worth and history. Work, for McGuane, is evidential: "My favorite concept is that the proof is in the pudding: what you do" (*An Outside Chance* 221). What counts is performance within a specific place; repeatedly in McGuane's fiction, characters are momentarily measured, transformed, redeemed by the work-rituals they prosecute. These work-rituals have their origins, their roots in the very old West that McGuane labors so hard to displace. If you are an outsider, you prove yourself by executing the native rituals, even while you work your changes upon the native culture. McGuane believes in the quality of these rituals, these significant remnants of the old West tradition, even though he sees the great part of that tradition as archaic, a brittle carapace slung upon the back of a new, less likeable creature.

This aesthetic pattern of ambivalence, of denial, and of confirmation repeats itself throughout McGuane's fiction, making itself most apparent, logically enough, in the novels and stories set in McGuane's Montana, in the Deadrock landscape. In *Nobody's Angel*, Patrick Fitzpatrick returns to the West a self-described "cowboy outsider," a fourth-generation Deadrocker still looking for ratification. He confronts a West that is at once familiar and perniciously alien, a West, on the one hand, filled with cowboy-gentlemen and Indian remains, and on the other, overrun with Cowboys for Christ and mock-cowboys from the Midwest and the Southwest ("the first part of the West with gangrene"). McGuane captures this outsized, inflated image in the caricature of Tio Burnett, the imitative would-be Westerner—threatening, pathetic, crude.

Balanced against this portrait is Fitzpatrick's grandfather, the man who is "too cowboy to play to nostalgia for anyone; though as a boy he had night-hawked on the biggest of the northern ranches, had seen gunfighters in their dotage, had run this ranch like an old-time cowman's outfit, built a handsome herd of cattle, raised his own bulls and abjured farm machinery" (61). Unlike his son and his grandson, Old Fitzpatrick has stayed behind, has lived the ranchlife, and now finds that life too much for his age and his aging will. But the power of his recollections, the clarity and force of his language, the past that he evokes and brings close for Patrick—all reveal the underlying ambivalence of McGuane's vision, his reluctance to let the old West go completely free.

The same ambivalence is revealed more directly in the descriptions of Patrick's horsemanship, where the narrative tone shifts markedly to one that is serious, matter-of-fact, plainly detailed. The descriptions reveal both McGuane's intimacy with the ritual, and his belief in the worth and measure of that ritual: "She was young. And when he pitched the saddle up on her, he held the cinch, girth and billets so that nothing would slap and start her pulling back. Today he tried her in a grazing bit to get her nose out a little; he had been riding her on a higher-ported bit, and she was collecting her head too much" (19). And once atop the horse, Patrick "proves his pudding," connects himself with the old West from his vantage point in the new:

> Patrick changed his weight from stirrup to stirrup, felt her compensate, then stopped her. She fidgeted a moment, waited, then let the tension go out of her muscles. He moved her out again to the right. All she gave him was her head; so he stopped her, drew her nose each way nearly to his boot, then made a serpentine track across the pasture, trying to get a gradual curve throughout her body in each of her turns. The rowels on his spurs were loose enough that they chinked with her gaits. Patrick used spurs like a pointing finger, pressing movement into a shape, never striking or gouging. On horseback, unlike any other area of his life, he never lost his temper, which, in horsemen, is the final mark of the amateur. (19-20)

There is nothing skittish, nothing flighty, nothing existentially cool about the language here; instead, there is detail

that is authoritative, realistic, unmediated by the distractions of Patrick's normal world: "I love this scene. It has no booze or women in it, he rejoiced."

In the end, Patrick cannot locate himself in this Deadrock world, cannot overcome the disjunctures of place and event and escapes to Spain, to an alternate vision, an alternate dream or myth. He abandons the West, or at least the new West, abandons his home ("he never came home again"), gives it up as lost to the ways of a culture more alien than the one he runs off to. But he carries with him those traces of the familial and regional past—family and region are inextricably bound up in one another—taking them as things of value, things worth the cost of transportation.

A similar pattern emerges in *Something to be Desired,* which describes Lucien Taylor's flight from self and from his past. Here, the "cowboy outsider" returns to a place at once his own and oddly inherited, a place dotted with images familiar, disturbing, evocative, a place (like Taylor) in flux. The ranch that becomes his, itself a reminder of the West that was, possesses its own living artifact, the hired hand, W. T. Austinberry, who walked "with one elbow held out from his body like the old-timers one saw when Lucien was a boy. He had jinglebobs on his spurs, which tinkled merrily as he went. How Lucien loved this vaguely ersatz air of the old days!" (37). Austinberry is a cowboy-manqué, a reproduction in living, breathing color of a past that Taylor (like his son) read about in those "true stories of the American West." It is sadly appropriate that Austinberry is seduced, and ultimately destroyed, by a figure of the New West, the New Age, the New Reality.

Taylor understands the disparity between what was and what is in the American space he inhabits, and thus his story is generally told in a voice that is mocking, and self-mocking. But the landscape of the West has its undeniable power. When Taylor and Austinberry ride out (note the vantage point—on horseback—the fulfillment of ritual) to "gather up some year-lings," they also ride *up* into the foothills, a perspective that allows them a certain distance and that allows Taylor to "lose his sense of irony":

The two men ascended to the flat top of the first bench. They could look down from here and see the broad plan of the ranch with clarity, as well as the ascent of the agrarian valley floor to the imperial rock of the Crazies. The whole thing was forged together by glacial buttresses and wedges of forested soil that climbed until stone or altitude discouraged the vegetation. In springtime the high wooded passes exhaled huge clouds of pollen like smoke from hidden fires, which in a sense they were. These sights seemed to draw Lucien's life together. (37)

Both the language and the experience illuminate; the discrete parts of Taylor's existence cohere in these moments of authentic, substantial wonder. Passages like these are moments of rest, of tonal pause where the reader, and McGuane's hero, can catch his breath, touch earth, reorient himself to what is real and permanent.

For the irony resumes; McGuane picks up his sharp satiric voice, turning Lucien Taylor from rancher to spa owner—another user of the landscape, another symbol of the new West mentality. The portrait of Taylor here is, importantly, satiric, blended of light and dark comedy; Taylor is a character in whom we both want and want not to believe. He fails the ranch and the tradition it represents, forfeits "what he had paid to be here alone," that price a little too high. With some reluctance and self-consciousness, Taylor transforms the old into the new-within-the-old, comically reconstructing from odds and ends a symbolic hybrid (his spa) that capitalizes on the old West myths and images Taylor once revered (and, to some degree, still does revere). Finally, Taylor desires only reduction; he covets "an island," something insular, a withdrawal from the American space he originally hoped to reclaim.

Most recently, in the stories in **To Skin a Cat,** McGuane has examined in particular detail life in the new West, examined it from many perspectives and in many voices. In **"Little Extras,"** a young fellow, newly married, caught amid the trappings of the new West—the doublewide trailer being the most evident symbol—loses just about everything worth having: woman, home, self. He learns the lesson of starting out on the new western frontier. In **"The Road Atlas,"** Bill Berryhill, his "gear, all New West," struggles against the intrusive influence of his Yuppie brothers—all Yuppie new West—at the same time that he tries to keep a hold on his ranch and a woman. Here, as in the Deadrock novels, McGuane betrays his affection for the old ways, the old labors that have maintained themselves in the lives of some new westerners; here, he describes Berryhill cutting a yearling out of a herd:

> The steer just stopped and took things in. The steer moved and Red [his horse] boiled over, squealing and running off. Bill took a light hold of him, rode him in a big circle, then back to the same place on the steer. This time, Red lowered himself and waited; and when the cow moved he sat right hard on his hocks, broke off, stopped hard, and came back inside the cow. Now he was working, his ears forward, his eyes bright. This little horse was such a cow horse, he sometimes couldn't stand the pressure he put on himself. The steer then threw a number nine in his tail and bolted. Red stopped it right in front of the herd. He was low all over, ready to move anywhere. Bill tipped his head and saw the glint of eye and the bright flare at his nostrils. (150)

Even though the language in the majority of these stories is noticeably more down-to-earth, more tempered and more confident and more *mature,* McGuane seems to tip his hand in such passages as these, as if he settles in to this kind of description, seats himself, finds a good purchase.

In other stories, elements of the old and the new West figure in various ways. In **"Partners,"** a story of the white-collar, Yuppie new West, the central character, Dean Robinson, finally "gets Western," his character built upon a proof in performance, upon a violent, physical proving of self. In **"Like a Leaf,"** an old rancher (who in some ways could be Patrick Fitzpatrick's grandfather) involves himself with a wild woman, a sort of sexual outlaw, an attractive Calamity Jane, and watches as that involvement grows crazy, outrageous, ultimately fatal. After she sexually buys her way into an old prison on the outskirts of Deadrock (a prison that once held "famous Western outlaws"), the woman takes on these new West desperadoes, services them, and then is shot by the old-timer, who acts out of an almost old West code of ethics: "The little homewrecker kneels at the end of the sandbar and washes herself over and over. When I am certain she feels absolutely clean, I let her have it. I roll her into the pool, where she becomes a ghost of the river trailing beautiful smoky cotton from a hole in her silly head" (54). This sort of ethical violence is countered by the amoral, free-wheeling violence of the title story, which is the story most akin to McGuane's pre-Montana-adoption fiction. Here, McGuane creates the familiar, darkly comic send-ups, from Bobby Decatur, the mock-cowboy from Deadrock who longs to be a pimp; to his mother, Emily, who lives in New York City and dresses like Dale Evans. The jazzed-up life of Decatur is a mess of deceit and abuse and egotistic nastiness, a life that seeks adventure but swirls downward into death, into a dismal, unheroic end in the symbol of all that is not-the-West-within-the-West: California.

Even when McGuane is not writing solely or particularly of the American West in his fiction, the influence of that geography works itself into that fiction. In *The Bushwhacked Piano,* for instance, Nicholas Payne, taking what he calls the "Rand McNally approach to self-discovery," occupies various portions of that American space, moving through Michigan, into Montana, and on to the South and to Florida. Payne is an escapee from these lesser regions, his character an awkward juxtaposition of the comic and the genuine; he pursues, he perceives, and occasionally he *does.* The Montana portion of his travels is filled with the same sort of ironic quality that infuses McGuane's fiction throughout: the Fitzgeralds' ranch, the Double Tepee, is a comic rendition of what a ranch should be; even its history is a commentary on the changes wrought in this part of the republic:

> The Fitzgeralds' Double Tepee Ranch, whose twin triangle brand aroused local cowboys to call it wishfully

the Squaw Tits, sat on a bench of fat bottom land in a bend of the Shields River somewhere between Bangtail Creek and Crazyhead Creek. It was one of the many big holdings whose sale was consummated through the pages of the *Wall Street Journal*. The ranch had been founded, under its present name, by Ansel Brayton, a drover from New Mexico who had brought the earliest herds this far north. It was sold—through the *Wall Street Journal*—by Ansel Brayton's grandson, a well-known Hialeah faggot. (68)

And Nicholas Payne sees other "curious things happening in the American West. For instance, at the foot of the Belt Mountains, a young man who had earlier committed the stirring murder of a visiting Kuwait oil baron, ate from a tin and marked '*mudder*' at his captors" (119). And when Payne goes to buy a pair of boots, he gets this spiel: "'Here's a number that sells real well here in Big Sky Country. It's all-American made from veal leather with that ole Buffalo Bill high stovepipe top. I can give you this boot in buff-ruff, natural kangaroo or antique gold—'" (49). This is not a place for the self-discoverer, at least not for one like Payne, who still holds to certain mythic conceptions of the West. No wonder that **The Bushwacked Piano,** the first book in which McGuane really touches down in Montana, offers the least sympathetic, the most ironic treatment of that terrain. And no wonder that Payne tires of this West, begins to "lose interest" and heads South. When he tires of Florida (or vice versa), his Hudson Hornet is headed toward the "interior of the continent," perhaps *back* to the high lonesome.

One of McGuane's finest comic send-ups of the new western character appears in **Ninety-Two in the Shade,** the novel least attached to the American West. McGuane gives us Olie Slatt, a loud but no-larger-than-life new westerner plunked down among the Florida Keys, bellowing a mock-folkloric, mock-heroic boast to the other contestants in the pie-eating competition:

> "*I am Olie Slatt. And don't you ever forget it. I mine for subbituminous low-sulphur coal in the Bull Mountains of Roundup, Montana, where they have to blast through twenty feet of sandstone to reach the vein. We have two spoils bands with eight slopes and four different strata arrangements. I'm damned proud of that and I'm going to win today. Don't you ever forget it.*" (92)

Slatt is a miner, the new and disreputable figure on the landscape of the American West; mining, in McGuane's West, is always the work of last resort, of least value.

What a significant irony, then, that Slatt is the final arbiter of justice when things get truly western between Thomas Skelton and Nichol Dance: Skelton, the would-be "horse-man of light," Dance, the latter-day incarnation of the American outlaw, a variation on Charlie Starkweather (the outlaw of the *new* American West) with his Nebraska outrage. In the end, when Dance, acting out his private, bizarre ethic, shoots Skelton, Slatt closes the novel by bringing in his "prize"—the Western lawman cleaning up his territory—hammering Dance's head to a pulp in the process (though shooting Dance is what Slatt "first thought he owed the republic").

This image of the outlaw is used with particular effect and purpose in **Panama,** a book set wholly in the Florida Keys, yet a book emphatically informed by western (both old and new western) images and influences. Although the locale is nonwestern, the novel's plot re-enacts an old West model. Charlie Pomeroy, dissipated, "exhausted" rock figure (a "performer" of sorts), looks to replay the cowboy role, constantly "trying to act like a cowboy," although realizing that "The real cowboys are all in drugstores" (145). At one and the same time, he is the do-gooding sheriff, running the old "get out of town" routine with the perverse agent; and he is the outlaw himself, pursued, harassed by "the law."

For a central symbol, McGuane appropriately borrows perhaps the quintessential western outlaw, Jesse James, who intrudes into McGuane's Florida with a striking, powerful directness. Pomeroy models himself on James, lives imitatively, makes judgments based on a confused notion of James's nature. Pomeroy must convince himself that James is not alive, that he died with the blast from Robert Ford's gun; he must also convince himself that his own father in fact lives, that the physical presence who calls himself Pomeroy's father is not the manifestation of Jesse James, but is instead the very real incarnation of family. The Jesse Jameses of this republic, of our historical West, are dead; what we have as replacements are the Charlie Starkweathers. The outlaw has become the mass murderer; the myth has become the unglamorous, brutal banality.

To accept the new West, says McGuane, we must first deny the complete, continued existence of the old. He does this in his fiction, moving in and out of regions, in and out of voices, but always trailing behind him a fond remembrance of and a partial reverence for the ways of that old West. "The West," writes McGuane again in **"Roping, from A to B,"** "is getting to be a number of things." Writing about the West also "is getting to be a number of things." There are writers who write seriously of the historical West, who examine and re-examine the figures, stories, myths of the old West, revising our sense of history. Some write of the contemporary West, in the light cast by their memory of the old West; others describe a new landscape peopled by new breeds of westerners, many of whom bear the legacy of that historical West. Still others describe new economies of being, new relationships between land and inhabitant, new histories being crafted. For these latter writers, especially, Thomas McGuane has made their work easier, in fact, made it possible. By struggling with his own ambivalence, by working through his own sense of connection and disconnection with the West and its baggage of myth and belief, and by removing the patina of our national, republican nostaglia, McGuane has opened up the West to reexploration and eventual reaffirmation by its newest fiction writers.

NOTES

1. For other considerations of McGuane's use of language, see Jerome Klinkowitz's *The New American Novel of Manners: The Fiction of Richard Yates, Dan Wakefield, and Thomas McGuane*; and Jon Wallace's "The Language Plot of Thomas McGuane's *Ninety-Two in the Shade.*" Klinkowitz argues that McGuane, among others, renders "the semiotics of a culture . . . artistically craftable by making use of the language of manners" (155). Wallace, on the other hand, focuses on McGuane's descriptions of technical tasks, seeing the technical language used in those descriptions as private "codes" that locate and reveal character.

WORKS CITED

Carter, Albert Howard III. "Thomas McGuane: An Interview." *fiction international*, 4/5, (1975): 50/62.

Kittredge, William, and Steven M. Krauzer. "Writers of the New West." *TriQuarterly* 48 (Spring 1980): 5-14.

Klinkowitz, Jerome. *The New American Novel of Manners: The Fiction of Richard Yates, Dan Wakefield, and Thomas McGuane*. Athens: U of Georgia P, 1986.

McGuane, Thomas. *An Outside Chance: Essays on Sport*. New York: Farrar, 1980.

——. *The Bushwhacked Piano*. New York: Simon, 1971.

——. *Ninety-Two in the Shade*. New York: Farrar, 1973.

——. *Nobody's Angel*. New York: Random, 1981.

——. *Panama*. New York: Farrar, 1978.

——. *Something to be Desired*. New York: Random, 1984.

——. *To Skin a Cat*. New York: Dutton, 1986.

Wallace, Jon. "The Language Plot of Thomas McGuane's *Ninety-Two in the Shade.*" *Critique* 29, 2 (1988): 111-20.

Brad Knickerbocker (review date 7 October 1992)

SOURCE: "Midlife Misery in Cow Country," in *Christian Science Monitor*, October 7, 1992.

[In t*he following review of* Nothing But Blue Skies, *Knickerbocker praises McGuane's characterizations, stating*"The strength of McGuane's characters is the compassion they elicit."]

Thomas McGuane writes like a dream . . . in a nightmarish world.

His characters are deep, real, funny, and intelligent. Their dialogue is sharp and sweet, clever (in the best sense) without being contrived. They move in a landscape of rich detail, in town and out, following a trout stream.

They are also desperate and at times out of control. Not out of McGuane's control but their own, on paths of painful discovery often verging on the self-destructive.

It is a path McGuane himself acknowledges having followed, before he stabilized into writing and ranching in Montana, which is no doubt why he reads so well the current manifestation of men's search for balance between action and intellect.

Nothing But Blue Skies centers on Frank Copenhaver, a successful, middle-aged entrepreneur in Montana real estate and cattle, who has managed to disprove his disapproving father's prediction that he would never rise above his carousing youth.

It's all falling apart now, starting with his marriage, and he's beginning to feel "that something inside had come completely undone." He chatters on about adjustable mortgages and arbitrage stock selling as he drives his wife of 20 years to the airport for the last time.

Alone now, his business begins to go to pot. His friends and brother are concerned but unable to stop his descent into desperate sex and alcohol-fueled craziness, which accelerate the spiral. "I have underestimated what a delicate thing life really is," he tells a woman friend.

It's not what he wants, and he moves on through the dream looking for solace and answers. He thinks the steadying rock in this turbulent flow is his college-student daughter, whom he has taught to fly-fish expertly. There is a day of heartbreaking father-child intimacy and love at a favorite trout stream in the Gallatin Valley with this sweet, strong, and wryly funny young woman:

> "'The only things that undermine my happiness are things I can't lay hands on,' [he tells his daughter].

'Like what?' said Holly.

'Oh, I don't know.'

'Just give me an example.'

'I can't.'

'Is regret one of them?'

'Sure.'

'Do you ever get lonely?'

'Of course. That's a bad one. It's not like other things that strengthen you. Loneliness makes you weaker, makes you worse. I'm guessing that enough of it makes you cruel.'

Two more pale morning duns and we can call it quits,' said Holly [referring to the dry flies used in trout fishing]. She turned and looked at her father in thought. She smiled. He shrugged. She laughed, reached over and squeezed his nose. 'Poor little friend,' she said."

Before long, that relationship too is challenged. The strength of McGuane's characters is the compassion they elicit, even the louts and leeches who are drawn attractively and with sympathy. They are not caricatures.

After Frank swipes and wrecks the truck of a romantic rival he encounters in a bar, he offers to buy the man a new pickup if the charges are dropped. Frank goes home to get his checkbook, then comes outside to find that the man has left:

"Darryl was gone and a note fluttered on the sidewalk gate: 'Forget it.'"

As disturbing and depressing as this book mostly is, there is also plenty of the kind of sharp and ironic humor McGuane concocted in earlier novels, short stories, and screenplays. Frank bumps into a buddy on the street and says:

"'I'm one of those guys you read about who's not really in touch with his feelings.'

'Hey, me either! [comes the reply.] I don't want to be in touch with my feelings. What a can of worms!'"

McGuane's own can of worms—at least the fictional one as depicted in *Blue Skies* and some of his earlier works—may be a bit raunchy for some tastes. One wonders if he could put together a story about, say, a marriage that is not dysfunctional, and make it interesting and worthwhile, more than a counterpoint to whatever disaster his antihero finds himself in.

But there's no doubting that he's one of the best fiction writers in the country today, proving at the very least that a guy who spends half his time raising cows 2,000 miles from New York has just as much to say—and can say it just as well—as anybody around.

William Kittredge (review date 11 October 1992)

SOURCE: "Get Real," in *Los Angeles Times Book Review*, October 11, 1992, pp. 1, 11.

[*In the following review of* Nothing But Blue Skies, *Kittredge praises McGuane's ability to evoke the pathos of the disappearing natural landscape of the American West.*]

Tom McGuane's work has always been vibrant with the pleasures of ironic language, play and chase, and quick with the kind of brokenhearted humor that mirrors large-scale fracturing inside our society. We can't stand behind many of our preconceptions any more. The so-called nuclear family, for instance, mom and dad and the kids, the mortgage, the old folks back home, is a kind of vanishing species. And in Montana, where McGuane's new novel, *Nothing But Blue Skies,* is set, sometimes we can't even fish the same old streams. They're just gone.

"The creek was gone . . . ferns were dying on the banks, and here and there were the remains of fish, picked over by birds and racoons. . . . Caterpillars with which the farmer had built up a broad dike to impound the stream were parked nearby. . . . Frank thought it was pretty unlucky to go fishing and find the stream had been stolen, particularly when you needed the stream for more than just fishing."

Frank Copenhaver is a boyish middle-aged entrepreneur who has drifted from aimlessness to venture capitalism, where he has found ways to meet his challenges with wit and boldness, and enjoy them. "In some ways he loved money; he certainly loved the sedative effects of pursuing it . . . he had been forced to conclude that nothing got him out of bed with the smooth surge of power—as the Chrysler ad used to say—like the pursuit of the almighty dollar."

Now Frank's having trouble doing business because his life has come unglued. His emotional beans have spilled. His wife Gracie, a sharp Cajun beauty, daughter of a furniture dealer from Bayou Teche in southern Louisiana, is leaving him (she once said he made her "feel invisible"), and Frank can't "bring himself to make his calls."

He's lost touch with his set of reasons why some things are more important than others. He's disoriented and suffering a malaise that certain psychology professionals call "Narrative Dysfunction" (the inability to define your own true story, which you ought to be inhabiting). "It was becoming hard for him to not think of work as something completely made up, no matter how remunerative."

While driving Gracie to the airport, Frank detours past his properties—the medical clinic, the historic but defunct Kid Royale Hotel, the mini-storage units—as if trying to reassure himself of his own existence (worth, actuality).

"Gracie," Frank says, "I just know you're going to hit the ground running."

It's Frank who's running. He climbs an apple tree in the night, and peeps at one of Gracie's friends, a travel agent named Lucy Dyer, as she undresses. "She dug her fingers into her scalp and pushed them up through her hair, loosening and letting it fall in a wonderful declaration of day's end. Frank sighed in his tree and rested his head against the trunk. This was serene."

Frank confesses his peeping. Lucy is as unmoored as he is. "'It's something how lonely life is,'" she says.

"Man, thought Frank, she just chirped that out."

They are soon to bed. His response to her, Lucy says, is "harder than Chinese arithmetic." Sex, it seems, is fine and actual. The trouble lies in thinking about it afterward.

But nothing is emotionally useful until Frank is driven to an accurate look at what's happening in his West, which might be called make-believe all around. Our reality, in the American West and everywhere, is being spun into a cloth all too virtual (read Disneylandish, false). Frank finds the same inauthenticity in his own life. Without purposes driven by love (politics), he is pointless.

"I want to make you *see*," Joseph Conrad wrote, in a famous pronouncement about the purposes of his storytelling. And making sense of what we see, we come to understand the story. Tom McGuane works in the same way, as in "A covey of partridges took to the air in an ivory rush, brown terrestrial birds against the blue of outer space." And, later on: "At the bend, the wild irises looked as if they would topple into the stream. The narrow band of mud at the base of the sedges revealed a well-used muskrat trail, and on this band stood a perfectly motionless blue heron, head back like the hammer of a gun. It flexed its legs slightly, croaked, sprang into wonderfully slow flight, a faint whistle of pinions, then disappeared over the top of the wall of grasses as though drawn down into its mass."

Such instances of flight constitute a motif which helps us respond—brown birds, blue sky, and then a blue heron and

sedges. They are examples of the care with which this story has been organized around its meanings (the world is splendid without us, so why can't we learn to fly, or figure a way to be just occasionally joyous).

At first Frank is infuriated by Western phoniness. Everybody, it seems, is looking for a life, as in "a picture of a movie star in *People* magazine who was attending a Crow Indian sun dance ceremony, hanging by thongs through his chest from the lodge-poles of a prodigious tepee." And it's not just the show-biz types. Frank typifies cowboys as "drunken, wife-beating, snoose-chewing geeks with big belt buckles and catfish mustaches. They spend all their time reading magazines about themselves. College Professors drive out and tell them they're a dying breed." Inhabiting fantasy.

When Frank's daughter and trout-fishing companion Holly takes up with a right-wing nitwit, Frank is driven to begin thinking politically. "More than anything, he heard the doleful howl of the saws in the shattered forest. He knew how the soul would be rent in hauling off the trees.... It was probably time, he thought, for Americans to learn to love pavement with all their hearts."

Sometimes spoiled and kicking, and as often honest and creative (typically American, we think), Frank is like a child. His graces (love of wife, friends, Holly, fishing, business) have always proceeded from the idea that life was properly play. Now his playpen has been trashed.

Frank may not be able to save much of his beloved fisherman's world. But, as we watch him think about trying, we come to at least encounter the notion that maybe we ought to do something about saving the pretty world we inhabit.

I've been acquainted with McGuane for at least a couple of decades (we live in the same state, even though his ranch is 250 miles away), and all that time he's been writing about our emotional dislocations like a crown prince of the language. I've pleasured in his wit, been jealous of his talent, and loved his storytelling. But I've never been so moved to admire his work as in this story that encourages us to realize the world is not only our playpen but also our sacred trust.

David Streitfield (essay date 25 October 1992)

SOURCE: "McGuane Mellows," in *Washington Post Book World*, Vol. XXII, No. 43, October 25, 1992, p. 15.

[*In the following essay, Streitfield discusses McGuane's current lifestyle on his Montana ranch with his wife and children, contrasting it with his long-time reputation as a drinker and womanizer.*]

Sometime in the past couple of years, Tom McGuane completed the transition from aging Bad Boy to youngish Grand Old Man. You can chart the transition by looking, first, at the back of his old 1978 novel, *Panama*: It's a photo of McGuane at the tiller of a boat, long hair askew, hunting for something, looking manic. Then examine the back of his latest, *Nothing But Blue Skies.* There the 52-year-old author is at rest, head propped on his arm. It's a portrait of a mature rancher in his Sunday best.

Panama was, as it happens, a key book for McGuane, the end of his early period. He had written three other novels by then—*The Sporting Club, The Bushwhacked Piano* and *Ninety-Two in the Shade*—three hat tricks that won him considerable fame in the early '70s.

The celebrity culture in this country was then still in its infancy, which was a good thing: A little more attention and McGuane might have been destroyed as a writer. As it was, his exploits with various women—actresses Elizabeth Ashley and Margot Kidder, for two—and taste for hijinks made for sensational copy.

"I had vivid good times then, and still do in other ways. But I'm not as newsworthy," says the writer. The reality never quite matched the reputation anyway. "I got a lot of work done then. I was writing all day everyday as I've been doing since I was a teenager.

"I had a spell of really being out in the streets, but I thought I noticed everybody else was out there, too," says McGuane. "I've never been that bold differentiating myself from the quotidian. It was just what everybody was doing, everyone I knew. Admittedly, I wasn't in Cleveland. . . . There was this thing called 'hanging out.' People don't really do that anymore, but then it was an official activity."

McGuane long ago got tired of talking about his past. For a while, it seemed all anyone wanted to know about. "I've been married to my wife for 16 years, and no one ever asks about her," he comments. "They want to pry about my ex-wife [Kidder], women I used to go out with. My poor old wife is never even inquired about."

So how is Laurie, anyway?

"She's fine."

Middle-period McGuane—four novels published over the last decade—takes place in the state he's been living in for the last two decades, Montana. "This has been a good milieu to a point," he says. "Sometimes I wish we had greater diversity of people where I live. Everyone's so laconic up there. When you get out, it seems pretty exciting because people are so wound up."

Why are they so quiet?

"They don't have conversational skills. It's not a valued thing. In fact, they're very suspicious of people who talk much. That's a problem for people who go out West from town to town with some new plan. The locals see some yammering guy from the East Coast and they're immediately suspicious."

Which must mean they're suspicious of writers, too.

"Yeah. They certainly don't think it's a real job. I'm always making excuses."

Montana, like most everywhere in the West, is the scene of a fair amount of environmental combat these days. McGuane has joined the fray, both in fiction (a key character in *Nothing But Blue Skies* wants to prevent all the rivers from leaving the state) and in real life. He's a member of the board of American Rivers, a D.C.-based organization dedicated to the wild and scenic rivers system as well as urban rivers, and to the preservation of riverine species.

"Aquatic species are crashing at much deeper rate than nonaquatic species. Rivers are really collecting all the bad things we're doing and intensifying them. It seems to be a real good place to focus on environmental issues. Plus, I'm just a river lover."

Nothing But Blue Skies is less, however, about the environment than an older war—the one between the sexes. The hero is a familiar McGuane type, a guy who can't co-exist with women and won't live without them.

"I don't think this relationship has ever been stable," McGuane says. "Certainly not in my experience, or my parents' or my aunts' or uncles'. It's always very charged. There are so few complacent relationships between lovers on any level—and if there were, they'd be inappropriate for fiction. Fiction is not about stability."

McGuane notes that "I have friends whose love lives are excruciatingly entropic. They're like people that have a vintage Jaguar that never really runs—it's a pretty idea, but you can't get to the store in it. They're always trying to fix these relationships, or being counseled, or trying separation, or trying a vacation. There doesn't seem to be any yield without a tremendous amount of energy input."

Robert M. Adams (review date 3 December 1992)

SOURCE: "Cornering the Market," in *New York Review of Books*, Vol. 39, No. 20, December 3, 1992, pp. 14-16.

[*In the following review, Adams gives* Nothing But Blue Skies *an unfavorable review, saying its similarity to McGuane's previous stories renders it unmemorable.*]

Thomas McGuane is mainly from Montana and has written, over the last twenty years, more than seven novels and several books of short stories set against this background. These are not cowboy-and-Indian novels, nor are they set in the familiar mean streets of the desert metropolis. The center of McGuane's universe is the good-sized town or small city of Deadrock, Montana, and his theme is the aching problem of the American male, what to do with himself. Perhaps it is McGuane's misfortune that he has written so many books, because after four or five the generic familiarity of the plots and the similarities of the heroes become very evident. McGuane's prose is swift and sharp, often belligerent. He can be very funny and also deeply disgusting. But he does write in a recognizable manner of speech.

McGuane's hero tends to be a self-conscious actor and rather proud of his reputation as a bad boy. The first novel, which set a pattern for many of the later ones, was titled *The Bushwacked Piano*. It followed the adventures of one Nicholas Payne, whose devotion to Ann Fitzgerald led him to break into her parents' house, and then to put forward a scheme for building outsized beehives that no one wanted. (A major aim of the people who invested in it was to get rid of the troublesome builder as quickly as possible.) These hilarious activities are interrupted by a major operation for hemorrhoids, described in painful detail. The novel *Something to be Desired* is similarly slam-bang, with the main character, Lucien Taylor, hung up between two girls, one with powerful impulses to homicide. He solves his problems by getting rid of both—which leaves the reader in doubt about his attachment in the first place to either. What they think of him as they depart we are not given to know. I have not found McGuane's tales various enough to be particularly memorable. Very often his narrative dashes from episode to episode, and the reader is as likely to wince at the end as to laugh.

The latest volume, *Nothing But Blue Skies,* deals with an older but still unsettled version of Nicholas Payne or Lucien Taylor. Frank Copenhaver rattles in much the same way as his predecessors around the dusty streets of Deadrock, Montana. He is a man of miscellaneous business interests, who has acquired by his middle years a string of assorted enterprises, such as a hotel, a medical clinic, a ranch and some cattle, as well as a mixed bag of stock-market holdings. He has a grown daughter in the state university at Missoula and a wife, Gracie, who, as the story opens, has just left him. This recent breakup of his marriage has left

Frank in a particularly truculent and touchy, as well as a randy, mood. He picks fights with cowboys and gets thrown for a time into jail. He drinks to excess; he smashes up a lot of earth-moving equipment in a midnight fight on a back-country road. He also manages to copulate with a goodly number of women he picks up, near and around Deadrock, Montana. The more of these diversions he indulges in, the more deeply his business affairs sink into disorder.

In other words, Frank Copenhaver appears to be suffering from a standard case of middle-aged jealousy based largely on a standard case of middle-class egocentricity. None of the people of Deadrock is particularly complex psychologically, but as the story works out, it appears that Frank had been using his multiple business interests to hold off his wife's efforts at intimacy. Meanwhile their daughter, sensing her parents' growing estrangement, had feigned interest in a loathsome suitor whom she knew her parents would unite in despising. Her calculations prove exactly right. The suitor is dispatched, her parents clinch. Too bad if it sounds like a plot put together with an Erector Set, but that's what it reads like.

Thomas McGuane with Deborah Houy (interview date January-February 1993)

SOURCE: "Thomas McGuane Speaks," in *Buzzworm*, Vol. V, No. 1, January-February, 1993, pp. 32, 34-35.

[*In the following interview, McGuane discusses his ideas about and activism in environmentalist issues as well as the "green" movement, which he claims is "the first sort of quasi-religious movement which cuts across class and economic lines."*]

Thomas McGuane—great American novelist, rancher and fly-fisherman—was in Denver recently on a promotional tour for his new novel, **Nothing But Blue Skies**. *McGuane is the author of eight novels, including* **The Sporting Club,** **Ninety-Two in the Shade** *and* **Keep the Change,** *as well as several screenplays (* **The Missouri Breaks, Tom Horn, Rancho Deluxe**). **Nothing But Blue Skies** *is set in near-millennial Montana, where members of the "granola underworld" and Wise Use fanatics are beginning to outnumber the cowboys and Indians. McGuane, who is on the board of the nonprofit conservation group American Rivers, spoke with* Buzzworm *Assistant Editor Deborah Houy.*

[*Buzzworm:*] *Your new book is wonderful. It has a lot of environmental . . .*

[McGuane:] Alertness to it, maybe? Good. Like a lot of other people in this country who have experienced the collapse of traditional religion, as well as other kinds of traditional values, my interest in conservation—as I like to call it, to keep from producing more volatility in Montana—my interest in *conservation*, I guess, has really replaced any other kind of religious presence in my life. I think I've been like that all my life, but I've started to codify that a little bit. I always make *that* the sort of over-arching spiritual presence of anything that I'm writing.

The kind of personal desperation of **Blue Skies'** principal character [a Montana businessman/rancher] and other characters in the book—well, it seems to me their *escape* from that emotional dead end is always seen in the natural world. I think that's been true of my writing since my first book, which came out in the 1960s.

Don't you think religion started as a reaction to the natural world?

I think it derives from observing the natural world. But I think that when you reach another plateau of spiritual bankruptcy—which we have in this country, discovering that entrepreneurial capitalism is not the way to personal happiness—we have to turn to something else. And I think, for a lot of people, it's not going to be traditional religion. And I am one of those people.

Do you think people are going to turn to something else? There's that great scene in **Blue Skies** *where Lance [a Wise Use fanatic] says, "How can we turn to something in Montana that hasn't worked in Russia?"*

I think capitalism is our system, and it's as viable a system as exists. I'm not opposed to that. But we have to understand the limitedness of our global environment, and start trying to do what we do in the context of understanding that. I think what we come up against as environmentalists is that kind of societal denial. These things are such banalities now, but an example is the Bush administration denying that there's a hole in the ozone layer . . . denying that global warming is a perceivable reality. All these things we've been through.

How can we save the environment if we have to keep expanding to keep the economy going? Do you buy Al Gore's argument that we can expand our economy by promoting solar power, for example?

Oh, I buy some of it. My problem is I don't buy any of the existing systems entirely, including Al Gore's. I think we have to learn to do with less. I think excessive materialism derives from spiritual desperation.

Filling the emptiness?

Yes. The other part of the situation—if I could, for example, just raise river consciousness, I think I would be adding my small part to allaying spiritual desperation, and combating materialism. I mean, it's famous that religiously fulfilled people are remarkable in their lack of materialism. And this has always been true.

How do you explain the kind of religion they had at the Republican National Convention?

I can't explain that. I guess—if I took a shot at it—I explain that as a form of addiction. We've been on one drug or another for a long time, and there's always a crash at the end and this period of spiritual desolation. We've just come out of the junk bond era and this wild enthusiastic materialism. We've never really put our shoulders to the wheel of materialism quite like we did in the 1980s. We just said: This is what everybody should be doing. Greed is great. We've never before just sort of stepped up to the plate and said: Let's all do it as hard as we can. And we hit a wall.

A wall, or an abyss? In your essay in **Heaven Is Under Our Feet** *[a collection of essays benefitting the Walden Woods Project], you say: "Abyss-front property is always popular." When you stare into the abyss, what do you see?*

Well, that's obviously an extremely ironic comment, and it can't be answered as a straight question.

Speaking of irony, when I read your novels, I never know whether to laugh or cry. Which are you doing while you're writing them?

Both. My earliest heroes were the Russian comic writers, particularly Gogol. And when you're reading Gogol, that's how you're supposed to be responding.

And how do you respond to life?

That way. It's hilarious, and I love the comic part of life, but there's always this kind of *gravitas* of mortality and delusion.

I always think your novels are a lot like Walker Percy's. Percy said that the question he tries to answer is: Why does man feel so sad in the 20th century? Is that the question you're trying to answer?

Well, I'm very flattered to be even momentarily compared to Walker Percy. Because I'm always being compared—without much point, I think—to Hemingway. I don't get that one at all.

You're much better than Hemingway.

Oh, good. Why is man so sad? Did you see in *Forbes*, of all things, a special issue called "Why do we feel so bad?" Alfred Kazin had a wonderful piece in there, and Saul Bellow had a very interesting piece. Why are we so sad? Well, I think that we're sad because we've dedicated ourselves to things that do not have a lot of long-term meaning. I just would like to think that my countrymen are smart enough to get onto that. Now there's a whole school of thought that they're too stupid to ever figure that out.

In **Nothing But Blue Skies,** *Frank is at a McDonald's restaurant, and he says: "We're down among them now." I assume that's an ironic comment. And there's another line where Frank says he hates the tone of his voice when he's "talking to the salt of the earth."*

Yeah. I'd have to see the context. I mean, I would never think that, and you would never think that. And I would never say it, and you would never say it, as a straight remark. Comic conventions have to be understood. To look at it humorlessly would be, really, to reverse its meaning and then make me responsible for it.

Okay. To get back to your point, people aren't following the road to happiness, not because they're too stupid, but because...?

I'm feeling—in this sense—optimistic, that increasingly people will see that what we've been doing for a long time is not going to work anymore. Now there's the doomsday time-table, which says: Yes, but they won't find it out in time. There's also the New Inquisition that says: Yes, but left to their own devices they won't find it out in time, so us cognoscenti are going to *tell* them what to do. That's the sort of new hipness I find extremely alarming. I am sort of a populist, and I wish that it would go faster, I wish people would understand some of the more permanent values that are available to us, in our backyards. But they weren't put on the planet to satisfy my sense of how rapidly things should occur.

I think there's a growing green movement in this country. And it won't surprise me a bit, if I live to a ripe old age, to find that being the dominant party. I actually believe that. It's the first sort of quasi-religious movement which cuts across class and economic lines. Not perfectly, but it does it better than the Episcopal church, for example. And it's a religious movement. It's a religious and a political movement, and it's very powerful. And it's a good movement, which is important.

Do you think the West is not so much a place as a destination—that what is important is getting there?

There's a great battle, you know, between the New Westerners, the Patty Limerick school—which is very interesting—who say that the West is not a process, it's a place. We know this argument very well. I think it's kind of both.

In **Blue Skies,** *Frank is a Montana rancher who talks about smelling the water in the sagebrush, and he says: "I love it here. At least it's a place to start." I agree, it's a place to start. And then where do you go from there?*

Well, I was thinking—vis-à-vis the previous question—about a wonderful thing that John Cheever said. He said that man is a better traveler than a farmer. I don't know if you've read Bruce Chatwin's *The Songlines*, but the sort of subtext of that book is that the wanderers are the happy people. You know, the wandering herdsmen of Africa. The Homeric Greek characters that were constantly on the move. The cruelties of the world are really generated by the farmers. Now we're in a time where we absolutely idealize the place on Earth kind of thing, where people don't move.

There's a scene in **Nothing But Blue Skies** *making fun of some academics who still believe that farmers are closer to Mother Earth. Don't you think they are?*

Some of them are, but some of them aren't. I have a grain farm up there in Montana—it really belongs to my children. A friend of mine sharecrops this thing—it just fascinates me how much of a businessman he has to be. He spends more time on paperwork than I do?

But don't you think farmers are still closer to the Earth than someone who lives in Manhattan?

Sure. But I think probably what I was doing was undercutting, sort of satirically, the self-righteousness, the hubristicness that fills the agricultural newspapers.

The Wise Use movement?

Well, not only that, but just the general chauvinism of farmers and ranchers—it's almost unbearable sometimes. And the fact that they look out from their piece of ground, and they see somebody with an out-of-state license plate and just *assume* a moral superiority, I have to fight that back a little bit.

Anthropologist Margaret Mead said that problems in modern society stem from the fact that for 99 percent of human history, we've lived in tribes of 30 people or less. And now we don't. Would you agree with that?

Just on my little book tour, I'm beginning to feel that independent bookstores are sort of tribal centers of some kind. I realize this doesn't stand up to *real* scrutiny, except that individual books collect societies around them. And particular kinds of bookstores come to be little societies, especially in urban areas.

But that's a self-selected tribe. That's the amazing thing about tribes—you have to learn to get along with everyone.

Whether you want to be in that tribe or not. I don't think we have tribes anymore. I think we have a lot of nostalgia for tribes. I remember vividly in the 1960s how everyone was searching for this tribalism, which was a little farfetched.

Who are your favorite writers?

Gogol, Chekhov, Turgenev, Saul Bellow.

Kurt Vonnegut says that most people can't use information for anything except entertainment. Do you agree?

No. Charles Olson says that sometimes people want tablets brought down from the mountain, and sometimes they want to go to the beach.

What are you going to do next? Another novel?

No. I plan to go get Mama, and the horse trailers, and be gone for about ten years.

Gregory McNamee (review date July-August 1993)

SOURCE: "The Spirit of the American West," in *Bloomsbury Review*, Vol. 13, No. 4, July-August, 1993, p. 14.

[*In the following favorable review of* Nothing But Blue Skies, *McNamee describes McGuane's novel as "a well-considered study of a man confronting mid-life crisis, and, in the end, overcoming it by sheer force of will."*]

Thomas McGuane has consciously carved out a niche in American literary history as our contemporary Hemingway, which includes tracing the old man's footsteps from place to place and adopting some of his poses: sports fisherman, footloose journalist. In the sixties and seventies he was associated with Key West, another Hemingway haunt, where McGuane kept a house and produced his earliest novels. He had a reputation as a hell-raiser then, seeking to match his distinguished literary ancestor drink for drink, book for book, spouse for spouse.

Twenty years have since passed, and McGuane has mellowed. He now lives on a ranch in the Paradise Valley of western Montana, where he devotes his time to raising cattle, reading, and writing. A mature man in his mid-50s, McGuane has abandoned most of his youthful pursuits, and his roman à clef *Nothing But Blue Skies* shows it.

Frank Copenhaver, the lonely hero—or antihero—of the novel, is a sorry sight to behold. He is lost on that great sea of grass verging on Montana's western mountains near Livingston, where his creator just happens to live. Montana may be the very definition of wide open spaces, but for Frank Copenhaver its vastness more and more resembles a prison with each passing day.

Copenhaver's world is unraveling before his eyes. He is well into his 50s, and the years aren't treating him well. His marriage of many years is imploding; as the novel opens his wife, Gracie, who runs a Cajun restaurant called Amazing Grease, is preparing to leave him for parts unknown. His neo-hippie daughter is dating a man his own age. Copenhaver has taken to driving down back roads screaming, "My empire is falling!" He has also lost connection to the world. A lover of fishing and wilderness, like any true Montanan, he spends his days and nights indoors, making business deals, sending faxes, and poring over *The Wall Street Journal*. All for naught, because—of course—his contracting business is falling to pieces along with the rest of his universe.

How Copenhaver extricates himself from the mess he's made of his life is the meat of McGuane's story. A fully fleshed, believable character, he makes a botch of nearly every attempt, as we all do. He picks barroom fights with big cowboys, taunts local politicians with cries of "fascist," and generally does things just the way he knows he should not. By twists and turns McGuane allows Copenhaver to grope his way to something approaching a happy ending, but not without major pratfalls.

Nothing But Blue Skies is appealing on any number of fronts, certainly more so than McGuane's last novel, *Something to Be Desired*. An especially fine touch is McGuane's respectful treatment of his women characters, another welcome sign of maturity. Copenhaver's wife is thoroughly likable, and he shows no rancor toward her for abandoning him. He has plenty of likable women friends as well, true friends and not mere objects of desire. The most intellectually attractive of them, June, isn't at all "astonished to find out that life was a fight," as the narrator observes. "So her feistiness lacked the indignation, the bruised quality, that gave relationships between men and women these days their peculiar smelliness."

McGuane's new novel is no tour de force, unlike his early novels: *Panama*, *The Sporting Club*, and *Ninety-Two in the Shade*. Youthfully exuberant and cocky, these books made his reputation and earned him those comparisons to

Hemingway in the first place. *Nothing But Blue Skies* is, however, a well-considered study of a man confronting midlife crisis and, in the end, overcoming it by sheer force of will. (In that regard it beats Robert Bly's weepy *Iron John* by a long shot. Frank Copenhaver despises poppsych solutions, remarking "I'm much too old for that sort of thing. The messages of my formative years all came from Little Richard, who never soiled himself with an inner journey.")

Ironic, precise, and in full command of his language, Tom McGuane delivers sharp observations on our deteriorating world, and his new novel is well worth reading.

David Ingram (essay date December 1995)

SOURCE: "Thomas McGuane: Nature, Environmentalism, and the American West," in *Journal of American Studies*, Vol. 29, No. 3, December, 1995, pp. 423-439.

[*In the following essay, Ingram discusses environmentalist themes in McGuane's fiction, stating "In McGuane's writings, nature gives an opportunity for his male protagonists to attempt to recover a sense of original purity and mastery beyond the compromises and power struggles of a competitive society."*]

The recent writings of Thomas McGuane show a particular interest in environmentalist concerns, examining the role played by inherited mythologies of the frontier in the ecology and politics of the contemporary American West. McGuane's explorations reveal complex and ambivalent responses to these subjects, in part liberal, radical and conservative.

This essay will discuss these issues in relation to contemporary American attitudes to nature. The basis for my approach will be to assume that conceptions of "nature" are socially constructed, and that "nature" and "culture" are separate but mutually interdependent. The relationship between human societies and the natural world will therefore be considered as an ongoing process in which the term "nature" must not be wholly subsumed under that of "culture." Environmental history is, as Donald Worster puts it, "a story of reciprocity and interaction rather than of culture replacing nature."[1]

Thomas McGuane's writings tend both to repeat and to question what may be called "traditional" or "Romantic" attitudes to nature. In particular, he combines both aesthetic and utilitarian perspectives: nature as a scene of spiritual restoration through the appreciation of beauty, and as the object of technological mastery and control. In practice, these two approaches are historically interrelated, in that they are both responses to, and constructions of, nature produced within an urban capitalist society. As Walter J. Ong has argued, a necessary precondition for Romantic attitudes to nature is a society that has confidence in its capacity to dominate nature, through the use of the very industrial technologies such attitudes ostensibly reject. In this way, even "when unacknowledged, the feeling of control over nature quiets old fears of being swallowed up by nature. Wordsworth's much advertised surrender to nature is to this extent a by-product of technology. Nature was under surveillance in his world."[2]

The interdependence of urban industrialism and non-utilitarian approaches to nature is a vital counter-argument to the anti-technological reflexes inherent in some ecological thought. Leo Marx's account of the "pastoral interlude" in American writing, for example, defines a "symbolic action which embodies values, attitudes, modes of thought and feeling *alternative* to those which characterize the dynamic, expansionary life-style of modern America"[3] (my italics). Yet, as Perry Miller has shown, a sentimental mystique of nature was not simply an *alternative* to the dominant utilitarian ideology of nineteenth century America, but also its by-product and alibi, in a society in which the natural world came to be seen increasingly as a resource for industrial capitalist exploitation.[4]

Industrialism both produces Romantic attitudes to nature, and is also, from an ecological perspective, a long term threat to its continued healthy existence. Central in this context is the founding American myth of nature as Garden of Eden. In *Under Western Skies*, Donald Worster makes an important break from this inherited mythology: "we can live without the old fantasy of a pristine, inviolate, edenic wilderness—it was, after all, never adequate to the reality of the natural world."[5] Yet the desire for a pristine nature, beyond the reach of human controls, persists in American culture, and is a central feature of Thomas McGuane's work, as his characters seek in nature an original purity in opposition to a corrupting modern civilization. Yet in McGuane's writings, the dangers of evasion implied by this need for pastoral retreat are acknowledged, as are the pleasures and seductions of urban life. As a result, he subjects the ongoing relationship between the human and natural world to skeptical inquiry and ironic disruptions.

II

The contemporary West is explored by McGuane as a site of capitalist competition and technological exploitation, dominated by agribusiness and the global flow of capital. Yet, within this context, the desire persists in his protagonists to experience nature as spiritually redemptive. McGuane's engagement with contemporary Montana also places preservationist politics within a recognition of both the dangers and the potentialities of myths inherited from the Old West.

In the essay **"Some Notes on Montana"** (1992), McGuane comments on the "competition for a prevailing idea of land use" between business interests, and those which favour recreation. The latter views, he argues, tend to be associated by "many ordinary Montanans" with "card-carrying interlopers" from outside the state.[6] McGuane sides with the "conciliatory, ordinary people" against exploitative business interests, the "backyard ward heelers" who eventually "work their polarizing harm" in Congress. In political terms, the essay attacks not so much capitalism itself, as the "entrepreneurial capitalism" promoted by the Reagan government in the 1980s, the "corporate crime wave" which was responsible for the further degradation of the Western environment. The rise in forest clear-cutting, for example, was a defensive reaction by small landowners against the "hostile takeovers" and "junk-bond-fueled gyrations" of the large corporations.[7] McGuane therefore argues from a liberal position against the abuses of a deregulated, *laissez-faire* form of capitalism.

McGuane's views on capitalism are elaborated further in his 1993 interview with *Buzzworm: The Environmental Journal*, in which he cautiously accepts capitalism as an apparently inevitable or unchangeable basis for American society: "I think capitalism is our system, and it's as viable a system as exists. I'm not opposed to that." However, this guarded response really shows his fundamental distrust of all systems—an attitude familiar in many American writers, reminiscent for example of the scepticism expressed in the "Cetology" chapter of *Moby-Dick* (1851). McGuane acknowledges that he does not "buy any of the existing systems entirely. . . ."

Again, McGuane's criticism tends to be not of capitalism *per se*, but of its deregulated form, as people in America discover that "*entrepreneurial* capitalism is not the way to personal happiness" (my italics). Yet this ambivalence is compounded as he goes on to endorse the "growing green movement in this country," which, he predicts, may in future become the dominant party in American politics. Hence there is a need "to understand the limitedness of our global environment," and accordingly to place limits on economic growth: "I think we have to learn to do with less." Yet this questioning of the necessity for economic growth attacks the very foundation of capitalist economics, thereby revealing a central uncertainty within McGuane's environmentalist politics, coming as it does after his earlier, albeit reluctant, acceptance of capitalism as "our system."[8]

This ambivalent and uncertain attitude to capitalism is also evident in the novel *Nothing But Blue Skies* (1993). McGuane's comment in *Buzzworm* that "excessive material-

ism derives from spiritual desperation" is a useful gloss on his most recent novel. Through the figure of Frank Copenhaven, McGuane explores the seductive pleasures and power thrills of the capitalist business world, as a form of second nature:

> In some ways, he loved money; he certainly loved the sedative effects of pursuing it, and if that was all money did for him at this point, it had much to be said for it. The year he tried to escape into bird-watching, into all the intricacies of spring warblers and the company of gentle people, he had been forced to conclude that nothing got him out of bed with quite the smooth surge of power—as the Chrysler ads used to say—like the pursuit of the almighty dollar.[9]

When visiting McDonald's, Frank is seduced by the gratifications and securities offered by conformist passivity: "Splendid to take what you are given." But this moment of acceptance and complicity is typically ironised, and quickly descends into a memory of childhood dependency and sentimental nostalgia:

> He smiled, felt the happiness go over the top of him. A long-ago day came back.
>
> "It's 1964 and news of Dad's hole in one has just shot through town."[10]

Frank's gradual disaffiliation from contemporary American society, his "coming adrift,"[11] leads him to question the invasive penetration of the economic and materialist as the ruling criteria of value in capitalist society. As he says to his insurance man and fellow ex-hippy, Dick Hoiness, "'You deal in values the world accepts or you'd be out of business. I pay you to insure things that are starting to have no value for me.'"[12] Yet there are no possibilities for radical social change in the novel. Frank's only option is to try to rejoin the society in which he has lost confidence. So he finds himself spying on homes in the suburbs:

> Frank wanted to be here among the families, to watch them in their ordinariness, that most elusive of qualities. To simply carry on and ignore all that is unthinkable seemed to require a special gift; and, in the end, the world belonged to those who never thought about nuclear holocaust, the collapse of the biosphere or even their own perfectly predictable deaths. Carry on! Who made the playoffs? Let's eat! Let's eat something![13]

In his desperation, Frank clings to an idealised image of American suburban life. These populist sentiments are the decadent nostalgia and bad faith of an outsider who has lost such securities, and quickly become an endorsement of the apolitical complacency and evasions of a consumer society.

Despite McGuane's endorsement of the Green movement in the *Buzzworm* interview, his writings show little belief in the possibilities of radical political change in American society. A way out of this impasse seems to be his recognition of the need for more local and piecemeal political action, in the pragmatic and compromised world of pressure group politics. In particular, McGuane has concentrated on preservationist issues concerning "wild river" protection. His 1993 *Audubon* piece, **"The Spell of Wild Rivers,"** is accordingly a defense of federal government intervention in environmental affairs, in particular the National Wild and Scenic Rivers Act, against pressures from those interests supporting states' rights. McGuane calls for a wider sense of community than that offered by the damaging ideology of individualism: "A rising tide of Americans are banding together and in the face of sloganeering about individual rights and antigovernmental posturing are concluding that wild rivers are indeed something we hold as a community."[14] McGuane's views are again informed by traditional attitudes to nature, a sense of the natural landscape as a source of patriotic pride, and as spiritually restorative: "I suppose many American families have had such days on our Wild and Scenic Rivers, days that are restorative not just to our beleagured constitutions but to our idealism as a people, to our capacity to dream." He is careful not to idealise his descriptions of nature, and recognises the political issues that inform them:

> The North Fork of the Flathead is an imperfect place. There are plenty of human disturbances preserved as part of the status quo, and plenty of new building. But these have been mitigated by a protective corridor and easements purchased by the federal government.[15]

Yet he adds: "A river like this ought to go through South-Central Los Angeles." This nostalgic element, claiming the purifications of nature as a solution to complex urban problems, is reminiscent of Thomas Jefferson via Frank Capra, and is evidence of the sentimentality that is a significant factor in McGuane's attachment to nature.

More serious as an argument is his defense of the role of the federal government in environmental matters, an issue explored in **Nothing to be Desired** through the figure of Lane Lawlor, leader of the organization "We, Montana." Lawlor represents McGuane's satirical attack on the vested interests of states' righters, and the disastrous impact that their politics have on the Western environment. Through this comic grotesque, McGuane shows how the perpetuation of the destructive myths of the Old West is a serious

constraint on contemporary possibilities. Lawlor's organization exhibits the right-wing, white supremacist assumptions of the central myths of the American West: "Frank especially remembered their Western Family archetypes: the John Wayne male and his bellicose, gun-toting woman, their cold-eyed, towheaded children."[16]

The policies of "We, Montana" are based on the use of big technology to master nature through acts of aggressive conquest. In the novel, the damming of a river to prevent water from leaving the state leads to the drying up of the stream where Frank and his daughter go fishing. This has consequences for Frank which go beyond simple utilitarian considerations: "Frank thought that it was pretty unlucky to go fishing and find the stream had been stolen, particularly when you needed the stream for more than just fishing."[17] The manipulation of nature for short-term economic and political purposes is shown to have destroyed other possible usages, in particular those responding to people's emotional and spiritual needs.

Lawlor rehabilitates frontier iconographies as political alibis for the actions of his pressure group, particularly those regarding the control of water: "'There's a way of looking at this world and this country and, more importantly, this state that begins with saddle leather and distance, unsolved distance. And water.'"[18] Frank recognises Lawlor's regional chauvinism and his politics of resentment as a selective interpretation of the history of the West: "The tone of the West had been set by the failure of the homesteads, not by the heroic cattle drives. The tone was in its bitter politics." Yet Frank himself also views the West through old myths, as the landscape inspires in him familiar thoughts of the West as a new start, and as future potentiality:

> There was something in its altitude and dryness and distances that he couldn't have lived without; and it was a good time to remember that. When he was walking in the hills and could see sundown begin about forty miles away, or smell running water in the bottom of a sagebrush ravine, or watch the harriers cup themselves to the curve of earth and slash through clouds of meadowlarks, he felt that thankfulness. It was always a starting point. He went to the mirror and watched himself say, "I love it here."[19]

Typically, however, the optimism of this traditional response to the Western landscape is given an ironic undertone in the final sentence here. The comically exaggerated self-consciousness, even narcissism, of Frank's final gesture suggests the complacency and over-confidence involved in putting too much faith in any mythic perceptions of the West.

Yet these fantasies are shown to persist out of an emotional need for an imaginary scene of unspoiled potentiality, a need which McGuane both respects and shows as limited and anachronistic. In *Something to be Desired* (1984), Lucien indulges in a reverie for a mythic Old West, as he rides along with W. T. Austinberry, the comically stereotypical cowboy: "How Lucien loved this vaguely ersatz air of the old days! Or better yet, that the frontier lingered in the draws where Indian spirits were as smoky and redolent as the pollen exhalations of the forest!" But there can be little place for such nostalgic fantasy in the modern West, as McGuane's bathos immediately shows: "They rode on and crossed a creek where W. T. Austinberry said that he had poured Clorox to kill a couple of hundred pounds of trout for his freezer."[20] The Western cowboy complacently takes for granted the abundance and permanence of nature, and his permissive actions damage the natural environment. Austinberry's actions raise the central issue of technology, an area explored by McGuane particularly in terms of the relationship between the mastery and control of nature and traditional forms of masculinity.

III

Ecological thought has provided a critique of some of the central assumptions of the modern scientific project, revealing it as founded upon a destructive and exploitative attitude to nature. As land came to be treated as a commodity to be bought and sold within a capitalist market economy, so, as Michel Serres puts it, "Our fundamental relationship with objects is summed up by war and property."[21] Serres calls for a new "natural contract" in which "our relationship to things would no longer involve mastery and possession, but an admiring stewardship, reciprocity, contemplation, and respect...."[22] This notion of a benign form of stewardship is an attempt to rehabilitate Christianity from its complicity, based on Genesis 1:28, in granting human beings permission for the destructive domination of nature.[23] The notion of human stewardship still clearly falls within an anthropocentric view of nature, seeking more benign forms of technological control. Serres' position may in this way be differentiated from the shift towards "biocentrism" evident in "deep ecological" thought, whereby human beings lose their assumed centrality in the world, and are relocated back into evolutionary nature as a species equal but not superior to other forms of life.[24] This attitude translates in its most extreme form into policies that seek to proscribe all utilitarian and even anthropocentric approaches to nature—even though this position is difficult to sustain on both political and epistemological grounds, in that any human action towards nature is inevitably anthropocentric, by definition.

McGuane's writings mostly favour an anthropocentric and interventionist approach to environmentalist issues, though he does recognise an emotional need for areas of nature left as far as possible beyond the reach of human technological mediation, or so-called "development." In a "beautifully farmed field . . . it was wonderful to see the sage-covered remains of buttes and old wild prairie that wouldn't submit to plowing."[25] Moreover, the very presence of human beings is seen on occasions to be inevitably destructive. In Argentina on a fishing trip, looking across "superb distances" to the Andes, "it was hard to avoid the feeling that the greatest thing man can do for the land is to stay off it."[26]

Yet this concern for wilderness preservation largely avoids the trap of a sentimental reflex against technology *per se*. There is, however, a clear antipathy towards big technology in McGuane's work. But as a rancher, hunter and fisherman, nature exists for careful human use, and the issue of domination and control is not a simplistic either-or choice. Indeed, McGuane's environmentalist interests show a pragmatic acknowledgment of the need to come to terms with human technological interventions.

In *Nothing But Blue Skies,* Frank experiences a thrill of omnipotence, when stealing an articulated log skidder: "This grand machine made its own road, and with their seats high above the destruction, they could feel some of the detached power that intoxicates those at war with the earth."[27] The scene recalls the sense of moral and political detachment experienced by the tractor driver, the "machine man," in *The Grapes of Wrath* (1939), who, as an extension of the destructive machine, is "contemptuous of the land and of himself."[28] McGuane's speculations on technology here give an insight into the seductiveness of big, destructive technologies, as he distances himself at this point from war as the central paradigm for technological controls, and from the dangers that arise from spurious notions of objectivity and detachment.

This attitude may be placed with evidence in McGuane's work of a more benign use of technology. His interest in angling may, in this context, be seen as an endorsement of a form of control of nature using small technology. Some modern techniques, especially the use of plastics and chemicals, are ruled out as excessive: "the latest teched-out fly-fishing, with its whirring split shot, 7X leaders, and transitional subaqueous life-forms imitated in experimental carpet fibers."[29] Indeed, McGuane extends such concerns to the technology of writing itself, in his rejection of large-scale epic structures, what he calls the "accretional monument-building" of much post-World War II American writing: "If you're building fishing rods or shotguns or yachts, the standard is lightness that is as much as possible commensurate with strength...."[30]

Yet a martial paradigm remains as the basis for angling, as for most sporting activities: mastery and control of the object are still the main end, only the tactical means have changed. In *Nothing But Blue Skies,* Frank recalls the fishing techniques of his grandfather, a successful businessman, whose approach was "too direct": "He tried to overpower trout, go straight at them. It was one of the many areas where fishing and life are not at all alike—or at least fishing and business."[31] So the paradigm of technology as war is not transcended here; rather, in a reformist move, the secret of successful dominance is shown to be an understanding of, and respect for, the object of control.

Indeed, the sense of war and competitive struggle as fundamental aspects of the human condition is central to McGuane. Ultimately, his work may be seen to assert an essentialist notion of human nature in an American society given over to brutal Darwinistic competitiveness, also viewed largely as a state of nature, unconditional and inevitable. As Frank Copenhaver comes to understand about the business world: "Any creature that goes in a straight line is an invitation to predators."[32] This sense of life as competitive struggle extends to sexual relationships. Hence Frank's admiration for his friend June: "She was a fighter. Unlike most women he knew, she wasn't astonished to find that life was a fight."[33]

McGuane's characters tend to be driven by their essential natures, their bodies' instinctual and sexual drives, as forces which they can control only ineffectively and temporarily. In the affair between Frank and Lucy, the latter finally manages to control these impulses. But for Frank, however, sexual desire is an overpowering appetite, involuntary and uncontrollable. McGuane's explorations of male sexuality here suggest many of the elements identified by Lynn Segal as falling within traditional discourses on masculinity, evident for example in the pseudo-science of "sexology" in the mid-nineteenth century.[34]

In this context, the issue of moral responsibility is crucial. As a tumescent Frank puts it: "'The worst hanging judge in the world doesn't penalize folks for that which is involuntary.'"[35] Yet the need for a sense of moral responsibility, as a means of reasserting control over nature, is a key preoccupation in McGuane's writings. Significantly, arguments about an involuntary human nature are used by his characters as alibis for their own moral failings. In *Something to be Desired,* when Lucien's father roughly throws out of his motel room a woman he has casually picked up, he then telephones his wife in the hope of being invited back home. In an attempt to justify his behaviour to his son, he draws on an argument from nature, by recalling the family pets he once bought for Lucien, "so you could learn about animals, about how we are all animals."[36] Yet this assertion of our animal nature is motivated by a desire to absolve himself of moral responsibility for his actions. Similarly, Lucien refers to his own act of desertion as an involuntary,

behaviouristic reflex: " . . . why can't I stop myself? I have the soul of a lab rat."[37] But Skinnerian behaviourism gives way to a Christian schema of guilt and punishment explored by the narrator independently of the character's point-of-view: "In any event, the process of stain had begun; he would not have known what to call it as it sank deeper inside him, nor been able to assess the turbulence and damage that was to come; but it was certainly shame."[38]

In McGuane's writings, nature becomes a scene of therapeutic healing in response to this ongoing sense of inadequacy, failure and guilt associated with living in a society based on competitive aggression. In particular, both the male protagonists of his novels and the autobiographical narrators of his fishing stories seek a renewed sense of mastery and control through contact with nature. Nature provides a scene in which competitive struggle, in sexual relationships and in the business world, may be momentarily transcended. In the following passage, Frank and his friend Phil Page attempt to leave behind the pressures of their failed marriages in a search for "purity" in nature. McGuane lightly satirises the sort of populist mysticism associated with angling in, for example, Norman Maclean's *A River Runs Through It* (1976), yet the emotional needs that inform such attitudes are also understood and respected. Phil Page is thinking about his cheating wife:

> "I guess that if we didn't have trout fishing, there'd be nothing you could really call pure in our lives at all."
>
> Frank stared at the road ahead, filling with joy at this inane but life-restoring thought. "I do like to feel one pull," he said.
>
> "Yes!" Phil shouted and pounded the dashboard.
>
> "Yes!" shouted Frank, and they both pounded happily on the dashboard.
>
> "Trout!" The volume knob fell off the radio. Phil dove down to look for it, muttering "Fuckin' douche bag" as he searched.[39]

Within McGuane's comedy, the attainment of a feeling of masculine mastery and control is transient, and characteristically falls prey to bathetic deflation.

As Jane Tompkins argues, the nurturing role attributed to the pastoral landscape by men in Western fictions suggests more than a simple substitute for the company of women. Rather, the Western landscape exists as a scene which displaces "heterosexual sexuality, the nuclear family, and a struggle for status among peers," in that the man "who leaves home and fireside and turns to the wilderness does so in search of something other than what they have to offer."[40] What McGuane's male characters seek tends to be a renewed sense of control over their lives through a meditative or epiphanic experience. Blood sports such as angling and hunting apparently become means of attaining a sense of the sacramental, and consequently a moment of healing. McGuane explores this aspect most fully in his essay on hunting, **"The Heart of the Game."**

The essay attempts to justify hunting in the light of the accompanying sense of "remorse" that "spins out almost before anything" with the act of killing the prey. McGuane's defense is initially a moral one: by involving himself directly in the killing of the animal, the hunter lacks the hypocrisy of those who buy meat in supermarkets and, as a result, try to avoid responsibility for the ugly realities of meat production in the industrial slaughterhouse. But McGuane adds: "and anyway, as Sitting Bull said, when the buffalo are gone, we will hunt mice, for we are hunters and we want our freedom."[41] There is an elision here from the "we" probably intended by Sitting Bull (the Sioux tribe), to a less specific "we" ("we" could refer to "men," "Americans," or "the human race"). Whatever the referent, the appeal is to an essential and therefore permanent human nature as an ultimate guarantor of permission ("we are hunters"). McGuane here is close to the arguments of sociobiologists, who posit what Stephen Jay Gould calls an "innate nature of human violence" which serves to confirm conservative, patriarchal power relationships by attempting "to fob off the responsibility for war and violence upon our presumably carnivorous ancestors."[42] Darwinism is invoked for the sense of boundless permission it can afford.

"The Heart of the Game" is ultimately concerned with metaphysics, as McGuane argues that hunting is socially necessary in that it provides a confrontation with death that reveals the sacramental in life. As he puts it, "A world in which a sacramental portion of food can be taken in an old way—hunting, fishing, farming, and gathering—has as much to do with societal sanity as a day's work for a day's pay."[43] McGuane describes a meal with his son, where they eat the antelope killed at the start of the story. As he informs his son of the death of his paternal grandfather, the meal provides the opportunity for a small act of communion, an attempt to heal the pain both of mortality, and of the awkward separation and repressed competitiveness between father and son. Human blood ties are strengthened through the spilling of the sacramental blood of the animal. McGuane's love of hunting in this way places him as a direct inheritor of those basic myths of the American West that assert the regenerative power of violence. As Richard Slotkin puts it, the violent male in Western mythology is "the lover of the spirit of the wilderness, and his acts of love and sacred affirmation are acts of violence against that spirit and her avatars."[44]

George Bataille's cross-cultural study of violence and the sacred analyses deep-seated psychological motivations for such desires for sacrifice. Death, ultimately unmasterable, is mastered symbolically and vicariously in violent sacrifice, where anxieties are projected onto the victim. Bataille locates such psychic needs in the biological separateness of human individuals, an unconditional effect of sexual reproduction. As such, their origin is asserted to be not in a socially constructed masculinity, but in an unchangeable human nature:

> We are discontinuous beings, individuals who perish in isolation in the midst of an incomprehensible adventure, but we yearn for our lost continuity. We find the state of affairs that binds us to our random and ephemeral individuality hard to bear. Along with our tormenting desire that evanescent things should last, there stands our obsession with a primal continuity linking us with everything that is.[45]

Ritual sacrifice allows for an ecstatic return to continuity, and a sense of control over the passing of time. In **"The Heart of the Game,"** hunting the deer provides not only a practical source of food, but also, in its irrational aspect, enacts a confrontation with mortality, recognised as our natural inheritance:

> As I took that step, I knew he was running. He wasn't in the browse at all, but angling into invisibility at the rock wall, racing straight into the elevation, bounding toward zero gravity, taking his longest arc into the bullet and the finality and terror of all you have made of the world, the finality you know that you share even with your babies with their inherited and ambiguous definition, the finality that any minute now you will meet as well.[46]

These "hand-to-mouth metaphysics"[47] show McGuane at his most conservative, nostalgic for traditional codes of masculinity as renewing a sense of potency and will through rituals of violent death. McGuane places his decision to hunt the deer within a speculation on the state of his life, within eighteen months of the deaths of his father and sister, and of the collapse of his marriage. In the context of these complex personal traumas, hunting takes on motivations associated with an embattled need for renewal, restoring a sense of mastery and control over his life:

> I didn't want to read and I didn't want to write or acknowledge the phone with its tendrils into the zombie enclaves. I didn't want the New Rugged; I wanted the Old Rugged and a pot to piss in. Otherwise, it's deteriorata, with mice undermin-

ing the wiring in my frame house, sparks jumping in the insulation, the dog turning queer, and a horned owl staring at the baby through the nursery window.[48]

The individual non-conformist stands out against the homogeneous mass ("the zombie enclaves"), and heterosexual machismo ("the dog turning queer") renews itself against the "deteriorata" of entropic collapse. Nature thus becomes a scene in which a declining sense of masculine power is restored. In McGuane, the masterful male hero often tends to persist as an absurd, self-deluding fantasy, rendered comic and absurd. Yet the figure is shown to have appeal as well as limitations.

This traditional sense of masculinity as involving the need for a man to prove himself in tests of prowess is a central preoccupation of McGuane's fishing stories for the men's magazine *Esquire*. **"The Bonefish in the Other Room"** begins characteristically with a sense of failure, as the narrator, with typically comic self-deprecation, describes his "wounded male vanity . . . " as he gets his fishing line caught in his back pocket. The mood of the writing then darkens: "I was in that state of mind perhaps not peculiar to angling when things seem to be in a steep curve of deterioration, and I had a fatal sense that I was not at the end of it."

McGuane recovers from this loss of control through a lesson in humility learned from his experience with the natural world. He watches the moon, appearing "as a fixed portion of the universe, while the clouds and weather of planet Earth poured over its face." The moon becomes a sign of the absolute, of a sublime element beyond human time. This decentring of the ego affords psychic relief: "Weather is one of the things that goes on without you, and after a certain amount of living, it is bracing to contemplate the many items not dependent upon you for their existence even if too many thinking reeds stalk the prairie." The final clause here suggests Malthusian-Darwinian fears of overpopulation as a threat to individual survival. Yet there is an overall feeling of confidence and mastery restored through contact with nature. Granted "a healthier view of loose fly line, the message from the moon, and my place in the universe . . . ," he successfully catches the bonefish, which "came to my fly at the end of a long cast. And I landed him."[49]

"The Bonefish in the Other Room" refers to the "ceremony of angling holding our minds on all the proper things."[50] In this respect, McGuane's deepest speculations move beyond the immediately political, into contemplations of a universalised human condition. In particular, mortality and loss exist in his work as inevitable facts to be confronted. The transience of human time, and experiences of separation, particularly those associated with generational differences, are healed by being set against the larger, cosmic times and "eternal" continuities of nature. Angling trips are often of interest to McGuane in the way that they provide opportunities for bridging generational differences:

> I think of the father and son, a month of fishing together; that is, day and night, life together at what might have been inflexible ages, a struggle for active intimacy late in life in a country where we were all strangers. The rest of us, men with fathers, living or dead, caught this out of the corners of our eyes.[51]

Having confronted the inevitabilities of time, mortality and separateness, the trip becomes "a permanent resource to this surviving son."[52] This need to overcome Oedipal rivalries is a key theme in McGuane's fiction. In *Nothing But Blue Skies,* Frank decides to become a businessman through a desire to prove himself to his father. This need for reconciliation between the generations extends to his daughter, Hollie, and significantly, it is an angling trip that provides the opportunity for their reunion.[53]

Many of McGuane's typical responses to nature are brought together in **"West Boulder Spring,"** a meditation on Thoreau published in aid of the Walden Woods Project. The essay locates human beings within a landscape that is gradually revealed as a site of predatory struggles for survival. An identification is made between human beings and animals: "Over the sere landscape, the creatures are chasing each other just like the children at the local junior high." As the essay begins to darken in tone, there is a growing recognition of disease, death and an aggressive competition for food: calves sick with pneumonia, a yearling buck eaten by coyotes. The piece ends with the narrator confronting death as an unconditional fact of nature:

> The face of creation takes in everything with a level stare. When I was younger, these manifestations of life's fury were comfortably free of premonition. Now there is a gravity that dignifies the hatchlings, the one-day lives of insects, the terrible slaughterhouse journey of livestock, and, of course, ourselves and our double handful of borrowed minerals.

Human beings are placed within a totalising metaphysic ("creation," "life's fury"), as part of an unconditional fate to which all living things are subject. However, this recognition tends to conflate what is natural ("the hatchlings, the one day lives of insects"), with what is more obviously culturally determined ("the terrible slaughterhouse journey of livestock"). This turning of culture into nature makes what is historical, and therefore potentially changeable, appear as inevitable and fixed. This is the basis of the pessimism that tends to permeate McGuane's writings, a sense of inevitabilities that cannot be transcended. **"West Boulder Spring"** ends accordingly with a search for spiritual consolation:

> The obsessive business Thoreau complained of is rooted in fear; fear of mortality, and then of pain and loss and separation. Only in the observation of nature can we recover that view of eternity that consoled our forebears. The remains of the young buck dead at the spring are sounded in the cliffs above our house in the calls of the young coyotes, testing the future with their brand new voices, under the stars of outer space.[54]

A sublime nature puts human beings in their place, cautious and humble before "eternity," and acknowledging a limit to ambitions. The passage ends with paradoxes of life-in-death, as the young coyotes embody springtime renewal amid death and decay. Time ("the future") and space ("the stars of outer space"), small and large, local and cosmic, the transient and the eternal, the living and the inert: the reconciliation of opposites in the final paragraph in McGuane at his most overtly transcendentalist, an epiphany that is significantly not undermined by irony. Similarly, in **Something to be Desired,** Lucien discovers, riding on horseback in Montana, that, "he could look out through the tall wild prairie grasses on the stream bank and start to lose his sense of irony."[55]

Typically in McGuane's novels, however, such attempts to find consolation and emotional escape in nature are treated more sceptically, as temporary evasions of moral responsibility. In **Nothing But Blue Skies,** after a night of drunkenness, involving the theft and destruction of a truck, Frank retreats to the countryside with his fishing gear. He looks up into the Big Sky of Montana:

> This seemed to him to be a grand and wholly acceptable arcade where his various sins were simply booths to be revisited with amusement . . . He joyously felt himself idling, an unreflective mood in which water was water, sky was sky, breeze was breeze. He knew it couldn't last.[56]

In a novel that also debunks psychiatry,[57] there is here a rejection of notions of therapeutic healing that appear to simplify the complexities of human experience in order to give false consolation. As Frank puts it, "the messages of my formative years all came from Little Richard, who has never soiled himself with an inner journey."[58]

Nothing But Blue Skies explores what McGuane calls a "plateau of spiritual bankruptcy"[59] without finding any easy solutions. Nature is seen as the site of possible renewal, but such a view is not allowed to become a system of belief beyond an ongoing spirit of skeptical inquiry. In McGuane's writings, nature gives an opportunity for his male protagonists to attempt to recover a sense of original purity and mastery beyond the compromises and power struggles of a competitive society. In the *Buzzworm* interview, McGuane described the "personal desperation" of his characters, and how their "*escape* from that emotional dead end is always seen in the natural world."[60] As such, his work confirms the recurrent element in American nature writing as identified by Peter Fritzell: "that deep, original desire to escape history or civilization, to return to Eden and become again an unthinking, unsinning part of nature. . . . "[61] Yet irony is a constantly disruptive force in McGuane's fiction, not allowing such moments of transcendence to evade radical questioning and doubt.

NOTES

1. Donald Worster, *Under Western Skies* (New York: Oxford University Press, 1992), 251.

2. Walter J. Ong, *Rhetoric, Romance and Technology* (London: Cornell University Press, 1971), 280.

3. Leo Marx, "Ecology and American Ideals," in *Environment and Americans*, ed. Roderick Nash (London: Holt, Richart and Winston, 1972), 100.

4. Perry Miller, *Errand into the Wilderness* (Cambridge: Belknap Press, Harvard University, 1956), ch. 9, "Nature and the National Ego."

5. Donald Worster, op. cit., 255.

6. Thomas McGuane, "Some Notes on Montana," *Architectural Digest* (June 1992), 45.

7. Ibid., 36.

8. "Thomas McGuane Speaks," interview with Deborah Houy, *Buzzworm: THE Environmental Journal*, Jan/Feb. 1993, 32-4.

9. McGuane, *Nothing But Blue Skies* (London: Minerva, 1993), 131.

10. Ibid., 48.

11. Ibid., 95.

12. Ibid., 95.

13. Ibid., 123.

14. McGuane, "The Spell of Wild Rivers," *Audubon*, Nov.-Dec. 1993, 63.

15. Ibid., 64.

16. McGuane, *Nothing But Blue Skies,* 206.

17. Ibid., 281.

18. Ibid., 208.

19. Ibid., 246.

20. McGuane, *Something to be Desired* (New York, Vintage Contemporaries, 1985), 37-8.

21. Michel Serres, "The Natural Contract," translated by Felicia McCarren *Critical Inquiry* (Autumn 1992), 6.

22. Ibid., II.

23. Lynn White, "The Historical Roots of our Ecological Crisis," *Science*, 155, (1967).

24. Kirkpatrick Sale, *The Green Revolution* (New York: Hill and Wang, 1993), 27.

25. McGuane, *Something to be Desired,* 54.

26. McGuane, "The Brown Trout at the Bottom of the World," *Esquire*, June 1992, 64.

27. McGuane, *Nothing But Blue Skies,* 230.

28. John Steinbeck, *The Grapes of Wrath* (1939; London: Mandarin, 1990), 133.

29. McGuane, "The F-word," *Esquire*, Dec. 1991, 81.

30. In, "Tom McGuane," Mark Harris, *Publishers Weekly,* 29 Sept. 1989, 50.

31. McGuane, *Nothing But Blue Skies,* 149.

32. Ibid., 273.

33. Ibid., 243.

34. Lynn Segal, *Slow Motion: Changing Masculinities, Changing Men* (London: Virago, 1990), 208ff.

35. McGuane, *Nothing But Blue Skies,* 223.

36. McGuane, *Something to be Desired,* 15.

37. Ibid., 28.

38. Ibid., 29.

39. McGuane, *Nothing But Blue Skies,* 82-3.

40. Jane Tompkins, *West of Everything* (Oxford: Oxford University Press, 1992), 82.

41. McGuane, "The Heart of the Game," in *An Outside Chance,* (Boston: Houghton Mifflin/Seymour Lawrence, 1990), 230-1.

42. Stephen Jay Gould, *Ever Since Darwin* (Harmondsworth: Penguin, 1991), 238-9.

43. McGuane, *An Outside Chance,* 234.

44. Richard Slotkin, *Regeneration Through Violence* (Middletown, Conn.: Wesleyan University Press, 1973), 22.

45. Georges Bataille, *Eroticism* (London: Boyars, 1987), 15.

46. McGuane, *An Outside Chance,* 239.

47. Ibid., 233.

48. Ibid., 236.

49. McGuane, "The Bonefish in the Other Room," *Esquire,* Feb. 1992, 56.

50. Ibid., 55.

51. McGuane, "Stupendous Vulgarities, Delicate Subjects," *Esquire*, Oct. 1991, 74.

52. Ibid., 76.

53. McGuane, *Nothing But Blue Skies,* 151ff.

54. McGuane, "West Boulder Spring," in *Heaven Is Under Our Feet*, ed. Don Henley and Dave Marsh, (New York: Berkley Books, 1992), 52.

55. McGuane, *Something to be Desired,* 36.

56. McGuane, *Nothing But Blue Skies,* 234.

57. Ibid., 127ff.

58. Ibid., 324.

59. "Thomas McGuane Speaks," *Buzzworm,* 32.

60. Ibid., 32.

61. Peter Frizell, *Nature Writing and America* (Ames: Iowa State University, 1990), 6.

James I. McClintock (essay date Winter 1997)

SOURCE: "'Unextended Selves' and 'Unformed Visions': Roman Catholicism in Thomas McGuane's Novels," in *Renascence*, Vol. IL, No. 2, Winter, 1997, pp. 139-52.

[*In the following essay, McClintock discusses Roman Catholic spirituality themes in McGuane's novels, particularly in* Panama *and* Nobody's Angel.]

Thomas McGuane's novels, short stories, essays, and screen plays place him among the best contemporary American writers. Reviewers have uniformly commented on his constant and redeeming wit in portraying suffering, alienated male protagonists, even though academic critics have neglected his work. For twenty-five years Thomas McGuane has employed a masterful range of language and comic imagination to write about these protagonists, adrift in a vulgar contemporary American culture, who are limited, furthermore, by their own "unformed visions" and "unextended selves."

Almost without exception, however, critics and reviewers have failed to notice that McGuane's topics, themes, and language are frequently, if not obviously, religious, and that McGuane belongs in the company of such writers as Walker Percy, Reynolds Price, and most notably Flannery O'Connor, as well as writers such as Jack Kerouac, J. P. Donleavy, and Robert Stone, all of whom in varying degrees explore fictional worlds shaped by their experiences with Roman Catholicism, whether broadly cultural or specifically liturgical. In a recently published interview with McGuane, Gregory L. Morris observes concerning the nearly invisible role of religion in McGuane's work that "You seem . . . to dismiss religion as a source of belief and affirmation in your work; religion is, in fact, scarcely visible in your fiction." McGuane responds that "I do have an inchoate pining for religion . . . In fact, I am very comfortable considering myself an Irish Catholic, implying, as it does to me, a superimposition of the life of Christ upon earth-worshipping pantheism." Despite the seemingly heretical yoking of Catholicism and pantheism and, in addition, recognizing McGuane's playfulness, this declaration should be taken seriously.[1] McGuane is like J. P. Donleavy and Jack Kerouac who, Paul Giles writes, "are by no means Catholic writers in any orthodox sense, but [who] emerged out of a culture of Catholicism that has continued to influence the shape and direction of their work" (394).

From the first of his novels, *The Sporting Club* (1969), to his most recent and seventh novel, *Nothing But Blue Skies* (1992), McGuane has turned repeatedly to generally Christian and, often, specifically Roman Catholic topics, themes, and language. In *The Sporting Club,* for instance, the novel's central, dangerous rivalry begins with the protagonist's statement that there is no God; and the novel's epigraph from Aristophanes indicates the central truth that if there is no God, then "Whirl is king." More peripherally, in the serio-comic *Nothing But Blue Skies,* the protagonist's hope throughout the novel is for the return of grace (his wife Gracie). The McGuane novels most preoccupied with religious subjects are, however, *Panama* (1978) and *Nobody's Angel* (1982), arguably his best, although reviewers savaged *Panama* and *Nobody's Angel* received a mixed reception. In these two novels McGuane elaborately explores religious themes, particularly the idea that his protagonists are in states of crisis that they, in some measure, have brought upon themselves by clinging to self-serving delusions while, at the same time, suffering from the victimization of living in a "fallen" and crushing American culture which offers them no succor. Chester Hunnicutt Pomeroy in *Panama* and Patrick Fitzgerald in *Nobody's Angel,* who are near spiritual death, are, by the novels' ends, minimally alive. While McGuane's protagonists have at best a limited grasp of its efficacy, the only alternative McGuane offers to spiritual extinction is a Christian existence. We can understand their desperate lives and marginally improved final states within the novels' persistent evocations of a Christian context larger than their own tormented lives and their culture's de-sacralized icons, whether in these instances rock-and-roll celebrities or Montana cowboys.

Chet Pomeroy is a burned-out rock-and-roll superstar notorious for outrageous stage performances. The poles of Pomeroy's spiritual life are that he is "discouraged as to finding a hot lead on the Altogether"; but, nonetheless, "like every other child of the century deluded enough to keep his head out of the noose" and not commit suicide, he "expect(s) God's Mercy in the end" (86). He is closer to the negative than the positive, believing that "anybody's refusal to commit suicide is a little fey" (86). He only wishes what we all wish for, he says, "a little light to live by. A start somewhere" (85). By the novel's end, he seems to have gotten his little light, a start, and a little of God's mercy. But his journey is excruciating.

Messianically, Chet Pomeroy had taken to the stage during the Nixon era of the Watergate coverup and subversion of the Constitution. At one point he says being called to the stage was like Ulysses S. Grant being summoned to save the nation: "It was an instance of a village crank being called by his Republic" (45). More frequently and persistently, he identifies himself with another historical figure, the outlaw folk hero Jesse James. Often, though, Pomeroy cannot distinguish Jesse James from Jesus Christ. That confusion allows Pomeroy to mythologize himself as an outlaw in a corrupted society which would victimize him, and as an actor in a historical drama of mythic and universal dimensions. Pomeroy believes he is actually related to Jesse James, and the last in a family in which everyone from Revolutionary times to the present has been outside the mainstream of

American history as a fighter against the Philistines, whom Pomeroy often refers to as "shitsuckers" (85). His stage crusade had been to awaken the country from its collective nightmare. "Your only shot," he explains, "is to tell everyone, to blow the whistle on the nightmare. It will work for a while; no one knows how long. The worse the dream, the more demonstrative you must become. I took to the stage" (89).

Pomeroy's most successful show was called *The Dog Ate the Part We Didn't Like* and his antics included appearing on stage dressed "in Revolutionary War throwaways and a top hat, much like an Iroquois going to Washington to ask the Great White Father to stop eating his babies. . . . I was a . . . strangely articulate shrieking misfit and I would go too damn far" (11, 14). Going too far in McGuane's overtly political novel includes as part of Pomeroy's act crawling "out of the ass of a frozen elephant" (the Republican party) and fighting a "duel in my underwear with a baseball batting practice machine" (the national pastime) (18). Pomeroy remarks that "it took me a little while to get the bugs out; and after that, I was lethal" (45).

The colloquial meaning of "lethal" signifies that his successes as a savior called upon by the endangered Republic coexist with the word's literal meaning of "deadly." Pomeroy becomes complicit in cultural destruction. Falling apart, near total collapse, he is advised by a friend that he "was having a destructive effect on all and sundry out in America . . . It is time . . . to go home; the dog is eating everything" (168). In **Panama,** as in other McGuane novels, the dog symbolizes malign forces which are the antithesis of human desires and hopes, a symbol evocative of the beast slouching toward Bethlehem. For McGuane, dogs are reminders of meaningless death as a prelude to purgatorial or, even, eternal suffering. The dog symbolizes McGuane's worst fears about contemporary America and lost possibilities for cultural and personal redemption. In an interview, he explicitly connects the beast with an American nightmare: "The America you see in public is a monster who crawls up to the door in the middle of the night and must be driven back to the end of the driveway" (McCaffery 206). Dogs haunt and menace the worlds of other McGuane novels. In **Nobody's Angel,** for instance, an enraged dog threatens a drunk Patrick Fitzgerald who thinks, "I must be close to death. . . . I always knew death would be a slobbering animal" (71). The "everything" the dog is eating in Pomeroy's friend's warning is not only the nation but Pomeroy himself. Pomeroy is deranged, and the cultural nightmare is enthralling.

Just as in McGuane's view, Pomeroy's life, the nation's, and a larger spiritual malaise are intertwined, so are they in Pomeroy's often deranged thoughts and emotions. He confuses his father, whom he insists is dead but who isn't, with Jesse James, whom he insists is alive but who isn't, and both—as well as himself—with Jesus. These confusions occur when he is in crisis; and he is in virtually continual crisis.

Jesse James is invoked regularly in Pomeroy's fantasies—Jesse will take revenge against those who threaten Pomeroy. Pomeroy often, though, thinks about Jesse James as Christians think of Jesus and God. When, for example, a detective hired by Pomeroy's beloved Catherine to help restore Pomeroy's memory tells him that Jesse James was shot by Bob Ford and threatens to hit Pomeroy in exasperation at Chet's refusal to accept the truth, Pomeroy prays, "Jesse, forgive them, for they know not what they do" (151). Shortly after, he reassures himself that he has certain truths to live by; for instance, "I know that Jesse robbed and killed and that he was lonely. I know that he was left behind, left for dead. But I know he rose again from the dead" (157-58). Defending himself from Catherine's exasperated sarcasm about his "rotten little Catholic heart" (and distancing her loving efforts to help him), he shouts, "There is no rotten little Catholic heart. There is only the Sacred Heart of Jesus and I have seen it shine in a Missouri tunic," which, of course, Jesse James had worn (167).

There are moments when Pomeroy sounds like Flannery O'Connor's Misfit in "A Good Man is Hard to Find," in which the Good Man of the title is Jesus even if others are mistaken as the good man, including the Misfit himself, who is actually a patricide. Pomeroy, in fact, more than once calls himself a "misfit" (14, 16, 28). Others describe him as "the most sleazed-out man in America," and he is the subject of a Paramount movie entitled "Chronicles of a Depraved Pervert" (94, 106). And, of course, he insists that his living father is dead. In another passage that could also be from a Flannery O'Connor story because of its comically grotesque surface and underlying Catholic dogmas, Pomeroy's father confronts his son: "I'm . . . running down my birdbrain, notorious son who refuses to admit I exist." In response to Chet's question "Why?" he answers simply, "Because it's all I want!" (101). A parallel with the Christian invitation to acknowledge a loving and forgiving Heavenly Father could not be more plain.

But Pomeroy defiantly denies his father's existence again. He rejects as necromancy, moreover, Catherine's efforts to help him acknowledge his father. Instead, he runs wildly down the street and tries unsuccessfully to buy a parrot "which said Jesus, Mary, Joseph at the trilling of a bell, the sign of a monstrance or a cracker" (143). Then, pursued by photographers, he "recited my Act of Contrition, genuflecting with enough sincerity that my knee could be heard against the sidewalk a hundred feet away" (144). These desperate, bizarre, and burlesque versions of Roman Catholic rituals do not help him even if they signal his best hope. He

should know the futility of the insanely parodic and burlesque, not only because of his stage act but because of
his earlier parody of the Crucifixion. In one of the novel's
most horrendous, even if most comic, scenes, Pomeroy
conflates Jesse James, Jesus, and himself by using a hammer to crucify himself by, as he says, "nail(ing) my left hand
to the door with Jesse's Colt" (24). He had lost the distinctions between savior and outlaw, between victim and vic-
timizer, and had egocentrically located them all in himself.

The most crucial distinction Pomeroy must make, before he
can move toward any kind of reconstructed selfhood that
expresses differently how he is a son of God, is the distinction between life and death. This is no simple matter of deciding whether to live or die—he has already stated that
"anybody's refusal to commit suicide is a little fey." Not only
is he confused about whether Jesse James and his father
are dead or alive, he is dying spiritually and wonders
whether, in fact, he himself is alive or dead.

Catherine, in a dream-like scene following her warning to
Pomeroy that his confusions about his father and Jesse
James and his denial of his father could have disastrous
consequences, asks who the old man was who went by in a
boat (Pomeroy's father), then dives into dark waters, perhaps to drown. Pomeroy searches frantically, finds her lying in the mud where an old man is moving off after
arranging her hair "like a sunburst." Her face pale, Catherine
stares into Chet's face and then asks the crucial question,
"Are we alive?" (114). He doesn't really know, of course.
For him "the living are skeletons in livery anyway," and he
had speculated that he, himself, "could be dead; could be
the kind of corpse that is sometimes described as 'fresh'"
(107, 8). Earlier, in fact, he had said simply, "I was dead" (4).

He does, finally, have some crucial insights into the realities of death and life. At his brother Jim's funeral, looking
into the coffin and into his brother's face, Chet has a "watershed" insight: "That's him all right and he's dead" (46).
Much later he has a "conversation" with his dead brother
who asks him to say aloud that their father is alive. Chet
says it, chokingly, and learns from Jim the essential, if dis-
tressing, truth that "I was among the living" (127). And, finally, he meets with and acknowledges his father. Marginally
sane, barely alive, abandoned by Catherine, Chet starts one
last time to mistake his father who has come to visit him for
Jesse James ("At twelve o'clock Jesse came, a cane in the
scabbard, his years at sea, the difficulties with the smokey
subways of Boston behind him"). His father says quietly,
"You know who I am . . . Can't you say hello?" The novel,
then, ends with a passage resonant with religious implications: Chet saying "the word" [father], at great risk, an act
of faith equivalent to his childhood "dive into the swimming
pool from the highest board on moonless nights, without
looking to see if there was water in the pool . . . I felt the

same blind arc through darkness when I spoke to my father"
(175).

That act may not be much of a beginning for Chet, but it is
a beginning nevertheless. He is still emotionally unstable,
but he is alive physically and spiritually; he is beyond nihilism.[2] The novel's religious overtones indicate that he is
healing. By the novel's conclusion, he has abandoned his
earlier messianic wish "to ache in the literal heart and chest
for all of us who had lost ourselves as parents lose children, to the horizon which is finally only overtaken in remorse and in death" for the dawning knowledge that he has
been a lost child himself and, thereby, eligible to receive
God's mercy (43). He has, at last, untangled the savior from
the one who needs salvation, savior from sinner. With childlike faith and the acknowledgement of his father, the most
fundamental of religious responses, he begins to find himself.

Nobody's Angel, McGuane's most overtly religious novel,
does not end as positively for its protagonist, Patrick
Fitzgerald, as even Chet Pomeroy's highly qualified success
in *Panama.* Still, *Nobody's Angel* is not nihilistic because
its themes, more sharply than *Panama's,* outline a spiritual
alternative, which the protagonist Patrick Fitzgerald may or
may not grasp but which the implied author defines. Patrick
Fitzgerald, like Chet Pomeroy, is a lost child and eligible to
receive God's mercy, but he chooses adulterous love over
salvation. Driven by the demands of an unsatisfied spirit.
Patrick attempts to "come home" but fails. The novel's epigraph from Malcolm Lowry's *Under the Volcano* captures
Patrick's spiritual condition: "I love hell. I can't wait to get
back."

Hell has multiple references: Fitzgerald's emotional states,
his domestic situation, the American West of Deadrock,
Montana, and the hell described in Catholic theology. Like
other McGuane protagonists, Fitzgerald is a "whiskey ad-
dict" of Irish-Catholic descent, who has not lived up to his
potential and is downwardly mobile. He is a well-intentioned
family member who, nevertheless, is on poor terms with his
family and the community at large, troubled particularly in
his affairs with women, and lost in sorrow and guilt. Patrick
is painfully aware of being adrift. He had left the army to
return to what was left of his family and to the family ranch,
to save them and himself, only to find that he continues to
suffer from "sadness-for-no-reason." Like Binx Bolling in
Walker Percy's *The Moviegoer* (1961), a novel McGuane
has said is for writers like himself what *The Sun Also Rises*
was for writers in the 1920s, Patrick Fitzgerald experiences
the pervasive "malaise" of alienation (McCaffery 211).
Patrick's love for his sister Mary, his grandfather, the
horses, and the place do not prevent his "waking nightmares," which reveal that these people and the place are
"edges" and there is "no middle" (56).

The center cannot hold. Fitzgerald suffers a spiritual debility which he mistakenly thinks can be cured by loving Claire, the beautiful wife of Tio Burnett, an unstable and volatile Oklahoma oilman. The day Patrick meets Claire, he determines to become "somebody's angel" (35). But in this anti-western, western novel, the pieties of popular fiction are inverted: good does not triumph over evil, the protagonist doesn't save the ranch, and he doesn't, ultimately, get the girl. He comes close to losing his soul.

Deadrock, Montana (originally "Deadlock—but renamed Deadrock out of some sad and irresolute boosterism meant to cure an early-day depression"), the locus of several other McGuane novels and stories, although featuring beautiful prairie and mountain landscapes, is hellish in its provincial narrowness (1). The West has a culture doomed by the Faulknerian sins of genocide against the Indians and pride in imposing ranching and farming on a landscape inhospitable to both. Fitzgerald's domestic situation is beyond repair, in part, McGuane suggests, because of his neglect—the ranch is moribund, his whiskey-soaked grandfather hostile, and his neglected sister mentally ill. Not that he alone is entirely responsible—one of the novel's major themes is abandonment by family. Patrick's father, a test pilot, died in a plane crash, an event which in variant forms begins, ends, and haunts the entire novel. His mother, when Patrick and Mary were children, had come to their room, drunk, and announced, "Why don't you two just get out? Why don't you just get the hell out and quit causing all this trouble?" (125). Patrick knew it was a turning point in his life. Patrick, in fact, feels unconnected with anyone or anything, having an "unremitting sense that there had never been connection, not with people and not with places" (126).

This is a sense of homelessness Paul Giles finds characteristic of contemporary Irish American, Catholic writers. J. P. Donleavy's "heroes are always looking for 'home,' but no place is home" and in Kerouac "the idea of travel and exile ultimately implies a sense of ontological loss, the expulsion from paradise." "The undermining of this fundamental notion of 'home,'" Giles concludes, "reduces these wayfarers to bedraggled pilgrims on the stony paths of postlapsarian life" (400). Patrick Fitzgerald's sense of alienation and dislocation is echoed besides in McGuane's own experience as an Irish American Catholic. In his interview with Larry McCaffery and Sinda Gregory, McGuane connected the significance of his Irish background to his fascination with "the figure of the outsider" in response to a question focusing on Patrick in *Nobody's Angel*:

> The outsider-stranger-bystander has always intrigued me in regard to my own family history. My family were all Irish immigrants. . . . People in Ireland feel like outsiders in their own country because the English have owned things for so long. . . .

When they immigrated to the East Coast (my family went to Massachusetts), they saw themselves as an enclave of outsiders in a Yankee Protestant world. My parents moved to the Midwest, and I can assure you that . . . we did not consider ourselves to be Midwesterners. We saw ourselves as Catholics surrounded by Protestant Midwesterners. . . . When I moved to Montana in my twenties, I felt myself to be an outsider in still another world (203).

McGuane finds these qualities also in F. Scott Fitzgerald, explaining why "so much of the magic of his fiction is his famous method of 'looking through the window.' And yet that mental quality, the glassy distance, is behind his craziness and his alcoholism. The vantage point of most authentic modern fiction is dislocation" (203-04).

There may be a religious consolation for this dislocation, alienation, isolation, and despair. *Nobody's Angel* is rife with religious language and overtones. Early in the novel, for example, Patrick leaves a bar, "a place where God was at bay," to seek information about his troubled sister Mary at a whorehouse where she sometimes worked. There, the prostitutes are watching an interview show about the "fetus's right to life." A nun on the talk-show panel repeatedly shouts, "*Sacred!*" and Patrick declares that "as he was a Catholic, he would kick in the set if the fetus lost" (7). Mary, it turns out, is unmarried and pregnant. Patrick, it turns out, is not a practicing Catholic.

The exchanges between Mary and Patrick most completely reveal the religious alternative to sadness-for-no-reason, although he is so fearful and repelled by her insane talk and bizarre behavior that he misses the spiritual opportunities. The novel's implied author, of course, is the agent presenting us with an unwed and pregnant Mary who is obsessed with religious experience that either repels or eludes Patrick. Sorting through Mary's deranged but nevertheless accurate admonitions about his irresponsibility, the forces of evil, and "the universe," Patrick realizes that she is "stuck on" Catholicism. Resisting "what he saw as her irrationality," however, he is blinded to the truths beyond the madness. To Mary's comment that "There-are-none-so-blind-as-those-who-will-not-see," Patrick responds, "Yeah, right." Because of his pride, Patrick can't hear the messages Mary brings him. He misses not only Mary's earlier warnings based on an underlying Catholicism about responsibility and evil but also her later warning in her ramblings about "mortal offenses" which Patrick half-listens to while noting without registering its significance that she is reading De Laclos's *Liaisons Dangereuses* (96).

Nevertheless, Mary's ideas do make Patrick spiritually uncomfortable, and he finds himself reflecting self-critically that in his mid-thirties he is still drawn to live by those "easy rules of an unextended self" (67). The Catholic antidote to Patrick's moral lassitude, sadness-for-no-reason, sense of abandonment, and spiritual obtuseness, is, nevertheless, near at hand. That antidote is suggested when Mary, just before she commits suicide, plays the Bud Powell jazz rendition she and Patrick love of "Someone to Watch over Me" (100). The song is a reminder that Patrick has failed in meeting his responsibilities to watch over Mary, but it is also a reminder that no Christian is abandoned. According to Catholic tradition, everyone has a guardian angel who protects and guides, as well as saints who hear petitions because they are watching over believers.

Before her death, Mary had been reading works by St. John of the Cross, whom Patrick did not recognize because he thought that "only Jesus was the one with the cross" (24). Patrick could have benefited from more knowledge of the Spanish saint and author of *The Dark Night of the Soul* as well as *The Living Flame*, mystical lyrics about purifying the soul through patient suffering and detachment. Mary also had been reading the Spanish St. Theresa of Avila's poems about the progress of the Christian soul toward God (23). More obscurely, McGuane is alluding to St. Theresa as the patron saint of aviators. This allusion has special meaning because the novel opens with Patrick locating a dead aviator who had crashed in the mountains and whose position "seemed the image of a man in receipt of a final sacrament" (4). The novel ends with the suicide death of Tio Burnett, the husband of Patrick's lover, in his helicopter (211). From the first death Patrick learns "that life doesn't just drag on" (the lesson Chet Pomeroy had learned at his brother's coffin) and from the last death that he is a sinner (as Pomeroy had learned by giving up his messianic illusions). Patrick, who wishes to be "somebody's angel" turns out to be "nobody's angel" because he had neglected looking out for his sister and had taken Claire as his lover after her husband had asked him "to be kind of a big brother" to her (53). Besides, as the colloquial meaning of "nobody's angel" indicates, he is not a good man, even if sympathetically portrayed. His father's death was "an archangelic semaphore more dignified than death itself," which Patrick cannot decipher, but which is, still, a message from the angels (5). The dead pilots had "someone to watch over" them—a patron saint, a guardian angel, and God.

Mary's ravings and the symbolism of the dead flyers are not the only religious messages Patrick doesn't hear and understand. Ironically, Patrick's adulterous relations with Claire are fraught with religious implications which Claire understands and mentions. From the beginning, Claire understands more than Patrick does of their souls' jeopardy. The first time he makes his sexual desire known to Claire, she is described as having some kind of "absolute revelation" and makes love to him "while his attempts to remember what it was he was doing, to determine what this meant, seemed to knock like pebbles dropped down a well, long lost from sight. He was gone into something blinding and it wasn't exactly love" (78). The sex is never right—Patrick experiences "mortal confusion" and Claire is "more martyred than loved" (211). It is, indeed, "mortal," not just "moral," confusion. In adolescence, Patrick had received traditional Catholic warnings about sexual impulses and behaviors; sex and sin, in fact, had been inextricable in Patrick's Catholic upbringing. He remembers his adolescent guilt and fear of purgatory, phoning Claire, even, to confess that he "fear(s) purgatory at the very least" (148, 169). But that fear is momentary since Patrick wants to believe that his feelings for Claire are sufficient justification for his behavior, that "sufficiency rather than salvation was at issue" (181).

McGuane establishes the connection between sex and mortal sin most dramatically in the conclusion of the novel after Tio commits suicide over Patrick's and Claire's affair. Claire, discussing sin in the face of Patrick's denial, summarizes what happened by asserting, "We fucked him to death." Lust and boredom, Patrick finally thinks, had "made thrill-killers of nice people" (211).

Catholicism has not failed; Patrick has failed. Early in the novel, when Claire asks if he is Catholic and he answers "I consider myself one," she understands that, "you mean you aren't practicing" (46). Moreover, the novel's religious language and allusions persistently evoke a spiritual alternative. When Claire and Patrick go dancing Saturday night at the Northbranch saloon, for instance, the band plays three cheating songs in a row as well as "The Window up Above" (the problem and the solution) (199). The saloon lights create an ecclesiastical atmosphere and remind Patrick of flames in the Bible, not just the flames of hell but the flames of divine love that purify the soul in St. John of the Cross' lyrics (198). There are "archangelic semaphores" everywhere.

In this charged atmosphere, Patrick tries but fails to create positive accounts of his motives and intentions in his affair with Claire, most notably a version in which he again portrays himself as a guardian angel protecting her from her husband. Tio: "Altruistic cowboy tank captain rescues princess of the Cimarron from mock-epileptic oil-and-gas-lease scoundrel" (199). But he is no one's rescuer, nobody's angel, and knows "the road to hell has seen more paving materials than the Appian Way, I-90 and A-1-A combined" (199). Ironically, and pathetically, having confused profane and sacred love, Patrick's lament to Claire is, "I thought love was all that mattered" (212).

Patrick, finally, returns to the army, buys a flat in Madrid as he had fantasized earlier and, as the last line of the novel says, he "never came home again" (214). A rumor heard by

Patrick's enemy, Deke Patwell, Deadrock's newspaper editor, is that Patrick is a blackout drinker living with an American woman named Marion Easterly.

What is to be made of Patrick Fitzgerald's final situation? Is he doomed to remain on the edges with no middle? Certainly that is possible, even likely. Commenting on Patrick's situation at the conclusion of *Nobody's Angel*, McGuane has said that "Patrick's situation is the modern situation: the adhesion of people to place has been lost. . . . [Y]ou either get out and do something else or the conditions will destroy you. I didn't think Patrick could win his war because his basics are fouled up, so he had to accept himself as an *isolato*" (McCaffery 203). Patrick, like so many of the protagonists Paul Giles finds in novels by Irish American Catholics, will never be "at home within any given setting" (400).

But allusions to Catholicism persist in evoking more positive possibilities for Patrick even though he has lost his connection to place and home. His last fantasy about living in Spain had been that "the question of smelly imbroglios starring oil-minded Southwesterners could not happen to him, stainless in Madrid." There "he'd go to the odd mass or two, not in *preparation*, as he might in the remorseless West; but in the healthy, ghoulish attendance of Spain, to stare at the wooden blood and pus on the old Stations of the Cross" (177). Referring to this passage about Spain, Jon Wallace concludes perceptively that despite the negative tone there is an "undercurrent of religious seriousness" through which McGuane can pay homage "to traditional religious values in a book written for a highly literate and spiritually skeptical audience" (298). Spain, we might remember in addition, was home for St. John of the Cross and St. Theresa of Avila.

The final mention of "Marion Easterly" is, moreover, ambiguously referential to both Patrick's escapism and a spiritual alternative, the dialectical poles of this novel. Marion Easterly was the fantasy girlfriend Patrick invented so as to hide his adolescent late-night carousing in town from his parents; later she became an extended fantasy of idealized womanhood which he indulges in "times of great tribulation" (175). "Beautiful in mind and spirit," Marion is entangled in Patrick's thoughts of other women, notably Claire and Mary (73, 113). Angry with Claire at one point, he puts her off by saying he's reading *The Life of Marion Easterly* "and it's by all three Brontë sisters" (204). But, surely, Marion Easterly is also a figure beyond adolescent idealization and lingering Victorianism. She is a promise of Christian possibilities in her name's evocation of both Mary and Easter, of divine love and the possibility of redemption, no matter how unredeemed Patrick seems. One hopes his sister Mary was more right than she knew when insisting that Marion Easterly is Patrick Fitzgerald's "greatest love" (175).

The religious preoccupations of *Panama* and *Nobody's Angel* are echoed in the several McGuane novels that precede and follow them: individual and social spiritual conditions are intertwined, a spiritual blight spreads, but some spiritual vitality may remain in Christianity, particularly Roman Catholicism. Christianity, in any case, whether moribund or efficacious, determines themes, topics, language, and outcomes in McGuane's novels. McGuane's protagonists are out of joint with themselves, their times, and "the universe." Nicholas Payne in *Bushwhacked Piano* (1971) speaks for them all when he observes, "Some varmint signed me up for a bum trip. And, quite honestly, I don't see why" (86). The culture isn't sustaining: Payne also says, if with a sense of his own melodrama, that "the U.S.A. is a floating crap game of strangling spiritual credit" (91). America has become "Hotcakesland" where "it is all for sale" (*Ninety-Two* 53).

McGuane's protagonists know, then, that something is radically wrong, but they lack the inner resources and vision to solve their problems—in fact, self-destructively, they contribute to them. Thomas Skelton, in *Ninety-Two in the Shade* (1973) has the "reflex to be a practicing Christian" but not the focus. Consequently, Skelton fails utterly, shot through the heart because of his pride. He has left "faith, hope and charity . . . largely untried" and has "an unformed vision of how he ought to live on earth with others" (22).

The central figures in McGuane's more recent novels grope toward spiritual renewal despite their unextended selves and unformed visions. At the conclusion of *Something to be Desired* (1984), for instance, Lucien Taylor gives a speech to his community about "his town and his country and his life." He talks about "children and the next world." His neighbors and friends cheer "with such merriment and accord and humanity that in it was a kind of sacrament between them all." Lucien couldn't "imagine where it was coming from" because earlier he, with a "battered soul," was "not sure the Savior actually got me off the long and lonely road" (167-68, 92, 94). Similarly, Joe Starling in *Keep the Change.* (1989), who "never quite . . . escaped [the feeling] that life had as one of its constant characteristics a strain of unbearable loneliness," learns at last that "somewhere in the abyss something shone," a gift of hope and faith (96, 215).

These spiritual preoccupations signify that Thomas McGuane's fiction belongs in discussions of contemporary writing shaped by Roman Catholicism. His identification with his Irish Catholic family history establishes for his novels a broad Roman Catholic perspective. Noting that in contemporary fiction by Catholics "formal Christianity and Catholicism resonate in various ways and in varying degrees of intensity," John F. Desmond sketches a broad category in which we can easily place McGuane's novels. For writers such as Louise Erdrich, Andre Dubus, and Tobias Wolf,

Desmond writes, Catholicism is mostly a "shadowy presence that haunts the pilgrims' journeys" (11).

Catholicism's shadowy presence in McGuane's fiction reveals itself in frequent authorial allusions to Catholic belief and ritual, as well as an array of themes clustering around such topics as guilt, judgment, and lives *in extremis*. It is revealed, too, by protagonists and narrators whose language, often ironically and many times comically, is the language of religion: heaven, hell, purgatory, salvation, damnation, Jesus, Mary, God, Devil, angel, sacrament, sacred, and so on. Like Flannery O'Connor's, Thomas McGuane's Irish Catholic heritage leads him to view the world as fallen, even purgatorial. But McGuane's comment that he "pines" for religion helps us understand that, unlike O'Connor's, his characters do not unequivocally experience or acknowledge grace's potential or reality. They are never free in the ways Saul Bellow's Henderson or Augie March are; they are more like Fitzgerald's, Kerouac's and Donleavy's protagonists. Unextended selves with unformed visions, McGuane's characters are not spiritually fit; but they do have souls whose journeys are not completed and whose destinies are not fully known. For them to succeed, some overarching authority, whether it is to be found in the Roman Catholic Church or not, or through Christ's redemptive sacrifice or not, is required beyond the will, intelligence, and actions of these suffering individuals. Behind McGuane's fiction is no absolute faith in communal renewal and solidarity through Roman Catholic sacraments, and no acceptance of the dogmas of Catholic orthodoxy. While reading McGuane's fiction, however, it is wise to be on the lookout for signs of possible grace and redemption.

NOTES

1. McGuane's "earth-worshipping pantheism" is too complex a subject to treat fully here. Some sense of its dimensions, however, can be gotten from his essay on bonefishing, "Close to the Bone" (*Chance*). On one hand, the consolation of bonefishing is that one visits another world, "a world whose cycles and conditions" are "serene to the addled twentieth-century angler." The angler "is searching less for recreation than for a kind of stillness" and finds in the bonefish a creature "radiant with nearly celestial beauty" (59). But if contact with the celestial is one dimension, the other is a more worldly boon, "the necessary, ecstatic resignation to the moment" ("The Longest Silence," *Chance* 21). And everywhere in McGuane's writing are catalogs of "sins" against nature.

2. In his interview with McCaffery and Gregory, McGuane commented that he identified himself with Pomeroy and his wife with Catherine. Pomeroy's loss of Catherine was "so absolutely agonizing that, unlaminated to something better, it was nihilistic. And I'm not a nihilist and didn't want this book to be nihilistic. . . . At that point in the end, when he's hit absolute rock bottom, the question becomes, Does he bounce, or does he flatten out and lie there? In my opinion he bounced. Slightly" (201).

WORKS CITED

Desmond, John F. "Catholicism in Contemporary American Fiction." *America* 170.17 (1994): 7-11.

Fisher. James T. *The Catholic Counterculture in America.* Chapel Hill: U of North Carolina P, 1989.

Giles, Paul, *American Catholic Arts and Fictions: Culture, Ideology, Aesthetics.* Cambridge: Cambridge UP, 1992.

McGuane, Thomas. *Bushwacked Piano*, 1971. New York: Vintage Books, 1984.

——. Interview with Gregory L. Morris. "Thomas McGuane." *Talking Up a Storm: Voices of the New West.* Lincoln: U of Nebraska P. 1994. 201-12.

——. Interview with Larry McCaffery and Sinda Gregory. "An Interview with Thomas McGuane." *Alive and Writing: Interviews with American Authors of the 1980s.* Urbana: U of Illinois P. 1987, 196-221.

——. *Keep the Change.* New York: Random House, 1989.

——. *Ninety-Two in the Shade.* 1973. New York: Penguin, 1980.

——. *Nobody's Angel.* 1981. New York: Ballantine, 1983.

——. *Nothing But Blue Skies.* New York: Houghton Mifflin/ Seymour Lawrence, 1992.

——. *An Outside Chance: Essays on Sport.* New York: Penguin, 1982.

——. *Panama.* 1978. New York: Penguin, 1979.

——. *Something to be Desired.* 1984. New York: Vintage, 1985.

——. *The Sporting Club.* 1969. New York: Penguin, 1979.

Wallace, Jon. "Speaking Against the Dark: Style as Theme in Thomas McGuane's *Nobody's Angel." Modern Fiction Studies* 33.3 (1987): 289-298.

FURTHER READING

Criticism

Garcia, Guy D. "He's Left No Stone Unturned." *Time*, 25 December 1989: pp. 70-2.

> Essay in which Garcia discusses McGuane's current lifestyle and writing habits as a "gentleman rancher and Marlboro Man of Letters."

Interview

Gregory, Sinda and Larry McCaffery. "The Art of Fiction LXXXIX: An Interview with Thomas McGuane." *Paris Review* 27, No. 97 (Fall 1985): 34-71.

> An in-depth interview in which McGuane discusses his early years as a writer, his writing methods, and his experiences as a director and screenwriter.

Additional coverage of McGuane's life and career is contained in the following sources publishes by Gale: *Authors in the News,* **Vol. 2;** *Contemporary Authors,* **Vols. 49-52;** *Contemporary Authors New Revision Series,* **Vols. 5, 24, 49;** *Dictionary of Literary Biography,* **Vols. 2, 212;** *Dictionary of Literary Biography Yearbook,* **Vol. 80;** *Major Twentieth-Century Writers,* **Vol. 1.**

Larry McMurtry

1936-

(Full name Larry Jeff McMurtry) American novelist, essayist, and screenwriter.

The following entry presents an overview of McMurtry's career through 1999. For further information on his life and works, see *CLC*, Volumes 2, 3, 7, 11, 27, and 44.

INTRODUCTION

McMurtry was known in the 1960s and 1970s as a regional author of distinction and acclaimed as a new voice from Texas. In his works, McMurtry reexamines the frontier myth, introducing more fully developed characters and a darker mood to the Western novel. However, with the publication of *Lonesome Dove* (1985)—his Pulitzer-Prize-winning, epic-length saga of a nineteenth-century cattle drive—McMurtry became a household name, praised by the public and critics alike. His works continue to focus on tensions between urbanization and the myth of the Texas frontier, as well as disillusionment among aging characters resistant to change. Many of McMurtry's novels, including *Horseman, Pass By* (1961), *The Last Picture Show* (1966), *Terms of Endearment* (1975), and *The Evening Star* (1992), have been made into successful films. McMurtry is known also for his essays that explore transitions in Texas literature and the nature of the film industry.

Biographical Information

McMurtry was born June 3, 1936, in Wichita Falls, Texas, to William Jefferson and Hazel Ruth McIver McMurtry. He grew up on his father's ranch, an experience from which he would draw material throughout his career. After graduating from Archer City High School in 1954, he attended North Texas State College where he earned a B.A. in 1958. He received an M.A. from Rice University in 1960 and studied under a Stegner Fellowship at Stanford University from 1960 to 1961. In 1959 he married Josephine Scot with whom he had one son; the couple divorced in 1966. McMurtry took numerous short-term teaching assignments at Texas colleges and universities during the 1960s while he wrote. He published *Horseman, Pass By* in 1961 to strong critical reviews. The book was adapted into a movie entitled *Hud* the following year and won two Academy Awards. McMurtry continued developing his reputation—albeit as a regional writer–and published *The Last Picture Show* in 1966. He won an Oscar in 1972 for his work on the screenplay of this movie. By the 1970s he left Texas, opening a rare bookshop in Washington D.C.; however, he continued to write about both rural and urban Texans. While McMurtry's reputation as a writer and his popularity grew, it was not until the publication of his novel, *Lonesome Dove*, that he received widespread national recognition. He won the 1986 Pulitzer Prize for Fiction for the novel and achieved greater acclaim when it was made into a popular television series. McMurtry has continued to write throughout the 1990s, publishing a sequel and two prequels in his *Lonesome Dove* series. In addition, he has collaborated with other writers on two fictional histories of real historical characters: Billy the Kid and Pretty Boy Floyd. He lives and writes in Arizona and Texas as well as managing his bookshop in Washington, D.C.

Major Works

McMurtry has published continuously and extensively throughout his career, writing several series of novels centering on common characters or places. His work is united by his themes, which include reluctance to face change, conflict between urbanization and Western myth, importance of place, and the role of the land. McMurtry's themes also include the emptiness of sex versus the promise of love, the void in marriage and family, the nostalgia of the past, emptiness of the present, and hopelessness of the future. In novels such as *Horseman, Pass By* and *The Last Picture Show*, McMurtry explores coming of age, as the youth of rural Texas face difficult choices, a lack of opportunities, needs which do not match resources, and disillusionment and loss of innocence. Throughout his career, McMurtry has explored these issues, following his characters throughout their lives. For instance, in his books about the mythical small town Thalia, Duane grows from an idealistic teen in love with the unobtainable Jacy in *The Last Picture Show* to the wealthy but unhappy middle-aged father in *Texasville* (1987) to the moody and eccentric individual depicted in *Duane's Depressed* (1999). His most famous series centers on Woodrow Call and Augustus McCrae, first introduced as two former rangers hired on a cross country cattle drive in *Lonesome Dove*. In this lengthy epic, McMurtry alters the traditional Western formula, depicting his characters as both heroic and human. In this novel, he also creates strong female characters, embodying the traditional plot of the trials and dangers of the frontier with deeper ideological issues. In his sequel and prequels *Streets of Laredo* (1993), *Dead Man's Walk* (1995), and *Comanche Moon* (1997), McMurtry expands the story of the central characters' lives from young and immature Texas Rangers to old and bitter men longing for the glory of their youth, unable to come to terms with the changes in Texas. In the 1990s McMurtry began to explore the fictionalization of historic figures in such novels as *Anything for Billy* (1987), a highly inventive tale of Billy the Kid which barely matches historical accounts. He also co-wrote *Pretty Boy Floyd* (1994), which was produced as a movie at the same time, along with *Crazy Horse* (1999), a book about the famous Sioux warrior.

Critical Reception

McMurtry received favorable critiques of his writing with his first novels even though he was relatively unknown and considered primarily a Western writer. In fact, scholars still list his first four books as some of his best work: *Horseman, Pass By*, *Leaving Cheyenne* (1963), *The Last Picture Show* and his collection of essays, *In a Narrow Grave* (1968). Critics such as John Leonard reviewing *Moving On* (1970), Ruth Prigozy writing about *All My Friends Are Going to Be Strangers* (1970) and Dorothy Rabinowitz in regards to *Terms of Endearment*, echo numerous other critiques in praising McMurtry's realistic and engaging dialogue, description of place, attention to detail, and entertaining sense of humor. These same reviewers argue that McMurtry is overindulgent, exaggerates, loses sight of his point with too much detail, and is too verbose. Nevertheless, most critics say the balance sways in favor of McMurtry, and argue that his wit and insight make up for the length and lack of focus in many of his works. Most scholars agree McMurtry's best work is *Lonesome Dove*, a novel they credit with reforming the Western genre. Reviewers praise the novel as a humorous but sincere tribute to the American West, full of rich detail and panoramic scenery. However, some reviewers have also noted that the novel is built on stereotypical characters and dubious historical accuracy. "*Lonesome Dove* is Larry McMurtry's loftiest novel, a wondrous work, drowned in love, melancholy, and yet, ultimately, exultant," said John Horne. McMurtry's work since *Lonesome Dove* is consistently compared to the novel, often unfavorably. Nevertheless, some critics note McMurtry's subsequent works still represent substantial accomplishments even though they lack in the scope and appeal of *Lonesome Dove*. Some critics have said that many of McMurtry's recent novels read like movie scripts. Others, however, praise his work, saying McMurtry brings the imagined West to life with his characters, attention to detail, and humor. In her review of *Streets of Laredo*, Denise Dwinnells said McMurtry is ". . . a man who writes as well about women as any American male ever has. . . ." McMurtry's work has mostly received an enthusiastic reception. "When a writer is as good as Mr. McMurtry is," Jack Butler said, "even a relatively minor book is a major event."

PRINCIPAL WORKS

Horseman, Pass By (novel) 1961
Leaving Cheyenne (novel) 1963
†*The Last Picture Show* (novel) 1966
In a Narrow Grave: Essays on Texas (essays) 1968
Moving On (novel) 1970
All My Friends Are Going to Be Strangers (novel) 1972
Terms of Endearment (novel) 1975
Somebody's Darling (novel) 1978
Cadillac Jack (novel) 1982
The Desert Rose (novel) 1983
Lonesome Dove (novel) 1985
Anything for Billy (novel) 1987
Film Flam: Essays on Hollywood (essays) 1987
‡*Texasville* (novel) 1987
Some Can Whistle (novel) 1989
Buffalo Girls (novel) 1990
The Evening Star (novel) 1992
Falling from Grace (screenplay) 1992
Streets of Laredo (novel) 1993
Pretty Boy Floyd [with Diana Ossana] (novel) 1994
Dead Man's Walk (novel) 1995
The Late Child (novel) 1995
Comanche Moon (novel) 1997
Zeke and Ned (novel) 1997
Crazy Horse (novel) 1999
Duane's Depressed (novel) 1999

*This novel was republished as *Hud* in 1963.

†The screenplay for *The Last Picture Show* (1971) was written by McMurtry and Peter Bogdanovich.

‡McMurtry wrote the screenplay for *Texasville* (1990).

CRITICISM

Walter Clemons (review date 15 August 1971)

SOURCE: "The Last Word: An Overlooked Novel," in *New York Times Book Review*, August 15, 1971, p. 39.

[*In the following review, Clemons praises* Leaving Cheyenne *as McMurtry's best work, lamenting its lack of popularity.*]

Edmund Wilson on one of life's pleasures: "There are few things I enjoy so much as talking to people about books which I have read and they haven't, and making them wish they had—preferably a book that is hard to get or in a language that they do not know." Earlier this summer there appeared an agreeable book called *Rediscoveries*, edited by David Madden, who enlisted 27 novelists to write about their favorite neglected works of fiction. Besides full-length essays such as Robert Penn Warren's on Andrew Lytle's *The Long Night*, Joyce Carol Oates on Harriette Arnow's *The Dollmaker*, and Evan S. Connell Jr. on Janet Lewis's *The Wife of Martin Guerre*, the book has a valuable checklist of 210 other ignored or out-of-fashion novels and short-story collections worth investigating.

Here I looked for a novel I like a lot, Larry McMurtry's ***Leaving Cheyenne***, but was not much surprised to find it unlisted. Not surprised, because though it's not exactly a secret that McMurtry is one of the two best writers to come out of Texas in the last ten years (Donald Barthelme's the other), he's been pigeon-holed as the creator of ***Hud***. The Paul Newman-Patricia Neal movie was based on McMurtry's first book, ***Horseman, Pass By*** (1961), of which he has since sternly written that it "has its moments, but they do not keep it from being a slight, confused, and sentimental first novel."

Leaving Cheyenne was his second novel. When Harper & Row published it in the fall of 1963, fewer than a thousand people bought it. At least five more read it and liked it in 1964, when I bought up five copies at a dollar each in Marboro and passed them out, but this funny, wonderful, heartbreaking book has been pretty thoroughly ignored. ***Horseman, Pass By*** is better than its author now says, but ***Leaving Cheyenne*** is better still; a rarity among second novels in its exhilarating ease, assurance and openness of feeling.

The title comes from a cowboy song:

My foot's in the stirrup,
My pony won't stand;
Goodbye, old partner,
I'm leaving Cheyenne.

This isn't Cheyenne, WY, nor are we reading a Western. A rather florid author's note (McMurtry was 27) explains; "The Cheyenne of this book is that part of the cowboy's day's circle which is earliest and best: his blood's country and his heart's pastureland." The book's actual locale is McMurtry's dry, West Texas Archer County. Here we meet, sometime around 1920, the three country people we follow until one of them dies 40 years later: Gideon Fry, a bothered, puritanical heir to his father's ranch and responsibilities; Johnny McCloud, his footloose cowboy friend; and the woman both of them love, Molly, who marries neither but bears each of them a son. The three take turns telling their story, with twenty-year gaps between the novel's three sections.

McMurtry is psychologically precise in tracing this three-sided relationship, which one Texan—nervously, I thought—denounced to me as "preposterous." "I know why you don't come to see me as much any more," Molly tells Gid at one point in their youth. "It's because Johnny's gone. You don't really care much about me, do you? You just like to spite Johnny." Gid adds: "She was wrong about that and we both knew it, but it was true that I got a little extra kick out of being with Molly when Johnny was around to notice it." We learn, too, that Molly has no women friends, she doesn't like them. Before we can formulate "She doesn't like herself," we learn this from Molly's own account of her relations with her brutal father and the worthless Eddie she marries: "He's the only one silly enough for me." The psychopathology is exactly charted; but McMurtry is interested in something else. Odd as the roots of this friendship may seem, there's enduring consideration and feeling in it. The story takes so many years to tell because feelings that last a lifetime are its subject.

In the telling, the self-conscious poeticism of that quoted author's note utterly disappears. There's nothing Larry McMurtry doesn't know about the way Texas people think and talk: for instance, that a cowboy moving into a fight, instead of uttering laconic threats, may respond in cheery mock-surprise "Goodness me" to his opponent's challenge. As a displanted Texan myself, I admit a bias here: the voices in the book make me sick for home. Yet I believe a reader from anywhere else will respond to delicacy and precision when he hears it. I like the book most of all because I like the people in it: each time I read it, I feel a wrench at leaving the first narrator and skipping twenty years to go on to the next, because I've forgotten that I'll like the second narrator so much I'll be sorry again when she finishes and the third voice takes up the story.

To cover so many years *Leaving Cheyenne* is a fairly short novel, with breathtaking foreshortenings—such as Molly's response to the news of a son's death in World War II: "They killed my last old boy." Here, economically, chillingly, we learn of the more hurtful loss of her other son. We don't quite believe her; we think we must have misunderstood; and then a few pages later it's confirmed.

Since *Leaving Cheyenne*, Larry McMurtry has published a good little novel, *The Last Picture Show* (1966) and a big not-so-good one, *Moving On* (1970). In between these two came his best book after *Leaving Cheyenne*, *In a Narrow Grave: Essays on Texas* (1968), which was published by a small press in Austin and has now been made available in paperback. In it we meet a salty, highly intelligent writer going his own way, and we learn some interesting things about what he's up to.

McMurtry comes from a family of ranchers and cowboys in northwest Texas, about whom he is, in a complicated way, admiring, sardonically funny and rudely, reluctantly acute. When he wrote these essays during the sixties, he was intent on sticking to his home ground and recording the shift from range to suburb: "Being a writer and a Texan is an amusing fate, one that gets funnier as one's sense of humor darkens. . . . The transition that is taking place is very difficult, and the situations it creates are very intense. Living here consciously uses a great deal of one's blood; it involves one at once in a birth, a death, and a bitter love affair."

A bitter love affair with the present is visible in McMurtry's latest novel, *Moving On*. In it, his eye and ear are as exact as before; nostalgia is quelled. He commits himself to the viewpoint of Patsy, an entirely believable, rather tiresome girl who cries, by my rough count, some 70 times during the book but when she isn't crying is stubbornly, acidly observant of ordinary, dully daylit scenes of contemporary Texas life. Though it's something of a chore to get through on a first try, it may turn out, like Philip Roth's sprawling *Letting Go*, to be a valuable step forward in its author's career. After finishing *Moving On*, McMurtry left Texas, I'm told, and now lives in the East. There isn't really any telling what he may yet do. A few years ago he took to wearing a black sweatshirt emblazoned MINOR REGIONAL NOVELIST, to his publishers' horror. Regional, he was; minor he's not. He's now all of 35.

James R. Giles (essay date Summer-Fall 1972)

SOURCE: "Larry McMurtry's *Leaving Cheyenne* and the Novels of John Rechy: Four Trips Along 'The Mythical Pecos'," in *Forum*, Vol. 10, No. 2, Summer-Fall, 1972, pp. 34-40.

[*In the following essay, Giles, a professor of American Literature at Northern Illinois University, considers the transformation of Texas literature and compares the work of McMurtry and John Rechy.*]

In the fall, 1969, issue of *Western American Literature*, the editor praises Larry McMurtry's collection of essays, *In a Narrow Grave*, for doing "two things very well. It assesses Texas culture and describes the quality of the life it has fostered. It explores the problems of a native Texas novelist in using creatively such traditions out of the past as the vanished god, the horseman, as well as life to the present moment that has been affected by that past."[1] This evaluation is undeniably correct. However the book represents more: first, it is a literary Declaration of Independence for the Texas writer from those restrictions of language and subject matter that so confined Dobie, Webb, and Bedichek (McMurtry is aware that this independence has been a *fait accompli* for some time); and, second, it develops a really complex theory about the relationship of the end of Texas' physical frontier and the present and future explorations into its literary frontiers. McMurtry ends his book with these words:

> Texas is rich in unredeemed dreams, and now that the dust of its herds is settling the writers will be out on their pencils, looking for them in the suburbs and along the mythical Pecos. And except to paper riders, the Pecos is a lonely and a bitter stream.
>
> I have that from men who rode it and who knew that country round—such as it was, such as it can never be again.[2]

He is asserting that the creative energy and imagination that went into settling the Texas frontier will, now that the frontier is gone, be channeled into literary attempts at comprehending the meaning of the Texas frontier heritage. McMurtry is also implying, of course, that much of this meaning, when discovered, will not be pretty—the *real* "Pecos is a lonely and a bitter stream." McMurtry's realization that this process of discovery and literary exploration is well under way is evident in the following wry lines from the essay **"Southwestern Literature:"**

> Nowadays, of course, Texas writers are scattered high, wide, and lonesome. The generation of which I am a member has barely got started, yet already a younger generation blossoms beneath our feet. A hastily constructed literary map of the state shows that novelists in veritable swarms have begun to emerge from the small towns. One notes the (to me) extraordinary fact that such communities as Chillicothe, Archer City, Stamford, Clarksville, Floydada, Groesbeck, Alvarado,

Abilene, and Dundee have produced novelists and can thus no longer be considered intellectually virgin. Some, of course, probably consider that they have been intellectually raped; but if we assume, as we must, that the writers who have published are merely the top of the iceberg (or let's say the ant-bed), the prospect is little short of terrifying. If these creative writing courses aren't stopped, every town in Texas will have its novelist within a decade, and the novelists will have to follow the lead of the oilman and apply for a depletion allowance.

(p. 53)

This growth of literary activity in Texas is astonishing. McMurtry believes, both in terms of its rapidity ("No fiction of interest was produced in Texas before the fifties" [p. 52], he unarguably states—the fifties being the decade in which Texas became a largely urbanized state) and its cosmopolitanism (he maintains that it was not until World War II "that Texas writers learned that they could leave the state without turning to dust at the borders" [p. 52]). Then in "a Maileresque glance at the talent in the room," he simply lists a group of twenty-nine Texas writers ranging from the fairly traditional stylist, William Humphrey, with his invariable Southwestern setting and subject matter, to such *avant garde* experimenters in technique as Donald Barthelme and Terry Southern, who are anything but *obviously* regional in their setting and subject matter. It is with the response to the loss of the frontier heritage on the part of McMurtry himself, who, of course, more closely resembles the Humphrey "side of the room," and with that of John Rechy, who is included in "the Maileresque glance" and who must be seated near Barthelme and Southern, that this essay is concerned. Moreover, the discussion in regard to McMurtry will be limited to his second novel, **Leaving Cheyenne**, because it, more than his other novels, primarily emphasizes the loss of the frontier heritage.

Although praised by the (London) *Times Literary Supplement*, by James Baldwin and by Herbert Gold, among other critics, and included in the list of significant contemporary writers in the Hills' anthology of current American fiction *How We Live*, John Rechy has the literary reputation of a major "underground novelist" because of his subject matter, the world of the male homosexual, particularly that of the "hustler." In the novels, *City of Night* (1963), *Numbers* (1967), and *This Day's Death* (1969), Rechy graphically depicts the lonely and ugly world of the compulsive male homosexual in a detail that is rare in American literature and unheard of in a Texas writer. Supporting McMurtry's thesis about cosmopolitanism, the setting of *City of Night* ranges from New York to Los Angeles to San Francisco to New Orleans; *Numbers* is largely set in Los Angeles; and *This Day's Death* shifts from El Paso to Los Angeles. Nevertheless, all

three novels center around a main character who considers himself to be a Texan. *City of Night* begins and ends in El Paso (Rechy's home), and *Numbers* opens with the main character just leaving Laredo on a significant journey to the West Coast. *This Day's Death* is about a native of El Paso facing a trial for homosexuality in Los Angeles. There are additional reasons for considering Rechy a Texas writer, one of the major ones being that an underlying theme in both novels is the "lonely and bitter" reality of the "Pecos" or Texas frontiers. Moreover, Rechy considers himself to be a Texas writer as he confirmed to me in an interview in January, 1972. He works basically out of El Paso, and he has contributed essays about Texas social problems to the *Texas Observer*. So, ready or not, Texas literature already has its Jean Genet. Thus, Rechy, like McMurtry himself, albeit in a *seemingly* quite different way, is an example of both McMurtry's assertions in **In a Narrow Grave** (he deals with subject matter that Dobie, Webb, and Bedichek would not have touched), and he personifies the new Texas writer who is reaching for creative, imaginative frontiers to replace the lost one and who realizes some of the ugliness involved in "the mythical Pecos."

As mentioned, McMurtry's treatment of these two related literary phenomena in **Leaving Cheyenne** is, on the surface, much more traditional and sentimental. Again, as in all McMurtry, there is a deeply felt regret at the end of the old way of life. Perhaps the passage which best exemplifies this sense of something having been lost forever occurs near the end of the novel when Gid Fry, the personification of the old idealistic Texas frontier traditions of duty, hard work, and Puritanism, complains to his lifelong friend, Johnny McCloud, the embodiment of frontier hedonism, about the growing number of restrictions being placed on the individual rancher by the federal government: "'Ten more years like this and it will strain a man to make an honest living in this country.'" Johnny, realistically aware of such things as oil-depletion allowances and related loopholes, answers simply: "'It strains the ones that make an honest living now, . . . but that don't affect the majority.'"[3] Gid's sense of "honesty" is emphasized throughout the novel; early in the book when he is "taken" in a cattle deal by a slicker, more experienced trader from South Texas, his reaction is predictable:

> I seen right then I was going to have to pay better attention if I was ever going to make a cattleman. Only I just gave up for that day. Losing that money kinda made me sick. I wanted to whip that South Texas bastard, but I didn't have a legitimate reason to. He had skinned me fair and square. It just left a bad taste in my mouth.

(p. 66)

This code of frontier honesty, as well as his sense of duty, has been inherited from his father. At one point in the novel,

Gid challenges his father's puritanical work drive with this comment:

> "Why, I think life's a damn sight more fun than that." "You ain't lived one," he said. Then he told me how much work we were going to get done that winter.
>
> (p. 78)

Gid's father realizes that he is an anachronism, and he commits suicide: his suicide note is perhaps the most touching example in the novel of the code of the dying way of life:

> Dear Gid:
>
> Miserable night. There's no profit in putting up with this.
>
> I think I'll go out on the hill and turn my horses free, or did you ever know that song. It's an old one.
>
> Take good care of the ranch, it's a dilly, and don't trust ever damn fool that comes up the road. Always work outside when you can, it's the healthiest thing.
>
> Tell Miss Molly I appreciated her coming and helping us, just tell her much obliged until she is better paid.
>
> Well, this is the longest letter I've written in ten years, it is too long. Be sure and get that windmill fixed, I guess you had better put in some new sucker rod.
>
> Your dad
>
> (p. 123)

The simple understatement of this letter is obviously modeled on one which McMurtry actually received from an uncle whose wife had been killed in an automobile accident. The novelist describes this letter, which he quotes in *In a Narrow Grave*, as "echt-cowboy." The letter, which is eleven paragraphs long, makes only this passing reference to the dead wife:

> Yes it was an awful tragedy to have Mint crushed in the smashup, my car was a total loss too.
>
> Things like that will just happen though. It is lonesome dreary out here in the backwoods by myself.
>
> (pp. 151-152)

It is fitting that Gid, every bit his father's son, dies still trying to fix the windmill mentioned in the father's suicide note. Before Gid falls from the windmill to his death, Johnny asks him why a man of his age and his money is "'still fighting a goddam windmill.'" He answers, "'Sometimes I wonder myself'" (p. 287). Then Johnny realizes, after the fall, that Gid had to try to fix the windmill for the same reason that, when he was a young man, he had to keep trying to ride a horse named Old Missouri which had thrown him six times. It's the code (p. 289). The Quixotic overtones are obvious; Gid dies still living by a code that has already become an anachronism. But it was a code that represented some beautiful and worth-while things.

It was a code that had its destructive side as well. As Charles D. Peavy points out in his article, "Coming of Age in Texas: The Novels of Larry McMurtry," it is the puritanism, the driving sense of duty, the always present sense of "right" and "wrong" of this code that prevent Gid from ever being able to give himself fully to Molly, the woman he loves.[4] The land must always come first. Peavy also correctly emphasizes the awesome importance of Molly Taylor in the novel: "So strongly does she dominate the actions of the book that it might well have been titled *Molly*" (176). Peavy's assertion that Molly's ability to love more than one man without ever giving herself irrevocably to any one does *not* represent "amorality on her part" is certainly true; however, his final analysis of Molly as representing "the Sanskrit message spoken by the thunder in Eliot's *Wasteland: datta, dayadhvam, damyata*" (176), while valid, seems to miss the main point.

Molly personifies the lost frontier. Gid and his father, the idealistic side of the old Texas myth, both love her, as does Johnny, the pragmatic side; and she loves *all* of them. But she gives herself in marriage finally to the worthless Eddie. Gid's father and, ultimately Gid himself, seem to sense what Molly represents. Early in the novel, his father warns Gid to forget Molly: "'. . . Molly, she don't want you'" (p. 76). And, in the closing fantasy dialogue between Johnny and the newly dead Gid, this exchange occurs:

> Johnny "You might have made the fortune, . . . But I'd just like to know what good it did you. Working like a Turk. Which one of us was satisfied?"
>
> Gid "Hell, that's easy, . . . Neither one. We neither one married her, did we?"
>
> (pp. 297-298)

Speaking from "the great Perhaps," Gid is telling Johnny symbolically that both of them, in their different ways, have had "a hell of a time," which, earlier, was his dying message. They were both frontiersmen living in a time when Texas was being populated by "the majority" who were interested in neither honestly working the land nor in living freely and hedonistically, but in finding loopholes in the government's limitations on their materialistic gains. Thus, Molly marries the worthless, unfeeling Eddie; the land marries "the majority"; the dream dies.

In *Leaving Cheyenne*, McMurtry has beautifully depicted the end of an era; he has utilized a freedom in language and subject matter that would have been totally foreign to Dobie, Webb, and Bedichek; and he has ridden "the mythical Pecos" and found it both beautiful and "lonely and bitter."

In *City of Night, Numbers*, and *This Day's Death* John Rechy develops the same themes in a different way. *City of Night* depicts, in Dantesque fashion, the descent of its main character into the nightmarish world of male homosexual prostitution from the time he initially leaves El Paso for New York until his total capitulation to degradation and despair in New Orleans during Mardi Gras. After the New York section, which in its tone of cold, unfeeling loneliness foreshadows the ending, there is a steady downward movement into horror. The Los Angeles section of the novel maintains some degree of comic relief because of the outrageous characterization of the "drag queen" Miss Destiny and her never daunted dream of being the bride in a big Hollywood wedding. However, even at the beginning of this part of the novel, Rechy hints at the tone which will conclude the novel:

> Southern California, which is shaped somewhat like a coffin, is a giant sanatorium with flowers where people come to be cured of life itself in whatever way. . . . This is the last stop before the sun gives up and sinks into the black, black ocean, and night—usually starless here—comes down.
>
> Along the coast. beaches stretch indifferently. *You can rot here without feeling it.*[5]

When the setting shifts to San Francisco, any relief is destroyed by the characterization of the masochist Neil, who finally tempts the central character into physically abusing him and, thereby, arouses feelings of permanent self-contempt in the anti-hero's heart. After this incident and a brief interlude in Chicago, the setting shifts to Mardi Gras and the final rung of Rechy's "inferno." The distance in mood covered in this novel can perhaps be best seen in a comparison of Miss Destiny in Los Angeles, pathetic yet comic at the same time, and the tragic figure of Kathy, the angelic appearing drag queen of New Orleans who is slowly dying of an unnamed disease. Kathy's disease is symbolic of all the characters in Rechy's homosexual hell—they are already dead as far as any hope of ever attaining contentment or peace of mind is concerned. That this fact is applicable to

the main character is chillingly brought home in the conclusion of the Mardi Gras section. After participating in a degrading homosexual orgy in a bar, he falls asleep in a dingy movie theater and wakens to find three cockroaches crawling on his arm and a man kneeling between his legs.

> And I was experiencing that only Death, which is the symbolic death of the soul. It's the death of the soul, not of the body—it's that which creates ghosts, and in those moments I felt myself becoming a ghost, drained of all that makes this journey to achieve some kind of salvation bearable under the universal sentence of death. And the body becomes cold because the heart and the soul, about to give up, are screaming for sustenance—from any source, even a remote voice on a telephone—and they drain the body in order to support themselves for that one last moment before the horror comes stifling out that already-dying spark.
>
> (pp. 408-409)

Shortly before his participation in the bar orgy, the main character has encountered Kathy on the street:

> Struggling through the crowd toward her, I said: "Kathy. . . . Kathy."
>
> "Yes, baby?"
>
> "Why are you smiling?"
>
> "Because," she said easily, "I'm going to die."
>
> (p. 405)

Despite the fact that it is primarily set in California and New Orleans, *City of Night* is relevant to Texas writing for more reasons than that John Rechy and the novel's main character are from El Paso. In the flashback sequences of the novel, the El Paso childhood of this main character is revealed as the cause of his compulsive attraction to the underground world of homosexuality. Rechy uses one incident in particular as a symbol of a traumatic childhood—the young boy has a pet dog named Winnie who is sick. A violent sand storm suddenly arises, and Winnie is left outside where the storm smothers her. The boy is then told by his mother that "'Dogs don't go to Heaven, they haven't got souls'" (p. 13); and, when he and his brother later dig Winnie up, he realizes the truth of what his mother has said:

> I had seen the decaying face of death. My mother was right. Soon Winnie will blend into the dirt. There was no soul, the body would rot, and there would be nothing left of Winnie.

(p. 14)

This incident haunts the main character the rest of his life. Throughout his existence in California and New Orleans, he has moments of wanting to return to El Paso, but then he remembers that storm:

> Often, too, the longing to return to El Paso would grasp me without warning. I would imagine my Mother standing before the glasscase in the living-room. Longingly, I remember the mountain I had climbed as a boy: the statue of Christ under that most beautiful sky in the world. . . . The memory of my father. . . . I would touch the ring he had given me.
>
> And then I would see El Paso racked by the savage wind.
>
> (p. 193)

The part that this incident plays in turning the main character to sexual abnormality is related to what life in El Paso has done to the boy's parents. The father had been a musical prodigy—"At the age of eight he had played a piano concert before the President of Mexico" (pp. 15-16)—until something in his environment destroyed his talent and subverted his artistic sensitivity into brutal perversion. It is the father who introduces the child to abnormal sexual behavior, and it is also the father who periodically flies into insane ranges during which he threatens the lives of all his family—once almost stabbing the child. It is also the father who then makes pathetic overtures to win back the boy's love, such as suddenly giving him a ring containing a ruby which had been the old man's most treasured possession for years; the boy's inability to respond to these gestures becomes a further torment to him. To compensate for the father's frightening instability, the boy's beautiful Mexican mother overwhelms him with a love so passionate that it terrifies the boy more than his father's fits of murderous insanity.

Rechy is depicting through the characterization of both father and son the terrifying impact of a hostile semi-frontier environment upon men of sensitive, artistic temperaments. The Texas wind which kills his dog and thus introduces the boy to death and decay is an excellent symbol for what Rechy is saying about what an environment like El Paso does to such men—it kills their souls and their spirits. The novel ends with the main character running to El Paso after his total degradation during Mardi Gras:

> It's impossible to escape the Wind. You can still hear it shrieking. You always know it's there. Waiting.

> And I know it will wait patiently for me, ineluctably, when inevitably, I'll leave this city.
>
> And the fierce wind is an echo of angry childhood and of a very scared boy looking out the window—remembering my dead dog outside by the mounded house as the gray Texas dust gradually covered her up—and thinking:
>
> It isn't fair! Why can't dogs go to Heaven?
>
> (p. 410)

Rechy has found what was left of "the mythical Pecos" to be a "lonely and bitter stream" indeed.

The irony of Rechy's statement about the Texas in which he was born is underscored by the main character's fellow hustler in Los Angeles, Chuck, who has perfected a cowboy facade. Everyone naturally assumes that Chuck is from Texas until he admit to the narrator that he is really from Georgia and his image of Texas is essentially based on the Western movies he saw as a kid. The main character's reaction to this confession is predictable:

> I smile now at the thought of his Texas and the Texas I had known: the city, not the plains of which he had dreamily conceived in Georgia, longing for Cowboy Country. The cactus-strewn desert . . . not the cactus which for me had grown in a feeble cluster outside that window, in that vacant lot. . . . The Texas I knew. . . . Memories of the wind . . . the dirt . . . tumbleweeds . . . my dead dog. . . . That wind blowing not freely across the plains but threateningly sweeping the paved streets into that injured house . . . El Paso . . . Texas . . . for me, not the great-stretching, wide-plained land of the movies—but the crushing city where I had been raised in stifling love and hatred.
>
> (p. 145)

As a kid, Chuck did hitchhike to Texas once and had the driver stop and let him out immediately when he saw the first horse roaming freely in the pastures. He jumped the fence and climbed on the horse and rode away, until he was stopped by the ranch workers, When he persisted in riding the horse, its owner had him arrested: "'So I left that place. . . . An what bugs me: I never said goodbye to my Horse. . . . And when I left, I think: Well, hell, it ain like in the movies'" (p. 152). The narrator accurately describes Chuck in the following passage: "He belongs on the range, I thought—on the frontier which disappeared long ago—existing now, ironically, only on those movie screens that had lured him as a child . . ." (pp. 153-154). Rechy implies that the frontier as Chuck views it never existed anywhere except "on those movie screens"—after all, even before the city arose, "that Wind" was always there.

Numbers has been viewed by most critics as a serious artistic lapse after the awesome power of *City of Night*: however, this analysis ignores the way in which Rechy's second novel should be read. It is about a main character named Johnny Rio who, after living "straight" for some years in Laredo, becomes terrified that his youth, looks, and ability to succeed as a male homosexual hustler have lessened. To reassure himself, he plans a ten-day trip to Los Angeles during which he is determined to have thirty homosexual "adventures." He does not really know how or why he has picked the number, thirty; and, after he has attained his goal, Johnny is puzzled by his lack of any deep feeling of triumph. It is then that a friend explains to him the significance of the printer's term 30, used at the bottom of a column of type to mean "The End." Then the spiritual meaninglessness of the past few days overwhelms Johnny; and he returns to The Park where most of the thirty "adventures" have taken place and, like the unnamed main character in *City of Night*, participates in a homosexual orgy that symbolizes spiritual suicide. *Numbers* must be read as a companion book to *City of Night*. In the first novel, the main character is never named; and, except in the El Paso flashback scenes and the climactic scenes in New Orleans, the narration is usually centered on some other character—Miss Destiny or Chuck or Kathy, for instance. In *Numbers*, the narration is centered from beginning to end upon Johnny Rio; and, despite the shift in hometowns from El Paso to Laredo, Johnny is obviously representative of the main character of *City of Night* grown slightly older and a great deal more frightened. Thus, *Numbers* should not be viewed as a literary lapse after *City of Night*, but as a companion novel to Rechy's earlier work. One must remember the warning contained in the last few pages of the first novel that "inevitably I'll leave this city (whether El Paso or Laredo does not matter) again."

The spiritual defeat which awaits Johnny Rio is symbolically foreshadowed at the beginning of the novel when he plays another game with "numbers"; as he speeds along the lonely highway from Texas to Los Angeles, he counts the number of bugs that smash to pieces against his windshield. The annihilation of the bugs leads Johnny into a metaphysical reverie in which he "imagines God poised behind an automatic rifle" cutting down each and every individual in the world when his "number comes up."[6] The image of God as the hidden rifleman waiting to "snipe each 'number' down" permeates the book. The resemblance of the symbolic pattern here to that of the classical Western is unmistakable. Johnny Rio, his name sounding like that of a Western hero, playing a "game of numbers" with homosexuality which can only end in his spiritual death—and his physical death when the unseen "sniper" is ready—is comparable to the classic

gunfighter notching victims on his gunhandle. Johnny, realizing the appeal of his Texas origins in the "game" he is playing, usually parks his car so that the Texas license plates show conspicuously when he is making homosexual contacts. This act is an echo, of course, of Chuck's Texas imitation in *City of Night*.

Little is told in *Numbers* about Johnny's Texas background except that he is part-Mexican and that he did try to live a "straight" life in the border town until his fear of approaching age and death drove him inevitably back to Los Angeles, the scene of his earlier homosexual triumphs. The reason for the omission of background is clear when one recalls that Johnny Rio is, for all practical purposes, the central character in *City of Night*: this information is all contained in the flashback scenes in the first novel. The main character does leave "this city again" with the identical tragic, soul-defiling results.

This Day's Death likewise utilizes some of the same motifs and images as *City of Night*. The novel opens with the main character, Jim Girard, remembering a traumatic experience from his childhood:

> *Once as a child six years old in a Southwest windstorm when the wind grasped at the sear Texas ground with swirling fingers a tumbleweed clawed furiously toward him and he dodged swiftly but the giant weed did too, thrusting itself against him, tearing at his face, arms, hands, ripping at him like a frantic animal until battling it with his clenched fists but the wind driving it with increasing force against him he felt surrounded by the dried twigs. Finally managing to wrench away from the path of the sweeping wind, he freed himself of the wiry clutch. The tumbleweed whirled away.*[7]

One is hardly surprised to learn that "he has always hated the wind since then" (p. 11). A tumbleweed transformed by the wind into a demon attacking a child is an even more graphic symbol of an alien environment than the storm which uncovers Winnie in *City of Night*. Throughout *This Day's Death*, the wind consistently maintains this symbolic value. When Miss Lucia, a strange Mexican woman whose dreams and visions personify primitive Mexican superstition and who is haunted by some never-disclosed sense of impending doom, arrives at the Girard home for the first time, she is escorted by the wind: "Jim opens the front door in response to the ringing of Miss Lucia. The revived wind attacks swiftly in gusts which came like stifled sighs" (p. 86).

Another evocation of *City of Night* is the characterization of Jim Girard's father, a sensitive and once successful lawyer reduced by his environment to a failure, plagued by violent paranoia. Like the father in the earlier novel, Mr. Girard falls into hysterical rages during which he threatens the lives of his wife and children and later futilely attempts to "make it up" with gifts. The relationship between Mr. Girard and Jim—at one point, they face each other with open Knives— also parallels that of the father and son in *City of Night.*

In Mrs. Girard, *This Day's Death* gives a complete description of the effect of this kind of marriage in this kind of environment on the wife, a theme only touched on in *City of Night* and completely ignored in *Numbers.* Like the mother in *City*, Mrs. Girard is of Spanish descent and, in compensation for the end of love with her husband, smothers her children in a terrifying passion. Jim feels that he and his mother are "at war" for the possession of his very being. His mother is suffering from some illness without a physical cause which demands constant attention from Jim, and one part of his mind suspects that the illness is merely a means to tie his life to his mother's forever. Thus, the love that he truly feels for his mother is "like sudden nausea" (p. 20); it is destroying his freedom and is therefore part hatred, but is still all-powerful. The novel ends with Jim still in his mother's absolute control.

Thus, through use of the wind again as a symbol for a hostile frontier atmosphere and through a more complete description than in the first two novels of the tragic effect of life in this environment on the female, Rechy brings his vision full circle. Mrs. Girard had two children who died tragically, a daughter of pneumonia, a son in World War II. One passage describes her regular pilgrimages on the Day of the Dead to the daughter's grave and to the desert on the outskirts of El Paso so that she can *peer west* toward that mysterious, far away place where her son died in the Pacific: "Her dark veil swirled about her in the wind—and it was always windy on that day. . . . Pulled by the wind, her veil was like a dark bird" (pp. 97-98). This passage epitomizes Rechy's frontier vision: the hostile environment of El Paso and Texas, symbolized by the wind, spiritually kills those sensitive people, such as Mr. Girard, Mrs. Girard, and Jim, whom it does not physically destroy.

McMurtry's *Leaving Cheyenne* and Rechy's novels illustrate the twin theses of *In a Narrow Grave*. The Texas writer now deals with subject matter that Dobie, Webb, and Bedichek would not have touched—the sexual promiscuity of Molly in *Leaving Cheyenne* and the Dantesque world of the homosexual "hustler" in Rechy. Of course, one is certain that the real cow men whom Dobie and Webb wrote about did know a few promiscuous women and undoubtedly had some experience with homosexuality as well, but the conservative literary climate in which they were writing and their own peculiarly romantic vision of "cow people" and Texas rangers made them unwilling to emphasize such distinctly realistic subject matter. One finds the movement

away from the Dobie and Webb romantic vision of Texas and the frontier not only in Rechy and McMurtry, but in Larry King, Tom Horn, William Brammer and other recent Southwestern novelists. These writers prove McMurtry correct in believing that the creative imagination which formerly went into the conquering of Texas' frontier will now be channeled into literary explorations of its loss. The "mythical Pecos" of *Leaving Cheyenne* is both idyllic and "lonely and bitter." Rechy's El Paso is that inescapable "wind" which perverts and destroys the soul of the sensitive man; and he strongly implies that, except "on those movie screens," the reality of the frontier always was like that. And it is probably true that the untamed West was never the best place for the delicate, artistic temperament.

NOTES

1. *Western American Literature*, IV, 246.

2. Larry McMurtry, *In a Narrow Grave* (Austin, 1968), p. 173. (All future references to his work will appear parenthetically in the text.)

3. Larry McMurtry, *Leaving Cheyenne* (New York, 1962), p. 230. (All future references to his work will appear parenthetically in the text.)

4. Charles D. Peavy, "Coming of Age in Texas: The Novels of Larry McMurtry," *WAL*, IV (Fall, 1969) 179. (Future references to this article will appear parenthetically in the text.)

5. John Rechy, *City of Night* (New York, 1963), pp. 95-96. (All future references to his work will appear parenthetically in the text.)

6. John Rechy, *Numbers* (New York, 1967), pp. 12-13. (All future references to his work will appear parenthetically in the text).

7. John Rechy, *This Day's Death* (New York, 1969), p. 11. (All future references to his work will appear parenthetically in the text.)

Raymond C. Phillips, Jr. (essay date Summer 1975)

SOURCE: "The Ranch as Place and Symbol in the Novels of Larry McMurtry," in *South Dakota Review*, Vol. 13, No. 2, Summer, 1975, pp. 27-47.

[In the following essay, Phillips explores the transition in McMurtry's portrayal of the Western frontier legend, exam-

ining the symbolic treatment of the ranch in the author's first five novels.]

In his essay on the contemporary literary heritage of the Southwest, Larry Goodwyn singles out Larry McMurtry as the young novelist "most embattled in terms of the frontier heritage."[1] By "frontier heritage" Goodwyn means treating the history of the Southwest as "the *unexamined* legend— the propagandistic Anglo-Saxon folk myth," which is pastoral, masculine, and racialistic.[2] Those writers who stay within this legend produce a literature of nostalgia that is largely affirmative, that perpetuates frontier romanticism. The newest generation of southwestern writers, however, has approached the legend and its myths in a skeptical mood; they "are asking radically different questions both about the nature of human experience and the functions of a received heritage in informing that experience."[3]

McMurtry, born in 1936 in Archer County, Texas, the author of five novels and a collection of essays, is very much representative of this new generation. That he is "embattled" can be seen by closely examining the significance that the ranch, both as place and as symbol, plays in his fiction. One finds that the ranch represents a stationary vortex, a cluster of values, about which everything moves. It is home, the place to revere, the place to protect, to flee from, to return to. It is the place to die. Usually peaceful and harmonious, offering psychological shelter, the ranch also can be the site of ultimate ineffectuality. It can be at the center of McMurtry's fictional world, or it can hover on the fringes. Finally, the ranch points up the ambivalence that McMurtry feels about the frontier legend.

Although written after the publication of his first three novels, McMurtry's essay **"Take My Saddle from the Wall: A Valediction"**[4] most clearly expresses his ambivalence about the Texas past and present. In the essay he remembers how "As a boy, riding across the lower field, I would sometimes look back at the speck of the ranch-house and imagine that I heard the old man's dinner call carrying across the flats" (p. 552). He recalls that the glory of the cowboy was his horsemanship; he writes of the cowboy's disgust with farming, his romanticizing of women, his stoical acceptance of life, his strength of character, his intolerance, his refusal to become domesticated, his violence, his pantheism, and, finally, his essential "dream of innocence and fullness never to be redeemed" (p. 569). The center of this world is not the Clarendon Country Club where in July, 1965, the heroic Uncle Johnny and the McMurtry clan held their last reunion, but the ranch that they built and lived on. McMurtry, who never could braid a rope, loves this world and the people in it, yet he wants his saddle taken from the wall. The problem, according to Goodwyn, is "the beguiling simplicity with which McMurtry takes down his saddle in his mind while his heart immediately replaces it." Goodwyn contends that "a writer

simply cannot afford such innocence in respect to his own point of view."[5] "Innocence," however may not be the accurate term for McMurtry's "embattled" position; instead, his career suggests an awareness of his ambivalence and some confusion as to how to come to grips with it.

Horseman, Pass By,[6] his first novel, shows McMurtry staking out the area in and around the imaginary north-central town of Thalia (really Archer City, his home town) as his fictional territory. Lonnie Bannon, the young narrator of the novel, writes very early in the novel that from his grandfather's ranch, "we could watch the cars zoom across the plains," that he could hear the trains fly by, that he "could see the airplane beacons flashing from the airport in Wichita Falls" (pp. 6-7). Lonnie dreams of the day "when I would have my own car, and could tear across the country to dances and rodeos" (p. 77). Very quickly, then, McMurtry introduces what becomes one of his crucial themes: the tension between the values centered in the ranch, the symbol of the Old West, values developed principally in Homer Bannon, and the values, the demands, and the expectancies of the more frenetic and transient world that lies beyond.

While later novels leave the immediate world of the ranch, ***Horseman, Pass By*** is set almost entirely on the Bannon Place, ruled over by old Homer Bannon, a life-long cattleman. Homer loves the land and, as Lonnie remembers, "was always studying it" (p. 138). Homer rejects the suggestion that he lease part of his ranch to the oil companies: "I guess I'm a queer, contrary old bastard, but there'll be no holes punched in this land while I'm here" (pp. 87-88). His love of the ranch is not sentimental: "There's so much shit in the world a man's gonna get in it sooner or later, whether he's careful or not" (p. 104). Very much aware that ranching has changed, Homer keeps an old Hereford bull and two longhorn steers around "to remind me how times was' (p. 45). Still, he does not dwell on the past: "If the times come when I get to spend my time lookin' back, why, I'd just as soon go under" (p. 103). Homer, the durable representative of the past, faces one of his greatest challenges when the hoof-and-mouth disease infects his herd. While waiting for the results of the tests that will determine the fate of his herd— the week or so that it takes for the verdict to come in emphasizes the inexorable winding down of all that he has built—he angrily refuses to follow Hud's suggestion that he unload the cattle on unsuspecting buyers. A decent man but one who has made mistakes, a man who has suffered through family tragedies, Homer retains his dignity until his death. At his funeral, the minister's lies and the undertaker's cosmetic skills cannot destroy that dignity, which grew out of his respect for life lived on the land.

Homer's feelings for the ranch are not shared by Hud, his stepson. Thirty-five years old, Hud resents Homer's ways. He would rather drive his Cadillac at high speeds through the night in search of sexual conquests. On being advised to stay home because of a storm warning, Hud snaps: "If I sat around an' waited for every little piss cloud to turn into a tornado, I never would go nowhere" (p. 12), a far cry from Homer's patient acceptance of life and nature. When he does stay home, Hud unnerves everyone who is about. At one point, he tries to rape Halmea, the Negro cook, an extreme example of the violence he exudes. Here, and elsewhere in McMurtry's fiction, a character embodies this sort of violence.[9] The violence of the nineteenth century West, patterned and ritualized in the literary and cinematic treatments of the frontier legend, gives way to a more subtle and ominous violence in McMurtry's work. More often than not, this contemporary violence is sexual, stemming in part from a loss of reverence for the land and the ensuing rootlessness.

Both Homer and Hud, the older and the middle generations, serve as models for young Lonnie to follow. Lonnie is attracted to both: when he rides his horse across the big valley pasture in the early morning he shares his grandfather's love of the land; on the other hand, he has an "itch to be off somewhere, with a crowd of laughers and courters and beer drinkers, to go somewhere past Thalia and Wichita and the oil towns and Sno-Cone stands, into country I'd never seen" (pp. 75, 21). Lonnie, restless and confused, senses the psychic disarray and gloom that has settled over the Bannon ranch, much in the same way that Huck Finn feels the cultural malaise along the Mississippi River. Lonnie, for instance, is disturbed by the moods of Jesse, the hired hand, who admits to having botched up his life because he "went all over his cow country, looking for the exact right place an' the right people" (p. 121) without ever finding it or them. Halmea's homelessness bothers Lonnie, too. She is both substitute mother and sexual woman for him, but when he tries to find her again after she leaves the ranch, she has gone north. At one point, Lonnie feels so pent up that he goes off in the night and shoots some animals, only to lament his senseless slaughter: "Things used to be better around here . . . I feel like I want something back" (p. 74).

What he wants back, of course, becomes impossible to have when his grandfather dies and when he realizes that nobody will be able to stop Hud from taking over the ranch. All that Lonnie has at the end is the warm and good memory of his grandfather, the horseman, passing by his window early in the morning, the horseman who "has always held the land, and would go on holding what he needed of it forever" (p. 140). As presented in the novel, then, the ranch is the good place as long as it was ruled over by Homer Bannon. It was no utopian retreat but a place where hard work, good luck, and patience yielded a life worth a man's living. What Hud will do with the ranch is problematical, of course, but it is doubtful whether he will cherish it the way Homer did. Lonnie, his traveling over, might be man enough and smart enough to right any damage that Hud might do. Perhaps his experiences outside of the ranch will temper his late adolescent enthusiasm for a good time. In any event, McMurtry's examination of the frontier legend succeeds; his characters embody the tensions inherent in the legend: primarily, the clash between those who love and respect the land and those who treat it unfeelingly.

Leaving Cheyenne,[10] McMurtry's second novel, treats ranch life from the early 1900s until about 1960. The setting is the same north-central cattle country as in **Horseman, Pass By**, the cast of characters is still fairly limited, and the ranch still functions as the central symbol of the story. That McMurtry is striving for a broad symbolic effect is apparent from the epigraphs that introduce each of the three sections of the novel. The epigraph for the whole novel, a four line verse about leaving Cheyenne refers to "that part of the cowboy's day's circle which is earliest and best: his blood's country and his heart's pastureland" (Foreword). These words suggest that near-magical attraction to the land, to Texas, that one finds in, say, Sara Orne Jewett's treatment of the Maine coast in *The Country of the Pointed Firs*. Such an attempt generally carries with it the risk of sentimentality, a risk avoided by McMurtry. *Leaving Cheyenne* has an understated, flat quality to it—the flatness often found in the old photographs of the family album. The pace of the novel is slow (again one is reminded of Jewett's novella); one expects more from the novel than it delivers, yet the "cowboy's blood country" is undeniably there. The second epigraph, immediately preceding Part One, which is tiled "The Blood's Country," refers to the "high lean country" that is "full of old stories" (Foreword). The land and the closely connected lives of three people, then, is what the novel is all about.

The epigraph for Part Two, from Shakespeare's Sonnet 64, emphasizes a major theme in McMurtry's fiction: the passing of time and the changes that ensure: "Ruin hath taught me thus to ruminate, / That Time will come and take my love way" (p. 135). Crucial to McMurtry's treatment of the Southwest is the presence of an eroded myth, but a myth that refuses to vanish no matter what the ruin of Time does to it. Two epigraphs introduce Part Three, one the Wife of Bath's bittersweet statement that although her youth is gone, she has had her world and will do the best she can: "The flour is goon, there is namoore to tell; / The bren, as I best kan, now moste I selle"; the other (Teddy Blue's request that when his life is over "go turn / my horses free" (p. 191). By quoting both from Chaucer and from a western folk source, McMurtry enriches the texture of his novel.

Leaving Cheyenne is the story of Gid, Molly, and Johnny, three Texans born around the turn of the century. In their late teens or early twenties when the novel begins, the three friends, evincing an uncommon love for and loyalty to each other, live out lives of mixed blessings and tragedy. Both men share the love of Molly, each fathering a son by her. Molly, with more than a bit of the Wife of Bath about her, possesses a resilience befitting her demotic background. "In some ways an updated version of the legendary dance-hall girls so familiar to lovers of the classic Western romance," the judgment of Thomas Landess,[11] Molly, nevertheless, emerges as a complex figure with an inner strength very closely dependent on her loyalty to her father and to the land on which she lives.

It is in Gid's section, Part One, that McMurtry develops the mystique of the ranch and the land. Old Mr. Fry, Gid's father, wants above all else to have his son perpetuate the ranch that he has spent his life building. He resents Gid's restlessness, his desire to go up to the Panhandle and do some cowboying: "Why, any damn fool can enjoy himself. What makes you think life's supposed to be enjoyed anyhow?" (p. 27). Mr. Fry, like Homer Bannon, knows the high price exacted in running a successful ranch. When he becomes too ill to continue, Mr. Fry kills himself. In his suicide note, he says "I think I'll go out on the hill and turn my horses free" (p. 107). By invoking the words of Teddy Blue, Mr. Fry places himself within the traditions of the past and he impresses them on his son. He ends his note with an order for Gid to fix the windmill, another way of ensuring that Gid remembers where his obligations lie—with continuing the existence of the ranch. That Gid fulfills his obligations is emphasized at the end of the novel when he insists that he and Johnny repair the same windmill; Gid, too old and ill for such hard work in the hot sun, falls and injures himself, dying a short time later. In the delirium before his death, Gid confuses the fall with being thrown from a horse years before, thereby linking his earlier skills in horsemanship with the demands his father placed upon him to keep the ranch going.

As a young man and before he becomes the rancher his father wants him to be, Gid suffers a great deal, not only because of his difficulty in winning Molly but also because of his longing to be a free roaming cowboy like Johnny. When the two young men go up to the Panhandle, Gid gets a taste of cowboying; on the Grinsom place, he breaks a string of eighteen horses in one day. He likes cowboying, but he soon becomes homesick: "I just minded feeling like I wasn't where I belonged. . . . The country might not be very nice and the people might be onry; but it was my country and my people, and no other country was" (pp. 93-94).

One attraction for Gid, of course, is Molly, who serves both men as lover and as confidant. Molly, quite ordinary in some ways, takes on an archetypal significance in several places in the novel, most clearly, perhaps, when she and either Gid or Johnny go fishing at the tank on the Fry ranch. The tank, along with the windmill a literal reminder of the cattleman's efforts to reckon with the aridity of the Southwest, is the idyllic retreat in most of McMurtry's fiction. It is here that Molly, now the Temptress, invites Gid to skinny-dip with her, in effect, to submerge and to lose his innocence beneath the life-giving water of the tank. He refuses because "I just know what's right and what ain't" (p. 32). Somewhat later, after finding out that Molly has married Eddie, an oil-field worker, Gid retreats to the tank to brood about his missed opportunity to win Molly for himself. Johnny also takes Molly to the tank to fish after she tells him about Jimmy's (Gid's son by Molly) decision to become a homosexual. In this scene, Molly, grieving for her lost sons (Johnny had been killed in the war), seems more the Earthmother now; "The tank was still as a mirror" (p. 180) and she and Johnny pass the long afternoon together. Molly sews a rip in Johnny's shirt while he sleeps, they swim, shoot at some cowchips, and finally, they eat. The entire scene has a slowed down, elegaic quality to it, but, at the same time, it is a powerful celebration of life and of the need to endure. Much of Molly's strength seems to emanate from the life-giving water of the tank. The tank, however, is but a part of the ranch, just as being able to go there very often is but a part of life.

Although the three characters live close to the land, it alone cannot sustain them. Both Gid and Molly suffer from loneliness. Gid misses Johnny when they are apart as young men, and after he marries Mabel, an ungenerous and overly proud woman, he continues to need Molly. Molly loses her father, to whom she was very close, a husband, and both of her sons. After visiting her, whether to sleep with her, to repair her windmill, or merely to talk to her, Gid says something like: "She always stood right where you left her, as long as she could see you. . . . Molly was just as permanent as my land" (p. 133). This picture of Molly, alone but enduring, one finds again and again in the novel. She has a remarkable ability to articulate her feelings. When her Bible-pounding son Johnny tries to make her feel guilty of adultery, she answers him in much the same way that the Rev. Casey explains his new ways in *The Grapes of Wrath*: "But words is one thing and loving a man is another" (p. 169). With such a simple power as this, Molly can fight her loneliness. Johnny, one of the men she sleeps with, is a cowboy-drifter who takes life easy. If he suffers from loneliness, we are not very aware of it. He has no desire to own land or to gain power. Sleeping with Molly presents him with no moral problems: "it's enjoyable . . . I ain't gonna bother to look no farther than that" (p. 189).

"The earth endures and the stars abide, but where are the old men," to paraphrase the earth-song in Emerson's "Hamatreya." So it is in *Leaving Cheyenne*. Gid, Molly, and Johnny grow old and, as Johnny complains to Molly, "Now we both just got yawny" (p. 234). While the passing of time is noticeable in Parts One and Two, it is most apparent in Part Three, the section narrated by Johnny. His narration seems almost too slack and rambling. Landess, for instance, in finding Johnny's drawn-out account of the automobile accident unjustified thematically, accuses McMurtry of wandering "into the tangled thicket of redundancy."[12] A defensible criticism, to be sure, but it is possible that McMurtry is trying to suggest the slowed down lives of the characters. Gid, his health growing poorer, reminisces and complains more. Molly also reflects about the passing of time; she recalls the time her father brought home a barrel of molasses only to have it accidentally spilled all over the ground.[13] Johnny humors Gid when he laments the passing of the West as they had known it, but Johnny also recalls the past with sadness. Both men realize they aren't as strong as they once were; in going out to round up a milk cow, they have trouble saddling their horses and then they muff the job. Gid, though greatly weakened after a stay in the hospital, insists on doing the chores about the ranch, but, as Johnny notes, he "wasn't the hand he used to be" (p. 241). Like his father, Gid stubbornly keeps on. When he becomes mortally hurt in falling from the windmill, he, in a sense, takes his own life. His half-delirious remark to Johnny on the way to the hospital—"Ain't this been a hell of a time?" (p. 246)—is a fitting remark for an old cattleman to make about his and Molly's and Johnny's lives on the land.

It is Molly, however, who dominates the last section of the novel and who most appropriately characterizes the spirit of the novel. After Gid's death, Johnny spends the night with Molly. He wakes up next to her in bed and is a bit nonplused to see that he has an erection. Molly, still the archetypal Earthmother, smiles at him and says: "That's nature. . . . And you better not waste it, either" (p. 249). With Molly, here and elsewhere in the novel, McMurtry reworks the "unexamined myth" of the West. He advances a woman to the forefront of what had usually been a man's world. Molly, her unabashed sexuality emulating the zest for living embodied in the Wife of Bath (remember the epigraph), challenges the ruin of time, the wearing down and the losses of her sixty-two years. Indomitable, she remains on her land and in her house, and when Johnny, at the end, remembers her sitting in her blue and white dress on the schoolhouse steps nearly a half century before, the novel comes full circle with the cowboy's "blood's country and his heart's pastureland" intact.

In his next novel, *The Last Picture Show,*[14] McMurtry turns from the ranch to the town of Thalia, to whom the novel is "lovingly dedicated." Thalia, as has been pointed out more than once, is the Greek Muse of comedy and pastoral poetry; the name comes from the Greek *Thaleia,* meaning "the blooming one." Thalia, Texas, however, does not bloom at all. In fact, as Sam the Lion says, "The oil fields are about to dry up and the cattle business looks like it's going to peter out" (p. 53). The inhabitants of Thalia, both young and old, find the place lonely and dreary. Sonny, the central

character, excuses a night of whoring and drinking at Ft. Worth with these words: "at least we got to go *somewhere*" (p. 56). Life is so bad sometimes that the boys of Thalia visit the stockpens to copulate with a heifer, an action hardly befitting the pastoral myth the town's name suggests. For Lois Farrow, the hard-drinking mother of Joey, the town's dream girl, Thalia and the land around it are "flat and empty, and there's nothing to do but spend money" (p. 42). McMurtry relentlessly hammers home the negative points of the town; Landess is correct in calling the novel a satire with one-dimensional and stylized characters which gives the book the flavor of Sinclair Lewis's novels.[15] Consider, for instance, Sonny's first girl friend, Charlene Duggs. Charlene, a bovine, gum-chewing girl, spends most of her time sitting in a beauty shop reading movie magazines. Full-breasted, Charlene is a flat character, sometimes amusing to the reader but hardly interesting.

Part of McMurtry's strategy in satirizing Thalia is the inclusion of a great many sexual, even scatological, passages. In his first two novels, to be sure, one finds sex, but beginning with *The Last Picture Show*, McMurtry stresses more and more the sexual manifestations of life in the West. I suggested earlier that violence is linked with sexuality; people commit violence against the integrity of someone else, and they do it sexually. Such is the case here. The boys of Thalia lead the unsuspecting half-witted Billy to Jimmie Sue Jones, the obese town whore. The wealthier teenagers from Wichita have nude swimming parties and "screw" each other; Coach Popper, a latent homosexual, cracks obscene jokes with his players; Lois Farrow sleeps with another man; and on and on it goes. In describing all of this, McMurtry uses very frank language (in his last two novels, the language is even more frank, causing discomfort to some readers).[16] Since most of the novel deals with high school students, a group that finds sex especially interesting, the language mostly rings true. The upshot of this heavy emphasis on sex is that it calls into doubt the sanctity of the West advanced in *Horseman, Pass By* and in *Leaving Cheyenne*.

Towering over everyone else in *The Last Picture Show* is Sam the Lion, the owner of the town's pool hall and movie house. Sam embodies whatever good is left in Thalia: he "took care of things" (p. 7), he always bets on the high school teams no matter how inept they are, he never goes to bed at night until Billy is safe, and, in general, he sympathizes with the young people who have to grow up in that town. The essential goodness of Sam's values is best seen in his reaction to the trick the boys play on Billy with the whore: "Scaring an unfortunate creature like Billy when there ain't no reason to scare him is just plain trashy behavior. I've seen a lifetime of it and I'm tired of putting up with it" (p. 92).[17] Sam belongs to the older generation that has roots in the land. He belongs with those other representatives of the frontier myth whose lives testify to the positive force of the West: Homer Bannon, Mr. Fry, and even Gid and Molly.

Every year or so, Sam would take Sonny and Billy out to a tank on land he once had owned to do some fishing. The last time he does this, he reminisces about the past; he tells Sonny of a day twenty years before when he had brought "a young lady swimming here. It was after my boys were already dead, my wife had lost her mind" (p. 123). The woman, we learn later, was Lois Farrow for whom Sam was the only good thing in her life. Once again a tank takes on symbolic importance. Although the ranch is gone, the values residing in it live on at the tank. Sonny's "pissing off the dam" (p. 122), just the way Sam once did, and his renewing the life of Ruth Popper, the coach's wife, just as Sam made Lois feel "worthwhile," offer the possibility that life in Thalia is not entirely hopeless after all, no matter how depressing and provincial it may seem. Sonny might take up the values of Sam, just as in **Horseman, Pass By** Lonnie holds out hope that Homer Bannon's life was not in vain. With his characterization of Sam the Lion and with his unmistakable elevation of the redemptive qualities of the ranch-tank, McMurtry keeps his saddle on the wall.

McMurtry's first three novels are geographically limited and rather sparsely peopled. Not so his fourth, **Moving On**,[18] a rambling story that moves over much of the West and that has some twenty important characters in its nearly 800 pages. One gets to know the people of the rodeo world, from Sonny Shanks, the World Champion horseman, to Peewee Raskin, a fledgling and usually inept bareback rider. Then, there is the Rice University graduate school circle presided over by Bill Duffin, an English professor. Joe Percy represents the Hollywood scene; Eleanor Guthrie, the wealthy Texan; Pasty's parents, the moderately wealthy; Roger Wagonner, the rural and the struggling; Stone, the spaced-out, beat San Francisco world; and fleetingly, other characters represent still more facets of the contemporary West. So immense and so panoramic is **Moving On** that it is impossible here to examine it thoroughly, yet so crucial is it to an understanding of McMurtry's attempts to deal with the frontier myth that I must present more details than was necessary before, commenting as I go along.

Moving On is primarily the story of Patsy Carpenter's search for a meaningful life in the modern West. Married but a year to Jim, a wealthy young man who is conducting his own search for a vocation, Pasty accompanies him on the rodeo circuit. Jim is trying to become a photographer; riding in an old Ford, the Carpenters encounter a world they have never known: fast sex, violence, different value systems altogether. Most perturbing to Pasty is Sonny Shanks, the champion cowboy, who, forsaking a horse except in the ring, drives from rodeo to rodeo in a white Cadillac hearse. Sonny uses the hearse for publicity but also as a place for his sexual conquests. With the hearse, McMurtry suggests the death of the cowboy as the frontier myth had pictured him, especially at the end of the novel when Sonny, high on amphetamines, dies in a freeway collision with a car full of hippies. In a way, Sonny's hearse is a ranch house on wheels, which moves over the land but which has no secure ties to it. Patsy comes to hate the rodeo world; when, for example, she hears of two cowboys almost killing an old man by mistake, she says: "It's not just two especially dangerous cowboys, it's some sort of insane violence this life seems to breed" (p. 170). Another from of violence encountered in the rodeo world is sexual; Sonny tries to seduce Pasty very soon after meeting her. Bored and lonely when she isn't afraid, Pasty finds one man on the circuit who impresses her favorably: Pete Tatum, a rodeo clown, but even he would like to take her to bed.

After two months of following the rodeos, Patsy and Jim return to Houston, where Jim, disenchanted with photography, enters graduate school at Rice University (where McMurtry himself studied and taught). Although they have no financial worries and even though Jim quickly becomes a favorite of Prof. Duffin, Patsy finds no self-fulfillment in Houston. In fact, she cries more in Book II than in any other part of the novel, on some twenty-one different occasions.[19] She does attract men easily: Flap Horton, her best friend's husband, Bill Duffin, Hank Mallory, all want to seduce her. Jim, his interests elsewhere, mostly ignores her, driving her finally to Hank, a graduate student friend of his. Book II has a wide variety of sexual activity and frank language in it. Flap and Emma Horton have sexual intercourse on the floor of their apartment; Clara Clark is known as a three orgasm girl; Bill Duffin fondles his wife in a very intimate way; Joe Percy, the screenwriter, tries but fails to copulate successfully with Patsy's Aunt Dixie; Hank works very hard in trying to convince Patsy to sleep with him; and so on. McMurtry spares the reader none of the vivid details of this sexual three-ring circus, Toward the end of Book II, Patsy and Jim have a baby boy, but not before Jim goes off to Mexico for a one night stand with a whore. It would take a team of social-psychologists to explain all of the reasons for this sex, but it seems that McMurtry is connecting the abundant sexuality here and elsewhere in the novel with the loss of meaningful values and the consequent malaise he finds existing in the contemporary West. That this may well be the case becomes probable by analyzing what happens to the ranch and its value system, but, first, a few more words about Patsy's search.

Book III opens with Patsy feeling a nameless restlessness. Jim is off in Amarillo helping Sonny Shanks make a movie, and, before too long, Patsy begins to sleep with Hank, who at least can make her feel like a woman sexually. While she and Jim grow more apart, McMurtry allows the reader brief glimpses into the other characters' lives. Jim, for instance, visits Eleanor Guthrie at her ranch (which is huge and efficiently managed), where each tries to seduce the other without success. Interestingly enough, her attempt to seduce him occurs at a tank on the ranch, which, in the context of *Moving On*, tends to subvert the positive image of the tank in the earlier novels. Eleanor's needs, though, are understandable: she realizes that she is aging and that Sonny, her lover, always thinks of himself first, of her second. By the end of Book III, then, the Carpenters' marriage is in near hopeless disarray with no positive values available to remedy it.

Things get worse in Book IV. Jim, discovering Patsy's affair with Hank, begins one of his own with Clara Clark, and they leave for Los Angeles, where Jim gets a job with IBM. Patsy and her son move into the Duffin house, which the Carpenters had bought in happier times, but all through the second winter in Houston, Patsy feels depressed. She next goes to California at the urging of her parents in order to rescue her sister Miri, who has become pregnant, probably by a black man. Patsy's frenetic few days in California allow McMurtry a chance to present what can only be described as a corrupt and debased world. Patsy finds Miri high on drugs, starving, and filthy. While tracking her down, Patsy sees a group of Hell's Angels and their women in a park openly fondling each other's sexual parts. A far cry from Hud's pinching Halmea's breast, this scene is part of a pattern that pictures the modern West as spiritually different from the romanticized and sentimentalized West of the "unexamined frontier legend." The novel closes with Patsy daydreaming about an imminent trip to Uncle Roger's ranch, which is northwest of Thalia and which earlier in the novel had been willed to her and to Jim: In other words, Patsy is still searching, still moving on, when the novel ends.

The above summary of *Moving On* has excluded any mention of Uncle Roger's ranch, not because it lacks importance but because it is so crucial to an understanding of McMurtry's reading of the modern West that it requires separate treatment. A highly mobile, sexually obsessed, often corrupt society as drawn by him, the West would seem to have no time and no room for the positive values of the frontier myth. Such is not the case. There all the time, in north-central Texas not too far from Thalia, sits Roger Waggoner's ranch. Roger, widowed eleven years before, lives alone. He admits to being "pore": "I been at it fifty years and get worse at it every year. Least that's the way it looks in the bankbook" (p. 51). His house is plain, he drives an ancient Chevrolet pickup, and, in Patsy's opinion, he fries his eggs hard as stones. A man of common sense, he speaks softly and simply. He lives close to the land, raises his cattle, endures stoically whatever life offers, and, above all else, remains loyal. Although the moral center of the novel, he does not strike heroic poses, nor does he exhibit any unusual facility with his words. Patsy visits the ranch four times: twice

with Jim, at the beginning of the novel and at the end of the rodeo section, then with her son Davey the following summer when Jim is in Amarillo making the movie, and, finally, to attend Roger's funeral. And, we remember, she is looking forward to visiting the place again when the novel ends.

These visits provide Patsy, the new woman of the West, with an opportunity to learn about the Texas that has closer and stronger ties with the old West. In the course of the novel Patsy travels thousands of miles; at the ranch the rhythms of life are slower. Roger gets up with the sun to feed the chickens and to milk his cow; Patsy, on her first visit, watches him from her bedroom window, much in the same way that Lonnie watches his grandfather ride beneath his window in *Horseman, Pass By*. The Waggoner house is filled with memories. Roger and his wife had argued for thirty-five years about salvation and sin, and through she has been dead for eleven years, Roger continues the argument: "In a way it's even better than having her here. I always win the argument" (p. 187). As one expects, Roger enjoys recalling the past; "After a while it seemed to Patsy that he was delivering an elegy" (p. 187), which saddens her. Because she finds him "a lovely man" (p. 190), Patsy, after the second visit, invites Roger to come to see her and Jim in Houston. At the end of Book II, he drives down to see Davey because he "always liked to keep tabs on my kin" (p. 384). That he would drive so far at his age in his old truck confirms the high opinion that Patsy has of him. He wants her to bring Davey to the ranch so he can "start 'em riding" (p. 387). Roger has a strong attachment to the ranching West, and he seems bent on maintaining this vital connection by teaching horsemanship, the highest skill in the old West, to little Davey.

By the time of her third visit to the ranch, Patsy's marriage is severely threatened and she has become involved with Hank Mallory: "She was alone with Davey and didn't really know where *she* was going . . . or what she was going to do" (p. 490). Soon after her arrival, Roger suggests that they go horseback riding; he brings out his wife's saddle for Patsy, and they go off across the fields, with Davey riding in front of Roger. The ride is a pastoral interlude; it is an idyllic affirmation of the Old West. Although an old man, Roger skillfully rounds up a stubborn cow that had wandered off. Patsy, impressed by his skill and struck by the beauty of the land and sky, feels a sense of great well-being. After supper, Roger tells her he would like to leave his ranch to her and Jim, "to keep it in the family somewhere" (p. 497). When he learns of the state of Patsy's marriage and of her relationship with Hank, Roger refuses to pass judgment or to advise her. All he wants to know is whether Hank is a scoundrel. Before Patsy leaves for home, Roger tells her to "Bring old Davey back to see me before he gets too old to ride double" (p. 500). Roger will never see Patsy and Davey again because he dies the following March. Although his presence quantitatively in the novel is small, Roger plays a very important role. His quiet resoluteness, his love for the land and for his family, and his sincerity stand in sharp contrast to the corruption and the machinations of the larger world beyond the ranch.

When Patsy returns to the ranch to attend the funeral and to take care of the affairs of the inheritance, she both affirms and denies the spirit of Roger's generosity. She realizes that his gift "had shown a faith in them [Patsy and Jim] that they had not lived up to" (p. 699). Nevertheless, she arranges for the disposition and care of the animals with the help of a neighbor. She eats the last of the peanut butter that she and Jim had bought on their first trip there; McMurtry mentions the peanut butter each time Patsy visits the ranch, thereby reminding us of the passing of time and, in an unobtrusive way, of the gulf between the Carpenter's lives and Roger's (he cannot understand anyone eating such food). Hank arrives the following morning (Patsy had invited him), and he and Patsy renew their sexual activities, first in the bedroom, then in the front seat of the Ford (the very car in which she and Jim had first kissed), and finally on Aunt Mary's couch. Their intercourse in the Ford takes place at a tank located on the ranch, which like, Eleanor Guthrie's attempted seduction of Jim earlier in the novel, amounts to a debasement of the positive values associated with the tanks in the other novels. Similarly, their use of Aunt Mary's couch violates the love and respect that had been Roger's and Mary's for over thirty years. After Hank leaves, Patsy cleans out the Ford, washes the dishes, and tidies up the house, suggesting, symbolically at least, her partial awareness that what she and Hank had done defiled Roger's memory. Patsy's inability to commit herself fully to the ranch and its values persists to the end of the novel; in contemplating another visit she wonders whether it would be better to go with Davey and share his delight at the cows or to go alone and meet Hank for another sexual spree. She cannot decide, and, it appears, neither can McMurtry. One thing is clear, what Goodwyn says: that "the frontier ethos, removed from the center of his work, continues to hover around the edges."[20]

Towards the end of *Moving On* Emma Horton tells Patsy of her brief affair with Danny Deck, a young writer who had lived in Houston for a time but who had disappeared and is presumed to be dead. McMurtry's most recent novel, *All My Friends Are Going to Be Strangers*[21] involves Danny's search for love as he wanders from Texas to California and back. The novel is set a year to two before *Moving On.* Danny, referred to as "the best young writer in the state' (p. 10), marries Sally, whom he has known but a couple weeks, has his first novel accepted, and then leaves Houston for California. Shortly afterwards, Danny and Sally split up, and Danny begins living alone in a grubby hotel. For diversion, he plays ping-pong with Wu, a Chinese friend

who is studying English literature. Next, Danny falls in love with Jill Peal, a girl who does drawings for animated cartoons. Their relationship is a good one, but it does not last. Following a night during which he gets high on some Mexican mushrooms, Danny drives back to Texas, where the rest of the action takes place. Up to this point, the novel is slack and not very interesting; the scene involving the flooded highway in Chapter 6 has a comic robustness about it, to be sure, but little else stands, out. McMurtry's language throughout the novel and the incidents he treats are quite salacious, frequently to the degree that one suspects him of pandering to the tastes of those who frequent the bus station paperback racks.[22] Whatever his designs in this regard, McMurtry does not give a very favorable view of the contemporary West. His characters are dislocated, loveless, lonely, hostile, unfaithful, or like Danny himself, living lives that "veer crazily one way and then another" (p. 51). In this way, *All My Friends* repeats the situations and moods of *Moving On.*

On his way back to Austin Danny decides to stop off at his Uncle Laredo's ranch near Van Horn. Since McMurtry has been describing a West where the frontier myth in any positive sense has been rendered irrelevant, we expect, especially if we have read his other works, that the ranch will be a place where the old values still hold. Danny's description of the Texas sky before he arrives at Uncle L's supports this expectation: "It had such depth and such spaciousness and such incredible compass, it took so much in and circled one with such a tremendous space that it was impossible not to feel more intensely with it above you" (p. 176). This promising sky, however, belies the state of things at the ranch. Danny finds his aged uncle (he is ninety-two) presiding over a madhouse. The ranch house itself is a blackened Victorian mansion, the living room of which still houses a grand piano and the musical instruments for a nine-piece orchestra, not to mention a stuffed lobo wolf, the last wolf killed in Pecos County. These images, and others like them, point up the demise of the Old West, its ineffectuality for today. When Danny drives up, he finds Uncle L digging a center-post hole; he has dug some 300 already. In case he ever decides to put up a fence, the holes will be ready. Danny theorizes that Uncle L really digs the holes in order to hurt the hateful earth (we recall that Homer Bannon would not allow the oil company to come in and deface his land).

Another bizarre incident occurs next. One of the Mexicans who works on the ranch throws himself on the mound of dirt next to the post hole and begins to copulate with it. Shortly thereafter, he does the same thing with the gas hole in an old, black pickup truck. Here is sexuality gone wild, comic but disgusting, as if McMurtry has become sickened of the West he has been describing earlier in the novel. Still another facet of Uncle L's incredible world is his camel herd, a vestige of the post-Civil War importation of camels into what at that time was called "the Great American Desert." There is more; piled behind the windmill are 300 manhole covers, and nearby stands Uncle L's junkyard: "twenty or thirty cars, two broken-down bulldozers, several tractors, a hay baler, a combine, and an old cattle truck" (p. 186). McMurtry's choice of images seems right out of the world of Nathanael West. The blackened house, the oversexed Mexican, the unused post holes, the manhole covers, the camels, and the junk all suggest that the frontier myth is no longer viable.

Danny provides a clue that this impression is correct. Seeing Uncle L's buffalo herd (another vestige from the past) reminds him of a story in which some reservation Indians come to Old Man Goodnight (the legendary cattleman who also kept a herd of buffalo) and asked for a buffalo. They got one and ran it down and killed it on the plains in front of Goodnight's house. Danny reflects: "To me it was the true end of the West. A few sad old Indians, on sad skinny ponies, wearing rags and scraps of white man's clothes and carrying old lances with a few pathetic feathers dangling from them, begging the Old Man of the West for a buffalo, one buffalo of the millions it had once been theirs to hunt. . . . From then on all they would have was their longing" (p. 191). It was all over for the Indians, and it seems to be finished for Uncle L and his friend Lorenzo, who both keep a nightly vigil for the reappearance of Zapata, the Mexican revolutionist, with whom they had fought. Uncle L, his mind addled by age, keeps a sack of gold in his jeep in case Zapata needs money when he comes back. In a sense, Uncle L and Lorenzo "had made life theirs" (p. 199), as Danny claims, but, in fact, they are but variants of McMurtry's Uncle Johnny, anachronistic guardians of the unexamined myth of the Old West. Suddenly Danny realizes that he never wants to visit the ranch again.

His disillusionment becomes clearer after he leaves the ranch. In Austin, for instance, he does violence to Geoffrey, "a little thing, in greasy Levi's" (pp. 207-208) because Geoffrey was bribing Godwin, a professor Danny had met earlier in the novel. Right before he hurts Geoffrey, Danny "felt strange and a little dangerous. Zapata was about to come out of the mountains" (p. 209). In other words, Danny's (and possibly McMurtry's) disgust at the debasement of the Old West explodes into violent outrage. The curious thing is that Danny invokes Zapata to express his feelings, testifying to the vitality of the frontier myth. A few chapters later, his autograph party in a Houston book store a flop, Danny drives south with Petey, a Mexican friend who has some dope with him. Two Texas Rangers (Uncle L had been a Ranger at one time) stop the pair, find the dope, and begin to needle the two men. They chide Danny because of his long hair, ask him if he is a homosexual, hit him, and finally, throw him over a fence onto a prickly pear cactus. The Ranger's violence further isolates Danny from the positive

parts of the frontier myth. A few pages later, he "gives" his car, which he has dubbed El Chevy, to an old couple who are hitchhiking. Divested of his "horse," the images of the past lost to him after his talk with Neville, an ex-movie actor, Danny renounces writing. He "drowns" the manuscript of his second novel in the Rio Grande, and he begins to walk farther and farther into the river, thinking to himself that "I didn't see the great scenes anymore, the Old Man riding, the Old Woman [Danny's grandmother who had endured the hardships of settling the Old West] standing on the ridge, the wild scenes from the past that I usually saw when I was walking some border of my own at night" (p. 285). The novel ends with Danny wanting, above all else, to flow with the fabled Rio Grande.

Whether Danny commits suicide or not, the point is clear: the frontier myth has failed him. The old cattlemen, Homer Bannon, Gid Fry, Sam the Lion, Roger Waggoner, the positive ties to a valid life and a viable legend, have given way either to the Huds, the Coach Poppers, the Sonny Shanks, the greasy runts on motorcycles, and the Texas Rangers or to the empty and absurd hungering for the past of Uncle L and Lorenzo. While Danny Deck himself falls short as an ideal heir of the Old West, he was attuned to its harmony and to its possibilities for art. His "death," and, if it is safe to speculate, McMurtry's move to Washington, D.C., suggest at least a temporary abandonment of the legend. Nevertheless, the ranch and the land may well endure in memory, if not in fact, to challenge not only the embattled McMurtry but also other writers both now and in the future.

NOTES

1. "The Frontier Myth and Southwestern Literature," *American Libraries*, 2 (1971), 363. Part I of this essay appears in February, 1971; Part II in April 1971.

2. Goodwyn, pp. 161-162.

3. Goodwyn, p. 363.

4. From *In a Narrow Grave: Essays on Texas* (Austin: The Encino Press, 1968), which is to be reprinted in the spring of 1974. A more available source and one cited in this article is *The Literature of the American West*, ed. J. Golden Taylor (Boston: Houghton Mifflin, 1971), pp. 550-569.

5. Goodwyn, pp. 364-365.

6. (New York: Harper and Row, 1961). I shall refer to the paperback edition: *Hud* (New York: Popular Library, 1961).

7. Except for Uncle L's ranch in *All My Friends Are Going to Be Strangers*, which is located south of Van Horn in

southwestern Texas, all of the ranches in McMurtry's novels are located around Thalia, the territory he knows best.

8. The titles of McMurtry's novels suggest his fascination with change and transience. Each novel, save one, has a verb in its title: *pass, leaving, moving, going to be*. The *Last* in *The Last Picture Show* implies the passing of time, the giving way to the present.

9. Few people, for instance, would want to tangle with Sonny Shanks, The Champion Cowboy, in *Moving On*.

10. (New York: Harper and Row, 1963). I shall refer to the paperback edition: *Leaving Cheyenne* (New York: The Popular Library, 1963).

11. *Larry McMurtry* (Austin: Stock-Vaughn, 1969), p. 22.

12. Landess, p. 19.

13 The molasses incident, along with many others in his novels, comes from McMurtry's family background. See "Take My Saddle from the Wall: A Valediction," pp. 561-562.

14. (New York: Dial, 1966). I shall refer to the paperback edition: *The Last Picture Show* (New York: Dell, 1966).

15. Landess, pp. 23-26.

16. In their literary history and bibliography, Mabel Major and T.M. Pearce find in *Moving On* that "the language used at all levels of society strains credibility with in coarseness." See *Southwest Heritage*, 3rd ed. (Albuquerque: University of New Mexico Press, 1972), p. 231.

17. Sam's words remind one of Nigger Jim's denunciation of Huck's actions in the fog in Chapter 15 of *Adventures of Huckleberry Finn*.

18. (New York: Simon and Shuster, 1970). I shall refer to the paperback edition: *Moving On* (New York: Avon, 1971).

19. Over the entire novel, Patsy cries about seventy times, often in moods of self-pity, often for silly reasons (see p. 15).

20. Goodwyn, p. 365.

21. (New York: Simon and Schuster, 1972).

22. See Reed Whittemore's review of the novel in *The New Republic* (April 1, 1972), pp 28-29, a somewhat facetious and inaccurate attack on McMurtry's fiction.

Patrick D. Morrow (essay date 1980)

SOURCE: "Larry McMurtry: The First Phase," in *Seasoned Authors for a New Season: The Search for Standards in Popular Writing*, edited by Louis Filler, Bowling Green University Popular Press, 1980, pp. 70-82.

[*In the following essay, Morrow, who teaches literature at Auburn University, evaluates the structure, purpose and style of* Hud *and* The Last Picture Show, *comparing them to McMurtry's subsequent works.*]

Larry McMurtry has now written six novels, and this seems a reasonable moment in time to examine and judge his artistry, to consider the question of his quality. McMurtry's first three novels were tales of nostalgia, satire, cultural criticism and barbed wire phrases that condemned the modern West. **Horseman, Pass By** (better known as **Hud**, 1961) and **Leaving Cheyenne** (1963) were both cowboy stories of initiation, disillusionment and generational conflict set in Texas. **The Last Picture Show** (1966) was thematically similar and also set in Texas, but small town life rather than ranch life, formed the center for this novel. All of McMurtry's novels have sold at least reasonably well, but **Hud** and **Picture Show** not only have been best-sellers and frequent college texts, but were made into distinguished and very successful films. After these early success, McMurtry may not have been a household name, but he was an established young writer—and a popular one too, especially with his skill at adapting his fiction into screenplay form.

Then, McMurtry's career took a surprising turn. Rather than continue writing screenplays, he retreated to Houston and then Washington, D.C. and during a low-profile past decade he has been engaged in writing a complex and lengthy trilogy. Demanding skill and time from the reader, the trilogy gradually revealed a chronicle—in panoramic vistas and through several generations—of the quest for moral maturity by a fascinating group of diverse Texans. These three thick volumes demonstrated an involved artistic consciousness, a well-wrought ambiguity in values, characterization and form. McMurtry has succeeded in producing a first-rate group of serious novels.

But appreciation for the magnitude of McMurtry's accomplishment in his trilogy was no means immediate. McMurtry's fiction has always polarized critics somewhat,[1] but the first volume in this new direction, **Moving On** (1970), drew intense critical scorn. Some reviewers damned the book's length (at 794 pages, **Moving On** is over five times **Hud's** length), and few critics could take seriously the protagonist—narrator, Patsy Carpenter. Quite pleased with the earlier short and schematic novels, many reviewers refused to believe that McMurtry could be capable of writing a profound statement on the human condition. Two short excerpts from many angered reviews indicate a pervasive sense of disappointment, perhaps even betrayal. "Tedious," "wrongly conceived," and "flat-surfaced" noted Elroy Bode in *Southwest Review*; "an obese catastrophy," claimed L. J. Davis in *Bookworld*.[2]

However, with the publication of the trilogy's second volume, wryly titled *All My Friends Are Going to Be Strangers* (1972), the critical crying out lessened in favor of some understanding praise. This was fortunate for the author because McMurtry clearly was not going to be deterred from writing a new kind of McMurtry novel. By the release of the last volume in the trilogy, *Terms of Endearment* (1975), critical acclaim was considerable. Leslie B. Mittleman's enthusiasm was by no means atypical. "In *Terms of Endearment* he [McMurtry] creates fully detailed, exuberant personalities who are so charged with the spontaneity of life that they seem to burst from the pages of the book. . . . Because of his concern for meaningful values, McMurtry is a writer whose best fiction teaches the reader how to live."[3]

McMurtry's literary reputation now has a reasonable amount of security with an increasingly widespread approval and understanding of his trilogy. The trilogy and McMurtry's earlier novels are so different in form and content that any lengthy comparison would be arbitrary and forced. Thus, the key question for this collection of essays appears to be: after some years for perspective, how high *does* the literary quality of his greatest popular successes, *Hud* and *The Last Picture Show*, measure now? This question deserves a fresh approach, and for an answer, two issues need to be explored: first, what was McMurtry's artistic strategy in these two popular novels; and second, where were his successes and failures in these books? Let us begin an exploration by a consideration of *Hud*.

Hud is a successful novel for a number of reasons. By an antiphony/response technique, the novel undercuts, without becoming mannered or silly, the all-time classic Western formula novel, Jack Schaefer's *Shane*. This technique enables McMurtry to maintain a tension between the ideal (past) dream and the nightmare (present) reality, all aimed toward the goal of dramatically rendering the theme of disintegration replacing progress in the modern, mechanical West. McMurtry also demonstrates in *Hud* a stunning talent for making the grotesque and the caricatured intensely, disturbingly real. (This talent has virtually become the author's trade mark.) Lonnie, the young narrator-protagonist of *Hud*, has a Holdon in a Chevy Pick-up quality, but an audience can still take this character seriously. He is an inventive and effective window into Texas as Hell.

Larger than life, villain Hud is an even more successful creation. He is entirely convincing as the Satanic figure who feeds his enormous appetite with an enormous greed. Hud

is Emersonian self-reliant man as destructive maniac in the pose of self-justified victim-rebel. He is one of several such figures to appear in anti-establishment novels of the 1950s and '60s; a group which includes Dean Moriarity (*On the Road*), Gnossos Pappadopoulis (*Been Down so Long It Looks Like Up to Me*), and Sebastian Dangerfield (*The Ginger Man*). *Hud*, then, may have been widely popular because McMurtry uniquely ranges into the tradition of mainstream literature while writing an essentially anti-formula novel. This technique is expanded upon even more successfully in the author's other great popular success, *The Last Picture Show* (1966).

In both form and theme, *Hud* is a direct attack on *Shane*. What Schaefer mythologizes McMurtry annihilates, and in such a punishingly extensive antiphony/response relationship that the parallels can hardly be accidental. The narrative mode of *Shane* is a dual first person voice. An older man (Bob Starrett) recollects from his childhood perspective an inspiring episode in the saga of how those 1880 era homesteaders won the West. This narrative voice, both on the scene and removed in time and space, creates a nostalgic mythology that views continuous masculine violence and continuous feminine security as the expected norm of life. *Hud* is also told in the first person, but the action is immediate and seen from the perspective of Lonnie, a sensitive, misfit adolescent. The beautiful in *Shane* has become the grotesque in *Hud*. *Shane* takes place in a long, lush valley at the base of Wyoming's breathtaking Grand Tetons. The air is clear, the weather bracing, the summer seemingly endless. The town in *Shane* is picturesque frontier frame, populated by helpful older businessmen and hard, tight-lipped ranch hands. *Hud* takes place on the depressing, arid expanses of wind-blown north Texas. It is the early 1950s, and the town consists of a few ramshackle buildings populated by a demoralized confederation of losers whose idea of good time is getting together for coffee, cherry pie, juke-box listening and reminiscing at a run-down roadside café.

Character parallels between *Shane* and *Hud* also exist in a similar golden to brazen antiphony/response. Among the minor characters, Chris in *Shane* and Jesse in *Hud* are parallel. Young and optimistic, Chris succeeds Shane as the hired hand on Starrett's expanding farm. Broken-down Jesse, mainstay of Homer Bannon and his collapsing ranch, has about reached the end of a long and undistinguished cowboy career. The major character parallels are even more pronounced. Joe and Marian Starrett are Bob's concerned, work ethic parents in *Shane*. Joe is mature and reliable while Marian couldn't be more pleased in her role of wife and mother. They are, after all, building their sacred dream on a new land. It is impossible to imagine Joe and Marian (even their names suggest holiness) having an argument. *Hud* presents no such idealized nuclear family. It is not that Lonnie's parents are evil; rather, he has no parents. The parental generation that should be controlling the novel's action and values has vanished or been killed off. A generation gap is emphasized with the entangled relationship of two widely separated groups—the old (Grandpa Bannon and Grandma) and the young (Hud and Lonnie). Grandma is sick, Grandpa is senile, Hud is greedy and Lonnie is confused. Tension, not nostalgia, establishes the tone of **Hud**.[4]

Both novels are strongly dominated by their leading male characters, Hud and Shane. Hud is a diabolical and vengeful bully, a clear-cut parallel and foil to Shane, whose heroism becomes increasingly Christ-like as the novel progresses. Shane is a mysterious stranger who arrives in the golden valley without explanation but with the ominous air and equipment of a professional gunfighter. However much a killer, he takes readily to home cooking and hard work at Starrett's place, although he insists on facing the front door while eating meals. A displaced Southerner (the true Western hero since Wister's Virginian), Shane is adored by Bob, supported by Marian and inspired by Joe. The symbolic Prodigal Son takes on a cause larger than himself in this novel as he endeavors to help Joe drive Fletcher's powerful and evil cattle monopoly out of the valley. In this parabolic conflict, Shane is reformed evil who restores the right of individual enterprise before vanishing back into the mountains. In the novel's climactic gunfight scene, Shane is wounded, but kills Wilson, Fletcher's hired killer. Wilson looks and dresses enough like Shane to be his double, but Wilson is self-serving, thus evil. (**Hud** reads a great deal like a sequel to *Shane* if Wilson had won the gunfight). *Shane* defines good in terms of just causes, with no amount of violence wrong in the service of such a cause.

However, violence is the means, not the end in *Shane*. The real substance of *Shane* rests in its theological vindication of the American Dream. Even Bob realizes that "What happened . . . was beyond me in those days."[5] As mysterious stranger, Shane is both martyr and savior, the final gun wound in his side establishing beyond doubt his selfless, Christ-like significance.[6] In a key passage, Shane explores his theology for Father Starrett:

> "I can't really explain it, Joe. But I just know that we're bound up in something bigger than any one of us, and that running away is the one thing that would make it worse than whatever might happen to us. There wouldn't be anything real ahead for us, any of us, maybe even for Bob, all the rest of our lives." (p. 93)

The sacred Manifest Destiny in jeopardy, Shane successfully rises to the rescue.

In **Hud**, villain and hero merge into one figure, the Western hero corrupted into the Western outlaw. *Shane* offers a posi-

tive parable of theologically-based Manifest Destiny, but in **Hud** the forces are daemonic, dominated by Hud himself. While Shane is a man of skill, few words and good intentions, loudmouth rebel Hud expresses resentment about what a rotten deal life, with its knaves and fools, has given him. When Grandpa Homer Bannon realizes the consequences of his ill-fated Mexican cattle investment, Hud unleashes his profane theology of a personal manifest destiny. His philosophy is, as he demonstrates in one instance: "Who gives a shit," Hud said. "I'm gonna be boss."[7] While Shane exemplifies the highest law of moral right, Hud operates, without persecution, beyond the law. Hardly the tight-lipped stoic, Hud feels that everyone has treated him unjustly, so he is owed the right to rip-off whatever he can get. Through the novel's course, Hud trades in his bronc for a smashed-up Cadillac, and hustles a distinctive Stetson, then a frizzy, rich blonde, in addition to obtaining a questionable deed to Homer's ranch.

Running through *Shane* is an undercurrent of sexual tension. Shane is attracted to more about Marian than her cooking, and Marian, bred to please, blushes, giggles and says of Shane. "I never saw a man quite like him before." (p.8) This issue reaches a climax when Shane, ready to fight for the homesteaders, knocks out the foolish Joe who is about to be ambushed by Fletcher. Shane turns to Marian. She says: "We have battered down words that might have been spoken between us and that was as it should be. But I have a right to know. . . .Are you doing this just for me?" (p. 105) Shane hesitates, and then ". . . he was looking only at mother and she was all that he could see. 'No, Marian. Could I separate you in my mind and afterwards be a man?' He pulled his eyes from her. . . . you were scarce aware that he was moving[;] he was gone into the outer darkness." (pp. 105-6)

Duty before dishonor is not, however, a theme in **Hud**. McMurtry uses sex and violence as the primary means for exploring man's capacity for evil in the modern, corrupt West.[8] In this latter-day frontier, justice is power, so Hud pretty much seizes what he wants. Hud rapes Halmea, the black, Dilsey-like housekeeper, explaining that she deserved it ("Now, you bitch. . ." [p. 93]), and that he alone had the guts to enact what the other young men were content to dream about.[9] Hud is also his own hired killer. In a state of total horror, Lonnie listens to Hud's justification for running over Homer, raving and helpless in a ditch, with his Cadillac;

> "You listen to me," he said." "No shit, it was best. I ain't lyin' now. Homer wanted it. . . . He was bad off, Lonnie . . . Tryin' to get to them goddamn dead people a his. I thought if he wanted to get to 'em so bad I'd just let him go. He always liked them better than us that was alive, anyhow. . . . He was just an old worn-out bastard." (pp. 128-29)

Shane ensured Bob's future, Hud successfully wipes out Lonnie's past and future.

Two contrasting, parallel scenes from *Shane* and *Hud* further illustrate the grotesque corruption of Western promise. Early in *Shane*, Starrett and Shane successfully remove an enormous stump which Starrett alone has failed to budge. The scene demonstrates the power of brotherhood, cooperative effort for the triumph of homesteading over nature. Starrett wants to clear the land for crops, and Shane wants hard work to redeem his past. Marian and Bob are an audience enthralled with their powerful men. This scene foreshadows, of course, the more important uprooting of Fletcher. Shane gives the final push that dislodges the stump, just as he gives the final push (killing Wilson) that rids the valley of the Fletcher menace. But in the contrasting analogous scene from *Hud*, Homer Bannon's cattle herd is plowed *into* the ground. In a blow of cosmic justice rendered as a Western formula fiction cliche, Homer learns that his entire herd is infected with hoof-and-mouth disease. No amount of noble intentions, productive hard work or brotherhood can establish success here. The benevolent forces in *Shane* have turned into impersonal, all-powerful and often hostile forces in *Hud*. Fate and the government conspire not only to destroy Homer and the herd, but also to wipe out the Western dream of progress through homesteading that *Shane* proffered. Under supervised governmental direction, Homer's final act as a rancher is to corral his cattle—even his aged prize longhorns—into an enormous pit and shoot every last one of them. "Don't take very long to kill things." Grandpa sadly philosophizes, "Not like it takes to grow." (p. 103)

A government agent offers an optimistic interpretation of this tragedy. The herd's destruction is actually a blessing in disguise because now Homer can convert his land into oil leases. But Homer reacts with absolute scorn because that is not his kind of money: "Piss on that kinda money." (p. 88) Leader in the impersonal new order of mechanical land rape for profit, Hud intends to do just what the government agent suggests.

While *Hud* is a jaundiced response to the ideal world of *Shane*, McMurtry does not limit himself to producing merely an anti-formula novel. Occasionally a sentimental moment or phrase drifts into the action of his novel. Certainly *Shane* and *Hud* share many of the same ideals, including a belief in individual freedom and the sacredness of the same ideals. But Schaefer stresses the notion that mankind is fundamentally good; that heroes will emerge, and that in a crisis they will bravely fight for their high ideals, ultimately gaining them. McMurtry studies man's depravity, not offering inspiring solutions, but posing disturbing questions. For example, most of Hud's criticisms against Homer are justified. Grandpa did want to make a cheap, easy, illegal deal on the Mexican cattle, and he was caught in the vice of a punishment far exceeding the crime. Hud continually shocks and intimidates Lonnie, but after Halmea is raped, Lonnie must admit that Hud *is* merely carrying out an action Lonnie has thought about many times. McMurtry's Texas is a brutal, mutilated world. Like Alex in *A Clockwork Orange*, Hud (the anti-Shane) acts on the premise that the only sane response to such a world is to be strong and self-serving, immune to feelings or weaknesses. These issues, explored in some depth and with a distinctive voice, along with the moving portrayal of Lonnie's painful adolescence, place *Hud* beyond the parameters of anti-formula writing.

Hud also has a definite dimension of literary self-consciousness beyond formula Westerns.[10] McMurtry positions the spectre of an aged William Butler Yeats hovering over his novel. Certainly Hud dramatically illustrates those famous lines from "The Second Coming": "The best lack all conviction while the worst / Are full of passionate intensity."[11] The original title of *Hud* was *Horseman, Pass By*, a phrase from Yeats' epitaph and the concluding lines of his poem "Under Ben Bulben." This original title brings to mind the Four Horsemen of the Apocalypse, a sense of the past's passing, and a plea for sanctuary, Yeats' words are an appropriate epitaph to he Western dream of the noble and successful self-made man.

The Last Picture Show is an even better book than *Hud*. Certainly *Hud* is successful, but the novel is more *tour de force* than substantial accomplishment. The anti-formula schemata is sometimes too much a self-conscious virtuoso piece of modeling; there is flight rather than growth on Lonnie's part; there is the triumph of evil Hud, who succeeds so easily because McMurtry has provided no competent, admirable foils. *Hud*'s one-dimensional characters and values are refreshing at first reading, but they pale with closer scrutiny. *Picture Show* reads as a much more complex and risky book. Something of a bantam black humor *Tom Jones*, this novel moves by the episodic and satirical to establish the moral growth and self-awareness of hero Sonny Crawford. Faced with some potent threats, including his own inadequacies, Sonny learns to perceive and accept his situation, rather than fleeing. Much of the ugly critical commentary against this book came about because it was misread as a filthy, funny and frightening tall tale posing as reality without any moral quest.

Considering McMurtry's career to date, we can see that *The Last Picture Show* is a transitional work, experimental and often exciting in its sense of self-discovery for author, protagonist and audience. The novel is also flawed with excess episodes—Joe Bob's morality trial seems repetitive as well as preposterous—and a failure to more fully realize thematic implications. But in another way, this is also McMurtry's most balanced book in its movement from anti-formula statement to personal statement, its blend of formula convention and artistic invention. In the mode of Kafka's *Trial* or Paddy Chayefsky's *Network*, McMurtry forces an audience into a confrontation with their values. *The Last Picture Show* convincingly dramatizes the idea that reality imitates art, that satire can be reality. McMurtry here establishes and sustains a marvelously comic tone.

While incident and plot development are emphasized in *Hud*, characterization dominates in *Picture Show* as it does in succeeding McMurtry novels. Set in a small isolated north Texas town in the early 1950s, *The Last Picture Show* bears little resemblance to the Sinclair Lewis-Sherwood Anderson school of small town exposes from the first quarter of this century. *Main Street* and *Winesburg, Ohio*, for example, depict their authors' outrage at the insensitivity and hypocrisy of the American small town. McMurtry points no accusing finger and only occasionally muckrakes with glee a dirty, smelly truth of rural reality underneath the American Dream. Rather, what Lewis and cohorts discovered, uncovered and made into a formula, McMurtry accepts in calm irony, articulating a comedy of further depravity with a fatigued shrug of "so it goes." The novel teases its audience: are we to take all this as modern realism, satire or some new hybrid?

McMurtry's characterization in *Picture Show* is more advanced than in *Hud*, both in terms of depth and range of types. It is primarily through characterization that McMurtry paradoxically compounds stereotypes to move beyond formula in *Picture Show*. Therefore, an ideal way to understand this novel is to trace its character development and interaction from simple beginning to complex finale. *Picture Show's* characters have the same division found in *Hud*—two conflicting groups, the adolescents and the adults—but this later novel centers on the problems of community involvements and conflicts, rather than problems with evil taking over on an isolated ranch.

The teens in *Picture Show* have their values and life styles built on an image of Hollywood celluloid, a vast romantic adventure played out in great sweeping heroic triumphs. The teens face two tragedies in *Picture Show*, the closing of the town's only movie theatre and the waning months of their senior year. As the novel progresses, this group becomes increasingly disoriented and disillusioned, a confusing on-going identity crisis which results in a bizarre series of shifting feuds and entangled alliances. The adults are set in their ways of disillusionment and impotence. Their problem is not recovering a lost or slipping romantic identity, but living out their mature years without becoming completely insane. They see motion pictures as a stimulating but cruel lie, and have turned to television, forcing the theatre's closing. The adults are happily tranquilized and addicted to this colorless narcotic as narcosis, much to the disgust of their

offspring. At the end of the novel, all but one of the adolescents have forsaken the town in search of a stage on which a lost Hollywood romanticism can be recovered and acted upon.

The Last Picture Show is told from an omniscient third person point of view and centers around the activities of several members of Thalia (Greek for paradise) High School's senior class of 1951, particularly one Sonny Crawford. The novel opens on a bitter cold day, the morning after Thalia High has lost the season's last football game. The novel's first sentence effectively sets the book's tone, a mixture of comedy, ignorance and self-pity: "Sometimes Sonny felt like he was the only human creature in town."[12] In the beginning he is a relatively carefree individual who attends school only because of the sports and that activity's correlative, the girls. Estranged from his alcoholic father, Sonny lives in a run-down rooming house with classmate-athlete star Duane Moore, his best friend. Sonny earns money by driving a butane truck for Frank Fartley. Sonny is dissatisfied with all his pasttimes.

Quarterback Duane's true love, Jacy Farrow, is the town's richest girl and the school beauty queen. Jacy, spoiled, selfish and madly in love with herself, ranks near the top of the list of recent literature's most frightening and insightful caricatures. She is first and foremost a performer, a show-off who hates to be considered "backward and country," whose largely realized ambitions are to be first in good looks, first in exciting experiences and first in the minds of admiring others. She is Daisy Miller reincarnated as an authentic mass media symptom—the would-be superstar.[13] Like her high school peers, Jacy is strongly theatrical, influenced most of all by what she sees in the movies.

A self-created "virtuous martyr," her greatest concern is her image, the construction around her person of a legend, an aura of wonder which will be secure for all time in Thalia. This means that Duane is to her little more than an extremely devoted but stupid tool. Sonny is a virtual nonentity. "He [Sonny] admired her extravagantly, but had no money and had not been in the backfield, so he really just didn't count." (p. 71)

The climatic senior class bus trip to San Francisco, wherein the Texas students are ironically cautioned by their teachers to be wary of "lurking preverts," (sic) is the occasion of Jacy's maidenhead sacrifice, said act motivated by her desire to participate fully in the revelry of her sophisticated friends in nearby Wichita Falls. She decides to use the hapless Duane to gain experience, planning to dump him when she returns home as a Woman of the World. She maps out her "seduction" with cunning ("It was the way things were done"), and when Duane's 2,000 mile case of anticipatory erection gives way to sudden impotence at the Crucial Moment, she is furious because her carefully laid plans seem thwarted. "What'll we say?. . . .The whole class knows what we were going to do!" (p. 147) Appearances must and can be preserved, so when the other girls eagerly come to her room afterwards for an account of the proceedings, Jacy lies in bed, "calm, replete, a little wasted even," and says. "I just can't describe it in words." (p. 148) She enacts reality into movie myth with golden articulation. Jacy's inability to talk about this experience establishes with total certainty for her audience the validity of her deeply-felt passion. Later in the trip Duane finally manages to perform, and to his bewilderment finds himself abandoned upon the return to Thalia. He had always felt that "you were supposed to get whoever you really loved. That was the way it worked in movies." (p. 150) Distraught, he leaves town at the end of the summer to join the army, trading Texas for Seoul and In-Chan.

The Romantic as rip-off artist, Jacy exploits all the reasonably attractive males in Thalia, then moves on to be a star performer with the fast rich set in Wichita Falls. But one night in Thalia, shortly before she takes off to conquer the college set at Southern Methodist, Jacy receives her comeuppance from the novel's best exploiter. This is the oil driller Abilene, an efficient mechanical extension of Hud. Abilene is probably the town's richest man by virtue of his nightly victories at the pool table, a battlefield over which he is so completely in command that his forays on it can only be considered mythically heroic. Extracting a total deference from everyone in Thalia, he epitomizes the modern cowboy after the conquest, the man in control whose hands and clothes never get dirty, and who never has to associate with horses and cattle. His freedoms have been redefined, and his personality and values have mutated from the ideal to fit these new freedoms. He specializes in cool insensitivity, getting what he wants, being exempt, and everyone fears, hates and envies him. Abilene is also the lover of Jacy's mother. On a warm, late summer evening, Jacy unwittingly allows Abilene to seduce her on top of a snooker table. "He played her out as recklessly as he had played the final ball, and when he did she scattered as the red balls had scattered when the white one had struck them so hard." (p. 174) Jacy is undone only for the moment by this well-rehearsed exhibition of Abilene's perfect technique and total disdain. It is Jacy's mother Lois who is really wounded.

Lois Farrow is the town's strongest person, admired and desired by all the men because of her good looks and wildness. A cynical alcoholic who is very bored and unhappy with her life, Lois uses her liquor as an anesthetic for her boredom; and because she is dependent on no one, she is able to dominate nearly all: "If there was anything in the world she was scared of no one knew what it was . . . she was not in the habit of walking around anyone." (p. 35) Prime time television makes the perfect complement to her alcoholism. As a young woman "she had more life than just

about anybody" but years of *ennui* have deadened her somewhat. She fails in her various attempts to implant some vestiges of reality into her daughter's plastic psyche. She enunciates the new ethos of the townsman, and her own, when she says that the land is too tough; that instead of "fighting the hell out of it" one merely acquiesces and does whatever one can to make existence more accommodating. The only thing for Lois to do is grow older and die, a process shunned and endured by everyone but Sam the Lion and Sonny. "Everything gets old if you do it long enough," she tells Jacy. (p. 43)

The book's wisest man, its "old order" representative, is Lois' one-time lover, Sam the Lion, venerable and grizzled owner of the pool hall and theatre (the town's main social centers), and guardian of the faithful and retarded adolescent, Billy. Much of Sam's mental acuity seems to have grown out of the terrible tragedy of his life: a well-known hell-raiser as a youth and later a prominent rancher, oilman and auto dealer, he has seen all three of his sons die violently, following which his wife went insane.[14] A traditional old-timer who fears the mechanical world which has repeatedly tried to destroy him (something like **Hud**'s Grandpa Bannon), Sam becomes known as "the man who took care of things, particularly of boys," (p. 7) and he emerges as Sonny's closest counselor. The latter asks, "Is growing up always miserable? Nobody seems to enjoy it much." Sam replies, "Oh, it ain't necessarily miserable. About eighty percent of the time, I guess." Growing old is one hundred percent miserable, however, and Sam's entreaties echo those of all the adults when he says, "Goddamit! Goddamit! I don't want to be old. It don't fit me!. . . . Being a decrepit old bag of bones is what's ridiculous." (pp. 123-4) Sam's sudden death, upon which Sonny inherits the pool hall, theatre and Billy, removes the last example of wisdom and perspective from Thalia.

Old or young, the issue of sex cements the generation gap. Sonny's sexual frustrations, while severe, do not drive him to the extreme of most of the other boys, for whom frequent public and private masturbation and regular couplings with heifers, sheep, dogs and even (for variety) geese are not uncommon. Instead, Sonny begins a chance affair with Ruth Popper, the homely wife of Thalia High's football coach. Her forty years of life and twenty years of marriage to this Good Ole Boy have left her devoid of either sexual or emotional fulfillment. Lonely, consumed by an unending depression, enduring an existence for which death would seem a welcome relief, Ruth eagerly jumps at the opportunity of an affair with Sonny because he can bring her companionship, can make her feel needed, wanted and useful. When they first meet she tells him, "Loneliness is like ice"(p. 102), but his presence melts that ice by allowing her—for the first time in her life—to feel a measure of happiness and satisfaction, even though she knows that Sonny comes to her only for sex. For Sonny, "it was an adventure to have slept with someone's wife . . . it was sort of a feather in his cap." (p. 98) He feels strangely pulled by her, is confused by the emotive processes of her awakenings, and is unable to communicate with her any way except physically. He becomes "everything" to her, what "made the days worth confronting," but after a time he begins feeling "washed out and restless" because he fears the responsibility that her dependence on him seems to imply. Sonny turns from Ruth to Jacy when the beauty queen suddenly becomes available and shows an interest in him. After their abortive elopement, a quite willing Sonny is seduced by Lois Farrow, who philosophizes: "Your mother and I sat next to one another in the first grade. . . . We graduated together. I sure didn't expect to sleep with her son. That's small town life for you." (p. 201)

Comedy and characterization are so successful in *The Last Picture Show* that some of the novel's other accomplishments may be overlooked. Similar to *Hud*, McMurtry places the hostile environment in the foreground. Few characters can forget that they are stuck and isolated in a vast, flat space and that the town is dying. An omnipresent wind emphasizes an irrecoverable loss. Symbol of angst and time, the "northers" blow everything away from Thalia except the adults, and none of them is in the twenty to forty age range except Abilene (cf. *Hud*). Winds of change accompany the several furtive trips the adolescents take in an attempt to escape the area's oppression and perplexing older generation. The wind motif works well in tandem with the major thematic pattern of illusion/reality, which centers around Sonny. This pattern is a more complex and versatile development of the antiphony/response sequence in *Hud*.

At first Sonny perceives this pattern in terms of bad fate, such as the theatre's closing, and the actions of other, more powerful characters upon him. Like also-ran Duane and others, Sonny has endured years of humiliation and resentment. Several incidents illustrate this victimization. One example would be the scene where, in a fit of rage, best friend Duane blinds Sonny's eye with a broken beer bottle. Duane becomes insanely angered not because Sonny is keeping company with Jacy, but because she revealed the secret that Duane is a woefully inept lover. Jacy also wounds Sonny by setting him up on the fake elopement that successfully enrages her parents enough to send her to chic, expensive Southern Methodist.

But in learning through this painful experience, Sonny outgrows being a pawn and scapegoat. Bright, sensitive and increasingly honest, Sonny gradually realizes that *he* is primarily responsible for his problems. Three episodes point to Sonny's increasing maturity. When he, Duane and several other boys publically humiliate Billy, it is Sonny who accepts Sam's punishment and seeks his forgiveness. Inheriting the pool hall upon Sam's death, Sonny is too slow to realize that this position involves more responsibility than opening, closing and presiding over the town's recreation center. Billy, sweeping the street at dawn when he should be inside and looked after, is run down by a semi loaded with cattle. Sorrowful beyond words, Sonny accepts his part in Billy's death.

Sonny must also take the blame for silently forsaking Ruth Popper who relapses into a helpless loneliness. In the most poignant scene in the novel, Sonny returns to Ruth. He gets no further than her dirty kitchen. Understandably bitter, overcome by betrayal and fast retreating into hopelessness, she cannot face being either happy or vulnerable again. In an angry denunciation she throws a coffeepot at Sonny, who remains calm, needing. Her anger dissolves into tears, and she makes the novel's finest statement in an ambiguous one: "Honey, never you mind. . . ." (p. 220) All the adolescents have made a mess of their lives, but only Sonny has the courage to stay, to see the pointlessness of leaving Thalia to escape himself and the consequences of his actions. Unlike Lonnie, who runs away at the end of *Hud*, Sonny remains behind, sliding into an unarticulated but admirable existential acceptance. He at least passively realizes that wherever he is he must accept his fate, and Thalia is a comfortable known evil. By the end of *Picture Show* a father-son reconciliation is no longer an impossibility. Sonny has been pointed in a direction McMurtry will pursue in much more depth and direction throughout his trilogy.

Perhaps McMurtry has always been more of a cult figure than a popular writer. Muted now, his mass appeal came not so much from its fiction as from two fine films based on his fiction, made some time ago. I would speculate that at present he is a cult figure of the Eastern literary establishment. If his trilogy turns into a successful film or television series, then his broad-based popularity may return. Assuming McMurtry was a cult figure before the film success and his initiation into the highest literary circles, who believed that *Hud* and *The Last Picture Show* were outstanding books? Certainly not the millions who adore Louis L'Amour. Probably not the readers, writers and critics of "serious" Western literature who typically prefer Edward Abbey, Frank Waters or even Eugene Manlove Rhodes as candidates for major recent Southwest writers. McMurtry just doesn't say much to us here," Tom Lyon, the editor of *Western American Literature* (based at Utah State University in Logan) wrote me some years back. Indeed.

Both *Hud* and *The Last Picture Show* can be seen as Westerns for people who have left the rural West (at least in spirit) in favor of urban life and values (anywhere). Perhaps guilty and unforgiving about their origins and amply large enough for a cult, such an audience would see, especially in *Picture Show*, a fine justification for "moving on," better than a summer vacation "back home" to renew their faith in how rotten their roots really were. Certainly Thalia bears little resemblance to, say, Petticoat Junction or Andy Griffith's Mayberry.[15] This anti-local color dimension may explain why so many urban readers of **Picture Show** I've encountered have been so taken with the novel's "amazing realism." **The Last Picture Show** successfully articulated a generation's feelings about their origins and youth, establishing a theme and tone which can be seen in *American Graffiti*, an imitation even more famous. But **Hud** and **The Last Picture Show**, although flawed, are also good works of literature that deserve serious, attentive reading. They are solidly in the twentieth century tradition of the experimental *bildungsroman* that has produced such great works as a Lawrence's *Sons and Lovers* and Joyce's *Portrait of the Artist as a Young Man*.

While it is to McMurtry's credit that his artistry markedly improved this past decade, he has also suffered an important loss. There is much to be said for those novels which have a mission to articulate—with a shock of recognition—our perception of the American scene, the American experience. Larry McMurtry has become the spokesman of his own vision at the expense of continuing his career as an authentic American *vox populi*. With the trilogy behind him, it would be fascinating to see what kind of a Western novel as cultural statement McMurtry could produce now.

NOTES

1. Critics tend to avoid impartiality with McMurtry in favor of either adulation or condemnation. Thus, most articles are justifications thinly disguised as explications, perhaps because the longest standard treatment of McMurtry is harsh. This is *Larry McMurtry* (Austin, Texas: Steck-Vaughn Southwest Writers Series, No. 23, 1969) by Thomas Landess.

2. Elroy Bode, "Moving On . . . and On . . . and On," *Southwest Review*, 55 (1970), p. 427; L.J. Davis," *Moving On* by Larry McMurtry," *Bookworld* (June 21, 1970), p. 6.

3. Leslie B. Mittleman, *"Terms of Endearment,"* in *Literary Annuals*, 1975, ed. Frank McGill (Englewood Cliffs, New Jersey: Salem Press, pp. 317, 320.

4. Is it coincidence or design that the late Brandon de Wilde played both Bob and Lonnie in the film version of these novels?

5. Jack Schaefer, *Shane* (Boston: Houghton-Mifflin Co., Riverside Reading Series, 1964), p. 84. Further page citations from this work appear in this text. *Shane* was first published in 1949.

6. For a full and excellent treatment of Shane as Messiah, see Michael T. Marsden, "Savior in the Saddle: The Sagebrush Testament," *Illinois Quarterly*, 36 (Dec., 1973), pp. 5-15. The definitive treatment of the religious impulse in Western literature is still Max Westbrook's 'The Practical Spirit; Sacrality and the American West," first published in *Western American Literature*, 3 (Fall, 1968), pp. 193-205.

7. Larry McMurtry, *Hud* (New York: The Popular Library, 1961), pp. 67-68. All subsequent page reference are from this edition and are included in the text. *Hud* was originally published by Harper & Row in 1961 under the title *Horseman, Pass By*.

8. McMurtry's frequent scenes of sexual explicitness may partially account for his popularity as well as, to some, his offensiveness.

9. The grim allegory of this scene was side-stopped in the screen version of *Hud*. There, the Halmea character won an Oscar as played by Patricia Neal, carefully made up in a whiter shade of pale.

10. As Eliot noted in "Tradition and the Individual Talent," one of the hallmarks of quality literature is its reliance upon past major works and recognition of innovation in genre development.

11. M.L. Rosenthal, ed., *Selected Poems of William Butler Yeats* (New York: The Macmillan Co., 1962), p.91.

12. Larry McMurtry, *The Last Picture Show* (New York: Dell, 1966), p. 5. Further important quotes from this novel will be identified by page numbers in the text. *Picture Show* was first published by The Dial Press in 1966.

13. Cybil Shepherd played Daisy and Jacy in film versions of these novels, both directed by Peter Bogdanovich. Ms. Shepherd, of course, is Jacy's projection of her ideal self, not what she actually is.

14. With the names, insanity, retardation, enslavement by the land and culture, *and* death of the older order, it is difficult to miss Faulkner's presence in *The Last Picture Show*.

15. The Pasadena of *Family* (ABC) might also qualify.

Charles Champlin (review date 16 August 1987)

SOURCE: A review of *Film Flam: Essays on Hollywood*, in *Los Angeles Times Book Review*, August 16, 1987, p. 12.

[*In the review below, Champlin praises McMurtry for his*

analysis of the emerging problems with the American film industry.]

Larry McMurtry, whose novels-into-films include **Hud**, **The Last Picture Show**, **Leaving Cheyenne** (filmed by Sidney Lumet as *Lovin' Molly*) and **Terms of Endearment**, knows his way around Hollywood and is not much enchanted by what he sees.

"With rare exceptions," he says in an introduction to **Film Flam**, "the pictures coming out of Hollywood today are the last resorts of the gutless. In my opinion, a little film flam is all such an industry deserves."

McMurtry contributed a column on movies and television to *American Film* magazine for a couple of years, then found that the prospect of going on was appalling—columinizing is "a perversion in which only the vain and/or the indigent indulge." Or the vainly indigent, he could have added.

The book is a collection of those columns and some free-standing pieces, including a lively account of a day spent wandering around Pasadena with Diane Keaton and her grandmother, Mary Alice Hall, that illuminates Keaton far better than the millions of words uttered elsewhere.

As with all such collections, the passage of time is evident, and the films under attack (as most are) have, like *The Deep* and *Lovin' Molly*, long since passed to their eternal rest, disturbed only for an occasional late-night ghost walk across the television screen.

But the untimeliness matters relatively little with McMurtry because his indictments of and observations about the industry are fairly timeless. He writes trenchantly.

Coming to Hollywood to help on **The Last Picture Show**, he says, "I felt that a novelist might, after all, be of some use in the creation of a movie script, if only as the guardian of valid motivation."

He discovered that screen writing was a particular craft for which the novelist was by no means inevitably well-suited. He realized that his novel had been written hastily (in six weeks) in unjustified bitterness toward his hometown. Peter Bogdanovich, imposing his gentler perceptions on the material, may have made a movie that was in some ways truer than the book. McMurtry admires good screen writers, but says: "The vast bulk of the industry's writing chores is still divided between smartassed amateurs (the novelists) and dullwitted hacks: in other words, between people who are given little chance to treat screenwriting as other than a joke, and the peons of the system, who can only treat it as a job."

He has words for the boxcar salaries paid to executives, stars and novelists (other than himself): "Big money has a way of convincing people they deserve it. . . . Being rich is an occupation in itself, particularly for people who arrive at it via parachute in middle life."

Like many a viewer, McMurtry laments the decline of stars: "The generation of actors and actresses who could interest us in a character simply by appearing on the screen . . . are slipping away fast, to be succeeded, for the most part, by a generation of dope freaks, pretty boys, and lazy ladies, some of whom are better actors than their predecessors but precious few of whom can make us like them."

Part of his lament for the generation of Bogart, Grant, Tracy, Wayne, Crawford and Bergman is what McMurtry finds to be the devaluation of grace (as embracing everything positive you might hope to find in a character).

"Grace is seen as insincere, probably phony, nearly always a cheat—or, at the very least, dumb." It bespeaks "a desperate distrust of polished people." The decline of grace parallels and is probably related to a decline of the love story and the romantic impulse, as against what he saw as a current diet of "Trivial comedy, torture, assassination, horror and star epics offering nothing but the inflations of personality."

McMurtry is, or was, happier with television, finding in *All in the Family*, *The Mary Tyler Moore Show*, and even in many of the cop shows and the mini-series a grasp of American realities and a gallery of middle-American portraits that the movies had for a whole complex of reasons forgotten how to do or chosen not to do.

A leading studio executive remarked at a luncheon recently that the movies were not much fun to be around anymore because the executives responsible for them hated them, or, at a minimum, found no joy in making movies and felt no passion for them.

The founding moguls may have had their monstrous moments, but they did have a passion for making movies, and for making movies that audiences would be eager to see. The latter-day chieftain and McMurtry would find much to agree on.

Driving across the country, McMurtry concluded that his **The Last Picture Show** had been all too prophetic, confirming "the long retreat of movies out of rural and in some cases even suburban life." Even in the six-theater complexes in the jazzy malls, "there is evidence of torpor," McMurtry says.

The movies, historically, have been unpredictable, living out a death wish, as it sometimes seems, but never quite getting to the last reel. New screens are going up by the hundreds and, quite surprisingly, the prevalence of VCRs appears to have sustained rather than hurt walk-in theater trade.

Yet a look at any day's movie ads seems to sustain McMurtry's snarling dismissal. The vitality in style and content, movies mirroring something of life as it is actually lived, seem to arise abroad or on the independent fringes of the American industry. *Film Flam* is rich in well-said clues why this should be true.

Robert Gish (review date 30 October 1988)

SOURCE: "Anything for Larry," in *Los Angeles Times Book Review*, October 30, 1988, pp. 1, 13.

[*In the review below, Gish, the author of* Frontier's End, *praises* Anything for Billy *as an intriguing example of a new type of Western.*]

There's much about the Old West and the Western novel that should stay dead and gone: the gun-slinging violence, the racism and sexism (all so predictable and stereotyped when "novelized"), the cussing and carousing—all the qualities that made the West so wild.

But the West (old and new), as every one knows, is a big place and its telling, remembering and imagining take many forms—in fiction and in fact. Moreover, it seems as if the Western novel may have recovered from its reported demise, dusted itself off and saddled up once again.

More than any other contemporary novelist, Larry McMurtry has been hard at work revitalizing the Western. Part of the interest and the urgency of his own artistic westering, his performance as his own (and our own) hero of the West as literary vision, is built into his novels. Even reluctant readers soon realize that these novels, these Westerns that he keeps turning out, deal with matters of some deep personal import. None of his tellings are trivia—as is always the case with true "entertainments." McMurtry established that early on with his first novels, *Horseman, Pass By* and *The Last Picture Show*.

Later, his Pulitzer Prize-winning *Lonesome Dove* revisited that epic narrative of the turn-of-the-century West, the trail drive. *Lonesome Dove*, defying classification, remains, paradox of paradoxes, a *modern* trail-drive novel. In *Texasville*, McMurtry took a years-later look at some of his earlier characters swaggering into middle age and the throes of modern living and world-crisis economics. Usually McMurtry's West as word is the West as Texas. But Hollywood and Ne-

vada—and points in between—also play a part in his staking out the larger landscape and idea called "the West."

Now, in *Anything for Billy*, comes the inevitable—McMurtry's attempts to account for Billy the Kid, the life and the legend of one of the West's most storied outlaws. It's a great, good book with everything in it to make readers think again about the real and the imagined West and the rendering of them in words.

Not surprisingly, the narrator of the story as we hear it, one Ben Sippy–a dime novelist and would-be train robber on the lam (with his mule, Rosy) from his boring wife, Dora, his nine daughters, and his monotonous Philadelphia life—is much more intriguing than William H. Bonney ever was. Here Bonney is cleverly called, for McMurtry's inventive and parodic purposes, Billy Bone.

Sippy–with his constant scribbling and his silly-titled "dimers"—is in many ways McMurtry's counterpart: the Western writer in thrall to character and landscape, history and story. In the New Mexico Territory, Sippy falls in with Billy and his loyal cowboy sidekick, Joe Lovelady (a Texas charmer if ever there was one), and rides with them up and down the territory and across the Rio Grande into Mexico in a month long traipse that sees Billy ruthlessly murder nine (usually) innocent people. It's all in a month's work for poor Billy, who seems all the more frightening because of his own fears and his inability to shoot straight (a failing which demands that he use a 10-gauge goose gun rather than the Colt "Peacemaker" revolver associated with Western heroes). Most demythologizing of all is Billy's downright dumbness.

Sippy, however, is ready to do just about anything for Billy. He follows him when he says ride. He gives him his mule when villainous old Whiskey Isinglass and his band of wild Texans have Billy and his gunslinging cronies cornered at Skunkwater Flats. He shares Billy's craving for sexual coupling with the macabre, crazed seductress Cecily Snow. He serves him, advises him, even writes about him, helping elevate him into legend by giving him the name Billy the Kid. And this is the nagging craw-sticker in the novel.

Sippy's sappiness stops short at the crucial time. His devotion to Billy is not as unqualified as that of Katie Garza, the half-breed bandit queen (one of Isinglass's many strange and exotic children) for her *chapito* Billy.

Like Katie, Joe Lovelady gives everything for Billy. What Joe and Katie give and what Ben Sippy withholds is what allows McMurtry to pose the haunting questing of the novel and of Billy Bone's misspent life—a question as much for the new West as for the old: When is a hero merely a celebrity?

Call it a Western against itself, an anti-Western, a gothic Western, an adult Western. Call it a tall tale that outdoes any previous telling about Billy the *bandito* boy of old New Mexico. Call it a parody of great purpose. Call it anything you like. But those who ride/read along with McMurtry, Billy, Sippy and the rest; those who like to dislike or dislike to like the West—what it was, is, might have been, or still might be—will say after this book, for sure, "Anything for Larry." Anything at all.

Barbara Kingsolver (review date 22 October 1989)

SOURCE: "Across Texas by Non Sequitor," in *New York Times*, October 22, 1989, p. 8.

[*In the following review, Kingsolver, a novelist and author of* The Bean Trees, *states that despite a weak ending,* Some Can Whistle *is engaging and entertaining.*]

A novel about a novelist is a narcissistic contraption at best—and, at worst, false advertising. If the truth must be known, we novelists are a pale, unglamourous lot, cowering behind our dictionaries. Few of us have wacky maids and the knack for stumbling on corpses; even fewer of us are rich. But Larry McMurtry can write about anything he wants, and most everything that breathes and is literate will beg for more. Mr. McMurtry's prose stands up and kicks fence posts. His cowboys are articulate, his petty criminals have grand potential, and in his latest book, *Some Can Whistle*, even a rich novelist is as complex as Hamlet, and as doomed.

The character in question is Danny Deck, whom we last saw some half-dozen novels ago (in *All My Friends Are Going to Be Strangers*) drowning a failed manuscript in the Rio Grande. Now Danny has become a sort of Walter Mitty in reverse; he's so wealthy that he discards his Mercedes when it balks rather than call a mechanic, yet he dreams of middle-class domesticity—a fantasy he once turned into a popular television series. At 51, with his sitcom days behind him, portly Danny now lives on the Texas prairie, moping around the house in a caftan, eternally revising the first sentence of his would-be next novel. He shares a testy solitude with Gladys, the cook, who stomps around in orange parachute pants but does not actually cook, and with Godwin, an equally uncheerful classics scholar and Lothario emeritus who amuses himself by picking up hitchhikers in a Volkswagen Danny and Gladys call the Aidsmobile.

Danny, by contrast, has numerous old flames, mostly European actresses, but he's intimate only with their answering machines. Twenty-two years ago, in what appears to have been his sole potent act, he sired a daughter he has thought of constantly but never seen. *Some Can Whistle* opens with her entrance into his life, a furious voice on the phone demanding, "Mister Deck, are you my stinkin' Daddy?" He is, and he rushes to Houston to collect her. Larry McMurtry's fiction sometimes leans toward what a friend of mine calls "the dirty sock novel," that alienated masculine genre where men are men and they don't do emotional responsibility or laundry. But it's redeemed by the author's extraordinary way with women. His heroines are the kind you want to love, listen to forever or at least have move in next door. Danny Deck's daughter, T. R. by name, turns out to be a beautiful, foul-mouthed mother of two whose personality has the bite of a good Texas salsa. She's so entrenched in life that Danny can't fetch her without carrying away a sizable entourage of children and friends, as well as a burglar boyfriend named Muddy—all of whom eye T. R. with bewilderment and adoration. They come into Danny's life the way a hurricane hits Galveston, leaving a trail of non sequiturs and broken toys all the way across Texas.

If T. R. is like salsa, her father resembles a loaf of bread, both in shape and ambition. He loves his daughter, but doesn't seem able to do anything about it beyond handing her rolls of hundred-dollar bills. During her brief stay with Danny, T. R. makes up for the holidays they missed, filling his house with people and possessions that are layered on one another like a lunatic birthday cake. In all the confusion, even Gladys the cook forgets her varicose veins long enough to fall in love with a security guard; they consummate their passion only minutes before he's killed. Gladys is inconsolable; she'll always regret that she didn't let him "do it." When Danny replies that he thought she had, Gladys says sadly, "Yeah, but he wanted to try for two . . . I thought that would be rushing things a little."

The book's setting is contemporary (as contemporary as Cabbage Patch dolls and pink hair, anyway), and it describes Danny's few woolly weeks as a family man, which are altered by a sudden act of violence. The last section of *Some Can Whistle* is an odd epilogue in which Danny quickly recounts the next two decades of his life, which seem to have taken place in the future. It's hard to follow and emotionally disengaged, like a rushed catch-up at a class reunion. This tagged-on anticlimax weakens the narrative, but it's apparently there to prove that Danny will never acquire his daughter's virtuosity for living. Even tragedy can't touch his inertia. Danny Deck is exasperating and entirely believable. Well-formed fictional characters always inspire something in us, and Danny, virtuoso of the missed opportunity, is inspirational in his failure. He cautiously camps outside life's fence, but the claws of the beast reach through and maul him anyway. His sad tale exhorts us, as Gladys puts it, to "try for two," since you're damned if you don't—and the moment you've got is all you're guaranteed.

Jim Sanderson (essay date Summer 1990)

SOURCE: "Old Corrals: Texas According to 80s Films and TV and Texas According to Larry McMurtry," in *Journal of American Culture*, Vol. 13, No. 2, Summer, 1990, pp. 63-73.

[In the following essay, Sanderson—in the context of considering modern Texan popular culture—critiques Anything for Billy, commenting on McMurtry's dual role as a writer reacting to and creating Texas myths.]

For several years now, in conversations at conventions and at cocktail parties, I have noticed Texans arguing about Texas literature. The same arguments have appeared in print from *Texas Monthly* to *The Texas Observer* to *The Concho River Review*. The more notorious of these articles raised literary dust across the state from the stamping of feet of angered Texas critics and writers. Palefaces, Redskins, and bridegrooms all have different and sometimes conflicting notions about what a Texas writer is and what Texas writing is. The Texas Institute of Letters annually awards cash money to the best Texas literature. But, as Jim Lee says in *Range Wars*, neither the institute, the prize winners, nor observers can figure out its rules for eligibility. No one seems to know what qualifies someone to be a Texas writer, although Clay Reynolds does a good job in his essay in *Range Wars*. (S.M.U Press). Texas critics and writers may be copying the same phrase that so many West Texans say about art: They don't know how to define Texas literature but they know what it is. Or, so they think.

The same sort of mist surrounds most things Texas. Few Texans can even agree about what a Texan is: a native, a native moved away, a New Yorker with sympathies, a naturalized Texan like my father who, nevertheless, after living in Texas nearly forty years claims not to be a Texan, or me. Texans seem to have an overemphasized love and hate for their territory; yet they don't want anyone other than a Texan telling them about Texas. On the other hand, the nation as a whole has a certain fascination with Texas, perhaps for the same reasons that Texans love it and hate it—the Cowboys (both wranglers and football players), rural poverty and oil wealth, tarball beaches and truly ugly West Texas emptiness. To the nation, Texas is an example of unrestrained Americaness, manifest destiny gone unchecked. Lyndon Johnson showing compassion by declaring war on poverty yet conducting an unpopular war from his toilet seat. I loved to hate Lyndon because of his embarrassing crudity, but I hated to love him because of his naturalness compared to the tight assed, Harvard-trained, Europeanized Kennedy men around him.

So, to say anything about Texas, a critic has to define whether he is talking about a national perception of Texas. Texans' perception of Texas, or some personal observations

about Texas. I want to discuss popular artistic portrayals of Texas. In this discussion, I'll address some national perceptions of Texas presented by a television series, a film, and a novel. I'll leave other art out since I don't know much about it and don't want to blatantly reveal my ignorance.

Since TV is the most pervasive American art form (the term *art* used here for lack of better term), I'll discuss a TV show. Because film is the most popular and dominate medium of the twentieth century, perhaps the form for folk art in this century, I'd like to discuss movies about Texas. And, since he is a bright guy and an icon, I'll discuss Larry McMurtry in regard to a recent book and his own wrestling with his identity to a national audience as a Texas writer. . . .

Sitting On The Corral In Anything For Billy

With his early successes, **Horseman Pass By** and **Leaving Cheyenne**, Larry McMurtry, perched up on the corral post in the dust jacket photo, saw the God of national acclaim and popular success. With the first movies—**Hud** and **The Last Picture Show**—then the academy awards raining down upon **Terms of Endearment**, McMurtry was nominated for beatification. With the Pulitzer Prize for **Lonesome Dove** and the following media event, the film of **Lonesome Dove**, "the" TV event of the 88-89 season, McMurtry achieved popular sainthood. As a result, no Texan discussing literature or Texas dare leave out McMurtry. But, as soon as any critics mention McMurtry, Texas readers sigh and groan. For, because of Archer City's golden boy, Texans can't talk about Texas without talking about McMurtry. And, McMurtry can no longer hope to ever escape being labeled a "Texas" writer.

I don't mean to imply that **Lonesome Dove** is not a good novel or TV show. McMurtry and his TV translators know about the cultural baggage in Americans' minds. Though bounded by the small screen that barely contains the livestock or the story, the mini-series has a visual and thematic complexity rarely seen from a living room sofa. Director Simon Wincer and Austin writer Bill Wittliff (another Texas/Australian writer/director team), understand filming open space and cattle and playing realism against myth.

So, in **Lonesome Dove** a viewer sees the aching realism of the desperately psychologically and materialistically impoverished 19th century Texas yet senses the mythic proportions in the physical and mental struggles in the film. Robert Duvall understands this tone and perhaps even Texas. As Gus McCrae and as the down and out country-western singer, Max Sledge, in *Tender Mercies* (a historical descendant but literary predecessor of Woodrow Call), Duvall shows the potential greatness in the moves, the physiques, and the voices of his Texas characters (Not that native Texan Tommy Lee Jones doesn't sit a horse and the role rather nicely, but wouldn't it have been something to see Duvall play both leads in *Lonesome Dove*?) So, Gus' crudity and savagery enable him to survive, yet his attempts at grandiose rhetoric, deeds, thought, and movement show the real becoming myth. Duvall gets the tone just right, but he got the idea for the tone from McMurtry's novel.

But, even with *Lonesome Dove's* high ratings, TV and moviemakers may not be able to find new explorations of the 19th century West that escape the audience's notions about how the 19th century West should look on film. The West or Texas as part of Western myth, then, is probably best presented so that the audience can't *see* it. McMurtry has readers and not viewers and thus doesn't have to deal with film apprehensions. But, even with print he has to deal with his audiences' mythic apprehensions. McMurtry, who stole from twentieth century film and fiction and nineteenth century legends, knows about film's and fiction's audiences' expectations. And, he knows what that expectation does to his artistic ambitions. He is, in the eyes of the country and even in the eyes of grouchy Texas critics, "a Texas writer" (who uses the term on what occasion determines whether it is derogatory or not).

Larry is now so closely associated with Texas that each time he picks up a pen or presses his fingers to any of his portable typewriters, he simultaneously comments about Texas, the country's ideas about Texas, and the ideas about Texas that he created. His fame and accompanying money and his own interests and instincts have brought him the freedom to dedicate himself to developing his craft yet put limits around what form that craft will take.

So, readers, mostly those who buy a novel to enjoy it rather than to critique it, fully expect to enter a Texas according to McMurtry when they fold back the spine of any recent McMurtry novel. This past year, after the Pulitzer, after *Texasville*, while *Lonesome Dove* was on the screen, readers were turning the pages of *Anything For Billy*, in which McMurtry perhaps consciously looks at his own dilemma. And, as reader and potential reviewer or commentator, I too am stuck in McMurtry's position.

McMurtry is primarily a realist. Not Barthleme or Barth, he is concerned with what he wishes his text to show rather than with the text itself. But, he at times becomes enamored of his text and pushes it far away from the worldly pastures where he starts. This tendency represents McMurtry at his worst and his best.

When he stays with his realism, he presents an ironic and laconic world and revels in its ordinariness and normality. He makes boredom, whether high plains travel or small town West Texas life, seem funny, touching, or pathetic. McMurtry's simple heroes aren't blessed with much intro-

spection, so they never develop much self awareness. Their own peculiar natures are intriguing to them and us because they never seem able to control themselves or understand themselves. They are caught between neurosis and psychopathy (Gus is McMurtry's freest character and most rounded psychopath and so is not like these characters. Call is like them).

Like the slow motion worked at *Lonesome Dove*, the dreary, dirty world at Greasy Corners in *Anything For Billy*'s New Mexico presents the figures we assume to be myth in their pre-mythic days. The gunfighters and buffalo hunters gathered at Greasy Corners are a bunch of heroes who are cognizant of their reputations but trapped by their own simpleness and the grittiness of their milieu. These characters thus develop an ironic, if cruel, acceptance of death. McMurtry's point is that this ironic view, hiding a barrel full of insecurities and irritated by a simple mind and hostile environment, sometimes looks heroic and can, with the right coloring, escalate into myth. But the myths, as Ben Sippy (McMurtry's narrator) observes, can never stand in for the specific characteristics of those "sweetheart's" at Greasy Corners:

> The dime novelists might portray gunfighters as a confident, satisfied lot—I'm guilty of that myself—but the truth is they were mainly disappointed men. They spent their lives in the rough barrooms of ugly towns: they ate terrible food and drank a vile grape of liquor: few of them managed to shoot the right people, and even fewer got to die gloriously in a shoot-out with a peer. The majority just got shot down by some bold stranger, like that drunk who killed the great Hickok.

McMurtry is at his traditional best in *Anything For Billy* when he positions his narrator in space and time to observe a shooting contest between Katerina Garza and his legendary gunfighter Hill Coe. Katerina Garza, like many of McMurtry's women, has the self assurance and conviction that his males so often lack. Even McMurtry's narrator can not quite figure out Katerina and is awed by the other female characters, including his own wife. She squats, takes careful aim, and shoots twenty bottles in a row. Next, Hill Coe will shoot his twenty. He misses the first one. Embarrassed and disgraced, Hill Coe falls into a whiskey bottle. Billy, the famous outlaw, then tries his hand and hits only two of the twenty. The Yankee narrator, who is seen as something of an ineffectual oaf in the West, nearly matches Katerina's marksmanship. The tone of this scene—the manner in which McMurtry, while letting his narrator revel, down-plays the skill and what we know about who will become myth and who will not—reveals McMurtry with his feet firmly planted in reality yet achingly dealing with a contrary myth.

With Billy, already a myth, McMurtry has to down-play the character because of the mythic baggage, so I delighted in Billy's normality, in fact his sub-normality. But when he goes about creating his own characters, McMurtry destroys his realistic tone by endowing these characters with god-like prowresses. It grew tired of Isinglass (clearly John Chisum), Lady Snow, and Mesty-Woolah. Too much seems exaggerated. McMurtry grows too extravagant. The trappings and architecture of Will Isinglass's ranch house, a castle-like creation; Will Isinglass' sexual appetites at age eighty-five; Lady Cecily Snow's icy and deadly character and expertise in botany; Mesty-Woolah's deadliness and red camel all seem like characters from Ben Sippy's imagination rather than from his observation. And, as all of the characters converge at once to observe Billy Bone's death, McMurtry seems to give in to Sippy's sense of melodrama. The characters stop the novel and stomp the delicate play between the ordinariness and simplicity of the characters and their future mythic proportions.

I have heard McMurtry say in his lectures that he writes for character and not plot. In the best Realistic tradition, he lets his characters lead his plot wherever it might go. Ironically, though, McMurtry's fondness for his extravagant characters (perhaps the creations that earned this literary and commercial success) leads his novels away from their realistic tone. It is as though, with his characters, he tries to jump out of the world that he observes and into some world of his creation. But, McMurtry can't jump as high as the magical realists. He sometimes ends up creating his own stereotypes. He spends perhaps needless pages describing these characters being characters. I put down *Terms of Endearment* several times because I got tired of Aurora Greenway and General Scot being eccentric. My first McMurtry Book, *All My Friends Are Going To Be Strangers*, first introduced me to this tendency when I read about Prof. Godwin Lloyd Jons, while naked, hanging on the bumper of a co-ed's car. I was amused but didn't know what end these characters and their scenes served.

These characters seem attempts to escape the myth, or McMurtry's liberating himself from the public's expectations of a "Texas" writer. So, these characters become "McMurtry" characters rather than the similarly grandiose "Texas" characters.

Ironically then Texas and the myths that cling to Texas provide McMurtry with the models for these characters. Even his extravagant non-Texans have this extravagant Texas-like feel to them. This extravagance stems from folklore. McMurtry has heard the Texas stories, jokes, and metaphors so that he is familiar with them. But, fiction requires more

restraint, and McMurtry is trying to figure out just how much restraint he needs to have.

The epic proportions of *Lonesome Dove* accommodated this extravagance. The thin narrative line of getting a herd to Montana kept him mostly on track with several detours so that the extravagance seemed to match the subject matter. But, in *Billy*, the characters seem extravagant for their own sake, for the sake of escaping yet staying within the corral that surrounds McMurtry. To American readers, McMurtry is like Dickens. He can create villains and super real characters that welcome parody or play against myth, but though they serve to show social or literary indignation, their very colorfulness makes them complete in themselves, loose from mythic or social relevance, so readers divorce these characters from substance. We delight in Dicken's or McMurtry's characters but don't ask what they mean.

But, I have yet to elaborate on what intent I sniff in the dust that McMurtry raises. In *Lonesome Dove*, McMurtry took on the cowboy myth; but with *Billy* he takes on a more specific legend. And perhaps, more than with *Lonesome Dove*, the specificity of this legend and its familiarity and popularity, particularly in films, create an even more formidable problem for McMurtry. So, to deal with this problem, he obscures historical facts, changes Billy Bonny's name to Billy Bone to buy poetic license yet keep us informed about whom he is really writing about, and most important, creates his middle-aged narrator, Ben Sippy.

With Ben Sippy, McMurtry has a foreign point of view to register the drama. Ben looks at occurrences with a mixture of sense of strangeness that a Philadelphia gentleman would have, yet with all the mundanity and banality of a participant. He is at his best in his discussion of the massacre at Skunkwater Flats:

> They've all made a study of it, you see, whereas I was just there. The very fact that I *was* there— it's about the only fact they can't dispute—just makes them edgy; in fact, it make them jealous and produces much resentment. They'd all like me better if I were dead, like the other mighty men who fell that day (pg. 220).

> They're part of legend now, the sweethearts who died at Skunkwater Flats: they died and were raised to glory: I lived and became deflated and old. It's a melancholy thing because, hard though they were, I liked those gunmen who died in that windy gully. They only warred on one another, as near as I can see, and they brought some spirit to the ragged business of living, a spirit I confess I miss (pg. 223).

McMurtry, through imagination and craft, must closely approximate the excitement of what really happened. A good history of Billy, one like Evan Connell's *Son of Morning Star* would be the most intriguing account of Billy because it would achieve a more factual rendering of his less than romantic reality. But, McMurtry is also interested in myth, and thus his fictive narrator also provides insights in myth.

Ben writes dime novels, so he helps create myths by distorting truth. In fact, Cecily and a nun read his novels that distort the reality that they are stuck in and find excitement and truth in his novels. So, Ben—when he discusses his life, observes his cowboy heroes, or tells us about his novels—constantly juxtaposes reality and myth and the tension between the two. Then, when we realize that Ben is myth or perhaps a potential myth because he is in a McMurtry book, we get real confused about which is more real, myth or reality. This is McMurtry's point.

But, McMurtry also uses Ben Sippy to comment about the effect of the tension between myth and reality on the mythmaker. In fact, Ben Sippy may be a device for self criticism, a means for McMurtry to criticize his own work. At the end of the novel, in 19th century fashion, is the writer's signature, but the signature is not Sippy's but McMurtry's. *Anything For Billy* is not just Sippy's reminiscences but McMurtry's novel. It is both realistic and reality shattering.

And Ben, now with Larry's signature, gives something of an eulogy to McMurtry's and all writers' careers and truths. McMurtry says in lectures that novel writing is a middle-aged activity, that the writer reaches literary maturity in middle age but exhausts it before he reaches old age. Ben Sippy discovers the "real" west and "human depth" in middle age during his trip to New Mexico but bumps into the limits, his own corral posts, in old age.

Sippy has seen the real Billy and Billy's real death and tried to write a real novel, which we should expect, because of Ben's style, is overwrought and overly dramatized. He, after all, coins the nickname *Billy the Kid*. Ben states that, despite his literary pretensions, he fails at literature and leaves only a few notable dime novels. He does find something of a resurrection with his nearly accidental collaboration with the movies. Like Ben Sippy and his version of the "White Star of the West" (Billy the Kid), McMurtry created grandiose character out of legends or mixtures of legends and imagination that in turn make McMurtry even more popular and more rich through the movies that they inspired. For, McMurtry's extravagant characters became great roles for stars wishing to act or character actors looking for better billing: Paul Newman, Patricia Neal, Ben Johnson, and Shirley McClaine. McMurtry cons both Ben and the movies. He shows us Ben's insight into "human depth" but failure to reproduce it in literature or to recapture the heart of

his recalcitrant wife, Dora. And, if Ben is the butt of these jokes and is a stand-in for McMurtry, perhaps, then McMurtry critiques his own sense of failure in dealing with a Texas or Western myth. McMurtry is perhaps his and his subject matter's best critic.

And finally Billy is like McMurtry's Texas background. Pre-programmed to be mythic by McMurtry's technique and his own legend, Billy just can't quite live up to anything. Everyone in the novel will do anything for him, but he is limited by his own ordinariness. For this reason, for his pathetic nature, I like him more than many of McMurtry's fully blown characters who beg to be myths. Ben Sippy loves Billy yet is disgusted by him, wants to dispel the myths about him but helps nurture them, desires to look at "human depth" within Billy (his ordinariness) but winds up fenced-in by the myth and the mythmakers. As Ben Sippy says, "I suppose they'll argue it forever—or until all the black dirt of life finally washes off Billy and leaves him a pure, clean legend" (315).

So, in *Anything For Billy*, McMurtry, perhaps consciously, complains about being trapped as a Texan, as a Texas writer, or as a myth. Unlike Benton and Zinberg et. al. from *The Yellow Rose*, he knows what he is up against. He hates his Texas roots, and he bitches about them in his two most uprooting essays, **"Southwestern Literature,"** and **"Ever A Bridegroom: Reflections On The Failure Of Texas Literature."** Yet, he loves the past as is evidence in *Lonesome Dove, Anything For Billy, Horseman Pass By*, and all the rest. Thus, a Texan is corralled because of the way the rest of the country sees him. He is corralled because of the way other Texans see him. He perhaps even corrals himself. Yet, he likes the old, scarred boards. So, any narrative about Texas—whatever Texas it deals with, whether myth, reality, nostalgia, old South, or Old West—must confront the myths and overcome them. What is real, what is myth, and what people think is myth and real get many storytellers lost.

The Texas corral encloses subject matter and audience expectation. It provides *Places In The Heart's* nostalgia and *The Yellow Rose's* attempt to show tension between past and present. But for some like McMurtry, who knows the arena and the fence around it, it is both resource and trap. In the old dust jacket photo, Larry sits on a Texas corral post and, like the Kid, looks to be just an ordinary guy stuck with his peculiar obsession. He has some virtue and some insight from his vantage point. But, he doesn't know whether to stay put, to jump into the middle, or to kick the damn thing down.

WORKS CITED

Abramowitz, David, story editor for *The Yellow Rose*, Warner Brothers Televisions. Telephone interview. 27 October 1965.

Bazin, Andre. "Theatre and Cinema," What is *Cinema?* Vol. 1. ed and trans. Hugh Gray. Berkeley: University of California Press, 1967, rpt. in *Film Theory and Criticism.* eds. Gerald Mast and Marshall Cobern, 3rd ed. New York: Oxford University Press, 1985, pp. 356-369.

Benton, Robert, writer and director *Places in the Heart.* Tri-Star Pictures, 1984.

Beresford, Bruce, director, and Horton Foote. writer, *Tender Mercies.* EMI Films, 1985.

Cawelti, John G. "*Chinatown* and Generic Transformation In Recent American Films." 1979, *Film Theory* and *Criticism* eds. Gerald Mast and Marshall Cohen, 3rd ed. New York: Oxford University Press, 1985, pp. 503-520.

Goodman, Bob. "Big Screen-Stars Turn to TV," *Family Weekly* 25 September 1965, pp. 4.8 (exact part of article).

Lee, Jim. "Arbiters of Texas Literary Taste" *Range Wars: Heated Debates, Sober Reflections, and Other Assessments of Texas*: Dallas: Southern Methodist University Press, 1989. pp. 125-136.

McMurtry, Larry. *Anything For Billy*, New York: Simon and Schuster, 1988.

————. Lectures. Sam Houston State University 27 February 1987 and The University of Texas of the Permian Basin. 5 April 1988.

————. *Lonesome Dove*, New York: Simon and Schuster, 1985.

Reynolds, Clay. "What Does It Take To Be A Texas Writer?" *Range Wars: Heated Debates, Sober Reflections, and Other.*

Schickel, Richard. "A Search for Connections." Time 24 September 1984, pp. 70-71.

Stewart, Bob. "Yellow Rose' Series Will Be Deep In The Heart of Texas." *TV Week, The San Antonio Light*, 2 October, 1983. p. 4T.

Wilder, John. *The Yellow Rose* (TV Script), Revised draft 14 March 1983.

Wincer, Simon, director, and Bill Wittliff, writer. *Lonesome Dove*, CBS Televisions, 1989

Zinberg, Michael and John Wilder, executive producers. *The Yellow Rose.* Warner Brother TV. 1983-1984

Susan Fromberg Schaeffer (review date 7 October 1990)

SOURCE: "Lonesome Jane," in *New York Times*, October 7, 1990, p. 3.

[*In the following review of* Buffalo Girls, *Schaeffer–also an author—praises McMurtry's work, saying the appeal of the novel stems from McMurtry's portrayal of an era at the cusp of change.*]

Twenty-five years ago, driving across the country for the first time and overwhelmed by the flatness and vast size of Nebraska, my husband and I rented a motel room in a small town just off the main highway. The proprietress wanted us to see two local treasures. One was her "Gone With the Wind" lamp; the other was what the town was known for: its stuffed animal museum. In this museum was a stuffed elk, a stuffed buffalo, several stuffed beavers and one towering stuffed grizzly bear. The size of the larger animals was stunning, the feeling they inspired one of terrible sadness. These animals were long dead, but they seemed to watch us as if they would speak, if only we knew how to listen. A part of the past that we no longer knew—the Wild West—was alive in them.

This past does comes alive in Larry McMurtry's *Buffalo Girls*, a lovely, moving and very funny novel that is first and foremost a work of resurrection, a book that rescues an important era of our country's saga both from that taxidermist, the history book, and from that waxwork beautifier, the myth machine, which changes and simplifies what were once living human beings, turning them into legends, and icons, names everyone knows, but whom no one thinks about or tries to understand.

The remarkable power of *Buffalo Girls* grows out of Mr. McMurtry's decision to bring his characters alive just as they, and the Wild West they personify, are about to die. The era chronicled in Mr. McMurtry's earlier novel, *Lonesome Dove*, is over; the Indian wars have ended; the buffalo and the beaver are almost gone. Slowly but surely, even the most independent and fractious of the mountain men and buffalo girls are beginning to settle down. Almost everyone in *Buffalo Girls* knows himself and his world to be on the verge of extinction; throughout the book, each character looks backward as often as he looks forward, and each finds that most of his life is behind him. As Mr. McMurtry's characters journey through the plains and mountains, they compose their own elegies—for themselves and their friends, for the Wild West they helped to create and destroy.

Western novels and films are often derogatorily referred to as horse operas, but *Buffalo Girls* is truly operatic. Although something happens on almost every page—a lover climbs his beloved's drainpipe, falls down and breaks his arm; another drifts off in a blizzard and is rescued by an earless Indian; still another finds love when her foot gets stuck in the mud—this book is really composed of interwoven arias, death songs in which each character sings about what he remembers best of his soon-to-be-ending life.

Buffalo Girls tells the story of "a little tribe" of friends, mountain men, whores and Indians (many of them based on actual people) who have grown with the Wild West—and a remarkable group they are, too. There is Calamity Jane, who seems to believe she has had a child with Wild Bill Hickok, although no one who knows her can recall that she spent any time with him. There is her friend Dora DuFran, who, after nearly starving on her family's Kansas ranch, buried her mother, her sisters and finally her father and, as a gawky teen-ager, walked into Abilene in her dead father's shoes and later prospered as the owner of a brothel. Mr. McMurtry's portrayal of her long love affair with the cowboy-turned-rancher T. Blue is one of the sweetest, saddest and grittiest I know of.

Also among the cast of characters are Jim Ragg and Bartle Bone, two mountain men who opened up the West and hunted together for almost 30 years, quarreling the entire time like an old married couple. There is also Buffalo Bill, proprietor of the Wild West Show that eventually brings Mr. McMurtry's characters to England. And, best of all, there is No Ears, an Indian over 80 years old, left for dead as a child, his ears cut off, when his tribe was massacred. He's an old man who can still see a dog lying down behind a bush two miles away, who can smell death approaching from even farther, and who functions as a kind of guardian angel to many of the other characters.

For all these people, the Wild West represents unprecedented freedom, an escape from the restricting codes of civilization. But as they grow older—as they tire of sleeping in bear and snake dens to escape blizzards, as they become too old to race one another, from one fort to another, simply for the adventure of it—they begin to question the supreme value they have put upon their freedom. As Dora DuFran says shortly after she marries and tries to settle down, "Freedom isn't something everybody needs for their whole lives. About all I did with my freedom was cry."

As Mr. McMurtry's people sense the passing of the Wild West, they begin to understand that they have outlived their time. The question then becomes whether they can find a new way to live, or at least a new meaning that will justify their lives. That most of them fail to do so should be no surprise, because the Wild West, as Mr. McMurtry seems to conceive it, is a period in the history of American that is similar to a time in the life of an individual: the Wild West was the childhood of our country and, like all childhoods, it

must pass. What makes Mr. McMurtry's characters—Sitting Bull, Calamity Jane, No Ears, Jim Ragg and Bartle Bone—so irresistible is that they are like children, captious, hilarious, unpredictable, irrepressible. They are never boring. Neither are they entirely adult. Like very-large children, they tend to break things, and so, when they reach adulthood, they cannot return to the things of their youth, for they themselves have destroyed them.

Calamity Jane realizes this early in the novel. Jim Ragg, she writes, "feels sorry for himself because the beaver got used up—and it was him and Bartle that helped use them up! You'll find plenty of cowboys like that, they'll cuss and complain because the country's all settled up when it was them that settled it! . . . Montana was just Indians when they started bringing in cattle, now look at it. The cowboys ruined it, now they're mad because it's ruined."

It is this discovery, that the making of the West was the breaking of the West, that finally breaks the characters' hearts. As Calamity says, "Lost is lost, why think of it?" When Jim Ragg finally hears the slap of a beaver tail again, the animals are in a zoo in London and he is performing in Buffalo Bill Cody's Wild West Show. For Jim, the beavers are the Wild West, but now they exist only in zoos—as, for most of us, the past exists only in our domestic zoos, our ubiquitous family photograph albums.

Oddly enough, it is those people who were least heroic during the heroic times who seem to prosper. Buffalo Bill Cody, criticized by many for running his "circus," the Wild West Show, eventually comes to be seen as something of a seer—if not by the other characters, at least by Mr. McMurtry. Cody understands faster than the others that the West is gone, and as a kind of artist, a parodic version of Mr. McMurtry himself, he can do more than lament what is passing. He can preserve it:

> "It sometimes seemed to him that he was the only one in the whole troupe who could see the greatness of the pageant they were part of: the pages of Passing History, they called it in the show. It seemed that he alone could feel the wonder of the past they had all lived, as it came alive in recreated scenes. . . . The story of the west was a great story. You had a wilderness won, red race against white race, nature red in tooth and claw, death to the loser, glory to the victor: what could ever make a nobler show?"

Buffalo Girls gives the reader a sense of how eras ebb and flow, how the world and time itself are too huge for any one consciousness to embrace. In the end, the reader is like No Ears on the ship taking the Wild West Show to England, contemplating the unexpected vastness of time and distance:

"Traveling on the ocean made No Ears realize that the world was far larger than he had supposed and that the destruction of the buffalo, and even of his people, was a smaller thing than it seemed to those who only knew the plains. . . . He himself had believed at one time that the world was all prairie. . . . After many days on the ocean, he was forced to think once again about the size of the world."

Before she dies, Calamity writes, "Now I am old and going blind, half the time I wander over the plains and don't even know what town I am looking for. Perhaps I am only looking for the past . . . how do you find the past?" Calamity cannot find it, but we can, amazingly alive, pulsing with energy but beginning its slide into oblivion—from which Larry McMurtry's elegant and moving elegy so wonderfully rescues it.

Diana H. Cox (essay date Summer 1991)

SOURCE: "*Anything for Billy*: A Fiction Stranger than Truth," in *Journal of American Culture*, Vol. 14, No. 2, Summer, 1991, pp. 75-81.

[*In the following essay, Cox compares the historic record of Billy the Kid with McMurtry's depiction of him in* Anything for Billy.]

When I was a little girl, about eight or nine years old, my granddaddy, who was one of the town characters (For example, when we remodeled his home in 1932, he put three bathrooms in it and everyone who lived in Humbler, Texas, talked about his decision.), took me into the middle bathroom, reached into a cabinet, and brought out something wrapped in what appeared to be a rag made from an old sheet. He gently, and carefully, removed the frayed cloth, and lo and behold held in his hand a pistol, one like those I had seen only in the Saturday afternoon westerns at the picture show. The Colt pistol in itself would have made this incident a lasting one, but the story he told me perhaps is, indirectly, why I have prepared this paper for the 1990 Texas/Southwest Popular Culture Association meeting. In his boyhood, he lived in the Oklahoma Territory, and one day when he was going home bareback on a big black and white horse, he came up out of a little gully and straight into a band of outlaws who commenced to shoot. Whether they were shooting at him, he never knew because, he said, he kicked that horse with his bare heels as hard as he could, fired his pistol into the air, and headed in the other direction, convinced that these desperadoes must be part of the James gang known to be riding in those parts. If my young eyes were opened at the sight of the pistol, they must have been

wider as his tale progressed. My own granddaddy was part of the history of the outlaws of the West. Today that Colt is part of my trappings, as is his story and so are my interests in that colorful era of the cowboy gunfighter. When I saw **Anything for Billy** in an airport book store, I surmised—who better could exemplify fact and fantasy than McMurtry with a subject like Billy the Kid.

The title of this paper represents how I looked at the persons, places, and things and compared the novel with only a fragment of the legends of this notorious and ever popular young man. Reading the novel roused my interest to learn more about what had been recorded because the McMurtry's story did not approximate any I had heard before; however, I had never really done any kind of research on Billy. Thus, at best my adventure with the novel, legend, and history has been sophomoric and cursory, and I view it as only entertaining, not scholarly. Since I read the novel and began work on this paper, I have been amazed at the current printed material about Billy in newspapers and magazines. In a motel room in Ruidoso, New Mexico, I found a magazine *New Mexico, 68th year* (Volume 68, Number 6) whose cover pictured the Kid in "Kid Fever." The fascination with Billy the Kid appears to me universally popular.

Persons

What McMurtry does with names has often intrigued me: for example, what a tongue-in-check name Moore for the central characters in **Texasville**, the saga of a Texas family once made oil rich and wanting more, more, and more. But Billy Bonney, alias Billy the Kid, became Billy Bone, a peculiar choice to my thinking. Bone conjures images of pirates, skull and crossbones, a bottle of poison, death. And, perhaps, those are the images that should be conjured: Billy was a land pirate in a long black coat, and as deadly a killer with his beloved double barrel shotgun as any arsenic so marked as deadly dangerous.

However, Billy Bonney, that is William H. Bonney, was not his only name: in fact, there is much speculation on his name—at least by me. Researcher James D. Horan states in *The Gunfighters: the Authentic Wild West* that the Kid's name was Henry McCarthy, son of Michael and Catharine McCarthy, and that he was born in of all places, New York City (10)! (Sounds like the Pace Picante sauce commercial, doesn't it?) Widowed, Catharine moved West with sons Henry (Billy) and Joseph and remarried one William Henry Antrim in the Presbyterian Church in Santa Fe, New Mexico, when Billy was fourteen (13). Whether Billy was ever called Henry Antrim is doubtful, though Horan states that he once was. What is interesting to me, however, is that both Stepfather Antrim's and Billy's given names were the same (William Henry), and both Billy and Antrim signed their names *William H.* (34-35). One story is that Billy changed his name to Bonney, an alias, so he would not bring disgrace to his family. Having pondered McMurtry's choice, I concluded, probably obvious to you from the first, that Bone is not Bone at all; it is Bon-e, thus pronounced, though not spelled the same as the outlaw's infamous name.

The title of McMurtry's book comes from a line in the first chapter when the narrator of the story, dime novelist Mister Ben Sippy, recalls his first meeting with the Kid:

> "Howdy, Mr. Sippy, are you from Mississippi?" he said, and burst out laughing. In those days Billy was always getting tickled at his own remarks. When he laughed at one of his own jokes you couldn't help liking him—he was just a winning kid.
>
> Though now, when I think of Billy Bone giggling at one of his own little sallies, I soon grow blind with tears—sentimental, I guess. But there was a time when I would have done *anything for Billy*.

The name Mister Sippy speaks for itself, as Billy ridiculed it. The character narrator is a middle-aged runaway who could no longer stand his boring plebeian life with wife Dora—a dumb Dora, perhaps—and his houseful of daughters. His initial escape was accomplished by his obsession with escape literature in the form of dime novels. His second, a physical one to the West, he narrates beginning with his Billy the Kid adventures. McMurtry must have known that the best selling version of the life of Billy was one with Sheriff Pat Garrett's name on it as the author: in truth, its ghost writer was a famous dime novelist, Ash Upton (Horan, 10).

Joe Lovelady, the good guy in the story who comes to a bad end, has a name that also speaks for itself. He is a melancholy man who lost his lady love to the grim reaper, and he is a good Joe. He cares for the neurotic Kid, but he does no wrong; his death at the hand of Mesty-Woolah, a seven-foot, black, camel-riding compadre of old Will Isinglass, stunned me as it did Sippy.

> Mesty-Woolah stopped when he saw me approaching. Isinglass and Joe Lovelady took another step or two, still chatting. . . .
>
> Joe Lovelady smiled when he looked up and saw me. . . .
>
> I was about to offer him a warm greeting . . . when something happened that to this day I can neither forget nor clearly remember. It happened in a second, so fast that I wonder if even the retina of genius . . . could have caught it; when I try to recover a memory of it now I only get confusing particles.
>
> Mesty-Woolah moved; perhaps he whirled: I remember the briefest flash, though I saw no sword; in none of my memories of the three men walking that morning do I remember Mesty-Woolah having a sword—not, that is, until he used it.
>
> There was just the briefest moment, a swish of sound: Joe Lovelady was still smiling at me, but there was something wrong with his head. The smile seemed suddenly to be coming from above his right shoulder. Then his body tilted slightly, swayed a little, and toppled toward the chicken house. A great fan of blood spread across the chicken-house wall; my clearest memory is of that perfect fan of blood, and then Joe's head was rolling past Isinglass, who put out this foot and stopped it.
>
> The old man looked at me perplexed.
>
> "The head always jumps to the right," he said. "You'd think as clean as Mesty cuts, it would just stay on the neck until the body falls down dead. But it don't—it jumps to the right."

Lovelady was most likely based on the real-life sidekick Tom O'Folliard (Horan, 41), but really he is a combination of all those who rode with Billy and some of McMurtry's makings, too.

Will Isinglass portrays a typical character of the West, the owner of the biggest ranch in the West; "in his heyday fifty thousand acres would not have pastured his remuda." Again he is a composite: John Chisum, John Tunstall, Alexander McSween, J. L. Murphy, and J. J. Dolan, principal characters in the Lincoln County war (Horan, 42). He got his nickname Old Whiskey from his cowboys "because of his habit of strapping a quart jar of whiskey to his saddle before he left his headquarters each morning . . . and if he happened to chance back by his ranch house around the lunch hour, he'd secure himself another quart for the afternoon." A Texan, "a short fellow with a drooping lip and a quarrelsome manner," once wised off at eighty-five year old Will in a saloon.

> Will didn't welcome the interruption. He looked around at the man and his old eyes held a chill.
>
> He stood up wearily, walked over to the Texan, and held out his hand.

"What do you want?" the Texan asked, surprised.

"Your rifle, I need it a minute," Isinglass said.

The man handed over the Winchester, looking somewhat puzzled, and before he could move Isinglass clubbed him with it. He didn't seem to move fast or swing hard. . . .

"I despise loud talk this early," Isinglass said. "In fact, loud talk is never welcome, but I do expect to be spared it on a peaceful morning when the sun is barely up."

Another of the Texans knelt by the fallen man.

"My god, John's dead," he said, "He's not drawing his breath no more."

"Good," said Isinglass, "He's spoilt my morning once too often, and another benefit is this [other] fellow here has a horse to sit on once we get around to hanging him."

At the age of "nearly one hundred," he bought a motorcar, "the first to be shipped to the eastern New Mexico plains," and reportedly "was emptying his gun into the motor, in a vain effort to kill the thing, when the car went off the cutbank" and crushed "the old plainsman" to death. He knew how to start it but not how to stop it, this "new buffalo" that "someday would cover the prairies in vast herds."

In McMurtry's story, Will had fathered a stranger brood: Katie Garza, who headed up a band of Mexican raiders: Bloody Feathers, an Indian whose name indicated his fetish; four retarded mutes—brothers to Cecily Snow—two of whom are shot by Billy and two of whom are presumed shot by Billy in this tale. Daughter Cecily tried to kill Will by putting ground glass made from wine glasses in, of course, his daily bowl of chili. Is this not a wild story?

The name of Cecily Snow stopped me in my tracks, I suppose because I related the name to Queen Elizabeth's sister Margaret's disastrous marriage to Lord Snowden. Although John Tunstall was the authentic Englishman who partnered with McSween, McMurtry's Lord Snow had been Isinglass' partner. Cecily, the stepdaughter of Will Isinglass and daughter of his wife Lady Snow, caustically sums up her past and present: "Mr. Isinglass robbed my father, destroyed my mother, exiled my brothers, and ruined me. If I catch him asleep I'll kill him." But instead she courted Billy to attempt Will's murder. Sippy commented:

The ways of women never cease to startle, I

guess. There Billy Bone sat: young, short, dirty, ugly, and violent—an American—a boy with no grace or learning, and yet the tall, brilliant, beautiful daughters of the Cavendishes and the Montstuarts had chosen to make him her paramour.

Katie Garza said that Billy "liked Cecily because she was white and clean." She lived in "a great granite pile, all turrets and towers, known as Wind's Hill" with a butler named Bertram, "who looked Egyptian," "a cherry wood table from the time of Charles I," an aquarium which provided terrapin for soup cooked by a coolie, and "an Irish laundry run by two old crones who spoke only Gaelic." Her talents lay in botanical sketching and sexual promiscuity. Pregnant, I presume by Will, she met her end in a snow storm escape from the tower where he had imprisoned her. Once when Will had bragged he had everything, she retorted "except a son with a chin," in reference to his deformed mute sons, and thus no heir to his fortune.

Tully Roebuck was the name McMurtry gave the Pat Garrett figure–a man who turned sheriff after a spotted past, who hunted Billy, and who authored with a ghost writer the successful, but prevaricated version of the Billy the Kid story. Sippy said that his own—*Billy the Kid or, the Wandering Boy's Doom*—was the only true version and that Tully stole the name Billy the Kid from him. Sippy was jealous of the success and felt justified when Tully died destitute. Tully had once cowboyed with Billy and left with him "out of loyalty" after Billy, "a dud as a cowboy, . . . got Joe fired." As sheriff of Lincoln County, "his gun was at the service of Will Isinglass": yet he warned Billy: "That old man's a troublesome neighbor . . . He don't let up. If I were you boys I'd scat for a while. Maybe a horse will fall on him and slow him down." But in the end, it is not Old Whiskey or Tully who kills Billy, but one of the Isinglass brood.

Places

McMurtry gave the name Whiskey Glass Ranch to parallel the real spread of cattle baron John Chisum, the Jinglebob. In San Jon, Sippy saw "towering stacks of cedar posts and thousands of huge coils of barbed wire—for it was Isinglass's aim to encircle the whole of [his] Whiskey Glass Ranch with barbed wire," reportedly three million acres. Sippy recalled an article he had read about

old Leon, the Mexican leader of Isinglass's fencing crew, who spent his entire adult life in an attempt to complete the fence around Whiskey Glass, toiling year after year on the long prairies with his mules, his men, his posthole diggers, and his wife only to have Old Whiskey acquire, by purchase or flat, another fifty square miles just as Leon thought his task was finally completed.

Joe Lovelady had been asked to be foreman of that ranch—"quite an honor"—but declined and rode off with Billy." 'I don't like to be bossing men who are older than me,' Joe later explained."

Part II of the novel, entitled "The Whiskey Glass War," references the Lincoln County War which Billy participated in. Its beginning is a place called Greasy Corners, particularly in the China Pond, "a dim smoky barroom," owned by Des Montaignes–"a little man in buckskins, with greasy black hair and rotting teeth—the very image of Black Nick." In this hangout for gunslingers and buffalo hunters, "all of them . . . were careful of Billy Bone, a boy with little experience, but a reckless eye." "'They don't know what Billy might do,' was Joe Lovelady's analysis. 'They don't and he don't neither.'" Billy respected Des' wife La Tulipe, an old crone who knew the past and future. When Des kicked her off a bar stool, Billy threatened him:" don't be mistreating the Tulip. . . . If you do I might decide to blow your brains out that back door." Personally, I preferred her emotionless retort at her husband: "A wolf will eat you and shit you out as a green puddle."

Unfortunately, Greasy Corners is on Isinglass land, and Old Whiskey decides to clean out Hill Coe and company because he believes they are rustling his cattle; why else? (Incidentally, there was a Coe ranch, one of the reasons for the Lincoln County War; its owner's name was George Coe.) Will appears to tell them to get out of town and uses Mesty's talents of swordsmanship—he disembowels a hotheaded gunslinger with one slice while approaching him on, of all things, a red camel. But the greatest threat is a trainload of gunfighters from South Texas whom Isinglass imports. I suppose Isinglass is a former Texan like Chisum! The Greasy Corners "gang" head for Lincoln while Billy and companions go to Tularosa to meet Katie Garza and her band.

"We spent that night at a place called Skunkwater Flats." In reality the place was Stinking Spring (Horan, 62), a place where Billy was captured and taken to Lincoln to be hanged. In the old cabin the fleeing gunfighters plus Joe Lovelady's horse bed down for the night in the middle of a sand storm believing the storm will hinder Isinglass' chase. The next morning when Barbecue Campbell goes out the door to relieve himself, he is shot and all hell breaks loose. Billy shoots the emissary who comes to parley, Joe puts on Billy's clothes, mounts his horse, and rides out in a cloud of dust while Billy snakes out on his belly to catch Sippy's mule and make his escape. All in the cabin were killed except for Sippy and one other who was killed the next day trying to escape. Sippy recalls:

> They're all part of legend now, the sweethearts who died at Skunkwater Flats: they died and were raised to glory . . . hard though they were, I liked those gunmen who died in that windy gully. They only warred on one another, as far as I can see . . . Hill Coe rose from disgrace to die as gallantly as the hosts at the Alamo . . . they're all gone where Hickok is, and Custer, those sweethearts, and where Napoleon is and Hector and the other great fallen. . . .

Since I have lived in the Panhandle of Texas, I have become familiar with some of the places in New Mexico mentioned in the novel. But the one that took my attention is Glorieta, presently a place where my Baptist friends have retreats and summer youth camps. In *Anything for Billy*, Sippy and Billy wander into this little town and meet up with "Sister Blandina, Billy's friend . . . a tiny nun." After she fed the pair, she admonished Billy to give up his "desperado life" and "be decent." Turning to Sippy, she asked his profession, and learning he was a writer, said, "Goodness me, are you *that* Sippy?" She was a dime novel fan of his who got her books from a "news agent in St. Louis." Note the words Goodness and St.!! Sippy had thought that nuns read only prayer books and catechism, not *Wedded but Not Won* or *A Tryst at Twilight*:

> . . . the nun of La Glorieta, after a busy day of butchering, plastering, cooking, praying, and teaching the heathen, would take a candle to her cell at night and fix her interest on . . . a tale of domestic strife among the privileged of Philadelphia.

> I suppose we all (said Sippy)—even nuns—dream of life other than the one we actually live on this indifferent earth.

Later in her honor Sippy penned "a half-dimer called *Sister of the Sangre*; or, *The Mission in the Mountains*, about a nun who robbed the rich.

In a subsequent chapter the little nun plays a part in the real legend, the jailing of the Kid in the Lincoln jail. She leads him with Sippy and the sheriff from the store to the jail through a mob yelling for his neck. In truth, Billy was jailed in Lincoln; I've seen the jail and the cell and the irons he was chained to in the floor. And true, he did escape to kill another day. The real story has a similar jailer who taunted him. As he escaped from Lincoln, he stood on the balcony of the jail and shot that man Bob Ollinger, as he ran from the saloon to the jail to see about the noise (Paul Trachtman, *The Old West; The Gunfighters*, 90). In both stories, Billy found a pistol in the privy; but in McMurtry's story, it was left there by Katie Garza; and after he shot his captor, then he rode off with Katie. His exit was not a solitary one on a horse that just happened to be tethered outside the jail, but on the exceptional mount Cecily Snow had given him.

Things

Nearly every western saga has a duel of some kind or another; in **Anything For Billy**, a shooting contest develops at Greasy Corners between gunslinger Hill Coe and Katie Garza. Every morning Coe practices, fifty rounds a day, "eighteen thousand bullets a year." One morning as he was doing an exhibition practice for the crew at Greasy Corners, Katie Garza said, "'I think I can outshoot you. . . . I've got a hundred dollars that thinks so, too.' Hill Coe looked dismayed; but after a moment he nodded politely to Katie. . . ." Each was to shoot at twenty bottles; if tied, "they would shoot bottle by bottle until someone missed. . . . Katie Garza shot first. She sat down, crossed her legs, rested her pistol across her forearm, and proceeded to shatter twenty bottles." Coe stepped up, "raised his pistol, as he had some eighteen thousand times a year for many years—and missed clean with his first and only shot." Dumbfounded, Coe looked "down at his pistol, a look of faint puzzlement on his face."

> Then Billy stepped up and *missed* eighteen—and of the two he hit, one was barely chipped. On some of the shots he would aim for two or three minutes and the bullet would still sing away.

> Joe Lovelady was deeply embarrassed for his friend. "He can't shoot a pistol," he said. "I don't know what makes him think he can."

Billy's marksmanship remains the subject of speculation. He bought an old Winchester in Tularosa and "practiced riflery, shooting at anything in sight." Joe related, "I never saw him hit anything with the Winchester." When Cecily and Billy plan Mesty-Woolah's murder, she asked Billy, "do you have a good rifle?' 'Uh, no,' Billy said. He looked embarrassed at having overlooked such an elementary thing. 'I guess I'll have to get close enough to shoot him with my shotgun,' he said." At sunrise when Mesty went out to pray, two shots rang out.

> The Historians and the legend makers still dispute this point, imputing to Billy Bone power of marksmanship that he never remotely possessed. It was more than one hundred yards from the corner of the barn where the shots were fired to Mesty Woolah's tower [where he was shot while praying outside]—and Billy Bone in all his life never killed a man who stood more than twenty feet from him. Billy was a blaster, not a marksman. It may even be that he was myopic, though

the truth of that will never be known. He seldom fired a rifle, and Cecily's gun was unfamiliar to him: I doubt he could have hit the tower itself twice in a row, much less Mesty-Woolah's heart.

"Volume, not accuracy was Billy Bone's skill." However, a ten-year old Indian boy, a friend of Joe, and the mutes fell victim to this killer who "would have been all day hitting a snake with his pistol." The famous picture of him shows him in a black coat with his rifle. On his first night in Skunkwater Flats, he threatens," 'If he [will] gets within shotgun range I'll blow his dern compass out the other side of his skull.' Then he wrapped his black coat around him a little tighter, and was soon asleep." Gunslinger, maybe: marksman, never.

"What brought you out here, Mr. Sippy?" [Billy] asked.

"Dime novels," I said . . . to a company of two people who couldn't even read.

"I doubt if anyone has caught a worse case of dime-novel mania than I had. First I read them, then I had to try to write them." And read and write them Sippy did. His reading list began with *Hurricane Nell, Queen of the Saddle and Lasso*, followed by *Mustang Merle's Mandate*, *The Kansas Kitten*, *Saul Sabberday*, and *Solemn Sam, the Sad Man from San Saba*. His writing began with *Sandycraw, Man of Grit*; his famous hero was Orson Oxx, that's with two x's. When his wife threw away his collection of dime novels, including his favorite, *Boiled in Yellowstone, or, Mustang Merle Amid the Geysers*, he left home, headed West, and there began his odyssey with the Kid. The books he wrote on his passage to Galveston—*Wedded, but not Won* and *The Butler's Sorrow* brought him fame and fortune; Galveston brought him the raw material for one of his best, *The Bug Oracle*. Mesty Woolah was the impetus for *The Negro of the Nile; or, Son of the Mahdi*, Will Isinglass, an avid fan of Orson Oxx, was startled when he learned that Sippy had written it. When he arrived at Wind's Hill, Cecily had just finished another of his works, *Did She Sin, or, The Desperate Game*. After Billy had killed her brother, Sippy wrote *Mutes of the Mesa; or, The Sheepherder's Remorse*—"easily the best thing . . . since *The Butler's Sorrow*." After Billy broke his leg in his escape from Lincoln, Sippy penned, *Lynched in Lincoln; or, the One-Legged Judge*. But it was his novelette *Billy the Kid; or, the Wandering Boy's Doom* that he loved the most and the public loved the least. ". . . it sold poorly. The only thing that caught on was the nickname: now that Billy's risen to legend . . . —it's the only phrase I contributed to the language, of all the millions I wrote, though the book it introduced is forgotten, and was never believed."

And what finally happens to this successful dime novelist? Why the same thing that has happened to author

McMurtry—he became a Hollywood script writer for "the biggest hit of 1908 "—*Sweethearts of Greasy Corners*!

Billy the Kid of the novel is moody, neurotic, and juvenile. He is also superstitious and scared. Early in the story he declares that he is afraid of water and later is warned by Tulipe not to cross any river. He goes to pieces when a thunderstorm hits one night. Terrified and shaking, he said he'd "rather be dead than go through" the lightning and thunder. Then he saw what he called "the Death Dog"; his teeth chattering, he declared that there is "no worse luck than to see the Death Dog in a lightning flash." "Any mention of death turned Billy white unless it was a death he was preparing to cause."

> The truth is, Billy Bone was delicate, a prey to sick headaches and sudden spells of weakness. . . . When a headache or bad spell seized him he could quickly look so wan you'd hardly expect him to survive.

> This happened as we stood around . . . in San Isidro. Billy suddenly turned so white and faint-looking I had to jump up and urge him to take my chair.

> "It's all right. Billy. . . . ," I said. "Sit down before you topple."

> He sat, his hands trembling.

> . . . "I'm getting one of those old headaches."

The death of Billy the Kid at the hand of Pat Garret is legend, but it is not Billy's death in this book.

> It was full dawn:. . . . Billy's old shirt hung open. . . . He awaited the approaching rider with half-awake curiosity; he seemed anything but scared.

> Then I saw the white mare come racing out of the long shadow of the south—Katie Garza almost ran past me before she checked her horse. The mare was flecked with sweat. I remember clearly how anxious Katie looked, as if fearful of having arrived too late. She had her gun in her hand.

> "Oh, dern!" Billy said, with a horrified glance at Katie. "This is gonna give me a headache."

> Katie swung off her mare, dropped the rein, and shot Billy before he could move. He didn't fall flat: he gripped the shotgun and slid into a seated position. Katie walked closer to him, her gun

cocked; I saw her glance at the ivory comb (belonging to Cecily) on the camp table.

> There was a spot of blood on Billy's breast—not much.

> "I guess it's one cure for a headache," he said, still clinging to his shotgun.

> Then, from the wind's four quarters, the losers in the race to kill him moved out of their hiding places. Isinglass stepped in view from behind the tent, Winchester in the crook of his arm. Tully Roebuck emerged from the China Pond, a pistol in each hand. Bloody Feathers stood atop the old, rotting pile of buffalo hides. . . . And a small weasel in a dark coat—it was Long Dog Hawkins—appeared practically at my elbow, carrying a hugh Colt. . . .

> "Hi Tully," Billy said in a weaker tone.

> He looked at Katie with a crooked smile.

> "You ought to let on that Tully got me," he said. "Tully's got politics to think of."

> "Hurry up and die, chapito," Katie said softly. "I've ridden a long way and I need to water this horse."

> . . . before my words were out, Billy Bone had obeyed her request.

> Katie Garza laid her hat over Billy's face. Then she stood up, broke into sobs and flung herself into her father's arms. Tully Roebuck—he really liked Billy—was crying too, and my own eyes were not dry.

People, places, things—a fiction stranger than truth—In Larry McMurtry's words: "I suppose they'll argue over it forever—or until all the black dirt of life finally washes off Billy and leaves him a pure, clean legend." I agree about the arguing.

WORKS CITED

Horan, James D. *The Authentic Wild West: The Gunfighters.* New York: Crown Publishers, Inc., 1976.

McMurtry, Larry. *Anything For Billy.* New York: Simon and Schuster, 1988.

Trachtman, Paul. *The Old West: The Gunfighters.* New York: Time-Life Books, 1974.

Michiko Kakutani (review date 12 May 1992)

SOURCE: "Books of the Times: McMurtry's Sequel to *Terms of Endearment*," in *New York Times*, May 12, 1992.

[*In the following review of* The Evening Star, *noted critic Kakutani states that while McMurtry's writing is not always balanced, he is skilled enough to overcome the novel's weaknesses and tell an entertaining story.*]

As Aurora Greenway thinks about her granddaughter, Melanie, leaving Texas for a new life in California, she feels her own spirits sink. "All around them," she thinks, "was evidence of what she knew in her own heart: that life was nothing but a matter of innumerable comings and goings, separations and separateness, of departures from which there might be no certain return." In short, "People left, they died, they didn't come back."

These melancholy thoughts pretty much sum up the dominant mood, not to mention the plot, of *The Evening Star*, Larry McMurtry's sequel to his 1975 novel, *Terms of Endearment*. Some 15 years have passed since Aurora's daughter, Emma (played by Debra Winger in James L. Brooks's 1983 movie adaptation), died of cancer, and Aurora (played by Shirley MacLaine in that movie) is now reluctantly entering her 70's.

She's still imperious, self-indulgent and impossible, and she's still adept at charming and manipulating her hapless suitors. Her main man is still the general, who at the age of 86 is more or less bedridden with a broken leg; and her main confidante is still Rosie, her loyal maid. Things in the Greenway clan have changed, however, and hardly for the better.

The general no longer has sex with Aurora, and Aurora has become fed up with her sometime boyfriend, Pascal. Rosie and her lover, C. C., aren't getting along particularly well either. In fact, all of them are felling old, frustrated and more and more susceptible to unexpected bouts of dread. Each, in his or her way, tries to cope: Rosie immerses herself in television news; the general flirts with nudism, and Aurora sets out to find herself some new admirers.

As for Emma's children, whom Aurora brought up, they, too, seem to have lost their way. Melanie is confused, lovelorn and pregnant. Teddy is recovering from a mental breakdown and living with a woman who has taken a female lover. And Tommy is serving a long jail sentence for fatally shooting his girlfriend. Aurora wonders what went wrong, whether Emma's death irrevocably damaged the children or whether she somehow failed in her maternal duties.

As in *Terms of Endearment*, Mr. McMurtry commutes back and forth between two narrative modes, the sentimental and the farcical. From time to time he goes overboard in one direction: a series of episodes in which the general exposes himself feels tasteless and repetitious, just as the series of romantic disasters that overtake members of the Greenway circle seems contrived and melodramatic. For the most part, though, Mr. McMurtry's fluency and poise as a writer smooth over such bumpy sections, seducing the reader and soothing away any lingering doubts. His quick, eager sympathy for his characters, his uncanny ability to zip in and out of all their minds and his effortless narrative inventiveness all combine to create a story that's as emotionally involving as it is entertaining.

Whenever it seems like things for Aurora and her family have settled into a predictable rut, something surprising happens. Aurora's determination to repair her relationship with the general through a visit to a psychiatrist turns into an unexpected new romance, which, in turn, gives way to an unlikely flirtation with a pair of brothers. And Rosie's troubles with C. C. are quickly superseded by problems with her new boyfriend, Willie, a heroin-addicted prison guard.

As the years rapidly slip by, Aurora begins to dwell more and more on the past: inspired by Proust, she embarks on what she calls her "memory project." She is determined, she says, to remember and document every day of her life. Yet even as the boundaries of Aurora's daily life contract, the lives of her grandchildren start to blossom: there are new careers and new partners and the arrival of several great-grandchildren. Aurora, once the indomitable queen bee, has the sense that things are moving on without her.

All of Larry McMurtry's novels, from *The Last Picture Show* and *Texasville* to *Lonesome Dove* and *Anything for Billy*, have radiated a certain wistfulness. Sadness, occasioned by loneliness and an awareness of the precariousness of life, runs though his oeuvre like a plaintive, insistent refrain. That emotion is heightened in *The Evening Star*, a novel that, like John Updike's last Rabbit novel (*Rabbit at Rest*), traces an aging character's attempts to grapple with the obdurate facts of mortality and loss.

The Evening Star is not ambitious the way *Rabbit at Rest* is. Mr. McMurtry isn't interested in using Aurora's story to comment on changes in America. He isn't interested in creating a chronicle of contemporary middle-class life. He's simply interested in telling a good story. What the novels do have in common is their success as sequels; while utterly satisfying on their own, they also give the longtime reader the pleasure of seeing a character mature through the decades. The result is not unlike growing old in the company of a favorite relative or friend.

Noel Perrin (review date 25 July 1993)

SOURCE: "Woodrow Call Rides Again," in *New York Times*, July 25, 1993.

[*In the following review, Perrin writes that while the dialogue in* Streets of Laredo *matches the high quality in* Lonesome Dove, *the rest of the novel falls short.*]

It turns out that the person who can write the best parody of Larry McMurtry is Larry McMurtry.

Eight years ago the Texan published what was instantly recognized as his masterpiece: the epic novel **Lonesome Dove**. Using every element of standard Western myth—cowboys, whores, outlaws, sheriffs—Mr. McMurtry tells the story of a great cattle drive from the Mexican border up to Montana around 1875. Leading it are two legendary heroes: Augustus McCrae and Woodrow F. Call, both former captains in the Texas Rangers. All is fresh and new in **Lonesome Dove**, as if no one had ever written a western before. So far as I know, no one ever had written a western with so many brilliantly articulate characters, and the dialogue has much to do with the book's greatness.

Now, Mr. McMurtry has taken the considerable risk of publishing a sequel. It is hard to think of sequels that live up to their originals. Even Shakespeare did less well in *Henry IV, Part 2* than he had in *Part 1*. Trollope lived up to earlier books once or twice in the *Barsetshire* series, and perhaps John Updike has done it with *Rabbit*. Alas, Larry McMurtry has not done it with *Streets of Laredo*.

In this novel the time seems to be about 1890. Captain McCrae is long dead, and Captain Call is an old man. Lorena, the blond whore who played such a spectacular role in **Lonesome Dove**, is now a married woman with five children. She teaches school.

As the book opens, Captain Call is waiting for the train at Amarillo. With him is a middle-aged accountant from Brooklyn. Call has been hired by the railroad to catch a young Mexican bandit who has robbed eight trains and killed 30-odd crew members and passengers so far, not to mention the 712 sheep on one stock train. The accountant is there—in his city clothes—because the railroad is paying Call on a fee-plus-expenses basis. The president of the line, back in New York, wants to be sure the old Ranger doesn't pad his expense account.

This two-man hunting party gradually grows. Pea Eye, another Ranger from **Lonesome Dove**, appears, though reluctantly, because he is now married to Lorena and the father of those five kids. He'd rather stay home and farm. Deputy Sheriff Plunkert of Laredo joins up. The old, old Indian tracker Famous Shoes comes along. And now there is an endless horseback ride in pursuit of the young bandit—whom Pea Eye eventually wounds and a totally unheroic Mexican butcher finishes off.

Don't think Texas's troubles are over, though. The book is loaded with killers and they pop up in front of Captain Call and party with great frequency. John Wesley Hardin (a real historical figure) shows up and so does the man known as Mox Mox. His passion is burning people alive, especially children. He's been doing it for years.

Here is a good example of Mr. McMurtry's self-parody. He has always liked picturesque forms of death, and in **Lonesome Dove** he draws a chilling portrait of the three Suggs brothers, killers who shoot a couple of settlers, then hang them and then on impulse douse the bodies with coal oil and burn them. It makes a powerful scene. But with Mox Mox, burning's a habit, so the power leaks away. Cartoon deaths don't count.

Or consider tracking. In **Lonesome Dove**, a black cowboy named Deets is the tracker, and he is very good indeed. But Famous Shoes here is something out of a comedy routine. The old Indian can glance at a bunch of horse tracks and announce that there are eight men with two extra horses. Impressive. But when he adds that three are "Mexicans who spur their horses too much," one is a Cherokee, and so on, the book topples into absurdity. Or into the western tall tale, anyway.

Even the rattlesnake-eating blue pigs of **Lonesome Dove** get inflated. Their representative in **Streets of Laredo** is a creature known as the "devil pig." It feeds exclusively on human corpses and is apparently immortal. It is definitely silly. The trouble is that tall tales and real human emotions don't readily mix, but Mr. McMurtry has shoved them together anyway. They keep separating, like salad dressing.

Streets of Laredo is by no means a complete failure. In one way at least it is the full equal of **Lonesome Dove**. Larry McMurtry remains a genius at dialogue. The scene where the seven whores start reminiscing about the first men in their lives is wonderful. So is the one where Call and a rancher named Goodnight have a discussion about counting sheep. You might not think that a promising subject, but it yields a page of superb conversation.

There are many such pages, but I'm afraid there are also

many on which Mr. McMurtry makes you wish he had left the characters of *Lonesome Dove* in peace.

Pauline Sarll   (essay date Summer 1994)

SOURCE: "Boundaries, Borders and Frontiers: A Revisionary Reading of Larry McMurtry's *Horseman, Pass By*," in *Journal of Popular Culture*, Vol. 28, No. 1, Summer, 1994, pp. 97-110.

[*In the following essay Sarll, a member of the Department of American and Canadian Studies at the University of Nottinham, discusses the way McMurtry juxtaposes conflicting ideas in* Horseman, Pass By.]

It is time for a reappraisal of Larry McMurtry's fiction, a reappraisal which recognizes the complexity of his work, acknowledges the serious cultural and literary issues he addresses, and is not tied exclusively to a 'Western' or 'regional' critique.[1] One approach which can encompass these issues is through the boundaries deeply embedded in his novels. Danny Deck, novelist protagonist of *All My Friends Are Going To Be Strangers* (1972), and perhaps the closest to a fictional self-projection in McMurtry's work, comments that the boundary, or borderline, is his peculiarly appropriate vantage point.

> It was always a borderland I had lived on . . . a thin little strip between the country of the normal and the country of the strange. Perhaps my true country was the borderland . . . (McMurtry, *Friends* 231)

Formal and thematic boundaries emerge in McMurtry's novels as the place where conventional oppositions collapse. Perceived boundaries between genres, between the rural American past and the urban present, between reality and imagination and between myth and history become a site of interrogation. Borders and boundaries are dynamic; they are areas of transgression, translation, transformation and clandestine activity, where power changes hands and conventional rules are revealed as arbitrary human constructs. In McMurtry's novels boundaries operate as multi-faceted signifiers denoting variously a compromised line, a marginal place, a geographical phenomenon or a psychological, social, cultural, political or historical construct. These boundaries, written, imagined, installed, transgressed or subverted, offer an expansive interpretative route into McMurtry's fiction. Though the theme of boundaries permeates all of McMurtry's work in many different forms, I want here to concentrate on three interrelated boundary themes as exemplified in his first novel, *Horseman, Pass By*. These concern the problematic boundaries between Old and New West,

between Homer Bannon as mythical frontiersman and Hud as 'modern cowboy,' and Lonnie Bannon's ambivalent progress from child to man.

Naming the Boundaries

McMurtry's debut novel has usually been discussed in terms of the initiation into manhood of its young narrator/protagonist, Lonnie Bannon,[2] as a regional novel concerned primarily with place and displacement[3] or as a "modern cowboy" novel (Reynolds 76). It is all of these, but it is also more. The assumed boundaries McMurtry problematizes within the text include those between past and present, youth and age, good and evil, authenticity and falsification, and stasis and movement. In the novel interrogation of generational, regional, proprietal, legal and representational boundaries combine with an engagement with many of the themes which come to characterize McMurtry's later work, including families, orphans and an interest in dying breeds. At the same time an examination of the novel reveals that McMurtry is also challenging canonical boundaries between 'high' and 'popular' literature. Such literary and generic categorizations are potentially reductive if provisional temporal or generic parameters are allowed to become static and exclusive. Russell Reising argues that the heterogeneity of American literature has until relatively recently been ". . . denied by the polarization of canonical/noncanonical, major/minor" categorizations (234). McMurtry has parodied such reductiveness in life, by the wearing of a sweatshirt emblazoned with the legend "Minor Regional Novelist." He also made ironic comment through Danny Deck who dreams when his first novel (a parallel to *Horseman, Pass By*) is published, "I could probably even be minor." Typically, McMurtry thus raises complex cultural and literary issues in a seemingly casual way.

Names are a crucial device used to echo such issues. Homer Bannon, the horseman of the novel's title, is, as his name implies, a rancher in the classic, heroic mould, one of a type whose time has ended, who must 'pass by.' Significantly Hud is rarely seen on a horse, a Cadillac being his more characteristic mode of transport, a crucial signal regarding the boundary between Old and New West. The days are numbered for the horseman of the title, both in the specific person of Homer, and in general, as the automobile replaces the horse. Lonnie, as befits his liminal position on the threshold of adulthood, inheritor of a new economic structure, is only a part-time horseman, riding out with his grandfather on Saturdays, but "on the weekdays riding the long road home . . . in the old yellow school bus" (5). The title's other referent subverts the potential boundary between 'high' literature and the Western genre: it is the last line of Yeats' poem 'Under Ben Bulben' which ends "Cast a cold eye / On life, on death. / Horseman, pass by."

McMurtry also carefully names the fictional Texan town which is the setting for his first novel, and several others, to raise similar intertextual issues, challenging the boundary between 'high' literature and the Western. Thalia is the name of the classical Greek muse, who came to be identified as the inspiration for comedy and pastoral poetry, from the Greek *thallein*, to bloom. Thalia is more than a metaphor for McMurtry's comic treatment of small-town and rural life, however, since she was the daughter of Zeus—remarkable for his extensive fatherhood—and Mnemosyne, meaning Memory. Thus, in the name Thalia are condensed references to some of McMurtry's major preoccupations, desire, history, and memory.

Old West Meets New West

As the epigraphs to this piece suggest, the meeting place between Old and New is always a locus of interest. If Buffalo Bill Cody stood on the boundary *between* savagery and civilization, he also *represented* both, each to the other. Frederick Jackson Turner defined the frontier in the same terms as Cody, as "the meeting point between savagery and civilization." But whose savagery, and what constitutes civilization? The most cursory study of the Westward expansion of the United States reveals that 'savagery' was by no means confined to Native Americans. The early 'civilization' that ensued was also problematic, with none of the cultural features or social institutions which normally define that condition. 'Savagery' and 'civilization,' 'nature' and 'culture' deconstruct as they collapse into each other at the frontier. 'Frontier' compresses associations with Westward progress ("*frontiersman*") and cultural regress ("*back* woodsman") (Fussell 15), along with time, space and notions of national and political boundaries.

Marshall McLuhan talks of the "between-ness" of borders, of the "world of the interval" (226-48). For him the national boundary between Canada and the United States is both line and space, interface and interval, difference and sameness, rather than an opposition of absolutes. Each side of any boundary differs from its opposing side but is simultaneously inseparable from it. Even national borders which have an apparent objective existence in cartographic and political terms, often owe more to the determinants of compromise and expediency than to logic and topography and divide peoples and areas whose similarities may be as striking as their differences. Thus any definition of 'boundary,' 'border' and 'frontier' shifts according to context.

Ostensibly in **Horseman, Pass By**, Homer is the representative of the Old West and Hud the representative of the new, and Lonnie must make an invidious choice between these two potential role models. However, an examination of the notional boundary between Homer and Hud reveals their similarities as well as their differences. Paradoxically, both

Homer and Hud represent aspects of old frontier values, blurring supposed oppositions between new and old ways of life. It is the aggressive Cadillac-driving Hud, symbol of modernity, who embodies the thrusting pragmatic 'frontier' values to an even greater extent than Homer who is temporally part of that frontier history. Homer abides by the legal requirements for diagnosis and disposal of his infected herd, while Hud advises evading the law and selling the cattle. Homer emerges as law-abiding, with social values inimical to the individualistic Hud. Homer's respect for the land is part of the value scheme on which the notion of frontier rests, but so is a belief in individual rights, which Homer disregards in favor of the communal good. Hud embodies the drive for primary exploitation of the land that characterized the early Westering process, the surface activities of logging, mining, fishing and trapping replaced in the twentieth century by drilling for oil. Homer has expressly forbidden any drilling on his ranch. "There'll be no holes punched in the land while I'm here" (McMurtry, **Horseman** 88). His statement turns out to be ironically prophetic, for he is dead before the exploitation of his land for oil begins, proprietal boundaries proving to be fragile and transitory human constructs.

Lonnie

The condensed referents of memory and desire, found in the name Thalia, emerge as the structuring principles the life of Lonnie, whose head is "full of old sights and half-dreams" (McMurtry, **Horseman** 59), and it is through memory and desire that oppositions are blurred to transgress conventional boundaries. In an essay collection McMurtry links memory and frontier to describe an internalized temporal boundary between past and present, a boundary unfixed, breached in a moment of historical consciousness,

> Myself, I dislike frontiers, and yet the sense that my own has vanished in me produces the strongest emotion I have felt.... It has embedded itself in the titles of each of my books, and just as I think I have worn out the emotion it seizes me again, usually at some unlikely moment. I see my son, aged five, riding a mechanical horse in front of a laundromat ... and the sight calls up my Uncle Johnny, when he was aged five, sitting on top of the McMurtry barn watching the last trail herd go by. (**Grave** xxii-xxiii)

Here 'frontier' connotes internal and external meanings, affirming its fluidity as a signifier. History of the 'frontier' days of the last trail herds merges with memory (that of his uncles, and his own memories of them), in emotive reactions. Unreliable, and inescapable, memory functions as a personal history which occurs in the present as internalized boundaries between past and present dissolve.

Horseman, Pass By is framed with an italicized epilogue and prologue. From the tone and tense of the prologue's opening words it is evident that Lonnie Bannon is looking back from the perspective of an unspecified later date, "I remember how green the . . . fields were, that year" (5). McMurtry does not, however, use the presumed enlarged experience of the narrator to intervene in, or explain, these earlier events from a more mature standpoint, but sticks to the uncertain viewpoint of a youthful narrator whose perceptions are limited by his youth and inexperience and his mediated access to the past. The narrator seemingly views the events with no more clarity than when he initially experienced them, a stance which questions the assumption that additional years necessarily give insight. The implication is that there is no simplistic boundary for him to cross into maturity, wisdom and understanding. Between the prologue and the epilogue the novel is presented as a memory and a personal history of a past time, but reader expectations of the conclusive function of an epilogue are subverted by McMurtry's refusal of its conventional opportunity to close the novel with totalizing summary and explanation.

The detailed evocation of the ranch, the landscape and the characters, in a vernacular given to straightforward spade-calling rather than genteel euphemisms, adds an air of authenticity to the text. Lonnie's discourse is that of a farm-boy, unabashed by bestiality ["half the boys in town had had a wild soiree with a blind heifer" (48)], or defecation ["Jesse . . . had to go where he could get the leverage on his bowels" (23)]. His candid first-person narrative implies that he is a 'reliable' narrator who will withhold nothing. Lonnie's ambivalent affection for his grandfather vies with the powerful attraction of the amoral Hud. Earlier, when seated in a car between Homer and Hud, emotionally torn by the conflict between them, Lonnie expresses his unease in a boundary metaphor, seeing himself poised on a dangerous edge ". . . like I was riding a horse along a high slippery ledge when it was raining. One splash of words in the wrong place and I didn't' know where we'd be" (64-65). Lonnie's reference to the danger of "words in the wrong place" is one of the few explicit indications of his reticence. Unsophisticated and apparently reliable as narrator, Lonnie withholds crucial information relating to the tragic history of the Bannon family, a tragedy which links Lonnie and Homer and blurs the boundary between the emotionally damaged youth and his grandfather. Lonnie's father accidentally shot his own mother, Homer's first wife, but the incident has never been fully discussed by Homer, nor has Lonnie asked him. This complicity of silence is reproduced in the narrative in which the reader discovers little about Lonnie's parents. Homer's reluctance to confront his emotions is reenacted by Lonnie near the book's end when he finds himself unable to utter the words confirming his grandfather's death. Asked "How is Mister Homer?", he prefers to avoid "a long conversation about it" and says merely "Mean as he ever was" (142).

Autobiographical connotations are accentuated by McMurtry's transgression of the textual boundaries between fiction and his own early life on his grandfather's Idiot Ridge ranch, near a small town with all of Thalia's limitations. Like McMurtry, who in his youth heard tales from his nine trail-driving uncles, Lonnie spends hours listening to the old-timers' stories, and for him "the best hour" (5) was the hour of dusk, the borderline where day blurs into night, when Homer tells Lonnie stories of the old days and Lonnie sits at his feet "taking in every word he said" (6). Presumed boundaries between day and night, past and present, youth and age, are elided in the fading light as Lonnie leaves the present and enters his grandfather's old world.

Though linked to Homer through blood relationship and memory, Lonnie begins to tire of the "old-timy stories" (21) he previously admired. Saying "Granddad and I were in such separate times and separate places" he seems unaware that he himself is already looking back to an idealized past in his "gradeschool days" of "frosty mornings" and "salty smells," when the ranch was fully functional and self-contained; ". . . now the beeves and hogs were in the locker plant in Thalia, and the smokehouse only held broken lawn mowers . . ." (21). Boundaries of time blur as Homer is involuntarily precipitated into the past when his mental health breaks down following the destruction of his herd, and family history and memories begin to crowd into his present. Lonnie's separation from his grandfather, intensified by Homer's increasing removal from reality, is metaphorically compared to a boundary fence. "I wanted to get out of the dark old house with its dreams and ghosts. Granddad was on the other side of a high barbed fence . . . and I couldn't go over it and I couldn't crawl through" (111).

Lonnie can no longer reach Homer who is fenced into his isolated world of "dreams and ghosts," through ironically this is exactly the situation that Lonnie is eventually left in.

Hud

The gentle, folksy mood established in the prologue is linguistically disrupted in the first chapter when Homer looks up from his whittling to ask his stepson Hud to take his used plate out to Halmea, the cook. Hud's reply, ". . . let the nigger bitch gather 'em up herself" (10), emblematically exposes a refusal of social norms which he later violently enacts in Halmea's rape and Homer's murder. The rejection of Homer's authority, and explicit racism and sexism of Hud's first statement, prefigure the conflict to come.

The adolescent Lonnie's awakening sexuality and frustration at the limitations of his small-town environment are multiplied by the brooding presence of Hud and the hostility between Hud and Homer. Hud's belief that Homer blighted his youth by refusing to allow him to go to college, but allowing him to serve in the Korean war, exacerbates Hud's contempt for Homer and his stubborn adherence to outdated values and serves as motivation for appropriation of the ranch. On the surface Homer and Hud suggest two possible role models for Lonnie, Homer the old values associated with the land and its nurture, and Hud the new way of exploitation for power, money and sex, values perhaps more often associated with the city. The generational boundaries are not, however, as clear-cut as they appear, and Lonnie has much in common with both Homer and Hud. All three are physically isolated, all borderers living outside of town on the margins of the community. All are psychologically isolated too, partly due to their inability to relate to women. Lonnie is an orphan whose solitariness eventually becomes alienation, "I felt lost from everybody . . . myself included" (117). Homer's second marriage, to a quarrelsome, querulous, ironically named Jewel, offers little joy to either. Symptomatically they listen simultaneously to a different program on separate radios in their living room: "They disagreed over the programs so much that they couldn't get along with just one" (70).

Ranch-hand Jesse recognizes that Hud must also contend with isolation. When Lonnie incredulously points out that Hud "can get more women company than anybody around here," Jesse says, "That ain't necessarily company" (70). Jesse sees that Hud exploits rather than relates to women as interpretation borne out by Hud's frequent references to woman as animals. Halmea is both "wild bitch" (93) and domestic milk cow, when Hud squeezes her breast "wanting a little choclate [sic] milk" (58). Hud also speculates that he could arouse a passing blonde woman to "make some cat tracks on the ceiling" (68). For Hud both the black and white female are commodities like livestock in a competitive masculine power game. Lonnie's terminology is similarly marked by animal referents. Halmea during the rape is "like a heifer Hud had thrown down to work over" (97). He describes a woman's hair as "curled like a colt's" (115) and another woman has "naked teats" rather than breasts (127). McMurtry draws clear similarities between Hud's and Lonnie's sexual desire, and its verbalization, but crucially they differ in desire's translation into action. Watching Hud, Lonnie realizes, "I had wanted to do pretty much the same thing to Halmea. I didn't want to do it mean, like Hud did everything, but I wanted to do it to her" (97). Hud seeks to assert his mastery over women as part of his bid for power, while Lonnie's sexual desire is inextricably complicated by other emotions. For Lonnie, motherless in a male world, Halmea is a conflicting amalgam of kindly mother figure, female friend and desirable sexual object.

Potential Escape Routes

The novel's musical referents resonate as temporal, generic and cultural signposts and also serve to heighten mood.

Lonnie's juke-box choices, *Folsom Prison Blues* and *I'm in the Jailhouse Now*, reflect his caged-in feelings and his alienation. Peter Thorpe suggests that the theme common to all country and western music is that of "escape from the complexities of adult life" (307-18), through means varying from the geographical (the road), physiological (drink), sociological (prison), religious, psychological (reversion to childhood dependence through crying), to the philosophical (simplification of life's complexity). He notes that while *Folsom Prison Blues* is "a vigorous attack on imprisonment . . . one senses an ambivalence between hating prison and feeling at home in it," nor is it coincidental that in prison there is also an escape from women. Lonnie's choice of songs reflect his ambivalence over the 'prison' of his current lifestyle, a simultaneous desire to transcend and remain within both adolescence and Thalia's boundaries. Typically about the past and about loss, the "worn-out words" (117) of the songs' lyrics and their mournful tunes are for Lonnie achingly emotive and "fit the night and the country and the way I was feeling," reminding him of all the boys he knows, who like him suffer from unfocused desire. "All of them wanted more and seemed to end up with less . . . whatever it was they wanted, that was what they ended up doing without" (117-18).

Lonnie's hazy desire, "an itch there's no way to scratch" (71), is sometimes sexual and sometimes expressed as a desire to emulate Jesse's mobility—an "itch to be off somewhere . . . past Thalia and Wichita . . . into country I'd never seen" (21). Jesse remembers lack well, particularly as accentuated by adolescent appetites, "When I was seventeen I never got enough of anything" (19). Through Jesse, McMurtry suggests that desire is doomed to be unfulfilled, that movement is deferment not solution. McMurtry installs Jesse as potential role model for Lonnie, then undercuts his appeal by an interrogation of the boundary between stasis and movement, home and the road. When asked by the action-hungry Lonnie about his adventurous life as ranch-hand and rodeo contestant, Jesse tiredly points out the unromantic reality.

> You boys think staying in one place is tiresome, just wait till you see that goddam road comin' at you ever mornin'. And still comin' late that evenin' and sometimes way into the night. I run that road for ten years and never caught up with nothing'. (78-79)

The cowboy's lifestyle—whether on the ranch or at the rodeo—is demythologized in the novel. Homer Bannon is scarred from a roping accident, Lonnie's friend is critically injured in his first rodeo appearance and Jesse has a limp, a "gimpy leg" from an old rodeo injury; yet, Lonnie remarks, "As cowboys go he was in good shape" (13). In contrast to the valorized romantic image of a vigorous, healthy cowboy, whose very name implies eternal youth, the prosaic realities of cow-punching were harsh, allowing an average of "seven years of active riding (Durham 294) before curtailment by physical injury.

Written texts are used in the novel as a mode of escape which may ameliorate desire and fill in the gaps of social and familial discourse. *From Here To Eternity* is read by Lonnie "over and over," partly for the voyeuristic thrill of vicarious sexual gratification, but also for reassurance: some parts "reminded me a lot of my nights in Fort Worth; the people in the book seemed a lot like the ones I saw" (22). Assuring him that a more exciting world exists, Lonnie's novel serves the same purpose as Halmea's *True Romances* magazine, offering escape from the controlling boundaries of place and time, and temporarily assuaging desire.

Another form of escape in the novel is film, and here McMurtry raises problems of historical authenticity. Lonnie and the ranch-hands watch a Gene Autry film, *The Streets of Laredo* (intriguingly, the title of McMurtry's latest novel), in which the hero uses a silver-mounted saddle. Lonzo guffaws "You couldn't lift that bastard on a horse with a goddam crane" (32). The ironic choice of Autry, a real-life war hero whose advent into the Western coincided with its decline to B-movie status, contests the boundary between the historical West and its imaginative representations into which history has popularly been subsumed. Autry inaugurated the moralizing, clean-living cowboy figure who lived by a ten-point cowboy code more appropriate to the Boy Scout. In McMurtry's modern West, Hud's conduct is unaffected by similar personal ethics, and neither individual nor judicial codes offer the prospect of moral or legal justice, as Lonnie knows. "I had seen a good many trials in Thalia, and I'd seen a lot dumber people than Hud get away with doing a lot worse things than he had done" (163). Lonnie believes that Hud, a member of the dominant white male elite, de facto owner of an extensive area of land, is unlikely to suffer much at the hands of the Texas Rangers.

Lonnie has access to his grandfather's history through oral texts, but perceives it through the filter of cinematic representation. Boundaries between the personal and the public are blurred when both are thus apparently accorded the same status by Lonnie. Lonnie has a dream portraying what Don Graham calls "a moment of sympathetic merger" with Homer.

> I dreamed that Granddad and I were out together, riding in the early morning. . . . We stopped our horses on the edge of a hill. . . . There below us was Texas . . . spread wide under the clear spread of sky like the opening scene in a big Western movie . . . we rode down together . . . toward some ranch I couldn't see, the Llano Estacado or the old Matador . . . (59-60)

The boundaries between Old and New West, between authenticity and simulacrum, between dream and reality, are simultaneously problematized by McMurtry. Graham notes that Lonnie can't see the Llano Estacado or the old Matador because "they are storied ranches of a bygone era" which "belong to the myths of the past." Lonnie's "lens of observation is modern, and Lonnie sees the landscape . . . as an open-ended frame in a "big Western movie" (Graham 343-55). Lonnie's memories and perceptions are infused with oral, written, musical and visual texts, compromised representations which are his only point of access to an irrecoverable past.

Fences and the Diminished Frontier

Merging with his grandfather in dreams, Lonnie attempts to physically identify with him. Borrowing Stranger, Homer's horse, Lonnie acts out a desire to become symbolic heir to Homer's values and horsemanship skills as well as his material property. He rides to Idiot Ridge, a high natural boundary. After viewing the ranch, its stock and the wildlife which acknowledges no human boundaries, Lonnie returns to the ranchhouse, but falls heavily at a fence. The territorial fence over which Lonnie tumbles is a visible boundary to the land, a tangible proof of ownership on Homer's mind the day after his infected herd is destroyed. He determines to work on his proprietal boundaries while the ranch is quarantined, an assertion of ownership in defiance of natural hazards, personal tragedy, governmental interference and Hud's threats of encroachment. Significantly, the ranch's fences are both a reduced image of the frontier, and part of the means of its reduction. It was with the invention of barbed wire in the 1880s that it became practicable to fence in large tracts of land, enclosing the formerly open range.

Complicity

Hud's intended violation of the land for oil-production reproduces the violation of Halmea's person in which Lonnie found himself guilty by association. Lonnie is also psychologically implicated in the death of his grandfather. Hud's murder or mercy killing of Homer adds to Lonnie's isolation, and he responds to the act with the words, "I needed him. . . . What will I do?" Hud's reply is also in terms of lack, "You'll do without like the rest of us" (129). The enigma surrounding Homer's death is not only due to doubt about Hud's motive, but to Lonnie's apparent prior complicity. When Homer shoots the longhorn steers, symbols of his whole life as a cattle rancher, and like Homer himself, representatives of a dying breed, Lonnie thinks his grandfather "might as well be dead with them, herd and herdsman together, in the dust" (105). Hud later enacts Lonnie's thought, claiming he shot Homer to put him out of his misery, ". . . it was the best thing. The pore old worn-out bastard" (128). Had Homer been capable he might well have agreed with

Hud. Homer had earlier indicated his aversion to sentiment and nostalgia, saying, "Hell. If the time's come when I got to spend my time lookin' back, why, I'd just as soon go under" (103). Taking upon himself the responsibility of shooting his beloved longhorns rather than allowing an anonymous government agent to do it, his own words and deeds seem to authorize Hud's action.

After Homer's murder Hud's "easy and peaceful smile" and overt assertion denote a moral self-approval, "Me and him fought many and many a round. . . . It's hard to say though. I helped him as much as he ever helped me, I believe that" (129). Does the ambiguous 'help' provided by Hud refer to the shooting, his helping Homer to die or to previous work on Homer's ranch? Lonnie cannot decide ". . . seeing that wild blood-smeared grin, I didn't know. It could have been for kindness or for meanness either" (30). In Homer's death, as in Halmea's rape, Hud takes the action that Lonnie had himself considered, crossing boundaries of socially acceptable norms. At Homer's funeral Lonnie longs to flout convention by ridiculing Brother Barstow's hypocritical sermon, and this time the wish that Hud should cross the boundary he dare not cross himself becomes explicit. "I wish I could have laughed out loud. . . . Or I wish Hud would have done it. But we didn't" (137).

Conclusion

In spite of its Texan setting, its horses and cowboys, **Horseman, Pass By** embodies few of the usual certainties of the Western genre. McMurtry challenges preconceptions by a careful presentation of complex characters who resist simplistic categorization as villain or hero. Homer, apparently of the mythic frontier tradition, arouses little affection or even respect, "There wasn't hardly anybody cared much for Granddad. Some liked him and some were scared of him and a good many hated his guts" (135). McMurtry deliberately undercuts expectations of Western stereotypes by adopting much of the genre's familiar imagery, but disrupting it linguistically. The funeral, a quintessential feature of the Western film, provides one such opportunity. The prototypical film funeral often involves sincere friends muttering poorly remembered but heartfelt words which conceal genuine emotion and reverence. At Homer's funeral Lonnie is unwilling to enter the church, with its "chicken-shit" preacher (134) and hypocritical strangers, until Hud takes his arm, in a role reversal in which Hud now publicly observes proprieties. Later Lonnie is appalled when he sees how the undertakers have falsified his dead grandfather's appearance with "slick oil" and "red paint," just as Brother Barstow's sermon falsified the text of Homer's life. Hud once more takes Lonnie's arm, overtly conforming to ritual social norms, but remaining violently oppositional in his language, "Let's get this shit over with" (139). Hud and Lonnie are united in their private disgust with the public cant at Homer's funeral.

With installation of a conventional situation, then subversion of reader expectations, McMurtry simultaneously remythologizes and demythologizes the Western tradition.

It could be argued that the novel is about Hud's, rather than Lonnie's, entry into manhood, a point of view implicitly endorsed by the emphasis on Hud in the eponymously retitled film. It is Hud who is the participant in bloody rituals of rape and murder, who ends his extended adolescence first by exercising *droit de seigneur* over Halmea, then by seizing ownership of the ranch and killing Homer, all actions which symbolize his entry into a brutal male power sphere. Initiation's intrinsic theme is that of crossing the boundary from one social or familiar role to another, and Hud's violently oppositional behavior ultimately transgresses familial, social, moral and legal boundaries, while Lonnie remains a confused observer and fails to cross the boundary into adulthood.

The epilogue shows Lonnie embarked on half-hearted physical escape. He packs his "clothes and paperbacks," ostensibly to pay a visit to his injured friend, but he is reluctant to leave. Poised on a boundary between stasis and movement he loiters in Thalia until dusk, that time of day charged with possibilities, the blurred boundary between day and night. Finally hitching a ride in a truck Lonnie has still not decided if his leaving is to be temporary or permanent. He physically crosses the region's boundaries, only to retain emotional baggage which transcends such spatio temporal markers. As the dashboard light penetrates the darkness, the blurred outline of the truck driver's face reminds Lonnie "of someone that I cared for, he reminded me of everyone I knew" (143).

The author has renounced **Horseman, Pass by** as a "slight, confused, and sentimental first novel" (McMurtry, **Grave** 17). On the contrary, it has a dense intertextuality which explores complex cultural concerns as it transgresses conventional generic boundaries. It avoids sentimentality by humor, robust language and a refusal to simplify. Ambivalent rather than confused, the novel has a resonance which arises largely from its focus on all types of boundaries. Oddly enough, some previous criticism of McMurtry's work has seen his ambivalence as a failing rather than one of his greatest strengths. Charles Peavy said in 1977 that McMurtry will remain "a regional novelist" until he overcomes "the unresolved tension he feels about his native soil" (Peavy 118), while Jim Sanderson complains that McMurtry "sits on a Texas corral" fence and "doesn't know whether to stay put, to jump in the middle, or to kick the damn thing down" (Sanderson 72). McMurtry's ambivalence (and by implication Lonnie's), arises from an intellectual rejection of the frontier myth which conflicts with a powerful emotional attraction. The boundary between educated response and emotive reaction can never be clear-cut, however convenient that might be for the critic. McMurtry's ambivalence gives rise to a literature which rejects the simplified unitary language of ideology and shows values in conflict with one another, across historical, literary, cultural, regional and textual boundaries. To paraphrase Marshal McLuhan, in McMurtry's fiction the boundary is where the action is.

NOTES

1. McMurtry is of course, in some sense, both a regional and Western writer, inasmuch as he hails from Texas and his characteristic setting is the fictional small town of Thalia, loosely based on his own home town, while his fictions have often utilized a cowboy motif.

2. For instance, Charles D. Peavy refers to initiation and rites of passage as major themes in the author's work in *Larry McMurtry*. Boston: G.K. Hall & Co., 1977.

3. See, for example, the study of McMurtry as "neoregionalist" in Raymond L. Neinstein's *Ghost Country*. Berkeley: Berkeley Creative Arts Book Co., 1976.

WORKS CITED

Durham, Philip. "The Negro Cowboy." *American Quarterly* 7.3 (1955).

Fussell, Edwin. *Frontier: American Literature and the American West*. Princeton, NJ: Princeton UP, 1965.

Graham, Don. "The Regionalist Imperative." *Taking Stock: A Larry McMurtry Casebook*. Ed. Clay Reynolds. Dallas: Southern Methodist UP, 1989.

MuLuhan, Marshall. "Canada: The Borderline Case." *The Canadian Imagination: Dimensions of a Literary Culture*, Ed. David Staines. Cambridge, MA: Harvard UP, 1977.

McMurtry, Larry. *All My Friends Are Going to Be Strangers*. 1972. New York: Touchstone, Simon & Schuster, Inc., 1989.

———. *In a Narrow Grave; Essays on Texas*. 1968. New York: Touchstone, Simon & Schuster Inc., 1989.

———. *Horseman, Pass By*. 1961. Rpt. *as Hud.* New York; Harper, 1963.

Peavy, Charles D. *Larry McMurtry*. Boston: G.K. Hall & Co., 1977.

Reising, Russell. *The Unusable Past: Theory and the Study of American Literature*. New York & London: Methuen, 1986.

Reynolds, Clay. "What Does It Take to Be a Texas Writer?" *Range Wars: Heated Debates, Sober Reflections, and Other Assessments of Texas Writing*. Eds. Craig Clifford and Tom Pilkington. Dallas: Southern Methodist UP, 1989.

Sanderson, Jim. "Old Corrals: Texas According to 80s Films and TV and Texas According to Larry McMurtry." *Journal of American Culture* 13.2 (1990).

Thorpe, Peter. "I'm Movin' On: The Escape Theme in Country and Western Music." *Western Humanities Review* 24.4 (1970).

Michiko Kakutani (review date 26 August 1994)

SOURCE: "Books of the Times: Deconstructionist Turns to Building," in *New York Times*, August 26, 1994.

[*In the following review of* Pretty Boy Floyd, *Kakutani argues that McMurtry and Diana Ossana embellish the myth of the character, but fail to make readers care about his fate.*]

The book, written in conjunction with a screenplay on the same subject, tells the story of the famous 1930's outlaw, Charles Arthur (Pretty Boy) Floyd, an Oklahoma bank robber who became such a folk hero that 20,000 people supposedly went to his funeral in 1934. As depicted by Mr. McMurtry and Ms. Ossana, Charley emerges as a charming bandit who more or less stumbles into a life of crime. He's portrayed as handsome, well mannered and boyishly sweet. He never shoots anyone unless his own life is in danger, and he's always polite to the bank tellers he robs. He's the sort of guy who says "Aw, applesauce" when he's angry.

In fact, while earlier McMurtry novels like **Lonesome Dove** and **Anything for Billy** effectively deconstructed the old frontier myths, **Pretty Boy Floyd** perpetuates and polishes the myth of the likable gangster. While Charley Floyd is not exactly glamorized in this book—his day-to-day existence is made to seem a rather drab, hand-to-mouth affair—he is romanticized as a charming, sympathetic and well-meaning hero.

His lies—to his wife, his girlfriends, the police—are shrugged off as the prevarications of an overgrown boy who really doesn't know any better. His crimes, including the murder of several police officers, are explained as the acts of someone who is simply trying to survive. Much is made of Charley's halfhearted efforts to go straight, and his generosity toward friends, neighbors and family is repeatedly mentioned. He is even referred to several times as a sort of modern-day Robin Hood.

"I was just a green country kid that got caught on a job that I didn't know much about," Charley tells a newspaper reporter, "but I guess that was the job that put its mark on me and I could never shake it off. I tried, though."

When we first meet Charley, he's a 21-year-old hick who is bored with the monotony and poor financial rewards of farming in Oklahoma. In a slapstick scene worthy of the Three Stooges, Charley and a friend somehow manage to pull off a bumbling stick-up: they hold up an armored car and make off with enough money for Charley to buy himself a fancy new suit, a robin's-egg-blue Studebaker, a garnet bracelet for his girlfriend, an 18-karat gold ring for his wife and some nifty toys for his 9-month-old son.

It's not long before the law is in hot pursuit of Charley. Indeed, he will spend the rest of his life on the run: pulling bank robberies and hiding from the police and the F.B.I. In the course of relating Charley's adventures, Mr. McMurtry and Ms. Ossana given us colorful sketches of the major players in Charley's life. To begin with, there's Ruby, his long-suffering wife, whom he abandons for months, even years at a time. Broke and worried about her son, Dempsey, Ruby tries to leave Charley: she divorces him and marries a sweet, supportive baker named Lenny, whom she realizes she does not love. It's not long before she's back with Charley, sitting in one drafty room or another, waiting for him to return for a day or two from his life on the road.

Though Charley says he's completely devoted to Ruby, he spends a considerable amount of time with two other women: Ma Ash, a feisty former whore who freely dispenses sex and maternal advice, and Beulah Baird, a bossy ex-waitress who loves to spend men's money on clothes and pretty trinkets.

Charley's partner in crime is a suave cowboy named George Birdwell, who shares his taste for philandering. George sees little of his wife, Bob, a hard-drinking dame who tries to conceal her loneliness with a lot of tough talk; he's not even terribly devoted to Red, his favorite whore, whom he's happy to cheat on with other pretty faces.

Mr. McMurtry and Ms. Ossana ask us to care about these not especially likable people by relating events from their point of view and by focusing on their private feelings rather than on the consequences of their actions. The narrative has the speed and lightness of a made-for-television movie; it dances quickly from incident to incident, pausing only here and there to cast a warm halo of sentimentality around its heroes.

As the novel progresses, Charley's bank robberies gradually recede into the background. Like so many recent McMurtry characters, Charley finds himself increasingly torn between the demands of his profession and his yearnings for domesticity. By the time he's at the top of the F.B.I.'s Most Wanted list, he wants only to settle down to a "normal" life with Ruby and their son.

For all Mr. McMurtry and Ms. Ossana's concerted efforts to make Charley and his pals sympathetic and engaging, it's hard not to feel that they deserve what they get.

Thomas Flanagan (review date 10 September 1995)

SOURCE: "*Lonesome Dove*: The Prequel," in *New York Times*, September 10, 1995.

[*In the following review, Flanagan compares* Dead Man's Walk *to* Lonesome Dove, *praising McMurtry handling of atmosphere and theme in both novels.*]

In the opening paragraph of Larry McMurtry's **Dead Man's Walk**, a whore named Matilda Jane Roberts, known throughout south Texas as the Great Western, walks, "naked as the air," up from the muddy Rio Grande and into an encampment of Texas Rangers, holding a snapping turtle by the tail. As Mr. McMurtry credibly reports, "the sight of a naked, 200-pound whore carrying a full-grown snapping turtle" captures the complete attention of the troop.

But it must be merely the piquant conjunction of whore and turtle the attracts them. Save perhaps for a few youngsters who have lied about their ages, everyone in the troop has seen Matilda naked more times than he can count. **Dead Man's Walk** is plumb chockablock with whores and turtles. The whores are used by the Rangers, and anybody else who can cough up six bits, with the remote, casual confidence one might feel toward a seasoned and reliable saddle. Turtles are a different matter—fit food perhaps for slaves and savages, but edible by white men only as a last, stomach-heaving remedy for starvation. Needless to say, especially to readers of **Lonesome Dove** (1985), they are soon driven to that extreme. When it comes to contriving tests of manhood, Mr. McMurtry knows no master.

Lonesome Dove, set in a more or less civilized post-Civil War West, had as its center an epic cattle drive from the Rio Grande to Montana, captained by two grizzled former Rangers named Woodrow Call and Gus McCrae, described by the publishers of **Dead Man's Walk** as "beloved," although for my part I would rather belove a snapping turtle. The modern world was closing in on Call and McCrae. They told themselves that they were turning cattlemen to make money, but of course they were trying to outrun modernity, to move back to a springtime world of tests of manhood. For a part of their trek, they were accompanied by a specific test of manhood—a whore with the requisite largeness of spirit and frame. She shared with them and most of the cowboys that gift for dry, laconic understatement that seems necessary for survival, if not in Texas, then surely on Mr. McMurtry's pages. His characters savor their own taciturnity, valuing it as an expression of virtue in a world where Gary Cooper would have been called gabby.

Dead Man's Walk is that novel's prequel, as such things are called—set in the days of the independent Republic of Texas, with McCrae and Call still in their early 20's. It is a stranger and a more ambitious book than its predecessor, ruthless in its disposition of characters, sparse and vivid in its creation of the inhuman landscapes of New Mexico and the plains.

Not that *Lonesome Dove* was not strange in some similar ways. Just about all the women were whores, never referred to in other terms. A few exceptions existed, but mostly for the purpose of being slaughtered by nonwhite malignants like Blue Duck, who tortured and killed out of pure cussedness. In the final pages, Blue Duck was captured and sentenced to die, at which point something happened that was the Texas equivalent of magic realism. Call went into Blue Duck's cell to look at him, and there he was, looking all baleful and bad, like Victor Jory in the 1930's film of *Tom Sawyer*. He told Call that he could fly. And damned if he couldn't: a bit later, as Call stood watching outside the courthouse, he saw Blue Duck hurling himself out the window, carrying a jailer with him. "He looked up and the hair on his neck rose, for Blue Duck was flying through the air in his chains."

In the line of fathomless cruelty, though, Blue Duck is an effete dandy compared with Buffalo Hump, the Comanche chief in *Dead Man's Walk*, or Gomez, the gruesome, merciless Apache. Some of the whites are awful too—Caleb Cobb, for example, an ex-pirate and self-appointed colonel who takes the Rangers on the goofy expedition to Santa Fe that supplies the novel with its plot. Chiefly, however, the book is held together by various tests of manhood, culminating in a 200-mile forced march across New Mexico's dread Jornada del Muerto, the dead man's walk. Cobb has various limitations of character and is accorded only a mild sympathy when the Comanches hamstring him and punch out his eyes with thorns. Even worse is Major Laroche, a Frenchman serving in the Mexican Army, given to twisting his curled and waxed mustaches, his thoughts doubtless on turtle soup. But they just aren't in the running. For a cruelty that is truly fathomless, one needs Comanches or Apaches, although in a pinch the unspeakable Kiowas will do.

Lonesome Dove and *Dead Man's Walk* are linked by the elements out of which Mr. McMurtry has created their world: an intense if unstated male bonding forged through suffering and an appetite for experience, a world of women who have passed into the sisterhood of whoredom, horizons of bleak and aching beauty and intimations of a transcendence that reveals itself in strange shapes—like Blue Duck in his chains, sailing through the Texas sky.

In *Dead Man's Walk*, the transcendence is more bizarre. Call, McCrae and three other surviving Rangers have been consigned to a leper colony near El Paso by the diabolical Major Laroche. They are rescued by an English aristocrat, Lady Carey, ravaged by leprosy but exquisite of manner and speech and gifted with a haunting soprano voice. The Rangers—and Matilda, the Great Western, who has strung along with them—are not quite sure how to behave in front of Lady Carey, and I don't think I would know how either. Suddenly one has passed into a blue-lighted grotto of Gothic theatricalities and lofty thought.

The shift of modalities is stunning, but not persuasive. On the novel's closing page, Matilda and the Rangers are standing on the pier at Galveston, and McCrae has never felt happier. He is safe, Mr. McMurtry says, "and the port of Galveston virtually teemed with whores. He had already visited five." Matilda, fortunately, is not the jealous type, and she must be bone-weary after the Jornada del Muerto, the leper colony and yet another Comanche attack led by the indefatigable Buffalo Hump. "I guess this is where I quit the rangering, boys," Long Bill Coleman, one of Call and McCrae's sidekicks, says. "It's rare sport, but it ain't quite safe." This should surely earn him the Walter Brennan Award for Most Laconic Understatement by a Supporting Character. And Mr. McMurtry's two novels, freestanding and yet linked, should surely earn an award of some kind, for carrying forward to their ultimate limit the themes and leather-tough atmospherics on which novels and films of the Texas frontier depend. Perhaps they should be called the Great Western.

Joyce Maynard (review date 19 January 1997)

SOURCE: "The Eve of Destruction," in *Los Angeles Times Book Review*, January 19, 1997, p. 6.

[*In the following review of* Zeke and Ned, *Maynard, a novelist, states that McMurtry and coauthor Diana Ossana have a created a rich, entertaining, embellished myth.*]

In his 20th novel [*Zeke and Ned*]—written in collaboration with Diana Ossana—Larry McMurtry gives us the characters of Zeke Proctor, a part-Cherokee farmer, husband and father, and his younger friend, Ned Christie, a full-blooded Cherokee now homesteading, like Zeke and his family, in the Cherokee territory known today as Oklahoma. If they make a movie out of this book (and it's not unlikely they will), the role of the romantic male lead goes, unquestionably, to the character of Ned—a smart, devastatingly handsome, hard-working and loyal man whose prowess as a sharpshooter is celebrated throughout the Cherokee Nation even before the events of this novel unfold.

Both Zeke and Ned are members of the Keetoowah Society, a group dedicated to the preservation of traditional Cherokee ways, formed in the aftermath of the forcible removal of 17,000 Cherokees from their native land, a march known as the Trail of Tears. When we meet Zeke and Ned, however, the Trail of Tears is well behind them. They and their families have spent years building new lives in the West, and this novel is the story of their gradual and increasingly inevitable destruction.

The writers favor a slow, leisurely pace to their storytelling: small talk about livestock and whiskey, crops, hunting, minor family feuds and women. You know as McMurtry and Ossana go into their windup that pretty soon hearts will break and bullets will fly. But the writers are in no hurry to get there.

Part of the pleasure comes from McMurtry and Ossana's obvious enjoyment of the small scene, the seemingly incidental details of daily life in the comings and goings of characters whose lives and world are all about to change dramatically. They give us a long, careful glimpse at how Ned shoots a squirrel or the traits of Zeke's dog; we get small talk down at the courthouse and over breakfast, recounted with a conversational authenticity and understated humor that is a McMurtry trademark.

Zeke and Ned has the tone of a yarn spun over a campfire with plenty of whiskey on hand and nobody in a rush to get anyplace quick. If a new character gets introduced—as several dozen do—the authors are apt to wander off with a side story or two concerning whatever odd trait or interesting piece of family history might be worth knowing.

Indeed, there's matter-of-fact bluntness to the storytelling that suits the bare-bones lives of the characters who inhabit the world of McMurtry and Ossana's novel. One minute Rebecca, Zeke's wife, is telling their 16-year-old daughter, Jewel, to snap beans for dinner. Not half an hour later, Ned has asked for and received her hand in marriage over that dinner of beans. Soon he's saddling up his horse, preparing to ride off with his bride-to-be.

Another writer might have made more of the moment, but the authors recognize that the events unfolding here are melodramatic enough without the insertion of drum rolls. Castrating a pig, marrying off a daughter, planting corn,

shooting your neighbor, burying a child: In the world of this novel, they're part of a day.

To be sure, *Zeke and Ned* is a story of grand-scale tragedy. But it's also about the way disaster grows out of seemingly small mistakes in judgment and flaws of character, infecting like a virus not just whole families but an entire population. The precipitating event is Zeke's attraction to a feisty woman named Polly Beck and his desire (after 17 years of marriage to the quiet, frail but strong-willed Rebecca) to take Polly as his second wife, as allowed by Cherokee tradition.

Recognizing Zeke's attentions to his wife, Polly's jealous husband, T. Spade, sells Zeke a load of corn into which he's shoveled weevils. Zeke seeks retribution but, instead of getting rid of Spade, he ends up shooting Polly, then seeking out Ned's aid to shield him from Polly's vengeful brothers.

When a trial in Cherokee court leads to more shootings (including that of the judge), President Ulysses S. Grant authorizes a party of marshals to hunt down Zeke and Ned. By the time the novel reaches its conclusion, the weevil incident has, at times indirectly, brought about not only murder in the double digits but also miscarriage, amputation by frostbite, blinding, beheading, drowning, rape, madness and suicide.

Recounted with even a trace of melodrama, this story would read like a soap opera. But McMurtry and Ossana favor a wry, matter-of-fact and more than faintly comical tone. In Zeke and Ned's brutal world, a significant character may be dispatched in a sentence or two. The authors know how to sustain a drama played out over a plate of corn and vinegar cobbler, and they do it well.

Consider, for instance, their deft handling of the minor character Cracky Bolen. Cracky's paying a visit to the home of an equally insignificant character, Marshal Dan Maples, and his wife, Wilma; he's trying to track down Zeke and Ned in the aftermath of a blood bath in which, he reports (as he's salting his corncob), 50 people were killed. Dan Maples "did not believe that figure for a moment, and he also did not believe it was the death figure that really interested Cracky Bolen," write Ossana and McMurtry. "The figure that interested Cracky was Wilma's figure, a generous, womanly figure by any standards, and particularly so by Cracky's standards, since his own wife, Myrtle Lou, was skinny as a weed and about as unfriendly."

Within a matter of pages, Maples is lying dead on the ground and the story moves along so fast we barely have a chance to catch the dust as he's biting it. But first, the writers linger for a page or two over the living Maples' obsessive suspicion that his shapely wife may be secretly selling eggs to buy herself hair ribbons. Nothing in this scene—or in the many other equally insignificant tales the writers pause to spin—plays a major or even minor role in furthering the saga of Zeke and Ned. But it's what brings this novel to life; the authors have filled their novel with minor stories and characters, giving as much weight to small human foibles as they do to the ultimate ruin of the characters who stand at its center.

As a sad history of the Cherokee, a fundamentally peaceful tribe destroyed by the white man and brutally transplanted to Oklahoma territory, *Zeke and Ned* is less than wholly successful. While Zeke and Ned belong to a Cherokee society and eventually go to war with the white man's law, there is little in the ways of these men or their families that enlightens the reader about the Cherokee people. Except for the sense of inevitable tragedy awaiting them, there's little here that identifies them as belonging to any particular culture.

But ultimately, the novel isn't diminished by that lack. For this isn't really a story about the downfall of the Cherokee; it's a more universal tale, a novel about bad luck that could happen in just about any culture where men covet women and carry guns. The Cherokee people, unluckier than many, don't hold the patent on that one.

Ultimately, *Zeke and Ned* is an enjoyable, richly entertaining reading experience. Pick up this novel in search of complex characters and subtle portrayals of human psychology, however, and you may be disappointed.

McMurtry and Ossana haven't exactly given us finely wrought, multilayered characters, but my guess is they never intended to. What they lay out instead is historical tapestry on the grand scale, wider than it is deep. In this book, a character is likely to exhibit one or two distinctive traits: an annoying talkativeness, a preoccupation with neatness of dress, a tendency toward lechery or bossiness or drunkenness, a suspicion that one's wife many be selling eggs on the side. No matter.

Even Ned is not exactly a fully formed figure of a man. Tall, handsome, brave and strong, he possesses all the virtues of a mythic hero and no discernible flaws. Much the same can be said about his wife, Zeke's daughter Jewel—a beautiful goddess of a woman, quiet and loyal unto death. They're archetypes, which is exactly what we want them to be.

What McMurtry and Ossana have given us here is a piece of semi-modern mythology—part folk song, part tall tale—set against the backdrop of the post-Civil War frontier. *Zeke and Ned* belongs less to literary tradition, perhaps, than to the oral tradition of wonderful, richly textured storytelling. If the novel were shorter, it would be a great one to read out loud, passed on, embellished further over time, in direct proportion no doubt to how much whiskey the teller's been consuming. You don't ask yourself, as the wagon bounces you along, whether the whole thing makes total sense. You simply enjoy the ride.

Ann Ronald (review date Winter 1998)

SOURCE: A Review of *Texasville*, in *Western American Literature*, Vol. 22, Winter, 1998, pp. 373-74.

[*In the review below, Ronald, a professor at the University of Nevada, argues that* Texasville *does not measure up to earlier novels in the series such as* The Last Picture Show.]

Few literary sequels live up to their critics' expectations. Still, we had high hopes for Larry McMurtry's *Texasville*. Its acclaimed predecessor, *The Last Picture Show*, gave us a rural Thalia in a '50s Texas setting, overlaid with nostalgia and populated by a variety of winsome people. *Texasville* gives us Thalia and her inhabitants thirty years later. The '80s haven't been kind, and the Thalians haven't aged well.

McMurtry's premise has potential. Texas, with oil dictating its economic ups and downs, has changed mightily during the past three decades. Thalia's citizens made fortunes. By the time of *Texasville*, however, the price of oil is plummeting toward five dollars a barrel, the local bank is closing its doors, and today's bankruptcy is threatening yesterday's millionaires. But where the premise suggests some provocative questions, few are answered. Rather than test his characters with genuine problems, McMurtry allows them (and himself) only self-indulgent maunderings.

Several things go amiss in *Texasville*. Because the characters aren't true to themselves, they annoy anyone who remembers their pasts. Sonny of *The Last Picture Show* is now a befuddled bachelor; Duane is an idle rich man with whom we're supposed to identify. Jacy is a reclusive refugee; Ruth, a well-adjusted seventy-year-old who jogs. If the names weren't the same, we would hardly recognize these folk.

We might recognize Thalia. We might even recognize parallel plots. Where the one book examined the growing pains of late adolescence, the other looks at so-called mid-life crises. Both uncover a Thalian psychological set. "I've lived here all my life," Sonny concludes. "If I'm crazy it must be because the town's done it to me. . . . I think we're all crazy now. There's not a sane person left in town. We should get up a class-action suit and sue the town for a lot of money." Duane's monosyllabic response clarifies the theme. "But we are the town," he replies. "If we're crazy, we made ourselves crazy. There's no point in suing ourselves."

When McMurtry is good, he is very very good. I thought *Lonesome Dove* was the finest western novel I had read in years. *Texasville* isn't. With superficial exchanges between characters whose own inertia underscores the motionless milieu of the entire tale, nothing much happens. "People are always racing out of this town," Duane remarks. "I guess they think they can go fast enough to escape gravity and get in orbit somewhere else. But mostly they just turn around and come back." Their return in *Texasville* seems rather unfortunate.

FURTHER READING

Criticism

Bode, Elroy. "Moving on . . . and on . . . and on." *Southwest Review* 55 (Autumn 1970): 427-31.
    Contends that *Moving On* fails to achieve the high quality of *Leaving Cheyenne* and *Horseman, Pass By*.

Cameron, Julia. "McMurtry Goes the Distance." *Los Angeles Times* (7 June 1992): 4, 7.
    Reviews *The Evening Star* and discusses McMurtry's writing style.

Dwinnells, Denise. "'Dove' Sequel Offers Action, Compassion." *Christian Science Monitor* 85, No. 193 (31 August 1993): 15.
    Favorably reviews *Streets of Laredo* and compares it to *Lonesome Dove*.

Jones, Malcolm. "The Ghost Writer at Home on the Range." *Newsweek* 122 (2 August 1993): 52-3.
    Favorably reviews *The Streets of Laredo*.

Mano, D. Keith. "Vegas Deserta." *National Review* XXXV, No. 23 (November 25, 1983): 1495-96.
    Unfavorable review of *The Desert Rose*. Mano criticizes the dialogue and argues that the female characters are such senseless victims that they are not believable.

Schmidtberger, Loren F. A Review of *The Late Child*, by Larry McMurtry. *America* 173, No. 16 (18 November 1995): 28-9.
    Compares the humor of the New York section of *The Late Child* with the somber but moving descriptions of Oklahoma.

Skow, John. "Been There, Done That." *Time* 150, No. 22 (24 November 1997): 106-7.
    Reviews *Comanche Moon* and places it in the context of the other novels in the *Lonesome Dove* series.

Zion, Sidney. "A Legend in J. Edgar Hoover's Time." *New York Times* (16 October 1994): 31.
    Argues that *Pretty Boy Floyd* is unworthy of McMurtry's stature.

Additional coverage of McMurtry's life and career is contained in the following sources published by Gale: *Authors and Artists for Young Adults*, **Vol. 15;** *Authors in the News*, **Vol. 2;** *Bestsellers*, **89:2;** *Concise Dictionary of American Literary Biography*, **1968-1988;** *Contemporary Authors*, **Vols. 5-8, revised edition;** *Contemporary Authors New Revision Series*, **Vols. 19, 43, 64;** *Dictionary of Literary Biography*, **Vols. 2, 143;** *Dictionary of Literary Biography Yearbook*, **1980, 1987;** *DISCovering Authors Modules*: *Novelists, Popular Fiction and Genre Authors*; **and** *Major 20th-Century Writers*, **Vols. 1, 2.**

Anaïs Nin

1903-1977

French-born American novelist, diarist, short story writer, essayist, and critic.

The following entry presents an overview of Nin's career. For further information on her life and works, see *CLC*, Volumes 1, 4, 8, 11, 14, and 60.

INTRODUCTION

Nin is best known for her erotica and seven volumes of diaries published from 1966 to 1981. Her other works, which include novels and short stories, are greatly influenced by surrealism. The surrealist movement was initiated in the 1920s by artists who explored irrationality and the subconscious, in addition to formal experiments of modernists such as D. H. Lawrence and Virginia Woolf, who used expressionistic and stream-of-consciousness narration. Rather than relying on a chronological ordering of events as in conventional narratives, Nin wrote in a poetic style using repetition, omission, and pastiche as organizing principles. As a result, Nin is credited by some feminist critics with embodying *écriture féminine*, or "women's" writing. Others, however, dispute this claim and argue that Nin's work—particularly her *Diary*—is overly self-conscious and written with an audience in mind.

Biographical Information

Nin was born in Paris, France, in 1903, and moved to the United States in 1914 with her mother and two brothers. Her father Joaquin Nin, a Spanish pianist and composer, abandoned the family when Nin was eleven. Shortly afterward, Nin began her diary, written as an extended letter to her father. In Europe, Nin's family was included in wealthy artistic circles because of her parents' musical careers. However, in New York City—for which Nin held a lifelong disdain—Nin and her family lived a comparatively poor life, and Nin helped support the family as a part-time model. At sixteen she dropped out of school after a teacher told her she had a stilted writing style. After dropping out of school, Nin educated herself by reading alphabetically through books in the public library. At twenty she married Hugh Guiler, a banker, and moved back to Paris with him. Nin began writing with publication in mind, but felt torn between her duties as a conservative banker's wife and her desire for artistic expression. Nevertheless, it was around this time that Nin published her first work, *D. H. Lawrence: An Unprofessional Study* (1932), which was well-received. Around this time, she met Henry Miller, then a struggling writer in Paris, through

her lawyer. Miller and his wife June associated with members of Paris's underworld of prostitutes, thieves, and drug addicts. Once introduced to this world, Nin felt her own life even more stifling. To resolve her inner conflicts she entered therapy with the prominent Parisian psychoanalyst Réné Allendy and, later, with Otto Rank. Eventually, Nin studied psychoanalysis under Rank, working in his practice in New York City. In her writing, Nin combined her knowledge of psychoanalysis with vivid depictions of the love triangle she entered with Henry and June Miller, creating her own highly acclaimed style of psychologically incisive erotica. Nin heavily edited her diaries before publication and, at her husband's request, removed all references to him. Nonetheless, the two remained legally married until her death. In the mid-to-late 1930s, Nin, Miller, and other writers in the Villa Seurat circle who experienced difficulty finding publishers founded Siana Editions to publish their own works. Nin in particular could find no one to publish her extended prose poem, *House of Incest* (1936). *House of Incest* and Nin's next book, *Winter of Artifice* (1939), were well-received in Europe. However, when Nin moved back to New York City in 1939 with her husband, she found American publishers even less receptive to her work than those in Europe initially were. Many publishers found Nin's open exploration of female sexuality scandalous and decadent. After several years of trying to place her works with American publishers, Nin bought a second-hand printing press and began to typeset and print her own books. Nin's work eventually caught the attention of critic Edmund Wilson, who praised her writing and helped Nin find an American publisher. It was Nin's *Diary*, however, that brought her the greatest success and critical acceptance. Nin never intended the two hundred manuscript volumes for publication, and many, including Miller, Rank, and Allendy, discouraged her obsessive diary writing. Others in her circle eventually persuaded her to publish the work, which is considered her magnum opus. Following publication of the multi-volume *Diary of Anaïs Nin*, the author became a controversial figure in the feminist movement. She was at once praised for her unflinching examination of the female psyche and vilified as someone who upheld archaic feminine stereotypes. Nevertheless, Nin remained in great demand as a lecturer at universities across the United States until she died of cancer in 1977.

Major Works

Most critics assess the seven published volumes of Nin's *Diary* as a story delineating the birth of Nin as an artist and the development of her feminine artistic temperament. Nin's diaries relate incidents in the present tense, featuring real people who appear as carefully rendered characters in fully realized settings. The diaries share many concerns expressed in Nin's fiction and are divided according to themes such as the life of the creative individual, the effectiveness of psychoanalysis, the relation between the inner and outer worlds, and the nature of sexuality. The volumes include photographs, conversations presented in dialogue form, and letters from Nin's personal correspondence, completing the impression of a thoughtfully orchestrated work of art rather than a spontaneous outpouring of emotions. Nin's first published work, *House of Incest*, is often considered a prose poem due to its intensely resonant narrative. Emphasizing psychological states rather than surface reality, *House* achieves a dream-like quality. *Winter of Artifice* contains three long stories, the first of which, "Djuna," concerns a love triangle that closely resembles the relationship Nin had with Henry and June Miller. *Under a Glass Bell* (1944), another collection of short stories, contains "Birth," one of Nin's most celebrated pieces. In this story, a woman undergoes an excruciating labor, bearing a stillborn child in an experience that symbolically frees her of her past. *This Hunger . . .* (1945), Nin's next collection of short fiction, extends her exploration of the female unconscious in psychoanalytic terms. *Cities of the Interior*, which Nin described as a "continuous novel," is often considered her most ambitious and critically successful project. Between 1946 and 1961, Nin published the work in four parts: *Ladders to Fire*,

Children of the Albatross, *The Four-Chambered Heart*, and *Seduction of the Minotaur*. Each of the four installments follows a female character through her journey to self-discovery. Much of Nin's notoriety is a result of the short erotic pieces she wrote for a patron while living in Paris in the 1940s. Collected in *Delta of Venus* (1977) and *Little Birds* (1979), these works have garnered much commentary regarding their status as literature.

Critical Reception

Nin gained wide acceptance among artists and writers when she first began publishing, largely because of the surrealist elements in her work. But publishers and critics were divided over the "decency" of her writing, which often contained psycho-sexual material. Feminist critics since the 1960s have also questioned the relevance of Nin's work to the women's rights movement and whether it represents support of the movement. On the issue of whether feminine nature is essential (in-born) or material (learned behavior), Nin believed the former. However, some critics point out that Nin's diaries were so heavily edited that they seem contrived. Nin's erotica—labeled by some as outright pornography—earned greater regard in the 1990s. Nin also gained a wider reputation as a brilliant recorder of the mind of a female artist in the twentieth century.

PRINCIPAL WORKS

D. H. Lawrence: An Unprofessional Study (criticism) 1932
House of Incest (prose poem) 1936
Winter of Artifice (short stories) 1939
Under a Glass Bell (short stories) 1944
This Hunger . . . (short stories) 1945
Ladders to Fire (novel) 1946
Realism and Reality (nonfiction) 1946
Children of the Albatross (novel) 1947
On Writing (nonfiction) 1947
The Four-Chambered Heart (novel) 1950
A Spy in the House of Love (novel) 1954
Solar Barque (novel) 1958
Cities of the Interior [contains *Ladders to Fire, Children of the Albatross, The Four-Chambered Heart*, and *Solar Barque*; republished under the same title with *Seduction of the Minotaur* replacing *Solar Barque*] (novels) 1959
Seduction of the Minotaur (novel) 1961
The Diary of Anaïs Nin. 7 Vols. (diaries) 1966-1981
The Novel of the Future (nonfiction) 1968
In Favor of the Sensitive Man and Other Essays (essays) 1976
Delta of Venus (short stories) 1977
Little Birds (short stories) 1979

CRITICISM

Wayne McEvilly (essay date Summer 1971)

SOURCE: "The Bread of Tradition: Reflections on the Diary of Anaïs Nin," in *Prairie Schooner*, Vol. XLV, No. 2, Summer 1971, pp. 161-67.

[*In the following essay, McEvilly interprets Nin's writing in her diary as a poetic examination of the self.*]

("I'm the alchemist, not the ego." Nin)

In the world of Proust the sound of the spoon and the taste of the madeleine were able to efface the ego and to allow the mysterious person—"that person," as Proust himself says, as though he were, in his ecstatic illumination, like those ancient Indian seers who when they had reached that level beneath the state of dreamless sleep could designate it only by the neutral, and yet quite fecund, word *That*, which in Sanskrit is even more neutral for it may be pronounced without the benefit of teeth, so that even an ancient seer in that final stage of physical dissolution which so fascinated Proust as he meditated on the devastation of the faces along the Guermantes Way, in the enchanted yet all-too-mortal environs of the Princess, could articulate the word with utter clarity: TAT.

In the world of Anaïs Nin we find a trust which makes the Proustian analytic unnecessary, superfluous, for it is as if she knew that every sound is the sound of the magic spoon, every taste that of the madeleine which restores to us that paradise which we had indeed inhabited but without the conscious realization that we were living it—and since this acute sensibility of the paradisiacal element of all experience is for Nin an abiding state and not merely one which hovers at the difficult and distant edges of experience, in her promised surprises as the Madam Venus of the House of Erotica there will be, indeed there already is, the reverberations of that eternal spoon. Or was it a fork? Those who have visited Proust's world know that it does not matter, whether fork or spoon, for it is the reverberation to which one must listen with Proust's delicately attuned ear, and Proust himself grew vague, saying sometimes spoon, sometimes fork, with what to a literalist would no doubt be a shocking lack of attendance to detail. Or was it simply music, the hidden harmony of objects which only the phenomenon of real music objectifies, music heard only perhaps by those who might be, as it were, deaf to certain other sounds, deaf to the concrete music of literal existence in order to hear. . . . To hear what? One would like to be able to clarify the relation of the art of Nin to the world of music, to articulate precisely how and that and why they are one, but this particular aspect of her world, so clear in the experience of

reading her art, continues to elude attempts at specific formulation, and one must finally content himself with a seemingly dogmatic utterance. The diary is music.

Beneath the surface sustained by the sense of a strong and bristling vividity the diary lives another life as a phenomenology of anguish. An entry for the Fall, 1943: "For many days I lived without my drug, my secret vice, my diary. And then I found this: I could not bear the loneliness." At times the concern with anxiety surfaces, becomes the specific subject under consideration, and the clairvoyant sensibility of the diarist reveals new depths here, also, as in the universal transmutation effected by art even the failures, horrors, fissures, witherings, and finally that most mysterious visitation of nothing itself which is the possession of the soul by absolute horror—that too is heroically transformed into poetry, into humanity, until out of the dread experience the diarist has forged a vision of the foundation of our brotherhood. When I feel anguish, there is nothing there—am I then feeling the subaqueous horror of others? Horrors we share, mute, vague, terrible? Is there a communion here? From nothing, nothing comes? Or from nothing all things are brought forth? "Pray, what was your father saying?—Nothing." Thus ends the first chapter of that most intimate of novels whose playful surface also masks a profound phenomenology of despair—*Tristram Shandy*. Anguish, anxiety—subtle horrors, but none the less real.

("*All one has must be shared, given—secrets, techniques.*" Nin)

The poet speaks of giving, and in doing so gives. Through words we come to discover the essential drama which has always been the same. Writing in service of *moksha*. Laurence Sterne, too, said it quite simply: "—for never do I hit upon any invention or device which tendeth to the furtherance of good writing, but I instantly make it public; willing that all mankind should write as well as myself.—Which they certainly will, when they think as little." Laurence Sterne—the bodhisattva in motley, with his fool's bells and his fool's black page (alas, poor Yorick!), his consciousness hiding consciousness, his subtlety masked as psychic-poetic fire-works, his own secret jewel in a lotus intricate as any passion flower, yet allows himself to say, all freely and openly, that his art is the sharing of secrets. Intimacy. The word ought to be whispered. *Sotto voce*.

The writer really at work writing—as opposed to reflecting on the craft, its dangers, despairs, relations to life, to art—is a lapidary whose creation is the jewel, that jewel which in Sanskrit is known as Vajra—immortal diamond, the illuminating thunderbolt of the gods around which, and into whose depths, meditations have been sustained in order to pierce certain essential secrets, in a quest for the absolute which never ends, never passes, that for which one might die in order to live, death having two faces, and writing itself being the disciplined formation of the jewel which is the penetrating and quickening light shining in the darkness of all psyches, all souls, in the darkness of the universal soul, the one, a light which comes to destroy the negative charms and spells of that most ineluctable and inescapable of dread facts—the passage of time. The jewel must be beautiful, if it is to effect its countermagic, its spell—and this for no mere matter of embellishment, adornment, no mere matter of plumage but of flesh, of life, of bread, and of death. Why must it be beautiful? (Our age has forgotten this.) Why is the writer's primary obligation to beauty? (Our age has forgotten this.) Because he must know, if he has seen what he must have seen in order to write a visionary work—for it is a matter, too, of vision—that the human creature is sufficiently and—yes, let me most insistently drum upon the bass notes here—quintessentially wounded that he will listen only to song.

The world must be loved because it is beautiful, not because it is real, which it may—who knows? Who could possibly know?—very well not be. And the poet is the lover of the world—a definition which Nin has taken upon herself, a definition which entails, appropriately enough, what one might have been tempted to have called obligation, were it not for the aesthetically misleading over-tones of that beleaguered word.

In the most recently published volume of the diaries, the third, there is the fulfilled promise of a change of scenery, a transition from tragedy to comedy, and the background is now an often mad Vanity Fair, a comic literary New York, comic even in its passions, its poverties, while the neurosis of a deaf dancer is placed barely within reach of the discriminating eye, at the back of the stage, where it joins the madness of Artaud, hospitals, asylums, the past, and the diarist writes in full self-consciousness but without a restricting self-involvement as the Madam Venus of a House of Erotica. The diary has moved freely from horror to ecstasy, following the pattern of life itself, and there is as strong a refusal to despair as there is a refusal to maintain a false sense of flight where everything is suffused with significance, there being here no high, no low. Sanity prevails— "Tranquillity is contagious, peace is contagious. One only thinks of the contagiousness of illness, but there is the contagion of serenity and joy. Neurosis is the real demon, the only real possession, the real evil force in the world. And it is curable" (Winter 1942).

Nin's is not a writer's notebook, a diary in the sense of standing aside from the art with the intention of commenting on more important matters. ("I'm the alchemist, not the ego.") It is itself the vast production sustained, one feels, by an utter silence concerning the matter most at hand, a matter which is at once all exquisitely hidden and all artfully revealed. One of the supreme values of fiction is the contextual transformation which it allows to otherwise hopelessly indelicate direct statements, a transformation which indeed puts wings on the commonplace and rids the world of excess weight, of the moral, for instance, of the practical, and we fly beyond good and evil, delighting in murder, one might say—and that to mention only one of many facets. "We should submit ourselves to an unknown fear." Without the transforming context, that is the statement of a tiresome moralist, yet the indelicacy of such a direct statement can be eradicated by the efficient adoption of a most happily convenient fiction. The King's a beggar. Now the play is done. Or, to be most indelicately direct, the diary is precisely that novel of the future about which Nin has spoken in her recent book of literary theory. It is a sustained image of dispersion which becomes, as those immediate things which it describes and reveals fade into oblivion, the agent which keeps before us life which has passed, and in so doing effectively denies that life itself passes, the revelation itself being of eternal poetic meaning.

Many great writers have kept diaries, some not being above a scribbling down of whatever might enter the head, yet there is a certain recognition of self which must always play havoc with the art—and by some mysterious extension of such an unclarified principle one might in a moment of all-too-fleeting clarity intuit something utterly vitiating in the habitual act of paying attention to a crude reality untransformed by vision, at the expense of what one might call, without having, of course, to bother defining the term, art. There might be a principle of composition lurking in the dense underbrush of thought to which such an intuition would no doubt have given a vigorous if veiled birth. That is to say, there are diaries which do not enter into the prerequisite intimacy which is perhaps alone sufficient to justify our speaking of the presence of fiction. Nin's diaries are fiction, even if true—as though the matter of corresponding truth were indeed not only inessential but magnificently, even joyfully, wide of the mark. The sense of reality is the artist's creation, and Nin writes the myth of cities, friends, domestic events, shoes and hats, dances, parties, poets, pets (an organ grinder's monkey leaps off the page, delighting children, for he is also Hanuman of the Ramayana), and the fact becomes the myth which it always was but which without the artist's—one is tempted to say compassionate—intervention and invention it would never have become. The world indeed cries out for the love of the poet, the touch of the poet, the speech of the poet, one of whose guises is that of Vishnu, the preserver.

("*I have given myself to the care of more mysterious anguish.*" Nin)

Out of the universal experience of human anguish, human bondage, the diarist fashions a literature of bread and a fellowship of the abandoned. There is a literature of the bread of the spirit which nourished us as the mystical wafer which is art, based upon an intimacy than which there is none greater, as between brother and sister, friend and friend, lover and beloved, parent and child—the fellowship of the abandoned, which is perhaps at once the most intimate and the most universal of human bonds, that which even in a last analysis could not be broken, for the basis of its being is not willed or chosen or invented or even created but rather woven into the fabric and texture of our existence. The warp might be hidden from sight, but with age, or violence, with disease, or sudden change, with the erosion of time or the disappearance of all texture, all substance, as in metaphysical insight of moments when the real is suddenly seen as illusory, the illusory as real, the illusory as illusory, when the shadow is seen as shadow of faded shadow, we fall back on the indestructible warp of the human condition as abandoned. Out of this arises the most poignant and at once the most ineradicable passion for communion. If this is not the theme of the diary, as of all our literature of bread, from Tristram and Quixote to the Wake and beyond, then I am at a loss as to what is and as to why we persist in going to literature as if it were food. "Feed on us before you bury us." That is the voice of the great diarist whose diary is fiction, but what she says has been said by every great writer of our—and let me pause here before the word which ought to be uttered with full consciousness of its meaning, indeed as though there were the air of a certain necessity, perhaps even, to speak in consonance with the consciousness of that princess who approached the ivory tower and adorned pagoda of The Golden Bowl, perhaps even the necessity, yes, of removing one's very shoes—our tradition. It is the only theme—"A single note. Yes."

Anaïs Nin with Barbara Freeman (interview date 1972)

SOURCE: "A Dialogue with Anaïs Nin," in *Chicago Review*, Vol. 24, No. 2, 1972, pp. 29-35.

[*In the following interview, Nin and Freeman discuss the nature of diary writing, in particular the lack of integrity of individual personality over a lifetime and differences between life as lived and as written, as well as criticism of one's own writing and that of others.*]

Although her works survived in relative isolation for many years, Anais Nin has now become a resonant voice for many readers, especially women, primarily through her published *Diaries*. The collage of her life in Louvouciennes and Paris (with Henry Miller, Artaud, and Lawrence Durrell among others), of her work as a lay analyst with Otto Rank in New York, and the world of writers and artists in America is the rich substrate for her novels.

The *Chicago Review* first took notice of Anais Nin in 1949 in Violet Lang's review of her short stories and *Winter of Artifice.* She spoke for the *Review* that year at the University of Chicago. She published her story **"Sabina"** in 1962 (*CR*, vol. 15, no. 3). This year, Miss Nin comes to Chicago again in November under the auspices of the *Chicago Review* Speaker Series.

Miss Freeman interviewed Anais Nin during her recent visit to the University of California, Berkeley.

[*Barbara Freeman:*] *Talking to you right now seems at the same time to be completely natural and yet . . . who am I talking to? There is a difference between a book and a person in the flesh . . .*

[Anais Nin:] There isn't very much with me, because I've always tried to match the work and the life. The thing that may be difficult for you, knowing the diaries as certain periods, is which period are we getting into? That's difficult for me, too. For instance, if you ask me about the childhood, or if you ask me about the period in France, if you ask me about the period in America, those are very distinct periods when I was a different self too. A different person. So *I* have difficulty, not you, and I sometimes ask, "which period are we in?" Are we in the French part of the life, are we in the period in America, or are we in the present? The present activities, or Volume Four, which is closer? That's my own thing, because in each period you do feel that it's a different self. I don't think the same way as I did when I was twenty . . . That's why I think the diary is so faithful. Because it's written at the moment. When I used to read it back I would say, "You mean, I really thought that at twenty?" I don't always approve, I didn't always agree with myself at thirty. That's why I'm sure that biography and memory are not faithful, because we rearrange those things. I look at myself with my eyes today at the eleven year old girl and I see it quite differently. But it wasn't that way at all and I have a proof of it in the diary where I say this and this and that. It's a very strange thing. It makes you think that memory is not to be relied on. Because it's my memory today, and you rearrange it. You don't mean to, but you reinterpret it, so I see myself at twenty quite differently, and then I read the diary and I said, "Oh, no, at twenty I had that feeling, I had rebellions and I had melancholia."

So it must be that when you edit the diaries, it must be almost like editing the diary of another person . . .

. . . Somebody else, and I must be very careful not to cheat. I mustn't cheat because that would ruin it completely. That's why there are things in the First Diary that embarrass me, that I would rather have changed. The narcissism when you're concerned with relationships. They're things I wish I could improve on. But that would have ruined the diary, which is evolution. So I'm enough of a scientist to think that I want to see the growth of it as it happened, with the mistakes, with the errors, and the stumblings and the fumblings.

When you were beginning to write, when you wrote **House of Incest** *and the two novels before it, did you show the novels to many friends, ask for criticism?*

Yes. Oh yes. I showed them to close friends. The first one was very bad, very bad. It was a D. H. Lawrence imitation. I left it to the students of Evanston because I wanted them to see that a writer can write a bad novel so they won't feel so awful about their first novels. Because usually they read you, when you have already become a good craftsman, and when they don't imagine that you could write a poor novel. But I did write a very, very bad novel. In the first place, I learned my English from the library; some of it was Victorian, some of it was modern, it was a jumble of English. And secondly, I was under the influence of D. H. Lawrence, so it sounded like a bad imitation of him.

Have you read any imitations of your novels . . . yet?

No. I don't think I'm easy to imitate. No, I can't say I have. It always used to worry me, in one way I was worried, in another way I was glad, that I didn't have any disciples in that sense. And I used to think, well, I didn't really influence my friends because my friends write very differently from me. So I can't say I have anybody who writes as if they had been trained by me. Or felt very close to my style. I don't know why that is, whether it's a good or a bad thing.

How do you want to touch your readers? If you had an "ideal reader" what would the response be?

Well, there are two answers to that. There's one reader who reads the diary, which is a direct and a human experience, and responds to that. But the response to the novels was a great disappointment to me, when they came out before the diaries. Because in the novels there was a myth, and I wanted that myth to raise the standard of our life a little bit, just above the ground, just a little bit above the daily facts and the things that oppress us and the heavy, daily contingencies. The novels were, in that sense, a little bit abstract. They're like poetry. And *that* people didn't read well. Now they do. But they didn't then—certainly not in the forties or the thirties. So there are two kinds of responses I would like . . . one, a response as to poetry or music; and the other a human one.

Except your novels are so human too . . .

Well, they didn't seem to be to critics so far.

Really? Still?

Yes, there is certainly a much stronger reaction to the diaries. And then when they have read the diaries, they're willing to go back, and then they find some completions in the novels, some interlocking.

It seems to me that in the continuous novels, Lillian's development is traced more completely.

Yes.

The others are left in process, not yet resolved . . .

These things are sometimes very unconscious and mysterious. The fact that Lillian was taken from a real person. In the novels, usually all my characters are taken from reality, they are all someone. And it happened that this one person had been associated with Mexico. And how do you know how those things happen? I went and got to know Mexico very well . . . But why I didn't pick Sabina, I know the reason. In Sabina, there wasn't really anything to develop . . . no. Now Djuna could have been developed into something else but I didn't do that. I really dropped the novels. In a sense they're not finished.

Well, when you were working on novels . . . when you started, how much of a definite story line, structure . . .

None whatever.

None . . .

None whatever, no. That's what I said in **The Novel of the Future,** following free association. That's why I can't answer you why I followed Lillian, and not the others. When you follow free association like that and it does come from some subconscious source, you don't, you can't plan ahead. I couldn't plan ahead, I didn't know what was going to happen to them. It happened as I lived, in a way. It would happen as I lived and saw something new, or discovered some other aspect of them or understood them with a different kind of vision. They would change with me. So there was really a happening in that sense.

You created these three women and then you followed their lives . . .

Yes. Well, I created them in part and took them in part from reality. And then I knew their lives, and I saw their lives differently as my vision changed. Time changed them too. So there was a constant change, which is keeping up with life

. . . Because our lives make a pattern. You don't know it but it does . . .

That's why I made the comment earlier about faith . . . (laugh) . . . backtracking with you, because it takes a great deal of trust in life to know that what happens to you makes a pattern.

Yes. There's a trust in your own understanding of life. In other words, things do happen and they seem accidental and they seem incidental but they're really not and the minute we have an understanding of them we say, "Of course that goes well, that would happen to this person and there is a pattern." It's not the usual pattern that people want. And this is what men find hard to read, believe me, men's objections . . .

They're brought up more to believe that they should control.

I've seen friends of mine design their whole plot, their whole story . . . Do you remember Zola making horoscopes of his characters? He would give them a birthday and then have their horoscope made, and that would be those characters. But that's sort of fun. That's one thing Miller and I had in common, that we both believed in writing without plan or structure.

When you're writing a novel, where are you? What is the balance between the dreamer and the critic who says, "I didn't describe this well enough"?

Well, let's put it this way. The critic is not involved at all in the writing. The writing is trusting, it's subconscious. The critic only comes afterwards, when I'm all through, when I begin to look over what I've done and see if it's right. Sometimes if you are following an association there are times when the writing is foggy and not very well focused. And so the critic comes in and says, "This part must come out." Usually, it ends up in my taking it out. It's like a poem almost. What doesn't come out right, there's something wrong with, basically, that can't be fixed, I think.

Do you feel there's any distinction between your life and your art?

No. No, they only feed each other. For instance, to put it in a humorous way, if my life isn't interesting, I worry that the Diary won't be interesting. They tyrannize over each other in a nice way, in a gentle way. There's a standard that I've set, that I want to live and work and write everything as closely together as possible. And so it works . . . You know, the only time I ever took LSD, once during the Huxley period, it worked into a synthesis of music, painting, words. It really made a complete, absolute unity, which shows that

that was my aim, and I work at that, it's not a conscious wish. It's something I need, to be in harmony, and the friends and the things you choose, everything to correspond to the meaning.

I think of that . . .

You agree with that?

Yes . . . for me, I think of that union of life and art, that marriage, as Lillian going home in **Seduction of the Minotaur** *. . . there are certain things, people, places, climates all through your life that attract you, architecture, styles, words . . . Often the books that I love most use certain words, words that all through my life I've pursued, followed and I've made lists of them.*

Yes. Do you have key words, too? I have key words. Remember I told you, they're all in the dictionary under "trans"?

Also, "intimacy" . . .

Yes . . . And the "trans" words I love very much. I just fall in love with those words—transform, transfigure, translucent, transpose. Transparent. Transparent. (Said together) (laughter)

I wonder why you more than other writers have been made into a myth, a legend to be worshipped. You seem to lend yourself to that . . .

It's very simple—I give others the desire to write and paint and do things, so they think there's something magical about me. And I think there's nothing more magical about it than the fact that I wish it. I wish others to write, I think them to be painting, to be doing music. The wish is there, and when I was sixteen, when I was being a model for the painters, they all used to send for me because they said they painted better. But they painted better because I was nothing more than that. It was that kind of magic. And that makes it seem like magic and a legendary thing, but it isn't . . . Most models just sit there, waiting for the time to pass, looking at the clock—and the painter feels it. But I was learning about colors and I was very interested and I think I knew if that one was going to be good and it really showed, that probably does something to other people.

You've said that you aren't writing the diary as such any more, that it is more now a record of your correspondence.

Yes, letters going back and forth. I'm not worried about it because I think that's another phase of the diary. It's a corresponding with the world, and that's what I must have wanted because I started it to connect with my father. So this is another kind of fulfillment. Now the diary volumes are really letters from everywhere. And I find that also very interesting.

I remember in **The Novel of the Future,** *you say, "the truest objectivity of all is to see what others see, to feel what others feel." Is that it?*

Not quite, no. I was thinking more of the completion of a character. I was thinking of the people in my diary as characters. And people used to tease me about it. Daniel Sterne said, "You're talking as if you're writing fiction, you're talking about characters." I think of them as completions. Does that add to them, does this complete them, is this necessary to their portrait and is it necessary also to my own? I'm doing two things—I'm portraying you and I'm portraying myself, so the choice lies much more in that.

When I write portraits, or when I write anything for that matter, it's weeks, months before I can go back and even ask those questions.

Yes, but that's very good. The best critic is time. The best critic is waiting. I often wait with articles, I really do. A week or two and then I re-read it, and that's the critic. (laugh) Why do you shake your head?

Oh, I'm always afraid to re-read my stuff.

But I think you are your best critic. You are the only one who knows what you intend to do. Nobody else really does that. And you're the only one who can ask: did I do what I intended to do. And you can answer that with time, because time makes you more objective.

It's always very hard for me to know . . . the tension between communication and self-expression . . . I always feel that I've expressed what I've wanted to express, but don't know if I've communicated it to anyone beside myself.

Yes, but then that's the confirmation . . . But then think of the writer . . . Well, I had to spend twenty years with complete silence about the novels, and still believe in them. Without confirmation from the critics or the world. I did have confirmation from close friends but sometimes you don't trust your friends because you think they are always in your favor.

We're getting back to some of the critical standards we were talking about in the kitchen before . . . I can feel that I have articulated something important to me, expressed some emotional truth, some essence, some view of a moment, but do you believe that if I've done that, that other people will find it of value, of meaning?

Yes. But you have to be ready for not having the right per-

son at that moment say, "Yes, you have done it, you have said it, and I understand it." You have to be ready not to find it instantly, which is what the writer dreams about. He writes and it comes out of the oven, it's warm, he goes to the stage and reads it and he knows, right away, whether he's good or not . . .

What more can you say about books then? "Does the author do what he sets out to do?" Is that all you can say, as a critic?

I think you can be honest, First of all, there are some writers who have done what they have done well. Even though you may not like it. The writers you respect but do not love.

Yes, like Virginia Woolf, say.

All right. Then you can put her in that group. But you can pay homage to that: it's beautifully written and visionary and she is a poet . . . Of course, you know, we don't get a very true picture of Virginia Woolf from her *Writer's Notebook* because it was so heavily edited by her husband to conceal her periods of disturbance and turbulence.

I don't want to judge destructively, because I have suffered so much from that. I don't want to say, "Burroughs is worth absolutely nothing," just because I don't enjoy his book. I will never say that. But I will say that it is not the book I want to read and keep by my bedside. And I think the best thing of all is how someone put it—"What I cannot love I leave alone." I just won't say anything about it.

The problem for me is getting to the deepest level where personal and universal merge. Because they do, and your work has shown that they do, but it can be damn hard to get there.

I know. It's hard. I think at this point it would be more important for you to write as an individual, than as a critic. Until you can reach that clear plateau where you can distinguish between what you love and what you don't love.

Unless criticism can be an articulation of why you love what you love and what you don't love, on the assumption that if it's real enough to you, it will connect with other's feelings too.

Well, there's still different kinds of connections. There are people who feel as William Burroughs does, and there are people who respond to that very cold sort of skeleton, the French school, that whole group with Grillet "le roman nouveau," the new novel, there are things for every taste. I didn't really care for that either, except Duras. Because the other is destructive. It's what so many critics do. If they don't understand you, they destroy you. And that's such a terrible thing. They've done that with Marguerite Young—the book was too big, they didn't understand it so they damn it and—you wouldn't do that? Just because a book didn't reach you?

Yes, being personal is not enough. The reviewer who gets into a tantrum because he does not understand the book is the wrong kind of personal reaction. You also have to learn to go beyond your prejudices or your limitations. The personal I mean is defined as one who *feels* and *responds* to the writer and can therefore penetrate his meaning more deeply.

Ekbert Jaas (essay date Winter 1978)

SOURCE: "'The Barbaric Friendship with Robert': A Biographical Palimpsest," in *Mosaic*, Vol. 11, No. 2, Winter 1978, pp. 141-52.

[*In the following essay, Jaas discusses Nin's influence on the poetic and personal explorations of the poet Robert Duncan, particularly in light of their respective diary-writing.*]

His portrait in the *Photographic Supplement to The Diary of Anaïs Nin*,[1] Robert Duncan remarked, shows him "posed with [his] eyes cast down in a revery with heavy eyelids and [his] mouth closed in some secret thought or dream."[2] There is an almost identical pose in an Anaïs Nin portrait from the same period—her eyes, again in Duncan's words, "cast down in a revery, her eyelids heavy as if in dream . . . her mouth at once sweet and reserved" (*Caesar's Gate*, p. xxx). The similarity between the two poses, however, is as striking as the contrast between the photograph of Duncan in question and the verbal portrait of him which Nin provided in the *Diary* itself: "Robert, *l'enfant terrible*, perverse and knowing. . . . His eyes are too widely opened, like a medium in a trance" (III. 170).

This description of Duncan, which he quotes and discusses in his introduction to a 1972 reprint of *Caesar's Gate*, occurs in Nin's journal notes for November, 1941, when, according to Duncan, she "had come to a revolting vision" of her previous friend. "Writing in her diary," Duncan comments, "she sees my sensuality as 'exasperated'. . . . Then there follows, as she writes to rid herself of the oppressive attendant I had become for her, even a vice, a vision of me as a whorish caricature of a possibility"; and he goes on to quote Nin:

> His face became that of the coquette, receiving
> flowers with a flutter of the eyelashes, oblique
> glances like the up-turned corner of a coverlet . . .

the stage bird's sharp turn of the head, the little dance of alertness, the petulance of the mouth pursed for small kisses that do not shatter the being, the flutter and perk of femininity, all adornment and change, a mockery of the evanescent, mysterious fluidities of woman, a mockery of her invitations, a burlesque of her gestures of alarm or promise.

> (*Caesar's Gate*, p. xxx; cf. *Diary* III, 92)

Duncan's quotations from Nin's *Diary* are as accurate as Nin's quotations from his unpublished journal often are not. But Duncan errs in claiming that Nin's description of him follows her other comment on his "exasperated" sensuality. Actually, the "coquette" passage appears in Nin's notes for January, 1941: that is, almost a year before the final break which supposedly led to her "revolting vision" of Duncan. And though it may well have helped Nin to rid herself of her "oppressive attendant," such exorcism is more likely to have taken place when she prepared her diary for publication, rather than in January, 1941.

What then could have motivated Nin to immortalize Duncan in a photograph so unlike the "whorish caricature" she describes and so like the portrait she included of herself? Was it by way of paying final tribute to a spiritual kinship with a friend who at one point in her life had stood "nearest" and "clearest" to her above all others? (*Diary* III, 82). Duncan's own suggestion—that in the photographic resemblance he "may be her ape" (*Caesar's Gate*, p. xxx)—seems to add to the mystery of their "barbaric friendship" (*Diary* III. 187) rather than to provide us with the answer. Although he accuses Nin of "smalltown bigotry," his own interpretation of his relationship with the older woman hardly gives us a more flattering portrait of his former self than that contained in Nin's *Diary*:

> I was, then, one of your *maricas*, Garcia Lorca, one of those "esclavos de la mujer" . . . ten years after your season in that city as hell, I sought to infect myself with the Fall itself. . . . In the New York of 1940 I roamed the streets and made the round of bars, like a soul making a round of lives, to find some adventure of love; but it was also nightly to find a place to sleep, for I was no more than a loiterer in the entourage of an obscurely celebrated would-be star, a kept ape, but for no more than the board—a hustler then, of a pariah sort, transient in my passions, seeking to take hold among more fortunate drifters.

> (*Caesar's Gate*, p. xxix, xxxii)

Duncan's unpublished notebooks, the letters he received from Nin, and my own extensive conversations with the poet have revealed yet another image of his youthful self which, beyond a few basic traits, has little in common with either Nin's or Duncan's own. They also disclosed a process of writing and rewriting, interpretation and reinterpretation, which has obscured the story of their relationship under several graphs of fictionalization.

To be sure, even an attempt to decipher the earliest traces of this palimpsest cannot touch the original facts of bodies and emotions, conversations, gestures and silences. All that survives, apart from a few photographs and drawings, are once more words on paper, most of them in diaries written for open display amongst friends and with the ineluctable portion of unconscious or even deliberate self-dramatization that Duncan's journals display throughout. What may emerge, then, in the following collage of quotations,[3] pieced together from the earliest versions of these legends, is but one more life-graph or bio-graph, itself to be superseded by yet another, in the form of a portrait of Anaïs Nin which Duncan, as he told me, plans to include in a yet to be written section of his *H.D. Book*.

When I first met Duncan in the summer of 1973, there was little in his commanding but rather remote and austere presence to prepare one for the subsequent disclosure of his youthful personality in the words of the poet himself, or Anaïs Nin, and others I have interviewed since then. Here is Nin's portrait of the young poet after their first meeting in Woodstock late in 1939: "a strikingly beautiful boy, who looked about seventeen, with regular features, abundant hair, a furnish expression" (*Diary* III, 16). The site of the meeting was a log cabin inhabited by James and Blanche Cooney who were the first in America to show interest in Nin's work and to publish some of her stories in the magazine *Phoenix*. As Nin remembers, Duncan read one of his poems, perhaps "Toward the Shaman," and "talked obsessionally, overintently, overwillfully, as if he wanted to hypnotize me" (*Diary* III, 159).

Duncan must have anticipated the encounter with some eagerness, for even before it took place Anaïs Nin had come to play an influential role in his life. As he mentioned to a friend in January, 1940, his feeling that there were "the same dynamics of love" in Nin's story **"Birth"** as in D. H. Lawrence's work had led him "to read more Anaïs Nin and then to discover in search for more Nin, *Phoenix* and Jimmy Cooney and Miller." The results were crucial ones in the poet's life. *The Phoenix* became the first magazine to publish Duncan outside the college journals, while his subsequent review of *Tropic of Capricorn*, in his own *Experimental Review* (November, 1940), won Miller's enthusiastic approval as the best criticism of his work published till then. It comes closer than any other, Miller wrote Duncan, "to expressing what I feel about my work myself. It puts you immeasurably above *all* American critics and also above

such nincompoops as Eliot and Pound and Huxley *et alia*" (Unpublished letter of 26 Dec. 1940).

Moreover, Nin's work had a more direct though problematic influence on the poet's. According to the **Diary, House of Incest** inspired Duncan "to state the visionary experience of the poet, his sense of ritual" and made him write "Arctics" after reading Nin's prose poem in the fall of 1939 (III, 18). As Duncan himself wrote to Nin in December, 1940, **House of Incest** also inspired "Toward the Shaman," a poem he had already come to see as "very limited" in its "range of perceptions": "My *Shaman* is an emanation of a cosmic myth world awakened by your **House of Incest**—it is my journey in the territories of the Saint of Persia . . . illuminated by the ways of consciousness made articulate through your work."

Then, of course, there was also the venture into "erotic" writing. After finding an old and wealthy client for her erotica in December, 1940, Nin instigated a veritable epidemic of "erotic journals" amongst her friends: "All of us need money, so we pool our stories. I could not turn them out fast enough, so I inserted some of Robert's, some of Virginia's, some of George Barker's," Those written by Duncan, who also offered "to test [their] inventions" (**Diary** III, 70), must have been of particular appeal, although not to the poet himself. When Nin, in the summer of 1941, had Virginia Admiral make a separate copy of Duncan's *Erotica*, the poet wondered "what sort of thing you can really make of it" given the fact that his "scenes have no real continuity."

It was quite a different matter with the journals proper, a literary pursuit which determined Duncan's creativity for several years. Although full of brilliant forays into diverse literary modes, they ultimately tell the story of an artistic impasse. Yet to their initiator they promised the very opposite. "I fell in love with the pages from the Journal," Anaïs wrote to Robert in December, 1940 (Unpublished undated letter). And even their first major quarrel, caused by Nin's rejection of Patchen, only seems to have enhanced this enthusiasm. "I am suffering, because you are afraid of Kenneth Patchen" (*cf.* **Diary** III, 81). Duncan shortly afterwards wrote to Nin, exhorting her to follow his example: "I am beginning to write more like Patchen . . . I am beginning to talk directly, brutally. . . . But I fear and hate you when I think that you have resolved to stay in the House of Incest . . . . YOU HAVE NEVER ESCAPED—together shall we destroy this bondage in this book? Every day I shall gain power because I have to discover for you a new door." After jotting them down in a feverish outburst of despair, Duncan hurried to hand his effusions to Nin who sent him the following reply:

> Robert, all you desired came true. "Every day I shall gain power because I have to discover for

you a new door." You have done this. You have freed me. You stand nearest and clearest. The miracle came with your diary. It was a complete emotional revelation, and as such a gift of the self. . . . I began to omit, retract, vanish. So I begin again. . . . Robert conquered me. He came first as a child—Enfant Terrible, perverse and knowing. But suddenly he grew large, strong, firm. . . . We never touch physically but I am under his spell. . . . Robert creates the enchantment in which I alone can live. . . . I think it is that I love him completely, whatever the form he takes. The part of him that is a woman I feel but as a double. I feel always the strength. Our complete knowledge of each other is so strong that we are beyond judgment, reservations and absolutions. We have penetrated each other. . . . I am out of the house of death. Robert saved me.

(Unpublished undated letter)

In contrast to Nin, Duncan never recovered the enthusiasm he had felt for his friend before this first quarrel. By mid-January, 1941, a sense of unreality began to surround his memory of their earlier relationship—"how we met always like figures on a stage—the touching was not real touching, the speeches were not real talking." And on January 23, he announced "the end of volume one of the Journal called *chez* Anaïs":

the spectral lovers are all gone and the volume closes the House of Anaïs.

During the same period he stopped reading Nin's diaries (see *Diary* III, 92) and decided against publishing his own—"at least not in the Experimental Review." But his subsequent announcement of the "END OF THE JOURNAL" and of "the return of the poem" from the beginning of February, 1941, proved to be self-deceptive. True enough, there are the first poetic traces of an impulse that some years later was to engender "An African Elegy." And, suddenly emerging from the prose, there are several pages of Whitmanesque rhythms anticipating the revolutionary thrust that was to erupt in *Howl*:

America, America—what a nest of old teeth, spectacle ruins, glasses without bottoms—the great dump yard—only the dump yards here have a soul. . . .

And the great body of this nation stuffed with straw. . . . Everyone here is stillborn. The women aren't fucked well enough. Our mothers are of a race that killed. . . . This nation without love, without hate—only greed. Greed, it has been written upon the brow of America, it is written indelibly

upon the lips, the breasts, the cunt, the ass. . . . This is the insane idiotic dance of America—this is the song of the completely slap-happy. I'M HAPPY AMERICA! the crosseyed eagle with nuts like a bull in July.

This impulse, prompted by the anxieties of his pre-draft period, seems to have been stifled during his actual three months stay in the army. And before Duncan managed to obtain a discharge for homosexuality in the summer of 1941, the old specter of the journal had recaptured his imagination in the guise of a new plan. As he announced to his painter friend, Virginia Admiral (and subsequently to Anaïs Nin), he now wanted to write a novel—"a sort of copulation of the Anatomy of Melancholy—Max Ernst and Boris Karloff, Cummings and the Commedia dell' Arte, The House of Incest and the Arabian Nights with the base line of the Journal."

More than anything else, the plan had the effect of launching him into a period of voracious novel reading, during which Dorothy Richardson, Virginia Woolf, Henry James and others gradually superseded Anaïs Nin as Duncan's literary models. Although the poet set about writing and partly rewriting pieces about his childhood, the Anaïs Nin period, or his subsequent marriage, the novel as a whole, originally planned for completion by the end of 1941, never developed beyond its initial conception. Even as late as August 28, 1946, however, telling a friend about his "years with Anaïs Nin and vividly recalling the turbulent display of these early journals," Duncan tried to map "the context in which [he] turn[ed] again to a journal." Yet by now his sense of a diary as fiction had reached an intensity strong enough to smother the autobiographical impulse in its own *reductio ad absurdum*, and there are few pages of such writing in the unpublished notebooks beyond the following statement: "This is the journal then of a young man . . . who concedes no order and consequently can make bold to create his 'order' [and] who conceives of himself as his own fiction."

It is tantalizing to speculate about the possible results had Duncan's plan to write a novel been realized. There is a lot in the notebooks that is derivative of Miller or James. There is more that is original to the extent of anticipating such writers as Jack Kerouac or Frank O'Hara. But nowhere, even at his most exhibitionist—

As I passed down the bar parading like a sexual pigeon—
Someone said—Hi—

—does the narrator's tough-minded candor and ironical self-detachment allow one to react with the revulsion that Anaïs Nin and, to a lesser extent, Robert Duncan himself came to feel towards his young self. Pauline Kael's marginal comments in the notebooks are an infallible guide to the best, and her enthusiasm about two such pages as the following, which she annotated as "wonderful," is well-founded:

> Then I was standing alone on the empty street at five in the morning with my little bag in hand.
>
> —I bet you got plenty of women—the fat man said—The folds of flesh hung from his pig-face. His eyes rolled stupidly under the fat lids. The soft flesh pushed out into a red deformity under his nose. . . .
>
> —I bet you get hard just to talk about it—he said looking at me out of the corners of his eyes.
>
> —I said nothing. I became frigid, ruthless. I was angry.
>
> —I bet you wake up in the morning with it hard—he said looking; I sat far over by the window. If he touches me I thought, I'll punch his flabby face in, like a puff-ball, like a soft blubber-puss.
>
> —I bet you get hard just with my talking—he leered hopefully. Peering to see if he might put his hand over a hard penis. —I bet if I keep talking you'll get hard. I'd better stop talking or you'll get hard.—
>
> —I don't get hard from talking about it—I said stonily.
>
> —I got a piss-hard-on—the monster bloated.— Guess I'd better piss and get over it.
>
> —I bet you got seven inches to show—he said after a silence.
>
> —The man is crazy, I thot—he kept going on in a hopeful way—every word seemed as if he were about to drag his pudgy cock out and slap it into my face. He had no energy—it was an impotent, unbearable affront as if he sat masturbating. I expected him to drag it out and jack away.—
>
> —How far are you going?—I said nervously.
>
> I stood on the open road in the morning and watched his car roar on toward my destination. The clear air lifted my head and my heart. The cold ground was hard and firm under my feet. I leaped into the air, I ran across the field.

Although Duncan never completed his own *Malte Laurids*

Brigge, the journal—however much of an impasse in itself—played a role in his life similar to that of this novel in Rilke's. While writing it, Rilke realized that he could "go on only through" his semi-autobiographical protagonist.[4] Yet once Malte's portrait "made out of [the poet's] dangers" (*Letters*, II, 32) was complete, it filled Rilke with something of the dread Duncan has apparently come to feel towards his own former self. In the words of the German poet: "I shudder a little when I think of all the violence I put through in Malte Laurids, how I landed him back of everything in consistent despair, back of death in a way, so that nothing more was possible, not even dying" (*Letters*, II, 17). In all this, both poets were driven by the attempt to make the horrible and repulsive a valid part of the poet's vision (*cf. Letters*, I, 314-15), a quest which finally turned out to be "not so much . . . a going under, rather [than] a singularly dark ascension into a remote neglected part of heaven" (*Letters*, II, 33) after which "almost all songs are possible" (*Letters*, I, 361). "I will work on a book out of the journal," Duncan wrote to Nin shortly before his discharge from the army: "I mean to whip the whole work into . . . a sort of a death of the soul, Bardo states—'for one lost it is, the writing of a map but of a country which is never located, which falls to pieces continually.' I am tired of my hell, I am destroying it."

Like another predecessor in this inferno, Duncan was to make himself a seer by "a long, gigantic and rational *derangement of all the senses*," resulting in a total transformation of his self. "It is wrong to say: I think," Rimbaud had written. "One ought to say: people think me . . . For *I* is someone else, ['Car JE est un autre.'] If brass wakes up a trumpet, it is not its fault . . . I am present at the birth of my thought; I watch it and listen to it."[5] Like Rilke, Rimbaud also seems to anticipate Duncan in the way he turned against his former ego as soon as this shamanistic quest for a new self was accomplished. In fact, the same attitude of shuddering incredulity towards their previous lives must be shared by many of the original shamans. For their initiation—"a symbolic return to Chaos . . . preparing a new Creation," often heralded by dance and song[6]—frequently leads through "complete disintegration of the personality and . . . madness." Yet however frightening in itself, this "psychic Chaos" is a clear sign "that the profane man," as Mircea Eliade puts it, "is being 'dissolved' and a new personality being prepared for birth."[7] Eliade's research freed such symptoms from the psychopathological labels attached to them by anthropologists working under the influence of early psychiatry. Present-day anti-psychiatry, by reinterpreting mental disturbances as a potential "*initiation* ceremonial" through self-distintegration towards "a new ego,"[8] now seems to point out the contemporary analogue of the shamanistic ritual, especially when applied to many modern artists. According to Laing, such a healing journey "entails in one way or another the dissolution of the normal ego, that false self competently adjusted to our alienated social reality: the emergence of the 'inner' archetypal mediators of divine power, and through this death a rebirth, and the eventual re-establishment of a new kind of ego-functioning, the ego now being the servant of the divine, no longer its betrayer" (p. 119).

With her hyper-sensitive responsiveness to the young poet, Anaïs Nin had been quick to notice the direction this "*initiation* ceremonial" was going to take in Duncan's life. "I must somehow get you the Book of the Dead, the Thibetan one," she wrote Duncan early in their friendship, "for very often it is those regions you are traversing" (Unpublished undated letter). Yet although she acted as his initiator, Nin was not to follow her friend on the actual journey herself. From early on she was repelled by some of Duncan's poems:

> There are parts which I like honestly for their direct thrust and naked utterance, some passages I like less because they are not naked but ugly as America is ugly, without the transformation. Nakedness is marvellous and part of the ritual you achieve so many times, but certain lines are ugly without the strength that is at times in ugliness and monstrosity. The poet you are has a greater struggle here.... as in "I see my mother too clearly" he touches concrete and clinical or that untransferred language which kills life.
>
> (Unpublished undated letter)

Such criticism, however, only confirmed Duncan in his "DESIRE TO INCLUDE EVERYTHING." And it was Nin, as we have seen, who for a while seemed ready to follow the poet's advice in trying to break out of the self-protective "House of Incest" in which Duncan saw her enclosed: "My poor Anaïs who stares out from her intricate prisons with wide eyes; they open wider—they are startled the soul inside is a child weeping because it is so helpless to love—her anguish because she cannot become real, free without destroying, without murdering."

Yet Nin was an unlikely person to share in Duncan's "anarchist 'experiments'" of trying to remove "the ego-personality barrier" or "perspective disease of personality." A diary entry of December 12, 1940, reports one of the "interlude[s] of terror" the poet and some of his other friends were staging at the time:

> After descending from a session in the attic in which Sanders, Jeff, Margaret, Alvin and I tried once more to open the doors "of fear"—we have a desire to go into the world on the other side of those doors. I said I wish there would be a knocking on the door and I don't mean *that* door—I said pointing to the front door—I mean that one—pointing to the attic trap door. At that there

was a loud knock (as if the attic door had been lifted and dropped)—Alvin was so terrified that his face actually turned white—and his heart was beating rapidly. Sanders and I immediately ascended to the attic again—the others followed—while we were quiet, waiting, and observing—waiting. But then after ten moments or so we relaxed and as we laughed and talked—I lay back on the floor—a growing presence came over us—As it reached a speedy peak—Margaret remarked on the change—everyone felt it—and Jeff, Margaret and Alvin went downstairs. Sanders and I stayed—there was another minor crest of fear which those downstairs felt also—but it passed and left us quite dispossessed.

Duncan describes the purpose of these sessions in the well-known terms of Rilke, whose *Duino Elegies*, in "that early edition" with "the wonderful notes and letters at the back,"[9] he had read sometime in 1938 or 1939: "to face our angels ... just as we must face the monsters of our inner worlds and the monsters of the inner world of all mankind."

Like Rilke, Duncan found psychoanalysis to be of little avail in this pursuit. In response to his wife Clara, who charged him with being afraid of it, the German poet concluded that psychoanalysis was really "too basic a help for [him]": "I rather shun this getting cleared out.... Something like a disinfected soul results from it, a monstrosity, alive, corrected in red like the page of a school notebook." What's more, "if one were to drive out [his] devils," Rilke felt, his "angels by some chance [might] leave as well" and destroy his work as a poet which was "really nothing but a self-treatment of the same sort" (*Letters*, II, 34-51).

Unlike Rilke, Duncan did not escape analysis, although he had similar misgivings about it. "The psychologist wants to erase the sado-masochistic cycle of Virginia's love life," he remarked in December, 1940. "yet that is the pure thing, the destructive and the creative thing. How little they understand what is going on in the soul—like the Marxists they want to render it neutral." At about the same time, however, Anaïs Nin introduced Duncan to a rich cousin who not only offered the young poet "a beach where they could ... embrace day and night, a paradise of caresses" (*Diary* III, 170), but who also volunteered to finance his lover's psychoanalysis, believing that the latter's preference for a younger competitor was a "mere phantom." Yet little did result from it, for from the very first day of treatment Duncan somehow managed to invert the patient-analyst relationship.

> "Why are you looking at me like that?" The analyst said—"do you look at everyone like that?"—his voice had been going on and on like a dull lecture on and on about money and I had been

staring at his face—at him—He was moving further away—his face receding and going flat—losing dimension—I was making him inhuman in an effort to search him out back to the human—you have prejudices—my mind was going on—like all the others.

Subsequent sessions followed the same pattern. After a fruitless attempt to make the analyst talk to him about magic ("the doctor did not understand about . . . the mechanism of it in the dream"), Duncan decided to switch to the subject of fear in the creative process, until on February 6, 1941, he was dismissed for not being unhappy enough to deserve analysis. The poor doctor had apparently learned his lesson: "You don't live—he said. Everything goes into the book. You are here not to tear yourself to pieces but to observe yourself torn to pieces. The artist thinks of *I* as a *he*, he says *I* and he is observing himself as a character in the drama of life. . . . He had discovered my secret—I kept thinking as I walked away."

If psychoanalysis had an effect on Duncan, it was mainly in making him recognize his vision as "the split vision of the paranoic." Yet such insight was reached with the pre-Laingian aplomb of someone who had come to see his madness as sanity by comparison with the "machinery for insanities which is called civilizations": "So it is that I live here—in this Journal which is my private Asylum—all the madness is a ruthless sanity. Outside I tell you there is real lunacy—the homicides hunt men like dogs in the street standing in the shadow, planning our final destruction, all our defeats, our tortures, our inquisitions." Psychoanalysis also resulted in a further estrangement from those who had tried to inflict it upon him. When Duncan, as Nin puts it, finally "broke away with cruelty" from the cousin, to go off and make love "to a girl" (*Diary,* III, 91-92)—who, incidentally, became his future wife—Duncan himself knew he had torn open a "wound in the body between Anaïs and [himself]." Yet Nin again hastened to send him assurances to the contrary:

> Robert there was no judgment or wound for the cruelty. When I acted for [my cousin] what you were unable to act. I knew then that your cruelty was an act of honesty. You acted more nakedly and naturally and deep down I loved this because it is the sign of the creator. I knew it is inhuman, but I knew it is an act of courage. I realized then my capacity for cruelty was my weakness and that in this you were the male tonic. And then I was glad that you were not going to live my life but that I failed to live in my life.
>
> (Unpublished undated letter)

Besides genuine good will, the letter also shows the author's

awareness of an irremediable rift which, according to all original evidence, was thus widened, not by Nin's "revolting vision of [Duncan's] character" following a sudden "revolution of her love" (*Caesar's Gate*, p. xxx), but rather by "the strain incurred by her devotions" which Duncan noted as early as February 16, 1941.

As Duncan began to withdraw from an active relationship with his friend, their former quarrels found a new battleground in the poet's unconscious. The following is one of several surrealist portraits which began to emerge in Duncan's journal while he was undergoing analysis:

> ANAÏS. My hands are covered with hair. The fingers grow like white tubers into her vagina. A mouth without lips has closed over my penis. I am attempting to turn her inside out.

The image seems like an unconscious projection of the poet's shamanistic "search for the self" beyond "the perspective disease of . . . personality." "[W]hen it is done," Duncan wrote a few weeks later, "the identity will be turned inside out—it will no longer stare inward but the eyes will be slipped to the surface of the world."

Duncan's full poetic stance did not mature till after he had met Charles Olson. But there are several notions—the outcome of this prior quest—which anticipate the new open form aesthetics that began to evolve after mid-century, led by such pioneers as Cage, Pollock, Olson and Duncan himself. Implicit in Duncan's early notion of the poet turning his identity "inside out" while conceiving "of himself as his own fiction," for instance, seems to be what Olson—paralleling Robbe-Grillet's "SUBJECTIVE TOTALE" of the narrator[10]—describes as the ultimate *coincidentia oppositorum* of the total narrator "IN" with the total narrator "OUT"—the narrator being "still, no more than—but just as much as—another 'thing,' and as such . . . in, inside or out."[11] Duncan also anticipated *nouveau roman* theorizing by insisting upon a self-reduction of the creative ego to the point where a narrator, for example, will turn himself into a mere medium, letting nature's cycles of creation and destruction reenact themselves through him in a "*double movement de création et de gommage.*"[12] According to Robbe-Grillet, a description, for instance, should leave no traces, so that when it ends "one realizes that it has left nothing behind itself still standing up: it has reified itself in a double movement of creation and erasure" (p. 160). Or as Duncan put it many years earlier: "Everything is completed in the Journal and destroyed," the writing of it being like "the writing of a map but of a country which is never located but which falls to pieces continually."

In an attempt to locate these "dynamics of . . . destruction and creation" in the creative act itself, Duncan again anticipated Olson, who, a professionally trained dancer himself, was to recognize "the kinetic as the end of life"[13] and dance as the essence of a new art no longer of "mimesis but [of] kinesis."[14] *Ionisation* (1931), by Edgar Varèse, a member of Nin's circle, provided Duncan with the music to realize such aesthetic principles in the dancing he loved to perform in front of others. Anaïs Nin gives a vivid account of such a performance in the *Diary*: "Robert came with a recording by Edgar Varèse. He danced for us. It was a creation. He invented a nonhuman, abstract dance, a war of elements, torn, resoldered, percussion gestures to the percussion sounds of Varèse. His face was like a mask" (III, 85). The dancer himself praised Varèse's "terrifying sounds beyond the human-movements that tear the body, that set the centers of the body into motion." But the final revelation came with the discovery of primitive music, through which Duncan reached what Olson, in a crucial programmatic formula, later called "the replacement of the Classical-representational by the *primitive-abstract*."[15] Swahili dance, in contrast to the "superficial disintegration" of Stravinsky's *Histoire du soldat*, Duncan found, "destroys the dancer completely": "There is only a body gone insane with it, crawling, jerking its head, shoulders, the whole body twitching back into the beginning Lemurian frenzy . . . My arms seemed to spring loose from their sockets, the beast and the shaman had reclaimed the human being."

Although Nin with her *House of Incest* had prompted Duncan to take his first steps "Toward the Shaman," his actual journey through the Bardo states of a self-destructive exposure to the horrific made him assume a stance that clearly passes beyond the reach of his previous initiator. An unusually comprehensive statement of poetics from the same period, although directed against a certain *type* of poetry lover to whom beauty is "a tasteless misty essence derived from the music of words and scorning the revelation of the phrase," may very well have been written with Anaïs Nin in mind: "There is in such followers no capacity for what the great artist does, for Rilke's corrosion of reality and the invasion of death. . . . This 'lover of poetry' feels that experience should be evaded, made 'dreamlike' at a time when we are trying to make even the dream unavoidable as experience." But this theoretical stance, partly an outgrowth of Duncan's "barbaric friendship" with Anaïs Nin, was not to turn into a major creative force till after World War II when, with the disappearance of the journal, Nin ceased to exert her in some ways deleterious but ultimately beneficial influence on the poet's development.

NOTES

1. *A Photographic Supplement to The Diary of Anaïs Nin* (New York and London, 1974).

2. Robert Duncan, *Caesar's Gate* (San Francisco, 1972), p. xxx: hereafter cited in the text as *Caesar's Gate*.

3. All quotations, if not otherwise identified, are from Robert Duncan's notebooks and other unpublished material housed in the Bancroft Library, University of California, Berkeley. Unpublished letters are identified as such within the text.

4. Rainer Maria Rilke, *Letters*, trans. J. B. Greene and M. D. Herter Norton, 2 vols. (New York, 1969), I, 337; hereafter cited in the text as *Letters*.

5. Arthur Rimbaud, *Complete Works*, ed. Wallace Fowlie (Chicago, 1966), pp. 303-07.

6. See Mircea Eliade, *Shamanism*: *Archaic Techniques of Ecstasy*, Bollingen Series LXXVI (Princeton, 1972), pp. 27-28: "The famous Yakut shaman Tüspüt (that is, 'fallen from the sky') had been ill at the age of twenty; he began to sing, and felt better. When Sieroszewski met him, he was sixty and displayed tireless energy. 'If necessary, he can drum, dance, jump all night.'" Further examples are to be found throughout the book; see also *Technicians of the Sacred*: *A Range of Poetries from Africa, America, Asia, & Oceania*, ed. J. Rothenberg (Garden City, N.Y., 1968).

7. Eliade, *Rites and Symbols of Initiation*: *The Mysteries of Birth and Rebirth* (New York, 1965), p. 89.

8. R. D. Laing, *The Politics of Experience* and *The Bird of Paradise* (Harmondsworth, 1975), p. 106.

9. See "An Interview," by George Bowering and Robert Hogg (Toronto, 1971), n.p.

10. Alain Robbe-Grillet, *Pour un nouveau roman* (Paris, 1963), p. 148.

11. Charles Olson, *Human Universe and Other Essays*, ed. D. Allen (New York, 1967), pp. 127-28.

12. Robbe-Grillet, p. 160.

13. "A Syllabary for a Dancer" (Featuring Charles Olson), *Maps*, 4 (1971), 12.

14. Charles Olson, *Selected Writings*, ed. Robert Creeley (New York, 1966), p. 148.

15. Olson, *Selected Writings*, p. 28.

Duane Schneider (essay date Winter 1978)

SOURCE: "Anaïs Nin in the *Diary*: The Creation and Development of a Persona," in *Mosaic*, Vol. 11, No. 2, Winter 1978, pp. 9-19.

[In the following essay, Schneider traces the evolution of the narrator in the Diary, *contrasting the persona therein with Nin herself and maintaining that the* Diary's *narrator is a literary creation more than an accurate and objective representation of Nin.]*

The intriguing and engaging narrator of Anaïs Nin's *Diary* has surely earned for herself a place among the great literary creations to appear in this century. Purporting to reveal aspects of her life (and the growth of her sensibilities) in selections from an autobiographical journal, the narrator knows and relates the truth about herself. In a series of volumes covering the years 1931-1966, the reader is allowed to trace the progress of this narrator/persona (called "Anaïs Nin") through a set of experiences that simulates the depth and variety of human life and achievement. The creation and development of this narrator unquestionably attest to the power and skill of Nin, the author, and it is therefore unfortunate that many readers have failed to appreciate the difference between the two.[1]

Such confusion is also difficult to understand, as there would seem to be ample directions in the prefatory material of the six volumes to deter us from assuming that Nin the author and Nin the narrator are uniform; since we are told that the published *Diary* represents only a fraction of the original, and since both the processes of selection and organization have taken place, we would seem led to conclude that the published versions (having been revised at least once) are carefully wrought works of literature, regardless of the apparent autobiographical nature of their origin.

In any case, Nin never forgot, even if some readers occasionally do, that it "was the fiction writer who edited the diary" (*Novel*, p. 85), and it ought to come as no surprise to find that the values and techniques she employed in her fiction are finely honed for use in the *Diary*. Psychological authenticity, which lies at the heart of all of Nin's work, is effected in the *Diary* as in the fiction through the manipulation of symbolism, dreams, and other dramatic devices which generate a sense of immediacy. Similarly, the *Diary* reveals a fine sense of timing, character development and selection, which Nin initiated and Gunther Stuhlmann aided; as in her fiction, but frequently with sustained concreteness, characters appear and reappear in multiple contexts, while typical of both the fiction and the *Diary* is the presence of a chief female character who is omnipresent—as a participant or as an observer—and whose development is presented through multiple exposures in a variety of contexts, through her own self-analysis, or through the responses she evokes from the satellite characters around her.

There is, however, one important difference between the material as it is presented in the fiction and as it is presented in the *Diary*; namely, the presence within the latter of a central consciousness—that of the persona—through whose mind all the characters and incidents are filtered, interpreted, and colored. Every detail she affords us tells us perhaps as much about herself as it does about the person or incident described. In contrast to the situation in Nin's fiction, therefore, narration in the *Diary* becomes simultaneously self-characterization. Under the appearance of a journal that records real-life situations and individuals, there have, in fact, been gathered a set of compelling "actors" in accordance with the literary principle of point of view. The result is neither fiction in the traditional sense nor diary in the conventional sense but rather something of a new art form—the journal-novel.

It is not difficult to describe the characteristics of the persona in each volume of the *Diary*; accounting for the narrator's development and the changes in her characterization, however, may be more problematic. For even if one grants that the "Nin" of the *Diary* is distinct from Nin, the real person, one must still, to a certain extent, take into consideration the way in which her own experiences influenced her editing of the original diary and her creation of a persona. Even if key questions cannot be answered they need to be posed. To what extent, for example, were the frustration and disappointment of her initial fiction-writing years factors in determining the kind of persona Nin chose to construct in the first volumes of the *Diary*? Did she perhaps need to compensate for rejection and disappointment by creating a narrator who, as we shall see, is helpful, attractive, perceptive and observant, one whom a number of colorful characters—Henry Miller, June, Dr. Allendy, Dr. Rank, Artaud, and others—turn toward for emotional nourishment? And did Nin's success in publishing the earlier volumes of the *Diary* and their enthusiastic reception in turn influence the conception of the narrator in the later volumes, where we find (finally) one who is more human, more relaxed, one who can admit errors and mistakes, and who allows for flaws in her characterization? Finally, in this context one should also notice that while the narrator is characterized as one who consistently trusts the truth of her own emotions and intuitions and who exhibits the kind of faith in herself that only a modernist could,[2] she nevertheless seldom appears to be hermetically sealed or incapable and uninterested in learning more about the human condition; rather she is characterized as one who benefits from insights which allow her and others to live more freely and honestly than before, and with less pain. The thematic truth that lies at the heart of the *Diary*, then, is inextricably connected with Nin's conception of the narrator who is compelled to tell her tale, and who in so doing becomes both the subject (teller) and the object (told about).

The narrator of Volume I (1931-1934) encounters a few special problems, and yet, interestingly enough, the problems of exposition that we might expect to be dealt with are largely left untouched. We are introduced to the protagonist, Anaïs Nin, fully developed in the Paris of 1931, with house and friends, but virtually no past. That it is an exciting time in the life of the narrator, the tone makes clear. The emotional intensity is reflected in her diction and descriptions: "Ordinary life does not interest me. I seek only the high moments. I am in accord with the surrealists, searching for the marvelous" (1,5). Infinity becomes an important dimension in the persona's life, as it tends to in many Romantics.

And yet the persona is distinctly different in practice from what she claims to be in theory; there are no surrealistic passages here, but rather a carefully-planned, lucid, detailed description of the narrator's encounters with Henry Miller, a Bohemian writer who revels in earthy living, and his wife June, a magnificent and attractive puzzle who tantalizes the narrator from the beginning. The discussions of June characterize her and introduce her to the reader long before she makes an appearance in these pages. And from the outset she serves as an effective contrast to the narrator, whose role at this time is characterized by fragility and vulnerability. Both the power of June's beauty and the attractiveness of Miller's spirit, awaken and kindle new life—life that was not known to exist—in the persona's psyche. The stage is set for high personal and emotional drama, the richest of all drama: that of self-revelation and penetration. And the simulation of reality gained through the first person narration gives the narrative added immediacy and interest for the reader.

The tale is told with artistry and efficiency, alternating between dialogue and observation. New characters appear, new situations arise, as the narrator makes her course along the three-year span covered in Volume I. With something very much like a plot, the narrator moves from the Miller/June encounter into the psychoanalytic episodes with Dr. René Allendy. With Miller and his circle, the narrator is able to witness at first hand a life of ugliness, violence and shabbiness; full of considerable ambivalence, she travels outward from her lacquered suburban home, with curiosity and trepidation, to experience this other side of life.

But is the narrator really participating in it all? Or is it all safely observed—the violence, the drunkenness, the sexuality? Actually, we are not told. And one of the great irritations to some is that the *Diary* leaves out, it seems, as much as it contains. As in some of Nin's novels, a portion of the context is missing or is deleted. But the enjoyment, the wonder, the pleasure, and the surprise of the persona all seem to be present, and the richness of life is felt even if it is not described in detail. The scenes between the narrator and June are masterpieces of literary control; Nin's sensitivity

to diction here is at its most delicate and discerning. None of Nin's works of fiction has a greater unity than this progress of the *Diary*'s heroine in her first public appearance; not seeking fortune, but looking for friendship, self-esteem and worthy productivity. It is an impressive character delineation that Nin sketches in Volume I: the persona moving from Miller to June to Dr. Allendy and Antonin Artaud (a fine set of characters), while in the background there is the painful contrast of her father's world, a world lost to the narrator both literally and figuratively. The persona is depicted as a questor who moves steadily toward levels of self-realization, and in Volume I it is as though each character she encounters somehow contributes to this quest.

However, the strength of Volume I is also its weakness. The character of the persona seems incomplete, unrounded—perhaps unreal. Certainly the narrator is relatively flawless. We soon realize, in fact, that she is depicted as the one who is needed, a kind of savior, and not merely one who needs. Those with whom she comes into contact—Miller, June, Dr. Allendy, Dr. Rank—eventually need her, as does her father. The roles are reversed time and time again. The inversion from being the helped to becoming the helper is made explicit; the persona becomes the Great Mother upon whom her many children depend. This motif, which is developed even more clearly in Volume II, begins to emerge when the diarist observes that she always loses her "guide halfway up the mountain, and he becomes [her] child" (I, 261). The persona who said that she wanted to live only for ecstasy and extravagance may have been speaking more openly than she knew, and for this narrator, at least, the description seems to be most appropriate in her urgent wish to appear heroic and needed. The new life—with many people needing her—is fittingly capped by the ending of Volume I, in which Otto Rank is portrayed as sending the narrator desperate letters to come and rescue him in the United States. "I may not become a saint," she notes, "but I am very full and very rich" (I, 360). And, we might add, very stylized and very incomplete.

The narrator of Volume II shares a great deal with that of Volume I, and the time of composition (editing, organizing and selecting) was probably close to that of the first volume, since Volume II appeared only a year later. Many motifs, themes and characters reappear in this volume, which covers the years 1934-1939. But because the advent of war dominates the scene here, this volume has both a political and social context that is lacking in Volume I. During these years the narrator develops significantly as a writer and forms close and important literary associations with a group made up of Henry Miller, Alfred Perlès, Lawrence Durrell and others. Of the new characters in the volume, the most remarkable are Gonzalo, a Peruvian Marxist, and Helba, his wife. The narrator's political initiation, and to some extent her portrayal as a person with a social conscience, is managed by Gonzalo. Again, however, the persona is incomplete, only partially revealed. The narrator does travel to the United States to help Otto Rank, but when she realizes the sacrifices she would need to make—chiefly sacrifices that would require her to give up her writing—she breaks with psychoanalysis in favor of art. Her opiate, the diary she keeps, continues to provide her with a direct connection to the world of writing, however, and when she returns to Europe and her friends, they determine to publish their own works and found a press, Siana Editions (Anaïs spelled backward).

These two themes—writing and politics—dominate Volume II, and just as psychoanalysis is given up by the narrator (not, of course, without having heightened her awareness), so does the narrator find herself forced to deal with political realities. She would prefer to ignore politics altogether and explore only her artistic inclinations, but faced with the reality of war and destruction, she finds that art cannot act as a substitute for life, and also finds her own sense of life and its preciousness considerably heightened.

Simultaneously, the narrator cultivates her image as nurturer and protectress—a pattern of self-characterization that echoes Volume I. She continues to be introspective. She recognizes that the constant need for "a mother, or a father, or a god (the same thing) is really immaturity" (II, 21); she also recognizes the need to provide love for those who seek it. And so the portrayal of the narrator as a benefactress emerges more and more, and indeed dominates the larger portion of the volume. Of her friends in Paris, 1935, she writes: "I am the young mother of the group in the sense that I am giving nourishment and creating life. All of them now in motion. When I look at the changes, the transformations, the expansions I created, I grow afraid, afraid to be left alone, as all mothers are ultimately left alone. To each I gave the strength to fly out of my world, and at times my world looks empty. But they come back" (II, 51). Born under the sign of Pisces, the giver, she continues to give at the same time that she pursues her literary career. Reflecting on the austere pasts of each of her friends, she feels more able to cope with her few possessions. She enjoys giving up self-indulgence, luxury, and travel: "I have to pay for Henry's rent, Gonzalo's rent, and to feed them all. No rest. No seashore, no travel, no vacation. Voilà. No Heine's beach costume, no mountain air, no sun on the body. But I get pleasure from seeing how my children live" (II, 201). With her literary companions, the narrator lives an exciting life of the mind, unmasking each other (she says), defending their varied approaches to literature.

And yet, the narrator herself seems more incomplete than ever, and Anaïs Nin, the author, is not unmasked, nor we feel, was meant to be. The persona is busily engaged with the rites of more self-analysis. Her self-esteem is nurtured by the testimonies of her friends, which the narrator repro-

duces, as though to convince herself of her own value. Her convictions, however, remain unaltered, and much that is the best of Anaïs Nin's liberality and humaneness is revealed, in spite of the author's apparent preoccupation with creating a persona who will appear to be flawless. When Gonzalo, for example, tries to impose Marxism upon the narrator, she resists, refusing to pass from one narrowminded concept to another, chiefly because she has fought for a spiritually honest and free life (II, 274). She allows, however, that social and political awareness may be necessary to improve the lives of many; yet even on that basis, she has reservations: "I have built a rich private world, but I fear I cannot help build the world outside. Deep down, I feel, nothing changes the nature of man. I know too well that man can only change himself psychologically, and that fear and greed make him inhuman, and it is only a change of roles we attain with each revolution, just a change of men in power, that is all. The evil remains. It is guilt, fear, impotence which makes men cruel, and no system will eliminate that" (II, 154-55).

The narrator's vision of the artist transforming the world constructively is a view that she clings to. On the personal level as well as on the cosmic scale, the function of the artist is a beneficial one, and above all, the persona is characterized as one who maintains these values in her personal relationships as well as in her own ideology, which she is forced to create. It may seem like a role that attracts too much self-aggrandizement, and some find it obnoxious because of the unreal consistent nobility with which the narrator characterizes herself or allows others to do for her.

Given the scope of Volume III—the years 1939-1944—one might assume that the selection dwells upon the Second World War. Not so. The war exists as a kind of backdrop, but it does not dominate nearly so much as it does in Volume II when the narrator must deal with Gonzalo, the Spanish Civil War, and the preparations for the greater war. With Volume III, the narrator is cast back into America and must cope with her artistic endeavors on American terms, a task that turns out to be difficult. Unable to find a suitable market for her works, she and Gonzalo turn to printing her stories and short novels themselves, tasteful works issued by the Gemor Press, largely unnoticed except amidst a coterie of friends and admirers, until one influential friend gives one book a good review in an important magazine: Edmund Wilson's review of *Under a Glass Bell* in *The New Yorker*, 1944.

With an agreeable symmetry, not unlike its predecessors, Volume III begins with difficulty and dislocation (also true of Volumes I and II), but ends with success and acceptance—true in Volume I, but only generally so in Volume II. The dovetailing and interweaving of character and motif continue: in time, part of the Paris circle that Nin regrets leaving—Miller, Gonzalo, Helba—appear on American shores.

The persona progresses in a logical fashion: the literary initiate of the first volume, who chooses art in the second, becomes the maverick and determined devotee of her own vision in the third volume. The problem she faces is: how does an avant garde writer establish contact with an American audience in 1940? Answer: with extreme difficulty, and never successfully. The persona's consciousness is almost entirely directed toward this problem, and the war lies far in the background. How the persona deals with the problem—another success story, so far as we can tell—perpetuates the pattern of the quest: the goal is established, the obstacles arise and are overcome in the face of great odds, the prize is won and the heroine acknowledged. The triumphs continue to be kept steadily before the reader, and are made all the more significant by the kinds of difficulties that the narrator needs to overcome (irresponsible friends, impossible demands made by others, the poor taste and insensitivity of the American publishing world). The stamina of the narrator is admirable; the cost of pain is not related in detail until later, in Volume VI.

The contrast between Paris and New York is made explicit in this volume. In Europe, the writer was comfortable among friends with whom she shared a number of values, and the cultured continent reflected these civilized values; in America she finds no intimacy, no café life, but rather opulence and decadence. The narrator's coming to terms with this new world gives a good deal of order—if not unity—to her quest for literary acceptance and recognition. The entire volume, in a sense, reflects the very kind of communication and relationship with readers that the narrator was seeking from the beginning of her career in Paris. To some extent, in the description of the quest, the narrator's quest is close to being achieved.

In view of the principles of literary value espoused in Volumes I and II (to some degree the values of D. H. Lawrence), the rejection by the American literati in the 1940's was predictable. But there is no pretense on the part of the persona that she could change her approach, or ought to. The idea of her writing something like *The Good Earth* is to her simply odious; her work, she implies, like herself, is "free and beyond nationalism" (III, 247). Miller's intolerance for American glitter reinforces the narrator's distaste for the country; so far as she can see, Americans are busy rejecting European values, while the isolationism Americans feel is being projected upon her work. The narrator whose value has in the past been unquestioned, now seems dispensable. And so, to save herself, and to triumph, she defies the publishers by printing and publishing her own works, ***Winter of Artifice*** and ***Under a Glass Bell.*** The publication of these modest volumes is apparently enough to hearten the narrator and her friends. But to survive financially, they write erotica.

Volume III, however, lacks a continuity that the first two volumes contain. Most of the characters introduced in this volume hold interest for the reader, but some seem superfluous. The narration seems for the first time broken at times, slightly desperate if not shrill. The narrator's problems and friendships are not always so engaging as the nature of her literary achievement. She feels abused because her spontaneity and Lawrencean values are not respected (by publishers, who ought to know better). The reward, of course, comes to the narrator in the end, when Edmund Wilson's review brings all sorts of benefits and attention, so long sought after. The writer is vindicated, and from this time on she knows that she will have a number of loyal supporters.

Although the details and emphases have changed, basically Anaïs Nin's depiction of the persona does not shift significantly in the first three volumes: generous, industrious, ambitious, respected by a core of admirers, the narrator pursues her vision of the feminine perception in her own unique kind of fiction. She does not reject psychoanalysis, but subordinates it to her art and vision. But the fully developed, human narrator, portrayed in her weaknesses and vulnerability, has yet to appear. The narrator in Volume III remains a literary creation, not a live human being. The author's defenses, it would seem, are still up.

The fourth volume, covering the years 1944-1947, represents to some degree the legacy earned from the years of the early 1940's. More fragmented than any earlier volume, it is not, however, weak or uninteresting, and contains some of Nin's finest and most poignant observations about life and literature. A number of familiar themes appear: the narrator continues to be concerned about her own artistic and psychological development, conscious of the restrictions imposed by guilt and neurosis, sensitive to those aspects of her existence which seem healthy and life-giving. Her literary life—printing, writing fiction—receives some fascinating attention here; her gravitation toward the young and her disappointment in the "mature" is dealt with in some detail. A strong sense of humanism emerges in this volume, a clear articulation—through the persona—of a vision of how life may be lived in an integrated fashion.

The sense or need of a persona—shall we say the author's?—also seems less urgent in Volume IV. For the first time the narrator does not have to succeed: she has succeeded. She is not fully rounded yet, but the heroics lie further in the background than ever before. The articulation of values is more explicit as well, and there is no compelling feeling that the narrator needs to be victorious. Her life is presented as one with a high degree of integration, and she sees herself as evolving and changing. Fusing her fiction with psychology, she understands the usefulness of focusing on the inner life, even if certain friends are trying to develop the "realist" in her. And with some pleasure, she notes that one of the great satisfactions of her life is that she lives "out what others only dream about, talk about, analyze. I want to go on living the uncensored dream, the free unconscious" (IV, 62). The attempt to free herself and others from the restrictions of neurosis means risk-taking for the narrator on the one hand, and her rejection of the dull, down-to-earth, and prosaic on the other hand. Increasingly she sees her life and her writing as inseparable, and the importance of sympathy, movement, and humaneness is made explicit time and time again in the fourth volume, perhaps with a bit of repetition in the tone. The authenticity and deep sincerity of key passages are impressive, and signify the increased development of a persona who seems human and alive.

It thus seems that the further Nin carried her open-ended *Diary,* the more comfortable she became in allowing for a free and open narrator, in place of the narrower persona who seemed to be created with specific roles and images in mind. Expansion, fulfillment and evolution become a manifestation of the narrator's success and acceptance as a fiction writer and lecturer; the dream has become reality. For Nin, the dream, if lived out, provided for more abundant life; but the dream could also become a tragic trap, for to live within the dream and not to bring it into reality could lead to disaster. "You discard realism," Frances Brown tells her, "but not reality" (IV, 70). The persona is thus chiefly an accomplished fiction writer in this volume, no longer an apprentice, no longer needing to publish her own work. Her depiction of emotional reality finally finds a greater outlet than ever before through New York publishers, and the harmony—the diminution of frustration—is reflected tonally in the *Diary*'s pages.

Nin organized and edited the materials for the fourth volume from the vantage point of 1970-1971; she had been able to see the immense success of the first three volumes, and in the text of Volume IV, she is less insistent on the value of the diary in the narrator's life. When we are told, however, that "the real Anaïs is in the diary" (IV, 105), we have no more concrete reflection of that complex author than we had in the earlier versions with their less developed persona. Nevertheless, the narrator is characterized as moving toward her dream of literary success and acceptance in a culture that she had deemed hostile, superficial, and under-developed in those qualities she valued most. The consistency of the narrator is kept steadily before us, sympathetic, humane, but controlled.

The fifth volume, which covers the years 1947-1955, is far different from the first four, and is more fragmented and less sustained even than Volume IV. Although familiar themes reappear—sympathy, analysis, fiction writing, travel—no clear focus emerges and no clear theme is developed. It contrasts most strikingly with a work like Volume I, with its dramatic and engaging characterizations that are developed in great detail. The incoherence of Volume V in fact mirrors the incoherence of the narrator's life at this time; more than in any other volume, the persona here is less stylized and artificial. Suffering from depression and attendant emotional problems, as well as physical illness, the narrator encounters difficulties of considerable proportions, not the least of which are the deaths of her parents and a strange kind of hostility on the part of critics and reviewers. For the first time the narrator is depicted as beginning seriously to turn to the diary as her major work, with an eye toward eventual publication. In all its fragmentation, it may well be that Volume V, edited carefully, stands as a masterpiece of organic form, imaging in its structure (with short, undeveloped passages) the disconnected nature of the narrator's life. It may have been at this time that Nin chose to redirect her characterization of the persona toward something less glamorous, less dramatic than she appeared in earlier volumes.

Travel, descriptive passages, the shift from fiction toward the diary, all give Volume V a new and different tone. In fact, however, the kind of literary success the narrator seeks continues to elude her. Her bitterness and sense of estrangement are verbalized with more despair than ever. She sees herself in the traditional artist's role, articulating what all people know and feel, but are unable to speak. And gradually she recognizes that the diary can serve her better, not as a secret retreat or as an opiate, but rather as her artistic *magnum opus.* The fiction writer begins to try to find a way of providing a flow in the diary "so that it may not seem like a diary but an inner monologue, a series of free associations accompanying the life of several characters" (V, 38). As the persona finds herself continually frustrated in her attempt to be an accepted fiction writer, the idea of capitalizing on the diary seems increasingly attractive. She writes to Maxwell Geismar, a critic with whom she maintained a most ambivalent friendship, asserting her commitment to the diary.

> I don't need to be published. I only need to continue my personal life, so beautiful and in full bloom, and to do my major work, which is the diary. I merely forgot for a few years what I had set out to do. . . . I have settled down to fill out, round out the diary. I am at work now on what I call the volume of superimpositions, which means that while I copy out volume 60, I write about the developments and conclusions which took place twenty years later. It all falls into place. It is a valuable contribution to the faith in the Freudian system. It can wait for publication (V. 217).

The tension evident here, between her quiet commitment and faith on the one hand, and her urge to press the diary into publication on the other hand, seems to resolve itself in the narrator's mind, however, when she declares: "I think what

I should do is devote the rest of my time to preparing diaries for publication, no more novels" (V, 237); but even in the life of the narrator it was to be eleven years and two novels later before the *Diary* came to be published.

To suggest that the writing of the diary—or the preparation of the diary for publication—emerges as the narrator's chief preoccupation in Volume V would be untrue, but one can see the shift in direction clearly enough, from novel writing and publishing toward diary writing, editing and success. The intensity of the pain that the persona (and Nin, the author) felt at the hands of the critics was considerable; the pleasure that attended the plans to publish was equally considerable, particularly in retrospect. The reader's knowledge that the venture to publish the *Diary*—the very book the reader is reading—would turn out to be a huge success helps to give this fragmentary volume a unity of concept and emotion. It does all fall into place, just as does a drama that we have seen performed before, knowing the pain and pleasure which will develop in the plot.

The sixth volume of the *Diary,* covering the years 1955-1966, contains more pages, deals with more years, and has far more balance and structure than earlier volumes. Some will say that it cannot rival the first two contributions to the series, which detail Nin's relationship with her literary associates in Paris; and yet Volume VI brings to the reader a narrator who is more open and relaxed than before. "I have decided to retire as the major character of this diary," she writes (VI, 319), and from that point on it was to be called *Journal des Autres* (Diary of Others). That the narrator had been the central character in the first five volumes will be readily acknowledged; that the persona herself can admit this fact openly in Volume VI is something new. The openness of the disclosure, however, is characteristic of the tone of the volume; the persona retires quietly in the background and the mood is at times relaxed. The narrator does not have to center the attention on herself, and when she speaks she seems to be candid and confident. The tensions and conflicts of the past have been resolved, she notes, and she now turns to the editing and copying of the diary, preparing it for publication. It might be said, in fact, that the diary itself now acquires the centrality and focus which the narrator is willing to abdicate.

Again, it is not that these years are totally dominated by the diary; it is a time when the narrator continues in psychoanalysis and assiduously pursues the composition, publication, and distribution of her fiction. The earlier defensiveness and bitterness have virtually vanished. "My connection with the world broke twice: the first time when my father left me. The second time when America slammed the door on my writing. What I have been busy reconstructing is my bridge to the world" (VI, 121). In 1966, finally, the narrative comes full circle, and the narrator is able to witness her triumph and acceptance in the United States as evidenced by the publication of the first volume of the *Diary.*

To summarize briefly, then, the *Diary,* in all its six volumes, details the movement of its narrator, from her first entrances into serious literary composition, through various successes and failures (of virtually every variety), until she finds the true voice that a readership in the United States wants to hear. The persona, created in many ways as a conventional literary heroine, increases in human qualities approximately midway through the narrative and in the final volume is most humanely realized and most fully human of all; narcissism and self-aggrandizement give way to a more balanced self-portrait, one that admits weaknesses along with strengths. As a character in this drama, the narrator becomes more and more unmasked; but we are never certain whether in the process the author also does or not, and we must not assume that the narrator is ever identical with Nin or an accurate representation of her, were such a representation possible.

The legendary *Diary* has, of course, become famous partly because—ironically as the result of the excellence of Nin's art—the narrator seems so "real": she develops, the complexities and nuances of her feelings are explored, and she finally succeeds in her attempt to arrive at a point in her life where she is both accepted and accepting. But the protagonist of the *Diary* is a literary creation, and our awareness of this fact, far from detracting from the quality, value, and interest of the *Diary,* should serve only to enhance our appreciation of Nin's—the author's—humanism and her powers of articulation.

NOTES

1. The persona's self-understanding, presented in the guise of self-revelation, is the one technique Nin never quite discovered—or rather, perfected—in her fiction. But in the *Diary* she managed it so skillfully that Leon Edel was lured into describing the work as Nin's way "of giving herself concrete proof of her own existence." See "Life Without Father," *Saturday Review,* 7 May 1966, p. 91.

2. Compare, for example, an ancient historian such as Thucydides who was unwilling to document an event at which he was an eye-witness without corroborating his information with other eye-witnesses.

Nancy Scholar   (essay date 1979)

SOURCE: "Anaïs Nin's *House of Incest* and Ingmar Bergman's *Persona*: Two Variations on a Theme," in *Literature and Film,* Vol. 7, No. 1, 1979, pp. 47-59.

[In the following essay, Scholar examines the nature of identity as it appears in Nin's House of Incest *and Ingmar Bergman's film* Persona.*]*

> So now we are inextricably woven . . .
> I AM THE OTHER FACE OF YOU
> Our faces are soldered together by soft hair,
>   soldered together,
> showing two profiles of the same soul.[1]

There is an intriguing congruence between this poetic description of merged identities in Anaïs Nin's prose-poem *House of Incest* (1936) and an identical visual image in Ingmar Bergman's film *Persona* (1966).[2] The similarity extends beyond an overlap of image. There are many commonalities between these disparate artists and works—as well as interesting differences—which are illuminated by this imagistic convergence. Both film and book present a "distillation" of the themes which haunted the artists in many other works. "It is the seed of all my work, the poem from which the novels were born,"[3] Nin has said about her first work of fiction. Bergman has also described *Persona* in poetic terms,[4] but this masterpiece came after more than twenty years of prolific filmmaking, and hence, has an artistic maturity which is lacking in Nin's first effort. Yet there is an intuitive, visionary quality to *House of Incest* which gives it an extraordinary luminosity.

Bergman has referred to *Persona*, along with *Through a Glass Darkly, Winter Light*, and *The Silence*, as a "chamber work." This description applies to *House of Incest* as well: "They are chamber music—music in which, with an extremely limited number of voices and figures, one explores the essence of a number of motifs. The backgrounds are extrapolated, put into a sort of fog. The rest is distillation."[5] Nin describes *House* as containing the "purest essence" of her meaning, the "distillation of her experience."[6] In this "EDIFICE WITHOUT DIMENSION," she focuses on a small number of figures and puts the background into a "fog." The same could be said for later works, including *Winter of Artifice* and the five-volume *Cities of the Interior*, but *House of Incest* is the most condensed and poetic.

It is also the most unconventional of Nin's books, and the least amenable to analysis and definition. The same is true for *Persona*, which marks a radical departure for Bergman from more traditional forms and subject matter. Both works may have discouraged critical approach, because they tend to resist analysis and definition, as part of their meaning. Nin and Bergman alike wish to explore a realm of experience below or beyond rationality; they attempt to break down and through the comfortable masks and surfaces by which most of us live. For such purposes, they both require forms which depart from the norm. Experimental themes and forms are

frightening to some, unsatisfactory to others. In addition, both film and book share a reputation for difficulty which has added to the confusion. Oliver Evans calls *House* the "most difficult of Miss Nin's books,"[7] and John Simon refers to *Persona* as "probably the most difficult film ever made."[8] It is hardly surprising, after such ominous warnings, that these works have not received as much recognition as they deserve.

II

The appearance of formlessness in the prose-poem is, to some extent, deceptive; each of the seven sections which compose the book has the underlying coherence of the dream. But the meaning of these "visionary symbolic dream sequences"[9] must be "unravelled" by the reader. Nin created *House* out of a record of her dreams which she kept for a year, so it is her unconscious—transformed, to be sure—which provides the deepest structure in this work. Jung's words were her inspiration: "To proceed from the dream outward."[10] But Nin herself doubted whether her dream exploration actually moved outward: "In *House of Incest* I describe what it is to be trapped in the dream, unable to relate it to life, unable to reach 'daylight.'"[11] Even though she may not have reached "daylight" in *House,* Nin was able to explore and suggest the rich potentiality of the dream terrain, which she continued to excavate in later writing.

Although there is no indication that Bergman created *Persona* out of personal dreams, he certainly seems to have been in a nightmarish state during its inception. He was confined to the hospital for two months with a disease of the inner ear which produced dizziness and a sensation of imbalance. "I was lying there," he says, "half dead, and suddenly I started to think of two faces, two intermingled faces, and that was the beginning, the place where it started."[12] Most of *Persona* takes place in that twilight zone between wakefulness and the dream state, life and death. It is difficult to separate dream and reality in the film, and this is another aspect of its reputed difficulty. Bergman has commented: "The reality we experience today is in fact as absurd, as horrible, and as obtrusive as our dreams . . . And one is strongly aware . . . that there are no boundaries between dream and reality today."[13]

But how much more difficult to recreate the wordless dream through language than through the visual image. Hence the use of photomontages in *House* to assist in this near-impossible task, and the reliance on hypnotic, incantatory language in the first sequence to facilitate reconstruction of a dream state. The barrage of images which flash rapidly on the screen during the first moments of *Persona* serve a similar function. They are both an effort to jolt the audience out of comfortable, ordinary existence and into a condition receptive to the unconscious, at the same time as they are a reflection of the artist's own unconscious creative process.

In other words, for Nin and Bergman alike, the unconscious is their own starting point, their subject matter, and their focus in the audience at once. As Bergman comments, "You sit in a dark room and you have this little bright, bright square before you . . . And of course, it goes right inside you and right down in your emotional mind—in your unconscious."[14] Nin is more explicit about audience involvement in this process in a discussion of Bergman's films:

It is the emotional, not the analytical, journey which brings deliverance from secret corrosions. Bergman's films have that intent; we should accept the fact of a profound emotional journey into mostly unexplored realms, into all we have not dared to feel, to say, to act, to embrace in life. It is a journey through dark regions. But it should stir in us all the unknown elements in ourselves . . . this is the world which Jung has called our shadow. Bergman presents the shadow of the selves we do not wish to acknowledge.[15]

III

House as well as *Persona* has the intent which Nin describes here. Jung's concept of shadow and persona are directly relevant to both works, and profoundly significant as a whole for Bergman and Nin. Bergman was reading Jung during the time he was working on the film, and has acknowledged the Jungian basis for its title.[16] "Persona" originally meant actor's mask, which Jung extended to the personality we construct to meet the world, "designed on the one hand to make a definite impression upon others, and, on the other hand, to conceal the true nature of the individual."[17] Nin summarizes the effects of developing this social mask in the fourth published diary:

The acceptance of this social role delivers us to the demands of the collective, and makes us a stranger to our own reality.

The consequent split in the personality may find the ego in agreement with general community expectations, while the repressed shadow turns dissenter.

Failure to acknowledge this dark alter ego creates the tendency to project it onto someone in the immediate environment, the mirror opposite to one's self.[18]

It is this split between the socially acceptable facade and the hidden shadow self projected outwards which is dramatized in both *House* and *Persona*. Persona, shadow, and double are prominent themes in the work of both Nin and Bergman, but in *House* and *Persona* they are more fully explored. The two women in each work can be seen as personifications of mask and shadow respectively, at the same time as they play out the drama of identification and projection between two selves. They are each dramas of division and isolation, both internal and external. Fusion within the self, resolution of the feelings of division, and unity between two selves, prove impossible to sustain, but it is this quest for wholeness which underlies both film and book.

From one perspective, Alma, the nurse in *Persona*, and the narrator in *House* represent the external, daily personality or persona. Elizabeth, the actress in the film, and Sabina in the prose poem personify the shadow figure. We first catch a glimpse of Elizabeth literally masked in theatrical make-up and playing the role of Electra. But in suddenly ceasing to speak or act, she seems to resign the artificiality of her customary pose. Yet she remains protected and concealed behind the silence she maintains almost undisturbed in the course of the film. The psychiatrist in the hospital where she is staying at the beginning of the film interprets her condition as the abyss between "what you are for others and what you are for yourself . . . the continual burning need to be unmasked. At last to be seen through, reduced, perhaps extinguished. Every tone of voice a lie, an act of treason. Every gesture false." But she warns her: "Your hiding place isn't watertight enough. Life starts leaking in everywhere. And you're forced to react. No one asks whether it's genuine or not, whether you're true or false." She suggests that Elizabeth's silence is but another role which she will play out until it loses interest for her.

Some of the fears which the psychiatrist points to in her analysis of Elizabeth are expressed by the characters in *House*. Jeanne, who embodies the shadow side of the narrator's personality in the fourth section of *House*, is a verbal counterpart to Elizabeth: "I have such a fear of finding another like myself, and such a desire to find one! I am so utterly lonely, but I also have such a fear that my isolation be broken through, and I no longer be the head and ruler of my universe. I am in great terror of your understanding by which you penetrate into my world; and then I stand revealed and I have to share my kingdom with you" (*HI*, 46-47). The desire to be known and fear of being known, the yearning for the protection of the mask, and the relief of stripping the mask: these universal dualities produce some of the tension and struggle in both works.

Persona and *House* reflect the ambivalent attitude of Nin and Bergman alike towards being understood: there is a purposeful obfuscation of meaning, at the same time as there is a revelation of deepest meaning. Both seem suspicious of the craving to scrutinize and penetrate which is characteristic of artist and critic. The writer in *Through a Glass Darkly* is shown to be guilty of this, as is Elizabeth in the film. Nin rails against this tendency in critics throughout her writing, including this passage in which she discusses the critics' reaction to Bergman: "The critics are annoyed by mystery. If significance eludes them they feel powerless . . . The one who seeks analytical clarity remains only a tourist, a spectator."[19] In place of critical detachment, Bergman and Nin alike demand immersion in the experience on the part of reader and audience.

The second section of *House*, which is the primary focus of this discussion, revolves around the narrator, who is a writer, and Sabina, a masked personage, who is her shadow self. The narrator, like Alma the nurse in *Persona*, is protected by the semblance of normality and wholeness which she presents at the start of the narrative: "Step out of your role and rest yourself on the core of your true desires . . . I will take them up" (*HI*, 27). Sabina is the more obviously disguised: "Sabina's face was suspended in the darkness of the garden . . . The luminous mask of her face, waxy, immobile, with eyes like sentinels" (*HI*, 18, 22). They are both masked figures, but the narrator's mask is her artistic persona, which enables her to play the role of integrator and nurturer, while Sabina's mask is her primeval sensuality. She embodies the shadow side of "proper" femininity. Nin describes her as sexually overpowering: "Every gesture she made quickened the rhythm of the blood and aroused a beat chant like the beat of the heart of the desert, a chant which was the sound of her feet treading down into the blood the imprint of her face" (*HI*, 18, 21). There is also an aspect of cruelty and power hunger in her: "Her necklace thrown around the world's neck, unmeltable. She carried it like a trophy wrung of groaning machinery, to match the inhuman rhythm of her march" (*HI*, 21).

Both Sabina and Elizabeth have an inhuman quality, related to their silence and waxy immobility. They represent the dreamed self, woman as OTHER. The mysterious, unformed aspect to both provide invitations for audience projection and fantasy. The narrator in *House* and Alma in *Persona* project onto this flexible image buried facets of themselves, both positive and negative. Alma identifies with the fantasy self she sees in the beautiful, successful actress, Elizabeth, and boasts that she could change herself into her if she tried hard. The narrator in *House* expresses her identification with the other in beautiful poetic language:

> Your beauty drowns me, drowns the core of me. When your beauty burns me I dissolve as I never dissolved before man. From all men I was different and myself, but I see in you that part of me which is you. I feel you in me; I feel my own voice becoming heavier, as if I were drinking you in, every delicate thread of resemblance being soldered by fire and one no longer detects the fissure (*HI*, 25-6).

The writer in *House* yearns to merge with her mirror-opposite, the physical embodiment of her dreamed self. Mirror love is a persistent theme in Nin's writing, which gains clarity over the years. In *Seduction of the Minotaur*, the last novel of *Cities of the Interior*, she summarizes the meaning of this attraction to Sabina:

> It was a desire for an impossible union: she wanted to lose herself in Sabina and BECOME Sabina. This wanting to BE Sabina she had mistaken for love of Sabina's night beauty. She wanted to lie beside her and become her and be one with her and both arise as ONE woman; she wanted to add herself to Sabina, re-enforce the woman in herself, the submerged woman, intensify this woman Lillian she could not liberate fully . . . She had loved in Sabina an unborn Lillian. By adding herself to Sabina she would become a more potent woman.[20]

The narrator's longing, from this perspective, is not so much for another person, as for the liberation of the buried parts of herself. This is one of the patterns which binds the dream fragments of *House* together, and for that matter, much of Nin's writing: woman's struggle to liberate the submerged aspects of herself, to resurrect and confront qualities considered socially unacceptable, such as overt sexuality and creative ambition. The dramas of twinship in this volume, and elsewhere in Nin, are variants on the theme of this drive towards self-fulfillment; but mirror love turns out not to be a satisfactory method of attaining that completion of self, since it leads to isolation, guilt, and self-division. Sabina is but a facet of the narrator's self-reflected image, and she is left confined in the coils of self-love: "Worlds self-made and self-nourished are so full of ghosts and monsters," she tells Jeanne (*HI*, 47). The writer in the last section of *House* cries out: "If only we could all escape from this house of incest, where we only love ourselves in the other" (*HI*, 70).

As unsatisfactory as this narcissistic form of love is shown to be in *House,* it may perhaps be a necessary stage of development, particularly for the artist who, almost by definition, must be self-reflective, self-absorbed, especially at the beginning of the creative process. From this vantage point, *House of Incest* is about the birth of an artist, just as it is about the birth of the artist's first work. In uniting with Sabina, the narrator hopes to attain the visibility as woman and artist that she lacked: "Sabina, you made your impression upon the world. I passed through it like a ghost . . . DOES ANYONE KNOW WHO I AM?" (*HI*, 26). Similarly, if Alma in the film is regarded as a projection of Elizabeth, the actress/artist, then the film, too, may be about her creative birth. Nin describes *Persona*, interestingly enough, as just that: "Part of the mystery is that he takes us into the act of birth, birth of a film as well as of a character."[21] Elizabeth's alienation from her roles as actress, wife, and mother also makes sense in terms of her conflicts as woman and artist, just as the narrator's struggles in **House** may be seen as a duel between the demands of the woman and artist within herself.

Although the same narcissistic impulse informs the film as the book, whether from Alma's or Elizabeth's perspective, it differs from **House** in that the dynamic between two women seems much more apparent, perhaps due to the greater tangibility of the figures in the visual medium. Alma's identification and projection onto Elizabeth is concretely displayed when she begins to dress and behave like her, until finally their images on the screen become inextricable. It is this loss of definition between the two selves which is at once feared and desired, as is the case in the book. Nin has commented about **House** and **Persona**: "In **House of Incest** I treated the theme of exchange of personalities, as Bergman did later in the film **Persona**. Sabina and the writer of the poem are in constant danger of identifying with each other and *becoming the other*."[22] Total identification in both cases leads to confusion and loss of identity, a sensation of drowning in the other. Alma's captivation by her mirror-opposite forces her into a confrontation with her own shadow self, and a loss of the comforts of her mask.

Gradually the protective coating of her nurse's uniform wears off, and she is revealed both to herself and to the audience. Elizabeth's silence forces her in upon herself, and this is the source of her terror and her desperation. She begins to reveal things about her past which she had long ago forgotten. She recounts an early sexual experience and a subsequent abortion. The next day, she discovers a letter from Elizabeth to her psychiatrist in which her psyche is discussed in abstract, analytic terms. She feels vulnerable and betrayed, and takes brutal revenge. Alma places a piece of broken glass in Elizabeth's path as retribution, and in that act the persona of the nurse is stripped bare. Bergman conveys this crack in her mask visually by having the image of her face through the window crack and burn immediately after this event. It is a powerful visual metaphor, suggesting the collapse of personality, reality, and art simultaneously.

After the film burns, there is a duplication of some of the same disturbing images Bergman used in the opening sequence of the film. Once again the audience is made aware that they are watching a film, at the same time as they are presented with an image which burns right through the surface of art, reality, and mask. When the camera refocuses, in place of Alma's face in the window, Elizabeth appears. The audience is unsettled; it is impossible to sort out exactly what is "real." There is an increasing confusion between the identities of Alma and Elizabeth, between imagined and actual events. Yet to attempt to untangle what is dream and what actually "happens" in the film is to miss

the point. Boundaries have been eradicated in both these works between real and dreamed events, between mask and shadow, and between the two women.

IV

The center of the drama in both film and book, and the point of convergence between visual and verbal image, comes at the moment of total identification between the two women. The fusion of the narrator and Sabina is described in words which provide a perfect counterpart to the screen variation on this theme: "So now we are inextricably woven . . . Our faces are soldered together by soft hair, soldered together, showing two profiles of the same soul" (**HI**, 28). In the film, the faces of the two women are literally merged into a single face, at first obviously off-kilter, then disturbingly integrated. It is an indelible image of integration and self-division at once, a picture of unity between mask and shadow, between Alma and Elizabeth, and of fragmentation and loss of self. There is a haunting terror and beauty in this image which is unmatched by any other shot in Bergman's impressive repertoire.

This visual fusion of identities comes after one of the most excruciating scenes in the film. Alma's identification with Elizabeth is at this point nearly total. She is dressed exactly like her, and appears to have absorbed her inner self as well. She discovers Elizabeth looking at the picture of her son which she had torn apart at the start of the film. Alma uncovers the picture which Elizabeth attempts to hide, and proceeds to tell Elizabeth how she felt before, during, and after her pregnancy. We watch Elizabeth's pained reaction as Alma reminds her of the social pressures that led Elizabeth to get pregnant to begin with (the accusation that she was not a complete woman, even though she was a successful artist), the hostile feelings she had towards the unborn child within her, and the disgust and hate she felt for the newborn infant. There is probably no deeper shadow Alma could reveal in Elizabeth: her lack of the "appropriate" motherly feelings. Bergman replays the exact same scene, only this time the camera focuses on Alma's face instead of Elizabeth's. The audience wonders how she could know these things about Elizabeth. Is she projecting her own deepest feelings? It is impossible to say, but the revelation of her own abortion suggests her involvement in the accusation. The two women are one in the overlap of their hidden selves. At the end of this scene, the two faces merge; they are inextricably woven.

The emotional intensity of this scene is accentuated by the intimacy of the camera shots. The faces of the two women fill the screen, and we are enveloped in their images. In this way, we are brought into the process taking place between them. If the film's full effectiveness is to be experienced, the audience must identify and project into the characters, just as they do with each other. The same invitation for audience participation takes place in *House.* At the high point in the merging of identities, the following words appear centered on the page:

I AM THE OTHER FACE OF YOU . . .
THIS IS THE BOOK YOU WROTE
AND YOU ARE THE WOMAN
I AM.

(*HI,* 28)

The interchange of identities between Sabina and the narrator is extended through this method to include the reader as well. We are encouraged to discover and lose ourselves at once in the narrator's words. Complete identification with the narrator may lead to a discovery of the hidden artist within us, or to a sense of unity and mergence with our shadow self. The meaning of this peak moment in both book and film is the product of a coalescence of artist, audience, and actors.

But the center does not hold. The moment disintegrates, perhaps because of the difficulty of maintaining a feeling of wholeness in a shattered world, or within a fragmented self. The dissolution of the bond also suggests the fear of intimacy, a powerful *leitmotif* in the work of both Nin and Bergman. At least as strong as this fear of closeness is the fear of homosexuality, which appears as an undercurrent in *Persona* and *House.* The erotic component in *Persona* is implied by visual innuendo, such as the night scene in which the two women embrace and their figures overlap in a dreamlike manner. The eroticism in the prose-poem is quite blatant: "Around my pulse she put a flat steel bracelet and my pulse beat . . . thumping like a savage in orgiastic frenzy" (*HI*, 23). The sexual suggestiveness in both *House* and *Persona* is shrouded with ambiguity, partly because of the dream atmosphere which pervades book and film. Whether the women touch in either case is irrelevant; what is significant is the potency of this buried fear which appears to surface at the moment of mergence. There is an immediate disintegration afterwards in both *House* and *Persona*, which is not remedied for the remainder of book or film, with the possible exception of the ambiguous endings.

In *House,* the narrator spins off into her "madness" as a result of this fusion and the concomitant fears. In one of the most effective passages in the book, she describes the feelings which have arisen from this mergence:

I am ill with the obstinacy of images, reflections in cracked mirrors. I am a woman with Siamese cat eyes smiling always behind my gravest words, mocking my own intensity. I smile because I listen to the OTHER and I believe the OTHER. I am a marionette pulled by unskilled fingers, pulled

apart, inharmoniously dislocated; one arm dead, the other rhapsodizing in mid-air. (*HI,* 29-30)

The narrator's sense of self has been "dislocated" by this total mergence with her mirror-opposite. The image of her health and normality has been cracked, and she is left uncertain of who she is. She is divided between the reflection of herself which she presents to please the OTHERS and the buried shadow which has appeared as a result of this identification. Nin continues to depict woman divided against herself in unforgettable language:

I see two women in me freakishly bound together, like circus twins. I see them tearing away from each other. I can hear the tearing, the anger and love, passion and pity. When the act of dislocation suddenly ceases—or when I cease to be aware of the sound—then the silence is more terrible because there is nothing but insanity around me, the insanity of things pulling, pulling within oneself, the roots tearing at each other to grow separately, the strain made to achieve unity. (*HI,* 30)

This is the nightmare of total duality: the desire for unity, intimacy, counterbalanced by the fear thereof; the outer woman, persona, at war with the shadow. The allusion to freakish circus twins suggests the spectral fear of "abnormality" which leads to conflict and anxiety. There is no distinguishing the "pulling within" and without; the outer "insanity of things" is incorporated within, the violence buried inside gets projected outwards. This is poetically stated here, and in *Persona*, dramatically demonstrated through a series of violent acts on the part of Alma towards Elizabeth, which mirror the cruelty of the outer world. Bergman also uses documentary evidence to make his point.

In the early part of the film, Elizabeth is in her hospital room and turns on the television, only to recoil in horror at a clip of a Buddhist monk immolating himself in protest against the Vietnam war. The camera focuses steadily on the monk; we are brought into Elizabeth's experience and feel the same horror that she feels. The "madness" of her silence throughout the film makes sense in the context of her revulsion from a world in which such violence regularly occurs.

Later in the film, we observe Elizabeth in one of her private moments in which she contemplates a photograph taken in the Warsaw ghetto, during the round-up of the Jews for the camps. The camera zeroes in on the pathetic figure of a little boy gazing in terror at the Nazis. The connection between private and societal breakdown is brilliantly revealed in this scene. Elizabeth's culpability in terms of her neglected child is suggested in her contemplation of the photograph.

Inner and outer nightmare converge for both Nin and Bergman, but the latter has a greater apprehension of external, political nightmares, and the former, at least in **House,** remains trapped in the inner nightmare, reluctant to "pass through the tunnel which led from the house into the world on the other side of the walls" (**HI,** 70). This difference between the two is reflected in their imaginative conceptions of transparent images. The window in the house of incest, for example, looks out on a "static sea, where immobile fishes had been glued to painted backgrounds" (**HI,** 51-52). The window in the summer house in *Persona* looks out on the world, reflects back to the characters and the audience woman's capacity for cruelty to others. The fissure in the window occurs directly after Alma places the piece of broken glass in Elizabeth's path. Images overlap once again: fragments of broken glass appear in **House** as well, but in that case, the writer is cut by her own book, perhaps in punishment for the "labyrinth of selflove," the prison of narcissism: "As I move within my book I am cut by pointed glass and broken bottles . . ." (**HI,** 62). This image suggests the guilt and pain involved in creation, particularly when the life and art are inseparable. The book becomes a mirror of the artist and reflects back to her a shadow image. It is interesting that Nin conceives of the image in a rather masochistic manner, and Bergman in more sadistic terms, perhaps in keeping with social conditioning.

Although there is more inter-play between the world perceived through the window and the reflection in the mirror in *Persona* than in **House,** it is the private, self-reflective struggle with the "monster who sleeps at the bottom of . . . [man's] brain"[23] which predominates in both *Persona* and **House.** This struggle between the shadow-monster and persona is an on-going process without resolution in either work. This is what unsettles so many about book and film: there are no certitudes, and the conclusions about the possibilities of real change are tentative. Alma boards a bus at the end of the film, presumably to return to her old life, but whether she has been changed by the experience we cannot be certain. We catch a glimpse of Elizabeth acting in *Electra* again, but whether this is past or future is impossible to say.[24] There is the suggestion in this image of her willingness to resign the mask of her silence and to return to "ordinary" existence. The film concludes with the same exposure to the film process with which it opened; once again, the audience is forced into an awareness of the gap between life and art, and of the limitations of the artistic process.

No such reminder takes place at the end of **House** which, in comparison, is more affirmative. The book concludes with a woman dancing "with the music and with the rhythm of earth's circles; she turned with the earth turning, like a disk, turning all faces to light and to darkness evenly, dancing towards daylight" (**HI,** 72). Perhaps this is a movement towards acceptance of the light and dark sides of the self, of mask and shadow; or, put another way, a movement in the direction of the world outside the self, "towards daylight." Nin ends the book, as she began it, in process, moving towards completion of her "uncompleted self" (**HI,** 15).

NOTES

1. Anaïs Nin, *House of Incest* (Chicago: Swallow Press, 1958), p. 28. (Originally published in Paris: Siana Editions, 1936). Subsequent references in the text will be to HI.

2. It should be understood from the start that I am not implying a case of influences here. As far as I know, Bergman is unaware of Nin's book.

3. Oliver Evans, *Anaïs Nin* (Carbondale: Southern Illinois University Press, 1968), p. 26.

4. Stig Björkman, Manns, Sima. *Bergman on Bergman* (New York: Simon and Schuster, 1973), p. 198.

5. Björkman, p. 168.

6. *The Diary of Anais Nin. Volume Two. 1934-1939* (New York: Harcourt Brace, 1967), p. 319.

7. Evans, p. 26.

8. *John Simon, Ingmar Bergman Directs* (New York: Harcourt Brace, 1972), p. 215.

9. Anaïs Nin, *The Novel of the Future* (New York: Macmillan, 1968), p. 119. Subsequent references to *Novel*.

10. *The Diary of Anaïs Nin. Volume One. 1931-1934* (New York: Harcourt Brace, 1966), p. 132.

11. *Novel*, p. 18.

12. Simon, p. 39.

13. Simon, p. 239.

14. Simon, p. 288.

15. Anaïs Nin, In *Favor of the Sensitive Man and Other Essays* (New York: Harcourt Brace, 1976), p. 116. Subsequent references to *In Favor*.

16. See Simon, p. 224; Björkman, p. 202.

17. C. G. Jung, *Two Essays on Analytical Psychology* (Cleveland: World Publishing Co., 1956), p. 203.

18. *The Diary of Anaïs Nin. Volume Four.* 1944-1947 (New York: Harcourt Brace, 1971), p. 59.

19. *In Favor*, p. 112.

20. Anaïs Nin, *Seduction of the Minotaur* (Chicago: Swallow Press, 1961), p. 125.

21. *In Favor*, p. 114.

22. *Novel*, pp. 122-123.

23. *The Diary of Anaïs Nin. Volume Two*, p. 347.

24. Bergman claims that Elizabeth has returned to the theatre, but this is not clear in the film. See Simon, pp. 31-32.

Smaro Kamboureli (essay date March 1984)

SOURCE: "Discourse and Intercourse, Design and Desire in the Erotica of Anaïs Nin," in *Journal of Modern Literature*, Vol. 11, No. 1, March 1984, pp. 143-58.

[*In the following essay, Kamboureli distinguishes between purveyors of erotica from those of pornography, attempting to establish Nin's* Erotica *as pornography wherein she focuses as much on poetry as on sexuality.*]

In the following excerpt from the "Preface" to *Little Birds*, Anaïs Nin distinguishes between erotica and pornography:

> It is one thing to include eroticism in a novel or a story and quite another to focus one's whole attention to it. The first is like life itself. It is, I might say, natural, sincere, as in the sensual pages of Zola or of Lawrence. But focusing wholly on the sexual life is not natural. It becomes something like the life of the prostitute, an abnormal activity that ends up turning the prostitute away from the sexual. Writers perhaps know this.[1]

While both erotica and pornography acknowledge the significance of sexuality and aim to arouse sexual feelings, they differ from each other insofar as their aesthetic and sociocultural perspectives are concerned.

Erotica deals primarily with the dialectics of desire: desire as the articulation of the tension that exists between a lover's emotions and the cravings of his body, and desire as the tendency to give aesthetic form to sexual experience. Erotics and aesthetics, then, depend on each other: as desire gives shape to man's life so does language enact or amplify the semantics of his sensual gestures. Sexuality is evoked both by the depiction of entangled naked bodies and by devices that enhance the lover's identity. Thus the sexual act in erotica is not an end in itself; it is only one of the forms that eroticism takes. Pornography, on the other hand, according to the *OED*, is about the "description of the life, manners, etc. of prostitutes and their patrons." Pornography reduces the ramifications of desire to one aspect of sexuality. Its material is located within a minimal context which not only undermines the complexities of sexuality, but also deprives man of the feelings necessary for the arousal of "natural" desire.[2]

These differences between erotica and pornography, as Nin is implicitly aware, make **Delta of Venus** and **Little Birds** more pornographic than erotic. In an oblique way, she advises her readers against comparing or confusing these stories with her other writings. In this respect, **Erotica,** the collective title of **Delta of Venus** and **Little Birds,** is a misleading index of their contents.[3] Yet Nin has deliberately chosen to call her pornographic stories erotic, for, as I intend to show, she is innovative within the genre of pornography. She creates a context where, even though the focus is exclusively on the sexual life, sexuality is far from being "not natural." Nin, however, does not allow her readers to wonder why she is engaged in an "abnormal activity."

The two volumes of her stories open with prefaces that both obfuscate and illuminate this engagement. The prefaces come as a surprise to a reader who has been already initiated into pornography or to a novice who is solely interested in titillating experiences. It is not conventional to find literary prefaces to pornographic stories or novels, first, because they cause a confusion of the pornographic genre with more serious literature and, second, and more importantly, because they delay the promised pleasure. A notable exception is Pauline Réage's *The Story of O* which bears a "Note" by its translator Sabine d'Estrée, a "Note" by the critic Mandiargues, and lastly a "Preface" by Jean Paulhan, a member of L'Académie Française. But this is in France, where erotica and pornography have a long and serious tradition, claiming, among others, George Bataille whose novels *Madame Edwarda, Histoire de l'Oeil* and his studies *L'Érotisme, Les Larmes d'Éros* and *La Literature et le Mal* deserve an important place in the history of sexuality as an expression of human nature.

Nin, having lived both in France and in the States, is familiar with the differences that characterize the traditions of the two countries in terms of perceiving, and writing about, sexuality. As she notes in her **Diary**,

> The joke on me is that France had a tradition of literary erotic writing, in fine elegant style, written by the best writers. When I first began to write for the collector I thought there was a simi-

lar tradition here, but found none at all. All I have seen is badly written, shoddy, and by second-rate writers. No fine writer seems ever to have tried his hand at erotica.[4]

In writing her *Erotica,* Nin confronts the established French tradition of erotic writing and the American tradition of pornography that makes no claim whatsoever as literature. She is conscious of addressing an American audience. Given this, the two prefaces reveal her intent to present *Delta of Venus* and *Little Birds* in a different light: they read as apologias and as disguised manifestos about pornography.

In the "Preface" to *Delta of Venus,* which is an excerpt from the third volume of the *Diary,* Nin provides us with the context that generated the writing of these stories. Henry Miller was writing erotica "at a dollar a page" for an old collector and one of his rich clients (vii). But because he found this "writing to order . . . a castrating occupation" (ix), he quit after a while and asked Nin, who also claimed to be in financial need, to continue. This incident constitutes not only the occasion of her pornographic stories, but also the beginning of her apologia.

In the "Preface" to *Little Birds* we read,

> In New York everything becomes harder, more cruel. I had many people to take care of, many problems, and since I was in character very much like George Sand, who wrote all night to take care of her children, lovers, friends, I had to find work. I became what I shall call the Madame of an unusual house of literary prostitution. It was a very artistic "maison". . . .
>
> Before I took up my new profession I was known as a poet, as a woman who was independent and wrote for her own pleasure. . . . Yet my real writing was put aside when I set out in search of the erotic. (*LB,* viii, ix)

Nin presents the conditions that led her to the writing of *Erotica* as the continuation of two cultural paradigms. The first one is, of course, New York City which, besides offering artists an exciting environment to live in, makes life "harder" for them. In short, Nin justifies herself by evoking the theme of survival: the poor artist sacrifices her moral principles for the sake of her altruism. The second cultural paradigm she employs is notably French again, that of George Sand. Nin is not alone in the game that "cruel" conditions force her to play. George Sand, a writer of status, was engaged in, more or less, the same activity. Nin feels that by writing pornography her reputation as a literary writer is at stake. The analogy she draws between herself and Sand and her statement that she put aside her "real writing" when

she "set out in search of the erotic" make her latent anxiety quite obvious.

Nin "prostitutes" herself by writing, as she claims, not for her "own pleasure," but for the pleasure of the collector. The result is that she becomes a "Madame" who is, paradoxically, not a lover or a friend, but a mother figure as "matron." J. S. Atherton, in his review of *Delta of Venus* titled "The Maternal Instinct," says that "it is rather unfortunate that the latest book by her to appear here [Britain] is a book of frankly dirty stories of which she herself disapproved and only produced *under pressure.*"[5] Atherton emphasizes, to a greater extent than Nin, the occasion of the stories in order to justify their "dirtiness." He has obviously read the "Preface" only as an apologia.

In the story of **"The Basque and Bijou,"** the madame of a house in a red-light district is described as "A maternal woman . . . but a maternal woman whose cold eyes travelled almost immediately to the man's shoes, for she judged from them how much he could afford to pay for his pleasure. Then for her own satisfaction, her eyes rested for a while on the trouser buttons" (*DV,* 159). The profession of this madame is apparently different from Nin's profession of "literary prostitution"; Nin does not apply this "maternal" image to herself. As a mother figure, she has different intentions.

Although Nin was undoubtedly taking care of her lovers and of her friends whenever needed, as her *Diary* testifies, she is obviously manipulating in the "Preface" the nurturing aspects of the maternal role because of their positive ethical connotations. Thus Nin exonerates herself socially.

As for her literary role, she makes it clear that she is the "madame" of a "very artistic 'maison.'" She is engaged in "literary prostitution." The word "literary" is revealing both of her intent to justify herself and of the changes she brings in the pornographic genre.

Even though Nin "hated" the old collector, and could not afford typing paper or the repairs of broken windows, and could not pay the expenses of Miller, Duncan, Gonzalo, etc., she could somehow afford the time for background research. She proceeded to write the stories in an almost scholarly fashion: she "spent days in the library studying the *Kama Sutra,* listened to friends' most extreme adventures" (*DV,* ix). In spite of her reservations, Nin is not writing pornography "tongue-in-cheek"; she "caricatur[es] sexuality," but she does so only to the extent that she makes it the single theme of *Delta of Venus* and *Little Birds* (*DV,* ix).

Nin's focus on sexuality emphasizes the pornographic aspect of *Erotica.* Yet the biographical elements that occasionally permeate her stories cause a shift of her gaze from the mere pornographic to a more inciting look at the sexual lives of people she knows. Nin is being deceptive when she says that "I did not want to give anything genuine, and decided to create a mixture of stories I had heard and inventions, pretending they were from the diary of a woman" (**DV,** ix). This straightforward statement becomes baffling when we see it in its original context which is the third volume of the *Diary.* In the same volume, we read about incidents which echo almost identical incidents in **Erotica.** I will limit myself to two examples of this kind:

(from *the* **Diary,** vol. III)

I visited Hugh and Brigitte Chisholm in their East River apartment. The place is so near the water that it gave me the illusion of a boat. The barges passed down the river while we talked. . . . Hugh is small in stature, with curly hair, soft greenish eyes, an impish air. He is a good poet.

As I enter they treat me like an *objet d'art.* . . .

She shines steadily, under any circumstance. Not intermittedly as I do, because I can only bloom in a certain . . . warmth. . . . That afternoon, in the warmth of their appreciation, I blossomed. . . .

From the objects I could divine their life in Rome, Paris, Florence; Brigitte's mother; the famous *haute couture* designer, Coco Chanel; *Vogue*; the pompousness of their family background and their effort to laugh at it. (22)

I knew no woman as easily persuaded to go to bed who had obtained so little from her play-acting. The extent of her frigidity appalled me, and I persuaded her it would get worse, and finally become incurable if she so deadened her contact with men. I gently took her by the hand and led her to an analyst.

But this woman, who could undress at the request of any man, make love with anyone, go to orgies, act as a call girl in a professional house, this Beth told me she found it actually difficult to *talk* about sex! (21-22, 24)

(from **"Mandra"** in *Little Birds*)

I am invited one night to the apartment of a young society couple, the Hs. It is like being on a boat because it is near the East River and the barges pass while we talk. . . . Her husband, Paul, is small and of the race of the imps. Not a man but a faun—a lyrical animal, quick and humorous. He thinks I am beautiful. He treats me like an objet

d'art. . . . She is a natural beauty, whereas I, an artificial one, need a setting and warmth to bloom successfully. . . .

Everything is touched with aristocratic impudence, through which I can sense the Hs' fabulous life in Florence; Miriam's frequent appearances in *Vogue* wearing Chanel dresses; the pompousness of their families; their efforts to be elegantly bohemian; and their obsession with the word that is the key to society—everything must be "amusing." (144)

She is being analyzed and has discovered what I sensed long ago: that she has never known a real orgasm, at thirty-four, after a sexual life that only an expert accountant could keep track of. I am discovering her pretenses. She is always smiling, gay, but underneath she feels unreal, remote, detached from experience. She acts as if she were asleep. . . .

Mary says, "It is very hard to talk about sex, I am so ashamed." She is not ashamed of doing anything at all, but she cannot talk about it. She can talk to me. We sit for hours in perfumed places where there is music. She likes places where actors go. (140-41)

The diary which Nin "pretends" to have invented is actually her published **Diary,** the edited version of the diaries she kept all her life. She uses some of its material concerning her friends practically verbatim, an act that suggests that she is far from writing a caricature of sexuality; she records in detail sensual settings and recollects the way sexuality manifests itself in her milieu. Reality is embedded in fantasy and vice versa.

But Nin does not limit herself to using only her friends' sexual adventures. What enhances her fusion of the real with the imaginary is her personal presence in **Erotica,** a presence hardly disguised. In **"Marcel"** we read about a woman who lives in a houseboat (**DV,** 250); in **"A Model"** we read about a young woman whose mother "had European ideas about young girls," who "had never read anything but literary novels" (**LB,** 67), who "knew languages," who also "knew Spanish dancing," who "had an exotic face" and "accent," who posed as a model for New York artists (**LB,** 68). A reader of Nin's **Diary** will recognize immediately Nin herself. I am not arguing here that **Delta of Venus** and **Little Birds** are Nin's disguised, or "anonymous" (**DV,** xii), autobiography. What is of great interest is that Nin does not distance herself from her pornographic writing, a distance she should have kept had she thought of her pornography in purely negative terms. Nin's self-portrait in **Erotica** is her signature as artist. It is a signature that falsifies her apologetic tone while it verifies her belief that her pornography is not completely devoid of art.

This brings us back to the occasion of **Erotica.** Nin has to comply with the collector's persistent demand: "leave out the poetry . . . [c]oncentrate on sex" (*DV*, ix). In Nin's words, he wants her to "exclude," from her writing her "own aphrodisiac—poetry" (*DV*, x). Here we have two different attitudes toward pornography. As D. H. Lawrence says, "What they are [pornography and obscenity] depends, as usual, entirely on the individual. What is pornography to one man is the laughter of genius to another."[6] The collector, in this respect, and his client (whether real or fabricated, he is an extra-textual device designed to create the occasion) deprive Nin of her sensuality. They collect (steal) her fantasies, her longings, her actual experiences. They deprive her of her memories, and of her imagination as a person and as an artist.

The collector wants Nin to reduce discourse to the level of mere intercourse. Yet, ironically, it is language he is solely interested in. He is not like Elena and Pierre in **"Elena"** whose reading of erotic books keeps them in touch with their bodies:

> He bought her erotic books, which they read together. . . . As they lay on the couch together and read, their hands wandered over each other's body, to the places described in the book. . . .
>
> They would lie on their stomachs, still dressed, open a new book and read together, with their hands caressing each other. They kissed over erotic pictures. (*DV*, 115-16)

The process of reading erotica amplifies Elena's and Pierre's desire. The real (Elena's and Pierre's lovemaking) merges with the imaginary (the content of the books). They not only re-enact what they read, but they also "embrace" the books themselves. Their response to erotica is different from the response of the pornographic reader, which usually results in vicarious sexuality.

In contrast, the collector represents one of the two stereotypes of the pornographic mind. He is the one who fears, and thus has to forget, the reality of the body. His stance toward sexuality divorces the body (eros) from the head (logos). Not being able (potent) to face the body naked, he wants the pornographic discourse to be naked instead, namely unadorned with poetry. By avoiding, therefore, an encounter with the presence of a real lover, the collector, or the stereotype he represents, destroys the flesh of the body: he goes to a skeletal outline which is a fabrication and as such empty of spirit. As Nin says when she addresses him

in the **Diary,** "You are shrinking your world of sensations. You are withering it, starving it, draining its blood" (*DV*, xiii). The collector is not like Donald who says to Elena that "[t]alking together is *a form* of intercourse" (*DV*, 104; my emphasis). The collector desires a discourse that will entirely replace intercourse.

The second stereotype of the pornographic mind is the lover who worships the body while, at the same time, wanting to silence it. Nin provides us with an example of this in **"The Queen."** The narrator of the story talks about a painter who sees women only as whores:

> He was saying "I like a whore best of all because I feel she will never cling to me, never get entangled with me. It makes me feel free. I do not have to make love to her. . . .
>
> "The women who are unabashedly sexual, with *the womb written all over their faces* . . . the women who throw their sex out at us, from the hair, the eyes, the nose, the *mouth*, the whole body—these are the women I love." (*LB*, 101, 104; my emphasis)

This character is receptive only to the sexuality of the body. His exclusive love for its sensual qualities erases all the features that give life and character to a woman. Unlike the collector, whose fear of the body makes him a lover of a surrogate body, the body of language, the painter of this story reduces discourse to one level only of signification, that of sex. Accordingly, the sexual act for him is solipsistic. This solipsism expresses the painter's narcissism as well as his reluctance to accept the presence of woman during the act of lovemaking. He is afraid of her feminine psyche.

This kind of pornographer, as Susan Griffin says in *Pornography and Silence*, "reduces a woman to a mere thing, to an entirely material object without a soul, who can only be 'loved' physically."[7] The painter, afraid of the loss of his freedom, kills the individuality of woman: he sees her mouth only as the surfacing of her sex. Yet this phenomenology of female sexuality and pleasure is deceptive. The mouth seen only as metaphor is reduced to an orifice, an orifice though that remains mute. Nin, aware of this, renounces this attitude toward pornography within the story itself: the painter's most favorite whore, Bijou, is "colder than a statue" (*LB*, 101); her sexuality is static; moreover, it is the painter who "clings" to her as he follows the "tiny trail of semen" that she leaves behind her from all the lovers she took, except him (*LB*, 106). The painter is betrayed both by his whore and by his own erotics of detachment.

Nin herself is a pornographer of a different kind. She transforms her contempt for those who focus "only on sexuality" into "violent explosions of poetry" (**DV**, xii). The metaphor of explosion is pertinent here. What is a physical orgasm for the pornographic mind is for Nin both a physical act and the release of poetic language. As Roland Barthes says in talking about Sade's writings, "there [is] no distinction between the structure of ejaculation and that of language."[8] Nin's fusion of discourse and intercourse is evident in most of the stories in **Delta of Venus** and **Little Birds**.

We read, for instance, in **"Linda"**:

> André had a particular passion for the mouth. In the street he looked at women's mouths. To him the mouth was indicative of the sex. A tightness of a lip, thinness, augured nothing rich or voluptuous. A full mouth promised an open, generous sex. . . .
>
> Linda's mouth had seduced him from the first. . . . There was something about the way she moved it, a passionate unfolding of the lips, promising a person who would lash around the beloved like a storm. When he first saw Linda, he was taken into her through this mouth, as if he were already making love to her. And so it was on their wedding night. (**DV**, 232-33)

There are some subtle differences here between André and the painter mentioned earlier. For André, the mouth is not a projection of the female sex, but the entrance itself into the being of a woman. The mouth as the source of language reveals a woman's potentiality both as a lover and as a person who can articulate her imaginings. Thus André does not see woman as a whore, as the painter does, but as a "beloved" who eventually becomes his wife.

What illustrates even better the relationship that Nin establishes between discourse and intercourse is, again, the story of **"Elena"**:

> She [Elena] moved quicker to bring the climax, and when he saw this, he hastened his motions inside of her and incited her to come with him, with *words*, with his *hands* caressing her, and finally with his *mouth* soldered to hers, so that the *tongues* moved in the same rhythm as the *womb* and *penis*, and the climax was spreading between her *mouth* and her *sex*, in *crosscurrents* of increasing pleasure, until she *cried out*, half *sob* and half *laughter*, from the overflow of *joy* through her body. (**DV**, 96; my emphasis)

Here erotics and poetics merge. The lovers' desire for each other engulfs their whole selves. Intercourse is not a mechanical operation but an act both of love and speech. As

George Steiner notes, "Sex is a profoundly semantic act."[9] The semantics of lovemaking communicates the lovers' sexuality in language that has a dialectic structure: it is the "crosscurrent" of the body (the sexual organs/the tongues) and of the spirit (the sob/the laughter/the joy); it is the expression of sexuality as it is contained in the psyche.

By presenting the sexual face of the psyche, Nin reveals the animal in man. The fiercer the desire of the lovers and the greater their abandonment, the closer they come to the instinctive world of the animals. Elena and Pierre reach this level of sexual existence:

> His caresses had a strange quality, at times soft and melting, at other times fierce, like the caresses she had expected when his eyes fixed on her, the caresses of a wild animal. There was something animallike about his hands, which he kept spread over each part of her body, and which took her sex and hair together as if he would tear them away from the body, as if he grasped earth and grass together. (**DV**, 94)

The two lovers *transgress* their consciousness as their animality manifests itself. They are dehumanized, becoming thus aware of their own limits and consequently of the limits of their sexuality. As Michael Foucault says in his discussion of sexuality and Bataille in the essay "Preface to Transgression," transgression "serves as a glorification of the nature it excludes: the limit opens violently onto the limitless, finds itself suddenly carried away by the content it had rejected and fulfilled by this alien plenitude which invades it to the core of its being."[10] The excess of Elena's and Pierre's desire, like that of most of the characters in Nin's **Erotica,** becomes the measure of a double recognition: they encounter their profanity and its limits, a profanity that designates the finitude of their consciousness, in other words, the effacement of their egos during the sexual act.

What further indicates the prominence of animal profanity and the absence of an overtly conscious self in Nin's **Delta of Venus** and **Little Birds** is her diction, which is pointedly different from the diction we see in traditional pornography. Nin never uses words like "cunt," "cock" and "fuck." Instead, she expresses the profanity of the sexual organs by describing them in terms of natural and animal imagery.

In **"Mathilde,"** Mathilde's sex is "like the gum plant leaf with its secret milk that the pressure of the finger could bring out, the odorous moisture that came like the moisture of the sea shells" (**DV**, 15). Similarly, we read in **"Two Sisters"** that "[t]he fur had opened to reveal her [Dorothy's] whole body, glowing, luminous, rich in the fur, like some jeweled animal. . . . John did not touch the body, he suckled at the breasts, sometimes stopping to feel the fur with his mouth, as if he were kissing a beautiful *animal*" (*LB*, 44).

The profanity of the body and its multifarious significance are further reinforced by Nin's usage of the word "ass," which is the most apparent word in her sexual discourse, pointing as it does to the boundary line between body and spirit. Octavio Paz in his *Conjunctions and Disjunctions* compares the face with the ass and thus illustrates the "soul-body dualism." He sees the conflict between the two as representing "the (repressive) reality principle and the (explosive) pleasure principle."[11] We find a good example of this dualism in **"Mathilde"**: "she lay on her left side and exposed her ass to the mirror" (*DV*, 15). As Paz says, "the mirror reflects the face of an image";[12] in Mathilde's case, then, the mirror image of her ass is symbolic of the "other" face of *homo eroticus*. Nin reconciles the profanity of the body and the unconscious power it imbues with the self-consciousness of the face.

Nin's sexual discourse avoids the vulgarity of hard-core pornography. Her lyrical language emphasizes the poetics of sexuality. She transgresses the limits of the body's anatomy by stressing its eroticism. The semantics of the sexual act, therefore, signifies the lovers' transgression of the boundary of the human as they enter the realm of the animal. We should not overlook at this point the paradox of the fact that the human element, even when it is transgressed, is quite often described in utterly civilized terms, for example, the fur of the animal is a sign of luxury, the woman that is a jeweled animal. This civilized form of sexuality indicates that the lovers in Nin's *Erotica* estrange themselves from the familiar (their egos) in order to discover a strangeness that reconciles them with their sexual instincts. Sexual transgression has now come full circle. To quote from Foucault again, "Sexuality points to nothing beyond itself. . . . It marks the limit within us and designates us as a limit."[13] As Elena says, "it [is] a strange transgression" (*DV*, 104).

Transgression destroys the relationship of ethics to sexuality. Foucault observes that "A rigorous language, as it arises from sexuality . . . will say that he [man] exists without God."[14] When Elena notes about Leila that she has "acquired a new sex by growing beyond man and woman," that she is like "a mythic figure, enlarged, magnified" (*DV*, 135), she describes a human condition that signifies the "death of God." The same concept is also implied by the "naked savage woman" that Reynolds talks about in **"A Model"** (*LB*, 84). According to Foucault, "it is excess that discovers that sexuality and the death of God are bound to the same experience."[15] Indeed it takes Leila's fierce desire to experience both male and female sensuality and the "panther" qualities of the "naked savage woman" to annul the unethical connotations of obscenity that make God unnecessary. As Henry Miller observes in *The World of Lawrence*,

> Obscenity is pure and springs from effervescence, excess vitality, joy of life, concord, unanimity, alliance with nature, indifference to God of the healthy sort that takes God down a peg or two in order to reexamine him. . . .
>
> Obscenity figures large and heavily, magnificently and awesomely, in all primitive peoples. . . . The savage is not a sick man. The savage retains his sense of awe, wonder, mystery, his love of action, his right to behave like the animal he is. . . .[16]

This "pure" nature of obscenity explains why Nin's characters, by crossing beyond their limits, challenge the existence of God.

Yet the "death of God" does not imply an absence of the sacred. The lover as transgressor creates his own version of the sacred out of the intensity of his profanity. This is what Elena has in mind when she says to herself, "I talk almost like a saint, to *burn* for love—for no mystic love, but for a ravaging sensual meeting" (*DV*, 144; my emphasis). The same "saintly" abandonment is expressed by the clairvoyant in **"The Basque and Bijou"**:

> His dance for the three women took place one evening when all the clients were gone. He stripped himself, showing his *gleaming golden-brown body*. To his waist he tied a fake penis modelled like his own and the same color.
>
> He said, "This is a dance from my own country. We do this for the women on *feast days*." . . . He jerked his body as if he were entering a woman. . . . The final spasm was wild, like that of a man *giving up his life in the act of sex*. (*DV*, 184; my emphasis)

The motif of sacrifice that we see in both cases is the natural consequence of the latent presence of the sacred. The light that surrounds the two lovers signifies that they have already gone beyond their profane limits and they are now ready to transgress another boundary, that of death. Sexual transgression as sacrifice reinstates God's presence, only now his presence inspires no awe, for he is experienced as a divine power that dwells within the body. Thus the body as a vehicle of the divine receives all the acts of worship offered to it.

The infliction of death on a lover during the sexual act is the most extreme blow that the lovers' sexual drive can direct against the prohibitions that our culture imposes on sexuality. Bataille, in discussing the nature of sexual prohibition, says,

What is forbidden urges transgression, without which such an action of transgression would not have had that evil glimmer that seduces. It is the transgression of what is forbidden that bewitches.

But this glimmer is not only one that radiates from eroticism. It lights up the religious life every time it involves an action of utter violence, an action which is triggered the moment death slits the throat of a victim.

Sacré!

But, as for me, the ultimate form of death brings a strange sense of victory. It bathes me in its light, and stirs within me an infinitely joyous laughter. This is the laughter that allows one to disappear![17]

The disappearance that Bataille talks about is the ultimate form of transgression, a sacred transgression this time, that transforms the sexual act into a miracle: what inhibits sexuality is forced to disappear by the power of sexual desire. It is not accidental, for instance, that Mathilde is given incense; "[i]n Lima she received much of it, it was part of the ritual. She was raised on a pedestal of poetry so that her falling into the final embrace might seem more of a miracle" (*DV*, 12). The incense that Mathilde receives and its rapturous effects present her as a "victim" because they cause her *fall* "into the final embrace." Contrary to what is observed in traditional pornography—an abuse of the myth of the fallen woman—Nin sees Mathilde's fall through different eyes: Mathilde's profane self disappears in order to emerge (to be "raised") as a source of joy and illumination. Accordingly, death, or orgasm seen as *une petite mort* by Bataille,[18] kills the lover while it restores the power and significance of sexuality.

Thus when Nin says that "[w]riting erotica became a road to sainthood rather than to debauchery" (*DV*, xii), she suggests that man does not necessarily blind himself when he focuses on sexuality if he manages to transgress the sexual limits prescribed by our culture. Transgression, in this context, is ultimately both positive and negative: sexual desire connects but its fulfillment separates.

It is obvious by now that Nin's treatment of pornography results in a sexuality that is considerably different, both in intent and content, from the sexuality described in traditional pornography. Nin explains this herself by saying that she "was intuitively using a woman's language, seeing sexual experience from a woman's point of view" (*DV*, xv). Most of the stories, indeed, display a woman's sensibility, and a number of them, when they are not narrated in the third person, which is usually the case, are told in a woman's voice. Nin

challenges the assumption that women repress their sexuality and that they do not like reading pornography. The point she tries to make, and I think that she does so successfully, is that there is a difference between pornography and, what I called earlier, the pornographic mind. Pornography as writing pertaining to prostitution, and erotica as writing pertaining to eroticism, can be appealing to both sexes when they take into account both man's and woman's points of view.

But I think that Nin's contribution to the genre of pornography owes less to her feminism and more to the fact that she is an artist. When she says that her own aphrodisiac is poetry and that her pornography consists of explosions of poetry, she announces, I believe, a new kind of pornography which links the lover with the artist and the body with the artist's creative work. The predominant artist figure in *Erotica* is the painter.

The world of the artists and their models in Nin's stories is both erotic and pornographic in the generic sense of the terms. One of the stories that illustrates that is **"A Model."** Nin works here with the paradox inherent in the male chauvinistic tradition that views woman as an object. The first-person narrator of the story is a young model who poses for New York artists. Some of them see and treat her as an aesthetic and sexual object. Others, like Reynolds, see her in aesthetic (object-I've) terms but in a manner that does not erase her individuality. On the whole, however, Nin's intent is to show that for the artist design and desire, like discourse and intercourse, go together. When the artist depersonalizes the model by focusing solely on the aesthetics of her body, he proves to have a pornographic mind. When, on the other hand, he interprets her external beauty in conjunction with her personal qualities, he is then an artist/lover for whom the aesthetics of his art reveals woman not as a sexual object but as an *objet d'art*. He sees her as subject matter, as a person out of whom art is made.

The story that illustrates this conflict of woman-as-object versus woman-as-subject is **"The Maya."** "The painter Novalis was newly married to Maria . . . with whom he had fallen in love because she resembled the painting he most loved, the *Maja Desnuda*, by Goya" (*LB*, 59). Novalis cannot make love with his wife because he sees her not as a real woman but as the projection of his favorite painting. What he asks of her is "not the caprice of a lover, but the desire of a painter, of an artist" (60). The result is that he can make love only to the paintings he makes of Maria. He is, in short, the artist as Pygmalion reversed.

Novalis' resistance to the real Maria derives from his belief that she is art personified. Besides evoking Goya's *Maya*, Maria is the muse who opens Novalis' way toward his desired subject-matter, namely herself. Nevertheless, the identification of these two orders of reality, art and life, is a form of fulfillment that threatens Novalis with the elimination of his concept of the muse as a figure that stands somehow outside the territories of life and art. Only when Maria unfolds her controlled sexuality does she manage to "efface the paintings from his emotions, to surpass them" (64).

Sexuality, as it is presented here, is the artist's inspiration. Yet the artist has to transgress the limits of his medium before he is able to realize this inspiration. He has to demystify the figure of the erotic muse by sacrificing it to his real lover. Moreover, he has to distinguish between the woman he paints and her image on the canvas. He has to destroy this frozen image in order to be able to embrace the real woman. The sacredness of sexuality is to be found at the point where the limits of the real and the imaginary meet. The artist must realize that his art is meaningful only when it is grounded in life.

Nin realizes this point by having many women characters evoke actual erotic paintings. In **"Pierre,"** the visitor to Pierre's mother who has to dry her clothes and thus takes off her stockings, evokes, for me, Courbet's *Woman with White Stockings*, Pierre, when he looks at her, discovers the "pose he had pictured. . . . [T]he first naked woman he had seen, so much like paintings he had studied in the museum" (**DV**, 208). In **"Elena,"** when Elena goes with Leila to an opium den which is like an "Arabian mosque," they hear the "voice of a woman which began what seemed to be at first a song, and then turned out to be another sort of vocalizing . . . a vaginal song" (**DV**, 128). Nin might have had in mind Ingres' *Odalisques with the Slave* which makes material the two pairs of concepts that she is working with in **Delta of Venus** and **Little Birds** discourse and intercourse and design and desire.

This intermingling of works of art with Nin's discourse amplifies her signature in **Erotica.** The allusions to Goya, Lawrence, Balzac, and Freud, to mention only a few, give to **Delta of Venus** and **Little Birds** a greater perspective than is normally given to pornographic writings. Had Nin been "exclusively" interested in the mechanics of the sexual act, she would neither have written in a lyrical language nor would she have made the artist the focus of her stories. As her own aphrodisiac is poetry, so her stories are exciting to her readers because their sexual content is enriched by her poetic sensibility.

NOTES

1. Anaïs Nin, *Little Birds* (Bantam Books, 1979), p. viii. All further references to this book, abbreviated *LB*, will hereafter appear parenthetically in the text.

2. See Peter Michelson, *The Aesthetics of Pornography* (Herder and Herder, 1971), for an indepth analysis of the genre. See also Cathy Schwichtenberg's semiotic analysis of Nin's *Delta of Venus*, "Erotica: The Semey Side of Semiotics," *Sub-Stance*, No. 32 (1981), pp. 26-38.

3. Nin's *Erotica* consists of two volumes, *Little Birds*, mentioned above, and *Delta of Venus* (Bantam Books, 1978), cited hereafter in the text under the abbreviation *DV*.

4. *The Diary of Anaïs Nin*, Vol. III, edited and with a preface by Gunther Stuhlmann (Harcourt Brace Jovanovich, Inc., 1969), p. 147. Further references to the book will appear in the text.

5. J. S. Atherton, "The Maternal Instinct," *Times Literary Supplement*, July 1978, p. 756.

6. D. H. Lawrence, "Pornography and Obscenity," in *Selected Literary Criticism*, ed. Anthony Beal (London: Mercury Books, 1956), p. 32.

7. Susan Griffin, *Pornography and Silence* (Harper and Row, 1981), p. 3.

8. Roland Barthes, *Sade, Fourier, Loyola*, trans. Richard Miller (Hill and Wang, 1976), p. 129.

9. George Steiner, *After Babel*: *Aspects of Language and Translation* (London: Oxford University Press, 1977), p. 38.

10. Michel Foucault, "Preface to Transgression," in *Language, Counter-Memory, Practice: Selected Essays and Interviews, ed.*, and introduction Donald F. Bouchard, trans. Donald F. Bouchard and Sherry Simon (1977; rpt (Cornell University Press, 1980), p. 34.

11. Octavio Paz, *Conjunctions and Disjunctions*, trans. Helen R. Lane (The Viking Press, 1974), p. 4. Paz's study has as its point of departure a woodcut by Jose Guadalupe Posada titled "The Phenomenon," which shows "a dwarf seen from the back, but with his face turned toward the spectator, and shown with another face down by his buttocks," and Francisco Quevedo's *Gracias y Degracias del Ojo del Culo* [*Graces and Disgraces of the Eye of the Ass*], which is "a long comparison between an ass and a face" (3).

12. Paz, p. 11. Paz uses here as a paradigm Velazquez's "Venus of the Mirror," and "a variant of the sex/face metaphor," in order to discuss the "miraculous concord" of the face and the ass.

13. Foucault, p. 30.

14. Foucault, p. 30.

15. Foucault, p. 33.

16. Henry Miller, *The World of Lawrence: A Passionate Appreciation*, ed. with an introduction and notes by Evelyn J. Hinz and John J. Teunissen (Capra Press, 1980), pp. 175-76.

17. Georges Bataille, *Les Larmes d'Eros* (Paris: Jean-Jacques Pauvert, 1964), p. 60 (my translation).

18. Bataille, p. 35.

Judson Klinger (essay date September 1990)

SOURCE: "Henry and June," in *American Film*, Vol. XV, No. 12, September 1990, pp. 22-29, 46-48.

[*In the following essay, Klinger talks with some major players in the production of the film* Henry and June, *the screenplay of which was adapted from an excerpt from Nin's* Diary.]

How would you react if you found out your wife was having sex with another man? Would it make any difference if she were only doing it for the money? What if the two of you were broke and starving? Or suppose you were an artist, and your wife's belief in your talent was so unrelenting that her adultery was a purely selfless act? Would you try to stop it? Would you look the other way? Or could you watch as it happens?

On a winter afternoon in Paris, a heavy snow is about to fall. Well, not exactly *snow*, but pounds of white, lighter-than-air guck (ground-up plastic foam, confetti, soap suds and mousse foam) with a half-life of around a century. And it isn't actually going to fall but, instead, will soon be blown blizzard-like out of air cannons across a dark Brooklyn rooftop. Not the *real* Brooklyn, but a detailed replica of a neighborhood that a young and unpublished writer named Henry Miller called home. This flash-back Brooklyn stands inside a soundstage at the Studios Eclair on the outskirts of Paris, where writer-director Philip Kaufman is shooting *Henry & June*.

Kaufman and his French crew wait behind a video monitor on the roof for a fairly simple shot: Fred Ward, who plays Miller, will scurry across the roof and down the fire escape, where he'll look in on his unfaithful bride, June (Uma Thurman). Kaufman, in old tennis shoes, jeans and a dark jacket, opens a small umbrella over his shoulder-length, graying hair and says, "Action."

The snowstorm blasts the roof; Ward crosses, head down, and lowers himself onto the fire escape. The whole thing takes about 10 seconds, then it's, "Cut." When the snow settles, Kaufman folds the umbrella. He smiles and looks pleased. But as a director whose offbeat sense of humor permeates even his most somber films, it's not clear whether he's happy about the scene or the fact that he's the only person on the roof who doesn't appear to be dusted with toxic levels of powdered sugar.

The film is based on the book *Henry & June*, culled from previously unpublished sections of **The Diary of Anaïs Nin.** When her diary was first published in 1966, Nin chose to edit out references to her personal life in order to protect her husband, Hugh Guiler. After Guiler's death, it was Nin's wish that the unexpurgated journals, written from October 1931 through October '32, be published. In 1986, Rupert Pole, the executor and trustee of Nin's estate, edited the material to focus on her relationships with Henry and June Miller and, with the publication of *Henry & June*, revealed the story that had been kept secret from the world for more than 50 years—that Anaïs Nin and Henry Miller had been lovers.

"They had a literary relationship that lasted a lifetime," says Kaufman. "It was really extraordinary to realize that they had this wild, passionate love affair, and that they chronicled it— the idea that the two most prominent writers who wrote about sexual freedom turned out to have been lovers."

The film's story, then, is really Nin's story, a journey of sexual awakening, liberation and experimentation. Happily married for seven years, Nin lives a comfortable life in suburban Paris. Then into her world steps Henry Miller, and within a year, all of their lives would be dramatically altered. "The whole film is about writers and writing and the creative urge," explains Kaufman, "the connection between their creative urges and sexual urges. In a way, it's an adventure story, an exploration. Three people who went on a creative adventure together."

Further complicating matters, before embarking on her odyssey with Miller, Nin becomes intrigued by the character he was writing about—his wife, June. When June arrives from New York, Nin soon finds herself uncontrollably drawn to June as well, setting the stage for an emotional love triangle.

In a way, the film becomes the story of two writers who are writing about the same woman—their stories revealed through the telling of the story of June. "These are two writers who, the great bulk of their writing was about the same woman," says Kaufman. "The one year that June entered both of their lives [1931-32] affected them for the rest of their lives. . . . June was their muse and their fixation. And a real troublemaker."

Wind whips the circus tent that serves as the crew's mess hall. I'm seated at a lunch table with Phil, his wife, Rose (with whom he cowrote the screenplay), and their son Peter, who's producing. As screenwriters, the Kaufmans have mastered the art of adapting impossibly complex and literate books into accessible mainstream films. But their previous experience, translating *The Wanderers, The Right Stuff* and *The Unbearable Lightness of Being* to the screen, didn't prepare them for the challenge of adapting a diary. The biggest problem was finding a way to dramatize events *as they happened*, moment to moment, without the analysis and reflection that comes when those events are described hours afterward in a diary.

"Nin's analysis tends to dehydrate things in some way," Phil admits. "And putting the juice back into the events was difficult. The way you do it is, you just sort of inhabit the atmosphere [of the book] and start dreaming about what's in there. You need to take three or four years between movies, and that's all you do, work on one movie."

But the idea of working on a single screenplay for several years sounds like heresy at a time when studio executives expect scripts in a matter of weeks.

Kaufman shakes his head. "You don't get to make that many films. That's part of the Hollywood syndrome, really—everyone is just pumping away and pumping away, and most of the films never have that sense of being lived in. There's nothing authentic about them." He pauses, then dovetails this position to the subject at hand. "Somewhere you have to make the decision to step aside, and that's what interests me about Henry Miller: He burned his bridges. He was 40 years old and unpublished. When I was younger and struggling and trying to be a writer, just the existence of that fact was a great thing. There was something about Henry's enthusiasm and energy that was encouraging and inspiring, that said you have to live with a different rhythm and a different sensibility."

Step aside. Live with a different rhythm. Life lessons Philip Kaufman learned early and well. Raised on the north side of Chicago, he attended the University of Chicago (class of '58), where he met Rose. They have a marriage as well as a working partnership—she has been intimately involved in most of his films and shares writing credit on two of them. "I'm with Rose *all* the time," he confesses. "We're always reading and talking about things."

Kaufman entered Harvard Law School but was so seduced by the liberating spirit of Miller's books, he dropped out and moved to Mill Valley, California, where he delivered mail and started work on a novel. During this period, the Kaufmans made a pilgrimage to Miller's home in Big Sur and spent an inspiring evening with the somewhat fragile, 68-year-old author. Shortly thereafter, the Kaufmans took off for Europe.

They hitchhiked around the continent while Phil taught at

American schools in Greece and Italy, drove a tractor on an Israeli kibbutz, and kept at his novel. But his head was turned again, this time by the emergence of New Wave cinema, particularly the first films of Godard, Truffaut and Pasolini. In 1962, he returned to Chicago with aspirations of becoming a filmmaker.

Later that year, Anaïs Nin came to the University of Chicago to promote her husband's experimental film, and Kaufman was introduced to another of his literary heroes. "I was very moved by Anaïs when I met her," he says. "I was just a guy struggling to make his first film. She'd never read anything I'd written, and yet she spent hours and hours talking to me and encouraging me."

Duly inspired, Kaufman—all of 26—wrote and directed two films on shoe-string budgets. *Goldstein* won the Prix de la Nouvelle Critique at the Cannes Film Festival; *Fearless Frank*, a comic-book satire starring Jon Voight, won Kaufman a contract with Universal Studios as a member of its young directors program. The Kaufmans moved to Los Angeles for what might best be described as a decade of discouragements.

In '68, Kaufman wrote the brilliant, revisionist Western, *The Great Northfield, Minnesota Raid*, then carried on a four-year fight with the studio to get it made and released. *The White Dawn* (1974), an Eskimo adventure shot on location in the Arctic, went unnoticed. He wrote *The Outlaw Josey Wales* (1976), but was replaced as the director by the film's star, Clint Eastwood. Scarred by the experience, to this day Kaufman avoids working with stars. "I'd rather work with actors who will stimulate me and be stimulated by me, and, unfortunately, I think most stars remove themselves from that interplay with the director. It has something to do with [stars'] salaries now—everyone's a millionaire."

Worse was yet to come. Kaufman spent eight months developing the first *Star Trek* movie, only to have a top Paramount executive tell him that there was no future in science fiction—a remark that predated the release of *Star Wars* by a few weeks. Around the same time, he bought the rights to Richard Price's teen novel *The Wanderers* and wrote the screenplay; the project was initially turned down everywhere on the belief that an audience for teen comedies was nonexistent.

Feeling trapped, the Kaufmans decided to return to the San Francisco Bay area, and, almost immediately, their luck changed. His next film, the darkly satiric, stylish remake of *Invasion of the Body Snatchers* (1978), shot in San Francisco, became his first box-office hit. On the heels of that success, he got *The Wanderers* made in 1979, then cowrote the story for *Raiders of the Lost Ark* with George Lucas. Next came the Oscar-winning astro-epic *The Right Stuff*

(1983) and then his erotic tour-de-force, *The Unbearable Lightness of Being.* By leaving L.A., remaining true to his iconoclastic tastes, and refusing to sell himself short for a check, he'd become an Oscar-nominated, A-list writer-director.

The most emotionally ambitious film Kaufman's ever attempted, *Henry & June* further explores the thematic terrain of *Unbearable*—the sexually charged interpersonal dramas between man and woman, woman and woman, husband and wife. The more deeply involved the characters become sexually, the deeper the film delves into the meaning of innocence. The moral outlook isn't that anyone who has sex loses innocence. It's not a film that takes place within a traditional morality. Kaufman once said, in reference to *Unbearable*, that love, sex, ecstasy and the links between them should be film's real subject.

Of *Henry & June*, he says, "That's exactly what this film is about. It's much more of an exploration into eroticism, love, marriage, literature."

> I am trapped between the beauty of June and the genius of Henry. I am devoted to both, a part of me goes out to each of them. Are we three immense egos fighting for domination, or for love, or are these things mixed?
>
> —Anaïs Nin

When you set out to make a movie that will serve as a personal payback for a lifetime of inspiration, finding the right actors to portray your heroes takes on a higher importance than usual. For Kaufman, casting *Henry & June* was a long, arduous process. He saw half the actresses on two continents in his search for Anaïs Nin, among them French star Isabelle Adjani. Hollywood's flavor-of-the-year, Alec Baldwin, was actually cast as Henry Miller, then backed out for personal reasons. Ultimately, Kaufman fell back on his career-long pattern of casting lesser-known performers.

To play Nin, he chose Maria de Medeiros, a young Portuguese actress with a hot theater reputation but no film work, and the buzz on the set was that he'd struck gold. "I was hoping she'd be good, but she was beyond any hopes I had. Maria is a genius. . . . She really became Anaïs Nin. She's an idea actress—she only would try to do what I really was after. She speaks four languages fluently, and in English, she could match Nin's accent exactly." And not that it necessarily mattered, but she happens to be a dead ringer for the petite, saucer-eyed diarist.

Kaufman surprised a lot of people by going against type when he cast Fred Ward as Miller. "Fred's an old friend of mine, and those of us who know him know that Fred has a literary side. He's a serious poet. During *The Right Stuff* [he played Gus Grissom], he'd always be the guy reading books between takes. [For months] he'd been writing me in Paris, saying how much he wanted to play Henry Miller—he lived in Big Sur, he's knocked around, he's lived the life."

Ward is virtually unrecognizable. More compact in person than he appears in the movies, with shaved head, glasses and period costume, he bears ample resemblance to Miller. Those on the set say that he perfected Henry's gruff, Brooklyn accent.

Though she is only a supporting character, the casting of June Miller was crucial. As the pivotal beauty who brings the two writers together and fuels their adventure, whoever got the part had to capture the innocence and deceit, the quirkiness and mystery that is June.

When Kaufman met Uma Thurman, who was impressive in supporting performances in *Dangerous Liaisons* and *The Adventures of Baron Munchausen*, she was a risky choice—an actress significantly younger than the character, with limited experience. But she made the decision easy for him. "Uma has an amazing quality," he says. "We couldn't find anyone who had that quality—that haunting, wonderful thing June had."

But when asked how she's doing in the film, Kaufman's voice becomes subdued. "Uma is a very good actress, and I'm very pleased by her. I think she gives a wonderful performance."

Back on the set, Ward has gone to the airport to meet his wife, and the actresses have the day off. A couple of crew guys are 50 feet up on a portable scaffold, adjusting equipment for what will amount to a four-second reverse angle from Henry's point-of-view, looking down from the fire escape. They're an hour away from completing the set-up, so Kaufman offers an impromptu tour.

The production design by Guy-Claude Francois was inspired by photographs of that period, especially a collection by Brassai titled *The Secret Paris of the '30s*. In some instances, sets have been decorated and lit in order to re-create a specific Brassai still.

Kaufman shows me his "Brassai wall"—a block-long exterior facsimile complete with cobblestone street—built with a downward slant to increase its illusion of depth. The same care was paid in re-creating Miller's squalid Paris apartment. Unwashed dishes, empty bottles, peeling wallpaper, bricks coming through worn-out linoleum floor (a detail unlikely to ever show up on film), and a desk with pages of longhand writing and pictures of June and Anaïs taped to the wall.

Kaufman takes great joy in getting the details right. Although it isn't necessary to know anything about Miller or Nin to follow their story in the film, the more you know about them, the more you'll appreciate the attention to authenticity. "There are so many things planted for you to see," says Kaufman. "These are the real metal boxes that Nin kept her journals in, sent to us by Rupert Pole. Nobody would have known that, but it gives the film the right feeling.

"We've shot quite a few sex scenes on that bed," he quips, gesturing at the dilapidated bunk in Miller's shabby bedroom. Asked if he is concerned about the possibility of an X rating, his voice grows a little tense. "Let's just say, I'm contractually bound to deliver an R."

"It was very painful writing this screenplay," he confesses later that day. "It took us well over a year. We had to go through not only *Henry & June* but the matching journal, which has the other half of the story. We read all the diaries, her novels, Miller's novels and their correspondence."

The production office bookcase bears him out. It's jammed with every conceivable book relating to Miller, Nin and Paris in the '30s, their pages marked with Post-its and 3-by-5 cards, painstakingly cross-referenced. The Kaufmans more likely spent *years*, not months, saturating themselves in the source material. "There's a scene in the film where Henry and Anaïs are going over each other's work and arguing about it," he says. "Rose and I had a similar experience writing this."

A publicist summons Kaufman to the set. The famous European producer Serge Silberman has come to Paris to have lunch with Uma Thurman. Thurman, in turn, has brought Silberman to the set to meet her director. The publicist informs me that this is not the right moment to meet Thurman. She'll be available later.

Stephen Frears, her director on *Dangerous Liaisons*, once remarked that he was amazed by her steady stream of visitors. "She seemed to have the most wonderful life going on. People would pass through Paris and see the Eiffel Tower and Uma."

Piles of black-and-white prints taken by the production's still photographer attest to the effectiveness of Kaufman's recreation of "wild Paris of the '30s." The mysterious neo-Brassai night scenarios, hundreds of semi-nude extras, freaks in a dark cold rain, a carnival of the absurd. Then come pictures of Uma Thurman, which call to mind one of Nin's descriptions of June Miller:

> A startling white face, burning eyes. . . . As she came toward me from the darkness . . . I saw for

the first time the most beautiful woman on earth. . . . Her beauty drowned me. As I sat in front of her I felt that I would do anything for her, anything she asked me. . . . She was color, brilliance, strangeness.

"We needed a goddess," Rose Kaufman says as I set down the pictures, "and we got one."

"People come in with their projection of who you are, and they expect you to match it," says Uma Thurman, explaining on the phone why she dislikes being interviewed. "It's entirely uncomfortable, top to bottom, and it all seems sort of irrelevant."

It is a rainy night in New York almost five months after Paris, and we are having our first conversation. We're setting up a time to meet for an interview, and although her voice is calm and polite, the wariness comes through loud and clear. With the release of *Liaisons* the year before, she experienced her first go-round with the entertainment press and was caught off guard.

"I mean, I was 18. It's an awkward position to be in, when you're still sort of discovering yourself, and to have, at the same time, serious people asking you serious questions.

"Basically, a lot of my attitudes about a lot of things were very adolescent—and probably still are. I learned that I get flippant, that I say foolish things. I learned that irony doesn't play in print particularly well."

Without the cachet of a major acting role or a previous incarnation as a supermodel, she landed the cover of *Rolling Stone's* 1989 "Hot Issue" and was named one of *Us* magazine's "10 Most Beautiful Women." *Mademoiselle* dubbed her "the thinking man's sex symbol." This kind of pop-culture attention seems to vaguely embarrass her.

I suggest we meet the next day and go for a walk around the Village. No serious questions.

No tape recorder in her face.

"Great," she says conspiratorially. "Instead of doing an interview, we'll just get together and talk off the record."

I order room service. A few minutes later, the phone rings. It's Thurman. "Hi. What are you doing right now?"

"Watching *Twin Peaks*."

"Everyone's watching *Twin Peaks*! I don't have television. Listen. Why don't you meet us in about a half-hour at Chelsea Billiards? We'll shoot pool, then afterwards go to a wrap party for my roommate's movie. This'll all be off the record, OK?''

I take a chair along the back wall under a photo-portrait of Minnesota Fats and wait for them to show. I expect to see someone like the voluptuous, oval-faced Venus of *Munchausen* or the hypnotic Cecile from *Liaisons*. A girl with loose bales of blonde hair, innocent gray-blue eyes and a tall neck, colorless as a milkwood vase. When she finally arrives, it's a different Uma Thurman.

Dressed in an ankle-length, loose silk over-coat, she arrives as unnoticed as any five-11 blonde can, cutting through rows of tables and low overhead lights. She hurries downstairs to a less crowded room and takes a table in the back corner, where, for the next two hours, no one will bother her, her boyfriend or her best friend and roommate, Galaxy Craze (a fellow actress and undergrad at Barnard).

Thurman opens a felt case and removes a beautiful new cue stick—a birthday gift of the week before, when she had officially escaped teenager status. Under her coat, she wears a loose black cashmere sweater tucked into black jeans. Black flats. Three loops of century-old steel beads from Ethiopia. No lipstick to draw attention to her full, pouty mouth. No makeup to hide the dark circles under her eyes. The glorious Uma hair chopped to shoulder-length, part of a recent effort, she explains, to downplay the sex-star thing, to try to avoid future appearances in such places as *Playboy*'s list of one-night-stand fantasies of the decade. She buys coffee (cream, no sugar) from a machine and lights the first of a chain of Marlboro Lights (in the box), then stretches her long-stemmed frame across the felt for a bank shot. She has a great stroke.

One thing you should know about Uma Thurman is that she's American. Because her two breakthrough films were mounted in Europe, there's a popular misconception that she's Scandinavian. And then there's the name: Uma Karuna Thurman. Her father, an Eastern Religions scholar and professor at Columbia University, took the name from Hindu mythology. *Uma* is a word that has meanings in Japanese, Sanskrit and Tibetan, but it doesn't mean a thing in Peoria.

An *Uma-nescent* dossier: born in Boston in 1970; grew up in New England and Woodstock, New York; her mother, a former model once married to acid guru Timothy Leary, is a psychotherapist in New York; has three brothers; attended Northfield Mount Hermon boarding school; moved to New York at 16 and lived alone in Hell's Kitchen; modeled to make ends meet; studied acting and auditioned relentlessly; appeared in the films *Kiss Daddy Goodnight, Johnny Be Good* and *Where the Heart Is*; lives in a duplex in Greenwich Village, but may soon move to the country; loves a cold bottle of beer.

What's the point of denying it? Hanging out with Uma Thurman is a blast. She is bright, frequently hilarious, intense and impossibly charming. She has a great group of loyal friends who are also fun to be around. She loves to talk (off the record) and will speak at length on an assortment of subjects, from religious iconography or architecture to Shakespeare. ("Don't say I'm reading *Hamlet*! It sounds like I'm promoting myself as an actor.") And when she's not carefully editing every thought, she's inclined to say something unpredictable. For instance, when the subject of her nude scenes in *Dangerous Liaisons* comes up, she remarks, "I don't know why it's so sensationalized. We're living in a country where 55 percent of the people think they've had a personal conversation with God—but that's not considered insane! So there's sex in a movie. What's the big deal?"

When she's completely at ease, her voice dissolves into a soft teenage purr, and she sounds like the archetypal Sensitive Girl from your high-school class. At such moments, she is most apt to describe one thing or another as "my very favorite thing"—as in, "*Dreaming* is my very favorite thing." Over two days, she labeled each of the following as her "very favorites": cooking for friends at her house, backgammon ("the Thurmans are very big on board games," says a close friend), reading, her industrial-strength juicer ("the one thing I'd save in a fire"), having Galaxy for a roommate, and the view of the trees in her backyard.

A movie goddess is often made up of disparate parts, qualities that might go unnoticed if you passed her on the street. Thurman is a good example. Her body doesn't go with her face; her nose isn't thin or perfect; she lacks the classic, neatly framed cuteness. But magnified a hundred times on the screen, these parts don't just work together, they work wonders.

The quality Kaufman and other directors talk about when they talk about Thurman is hard to describe, but they know it's there. It's the quintessence of what we stand in line and pay $7 to see in a theater. So, while she optimistically searches for the next worthy project, she tries to discount the fear that, in some measure, her early success is based on ethereality—more on a body than a body of work.

One famous actor who's worked with her notes, "The recognition of great talent isn't as easy to see without the body of work. With Uma, it hasn't come yet, so people look for a way to define what they're attracted to; they scrutinize what isn't there yet. The whole thing starts to become kind of sexist—defining her success in terms of body parts."

She settles into an easy chair in her living room, sips coffee from à crystal goblet and talks about how she prepared to play June Miller. She hired a dialect coach and worked on a Brooklyn accent months before leaving for Paris, while spending hundreds of hours studying Nin's diaries and a half-dozen of Miller's novels.

"I want to qualify this by saying that I'm not a great authority on Miller, but in reading those books for the purpose of trying to excavate June, I found a tricky and dangerous path. I felt that Henry boxed her into his projections.

"Phil once said that people attack Henry Miller for being a narcissist. Well, it's very hard for a narcissist to deal with uncontrollable love for someone besides himself; it's hard for him to be at someone's mercy on an emotional level. In a lot that he wrote about her, there was the strange tone of a desperate need to capture her, tie her down to paper. His life's work.

"This is my belief, the thing that lead me in playing the character: I don't think either of them could ever take from her what she had. I believe she had a magic in life that couldn't be described or encapsulated."

Her wide eyes mist over, and she momentarily looks away. Her voice drifts off to a whisper filled with emotion. "June needed a great deal. She was sort of an unquenched thirst. She had a great longing and a painful self-reliance. She was a tragic character.

"I don't know if it comes off, 'cause I haven't seen the film, but I know June Miller put a knife in my heart. I know that through my empathy for June, I despised Anaïs Nin. I thought she was full of shit."

Counting down to the summer movie season, two topics— money and sex—are being debated on car phones all over L.A. The talk is about which pictures in a crowded field of action blockbusters and can't-miss sequels will ride to glory in the box-office sweepstakes, and about what's going on with the MPAA ratings board, which had recently slapped an X on four controversial but high-minded films.

These subjects haven't escaped the attention of Kaufman, looking rested and relaxed in the office of his postproduction center in the North Beach district of San Francisco. The irony is bittersweet: For nearly 30 years, Henry Miller's books were labeled obscene and banned from circulation in this country. Kaufman himself had smuggled a few of Miller's novels through customs on his return from Europe in '62. Now once more, the specter of censorship is looming over the passions of Miller's world.

The board's reasoning seems so subjective, its decision is impossible to predict. "I think it is censorship, and it's a dangerous thing," says Kaufman. "Our film is stimulating. It sets the mind working. But those are the areas of the mind that I feel should be stimulated. I think that the expansion of the libidinous side of our brain is somehow connected with the creative [process].

"I don't know what's going to happen. Supposedly, this is a new [ratings] board, but I'm against that form of censorship." He stops to laugh. "I mean, I'd like to see some standards applied to stupidity. . . . There's an hysteria loose in Hollywood—connected with money—that no one has fully been able to analyze. It defies analysis, because it's so boring."

This may look patronizing in print but, coming from Kaufman, it sounds funny. It's the same mocking sense of humor that shows up in his films and undoubtedly helps carry him through the years of intense work he puts into each project. But what's no laughing matter to him is the industry's obsession with profits.

"The thing that money creates is a separateness from society. It's a tragedy, and it happens to directors and writers and producers as well. *Making money* becomes an excuse for all sorts of bad movies—'I took the job because I had to support the house.' It used to be that those justifications didn't count."

He gives me a tour of the shop. Wide-open rooms with lots of windows peering down on tree-lined streets and aromatic Italian restaurants. It's a refreshing environment for work that is often tedious, and the editors I'm introduced to appear to appreciate their situation.

"I try to avoid working with people who become perverse," explains Kaufman. "I think the atmosphere comes through in the project. If there's an ornery atmosphere in the cutting room, you may not give something to the scene that's there. If you're angry, anger takes the magic out of things."

Outside, the noonday sidewalks, brimming with people, attest to the vitality of the community that surrounds. "You don't get this in Los Angeles," Kaufman observes. "Here, it isn't people isolated in cars, with their car phones. That's such a tense environment.

"Life is difficult enough, but the film business is *tremendously* difficult for everyone involved. There are a few people who have stunning early successes, but even they learn that this business is a battleground. It's important that we know how to revive ourselves and keep our innocence. That we have a freshness."

Kaufman, no doubt, has found his way. As someone who holds a spiritual kinship with Henry Miller—an artist who valued individuality and the indulgence in one's passions over the brace of conformity, who, above all, celebrated life—it's as simple as walking down the street and replenishing himself in this momentary nexus with humanity.

Lynette Felber (essay date Fall 1995)

SOURCE: "The Three Faces of June: Anaïs Nin's Appropriation of Feminine Writing," in *Tulsa Studies in Women's Literature*, Vol. 14, Fall 1995, pp. 309-24.

[*In the following essay, Felber examines Nin's assertion that she wrote "as a woman only," particularly in her fictionalized portraits of June.*]

As early as the 1930s, Anaïs Nin described her objective as that of writing "as a woman, and as a woman only" in the prose poem *House of Incest,*[1] purportedly composed after Henry Miller stole ideas from her unpublished diary for his own work. The subsequent claims by Nin and her circle throughout her career that she was writing a new feminine prose might be dismissed as merely a marketing technique. Miller's pronouncement that her diary provides "the first female writing I have ever seen," revealing "the opium world of woman's physiological being, a sort of cinematic show put on inside the genito-urinary tract"[2] might be viewed as an effort to associate her work with the commercial success of his own Rabelaisian excesses. Similarly, Nin's assertion in a postscript to the reprinting of *Delta of Venus* that she is "intuitively using a woman's language, seeing sexual experience from a woman's point of view"[3] might be motivated by a desire to promote and legitimate her erotica. The sales of Nin's books in the 1970s suggest that the marketing of a feminine writing, coinciding with the Women's Liberation Movement of the late '60s and early '70s, was indeed astute merchandising. Yet in the wake of recent discoveries of "lost" and "minor" women writers such as Kate Chopin or Zora Neale Hurston and their inscription into a new feminized canon, Nin herself has been denied entry. By choosing to cultivate the identity of a feminine writer, Nin may have relegated herself to the status of a vogue writer and contributed to her own *literary* marginality with both male critics, for whom "feminine" is a term of denigration or condescension, and feminist critics, who in the 1980s and '90s often dismiss the self-proclaimed feminine writer as essentialist.

In the context of the French feminists' call in the late 1970s and '80s for a writing that would inscribe the female body, however, Nin's oft-repeated assertions deserve further consideration. Many of Nin's claims to be experimenting with a feminine writing were made in reference to the "June" portraits based on her encounters with Miller's second wife, June Miller, or Mansfield, as she is sometimes called. Nin's accounts of her efforts to capture the enigmatic June in writ-

ing read as a plea for a feminine discourse. Through her experimentation with a self-proclaimed feminine language in the June portraits, Nin anticipates both contemporary French arguments for an *écriture féminine* and feminist psychoanalytic revisions of the process by which gender identity is formed.[4] These accumulated portraits, revising the same material over a period of more than thirty-five years, work through the process and conflicts inherent in acquiring a female identity and a feminine aesthetic. These portraits also demonstrate, however, that Nin moved through and beyond *écriture féminine* to produce a double discourse. Ultimately, I will argue, Nin revealed the daughter's competence in two languages, the masculine and the feminine.

A comparison of the portraits Nin creates in the first *Diary* volume, in *House of Incest,* and in *Henry and June* shows her self-consciously experimenting with language she calls feminine. The interrelations of the three portraits are complicated by the discrepancy between order of composition and publication as well as the repetition and overlap of material in Nin's works. The source material or intertext for all three is her unpublished diary of over 150 volumes. The 1931-34 *Diary,* volume one (published in 1966), and *Henry and June* (published in 1986), are both edited and excerpted versions of the original diary. The 1966 *Diary* was edited to delete passages about Nin's lovers, her husband, and others who did not want to be named. *Henry and June* was edited to restore most deleted passages focusing on Henry and June Miller and to exclude those already published in 1966. *House of Incest* appeared in 1936, and Nin records her struggles with the composition of this prose poem in the first volume of the *Diary,* which was of course originally composed contemporaneously.[5]

Nin's use of the diary, a purportedly nonfiction genre, further complicates the interrelations of these texts as it raises issues of art and truth in autobiography, in this case rendered in both fictional and nonfictional genres.[6] Because her published diaries are selective and edited, I consider their narrators, as well as the narrator of *House of Incest,* as textual personae, named Anaïs Nin in the diaries, but unnamed in the prose poem. That both the prose poem and the *Diary* were influenced by male editors and colleagues also complicates discussion of gendered discourse in these texts; Miller, for example, tried to rewrite *House of Incest* but gave it up as "presumptuous" (*Diary,* p. 117).[7] In 1968 in *The Novel of the Future,* however, Nin denied the influence of male colleagues on her early development as a writer,[8] and ultimately as author she is accountable for the versions of works published in her lifetime.

The portraits of June are elaborated throughout the 1931-34 *Diary, House of Incest,* and *Henry and June,* but I will concentrate on representative expository passages that establish the qualities of this enigmatic figure in an almost incantatory fashion. Nin's initial portrait of June in the 1931-34 **Diary** renders her response to their first meeting:

Henry came to Louveciennes with June.

As June walked towards me from the darkness of the garden and into the light of the door, I saw for the first time the most beautiful woman on earth. A startlingly white face, burning dark eyes, a face so alive I felt it would consume itself before my eyes. Years ago I tried to imagine a true beauty; I created in my mind an image of just such a woman. I had never seen her until last night. Yet I knew long ago the phosphorescent color of her skin, her huntress profile, the evenness of her teeth. She is bizarre, fantastic, nervous, like someone in a high fever. Her beauty drowned me. As I sat before her, I felt I would do anything she asked of me. Henry suddenly faded. She was color and brilliance and strangeness. By the end of the evening I had extricated myself from her power. She killed my admiration by her talk. Her talk. The enormous ego, false, weak, posturing. She lacks the courage of her personality, which is sensual, heavy with experience. Her role alone preoccupies her. She invents dramas in which she always stars. I am sure she creates genuine chaos and whirlpools of feelings, but I feel that her share in it is a pose. That night, in spite of my response to her, she sought to be whatever she felt I wanted her to be. She is an actress every moment. I cannot grasp the core of June. (p. 20)

This portrait emphasizes the qualities of the femme fatale—June's dangerously attractive but predatory and consuming nature.[9] She is an enigmatic menace, typical of the femme fatale archetype, as Mary Ann Doane describes it, whose "most striking characteristic, perhaps, is the fact that she never really is what she seems to be. She harbors a threat which is not entirely legible, predictable, or manageable . . . a secret . . . which must be aggressively revealed, unmasked, discovered. . . ."[10] While the beginning of the passage echoes the masculine perception of this literary archetype, it presents a significant variation on the usual depiction of the male gaze fixed upon the female object. The short declarative sentence-paragraph that introduces the portrait establishes that it is Miller, the male, who delivers the femme fatale for Nin's *female* gaze.

What does it mean when the gaze is female, when woman gazes upon woman? Teresa de Lauretis argues that "for women spectators . . . we cannot assume identification to be single or simple. For one thing, identification is itself a movement, a subject-process, a relation: the identification

(of oneself) with something other (than oneself)."[11] Significantly, the female gaze seizing upon female image provides an experience of identity *and* difference, discovery of self *and* other. It differs from the male gaze/female spectacle in both the identity (sameness) and the (slighter) extent of difference perceived. Initially, the female narrator participates in the male attraction to the femme fatale, insisting on her own difference and sharing the compulsion to "unmask" and expose June. She defines her function as an active translator of an inarticulate force: "Poor June is not like me, able to make her own portrait" (**Diary**, p. 16). Together Nin and Miller ambivalently admire and fear the vortex of June, for, as Doane says, the "power accorded to the femme fatale is a function of fears linked to the notions of uncontrollable drives, the fading of subjectivity, and the loss of conscious agency."[12] Drawn in by the attractions of the femme fatale, Nin nevertheless differs from Miller in sharing the gender of the femme fatale, an identification that offers her a kind of protection: if she loses herself in June, she has merely succumbed to her own drives. The femme fatale is primarily an archetype in male-authored fiction because she represents, according to Doane, "an articulation of fears surrounding the loss of stability and centrality of the self, the 'I,' the ego. These anxieties appear quite explicitly in the process of her representation as castration anxiety."[13] Because her relationship with June is one of gender identification, however, Nin is not threatened by her in the same way as Miller. There can be no loss of "I," because there is no threat of castration, no oedipal separation from the mother.[14]

Nin's gaze and her representation of June differ from the male strategy for dealing with the femme fatale because she emphasizes understanding; Nin insists repeatedly that Miller asks the wrong questions about June, neglecting to ask *why* she feels she must fabricate and lie. Hélène Cixous argues that man's view of woman as Sphinx is a strategy for keeping her outside the dominant culture: "And so they want to keep woman in the place of mystery, consign her to mystery, as they say 'keep her in her place,' keep her at a distance: she's always not quite there . . . but no one knows exactly where she is."[15] The male fascination with the femme fatale is rooted, paradoxically, in the simultaneous compulsion to unmask her and the futility of doing so. If the function of the male gaze is to compensate for the loss of the mother's gaze while reinforcing his difference, when the woman is onlooker the process is not one of compensation and mastery over another, but rather one of reconnection and mastery of self.

Kent Ekberg claims that the "triangular relationship" of Anaïs, June, and Henry is a "re-enactment of the Oedipal triangle that Nin confronts in her **Diary**."[16] This statement seems to suggest a Freudian interpretation emphasizing the daughter's development as womanly seductress in relation to the father and an autobiographical interpretation stressing Nin's traumatic childhood abandonment by her father. Yet Miller (the father) is a secondary figure in this portion of the diary; his appearance precedes June's, but she quickly displaces him as the focus of the narrator's interest.[17] Thus, it may be more appropriate to view the ***Diary*** portrait of June as an account of female identity acquisition in relation to a mother figure, an illustration of the views of Nancy Chodorow, Margaret Homans, and other feminist psychoanalysts and literary critics who focus on the mother-daughter dyad. As Nin revives the memory of the forgotten mother through her encounter with June, the immediacy of Miller, the male lover, "suddenly fade[s]," and the narrator establishes a direct and symmetrical relationship with June, who personifies an "image" she had previously "created."

For Nin, she represents the long-repressed presymbolic mother, someone "I knew long ago." The relationship, as in the revised mother-daughter dyad, is symmetrical, the emphasis on knowledge of self through the female other. Margaret Homans says, "because of various consequences of the daughter's likeness to her mother, she does not enter the symbolic order as wholeheartedly or exclusively as does the son."[18] The result of this process, according to Homans, is that women remain in contact with the literal, presymbolic language of the mother-daughter dyad: the female retains a literal language while the male develops a figurative one. Accordingly, in the ***Diary*** account, Nin learns from the experience with June, whose talk is "unconscious" (p. 27), an "underworld language" (p. 28).[19] The process of identification is clarified as Nin claims, "When I talk now, I feel June's voice in me" (p. 29). To articulate June is to understand her, a stage in female identity acquisition of which language is one manifestation. In the expository passage quoted above, literal and direct statement function to pinpoint the nature of June. Nin's stylistic technique uses declarative sentences and series of adjectives that are generally synonyms ("false, weak, and posturing," "color and brilliance"). Even when Nin resorts to figurative language, describing June with the simile "like someone in a high fever," its purpose is to define and elucidate by qualifying the clause before it.[20]

The narrator's response in the ***Diary*** portrait of June vacillates, however, between identification with the mother-figure and conspiracy with the male in exposing her. Midway in the introductory passage, the emphasis shifts from admiration to rejection. With the transitional sentence "By the end of the evening," the narrator claims to have "extricated" herself from June's "power."[21] This summary statement is in actuality prophetic rather than conclusive, for the June sequence continues for sixty pages further in the ***Diary*** before the emphasis shifts to René Allendy, Otto Rank, Antonin Artaud, and other significant figures from Nin's life during this era. Yet this premonitory passage encapsulates the narrator's eventual reaction to June: the sequence finally ends with the narrator's judgment and rejection of June.

It is also significant that Nin experiments with different genres for her various portraits of June. Ellen G. Friedman associates Nin's acceptance of patriarchal forms with her use of the incest trope, which "speaks not only to woman's relationship to man but also to the woman artist's relationship to traditional forms of expression."[22] Thus, Nin's struggle to retain the diary, a subgenre often considered feminine and stigmatized accordingly, is a rebellious act of feminine identity. Nin's male associates, Miller and her two analysts during this period, Dr. Otto Rank in particular, try to wean her from the diary, arguing that it diffuses artistic energy she could direct into her fiction. Curiously, Rank wanted Nin simultaneously to give up the diary and live by herself (***Diary***, p. 280). Like a jealous lover, he accuses her of being "kept by the Diary" (***Diary***, p. 289). Rank also associates women's diaries with a realism he denigrates. Of one of their sessions Nin reports, "Then we talked about the realism of women, and Rank said that perhaps that was why women had never been great artists. They invented nothing" (***Diary***, p. 291). What seems most troublesome to Rank is that the diary is a *feminine* form; since women cannot invent, it cannot be art. Viewed more positively, however, the diary may be associated with the literal, the presymbolic, a time when direct contact makes the fictional text "superfluous."[23]

Rank and Miller would like to see Nin leave the literal language of the diary in order to fulfill their image of a writer, the male who uses symbolic language. Miller's ambivalence about the diary form is evident in his alternate efforts to help Nin get her diary published and to get her to "drop [the] god-damned diary."[24] Although he praised Nin's diary and wrote to publisher William Bradley in 1933 to argue for its publication,[25] at the same time Miller claimed that "journal writing is a disease" (***Henry and June***, p. 137). Notably, when he tries to legitimate the literary quality of Nin's diary, he associates it with the male confessional tradition of "St. Augustine, Petronious, Abélard, Rousseau, Proust" (***Diary***, p. v).

While Nin made some fleeting attempts to direct her energy to fiction, it was less persuasion than necessity that led to her creation of June in the prose poem ***House of Incest***. After Miller took her ideas about June for his own work, Nin protested against his theft in her ***Diary***, claiming that all that remained was for her "to write as a woman, and as a woman only," resulting in the portrait of Sabina in ***House of Incest***.

> While I was working, I was in despair. I discovered that I had given away to Henry all my insights into June, and that he is using them. He has taken all my sketches for her portrait. I feel empty-handed, and he knows it, because he writes me that he 'feels like a crook.' And what have I

left to work with? He is deepening his portrait with all the truths I have given him.

What was left for me to do? To go where Henry cannot go, into the Myth, into June's dreams, fantasies, into the poetry of June. To write as a woman, and as a woman only. I begin with dreams, hers and mine. It is taking a symbolic shape, closer to Rimbaud than to a novel. (p. 128)

Thus, *House of Incest* is born out of the writer's need to answer the claim that the *Diary* keeps her from "real" writing and, more immediately, out of her need to recast her material in a mode that her male literary colleague and rival, Henry Miller, cannot steal. Significantly, Nin's reworking of the June material in the prose poem shows her grappling again with the same conflict, torn between identification with the mother-figure and communication with the male.

House of Incest is divided into seven parts, dramatizing different kinds of incestuous love. The opening sequence of the prose poem, which precedes the introduction of Sabina, is a narrative account of the daughter's "first birth," an encounter with the presymbolic regained through the medium of the dream:

All round me a sulphurous transparency and my bones move as if made of rubber. I sway and float, stand on boneless toes listening for distant sounds, sounds beyond the reach of human ears, see things beyond the reach of human eyes. Born full of memories of the bells of the Atlantide. Always listening for lost sounds and searching for lost colors, standing forever on the threshold like one troubled with memories. (p. 15)

The passage is much more explicit than the *Diary* in recreating the presymbolic through the encounter with Sabina. Nin's self-proclaimed woman's "myth" associates Sabina and the narrator (June and Anaïs) with the preoedipal state of mother-child fusion that initiates the process of gender identity and prefigures Lacan's account of the narcissistic "mirror-stage." Replete with fluid, feminine images suggestive of Kristeva's semiotic chora, the *House of Incest* sequence places the narrator, an "uncompleted self" (p. 15), in the maternal "giant bosom" of the sea. Her state of mind is preanalytic, in direct physical contact with the mother: "There were no currents of thoughts, only the caress of flow and desire mingling, touching, travelling, withdrawing, wandering" (p. 17). At one with the maternal, she is "loving without knowingness" (p. 17). The transitional passage preceding the first description of Sabina depicts the narrator "falling in between not knowing on which layer I was resting" (p. 18) and the narrator's symbolic birth, "I awoke at dawn, thrown up on a rock" (p. 17). Thus, it dramatizes

both the mother-daughter bond and the formative stage of acquiring separate identity, "moving into the body of another" (p. 17).

Through Sabina and her relation to the narrator, Nin again evokes the preoedipal "phallic" mother. In contrast to the *Diary* portrait, the dramatization in *House of Incest* contains less of the mysterious femme fatale and more emphasis on bonding of the mother-daughter. On one hand, Sabina is the destructive warrior woman, a powerful role model for the daughter: "The steel necklace on her throat flashed like summer lightning and the sound of the steel was like the clashing of swords. . . . Her necklace thrown around the world's neck, unmeltable" (p. 21). But at the same time, she embodies maternal qualities: "There is no mockery between women. One lies down at peace as on one's own breast" (p. 24). In *House of Incest,* as in the 1931-34 *Diary,* the narrator recognizes a feminine self she had not previously acknowledged: "From all men I was different, and myself, but I see in you that part of me which is you. I feel you in me; I feel my own voice becoming heavier . . . " (p. 26). The images are those of doubles and mirroring because as a woman, the narrator is acquiring both a sense of self and sense of self-as-other, and both are feminine: "Deep into each other we turned our harlot eyes" (p. 22). Thus, the Sabina sequence allegorically represents the daughter's discovery of her *gendered* identity.

Sharon Spencer has described Nin's prose as an *écriture féminine* using Nin's own phrase, a "language of the womb," to describe a lyrical and "flowing" language centered on women's (often tabooed) experiences.[26] In different ways, both the diaries and *House of Incest* correspond to recent definitions of *écriture féminine,* inspired by French feminists such as Cixous (who generally promote a feminine writing while refusing to define it). Christiane Makward succinctly defines the stylistic features of this discourse as "open, non-linear, unfinished, fluid, exploded, fragmented, polysemic, attempting to 'speak the body,' i.e. the unconscious, involving silence, incorporating the simultanity of life as opposed to or clearly different from logical, nonambiguous, so-called 'transparent' or functional language."[27] This definition is exemplified by Nin's diary and the prose poem, but as she distills the portrait of June in *House of Incest* Nin intensifies many features of this feminine, presymbolic discourse. The fragmentation of the diary is accelerated in the prose poem; the unconscious is not merely given expression, as in the diaries, but visually represented in the "house of incest"; the preface announces the writer's intent to write her body as she disgorges, simultaneously, her book and her heart. Moreover, the texts are, in different senses, "unfinished": Nin continued to write her diary until the end, but requested that the final volumes, detailing her fight with cancer, remain unpublished. The prose poem is eternally "unfinished" through its ambiguous final passages.

At the same time, the prose poem modifies the literal account of June from the *Diary*, and Nin mediates between what are conventionally perceived as masculine and feminine languages. Even the "symbolic shape" she describes in the *Diary* is a blend, a "prose poem," at once novel and poem, combining genres associated with the feminine (novelistic) and masculine (poetic) traditions. Nin's choice of genre is evidence of the kind of double "both/and" thinking Rachel Blau DuPlessis describes as feminine in "For the Etruscans," expansive in contrast to the masculine "either/or."[28] Nin does not conform to rigid literary categories; the innovation of her experimental forms challenges the boundaries of established genres. However, although Nin's self-proclaimed purpose is to write as a woman, *House of Incest* was, in one sense, also written for men, in an effort to placate Miller and Rank, who complained that the diary was diffusing her energy as a writer.[29] Within *House of Incest* the narrator claims to be writing Sabina for men: "The soft secret yielding of woman I carved into men's brains with copper words; her image I tattooed in their eyes. They were consumed by the fever of their entrails" (p. 22). In a major contrast from the literal diary presentation, Nin attempts to communicate with men by delivering a woman in symbolic language to which they can respond.

In the prose poem, Nin echoes the associations established in her diary portrait but modifies the literal account of June with figurative language. Nin often transforms the literal with surreal qualities: "[Sabina's] face was *suspended* in the darkness of the garden" (p. 18, emphasis mine). Her surreal images do not say what Sabina is *like* (simile), but metaphorically render the essence defined by the unconscious and the dream. As with June in the *Diary*, Sabina represents the primordial woman, goddess and mother, with her "ancient stare, heavy luxuriant centuries flickering in deep processions" (p. 18). Nin also tries to explain Sabina by implied comparisons; her primary technique for this in the prose poem is metaphor, a form of figuration close to literal language: metaphor "fuse[s] its terms" in comparison with simile, which "insist[s] that the terms are discrete."[30] Much of the linguistic tension in *House of Incest* results from Nin's attempt, simultaneously, to depict June in a feminine language appropriate for a woman's myth and to bridge the gap of gendered discourse by representing her in poetic or symbolic language.

In both the 1931-34 *Diary* and in *House of Incest,* Nin presents the encounter with June as a metaphoric flirtation with lesbianism, which she finally rejects as incestuous, a narcissistic love of the self in the other. Prior to this ultimate rejection, however, the woman-to-woman identification is presented as more literally lesbian and thus exclusively feminine in an erotic scene that is included—with significant variations—in both the diary published in 1966 and in *Henry and June.* Both versions recount Nin's visit to a brothel at 32 rue Blondel for an "exhibition" of two female prostitutes making love. In the *Diary* account, as in its earlier scene introducing June to Anaïs, it is Henry who suggests the entertainment and accompanies her. In *Henry and June,* however, Nin takes a much more active role, suggesting the visit to her husband Hugo, choosing the prostitutes herself, and requesting "lesbian poses" (p. 71). The framing of the scene in the *Diary* provides another significant variation. Although the *Diary* lacks transitions between entries, their juxtaposition often creates a complex context. In the passage directly preceding the visit, Nin tells Miller that his "relentless analysis of June leaves something out" and wonders if he'll ever "see the world as I do" (p. 58). The brothel incident reveals what his patriarchal view omits: the woman-woman bond.

The episode recasts the June/Anaïs, mother/daughter dyad into an erotic fantasy in which the male role, even as gazer, is diminished. The participants and observers enter a vaginal, womb-like room: "like a velvet-lined jewel casket. The walls are covered with red velvet" (*Diary,* p.59). According to Nin, the prostitutes are "like mother and daughter" (*Diary,* p.59). The contrasting appearance of the two prostitutes—one "vivid, fat, coarse" and the other "small, feminine, almost timid" (p. 70)—exaggerates and parodies the antithetical features of June and Anaïs, a contrast accentuated in Philip Kaufman's cinematic depiction of the scene, in which the "vivid" prostitute is a near double of the actress who plays June and whom Nin seeks out alone, unsuccessfully, in a later scene. Although the lesbian sex scene with a male voyeur is a set piece in male-directed pornography, the traditional function of the male role is that of subject, suggesting that love between women exists for *his* titillation. In this episode, however, Nin breaks out of the convention to the extent that she adds a new figure, the female voyeur, whose primacy contests his role: she insists it is *"my* evening"; the *patronne* reassures them that although there will be no man in the exhibition, they will "see *everything*" (*Henry and June,* p. 71, emphases mine). Both versions make clear, in different ways, that the visit is an initiation into an exclusively woman's sexuality, one from which men are excluded.

Thus the two accounts of the scene emphasize rejection of the "third term" of the oedipal triangle, the patriarchal obstacle to the mother-daughter relation. When the big woman ties on a rubber penis, the exhibition's poses of love teach "nothing new" to Nin (*Henry and June,* p. 71). The phallus is "a rosy thing, a caricature"; but when it is discarded, the "little woman loves [the caresses], loves it better than the man's approach" (p. 71). From the encounter Nin learns "a source of a new joy, which I had sometimes sensed but never definitely—that small core at the opening of the woman's lips, *just what the man passes by*" (*Henry and June,* p. 72, emphasis mine).

This scene, in which the gazer gazes upon herself (the "little woman") in a union with the preoedipal mother, also functions to reverse the usual psychoanalytical conception of the daughter's discovery of her mother's "castration." As Chodorow explains, "[the daughter's] common genital arrangement with her mother does not work to her advantage in forming a bond with her mother. . . . her mother prefers people like her father . . . who have penises"; accordingly, "She comes to want a penis, then, in order to win her mother's love. . . ."[31] Chodorow softens the Freudian interpretation, reinterpreting the phallus's value as an instrument to gain the mother's affection. Nin's revision of the oedipal triangle goes even further: the phallus is now extraneous. Freed from the obstacle of the phallus, the woman-woman gaze produces not castration fear (as for the male gazer) but the acquisition first of gender identity, and then of libido, as discussion of a further scene will demonstrate.

The feminist revision of Freud and Lacan inherent in the 32 rue Blondel sequence and the deprivileging of the male become even more explicit in a scene included in *Henry and June* but excluded from the diary published in 1966. Significantly, the expurgated experience takes the form of a dream Nin recounts:

> I begged [June] to undress. Piece by piece I discovered her body, with cries of admiration, but in the nightmare I saw the defects of it, strange deformations. Still, she seemed altogether desirable. I begged her to let me see between her legs. She opened them and raised them, and there I saw flesh thickly covered with hard black hair, like a man's but then the very tip of her flesh was snow-white. What horrified me was that she was moving frenziedly, and that the lips were opening and closing quickly like the mouth of the goldfish in the pool when he eats. I just watched her, fascinated and repulsed, and then I threw myself on her and said, 'Let me put my tongue there,' and she let me but she did not seem satisfied while I flicked at her. She seemed cold and restless. Suddenly she sat up, threw me down, and leaned over me, and as she lay over me I felt a penis touching me. I questioned her and she answered triumphantly, 'Yes, I have a little one; aren't you glad?' (p. 91)

This encounter with June suggests the daughter's discovery of her mother's "lack," accompanied by the traditional threat of castration, but as the dream progresses Nin rewrites the Freudian scenario of the daughter's supposed horror at finding that her mother has no penis. According to Freud, of course, this discovery—and the daughter's return to the mother, a movement toward identification—would be accompanied by the daughter's desire to have a baby as compensation for the absent penis. Anticipating Chodorow's revision of Freud, however, Nin enacts in the dream the daughter's wish to satisfy the mother's desire, as well as the impulse to be the object of the mother's desire. Through a process of contestation for erotic dominance ("she . . . threw me down") with the phallic mother, Nin discovers instead that the mother has a clitoris, "a little one," of her own. For Nin, the dream encounter with June, the preoedipal mother, results in a discovery of her own previously unrecognized sexuality and an identification with her mother's desire. In *Henry and June,* the encounter with June reveals to Nin a female sexuality that is symbolized as presence, not absence; she discovers not lack but the potentiality of her own genitalia, asserting the "triumphant" presence of the clitoris.

The diminishment of the male role in the rue Blondel sequence and his virtual exclusion in the erotic dream in *Henry and June* suggest the inevitable isolation of men and women as a result of the asymmetry of the oedipal triangle and gender difference: the child can never identify with both parents in the same way; concomitantly, there are certain gendered and linguistic experiences that men and women can never share. The scenes reveal, ultimately, the futility of Nin's self-assigned role as aesthetic mediator between the sexes. At the same time, her persistent insistence on including the male reveals her humanistic refusal to abandon men. Only in the dream (the feminine subconscious) is man excluded. Her aesthetic commitment to both sexes is echoed in one of Nin's typical statements about the feminist movement:

> There is far too much imitation of man in the Women's Movement. That is merely a displacement of power. Woman's definition of power should be different. It should be based on relation to others. The women who truly identify with their oppressor as the cliché phrase goes, are the women who are acting like men, masculinizing themselves, not those who seek to convert or transform man.[32]

Politically and aesthetically, Nin insists on seemingly contradictory objectives, emphasizing both the difference of the sexes and the mediating role of the woman.

In the diary published in 1966, Nin denies any "lesbian" impulse and vows to "collaborate" with Miller in "understanding June" (pp. 41-42). This decision functions as an explanation for the stylistic and generic changes Nin makes when she recreates June in *House of Incest.* Her denial of "lesbian" impulses represents a recognition that to write in feminine language, to write for women only, is to relinquish the opportunity to help man understand woman and to abandon woman to the male gaze. Nin's announced objective of collaboration is both an act of mastery as a woman writer and an act of mediation to articulate woman for man. In the **Diary,** Nin dramatizes the conflicting impulses of the woman writer: she views literal language as her natural style, yet to write in this exclusively feminine language is to place herself outside of communication, incommunicado as it were, with the literary community at large, leaving it to them to write women for themselves and retaining the status quo, the patriarchal literary tradition. Similarly, to identify fully with June, the phallic mother, is to remain inarticulately within the presymbolic. Nin attempts in **House of Incest** both to articulate her intuitive, feminine understanding of June and to communicate it to Everyman—or Henry Miller—representative of the symbolic discourse community. **House of Incest** is a double discourse, containing features of the languages Homans defines as feminine and masculine, revealing the daughter's ability to speak two languages. Nin's prose poem reveals that her dilemma is that of the daughter in the dyad Homans describes; as a woman writer, she is "caught between her own interests in a literal mother-daughter language and her desire at once to placate and to enter the symbolic realm of literary language."[33]

Anaïs Nin's contribution has often been denigrated for perpetuating the feminine mystique or an essential femininity. Her effort to dish up a creation that would please men, articulated by means of a feminine aesthetic, could be seen as producing a major contradiction in her work.[34] Her complicity with male desire and language leads her to create for herself an ultra feminine persona that has been detrimental to her reception by late second-wave feminists. Yet, in contrast to male-authored accounts, Nin's do not exclude and marginalize the female through the male gaze but establish a bond between subject-object through woman-to-woman identification.

The June portraits suggest the inevitable complexity of the woman writer's acquisition of identity within a gendered discourse community. Nin's experiments with language and genre in these three June portraits reveal the woman writer's uncomfortable stance: a Colossus of gendered discourse, she straddles the gap between masculine and feminine language. The irony of Nin's individual plight is that in assuming the identity of a feminine writer she may have excluded her writing from both the established (male) canon and the revisionist canon of women's writing.

NOTES

1. Anaïs Nin, *The Diary of Anaïs Nin,* 1931-34, ed. Gunther Stuhlmann (New York: Harcourt, 1966), p. 128; *House of Incest* (Athens: Ohio University Press, 1958). Subsequent citations to both the *Diary* and *House of Incest* will appear parenthetically in the text.

2. Henry Miller, "Un Etre Eroilique," in *The Cosmological Eye* (Norfolk, Connecticut: New Directions, 1939), p. 289.

3. Anaïs Nin, *Delta of Venus* (New York: Harcourt Brace Jovanovich, 1977), p. xvi. This work is copyrighted 1969 and was posthumously published in 1977.

4. Three of Nin's critics have noted her anticipation of French feminism. See Ellen G. Friedman, "Anaïs Nin," in *Modern American Women Writers,* consulting ed. Elaine Showalter (New York: Scribner's, 1991), p. 347. Also see Margret Andersen, "Critical Approaches to Anaïs Nin," *The Canadian Review of American Studies,* 10, No. 2 (1979), 263, and Sharon Spencer, "Anaïs Nin's 'Feminine' Writing," in *Breaking the Sequence: Women's Experimental Fiction,* ed. Friedman and Miriam Fuchs (Princeton: Princeton University Press, 1989), pp. 165, 171.

5. Nin used the June archetype—variously named—for many women characters in her fiction. I have chosen, however, to analyze the most accessible, published versions of the June story. In addition to these versions and the unpublished diary manuscripts at UCLA, June material appeared in Nin's letters and in the 1939 Obelisk Press edition of *Winter of Artifice;* see Noël Riley Fitch, *Anaïs: The Erotic Life of Anaïs Nin* (Boston: Little, Brown, 1993), p. 252. According to Fitch, the novella "Djuna" was omitted from later editions of *Winter of Artifice* because it revealed too much of the Anaïs-June-Henry relationship (p. 252).

6. See Joan Bobbitt, "Truth and Artistry in the *Diary of Anaïs Nin,*" *Journal of Modern Literature,* 9, No. 2 (1982), 267-76, for a detailed analysis of Nin's "calculated artistry" in presenting the edited diary as nonfiction.

7. Determining the amount and kind of influence these official and unofficial editors had on Nin's work is important scholarly work yet to be done. According to Fitch, Miller's influence (as well as Nin's on Miller) was extensive (p. 119). Not only did Miller make detailed suggestions on Nin's draft of *House of Incest,* but Otto Rank proposed its conclusion (pp. 161-62, 181). Regarding Stuhlmann's revisions of Nin's published diaries, Fitch claims that the "presence of his name on the title page and cover of each diary" reveals its extent, and the revisions were so drastic as to "reduc[e] [Nin] to tears" (pp. 375, 368).

8. Nin, *The Novel of the Future* (New York: Macmillan, 1968), p. 146.

9. Critics have been as puzzled by the writers' depictions of June as Nin and Miller were by June herself: most see her as a femme fatale—fascinating, elusive, and deadly. For Gary Sayre, Sabina, the June character in *House of Incest,* embodies a "carnivorous, incestuous" desire, which would destroy

the narrator if she continued to identify with her, in "*House of Incest*: Two Interpretations," in *Anaïs, Art and Artists: A Collection of Essays*, ed. Sharon Spencer (Greenwood, Florida: Penkevill, 1986), p. 47. Oliver Evans sees Sabina as "*naturally*" destructive in contrast to the narrator, the "earth-mother archetype," in *Anaïs Nin* (Carbondale: Southern Illinois University Press, 1968), p. 31. According to Evelyn Hinz, the diary's June is one half of Nin's literary dilemma: June is the half that creates illusion; Miller the half that exposes it, in *The Mirror and the Garden: Realism and Reality in the Writings of Anaïs Nin* (New York: Harcourt, 1973), p. 102. Marie-Line Pétrequin argues that June represents Nin's repressed desires and a "'male' quality," in "The Magic Spell of June Miller," trans. Gunther Stuhlmann, Anaïs, 6 (1988), 49. The maternal qualities I emphasize in this essay are to some extent, though in an archetypal rather than a psychoanalytical context, remarked upon by Stephanie Demetrakopoulis, who describes June as both "an aspect of archetypal femininity, which is implicit in [Nin]," and Erich Neumann's "'Terrible Mother,'" in "Archetypal Constellations of Feminine Consciousness in Nin's First Diary," *Mosaic*, 11, No. 2 (1978), 124-26.

10. Mary Ann Doane, *Femmes Fatales: Feminism, Film Theory, Psychoanalysis* (New York: Routledge, 1991), p. 1.

11. Teresa de Lauretis, *Alice Doesn't: Feminism, Semiotics, Cinema* (Bloomington: Indiana University Press, 1984), p. 141.

12. Doane, p. 2.

13. Doane, p. 2.

14. In her study of Nin's erotica, Karen Brennan makes a similar point about Nin's comfort, relative to that of Henry Miller, in being herself "a spectacle for the gaze of a man" as she performs (i.e., writes) for the collector after Miller refuses, in "Anaïs Nin: Author(iz)ing the Erotic Body," *Genders*, 14 (Fall 1992), 67-74. Brennan's discussion of the "paradox of the female writing spectacle" (p. 67) and gendered authorship as it draws upon the issues of the female gaze, "double-identification" (p. 69), and voyeurism, as well as Nin's ambivalent complicity, intersects in significant ways with my argument although her primary text and conclusions differ markedly.

15. Hélène Cixous, "Castration or Decapitation?" trans. Annette Kuhn, *Signs: Journal of Women in Culture and Society*, 7, No. 1 (1981), 49.

16. Kent Ekberg, "Studio 28: The Influence of Surrealist Cinema on the Early Fiction of Anaïs Nin and Henry Miller," *The Lawrence Durrell Newsletter*, 4, No. 3 (1981), 4.

17. In her original sequence of diaries, the volume entitled "June" apparently preceded that entitled "Henry." See Rupert Pole's preface to Nin's *Henry and June: From the Unexpurgated Diary of Anaïs Nin* (San Diego: Harcourt, 1986). All subsequent references to this work will appear parenthetically in the text.

18. Margaret Homans, *Bearing the Word: Language and Female Experience in Nineteenth-Century Women's Writing* (Chicago: University of Chicago Press, 1986), p. 12.

19. Rachel Blau DuPlessis also makes this point in associating their language, with the lost Etruscan language, in "For the Etruscans," in *The New Feminist Criticism*, ed. Showalter (New York: Pantheon, 1985), p. 275.

20. In contrast to Nin's similes, Miller's attempt to define June by comparison is extended through qualifiers that modify the vehicle of his similes: "At first she was big and velvety, like the jaguar, with that silky, deceptive strength of the feline species, the crouch, the spring, the pounce; then she grew emaciated, fragile, delicate, almost like a cornflower, and with each change thereafter she went through the subtlest modulations—of skin, muscle, color, posture, odor, gait, gesture, et cetera. She changed like a chameleon. Nobody would say what she really was like because with each one she was an entirely different person. After a time she didn't even know herself what she was like," in *Tropic of Capricorn* (New York: Grove, 1961), p. 237. In describing the June character's feline attributes, he qualifies "jaguar" rather than "she," moving farther and farther from the tenor, the woman herself. Miller is the son Homans describes "in flight" from literal representation through the characteristic separation of male from the mother after his entrance into the symbolic order (*Bearing the Word*, p. 14). His emphasis in describing June is on defining "what she was really *like*" (emphasis mine). The real woman is distanced and finally absent.

21. The version of the encounter published in *Henry and June* is very similar to this passage. The major differences are that the passage is broken up into short paragraphs in *Henry and June* and the judgmental sentence "She killed my admiration by her talk" is not present, suggesting it may have been added when the original diary was edited for publication in 1966. Another significant difference is that in the final paragraph of *Henry and June*, the narrator claims she is "like a man" in loving June's "face and body" (p. 14). Although the editor, Nin's literary executor Rupert Pole, claims the volume is edited to focus on Henry and June, the degree to which the editing might have altered this kind of passage remains unclear.

22. Friedman, "Anaïs Nin," p. 342.

23. Homans, p. 4.

24. Nin, *A Literate Passion: Letters of Anaïs Nin and Henry Miller*, 1932-53, ed. and intro. Stuhlmann (San Diego: Harcourt, 1987), p. 223.

25. Nin, *A Literate Passion*, p. 98.

26. Spencer, p. 165.

27. Christiane Makward, "To Be or Not to Be . . . A Feminist Speaker," trans. Marlène Barsoum, Alice Jardine, and Hester Eisenstein, ed. Eisenstein and Jardine, in *The Future of Difference* (New Brunswick: Rutgers University Press, 1985), p. 96.

28. DuPlessis, p. 276.

29. Friedman makes this point about both *House of Incest* and *Winter of Artifice*, in "Anaïs Nin," p. 345.

30. Earl Wasserman, "Mont Blanc," in *Shelley: A Collection of Critical Essays*, ed. George M. Ridenour (Englewood Cliffs: Prentice-Hall, 1965), p. 78.

31. Nancy Chodorow, *The Reproduction of Mothering: Psychoanalysis and the Sociology of Gender* (Berkeley: University of California Press, 1979), p. 125.

32. Nin, "Notes on Feminism," *Massachusetts Review*, 13, Nos. 1 and 2 (1972), 28.

33. Homans, p. 38.

34. DuPlessis believes this contradiction, "between the desire to please, making woman an object, and the desire to reveal, making her a subject," is resolved by the diary "as form and process" (p. 280).

Barry Unsworth

1930-

(Full name Barry Forster Unsworth) English novelist.

The following entry presents an overview of Unsworth's career through 1997. For further information on his life and works, see *CLC*, Vol. 76.

INTRODUCTION

Unsworth is widely respected for his historical novels that range in setting from medieval Yorkshire to early twentieth-century Turkey. Using the past as a springboard to explore larger universal themes of greed, betrayal, and the function and effect of art in human life, Unsworth concentrates on moral ambiguities and hidden complexities of seemingly minor decisions.

Biographical Information

Unsworth was born in Durham, England, in 1930. He graduated with an English degree from the University of Manchester in 1951. In the 1960s he moved his family to Greece and Turkey, where he worked as an English lecturer for the British Council at the Universities of Athens and Istanbul. Unsworth moved back to England in 1970 to teach at the Lennox Cook School of English, a private school that provided English classes to non-English speakers. In the late 1970s Unsworth earned a creative writing fellowship from Charlotte Mason College, Ambleside. In 1982 he was appointed Northern Arts Literary Fellow at the Universities of Durham and Newcastle. From 1984 to 1985 Unsworth was writer in residence at Liverpool University. In the early 1980s Unsworth visited Venice, Italy, to do research for his novel, *Stone Virgin* (1985). Later in the decade he moved to Scandinavia, living first in Sweden and then Finland, where he finished his Booker Prize-winning novel, *Sacred Hunger* (1992). After *Sacred Hunger* was published, Unsworth moved to the Umbrian countryside in Italy, where he still lives.

Major Works

Unsworth gained critical success with his novel *Mooncranker's Gift* (1973), winning the Heinemann Fiction Award. Told mostly in flashback, *Mooncranker's Gift* is the story of James Farnaby, who, in the midst of an adolescent religious obsession, is given the gift of a crucifix made of sausages by his middle-aged neighbor, Mooncranker. After masturbating in the garden one day, Farnaby sees the crucifix, rotting and infested with worms.

His horror at the sight haunts him for years, until he encounters Mooncranker ten years later in Istanbul. Unsworth continued his critical success in 1980 with *Pascali's Island*, his first effort in the historical novel genre. Set on an island in the Aegean at the end of the Ottoman Empire in 1908, *Pascali's Island* is told as a monthly report from Basil Pascali, an agent working undercover for the last Ottoman sultan. As he writes his report, he embellishes certain aspects of his efforts and confesses various professional trangressions, eventually realizing that the work he has devoted eighteen years to is futile. In *Rage of the Vulture* (1982) Unsworth again explored events at the fall of the Ottoman Empire, but from the perspectives of the sultan and the British Captain Robert Markham and his young son, Henry. Unsworth's next novel, *Stone Virgin* (1985) explores the impact of a Venetian statue of the Virgin Mary on three men who encounter her between 1432 and 1972. Again using various points of view, Unsworth examined the relationship between art and life. *Sugar and Rum* (1988) is a quasi-historical work about an author suffering from writer's block while working on a novel about the slave trade. In 1992 Unsworth published his most successful and critically acclaimed novel, *Sacred Hunger,* which is about a slave ship in the eighteenth century that his fictional protagonist in *Sugar and Rum* was researching. *Morality Play* (1995) also was highly successful and nominated for the Booker Prize. Set in medieval Yorkshire, *Morality Play* is a murder mystery and complex discussion about art's place in life. Principle characters in the novel produce a play acting out the murder to solve the mystery. In *After Hannibal* (1996) Unsworth left the historical genre behind to examine backbiting and treachery among a group of expatriate neighbors fighting for property in Italy's Umbrian countryside.

Critical Reception

Response to Unsworth's work has varied, ranging from the relative indifferent reception that greeted *Sugar and Rum* after its publication to the nearly unanimous praise earned by *Sacred Hunger,* which shared the prestigious Booker Prize for literature. *Morality Play* was also nominated for the Booker, and *Pascali's Island* was widely admired for its take on the theme of creating a personal utopia. Unsworth's work has experienced a resurgence of interest during recent years with several new paperback editions of his novels.

PRINCIPAL WORKS

The Partnership (novel) 1966
The Greeks Have a Word for It (novel) 1967
The Hide (novel) 1970; reprinted 1996
Mooncranker's Gift (novel) 1973
The Big Day (novel) 1976
Pascali's Island (novel) 1980; published in America as
    The Idol Hunter, 1980
The Rage of the Vulture (novel) 1982
Stone Virgin (novel) 1985
Sugar and Rum (novel) 1988
Sacred Hunger (novel) 1992
Morality Play (novel) 1995
After Hannibal (novel) 1996; also published as *Umbrian
    Mosaic,* 1997

CRITICISM

Anatole Broyard (review date 9 October 1977)

SOURCE: "Painted into Opposite Corners," in *New York Times Book Review,* Vol. LXXXII, No. 41, October 9, 1977, p. 14.

[*In the following review, Broyard compares Unsworth's*

The Big Day to MacDonald Harris' Yukiko. *Though his critical evaluation focuses more on* Yukiko, *Broyard uses it to illustrate why he finds* The Big Day *a disappointing follow-up to* Mooncranker's Gift.]

Yukiko and ***The Big Day*** illustrate, all too neatly in my opinion, two contrasting attitudes toward the novel, two unrewarding corners into which quite a few authors have painted themselves. MacDonald Harris writes a dogged, log-ahead prose under the assumption that his story is irresistible enough to grip and hold the reader. Barry Unsworth offers impressive style and technique that overwhelm the thin and rather stale idea behind his novel. Mr. Harris's style, his novelist's equipment, seem to be virtually forgotten in his preoccupation with his subject. His diction is deadpan, and there is hardly a memorable sentence in the book. His tone seems solemnified by the grandeur of what he is attempting. He has no time for frivolity, for bandying words or digressing into the psychological complexities of his characters. He is a bringer of a message, a purveyor of profundity.

Compared to him, Mr. Unsworth strikes me as a literary playboy. He enjoys the run and rhythm of a sentence, the happy impact of a well-chosen word. He has such a consummate talent for getting inside his characters' obsessions, he so blurs the figure-ground boundaries, that his characters spill like wine over the table he has set. It is, however, merely a platter of hors d'oeuvre.

Yukiko concerns four men, three American soldiers and a Japanese-American interpreter, who land on the island of Hokkaido in August of 1945. Their original mission was to deliver Havenmeyer, a commando, and his interpreter Ikeda to the island by submarine so that he might blow up a heavy-water plant. Under ambiguous circumstances, the submarine runs aground on a reef, and Gus, the sub commander, and Angelo, his navigator, are forced ashore with the other two.

Havenmeyer is a caricature, a destructive machine. Ikeda is a shadow, a mere decoder of language. Gus, the narrator, seems to have been hired, as one hires a butler, to bring a wry, humanistic perspective to the proceedings. Against all these predictable elements, Angelo embodies the unpredictable. He is moody, ironic, laconic, mysterious, forever saying things the others fail to understand. This deliberate inscrutibility, one supposes, is meant to create an aura of ominousness, of more-than-meets-the-eye, of suspended tensions.

When Gus asks Angelo whether he deliberately ran the submarine aground, Angelo will not talk about it, even though they have been friends and fellow officers for several years, even though four men were drowned as a result of Angelo's "mistake." It is not "healthy," Angelo says, to dwell on such things. He is not traumatized by the incident: he just does not feel in the mood to discuss it. He is, in other words, a prototype of contemporary fiction.

It may seem that I am laboring the point, but in fact most of the action in the book is of this nature. Mr. Harris is forever retreating into coy obscurity. There is no reason, for example, for Gus and Angelo to accompany Havenmeyer on his suicidal mission. The war is almost over, they point out. Under the circumstances, the mission is not only suicidal, but pointless. Havenmeyer invited them to leave, adding that they are useless anyway—yet they tag along with him, more obedient to the author or the plot than to their own convictions.

Sensei, Havenmeyer's local contact, is a school-teacher. His name, in fact, means teacher. He is an Ainu, one of a tall, pale, hairy, primitive people who are discriminated against by the Japanese. Sensei's behavior is consistently baffling, beginning with his mirrored sunglasses. After speaking of the novels of D. H. Lawrence, which he has puzzled out with a dictionary, Sensei delivers a homily on love, which he follows up, like a true teacher, by presenting to the group an "Air Fairy," a remarkably lifelike rubber doll that they are invited to employ for whatever kind of communion best suits their individual needs.

Why does Sensei introduce this doll? What does it have to do with Havenmeyer's mission, which he is supposed to assist? Is this some sort of psychological test? Is he practicing Ainu voodoo on them? Havenmeyer and Ikeda use the doll, which is named Yukiko, for simple masturbatory purposes. Gus has a vague but more complex attitude toward it. Angelo turns away in disgust.

Sensei consistently refuses to advance the mission or to clarify his position relative to the Americans. Everything he says must be filtered through the stumbling translation of Ikeda, which makes for considerable monotony and causes Sensei to seem even more stilted and removed than he already is. When he takes Gus on a dangerous eight-hour boat trip for the sole purpose of having him photographed in the nude—a preliminary step for the manufacture of a rubber doll in his image—Gus never even asks Sensei why they are doing this.

After a couple of hundred pages of undistinguished conversation and little action, all five characters come to seem like zombies, passive creatures of the author's will, simply waiting for him to put them to work. Now, it has always been my feeling that a good character occasionally overflows the author's intention and appears to speak to us directly. He takes on autonomy and denies that he is only part of someone else's "story." A character who is tranquilized by the author, who is held in thrall to a preordained plot, is nothing but a doll like Yukiko.

At the end of *Yukiko*, it is not Havenmeyer who blows up the heavy-water plant, but Navy dive bombers. If it is possible for them to do this, why was Havenmeyer sent in the first place? The point I am making is that there is a gratuitous looseness of thinking here that has tended to become an accepted convention. As I see it, one of the functions of a novel is to usher us into the presence of mystery, to frame, reaffirm and perhaps even celebrate certain indissoluble tensions that we all share. But this is not the same as making mysteries out of everything and nothing.

In the name of the social order, the Victorian novel tied up every loose end, but the novel of the 70's, in a belated backlash, seems determined to untie them. Only connect, E. M. Forster said; and now it has become only disconnect. Disorder is our pride. Romanticism has degenerated from the extravagant to the random.

Readers seem to have accepted the situation with a remarkable complacency. The willing suspension of disbelief was never more willing. Familiarity breeds contempt: if a character's behavior does not contradict every expectation, he is the worst sort of conformist. The melancholy result of this fashion is that the true mysteries—love, loneliness, the fear of death, the need for a structure of some kind—are lost in a welter of trendy improvisation, of scare-crows dressed in Samuel Beckett's clothes.

While Mr. Harris attempts to "rivet" us, Mr. Unsworth is content merely to entertain us. Cuthbertson, his protagonist, has founded a bogus school that confers "degrees" on those who cannot get them elsewhere, particularly foreigners who have not mastered English. There is a good deal of talented parody of this last group, and I am reminded of Malcolm Bradbury's witty novel, *Eating People Is Wrong*, which was written at least 15 years ago. There are echoes of Kingsley Amis's *Lucky Jim*, too, but faint ones.

The Big Day seems to have a very limited ambition. Most of Mr. Unsworth's considerable talent is expended on the disintegration of Cuthbertson, and while his is a brilliantly rendered decline, it is not enough. Cuthbertson, a rigid character, is undone by such influences as the shifting patterns of light on his highly polished desk, by the odor of hyacinths that an overzealous assistant has concealed in his office, by his attempt to persuade himself that his school is an honest attempt at education, by his emancipated wife's importunities. No one can suggest better than Mr. Unsworth the panicked floundering of a consciousness about to drown in its own elements. Like the rubber doll in *Yukiko*, ***The Big Day*** is a skillfully crafted but lifeless artifact.

Cuthbertson has no more personality than Yukiko. He is only a vehicle for a certain kind of exercise.

Mr. Harris's previous novel, *The Balloonist*, was nominated for the National Book Award in 1976. Mr. Unsworth's last novel, *Mooncranker's Gift,* was one of the best books I read in 1974. If I were asked to explain why these two authors have not done better here, I would be tempted to answer that the reading public has not sufficiently moved them to exert themselves. A cynic whose name I forget said that people deserve what they inspire. I think that readers certainly do.

Michael Malone (review date 11 January 1981)

SOURCE: "Other Times and Places," in *New York Times Book Review*, January 1, 1981, p. 10.

[*In the following review, Malone provides an appreciative assessment of Unsworth's main character in* The Idol Hunter.]

In 1908 on an irrelevant Greek island of the crumbling Ottoman Empire, the Levantine spy Basil Pascali writes his 216th irrelevant report to Constantinople, this time to the Sultan himself. Monthly, for 20 changeless years, the fat shabby informer has received for his services the same sum but never the slightest response to these millions of words poured into an Imperial void. In the silence he has written his life away and in so doing has fashioned it into the marvelous lapidary creation that constitutes British novelist Barry Unsworth's *The Idol Hunter.* Esthetic, solipsistic, constrained to see himself from the viewpoint of others as an obsequious, cowardly buffoon wretchedly cavorting for cadged meals, Our Man in Asia Minor is a spy Graham Greene could appreciate, George Smiley would employ and Peter Ustinov should play. He is a wifeless, homeless, drugged Ulysses abandoned to live by trickery on a foreign island.

By 1908 Turkish dominions have contracted to a moribund core of corruption and clogged bureaucracy, which exists only by the inertia that pays Pascali's salary and that keeps immobile the old emigres who sit hearing Offenbach and reading frayed Figaros in the pink rattan chairs of the island's Hotel Metropole while rebels collect in the hills. In fact, the Young Turks soon will depose the Sultan, Balkan wars will remap Europe, a World War will re-create the world. Poised at this abyss, Pascali yearns both for the past's "fixity of perfect balance" and for the "gesture that shatters the glass." The world awaits new idols.

Waiting too, this scrounger and clown who studies

Parmenides and quotes Mallarme, who squires paying American widows and saves up for fortnightly visits to a boy prostitute, this observer of nuance and gesture who has always falsified his reports "for the sake of color and variety," this artist has created an island. Its opaline blue gashed with white, its jumble of jasmine and dark tobacco, of Roman harbors, Moslem mosques and Crusaders' castles, its Greeks, Turks, Jews and Armenians, the woman painter he desires, the English adventurer with whom he attempts a deadly con game—all are caught like exotic fish in the net of Pascali's unanswered words.

Christopher Lehmann-Haupt (review date 7 February 1983)

SOURCE: "Books of the Times," in *New York Times Book Review*, February 7, 1983, p. 15.

[*In the following review, Lehmann-Haupt offers praise for Unsworth's evocation of the Middle East in the early twentieth century in* The Rage of the Vulture.]

In Barry Unsworth's latest novel, *The Rage of the Vulture,* Capt. Robert Markham—a British infantry officer posted to Constantinople during the final years of the Ottoman Empire—is a complicated and not very sympathetic protagonist. He regards his 10-year-old son, Henry, mainly as a rival for his wife's affection.

He resents his wife for her failure to understand a secret thing about him, which secret, paradoxically enough, he refuses to reveal to her just because of that resentment. Convinced that Henry's governess can understand him, he all but rapes her and then rejects her for understanding him too easily.

He has a facility for surpassing in unpleasantness even the worst of the novel's other characters. In one of Mr. Unsworth's more bitter scenes, an English visitor named Miss Munro, who finds Constantinople "romantic," asks Markham to accompany her on an interview she has arranged with one of the Sultan's eunuchs. She has had great success with a series for an English magazine on Turkey during the 1908 revolution and wants to see "what the experience has meant to people. The guardsman, the concubine, the pageboy." "'Ordinary people,' Markham said, but Miss Munro was too absorbed in her subject to notice the irony."

When the liberal Miss Munro inadvertently prompts the eunuch to describe his castration, Markham savagely translates the horrifying description while Miss Munro tries to stop her ears. We actually end up feeling sorry for the petty-minded creature. Why then, you might ask, does one continue to put up with Markham as he makes his way through Barry Unsworth's dazzling and complex portrait of Constantinople in the year 1908? Why does one continue reading *The Rage of the Vulture,* whose title is taken from Canto I of Lord Byron's "The Bride of Abydos": "Know ye the land where the cypress and myrtle / Are emblems of deeds that are done in their clime? / Where the rage of the vulture, the love of the turtle, / Now melt into sorrow, now madden to crime." Why does one go on? For one thing, because Robert Markham's secret is a plausible reason for his complicated behavior. He had been in Constantinople 12 years earlier, about to marry an Armenian girl, when the Turkish massacre of the Armenians began to spread throughout the city. At their engagement party, Markham's fiancee was raped and murdered while he stood by, protesting to her tormentors: "I am an Englishman. I am an Englishman." The shame of the incident has unmanned him, which, of course, is why he translates the eunuch's experience for Miss Munro with such savage relish. Now, in the novel's present, he is determined somehow to make amends for his shame.

Of course he cannot. As a young Armenian nationalist tells him, "The suffering of individuals is not important." He continues, "You lost your fiancee. You think: They did this to me, to me! You nurse what they did to you. You think of yourself as an outraged individual. You are alone with yourself. There are two million Armenians in Turkey, Captain Markham. The very great majority of them have no leisure to cultivate their personal sense of outrage in that way."

What is more, the reader knows from actual history that whatever Markham may accomplish by way of revenge or self-punishment, the Armenians in Turkey will eventually suffer far more widespread massacres.

Still, Markham will pursue his own degradation all the way to the Sultan's personal torture chamber. And if he accomplishes little more than to have his English pride and individuality beaten out of him, he serves along the way as the reader's witness to the splendors of exotic Constantinople. Many of Mr. Unsworth's spectacles, such as the celebration of a holy day in the interior of the Hagia Sophia, are heightened in their effect by being made an integral part of the plot. But even when he is merely sightseeing, his scenery is often spectacular.

Markham's eventual defeat transports him into a state of eccentricity somehow peculiar to the English. In the novel's epilogue, set toward the end of World War I, we find him back in England, living once again with his wife, though at a somewhat chilling remove. He has taken up beekeeping, as well as writing a massive book whose thesis it is that in keeping with the tendency of certain races to "take

on an excitatory role in history," it has been the fate of the Armenians to stimulate "the atrocity glands, that was their collective historical role."

As the conclusion to a heroic quest, this is not very satisfying. But it is an altogether fitting end to this curiously crabbed and obsessive adventure, in which Barry Unsworth once again, just as he did earlier in such accomplished novels as *Mooncranker's Gift* and *The Idol Hunter,* has exercised his strange fascination with Turkey and the Middle East during the early years of this century, and has thereby succeeded in fascinating his readers.

Thomas R. Edwards (review date 13 March 1983)

SOURCE: "Atonement in Turkey," in *New York Times Book Review*, March 13, 1983, p. 7.

[*In the following review, Edwards finds* The Rage of the Vulture *an admirable attempt to reveal personal conflict amid catastrophic world events.*]

The recent conquest of America's television screens by *The Winds of War* is the latest evidence of our desire to know the origins of the cataclysms the 20th century has made so commonplace. Or since such entertainments conceal as much as they reveal, maybe it is our desire not to know these origins too accurately, on the not unreasonable assumption that the whole truth might be more than we could handle.

The Rage of the Vulture, the sixth novel by the British writer Barry Unsworth, could also be made into a pretty good television spectacle but only by excising most of what makes it impressive as a novel; it comes not to conceal but, like any serious work of imagination, to tell us more than we are morally prepared to know. Mr. Unsworth's story is set in Turkey in 1908, when "the sick man of Europe" at last lay dying while its racially and religiously fragmented populace was in turmoil and the European powers sought to extend their spheres of influence. These struggles would become more public in August 1914.

As the novel begins, the aged Sultan Abdul Hamid II, rightly fearful that his cruel reign has brought retribution close to his door, studies Constantinople through a telescope from his hilltop palace while, within his field of vision and deeply aware of being so, Capt. Robert Markham of the British Military Mission gives a garden party for members of the European community. Farther away rebellion is stirring in Macedonia, led by the Young Turk dissidents in the army, avowedly bent on European-style modernization and liberalization. Ethnic and religious animosities in the diverse populace, relatively quiet since the massacres of Armenians in the 1890's, are on the rise. And the other major powers are maneuvering to block the ominous growth of German influence in the region.

Observing a primary convention of historical fiction, Mr. Unsworth places a minor personal experience at the center of the public drama. In the eyes of his British colleagues Robert Markham is rather a difficult sort. Clever, sensitive, aloof, "erratic," he lives with his wife and 10-year old son, Henry, in a non-European quarter of the capital. He seems puzzlingly "proprietorial" about Turkey, with a most un-British interest in its political and cultural subtleties, and it alerts him to an impending revolutionary change to which his hidebound colleagues are quite oblivious.

The reader learns that Markham has a secret concealed even from his wife. He was in Turkey 12 years earlier, when he was compelled to witness the rape and murder of Miriam, his Armenian financee, during the Armenian massacre of 1896. He saved himself by telling her killers that he was English, asserting a detachment from the horrible event that has haunted him ever since; his return to Turkey seems in some way meant as atonement. As Markham enters the unknown depths of official and underground politics that involve both Turks and Armenians, his son, in a delicate echo of his father's initiation, begins a childish but incipiently sexual relationship with the little Turkish girl next door.

Markham's search for self-respect provides both a gripping story of adventure and intrigue and a deeper portrait of an interesting mind puzzled and thwarted by its own experience. As events compel the Sultan to accept the constraints of constitutional monarchy, Markham's suspicions about Colonel Nesbitt, a senior colleague who seems closer to Turkish Intelligence than he should be, lead him into a secret world of subversion where a faction of Armenian nationalists and Young Turks guardedly conspires against the old regime. At home, needing someone to hear his confession about Miriam, Markham makes a rather predatory conquest of Miss Taverner, his son's young English governess, which Henry (something of a spy himself) witnesses and later deliriously reveals when stricken with typhoid fever.

This domestic disaster—his wife and son and Miss Taverner quickly return to England—brings Markham the physical and moral solitude his quest for personal and political understanding requires. And a pattern begins to emerge from his experience: He seeks in effect to be a man, not merely an Englishman (the identity that protected him from Miriam's fate), not a husband or father or lover or soldier, not subject to terms of existence narrower than those of full humanity. But this desire is enclosed by history, with (as T. S. Eliot wrote) its "many cunning passages, contrived corridors / And issues." And Markham's search for his own

humanity through the physical and moral labyrinth of pre-war Constantinople is ironically shadowed by the novel's depiction of the maze of secret corridors and exits the doomed Sultan keeps rebuilding in his palace to foil assassins.

Markham's effort to participate meaningfully in history, to know and assist those who would bring down a brutal regime, causes him to shed his European selfhood even as he physically assumes native identities. He takes refuge with gypsies, dresses as a Turk and finally enters the palace in disguise as the Sultan is at last being deposed, for an oblique but personally decisive encounter with the tyrant who has obsessed his mind for so long. But the ironies of history cunningly persist and triumph. Markham's assertion of his humanity by revealing his moral guilt to others is compromised by his unrecognized need to dominate, even destroy, those to whom he reveals it. His sympathetic approach to the Armenian cause, to the achievement of a national homeland, makes him a useful pawn of extremists in that cause who would provoke new massacres to dramatize their plight. Provoked or unprovoked, massacres did indeed take place in 1915, after the "liberal" new regime replaced the Sultanate.

The Rage of the Vulture is in many ways a curious novel for these days. Eloquently, even poetically, written, it still does not pursue ambitiously "literary" effects, meanings noticeably larger than its material suggests. Though its chief concern is coherent narrative, it isn't really an espionage-intrigue tale or a historical novel in the popular mode. (Devotees of those genres ought nevertheless to enjoy it.) Nor, despite its potential resonance with religious and racial horrors still abroad in the Middle East (and elsewhere), is it a parable about contemporary history. It is a beautifully honest story of how a life is both given point and thwarted by its concern for self-definition through political commitment, and I admire Barry Unsworth very much for having told it so scrupulously and vividly.

John Clute (review date 16 August 1985)

SOURCE: "Death in Venice," in *New Statesman*, Vol. 110, No. 2839, August 16, 1985, p. 28.

[*In the following review, Clute finds the meaning of* Stone Virgin *somewhat confusing but appreciates Unsworth's depiction of Venice.*]

Bulging like a teardrop into its poisonous lagoon, Venice boasts a geography so graspable for purposes of art that it comes as a surprise not that so many stories are set there, but so few. In its fatal intercourse with the sea, the city models an inherent tendency of the Western mind to see the world as a series of dire consequences: the old familiar marriages of love and death, art and decay, power and corruption, sex and drowning.

Stone Virgin, a tale of love and death, art and decay, power and corruption and sex and drowning, has been set by Barry Unsworth, who is a deft and canny teller of tales, in the best place possible to add depth and a sense of the sorrows of time to a story that might otherwise seem marginally overblown. Conservation expert Simon Raikes has been called to Venice to restore a 15th-century Madonna, almost instantly to be haunted by the intricate circumambient city whose every vista seems to embody and to intensify his veil-rending obsessions. For he is an epileptic and, succumbing to seizures in the Virgin's presence, catches glimpses of an epiphanic Venetian past: bodies in clean rapture; hints of events that must have occurred when the sculpture was whole; a light as golden as childhood.

While this is going on, Unsworth omnisciently weaves into the main text two smaller narratives, the story of the artist who carved the Virgin in 1432 and of an 18th-century rake who seduced a woman in her shadow. Raikes's visions are of events from these two narratives. It seems that we are in the world—it is not an ignoble one—of the Venetian tales of Vernon Lee and Daphne du Maurier, for Raikes's visions can only be supernaturally derived. It is precisely at this point, however, that ***Stone Virgin*** slips into a slightly tedious mundanity—for Unsworth is clearly unwilling to give his novel any supernatural warrant.

The ending isn't much helped, either, by this refusal to tie the knots. Raikes falls in love with a woman whose family has been darkly involved with the Virgin throughout its history and it begins to look as though he's destined to reenact the same fatal sequence of passions that uplifted but then destroyed his predecessors. Perhaps wittingly, she has involved him in the death by the drowning of her artist husband; he is in sexual thrall to her—in thrall, also, to Venice. Unfortunately, through omniscience, we know rather more about Raikes's situation than Raikes does. Even so, because the novel has lost some of its coherence by this point, when Raikes does reconcile himself to her, goes to her isolated islet and watches her 'pale gold, glistening form emerge' like Aphrodite from the sea, we do not know if she is meant to be redeemed, redeeming or merely wet.

All the same, Unsworth's lovingly detailed Venice resonates with all her old beauty, her old desolate hints that time will not have a stop. She saves ***Stone Virgin.***

Katha Pollitt (review date 6 April 1986)

SOURCE: "A Sexual Rectangle," in *New York Times Book Review*, April 6, 1986, p. 27.

[*In the following review, Pollitt considers Unsworth's figure of the Madonna in* Stone Virgin *more interesting than his depiction of his human characters.*]

Just when I thought I couldn't stand to read another semi-autobiographical novel about a failing marriage, a blocked writer or a young man on drugs and the make, along comes the British novelist Barry Unsworth (***Mooncranker's Gift***) with a book that makes me think of that old *Monty Python* line "And now for something completely different." ***Stone Virgin*** is certainly that. Set in Venice in three different centuries, it's the only novel I can think of besides *The Picture of Dorian Gray* whose central figure and most interesting character is a work of art—a late Gothic statue of the Virgin of the Annunciation that seems to glow, may have supernatural powers and is definitely associated with murder, treachery, vengeance and high erotic doings down through the ages. There are problems with having a statue upstage the human characters, and I'll get to them in a bit, but give Mr. Unsworth credit: one couldn't be farther from the Upper West Side.

The main line of the story, set in 1972, gives us the British art restorer Simon Raikes, who has come to Venice to clean a sadly corroded Madonna as part of an international effort to rescue Venetian art treasures from the ravages of acid rain and air pollution. Raikes becomes obsessed with tracking down the statue's lost history: who was its sculptor, and what happened to him? Why was it installed in a church only in 1743, and where was it before? More to the point, why is Raikes, a rather tepid and tweedy sort of fellow, suddenly tormented by sexual desire and hallucinatory visions? In pursuit of the answers to all these questions, Raikes becomes involved with Lattimer, a sinister collector of artistic and sexual trophies, and Chiara, elusive wife of the gloomy sculptor Litsov.

If Raikes soon finds himself enmeshed in a rectangular drama of adultery, art theft and possibly murder, it comes as no surprise. Flashbacks set in 1432 show us the Madonna's creator, Girolamo, framed for the murder of the beautiful prostitute who served as his model. "Interludes" dated 1793 present Ziani, an aged aristocratic rake in whose salacious memoirs the Madonna, demoted to garden statue, plays a starring role. Both these men end up badly, and so, almost, does Raikes.

Mr. Unsworth has lavished a great deal of ingenuity—not to mention historical research—on his plot, carefully placing motifs and settings and incidents that echo back and forth in time. Yet I have to say that rarely have I read a novel with so little suspense. Part of the problem is that since we already know the Madonna's story through the flash-backs, it's boring to watch poor Raikes piece it together all over again from documents. And part of the problem is the prose. Mr. Unsworth offers touching desperation in the Girolamo chapters and elegant pastiche in the Ziani ones ("The airs of the past came to him, warm with malice, spiced with lechery, scented with self-congratulation"). But he also writes too many sentences like "Time and the world stood still for Raikes" and "Was this the burning creature of the night?"

Mostly, though, the problem is the characters. Lattimer is too creepy, Chiara too wise, Litsov too solemn and Raikes too flat to make us want to believe their rather improbable story. Never mind whether Raikes's visions are epileptic symptoms or psychic tremors from the Madonna's past. What I really wanted to know was what on earth Chiara, the pagan goddess of love and sex, sees in a morose young man who has never been in love and abandoned his sculpting ambitions out of cowardice. The minor characters are national stereotypes—the Italians dangerous and passionate, the English hyperrational and cool and furtively kinky. It would be fun to see the stereotypes reversed for a change—are there no fierce, licentious Englishmen, no shy, cerebral Italians? But that would require a writer with more of a sense of humor than the author cares to display here. Mr. Unsworth, moreover, is in the grip of a large idea. Men, he is out to demonstrate, see women not as complex human beings but as sex objects, to be worshiped as Madonnas if unattainable and despised as Jezebels if won. This is perhaps not as large an idea as he thinks, but virtually every character and every situation in **Stone Virgin** is set up to bear it out. Girolamo and Ziani are destroyed because they think their mistresses are playthings; Raikes almost loses Chiara because he confuses her sexual autonomy with a propensity for murder. Litsov possesses his wife through his sculpture; Lattimer collects pornographic souvenirs; all of Raikes's male colleagues are obsessed with the beautiful breasts of Miss Greenaway, the boiler-suited Titian expert. "It is you who are interested in fetishes, not us," Chiara tells Raikes, just in case we've missed the point; "you, all these dirty little boys who cannot grow up."

Against such a human backdrop, the Madonna looms steadily larger. Posed for by a prostitute and commissioned by an order of flagellant monks, Girolamo's statue embodies both sides of men's attitudes toward women, yet her strange luminosity, her otherworldly smile and her semierotic pose lift her beyond categories. I felt sorrier about the "badger stripe" of pollution across her face than about the travails of all the humans put together, and I held my breath when Raikes lifts his cleaning tool for the last, supremely dangerous touches, as I did for none of the murders, couplings and betrayals, past or present. Mr. Unsworth's people may lack reality, but if I ever visit

Venice, I fully expect to see Girolamo's Madonna smiling down at me from a church front. And if I don't, I'll be disappointed indeed.

Barry Unsworth with Phil Hogan (interview date 18 October 1992)

SOURCE: "Standing outside England and Looking In," in *London Observer*, No. 10,488, October 18, 1992, p. 59.

[*In the following interview, Unsworth reflects on his childhood and literary influences as well as on winning the prestigious Booker Prize for* Sacred Hunger.]

On balance, Barry Unsworth is in favour of literary prizes, even if he has to share one.

'I'm glad enough to have trousered the money,' he says, smiling diffidently—as much at his turn of phrase as at the sudden novelty of being £10,000 better off. 'And if the judges were genuinely at loggerheads between myself and Ondaatje, it was better to divide the prize than settling on a third who might not have been the first choice of anyone.'

In a posh suite on the tenth floor of the Royal Garden Hotel in Kensington, Unsworth pours a second cup of morning coffee after the night's celebrations. Cheerful and attentive, he's too polite to burden strangers with details of his hangover, though he is noticeably wary of the Danish pastries.

The prize will come in handy. After several years' residence in Finland—where people go to bed early—he and his second wife are currently converting the pigsty of a 100-year-old Umbrian farmhouse into a habitation fit for a newly prominent novelist. 'It costs money,' he explains. But if previous Booker form is anything to go by, worldwide earnings for **Sacred Hunger** will pay for an embarrassment of pigsties. And the lira is cheap at the moment.

This move is the latest of many. Unsworth has led a nomadic life since fleeing the coalfields of County Durham 40 years ago—Greece and Turkey in the Sixties and Seventies, Liverpool and Cambridge in the Eighties—eking out his royalties by teaching, and taking whatever scholarships or reviewing work came his way.

Unsworth broke loose from the North-east after his parents died in the early Fifties. His father—'an intelligent and energetic man'—had worked down the pit; his children did not. Determined to be a writer, Unsworth junior donned a black polo-neck jumper and moved to Cornwall, whose craggy scenery and wild aspects—it has to be imagined without the cream teas—attracted all manner of bohemian types. Ensconced in a cliff-top cottage Unsworth dispatched dozens of short stories to publishers in return for dozens of rejection slips.

While he admits that Cornwall was an awfully romantic idea, he points out that to a lad from Stockton-on-Tees—a place where ownership of an umbrella was an affectation punishable by public ridicule—it was the pinnacle of sophistication. It's not difficult to imagine the young Unsworth on that clifftop. The strain of idealism survives in *Sacred Hunger,* his epic tale of life aboard an eighteenth-century slave ship. For all its portrayal of brutality and corruption, there lies at its heart a niggling argument for man's capacity for good. Rationalist ideas—Rousseauesque philosophy, pre-Darwinian inklings—battle against the prevailing moral orthodoxies born of mercantile expedience. The book resonates with glimpsed Utopias—like Unsworth's Cornwall—amid the despair and degradation.

But when at one point the narrator speaks of 'wealth creation' as a sacred duty, it rings a bell closer to home. Unsworth is unrepentant about using this buzzword from the Thatcherite Eighties—the point being made is identical, he says. 'It was impossible to live in the Eighties without being affected by the sanctification of greed. My image of the slave ship was based on the desire to find the perfect symbol for that entrepreneurial spirit. The arguments used to justify it are the same used now to justify the closure of these pits and the throwing out of work of all these miners. I used the term "wealth creation" deliberately. I knew it was anachronistic.'

Unsworth's narrator pops up in other places to prod us with some pointed aphorism. One doesn't want to press the point too much, but where exactly is that authorial voice coming from? Which century? This is one of those awful postmodernist things. Unsworth looks thoughtful, even perturbed. 'I'm not sure. When I started, I wanted a narrator who would be like some grandmother who sits by the fireside moralising and throwing in little axioms and proverbs and homely sayings. She would tell a story that she knew and at the same time reflect upon it.'

As a child, Unsworth worked his way through his father's shelf of Victorian novels—George Eliot, Dickens, Wilkie Collins. Is this the kind of narrator he's talking about? 'I know Henry James and Flaubert have intervened since those days. But it is possible to regard the modernist aesthetic as an aberration. One doesn't need to apologise for not having a centre of consciousness or an exclusive viewpoint. My own daughters took to George Eliot at an age when you

would have expected them to be involved with . . . what was he called, big *ears* . . .'

Er, Prince Charles? 'Enid Blyton, you *know.*' Oh, *Noddy.*

Will Unsworth ever come back home for good? His adherence to traditional storytelling and his uncluttered moral vision is at odds with the intellectual cladding that has become the *sine qua non* of 'smart' contemporary fiction. 'It's become a habit now to be a bit on the outside looking in. I do love England and I hope to live here eventually but I wouldn't like to be too much in the swim.'

He's talking about London's literary clans: 'I don't think I'm built for that. I would get impatient with it. It is too incestuous, too . . .' He trails off, diplomatically, *decently.* But you know what he means.

Herbert Mitgang (review date 23 December 1992)

SOURCE: "Books of the Times: Trading in Misery on a Doomed Slave Ship," in *New York Times Book Review*, December 23, 1992.

[*In the following review, Mitgang calls* Sacred Hunger *"a remarkable novel in every way."*]

Reading *Sacred Hunger,* Barry Unsworth's long and beautifully written novel, you know you are in the hands of a master craftsman when you find yourself slowing down on page after page to savor his thoughts and words.

A hypocritical shipowner engaged in the slave trade: "Wealth had not dimmed his need to be liked, his desire to appear knowledgeable."

The shipowner's self-praise for including a doctor on his slaver's roster: "God balanced the ledgers. Nothing went unrecognized. A good deed was an entry on the credit side, a bill drawn on destiny which could not fail to be met one day."

The slave ship's cruel captain: "He felt the beginnings of rage, always his willing confederate."

Before setting sail to Africa from Liverpool, the captain and the doctor, his nephew, "touched glasses and drank, but it was the spirit of enmity they imbibed that afternoon, and both of them knew it."

He writes of a half-blind former slave in New Orleans, "He was small-boned and delicately made and he had a way of tilting his head up when he spoke, as if seeking to admit more light to the curdled crystals of his eyes."

Sacred Hunger can be read as a straightforward story of the British slave trade in the middle of the 18th century. Right down to the last impressed seaman and knotted lash, the novel's specificity is so detailed that you accept the characters as true to life and the horrible scenes as an accurate picture of the trade in human beings. But in this brilliant narrative, it is impossible not to feel that Mr. Unsworth's characters represent something larger: the eternal clash between good and greed—sometimes within the same person—and the dream of an Arcadian life where people live free and equal in peace.

A slave ship is being built for a proud Liverpudlian businessman, a member of the newly formed Company of Merchants Trading to Africa, created for what is known as the triangular trade. Goods, muskets and cheap trinkets are traded in Africa in exchange for blacks from other raiding blacks; the slaves are carried to America or the West Indies and sold there; tobacco, rum and sugar are then bought with the proceeds and resold in England.

The slave ship, called the Liverpool Merchant, has certain special features. The swivel guns on its quarterdecks are mounted so they can be trained down to quell slave revolts. The ship's rails are thickened to make death leaps more difficult. In the hold, at the lowest level of the ship, there is room for 200 slaves, tightly packed together. In language that echoes Joseph Conrad, the author describes the ship's maiden voyage on the first leg of the triangular trade:

> And so, in the course of that morning, the Liverpool Merchant was turned loose into the Irish Sea. With her mainsails set and a fair wind from the southeast, released from tethering rope and umbilical cable, she was for the first time in her life unfettered, free—save for her own groaning tensions—between wind and current.

On board is the novel's hero, the scholarly young doctor. While unsympathetic to the barbarities of buying and selling the human goods that have enriched his uncle, he has his own reasons for taking a job on the Liverpool Merchant. Having served a prison term on vague grounds of defending free speech, and because his wife and infant have recently died, he is seeking a new life.

But the Queeg-like captain, an experienced professional in the slave trade, quickly recognizes the young doctor as his enemy. He doesn't want the waterfront dregs who make up the ship's crew to be treated for illnesses and beatings; the doctor's role is only to keep them healthy enough to work and pay off their drinking debts. When the enslaved families, made servile by their nakedness, are bought on the

western coast of Africa, their treatment is even more demeaning. With a hot iron, the slaves are branded like cattle with the initial of the ship's owner: the men on their chests, the women on their buttocks. A smell of burned flesh hangs in the air over the Liverpool Merchant.

Again and again, the captain tells the doctor that a prime male slave is worth hard cash on the auction block in Jamaica or Virginia, and that a gentleman can live well in England for a year on the proceeds brought by a single slave. Watching the slaves stripped and branded, humiliated and whipped, the doctor finds that he too is becoming degraded.

While the Liverpool Merchant is crossing the Atlantic, the author keeps a secondary story spinning in Liverpool itself. The shipowner's son has fallen in love with an amateur actress, part of a young circle of friends who are rehearsing a play. And which of Shakespeare's dramas has Mr. Unsworth so cleverly chosen to remind the reader of the two different, but parallel lives, led by the two cousins: one on the perilous high seas, the other safely at home? *The Tempest*, with its shipboard scenes, inferno, storm, shipwreck and attempt to enjoy an idyllic life on a desert island.

Without straining too hard, the rehearsal of *The Tempest* can be read as a metaphor for what occurs in the harsh reality of *Sacred Hunger*. Prospero's line "Abhorred slave!" brings together the events in the play and the novel. But it isn't necessary for a reader to do so because Mr. Unsworth's main story is propelled by its own strong narrative engine.

In *Sacred Hunger,* disease spreads, the crew mutinies, the captain goes to his just reward and the Liverpool Merchant ends up shipwrecked on the coast of Florida. There a secret community is formed by the doctor, the sailors and the slaves, living together in what is an uninhabited land only lightly under the domination of Spain. But the story is not yet over; the two cousins, one driven by greed and revenge, the other by a dream, living on opposites sides of the world, will meet again.

Mr. Unsworth's book, which this year shared Britain's top fiction award, the Booker Prize, with *The English Patient*, by Michael Ondaatje, is a remarkable novel in every way.

Sybil S. Steinberg (review date 21 August 1995)

SOURCE: Review of *Morality Play*, in *Publisher's Weekly*, August 21, 1995, p. 43-44.

[*In the following review, Steinberg praises* Morality Play

as a "gripping" examination of the tension between appearances and reality.]

A portentous opening sentence—"It was a death that began it all and another death that led us on"—sets the tone for Booker Prize winner Unsworth's (*Sacred Hunger*) gripping story [*Morality Play*]. Indeed, a larger spectre than those two deaths hangs over this tale set in 14th-century England. The Black Plague is abroad in the land, and here it also symbolizes the corruption of the Church and of the nobility. One bleak December day, young Nicholas Barber, a fugitive priest who has impulsively decamped from Lincoln Cathedral, comes upon a small band of traveling players who are burying one of their crew. He pleads to join them, despite the fact that playing on a public stage is expressly forbidden to clergy. His guilt and brooding fear of retribution pervade this taut, poetic narrative. Footsore, hungry, cold and destitute, the members of the troupe are vividly delineated: each has strengths and weaknesses that determine his behavior when their leader, Martin, suggests a daring plan. In the next town they reach, a young woman has been convicted of murdering a 12-year-old boy, on evidence supplied by a Benedictine monk. Desperate to assemble an audience, Martin suggests that they enact the story of the crime. This is a revolutionary idea in a time when custom dictates that players animate only stories from the Bible. As the troupe presents their drama, many questions about the murder become obvious, and they improvise frantically, gradually uncovering the true situation. This, in turn, leads to their imprisonment in the castle of the reigning lord and their involvement in a melodrama equal to the one they have acted. Among the strengths of this suspenseful narrative are Unsworth's marvelously atmospheric depiction of the poverty, misery and pervasive stench of village life and his demonstrations of the strict rules and traditions governing the acting craft; underlying everything is the mixture of piety and superstition that governs all strata of society. Though sometimes he strays into didactic explanations, Unsworth searchingly examines the chasm between appearance and reality and the tenuous influence of morality on human conduct.

Janet Burroway (review date 12 November 1995)

SOURCE: "The Great Pretenders," in *New York Times Book Review*, November 12, 1995, pp. 11+.

[*In the following review, Burroway cites minor flaws in* Morality Play, *but otherwise praises the novel's deft universality of theme.*]

In a bitter winter in 14th-century England, a young scholar-priest comes upon a troupe of traveling players. These are

violent times, when victims of the plague are heaped in common pits and "the spirit of murder is never far." Nicholas Barber is in several sorts of flight: from the verbosity of the Latin manuscripts he has been set to copy, from the wrath of the bishop whose kindness he has betrayed and from the husband of the (most recent) woman he has toppled. Characteristically, the engaging hero of Barry Unsworth's new novel, *Morality Play,* is walking not on the road but in the shadows. From his hiding place, he witnesses the actors in a real-world death scene, gathered around one of their number. We know at once that Nicholas will join the troupe, taking the dead man's place.

One of the things that distinguish Mr. Unsworth's fiction is a sense of community that is warm without being sentimental. In *Sacred Hunger,* which won the Booker Prize in 1992, Mr. Unsworth created a leaderless band of former slaves and sailors in a credible utopia. In *Morality Play,* he offers a rich mix of squabbling, prideful players: the leader, Martin Bell; pale Straw, the mime; old Tobias; Stephen, whose deep-voiced dignity earns him the part of God in the morality plays; Springer, the boy who plays the women; and slatternly Margaret Cornwall, who looks after the mending and the money basket.

This band is en route to a performance at Durham, arranged as a Christmas gift from their patron to a relative. Determined to give their dead comrade a Christian burial, they make their way to the nearest town, now with Nicholas as well as the ripening corpse. But the cost of rent and rites is high, perhaps exorbitant. To raise the money, they must ply their trade; and, the drawing power of live theater being what it is, the take is hardly enough to offer rest to any of them, alive or dead.

Very soon it becomes clear that the town has another drama on its mind. A peasant boy has been murdered, and has been buried with strange alacrity. A beautiful deaf girl, who cannot speak, is being brought to justice with a speed also perhaps too deliberate. Listening to the town's gossip, the "greatly gifted" Martin, with his "zealot's face," comes up with the idea of docudrama. If we play their play, he tells the troupe, they will come; and, of course, he is right—although, then as now, the process involves both legal and spiritual pitfalls. Nicholas, too uneasy in his new profession to resist, at least knows with shame that "our profit would come from the shedding of a child's blood."

In order to plot their play, the actors skulk and interview and theorize. They become investigative journalists whose media are rhyme and dumb show. Yet it is in the feigning of the murder that they are led to the truth, not so much stumbling upon it as entering into it through the minds of their half-invented characters. Martin is most possessed by the enterprise, unable to detour from either his artistic insights or his role as savior of the girl, even at the threat to all their lives.

Historical genre fiction wants to amaze us with exotica: with dazzling costumes, splendid pageantry, feats of daring. In such fiction, any modern note reads as an anachronism, often unintentionally comic. But Mr. Unsworth has the art to enter the sensibility of a period—its attitudes, assumptions and turns of phrase—so convincingly that he is able to suggest subtle yet essential parallels between an earlier era and our own. The sailors of *Sacred Hunger* fought scurvy and foul weather and a cruel captain, familiar struggles all, in a way that made no concessions to Hollywood. In *Morality Play,* Mr. Unsworth has devised for his sinner-priest a voice that is sweetly pious, logical in a slightly literal-minded way and full of medieval-seeming wonder. Nicholas is a man well acquainted with the smell of death and muck but riven with fear that "if we make our own meanings, God will oblige us to answer our own questions."

Nicholas's wide-eyed explorations illuminate a range of current issues, seen in a new light by way of this unexpected context: the plight of women, the general abuse of children and the disabled, the fear and ignorance that surround a plague, the showy cynicism of the law, the social and political corruption that is found to spread farther and higher than could at first have been imagined. Even jousting, like today's prime-time sports, represents an expensive nostalgia for battle.

Embedded in Nicholas's tale is a variety of speculations about the nature of art and its uncomfortable fit in the "real" world of commerce, power, will, greed and intrigue. He delineates the subtle tyrannies of patronage and the preference of the populace for the crude entertainment of a dancing bear over the careful skills of an actor. He is full of Pirandellian reflections on the dangerous freedom the actors acquire with their roles, and the masks to which all return in their daily functioning, "playing parts even when there was no one by but themselves."

The little band makes a trap of Hamlet's kind, the play being the thing to catch the murderer. When Martin teaches Nicholas the prescribed theatrical gestures, we sense the mismatch between immediate matter and formal style—like the mismatch between Chekhov's realism and the rhetorical acting style before Stanislavsky. There is even an echo of Beckett's Vladimir, seeing the suffering world as the dream/drama of some greater being.

Occasionally, Mr. Unsworth nudges us a bit too hard. It is very convenient in a story so full of disguises that the lord of the locale is named de Guise, and that when the players finally confront him his face is "obscured from us by the brim of his hat and the plume set in it at the side." It undermines our readerly cleverness when Martin declares, "This is the way that plays will be made in the times to come." Nicholas's foreshadowing also hints at a doom that never materializes, so the novel's ending seems slightly askew, given the preparation that has come before it.

But these are minor cavils. *Morality Play* is a bravura performance, sparkling with the author's and the players' invention and mined with small ironies, like the description of Tobias, "who played Mankind and doubled the small parts and did attendant demons." The novel is a thought-provoking comedy on the eternal sameness of disaster and the recurrent uses we put it to in art. On the way, we toy with morality and also play our way to truth.

Charles Nicholl (review date 12 November 1995)

SOURCE: "All the Stage Is a World," in *Los Angeles Times Book Review,* November 12, 1995, pp. 2, 7.

[*In the following review, Nicholl presents an appreciative assessment of* Morality Play, *maintaining that the novel is a worthy successor to Unsworth's prior works.*]

It is three years since Barry Unsworth's last novel, *Sacred Hunger,* won plaudits and prizes (including the United Kingdom's prestigious Booker Prize) for its rich, harrowing portrayal of lives aboard an 18th-Century English slaving-ship.

The setting of his new book is very different, and the tone of it even more so. *Morality Play* tells the story of a troupe of players on the road in late 14th-Century England. The action unfolds over a few days and features a tight ensemble of characters. Most of it takes place in a small, unnamed Yorkshire town where the actors arrive, in the deep midwinter, and set up their stage in the inn yard. After the epic sweep of *Sacred Hunger,* this is a spare and sharply focused piece. It has the deceptive conciseness of a parable, or indeed a medieval morality play, in which the complexity lies not in the telling of the story but in the meanings and resonance that echo in the mind after it is told.

If this makes it sound rather austere, I should straightaway add that it is also an intriguing murder mystery, which keeps you guessing until almost the last page.

The story is narrated by a young man called Nicholas Barber. "A poor scholar, open-breeched to the winds of heaven," he has run away from his tedious studies as a subdeacon at Lincoln Cathedral and taken to the open road. Cold and hungry and full of remorse, he falls in with a troupe of strolling players. They have recently lost one of their members, the comic Brendan; Nicholas is taken on as a replacement; "it was a death that began it all and another death that led us on."

The players, led by the pale, charismatic Martin, are en route to Durham, to entertain at a nobleman's Christmas. Somewhere in Yorkshire they stop off to bury Brendan and to eke out a few shillings with a performance of the "Play of Adam." Nicholas makes his debut—as an attendant demon with a horned mask and a rope tail and a trident "for roasting the damned"—and learns the dangerous excitement of the stage: "A mask confers the terror of freedom, it is very easy to forget who you are. I felt it now, this slipping of the soul."

Unsworth handles the playing scenes with quiet relish: the repertoire of gestures and symbolic costumes; the drums and the torchlight and the alarming masks; the appearance of God on stilts. He catches that vividly makeshift quality of early drama.

Then the story begins to darken. They learn of the recent murder of a 12-year-old boy, Thomas Wells. A young woman, a weaver's daughter, has been charged and—rather hastily, it seems—condemned to hang. The circumstances are shady, and become more complex as the players start to inquire about them.

There is a key scene, beautifully written, in which Martin broaches the idea that they should perform a play about the murder. To the others, this idea of representing a real event, rather than the stock themes and figures of the moralities, is extraordinary. They are nonplused. "Who plays things that are done in the world?" asks one. "It was finished when it was done. How can men play a thing that is only done once? Where are the words for it?"

As their "Play of Thomas Wells" becomes, in itself, a form of detection and inquiry, and as the finger of suspicion points ever higher toward the household of the local feudal magnate, Richard de Guise, one sees that Unsworth's story is about the capacity of art—and particularly the live, momentary art of theater—to create new meanings, and thereby new possibilities, in the lives of its audience.

Their performance is contrasted with the chivalric jousts and tourneys that also feature in the story. In these the knights and ladies play their parts in a performance that reinforces the hierarchies and assumptions of feudal society. The play does something different. It questions and explores, and within the marked-out boundaries of the stage, and with the active collusion of its audience, creates an area of comment and debate.

As a medieval murder mystery, **Morality Play** invites comparison with Eco's *Name of the Rose*, and to admirers of the latter it will perhaps seem somewhat skimpy. I personally find its cool, lapidary style something of a relief. This is not a historical novel that depends on texture—that brothy accumulation of period detail, picturesque squalor and archaic turns of phrase—to achieve a sense of the past. Even the best practitioners, like the late Anthony Burgess, tend toward this rhetorical construction of history. Too often a historical novel seems like a piece of repro furniture deliberately "distressed" to make it look like an antique.

Unsworth's story wears its authenticity lightly, and his dialogue is entirely free of "gadzookery." The social setting is cleverly evoked: wintry scenes, hard-bitten lives etched against a background of frost and snow. There is a sense of confinement and control—the presence of hunger and plague; the daily oppression of feudal society. **Morality Play** is a book of subtlety, compassion and skill, and it confirms Barry Unsworth's position as a master craftsman of contemporary British fiction.

Adam Begley (review date 24 December 1995)

SOURCE: "Barry Unsworth Rescues 'All the World's a Stage' from Cliche," in *Chicago Tribune Books*, December 24, 1995, pp. 3, 6.

[*In the following review, Begley praises Unsworth's deft handling of the historical novel genre and his thought-provoking themes in* Morality Play.]

Morality Play, a fine new novel by Barry Unsworth, who won the 1992 Booker Prize for his **Sacred Hunger,** works brilliantly on three levels. It's an accurate, carefully imagined historical novel, set in 14th Century England; a dark and suspenseful murder mystery; and a provocative meditation on the birth of a new art form. Each layer adds a different flavor and texture. Binding the whole is Unsworth's understated, unerringly precise prose, and his narrator, a priest on the lam, very young and very poor, named Nicholas Barber.

We meet Nicholas as he's running out of a house without his cloak, running from the rage of a jealous husband. A priest caught in the act of adultery? Nicholas is wayward and weak-willed, but engagingly honest in his confessions: "[I]t was not lust but hunger drove me, a lesser sin, I was hoping she would give me to eat, but she was too hasty and hot. Then by ill luck the husband returned before expected and I had to escape through the cowshed and left my good cloak behind in that bitter December weather."

Nicholas runs straight into a band of traveling players, also poor, and short a man, too: One of their company is breathing his last just as Nicholas appears. Desperate, and again a little weak, Nicholas joins them, though it is expressly forbidden for clerics to perform on a public stage and players are thought of as little better than vagabonds.

Bound for Durham, where they are meant to perform Christmas plays for their patron's cousin, the players are forced to stop in a strange town to bury their comrade. They also hope to replenish their common purse by staging the "Play of Adam." But the burial is unexpectedly expensive, the audience for the play unexpectedly small. The town is distracted, full of odd tension. There has been a murder—a young boy strangled. A woman has been swiftly tried and found guilty, sentenced to hang. Unsettling questions linger.

Martin, the master-player of the company, a man intensely devoted to his craft and skilled in uncanny ways, hatches a plan the others rightly fear: He wants to stage a play about the boy's murder. To act out secular events, the news of the moment, is a staggering proposition in an age when religious pageant and morality plays are the only sanctioned, the only known forms of theater. The other players are scandalized by Martin's subversive suggestion. And yet Martin wins them over, thanks in part to the force of his conviction.

To prepare the play they must learn more about the murder. They become detectives, and soon the clues are pointing away from the condemned woman. Her accuser is a Benedictine monk, confessor of the powerful lord whose castle looms above the town. The mystery deepens and the danger grows even as the players rehearse their parts.

Against the backdrop of cleverly plotted suspense, Nicholas engages in nervous speculation about the consequence of their audacious enterprise. He understands how this new kind of play turns everything topsy-turvy: "[I]f we make our own meanings, God will oblige us to answer our own questions, He will leave us in the void without the comfort of His Word." If man by his art manages to piece together some kind of truth, that truth may prove comfortless.

Part of the beauty of **Morality Play** is the way the mystery and the metaphysics come together. If the players can indeed find out truth by crafting a faithful representation of reality, then the murder will be all but solved. If not, their player's pride has led them sadly astray. There's a further twist, too. If, as they suspect, the murderer is still at large, then the better the play, the more danger for the players. Truth is deadlier than fiction.

Most historical novels are loaded down with too many pe-

riod details. Obsolete and dated doodads choke the flow of narrative and reveal the author's anxiety about making it all seem at once old and real. In this respect, Unsworth travels light, giving the reader just enough to suggest a coherent world very different from our own.

The historical detail gets technical only when it comes to the players' acting methods. Nicholas is initiated into a secret language of hidden signs and a public language of ritual gesture. When they speak among themselves the players mix words, signs and gestures: "[H]e made the sign of money, which is done by opening and closing the hand very rapidly."

Unsworth makes wonderfully efficient use of this for color, comic relief, characterization (each player has his own repertoire of gestures), and also to underscore the exotic element—it *is* strange to travel in this motley company.

Nicholas learns to act. He makes an unexpected discovery: "[T]he player is always trapped in his own play but he must never allow the spectators to suspect this, they must always think that he is free. Thus the great art of the player is not in showing but in concealing." He learns to see the world through a mask, and to see the machinations of others as elements in a larger drama.

Shakespeare's "All the world's a stage, / And all the men and women merely players" is worn thin from overuse; **Morality Play** gives it new life. Unsworth shows us the moment in Nicholas's education—and the moment in history—when it becomes possible to see in all the earnest bustle of mankind a gaudy pageant, footlights, costumes, greasepaint, props.

Richard Bernstein (review date 17 January 1996)

SOURCE: "When Someone Zigs Instead of Zags," in *New York Times Book Review*, January 17, 1996, p. C16.

[*In the following review, Bernstein praises Unsworth's "tightly constructed murder mystery" and the evocative details with which he builds his story in* Morality Play.]

The first few sentences of this cunning, suspenseful medieval murder mystery by Barry Unsworth [**Morality Play**] are a model of literary compression and an illustration of the artfulness that adorns the novel's every page. With quick strokes of the pen, Mr. Unsworth introduces his narrator, Nicholas Barber, as a priest who in the recent past was searching for a meal but ended up in an act of adultery from which he had to make a quick escape. This, in turn, put him in the woods, rather than on the open road, and it was in the woods that he ran into a troupe of itinerant players standing mournfully over the corpse of a recently deceased fellow. And this warrants the first half of Mr. Unsworth's opening line: "It was a death that began it all and another death that led us on."

At the heart of *Morality Play* is the fascinating logic obeyed by the chain of circumstance, whereby tiny, ordinary events lead to unforeseen large and life-changing ones. There is a theological statement here someplace about the role of free will and accident in human affairs, about the things that are predetermined and the things that are governed by a kind of 14th-century chaos theory, the contribution of the butterfly's wing to the movements of the atmosphere. *Morality Play* is constructed like a lesson in butterfly-wing complexity, showing the way in which one small decision about an obscure death in the forest later comes to intrude into the life of the lord's castle in town.

Morality Play, Mr. Unsworth's first book since his *Sacred Hunger* won the Booker Prize in England in 1992, is not theological. It is a learned, witty, satisfying entertainment set in medieval England. (The dust jacket says the 14th century, but this is not specified in the actual text.) Mr. Unsworth's not-too-pious priest—who is nonetheless concerned about his moral bookkeeping—joins a debate among the players in the woods over how to dispose of their recently deceased fellow actor.

They are on their way to perform for a relative of the lord who owns them, and since they are in a hurry it would be expedient for them to leave the body in the woods, where Nicholas, fleeing an irate husband, first sees them. The ground being frozen, however, and the dead player's friends eager to give him a proper burial, the troupe decides to take him along, and Nicholas too. And so, the priest's hunger determines his encounter with the troupe, and the company's compassion for the dead determines everything else, including a detour into an unknown town. There, in accordance with Mr. Unsworth's first-page hint, the actors learn of another death, and the tightly constructed murder mystery unfolds.

A story like this depends on the power of the payoff at the end, of course, and here is perhaps a minor weakness in Mr. Unsworth's book. Some readers will guess the secret of the plot well before it is disclosed in the final chapters. Moreover, Mr. Unsworth gets his characters out of the scrape their actions have led them into by creating a character whose presence on the scene is a somewhat too lucky coincidence.

Still, what *Morality Play* loses in climactic surprise, it gains by its originality as a mystery story and the persuasive strangeness of the 14th century in which it is set. The detective story unfolds through the activities of the players. They create a play intended to depict the murder—according to the official account of it by the authorities—to local townsfolk. They do this piece of pioneering theatrical work not to solve the crime but to make money.

"It has been in my mind for years now that we can make plays from stories that happen in our lives," says one member of the troupe, foreshadowing the made-for-television movie of half a millennium later. "I believe this is the way that plays will be made in the times to come."

As they rehearse, the players begin to see flaws in the official version of events. They come to see that nothing about the crime is what it first appeared to be. The play in this sense does not catch the conscience of a king, but it allows for the exploration of reality. "The player is himself and another," Nicholas explains at the end. "When he looks at the others in the play he knows he is part of their dreaming just as they are part of his. From this come thoughts and words that outside the play he would not readily admit to his mind."

Meanwhile, Mr. Unsworth evokes a believable 14th century, a time of religious conflict, of the struggle for power between the king and the country's great lords, of pervasive barnyard smells and the Black Death, which turns out, like everything else in Mr. Unsworth's plot, to play an indispensable role. The narrator speaks convincingly as one imagines narrators to have spoken in 14th-century England, and within that framework, Mr. Unsworth creates many scenes of graphic beauty.

"The yolk of the egg made a yellow smear on the snow and a rawboned dog saw it at the same time as the beggar did and both made for it and the beggar kicked the dog, which yelped and held back but did not run, hunger making him bold," Mr. Unsworth writes of a scene in the market. "The beggar cupped his hands and scooped up the egg in the snow and took it into his mouth and ate all together, the egg and the fragments of shell and the snow. He saw me watching him and smiled the same smile, with the wet of the snow and egg glistening on his innocent face."

Nicholas Barber seems too good a narrator to let go after just one short book. Perhaps Mr. Unsworth will write "Morality Play, Part II," in which Nicholas tells us another savory story.

Anthony Quinn (review date 4 August 1996)

SOURCE: "Creepy Crawling, Heavy Breathing," in *New York Times Book Review*, August 4, 1996, p. 12.

[*In the following review, Quinn offers praise for the reprint edition of* The Hide.]

Better known for his potent fictional reconstructions of time past—most memorably the slave trade epic **Sacred Hunger,** which shared the Booker Prize in 1992—Barry Unsworth reveals in this early novel, first published in Britain in 1970, an equally assured grasp of the modern world. Bristling with menace, **The Hide** is a superbly modulated study of the blighting of an innocent. While the canvas is somewhat narrower than one might expect from Mr. Unsworth, the texture of the prose is easily recognizable. And it is as dense and dark as the overgrown estate that furnishes the novel's setting.

The Hide is laid out as a dual narrative. Simon, who speaks to us in half the chapters, is a creature of the underground, obsessively patrolling the wild acreage of his sister's estate while he digs an elaborate system of hidden trenches, a "hide" from which he can watch "girls cycling past at weekends, careless of their skirts on the empty road." With his heavy binoculars and his heavy breathing, Simon likes nothing better than to spy on the woman in the bungalow across the way, priding himself on the discipline and stealth required for this perverted surveillance. He feels his secret domain coming under threat, however, when his sister, Audrey, hires a gardener. Terrified that the interloper will expose his subterranean labyrinth, he immediately embarks on a plan of defense.

The gardener, 20-year-old Josh, is the book's other narrator, as open and innocent as Simon is furtive and scheming. Their voices are also markedly different. Where Simon's is fastidious, precise and braced with an almost Nabokovian disdain ("I see the bright frizz of her hair in the sunshine—she will inflict on herself these unbecoming home-perms"), Josh's is untutored and countrified, couched in an ungrammatical idiom that Mr. Unsworth catches beautifully ("She would never of tried to catch me out or show me up like").

Josh has been used to a peripatetic life—though he is touchy about any references to being a Gypsy—and while working at a seaside fairground falls in with Mortimer, an older man whose influence on him is, we soon learn, quietly pernicious. As Mortimer's brand of unsentimental education takes hold, distant but ominous alarms begin to sound in the reader's mind:

> He said blokes like that, cripples and blokes without their faculties, should be kept away from healthy people. . . . It is no use trying to feel what a dumb bloke

feels, Mortimer said, and his eyes got bigger because I was arguing like, he hates to be argued with. Well I got scared when I seen that, I hate Mortimer to be angry with me, he might just decide to stop being my friend and once he did that I know he'd never change, it would be for good. You are taking the sentimentalist line, he said. Haven't you heard of neecher? Neecher? I said. . . . Slave morality, he said, looking at me with those big eyes.

Meanwhile Josh himself has had a conspicuous and half-unwitting effect on the novel's two women characters. Audrey, a Brooknerish widow somewhat past her prime, seeks to relieve her loneliness in his company. She mistakenly assumes that her affections are returned when Josh makes her a gift of a toy horse he has carved. Unbeknown to her, Josh is already involved with her young housekeeper, Marion, a romance in which both Simon and Mortimer take a keen interest. The former sees it as a chance to compromise Josh and effect his dismissal; the latter has more sinister designs.

Mr. Unsworth sustains the motif of concealment: Simon's "hide" symbolizes the narrative's complex network of secret alliances and motives. It also yields a wonderfully grotesque set piece when Audrey has the local Dramatic Society round for a supper party. Simon, in revenge for his sister's appointment of the gardener, conceals his false teeth in the chocolate mousse and watches in an agony of excitement as the guests begin to help themselves:

> The teeth are already served then, already dished out. Perhaps, perhaps in mine. I return to my place in the corner, attack the mousse immediately, nothing, nothing at all. The glutinous stuff, darkly glistening, mocks my spoon with its lack of resistance, sweetly dissolves against my toothless gums. I see Mrs. King finishing off her mousse with dainty licks, nothing there either. . . . It is like seeing humanity for these few moments sub specie aeternitatis. We are all doomed, of course, but one of us is more immediately singled out.

Mr. Unsworth demonstrates throughout a steely command of technique. His patience in detailing the shifting nuances of a relationship is exemplary, but even more impressive is the suggestion of unspoken—hidden—feelings desperately contained. Moment by moment, we feel Josh's progress from puzzled ingenue to reluctant accomplice, a corruption no less agonizing for being inevitable. It is remarkable how much has been packed into so slight a novel. The most obviously compelling aspect of **The Hide** is in the characterization of Mortimer, an individual of unregenerate malignity. Yet in the novel's glancing depictions of seafront shabbiness, of the tight-lipped politesse of county society, of the exploitation of a luckless itinerant, Mr. Unsworth also offers us a bitter little slice of England.

Richard Eder (review date 9 March 1997)

SOURCE: "The Weight of History," in *Los Angeles Time Book Review*, March 9, 1997, p. 2.

[*In the following review, Eder considers* After Hannibal *a "dazzling" exploration of history, greed, and betrayal.*]

"Do you know the land where the lemontrees flower?" Goethe wrote in a poem that helped shift the elevation angle at which the Romantics regarded earthly salvation. Instead of going upward to heaven, you went sideways to Italy.

Since then, untold hundreds of thousands have traveled from Northern Europe, the United States and elsewhere, not so much for the sun as to follow a grand line of beauty and aesthetic order that shifted from Greece to Rome, sheltered in the medieval abbeys and burst forth in the Renaissance. Above all, it went beyond works of art to show itself at the turn of a street, to blossom almond-white in a restaurant's courtyard and to stretch over patterned hills, olive groves and terra cotta roofs, as if that same art had formed them all.

Increasingly, when the grand hotel gave way to the *pensione* and then to the dream of the perfect villa or a month's apartment rental, the sense grew that you could do more than follow the line. You could join it; you could become part of the beauty. You could change your life, have breakfast in the painting, wash dishes in the three stanzas retained from college Dante. Literary adjectives would climb off the shelf and enlist as daily household help. "Crystalline" might overdo it, but water would be more than water when you turned the tap.

Or less—and when a plumber finally came, he might go away without fixing it, overcharge and get mysteriously angry. Baffling notices would slide under the door; a routine bank errand turn into an inexplicable crisis. The cheerfully talkative butcher would fling an indifferent piece of meat across the counter and go taciturn.

The literature of Mediterranean illusion and disillusion is vast. A lot is bad—most recently, the smarminess of Peter Mayles' exploitative romancing about food and the picturesque in Provence. Much of it, honest enough, keeps to the ruefully light. But there is a literary tradition—a leading one, in fact—of great writing: Henry James, E. M. Forster, D. H. Lawrence, John Cheever, Penelope Fitzgerald and

William Trevor are a few of the very different names that come to mind.

After Hannibal, by the British writer Barry Unsworth, is a vivid, sinuous, profound and entirely beguiling venture at squaring their same circle: How do we balance our need for the Mediterranean illusion, the reality in the illusion and the reality of that reality?

The first leads to an exploration of ourselves, the second to an evocation of the power of art and beauty over time—a power as real as war and plague. The third brings in the war and plague and confronts the first two with the harshness of how people actually struggle and live. We are ravished by the beauty of hill-town walls and facades; we do not know how to reconcile it with the smell of bloodshed so copiously in building, assaulting and defending them.

Unsworth weaves these things together in a polyphony as acrid as a Gesualdo madrigal and playful as a tavern catch. He interweaves the stories of four couples—two Italian, one English, one American—and a single German, who own small villas along a common dirt road in the Umbrian countryside outside Perugia. Each is there after some illusion or fulfillment. Each comes up differently against the consequences of history, stretching back 2,000 years and affecting, right to the present day, the way that people behave and the way the very grass blades grow.

Not far from the dead-end dirt road, Hannibal's troops hid in the fogged-in hills above Lake Trasimeno and swept down to massacre the Roman legions, unfamiliar with the landscape and struggling in the lakeside marsh. Unfamiliarity with the landscape or, in the case of the Italians, with the history that seeps through it, is one of the themes that runs through Unsworth's dazzling novel.

There is Harold Chapman, a blustering, prosperous English developer, and his art-loving wife, Cecilia. She had hoped that an Umbrian villa and lots of culture would bring them together; for Harold, acquiring culture is a war of conquest like any other. He gets into a feud with a peasant family—not in the least picturesque and quite as greedy as he—who wants him to pay for the collapse of their rickety wall after the Chapman's construction trucks have rumbled through. When they hammer in stakes to block the road, Chapman sallies into Perugia to enlist Mancini, the lawyer.

There is Fabio, a former racing-car champion, and his male lover, Arturo, whom he has plucked from a life of prostitution. Benefaction and tyranny are hard to distinguish, though; Fabio insists on meticulous order and labor to embellish their small paradise of a villa. Outwardly compliant, Arturo seduces Fabio into signing the property over to him, arguing tax and other advantages. He then decamps and brings an eviction action. "I will kill him," Fabio rages, but he too goes to Mancini.

There are the Greens, two retired American art teachers who have invested their savings in a broken-down villa, hoping to turn it into a retirement dream. They are hopelessly bilked by Blemish, an English con man who sets himself up in the vicinity as a kind of super-contractor.

Blemish and his stout wife are a wonderfully loving pair. After his day of swindles and hers of frying up rich pastries, they don Restoration costumes and play galumphing sex games. They are a high order of low comedy and sharp as shark's teeth. Blemish's dealings with the sweetly and insufferably innocent Greens are an agonizingly expert course in how to be fooled. Rallying eventually, they arrive at Mancini's rapidly filling waiting-room—of which more in a moment.

Connected in a more ghostly fashion to the story is Ritter, a German translator who has broken down remembering his father, an army officer who took part in the Ardeatine Caves massacre of 335 Italian hostages. The father's self-exculpatory explanations work like slow poison in a son whose profession is words. He labors to clear his five acres of scrub, a wordless image for his battle with the tangled lies of the past.

Finally there is Monti, a historian whose wife has just left him for another man. Puzzling out her betrayal, he pursues his research into the bloody and treacherous conflict of Renaissance Perugia with the papacy. Monti's travels to nearby villages, in order to put together the story of the particularly carnivorous Baglioni family, is one of two silken threads that bind his neighbors' stories together. The gentle Monti learns from the history he unearths; it teaches the futility of revenge and, instead of burdening his grievance, lightens it.

The second thread is provided by the much-solicited Mancini. Angelically devious, he leads his tormented clients through the entirely divergent complexities of Italian law and Italian practice. As a young man, he explains, legal solutions seemed to be straight lines. Not so; they are a web.

This benevolent spider bends his clients' quests for linear justice through the prism of a millennial history. Law is not a sword in Italy—too many righteous causes have been pursued too long and horribly. Instead, it is a cloudiness, under cover of which one can devise advances, retreats, feints, traps and finally, if possible, a solution. The tactics he proposes are hilariously twisted, while serving, strangely, time's long-drawn approximate justice.

Each of the stories achieves indeterminate balances of satisfaction and frustration, thanks in part to the lawyer's tutelage and in part to that of a fortuitous earthquake. History (researched by Monti, applied by Mancini) and the unstable landscape: These are the regulators of the dozen turbulent and comically detailed passions that Unsworth has so finely set in motion.

Hilary Mantel (review date 9 March 1997)

SOURCE: "Etrurian Shades," in *New York Times Book Review*, March 9, 1997, p. 30.

[*In the following review, Mantel finds* After Hannibal *uneven in structure and character and overly formal in language.*]

Barry Unsworth's latest novel [*After Hannibal*] is a sad comedy of cheats and fools, a story of unbounded beauty and blighted hopes, of multiple and layered betrayals, "a regression of falsehoods and deceptions going back through all the generations to the original agreement, God's pact with Adam." Its setting is the Umbrian countryside, "the hills that Perugino and Piero della Francesca looked at," and the little hill towns with their art treasures and their frequently bloody history. What lies beneath the promise of the spring landscape, the poplars gently unfurling, the peach trees in bud? The answer is there in the place names: "Sepoltaglia, burial ground, Sanguineto, where the blood ran, Ossaia, place of bones."

Mr. Unsworth's characters are linked by the road that runs past their houses. "They are called strade vicinali, neighborhood roads. . . . Dusty in summer, muddy in winter, there are thousands of miles of them wandering over the face of rural Italy. When such a road has reached your door it has no necessary further existence." These roads are marked on maps, but the maps make no distinction between broad highways and rutted tracks, between roads that are useful and roads that are merely notional. The cost of their upkeep falls on those whose doors they pass. It is a dispute about the maintenance of a wall adjoining one particular strada vicinale that embroils a British couple named Harold and Cecilia Chapman in a quarrel with the Checchetti family, who are just as coarse and cunning as peasants in literature can possibly be.

Not that the reader is on the side of the English couple. Harold is a blusterer, his wife a bore. Their other neighbors are a strange German, Ritter, who has suffered a mental breakdown and lives in isolation in the hills above; an ingenuous American couple, the Greens, soon to become the dupes of a British "project manager" who will wreck their house instead of renovating it; two Italian homosexuals, whose personalities are hardly established before the younger one runs away, having first persuaded his partner to sign over the house to him.

There is also the morose figure of Monti, an Italian historian whose wife has recently left him. Here is a personal betrayal to add to the historical betrayals on which Monti's mind dwells. His function in the plot is that of matchmaker between the past and the present. The history he teaches his students seems old-fashioned, quaint and anecdotal, and the reader may not have much confidence in his judgment. Did Gibbon really find the era of ancient Rome "a period as remote from him in its manners and morals as the time before the Flood"?

In addition to the strada vicinale there is another link between these characters. It is Mancini, the cunning and enigmatic lawyer whom most of them find reason to consult. Mancini seems to be of no particular age. Has he a beginning and an end? His clients, with their childlike notions about justice, merely furnish him with entertainment. He seems to be in possession of some truth—but what is the truth Mr. Unsworth offers us? Houses fall down. They are razed. Earthquakes and enemies blitz them. We are all exposed, sooner or later: "no walls left standing to shelter our illusions."

After Hannibal does not earn the right even to this glib, routine pessimism. Mr. Unsworth himself lives in Umbria. He writes tenderly about fig trees and nightingales, frescoes and stained glass, and particularly about the lovely light of the area: "The experience of it was like the experience of understanding something." Sometimes he seems to be describing the terrain just to cheer us up—after all, there is not much in the characters or plot to please us— and at these times the novel reads like a very superior guidebook. Elsewhere, descriptions carry a heavy weight of symbolism, and this makes the writing seem inauthentic. When Mr. Unsworth's characters have a crisis, they go off to view a ruin; under stress, they urgently examine an altarpiece.

Occasional flashes of acid observation are welcome. (Harold Chapman "was given to the counting of blessings, which in practice meant the listing of assets.") And Mr. Unsworth writes well about how we hate the people we cheat, how betrayal changes the nature of the past by poisoning memory. The interplay of the individual stories is neat and ingenious, but the structure does not allow narrative tension to build.

Mr. Unsworth's intimate knowledge and delight in his territory gives the prose life and beauty, but expatriation may also be undermining him. He has never been a writer who followed the fashion; with admirable integrity, he has plowed his own furrow. But it isn't wise to become estranged from how people in the street use your native language; you should know about it, even if you don't use the knowledge. This is not just a matter of vocabulary, it's a matter of rhythm and speed. In this novel, Mr. Unsworth's idiom is stiff, like that of an old-fashioned schoolmaster. Studied, literary inversions are dotted throughout the text. ("Those we have pardoned do we always underrate?") Some readers may value the elegance of expression, but when this degree of formality is applied not just in narrative but in dialogue, the effect is to make the characters into a ventriloquist's dolls.

There is, too, a problem of register. Ritter, the German, contends with welling memories of a World War II atrocity in which his father was implicated. Blemish, the project manager, is—as his name suggests—a vehicle for broad farce. It is possible that one story could accommodate Ritter's anguish and Blemish's silliness, but it is surprising that an author writing his 11th novel should toss them together so casually, without seeing that something strong and cunning in terms of authorial control must be exercised if one is not to negate the other.

Mr. Unsworth may be a victim of his own recent triumphs. *Sacred Hunger,* his novel about the slave trade, won the 1992 Booker Prize in Britain and was greeted by many critics as an instant classic. It is a massive work, very different from its quicksilver successor, *Morality Play,* which was a finalist for the Booker in 1995. Scorned by the imperceptive as a medieval whodunit, *Morality Play* was a near-perfect novel, with a diamond's glitter and a diamond's hardness: a profound meditation on the nature of justice and the transforming power of art. By contrast, *After Hannibal* seems a book made up of other books: the commonplace book, the scrapbook.

Miranda Schwartz (review date 9 March 1997)

SOURCE: "Meet the Neighbors," in *Chicago Tribune Books,* March 9, 1997, p. 4.

[*In the following review, Schwartz finds the characterizations in* After Hannibal *particularly intriguing and rewarding to the reader.*]

After Hannibal, the latest novel from Booker Prize-winner Barry Unsworth (*Morality Play, Sacred Hunger*), is a deliciously keen observation of strangers in a strange land.

deliciously keen observation of strangers in a strange land. Unsworth reminds the reader of Muriel Spark and Barbara Pym; he shares their understated wit and their talent for clean and stylish description. This contemporary novel even owes debt to E. M. Forster in its portrayal of foreigners at sea in Italy. While Forster may go deeper into the minds of his creations, Unsworth seems to have more fun gleefully setting his characters loose on one another and recounting the ensuing havoc: marriages broken, alliances formed, houses destroyed, secrets unburied.

Unsworth's people live near Perugia's Lake Trasimeno, on a small neighborhood road about which he writes, "the important thing, really, about roads like this, is not where they end but the lives they touch on the way." The inhabitants along this road include a comically mismatched British couple, two gay Italians, a slightly naive American couple and an Italian medievalist whose wife has just left him.

As Unsworth explores the lives touched by this road, he slowly reveals the background of his characters—the detours made, the signposts missed. He is not above poking a bit of fun at his creations ("He was given to the counting of blessings, which in practice meant the listing of assets"), yet they are durable enough to retain a measure of dignity and realism.

Unsworth is most intrigued by the relations between incompatible couples—the constant give and take, the outpourings of the soul versus the lies of omission—all exemplified perfectly here by the supremely incompatible Brits: Harold is a money-grubber feigning refinement, while Cecilia is a dreamy, poetic soul; the tracks of their inner lives will never merge. The gay couple are ill-matched as well, the older man oblivious to his lover's restlessness and duplicity.

The only good, happy people are the Greens, retired American art teachers who, like the abstracted Cecilia, truly appreciate the beautiful Italian landscape and the timeless inheritance of the great Renaissance artists. But the Greens' happiness in themselves, their newly purchased villa and the country is threatened by a dishonest English building supervisor who preys upon newcomers to Italy.

Only one individual rises above the hodgepodge of life—Mancini, a lawyer consulted by the neighbors as they thread their way through treacherous attachments and feuds. Serene and sagacious, he has a hand in every pot bubbling in Perugia and its outskirts; he knows everyone and divines all motivations.

At first Unsworth cloaks Mancini in mystery: It's uncertain if he is desirous of helping the good and thwarting the bad, or merely a detached and amused observer—and much hangs on this tantalizing question. But thankfully, the cagey

Mancini is a seeker after both inner beauty and outer order; he serves as a kind of spiritual-legal traffic cop on the road of life. With his guidance, the characters begin to see a path out of the chaos in and around them.

Patricia Lothrop-Green (review date September 1997)

SOURCE: "It's Hip! It's Contemporary! It's Literature!," in *School Library Journal*, Vol. 43, No. 9, September 1997, pp. 128-29.

[*In the following review, Lothrop-Green provides a brief overview of the plot of* Morality Play *and praises the novel's exploration of the role of art in revealing universal truths.*]

Barry Unsworth's *Morality Play* (Norton, 1995) was praised by novelist Hilary Mantel (in the *New York Times Book Review*) as "a near-perfect novel, with a diamond's glitter and a diamond's hardness: a profound meditation on the nature of justice and the transforming power of art." It is also a gripping mystery, a coming-of-age story, and a fascinating road trip through 14th-century England. Nicholas is a young cleric on the run from his boring desk job (copying Latin manuscripts). He sees a troupe of traveling players grouped around a death bed; characteristically, Nicholas fails to do his duty and absolve the dying man. The troupe could disguise his fugitive status, however, so he persuades the players to let him wear the dead man's clothes—both literally and figuratively. As he (and readers) learn about the life of the group and the nature of the morality play, issues bridging that time and ours are raised: the role of women, social roles generally, prejudice and fear, the arrogance of privilege and the cynicism of power, and the piety or nostalgia that conceal corruption. Questions of identity and purpose underline the actors masking, disguises, and role-playing (Follow this novel with a discussion of masking in Shakespeare's *Much Ado about Nothing*). When the troupe stops to raise money for the funeral of the dead man, they are caught in another death. Why has a young boy been so hastily buried? What does a father's radical politics have to do with the accusation against his mute daughter? The players' leader decides to make a daringly original move: to improvise a play about the murder. Like a mask, art conceals but can thereby reveal the truth.

FURTHER READING

Criticism

Altinel, Savkar. "Trinitarian Tanglings." *Times Literary Supplement* (30 August 1985): 946.

Altinel finds *Stone Virgin* disappointing as the final volume in Unsworth's literary triptych.

Bernard O'Donoghue, Bernard. "Medieval Mysteries." *Times Literary Supplement* (8 September 1995): 7.
    O'Donoghue maintains that *Morality Play* is Unsworth's best book to date.

Colegate, Isabel. "Dreams of Umbria." in *Times Literary Supplement* (30 August 1996): 24.
    Colegate finds *After Hannibal* "a skillfully composed and beautifully written novel" about the after effects of treachery and betrayal.

Fitton, Toby. "A Slave to Symbols." *Times Literary Supplement* (16-22 September 1988): 1014.
    Fitton praises the originality of *Sugar and Rum* de

spite what he considers some stereotypical episodes.

Godwin, Gail. "Three Troubled Lives." *New York Times Book Review* (7 April 1974): 31.
    Godwin praises Unsworth's dexterity with presenting moral ambiguities in *Mooncranker's Gift.*

Goldsmith, Francesca. A review of *After Hannibal. Library Journal* 122, No. 2 (1 February 1997): 108-9.
    Goldsmith presents a brief overview of the plot and major themes of *After Hannibal.*

Ross, Maria. "Profit at Any Cost." *Books* 6, No. 2, (March-April 1992): 5.
    An interview in which Unsworth discusses his research for *Sacred Hunger,* particularly issues related to capitalism, trade, and morality.

Additional coverage of Unsworth's life and career can be found in the following sources published by Gale: *Contemporary Authors*, **Vols. 25-28R;** *Contemporary Authors New Revision Series*, **Vols. 30, 54;** *Dictionary of Literary Biography*, **Vol. 194.**

☐ Contemporary Literary Criticism

Indexes

Literary Criticism Series
Cumulative Author Index
Cumulative Topic Index
Cumulative Nationality Index
Title Index, Volume 127

How to Use This Index

The main references

Camus, Albert
1913-1960 . . . . . . .CLC 1, 2, 4, 9, 11,
14, 32, 69; DA; DAB; DAC; DAM
DRAM, MST, NOV; DC2; SSC 9;
WLC

list all author entries in the following Gale Literary Criticism series:

BLC = *Black Literature Criticism*
BLCS = *Black Literature Criticism Supplement*
CLC = *Contemporary Literary Criticism*
CLR = *Children's Literature Review*
CMLC = *Classical and Medieval Literature Criticism*
DA = *DISCovering Authors*
DAB = *DISCovering Authors: British*
DAC = *DISCovering Authors: Canadian*
DAM = *DISCovering Authors Modules*
  DRAM = *dramatists;* **MST** = *most-studied
  authors;* **MULT** = *multicultural authors;* **NOV** =
  novelists; **POET** = *poets;* **POP** = *popular/genre
  writers;* **DC** = *Drama Criticism*
HLC = *Hispanic Literature Criticism*
LC = *Literature Criticism from 1400 to 1800*
NCLC = *Nineteenth-Century Literature Criticism*
PC = *Poetry Criticism*
SSC = *Short Story Criticism*
TCLC = *Twentieth-Century Literary Criticism*
WLC = *World Literature Criticism, 1500 to the Present*
WLCS = *World Literature Criticism Supplement*

The cross-references

See also CA 89-92; DLB 72; MTCW

list all author entries in the following Gale biographical and literary sources:

AAYA = *Authors & Artists for Young Adults*
AITN = *Authors in the News*
BEST = *Bestsellers*
BW = *Black Writers*
CA = *Contemporary Authors*
CAAS = *Contemporary Authors Autobiography Series*
CABS = *Contemporary Authors Bibliographical Series*
CANR = *Contemporary Authors New Revision Series*
CAP = *Contemporary Authors Permanent Series*
CDALB = *Concise Dictionary of American Literary
Biography*
CDBLB = *Concise Dictionary of British Literary
Biography*

DLB = *Dictionary of Literary Biography*
DLBD = *Dictionary of Literary Biography
Documentary Series*
DLBY = *Dictionary of Literary Biography Yearbook*
HW = *Hispanic Writers*
JRDA = *Junior DISCovering Authors*
MAICYA = *Major Authors and Illustrators for
Children and Young Adults*
MTCW = *Major 20th-Century Writers*
NNAL = *Native North American Literature*
SAAS = *Something about the Author Autobiography
Series*
SATA = *Something about the Author*
YABC = *Yesterday's Authors of Books for Children*

Androvar
See Prado (Calvo), Pedro

Angelique, Pierre
See Bataille, Georges

Angell, Roger 1920- .... **CLC 26**
See also CA 57-60; CANR 13, 44, 70; DLB 171, 185

Angelou, Maya 1928-**CLC 12, 35, 64, 77; BLC 1; DA; DAB; DAC; DAM MST, MULT, POET, POP; WLCS**
See also AAYA 7, 20; BW 2, 3; CA 65-68; CANR 19, 42, 65; CDALBS; CLR 53; DA3; DLB 38; MTCW 1, 2; SATA 49

Anna Comnena 1083-1153 .... **CMLC 25**

Annensky, Innokenty (Fyodorovich) 1856-1909 **TCLC 14**
See also CA 110; 155

Annunzio, Gabriele d'
See D'Annunzio, Gabriele

Anodos
See Coleridge, Mary E(lizabeth)

Anon, Charles Robert
See Pessoa, Fernando (Antonio Nogueira)

Anouilh, Jean (Marie Lucien Pierre) 1910-1987 **CLC 1, 3, 8, 13, 40, 50; DAM DRAM; DC 8**
See also CA 17-20R; 123; CANR 32; MTCW 1, 2

Anthony, Florence
See Ai

Anthony, John
See Ciardi, John (Anthony)

Anthony, Peter
See Shaffer, Anthony (Joshua); Shaffer, Peter (Levin)

Anthony, Piers 1934- .... **CLC 35; DAM POP**
See also AAYA 11; CA 21-24R; CANR 28, 56, 73; DLB 8; MTCW 1, 2; SAAS 22; SATA 84

Anthony, Susan B(rownell) 1916-1991 **TCLC 84**
See also CA 89-92; 134

Antoine, Marc
See Proust, (Valentin-Louis-George-Eugene-) Marcel

Antoninus, Brother
See Everson, William (Oliver)

Antonioni, Michelangelo 1912- .... **CLC 20**
See also CA 73-76; CANR 45, 77

Antschel, Paul 1920-1970
See Celan, Paul
See also CA 85-88; CANR 33, 61; MTCW 1

Anwar, Chairil 1922-1949 .... **TCLC 22**
See also CA 121

Anzaldua, Gloria 1942-
See also CA 175; DLB 122; HLCS 1

Apess, William 1798-1839(?) ... **NCLC 73; DAM MULT**
See also DLB 175; NNAL

Apollinaire, Guillaume 1880-1918**TCLC 3, 8, 51; DAM POET; PC 7**
See also Kostrowitzki, Wilhelm Apollinaris de
See also CA 152; MTCW 1

Appelfeld, Aharon 1932- .... **CLC 23, 47**
See also CA 112; 133; CANR 86

Apple, Max (Isaac) 1941- .... **CLC 9, 33**
See also CA 81-84; CANR 19, 54; DLB 130

Appleman, Philip (Dean) 1926- .... **CLC 51**
See also CA 13-16R; CAAS 18; CANR 6, 29, 56

Appleton, Lawrence
See Lovecraft, H(oward) P(hillips)

Apteryx
See Eliot, T(homas) S(tearns)

Apuleius, (Lucius Madaurensis) 125(?)-175(?) **CMLC 1**
See also DLB 211

Aquin, Hubert 1929-1977 .... **CLC 15**

See also CA 105; DLB 53

Aquinas, Thomas 1224(?)-1274 .... **CMLC 33**
See also DLB 115

Aragon, Louis 1897-1982**CLC 3, 22; DAM NOV, POET**
See also CA 69-72; 108; CANR 28, 71; DLB 72; MTCW 1, 2

Arany, Janos 1817-1882 .... **NCLC 34**

Aranyos, Kakay
See Mikszath, Kalman

Arbuthnot, John 1667-1735 .... **LC 1**
See also DLB 101

Archer, Herbert Winslow
See Mencken, H(enry) L(ouis)

Archer, Jeffrey (Howard) 1940- .. **CLC 28; DAM POP**
See also AAYA 16; BEST 89:3; CA 77-80; CANR 22, 52; DA3; INT CANR-22

Archer, Jules 1915- .... **CLC 12**
See also CA 9-12R; CANR 6, 69; SAAS 5; SATA 4, 85

Archer, Lee
See Ellison, Harlan (Jay)

Arden, John 1930- **CLC 6, 13, 15; DAM DRAM**
See also CA 13-16R; CAAS 4; CANR 31, 65, 67; DLB 13; MTCW 1

Arenas, Reinaldo 1943-1990**CLC 41; DAM MULT; HLC 1**
See also CA 124; 128; 133; CANR 73; DLB 145; HW 1; MTCW 1

Arendt, Hannah 1906-1975 .... **CLC 66, 98**
See also CA 17-20R; 61-64; CANR 26, 60; MTCW 1, 2

Aretino, Pietro 1492-1556 .... **LC 12**

Arghezi, Tudor 1880-1967 .... **CLC 80**
See also Theodorescu, Ion N.
See also CA 167

Arguedas, Jose Maria 1911-1969 .. **CLC 10, 18; HLCS 1**
See also CA 89-92; CANR 73; DLB 113; HW 1

Argueta, Manlio 1936- .... **CLC 31**
See also CA 131; CANR 73; DLB 145; HW 1

Arias, Ron(ald Francis) 1941-
See also CA 131; CANR 81; DAM MULT; DLB 82; HLC 1; HW 1, 2; MTCW 2

Ariosto, Ludovico 1474-1533 .... **LC 6**

Aristides
See Epstein, Joseph

Aristophanes 450B.C.-385B.C. .... **CMLC 4; DA; DAB; DAC; DAM DRAM, MST; DC 2; WLCS**
See also DA3; DLB 176

Aristotle 384B.C.-322B.C. **CMLC 31; DA; DAB; DAC; DAM MST; WLCS**
See also DA3; DLB 176

Arlt, Roberto (Godofredo Christophersen) 1900-1942 .... **TCLC 29; DAM MULT; HLC 1**
See also CA 123; 131; CANR 67; HW 1, 2

Armah, Ayi Kwei 1939-**CLC 5, 33; BLC 1; DAM MULT, POET**
See also BW 1; CA 61-64; CANR 21, 64; DLB 117; MTCW 1

Armatrading, Joan 1950- .... **CLC 17**
See also CA 114

Arnette, Robert
See Silverberg, Robert

Arnim, Achim von (Ludwig Joachim von Arnim) 1781-1831 .... **NCLC 5; SSC 29**
See also DLB 90

Arnim, Bettina von 1785-1859 .... **NCLC 38**
See also DLB 90

Arnold, Matthew 1822-1888 .... **NCLC 6, 29; DA; DAB; DAC; DAM MST, POET; PC 5; WLC**
See also CDBLB 1832-1890; DLB 32, 57

Arnold, Thomas 1795-1842 .... **NCLC 18**
See also DLB 55

Arnow, Harriette (Louisa) Simpson 1908-1986 **CLC 2, 7, 18**
See also CA 9-12R; 118; CANR 14; DLB 6; MTCW 1, 2; SATA 42; SATA-Obit 47

Arouet, François-Marie
See Voltaire

Arp, Hans
See Arp, Jean

Arp, Jean 1887-1966 .... **CLC 5**
See also CA 81-84; 25-28R; CANR 42, 77

Arrabal
See Arrabal, Fernando

Arrabal, Fernando 1932- .... **CLC 2, 9, 18, 58**
See also CA 9-12R; CANR 15

Arreola, Juan Jose 1918-
See also CA 113; 131; CANR 81; DAM MULT; DLB 113; HLC 1; HW 1, 2

Arrick, Fran .... **CLC 30**
See also Gaberman, Judie Angell

Artaud, Antonin (Marie Joseph) 1896-1948**TCLC 3, 36; DAM DRAM**
See also CA 104; 149; DA3; MTCW 1

Arthur, Ruth M(abel) 1905-1979 .... **CLC 12**
See also CA 9-12R; 85-88; CANR 4; SATA 7, 26

Artsybashev, Mikhail (Petrovich) 1878-1927 **TCLC 31**
See also CA 170

Arundel, Honor (Morfydd) 1919-1973 ... **CLC 17**
See also CA 21-22; 41-44R; CAP 2; CLR 35; SATA 4; SATA-Obit 24

Arzner, Dorothy 1897-1979 .... **CLC 98**

Asch, Sholem 1880-1957 .... **TCLC 3**
See also CA 105

Ash, Shalom
See Asch, Sholem

Ashbery, John (Lawrence) 1927-**CLC 2, 3, 4, 6, 9, 13, 15, 25, 41, 77, 125; DAM POET; PC 26**
See also CA 5-8R; CANR 9, 37, 66; DA3; DLB 5, 165; DLBY 81; INT CANR-9; MTCW 1, 2

Ashdown, Clifford
See Freeman, R(ichard) Austin

Ashe, Gordon
See Creasey, John

Ashton-Warner, Sylvia (Constance) 1908-1984 **CLC 19**
See also CA 69-72; 112; CANR 29; MTCW 1, 2

Asimov, Isaac 1920-1992 **CLC 1, 3, 9, 19, 26, 76, 92; DAM POP**
See also AAYA 13; BEST 90:2; CA 1-4R; 137; CANR 2, 19, 36, 60; CLR 12; DA3; DLB 8; DLBY 92; INT CANR-19; JRDA; MAICYA; MTCW 1, 2; SATA 1, 26, 74

Assis, Joaquim Maria Machado de
See Machado de Assis, Joaquim Maria

Astley, Thea (Beatrice May) 1925- .... **CLC 41**
See also CA 65-68; CANR 11, 43, 78

Aston, James
See White, T(erence) H(anbury)

Asturias, Miguel Angel 1899-1974**CLC 3, 8, 13; DAM MULT, NOV; HLC 1**
See also CA 25-28; 49-52; CANR 32; CAP 2; DA3; DLB 113; HW 1; MTCW 1, 2

Atares, Carlos Saura
See Saura (Atares), Carlos

Atheling, William
See Pound, Ezra (Weston Loomis)

Atheling, William, Jr.
See Blish, James (Benjamin)

Atherton, Gertrude (Franklin Horn) 1857-1948 **TCLC 2**
See also CA 104; 155; DLB 9, 78, 186

Atherton, Lucius
  See Masters, Edgar Lee
Atkins, Jack
  See Harris, Mark
Atkinson, Kate .... **CLC 99**
  See also CA 166
Attaway, William (Alexander) 1911-1986**CLC 92; BLC 1; DAM MULT**
  See also BW 2, 3; CA 143; CANR 82; DLB 76
Atticus
  See Fleming, Ian (Lancaster); Wilson, (Thomas) Woodrow
Atwood, Margaret (Eleanor) 1939-**CLC 2, 3, 4, 8, 13, 15, 25, 44, 84; DA; DAB; DAC; DAM MST, NOV, POET; PC 8; SSC 2; WLC**
  See also AAYA 12; BEST 89:2; CA 49-52; CANR 3, 24, 33, 59; DA3; DLB 53; INT CANR-24; MTCW 1, 2; SATA 50
Aubigny, Pierre d'
  See Mencken, H(enry) L(ouis)
Aubin, Penelope 1685-1731(?) .... **LC 9**
  See also DLB 39
Auchincloss, Louis (Stanton) 1917- **CLC 4, 6, 9, 18, 45; DAM NOV; SSC 22**
  See also CA 1-4R; CANR 6, 29, 55; DLB 2; DLBY 80; INT CANR-29; MTCW 1
Auden, W(ystan) H(ugh) 1907-1973**CLC 1, 2, 3, 4, 6, 9, 11, 14, 43; DA; DAB; DAC; DAM DRAM, MST, POET; PC 1; WLC**
  See also AAYA 18; CA 9-12R; 45-48; CANR 5, 61; CDBLB 1914-1945; DA3; DLB 10, 20; MTCW 1, 2
Audiberti, Jacques 1900-1965 ..... **CLC 38; DAM DRAM**
  See also CA 25-28R
Audubon, John James 1785-1851 .... **NCLC 47**
Auel, Jean M(arie) 1936-**CLC 31, 107; DAM POP**
  See also AAYA 7; BEST 90:4; CA 103; CANR 21, 64; DA3; INT CANR-21; SATA 91
Auerbach, Erich 1892-1957 .... **TCLC 43**
  See also CA 118; 155
Augier, Emile 1820-1889 .... **NCLC 31**
  See also DLB 192
August, John
  See De Voto, Bernard (Augustine)
Augustine 354-430 . **CMLC 6; DA; DAB; DAC; DAM MST; WLCS**
  See also DA3; DLB 115
Aurelius
  See Bourne, Randolph S(illiman)
Aurobindo, Sri
  See Ghose, Aurabinda
Austen, Jane 1775-1817**NCLC 1, 13, 19, 33, 51, 81; DA; DAB; DAC; DAM MST, NOV; WLC**
  See also AAYA 19; CDBLB 1789-1832; DA3; DLB 116
Auster, Paul 1947- .... **CLC 47**
  See also CA 69-72; CANR 23, 52, 75; DA3; MTCW 1
Austin, Frank
  See Faust, Frederick (Schiller)
Austin, Mary (Hunter) 1868-1934 .... **TCLC 25**
  See also CA 109; 178; DLB 9, 78, 206
Averroes 1126-1198 .... **CMLC 7**
  See also DLB 115
Avicenna 980-1037 .... **CMLC 16**
  See also DLB 115
Avison, Margaret 1918-**CLC 2, 4, 97; DAC; DAM POET**
  See also CA 17-20R; DLB 53; MTCW 1
Axton, David
  See Koontz, Dean R(ay)
Ayckbourn, Alan 1939-**CLC 5, 8, 18, 33, 74; DAB;**

DAM DRAM
  See also CA 21-24R; CANR 31, 59; DLB 13; MTCW 1, 2
Aydy, Catherine
  See Tennant, Emma (Christina)
Ayme, Marcel (Andre) 1902-1967 .... **CLC 11**
  See also CA 89-92; CANR 67; CLR 25; DLB 72; SATA 91
Ayrton, Michael 1921-1975 .... **CLC 7**
  See also CA 5-8R; 61-64; CANR 9, 21
Azorin .... **CLC 11**
  See also Martinez Ruiz, Jose
Azuela, Mariano 1873-1952**TCLC 3; DAM MULT; HLC 1**
  See also CA 104; 131; CANR 81; HW 1, 2; MTCW 1, 2
Baastad, Babbis Friis
  See Friis-Baastad, Babbis Ellinor
Bab
  See Gilbert, W(illiam) S(chwenck)
Babbis, Eleanor
  See Friis-Baastad, Babbis Ellinor
Babel, Isaac
  See Babel, Isaak (Emmanuilovich)
Babel, Isaak (Emmanuilovich) 1894-1941(?) **TCLC 2, 13; SSC 16**
  See also CA 104; 155; MTCW 1
Babits, Mihaly 1883-1941 .... **TCLC 14**
  See also CA 114
Babur 1483-1530 .... **LC 18**
Baca, Jimmy Santiago 1952-
  See also CA 131; CANR 81; DAM MULT; DLB 122; HLC 1; HW 1, 2
Bacchelli, Riccardo 1891-1985 .... **CLC 19**
  See also CA 29-32R; 117
Bach, Richard (David) 1936-**CLC 14; DAM NOV, POP**
  See also AITN 1; BEST 89:2; CA 9-12R; CANR 18; MTCW 1; SATA 13
Bachman, Richard
  See King, Stephen (Edwin)
Bachmann, Ingeborg 1926-1973 .... **CLC 69**
  See also CA 93-96; 45-48; CANR 69; DLB 85
Bacon, Francis 1561-1626 .... **LC 18, 32**
  See also CDBLB Before 1660; DLB 151
Bacon, Roger 1214(?)-1292 .... **CMLC 14**
  See also DLB 115
Bacovia, George .... **TCLC 24**
  See also Vasiliu, Gheorghe
  See also DLB 220
Badanes, Jerome 1937- .... **CLC 59**
Bagehot, Walter 1826-1877 .... **NCLC 10**
  See also DLB 55
Bagnold, Enid 1889-1981 **CLC 25; DAM DRAM**
  See also CA 5-8R; 103; CANR 5, 40; DLB 13, 160, 191; MAICYA; SATA 1, 25
Bagritsky, Eduard 1895-1934 .... **TCLC 60**
Bagrjana, Elisaveta
  See Belcheva, Elisaveta
Bagryana, Elisaveta 1893-1991 .... **CLC 10**
  See also Belcheva, Elisaveta
  See also CA 178; DLB 147
Bailey, Paul 1937- .... **CLC 45**
  See also CA 21-24R; CANR 16, 62; DLB 14
Baillie, Joanna 1762-1851 .... **NCLC 71**
  See also DLB 93
Bainbridge, Beryl (Margaret) 1933-**CLC 4, 5, 8, 10, 14, 18, 22, 62; DAM NOV**
  See also CA 21-24R; CANR 24, 55, 75; DLB 14; MTCW 1, 2
Baker, Elliott 1922- .... **CLC 8**
  See also CA 45-48; CANR 2, 63
Baker, Jean H. .... **TCLC 3, 10**

  See also Russell, George William
Baker, Nicholson 1957- ..... **CLC 61; DAM POP**
  See also CA 135; CANR 63; DA3
Baker, Ray Stannard 1870-1946 .... **TCLC 47**
  See also CA 118
Baker, Russell (Wayne) 1925- .... **CLC 31**
  See also BEST 89:4; CA 57-60; CANR 11, 41, 59; MTCW 1, 2
Bakhtin, M.
  See Bakhtin, Mikhail Mikhailovich
Bakhtin, M. M.
  See Bakhtin, Mikhail Mikhailovich
Bakhtin, Mikhail
  See Bakhtin, Mikhail Mikhailovich
Bakhtin, Mikhail Mikhailovich 1895-1975 **C L C 83**
  See also CA 128; 113
Bakshi, Ralph 1938(?)- .... **CLC 26**
  See also CA 112; 138
Bakunin, Mikhail (Alexandrovich) 1814-1876 **NCLC 25, 58**
Baldwin, James (Arthur) 1924-1987 **CLC 1, 2, 3, 4, 5, 8, 13, 15, 17, 42, 50, 67, 90, 127; BLC 1; DA; DAB; DAC; DAM MST, MULT, NOV, POP; DC 1; SSC 10, 33; WLC**
  See also AAYA 4; BW 1; CA 1-4R; 124; CABS 1; CANR 3, 24; CDALB 1941-1968; DA3; DLB 2, 7, 33; DLBY 87; MTCW 1, 2; SATA 9; SATA-Obit 54
Ballard, J(ames) G(raham) 1930- **CLC 3, 6, 14, 36; DAM NOV, POP; SSC 1**
  See also AAYA 3; CA 5-8R; CANR 15, 39, 65; DA3; DLB 14, 207; MTCW 1, 2; SATA 93
Balmont, Konstantin (Dmitriyevich) 1867-1943 **TCLC 11**
  See also CA 109; 155
Baltausis, Vincas
  See Mikszath, Kalman
Balzac, Honore de 1799-1850**NCLC 5, 35, 53; DA; DAB; DAC; DAMMST, NOV; SSC 5; WLC**
  See also DA3; DLB 119
Bambara, Toni Cade 1939-1995**CLC 19, 88; BLC 1; DA; DAC; DAM MST, MULT; SSC 35; WLCS**
  See also AAYA 5; BW 2, 3; CA 29-32R; 150; CANR 24, 49, 81; CDALBS; DA3; DLB 38; MTCW 1, 2
Bamdad, A.
  See Shamlu, Ahmad
Banat, D. R.
  See Bradbury, Ray (Douglas)
Bancroft, Laura
  See Baum, L(yman) Frank
Banim, John 1798-1842 .... **NCLC 13**
  See also DLB 116, 158, 159
Banim, Michael 1796-1874 .... **NCLC 13**
  See also DLB 158, 159
Banjo, The
  See Paterson, A(ndrew) B(arton)
Banks, Iain
  See Banks, Iain M(enzies)
Banks, Iain M(enzies) 1954- .... **CLC 34**
  See also CA 123; 128; CANR 61; DLB 194; INT 128
Banks, Lynne Reid .... **CLC 23**
  See also Reid Banks, Lynne
  See also AAYA 6
Banks, Russell 1940- .... **CLC 37, 72**
  See also CA 65-68; CAAS 15; CANR 19, 52, 73; DLB 130
Banville, John 1945- .... **CLC 46, 118**
  See also CA 117; 128; DLB 14; INT 128
Banville, Theodore (Faullain) de 1832-1891**NCLC**

MAICYA; SAAS 9; SATA 6

Becque, Henri 1837-1899 .... **NCLC 3**
　See also DLB 192

Becquer, Gustavo Adolfo 1836-1870
　See also DAM MULT; HLCS 1

Beddoes, Thomas Lovell 1803-1849 ...... **NCLC 3**
　See also DLB 96

Bede c. 673-735 .... **CMLC 20**
　See also DLB 146

Bedford, Donald F.
　See Fearing, Kenneth (Flexner)

Beecher, Catharine Esther 1800-1878 **NCLC 30**
　See also DLB 1

Beecher, John 1904-1980 .... **CLC 6**
　See also AITN 1; CA 5-8R; 105; CANR 8

Beer, Johann 1655-1700 .... **LC 5**
　See also DLB 168

Beer, Patricia 1924- .... **CLC 58**
　See also CA 61-64; CANR 13, 46; DLB 40

Beerbohm, Max
　See Beerbohm, (Henry) Max(imilian)

Beerbohm, (Henry) Max(imilian) 1872-1956
　TCLC 1, 24
　See also CA 104; 154; CANR 79; DLB 34, 100

Beer-Hofmann, Richard 1866-1945 .... **TCLC 60**
　See also CA 160; DLB 81

Begiebing, Robert J(ohn) 1946- ....:...... **CLC 70**
　See also CA 122; CANR 40

Behan, Brendan 1923-1964 **CLC 1, 8, 11, 15, 79;**
　DAM DRAM
　See also CA 73-76; CANR 33; CDBLB 1945-1960;
　DLB 13; MTCW 1, 2

Behn, Aphra 1640(?)-1689 **LC 1, 30, 42; DA; DAB;**
　DAC; DAM DRAM, MST, NOV, POET; DC
　4; PC 13; WLC
　See also DA3; DLB 39, 80, 131

Behrman, S(amuel) N(athaniel) 1893-1973 **C L C**
　40
　See also CA 13-16; 45-48; CAP 1; DLB 7, 44

Belasco, David 1853-1931 .... **TCLC 3**
　See also CA 104; 168; DLB 7

Belcheva, Elisaveta 1893- .... **CLC 10**
　See also Bagryana, Elisaveta

Beldone, Phil "Cheech"
　See Ellison, Harlan (Jay)

Beleno
　See Azuela, Mariano

Belinski, Vissarion Grigoryevich 1811-1848
　NCLC 5
　See also DLB 198

Belitt, Ben 1911- .... **CLC 22**
　See also CA 13-16R; CAAS 4; CANR 7, 77; DLB
　5

Bell, Gertrude (Margaret Lowthian) 1868-1926
　TCLC 67
　See also CA 167; DLB 174

Bell, J. Freeman
　See Zangwill, Israel

Bell, James Madison 1826-1902 **TCLC 43; BLC 1;**
　DAM MULT
　See also BW 1; CA 122; 124; DLB 50

Bell, Madison Smartt 1957- .... **CLC 41, 102**
　See also CA 111; CANR 28, 54, 73; MTCW 1

Bell, Marvin (Hartley) 1937- .. **CLC 8, 31; DAM**
　POET
　See also CA 21-24R; CAAS 14; CANR 59; DLB
　5; MTCW 1

Bell, W. L. D.
　See Mencken, H(enry) L(ouis)

Bellamy, Atwood C.
　See Mencken, H(enry) L(ouis)

Bellamy, Edward 1850-1898 .... **NCLC 4**
　See also DLB 12

Belli, Gioconda 1949-
　See also CA 152; HLCS 1

Bellin, Edward J.
　See Kuttner, Henry

Belloc, (Joseph) Hilaire (Pierre Sebastien Rene
　Swanton) 1870-1953 ..... **TCLC 7, 18; DAM**
　POET; PC 24
　See also CA 106; 152; DLB 19, 100, 141, 174;
　MTCW 1; YABC 1

Belloc, Joseph Peter Rene Hilaire
　See Belloc, (Joseph) Hilaire (Pierre Sebastien
　Rene Swanton)

Belloc, Joseph Pierre Hilaire
　See Belloc, (Joseph) Hilaire (Pierre Sebastien
　Rene Swanton)

Belloc, M. A.
　See Lowndes, Marie Adelaide (Belloc)

Bellow, Saul 1915- **CLC 1, 2, 3, 6, 8, 10, 13, 15, 25,**
　33, 34, 63, 79; DA; DAB; DAC; DAM MST,
　NOV, POP; SSC 14; WLC
　See also AITN 2; BEST 89:3; CA 5-8R; CABS 1;
　CANR 29, 53; CDALB 1941-1968; DA3; DLB
　2, 28; DLBD 3; DLBY 82; MTCW 1, 2

Belser, Reimond Karel Maria de 1929-
　See Ruyslinck, Ward
　See also CA 152

Bely, Andrey .... **TCLC 7; PC 11**
　See also Bugayev, Boris Nikolayevich
　See also MTCW 1

Belyi, Andrei
　See Bugayev, Boris Nikolayevich

Benary, Margot
　See Benary-Isbert, Margot

Benary-Isbert, Margot 1889-1979 .... **CLC 12**
　See also CA 5-8R; 89-92; CANR 4, 72; CLR 12;
　MAICYA; SATA 2; SATA-Obit 21

Benavente (y Martinez), Jacinto 1866-1954 **TCLC**
　3; DAM DRAM, MULT; HLCS 1
　See also CA 106; 131; CANR 81; HW 1, 2;
　MTCW 1, 2

Benchley, Peter (Bradford) 1940- **CLC 4, 8; DAM**
　NOV, POP
　See also AAYA 14; AITN 2; CA 17-20R; CANR
　12, 35, 66; MTCW 1, 2; SATA 3, 89

Benchley, Robert (Charles) 1889-1945 **TCLC 1, 55**
　See also CA 105; 153; DLB 11

Benda, Julien 1867-1956 .... **TCLC 60**
　See also CA 120; 154

Benedict, Ruth (Fulton) 1887-1948 ..... **TCLC 60**
　See also CA 158

Benedict, Saint c. 480-c. 547 .... **CMLC 29**

Benedikt, Michael 1935- .... **CLC 4, 14**
　See also CA 13-16R; CANR 7; DLB 5

Benet, Juan 1927- .... **CLC 28**
　See also CA 143

Benet, Stephen Vincent 1898-1943 **TCLC 7; DAM**
　POET; SSC 10
　See also CA 104; 152; DA3; DLB 4, 48, 102; DLBY
　97; MTCW 1; YABC 1

Benet, William Rose 1886-1950 **TCLC 28; DAM**
　POET
　See also CA 118; 152; DLB 45

Benford, Gregory (Albert) 1941- .... **CLC 52**
　See also CA 69-72; 175; CAAE 175; CAAS 27;
　CANR 12, 24, 49; DLBY 82

Bengtsson, Frans (Gunnar) 1894-1954 **TCLC 48**
　See also CA 170

Benjamin, David
　See Slavitt, David R(ytman)

Benjamin, Lois
　See Gould, Lois

Benjamin, Walter 1892-1940 .... **TCLC 39**
　See also CA 164

Benn, Gottfried 1886-1956 .... **TCLC 3**
　See also CA 106; 153; DLB 56

Bennett, Alan 1934- **CLC 45, 77; DAB; DAM MST**
　See also CA 103; CANR 35, 55; MTCW 1, 2

Bennett, (Enoch) Arnold 1867-1931 **TCLC 5, 20**
　See also CA 106; 155; CDBLB 1890-1914; DLB
　10, 34, 98, 135; MTCW 2

Bennett, Elizabeth
　See Mitchell, Margaret (Munnerlyn)

Bennett, George Harold 1930-
　See Bennett, Hal
　See also BW 1; CA 97-100

Bennett, Hal .... **CLC 5**
　See also Bennett, George Harold
　See also DLB 33

Bennett, Jay 1912- .... **CLC 35**
　See also AAYA 10; CA 69-72; CANR 11, 42, 79;
　JRDA; SAAS 4; SATA 41, 87; SATA-Brief 27

Bennett, Louise (Simone) 1919- **CLC 28; BLC 1;**
　DAM MULT
　See also BW 2, 3; CA 151; DLB 117

Benson, E(dward) F(rederic) 1867-1940 **TCLC 27**
　See also CA 114; 157; DLB 135, 153

Benson, Jackson J. 1930- .... **CLC 34**
　See also CA 25-28R; DLB 111

Benson, Sally 1900-1972 .... **CLC 17**
　See also CA 19-20; 37-40R; CAP 1; SATA 1, 35;
　SATA-Obit 27

Benson, Stella 1892-1933 .... **TCLC 17**
　See also CA 117; 155; DLB 36, 162

Bentham, Jeremy 1748-1832 .... **NCLC 38**
　See also DLB 107, 158

Bentley, E(dmund) C(lerihew) 1875-1956 **TCLC 12**
　See also CA 108; DLB 70

Bentley, Eric (Russell) 1916- .... **CLC 24**
　See also CA 5-8R; CANR 6, 67; INT CANR-6

Beranger, Pierre Jean de 1780-1857 .. **NCLC 34**

Berdyaev, Nicolas
　See Berdyaev, Nikolai (Aleksandrovich)

Berdyaev, Nikolai (Aleksandrovich) 1874-1948
　TCLC 67
　See also CA 120; 157

Berdyayev, Nikolai (Aleksandrovich)
　See Berdyaev, Nikolai (Aleksandrovich)

Berendt, John (Lawrence) 1939- .... **CLC 86**
　See also CA 146; CANR 75; DA3; MTCW 1

Beresford, J(ohn) D(avys) 1873-1947 .. **TCLC 81**
　See also CA 112; 155; DLB 162, 178, 197

Bergelson, David 1884-1952 .... **TCLC 81**

Berger, Colonel
　See Malraux, (Georges-)Andre

Berger, John (Peter) 1926- .... **CLC 2, 19**
　See also CA 81-84; CANR 51, 78; DLB 14, 207

Berger, Melvin H. 1927- .... **CLC 12**
　See also CA 5-8R; CANR 4; CLR 32; SAAS 2;
　SATA 5, 88

Berger, Thomas (Louis) 1924- **CLC 3, 5, 8, 11, 18,**
　38; DAM NOV
　See also CA 1-4R; CANR 5, 28, 51; DLB 2; DLBY
　80; INT CANR-28; MTCW 1, 2

Bergman, (Ernst) Ingmar 1918- ..... **CLC 16, 72**
　See also CA 81-84; CANR 33, 70; MTCW 2

Bergson, Henri(-Louis) 1859-1941 ..... **TCLC 32**
　See also CA 164

Bergstein, Eleanor 1938- .... **CLC 4**
　See also CA 53-56; CANR 5

Berkoff, Steven 1937- .... **CLC 56**
　See also CA 104; CANR 72

Bermant, Chaim (Icyk) 1929- .... **CLC 40**
　See also CA 57-60; CANR 6, 31, 57

Bern, Victoria
　See Fisher, M(ary) F(rances) K(ennedy)

Bernanos, (Paul Louis) Georges 1888-1948

TCLC 3
See also CA 104; 130; DLB 72
Bernard, April 1956- .... **CLC 59**
See also CA 131
Berne, Victoria
See Fisher, M(ary) F(rances) K(ennedy)
Bernhard, Thomas 1931-1989 ..... **CLC 3, 32, 61**
See also CA 85-88; 127; CANR 32, 57; DLB 85,
124; MTCW 1
Bernhardt, Sarah (Henriette Rosine) 1844-1923
TCLC 75
See also CA 157
Berriault, Gina 1926- ..... **CLC 54, 109; SSC 30**
See also CA 116; 129; CANR 66; DLB 130
Berrigan, Daniel 1921- .... **CLC 4**
See also CA 33-36R; CAAS 1; CANR 11, 43, 78;
DLB 5
Berrigan, Edmund Joseph Michael, Jr. 1934-1983
See Berrigan, Ted
See also CA 61-64; 110; CANR 14
Berrigan, Ted .... **CLC 37**
See also Berrigan, Edmund Joseph Michael, Jr.
See also DLB 5, 169
Berry, Charles Edward Anderson 1931-
See Berry, Chuck
See also CA 115
Berry, Chuck .... **CLC 17**
See also Berry, Charles Edward Anderson
Berry, Jonas
See Ashbery, John (Lawrence)
Berry, Wendell (Erdman) 1934- **CLC 4, 6, 8, 27,
46; DAM POET; PC 28**
See also AITN 1; CA 73-76; CANR 50, 73; DLB
5, 6; MTCW 1
Berryman, John 1914-1972**CLC 1, 2, 3, 4, 6, 8, 10,
13, 25, 62; DAM POET**
See also CA 13-16; 33-36R; CABS 2; CANR 35;
CAP 1; CDALB 1941-1968; DLB 48; MTCW
1, 2
Bertolucci, Bernardo 1940- .... **CLC 16**
See also CA 106
Berton, Pierre (Francis Demarigny) 1920- **C L C
104**
See also CA 1-4R; CANR 2, 56; DLB 68; SATA
99
Bertrand, Aloysius 1807-1841 .... **NCLC 31**
Bertran de Born c. 1140-1215 .... **CMLC 5**
Besant, Annie (Wood) 1847-1933 .... **TCLC 9**
See also CA 105
Bessie, Alvah 1904-1985 .... **CLC 23**
See also CA 5-8R; 116; CANR 2, 80; DLB 26
Bethlen, T. D.
See Silverberg, Robert
Beti, Mongo .... **CLC 27; BLC 1; DAM MULT**
See also Biyidi, Alexandre
See also CANR 79
Betjeman, John 1906-1984 **CLC 2, 6, 10, 34, 43;
DAB; DAM MST, POET**
See also CA 9-12R; 112; CANR 33, 56; CDBLB
1945-1960; DA3; DLB 20; DLBY84; MTCW 1,
2
Bettelheim, Bruno 1903-1990 .... **CLC 79**
See also CA 81-84; 131; CANR 23, 61; DA3;
MTCW 1, 2
Betti, Ugo 1892-1953 .... **TCLC 5**
See also CA 104; 155
Betts, Doris (Waugh) 1932- .... **CLC 3, 6, 28**
See also CA 13-16R; CANR 9, 66, 77; DLBY 82;
INT CANR-9
Bevan, Alistair
See Roberts, Keith (John Kingston)
Bey, Pilaff
See Douglas, (George) Norman

Bialik, Chaim Nachman 1873-1934 .... **TCLC 25**
See also CA 170
Bickerstaff, Isaac
See Swift, Jonathan
Bidart, Frank 1939- .... **CLC 33**
See also CA 140
Bienek, Horst 1930- .... **CLC 7, 11**
See also CA 73-76; DLB 75
Bierce, Ambrose (Gwinett) 1842-1914(?)**TCLC 1,
7, 44; DA; DAC; DAM MST; SSC 9; WLC**
See also CA 104; 139; CANR 78; CDALB 1865-
1917; DA3; DLB 11, 12, 23, 71, 74, 186
Biggers, Earl Derr 1884-1933 .... **TCLC 65**
See also CA 108; 153
Billings, Josh
See Shaw, Henry Wheeler
Billington, (Lady) Rachel (Mary) 1942- **CLC 43**
See also AITN 2; CA 33-36R; CANR 44
Binyon, T(imothy) J(ohn) 1936- .... **CLC 34**
See also CA 111; CANR 28
Bioy Casares, Adolfo 1914-1999**CLC 4, 8, 13, 88;
DAM MULT; HLC 1; SSC 17**
See also CA 29-32R; 177; CANR 19, 43, 66; DLB
113; HW 1, 2; MTCW 1, 2
Bird, Cordwainer
See Ellison, Harlan (Jay)
Bird, Robert Montgomery 1806-1854 ... **NCLC 1**
See also DLB 202
Birkerts, Sven 1951- .... **CLC 116**
See also CA 128; 133; 176; CAAE 176; CAAS
29; INT 133
Birney, (Alfred) Earle 1904-1995**CLC 1, 4, 6, 11;
DAC; DAM MST, POET**
See also CA 1-4R; CANR 5, 20; DLB 88; MTCW
1
Biruni, al 973-1048(?) .... **CMLC 28**
Bishop, Elizabeth 1911-1979 **CLC 1, 4, 9, 13, 15,
32; DA; DAC; DAM MST, POET; PC 3**
See also CA 5-8R; 89-92; CABS 2; CANR 26, 61;
CDALB 1968-1988; DA3; DLB 5, 169; MTCW
1, 2; SATA-Obit 24
Bishop, John 1935- .... **CLC 10**
See also CA 105
Bissett, Bill 1939- .... **CLC 18; PC 14**
See also CA 69-72; CAAS 19; CANR 15; DLB
53; MTCW 1
Bissoondath, Neil (Devindra) 1955- .. **CLC 120;
DAC**
See also CA 136
Bitov, Andrei (Georgievich) 1937- .... **CLC 57**
See also CA 142
Biyidi, Alexandre 1932-
See Beti, Mongo
See also BW 1, 3; CA 114; 124; CANR 81; DA3;
MTCW 1, 2
Bjarme, Brynjolf
See Ibsen, Henrik (Johan)
Bjoernson, Bjoernstjerne (Martinius) 1832-1910
TCLC 7, 37
See also CA 104
Black, Robert
See Holdstock, Robert P.
Blackburn, Paul 1926-1971 .... **CLC 9, 43**
See also CA 81-84; 33-36R; CANR 34; DLB 16;
DLBY 81
Black Elk 1863-1950 ..... **TCLC 33; DAM MULT**
See also CA 144; MTCW 1; NNAL
Black Hobart
See Sanders, (James) Ed(ward)
Blacklin, Malcolm
See Chambers, Aidan
Blackmore, R(ichard) D(oddridge) 1825-1900
TCLC 27

See also CA 120; DLB 18
Blackmur, R(ichard) P(almer) 1904-1965**CLC 2,
24**
See also CA 11-12; 25-28R; CANR 71; CAP 1;
DLB 63
Black Tarantula
See Acker, Kathy
Blackwood, Algernon (Henry) 1869-1951**TCLC 5**
See also CA 105; 150; DLB 153, 156, 178
Blackwood, Caroline 1931-1996 .. **CLC 6, 9, 100**
See also CA 85-88; 151; CANR 32, 61, 65; DLB
14, 207; MTCW 1
Blade, Alexander
See Hamilton, Edmond; Silverberg, Robert
Blaga, Lucian 1895-1961 .... **CLC 75**
See also CA 157
Blair, Eric (Arthur) 1903-1950
See Orwell, George
See also CA 104; 132; DA; DAB; DAC; DAM
MST, NOV; DA3; MTCW 1, 2; SATA 29
Blair, Hugh 1718-1800 .... **NCLC 75**
Blais, Marie-Claire 1939- .. **CLC 2, 4, 6, 13, 22;
DAC; DAM MST**
See also CA 21-24R; CAAS 4; CANR 38, 75; DLB
53; MTCW 1, 2
Blaise, Clark 1940- .... **CLC 29**
See also AITN 2; CA 53-56; CAAS 3; CANR 5,
66; DLB 53
Blake, Fairley
See De Voto, Bernard (Augustine)
Blake, Nicholas
See Day Lewis, C(ecil)
See also DLB 77
Blake, William 1757-1827**NCLC 13, 37, 57; DA;
DAB; DAC; DAM MST, POET; PC 12; WLC**
See also CDBLB 1789-1832; CLR 52; DA3; DLB
93, 163; MAICYA; SATA 30
Blasco Ibanez, Vicente 1867-1928**TCLC 12; DAM
NOV**
See also CA 110; 131; CANR 81; DA3; HW 1, 2;
MTCW 1
Blatty, William Peter 1928- . **CLC 2; DAM POP**
See also CA 5-8R; CANR 9
Bleeck, Oliver
See Thomas, Ross (Elmore)
Blessing, Lee 1949- .... **CLC 54**
Blish, James (Benjamin) 1921-1975 ..... **CLC 14**
See also CA 1-4R; 57-60; CANR 3; DLB 8;
MTCW 1; SATA 66
Bliss, Reginald
See Wells, H(erbert) G(eorge)
Blixen, Karen (Christentze Dinesen) 1885-1962
See Dinesen, Isak
See also CA 25-28; CANR 22, 50; CAP 2; DA3;
MTCW 1, 2; SATA 44
Bloch, Robert (Albert) 1917-1994 .... **CLC 33**
See also AAYA 29; CA 5-8R; 179; 146; CAAE
179; CAAS 20; CANR 5, 78; DA3; DLB 44;
INT CANR-5; MTCW 1; SATA 12; SATA-
Obit 82
Blok, Alexander (Alexandrovich) 1880-1921
TCLC 5; PC 21
See also CA 104
Blom, Jan
See Breytenbach, Breyten
Bloom, Harold 1930- .... **CLC 24, 103**
See also CA 13-16R; CANR 39, 75; DLB 67;
MTCW 1
Bloomfield, Aurelius
See Bourne, Randolph S(illiman)
Blount, Roy (Alton), Jr. 1941- .... **CLC 38**
See also CA 53-56; CANR 10, 28, 61; INT CANR-
28; MTCW 1, 2

See also BW 1, 3; CA 85-88; 127; CANR 26; DA3;
DLB 48, 51, 63; MTCW 1, 2

Brown, Will
See Ainsworth, William Harrison

Brown, William Wells 1813-1884 **NCLC 2; BLC
1; DAM MULT; DC 1**
See also DLB 3, 50

Browne, (Clyde) Jackson 1948(?)- .... **CLC 21**
See also CA 120

Browning, Elizabeth Barrett 1806-1861 **NCLC 1,
16, 61, 66; DA; DAB; DAC; DAM MST,
POET; PC 6; WLC**
See also CDBLB 1832-1890; DA3; DLB 32, 199

Browning, Robert 1812-1889 **NCLC 19, 79; DA;
DAB; DAC; DAM MST, POET; PC 2; WLCS**
See also CDBLB 1832-1890; DA3; DLB 32, 163;
YABC 1

Browning, Tod 1882-1962 .... **CLC 16**
See also CA 141; 117

Brownson, Orestes Augustus 1803-1876 **NCLC
50**
See also DLB 1, 59, 73

Bruccoli, Matthew J(oseph) 1931- .... **CLC 34**
See also CA 9-12R; CANR 7; DLB 103

Bruce, Lenny .... **CLC 21**
See also Schneider, Leonard Alfred

Bruin, John
See Brutus, Dennis

Brulard, Henri
See Stendhal

Brulls, Christian
See Simenon, Georges (Jacques Christian)

Brunner, John (Kilian Houston) 1934-1995 **C L C
8, 10; DAM POP**
See also CA 1-4R; 149; CAAS 8; CANR 2, 37;
MTCW 1, 2

Bruno, Giordano 1548-1600 .... **LC 27**

Brutus, Dennis 1924- .... **CLC 43; BLC 1; DAM
MULT, POET; PC 24**
See also BW 2, 3; CA 49-52; CAAS 14; CANR 2,
27, 42, 81; DLB 117

Bryan, C(ourtlandt) D(ixon) B(arnes) 1936- **CLC
29**
See also CA 73-76; CANR 13, 68; DLB 185; INT
CANR-13

Bryan, Michael
See Moore, Brian

Bryan, William Jennings 1860-1925 .. **TCLC 99**

Bryant, William Cullen 1794-1878 **NCLC 6, 46;
DA; DAB; DAC; DAM MST, POET; PC 20**
See also CDALB 1640-1865; DLB 3, 43, 59, 189

Bryusov, Valery Yakovlevich 1873-1924 **TCLC 10**
See also CA 107; 155

Buchan, John 1875-1940 **TCLC 41; DAB; DAM
POP**
See also CA 108; 145; DLB 34, 70, 156; MTCW 1;
YABC 2

Buchanan, George 1506-1582 .... **LC 4**
See also DLB 152

Buchheim, Lothar-Guenther 1918- .... **CLC 6**
See also CA 85-88

Buchner, (Karl) Georg 1813-1837 ...... **NCLC 26**

Buchwald, Art(hur) 1925- .... **CLC 33**
See also AITN 1; CA 5-8R; CANR 21, 67; MTCW
1, 2; SATA 10

Buck, Pearl S(ydenstricker) 1892-1973 **CLC 7,
11, 18, 127; DA; DAB; DAC; DAM MST,
NOV**
See also AITN 1; CA 1-4R; 41-44R; CANR 1, 34;
CDALBS; DA3; DLB 9, 102; MTCW 1, 2;
SATA 1, 25

Buckler, Ernest 1908-1984 **CLC 13; DAC; DAM
MST**

See also CA 11-12; 114; CAP 1; DLB 68; SATA
47

Buckley, Vincent (Thomas) 1925-1988 . **CLC 57**
See also CA 101

Buckley, William F(rank), Jr. 1925- **CLC 7, 18,
37; DAM POP**
See also AITN 1; CA 1-4R; CANR 1, 24, 53; DA3;
DLB 137; DLBY 80; INT CANR-24; MTCW 1,
2

Buechner, (Carl) Frederick 1926- **CLC 2, 4, 6, 9;
DAM NOV**
See also CA 13-16R; CANR 11, 39, 64; DLBY 80;
INT CANR-11; MTCW 1, 2

Buell, John (Edward) 1927- .... **CLC 10**
See also CA 1-4R; CANR 71; DLB 53

Buero Vallejo, Antonio 1916- .... **CLC 15, 46**
See also CA 106; CANR 24, 49, 75; HW 1;
MTCW 1, 2

Bufalino, Gesualdo 1920(?)- .... **CLC 74**
See also DLB 196

Bugayev, Boris Nikolayevich 1880-1934 **TCLC 7;
PC 11**
See also Bely, Andrey
See also CA 104; 165; MTCW 1

Bukowski, Charles 1920-1994 **CLC 2, 5, 9, 41, 82,
108; DAM NOV, POET; PC 18**
See also CA 17-20R; 144; CANR 40, 62; DA3;
DLB 5, 130, 169; MTCW 1, 2

Bulgakov, Mikhail (Afanas'evich) 1891-1940
TCLC 2, 16; DAM DRAM, NOV; SSC 18
See also CA 105; 152

Bulgya, Alexander Alexandrovich 1901-1956
TCLC 53
See also Fadeyev, Alexander
See also CA 117; 181

Bullins, Ed 1935- ..... **CLC 1, 5, 7; BLC 1; DAM
DRAM, MULT; DC 6**
See also BW 2, 3; CA 49-52; CAAS 16; CANR
24, 46, 73; DLB 7, 38; MTCW 1, 2

Bulwer-Lytton, Edward (George Earle Lytton)
1803-1873 .... **NCLC 1, 45**
See also DLB 21

Bunin, Ivan Alexeyevich 1870-1953 **TCLC 6; SSC
5**
See also CA 104

Bunting, Basil 1900-1985 **CLC 10, 39, 47; DAM
POET**
See also CA 53-56; 115; CANR 7; DLB 20

Bunuel, Luis 1900-1983 **CLC 16, 80; DAM MULT;
HLC 1**
See also CA 101; 110; CANR 32, 77; HW 1

Bunyan, John 1628-1688 **LC 4; DA; DAB; DAC;
DAM MST; WLC**
See also CDBLB 1660-1789; DLB 39

Burckhardt, Jacob (Christoph) 1818-1897 **NCLC
49**

Burford, Eleanor
See Hibbert, Eleanor Alice Burford

Burgess, Anthony **CLC 1, 2, 4, 5, 8, 10, 13, 15, 22,
40, 62, 81, 94; DAB**
See also Wilson, John (Anthony) Burgess
See also AAYA 25; AITN 1; CDBLB 1960 to
Present; DLB 14, 194; DLBY 98; MTCW 1

Burke, Edmund 1729(?)-1797 **LC 7, 36; DA; DAB;
DAC; DAM MST; WLC**
See also DA3; DLB 104

Burke, Kenneth (Duva) 1897-1993 .... **CLC 2, 24**
See also CA 5-8R; 143; CANR 39, 74; DLB 45, 63;
MTCW 1, 2

Burke, Leda
See Garnett, David

Burke, Ralph
See Silverberg, Robert

Burke, Thomas 1886-1945 .... **TCLC 63**
See also CA 113; 155; DLB 197

Burney, Fanny 1752-1840 .... **NCLC 12, 54, 81**
See also DLB 39

Burns, Robert 1759-1796 **LC 3, 29, 40; DA; DAB;
DAC; DAM MST, POET; PC 6; WLC**
See also CDBLB 1789-1832; DA3; DLB 109

Burns, Tex
See L'Amour, Louis (Dearborn)

Burnshaw, Stanley 1906- .... **CLC 3, 13, 44**
See also CA 9-12R; DLB 48; DLBY 97

Burr, Anne 1937- .... **CLC 6**
See also CA 25-28R

Burroughs, Edgar Rice 1875-1950 **TCLC 2, 32;
DAM NOV**
See also AAYA 11; CA 104; 132; DA3; DLB 8;
MTCW 1, 2; SATA 41

Burroughs, William S(eward) 1914-1997 **CLC 1,
2, 5, 15, 22, 42, 75, 109; DA; DAB; DAC;
DAM MST, NOV, POP; WLC**
See also AITN 2; CA 9-12R; 160; CANR 20, 52;
DA3; DLB 2, 8, 16, 152; DLBY 81, 97; MTCW
1, 2

Burton, Sir Richard F(rancis) 1821-1890 **NCLC
42**
See also DLB 55, 166, 184

Busch, Frederick 1941- .... **CLC 7, 10, 18, 47**
See also CA 33-36R; CAAS 1; CANR 45, 73; DLB
6

Bush, Ronald 1946- .... **CLC 34**
See also CA 136

Bustos, F(rancisco)
See Borges, Jorge Luis

Bustos Domecq, H(onorio)
See Bioy Casares, Adolfo; Borges, Jorge Luis

Butler, Octavia E(stelle) 1947- ..... **CLC 38, 121;
BLCS; DAM MULT, POP**
See also AAYA 18; BW 2, 3; CA 73-76; CANR
12, 24, 38, 73; DA3; DLB 33; MTCW 1, 2;
SATA 84

Butler, Robert Olen (Jr.) 1945- .. **CLC 81; DAM
POP**
See also CA 112; CANR 66; DLB 173; INT 112;
MTCW 1

Butler, Samuel 1612-1680 .... **LC 16, 43**
See also DLB 101, 126

Butler, Samuel 1835-1902 **TCLC 1, 33; DA; DAB;
DAC; DAM MST, NOV; WLC**
See also CA 143; CDBLB 1890-1914; DA3; DLB
18, 57, 174

Butler, Walter C.
See Faust, Frederick (Schiller)

Butor, Michel (Marie Francois) 1926- **CLC 1, 3,
8, 11, 15**
See also CA 9-12R; CANR 33, 66; DLB 83;
MTCW 1, 2

Butts, Mary 1892(?)-1937 .... **TCLC 77**
See also CA 148

Buzo, Alexander (John) 1944- .... **CLC 61**
See also CA 97-100; CANR 17, 39, 69

Buzzati, Dino 1906-1972 .... **CLC 36**
See also CA 160; 33-36R; DLB 177

Byars, Betsy (Cromer) 1928- .... **CLC 35**
See also AAYA 19; CA 33-36R; CANR 18, 36, 57;
CLR 1, 16; DLB 52; INT CANR-18; JRDA;
MAICYA; MTCW 1; SAAS 1; SATA 4, 46,
80; SATA-Essay 108

Byatt, A(ntonia) S(usan Drabble) 1936- **CLC 19,
65; DAM NOV, POP**
See also CA 13-16R; CANR 13, 33, 50, 75; DA3;
DLB 14, 194; MTCW 1, 2

Byrne, David 1952- .... **CLC 26**
See also CA 127

Byrne, John Keyes 1926-
See Leonard, Hugh
See also CA 102; CANR 78; INT 102
Byron, George Gordon (Noel) 1788-1824**NCLC 2, 12; DA; DAB; DAC; DAM MST, POET; PC 16; WLC**
See also CDBLB 1789-1832; DA3; DLB 96, 110
Byron, Robert 1905-1941 .... **TCLC 67**
See also CA 160; DLB 195
C. 3. 3.
See Wilde, Oscar
Caballero, Fernan 1796-1877 ....**NCLC 10**
Cabell, Branch
See Cabell, James Branch
Cabell, James Branch 1879-1958 .... **TCLC 6**
See also CA 105; 152; DLB 9, 78; MTCW 1
Cable, George Washington 1844-1925 . **TCLC 4; SSC 4**
See also CA 104; 155; DLB 12, 74; DLBD 13
Cabral de Melo Neto, Joao 1920- **CLC 76; DAM MULT**
See also CA 151
Cabrera Infante, G(uillermo) 1929-**CLC 5, 25, 45, 120; DAM MULT; HLC 1**
See also CA 85-88; CANR 29, 65; DA3; DLB 113; HW 1, 2; MTCW 1, 2
Cade, Toni
See Bambara, Toni Cade
Cadmus and Harmonia
See Buchan, John
Caedmon fl. 658-680 .... **CMLC 7**
See also DLB 146
Caeiro, Alberto
See Pessoa, Fernando (Antonio Nogueira)
Cage, John (Milton, Jr.) 1912-1992 .... **CLC 41**
See also CA 13-16R; 169; CANR 9, 78; DLB 193; INT CANR-9
Cahan, Abraham 1860-1951 .... **TCLC 71**
See also CA 108; 154; DLB 9, 25, 28
Cain, G.
See Cabrera Infante, G(uillermo)
Cain, Guillermo
See Cabrera Infante, G(uillermo)
Cain, James M(allahan) 1892-1977**CLC 3, 11, 28**
See also AITN 1; CA 17-20R; 73-76; CANR 8, 34, 61; MTCW 1
Caine, Hall 1853-1931 .... **TCLC 99**
Caine, Mark
See Raphael, Frederic (Michael)
Calasso, Roberto 1941- .... **CLC 81**
See also CA 143
Calderon de la Barca, Pedro 1600-1681 . **LC 23; DC 3; HLCS 1**
Caldwell, Erskine (Preston) 1903-1987**CLC 1, 8, 14, 50, 60; DAM NOV; SSC 19**
See also AITN 1; CA 1-4R; 121; CAAS 1; CANR 2, 33; DA3; DLB 9, 86; MTCW 1, 2
Caldwell, (Janet Miriam) Taylor (Holland) 1900-1985 .... **CLC 2, 28, 39; DAM NOV, POP**
See also CA 5-8R; 116; CANR 5; DA3; DLBD 17
Calhoun, John Caldwell 1782-1850 ..... **NCLC 15**
See also DLB 3
Calisher, Hortense 1911- **CLC 2, 4, 8, 38; DAM NOV; SSC 15**
See also CA 1-4R; CANR 1, 22, 67; DA3; DLB 2; INT CANR-22; MTCW 1, 2
Callaghan, Morley Edward 1903-1990**CLC 3, 14, 41, 65; DAC; DAM MST**
See also CA 9-12R; 132; CANR 33, 73; DLB 68; MTCW 1, 2
Callimachus c. 305B.C.-c. 240B.C. ..... **CMLC 18**
See also DLB 176
Calvin, John 1509-1564 .... **LC 37**

Calvino, Italo 1923-1985**CLC 5, 8, 11, 22, 33, 39, 73; DAM NOV; SSC 3**
See also CA 85-88; 116; CANR 23, 61; DLB 196; MTCW 1, 2
Cameron, Carey 1952- .... **CLC 59**
See also CA 135
Cameron, Peter 1959- .... **CLC 44**
See also CA 125; CANR 50
Camoens, Luis Vaz de 1524(?)-1580
See also HLCS 1
Camoes, Luis de 1524(?)-1580
See also HLCS 1
Campana, Dino 1885-1932 .... **TCLC 20**
See also CA 117; DLB 114
Campanella, Tommaso 1568-1639 .... **LC 32**
Campbell, John W(ood, Jr.) 1910-1971 . **CLC 32**
See also CA 21-22; 29-32R; CANR 34; CAP 2; DLB 8; MTCW 1
Campbell, Joseph 1904-1987 .... **CLC 69**
See also AAYA 3; BEST 89:2; CA 1-4R; 124; CANR 3, 28, 61; DA3; MTCW 1, 2
Campbell, Maria 1940- .... **CLC 85; DAC**
See also CA 102; CANR 54; NNAL
Campbell, (John) Ramsey 1946-**CLC 42; SSC 19**
See also CA 57-60; CANR 7; INT CANR-7
Campbell, (Ignatius) Roy (Dunnachie) 1901-1957 **TCLC 5**
See also CA 104; 155; DLB 20; MTCW 2
Campbell, Thomas 1777-1844 .... **NCLC 19**
See also DLB 93; 144
Campbell, Wilfred .... **TCLC 9**
See also Campbell, William
Campbell, William 1858(?)-1918
See Campbell, Wilfred
See also CA 106; DLB 92
Campion, Jane .... **CLC 95**
See also CA 138
Campos, Alvaro de
See Pessoa, Fernando (Antonio Nogueira)
Camus, Albert 1913-1960 **CLC 1, 2, 4, 9, 11, 14, 32, 63, 69, 124; DA; DAB; DAC; DAM DRAM, MST, NOV; DC 2; SSC 9; WLC**
See also CA 89-92; DA3; DLB 72; MTCW 1, 2
Canby, Vincent 1924- .... **CLC 13**
See also CA 81-84
Cancale
See Desnos, Robert
Canetti, Elias 1905-1994 .. **CLC 3, 14, 25, 75, 86**
See also CA 21-24R; 146; CANR 23, 61, 79; DA3; DLB 85, 124; MTCW 1, 2
Canfield, Dorothea F.
See Fisher, Dorothy (Frances) Canfield
Canfield, Dorothea Frances
See Fisher, Dorothy (Frances) Canfield
Canfield, Dorothy
See Fisher, Dorothy (Frances) Canfield
Canin, Ethan 1960- .... **CLC 55**
See also CA 131; 135
Cannon, Curt
See Hunter, Evan
Cao, Lan 1961- .... **CLC 109**
See also CA 165
Cape, Judith
See Page, P(atricia) K(athleen)
Capek, Karel 1890-1938 **TCLC 6, 37; DA; DAB; DAC; DAM DRAM, MST, NOV; DC 1; SSC 36; WLC**
See also CA 104; 140; DA3; MTCW 1
Capote, Truman 1924-1984**CLC 1, 3, 8, 13, 19, 34, 38, 58; DA; DAB; DAC; DAM MST, NOV; POP; SSC 2; WLC**
See also CA 5-8R; 113; CANR 18, 62; CDALB 1941-1968; DA3; DLB 2, 185; DLBY 80, 84;

MTCW 1, 2; SATA 91
Capra, Frank 1897-1991 .... **CLC 16**
See also CA 61-64; 135
Caputo, Philip 1941- .... **CLC 32**
See also CA 73-76; CANR 40
Caragiale, Ion Luca 1852-1912 .... **TCLC 76**
See also CA 157
Card, Orson Scott 1951- **CLC 44, 47, 50; DAM POP**
See also AAYA 11; CA 102; CANR 27, 47, 73; DA3; INT CANR-27; MTCW 1, 2; SATA 83
Cardenal, Ernesto 1925- . **CLC 31; DAM MULT, POET; HLC 1; PC 22**
See also CA 49-52; CANR 2, 32, 66; HW 1, 2; MTCW 1, 2
Cardozo, Benjamin N(athan) 1870-1938**TCLC 65**
See also CA 117; 164
Carducci, Giosue (Alessandro Giuseppe) 1835-1907 .... **TCLC 32**
See also CA 163
Carew, Thomas 1595(?)-1640 .... **LC 13**
See also DLB 126
Carey, Ernestine Gilbreth 1908- .... **CLC 17**
See also CA 5-8R; CANR 71; SATA 2
Carey, Peter 1943- .... **CLC 40, 55, 96**
See also CA 123; 127; CANR 53, 76; INT 127; MTCW 1, 2; SATA 94
Carleton, William 1794-1869 .... **NCLC 3**
See also DLB 159
Carlisle, Henry (Coffin) 1926- .... **CLC 33**
See also CA 13-16R; CANR 15, 85
Carlsen, Chris
See Holdstock, Robert P.
Carlson, Ron(ald F.) 1947- .... **CLC 54**
See also CA 105; CANR 27
Carlyle, Thomas 1795-1881**NCLC 70; DA; DAB; DAC; DAM MST**
See also CDBLB 1789-1832; DLB 55; 144
Carman, (William) Bliss 1861-1929**TCLC 7; DAC**
See also CA 104; 152; DLB 92
Carnegie, Dale 1888-1955 .... **TCLC 53**
Carossa, Hans 1878-1956 .... **TCLC 48**
See also CA 170; DLB 66
Carpenter, Don(ald Richard) 1931-1995 **CLC 41**
See also CA 45-48; 149; CANR 1, 71
Carpenter, Edward 1844-1929 .... **TCLC 88**
See also CA 163
Carpentier (y Valmont), Alejo 1904-1980**CLC 8, 11, 38, 110; DAM MULT; HLC 1; SSC 35**
See also CA 65-68; 97-100; CANR 11, 70; DLB 113; HW 1, 2
Carr, Caleb 1955(?)- .... **CLC 86**
See also CA 147; CANR 73; DA3
Carr, Emily 1871-1945 .... **TCLC 32**
See also CA 159; DLB 68
Carr, John Dickson 1906-1977 .... **CLC 3**
See also Fairbairn, Roger
See also CA 49-52; 69-72; CANR 3, 33, 60; MTCW 1, 2
Carr, Philippa
See Hibbert, Eleanor Alice Burford
Carr, Virginia Spencer 1929- .... **CLC 34**
See also CA 61-64; DLB 111
Carrere, Emmanuel 1957- .... **CLC 89**
Carrier, Roch 1937- ... **CLC 13, 78; DAC; DAM MST**
See also CA 130; CANR 61; DLB 53; SATA 105
Carroll, James P. 1943(?)- .... **CLC 38**
See also CA 81-84; CANR 73; MTCW 1
Carroll, Jim 1951- .... **CLC 35**
See also AAYA 17; CA 45-48; CANR 42
Carroll, Lewis .... **NCLC 2, 53; PC 18; WLC**
See also Dodgson, Charles Lutwidge

See also CA 120; 155

Crockett, David 1786-1836 .... **NCLC 8**
See also DLB 3, 11

Crockett, Davy
See Crockett, David

Crofts, Freeman Wills 1879-1957 ...... **TCLC 55**
See also CA 115; DLB 77

Croker, John Wilson 1780-1857 .... **NCLC 10**
See also DLB 110

Crommelynck, Fernand 1885-1970 .... **CLC 75**
See also CA 89-92

Cromwell, Oliver 1599-1658 .... **LC 43**

Cronin, A(rchibald) J(oseph) 1896-1981 **CLC 32**
See also CA 1-4R; 102; CANR 5; DLB 191; SATA 47; SATA-Obit 25

Cross, Amanda
See Heilbrun, Carolyn G(old)

Crothers, Rachel 1878(?)-1958 .... **TCLC 19**
See also CA 113; DLB 7

Croves, Hal
See Traven, B.

Crow Dog, Mary (Ellen) (?)- .... **CLC 93**
See also Brave Bird, Mary
See also CA 154

Crowfield, Christopher
See Stowe, Harriet (Elizabeth) Beecher

Crowley, Aleister .... **TCLC 7**
See also Crowley, Edward Alexander

Crowley, Edward Alexander 1875-1947
See Crowley, Aleister
See also CA 104

Crowley, John 1942- .... **CLC 57**
See also CA 61-64; CANR 43; DLBY 82; SATA 65

Crud
See Crumb, R(obert)

Crumarums
See Crumb, R(obert)

Crumb, R(obert) 1943- .... **CLC 17**
See also CA 106

Crumbum
See Crumb, R(obert)

Crumski
See Crumb, R(obert)

Crum the Bum
See Crumb, R(obert)

Crunk
See Crumb, R(obert)

Crustt
See Crumb, R(obert)

Cruz, Victor Hernandez 1949-
See also BW 2; CA 65-68; CAAS 17; CANR 14, 32, 74; DAM MULT, POET; DLB 41; HLC 1; HW 1, 2; MTCW 1

Cryer, Gretchen (Kiger) 1935- .... **CLC 21**
See also CA 114; 123

Csath, Geza 1887-1919 .... **TCLC 13**
See also CA 111

Cudlip, David R(ockwell) 1933- .... **CLC 34**
See also CA 177

Cullen, Countee 1903-1946 **TCLC 4, 37; BLC 1; DA; DAC; DAM MST, MULT, POET; PC 20; WLCS**
See also BW 1; CA 108; 124; CDALB 1917-1929; DA3; DLB 4, 48, 51; MTCW 1, 2; SATA 18

Cum, R.
See Crumb, R(obert)

Cummings, Bruce F(rederick) 1889-1919
See Barbellion, W. N. P.
See also CA 123

Cummings, E(dward) E(stlin) 1894-1962 **CLC 1, 3, 8, 12, 15, 68; DA; DAB; DAC; DAM MST, POET; PC 5; WLC**

See also CA 73-76; CANR 31; CDALB 1929-1941; DA3; DLB 4, 48; MTCW 1, 2

Cunha, Euclides (Rodrigues Pimenta) da 1866-1909 **TCLC 24**
See also CA 123

Cunningham, E. V.
See Fast, Howard (Melvin)

Cunningham, J(ames) V(incent) 1911-1985 **C L C 3, 31**
See also CA 1-4R; 115; CANR 1, 72; DLB 5

Cunningham, Julia (Woolfolk) 1916- .. **CLC 12**
See also CA 9-12R; CANR 4, 19, 36; JRDA; MAICYA; SAAS 2; SATA 1, 26

Cunningham, Michael 1952- .... **CLC 34**
See also CA 136

Cunninghame Graham, R(obert) B(ontine) 1852-1936 .... **TCLC 19**
See also Graham, R(obert) B(ontine) Cunninghame
See also CA 119; DLB 98

Currie, Ellen 19(?)- .... **CLC 44**

Curtin, Philip
See Lowndes, Marie Adelaide (Belloc)

Curtis, Price
See Ellison, Harlan (Jay)

Cutrate, Joe
See Spiegelman, Art

Cynewulf c. 770-c. 840 .... **CMLC 23**

Czaczkes, Shmuel Yosef
See Agnon, S(hmuel) Y(osef Halevi)

Dabrowska, Maria (Szumska) 1889-1965 **CLC 15**
See also CA 106

Dabydeen, David 1955- .... **CLC 34**
See also BW 1; CA 125; CANR 56

Dacey, Philip 1939- .... **CLC 51**
See also CA 37-40R; CAAS 17; CANR 14, 32, 64; DLB 105

Dagerman, Stig (Halvard) 1923-1954 .. **TCLC 17**
See also CA 117; 155

Dahl, Roald 1916-1990 .. **CLC 1, 6, 18, 79; DAB; DAC; DAM MST, NOV, POP**
See also AAYA 15; CA 1-4R; 133; CANR 6, 32, 37, 62; CLR 1, 7, 41; DA3; DLB 139; JRDA; MAICYA; MTCW 1, 2; SATA 1, 26, 73; SATA-Obit 65

Dahlberg, Edward 1900-1977 .... **CLC 1, 7, 14**
See also CA 9-12R; 69-72; CANR 31, 62; DLB 48; MTCW 1

Daitch, Susan 1954- .... **CLC 103**
See also CA 161

Dale, Colin .... **TCLC 18**
See also Lawrence, T(homas) E(dward)

Dale, George E.
See Asimov, Isaac

Dalton, Roque 1935-1975
See also HLCS 1; HW 2

Daly, Elizabeth 1878-1967 .... **CLC 52**
See also CA 23-24; 25-28R; CANR 60; CAP 2

Daly, Maureen 1921- .... **CLC 17**
See also AAYA 5; CANR 37, 83; JRDA; MAICYA; SAAS 1; SATA 2

Damas, Leon-Gontran 1912-1978 .... **CLC 84**
See also BW 1; CA 125; 73-76

Dana, Richard Henry Sr. 1787-1879 ... **NCLC 53**

Daniel, Samuel 1562(?)-1619 .... **LC 24**
See also DLB 62

Daniels, Brett
See Adler, Renata

Dannay, Frederic 1905-1982 **CLC 11; DAM POP**
See also Queen, Ellery
See also CA 1-4R; 107; CANR 1, 39; DLB 137; MTCW 1

D'Annunzio, Gabriele 1863-1938 .... **TCLC 6, 40**

See also CA 104; 155

Danois, N. le
See Gourmont, Remy (-Marie-Charles) de

Dante 1265-1321 **CMLC 3, 18; DA; DAB; DAC; DAM MST, POET; PC 21; WLCS**
See also DA3

d'Antibes, Germain
See Simenon, Georges (Jacques Christian)

Danticat, Edwidge 1969- .... **CLC 94**
See also AAYA 29; CA 152; CANR 73; MTCW 1

Danvers, Dennis 1947- .... **CLC 70**

Danziger, Paula 1944- .... **CLC 21**
See also AAYA 4; CA 112; 115; CANR 37; CLR 20; JRDA; MAICYA; SATA 36, 63, 102; SATA-Brief 30

Da Ponte, Lorenzo 1749-1838 .... **NCLC 50**

Dario, Ruben 1867-1916 . **TCLC 4; DAM MULT; HLC 1; PC 15**
See also CA 131; CANR 81; HW 1, 2; MTCW 1, 2

Darley, George 1795-1846 .... **NCLC 2**
See also DLB 96

Darrow, Clarence (Seward) 1857-1938 **TCLC 81**
See also CA 164

Darwin, Charles 1809-1882 .... **NCLC 57**
See also DLB 57, 166

Daryush, Elizabeth 1887-1977 .... **CLC 6, 19**
See also CA 49-52; CANR 3, 81; DLB 20

Dasgupta, Surendranath 1887-1952 ... **TCLC 81**
See also CA 157

Dashwood, Edmee Elizabeth Monica de la Pasture 1890-1943
See Delafield, E. M.
See also CA 119; 154

Daudet, (Louis Marie) Alphonse 1840-1897 **NCLC 1**
See also DLB 123

Daumal, Rene 1908-1944 .... **TCLC 14**
See also CA 114

Davenant, William 1606-1668 .... **LC 13**
See also DLB 58, 126

Davenport, Guy (Mattison, Jr.) 1927- **CLC 6, 14, 38; SSC 16**
See also CA 33-36R; CANR 23, 73; DLB 130

Davidson, Avram (James) 1923-1993
See Queen, Ellery
See also CA 101; 171; CANR 26; DLB 8

Davidson, Donald (Grady) 1893-1968 **CLC 2, 13, 19**
See also CA 5-8R; 25-28R; CANR 4, 84; DLB 45

Davidson, Hugh
See Hamilton, Edmond

Davidson, John 1857-1909 .... **TCLC 24**
See also CA 118; DLB 19

Davidson, Sara 1943- .... **CLC 9**
See also CA 81-84; CANR 44, 68; DLB 185

Davie, Donald (Alfred) 1922-1995 **CLC 5, 8, 10, 31**
See also CA 1-4R; 149; CAAS 3; CANR 1, 44; DLB 27; MTCW 1

Davies, Ray(mond Douglas) 1944- .... **CLC 21**
See also CA 116; 146

Davies, Rhys 1901-1978 .... **CLC 23**
See also CA 9-12R; 81-84; CANR 4; DLB 139, 191

Davies, (William) Robertson 1913-1995 **CLC 2, 7, 13, 25, 42, 75, 91; DA; DAB; DAC; DAM MST, NOV, POP; WLC**
See also BEST 89:2; CA 33-36R; 150; CANR 17, 42; DA3; DLB 68; INT CANR-17; MTCW 1, 2

Davies, Walter C.
See Kornbluth, C(yril) M.

Davies, William Henry 1871-1940 .... **TCLC 5**
See also CA 104; 179; DLB 19, 174

Davis, Angela (Yvonne) 1944- ..... **CLC 77; DAM MULT**
See also BW 2, 3; CA 57-60; CANR 10, 81; DA3

Davis, B. Lynch
See Bioy Casares, Adolfo; Borges, Jorge Luis

Davis, B. Lynch
See Bioy Casares, Adolfo

Davis, H(arold) L(enoir) 1894-1960 .... **CLC 49**
See also CA 178; 89-92; DLB 9, 206

Davis, Rebecca (Blaine) Harding 1831-1910 **TCLC 6**
See also CA 104; 179; DLB 74

Davis, Richard Harding 1864-1916 ..... **TCLC 24**
See also CA 114; 179; DLB 12, 23, 78, 79, 189; DLBD 13

Davison, Frank Dalby 1893-1970 .... **CLC 15**
See also CA 116

Davison, Lawrence H.
See Lawrence, D(avid) H(erbert Richards)

Davison, Peter (Hubert) 1928- .... **CLC 28**
See also CA 9-12R; CAAS 4; CANR 3, 43, 84; DLB 5

Davys, Mary 1674-1732 .... **LC 1, 46**
See also DLB 39

Dawson, Fielding 1930- .... **CLC 6**
See also CA 85-88; DLB 130

Dawson, Peter
See Faust, Frederick (Schiller)

Day, Clarence (Shepard, Jr.) 1874-1935 **TCLC 25**
See also CA 108; DLB 11

Day, Thomas 1748-1789 .... **LC 1**
See also DLB 39; YABC 1

Day Lewis, C(ecil) 1904-1972 **CLC 1, 6, 10; DAM POET; PC 11**
See also Blake, Nicholas
See also CA 13-16; 33-36R; CANR 34; CAP 1; DLB 15, 20; MTCW 1, 2

Dazai Osamu 1909-1948 .... **TCLC 11**
See also Tsushima, Shuji
See also CA 164; DLB 182

de Andrade, Carlos Drummond 1892-1945
See Drummond de Andrade, Carlos

Deane, Norman
See Creasey, John

Deane, Seamus (Francis) 1940- .... **CLC 122**
See also CA 118; CANR 42

de Beauvoir, Simone (Lucie Ernestine Marie Bertrand)
See Beauvoir, Simone (Lucie Ernestine Marie Bertrand) de

de Beer, P.
See Bosman, Herman Charles

de Brissac, Malcolm
See Dickinson, Peter (Malcolm)

de Chardin, Pierre Teilhard
See Teilhard de Chardin, (Marie Joseph) Pierre

Dee, John 1527-1608 .... **LC 20**

Deer, Sandra 1940- .... **CLC 45**

De Ferrari, Gabriella 1941- .... **CLC 65**
See also CA 146

Defoe, Daniel 1660(?)-1731 **LC 1, 42; DA; DAB; DAC; DAM MST, NOV; WLC**
See also AAYA 27; CDBLB 1660-1789; CLR 61; DA3; DLB 39, 95, 101; JRDA; MAICYA; SATA 22

de Gourmont, Remy(-Marie-Charles)
See Gourmont, Remy (-Marie-Charles) de

de Hartog, Jan 1914- .... **CLC 19**
See also CA 1-4R; CANR 1

de Hostos, E. M.
See Hostos (y Bonilla), Eugenio Maria de

de Hostos, Eugenio M.
See Hostos (y Bonilla), Eugenio Maria de

Deighton, Len .... **CLC 4, 7, 22, 46**
See also Deighton, Leonard Cyril
See also AAYA 6; BEST 89:2; CDBLB 1960 to Present; DLB 87

Deighton, Leonard Cyril 1929-
See Deighton, Len
See also CA 9-12R; CANR 19, 33, 68; DAM NOV, POP; DA3; MTCW 1, 2

Dekker, Thomas 1572(?)-1632 ...... **LC 22; DAM DRAM**
See also CDBLB Before 1660; DLB 62, 172

Delafield, E. M. 1890-1943 .... **TCLC 61**
See also Dashwood, Edmee Elizabeth Monica de la Pasture
See also DLB 34

de la Mare, Walter (John) 1873-1956 **TCLC 4, 53; DAB; DAC; DAM MST, POET; SSC 14; WLC**
See also CA 163; CDBLB 1914-1945; CLR 23; DA3; DLB 162; MTCW 1; SATA 16

Delaney, Franey
See O'Hara, John (Henry)

Delaney, Shelagh 1939-. **CLC 29; DAM DRAM**
See also CA 17-20R; CANR 30, 67; CDBLB 1960 to Present; DLB 13; MTCW 1

Delany, Mary (Granville Pendarves) 1700-1788 **LC 12**

Delany, Samuel R(ay, Jr.) 1942-. **CLC 8, 14, 38; BLC 1; DAM MULT**
See also AAYA 24; BW 2, 3; CA 81-84; CANR 27, 43; DLB 8, 33; MTCW 1, 2

De La Ramee, (Marie) Louise 1839-1908
See Ouida
See also SATA 20

de la Roche, Mazo 1879-1961 .... **CLC 14**
See also CA 85-88; CANR 30; DLB 68; SATA 64

De La Salle, Innocent
See Hartmann, Sadakichi

Delbanco, Nicholas (Franklin) 1942- **CLC 6, 13**
See also CA 17-20R; CAAS 2; CANR 29, 55; DLB 6

del Castillo, Michel 1933- .... **CLC 38**
See also CA 109; CANR 77

Deledda, Grazia (Cosima) 1875(?)-1936 **TCLC 23**
See also CA 123

Delgado, Abelardo B(arrientos) 1931-
See also CA 131; CAAS 15; DAM MST, MULT; DLB 82; HLC 1; HW 1, 2

Delibes, Miguel .... **CLC 8, 18**
See also Delibes Setien, Miguel

Delibes Setien, Miguel 1920-
See Delibes, Miguel
See also CA 45-48; CANR 1, 32; HW 1; MTCW 1

DeLillo, Don 1936- **CLC 8, 10, 13, 27, 39, 54, 76; DAM NOV, POP**
See also BEST 89:1; CA 81-84; CANR 21, 76; DA3; DLB 6, 173; MTCW 1, 2

de Lisser, H. G.
See De Lisser, H(erbert) G(eorge)
See also DLB 117

De Lisser, H(erbert) G(eorge) 1878-1944 **TCLC 12**
See also de Lisser, H. G.
See also BW 2; CA 109; 152

Deloney, Thomas 1560(?)-1600 .... **LC 41**
See also DLB 167

Deloria, Vine (Victor), Jr. 1933- . **CLC 21, 122; DAM MULT**
See also CA 53-56; CANR 5, 20, 48; DLB 175; MTCW 1; NNAL; SATA 21

Del Vecchio, John M(ichael) 1947- ...... **CLC 29**
See also CA 110; DLBD 9

de Man, Paul (Adolph Michel) 1919-1983 **CLC 55**
See also CA 128; 111; CANR 61; DLB 67; MTCW 1, 2

De Marinis, Rick 1934- .... **CLC 54**
See also CA 57-60; CAAS 24; CANR 9, 25, 50

Dembry, R. Emmet
See Murfree, Mary Noailles

Demby, William 1922- ... **CLC 53; BLC 1; DAM MULT**
See also BW 1, 3; CA 81-84; CANR 81; DLB 33

de Menton, Francisco
See Chin, Frank (Chew, Jr.)

Demetrius of Phalerum c. 307B.C.- .. **CMLC 34**

Demijohn, Thom
See Disch, Thomas M(ichael)

de Molina, Tirso 1580-1648
See also HLCS 2

de Montherlant, Henry (Milon)
See Montherlant, Henry (Milon) de

Demosthenes 384B.C.-322B.C. .... **CMLC 13**
See also DLB 176

de Natale, Francine
See Malzberg, Barry N(athaniel)

Denby, Edwin (Orr) 1903-1983 .... **CLC 48**
See also CA 138; 110

Denis, Julio
See Cortazar, Julio

Denmark, Harrison
See Zelazny, Roger (Joseph)

Dennis, John 1658-1734 .... **LC 11**
See also DLB 101

Dennis, Nigel (Forbes) 1912-1989 .... **CLC 8**
See also CA 25-28R; 129; DLB 13, 15; MTCW 1

Dent, Lester 1904(?)-1959 .... **TCLC 72**
See also CA 112; 161

De Palma, Brian (Russell) 1940- .... **CLC 20**
See also CA 109

De Quincey, Thomas 1785-1859 .... **NCLC 4**
See also CDBLB 1789-1832; DLB 110; 144

Deren, Eleanora 1908(?)-1961
See Deren, Maya
See also CA 111

Deren, Maya 1917-1961 .... **CLC 16, 102**
See also Deren, Eleanora

Derleth, August (William) 1909-1971 .. **CLC 31**
See also CA 1-4R; 29-32R; CANR 4; DLB 9; DLBD 17; SATA 5

Der Nister 1884-1950 .... **TCLC 56**

de Routisie, Albert
See Aragon, Louis

Derrida, Jacques 1930- .... **CLC 24, 87**
See also CA 124; 127; CANR 76; MTCW 1

Derry Down Derry
See Lear, Edward

Dersonnes, Jacques
See Simenon, Georges (Jacques Christian)

Desai, Anita 1937- **CLC 19, 37, 97; DAB; DAM NOV**
See also CA 81-84; CANR 33, 53; DA3; MTCW 1, 2; SATA 63

Desai, Kiran 1971- .... **CLC 119**
See also CA 171

de Saint-Luc, Jean
See Glassco, John

de Saint Roman, Arnaud
See Aragon, Louis

Descartes, Rene 1596-1650 .... **LC 20, 35**

De Sica, Vittorio 1901(?)-1974 .... **CLC 20**
See also CA 117

Desnos, Robert 1900-1945 .... **TCLC 22**
See also CA 121; 151

Destouches, Louis-Ferdinand 1894-1961 **CLC 9, 15**
See also Celine, Louis-Ferdinand

See Betjeman, John

Fassbinder, Rainer Werner 1946-1982 . **CLC 20**
See also CA 93-96; 106; CANR 31

Fast, Howard (Melvin) 1914-**CLC 23; DAM NOV**
See also AAYA 16; CA 1-4R, 181; CAAE 181;
CAAS 18; CANR 1, 33, 54, 75; DLB 9; INT
CANR-33; MTCW 1; SATA 7; SATA-Essay
107

Faulcon, Robert
See Holdstock, Robert P.

Faulkner, William (Cuthbert) 1897-1962**CLC 1,
3, 6, 8, 9, 11, 14, 18, 28, 52, 68; DA; DAB;
DAC; DAM MST, NOV; SSC 1, 35; WLC**
See also AAYA 7; CA 81-84; CANR 33; CDALB
1929-1941; DA3; DLB 9, 11, 44, 102; DLBD 2;
DLBY 86, 97; MTCW 1, 2

Fauset, Jessie Redmon 1884(?)-1961**CLC 19, 54;
BLC 2; DAM MULT**
See also BW 1; CA 109; CANR 83; DLB 51

Faust, Frederick (Schiller) 1892-1944(?) **T C L C
49; DAM POP**
See also CA 108; 152

Faust, Irvin 1924- .... **CLC 8**
See also CA 33-36R; CANR 28, 67; DLB 2, 28;
DLBY 80

Fawkes, Guy
See Benchley, Robert (Charles)

Fearing, Kenneth (Flexner) 1902-1961 . **CLC 51**
See also CA 93-96; CANR 59; DLB 9

Fecamps, Elise
See Creasey, John

Federman, Raymond 1928- .... **CLC 6, 47**
See also CA 17-20R; CAAS 8; CANR 10, 43, 83;
DLBY 80

Federspiel, J(uerg) F. 1931- .... **CLC 42**
See also CA 146

Feiffer, Jules (Ralph) 1929- **CLC 2, 8, 64; DAM
DRAM**
See also AAYA 3; CA 17-20R; CANR 30, 59; DLB
7, 44; INT CANR-30; MTCW 1; SATA 8, 61,
111

Feige, Hermann Albert Otto Maximilian
See Traven, B.

Feinberg, David B. 1956-1994 .... **CLC 59**
See also CA 135; 147

Feinstein, Elaine 1930- .... **CLC 36**
See also CA 69-72; CAAS 1; CANR 31, 68; DLB
14, 40; MTCW 1

Feldman, Irving (Mordecai) 1928- .... **CLC 7**
See also CA 1-4R; CANR 1; DLB 169

Felix-Tchicaya, Gerald
See Tchicaya, Gerald Felix

Fellini, Federico 1920-1993 .... **CLC 16, 85**
See also CA 65-68; 143; CANR 33

Felsen, Henry Gregor 1916-1995 .... **CLC 17**
See also CA 1-4R; 180; CANR 1; SAAS 2; SATA
1

Fenno, Jack
See Calisher, Hortense

Fenollosa, Ernest (Francisco) 1853-1908**TCLC 91**

Fenton, James Martin 1949- .... **CLC 32**
See also CA 102; DLB 40

Ferber, Edna 1887-1968 .... **CLC 18, 93**
See also AITN 1; CA 5-8R; 25-28R; CANR 68;
DLB 9, 28, 86; MTCW 1, 2; SATA 7

Ferguson, Helen
See Kavan, Anna

Ferguson, Samuel 1810-1886 .... **NCLC 33**
See also DLB 32

Fergusson, Robert 1750-1774 .... **LC 29**
See also DLB 109

Ferling, Lawrence
See Ferlinghetti, Lawrence (Monsanto)

Ferlinghetti, Lawrence (Monsanto) 1919(?)-**CLC
2, 6, 10, 27, 111; DAM POET; PC 1**
See also CA 5-8R; CANR 3, 41, 73; CDALB 1941-
1968; DA3; DLB 5, 16; MTCW 1, 2

Fernandez, Vicente Garcia Huidobro
See Huidobro Fernandez, Vicente Garcia

Ferre, Rosario 1942- .... **SSC 36; HLCS 1**
See also CA 131; CANR 55, 81; DLB 145; HW 1,
2; MTCW 1

Ferrer, Gabriel (Francisco Victor) Miro
See Miro (Ferrer), Gabriel (Francisco Victor)

Ferrier, Susan (Edmonstone) 1782-1854**NCLC 8**
See also DLB 116

Ferrigno, Robert 1948(?)- .... **CLC 65**
See also CA 140

Ferron, Jacques 1921-1985 .... **CLC 94; DAC**
See also CA 117; 129; DLB 60

Feuchtwanger, Lion 1884-1958 .... **TCLC 3**
See also CA 104; DLB 66

Feuillet, Octave 1821-1890 .... **NCLC 45**
See also DLB 192

Feydeau, Georges (Leon Jules Marie) 1862-1921
TCLC 22; DAM DRAM
See also CA 113; 152; CANR 84; DLB 192

Fichte, Johann Gottlieb 1762-1814 ...... **NCLC 62**
See also DLB 90

Ficino, Marsilio 1433-1499 .... **LC 12**

Fiedeler, Hans
See Doeblin, Alfred

Fiedler, Leslie A(aron) 1917- ...... **CLC 4, 13, 24**
See also CA 9-12R; CANR 7, 63; DLB 28, 67;
MTCW 1, 2

Field, Andrew 1938- .... **CLC 44**
See also CA 97-100; CANR 25

Field, Eugene 1850-1895 ....**NCLC 3**
See also DLB 23, 42, 140; DLBD 13; MAICYA;
SATA 16

Field, Gans T.
See Wellman, Manly Wade

Field, Michael 1915-1971 .... **TCLC 43**
See also CA 29-32R

Field, Peter
See Hobson, Laura Z(ametkin)

Fielding, Henry 1707-1754 **LC 1, 46; DA; DAB;
DAC; DAM DRAM, MST, NOV; WLC**
See also CDBLB 1660-1789; DA3; DLB 39, 84,
101

Fielding, Sarah 1710-1768 .... **LC 1, 44**
See also DLB 39

Fields, W. C. 1880-1946 .... **TCLC 80**
See also DLB 44

Fierstein, Harvey (Forbes) 1954- **CLC 33; DAM
DRAM, POP**
See also CA 123; 129; DA3

Figes, Eva 1932- .... **CLC 31**
See also CA 53-56; CANR 4, 44, 83; DLB 14

Finch, Anne 1661-1720 .... **LC 3; PC 21**
See also DLB 95

Finch, Robert (Duer Claydon) 1900- .... **CLC 18**
See also CA 57-60; CANR 9, 24, 49; DLB 88

Findley, Timothy 1930-**CLC 27, 102; DAC; DAM
MST**
See also CA 25-28R; CANR 12, 42, 69; DLB 53

Fink, William
See Mencken, H(enry) L(ouis)

Firbank, Louis 1942-
See Reed, Lou
See also CA 117

Firbank, (Arthur Annesley) Ronald 1886-1926
TCLC 1
See also CA 104; 177; DLB 36

Fisher, Dorothy (Frances) Canfield 1879-1958
TCLC 87

See also CA 114; 136; CANR 80; DLB 9, 102;
MAICYA; YABC 1

Fisher, M(ary) F(rances) K(ennedy) 1908-1992
CLC 76, 87
See also CA 77-80; 138; CANR 44; MTCW 1

Fisher, Roy 1930- .... **CLC 25**
See also CA 81-84; CAAS 10; CANR 16; DLB 40

Fisher, Rudolph 1897-1934**TCLC 11; BLC 2; DAM
MULT; SSC 25**
See also BW 1, 3; CA 107; 124; CANR 80; DLB
51, 102

Fisher, Vardis (Alvero) 1895-1968 .... **CLC 7**
See also CA 5-8R; 25-28R; CANR 68; DLB 9, 206

Fiske, Tarleton
See Bloch, Robert (Albert)

Fitch, Clarke
See Sinclair, Upton (Beall)

Fitch, John IV
See Cormier, Robert (Edmund)

Fitzgerald, Captain Hugh
See Baum, L(yman) Frank

FitzGerald, Edward 1809-1883 .... **NCLC 9**
See also DLB 32

Fitzgerald, F(rancis) Scott (Key) 1896-1940
**TCLC 1, 6, 14, 28, 55; DA; DAB; DAC; DAM
MST, NOV; SSC 6, 31; WLC**
See also AAYA 24; AITN 1; CA 110; 123; CDALB
1917-1929; DA3; DLB 4, 9, 86; DLBD 1, 15, 16;
DLBY 81, 96; MTCW 1, 2

Fitzgerald, Penelope 1916- .... **CLC 19, 51, 61**
See also CA 85-88; CAAS 10; CANR 56, 86; DLB
14, 194; MTCW 2

Fitzgerald, Robert (Stuart) 1910-1985 .. **CLC 39**
See also CA 1-4R; 114; CANR 1; DLBY 80

FitzGerald, Robert D(avid) 1902-1987 ... **CLC 19**
See also CA 17-20R

Fitzgerald, Zelda (Sayre) 1900-1948 ... **TCLC 52**
See also CA 117; 126; DLBY 84

Flanagan, Thomas (James Bonner) 1923- .. **C L C
25, 52**
See also CA 108; CANR 55; DLBY 80; INT 108;
MTCW 1

Flaubert, Gustave 1821-1880**NCLC 2, 10, 19, 62,
66; DA; DAB; DAC; DAM MST, NOV; SSC
11; WLC**
See also DA3; DLB 119

Flecker, Herman Elroy
See Flecker, (Herman) James Elroy

Flecker, (Herman) James Elroy 1884-1915**TCLC
43**
See also CA 109; 150; DLB 10, 19

Fleming, Ian (Lancaster) 1908-1964 **CLC 3, 30;
DAM POP**
See also AAYA 26; CA 5-8R; CANR 59; CDBLB
1945-1960; DA3; DLB 87, 201; MTCW 1, 2;
SATA 9

Fleming, Thomas (James) 1927- .... **CLC 37**
See also CA 5-8R; CANR 10; INT CANR-10;
SATA 8

Fletcher, John 1579-1625 .... **LC 33; DC 6**
See also CDBLB Before 1660; DLB 58

Fletcher, John Gould 1886-1950 .... **TCLC 35**
See also CA 107; 167; DLB 4, 45

Fleur, Paul
See Pohl, Frederik

Flooglebuckle, Al
See Spiegelman, Art

Flying Officer X
See Bates, H(erbert) E(rnest)

Fo, Dario 1926-**CLC 32, 109; DAM DRAM; DC 10**
See also CA 116; 128; CANR 68; DA3; DLBY 97;
MTCW 1, 2

Fogarty, Jonathan Titulescu Esq.

See Farrell, James T(homas)

Follett, Ken(neth Martin) 1949- .. **CLC 18; DAM NOV, POP**
See also AAYA 6; BEST 89:4; CA 81-84; CANR 13, 33, 54; DA3; DLB 87; DLBY 81; INT CANR-33; MTCW 1

Fontane, Theodor 1819-1898 .... **NCLC 26**
See also DLB 129

Foote, Horton 1916- .. **CLC 51, 91; DAM DRAM**
See also CA 73-76; CANR 34, 51; DA3; DLB 26; INT CANR-34

Foote, Shelby 1916- .. **CLC 75; DAM NOV, POP**
See also CA 5-8R; CANR 3, 45, 74; DA3; DLB 2, 17; MTCW 2

Forbes, Esther 1891-1967 .... **CLC 12**
See also AAYA 17; CA 13-14; 25-28R; CAP 1; CLR 27; DLB 22; JRDA; MAICYA; SATA 2, 100

Forche, Carolyn (Louise) 1950- **CLC 25, 83, 86; DAM POET; PC 10**
See also CA 109; 117; CANR 50, 74; DA3; DLB 5, 193; INT 117; MTCW 1

Ford, Elbur
See Hibbert, Eleanor Alice Burford

Ford, Ford Madox 1873-1939 **TCLC 1, 15, 39, 57; DAM NOV**
See also CA 104; 132; CANR 74; CDBLB 1914-1945; DA3; DLB 162; MTCW 1, 2

Ford, Henry 1863-1947 .... **TCLC 73**
See also CA 115; 148

Ford, John 1586-(?) .... **DC 8**
See also CDBLB Before 1660; DAM DRAM; DA3; DLB 58

Ford, John 1895-1973 .... **CLC 16**
See also CA 45-48

Ford, Richard 1944- .... **CLC 46, 99**
See also CA 69-72; CANR 11, 47, 86; MTCW 1

Ford, Webster
See Masters, Edgar Lee

Foreman, Richard 1937- .... **CLC 50**
See also CA 65-68; CANR 32, 63

Forester, C(ecil) S(cott) 1899-1966 .... **CLC 35**
See also CA 73-76; 25-28R; CANR 83; DLB 191; SATA 13

Forez
See Mauriac, Francois (Charles)

Forman, James Douglas 1932- .... **CLC 21**
See also AAYA 17; CA 9-12R; CANR 4, 19, 42; JRDA; MAICYA; SATA 8, 70

Fornes, Maria Irene 1930- **CLC 39, 61; DC 10; HLCS 1**
See also CA 25-28R; CANR 28, 81; DLB 7; HW 1, 2; INT CANR-28; MTCW 1

Forrest, Leon (Richard) 1937-1997 **CLC 4; BLCS**
See also BW 2; CA 89-92; 162; CAAS 7; CANR 25, 52; DLB 33

Forster, E(dward) M(organ) 1879-1970 **CLC 1, 2, 3, 4, 9, 10, 13, 15, 22, 45, 77; DA; DAB; DAC; DAM MST, NOV; SSC 27; WLC**
See also AAYA 2; CA 13-14; 25-28R; CANR 45; CAP 1; CDBLB 1914-1945; DA3; DLB 34, 98, 162, 178, 195; DLBD 10; MTCW 1, 2; SATA 57

Forster, John 1812-1876 .... **NCLC 11**
See also DLB 144, 184

Forsyth, Frederick 1938- ... **CLC 2, 5, 36; DAM NOV, POP**
See also BEST 89:4; CA 85-88; CANR 38, 62; DLB 87; MTCW 1, 2

Forten, Charlotte L. .... **TCLC 16; BLC 2**
See also Grimke, Charlotte L(ottie) Forten
See also DLB 50

Foscolo, Ugo 1778-1827 .... **NCLC 8**

Fosse, Bob .... **CLC 20**

See also Fosse, Robert Louis

Fosse, Robert Louis 1927-1987
See Fosse, Bob
See also CA 110; 123

Foster, Stephen Collins 1826-1864 ..... **NCLC 26**

Foucault, Michel 1926-1984 ...... **CLC 31, 34, 69**
See also CA 105; 113; CANR 34; MTCW 1, 2

Fouque, Friedrich (Heinrich Karl) de la Motte 1777-1843 .... **NCLC 2**
See also DLB 90

Fourier, Charles 1772-1837 .... **NCLC 51**

Fournier, Pierre 1916- .... **CLC 11**
See also Gascar, Pierre
See also CA 89-92; CANR 16, 40

Fowles, John (Philip) 1926- **CLC 1, 2, 3, 4, 6, 9, 10, 15, 33, 87; DAB; DAC; DAM MST; SSC 33**
See also CA 5-8R; CANR 25, 71; CDBLB 1960 to Present; DA3; DLB 14, 139, 207; MTCW 1, 2; SATA 22

Fox, Paula 1923- .... **CLC 2, 8, 121**
See also AAYA 3; CA 73-76; CANR 20, 36, 62; CLR 1, 44; DLB 52; JRDA; MAICYA; MTCW 1; SATA 17, 60

Fox, William Price (Jr.) 1926- .... **CLC 22**
See also CA 17-20R; CAAS 19; CANR 11; DLB 2; DLBY 81

Foxe, John 1516(?)-1587 .... **LC 14**
See also DLB 132

Frame, Janet 1924- **CLC 2, 3, 6, 22, 66, 96; SSC 29**
See also Clutha, Janet Paterson Frame

France, Anatole .... **TCLC 9**
See also Thibault, Jacques Anatole Francois
See also DLB 123; MTCW 1

Francis, Claude 19(?)- .... **CLC 50**

Francis, Dick 1920- . **CLC 2, 22, 42, 102; DAM POP**
See also AAYA 5, 21; BEST 89:3; CA 5-8R; CANR 9, 42, 68; CDBLB 1960 to Present; DA3; DLB 87; INT CANR-9; MTCW 1, 2

Francis, Robert (Churchill) 1901-1987 **CLC 15**
See also CA 1-4R; 123; CANR 1

Frank, Anne(lies Marie) 1929-1945 **TCLC 17; DA; DAB; DAC; DAM MST; WLC**
See also AAYA 12; CA 113; 133; CANR 68; DA3; MTCW 1, 2; SATA 87; SATA-Brief 42

Frank, Bruno 1887-1945 .... **TCLC 81**
See also DLB 118

Frank, Elizabeth 1945- .... **CLC 39**
See also CA 121; 126; CANR 78; INT 126

Frankl, Viktor E(mil) 1905-1997 .... **CLC 93**
See also CA 65-68; 161

Franklin, Benjamin
See Hasek, Jaroslav (Matej Frantisek)

Franklin, Benjamin 1706-1790 **LC 25; DA; DAB; DAC; DAM MST; WLCS**
See also CDALB 1640-1865; DA3; DLB 24, 43, 73

Franklin, (Stella Maria Sarah) Miles (Lampe) 1879-1954 .... **TCLC 7**
See also CA 104; 164

Fraser, (Lady) Antonia (Pakenham) 1932- . **C L C 32, 107**
See also CA 85-88; CANR 44, 65; MTCW 1, 2; SATA-Brief 32

Fraser, George MacDonald 1925- .... **CLC 7**
See also CA 45-48; 180; CAAE 180; CANR 2, 48, 74; MTCW 1

Fraser, Sylvia 1935- .... **CLC 64**
See also CA 45-48; CANR 1, 16, 60

Frayn, Michael 1933- ... **CLC 3, 7, 31, 47; DAM DRAM, NOV**
See also CA 5-8R; CANR 30, 69; DLB 13, 14, 194; MTCW 1, 2

Fraze, Candida (Merrill) 1945- .... **CLC 50**
See also CA 126

Frazer, J(ames) G(eorge) 1854-1941 ... **TCLC 32**
See also CA 118

Frazer, Robert Caine
See Creasey, John

Frazer, Sir James George
See Frazer, J(ames) G(eorge)

Frazier, Charles 1950- .... **CLC 109**
See also CA 161

Frazier, Ian 1951- .... **CLC 46**
See also CA 130; CANR 54

Frederic, Harold 1856-1898 .... **NCLC 10**
See also DLB 12, 23; DLBD 13

Frederick, John
See Faust, Frederick (Schiller)

Frederick the Great 1712-1786 .... **LC 14**

Fredro, Aleksander 1793-1876 .... **NCLC 8**

Freeling, Nicolas 1927- .... **CLC 38**
See also CA 49-52; CAAS 12; CANR 1, 17, 50, 84; DLB 87

Freeman, Douglas Southall 1886-1953 **TCLC 11**
See also CA 109; DLB 17; DLBD 17

Freeman, Judith 1946- .... **CLC 55**
See also CA 148

Freeman, Mary E(leanor) Wilkins 1852-1930 **TCLC 9; SSC 1**
See also CA 106; 177; DLB 12, 78

Freeman, R(ichard) Austin 1862-1943 **TCLC 21**
See also CA 113; CANR 84; DLB 70

French, Albert 1943- .... **CLC 86**
See also BW 3; CA 167

French, Marilyn 1929- ... **CLC 10, 18, 60; DAM DRAM, NOV, POP**
See also CA 69-72; CANR 3, 31; INT CANR-31; MTCW 1, 2

French, Paul
See Asimov, Isaac

Freneau, Philip Morin 1752-1832 .... **NCLC 1**
See also DLB 37, 43

Freud, Sigmund 1856-1939 .... **TCLC 52**
See also CA 115; 133; CANR 69; MTCW 1, 2

Friedan, Betty (Naomi) 1921- .... **CLC 74**
See also CA 65-68; CANR 18, 45, 74; MTCW 1, 2

Friedlander, Saul 1932- .... **CLC 90**
See also CA 117; 130; CANR 72

Friedman, B(ernard) H(arper) 1926- ...... **CLC 7**
See also CA 1-4R; CANR 3, 48

Friedman, Bruce Jay 1930- .... **CLC 3, 5, 56**
See also CA 9-12R; CANR 25, 52; DLB 2, 28; INT CANR-25

Friel, Brian 1929- .....**CLC 5, 42, 59, 115; DC 8**
See also CA 21-24R; CANR 33, 69; DLB 13; MTCW 1

Friis-Baastad, Babbis Ellinor 1921-1970 **CLC 12**
See also CA 17-20R; 134; SATA 7

Frisch, Max (Rudolf) 1911-1991 **CLC 3, 9, 14, 18, 32, 44; DAM DRAM, NOV**
See also CA 85-88; 134; CANR 32, 74; DLB 69, 124; MTCW 1, 2

Fromentin, Eugene (Samuel Auguste) 1820-1876 **NCLC 10**
See also DLB 123

Frost, Frederick
See Faust, Frederick (Schiller)

Frost, Robert (Lee) 1874-1963 **CLC 1, 3, 4, 9, 10, 13, 15, 26, 34, 44; DA; DAB; DAC; DAM MST, POET; PC 1; WLC**
See also AAYA 21; CA 89-92; CANR 33; CDALB 1917-1929; DA3; DLB 54; DLBD 7; MTCW 1, 2; SATA 14

Froude, James Anthony 1818-1894 ..... **NCLC 43**
See also DLB 18, 57, 144

DAM MULT
See also BW 2, 3; CA 109; CANR 25, 53, 75;
DA3; DLB 67; MTCW 1

Gautier, Theophile 1811-1872 **NCLC 1, 59; DAM
POET; PC 18; SSC 20**
See also DLB 119

Gawsworth, John
See Bates, H(erbert) E(rnest)

Gay, John 1685-1732 .... **LC 49; DAM DRAM**
See also DLB 84, 95

Gay, Oliver
See Gogarty, Oliver St. John

Gaye, Marvin (Penze) 1939-1984 .... **CLC 26**
See also CA 112

Gebler, Carlo (Ernest) 1954- .... **CLC 39**
See also CA 119; 133

Gee, Maggie (Mary) 1948- .... **CLC 57**
See also CA 130; DLB 207

Gee, Maurice (Gough) 1931- .... **CLC 29**
See also CA 97-100; CANR 67; CLR 56; SATA
46, 101

Gelbart, Larry (Simon) 1923- .... **CLC 21, 61**
See also CA 73-76; CANR 45

Gelber, Jack 1932- .... **CLC 1, 6, 14, 79**
See also CA 1-4R; CANR 2; DLB 7

Gellhorn, Martha (Ellis) 1908-1998 **CLC 14, 60**
See also CA 77-80; 164; CANR 44; DLBY 82, 98

Genet, Jean 1910-1986 **CLC 1, 2, 5, 10, 14, 44, 46;
DAM DRAM**
See also CA 13-16R; CANR 18; DA3; DLB 72;
DLBY 86; MTCW 1, 2

Gent, Peter 1942- .... **CLC 29**
See also AITN 1; CA 89-92; DLBY 82

Gentile, Giovanni 1875-1944 .... **TCLC 96**
See also CA 119

Gentlewoman in New England, A
See Bradstreet, Anne

Gentlewoman in Those Parts, A
See Bradstreet, Anne

George, Jean Craighead 1919- .... **CLC 35**
See also AAYA 8; CA 5-8R; CANR 25; CLR 1;
DLB 52; JRDA; MAICYA; SATA 2, 68

George, Stefan (Anton) 1868-1933 .. **TCLC 2, 14**
See also CA 104

Georges, Georges Martin
See Simenon, Georges (Jacques Christian)

Gerhardi, William Alexander
See Gerhardie, William Alexander

Gerhardie, William Alexander 1895-1977 **CLC 5**
See also CA 25-28R; 73-76; CANR 18; DLB 36

Gerstler, Amy 1956- .... **CLC 70**
See also CA 146

Gertler, T. .... **CLC 34**
See also CA 116; 121; INT 121

Ghalib .... **NCLC 39, 78**
See also Ghalib, Hsadullah Khan

Ghalib, Hsadullah Khan 1797-1869
See Ghalib
See also DAM POET

Ghelderode, Michel de 1898-1962 **CLC 6, 11; DAM
DRAM**
See also CA 85-88; CANR 40, 77

Ghiselin, Brewster 1903- .... **CLC 23**
See also CA 13-16R; CAAS 10; CANR 13

Ghose, Aurabinda 1872-1950 .... **TCLC 63**
See also CA 163

Ghose, Zulfikar 1935- .... **CLC 42**
See also CA 65-68; CANR 67

Ghosh, Amitav 1956- .... **CLC 44**
See also CA 147; CANR 80

Giacosa, Giuseppe 1847-1906 .... **TCLC 7**
See also CA 104

Gibb, Lee

See Waterhouse, Keith (Spencer)

Gibbon, Lewis Grassic .... **TCLC 4**
See also Mitchell, James Leslie

Gibbons, Kaye 1960- ..... **CLC 50, 88; DAM POP**
See also CA 151; CANR 75; DA3; MTCW 1

Gibran, Kahlil 1883-1931 **TCLC 1, 9; DAM POET,
POP; PC 9**
See also CA 104; 150; DA3; MTCW 2

Gibran, Khalil
See Gibran, Kahlil

Gibson, William 1914- **CLC 23; DA; DAB; DAC;
DAM DRAM, MST**
See also CA 9-12R; CANR 9, 42, 75; DLB 7;
MTCW 1; SATA 66

Gibson, William (Ford) 1948- **CLC 39, 63; DAM
POP**
See also AAYA 12; CA 126; 133; CANR 52; DA3;
MTCW 1

Gide, Andre (Paul Guillaume) 1869-1951 **TCLC 5,
12, 36; DA; DAB; DAC; DAM MST, NOV;
SSC 13; WLC**
See also CA 104; 124; DA3; DLB 65; MTCW 1, 2

Gifford, Barry (Colby) 1946- .... **CLC 34**
See also CA 65-68; CANR 9, 30, 40

Gilbert, Frank
See De Voto, Bernard (Augustine)

Gilbert, W(illiam) S(chwenck) 1836-1911 **T C L C
3; DAM DRAM, POET**
See also CA 104; 173; SATA 36

Gilbreth, Frank B., Jr. 1911- .... **CLC 17**
See also CA 9-12R; SATA 2

Gilchrist, Ellen 1935- . **CLC 34, 48; DAM POP;
SSC 14**
See also CA 113; 116; CANR 41, 61; DLB 130;
MTCW 1, 2

Giles, Molly 1942- .... **CLC 39**
See also CA 126

Gill, Eric 1882-1940 .... **TCLC 85**

Gill, Patrick
See Creasey, John

Gilliam, Terry (Vance) 1940- .... **CLC 21**
See also Monty Python
See also AAYA 19; CA 108; 113; CANR 35; INT
113

Gillian, Jerry
See Gilliam, Terry (Vance)

Gilliatt, Penelope (Ann Douglass) 1932-1993 **CLC
2, 10, 13, 53**
See also AITN 2; CA 13-16R; 141; CANR 49;
DLB 14

Gilman, Charlotte (Anna) Perkins (Stetson) 1860-
1935 .... **TCLC 9, 37; SSC 13**
See also CA 106; 150; MTCW 1

Gilmour, David 1949- .... **CLC 35**
See also CA 138, 147

Gilpin, William 1724-1804 .... **NCLC 30**

Gilray, J. D.
See Mencken, H(enry) L(ouis)

Gilroy, Frank D(aniel) 1925- .... **CLC 2**
See also CA 81-84; CANR 32, 64, 86; DLB 7

Gilstrap, John 1957(?)- .... **CLC 99**
See also CA 160

Ginsberg, Allen 1926-1997 **CLC 1, 2, 3, 4, 6, 13,
36, 69, 109; DA; DAB; DAC; DAM MST,
POET; PC 4; WLC**
See also AITN 1; CA 1-4R; 157; CANR 2, 41, 63;
CDALB 1941-1968; DA3; DLB 5, 16, 169;
MTCW 1, 2

Ginzburg, Natalia 1916-1991 . **CLC 5, 11, 54, 70**
See also CA 85-88; 135; CANR 33; DLB 177;
MTCW 1, 2

Giono, Jean 1895-1970 .... **CLC 4, 11**
See also CA 45-48; 29-32R; CANR 2, 35; DLB 72;

MTCW 1

Giovanni, Nikki 1943- **CLC 2, 4, 19, 64, 117; BLC
2; DA; DAB; DAC; DAM MST, MULT, POET;
PC 19; WLCS**
See also AAYA 22; AITN 1; BW 2, 3; CA 29-
32R; CAAS 6; CANR 18, 41, 60; CDALBS;
CLR 6; DA3; DLB 5, 41; INT CANR-18;
MAICYA; MTCW 1, 2; SATA 24, 107

Giovene, Andrea 1904- .... **CLC 7**
See also CA 85-88

Gippius, Zinaida (Nikolayevna) 1869-1945
See Hippius, Zinaida
See also CA 106

Giraudoux, (Hippolyte) Jean 1882-1944 **TCLC 2, 7;
DAM DRAM**
See also CA 104; DLB 65

Gironella, Jose Maria 1917- .... **CLC 11**
See also CA 101

Gissing, George (Robert) 1857-1903 **TCLC 3, 24,
47; SSC 37**
See also CA 105; 167; DLB 18, 135, 184

Giurlani, Aldo
See Palazzeschi, Aldo

Gladkov, Fyodor (Vasilyevich) 1883-1958 **TCLC 27**
See also CA 170

Glanville, Brian (Lester) 1931- .... **CLC 6**
See also CA 5-8R; CAAS 9; CANR 3, 70; DLB
15, 139; SATA 42

Glasgow, Ellen (Anderson Gholson) 1873-1945
TCLC 2, 7; SSC 34
See also CA 104; 164; DLB 9, 12; MTCW 2

Glaspell, Susan 1882(?)-1948 . **TCLC 55; DC 10**
See also CA 110; 154; DLB 7, 9, 78; YABC 2

Glassco, John 1909-1981 .... **CLC 9**
See also CA 13-16R; 102; CANR 15; DLB 68

Glasscock, Amnesia
See Steinbeck, John (Ernst)

Glasser, Ronald J. 1940(?)- .... **CLC 37**

Glassman, Joyce
See Johnson, Joyce

Glendinning, Victoria 1937- .... **CLC 50**
See also CA 120; 127; CANR 59; DLB 155

Glissant, Edouard 1928- **CLC 10, 68; DAM MULT**
See also CA 153

Gloag, Julian 1930- .... **CLC 40**
See also AITN 1; CA 65-68; CANR 10, 70

Glowacki, Aleksander
See Prus, Boleslaw

Gluck, Louise (Elisabeth) 1943- **CLC 7, 22, 44, 81;
DAM POET; PC 16**
See also CA 33-36R; CANR 40, 69; DA3; DLB 5;
MTCW 2

Glyn, Elinor 1864-1943 .... **TCLC 72**
See also DLB 153

Gobineau, Joseph Arthur (Comte) de 1816-1882
NCLC 17
See also DLB 123

Godard, Jean-Luc 1930- .... **CLC 20**
See also CA 93-96

Godden, (Margaret) Rumer 1907-1998 . **CLC 53**
See also AAYA 6; CA 5-8R; 172; CANR 4, 27, 36,
55, 80; CLR 20; DLB 161; MAICYA; SAAS
12; SATA 3, 36; SATA-Obit 109

Godoy Alcayaga, Lucila 1889-1957
See Mistral, Gabriela
See also BW 2; CA 104; 131; CANR 81; DAM
MULT; HW 1, 2; MTCW 1, 2

Godwin, Gail (Kathleen) 1937- **CLC 5, 8, 22, 31,
69, 125; DAM POP**
See also CA 29-32R; CANR 15, 43, 69; DA3; DLB
6; INT CANR-15; MTCW 1, 2

Godwin, William 1756-1836 .... **NCLC 14**
See also CDBLB 1789-1832; DLB 39, 104, 142,

DAC; DAM MST; PC 2; WLC
See also CDBLB 1660-1789; DA3; DLB 109

Grayson, David
See Baker, Ray Stannard

Grayson, Richard (A.) 1951- .... **CLC 38**
See also CA 85-88; CANR 14, 31, 57

Greeley, Andrew M(oran) 1928- . **CLC 28; DAM POP**
See also CA 5-8R; CAAS 7; CANR 7, 43, 69; DA3; MTCW 1, 2

Green, Anna Katharine 1846-1935 ..... **TCLC 63**
See also CA 112; 159; DLB 202

Green, Brian
See Card, Orson Scott

Green, Hannah
See Greenberg, Joanne (Goldenberg)

Green, Hannah 1927(?)-1996 .... **CLC 3**
See also CA 73-76; CANR 59

Green, Henry 1905-1973 .... **CLC 2, 13, 97**
See also Yorke, Henry Vincent
See also CA 175; DLB 15

Green, Julian (Hartridge) 1900-1998
See Green, Julien
See also CA 21-24R; 169; CANR 33; DLB 4, 72; MTCW 1

Green, Julien .... **CLC 3, 11, 77**
See also Green, Julian (Hartridge)
See also MTCW 2

Green, Paul (Eliot) 1894-1981 ..... **CLC 25; DAM DRAM**
See also AITN 1; CA 5-8R; 103; CANR 3; DLB 7, 9; DLBY 81

Greenberg, Ivan 1908-1973
See Rahv, Philip
See also CA 85-88

Greenberg, Joanne (Goldenberg) 1932- . **CLC 7, 30**
See also AAYA 12; CA 5-8R; CANR 14, 32, 69; SATA 25

Greenberg, Richard 1959(?)- .... **CLC 57**
See also CA 138

Greene, Bette 1934- .... **CLC 30**
See also AAYA 7; CA 53-56; CANR 4; CLR 2; JRDA; MAICYA; SAAS 16; SATA 8, 102

Greene, Gael .... **CLC 8**
See also CA 13-16R; CANR 10

Greene, Graham (Henry) 1904-1991 **CLC 1, 3, 6, 9, 14, 18, 27, 37, 70, 72, 125; DA; DAB; DAC; DAM MST, NOV; SSC 29; WLC**
See also AITN 2; CA 13-16R; 133; CANR 35, 61; CDBLB 1945-1960; DA3; DLB 13, 15, 77, 100, 162, 201, 204; DLBY 91; MTCW 1, 2; SATA 20

Greene, Robert 1558-1592 .... **LC 41**
See also DLB 62, 167

Greer, Richard
See Silverberg, Robert

Gregor, Arthur 1923- .... **CLC 9**
See also CA 25-28R; CAAS 10; CANR 11; SATA 36

Gregor, Lee
See Pohl, Frederik

Gregory, Isabella Augusta (Persse) 1852-1932 **TCLC 1**
See also CA 104; DLB 10

Gregory, J. Dennis
See Williams, John A(lfred)

Grendon, Stephen
See Derleth, August (William)

Grenville, Kate 1950- .... **CLC 61**
See also CA 118; CANR 53

Grenville, Pelham
See Wodehouse, P(elham) G(renville)

Greve, Felix Paul (Berthold Friedrich) 1879-1948

See Grove, Frederick Philip
See also CA 104; 141, 175; CANR 79; DAC; DAM MST

Grey, Zane 1872-1939 .... **TCLC 6; DAM POP**
See also CA 104; 132; DA3; DLB 212; MTCW 1, 2

Grieg, (Johan) Nordahl (Brun) 1902-1943 **TCLC 10**
See also CA 107

Grieve, C(hristopher) M(urray) 1892-1978 **CLC 11, 19; DAM POET**
See also MacDiarmid, Hugh; Pteleon
See also CA 5-8R; 85-88; CANR 33; MTCW 1

Griffin, Gerald 1803-1840 .... **NCLC 7**
See also DLB 159

Griffin, John Howard 1920-1980 .... **CLC 68**
See also AITN 1; CA 1-4R; 101; CANR 2

Griffin, Peter 1942- .... **CLC 39**
See also CA 136

Griffith, D(avid Lewelyn) W(ark) 1875(?)-1948 **TCLC 68**
See also CA 119; 150; CANR 80

Griffith, Lawrence
See Griffith, D(avid Lewelyn) W(ark)

Griffiths, Trevor 1935- .... **CLC 13, 52**
See also CA 97-100; CANR 45; DLB 13

Griggs, Sutton Elbert 1872-1930(?) .... **TCLC 77**
See also CA 123; DLB 50

Grigson, Geoffrey (Edward Harvey) 1905-1985 **CLC 7, 39**
See also CA 25-28R; 118; CANR 20, 33; DLB 27; MTCW 1, 2

Grillparzer, Franz 1791-1872 . **NCLC 1; SSC 37**
See also DLB 133

Grimble, Reverend Charles James
See Eliot, T(homas) S(tearns)

Grimke, Charlotte L(ottie) Forten 1837(?)-1914
See Forten, Charlotte L.
See also BW 1; CA 117; 124; DAM MULT, POET

Grimm, Jacob Ludwig Karl 1785-1863 **NCLC 3, 77; SSC 36**
See also DLB 90; MAICYA; SATA 22

Grimm, Wilhelm Karl 1786-1859 ..**NCLC 3, 77; SSC 36**
See also DLB 90; MAICYA; SATA 22

Grimmelshausen, Johann Jakob Christoffel von 1621-1676 .... **LC 6**
See also DLB 168

Grindel, Eugene 1895-1952
See Eluard, Paul
See also CA 104

Grisham, John 1955- .... **CLC 84; DAM POP**
See also AAYA 14; CA 138; CANR 47, 69; DA3; MTCW 2

Grossman, David 1954- .... **CLC 67**
See also CA 138

Grossman, Vasily (Semenovich) 1905-1964 **CLC 41**
See also CA 124; 130; MTCW 1

Grove, Frederick Philip .... **TCLC 4**
See also Greve, Felix Paul (Berthold Friedrich)
See also DLB 92

Grubb
See Crumb, R(obert)

Grumbach, Doris (Isaac) 1918- . **CLC 13, 22, 64**
See also CA 5-8R; CAAS 2; CANR 9, 42, 70; INT CANR-9; MTCW 2

Grundtvig, Nicolai Frederik Severin 1783-1872 **NCLC 1**

Grunge
See Crumb, R(obert)

Grunwald, Lisa 1959- .... **CLC 44**
See also CA 120

Guare, John 1938- **CLC 8, 14, 29, 67; DAM DRAM**
See also CA 73-76; CANR 21, 69; DLB 7; MTCW 1, 2

Gudjonsson, Halldor Kiljan 1902-1998
See Laxness, Halldor
See also CA 103; 164

Guenter, Erich
See Eich, Guenter

Guest, Barbara 1920- .... **CLC 34**
See also CA 25-28R; CANR 11, 44, 84; DLB 5, 193

Guest, Edgar A(lbert) 1881-1959 .... **TCLC 95**
See also CA 112; 168

Guest, Judith (Ann) 1936- **CLC 8, 30; DAM NOV, POP**
See also AAYA 7; CA 77-80; CANR 15, 75; DA3; INT CANR-15; MTCW 1, 2

Guevara, Che .... **CLC 87; HLC 1**
See also Guevara (Serna), Ernesto

Guevara (Serna), Ernesto 1928-1967 ... **CLC 87; DAM MULT; HLC 1**
See also Guevara, Che
See also CA 127; 111; CANR 56; HW 1

Guicciardini, Francesco 1483-1540 .... **LC 49**

Guild, Nicholas M. 1944- .... **CLC 33**
See also CA 93-96

Guillemin, Jacques
See Sartre, Jean-Paul

Guillen, Jorge 1893-1984 **CLC 11; DAM MULT, POET; HLCS 1**
See also CA 89-92; 112; DLB 108; HW 1

Guillen, Nicolas (Cristobal) 1902-1989 **CLC 48, 79; BLC 2; DAM MST, MULT, POET; HLC 1; PC 23**
See also BW 2; CA 116; 125; 129; CANR 84; HW 1

Guillevic, (Eugene) 1907- .... **CLC 33**
See also CA 93-96

Guillois
See Desnos, Robert

Guillois, Valentin
See Desnos, Robert

Guimaraes Rosa, Joao 1908-1967
See also CA 175; HLCS 2

Guiney, Louise Imogen 1861-1920 ...... **TCLC 41**
See also CA 160; DLB 54

Guiraldes, Ricardo (Guillermo) 1886-1927 **TCLC 39**
See also CA 131; HW 1; MTCW 1

Gumilev, Nikolai (Stepanovich) 1886-1921 **TCLC 60**
See also CA 165

Gunesekera, Romesh 1954- .... **CLC 91**
See also CA 159

Gunn, Bill .... **CLC 5**
See also Gunn, William Harrison
See also DLB 38

Gunn, Thom(son William) 1929- **CLC 3, 6, 18, 32, 81; DAM POET; PC 26**
See also CA 17-20R; CANR 9, 33; CDBLB 1960 to Present; DLB 27; INT CANR-33; MTCW 1

Gunn, William Harrison 1934(?)-1989
See Gunn, Bill
See also AITN 1; BW 1, 3; CA 13-16R; 128; CANR 12, 25, 76

Gunnars, Kristjana 1948- .... **CLC 69**
See also CA 113; DLB 60

Gurdjieff, G(eorgei) I(vanovich) 1877(?)-1949 **TCLC 71**
See also CA 157

Gurganus, Allan 1947- .... **CLC 70; DAM POP**
See also BEST 90:1; CA 135

Gurney, A(lbert) R(amsdell), Jr. 1930- **CLC 32,**

Harper, Frances Ellen Watkins 1825-1911**TCLC 14; BLC 2; DAM MULT, POET; PC 21**
See also BW 1, 3; CA 111; 125; CANR 79; DLB 50

Harper, Michael S(teven) 1938- .... **CLC 7, 22**
See also BW 1; CA 33-36R; CANR 24; DLB 41

Harper, Mrs. F. E. W.
See Harper, Frances Ellen Watkins

Harris, Christie (Lucy) Irwin 1907- ..... **CLC 12**
See also CA 5-8R; CANR 6, 83; CLR 47; DLB 88; JRDA; MAICYA; SAAS 10; SATA 6, 74

Harris, Frank 1856-1931 .... **TCLC 24**
See also CA 109; 150; CANR 80; DLB 156, 197

Harris, George Washington 1814-1869**NCLC 23**
See also DLB 3, 11

Harris, Joel Chandler 1848-1908**TCLC 2; SSC 19**
See also CA 104; 137; CANR 80; CLR 49; DLB 11, 23, 42, 78, 91; MAICYA; SATA 100; YABC 1

Harris, John (Wyndham Parkes Lucas) Beynon 1903-1969
See Wyndham, John
See also CA 102; 89-92; CANR 84

Harris, MacDonald .... **CLC 9**
See also Heiney, Donald (William)

Harris, Mark 1922- .... **CLC 19**
See also CA 5-8R; CAAS 3; CANR 2, 55, 83; DLB 2; DLBY 80

Harris, (Theodore) Wilson 1921- .... **CLC 25**
See also BW 2, 3; CA 65-68; CAAS 16; CANR 11, 27, 69; DLB 117; MTCW 1

Harrison, Elizabeth Cavanna 1909-
See Cavanna, Betty
See also CA 9-12R; CANR 6, 27, 85

Harrison, Harry (Max) 1925- .... **CLC 42**
See also CA 1-4R; CANR 5, 21, 84; DLB 8; SATA 4

Harrison, James (Thomas) 1937-**CLC 6, 14, 33, 66; SSC 19**
See also CA 13-16R; CANR 8, 51, 79; DLBY 82; INT CANR-8

Harrison, Jim
See Harrison, James (Thomas)

Harrison, Kathryn 1961- .... **CLC 70**
See also CA 144; CANR 68

Harrison, Tony 1937- .... **CLC 43**
See also CA 65-68; CANR 44; DLB 40; MTCW 1

Harriss, Will(ard Irvin) 1922- .... **CLC 34**
See also CA 111

Harson, Sley
See Ellison, Harlan (Jay)

Hart, Ellis
See Ellison, Harlan (Jay)

Hart, Josephine 1942(?)- .... **CLC 70; DAM POP**
See also CA 138; CANR 70

Hart, Moss 1904-1961 ..... **CLC 66; DAM DRAM**
See also CA 109; 89-92; CANR 84; DLB 7

Harte, (Francis) Bret(t) 1836(?)-1902**TCLC 1, 25; DA; DAC; DAM MST; SSC 8; WLC**
See also CA 104; 140; CANR 80; CDALB 1865-1917; DA3; DLB 12, 64, 74, 79, 186; SATA 26

Hartley, L(eslie) P(oles) 1895-1972 ... **CLC 2, 22**
See also CA 45-48; 37-40R; CANR 33; DLB 15, 139; MTCW 1, 2

Hartman, Geoffrey H. 1929- .... **CLC 27**
See also CA 117; 125; CANR 79; DLB 67

Hartmann, Eduard von 1842-1906 .... **TCLC 97**

Hartmann, Sadakichi 1867-1944 .... **TCLC 73**
See also CA 157; DLB 54

Hartmann von Aue c. 1160-c. 1205 ..... **CMLC 15**
See also DLB 138

Hartmann von Aue 1170-1210 .... **CMLC 15**

Haruf, Kent 1943- .... **CLC 34**

See also CA 149

Harwood, Ronald 1934- .. **CLC 32; DAM DRAM, MST**
See also CA 1-4R; CANR 4, 55; DLB 13

Hasegawa Tatsunosuke
See Futabatei, Shimei

Hasek, Jaroslav (Matej Frantisek) 1883-1923 **TCLC 4**
See also CA 104; 129; MTCW 1, 2

Hass, Robert 1941- .... **CLC 18, 39, 99; PC 16**
See also CA 111; CANR 30, 50, 71; DLB 105, 206; SATA 94

Hastings, Hudson
See Kuttner, Henry

Hastings, Selina .... **CLC 44**

Hathorne, John 1641-1717 .... **LC 38**

Hatteras, Amelia
See Mencken, H(enry) L(ouis)

Hatteras, Owen .... **TCLC 18**
See also Mencken, H(enry) L(ouis); Nathan, George Jean

Hauptmann, Gerhart (Johann Robert) 1862-1946 **TCLC 4; DAM DRAM; SSC 37**
See also CA 104; 153; DLB 66, 118

Havel, Vaclav 1936-**CLC 25, 58, 65; DAM DRAM; DC 6**
See also CA 104; CANR 36, 63; DA3; MTCW 1, 2

Haviaras, Stratis .... **CLC 33**
See also Chaviaras, Strates

Hawes, Stephen 1475(?)-1523(?) .... **LC 17**
See also DLB 132

Hawkes, John (Clendennin Burne, Jr.) 1925-1998 **CLC 1, 2, 3, 4, 7, 9, 14, 15; 27, 49**
See also CA 1-4R; 167; CANR 2, 47, 64; DLB 2, 7; DLBY 80, 98; MTCW 1, 2

Hawking, S. W.
See Hawking, Stephen W(illiam)

Hawking, Stephen W(illiam) 1942-**CLC 63, 105**
See also AAYA 13; BEST 89:1; CA 126; 129; CANR 48; DA3; MTCW 2

Hawkins, Anthony Hope
See Hope, Anthony

Hawthorne, Julian 1846-1934 .... **TCLC 25**
See also CA 165

Hawthorne, Nathaniel 1804-1864 **NCLC 39; DA; DAB; DAC; DAM MST, NOV; SSC 3, 29; WLC**
See also AAYA 18; CDALB 1640-1865; DA3; DLB 1, 74; YABC 2

Haxton, Josephine Ayres 1921-
See Douglas, Ellen
See also CA 115; CANR 41, 83

Hayaseca y Eizaguirre, Jorge
See Echegaray (y Eizaguirre), Jose (Maria Waldo)

Hayashi, Fumiko 1904-1951 .... **TCLC 27**
See also CA 161; DLB 180

Haycraft, Anna 1932-
See Ellis, Alice Thomas
See also CA 122; CANR 85; MTCW 2

Hayden, Robert E(arl) 1913-1980**CLC 5, 9, 14, 37; BLC 2; DA; DAC; DAM MST, MULT, POET; PC 6**
See also BW 1, 3; CA 69-72; 97-100; CABS 2; CANR 24, 75, 82; CDALB 1941-1968; DLB 5, 76; MTCW 1, 2; SATA 19; SATA-Obit 26

Hayford, J(oseph) E(phraim) Casely
See Casely-Hayford, J(oseph) E(phraim)

Hayman, Ronald 1932- .... **CLC 44**
See also CA 25-28R; CANR 18, 50; DLB 155

Haywood, Eliza (Fowler) 1693(?)-1756 . **LC 1, 44**
See also DLB 39

Hazlitt, William 1778-1830 .... **NCLC 29, 82**
See also DLB 110, 158

Hazzard, Shirley 1931- .... **CLC 18**
See also CA 9-12R; CANR 4, 70; DLBY 82; MTCW 1

Head, Bessie 1937-1986**CLC 25, 67; BLC 2; DAM MULT**
See also BW 2, 3; CA 29-32R; 119; CANR 25, 82; DA3; DLB 117; MTCW 1, 2

Headon, (Nicky) Topper 1956(?)- .... **CLC 30**

Heaney, Seamus (Justin) 1939-**CLC 5, 7, 14, 25, 37, 74, 91; DAB; DAM POET; PC 18; WLCS**
See also CA 85-88; CANR 25, 48, 75; CDBLB 1960 to Present; DA3; DLB 40; DLBY 95; MTCW 1, 2

Hearn, (Patricio) Lafcadio (Tessima Carlos) 1850-1904 .... **TCLC 9**
See also CA 105; 166; DLB 12, 78, 189

Hearne, Vicki 1946- .... **CLC 56**
See also CA 139

Hearon, Shelby 1931- .... **CLC 63**
See also AITN 2; CA 25-28R; CANR 18, 48

Heat-Moon, William Least .... **CLC 29**
See also Trogdon, William (Lewis)
See also AAYA 9

Hebbel, Friedrich 1813-1863 .... **NCLC 43; DAM DRAM**
See also DLB 129

Hebert, Anne 1916- **CLC 4, 13, 29; DAC; DAM MST, POET**
See also CA 85-88; CANR 69; DA3; DLB 68; MTCW 1, 2

Hecht, Anthony (Evan) 1923-**CLC 8, 13, 19; DAM POET**
See also CA 9-12R; CANR 6; DLB 5, 169

Hecht, Ben 1894-1964 .... **CLC 8**
See also CA 85-88; DLB 7, 9, 25, 26, 28, 86

Hedayat, Sadeq 1903-1951 .... **TCLC 21**
See also CA 120

Hegel, Georg Wilhelm Friedrich 1770-1831 **NCLC 46**
See also DLB 90

Heidegger, Martin 1889-1976 .... **CLC 24**
See also CA 81-84; 65-68; CANR 34; MTCW 1, 2

Heidenstam, (Carl Gustaf) Verner von 1859-1940 **TCLC 5**
See also CA 104

Heifner, Jack 1946- .... **CLC 11**
See also CA 105; CANR 47

Heijermans, Herman 1864-1924 .... **TCLC 24**
See also CA 123

Heilbrun, Carolyn G(old) 1926- .... **CLC 25**
See also CA 45-48; CANR 1, 28, 58

Heine, Heinrich 1797-1856 . **NCLC 4, 54; PC 25**
See also DLB 90

Heinemann, Larry (Curtiss) 1944- .... **CLC 50**
See also CA 110; CAAS 21; CANR 31, 81; DLBD 9; INT CANR-31

Heiney, Donald (William) 1921-1993
See Harris, MacDonald
See also CA 1-4R; 142; CANR 3, 58

Heinlein, Robert A(nson) 1907-1988**CLC 1, 3, 8, 14, 26, 55; DAM POP**
See also AAYA 17; CA 1-4R; 125; CANR 1, 20, 53; DA3; DLB 8; JRDA; MAICYA; MTCW 1, 2; SATA 9, 69; SATA-Obit 56

Helforth, John
See Doolittle, Hilda

Hellenhofferu, Vojtech Kapristian z
See Hasek, Jaroslav (Matej Frantisek)

Heller, Joseph 1923- **CLC 1, 3, 5, 8, 11, 36, 63; DA; DAB; DAC; DAM MST, NOV, POP; WLC**

Hiraoka, Kimitake 1925-1970
See Mishima, Yukio
See also CA 97-100; 29-32R; DAM DRAM; DA3;
MTCW 1, 2

Hirsch, E(ric) D(onald), Jr. 1928- .... **CLC 79**
See also CA 25-28R; CANR 27, 51; DLB 67; INT
CANR-27; MTCW 1

Hirsch, Edward 1950- .... **CLC 31, 50**
See also CA 104; CANR 20, 42; DLB 120

Hitchcock, Alfred (Joseph) 1899-1980 .. **CLC 16**
See also AAYA 22; CA 159; 97-100; SATA 27;
SATA-Obit 24

Hitler, Adolf 1889-1945 .... **TCLC 53**
See also CA 117; 147

Hoagland, Edward 1932- .... **CLC 28**
See also CA 1-4R; CANR 2, 31, 57; DLB 6; SATA
51

Hoban, Russell (Conwell) 1925-**CLC 7, 25; DAM
NOV**
See also CA 5-8R; CANR 23, 37, 66; CLR 3; DLB
52; MAICYA; MTCW 1, 2; SATA 1, 40, 78

Hobbes, Thomas 1588-1679 .... **LC 36**
See also DLB 151

Hobbs, Perry
See Blackmur, R(ichard) P(almer)

Hobson, Laura Z(ametkin) 1900-1986 **CLC 7, 25**
See also CA 17-20R; 118; CANR 55; DLB 28;
SATA 52

Hochhuth, Rolf 1931-**CLC 4, 11, 18; DAM DRAM**
See also CA 5-8R; CANR 33, 75; DLB 124; MTCW
1, 2

Hochman, Sandra 1936- .... **CLC 3, 8**
See also CA 5-8R; DLB 5

Hochwaelder, Fritz 1911-1986 ..... **CLC 36; DAM
DRAM**
See also CA 29-32R; 120; CANR 42; MTCW 1

Hochwalder, Fritz
See Hochwaelder, Fritz

Hocking, Mary (Eunice) 1921- .... **CLC 13**
See also CA 101; CANR 18, 40

Hodgins, Jack 1938- .... **CLC 23**
See also CA 93-96; DLB 60

Hodgson, William Hope 1877(?)-1918 **TCLC 13**
See also CA 111; 164; DLB 70, 153, 156, 178;
MTCW 2

Hoeg, Peter 1957- .... **CLC 95**
See also CA 151; CANR 75; DA3; MTCW 2

Hoffman, Alice 1952- .... **CLC 51; DAM NOV**
See also CA 77-80; CANR 34, 66; MTCW 1, 2

Hoffman, Daniel (Gerard) 1923- . **CLC 6, 13, 23**
See also CA 1-4R; CANR 4; DLB 5

Hoffman, Stanley 1944- .... **CLC 5**
See also CA 77-80

Hoffman, William M(oses) 1939- .... **CLC 40**
See also CA 57-60; CANR 11, 71

Hoffmann, E(rnst) T(heodor) A(madeus) 1776-1822
NCLC 2; SSC 13
See also DLB 90; SATA 27

Hofmann, Gert 1931- .... **CLC 54**
See also CA 128

Hofmannsthal, Hugo von 1874-1929 ... **TCLC 11;
DAM DRAM; DC 4**
See also CA 106; 153; DLB 81, 118

Hogan, Linda 1947- .... **CLC 73; DAM MULT**
See also CA 120; CANR 45, 73; DLB 175; NNAL

Hogarth, Charles
See Creasey, John

Hogarth, Emmett
See Polonsky, Abraham (Lincoln)

Hogg, James 1770-1835 .... **NCLC 4**
See also DLB 93, 116, 159

Holbach, Paul Henri Thiry Baron 1723-1789 **L C
14**

Holberg, Ludvig 1684-1754 .... **LC 6**

Holden, Ursula 1921- .... **CLC 18**
See also CA 101; CAAS 8; CANR 22

Holderlin, (Johann Christian) Friedrich 1770-1843
NCLC 16; PC 4

Holdstock, Robert
See Holdstock, Robert P.

Holdstock, Robert P. 1948- .... **CLC 39**
See also CA 131; CANR 81

Holland, Isabelle 1920- .... **CLC 21**
See also AAYA 11; CA 21-24R, 181; CAAE 181;
CANR 10, 25, 47; CLR 57; JRDA; MAICYA;
SATA 8, 70; SATA-Essay 103

Holland, Marcus
See Caldwell, (Janet Miriam) Taylor (Holland)

Hollander, John 1929- .... **CLC 2, 5, 8, 14**
See also CA 1-4R; CANR 1, 52; DLB 5; SATA 13

Hollander, Paul
See Silverberg, Robert

Holleran, Andrew 1943(?)- .... **CLC 38**
See also CA 144

Hollinghurst, Alan 1954- .... **CLC 55, 91**
See also CA 114; DLB 207

Hollis, Jim
See Summers, Hollis (Spurgeon, Jr.)

Holly, Buddy 1936-1959 .... **TCLC 65**

Holmes, Gordon
See Shiel, M(atthew) P(hipps)

Holmes, John
See Souster, (Holmes) Raymond

Holmes, John Clellon 1926-1988 .... **CLC 56**
See also CA 9-12R; 125; CANR 4; DLB 16

Holmes, Oliver Wendell, Jr. 1841-1935**TCLC 77**
See also CA 114

Holmes, Oliver Wendell 1809-1894**NCLC 14, 81**
See also CDALB 1640-1865; DLB 1, 189; SATA
34

Holmes, Raymond
See Souster, (Holmes) Raymond

Holt, Victoria
See Hibbert, Eleanor Alice Burford

Holub, Miroslav 1923-1998 .... **CLC 4**
See also CA 21-24R; 169; CANR 10

Homer c. 8th cent. B.C.-**CMLC 1, 16; DA; DAB;
DAC; DAM MST, POET; PC 23; WLCS**
See also DA3; DLB 176

Hongo, Garrett Kaoru 1951- .... **PC 23**
See also CA 133; CAAS 22; DLB 120

Honig, Edwin 1919- .... **CLC 33**
See also CA 5-8R; CAAS 8; CANR 4, 45; DLB 5

Hood, Hugh (John Blagdon) 1928- .. **CLC 15, 28**
See also CA 49-52; CAAS 17; CANR 1, 33; DLB
53

Hood, Thomas 1799-1845 .... **NCLC 16**
See also DLB 96

Hooker, (Peter) Jeremy 1941- .... **CLC 43**
See also CA 77-80; CANR 22; DLB 40

hooks, bell .... **CLC 94; BLCS**
See also Watkins, Gloria
See also MTCW 2

Hope, A(lec) D(erwent) 1907- .... **CLC 3, 51**
See also CA 21-24R; CANR 33, 74; MTCW 1, 2

Hope, Anthony 1863-1933 .... **TCLC 83**
See also CA 157; DLB 153, 156

Hope, Brian
See Creasey, John

Hope, Christopher (David Tully) 1944- . **CLC 52**
See also CA 106; CANR 47; SATA 62

Hopkins, Gerard Manley 1844-1889 . **NCLC 17;
DA; DAB; DAC; DAM MST, POET; PC 15;
WLC**
See also CDBLB 1890-1914; DA3; DLB 35, 57

Hopkins, John (Richard) 1931-1998 .... **CLC 4**
See also CA 85-88; 169

Hopkins, Pauline Elizabeth 1859-1930**TCLC 28;
BLC 2; DAM MULT**
See also BW 2, 3; CA 141; CANR 82; DLB 50

Hopkinson, Francis 1737-1791 .... **LC 25**
See also DLB 31

Hopley-Woolrich, Cornell George 1903-1968
See Woolrich, Cornell
See also CA 13-14; CANR 58; CAP 1; MTCW 2

Horatio
See Proust, (Valentin-Louis-George-Eugene-)
Marcel

Horgan, Paul (George Vincent O'Shaughnessy)
1903-1995 .... **CLC 9, 53; DAM NOV**
See also CA 13-16R; 147; CANR 9, 35; DLB 212;
DLBY 85; INT CANR-9; MTCW 1, 2; SATA
13; SATA-Obit 84

Horn, Peter
See Kuttner, Henry

Hornem, Horace Esq.
See Byron, George Gordon (Noel)

Horney, Karen (Clementine Theodore Danielsen)
1885-1952 .... **TCLC 71**
See also CA 114; 165

Hornung, E(rnest) W(illiam) 1866-1921**TCLC 59**
See also CA 108; 160; DLB 70

Horovitz, Israel (Arthur) 1939- ..**CLC 56; DAM
DRAM**
See also CA 33-36R; CANR 46, 59; DLB 7

Horvath, Odon von
See Horvath, Oedoen von
See also DLB 85, 124

Horvath, Oedoen von 1901-1938 .... **TCLC 45**
See also Horvath, Odon von
See also CA 118

Horwitz, Julius 1920-1986 .... **CLC 14**
See also CA 9-12R; 119; CANR 12

Hospital, Janette Turner 1942- .... **CLC 42**
See also CA 108; CANR 48

Hostos, E. M. de
See Hostos (y Bonilla), Eugenio Maria de

Hostos, Eugenio M. de
See Hostos (y Bonilla), Eugenio Maria de

Hostos, Eugenio Maria
See Hostos (y Bonilla), Eugenio Maria de

Hostos (y Bonilla), Eugenio Maria de 1839-1903
TCLC 24
See also CA 123; 131; HW 1

Houdini
See Lovecraft, H(oward) P(hillips)

Hougan, Carolyn 1943- .... **CLC 34**
See also CA 139

Household, Geoffrey (Edward West) 1900-1988
CLC 11
See also CA 77-80; 126; CANR 58; DLB 87;
SATA 14; SATA-Obit 59

Housman, A(lfred) E(dward) 1859-1936 **TCLC 1,
10; DA; DAB; DAC; DAM MST, POET; PC
2; WLCS**
See also CA 104; 125; DA3; DLB 19; MTCW 1, 2

Housman, Laurence 1865-1959 .... **TCLC 7**
See also CA 106; 155; DLB 10; SATA 25

Howard, Elizabeth Jane 1923- .... **CLC 7, 29**
See also CA 5-8R; CANR 8, 62

Howard, Maureen 1930- .... **CLC 5, 14, 46**
See also CA 53-56; CANR 31, 75; DLBY 83; INT
CANR-31; MTCW 1, 2

Howard, Richard 1929- .... **CLC 7, 10, 47**
See also AITN 1; CA 85-88; CANR 25, 80; DLB
5; INT CANR-25

Howard, Robert E(rvin) 1906-1936 .... **TCLC 8**
See also CA 105; 157

Howard, Warren F.

See Wojciechowska, Maia (Teresa)

Larkin, Philip (Arthur) 1922-1985**CLC 3, 5, 8, 9, 13, 18, 33, 39, 64; DAB; DAM MST, POET; PC 21**
See also CA 5-8R; 117; CANR 24, 62; CDBLB 1960 to Present; DA3; DLB 27; MTCW 1, 2

Larra (y Sanchez de Castro), Mariano Jose de 1809-1837 ....**NCLC 17**

Larsen, Eric 1941- ....**CLC 55**
See also CA 132

Larsen, Nella 1891-1964 **CLC 37; BLC 2; DAM MULT**
See also BW 1; CA 125; CANR 83; DLB 51

Larson, Charles R(aymond) 1938- ....**CLC 31**
See also CA 53-56; CANR 4

Larson, Jonathan 1961-1996 ....**CLC 99**
See also AAYA 28; CA 156

Las Casas, Bartolome de 1474-1566 ....**LC 31**

Lasch, Christopher 1932-1994 ....**CLC 102**
See also CA 73-76; 144; CANR 25; MTCW 1, 2

Lasker-Schueler, Else 1869-1945 ....**TCLC 57**
See also DLB 66, 124

Laski, Harold 1893-1950 ....**TCLC 79**

Latham, Jean Lee 1902-1995 ....**CLC 12**
See also AITN 1; CA 5-8R; CANR 7, 84; CLR 50; MAICYA; SATA 2, 68

Latham, Mavis
See Clark, Mavis Thorpe

Lathen, Emma ....**CLC 2**
See also Hennissart, Martha; Latsis, Mary J(ane)

Lathrop, Francis
See Leiber, Fritz (Reuter, Jr.)

Latsis, Mary J(ane) 1927(?)-1997
See Lathen, Emma
See also CA 85-88; 162

Lattimore, Richmond (Alexander) 1906-1984**CLC 3**
See also CA 1-4R; 112; CANR 1

Laughlin, James 1914-1997 ....**CLC 49**
See also CA 21-24R; 162; CAAS 22; CANR 9, 47; DLB 48; DLBY 96, 97

Laurence, (Jean) Margaret (Wemyss) 1926-1987 **CLC 3, 6, 13, 50, 62; DAC; DAM MST; SSC 7**
See also CA 5-8R; 121; CANR 33; DLB 53; MTCW 1, 2; SATA-Obit 50

Laurent, Antoine 1952- ....**CLC 50**

Lauscher, Hermann
See Hesse, Hermann

Lautreamont, Comte de 1846-1870**NCLC 12; SSC 14**

Laverty, Donald
See Blish, James (Benjamin)

Lavin, Mary 1912-1996 ....**CLC 4, 18, 99; SSC 4**
See also CA 9-12R; 151; CANR 33; DLB 15; MTCW 1

Lavond, Paul Dennis
See Kornbluth, C(yril) M.; Pohl, Frederik

Lawler, Raymond Evenor 1922- ....;......**CLC 58**
See also CA 103

Lawrence, D(avid) H(erbert Richards) 1885-1930 **TCLC 2, 9, 16, 33, 48, 61, 93; DA; DAB; DAC; DAM MST, NOV, POET; SSC 4, 19; WLC**
See also CA 104; 121; CDBLB 1914-1945; DA3; DLB 10, 19, 36, 98, 162, 195; MTCW 1, 2

Lawrence, T(homas) E(dward) 1888-1935 **TCLC 18**
See also Dale, Colin
See also CA 115; 167; DLB 195

Lawrence of Arabia
See Lawrence, T(homas) E(dward)

Lawson, Henry (Archibald Hertzberg) 1867-1922

TCLC 27; SSC 18
See also CA 120; 181

Lawton, Dennis
See Faust, Frederick (Schiller)

Laxness, Halldor ....**CLC 25**
See also Gudjonsson, Halldor Kiljan

Layamon fl. c. 1200- ....**CMLC 10**
See also DLB 146

Laye, Camara 1928-1980**CLC 4, 38; BLC 2; DAM MULT**
See also BW 1; CA 85-88; 97-100; CANR 25; MTCW 1, 2

Layton, Irving (Peter) 1912- .. **CLC 2, 15; DAC; DAM MST, POET**
See also CA 1-4R; CANR 2, 33, 43, 66; DLB 88; MTCW 1, 2

Lazarus, Emma 1849-1887 ....**NCLC 8**

Lazarus, Felix
See Cable, George Washington

Lazarus, Henry
See Slavitt, David R(ytman)

Lea, Joan
See Neufeld, John (Arthur)

Leacock, Stephen (Butler) 1869-1944 . **TCLC 2; DAC; DAM MST**
See also CA 104; 141; CANR 80; DLB 92; MTCW 2

Lear, Edward 1812-1888 ....**NCLC 3**
See also CLR 1; DLB 32, 163, 166; MAICYA; SATA 18, 100

Lear, Norman (Milton) 1922- ....**CLC 12**
See also CA 73-76

Leautaud, Paul 1872-1956 ....**TCLC 83**
See also DLB 65

Leavis, F(rank) R(aymond) 1895-1978 .. **CLC 24**
See also CA 21-24R; 77-80; CANR 44; MTCW 1, 2

Leavitt, David 1961- ....**CLC 34; DAM POP**
See also CA 116; 122; CANR 50, 62; DA3; DLB 130; INT 122; MTCW 2

Leblanc, Maurice (Marie Emile) 1864-1941**TCLC 49**
See also CA 110

Lebowitz, Fran(ces Ann) 1951(?)- .... **CLC 11, 36**
See also CA 81-84; CANR 14, 60, 70; INT CANR-14; MTCW 1

Lebrecht, Peter
See Tieck, (Johann) Ludwig

le Carre, John ....**CLC 3, 5, 9, 15, 28**
See also Cornwell, David (John Moore)
See also BEST 89:4; CDBLB 1960 to Present; DLB 87; MTCW 2

Le Clezio, J(ean) M(arie) G(ustave) 1940- . **C L C 31**
See also CA 116; 128; DLB 83

Leconte de Lisle, Charles-Marie-Rene 1818-1894 **NCLC 29**

Le Coq, Monsieur
See Simenon, Georges (Jacques Christian)

Leduc, Violette 1907-1972 ....**CLC 22**
See also CA 13-14; 33-36R; CANR 69; CAP 1

Ledwidge, Francis 1887(?)-1917 ....**TCLC 23**
See also CA 123; DLB 20

Lee, Andrea 1953-**CLC 36; BLC 2; DAM MULT**
See also BW 1, 3; CA 125; CANR 82

Lee, Andrew
See Auchincloss, Louis (Stanton)

Lee, Chang-rae 1965- ....**CLC 91**
See also CA 148

Lee, Don L. ....**CLC 2**
See also Madhubuti, Haki R.

Lee, George W(ashington) 1894-1976 . **CLC 52; BLC 2; DAM MULT**

See also BW 1; CA 125; CANR 83; DLB 51

Lee, (Nelle) Harper 1926-**CLC 12, 60; DA; DAB; DAC; DAM MST, NOV; WLC**
See also AAYA 13; CA 13-16R; CANR 51; CDALB 1941-1968; DA3; DLB 6; MTCW 1, 2; SATA 11

Lee, Helen Elaine 1959(?)- ....**CLC 86**
See also CA 148

Lee, Julian
See Latham, Jean Lee

Lee, Larry
See Lee, Lawrence

Lee, Laurie 1914-1997**CLC 90; DAB; DAM POP**
See also CA 77-80; 158; CANR 33, 73; DLB 27; MTCW 1

Lee, Lawrence 1941-1990 ....**CLC 34**
See also CA 131; CANR 43

Lee, Li-Young 1957- ....**PC 24**
See also CA 153; DLB 165

Lee, Manfred B(ennington) 1905-1971 .. **CLC 11**
See also Queen, Ellery
See also CA 1-4R; 29-32R; CANR 2; DLB 137

Lee, Shelton Jackson 1957(?)-**CLC 105; BLCS; DAM MULT**
See also Lee, Spike
See also BW 2, 3; CA 125; CANR 42

Lee, Spike
See Lee, Shelton Jackson
See also AAYA 4, 29

Lee, Stan 1922- ....**CLC 17**
See also AAYA 5; CA 108; 111; INT 111

Lee, Tanith 1947- ....**CLC 46**
See also AAYA 15; CA 37-40R; CANR 53; SATA 8, 88

Lee, Vernon ....**TCLC 5; SSC 33**
See also Paget, Violet
See also DLB 57, 153, 156, 174, 178

Lee, William
See Burroughs, William S(eward)

Lee, Willy
See Burroughs, William S(eward)

Lee-Hamilton, Eugene (Jacob) 1845-1907 **TCLC 22**
See also CA 117

Leet, Judith 1935- ....**CLC 11**

Le Fanu, Joseph Sheridan 1814-1873**NCLC 9, 58; DAM POP; SSC 14**
See also DA3; DLB 21, 70, 159, 178

Leffland, Ella 1931- ....**CLC 19**
See also CA 29-32R; CANR 35, 78, 82; DLBY 84; INT CANR-35; SATA 65

Leger, Alexis
See Leger, (Marie-Rene Auguste) Alexis Saint-Leger

Leger, (Marie-Rene Auguste) Alexis Saint-Leger 1887-1975**CLC 4, 11, 46; DAM POET; PC 23**
See also CA 13-16R; 61-64; CANR 43; MTCW 1

Leger, Saintleger
See Leger, (Marie-Rene Auguste) Alexis Saint-Leger

Le Guin, Ursula K(roeber) 1929- **CLC 8, 13, 22, 45, 71; DAB; DAC; DAM MST, POP; SSC 12**
See also AAYA 9, 27; AITN 1; CA 21-24R; CANR 9, 32, 52, 74; CDALB 1968-1988; CLR 3, 28; DA3; DLB 8, 52; INT CANR-32; JRDA; MAICYA; MTCW 1, 2; SATA 4, 52, 99

Lehmann, Rosamond (Nina) 1901-1990 .. **CLC 5**
See also CA 77-80; 131; CANR 8, 73; DLB 15; MTCW 2

Leiber, Fritz (Reuter, Jr.) 1910-1992 .... **CLC 25**
See also CA 45-48; 139; CANR 2, 40, 86; DLB 8; MTCW 1, 2; SATA 45; SATA-Obit 73

See also CA 81-84; 147; CANR 72; DLB 13
Lunar, Dennis
See Mungo, Raymond
Lurie, Alison 1926- .... **CLC 4, 5, 18, 39**
See also CA 1-4R; CANR 2, 17, 50; DLB 2; MTCW 1; SATA 46
Lustig, Arnost 1926- .... **CLC 56**
See also AAYA 3; CA 69-72; CANR 47; SATA 56
Luther, Martin 1483-1546 .... **LC 9, 37**
See also DLB 179
Luxemburg, Rosa 1870(?)-1919 .... **TCLC 63**
See also CA 118
Luzi, Mario 1914- .... **CLC 13**
See also CA 61-64; CANR 9, 70; DLB 128
Lyly, John 1554(?)-1606 **LC 41; DAM DRAM; DC 7**
See also DLB 62, 167
L'Ymagier
See Gourmont, Remy (-Marie-Charles) de
Lynch, B. Suarez
See Bioy Casares, Adolfo
Lynch, B. Suarez
See Bioy Casares, Adolfo; Borges, Jorge Luis
Lynch, David (K.) 1946- .... **CLC 66**
See also CA 124; 129
Lynch, James
See Andreyev, Leonid (Nikolaevich)
Lynch Davis, B.
See Bioy Casares, Adolfo; Borges, Jorge Luis
Lyndsay, Sir David 1490-1555 .... **LC 20**
Lynn, Kenneth S(chuyler) 1923- .... **CLC 50**
See also CA 1-4R; CANR 3, 27, 65
Lynx
See West, Rebecca
Lyons, Marcus
See Blish, James (Benjamin)
Lyre, Pinchbeck
See Sassoon, Siegfried (Lorraine)
Lytle, Andrew (Nelson) 1902-1995 .... **CLC 22**
See also CA 9-12R; 150; CANR 70; DLB 6; DLBY 95
Lyttelton, George 1709-1773 .... **LC 10**
Maas, Peter 1929- .... **CLC 29**
See also CA 93-96; INT 93-96; MTCW 2
Macaulay, Rose 1881-1958 .... **TCLC 7, 44**
See also CA 104; DLB 36
Macaulay, Thomas Babington 1800-1859**NCLC 42**
See also CDBLB 1832-1890; DLB 32, 55
MacBeth, George (Mann) 1932-1992 **CLC 2, 5, 9**
See also CA 25-28R; 136; CANR 61, 66; DLB 40; MTCW 1; SATA 4; SATA-Obit 70
MacCaig, Norman (Alexander) 1910- . **CLC 36; DAB; DAM POET**
See also CA 9-12R; CANR 3, 34; DLB 27
MacCarthy, Sir(Charles Otto) Desmond 1877-1952 **TCLC 36**
See also CA 167
MacDiarmid, Hugh .. **CLC 2, 4, 11, 19, 63; PC 9**
See also Grieve, C(hristopher) M(urray)
See also CDBLB 1945-1960; DLB 20
MacDonald, Anson
See Heinlein, Robert A(nson)
Macdonald, Cynthia 1928- .... **CLC 13, 19**
See also CA 49-52; CANR 4, 44; DLB 105
MacDonald, George 1824-1905 .... **TCLC 9**
See also CA 106; 137; CANR 80; DLB 18, 163, 178; MAICYA; SATA 33, 100
Macdonald, John
See Millar, Kenneth
MacDonald, John D(ann) 1916-1986 . **CLC 3, 27, 44; DAM NOV, POP**
See also CA 1-4R; 121; CANR 1, 19, 60; DLB 8; DLBY 86; MTCW 1, 2

Macdonald, John Ross
See Millar, Kenneth
Macdonald, Ross .... **CLC 1, 2, 3, 14, 34, 41**
See also Millar, Kenneth
See also DLBD 6
MacDougal, John
See Blish, James (Benjamin)
MacEwen, Gwendolyn (Margaret) 1941-1987**CLC 13, 55**
See also CA 9-12R; 124; CANR 7, 22; DLB 53; SATA 50; SATA-Obit 55
Macha, Karel Hynek 1810-1846 .... **NCLC 46**
Machado (y Ruiz), Antonio 1875-1939 .. **TCLC 3**
See also CA 104; 174; DLB 108; HW 2
Machado de Assis, Joaquim Maria 1839-1908 **TCLC 10; BLC 2; HLCS 2; SSC 24**
See also CA 107; 153
Machen, Arthur .... **TCLC 4; SSC 20**
See also Jones, Arthur Llewellyn
See also CA 179; DLB 36, 156, 178
Machiavelli, Niccolo 1469-1527 .. **LC 8, 36; DA; DAB; DAC; DAM MST; WLCS**
MacInnes, Colin 1914-1976 .... **CLC 4, 23**
See also CA 69-72; 65-68; CANR 21; DLB 14; MTCW 1, 2
MacInnes, Helen (Clark) 1907-1985**CLC 27, 39; DAM POP**
See also CA 1-4R; 117; CANR 1, 28, 58; DLB 87; MTCW 1, 2; SATA 22; SATA-Obit 44
Mackenzie, Compton (Edward Montague) 1883-1972 .... **CLC 18**
See also CA 21-22; 37-40R; CAP 2; DLB 34, 100
Mackenzie, Henry 1745-1831 .... **NCLC 41**
See also DLB 39
Mackintosh, Elizabeth 1896(?)-1952
See Tey, Josephine
See also CA 110
MacLaren, James
See Grieve, C(hristopher) M(urray)
Mac Laverty, Bernard 1942- .... **CLC 31**
See also CA 116; 118; CANR 43; INT 118
MacLean, Alistair (Stuart) 1922(?)-1987 **CLC 3, 13, 50, 63; DAM POP**
See also CA 57-60; 121; CANR 28, 61; MTCW 1; SATA 23; SATA-Obit 50
Maclean, Norman (Fitzroy) 1902-1990 . **CLC 78; DAM POP; SSC 13**
See also CA 102; 132; CANR 49; DLB 206
MacLeish, Archibald 1892-1982**CLC 3, 8, 14, 68; DAM POET**
See also CA 9-12R; 106; CANR 33, 63; CDALBS; DLB 4, 7, 45; DLBY 82; MTCW 1, 2
MacLennan, (John) Hugh 1907-1990 **CLC 2, 14, 92; DAC; DAM MST**
See also CA 5-8R; 142; CANR 33; DLB 68; MTCW 1, 2
MacLeod, Alistair 1936- .. **CLC 56; DAC; DAM MST**
See also CA 123; DLB 60; MTCW 2
Macleod, Fiona
See Sharp, William
MacNeice, (Frederick) Louis 1907-1963**CLC 1, 4, 10, 53; DAB; DAM POET**
See also CA 85-88; CANR 61; DLB 10, 20; MTCW 1, 2
MacNeill, Dand
See Fraser, George MacDonald
Macpherson, James 1736-1796 .... **LC 29**
See also Ossian
See also DLB 109
Macpherson, (Jean) Jay 1931- .... **CLC 14**
See also CA 5-8R; DLB 53
MacShane, Frank 1927- .... **CLC 39**

See also CA 9-12R; CANR 3, 33; DLB 111
Macumber, Mari
See Sandoz, Mari(e Susette)
Madach, Imre 1823-1864 .... **NCLC 19**
Madden, (Jerry) David 1933- .... **CLC 5, 15**
See also CA 1-4R; CAAS 3; CANR 4, 45; DLB 6; MTCW 1
Maddern, Al(an)
See Ellison, Harlan (Jay)
Madhubuti, Haki R. 1942- ... **CLC 6, 73; BLC 2; DAM MULT, POET; PC 5**
See also Lee, Don L.
See also BW 2, 3; CA 73-76; CANR 24, 51, 73; DLB 5, 41; DLBD 8; MTCW 2
Maepenn, Hugh
See Kuttner, Henry
Maepenn, K. H.
See Kuttner, Henry
Maeterlinck, Maurice 1862-1949 **TCLC 3; DAM DRAM**
See also CA 104; 136; CANR 80; DLB 192; SATA 66
Maginn, William 1794-1842 .... **NCLC 8**
See also DLB 110, 159
Mahapatra, Jayanta 1928- **CLC 33; DAM MULT**
See also CA 73-76; CAAS 9; CANR 15, 33, 66
Mahfouz, Naguib (Abdel Aziz Al-Sabilgi) 1911(?)-
See Mahfuz, Najib
See also BEST 89:2; CA 128; CANR 55; DAM NOV; DA3; MTCW 1, 2
Mahfuz, Najib .... **CLC 52, 55**
See also Mahfouz, Naguib (Abdel Aziz Al-Sabilgi)
See also DLBY 88
Mahon, Derek 1941- .... **CLC 27**
See also CA 113; 128; DLB 40
Mailer, Norman 1923-**CLC 1, 2, 3, 4, 5, 8, 11, 14, 28, 39, 74, 111; DA; DAB; DAC; DAM MST, NOV, POP**
See also AAYA 31; AITN 2; CA 9-12R; CABS 1; CANR 28, 74, 77; CDALB 1968-1988; DA3; DLB 2, 16, 28, 185; DLBD 3; DLBY 80, 83; MTCW 1, 2
Maillet, Antonine 1929- ...... **CLC 54, 118; DAC**
See also CA 115; 120; CANR 46, 74, 77; DLB 60; INT 120; MTCW 2
Mais, Roger 1905-1955 .... **TCLC 8**
See also BW 1, 3; CA 105; 124; CANR 82; DLB 125; MTCW 1
Maistre, Joseph de 1753-1821 .... **NCLC 37**
Maitland, Frederic 1850-1906 .... **TCLC 65**
Maitland, Sara (Louise) 1950- .... **CLC 49**
See also CA 69-72; CANR 13, 59
Major, Clarence 1936- .. **CLC 3, 19, 48; BLC 2; DAM MULT**
See also BW 2, 3; CA 21-24R; CAAS 6; CANR 13, 25, 53, 82; DLB 33
Major, Kevin (Gerald) 1949- .... **CLC 26; DAC**
See also AAYA 16; CA 97-100; CANR 21, 38; CLR 11; DLB 60; INT CANR-21; JRDA; MAICYA; SATA 32, 82
Maki, James
See Ozu, Yasujiro
Malabaila, Damiano
See Levi, Primo
Malamud, Bernard 1914-1986**CLC 1, 2, 3, 5, 8, 9, 11, 18, 27, 44, 78, 85; DA; DAB; DAC; DAM MST, NOV, POP; SSC 15; WLC**
See also AAYA 16; CA 5-8R; 118; CABS 1; CANR 28, 62; CDALB 1941-1968; DA3; DLB 2, 28, 152; DLBY 80, 86; MTCW 1, 2
Malan, Herman
See Bosman, Herman Charles; Bosman, Herman

DLB 14

Middleton, Thomas 1580-1627 .... **LC 33; DAM DRAM, MST; DC 5**
See also DLB 58

Migueis, Jose Rodrigues 1901- .... **CLC 10**

Mikszath, Kalman 1847-1910 .... **TCLC 31**
See also CA 170

Miles, Jack .... **CLC 100**

Miles, Josephine (Louise) 1911-1985 . **CLC 1, 2, 14, 34, 39; DAM POET**
See also CA 1-4R; 116; CANR 2, 55; DLB 48

Militant
See Sandburg, Carl (August)

Mill, John Stuart 1806-1873 .... **NCLC 11, 58**
See also CDBLB 1832-1890; DLB 55, 190

Millar, Kenneth 1915-1983 . **CLC 14; DAM POP**
See Macdonald, Ross
See also CA 9-12R; 110; CANR 16, 63; DA3; DLB 2; DLBD 6; DLBY 83; MTCW 1, 2

Millay, E. Vincent
See Millay, Edna St. Vincent

Millay, Edna St. Vincent 1892-1950 **TCLC 4, 49; DA; DAB; DAC; DAM MST, POET; PC 6; WLCS**
See also CA 104; 130; CDALB 1917-1929; DA3; DLB 45; MTCW 1, 2

Miller, Arthur 1915-**CLC 1, 2, 6, 10, 15, 26, 47, 78; DA; DAB; DAC; DAM DRAM, MST; DC 1; WLC**
See also AAYA 15; AITN 1; CA 1-4R; CABS 3; CANR 2, 30, 54, 76; CDALB 1941-1968; DA3; DLB 7; MTCW 1, 2

Miller, Henry (Valentine) 1891-1980**CLC 1, 2, 4, 9, 14, 43, 84; DA; DAB; DAC; DAM MST, NOV; WLC**
See also CA 9-12R; 97-100; CANR 33, 64; CDALB 1929-1941; DA3; DLB 4, 9; DLBY 80; MTCW 1, 2

Miller, Jason 1939(?)- .... **CLC 2**
See also AITN 1; CA 73-76; DLB 7

Miller, Sue 1943- .... **CLC 44; DAM POP**
See also BEST 90:3; CA 139; CANR 59; DA3; DLB 143

Miller, Walter M(ichael, Jr.) 1923- .. **CLC 4, 30**
See also CA 85-88; DLB 8

Millett, Kate 1934- .... **CLC 67**
See also AITN 1; CA 73-76; CANR 32, 53, 76; DA3; MTCW 1, 2

Millhauser, Steven (Lewis) 1943-**CLC 21, 54, 109**
See also CA 110; 111; CANR 63; DA3; DLB 2; INT 111; MTCW 2

Millin, Sarah Gertrude 1889-1968 .... **CLC 49**
See also CA 102; 93-96

Milne, A(lan) A(lexander) 1882-1956**TCLC 6, 88; DAB; DAC; DAM MST**
See also CA 104; 133; CLR 1, 26; DA3; DLB 10, 77, 100, 160; MAICYA; MTCW 1, 2; SATA 100; YABC 1

Milner, Ron(ald) 1938- .. **CLC 56; BLC 3; DAM MULT**
See also AITN 1; BW 1; CA 73-76; CANR 24, 81; DLB 38; MTCW 1

Milnes, Richard Monckton 1809-1885 **NCLC 61**
See also DLB 32, 184

Milosz, Czeslaw 1911-**CLC 5, 11, 22, 31, 56, 82; DAM MST, POET; PC 8; WLCS**
See also CA 81-84; CANR 23, 51; DA3; MTCW 1, 2

Milton, John 1608-1674**LC 9, 43; DA; DAB; DAC; DAM MST, POET; PC 19; WLC**
See also CDBLB 1660-1789; DA3; DLB 131, 151

Min, Anchee 1957- .... **CLC 86**
See also CA 146

Minehaha, Cornelius
See Wedekind, (Benjamin) Frank(lin)

Miner, Valerie 1947- .... **CLC 40**
See also CA 97-100; CANR 59

Minimo, Duca
See D'Annunzio, Gabriele

Minot, Susan 1956- .... **CLC 44**
See also CA 134

Minus, Ed 1938- .... **CLC 39**

Miranda, Javier
See Bioy Casares, Adolfo

Miranda, Javier
See Bioy Casares, Adolfo

Mirbeau, Octave 1848-1917 .... **TCLC 55**
See also DLB 123, 192

Miro (Ferrer), Gabriel (Francisco Victor) 1879-1930 .... **TCLC 5**
See also CA 104

Mishima, Yukio 1925-1970**CLC 2, 4, 6, 9, 27; DC 1; SSC 4**
See also Hiraoka, Kimitake
See also DLB 182; MTCW 2

Mistral, Frederic 1830-1914 .... **TCLC 51**
See also CA 122

Mistral, Gabriela .... **TCLC 2; HLC 2**
See also Godoy Alcayaga, Lucila
See also MTCW 2

Mistry, Rohinton 1952- .... **CLC 71; DAC**
See also CA 141; CANR 86

Mitchell, Clyde
See Ellison, Harlan (Jay); Silverberg, Robert

Mitchell, James Leslie 1901-1935
See Gibbon, Lewis Grassic
See also CA 104; DLB 15

Mitchell, Joni 1943- .... **CLC 12**
See also CA 112

Mitchell, Joseph (Quincy) 1908-1996 ... **CLC 98**
See also CA 77-80; 152; CANR 69; DLB 185; DLBY 96

Mitchell, Margaret (Munnerlyn) 1900-1949 **TCLC 11; DAM NOV, POP**
See also AAYA 23; CA 109; 125; CANR 55; CDALBS; DA3; DLB 9; MTCW 1, 2

Mitchell, Peggy
See Mitchell, Margaret (Munnerlyn)

Mitchell, S(ilas) Weir 1829-1914 .... **TCLC 36**
See also CA 165; DLB 202

Mitchell, W(illiam) O(rmond) 1914-1998**CLC 25; DAC; DAM MST**
See also CA 77-80; 165; CANR 15, 43; DLB 88

Mitchell, William 1879-1936 .... **TCLC 81**

Mitford, Mary Russell 1787-1855 .... **NCLC 4**
See also DLB 110, 116

Mitford, Nancy 1904-1973 .... **CLC 44**
See also CA 9-12R; DLB 191

Miyamoto, (Chujo) Yuriko 1899-1951 . **TCLC 37**
See also CA 170, 174; DLB 180

Miyazawa, Kenji 1896-1933 .... **TCLC 76**
See also CA 157

Mizoguchi, Kenji 1898-1956 .... **TCLC 72**
See also CA 167

Mo, Timothy (Peter) 1950(?)- .... **CLC 46**
See also CA 117; DLB 194; MTCW 1

Modarressi, Taghi (M.) 1931- .... **CLC 44**
See also CA 121; 134; INT 134

Modiano, Patrick (Jean) 1945- .... **CLC 18**
See also CA 85-88; CANR 17, 40; DLB 83

Moerck, Paal
See Roelvaag, O(le) E(dvart)

Mofolo, Thomas (Mokopu) 1875(?)-1948**TCLC 22; BLC 3; DAM MULT**
See also CA 121; 153; CANR 83; MTCW 2

Mohr, Nicholasa 1938-**CLC 12; DAM MULT; HLC**

2
See also AAYA 8; CA 49-52; CANR 1, 32, 64; CLR 22; DLB 145; HW 1, 2; JRDA; SAAS 8; SATA 8, 97

Mojtabai, A(nn) G(race) 1938- **CLC 5, 9, 15, 29**
See also CA 85-88

Moliere 1622-1673 **LC 10, 28; DA; DAB; DAC; DAM DRAM, MST; WLC**
See also DA3

Molin, Charles
See Mayne, William (James Carter)

Molnar, Ferenc 1878-1952**TCLC 20; DAM DRAM**
See also CA 109; 153; CANR 83

Momaday, N(avarre) Scott 1934- **CLC 2, 19, 85, 95; DA; DAB; DAC; DAM MST, MULT, NOV, POP; PC 25; WLCS**
See also AAYA 11; CA 25-28R; CANR 14, 34, 68; CDALBS; DA3; DLB 143, 175; INT CANR-14; MTCW 1, 2; NNAL; SATA 48; SATA-Brief 30

Monette, Paul 1945-1995 .... **CLC 82**
See also CA 139; 147

Monroe, Harriet 1860-1936 .... **TCLC 12**
See also CA 109; DLB 54, 91

Monroe, Lyle
See Heinlein, Robert A(nson)

Montagu, Elizabeth 1720-1800 .... **NCLC 7**

Montagu, Elizabeth 1917- .... **NCLC 7**
See also CA 9-12R

Montagu, Mary (Pierrepont) Wortley 1689-1762 **LC 9; PC 16**
See also DLB 95, 101

Montagu, W. H.
See Coleridge, Samuel Taylor

Montague, John (Patrick) 1929- ..... **CLC 13, 46**
See also CA 9-12R; CANR 9, 69; DLB 40; MTCW 1

Montaigne, Michel (Eyquem) de 1533-1592**LC 8; DA; DAB; DAC; DAM MST; WLC**

Montale, Eugenio 1896-1981**CLC 7, 9, 18; PC 13**
See also CA 17-20R; 104; CANR 30; DLB 114; MTCW 1

Montesquieu, Charles-Louis de Secondat 1689-1755 .... **LC 7**

Montgomery, (Robert) Bruce 1921(?)-1978
See Crispin, Edmund
See also CA 179; 104

Montgomery, L(ucy) M(aud) 1874-1942**TCLC 51; DAC; DAM MST**
See also AAYA 12; CA 108; 137; CLR 8; DA3; DLB 92; DLBD 14; JRDA; MAICYA; MTCW 2; SATA 100; YABC 1

Montgomery, Marion H., Jr. 1925- .... **CLC 7**
See also AITN 1; CA 1-4R; CANR 3, 48; DLB 6

Montgomery, Max
See Davenport, Guy (Mattison, Jr.)

Montherlant, Henry (Milon) de 1896-1972**CLC 8, 19; DAM DRAM**
See also CA 85-88; 37-40R; DLB 72; MTCW 1

Monty Python
See Chapman, Graham; Cleese, John (Marwood); Gilliam, Terry (Vance); Idle, Eric; Jones, Terence Graham Parry; Palin, Michael (Edward)
See also AAYA 7

Moodie, Susanna (Strickland) 1803-1885 **NCLC 14**
See also DLB 99

Mooney, Edward 1951-
See Mooney, Ted
See also CA 130

Mooney, Ted .... **CLC 25**
See also Mooney, Edward

Moorcock, Michael (John) 1939-**CLC 5, 27, 58**
See also Bradbury, Edward P.
See also AAYA 26; CA 45-48; CAAS 5; CANR 2, 17, 38, 64; DLB 14; MTCW 1, 2; SATA 93

Moore, Brian 1921-1999**CLC 1, 3, 5, 7, 8, 19, 32, 90; DAB; DAC; DAM MST**
See also CA 1-4R; 174; CANR 1, 25, 42, 63; MTCW 1, 2

Moore, Edward
See Muir, Edwin

Moore, G. E. 1873-1958 .... **TCLC 89**

Moore, George Augustus 1852-1933**TCLC 7; SSC 19**
See also CA 104; 177; DLB 10, 18, 57, 135

Moore, Lorrie .... **CLC 39, 45, 68**
See also Moore, Marie Lorena

Moore, Marianne (Craig) 1887-1972**CLC 1, 2, 4, 8, 10, 13, 19, 47; DA; DAB; DAC; DAM MST, POET; PC 4; WLCS**
See also CA 1-4R; 33-36R; CANR 3, 61; CDALB 1929-1941; DA3; DLB 45; DLBD 7; MTCW 1, 2; SATA 20

Moore, Marie Lorena 1957-
See Moore, Lorrie
See also CA 116; CANR 39, 83

Moore, Thomas 1779-1852 .... **NCLC 6**
See also DLB 96, 144

Mora, Pat(ricia) 1942-
See also CA 129; CANR 57, 81; CLR 58; DAM MULT; DLB 209; HLC 2; HW 1, 2; SATA 92

Moraga, Cherríe 1952- . **CLC 126; DAM MULT**
See also CA 131; CANR 66; DLB 82; HW 1, 2

Morand, Paul 1888-1976 .... **CLC 41; SSC 22**
See also CA 69-72; DLB 65

Morante, Elsa 1918-1985 .... **CLC 8, 47**
See also CA 85-88; 117; CANR 35; DLB 177; MTCW 1, 2

Moravia, Alberto 1907-1990**CLC 2, 7, 11, 27, 46; SSC 26**
See also Pincherle, Alberto
See also DLB 177; MTCW 2

More, Hannah 1745-1833 .... **NCLC 27**
See also DLB 107, 109, 116, 158

More, Henry 1614-1687 .... **LC 9**
See also DLB 126

More, Sir Thomas 1478-1535 .... **LC 10, 32**

Moreas, Jean .... **TCLC 18**
See also Papadiamantopoulos, Johannes

Morgan, Berry 1919- .... **CLC 6**
See also CA 49-52; DLB 6

Morgan, Claire
See Highsmith, (Mary) Patricia

Morgan, Edwin (George) 1920- .... **CLC 31**
See also CA 5-8R; CANR 3, 43; DLB 27

Morgan, (George) Frederick 1922- ...... **CLC 23**
See also CA 17-20R; CANR 21

Morgan, Harriet
See Mencken, H(enry) L(ouis)

Morgan, Jane
See Cooper, James Fenimore

Morgan, Janet 1945- .... **CLC 39**
See also CA 65-68

Morgan, Lady 1776(?)-1859 .... **NCLC 29**
See also DLB 116, 158

Morgan, Robin (Evonne) 1941- .... **CLC 2**
See also CA 69-72; CANR 29, 68; MTCW 1; SATA 80

Morgan, Scott
See Kuttner, Henry

Morgan, Seth 1949(?)-1990 .... **CLC 65**
See also CA 132

Morgenstern, Christian 1871-1914 ...... **TCLC 8**

See also CA 105

Morgenstern, S.
See Goldman, William (W.)

Moricz, Zsigmond 1879-1942 .... **TCLC 33**
See also CA 165

Morike, Eduard (Friedrich) 1804-1875 **NCLC 10**
See also DLB 133

Moritz, Karl Philipp 1756-1793 .... **LC 2**
See also DLB 94

Morland, Peter Henry
See Faust, Frederick (Schiller)

Morley, Christopher (Darlington) 1890-1957 **TCLC 87**
See also CA 112; DLB 9

Morren, Theophil
See Hofmannsthal, Hugo von

Morris, Bill 1952- .... **CLC 76**

Morris, Julian
See West, Morris L(anglo)

Morris, Steveland Judkins 1950(?)-
See Wonder, Stevie
See also CA 111

Morris, William 1834-1896 .... **NCLC 4**
See also CDBLB 1832-1890; DLB 18, 35, 57, 156, 178, 184

Morris, Wright 1910-1998 .. **CLC 1, 3, 7, 18, 37**
See also CA 9-12R; 167; CANR 21, 81; DLB 2, 206; DLBY 81; MTCW 1, 2

Morrison, Arthur 1863-1945 .... **TCLC 72**
See also CA 120; 157; DLB 70, 135, 197

Morrison, Chloe Anthony Wofford
See Morrison, Toni

Morrison, James Douglas 1943-1971
See Morrison, Jim
See also CA 73-76; CANR 40

Morrison, Jim .... **CLC 17**
See also Morrison, James Douglas

Morrison, Toni 1931- **CLC 4, 10, 22, 55, 81, 87; BLC 3; DA; DAB; DAC; DAM MST, MULT, NOV, POP**
See also AAYA 1, 22; BW 2, 3; CA 29-32R; CANR 27, 42, 67; CDALB 1968-1988; DA3; DLB 6, 33, 143; DLBY 81; MTCW 1, 2; SATA 57

Morrison, Van 1945- .... **CLC 21**
See also CA 116; 168

Morrissy, Mary 1958- .... **CLC 99**

Mortimer, John (Clifford) 1923- .... **CLC 28, 43; DAM DRAM, POP**
See also CA 13-16R; CANR 21, 69; CDBLB 1960 to Present; DA3; DLB 13; INT CANR-21; MTCW 1, 2

Mortimer, Penelope (Ruth) 1918- .... **CLC 5**
See also CA 57-60; CANR 45

Morton, Anthony
See Creasey, John

Mosca, Gaetano 1858-1941 .... **TCLC 75**

Mosher, Howard Frank 1943- .... **CLC 62**
See also CA 139; CANR 65

Mosley, Nicholas 1923- .... **CLC 43, 70**
See also CA 69-72; CANR 41, 60; DLB 14, 207

Mosley, Walter 1952- ..... **CLC 97; BLCS; DAM MULT, POP**
See also AAYA 17; BW 2; CA 142; CANR 57; DA3; MTCW 2

Moss, Howard 1922-1987**CLC 7, 14, 45, 50; DAM POET**
See also CA 1-4R; 123; CANR 1, 44; DLB 5

Mossgiel, Rab
See Burns, Robert

Motion, Andrew (Peter) 1952- .... **CLC 47**
See also CA 146; DLB 40

Motley, Willard (Francis) 1909-1965 .... **CLC 18**

See also BW 1; CA 117; 106; DLB 76, 143

Motoori, Norinaga 1730-1801 .... **NCLC 45**

Mott, Michael (Charles Alston) 1930-**CLC 15, 34**
See also CA 5-8R; CAAS 7; CANR 7, 29

Mountain Wolf Woman 1884-1960 .... **CLC 92**
See also CA 144; NNAL

Moure, Erin 1955- .... **CLC 88**
See also CA 113; DLB 60

Mowat, Farley (McGill) 1921- .... **CLC 26; DAC; DAM MST**
See also AAYA 1; CA 1-4R; CANR 4, 24, 42, 68; CLR 20; DLB 68; INT CANR-24; JRDA; MAICYA; MTCW 1, 2; SATA 3, 55

Mowatt, Anna Cora 1819-1870 .... **NCLC 74**

Moyers, Bill 1934- .... **CLC 74**
See also AITN 2; CA 61-64; CANR 31, 52

Mphahlele, Es'kia
See Mphahlele, Ezekiel
See also DLB 125

Mphahlele, Ezekiel 1919-**CLC 25; BLC 3; DAM MULT**
See also Mphahlele, Es'kia
See also BW 2, 3; CA 81-84; CANR 26, 76; DA3; MTCW 2

Mqhayi, S(amuel) E(dward) K(rune Loliwe) 1875-1945 .... **TCLC 25; BLC 3; DAM MULT**
See also CA 153

Mrozek, Slawomir 1930- .... **CLC 3, 13**
See also CA 13-16R; CAAS 10; CANR 29; MTCW 1

Mrs. Belloc-Lowndes
See Lowndes, Marie Adelaide (Belloc)

Mtwa, Percy (?)- .... **CLC 47**

Mueller, Lisel 1924- .... **CLC 13, 51**
See also CA 93-96; DLB 105

Muir, Edwin 1887-1959 .... **TCLC 2, 87**
See also CA 104; DLB 20, 100, 191

Muir, John 1838-1914 .... **TCLC 28**
See also CA 165; DLB 186

Mujica Lainez, Manuel 1910-1984 .... **CLC 31**
See also Lainez, Manuel Mujica
See also CA 81-84; 112; CANR 32; HW 1

Mukherjee, Bharati 1940- . **CLC 53, 115; DAM NOV**
See also BEST 89:2; CA 107; CANR 45, 72; DLB 60; MTCW 1, 2

Muldoon, Paul 1951- . **CLC 32, 72; DAM POET**
See also CA 113; 129; CANR 52; DLB 40; INT 129

Mulisch, Harry 1927- .... **CLC 42**
See also CA 9-12R; CANR 6, 26, 56

Mull, Martin 1943- .... **CLC 17**
See also CA 105

Muller, Wilhelm .... **NCLC 73**

Mulock, Dinah Maria
See Craik, Dinah Maria (Mulock)

Munford, Robert 1737(?)-1783 .... **LC 5**
See also DLB 31

Mungo, Raymond 1946- .... **CLC 72**
See also CA 49-52; CANR 2

Munro, Alice 1931-**CLC 6, 10, 19, 50, 95; DAC; DAM MST, NOV; SSC 3; WLCS**
See also AITN 2; CA 33-36R; CANR 33, 53, 75; DA3; DLB 53; MTCW 1, 2; SATA 29

Munro, H(ector) H(ugh) 1870-1916
See Saki
See also CA 104; 130; CDBLB 1890-1914; DA; DAB; DAC; DAM MST, NOV; DA3; DLB 34, 162; MTCW 1, 2; WLC

Murdoch, (Jean) Iris 1919-1999**CLC 1, 2, 3, 4, 6, 8, 11, 15, 22, 31, 51; DAB; DAC; DAM MST, NOV**
See also CA 13-16R; 179; CANR 8, 43, 68; CDBLB

1960 to Present; DA3; DLB 14, 194; INT CANR-8; MTCW 1, 2

Murfree, Mary Noailles 1850-1922 .... **SSC 22**
See also CA 122; 176; DLB 12, 74

Murnau, Friedrich Wilhelm
See Plumpe, Friedrich Wilhelm

Murphy, Richard 1927- .... **CLC 41**
See also CA 29-32R; DLB 40

Murphy, Sylvia 1937- .... **CLC 34**
See also CA 121

Murphy, Thomas (Bernard) 1935- .... **CLC 51**
See also CA 101

Murray, Albert L. 1916- .... **CLC 73**
See also BW 2; CA 49-52; CANR 26, 52, 78; DLB 38

Murray, Judith Sargent 1751-1820 ..... **NCLC 63**
See also DLB 37, 200

Murray, Les(lie) A(llan) 1938- .... **CLC 40; DAM POET**
See also CA 21-24R; CANR 11, 27, 56

Murry, J. Middleton
See Murry, John Middleton

Murry, John Middleton 1889-1957 ...... **TCLC 16**
See also CA 118; DLB 149

Musgrave, Susan 1951- .... **CLC 13, 54**
See also CA 69-72; CANR 45, 84

Musil, Robert (Edler von) 1880-1942 **TCLC 12, 68; SSC 18**
See also CA 109; CANR 55, 84; DLB 81, 124; MTCW 2

Muske, Carol 1945- .... **CLC 90**
See also Muske-Dukes, Carol (Anne)

Muske-Dukes, Carol (Anne) 1945-
See Muske, Carol
See also CA 65-68; CANR 32, 70

Musset, (Louis Charles) Alfred de 1810-1857 **NCLC 7**
See also DLB 192

Mussolini, Benito (Amilcare Andrea) 1883-1945 **TCLC 96**
See also CA 116

My Brother's Brother
See Chekhov, Anton (Pavlovich)

Myers, L(eopold) H(amilton) 1881-1944 **TCLC 59**
See also CA 157; DLB 15

Myers, Walter Dean 1937- **CLC 35; BLC 3; DAM MULT, NOV**
See also AAYA 4, 23; BW 2; CA 33-36R; CANR 20, 42, 67; CLR 4, 16, 35; DLB 33; INT CANR-20; JRDA; MAICYA; MTCW 2; SAAS 2; SATA 41, 71, 109; SATA-Brief 27

Myers, Walter M.
See Myers, Walter Dean

Myles, Symon
See Follett, Ken(neth Martin)

Nabokov, Vladimir (Vladimirovich) 1899-1977 **CLC 1, 2, 3, 6, 8, 11, 15, 23, 44, 46, 64; DA; DAB; DAC; DAM MST, NOV; SSC 11; WLC**
See also CA 5-8R; 69-72; CANR 20; CDALB 1941-1968; DA3; DLB 2; DLBD 3; DLBY 80, 91; MTCW 1, 2

Naevius c. 265B.C.-201B.C. .... **CMLC 37**
See also DLB 211

Nagai Kafu 1879-1959 .... **TCLC 51**
See also Nagai Sokichi
See also DLB 180

Nagai Sokichi 1879-1959
See Nagai Kafu
See also CA 117

Nagy, Laszlo 1925-1978 .... **CLC 7**
See also CA 129; 112

Naidu, Sarojini 1879-1943 .... **TCLC 80**

Naipaul, Shiva(dhar Srinivasa) 1945-1985 . **C L C**
32, 39; DAM NOV
See also CA 110; 112; 116; CANR 33; DA3; DLB 157; DLBY 85; MTCW 1, 2

Naipaul, V(idiadhar) S(urajprasad) 1932- **CLC 4, 7, 9, 13, 18, 37, 105; DAB; DAC; DAM MST, NOV**
See also CA 1-4R; CANR 1, 33, 51; CDBLB 1960 to Present; DA3; DLB 125, 204, 206; DLBY 85; MTCW 1, 2

Nakos, Lilika 1899(?)- .... **CLC 29**

Narayan, R(asipuram) K(rishnaswami) 1906- **CLC 7, 28, 47, 121; DAM NOV; SSC 25**
See also CA 81-84; CANR 33, 61; DA3; MTCW 1, 2; SATA 62

Nash, (Frediric) Ogden 1902-1971 **CLC 23; DAM POET; PC 21**
See also CA 13-14; 29-32R; CANR 34, 61; CAP 1; DLB 11; MAICYA; MTCW 1, 2; SATA 2, 46

Nashe, Thomas 1567-1601 .... **LC 41**

Nashe, Thomas 1567-1601(?) .... **LC 41**
See also DLB 167

Nathan, Daniel
See Dannay, Frederic

Nathan, George Jean 1882-1958 .... **TCLC 18**
See also Hatteras, Owen
See also CA 114; 169; DLB 137

Natsume, Kinnosuke 1867-1916
See Natsume, Soseki
See also CA 104

Natsume, Soseki 1867-1916 .... **TCLC 2, 10**
See also Natsume, Kinnosuke
See also DLB 180

Natti, (Mary) Lee 1919-
See Kingman, Lee
See also CA 5-8R; CANR 2

Naylor, Gloria 1950- .. **CLC 28, 52; BLC 3; DA; DAC; DAM MST, MULT, NOV, POP; WLCS**
See also AAYA 6; BW 2, 3; CA 107; CANR 27, 51, 74; DA3; DLB 173; MTCW 1, 2

Neihardt, John Gneisenau 1881-1973 ... **CLC 32**
See also CA 13-14; CANR 65; CAP 1; DLB 9, 54

Nekrasov, Nikolai Alekseevich 1821-1878 **NCLC 11**

Nelligan, Emile 1879-1941 .... **TCLC 14**
See also CA 114; DLB 92

Nelson, Willie 1933- .... **CLC 17**
See also CA 107

Nemerov, Howard (Stanley) 1920-1991 **CLC 2, 6, 9, 36; DAM POET; PC 24**
See also CA 1-4R; 134; CABS 2; CANR 1, 27, 53; DLB 5, 6; DLBY 83; INT CANR-27; MTCW 1, 2

Neruda, Pablo 1904-1973 **CLC 1, 2, 5, 7, 9, 28, 62; DA; DAB; DAC; DAM MST, MULT, POET; HLC 2; PC 4; WLC**
See also CA 19-20; 45-48; CAP 2; DA3; HW 1; MTCW 1, 2

Nerval, Gerard de 1808-1855 **NCLC 1, 67; PC 13; SSC 18**

Nervo, (Jose) Amado (Ruiz de) 1870-1919 **TCLC 11; HLCS 2**
See also CA 109; 131; HW 1

Nessi, Pio Baroja y
See Baroja (y Nessi), Pio

Nestroy, Johann 1801-1862 .... **NCLC 42**
See also DLB 133

Netterville, Luke
See O'Grady, Standish (James)

Neufeld, John (Arthur) 1938- .... **CLC 17**
See also AAYA 11; CA 25-28R; CANR 11, 37, 56; CLR 52; MAICYA; SAAS 3; SATA 6, 81

Neville, Emily Cheney 1919- .... **CLC 12**
See also CA 5-8R; CANR 3, 37, 85; JRDA;

MAICYA; SAAS 2; SATA 1

Newbound, Bernard Slade 1930-
See Slade, Bernard
See also CA 81-84; CANR 49; DAM DRAM

Newby, P(ercy) H(oward) 1918-1997 . **CLC 2, 13; DAM NOV**
See also CA 5-8R; 161; CANR 32, 67; DLB 15; MTCW 1

Newlove, Donald 1928- .... **CLC 6**
See also CA 29-32R; CANR 25

Newlove, John (Herbert) 1938- .... **CLC 14**
See also CA 21-24R; CANR 9, 25

Newman, Charles 1938- .... **CLC 2, 8**
See also CA 21-24R; CANR 84

Newman, Edwin (Harold) 1919- .... **CLC 14**
See also AITN 1; CA 69-72; CANR 5

Newman, John Henry 1801-1890 .... **NCLC 38**
See also DLB 18, 32, 55

Newton, (Sir) Isaac 1642-1727 .... **LC 35, 52**

Newton, Suzanne 1936- .... **CLC 35**
See also CA 41-44R; CANR 14; JRDA; SATA 5, 77

Nexo, Martin Andersen 1869-1954 ..... **TCLC 43**

Nezval, Vitezslav 1900-1958 .... **TCLC 44**
See also CA 123

Ng, Fae Myenne 1957(?)- .... **CLC 81**
See also CA 146

Ngema, Mbongeni 1955- .... **CLC 57**
See also BW 2; CA 143; CANR 84

Ngugi, James T(hiong'o) .... **CLC 3, 7, 13**
See also Ngugi wa Thiong'o

Ngugi wa Thiong'o 1938- **CLC 36; BLC 3; DAM MULT, NOV**
See also Ngugi, James T(hiong'o)
See also BW 2; CA 81-84; CANR 27, 58; DLB 125; MTCW 1, 2

Nichol, B(arrie) P(hillip) 1944-1988 ..... **CLC 18**
See also CA 53-56; DLB 53; SATA 66

Nichols, John (Treadwell) 1940- .... **CLC 38**
See also CA 9-12R; CAAS 2; CANR 6, 70; DLBY 82

Nichols, Leigh
See Koontz, Dean R(ay)

Nichols, Peter (Richard) 1927- ... **CLC 5, 36, 65**
See also CA 104; CANR 33, 86; DLB 13; MTCW 1

Nicolas, F. R. E.
See Freeling, Nicolas

Niedecker, Lorine 1903-1970 **CLC 10, 42; DAM POET**
See also CA 25-28; CAP 2; DLB 48

Nietzsche, Friedrich (Wilhelm) 1844-1900 **TCLC 10, 18, 55**
See also CA 107; 121; DLB 129

Nievo, Ippolito 1831-1861 .... **NCLC 22**

Nightingale, Anne Redmon 1943-
See Redmon, Anne
See also CA 103

Nightingale, Florence 1820-1910 .... **TCLC 85**
See also DLB 166

Nik. T. O.
See Annensky, Innokenty (Fyodorovich)

Nin, Anais 1903-1977 **CLC 1, 4, 8, 11, 14, 60, 127; DAM NOV, POP; SSC 10**
See also AITN 2; CA 13-16R; 69-72; CANR 22, 53; DLB 2, 4, 152; MTCW 1, 2

Nishida, Kitaro 1870-1945 .... **TCLC 83**

Nishiwaki, Junzaburo 1894-1982 .... **PC 15**
See also CA 107

Nissenson, Hugh 1933- .... **CLC 4, 9**
See also CA 17-20R; CANR 27; DLB 28

Niven, Larry .... **CLC 8**
See also Niven, Laurence Van Cott

See also AAYA 27; DLB 8

Niven, Laurence Van Cott 1938-
See Niven, Larry
See also CA 21-24R; CAAS 12; CANR 14, 44, 66; DAM POP; MTCW 1, 2; SATA 95

Nixon, Agnes Eckhardt 1927- .... **CLC 21**
See also CA 110

Nizan, Paul 1905-1940 .... **TCLC 40**
See also CA 161; DLB 72

Nkosi, Lewis 1936-**CLC 45; BLC 3; DAM MULT**
See also BW 1, 3; CA 65-68; CANR 27, 81; DLB 157

Nodier, (Jean) Charles (Emmanuel) 1780-1844
NCLC 19
See also DLB 119

Noguchi, Yone 1875-1947 .... **TCLC 80**

Nolan, Christopher 1965- .... **CLC 58**
See also CA 111

Noon, Jeff 1957- .... **CLC 91**
See also CA 148; CANR 83

Norden, Charles
See Durrell, Lawrence (George)

Nordhoff, Charles (Bernard) 1887-1947**TCLC 23**
See also CA 108; DLB 9; SATA 23

Norfolk, Lawrence 1963- .... **CLC 76**
See also CA 144; CANR 85

Norman, Marsha 1947-**CLC 28; DAM DRAM; DC 8**
See also CA 105; CABS 3; CANR 41; DLBY 84

Normyx
See Douglas, (George) Norman

Norris, Frank 1870-1902 .... **SSC 28**
See also Norris, (Benjamin) Frank(lin, Jr.)
See also CDALB 1865-1917; DLB 12, 71, 186

Norris, (Benjamin) Frank(lin, Jr.) 1870-1902
TCLC 24
See also Norris, Frank
See also CA 110; 160

Norris, Leslie 1921- .... **CLC 14**
See also CA 11-12; CANR 14; CAP 1; DLB 27

North, Andrew
See Norton, Andre

North, Anthony
See Koontz, Dean R(ay)

North, Captain George
See Stevenson, Robert Louis (Balfour)

North, Milou
See Erdrich, Louise

Northrup, B. A.
See Hubbard, L(afayette) Ron(ald)

North Staffs
See Hulme, T(homas) E(rnest)

Norton, Alice Mary
See Norton, Andre
See also MAICYA; SATA 1, 43

Norton, Andre 1912- .... **CLC 12**
See also Norton, Alice Mary
See also AAYA 14; CA 1-4R; CANR 68; CLR 50; DLB 8, 52; JRDA; MTCW 1; SATA 91

Norton, Caroline 1808-1877 .... **NCLC 47**
See also DLB 21, 159, 199

Norway, Nevil Shute 1899-1960
See Shute, Nevil
See also CA 102; 93-96; CANR 85; MTCW 2

Norwid, Cyprian Kamil 1821-1883 ...... **NCLC 17**

Nosille, Nabrah
See Ellison, Harlan (Jay)

Nossack, Hans Erich 1901-1978 .... **CLC 6**
See also CA 93-96; 85-88; DLB 69

Nostradamus 1503-1566 .... **LC 27**

Nosu, Chuji
See Ozu, Yasujiro

Notenburg, Eleanora (Genrikhovna) von

See Guro, Elena

Nova, Craig 1945- .... **CLC 7, 31**
See also CA 45-48; CANR 2, 53

Novak, Joseph
See Kosinski, Jerzy (Nikodem)

Novalis 1772-1801 .... **NCLC 13**
See also DLB 90

Novis, Emile
See Weil, Simone (Adolphine)

Nowlan, Alden (Albert) 1933-1983**CLC 15; DAC; DAM MST**
See also CA 9-12R; CANR 5; DLB 53

Noyes, Alfred 1880-1958 .... **TCLC 7; PC 27**
See also CA 104; DLB 20

Nunn, Kem .... **CLC 34**
See also CA 159

Nye, Robert 1939- .... **CLC 13, 42; DAM NOV**
See also CA 33-36R; CANR 29, 67; DLB 14; MTCW 1; SATA 6

Nyro, Laura 1947- .... **CLC 17**

Oates, Joyce Carol 1938-**CLC 1, 2, 3, 6, 9, 11, 15, 19, 33, 52, 108; DA; DAB; DAC; DAM MST, NOV, POP; SSC 6; WLC**
See also AAYA 15; AITN 1; BEST 89:2; CA 5-8R; CANR 25, 45, 74; CDALB 1968-1988; DA3; DLB 2, 5, 130; DLBY 81; INT CANR-25; MTCW 1, 2

O'Brien, Darcy 1939-1998 .... **CLC 11**
See also CA 21-24R; 167; CANR 8, 59

O'Brien, E. G.
See Clarke, Arthur C(harles)

O'Brien, Edna 1936-**CLC 3, 5, 8, 13, 36, 65, 116; DAM NOV; SSC 10**
See also CA 1-4R; CANR 6, 41, 65; CDBLB 1960 to Present; DA3; DLB 14; MTCW 1, 2

O'Brien, Fitz-James 1828-1862 .... **NCLC 21**
See also DLB 74

O'Brien, Flann .... **CLC 1, 4, 5, 7, 10, 47**
See also O Nuallain, Brian

O'Brien, Richard 1942- .... **CLC 17**
See also CA 124

O'Brien, (William) Tim(othy) 1946- **CLC 7, 19, 40, 103; DAM POP**
See also AAYA 16; CA 85-88; CANR 40, 58; CDALBS; DA3; DLB 152; DLBD 9; DLBY 80; MTCW 2

Obstfelder, Sigbjoern 1866-1900 .... **TCLC 23**
See also CA 123

O'Casey, Sean 1880-1964**CLC 1, 5, 9, 11, 15, 88; DAB; DAC; DAMDRAM, MST; WLCS**
See also CA 89-92; CANR 62; CDBLB 1914-1945; DA3; DLB 10; MTCW 1, 2

O'Cathasaigh, Sean
See O'Casey, Sean

Ochs, Phil 1940-1976 .... **CLC 17**
See also CA 65-68

O'Connor, Edwin (Greene) 1918-1968 .. **CLC 14**
See also CA 93-96; 25-28R

O'Connor, (Mary) Flannery 1925-1964**CLC 1, 2, 3, 6, 10, 13, 15, 21, 66, 104; DA; DAB; DAC; DAM MST, NOV; SSC 1, 23; WLC**
See also AAYA 7; CA 1-4R; CANR 3, 41; CDALB 1941-1968; DA3; DLB 2, 152; DLBD 12; DLBY 80; MTCW 1, 2

O'Connor, Frank .... **CLC 23; SSC 5**
See also O'Donovan, Michael John
See also DLB 162

O'Dell, Scott 1898-1989 .... **CLC 30**
See also AAYA 3; CA 61-64; 129; CANR 12, 30; CLR 1, 16; DLB 52; JRDA; MAICYA; SATA 12, 60

Odets, Clifford 1906-1963   **CLC 2, 28, 98; DAM DRAM; DC 6**

See also CA 85-88; CANR 62; DLB 7, 26; MTCW 1, 2

O'Doherty, Brian 1934- .... **CLC 76**
See also CA 105

O'Donnell, K. M.
See Malzberg, Barry N(athaniel)

O'Donnell, Lawrence
See Kuttner, Henry

O'Donovan, Michael John 1903-1966 ... **CLC 14**
See also O'Connor, Frank
See also CA 93-96; CANR 84

Oe, Kenzaburo 1935-**CLC 10, 36, 86; DAM NOV; SSC 20**
See also CA 97-100; CANR 36, 50, 74; DA3; DLB 182; DLBY 94; MTCW 1, 2

O'Faolain, Julia 1932- .... **CLC 6, 19, 47, 108**
See also CA 81-84; CAAS 2; CANR 12, 61; DLB 14; MTCW 1

O'Faolain, Sean 1900-1991**CLC 1, 7, 14, 32, 70; SSC 13**
See also CA 61-64; 134; CANR 12, 66; DLB 15, 162; MTCW 1, 2

O'Flaherty, Liam 1896-1984 .. **CLC 5, 34; SSC 6**
See also CA 101; 113; CANR 35; DLB 36, 162; DLBY 84; MTCW 1, 2

Ogilvy, Gavin
See Barrie, J(ames) M(atthew)

O'Grady, Standish (James) 1846-1928 .. **TCLC 5**
See also CA 104; 157

O'Grady, Timothy 1951- .... **CLC 59**
See also CA 138

O'Hara, Frank 1926-1966**CLC 2, 5, 13, 78; DAM POET**
See also CA 9-12R; 25-28R; CANR 33; DA3; DLB 5, 16, 193; MTCW 1, 2

O'Hara, John (Henry) 1905-1970 **CLC 1, 2, 3, 6, 11, 42; DAM NOV; SSC 15**
See also CA 5-8R; 25-28R; CANR 31, 60; CDALB 1929-1941; DLB 9, 86; DLBD 2; MTCW 1, 2

O Hehir, Diana 1922- .... **CLC 41**
See also CA 93-96

Ohiyesa
See Eastman, Charles A(lexander)

Okigbo, Christopher (Ifenayichukwu) 1932-1967
CLC 25, 84; BLC 3; DAM MULT, POET; PC 7
See also BW 1, 3; CA 77-80; CANR 74; DLB 125; MTCW 1, 2

Okri, Ben 1959- .... **CLC 87**
See also BW 2, 3; CA 130; 138; CANR 65; DLB 157; INT 138; MTCW 2

Olds, Sharon 1942-**CLC 32, 39, 85; DAM POET; PC 22**
See also CA 101; CANR 18, 41, 66; DLB 120; MTCW 2

Oldstyle, Jonathan
See Irving, Washington

Olesha, Yuri (Karlovich) 1899-1960 .... **CLC 8**
See also CA 85-88

Oliphant, Laurence 1829(?)-1888 .... **NCLC 47**
See also DLB 18, 166

Oliphant, Margaret (Oliphant Wilson) 1828-1897
NCLC 11, 61; SSC 25
See also DLB 18, 159, 190

Oliver, Mary 1935- .... **CLC 19, 34, 98**
See also CA 21-24R; CANR 9, 43, 84; DLB 5, 193

Olivier, Laurence (Kerr) 1907-1989 ..... **CLC 20**
See also CA 111; 150; 129

Olsen, Tillie 1912- . **CLC 4, 13, 114; DA; DAB; DAC; DAM MST; SSC 11**
See also CA 1-4R; CANR 1, 43, 74; CDALBS; DA3; DLB 28, 206; DLBY 80; MTCW 1, 2

Olson, Charles (John) 1910-1970**CLC 1, 2, 5, 6, 9,**

11, 29; DAM POET; PC 19
See also CA 13-16; 25-28R; CABS 2; CANR 35, 61; CAP 1; DLB 5, 16, 193; MTCW 1, 2

Olson, Toby 1937- .... **CLC 28**
See also CA 65-68; CANR 9, 31, 84

Olyesha, Yuri
See Olesha, Yuri (Karlovich)

Ondaatje, (Philip) Michael 1943-**CLC 14, 29, 51, 76; DAB; DAC; DAM MST; PC 28**
See also CA 77-80; CANR 42, 74; DA3; DLB 60; MTCW 2

Oneal, Elizabeth 1934-
See Oneal, Zibby
See also CA 106; CANR 28, 84; MAICYA; SATA 30, 82

Oneal, Zibby .... **CLC 30**
See also Oneal, Elizabeth
See also AAYA 5; CLR 13; JRDA

O'Neill, Eugene (Gladstone) 1888-1953**TCLC 1, 6, 27, 49; DA; DAB; DAC; DAM DRAM, MST; WLC**
See also AITN 1; CA 110; 132; CDALB 1929-1941; DA3; DLB 7; MTCW 1, 2

Onetti, Juan Carlos 1909-1994 **CLC 7, 10; DAM MULT, NOV; HLCS 2; SSC 23**
See also CA 85-88; 145; CANR 32, 63; DLB 113; HW 1, 2; MTCW 1, 2

O Nuallain, Brian 1911-1966
See O'Brien, Flann
See also CA 21-22; 25-28R; CAP 2

Ophuls, Max 1902-1957 .... **TCLC 79**
See also CA 113

Opie, Amelia 1769-1853 .... **NCLC 65**
See also DLB 116, 159

Oppen, George 1908-1984 .... **CLC 7, 13, 34**
See also CA 13-16R; 113; CANR 8, 82; DLB 5, 165

Oppenheim, E(dward) Phillips 1866-1946 **TCLC 45**
See also CA 111; DLB 70

Opuls, Max
See Ophuls, Max

Origen c. 185-c. 254 .... **CMLC 19**

Orlovitz, Gil 1918-1973 .... **CLC 22**
See also CA 77-80; 45-48; DLB 2, 5

Orris
See Ingelow, Jean

Ortega y Gasset, Jose 1883-1955 **TCLC 9; DAM MULT; HLC 2**
See also CA 106; 130; HW 1, 2; MTCW 1, 2

Ortese, Anna Maria 1914- .... **CLC 89**
See also DLB 177

Ortiz, Simon J(oseph) 1941- .... **CLC 45; DAM MULT, POET; PC 17**
See also CA 134; CANR 69; DLB 120, 175; NNAL

Orton, Joe .... **CLC 4, 13, 43; DC 3**
See also Orton, John Kingsley
See also CDBLB 1960 to Present; DLB 13; MTCW 2

Orton, John Kingsley 1933-1967
See Orton, Joe
See also CA 85-88; CANR 35, 66; DAM DRAM; MTCW 1, 2

Orwell, George TCLC 2, 6, 15, 31, 51; DAB; WLC
See also Blair, Eric (Arthur)
See also CDBLB 1945-1960; DLB 15, 98, 195

Osborne, David
See Silverberg, Robert

Osborne, George
See Silverberg, Robert

Osborne, John (James) 1929-1994**CLC 1, 2, 5, 11, 45; DA; DAB; DAC; DAM DRAM, MST; WLC**

See also CA 13-16R; 147; CANR 21, 56; CDBLB 1945-1960; DLB 13; MTCW 1, 2

Osborne, Lawrence 1958- .... **CLC 50**

Osbourne, Lloyd 1868-1947 .... **TCLC 93**

Oshima, Nagisa 1932- .... **CLC 20**
See also CA 116; 121; CANR 78

Oskison, John Milton 1874-1947**TCLC 35; DAM MULT**
See also CA 144; CANR 84; DLB 175; NNAL

Ossian c. 3rd cent. - .... **CMLC 28**
See also Macpherson, James

Ostrovsky, Alexander 1823-1886 .. **NCLC 30, 57**

Otero, Blas de 1916-1979 .... **CLC 11**
See also CA 89-92; DLB 134

Otto, Rudolf 1869-1937 .... **TCLC 85**

Otto, Whitney 1955- .... **CLC 70**
See also CA 140

Ouida .... **TCLC 43**
See also De La Ramee, (Marie) Louise
See also DLB 18, 156

Ousmane, Sembene 1923- .... **CLC 66; BLC 3**
See also BW 1, 3; CA 117; 125; CANR 81; MTCW 1

Ovid 43B.C.-17 ...... **CMLC 7; DAM POET; PC 2**
See also DA3; DLB 211

Owen, Hugh
See Faust, Frederick (Schiller)

Owen, Wilfred (Edward Salter) 1893-1918 **TCLC 5, 27; DA; DAB; DAC; DAM MST, POET; PC 19; WLC**
See also CA 104; 141; CDBLB 1914-1945; DLB 20; MTCW 2

Owens, Rochelle 1936- .... **CLC 8**
See also CA 17-20R; CAAS 2; CANR 39

Oz, Amos 1939- **CLC 5, 8, 11, 27, 33, 54; DAM NOV**
See also CA 53-56; CANR 27, 47, 65; MTCW 1, 2

Ozick, Cynthia 1928-**CLC 3, 7, 28, 62; DAM NOV, POP; SSC 15**
See also BEST 90:1; CA 17-20R; CANR 23, 58; DA3; DLB 28, 152; DLBY 82; INT CANR-23; MTCW 1, 2

Ozu, Yasujiro 1903-1963 .... **CLC 16**
See also CA 112

Pacheco, C.
See Pessoa, Fernando (Antonio Nogueira)

Pacheco, Jose Emilio 1939-
See also CA 111; 131; CANR 65; DAM MULT; HLC 2; HW 1, 2

Pa Chin .... **CLC 18**
See also Li Fei-kan

Pack, Robert 1929- .... **CLC 13**
See also CA 1-4R; CANR 3, 44, 82; DLB 5

Padgett, Lewis
See Kuttner, Henry

Padilla (Lorenzo), Heberto 1932- .... **CLC 38**
See also AITN 1; CA 123; 131; HW 1

Page, Jimmy 1944- .... **CLC 12**

Page, Louise 1955- .... **CLC 40**
See also CA 140; CANR 76

Page, P(atricia) K(athleen) 1916- .... **CLC 7, 18; DAC; DAM MST; PC 12**
See also CA 53-56; CANR 4, 22, 65; DLB 68; MTCW 1

Page, Thomas Nelson 1853-1922 .... **SSC 23**
See also CA 118; 177; DLB 12, 78; DLBD 13

Pagels, Elaine Hiesey 1943- .... **CLC 104**
See also CA 45-48; CANR 2, 24, 51

Paget, Violet 1856-1935
See Lee, Vernon
See also CA 104; 166

Paget-Lowe, Henry
See Lovecraft, H(oward) P(hillips)

Paglia, Camille (Anna) 1947- .... **CLC 68**
See also CA 140; CANR 72; MTCW 2

Paige, Richard
See Koontz, Dean R(ay)

Paine, Thomas 1737-1809 .... **NCLC 62**
See also CDALB 1640-1865; DLB 31, 43, 73, 158

Pakenham, Antonia
See Fraser, (Lady) Antonia (Pakenham)

Palamas, Kostes 1859-1943 .... **TCLC 5**
See also CA 105

Palazzeschi, Aldo 1885-1974 .... **CLC 11**
See also CA 89-92; 53-56; DLB 114

Pales Matos, Luis 1898-1959
See also HLCS 2; HW 1

Paley, Grace 1922-**CLC 4, 6, 37; DAM POP; SSC 8**
See also CA 25-28R; CANR 13, 46, 74; DA3; DLB 28; INT CANR-13; MTCW 1, 2

Palin, Michael (Edward) 1943- .... **CLC 21**
See also Monty Python
See also CA 107; CANR 35; SATA 67

Palliser, Charles 1947- .... **CLC 65**
See also CA 136; CANR 76

Palma, Ricardo 1833-1919 .... **TCLC 29**
See also CA 168

Pancake, Breece Dexter 1952-1979
See Pancake, Breece D'J
See also CA 123; 109

Pancake, Breece D'J .... **CLC 29**
See also Pancake, Breece Dexter
See also DLB 130

Panko, Rudy
See Gogol, Nikolai (Vasilyevich)

Papadiamantis, Alexandros 1851-1911 **TCLC 29**
See also CA 168

Papadiamantopoulos, Johannes 1856-1910
See Moreas, Jean
See also CA 117

Papini, Giovanni 1881-1956 .... **TCLC 22**
See also CA 121; 180

Paracelsus 1493-1541 .... **LC 14**
See also DLB 179

Parasol, Peter
See Stevens, Wallace

Pardo Bazan, Emilia 1851-1921 .... **SSC 30**

Pareto, Vilfredo 1848-1923 .... **TCLC 69**
See also CA 175

Parfenie, Maria
See Codrescu, Andrei

Parini, Jay (Lee) 1948- .... **CLC 54**
See also CA 97-100; CAAS 16; CANR 32

Park, Jordan
See Kornbluth, C(yril) M.; Pohl, Frederik

Park, Robert E(zra) 1864-1944 .... **TCLC 73**
See also CA 122; 165

Parker, Bert
See Ellison, Harlan (Jay)

Parker, Dorothy (Rothschild) 1893-1967**CLC 15, 68; DAM POET; PC 28; SSC 2**
See also CA 19-20; 25-28R; CAP 2; DA3; DLB 11, 45, 86; MTCW 1, 2

Parker, Robert B(rown) 1932- .... **CLC 27; DAM NOV, POP**
See also AAYA 28; BEST 89:4; CA 49-52; CANR 1, 26, 52; INT CANR-26; MTCW 1

Parkin, Frank 1940- .... **CLC 43**
See also CA 147

Parkman, Francis Jr., Jr. 1823-1893 .. **NCLC 12**
See also DLB 1, 30, 186

Parks, Gordon (Alexander Buchanan) 1912-**CLC 1, 16; BLC 3; DAM MULT**
See also AITN 2; BW 2, 3; CA 41-44R; CANR 26, 66; DA3; DLB 33; MTCW 2; SATA 8, 108

Parmenides c. 515B.C.-c. 450B.C. **C M L C 22**
See also DLB 176

Parnell, Thomas 1679-1718 .... **LC 3**
See also DLB 94

Parra, Nicanor 1914- **CLC 2, 102; DAM MULT; HLC 2**
See also CA 85-88; CANR 32; HW 1; MTCW 1

Parra Sanojo, Ana Teresa de la 1890-1936
See also HLCS 2

Parrish, Mary Frances
See Fisher, M(ary) F(rances) K(ennedy)

Parson
See Coleridge, Samuel Taylor

Parson Lot
See Kingsley, Charles

Partridge, Anthony
See Oppenheim, E(dward) Phillips

Pascal, Blaise 1623-1662 .... **LC 35**

Pascoli, Giovanni 1855-1912 .... **TCLC 45**
See also CA 170

Pasolini, Pier Paolo 1922-1975 **CLC 20, 37, 106; PC 17**
See also CA 93-96; 61-64; CANR 63; DLB 128, 177; MTCW 1

Pasquini
See Silone, Ignazio

Pastan, Linda (Olenik) 1932- ..... **CLC 27; DAM POET**
See also CA 61-64; CANR 18, 40, 61; DLB 5

Pasternak, Boris (Leonidovich) 1890-1960 **C L C 7, 10, 18, 63; DA; DAB; DAC; DAM MST, NOV, POET; PC 6; SSC 31; WLC**
See also CA 127; 116; DA3; MTCW 1, 2

Patchen, Kenneth 1911-1972 **CLC 1, 2, 18; DAM POET**
See also CA 1-4R; 33-36R; CANR 3, 35; DLB 16, 48; MTCW 1

Pater, Walter (Horatio) 1839-1894 .... **NCLC 7**
See also CDBLB 1832-1890; DLB 57, 156

Paterson, A(ndrew) B(arton) 1864-1941 **TCLC 32**
See also CA 155; SATA 97

Paterson, Katherine (Womeldorf) 1932- **CLC 12, 30**
See also AAYA 1, 31; CA 21-24R; CANR 28, 59; CLR 7, 50; DLB 52; JRDA; MAICYA; MTCW 1; SATA 13, 53, 92

Patmore, Coventry Kersey Dighton 1823-1896 **NCLC 9**
See also DLB 35, 98

Paton, Alan (Stewart) 1903-1988 **CLC 4, 10, 25, 55, 106; DA; DAB; DAC; DAM MST, NOV; WLC**
See also AAYA 26; CA 13-16; 125; CANR 22; CAP 1; DA3; DLBD 17; MTCW 1, 2; SATA 11; SATA-Obit 56

Paton Walsh, Gillian 1937-
See Walsh, Jill Paton
See also CANR 38, 83; JRDA; MAICYA; SAAS 3; SATA 4, 72, 109

Patton, George S. 1885-1945 .... **TCLC 79**

Paulding, James Kirke 1778-1860 .... **NCLC 2**
See also DLB 3, 59, 74

Paulin, Thomas Neilson 1949-
See Paulin, Tom
See also CA 123; 128

Paulin, Tom .... **CLC 37**
See also Paulin, Thomas Neilson
See also DLB 40

Pausanias c. 1st cent. - .... **CMLC 36**

Paustovsky, Konstantin (Georgievich) 1892-1968 **CLC 40**
See also CA 93-96; 25-28R

Pavese, Cesare 1908-1950 **TCLC 3; PC 13; SSC 19**
See also CA 104; 169; DLB 128, 177

Pavic, Milorad 1929- .... **CLC 60**
See also CA 136; DLB 181

Pavlov, Ivan Petrovich 1849-1936 .... **TCLC 91**
See also CA 118; 180

Payne, Alan
See Jakes, John (William)

Paz, Gil
See Lugones, Leopoldo

Paz, Octavio 1914-1998 **CLC 3, 4, 6, 10, 19, 51, 65, 119; DA; DAB; DAC; DAM MST, MULT, POET; HLC 2; PC 1; WLC**
See also CA 73-76; 165; CANR 32, 65; DA3; DLBY 90, 98; HW 1, 2; MTCW 1, 2

p'Bitek, Okot 1931-1982 **CLC 96; BLC 3; DAM MULT**
See also BW 2, 3; CA 124; 107; CANR 82; DLB 125; MTCW 1, 2

Peacock, Molly 1947- .... **CLC 60**
See also CA 103; CAAS 21; CANR 52, 84; DLB 120

Peacock, Thomas Love 1785-1866 ...... **NCLC 22**
See also DLB 96, 116

Peake, Mervyn 1911-1968 .... **CLC 7, 54**
See also CA 5-8R; 25-28R; CANR 3; DLB 15, 160; MTCW 1; SATA 23

Pearce, Philippa .... **CLC 21**
See also Christie, (Ann) Philippa
See also CLR 9; DLB 161; MAICYA; SATA 1, 67

Pearl, Eric
See Elman, Richard (Martin)

Pearson, T(homas) R(eid) 1956- .... **CLC 39**
See also CA 120; 130; INT 130

Peck, Dale 1967- .... **CLC 81**
See also CA 146; CANR 72

Peck, John 1941- .... **CLC 3**
See also CA 49-52; CANR 3

Peck, Richard (Wayne) 1934- .... **CLC 21**
See also AAYA 1, 24; CA 85-88; CANR 19, 38; CLR 15; INT CANR-19; JRDA; MAICYA; SAAS 2; SATA 18, 55, 97; SATA-Essay 110

Peck, Robert Newton 1928- **CLC 17; DA; DAC; DAM MST**
See also AAYA 3; CA 81-84, 182; CAAE 182; CANR 31, 63; CLR 45; JRDA; MAICYA; SAAS 1; SATA 21, 62, 111; SATA-Essay 108

Peckinpah, (David) Sam(uel) 1925-1984 **CLC 20**
See also CA 109; 114; CANR 82

Pedersen, Knut 1859-1952
See Hamsun, Knut
See also CA 104; 119; CANR 63; MTCW 1, 2

Peeslake, Gaffer
See Durrell, Lawrence (George)

Peguy, Charles Pierre 1873-1914 .... **TCLC 10**
See also CA 107

Peirce, Charles Sanders 1839-1914 ... **TCLC 81**

Pellicer, Carlos 1900(?)-1977
See also CA 153; 69-72; HLCS 2; HW 1

Pena, Ramon del Valle y
See Valle-Inclan, Ramon (Maria) del

Pendennis, Arthur Esquir
See Thackeray, William Makepeace

Penn, William 1644-1718 .... **LC 25**
See also DLB 24

PEPECE
See Prado (Calvo), Pedro

Pepys, Samuel 1633-1703 **LC 11; DA; DAB; DAC; DAM MST; WLC**
See also CDBLB 1660-1789; DA3; DLB 101

Percy, Walker 1916-1990 **CLC 2, 3, 6, 8, 14, 18, 47, 65; DAM NOV, POP**
See also CA 1-4R; 131; CANR 1, 23, 64; DA3;

DLB 2; DLBY 80, 90; MTCW 1, 2

Percy, William Alexander 1885-1942 . **TCLC 84**
See also CA 163; MTCW 2

Perec, Georges 1936-1982 .... **CLC 56, 116**
See also CA 141; DLB 83

Pereda (y Sanchez de Porrua), Jose Maria de 1833-1906 .... **TCLC 16**
See also CA 117

Pereda y Porrua, Jose Maria de
See Pereda (y Sanchez de Porrua), Jose Maria de

Peregoy, George Weems
See Mencken, H(enry) L(ouis)

Perelman, S(idney) J(oseph) 1904-1979 **CLC 3, 5, 9, 15, 23, 44, 49; DAM DRAM; SSC 32**
See also AITN 1, 2; CA 73-76; 89-92; CANR 18; DLB 11, 44; MTCW 1, 2

Peret, Benjamin 1899-1959 .... **TCLC 20**
See also CA 117

Peretz, Isaac Loeb 1851(?)-1915 **TCLC 16; SSC 26**
See also CA 109

Peretz, Yitzkhok Leibush
See Peretz, Isaac Loeb

Perez Galdos, Benito 1843-1920 **TCLC 27; HLCS 2**
See also CA 125; 153; HW 1

Peri Rossi, Cristina 1941-
See also CA 131; CANR 59, 81; DLB 145; HLCS 2; HW 1, 2

Perrault, Charles 1628-1703 .... **LC 3, 52**
See also MAICYA; SATA 25

Perry, Anne 1938- .... **CLC 126**
See also CA 101; CANR 22, 50, 84

Perry, Brighton
See Sherwood, Robert E(mmet)

Perse, St.-John
See Leger, (Marie-Rene Auguste) Alexis Saint-Leger

Perutz, Leo(pold) 1882-1957 .... **TCLC 60**
See also CA 147; DLB 81

Peseenz, Tulio F.
See Lopez y Fuentes, Gregorio

Pesetsky, Bette 1932- .... **CLC 28**
See also CA 133; DLB 130

Peshkov, Alexei Maximovich 1868-1936
See Gorky, Maxim
See also CA 105; 141; CANR 83; DA; DAC; DAM DRAM, MST, NOV; MTCW 2

Pessoa, Fernando (Antonio Nogueira) 1888-1935 **TCLC 27; DAM MULT; HLC 2; PC 20**
See also CA 125

Peterkin, Julia Mood 1880-1961 .... **CLC 31**
See also CA 102; DLB 9

Peters, Joan K(aren) 1945- .... **CLC 39**
See also CA 158

Peters, Robert L(ouis) 1924- .... **CLC 7**
See also CA 13-16R; CAAS 8; DLB 105

Petofi, Sandor 1823-1849 .... **NCLC 21**

Petrakis, Harry Mark 1923- .... **CLC 3**
See also CA 9-12R; CANR 4, 30, 85

Petrarch 1304-1374 **CMLC 20; DAM POET; PC 8**
See also DA3

Petronius c. 20-66 .... **CMLC 34**
See also DLB 211

Petrov, Evgeny .... **TCLC 21**
See also Kataev, Evgeny Petrovich

Petry, Ann (Lane) 1908-1997 .... **CLC 1, 7, 18**
See also BW 1, 3; CA 5-8R; 157; CAAS 6; CANR 4, 46; CLR 12; DLB 76; JRDA; MAICYA; MTCW 1; SATA 5; SATA-Obit 94

Petursson, Halligrimur 1614-1674 .... **LC 8**

Peychinovich
See Vazov, Ivan (Minchov)

Phaedrus c. 18B.C.-c. 50 .... **CMLC 25**

See also DLB 211

Philips, Katherine 1632-1664 .... **LC 30**
See also DLB 131

Philipson, Morris H. 1926- .... **CLC 53**
See also CA 1-4R; CANR 4

Phillips, Caryl 1958-**CLC 96; BLCS; DAM MULT**
See also BW 2; CA 141; CANR 63; DA3; DLB
157; MTCW 2

Phillips, David Graham 1867-1911 ...... **TCLC 44**
See also CA 108; 176; DLB 9, 12

Phillips, Jack
See Sandburg, Carl (August)

Phillips, Jayne Anne 1952-**CLC 15, 33; SSC 16**
See also CA 101; CANR 24, 50; DLBY 80; INT
CANR-24; MTCW 1, 2

Phillips, Richard
See Dick, Philip K(indred)

Phillips, Robert (Schaeffer) 1938- .... **CLC 28**
See also CA 17-20R; CAAS 13; CANR 8; DLB
105

Phillips, Ward
See Lovecraft, H(oward) P(hillips)

Piccolo, Lucio 1901-1969 .... **CLC 13**
See also CA 97-100; DLB 114

Pickthall, Marjorie L(owry) C(hristie) 1883-1922
TCLC 21
See also CA 107; DLB 92

Pico della Mirandola, Giovanni 1463-1494**LC 15**

Piercy, Marge 1936- .... **CLC 3, 6, 14, 18, 27, 62**
See also CA 21-24R; CAAS 1; CANR 13, 43, 66;
DLB 120; MTCW 1, 2

Piers, Robert
See Anthony, Piers

Pieyre de Mandiargues, Andre 1909-1991
See Mandiargues, Andre Pieyre de
See also CA 103; 136; CANR 22, 82

Pilnyak, Boris .... **TCLC 23**
See also Vogau, Boris Andreyevich

Pincherle, Alberto 1907-1990 **CLC 11, 18; DAM
NOV**
See Moravia, Alberto
See also CA 25-28R; 132; CANR 33, 63; MTCW
1

Pinckney, Darryl 1953- .... **CLC 76**
See also BW 2, 3; CA 143; CANR 79

Pindar 518B.C.-446B.C. .... **CMLC 12; PC 19**
See also DLB 176

Pineda, Cecile 1942- .... **CLC 39**
See also CA 118

Pinero, Arthur Wing 1855-1934**TCLC 32; DAM
DRAM**
See also CA 110; 153; DLB 10

Pinero, Miguel (Antonio Gomez) 1946-1988**C L C
4, 55**
See also CA 61-64; 125; CANR 29; HW 1

Pinget, Robert 1919-1997 .... **CLC 7, 13, 37**
See also CA 85-88; 160; DLB 83

Pink Floyd
See Barrett, (Roger) Syd; Gilmour, David; Mason, Nick; Waters, Roger; Wright, Rick

Pinkney, Edward 1802-1828 .... **NCLC 31**

Pinkwater, Daniel Manus 1941- .... **CLC 35**
See also Pinkwater, Manus
See also AAYA 1; CA 29-32R; CANR 12, 38; CLR
4; JRDA; MAICYA; SAAS 3; SATA 46, 76

Pinkwater, Manus
See Pinkwater, Daniel Manus
See also SATA 8

Pinsky, Robert 1940-**CLC 9, 19, 38, 94, 121; DAM
POET; PC 27**
See also CA 29-32R; CAAS 4; CANR 58; DA3;
DLBY 82, 98; MTCW 2

Pinta, Harold

See Pinter, Harold

Pinter, Harold 1930-**CLC 1, 3, 6, 9, 11, 15, 27, 58,
73; DA; DAB; DAC; DAM DRAM, MST;
WLC**
See also CA 5-8R; CANR 33, 65; CDBLB 1960 to
Present; DA3; DLB 13; MTCW 1, 2

Piozzi, Hester Lynch (Thrale) 1741-1821 **NCLC
57**
See also DLB 104, 142

Pirandello, Luigi 1867-1936 ... **TCLC 4, 29; DA;
DAB; DAC; DAM DRAM, MST; DC 5; SSC
22; WLC**
See also CA 104; 153; DA3; MTCW 2

Pirsig, Robert M(aynard) 1928- .. **CLC 4, 6, 73;
DAM POP**
See also CA 53-56; CANR 42, 74; DA3; MTCW
1, 2; SATA 39

Pisarev, Dmitry Ivanovich 1840-1868 ..**NCLC 25**

Pix, Mary (Griffith) 1666-1709 .... **LC 8**
See also DLB 80

Pixerecourt, (Rene Charles) Guilbert de 1773-1844
NCLC 39
See also DLB 192

Plaatje, Sol(omon) T(shekisho) 1876-1932**T C L C
73; BLCS**
See also BW 2, 3; CA 141; CANR 79

Plaidy, Jean
See Hibbert, Eleanor Alice Burford

Planche, James Robinson 1796-1880 ..**NCLC 42**

Plant, Robert 1948- .... **CLC 12**

Plante, David (Robert) 1940-**CLC 7, 23, 38; DAM
NOV**
See also CA 37-40R; CANR 12, 36, 58, 82; DLBY
83; INT CANR-12; MTCW 1

Plath, Sylvia 1932-1963 **CLC 1, 2, 3, 5, 9, 11, 14,
17, 50, 51, 62, 111; DA; DAB; DAC; DAM
MST, POET; PC 1; WLC**
See also AAYA 13; CA 19-20; CANR 34; CAP 2;
CDALB 1941-1968; DA3; DLB 5, 6, 152;
MTCW 1, 2; SATA 96

Plato 428(?)B.C.-348(?)B.C. **CMLC 8; DA; DAB;
DAC; DAM MST; WLCS**
See also DA3; DLB 176

Platonov, Andrei .... **TCLC 14**
See also Klimentov, Andrei Platonovich

Platt, Kin 1911- .... **CLC 26**
See also AAYA 11; CA 17-20R; CANR 11; JRDA;
SAAS 17; SATA 21, 86

Plautus c. 251B.C.-184B.C. ...... **CMLC 24; DC 6**
See also DLB 211

Plick et Plock
See Simenon, Georges (Jacques Christian)

Plimpton, George (Ames) 1927- .... **CLC 36**
See also AITN 1; CA 21-24R; CANR 32, 70; DLB
185; MTCW 1, 2; SATA 10

Pliny the Elder c. 23-79 .... **CMLC 23**
See also DLB 211

Plomer, William Charles Franklin 1903-1973
CLC 4, 8
See also CA 21-22; CANR 34; CAP 2; DLB 20,
162, 191; MTCW 1; SATA 24

Plowman, Piers
See Kavanagh, Patrick (Joseph)

Plum, J.
See Wodehouse, P(elham) G(renville)

Plumly, Stanley (Ross) 1939- .... **CLC 33**
See also CA 108; 110; DLB 5, 193; INT 110

Plumpe, Friedrich Wilhelm 1888-1931**TCLC 53**
See also CA 112

Po Chu-i 772-846 .... **CMLC 24**

Poe, Edgar Allan 1809-1849 **NCLC 1, 16, 55, 78;
DA; DAB; DAC; DAM MST, POET; PC 1;
SSC 34; WLC**

See also AAYA 14; CDALB 1640-1865; DA3;
DLB 3, 59, 73, 74; SATA 23

Poet of Titchfield Street, The
See Pound, Ezra (Weston Loomis)

Pohl, Frederik 1919- .... **CLC 18; SSC 25**
See also AAYA 24; CA 61-64; CAAS 1; CANR
11, 37, 81; DLB 8; INT CANR-11; MTCW 1, 2;
SATA 24

Poirier, Louis 1910-
See Gracq, Julien
See also CA 122; 126

Poitier, Sidney 1927- .... **CLC 26**
See also BW 1; CA 117

Polanski, Roman 1933- .... **CLC 16**
See also CA 77-80

Poliakoff, Stephen 1952- .... **CLC 38**
See also CA 106; DLB 13

Police, The
See Copeland, Stewart (Armstrong); Summers,
Andrew James; Sumner, Gordon Matthew

Polidori, John William 1795-1821 ...... **NCLC 51**
See also DLB 116

Pollitt, Katha 1949- .... **CLC 28, 122**
See also CA 120; 122; CANR 66; MTCW 1, 2

Pollock, (Mary) Sharon 1936- ... **CLC 50; DAC;
DAM DRAM, MST**
See also CA 141; DLB 60

Polo, Marco 1254-1324 .... **CMLC 15**

Polonsky, Abraham (Lincoln) 1910- ..... **CLC 92**
See also CA 104; DLB 26; INT 104

Polybius c. 200B.C.-c. 118B.C. .... **CMLC 17**
See also DLB 176

Pomerance, Bernard 1940-**CLC 13; DAM DRAM**
See also CA 101; CANR 49

Ponge, Francis (Jean Gaston Alfred) 1899-1988
CLC 6, 18; DAM POET
See also CA 85-88; 126; CANR 40, 86

Poniatowska, Elena 1933-
See also CA 101; CANR 32, 66; DAM MULT;
DLB 113; HLC 2; HW 1, 2

Pontoppidan, Henrik 1857-1943 .... **TCLC 29**
See also CA 170

Poole, Josephine .... **CLC 17**
See also Helyar, Jane Penelope Josephine
See also SAAS 2; SATA 5

Popa, Vasko 1922-1991 .... **CLC 19**
See also CA 112; 148; DLB 181

Pope, Alexander 1688-1744**LC 3; DA; DAB; DAC;
DAM MST, POET; PC 26; WLC**
See also CDBLB 1660-1789; DA3; DLB 95, 101

Porter, Connie (Rose) 1959(?)- .... **CLC 70**
See also BW 2, 3; CA 142; SATA 81

Porter, Gene(va Grace) Stratton 1863(?)-1924
TCLC 21
See also CA 112

Porter, Katherine Anne 1890-1980 . **CLC 1, 3, 7,
10, 13, 15, 27, 101; DA; DAB; DAC; DAM
MST, NOV; SSC 4, 31**
See also AITN 2; CA 1-4R; 101; CANR 1, 65;
CDALBS; DA3; DLB 4, 9, 102; DLBD 12;
DLBY 80; MTCW 1, 2; SATA 39; SATA-Obit
23

Porter, Peter (Neville Frederick) 1929- . **CLC 5,
13, 33**
See also CA 85-88; DLB 40

Porter, William Sydney 1862-1910
See Henry, O.
See also CA 104; 131; CDALB 1865-1917; DA;
DAB; DAC; DAM MST; DA3;DLB 12, 78, 79;
MTCW 1, 2; YABC 2

Portillo (y Pacheco), Jose Lopez
See Lopez Portillo (y Pacheco), Jose

Portillo Trambley, Estela 1927-1998

See also CANR 32; DAM MULT; DLB 209;
   HLC 2; HW 1
Post, Melville Davisson 1869-1930 ...... **TCLC 39**
   See also CA 110
Potok, Chaim 1929-**CLC 2, 7, 14, 26, 112; DAM
   NOV**
   See also AAYA 15; AITN 1, 2; CA 17-20R; CANR
   19, 35, 64; DA3; DLB 28, 152; INT CANR-19;
   MTCW 1, 2; SATA 33, 106
Potter, Dennis (Christopher George) 1935-1994
   CLC 58, 86
   See also CA 107; 145; CANR 33, 61; MTCW 1
Pound, Ezra (Weston Loomis) 1885-1972 **CLC 1,
   2, 3, 4, 5, 7, 10, 13, 18, 34, 48, 50, 112; DA;
   DAB; DAC; DAM MST, POET; PC 4; WLC**
   See also CA 5-8R; 37-40R; CANR 40; CDALB
   1917-1929; DA3; DLB 4, 45, 63; DLBD 15;
   MTCW 1, 2
Povod, Reinaldo 1959-1994 .... **CLC 44**
   See also CA 136; 146; CANR 83
Powell, Adam Clayton, Jr. 1908-1972 ... **CLC 89;
   BLC 3; DAM MULT**
   See also BW 1, 3; CA 102; 33-36R; CANR 86
Powell, Anthony (Dymoke) 1905- **CLC 1, 3, 7, 9,
   10, 31**
   See also CA 1-4R; CANR 1, 32, 62; CDBLB 1945-
   1960; DLB 15; MTCW 1, 2
Powell, Dawn 1897-1965 .... **CLC 66**
   See also CA 5-8R; DLBY 97
Powell, Padgett 1952- .... **CLC 34**
   See also CA 126; CANR 63
Power, Susan 1961- .... **CLC 91**
Powers, J(ames) F(arl) 1917-1999**CLC 1, 4, 8, 57;
   SSC 4**
   See also CA 1-4R; 181; CANR 2, 61; DLB 130;
   MTCW 1
Powers, John J(ames) 1945-
   See Powers, John R.
   See also CA 69-72
Powers, John R. .... **CLC 66**
   See also Powers, John J(ames)
Powers, Richard (S.) 1957- .... **CLC 93**
   See also CA 148; CANR 80
Pownall, David 1938- .... **CLC 10**
   See also CA 89-92, 180; CAAS 18; CANR 49;
   DLB 14
Powys, John Cowper 1872-1963**CLC 7, 9, 15, 46,
   125**
   See also CA 85-88; DLB 15; MTCW 1, 2
Powys, T(heodore) F(rancis) 1875-1953 **TCLC 9**
   See also CA 106; DLB 36, 162
Prado (Calvo), Pedro 1886-1952 .... **TCLC 75**
   See also CA 131; HW 1
Prager, Emily 1952- .... **CLC 56**
Pratt, E(dwin) J(ohn) 1883(?)-1964**CLC 19; DAC;
   DAM POET**
   See also CA 141; 93-96; CANR 77; DLB 92
Premchand .... **TCLC 21**
   See also Srivastava, Dhanpat Rai
Preussler, Otfried 1923- .... **CLC 17**
   See also CA 77-80; SATA 24
Prevert, Jacques (Henri Marie) 1900-1977 **CLC
   15**
   See also CA 77-80; 69-72; CANR 29, 61; MTCW
   1; SATA-Obit 30
Prevost, Abbe (Antoine Francois) 1697-1763**LC 1**
Price, (Edward) Reynolds 1933-**CLC 3, 6, 13, 43,
   50, 63; DAM NOV; SSC 22**
   See also CA 1-4R; CANR 1, 37, 57; DLB 2; INT
   CANR-37
Price, Richard 1949- .... **CLC 6, 12**
   See also CA 49-52; CANR 3; DLBY 81
Prichard, Katharine Susannah 1883-1969 . **C L C**
   46
   See also CA 11-12; CANR 33; CAP 1; MTCW 1;
   SATA 66
Priestley, J(ohn) B(oynton) 1894-1984 **CLC 2, 5,
   9, 34; DAM DRAM, NOV**
   See also CA 9-12R; 113; CANR 33; CDBLB 1914-
   1945; DA3; DLB 10, 34, 77, 100, 139; DLBY 84;
   MTCW 1, 2
Prince 1958(?)- .... **CLC 35**
Prince, F(rank) T(empleton) 1912- ...... **CLC 22**
   See also CA 101; CANR 43, 79; DLB 20
Prince Kropotkin
   See Kropotkin, Peter (Aleksieevich)
Prior, Matthew 1664-1721 .... **LC 4**
   See also DLB 95
Prishvin, Mikhail 1873-1954 .... **TCLC 75**
Pritchard, William H(arrison) 1932-... **CLC 34**
   See also CA 65-68; CANR 23; DLB 111
Pritchett, V(ictor) S(awdon) 1900-1997**CLC 5, 13,
   15, 41; DAM NOV; SSC 14**
   See also CA 61-64; 157; CANR 31, 63; DA3; DLB
   15, 139; MTCW 1, 2
Private 19022
   See Manning, Frederic
Probst, Mark 1925- .... **CLC 59**
   See also CA 130
Prokosch, Frederic 1908-1989 .... **CLC 4, 48**
   See also CA 73-76; 128; CANR 82; DLB 48;
   MTCW 2
Propertius, Sextus c. 50B.C.-c. 16B.C.**CMLC 32**
   See also DLB 211
Prophet, The
   See Dreiser, Theodore (Herman Albert)
Prose, Francine 1947- .... **CLC 45**
   See also CA 109; 112; CANR 46; SATA 101
Proudhon
   See Cunha, Euclides (Rodrigues Pimenta) da
Proulx, Annie
   See Proulx, E(dna) Annie
Proulx, E(dna) Annie 1935- **CLC 81; DAM POP**
   See also CA 145; CANR 65; DA3; MTCW 2
Proust, (Valentin-Louis-George-Eugene-) Marcel
   1871-1922**TCLC 7, 13, 33; DA; DAB; DAC;
   DAM MST, NOV; WLC**
   See also CA 104; 120; DA3; DLB 65; MTCW 1, 2
Prowler, Harley
   See Masters, Edgar Lee
Prus, Boleslaw 1845-1912 .... **TCLC 48**
Pryor, Richard (Franklin Lenox Thomas) 1940-
   CLC 26
   See also CA 122; 152
Przybyszewski, Stanislaw 1868-1927 . **TCLC 36**
   See also CA 160; DLB 66
Pteleon
   See Grieve, C(hristopher) M(urray)
   See also DAM POET
Puckett, Lute
   See Masters, Edgar Lee
Puig, Manuel 1932-1990 ... **CLC 3, 5, 10, 28, 65;
   DAM MULT; HLC 2**
   See also CA 45-48; CANR 2, 32, 63; DA3; DLB
   113; HW 1, 2; MTCW 1, 2
Pulitzer, Joseph 1847-1911 .... **TCLC 76**
   See also CA 114; DLB 23
Purdy, A(lfred) W(ellington) 1918-**CLC 3, 6, 14,
   50; DAC; DAM MST, POET**
   See also CA 81-84; CAAS 17; CANR 42, 66; DLB
   88
Purdy, James (Amos) 1923- **CLC 2, 4, 10, 28, 52**
   See also CA 33-36R; CAAS 1; CANR 19, 51; DLB
   2; INT CANR-19; MTCW 1
Pure, Simon
   See Swinnerton, Frank Arthur

Pushkin, Alexander (Sergeyevich) 1799-1837
   **NCLC 3, 27, 83; DA; DAB; DAC; DAM
   DRAM, MST, POET; PC 10; SSC 27; WLC**
   See also DA3; DLB 205; SATA 61
P'u Sung-ling 1640-1715 .... **LC 49; SSC 31**
Putnam, Arthur Lee
   See Alger, Horatio Jr., Jr.
Puzo, Mario 1920-1999**CLC 1, 2, 6, 36, 107; DAM
   NOV, POP**
   See also CA 65-68; CANR 4, 42, 65; DA3; DLB 6;
   MTCW 1, 2
Pygge, Edward
   See Barnes, Julian (Patrick)
Pyle, Ernest Taylor 1900-1945
   See Pyle, Ernie
   See also CA 115; 160
Pyle, Ernie 1900-1945 .... **TCLC 75**
   See also Pyle, Ernest Taylor
   See also DLB 29; MTCW 2
Pyle, Howard 1853-1911 .... **TCLC 81**
   See also CA 109; 137; CLR 22; DLB 42, 188;
   DLBD 13; MAICYA; SATA 16, 100
Pym, Barbara (Mary Crampton) 1913-1980 **C L C
   13, 19, 37, 111**
   See also CA 13-14; 97-100; CANR 13, 34; CAP 1;
   DLB 14, 207; DLBY 87; MTCW 1, 2
Pynchon, Thomas (Ruggles, Jr.) 1937-**CLC 2, 3,
   6, 9, 11, 18, 33, 62, 72; DA; DAB; DAC; DAM
   MST, NOV, POP; SSC 14; WLC**
   See also BEST 90:2; CA 17-20R; CANR 22, 46,
   73; DA3; DLB 2, 173; MTCW 1, 2
Pythagoras c. 570B.C.-c. 500B.C. .... **CMLC 22**
   See also DLB 176
Q
   See Quiller-Couch, SirArthur (Thomas)
Qian Zhongshu
   See Ch'ien Chung-shu
Qroll
   See Dagerman, Stig (Halvard)
Quarrington, Paul (Lewis) 1953- .... **CLC 65**
   See also CA 129; CANR 62
Quasimodo, Salvatore 1901-1968 .... **CLC 10**
   See also CA 13-16; 25-28R; CAP 1; DLB 114;
   MTCW 1
Quay, Stephen 1947- .... **CLC 95**
Quay, Timothy 1947- .... **CLC 95**
Queen, Ellery .... **CLC 3, 11**
   See also Dannay, Frederic; Davidson, Avram
   (James); Lee, Manfred B(ennington);
   Marlowe, Stephen; Sturgeon, Theodore
   (Hamilton); Vance, John Holbrook
Queen, Ellery, Jr.
   See Dannay, Frederic; Lee, Manfred
   B(ennington)
Queneau, Raymond 1903-1976 **CLC 2, 5, 10, 42**
   See also CA 77-80; 69-72; CANR 32; DLB 72;
   MTCW 1, 2
Quevedo, Francisco de 1580-1645 .... **LC 23**
Quiller-Couch, SirArthur (Thomas) 1863-1944
   TCLC 53
   See also CA 118; 166; DLB 135, 153, 190
Quin, Ann (Marie) 1936-1973 .... **CLC 6**
   See also CA 9-12R; 45-48; DLB 14
Quinn, Martin
   See Smith, Martin Cruz
Quinn, Peter 1947- .... **CLC 91**
Quinn, Simon
   See Smith, Martin Cruz
Quintana, Leroy V. 1944-
   See also CA 131; CANR 65; DAM MULT; DLB
   82; HLC 2; HW 1, 2
Quiroga, Horacio (Sylvestre) 1878-1937 . **T C L C
   20; DAM MULT; HLC 2**

See also CA 117; 131; HW 1; MTCW 1

Quoirez, Francoise 1935- .... **CLC 9**
  See also Sagan, Francoise
  See also CA 49-52; CANR 6, 39, 73; MTCW 1, 2

Raabe, Wilhelm (Karl) 1831-1910 ...... **TCLC 45**
  See also CA 167; DLB 129

Rabe, David (William) 1940-**CLC 4, 8, 33; DAM DRAM**
  See also CA 85-88; CABS 3; CANR 59; DLB 7

Rabelais, Francois 1483-1553 . **LC 5; DA; DAB; DAC; DAM MST; WLC**

Rabinovitch, Sholem 1859-1916
  See Aleichem, Sholom
  See also CA 104

Rabinyan, Dorit 1972- .... **CLC 119**
  See also CA 170

Rachilde 1860-1953 .... **TCLC 67**
  See also DLB 123, 192

Racine, Jean 1639-1699**LC 28; DAB; DAM MST**
  See also DA3

Radcliffe, Ann (Ward) 1764-1823 .... **NCLC 6, 55**
  See also DLB 39, 178

Radiguet, Raymond 1903-1923 .... **TCLC 29**
  See also CA 162; DLB 65

Radnoti, Miklos 1909-1944 .... **TCLC 16**
  See also CA 118

Rado, James 1939- .... **CLC 17**
  See also CA 105

Radvanyi, Netty 1900-1983
  See Seghers, Anna
  See also CA 85-88; 110; CANR 82

Rae, Ben
  See Griffiths, Trevor

Raeburn, John (Hay) 1941- .... **CLC 34**
  See also CA 57-60

Ragni, Gerome 1942-1991 .... **CLC 17**
  See also CA 105; 134

Rahv, Philip 1908-1973 .... **CLC 24**
  See also Greenberg, Ivan
  See also DLB 137

Raimund, Ferdinand Jakob 1790-1836 **NCLC 69**
  See also DLB 90

Raine, Craig 1944- .... **CLC 32, 103**
  See also CA 108; CANR 29, 51; DLB 40

Raine, Kathleen (Jessie) 1908- .... **CLC 7, 45**
  See also CA 85-88; CANR 46; DLB 20; MTCW 1

Rainis, Janis 1865-1929 .... **TCLC 29**
  See also CA 170

Rakosi, Carl 1903- .... **CLC 47**
  See also Rawley, Callman
  See also CAAS 5; DLB 193

Raleigh, Richard
  See Lovecraft, H(oward) P(hillips)

Raleigh, Sir Walter 1554(?)-1618 ...... **LC 31, 39**
  See also CDBLB Before 1660; DLB 172

Rallentando, H. P.
  See Sayers, Dorothy L(eigh)

Ramal, Walter
  See de la Mare, Walter (John)

Ramana Maharshi 1879-1950 .... **TCLC 84**

Ramoacn y Cajal, Santiago 1852-1934 **TCLC 93**

Ramon, Juan
  See Jimenez (Mantecon), Juan Ramon

Ramos, Graciliano 1892-1953 .... **TCLC 32**
  See also CA 167; HW 2

Rampersad, Arnold 1941- .... **CLC 44**
  See also BW 2, 3; CA 127; 133; CANR 81; DLB 111; INT 133

Rampling, Anne
  See Rice, Anne

Ramsay, Allan 1684(?)-1758 .... **LC 29**
  See also DLB 95

Ramuz, Charles-Ferdinand 1878-1947 **TCLC 33**

See also CA 165

Rand, Ayn 1905-1982**CLC 3, 30, 44, 79; DA; DAC; DAM MST, NOV, POP; WLC**
  See also AAYA 10; CA 13-16R; 105; CANR 27, 73; CDALBS; DA3; MTCW 1, 2

Randall, Dudley (Felker) 1914- **CLC 1; BLC 3; DAM MULT**
  See also BW 1, 3; CA 25-28R; CANR 23, 82; DLB 41

Randall, Robert
  See Silverberg, Robert

Ranger, Ken
  See Creasey, John

Ransom, John Crowe 1888-1974 **CLC 2, 4, 5, 11, 24; DAM POET**
  See also CA 5-8R; 49-52; CANR 6, 34; CDALBS; DA3; DLB 45, 63; MTCW 1, 2

Rao, Raja 1909- .... **CLC 25, 56; DAM NOV**
  See also CA 73-76; CANR 51; MTCW 1, 2

Raphael, Frederic (Michael) 1931- ... **CLC 2, 14**
  See also CA 1-4R; CANR 1, 86; DLB 14

Ratcliffe, James P.
  See Mencken, H(enry) L(ouis)

Rathbone, Julian 1935- .... **CLC 41**
  See also CA 101; CANR 34, 73

Rattigan, Terence (Mervyn) 1911-1977 .. **CLC 7; DAM DRAM**
  See also CA 85-88; 73-76; CDBLB 1945-1960; DLB 13; MTCW 1, 2

Ratushinskaya, Irina 1954- .... **CLC 54**
  See also CA 129; CANR 68

Raven, Simon (Arthur Noel) 1927- .... **CLC 14**
  See also CA 81-84; CANR 86

Ravenna, Michael
  See Welty, Eudora

Rawley, Callman 1903-
  See Rakosi, Carl
  See also CA 21-24R; CANR 12, 32

Rawlings, Marjorie Kinnan 1896-1953 . **TCLC 4**
  See also AAYA 20; CA 104; 137; CANR 74; DLB 9, 22, 102; DLBD 17; JRDA; MAICYA; MTCW 2; SATA 100; YABC 1

Ray, Satyajit 1921-1992**CLC 16, 76; DAM MULT**
  See also CA 114; 137

Read, Herbert Edward 1893-1968 .... **CLC 4**
  See also CA 85-88; 25-28R; DLB 20, 149

Read, Piers Paul 1941- .... **CLC 4, 10, 25**
  See also CA 21-24R; CANR 38, 86; DLB 14; SATA 21

Reade, Charles 1814-1884 .... **NCLC 2, 74**
  See also DLB 21

Reade, Hamish
  See Gray, Simon (James Holliday)

Reading, Peter 1946- .... **CLC 47**
  See also CA 103; CANR 46; DLB 40

Reaney, James 1926- **CLC 13; DAC; DAM MST**
  See also CA 41-44R; CAAS 15; CANR 42; DLB 68; SATA 43

Rebreanu, Liviu 1885-1944 .... **TCLC 28**
  See also CA 165

Rechy, John (Francisco) 1934- **CLC 1, 7, 14, 18, 107; DAM MULT; HLC 2**
  See also CA 5-8R; CAAS 4; CANR 6, 32, 64; DLB 122; DLBY 82; HW 1, 2; INT CANR-6

Redcam, Tom 1870-1933 .... **TCLC 25**

Reddin, Keith .... **CLC 67**

Redgrove, Peter (William) 1932- ...... **CLC 6, 41**
  See also CA 1-4R; CANR 3, 39, 77; DLB 40

Redmon, Anne .... **CLC 22**
  See also Nightingale, Anne Redmon
  See also DLBY 86

Reed, Eliot
  See Ambler, Eric

Reed, Ishmael 1938- . **CLC 2, 3, 5, 6, 13, 32, 60; BLC 3; DAM MULT**
  See also BW 2, 3; CA 21-24R; CANR 25, 48, 74; DA3; DLB 2, 5, 33, 169; DLBD 8; MTCW 1, 2

Reed, John (Silas) 1887-1920 .... **TCLC 9**
  See also CA 106

Reed, Lou .... **CLC 21**
  See also Firbank, Louis

Reeve, Clara 1729-1807 .... **NCLC 19**
  See also DLB 39

Reich, Wilhelm 1897-1957 .... **TCLC 57**

Reid, Christopher (John) 1949- .... **CLC 33**
  See also CA 140; DLB 40

Reid, Desmond
  See Moorcock, Michael (John)

Reid Banks, Lynne 1929-
  See Banks, Lynne Reid
  See also CA 1-4R; CANR 6, 22, 38; CLR 24; JRDA; MAICYA; SATA 22, 75, 111

Reilly, William K.
  See Creasey, John

Reiner, Max
  See Caldwell, (Janet Miriam) Taylor (Holland)

Reis, Ricardo
  See Pessoa, Fernando (Antonio Nogueira)

Remarque, Erich Maria 1898-1970**CLC 21; DA; DAB; DAC; DAM MST, NOV**
  See also AAYA 27; CA 77-80; 29-32R; DA3; DLB 56; MTCW 1, 2

Remington, Frederic 1861-1909 .... **TCLC 89**
  See also CA 108; 169; DLB 12, 186, 188; SATA 41

Remizov, A.
  See Remizov, Aleksei (Mikhailovich)

Remizov, A. M.
  See Remizov, Aleksei (Mikhailovich)

Remizov, Aleksei (Mikhailovich) 1877-1957 **TCLC 27**
  See also CA 125; 133

Renan, Joseph Ernest 1823-1892 .... **NCLC 26**

Renard, Jules 1864-1910 .... **TCLC 17**
  See also CA 117

Renault, Mary .... **CLC 3, 11, 17**
  See also Challans, Mary
  See also DLBY 83; MTCW 2

Rendell, Ruth (Barbara) 1930-**CLC 28, 48; DAM POP**
  See also Vine, Barbara
  See also CA 109; CANR 32, 52, 74; DLB 87; INT CANR-32; MTCW 1, 2

Renoir, Jean 1894-1979 .... **CLC 20**
  See also CA 129; 85-88

Resnais, Alain 1922- .... **CLC 16**

Reverdy, Pierre 1889-1960 .... **CLC 53**
  See also CA 97-100; 89-92

Rexroth, Kenneth 1905-1982 **CLC 1, 2, 6, 11, 22, 49, 112; DAM POET; PC 20**
  See also CA 5-8R; 107; CANR 14, 34, 63; CDALB 1941-1968; DLB 16, 48, 165, 212; DLBY 82; INT CANR-14; MTCW 1, 2

Reyes, Alfonso 1889-1959 ... **TCLC 33; HLCS 2**
  See also CA 131; HW 1

Reyes y Basoalto, Ricardo Eliecer Neftali
  See Neruda, Pablo

Reymont, Wladyslaw (Stanislaw) 1868(?)-1925 **TCLC 5**
  See also CA 104

Reynolds, Jonathan 1942- .... **CLC 6, 38**
  See also CA 65-68; CANR 28

Reynolds, Joshua 1723-1792 .... **LC 15**
  See also DLB 104

Reynolds, Michael Shane 1937- .... **CLC 44**
  See also CA 65-68; CANR 9

Reznikoff, Charles 1894-1976 .... **CLC 9**

See Séjour, Victor

Selby, Hubert, Jr. 1928- **CLC 1, 2, 4, 8; SSC 20**
  See also CA 13-16R; CANR 33, 85; DLB 2

Selzer, Richard 1928- .... **CLC 74**
  See also CA 65-68; CANR 14

Sembene, Ousmane
  See Ousmane, Sembene

Senancour, Etienne Pivert de 1770-1846**NCLC 16**
  See also DLB 119

Sender, Ramon (Jose) 1902-1982 .. **CLC 8; DAM MULT; HLC 2**
  See also CA 5-8R; 105; CANR 8; HW 1; MTCW 1

Seneca, Lucius Annaeus c. 1-c. 65**CMLC 6; DAM DRAM; DC 5**
  See also DLB 211

Senghor, Leopold Sedar 1906- **CLC 54; BLC 3; DAM MULT, POET; PC 25**
  See also BW 2; CA 116; 125; CANR 47, 74; MTCW 1, 2

Senna, Danzy 1970- .... **CLC 119**
  See also CA 169

Serling, (Edward) Rod(man) 1924-1975 **CLC 30**
  See also AAYA 14; AITN 1; CA 162; 57-60; DLB 26

Serna, Ramon Gomez de la
  See Gomez de la Serna, Ramon

Serpieres
  See Guillevic, (Eugene)

Service, Robert
  See Service, Robert W(illiam)
  See also DAB; DLB 92

Service, Robert W(illiam) 1874(?)-1958**TCLC 15; DA; DAC; DAM MST, POET; WLC**
  See also Service, Robert
  See also CA 115; 140; CANR 84; SATA 20

Seth, Vikram 1952- ... **CLC 43, 90; DAM MULT**
  See also CA 121; 127; CANR 50, 74; DA3; DLB 120; INT 127; MTCW 2

Seton, Cynthia Propper 1926-1982 .... **CLC 27**
  See also CA 5-8R; 108; CANR 7

Seton, Ernest (Evan) Thompson 1860-1946**TCLC 31**
  See also CA 109; CLR 59; DLB 92; DLBD 13; JRDA; SATA 18

Seton-Thompson, Ernest
  See Seton, Ernest (Evan) Thompson

Settle, Mary Lee 1918- .... **CLC 19, 61**
  See also CA 89-92; CAAS 1; CANR 44; DLB 6; INT 89-92

Seuphor, Michel
  See Arp, Jean

Sevigne, Marie (de Rabutin-Chantal) Marquise de 1626-1696 .... **LC 11**

Sewall, Samuel 1652-1730 .... **LC 38**
  See also DLB 24

Sexton, Anne (Harvey) 1928-1974 **CLC 2, 4, 6, 8, 10, 15, 53; DA; DAB; DAC; DAM MST, POET; PC 2; WLC**
  See also CA 1-4R; 53-56; CABS 2; CANR 3, 36; CDALB 1941-1968; DA3; DLB 5, 169; MTCW 1, 2; SATA 10

Shaara, Jeff 1952- .... **CLC 119**
  See also CA 163

Shaara, Michael (Joseph, Jr.) 1929-1988**CLC 15; DAM POP**
  See also AITN 1; CA 102; 125; CANR 52, 85; DLBY 83

Shackleton, C. C.
  See Aldiss, Brian W(ilson)

Shacochis, Bob .... **CLC 39**
  See also Shacochis, Robert G.

Shacochis, Robert G. 1951-
  See Shacochis, Bob
  See also CA 119; 124; INT 124

Shaffer, Anthony (Joshua) 1926- **CLC 19; DAM DRAM**
  See also CA 110; 116; DLB 13

Shaffer, Peter (Levin) 1926-**CLC 5, 14, 18, 37, 60; DAB; DAM DRAM, MST; DC 7**
  See also CA 25-28R; CANR 25, 47, 74; CDBLB 1960 to Present; DA3; DLB 13; MTCW 1, 2

Shakey, Bernard
  See Young, Neil

Shalamov, Varlam (Tikhonovich) 1907(?)-1982 **CLC 18**
  See also CA 129; 105

Shamlu, Ahmad 1925- .... **CLC 10**

Shammas, Anton 1951- .... **CLC 55**

Shange, Ntozake 1948- **CLC 8, 25, 38, 74, 126; BLC 3; DAM DRAM, MULT; DC 3**
  See also AAYA 9; BW 2; CA 85-88; CABS 3; CANR 27, 48, 74; DA3; DLB 38; MTCW 1, 2

Shanley, John Patrick 1950- .... **CLC 75**
  See also CA 128; 133; CANR 83

Shapcott, Thomas W(illiam) 1935- ...... **CLC 38**
  See also CA 69-72; CANR 49, 83

Shapiro, Jane .... **CLC 76**

Shapiro, Karl (Jay) 1913-**CLC 4, 8, 15, 53; PC 25**
  See also CA 1-4R; CAAS 6; CANR 1, 36, 66; DLB 48; MTCW 1, 2

Sharp, William 1855-1905 .... **TCLC 39**
  See also CA 160; DLB 156

Sharpe, Thomas Ridley 1928-
  See Sharpe, Tom
  See also CA 114; 122; CANR 85; INT 122

Sharpe, Tom .... **CLC 36**
  See also Sharpe, Thomas Ridley
  See also DLB 14

Shaw, Bernard .... **TCLC 45**
  See also Shaw, George Bernard
  See also BW 1; MTCW 2

Shaw, G. Bernard
  See Shaw, George Bernard

Shaw, George Bernard 1856-1950**TCLC 3, 9, 21; DA; DAB; DAC; DAM DRAM, MST; WLC**
  See also Shaw, Bernard
  See also CA 104; 128; CDBLB 1914-1945; DA3; DLB 10, 57, 190; MTCW 1, 2

Shaw, Henry Wheeler 1818-1885 .... **NCLC 15**
  See also DLB 11

Shaw, Irwin 1913-1984 ...... **CLC 7, 23, 34; DAM DRAM, POP**
  See also AITN 1; CA 13-16R; 112; CANR 21; CDALB 1941-1968; DLB 6, 102; DLBY 84; MTCW 1, 21

Shaw, Robert 1927-1978 .... **CLC 5**
  See also AITN 1; CA 1-4R; 81-84; CANR 4; DLB 13, 14

Shaw, T. E.
  See Lawrence, T(homas) E(dward)

Shawn, Wallace 1943- .... **CLC 41**
  See also CA 112

Shea, Lisa 1953- .... **CLC 86**
  See also CA 147

Sheed, Wilfrid (John Joseph) 1930-**CLC 2, 4, 10, 53**
  See also CA 65-68; CANR 30, 66; DLB 6; MTCW 1, 2

Sheldon, Alice Hastings Bradley 1915(?)-1987
  See Tiptree, James, Jr.
  See also CA 108; 122; CANR 34; INT 108; MTCW 1

Sheldon, John
  See Bloch, Robert (Albert)

Shelley, Mary Wollstonecraft (Godwin) 1797-1851 **NCLC 14, 59; DA; DAB; DAC; DAM MST, NOV; WLC**
  See also AAYA 20; CDBLB 1789-1832; DA3; DLB 110, 116, 159, 178; SATA 29

Shelley, Percy Bysshe 1792-1822**NCLC 18; DA; DAB; DAC; DAM MST, POET; PC 14; WLC**
  See also CDBLB 1789-1832; DA3; DLB 96, 110, 158

Shepard, Jim 1956- .... **CLC 36**
  See also CA 137; CANR 59; SATA 90

Shepard, Lucius 1947- .... **CLC 34**
  See also CA 128; 141; CANR 81

Shepard, Sam 1943-**CLC 4, 6, 17, 34, 41, 44; DAM DRAM; DC 5**
  See also AAYA 1; CA 69-72; CABS 3; CANR 22; DA3; DLB 7, 212; MTCW 1, 2

Shepherd, Michael
  See Ludlum, Robert

Sherburne, Zoa (Lillian Morin) 1912-1995 **CLC 30**
  See also AAYA 13; CA 1-4R; 176; CANR 3, 37; MAICYA; SAAS 18; SATA 3

Sheridan, Frances 1724-1766 .... **LC 7**
  See also DLB 39, 84

Sheridan, Richard Brinsley 1751-1816**NCLC 5; DA; DAB; DAC; DAM DRAM, MST; DC 1; WLC**
  See also CDBLB 1660-1789; DLB 89

Sherman, Jonathan Marc .... **CLC 55**

Sherman, Martin 1941(?)- .... **CLC 19**
  See also CA 116; 123; CANR 86

Sherwin, Judith Johnson 1936-
  See Johnson, Judith (Emlyn)
  See also CANR 85

Sherwood, Frances 1940- .... **CLC 81**
  See also CA 146

Sherwood, Robert E(mmet) 1896-1955 . **TCLC 3; DAM DRAM**
  See also CA 104; 153; CANR 86; DLB 7, 26

Shestov, Lev 1866-1938 .... **TCLC 56**

Shevchenko, Taras 1814-1861 .... **NCLC 54**

Shiel, M(atthew) P(hipps) 1865-1947 .... **TCLC 8**
  See also Holmes, Gordon
  See also CA 106; 160; DLB 153; MTCW 2

Shields, Carol 1935- .... **CLC 91, 113; DAC**
  See also CA 81-84; CANR 51, 74; DA3; MTCW 2

Shields, David 1956- .... **CLC 97**
  See also CA 124; CANR 48

Shiga, Naoya 1883-1971 .... **CLC 33; SSC 23**
  See also CA 101; 33-36R; DLB 180

Shikibu, Murasaki c. 978-c. 1014 .... **CMLC 1**

Shilts, Randy 1951-1994 .... **CLC 85**
  See also AAYA 19; CA 115; 127; 144; CANR 45; DA3; INT 127; MTCW 2

Shimazaki, Haruki 1872-1943
  See Shimazaki Toson
  See also CA 105; 134; CANR 84

Shimazaki Toson 1872-1943 .... **TCLC 5**
  See also Shimazaki, Haruki
  See also DLB 180

Sholokhov, Mikhail (Aleksandrovich) 1905-1984 **CLC 7, 15**
  See also CA 101; 112; MTCW 1, 2; SATA-Obit 36

Shone, Patric
  See Hanley, James

Shreve, Susan Richards 1939- .... **CLC 23**
  See also CA 49-52; CAAS 5; CANR 5, 38, 69; MAICYA; SATA 46, 95; SATA-Brief 41

Shue, Larry 1946-1985 ... **CLC 52; DAM DRAM**
  See also CA 145; 117

Shu-Jen, Chou 1881-1936
  See Lu Hsun

See also CA 104

Shulman, Alix Kates 1932- .... **CLC 2, 10**
See also CA 29-32R; CANR 43; SATA 7

Shuster, Joe 1914- .... **CLC 21**

Shute, Nevil .... **CLC 30**
See also Norway, Nevil Shute
See also MTCW 2

Shuttle, Penelope (Diane) 1947- .... **CLC 7**
See also CA 93-96; CANR 39, 84; DLB 14, 40

Sidney, Mary 1561-1621 .... **LC 19, 39**

Sidney, Sir Philip 1554-1586 **LC 19, 39; DA; DAB; DAC; DAM MST, POET**
See also CDBLB Before 1660; DA3; DLB 167

Siegel, Jerome 1914-1996 .... **CLC 21**
See also CA 116; 169; 151

Siegel, Jerry
See Siegel, Jerome

Sienkiewicz, Henryk (Adam Alexander Pius) 1846-1916 .... **TCLC 3**
See also CA 104; 134; CANR 84

Sierra, Gregorio Martinez
See Martinez Sierra, Gregorio

Sierra, Maria (de la O'LeJarraga) Martinez
See Martinez Sierra, Maria (de la O'LeJarraga)

Sigal, Clancy 1926- .... **CLC 7**
See also CA 1-4R; CANR 85

Sigourney, Lydia Howard (Huntley) 1791-1865 **NCLC 21**
See also DLB 1, 42, 73

Siguenza y Gongora, Carlos de 1645-1700 **LC 8; HLCS 2**

Sigurjonsson, Johann 1880-1919 .... **TCLC 27**
See also CA 170

Sikelianos, Angelos 1884-1951 .... **TCLC 39**

Silkin, Jon 1930- .... **CLC 2, 6, 43**
See also CA 5-8R; CAAS 5; DLB 27

Silko, Leslie (Marmon) 1948- **CLC 23, 74, 114; DA; DAC; DAM MST, MULT, POP; SSC 37; WLCS**
See also AAYA 14; CA 115; 122; CANR 45, 65, DA3; DLB 143, 175; MTCW 2; NNAL

Sillanpaa, Frans Eemil 1888-1964 .... **CLC 19**
See also CA 129; 93-96; MTCW 1

Sillitoe, Alan 1928- .... **CLC 1, 3, 6, 10, 19, 57**
See also AITN 1; CA 9-12R; CAAS 2; CANR 8, 26, 55; CDBLB 1960 to Present; DLB 14, 139; MTCW 1, 2; SATA 61

Silone, Ignazio 1900-1978 .... **CLC 4**
See also CA 25-28; 81-84; CANR 34; CAP 2; MTCW 1

Silver, Joan Micklin 1935- .... **CLC 20**
See also CA 114; 121; INT 121

Silver, Nicholas
See Faust, Frederick (Schiller)

Silverberg, Robert 1935- ...... **CLC 7; DAM POP**
See also AAYA 24; CA 1-4R; CAAS 3; CANR 1, 20, 36, 85; CLR 59; DLB 8; INT CANR-20; MAICYA; MTCW 1, 2; SATA 13, 91; SATA-Essay 104

Silverstein, Alvin 1933- .... **CLC 17**
See also CA 49-52; CANR 2; CLR 25; JRDA; MAICYA; SATA 8, 69

Silverstein, Virginia B(arbara Opshelor) 1937- **CLC 17**
See also CA 49-52; CANR 2; CLR 25; JRDA; MAICYA; SATA 8, 69

Sim, Georges
See Simenon, Georges (Jacques Christian)

Simak, Clifford D(onald) 1904-1988 . **CLC 1, 55**
See also CA 1-4R; 125; CANR 1, 35; DLB 8; MTCW 1; SATA-Obit 56

Simenon, Georges (Jacques Christian) 1903-1989 **CLC 1, 2, 3, 8, 18, 47; DAM POP**

See also CA 85-88; 129; CANR 35; DA3; DLB 72; DLBY 89; MTCW 1, 2

Simic, Charles 1938- **CLC 6, 9, 22, 49, 68; DAM POET**
See also CA 29-32R; CAAS 4; CANR 12, 33, 52, 61; DA3; DLB 105; MTCW 2

Simmel, Georg 1858-1918 .... **TCLC 64**
See also CA 157

Simmons, Charles (Paul) 1924- .... **CLC 57**
See also CA 89-92; INT 89-92

Simmons, Dan 1948- .... **CLC 44; DAM POP**
See also AAYA 16; CA 138; CANR 53, 81

Simmons, James (Stewart Alexander) 1933- **CLC 43**
See also CA 105; CAAS 21; DLB 40

Simms, William Gilmore 1806-1870 .... **NCLC 3**
See also DLB 3, 30, 59, 73

Simon, Carly 1945- .... **CLC 26**
See also CA 105

Simon, Claude 1913-1984 **CLC 4, 9, 15, 39; DAM NOV**
See also CA 89-92; CANR 33; DLB 83; MTCW 1

Simon, (Marvin) Neil 1927- **CLC 6, 11, 31, 39, 70; DAM DRAM**
See also AAYA 32; AITN 1; CA 21-24R; CANR 26, 54; DA3; DLB 7; MTCW 1, 2

Simon, Paul (Frederick) 1941(?)- .... **CLC 17**
See also CA 116; 153

Simonon, Paul 1956(?)- .... **CLC 30**

Simpson, Harriette
See Arnow, Harriette (Louisa) Simpson

Simpson, Louis (Aston Marantz) 1923- **CLC 4, 7, 9, 32; DAM POET**
See also CA 1-4R; CAAS 4; CANR 1, 61; DLB 5; MTCW 1, 2

Simpson, Mona (Elizabeth) 1957- .... **CLC 44**
See also CA 122; 135; CANR 68

Simpson, N(orman) F(rederick) 1919- . **CLC 29**
See also CA 13-16R; DLB 13

Sinclair, Andrew (Annandale) 1935- **CLC 2, 14**
See also CA 9-12R; CAAS 5; CANR 14, 38; DLB 14; MTCW 1

Sinclair, Emil
See Hesse, Hermann

Sinclair, Iain 1943- .... **CLC 76**
See also CA 132; CANR 81

Sinclair, Iain MacGregor
See Sinclair, Iain

Sinclair, Irene
See Griffith, D(avid Lewelyn) W(ark)

Sinclair, Mary Amelia St. Clair 1865(?)-1946
See Sinclair, May
See also CA 104

Sinclair, May 1863-1946 .... **TCLC 3, 11**
See also Sinclair, Mary Amelia St. Clair
See also CA 166; DLB 36, 135

Sinclair, Roy
See Griffith, D(avid Lewelyn) W(ark)

Sinclair, Upton (Beall) 1878-1968 **CLC 1, 11, 15, 63; DA; DAB; DAC; DAM MST, NOV; WLC**
See also CA 5-8R; 25-28R; CANR 7; CDALB 1929-1941; DA3; DLB 9; INT CANR-7; MTCW 1, 2; SATA 9

Singer, Isaac
See Singer, Isaac Bashevis

Singer, Isaac Bashevis 1904-1991 **CLC 1, 3, 6, 9, 11, 15, 23, 38, 69, 111; DA; DAB; DAC; DAM MST, NOV; SSC 3; WLC**
See also AAYA 32; AITN 1, 2; CA 1-4R; 134; CANR 1, 39; CDALB 1941-1968; CLR 1; DA3; DLB 6, 28, 52; DLBY 91; JRDA; MAICYA; MTCW 1, 2; SATA 3, 27; SATA-Obit 68

Singer, Israel Joshua 1893-1944 .... **TCLC 33**

See also CA 169

Singh, Khushwant 1915- .... **CLC 11**
See also CA 9-12R; CAAS 9; CANR 6, 84

Singleton, Ann
See Benedict, Ruth (Fulton)

Sinjohn, John
See Galsworthy, John

Sinyavsky, Andrei (Donatevich) 1925-1997 **CLC 8**
See also CA 85-88; 159

Sirin, V.
See Nabokov, Vladimir (Vladimirovich)

Sissman, L(ouis) E(dward) 1928-1976 **CLC 9, 18**
See also CA 21-24R; 65-68; CANR 13; DLB 5

Sisson, C(harles) H(ubert) 1914- .... **CLC 8**
See also CA 1-4R; CAAS 3; CANR 3, 48, 84; DLB 27

Sitwell, Dame Edith 1887-1964 **CLC 2, 9, 67; DAM POET; PC 3**
See also CA 9-12R; CANR 35; CDBLB 1945-1960; DLB 20; MTCW 1, 2

Siwaarmill, H. P.
See Sharp, William

Sjoewall, Maj 1935- .... **CLC 7**
See also CA 65-68; CANR 73

Sjowall, Maj
See Sjoewall, Maj

Skelton, John 1463-1529 .... **PC 25**

Skelton, Robin 1925-1997 .... **CLC 13**
See also AITN 2; CA 5-8R; 160; CAAS 5; CANR 28; DLB 27, 53

Skolimowski, Jerzy 1938- .... **CLC 20**
See also CA 128

Skram, Amalie (Bertha) 1847-1905 .... **TCLC 25**
See also CA 165

Skvorecky, Josef (Vaclav) 1924- **CLC 15, 39, 69; DAC; DAM NOV**
See also CA 61-64; CAAS 1; CANR 10, 34, 63; DA3; MTCW 1, 2

Slade, Bernard .... **CLC 11, 46**
See also Newbound, Bernard Slade
See also CAAS 9; DLB 53

Slaughter, Carolyn 1946- .... **CLC 56**
See also CA 85-88; CANR 85

Slaughter, Frank G(ill) 1908- .... **CLC 29**
See also AITN 2; CA 5-8R; CANR 5, 85; INT CANR-5

Slavitt, David R(ytman) 1935- .... **CLC 5, 14**
See also CA 21-24R; CAAS 3; CANR 41, 83; DLB 5, 6

Slesinger, Tess 1905-1945 .... **TCLC 10**
See also CA 107; DLB 102

Slessor, Kenneth 1901-1971 .... **CLC 14**
See also CA 102; 89-92

Slowacki, Juliusz 1809-1849 .... **NCLC 15**

Smart, Christopher 1722-1771 **LC 3; DAM POET; PC 13**
See also DLB 109

Smart, Elizabeth 1913-1986 .... **CLC 54**
See also CA 81-84; 118; DLB 88

Smiley, Jane (Graves) 1949- **CLC 53, 76; DAM POP**
See also CA 104; CANR 30, 50, 74; DA3; INT CANR-30

Smith, A(rthur) J(ames) M(arshall) 1902-1980 **CLC 15; DAC**
See also CA 1-4R; 102; CANR 4; DLB 88

Smith, Adam 1723-1790 .... **LC 36**
See also DLB 104

Smith, Alexander 1829-1867 .... **NCLC 59**
See also DLB 32, 55

Smith, Anna Deavere 1950- .... **CLC 86**
See also CA 133

Smith, Betty (Wehner) 1896-1972 .... **CLC 19**

See also DLB 3
Tindall, Gillian (Elizabeth) 1938- .... **CLC 7**
　　See also CA 21-24R; CANR 11, 65
Tiptree, James, Jr. .... **CLC 48, 50**
　　See also Sheldon, Alice Hastings Bradley
　　See also DLB 8
Titmarsh, Michael Angelo
　　See Thackeray, William Makepeace
**Tocqueville, Alexis (Charles Henri Maurice Clerel,
　　Comte) de** 1805-1859
　　... **NCLC 7, 63**
Tolkien, J(ohn) R(onald) R(euel) 1892-1973 **C L C
　　1, 2, 3, 8, 12, 38; DA; DAB; DAC; DAM MST,
　　NOV, POP; WLC**
　　See also AAYA 10; AITN 1; CA 17-18; 45-48;
　　CANR 36; CAP 2; CDBLB 1914-1945; CLR 56;
　　DA3; DLB 15, 160; JRDA; MAICYA; MTCW
　　1, 2; SATA 2, 32, 100; SATA-Obit 24
Toller, Ernst 1893-1939 .... **TCLC 10**
　　See also CA 107; DLB 124
Tolson, M. B.
　　See Tolson, Melvin B(eaunorus)
Tolson, Melvin B(eaunorus) 1898(?)-1966 .. **C L C
　　36, 105; BLC 3; DAM MULT, POET**
　　See also BW 1, 3; CA 124; 89-92; CANR 80; DLB
　　48, 76
Tolstoi, Aleksei Nikolaevich
　　See Tolstoy, Alexey Nikolaevich
Tolstoy, Alexey Nikolaevich 1882-1945 **TCLC 18**
　　See also CA 107; 158
Tolstoy, Count Leo
　　See Tolstoy, Leo (Nikolaevich)
Tolstoy, Leo (Nikolaevich) 1828-1910 **TCLC 4, 11,
　　17, 28, 44, 79; DA; DAB; DAC; DAM MST,
　　NOV; SSC 9, 30; WLC**
　　See also CA 104; 123; DA3; SATA 26
Tomasi di Lampedusa, Giuseppe 1896-1957
　　See Lampedusa, Giuseppe (Tomasi) di
　　See also CA 111
Tomlin, Lily .... **CLC 17**
　　See also Tomlin, Mary Jean
Tomlin, Mary Jean 1939(?)-
　　See Tomlin, Lily
　　See also CA 117
Tomlinson, (Alfred) Charles 1927- **CLC 2, 4, 6,
　　13, 45; DAM POET; PC 17**
　　See also CA 5-8R; CANR 33; DLB 40
Tomlinson, H(enry) M(ajor) 1873-1958 **TCLC 71**
　　See also CA 118; 161; DLB 36, 100, 195
Tonson, Jacob
　　See Bennett, (Enoch) Arnold
Toole, John Kennedy 1937-1969 ...... **CLC 19, 64**
　　See also CA 104; DLBY 81; MTCW 2
Toomer, Jean 1894-1967 **CLC 1, 4, 13, 22; BLC 3;
　　DAM MULT; PC 7; SSC 1; WLCS**
　　See also BW 1; CA 85-88; CDALB 1917-1929;
　　DA3; DLB 45, 51; MTCW 1, 2
Torley, Luke
　　See Blish, James (Benjamin)
Tornimparte, Alessandra
　　See Ginzburg, Natalia
Torre, Raoul della
　　See Mencken, H(enry) L(ouis)
Torrence, Ridgely 1874-1950 .... **TCLC 97**
　　See also DLB 54
Torrey, E(dwin) Fuller 1937- .... **CLC 34**
　　See also CA 119; CANR 71
Torsvan, Ben Traven
　　See Traven, B.
Torsvan, Benno Traven
　　See Traven, B.
Torsvan, Berick Traven
　　See Traven, B.

Torsvan, Berwick Traven
　　See Traven, B.
Torsvan, Bruno Traven
　　See Traven, B.
Torsvan, Traven
　　See Traven, B.
Tournier, Michel (Edouard) 1924- **CLC 6, 23, 36,
　　95**
　　See also CA 49-52; CANR 3, 36, 74; DLB 83;
　　MTCW 1, 2; SATA 23
Tournimparte, Alessandra
　　See Ginzburg, Natalia
Towers, Ivar
　　See Kornbluth, C(yril) M.
Towne, Robert (Burton) 1936(?)- .... **CLC 87**
　　See also CA 108; DLB 44
Townsend, Sue .... **CLC 61**
　　See also Townsend, Susan Elaine
　　See also AAYA 28; SATA 55, 93; SATA-Brief 48
Townsend, Susan Elaine 1946-
　　See Townsend, Sue
　　See also CA 119; 127; CANR 65; DAB; DAC;
　　DAM MST
Townshend, Peter (Dennis Blandford) 1945- **CLC
　　17, 42**
　　See also CA 107
Tozzi, Federigo 1883-1920 .... **TCLC 31**
　　See also CA 160
Traill, Catharine Parr 1802-1899 .... **NCLC 31**
　　See also DLB 99
Trakl, Georg 1887-1914 .... **TCLC 5; PC 20**
　　See also CA 104; 165; MTCW 2
Transtroemer, Tomas (Goesta) 1931- **CLC 52, 65;
　　DAM POET**
　　See also CA 117; 129; CAAS 17
Transtromer, Tomas Gosta
　　See Transtroemer, Tomas (Goesta)
Traven, B. (?)-1969 .... **CLC 8, 11**
　　See also CA 19-20; 25-28R; CAP 2; DLB 9, 56;
　　MTCW 1
Treitel, Jonathan 1959- .... **CLC 70**
Tremain, Rose 1943- .... **CLC 42**
　　See also CA 97-100; CANR 44; DLB 14
Tremblay, Michel 1942- **CLC 29, 102; DAC; DAM
　　MST**
　　See also CA 116; 128; DLB 60; MTCW 1, 2
Trevanian .... **CLC 29**
　　See also Whitaker, Rod(ney)
Trevor, Glen
　　See Hilton, James
Trevor, William 1928- **CLC 7, 9, 14, 25, 71, 116;
　　SSC 21**
　　See also Cox, William Trevor
　　See also DLB 14, 139; MTCW 2
Trifonov, Yuri (Valentinovich) 1925-1981 **CLC 45**
　　See also CA 126; 103; MTCW 1
Trilling, Lionel 1905-1975 .... **CLC 9, 11, 24**
　　See also CA 9-12R; 61-64; CANR 10; DLB 28, 63;
　　INT CANR-10; MTCW 1, 2
Trimball, W. H.
　　See Mencken, H(enry) L(ouis)
Tristan
　　See Gomez de la Serna, Ramon
Tristram
　　See Housman, A(lfred) E(dward)
Trogdon, William (Lewis) 1939-
　　See Heat-Moon, William Least
　　See also CA 115; 119; CANR 47; INT 119
Trollope, Anthony 1815-1882 .. **NCLC 6, 33; DA;
　　DAB; DAC; DAM MST, NOV; SSC 28; WLC**
　　See also CDBLB 1832-1890; DA3; DLB 21, 57,
　　159; SATA 22
Trollope, Frances 1779-1863 .... **NCLC 30**

See also DLB 21, 166
Trotsky, Leon 1879-1940 .... **TCLC 22**
　　See also CA 118; 167
Trotter (Cockburn), Catharine 1679-1749 **LC 8**
　　See also DLB 84
Trotter, Wilfred 1872-1939 .... **TCLC 99**
Trout, Kilgore
　　See Farmer, Philip Jose
Trow, George W. S. 1943- .... **CLC 52**
　　See also CA 126
Troyat, Henri 1911- .... **CLC 23**
　　See also CA 45-48; CANR 2, 33, 67; MTCW 1
Trudeau, G(arretson) B(eekman) 1948-
　　See Trudeau, Garry B.
　　See also CA 81-84; CANR 31; SATA 35
Trudeau, Garry B. .... **CLC 12**
　　See also Trudeau, G(arretson) B(eekman)
　　See also AAYA 10; AITN 2
Truffaut, Francois 1932-1984 .... **CLC 20, 101**
　　See also CA 81-84; 113; CANR 34
Trumbo, Dalton 1905-1976 .... **CLC 19**
　　See also CA 21-24R; 69-72; CANR 10; DLB 26
Trumbull, John 1750-1831 .... **NCLC 30**
　　See also DLB 31
Trundlett, Helen B.
　　See Eliot, T(homas) S(tearns)
Tryon, Thomas 1926-1991 **CLC 3, 11; DAM POP**
　　See also AITN 1; CA 29-32R; 135; CANR 32, 77;
　　DA3; MTCW 1
Tryon, Tom
　　See Tryon, Thomas
Ts'ao Hsueh-ch'in 1715(?)-1763 .... **LC 1**
Tsushima, Shuji 1909-1948
　　See Dazai Osamu
　　See also CA 107
Tsvetaeva (Efron), Marina (Ivanovna) 1892-1941
　　TCLC 7, 35; PC 14
　　See also CA 104; 128; CANR 73; MTCW 1, 2
Tuck, Lily 1938- .... **CLC 70**
　　See also CA 139
Tu Fu 712-770 .... **PC 9**
　　See also DAM MULT
Tunis, John R(oberts) 1889-1975 .... **CLC 12**
　　See also CA 61-64; CANR 62; DLB 22, 171;
　　JRDA; MAICYA; SATA 37; SATA-Brief 30
Tuohy, Frank .... **CLC 37**
　　See also Tuohy, John Francis
　　See also DLB 14, 139
Tuohy, John Francis 1925-1999
　　See Tuohy, Frank
　　See also CA 5-8R; 178; CANR 3, 47
Turco, Lewis (Putnam) 1934- .... **CLC 11, 63**
　　See also CA 13-16R; CAAS 22; CANR 24, 51;
　　DLBY 84
Turgenev, Ivan 1818-1883　**NCLC 21; DA; DAB;
　　DAC; DAM MST, NOV; DC 7; SSC 7; WLC**
Turgot, Anne-Robert-Jacques 1727-1781 **LC 26**
Turner, Frederick 1943- .... **CLC 48**
　　See also CA 73-76; CAAS 10; CANR 12, 30, 56;
　　DLB 40
Tutu, Desmond M(pilo) 1931- .. **CLC 80; BLC 3;
　　DAM MULT**
　　See also BW 1, 3; CA 125; CANR 67, 81
Tutuola, Amos 1920-1997 **CLC 5, 14, 29; BLC 3;
　　DAM MULT**
　　See also BW 2, 3; CA 9-12R; 159; CANR 27, 66;
　　DA3; DLB 125; MTCW 1, 2
**Twain, Mark TCLC 6, 12, 19, 36, 48, 59; SSC 34;
　　WLC**
　　See also Clemens, Samuel Langhorne
　　See also AAYA 20; CLR 58, 60; DLB 11, 12, 23,
　　64, 74
Tyler, Anne 1941- **CLC 7, 11, 18, 28, 44, 59, 103;**

DAM NOV, POP
  See also AAYA 18; BEST 89:1; CA 9-12R; CANR
    11, 33, 53; CDALBS; DLB 6, 143; DLBY 82;
    MTCW 1, 2; SATA 7, 90
Tyler, Royall 1757-1826 .... **NCLC 3**
  See also DLB 37
Tynan, Katharine 1861-1931 .... **TCLC 3**
  See also CA 104; 167; DLB 153
Tyutchev, Fyodor 1803-1873 .... **NCLC 34**
Tzara, Tristan 1896-1963 **CLC 47; DAM POET;**
    PC 27
  See also CA 153; 89-92; MTCW 2
Uhry, Alfred 1936- **CLC 55; DAM DRAM, POP**
  See also CA 127; 133; DA3; INT 133
Ulf, Haerved
  See Strindberg, (Johan) August
Ulf, Harved
  See Strindberg, (Johan) August
Ulibarri, Sabine R(eyes) 1919- ... **CLC 83; DAM**
    MULT; HLCS 2
  See also CA 131; CANR 81; DLB 82; HW 1, 2
Unamuno (y Jugo), Miguel de 1864-1936**TCLC 2,**
    9; DAM MULT, NOV; HLC 2; SSC 11
  See also CA 104; 131; CANR 81; DLB 108; HW
    1, 2; MTCW 1, 2
Undercliffe, Errol
  See Campbell, (John) Ramsey
Underwood, Miles
  See Glassco, John
Undset, Sigrid 1882-1949 ... **TCLC 3; DA; DAB;**
    DAC; DAM MST, NOV; WLC
  See also CA 104; 129; DA3; MTCW 1, 2
Ungaretti, Giuseppe 1888-1970 ... **CLC 7, 11, 15**
  See also CA 19-20; 25-28R; CAP 2; DLB 114
Unger, Douglas 1952- .... **CLC 34**
  See also CA 130
Unsworth, Barry (Forster) 1930- .. **CLC 76, 127**
  See also CA 25-28R; CANR 30, 54; DLB 194
Updike, John (Hoyer) 1932- **CLC 1, 2, 3, 5, 7, 9,**
    13, 15, 23, 34, 43, 70; DA; DAB; DAC; DAM
    MST, NOV, POET, POP; SSC 13, 27; WLC
  See also CA 1-4R; CABS 1; CANR 4, 33, 51;
    CDALB 1968-1988; DA3; DLB 2, 5, 143; DLBD
    3; DLBY 80, 82, 97; MTCW 1, 2
Upshaw, Margaret Mitchell
  See Mitchell, Margaret (Munnerlyn)
Upton, Mark
  See Sanders, Lawrence
Upward, Allen 1863-1926 .... **TCLC 85**
  See also CA 117; DLB 36
Urdang, Constance (Henriette) 1922- .. **CLC 47**
  See also CA 21-24R; CANR 9, 24
Uriel, Henry
  See Faust, Frederick (Schiller)
Uris, Leon (Marcus) 1924-**CLC 7, 32; DAM NOV,**
    POP
  See also AITN 1, 2; BEST 89:2; CA 1-4R; CANR
    1, 40, 65; DA3; MTCW 1, 2; SATA 49
Urista, Alberto H. 1947-
  See Alurista
  See also CA 45-48, 182; CANR 2, 32; HLCS 1;
    HW 1
Urmuz
  See Codrescu, Andrei
Urquhart, Guy
  See McAlmon, Robert (Menzies)
Urquhart, Jane 1949- .... **CLC 90; DAC**
  See also CA 113; CANR 32, 68
Usigli, Rodolfo 1905-1979
  See also CA 131; HLCS 1; HW 1
Ustinov, Peter (Alexander) 1921- .... **CLC 1**
  See also AITN 1; CA 13-16R; CANR 25, 51; DLB
    13; MTCW 2

U Tam'si, Gerald Felix Tchicaya
  See Tchicaya, Gerald Felix
U Tam'si, Tchicaya
  See Tchicaya, Gerald Felix
Vachss, Andrew (Henry) 1942- .... **CLC 106**
  See also CA 118; CANR 44
Vachss, Andrew H.
  See Vachss, Andrew (Henry)
Vaculik, Ludvik 1926- .... **CLC 7**
  See also CA 53-56; CANR 72
Vaihinger, Hans 1852-1933 .... **TCLC 71**
  See also CA 116; 166
Valdez, Luis (Miguel) 1940-**CLC 84; DAM MULT;**
    DC 10; HLC 2
  See also CA 101; CANR 32, 81; DLB 122; HW 1
Valenzuela, Luisa 1938- ..... **CLC 31, 104; DAM**
    MULT; HLCS 2; SSC 14
  See also CA 101; CANR 32, 65; DLB 113; HW 1,
    2
Valera y Alcala-Galiano, Juan 1824-1905 **TCLC**
    10
  See also CA 106
Valery, (Ambroise) Paul (Toussaint Jules) 1871-
    1945 .... **TCLC 4, 15; DAM POET; PC 9**
  See also CA 104; 122; DA3; MTCW 1, 2
Valle-Inclan, Ramon (Maria) del 1866-1936**TCLC**
    5; DAM MULT; HLC 2
  See also CA 106; 153; CANR 80; DLB 134; HW 2
Vallejo, Antonio Buero
  See Buero Vallejo, Antonio
Vallejo, Cesar (Abraham) 1892-1938**TCLC 3, 56;**
    DAM MULT; HLC 2
  See also CA 105; 153; HW 1
Valles, Jules 1832-1885 .... **NCLC 71**
  See also DLB 123
Vallette, Marguerite Eymery
  See Rachilde
Valle Y Pena, Ramon del
  See Valle-Inclan, Ramon (Maria) del
Van Ash, Cay 1918- .... **CLC 34**
Vanbrugh, Sir John 1664-1726 ..... **LC 21; DAM**
    DRAM
  See also DLB 80
Van Campen, Karl
  See Campbell, John W(ood, Jr.)
Vance, Gerald
  See Silverberg, Robert
Vance, Jack .... **CLC 35**
  See also Kuttner, Henry; Vance, John Holbrook
  See also DLB 8
Vance, John Holbrook 1916-
  See Queen, Ellery; Vance, Jack
  See also CA 29-32R; CANR 17, 65; MTCW 1
Van Den Bogarde, Derek Jules Gaspard Ulric
    Niven 1921-1999
  See Bogarde, Dirk
  See also CA 77-80; 179
Vandenburgh, Jane .... **CLC 59**
  See also CA 168
Vanderhaeghe, Guy 1951- .... **CLC 41**
  See also CA 113; CANR 72
van der Post, Laurens (Jan) 1906-1996 .. **CLC 5**
  See also CA 5-8R; 155; CANR 35; DLB 204
van de Wetering, Janwillem 1931- .... **CLC 47**
  See also CA 49-52; CANR 4, 62
Van Dine, S. S. .... **TCLC 23**
  See also Wright, Willard Huntington
Van Doren, Carl (Clinton) 1885-1950 . **TCLC 18**
  See also CA 111; 168
Van Doren, Mark 1894-1972 .... **CLC 6, 10**
  See also CA 1-4R; 37-40R; CANR 3; DLB 45;
    MTCW 1, 2
Van Druten, John (William) 1901-1957 **TCLC 2**

  See also CA 104; 161; DLB 10
Van Duyn, Mona (Jane) 1921-**CLC 3, 7, 63, 116;**
    DAM POET
  See also CA 9-12R; CANR 7, 38, 60; DLB 5
Van Dyne, Edith
  See Baum, L(yman) Frank
van Itallie, Jean-Claude 1936- .... **CLC 3**
  See also CA 45-48; CAAS 2; CANR 1, 48; DLB 7
van Ostaijen, Paul 1896-1928 .... **TCLC 33**
  See also CA 163
Van Peebles, Melvin 1932-**CLC 2, 20; DAM MULT**
  See also BW 2, 3; CA 85-88; CANR 27, 67, 82
Vansittart, Peter 1920- .... **CLC 42**
  See also CA 1-4R; CANR 3, 49
Van Vechten, Carl 1880-1964 .... **CLC 33**
  See also CA 89-92; DLB 4, 9, 51
Van Vogt, A(lfred) E(lton) 1912- .... **CLC 1**
  See also CA 21-24R; CANR 28; DLB 8; SATA 14
Varda, Agnes 1928- .... **CLC 16**
  See also CA 116; 122
Vargas Llosa, (Jorge) Mario (Pedro) 1936-**C L C**
    3, 6, 9, 10, 15, 31, 42, 85; DA; DAB; DAC;
    DAM MST, MULT, NOV; HLC 2
  See also CA 73-76; CANR 18, 32, 42, 67; DA3;
    DLB 145; HW 1, 2; MTCW 1, 2
Vasiliu, Gheorghe 1881-1957
  See Bacovia, George
  See also CA 123
Vassa, Gustavus
  See Equiano, Olaudah
Vassilikos, Vassilis 1933- .... **CLC 4, 8**
  See also CA 81-84; CANR 75
Vaughan, Henry 1621-1695 .... **LC 27**
  See also DLB 131
Vaughn, Stephanie .... **CLC 62**
Vazov, Ivan (Minchov) 1850-1921 .... **TCLC 25**
  See also CA 121; 167; DLB 147
Veblen, Thorstein B(unde) 1857-1929 **TCLC 31**
  See also CA 115; 165
Vega, Lope de 1562-1635 .... **LC 23; HLCS 2**
Venison, Alfred
  See Pound, Ezra (Weston Loomis)
Verdi, Marie de
  See Mencken, H(enry) L(ouis)
Verdu, Matilde
  See Cela, Camilo Jose
Verga, Giovanni (Carmelo) 1840-1922 . **TCLC 3;**
    SSC 21
  See also CA 104; 123
Vergil 70B.C.-19B.C. **CMLC 9; DA; DAB; DAC;**
    DAM MST, POET; PC 12; WLCS
  See also Virgil
  See also DA3
Verhaeren, Emile (Adolphe Gustave) 1855-1916
    TCLC 12
  See also CA 109
Verlaine, Paul (Marie) 1844-1896 ..**NCLC 2, 51;**
    DAM POET; PC 2
Verne, Jules (Gabriel) 1828-1905 ... **TCLC 6, 52**
  See also AAYA 16; CA 110; 131; DA3; DLB 123;
    JRDA; MAICYA; SATA 21
Very, Jones 1813-1880 .... **NCLC 9**
  See also DLB 1
Vesaas, Tarjei 1897-1970 .... **CLC 48**
  See also CA 29-32R
Vialis, Gaston
  See Simenon, Georges (Jacques Christian)
Vian, Boris 1920-1959 .... **TCLC 9**
  See also CA 106; 164; DLB 72; MTCW 2
Viaud, (Louis Marie) Julien 1850-1923
  See Loti, Pierre
  See also CA 107
Vicar, Henry

See also AAYA 11; CLR 2; DLB 161; SAAS 3

Walter, Villiam Christian
See Andersen, Hans Christian

Wambaugh, Joseph (Aloysius, Jr.) 1937- **CLC 3, 18; DAM NOV, POP**
See also AITN 1; BEST 89:3; CA 33-36R; CANR 42, 65; DA3; DLB 6; DLBY 83; MTCW 1, 2

Wang Wei 699(?)-761(?) .... **PC 18**

Ward, Arthur Henry Sarsfield 1883-1959
See Rohmer, Sax
See also CA 108; 173

Ward, Douglas Turner 1930- .... **CLC 19**
See also BW 1; CA 81-84; CANR 27; DLB 7, 38

Ward, E. D.
See Lucas, E(dward) V(errall)

Ward, Mary Augusta
See Ward, Mrs. Humphry

Ward, Mrs. Humphry 1851-1920 .... **TCLC 55**
See also DLB 18

Ward, Peter
See Faust, Frederick (Schiller)

Warhol, Andy 1928(?)-1987 .... **CLC 20**
See also AAYA 12; BEST 89:4; CA 89-92; 121; CANR 34

Warner, Francis (Robert le Plastrier) 1937- **CLC 14**
See also CA 53-56; CANR 11

Warner, Marina 1946- .... **CLC 59**
See also CA 65-68; CANR 21, 55; DLB 194

Warner, Rex (Ernest) 1905-1986 .... **CLC 45**
See also CA 89-92; 119; DLB 15

Warner, Susan (Bogert) 1819-1885 .... **NCLC 31**
See also DLB 3, 42

Warner, Sylvia (Constance) Ashton
See Ashton-Warner, Sylvia (Constance)

Warner, Sylvia Townsend 1893-1978 **CLC 7, 19; SSC 23**
See also CA 61-64; 77-80; CANR 16, 60; DLB 34, 139; MTCW 1, 2

Warren, Mercy Otis 1728-1814 .... **NCLC 13**
See also DLB 31, 200

Warren, Robert Penn 1905-1989 . **CLC 1, 4, 6, 8, 10, 13, 18, 39, 53, 59; DA; DAB; DAC; DAM MST, NOV, POET; SSC 4; WLC**
See also AITN 1; CA 13-16R; 129; CANR 10, 47; CDALB 1968-1988; DA3; DLB 2, 48, 152; DLBY 80, 89; INT CANR-10; MTCW 1, 2; SATA 46; SATA-Obit 63

Warshofsky, Isaac
See Singer, Isaac Bashevis

Warton, Thomas 1728-1790 **LC 15; DAM POET**
See also DLB 104, 109

Waruk, Kona
See Harris, (Theodore) Wilson

Warung, Price 1855-1911 .... **TCLC 45**

Warwick, Jarvis
See Garner, Hugh

Washington, Alex
See Harris, Mark

Washington, Booker T(aliaferro) 1856-1915 **TCLC 10; BLC 3; DAM MULT**
See also BW 1; CA 114; 125; DA3; SATA 28

Washington, George 1732-1799 .... **LC 25**
See also DLB 31

Wassermann, (Karl) Jakob 1873-1934 . **TCLC 6**
See also CA 104; 163; DLB 66

Wasserstein, Wendy 1950- **CLC 32, 59, 90; DAM DRAM; DC 4**
See also CA 121; 129; CABS 3; CANR 53, 75; DA3; INT 129; MTCW 2; SATA 94

Waterhouse, Keith (Spencer) 1929- ..... **CLC 47**
See also CA 5-8R; CANR 38, 67; DLB 13, 15; MTCW 1, 2

Waters, Frank (Joseph) 1902-1995 .... **CLC 88**
See also CA 5-8R; 149; CAAS 13; CANR 3, 18, 63; DLB 212; DLBY 86

Waters, Roger 1944- .... **CLC 35**

Watkins, Frances Ellen
See Harper, Frances Ellen Watkins

Watkins, Gerrold
See Malzberg, Barry N(athaniel)

Watkins, Gloria 1955(?)-
See hooks, bell
See also BW 2; CA 143; MTCW 2

Watkins, Paul 1964- .... **CLC 55**
See also CA 132; CANR 62

Watkins, Vernon Phillips 1906-1967 .... **CLC 43**
See also CA 9-10; 25-28R; CAP 1; DLB 20

Watson, Irving S.
See Mencken, H(enry) L(ouis)

Watson, John H.
See Farmer, Philip Jose

Watson, Richard F.
See Silverberg, Robert

Waugh, Auberon (Alexander) 1939- .... **CLC 7**
See also CA 45-48; CANR 6, 22; DLB 14, 194

Waugh, Evelyn (Arthur St. John) 1903-1966 **CLC 1, 3, 8, 13, 19, 27, 44, 107; DA; DAB; DAC; DAM MST, NOV, POP; WLC**
See also CA 85-88; 25-28R; CANR 22; CDBLB 1914-1945; DA3; DLB 15, 162, 195; MTCW 1, 2

Waugh, Harriet 1944- .... **CLC 6**
See also CA 85-88; CANR 22

Ways, C. R.
See Blount, Roy (Alton), Jr.

Waystaff, Simon
See Swift, Jonathan

Webb, Beatrice (Martha Potter) 1858-1943 **TCLC 22**
See also CA 117; 162; DLB 190

Webb, Charles (Richard) 1939- .... **CLC 7**
See also CA 25-28R

Webb, James H(enry), Jr. 1946- .... **CLC 22**
See also CA 81-84

Webb, Mary Gladys (Meredith) 1881-1927 **TCLC 24**
See also CA 182; 123; DLB 34

Webb, Mrs. Sidney
See Webb, Beatrice (Martha Potter)

Webb, Phyllis 1927- .... **CLC 18**
See also CA 104; CANR 23; DLB 53

Webb, Sidney (James) 1859-1947 .... **TCLC 22**
See also CA 117; 163; DLB 190

Webber, Andrew Lloyd .... **CLC 21**
See also Lloyd Webber, Andrew

Weber, Lenora Mattingly 1895-1971 ..... **CLC 12**
See also CA 19-20; 29-32R; CAP 1; SATA 2; SATA-Obit 26

Weber, Max 1864-1920 .... **TCLC 69**
See also CA 109

Webster, John 1579(?)-1634(?) **LC 33; DA; DAB; DAC; DAM DRAM, MST; DC 2; WLC**
See also CDBLB Before 1660; DLB 58

Webster, Noah 1758-1843 .... **NCLC 30**
See also DLB 1, 37, 42, 43, 73

Wedekind, (Benjamin) Frank(lin) 1864-1918 **TCLC 7; DAM DRAM**
See also CA 104; 153; DLB 118

Weidman, Jerome 1913-1998 .... **CLC 7**
See also AITN 2; CA 1-4R; 171; CANR 1; DLB 28

Weil, Simone (Adolphine) 1909-1943 .. **TCLC 23**
See also CA 117; 159; MTCW 2

Weininger, Otto 1880-1903 .... **TCLC 84**

Weinstein, Nathan

See West, Nathanael

Weinstein, Nathan von Wallenstein
See West, Nathanael

Weir, Peter (Lindsay) 1944- .... **CLC 20**
See also CA 113; 123

Weiss, Peter (Ulrich) 1916-1982 **CLC 3, 15, 51; DAM DRAM**
See also CA 45-48; 106; CANR 3; DLB 69, 124

Weiss, Theodore (Russell) 1916- ..**CLC 3, 8, 14**
See also CA 9-12R; CAAS 2; CANR 46; DLB 5

Welch, (Maurice) Denton 1915-1948 .. **TCLC 22**
See also CA 121; 148

Welch, James 1940- **CLC 6, 14, 52; DAM MULT, POP**
See also CA 85-88; CANR 42, 66; DLB 175; NNAL

Weldon, Fay 1931- **CLC 6, 9, 11, 19, 36, 59, 122; DAM POP**
See also CA 21-24R; CANR 16, 46, 63; CDBLB 1960 to Present; DLB 14, 194; INT CANR-16; MTCW 1, 2

Wellek, Rene 1903-1995 .... **CLC 28**
See also CA 5-8R; 150; CAAS 7; CANR 8; DLB 63; INT CANR-8

Weller, Michael 1942- .... **CLC 10, 53**
See also CA 85-88

Weller, Paul 1958- .... **CLC 26**

Wellershoff, Dieter 1925- .... **CLC 46**
See also CA 89-92; CANR 16, 37

Welles, (George) Orson 1915-1985 **CLC 20, 80**
See also CA 93-96; 117

Wellman, John McDowell 1945-
See Wellman, Mac
See also CA 166

Wellman, Mac 1945- .... **CLC 65**
See also Wellman, John McDowell; Wellman, John McDowell

Wellman, Manly Wade 1903-1986 .... **CLC 49**
See also CA 1-4R; 118; CANR 6, 16, 44; SATA 6; SATA-Obit 47

Wells, Carolyn 1869(?)-1942 .... **TCLC 35**
See also CA 113; DLB 11

Wells, H(erbert) G(eorge) 1866-1946 **TCLC 6, 12, 19; DA; DAB; DAC; DAM MST, NOV; SSC 6; WLC**
See also AAYA 18; CA 110; 121; CDBLB 1914-1945; DA3; DLB 34, 70, 156, 178; MTCW 1, 2; SATA 20

Wells, Rosemary 1943- .... **CLC 12**
See also AAYA 13; CA 85-88; CANR 48; CLR 16; MAICYA; SAAS 1; SATA 18, 69

Welty, Eudora 1909- **CLC 1, 2, 5, 14, 22, 33, 105; DA; DAB; DAC; DAM MST, NOV; SSC 1, 27; WLC**
See also CA 9-12R; CABS 1; CANR 32, 65; CDALB 1941-1968; DA3; DLB 2, 102, 143; DLBD 12; DLBY 87; MTCW 1, 2

Wen I-to 1899-1946 .... **TCLC 28**

Wentworth, Robert
See Hamilton, Edmond

Werfel, Franz (Viktor) 1890-1945 .... **TCLC 8**
See also CA 104; 161; DLB 81, 124

Wergeland, Henrik Arnold 1808-1845 . **NCLC 5**

Wersba, Barbara 1932- .... **CLC 30**
See also AAYA 2, 30; CA 29-32R, 182; CAAE 182; CANR 16, 38; CLR 3; DLB 52; JRDA; MAICYA; SAAS 2; SATA 1, 58; SATA-Essay 103

Wertmueller, Lina 1928- .... **CLC 16**
See also CA 97-100; CANR 39, 78

Wescott, Glenway 1901-1987 .. **CLC 13; SSC 35**
See also CA 13-16R; 121; CANR 23, 70; DLB 4, 9, 102

Author Index

Literary Criticism Series
Cumulative Topic Index

This index lists all topic entries in Gale's *Classical and Medieval Literature Criticism, Contemporary Literary Criticism, Literature Criticism from 1400 to 1800, Nineteenth-Century Literature Criticism,* and *Twentieth-Century Literary Criticism.*

Topic Index

Topic Index

Topic Index

Contemporary Literary Criticism
Cumulative Nationality Index

Nationality Index

Nationality Index

Nationality Index

Nationality Index

Nationality Index

ISBN 0-7876-3202-3